LL 60

AUTHOR	CLASS
FRIAR, S.	

TITLE
The local history companion

The Local History Companion

STEPHEN FRIAR

'It is better to know a little bit of the world remarkably well,
than to know a great part remarkably little.'
Thomas Hardy

SUTTON PUBLISHING

First published in this revised edition in the United Kingdom in 2001 by
Sutton Publishing Limited
Phoenix Mill · Thrupp · Stroud · Gloucestershire

British Library Cataloguing in Publication Data

A catalogue record for this book is available from the British Library

ISBN 0-7509-2722-4

Title-page illustration: *Rebus of Abbot William of Milton, Dorset.*

08603898

Other books by the author:

A New Dictionary of Heraldry (Alphabooks/A & C Black, 1987)
The Batsford Companion to Local History (B.T. Batsford, 1991)
Heraldry for the Local Historian and Genealogist (Sutton, 1992; paperback, with revisions, 1996)
Basic Heraldry (The Herbert Press, 1993; paperback, with revisions, 1999)
A Companion to the English Parish Church (Sutton Publishing, 1996)

Typeset in 9/10 Times.
Typesetting and origination by
Sutton Publishing Limited.
Printed and bound in Great Britain by
J.H. Haynes & Co. Ltd, Sparkford, England.

ACKNOWLEDGEMENTS

The author acknowledges with gratitude the invaluable assistance of G.W. Bennett, Melanie Birdsall, Clare Bishop, Arthur Blackham, Peter Clifford, Christopher Feeney, John Ferguson, Kate Friar, Tom Friar, Roger Guttridge, Tony Harris, Revd Derek Hillier, Rosemary Humphreys, Jenifer Keeling, Roger Lovibond, John Mennell, Dr Mike Osborne, Roger Peers, Adrian Room, Tony Seward, Margaret and David Sibley, Howard Thomas, Catherine Watson, Geoffrey Wheeler and Vera and John Worledge in the preparation of this book.

The author and publisher would like to thank the following for their permission to reproduce illustrations:

Aerofilms: 43; Michael J. Allen Photography: colour plate 14; Ashmolean Museum, Oxford: 26, 440; B.T. Batsford Limited: 28, 34, 36, 52 (Alan Sorrell), 53 (Alan Sorrell), 59, 68, 75, 92, 93, 107, 120, 135, 156, 171, 178, 194, 211, 213, 222, 230, 247, 258, 261 (MS 39810; British Library), 285 (Alan Sorrell), 290, 297, 300, 306, 334, 347, 359, 361 (Alan Sorrell), 368, 386 (right), 408, 412, 420, 422, 432, 433, 447, 448, 452, 464, 472, 482; Ivan J. Belcher: colour plate 2; Jonathan Berg/Birmingham Picture Library: colour plate 7; Bournville Village Trust; colour plate 15; British Library, London/Bridgeman Art Library, London/New York: 429 (Roy 20 C VII f. 42v, Arrest of the Templars, 1308); Cambridge University Committee for Aerial Photography: 207; Paul Collins/Dudley Teachers' Centre: 47; Hugh Collinson: 201; Dorset County Museum: 109, 354 (bottom), 392; National Museum of Ireland, Dublin: 42; English Heritage: 342; John Ferguson: 340 (top), 345, 425, 475; Stephen Friar: vi, 39, 73, 89, 106, 123, 124, 125, 137, 143, 202, 239, 295, 328 (bottom), 383, 389, 419, 423, 434, 443; Tom Friar: 25, 61; The Dean and Chapter of Hereford Cathedral and the Hereford Mappa Mundi Trust: colour plate 4; Ironbridge Gorge Museum Trust: colour plate 9; A.F. Kersting: colour plates 10, 11, 12, 13; Martin Latham: colour plate 8; Map House, London, UK/Bridgeman Art Library: colour plate 5; John Mennell: 4, 6, 19, 79, 83, 102, 118, 126, 162, 167, 180, 182, 204, 225, 249, 250, 254, 266, 288, 313, 326, 331, 364, 373, 374 (left), 376, 406, 407, 442, 469; L.E. Milton: 463; Florence Morris: i, 294, 304, 311, 354 (top), 403 (top), 415, 424, 471; The Royal Collection © 2001 Her Majesty the Queen: 315; By permission of RCAHMS: 108 Crown copyright reserved, 317; Rural History Centre, University of Reading: 151 (35/27310), 153 (35/13487), 154 (35/30697); Ulster Folk and Transport Museum, W.A. Green Collection: 229, 417; Ulster Museum, Welch Collection: 121; Oliver Watts: 141; Geoffrey Wheeler: 95, 139, 144, 245, 283, 340 (bottom), 388, 410, 437, 479; colour plate 6; Geoffrey Williams: 269, 318, 357, 366, 370, 403 (bottom); colour plates 1 and 3; Doreen Yarwood: 189. All other line drawings are by John Ferguson.

INTRODUCTION

In recent years local history has become a major leisure activity. Courses arranged by university extra-mural departments and education authorities have encouraged the formation of local research groups and filled the county record offices with crowds of eager amateurs, searching anxiously for documentary fragments from which to piece together the patchwork of a village history. And yet, while their contribution to our understanding of the past is inestimable, such people are few in number by comparison with those who claim no academic distinction but acknowledge instinctively the potency of their heritage: that multitude of visitors to our parish churches, cathedrals, medieval castles and stately homes; those who at weekends may be found rambling along ancient trackways or traversing the ramparts of lonely hill forts; young people engaged in research projects in our schools and colleges and innumerable fireside historians who, in an increasingly materialistic world, continue to draw comfort from the past.

Thomas Hardy wrote 'It is better to know a little bit of the world remarkably well, than to know a great part remarkably little'. Anyone who takes more than a passing interest in his or her surroundings is a local historian and it is hoped that this book will provide them with as much pleasure as it will the more practised and erudite researcher.

The *Companion* is arranged alphabetically and consists of a number of primary entries (e.g. CHURCHES) from which cross-references lead on to a larger number of secondary entries (e.g. CHANTRY CHAPELS, EFFIGIES, HATCHMENTS, ROOD SCREENS, etc.). Many of the terms encountered in local history research are also included, either as short individual entries or by cross-referencing. These include the terminology of associated subjects, such as architecture and heraldry, and place-name elements. Entries on subjects such as EDUCATION, ANCIENT KINGDOMS, VIKINGS, WALES, etc., are intended to assist in placing local research in a wider historical context.

Cross-references are indicated by CAPITAL LETTERS and these are picked out in *italic letters* in the entry to which the reader is referred.

The addresses of organisations referred to in the text will be found listed in APPENDIX I and suggestions for further reading are provided in APPENDIX II.

This book is for my parents who taught me to rejoice in such things.

Stephen Friar
Folke, Dorset
January 2001

A

ABANDONED SETTLEMENTS *see* DESERTED VILLAGES

ABBESS The superior of certain communities of nuns within the Benedictine orders and of orders of canonesses, especially those of the Franciscan Order (the Poor Clares). With the exception of the latter, the office is usually held for life.

ABBEY Ostensibly a major monastic establishment of the Benedictine orders or certain orders of the Canons Regular and superior to a PRIORY, though in practice several priories attained religious and economic prosperity which greatly exceeded that of many abbeys, the most obvious example being that of the cathedral priory of Durham.
See also MONASTERIES

ABBOT The official title of the superior of a major religious establishment of one of the Benedictine orders or of certain orders of the Canons Regular. Normally elected for life by the monks of his abbey, an abbot exercises considerable powers in its governance. Since 1893 the head of the Benedictine Order has been termed the Abbot Primate (*see* MONASTERIES).

ABJURATION OF THE REALM *see* SANCTUARY

ABRAIDING *see* STAINED GLASS

ABUTMENT A mass of masonry or brickwork against which an arch abuts or from which it springs. Structurally an abutment resists the lateral thrust of an arch and may be a pier, wall or BUTTRESS.
See also VAULTING

ACCOLLÉ *see* HATCHMENT

ACHIEVEMENT OF ARMS An arrangement of armorial devices (*see* ARMORY, FUNERAL HERALDRY *and* HATCHMENT).

ACOUSTIC CHAMBERS *see* AMPLIFIERS

ACRE From *aecer*, meaning a piece of land of unspecified size. The term was originally used to imply a piece of land cleared for ploughing or grazing and later as a strip of open field, sufficiently large to be ploughed by a yoke of oxen in a day. Edward I standardized the acre as an area of land 40 rods long by 4 rods wide: a rod was 5½ yards (5.4 metres). However, variations will be found, particularly in Scotland, Ireland and northern England where the area of an acre was substantially larger than this. The Old English *acreman* was a farmer, a medieval term for one paying a *firma* or fixed rent.
See also CHAIN, FURLONG *and* ROOD

ACREMAN (AKERMAN) One who rented an ACRE of land. Commonly found as a place or street name.

ADDRESSES *see* APPENDIX I

ADULTERINE *see* CASTLES (MEDIEVAL)

ADVENAE Norman and English feudal lords who held lands in the Welsh Marches (often described as 'adventurers' in Welsh manuscripts), together with the retainers, officials, merchants and burgesses who accompanied them.
See also MARCH

ADVOWSON The right of appointing a priest to an ecclesiastical benefice. An advowson is held by a *patron*, which may be an individual or institution, who presents the priest to the appropriate bishop for institution and induction.

AFFEEROR Manorial official responsible for determining the amount of a fine (*see* MANOR).

AFFIDAVIT A written statement confirmed by an oath.

AFTERGRASS *see* MEADS

AFTERMATH The remnant of a hay crop used for grazing.

AGGER The raised foundation and drainage ditches of a ROMAN ROAD.

AGISTMENT *see* COMMONS

AGNUS DEI (PASCHAL LAMB) A Christian symbol depicting a lamb with a halo or *nimbus* round its head and holding a staff at the upper end of which are both a cross and a white pennon charged with a red cross (*see* CHRISTIAN SYMBOLS).

AGRARIAN REVOLUTION Eighteenth-century transformation of British agriculture characterized by the acceleration of ENCLOSURES and the consequent decline of the system of OPEN FIELDS, together with rapid technological innovation (e.g. the seed drill) which often met with stubborn resistance from agricultural labourers.
See also FARMING

AGRICULTURE *see* FARMING

AILETTES *see* BRASSES (MONUMENTAL)

AISLED HALL *see* HALL

AKERMAN *see* ACREMAN

ALABASTER Calcium sulphate, a form of gypsum, found in certain strata of rocks in the North Midlands, the Isle of Purbeck in Dorset and elsewhere, and used in medieval sculpture (particularly in EFFIGIES) because of the ease and speed with which it could be carved. Dressed alabaster is exceptionally smooth to the touch and is white with occasional flecks of red, though most tombs were originally coloured and gilded.
See also PLASTERWORK

ALAE *see* ROMAN FORTS AND CAMPS

ALDER Now a rare tree, alders once prospered on the banks of streams and rivers and provided excellent waterproof material for clogs and kitchen boards, as well as the best charcoal for gunpowder. Concentrations of scarlet withies found by streams in the north of England are usually indicative of a profusion of alders that have been cut and not replaced.

ALDERMAN (i) Formerly a senior member of an English county or borough council elected by fellow councillors and in rank next below mayor.
(ii) An elected governor of a city.
(iii) The head of a guild or fraternity.
See also EALDORMAN

ALE-TASTER A manorial official responsible for testing the quality and measurement of ale and, sometimes, of bread (*see* MANOR).

ALIENATION The transfer of property (*see* MANOR).

ALL HALLOWS *see* SAINTS' DAYS AND FEAST-DAYS

ALLOD Estate held without feudal obligation.

ALLOTMENTS The 700,000 Englishmen who in 1975 grew their vegetables and fruit on allotments were the descendants of the medieval villein, who cultivated strips of land in the open field and enjoyed common grazing rights in return for manorial service. These rights began to disappear in the sixteenth century with the enclosure of common land and in compensation the peasant was provided with a small 'allotment' of ground, which was usually attached to his cottage. In the next century some landowners permitted their labourers to grow crops on 'potato patches' as part of their wages, but parliamentary ENCLOSURE of the eighteenth and nineteenth centuries effectively removed any such opportunities for subsistence farming from what was then known as 'the labouring poor'. In the early nineteenth century, a small number of landowners provided allotments for this purpose and by an act of parliament parish wardens were able to rent out parcels of parish land. But, for the most part, opposition to the provision of allotments was overwhelming. Farmers in particular felt that men would spend all their time and energies on their allotments instead of labouring in their employment. Extreme conditions were often applied to the few allotments that were available: in one instance, labourers were not permitted to work on the allotments on Sundays or on weekdays between 6 a.m. and 6 p.m. The General Enclosure Act of 1845 established that 'field gardens' of not more than a quarter of an acre (1,000 square metres) could be provided, but as most of the land had already been enclosed the legislation came too late.

The Act itself was intended as a means of keeping 'a man at home from the alehouse' rather than helping him to supplement his meagre income with a few vegetables. Nevertheless, the allotments movement grew rapidly, especially in the burgeoning towns of the Industrial Revolution, and by the end of the nineteenth century there were nearly ½ million allotments. Following the First World War (1914–18) this number increased to 1¼ million.

Vegetables were expensive and men returning from the war with no prospect of work were applying for allotments at the rate of 7,000 a week. This was followed by a period of decline, the government-inspired requisition of land for the unemployed during the depression of the early 1930s being short-lived. The 'Dig for Victory' campaign of the Second World War (1939–45) resulted in a further increase but in the following five years the number of allotments under cultivation again fell to just over 1 million. Since 1975, when there were still nearly 700,000 allotments and a substantial waiting list, the soaring value of potential development land (especially in urban areas) and increasing affluence have effected a considerable reduction in the number of allotments.
See also GARDENS

ALLUSIVE ARMS *see* CANTING ARMS

ALMONER *see* MONASTERIES

ALMSHOUSES Many almshouses date from the Middle Ages when they were established as charitable foundations to care for the elderly, poor and infirm and wayfarers such as pilgrims. Each would have a warden, master or prior and would comprise an infirmary hall and chapel, similar in plan to a monastic infirmary. Known as hospitals, *bede houses* or *maisons dieu*, some were devoted to the care of lepers or lazars (such as the lazar houses of the Order of St Lazarus) and these would be divided into small cells or separate cottages instead of a corporate infirmary (*see also* HOSPITALS). In the later Middle Ages, many 'spitals' became permanent homes for the poor and elderly, and in 1547 most were dissolved as places of worship. The Elizabethans, however, re-established many old hospitals as almshouses and, encouraged by their example, the wealthy and charitable of the seventeenth and eighteenth centuries founded new establishments, the inmates of which were carefully selected for their unquestionable virtue. Several of our great hospitals, such as those of St Bartholomew and St Thomas in London, have medieval foundations. Typical of a number of medieval foundations which continue to operate today are the almshouses at Sherborne in Dorset, built in 1437 under royal licence at a cost of £80 raised (unusually) by public subscription. They were intended for 'twelve pore feeble and ympotent old men and four old women', cared for by a housewife who was required to share in the meals of the residents, presumably to ensure that they were properly fed.

ALPHYN *see* BEASTS (HERALDIC)

ALTARS The earliest altars were free-standing and made of wood but from 509 altars were constructed of stone slabs and often placed above the interred relics of a saint or with a recess in which the relics were placed. The altar usually stood to the east end of the chancel on a *predella* or raised step, and the front was covered by a decorative cloth or carved and painted panel known as the *antependium*. A *retable* may also have been fitted above the back of the altar. This was a decorative panel or shelf on which ornaments could be placed. The REREDOS was a richly carved and decorated screen, which rose behind and above the altar, often covering the wall with elaborate ornamentation and sometimes containing niches in which sculpted figures were placed. In the Middle Ages the high altar, where the priest celebrated the Sacrifice of the Mass, was concealed from the laity in the nave by the ROOD SCREEN. CHANTRY altars were enclosed by the *parclose*, an ornamental railing or fretted screen of stone or timber, within which private requiems were held. The medieval concept of the mystery of the *inner sanctum* was rejected by the Tudor reformers, who effectively brought the congregation into the chancel, where the Eucharist was shared as a family at 'God's Board', or moved the altar into the nave.

In 1505 an Act of Edward VI required that all altar stones were to be removed and destroyed. In many cases, the stones were hidden by Catholics in anticipation of better times and a few have been found intact and restored. The only stone altar to have survived *in situ* is that at the thirteenth-century Chapel of St Bartholomew at Corton in Dorset (*see* CHAPELS). The accessibility of the new altars caused problems, however, particularly from stray dogs, and rails to prevent profanation were widely introduced in churches from the early years of Elizabeth I's reign. These were disliked by the Puritans but were often restored following the Restoration and became known as *communion rails*. Many rood screens were removed during the Victorian period and recent liturgical changes in the Church of England have resulted in the removal of communion rails and the re-siting of the communion table so that it may be more accessible to the congregation.

ALTAR TOMBS *see* TABLE TOMBS

AMBO Latinized place-name element meaning 'both'. Usually found added to the name of a single parish or village which was once two parishes or hamlets (*see* LATIN).

Saxon altar at the church of St Laurence, Bradford-on-Avon in Wiltshire.

AMBULATORY A covered way for walking; specifically, the passageway in a church behind the high altar.

AMERCEMENT Once convicted, a man was 'at the king's mercy' (*amerced*) and liable for a monetary payment.

AMPHISBAENA A symbol of evil and the devil, this allegorical beast has dragon-like wings and a head at both ends of its scaly body, thereby enabling it to move with cunning in either direction. Found in medieval carving but rarely in armory.

AMPLIFIERS Earthenware vessels, usually set in the eastern face of a chancel wall in order to amplify the voice of the priest during the Mass. A set at Tarrant Rushton church in Dorset dates from *c.* 1458 and must have been effective for, in 1541, the churchwardens' accounts of nearby Wimborne Minster record: 'payd for 2 potts of cley for the wyndfylling of the Church 8p'. In many monastic churches, *acoustic chambers* were intended to provide extra resonance and amplification during the singing of plainsong and to make 'hauteyn speche ring out as round as gooth a belle'. Those at Fountains Abbey in Yorkshire consisted simply of rows of ceramic jars laid on their sides, but elsewhere sophisticated drain-like series of boxes were constructed beneath choir stalls for the same purpose. The twelfth-century set of acoustic chambers at St Gregory's Priory in Canterbury, Kent, is 1 metre wide (3 feet) and 0.6 metres deep (2 feet), with tiled floors and walls mortared with chalk and flint. They were built to allow the low notes of male voices to reverberate, and supposedly added lustre to the voices. Acoustic chambers were clearly *de rigueur* in the Middle Ages though it is doubtful whether they were really effective.

ANCHORAGE An anchorite's dwelling, often an endowed cell within a church or churchyard and usually inferior to that of a HERMIT.

ANCHORITE (*Fem.* ANCHORESS) A religious recluse living a solitary life of silence, prayer and

mortification. Anchorites often lived by means of an endowment: the Black Prince maintained an anchorite, in the park of Restormel Castle above the Fowey river in Cornwall, who said masses for the souls of the Prince's ancestors.
See also HERMIT

ANCIENT (i) Descriptive of the original coat of arms of a family who have subsequently been granted an additional or alternative coat.
(ii) A military officer responsible for the maintenance of the medieval STANDARD.

ANCIENT COUNTRYSIDE *see* COUNTRYSIDE

ANCIENT DEEDS Documents at the PUBLIC RECORD OFFICE, mostly drawn from monastic and private muniments, relating to conveyances of land, covenants, bonds, wills etc. 'earlier in date than the end of Elizabeth I's reign' (1603).
Further information: *Descriptive Catalogue of Ancient Deeds*, 6 Vols., HMSO, and publications of the List and Index Society (*see* APPENDIX I)

ANCIENT DEMESNE *see* TALLAGE

ANCIENT KINGDOMS *see* KINGDOMS (ANCIENT)

ANCIENT USER A legal claim based on constant use or custom since 'time immemorial', otherwise known as 'time out of mind'. In common law this is deemed to be 1189, although in the Court of Chivalry it has been argued that the Norman Conquest (1066) should be regarded as the limit of legal memory. During the HERALDS' VISITATIONS of the seventeenth century, a claim with proof of a prescriptive use of arms from the beginning of the reign of Elizabeth I (1558) was considered to be sufficient.

ANDIRON *see* FIREDOGS

ANGEL *see* COINAGE

ANGELS In the early Church, interest in angels was largely concerned with matters hierarchical and, in *c.* 500, the celestial host was arranged in three orders of three choirs each: Seraphim, Cherubim and Thrones; Dominations, Virtues and Powers; Principalities, Archangels and Angels.
The depiction, in Saxon and medieval churches, of angels in stone, wood and glass was intended to be a constant reminder of their invisible presence at the

Sacrifice of the Mass and, in particular, in the chancel around the high altar.
For the Nine Orders *see* CHRISTIAN SYMBOLS

ANGLE A member of a north German tribe originally located in what is now Schleswig-Holstein. Together with the SAXONS and JUTES they conquered and colonized much of England in the fifth century, founding kingdoms in Mercia, Northumbria and East Anglia. From their name is derived England and the English.
See also ANGLO-SAXON *and* OLD ENGLISH

ANGLO-SAXON Anglo-Saxon buildings in England date from two distinct periods with the calamitous Viking raids of the late eighth and ninth centuries intervening and effectively destroying earlier Saxon culture.
The work of the seventh and early eighth centuries was concentrated in two areas: a Celtic tradition based in Northumberland and an Augustinian school in the Canterbury area. Most Anglo-Saxon work was of wood and wattle and daub construction, stone being used only for MONASTERIES, MINSTERS and other important CHURCHES. The church of St Andrew at Greensted in Essex is believed to date from the mid-ninth century and is the only surviving example of an Anglo-Saxon wooden church with walls of solid oak. It is known that in 1013 the body of King Edmund rested there on its journey to Bury St Edmunds; recent tests, however, suggest that the church, with its nave of split oak logs fixed to a wooden sill, may have been constructed 150 years earlier. (The present sill and plinth of brick date from a restoration of 1848.) The first Northumbrian churches had tall naves without aisles and simple rectangular chancels, as at Escomb in County Durham. Following the Synod of Whitby in 664, monasticism and architecture followed the Roman pattern and by the end of that century great churches were being constructed on the BASILICAN plan, such as those at Hexham, Ripon and York. This was the plan already adopted for the construction of seventh-century churches in the south of England, though, because of the inexperience of the builders, these were comparatively simple in form. Instead of aisles separated from the nave by arcades of columns, walls were plain and pierced by a single opening which led to a series of chambers, with an apsidal chancel at the east and a corresponding vestibule at the west. The churches of St Peter and St Paul, Canterbury, and St Peter-on-the-Walls at Bradwell in Essex are two examples.

The Saxon church of St Laurence at Bradford-on-Avon in Wiltshire. Founded by St Aldhelm (639–709), the church was discovered within a stone's throw of the medieval parish church as recently as 1856.

The mid-tenth century saw a flowering of Anglo-Saxon culture and the rejuvenation of large-scale monasticism in England – a development that was to affect profoundly the subsequent nature of medieval society. Supported by the Anglo-Saxon monarchy, the Church was purged and strict Benedictine rule imposed by Ethelwold (*c.* 908–84), bishop of Winchester from 963. A singularly powerful and influential cleric, ecclesiastically puritanical and yet an enthusiastic patron of the tenth-century artistic renaissance, Ethelwold's reformed monastic houses evolved into one of the wealthiest and most powerful forces in England, and under his influence, Winchester became the political and cultural centre of Anglo-Saxon society.

Numerous Anglo-Saxon churches date from this later period, though of the thirty Benedictine monasteries built during the tenth and early eleventh centuries most were rebuilt by the NORMANS and little Saxon work is extant above foundation level. Of the many remaining smaller churches, several were remodelled following Viking incursions, and most comprise a simple high nave with a narrow arch leading to a rectangular chancel, such as the church of St Laurence at Bradford-on-Avon,

Wiltshire. Some were also built with apsidal chancels, for example at Deerhurst in Gloucestershire. Anglo-Saxon work may be recognized by decorative pilaster strips, particularly in towers; long-and-short work, a primitive method of strengthening corners by inserting long vertical slabs between shorter horizontal ones; thin masonry or rubble walls without buttressing and doorway and window openings (these sometimes in pairs) with flat lintels or crude semi-circular or triangular heads. East Anglia has the largest collection of Anglo-Saxon churches, many with distinctive round towers (*see* CHURCH TOWERS) that may have been built as refuges against Viking incursions.

Anglo-Saxon society was highly stratified, with the king and his *gesiths* or *thanes* (the military élite and members of royal or magnatial households) at the top and a nominally free peasantry and substantial slave class at the bottom. The difference between free peasant and slave was not simply one of class, it was also one of race. The majority of slaves were indigenous Celts whose ancestors had lost their freedom during the Anglo-Saxon colonization of Britain in the fifth and sixth centuries AD. Indeed, the Anglo-Saxon word for 'slave' and 'Celt' was the same: *Wealh*, from which derives the word 'Welsh'.

ANNEALING OVEN *see* GLASS

ANNIVELLAR A chantry priest who said masses for the souls of benefactors on the anniversaries of their deaths. The fifteenth-century Annivellars' Refectory at Exeter has survived as commercial premises.

ANTENAVE *see* NARTHEX

ANTEPENDIUM *see* ALTARS

ANTONINE WALL *see* ROMAN FORTS AND CAMPS

AP In the Welsh, 'son of', e.g. Llywelyn ap Gruffydd.

APES Although the representation of apes in the fabric of churches is usually allegorical, reminding medieval man of his false pretensions by depicting apes as men pretending to acts of virtue, their appearance in ARMORY is not unknown. In the crest of the fourteenth-century Martyns of Athelhampton in Dorset, an ape is depicted admiring himself in a mirror. The family motto was 'He who looks on Martyn's Ape so Martyn's Ape shall look on Him'.

APPANAGE (*also* **APANAGE**) (i) Provision for maintenance, especially of a sovereign's younger child.
(ii) A dependent territory.
(iii) A perquisite.

APPROPRIATION The annexation of parish tithes and other endowments to a monastic house.

APPROVER Particularly in the Saxon and Norman periods, a criminal who obtained a pardon by becoming an informer was required to undergo *Trial by Battle*, a custom (based on the notion of divine intervention) which had largely disappeared by the fifteenth century and was finally abolished in 1819. The accuser was usually expected to fight the accused five times and was hanged if he lost. In civil cases, a *champion* could be nominated as substitute. *For* Trial by Ordeal *see* LAW

APSE A polygonal or semi-circular recess characteristic of the early basilicas of the Christian Church and introduced into Anglo-Saxon architecture by missionaries from Rome at the end of the sixth century. The apse was widely used by the Normans, in both domestic and ecclesiastical buildings, but was abandoned by the Cistercians of the twelfth century in favour of the square-ended chancel or chapel.

APSIDAL Having the form of an APSE.

AQUEDUCTS An aqueduct is a conduit for conducting water, from the Latin *aquae* ('water') and *ducere* ('lead'). Aqueducts in Britain date from the Roman period, when water was conducted from springs and rivers to towns, forts and industrial sites by means of stone channels or open leats. A good example is that at Dorchester, Dorset, where an aqueduct carried 13 million gallons of water a day from the River Frome to within the fortifications of Durnovaria, a distance of 9.5 km (6 miles) with a fall of 7.6 metres (25 feet). Traces of the aqueduct are preserved to the north-west of the town, though the reservoir has not been located. Water was brought from Dartmoor to Plymouth in Devon by a 38 km (24 miles) aqueduct built in 1585–7 and the Hobson's Conduit, built 1610–14, carried water from Nine Wells, near Trumpington, to Cambridge.

The massive urban expansion of the nineteenth century outpaced the ability of private companies to provide adequate water supplies and many towns established their own municipal water authorities and obtained the authority of Parliament to impede and extract water. With typical Victorian ingenuity, cities like Manchester, Liverpool and Birmingham, which did not have a sufficient local supply, constructed dams and artificial lakes and pumped water great distances along enclosed aqueducts that were remarkable feats of engineering. The first to do so, in the 1870s, was Manchester Corporation, which created reservoirs in the Etherow Valley in the Pennines and a 24 km (15 miles) aqueduct. This supply was soon to prove insufficient and a decade later a second 128 km (80 miles) aqueduct was constructed from Thirlmere in the Lake District. Between 1881 and 1882 Liverpool Corporation created Lake Vyrnwy (in what is now Powys), then the largest artifical lake in Europe, and a 104 km (65 miles) aqueduct. By an act of parliament in 1892, Birmingham Corporation acquired the upper waters of the river Elan above Rhayader in mid-Wales and between 1893 and 1904 constructed a series of reservoirs and a superbly engineered aqueduct carrying the water to the heart of the Midlands, some 117 km (73 miles) to the east. The dams in the Elan Valley possess a Wagnerian quality: giant waterfalls whose man-made origins are evident only in their perfect symmetry. Equally spectacular is the rugged solidity of the dams, valve houses and straining houses of the northern reservoirs, such as the castellated straining house at Thirlmere and the elegant serpentine water-spill at Abbeystead in Lancashire. But magnificent masonry was not simply an expression of Victorian romanticism: the bursting of the Holmfirth Dam in 1852 (with 81 fatalities) and the Dale Dyke Disaster of 1864 (in which there had been 244 deaths) had seriously damaged public confidence. The dams that followed were deliberately endowed with a reassuring sense of permanence and solidity. At Vyrnwy, for example, the first large masonry dam to be built in Britain was begun in 1881, its straining tower designed to look like a turreted medieval fortress rising from the waters of the lake and placed well away from the shore to secure the purest water. The tower is 52 metres high (170 feet), with its lower 18 metres (60 feet) below water. The inlet valves were located immediately below the surface and the water was strained inside the tower, the lower part of which provided a sump for foul water, which was periodically ejected by air pump.

The Industrial Revolution also brought with it the rapid expansion of the canal network and the spectacular water bridges of Thomas Telford and his

contemporaries, to which the term 'aqueduct' is generally applied. The first stone aqueduct, 12 metres high (39 feet) and carrying boats across the Irwell at Barton in Lancashire, was opened in 1761. But Telford's iron and sandstone aqueducts on the Shropshire Union canal (the Ellesmere Canal) in North Wales are undoubtedly the most glorious examples. The shorter is the Chirk Aqueduct, completed in 1801. This carries the canal in an iron trough, supported on ten arches, 21 metres (70 feet) above the Vale of Ceiriog. The canal passes through a tunnel and emerges at the magnificent Pont-y-cysylltau Aqueduct near Llangollen. This was opened in 1805 and crosses the River Dee on another iron trough, supported by nineteen arches with slender stone columns, 36 metres (120 feet) above the valley floor. Numerous industrial leats may be found, carrying water to (or from) mines, mills and other industrial sites. In the Forest of Dean, for example, there are leats dating from nearly every period of history, culminating in an impressive system of aqueducts servicing the coal and iron industries of the last century.
See also CANALS, PUBLIC UTILITIES, PUMPING HOUSES, WATER-MILLS *and* WEIRS

AQUITAINE An ancient province of south-western France, at times comprising the entire country from the Loire to the Pyrenees, though a permanent delineation of its boundaries was never feasible. By the marriage of Eleanor of Aquitaine to Henry II (1133–89) the province became one of the English possessions in France. In the thirteenth century, the terms Aquitaine, Gascony and Guyenne were effectively synonymous. The term Gascony was generally used to designate territory in south-western France that was actually held by the English. By 1224 the English had lost most of the northern part of the old Duchy of Aquitaine, though the title of duke was not relinquished. As Duke of Aquitaine, the King of England had to recognize the King of France as his feudal overlord in Gascony.

ARABIC NUMERALS Over the west door of Piddletrenthide church in Dorset are written the words: 'Est pydeltrenth villa in dorsedie comitatu Nascitur in illa quam rexit Vicariatu 1487'. It is remarkable that in such a remote village Arabic numerals were used when elsewhere Roman figures continued in use for at least another century.

ARCADE A range of arches resting on piers or columns. A *blind arcade* is an arcade attached to a wall.
See also NAVE

ARCH A curved series of radiating wedge-shaped bricks or blocks of stone (*voussoirs*) so arranged above an opening that they support one another and are capable of carrying a considerable weight (*see also* LINTEL). The uppermost central block is the *keystone*, and the pair of horizontal blocks from which the arch rises on either side of an opening are the *springers*. Between the springers is the notional *springing line*, which determines the geometry of the different types of arch. The walling or support on or against which an arch rests is the *abutment* and the width between abutments is termed the *span*. The under-surface of an arch is the *soffit* and the height of the arch, measured between the soffit of the keystone and the centre of the springing line, is known as the *rise*.

Saxon arches were usually of the *triangular* or *mitre* type, formed by a pair of stone slabs joined in a mitre at the top. From the semicircular *classical arch* of ancient Rome derived the ROMANESQUE arch of the early medieval period (popularly known as the 'Norman arch'), which was either semicircular (with its centre on the springing line), *segmental* (with its centre below the springing line) or *stilted* (with its centre above the springing line). The classical arch is also found in Renaissance and BAROQUE architecture. The essence of GOTHIC ARCHITECTURE was the *pointed arch* (the French *arc brisé* or 'broken arch'), which originated in the Middle East and reached western Europe by the twelfth century (*see* VAULTING). Its principal forms were the tall, narrow *lancet arch*, associated with the Early English style of Gothic architecture; the *equilateral arch*, the radii of which were equal to the span; the *obtuse arch*, with a span greater than its radius; the *ogee arch*, characteristic of the fourteenth century; and the *four-centred arch*, which is commonly found in buildings dating from the late medieval and Tudor periods. A *strainer* is an arch which spans an internal space to prevent walls from leaning (the finest examples are those above the crossing at Gloucester Cathedral); *interlacing* consists of semicircular arches which interlace and overlap, especially in Romanesque blind arcading (*see* ARCADING); the *Tudor arch* is an extreme form of the late fifteenth-century four-centre arch in which the upper curves are almost flat; and the *straight arch* is a rectangular opening, the lintel of which is composed of radiating *voussoirs*. There are, of course, numerous other variations including the *rampant arch*, in which the springing at either side of the opening is at different levels.

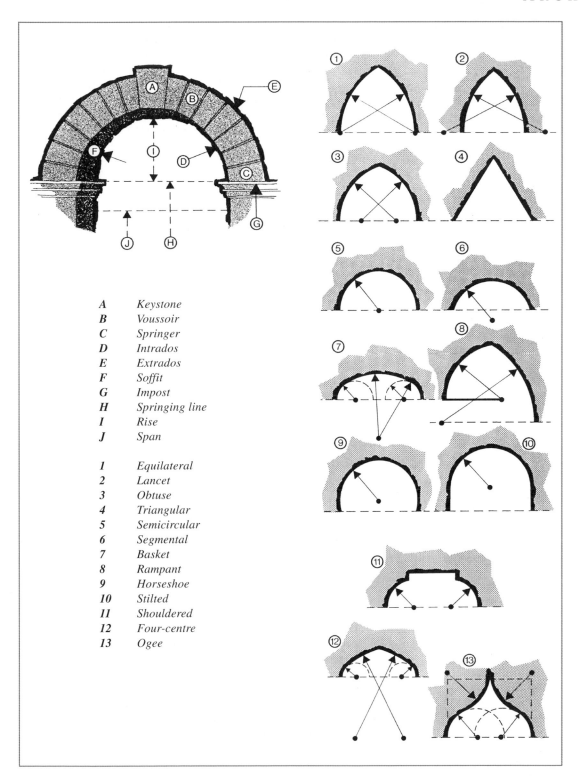

A	Keystone
B	Voussoir
C	Springer
D	Intrados
E	Extrados
F	Soffit
G	Impost
H	Springing line
I	Rise
J	Span

1	Equilateral
2	Lancet
3	Obtuse
4	Triangular
5	Semicircular
6	Segmental
7	Basket
8	Rampant
9	Horseshoe
10	Stilted
11	Shouldered
12	Four-centre
13	Ogee

ARCHAEOLOGY Archaeology, as opposed to antiquarian curiosity, is little more than a century old. Major advances in methodology in the second half of the nineteenth century provided the foundation for a scientific approach to archaeology which has subsequently developed at an increasing rate. Excavation, once practiced in order to unearth artefacts, is now directed at the recovery of new evidence. There is no longer an assumption which equates age and rarity with importance. A Victorian chancel is, therefore, of equal significance to the modern archaeologist as a building's Anglo-Saxon foundations: each demands the same degree of meticulous investigation and recording. The practice of concentrating effort and resources on the earliest evidence, to the exclusion of the recent past, is no longer tenable. It is now acknowledged that it is rare for work of any period, no matter how recent, not to reflect influences from the past – including earlier features that have not survived. Archaeology is now the 'total study of the material past'. To consider the evolution of a site by studying the earliest evidence first invites the adoption of errors and omissions that may become apparent only in the later stages of an investigation. By beginning with the present and working back, by peeling away successive layers of history, and by devoting equal care and resources to each layer, the archaeologist may arrive at a significantly more complete and accurate picture of a site's development. But while stratigraphy reveals evidence of sequence, it should be remembered that an undisturbed series of layers, with the oldest at the bottom and the most recent at the top, is rare. More typical is a sequence which provides evidence of phases of rebuilding and periods of abandonment. Context, a term used by archaeologists to describe the position of a particular find in relation to other material, is of prime importance since it is only when such relationships are understood that progress can be made. And this approach is now applied not only to archaeological excavations, but to all aspects of site investigation – to structures above ground level, to decorative features, furnishings and artefacts, and to documentary and other historical evidence. Furthermore, typology (the study of changes in the forms of tools, pottery, etc.) may link artefacts from one site with those of another, and the sciences of palaeontology (the study of life-forms in the geological past), palaeobotany (the study of vegetation), dendrochronology (growth-ring dating in timber), environmental archaeology (botany, zoology and ecology) and geophysics (notably magnetometry, by which the earth's magnetic field is measured together with any effect that buried structures may have on it, and resistivity, by which the electrical resistance of the soil and any buried features are measured) contribute to the location, dating and interpretation of evidence, as do the techniques of radio-carbon dating, CAD (computer-aided design), photography (aerial, digital, and infra-red), EDM (electronic distance measurer) and, most recently, DNA (genetic fingerprinting).

But while archaeology is not for the amateur, unless he or she is prepared to work under the direction of an expert at an authorized site, *field-walking* is an invaluable method of adding to one's understanding of the past. Since prehistory, domestic debris, particularly the *sherds* of broken pots, has been accumulated in muck-heaps and casually distributed with manure on the ploughed fields. Concentrations of pot fragments often indicate former settlement sites which may be dated from the distinctive qualities of the different types of pottery found. Continuity of occupation, of expansion and decline, may also be deduced from the discovery in one place of fragments dating from several centuries. All this requires study and the advice of experts at local museums, who may be able to identify fragments or provide samples of complete pots for comparison. A variety of early artefacts, such as worked flint, arrow-heads, stone or clay sling-shot and axes of flint or bronze, may also be found, as may the broken shafts of clay pipes and the familiar blue and white glazed pottery of the Victorian era. A field should be searched slowly and methodically, using a grid system, and it goes without saying that the landowner's permission should always be obtained before entering a field, which will invariably contain a growing crop as it is only arable land which is of interest to the field-walker. The most favourable conditions for field-walking are immediately after harrowing, especially if there has been a shower of rain.
See also TREASURE TROVE

ARCHBISHOP *see* CLERGY (CHURCH OF ENGLAND) *and* SIGNATURES, ARCHBISHOPS AND BISHOPS

ARCH BRACE *see* ROOFS

ARCHDEACON *see* CLERGY (CHURCH OF ENGLAND)

ARCHITECTURE *see* ANGLO-SAXON, BAROQUE, CLASSICAL ARCHITECTURE, ELIZABETHAN AND JACOBEAN ARCHITECTURE, GOTHIC ARCHITECTURE, GOTHIC

REVIVAL, PALLADIAN, REGENCY ARCHI-
TECTURE, ROCOCO, ROMANESQUE (Norman),
TUDOR ARCHITECTURE *and* VICTORIAN
ARCHITECTURE

ARCHITRAVE A horizontal beam resting on the
tops of columns. A moulded frame round a window
or door.

ARCHIVES *see* DOCUMENTARY SOURCES

ARDEN COUNTRYSIDE *see* COUNTRYSIDE

ARMARIUM A recessed cupboard for storing
books.

ARMED POND An artificial or modified natural
pond of stelliform shape provided for the watering
of livestock. The 'arms' of such ponds often extend
beyond a field boundary so that animals in adjacent
fields may also drink.

ARMIGEROUS An armiger is one who bears a
coat of arms by lawful authority and is therefore
armigerous.

ARMORY (i) A system of personal identification
by means of hereditary devices placed on, or
associated with, a shield. Armory is generally (and
erroneously) referred to as HERALDRY.
(ii) Also a dictionary of coats of arms listed
alphabetically by surname, notably Sir Bernard
Burke's *General Armory of England, Ireland,
Scotland and Wales*, published in 1842 and reprinted
by Heraldry Today in 1984.

It is quite extraordinary that historians should so
consistently undervalue a subject which was held in
such esteem by the medieval and Tudor
establishment. Coats of arms, badges and other
armorial devices are ubiquitous in the architecture
and decoration of domestic and ecclesiastical
buildings, in illuminated manuscripts and official
documents, and on seals, monuments, tombs and
memorials. Such devices provide not only an insight
into the medieval mind, but also a rich source of
genealogical and historical information.

The origins of armory are obscure. The
conventional theory is that the use of symbols on
shield, surcoat and banner developed during the
twelfth century in response to the need for
identification in battle. However, the use of symbols,
particularly on flags, to denote dynastic and
seignoral allegiance and territorial authority pre-

dates medieval European armory by several
thousand years:

> *And the children of Israel . . . pitched by their
> standards, and so they set forward, every one
> after their families, according to the house of
> their fathers.*
> (The Book of Numbers Ch. 2, v. 34)

There is evidence that flags, bearing charges
common to families or groups linked by blood or
feudal tenure, were in use in eleventh century
Europe, notably in Flanders. But devices on shields
do not seem to have possessed any such significance
at that time and we must look to what is now known
as the Twelfth-Century Renaissance in order to
understand the development of western European
armory which, unlike other systems, is essentially
hereditary and based on the shield. The exuberance
of spirit inspired by this movement expressed itself
in a self-confident delight in adornment and visual
decoration of which the adoption of personal
symbols and colours was an obvious manifestation.
The emergence of the hereditary principle is said to
date from 1127, when Henry I of England invested
his son-in-law, Geoffrey Plantagenet, with a blue
shield charged with gold lions. The same shield later
appears on the tomb (at Salisbury Cathedral) of
Geoffrey's bastard grandson, William Longespée,
Earl of Salisbury (d.1226), and the device would
therefore seem to have acquired an hereditary
significance.

It is clear that from these earliest times the use of
armorial devices was considered to be the exclusive
right of the knightly class. Pride in the possession of
arms, and of the status of *armiger* that such a
privilege implied, was undoubtedly of greater
significance in the development of armory than was
its practical application in the field of battle. The
pageantry of the tournament was the perfect
manifestation of this ethos, for participation was
restricted to those of knightly rank and was
enormously expensive, and it was at the tournament
that the CREST was most in evidence, as a
flamboyant confirmation of the participants' social
superiority. Brilliantly emblazoned CHANTRY
CHAPELS, MEMORIALS, TOMBS and WINDOW
GLASS declared a medieval magnate's
magnificence; his retainers mustered at his
STANDARDS, fought in battle beneath his
GUIDONS, and, by their liveries and household
badges, proclaimed his authority. During the latter
part of the thirteenth century, armorial devices began
to be ordered and displayed to denote marriage

alliances and the acquisition or inheritance of lordships (*see* MARSHALLING). But by the fifteenth century, 'the bearing of coat armor' was so widely abused that HERALDS' VISITATIONS were necessary in order to ascertain precisely who was entitled to use arms. Many claimed the right of ANCIENT USER, while others paid hefty fines to the officers of arms by whom their devices were confirmed. Visitations continued throughout the Tudor period, which witnessed a proliferation of grants of arms and crests to the new establishment: gentlemen who were concerned more with the administration of the state and the development of commerce than with the tournament or battlefield. The ancient nobility, jealous of their status as *armigers*, established the practice of adding SUPPORTERS to their arms. These were generally chimerical creatures, many of which originated in SEALS and, in the medieval period, had been translated into badges and crests.

During the late and post-Tudor period (now known as The Heraldry of the Decadence), armorial practice degenerated. The practical application of armory in the battlefield and tournament was replaced by exaggerated ceremonial, and coats of arms became stylized and extravagant. The Industrial Revolution of the nineteenth century created a new élite, anxious to acquire the trappings of gentility and with a voracious appetite for matters genealogical and armorial. This is reflected in the plethora of heraldic 'manuals' of the period, and a quite extraordinary level of genealogical activity exemplified by the works of the ubiquitous Sir Bernard Burke.

Welsh armory is fundamentally different in that its purpose is to proclaim ancestry. The majority of the Welsh nation consists of a pedigreed population, a distinct caste, descended from the native Welsh aristocracy, warrior farmers and ADVENAE. The ancient social system of the Welsh, in which so many rights and obligations were dependent on membership of a tribe, conditioned them to regard a pedigree as of the utmost importance. In Wales, there was no such person as an 'armigerous gentleman', as there was in England, for a man was 'gentle' by virtue of his genealogy and 'gentility followed the blood'. Although the Welsh had been acquainted with medieval armory, it was not until the early Tudor period that they produced a system. Those Welshmen who already bore arms were assumed to have inherited them from tribal ancestors, while new arms were attributed to the ancestors of other, non-armigerous families. For example, the numerous descendants of Hywel Dda,

who lived in the tenth century, of Cadwaladr, who lived in the seventh, of Cunedda, who lived in the fifth and of Beli Mawr, who probably never lived at all, all received retrospective coats of arms which they hurriedly registered with the English heralds of the new Tudor dynasty.

Civic armory dates from the late twelfth century when officials of boroughs and other towns made use of seals carrying devices. Initially, these were rarely depicted on shields and were simply religious or other emblems of local significance, or seignoral devices indicative of feudal allegiance or benefaction, contained within an inscribed border. With the gradual development of corporate authority in the Middle Ages came a corresponding desire to assert corporate identity in a form which could be equated with that of the feudal magnate, and by the fourteenth century many towns, guilds and corporations had adopted the devices of their seals as coats of arms, simply by depicting them in colour on a shield, and sometimes rearranging charges to conform with armorial conventions. In the sixteenth and seventeenth centuries, several corporations took advantage of the heralds' visitations to record their previously unauthorized arms. Others retained their original emblems, many of which are still used today.

See also ATTRIBUTED ARMS, AUGMENTATION OF HONOUR, BLAZON, CADENCY, FUNERAL HERALDRY, HATCHMENTS, INN-SIGNS, ROLLS OF ARMS, ROYAL ARMS IN CHURCHES *and* TINCTURES

For the addresses of The Heraldry Society of Ireland; The Heraldry Society, London; The Heraldry Society of Scotland; The Chief Herald of Ireland's Office, Dublin; The College of Arms, London; The Court of Lord Lyon, Edinburgh *and* The Harleian Society *see* APPENDIX I

ARROW-HEAD BASTION *see* TUDOR COASTAL FORTS

ARROW SLITS (*also* **ARROW LOOPS**) Medieval castles were initially defended by means of the longbow and crossbow, each of which had different characteristics and required different types of loop. Arrows were released from the standing position through arrow loops in the towers and curtain walls, the massive thickness of which enabled the castle builders to provide both comparative safety for the defending archer and a wide range of view. This was achieved by constructing an embrasure on the inside of the wall which narrowed to a vertical 'slit' in the exterior masonry. Sometimes (as at Caernarfon Castle, Gwynedd) multiple embrasures vented into the same arrow loop. Because of its weight, a crossbow was more effective when held in the kneeling position, and arrow loops were often modified by the provision of a small circular opening at the foot of the slit. Later loops were sometimes cruciform in shape, each limb having a circular hole through which the bolts were released.

See also GUNPORTS

ARTHURIAN BRITAIN When the legions of Rome withdrew from Britain at the beginning of the fifth century they left a Romanized, nominally Christian society of Celtic people to defend themselves against the Irish from the west and the Picts and Scots from the north. Vortigern, a dominant fifth-century British ruler, responded by inviting mercenaries – Angles, Saxons and Jutes – to assist in the defence his kingdom, a practice which had been employed successfully by the Romans but which collapsed when Vortigern's resources were stretched to the limit and he could no longer pay his troops. The ensuing wave of carnage and devastation encouraged further Saxon invasion and resulted in the disintegration of Britain into a number of minor kingdoms. Gildas, writing in the sixth century, credits one Ambrosius Aurelianus, a Romano-British *imperator*, with a series of victories over the Saxons and the re-unification of the south and west, and in contemporary chronicles a man called Artos, or Arthur, also begins to emerge as a significant soldier and leader – uniting the squabbling, petty kings of Britain against the common enemy.

Artos was the Celtic form of the Roman *Artorius* and suggests that Arthur was a noble Celt whose family had grown to prominence during the Roman occupation. Until the fifth century there is no recorded instance of the name, yet in the hundred years following his supposed death it became extraordinarily popular: indicative of the breadth of Arthur's fame.

The first reference to Arthur's military prowess is found in an elegy called the *Gododin*, written by a Welsh bard, Aneurin, in *c.* 600 AD. Nennius, a monk at Bangor writing at the end of the eighth century, describes Arthur as the *dux bellorum* and enumerates twelve of his battles in the *Historia Britonum*. The *Annales Cambriae*, the ancient annals of Wales, dating from the second half of the tenth century, tell of the 'Battle of Badon' in 518, in which Arthur carried the cross of Christ on his shoulders, and the 'Battle of Camlann' in 539, 'in which Arthur and Medraut fell . . .'. There are few references to Arthur

in contemporary ecclesiastical records: the Celtic monks were generally antagonistic towards him, for his men are known to have plundered monasteries in their efforts to maintain supplies.

The rapidity with which Arthur and his guerrillas moved about the country suggests that they were organized in light cavalry units and enjoyed a mobility that could not be matched by the Saxons who rarely fought on horseback. Here, perhaps, is the foundation of the chivalric, knightly élite that flourished in Europe through the triumphs of the Norman and Flemish cavalry in the eleventh century, was manifest in the great orders of chivalry and the ceremonial tournaments of the high Middle Ages, and remains today in the glamour and tradition of the mounted regiments.

Arthur and several other characters may also be traced to figures in ancient Celtic mythology, but it was the 'Matter of Britain', the legend cycle that evolved from Geoffrey of Monmouth's highly imaginative twelfth-century chronical *Historia Regium Britanniae* (c. 1138), through Robert Wace's *Geste des Bretons* (c. 1154) and the early medieval European verse and prose romances (notably those of Chrétien de Troyes), that succeeded in raising an obscure and shadowy *chieftain* to the patriot-king of the Arthurian legends, familiar in such works as the anonymous *Sir Gawain and the Green Knight* (1360–70) and Malory's *Morte d'Arthur* (1469).

The ideals of the Fellowship of the Round Table (first introduced by Wace) were precisely those of the medieval chivalric code and the Quest for the Holy Grail by Galahad, the perfect knight, its highest achievement. Although destroyed by infidelity, disloyalty and treachery, the Fellowship became the object of an international cult and the model for the medieval orders of chivalry.

The Plantagenets clearly recognized the political advantages of association with such an illustrious British 'king'. 'Round Tables', festive pageants and tournaments were held throughout the reigns of Edward I and his successors. Edward III had a circular house built at Windsor Castle to accommodate a round table and, at the conclusion of a great tournament held there in 1344, he took a solemn oath that in time he would follow in the footsteps of King Arthur and create a round table for his knights. In 1348 the Order of the Garter was founded, comprising twenty-six knights companion, including the sovereign and his eldest son. The Welsh Henry Tudor, who became Henry VII in 1485, claimed he had restored the true 'British' royal line by his descent from Arthur through the Welsh princes. The Celtic legend, suppressed by the

Plantagenets, that Arthur had not died but 'sleeps on until the day shall come for that Golden Age to be restored' was used as justification for his usurpation – he was to be the instrument by which the Tudor dynasty was to create a new Golden Age. Henry ordained that his son (also Arthur) should be born at Winchester, the ancient capital of Wessex, where the legendary Round Table hung in the Great Hall of the castle as it does today. In Henry VIII's reign, the table was repaired in 1516–17 and re-painted in anticipation of the visit of the Holy Roman Emperor, Charles V in 1522. The table, which is of oak and measures 5.5 metres in diameter (18 feet), was painted in twenty-four segments, alternatively white and green (the Tudor livery colours), radiating from a central Tudor Rose, the figure of the sovereign himself occupying a further two. Each segment represents one *seige* or place for each of the twenty-six Garter knights. According to the chronicler John Hardynge the table was already in position on the wall of the Great Hall in *c.* 1463. Radio-carbon dating carried out in 1976 indicated that the felling date of the youngest tree used in its construction was *c.* 1255. A further test using tree-ring dating suggested that the table was made some time between 1250 and 1280 during the reigns of Henry III and Edward I.

There are numerous topographical references to Arthurian legend throughout Britain, particularly in evidence in the names of unusual physical features and megaliths, to which our ancestors ascribed mystical properties, such as Arthur's Chair, Arthur's Table, Arthur's Kitchen and Arthur's Finger. Many caves in Wales, Cumbria and Northumberland are said to contain the sleeping Arthur and his knights; two islets of the Scilly Isles are called Great and Little Arthur; and in Scotland are Arthur's Seat at Edinburgh and Ben Arthur in the Highlands. Then there is the Arthurian landscape on which has been superimposed that of the archaeologist. Of the twelve battles listed by Nennius few have been identified, though the site of Mount Badon, the decisive battle of *c.* 518 AD that was to delay the Saxon advance for a quarter of a century, is thought to have been Liddington Castle near Swindon in Wiltshire or Badbury Rings near Wimborne in Dorset. Most legends associate Arthur with the West Country, to which the Celt, Artos, is said to have retired. Tintagel, now a Cornish tourist village, is reputed to be the place of Arthur's birth, and though the first Norman castle on the site dates from 1141 there is also evidence of an earlier fifth-century fortification. Geoffrey of Monmouth located Arthur's Camelot at Caerleon-on-Usk in Newport,

the Roman legionary fortress of *Isca*; however, Cadbury Castle on the Somerset–Dorset border near Sherborne is a sixth-century stronghold of considerable military and administrative significance and, while it was never the romantic, many-towered Camelot of legend, it was undoubtedly the headquarters of an important *dux bellorum* and has no archaeological equivalent in Britain. Nineteen kilometres (12 miles) to the north of Cadbury, at Glastonbury – the *Isle of Avalon* – in the Somerset Levels, is the abbey where in 1190 the monks claim to have exhumed a hollow log coffin containing the bones of Arthur and his queen, Guinevere. It is said that Arthur was buried here in the greatest secrecy so that the Saxons should not be encouraged by his death, and mystery has surrounded the place ever since. Recent research has shown that although there was once a deep grave of the correct period and type at the location indicated by the monks, the 'discovery' was probably a hoax. It is certainly true that the discovery greatly enhanced the Abbey's prestige and the increased income from pilgrims enabled the monks to finance the rebuilding of the church and domestic buildings which had been destroyed by fire in 1184. Whatever the truth of the matter, the ground on which the present ruins stand is one of the most sacred, historic and mysterious sites in Britain.

ARTIFICIAL RUINS Most artificial ruins, façades and gateways date from the eighteenth century when they were constructed as Gothic '*eye-catchers*': focal points in landscaped parklands. These ornamental ruins, with their chivalric overtones, correspond to the Gothic Revival of domestic architecture and the Romantic Movement in literature, in which 'the classical, intellectual attitude gave way to . . . claims of passion and emotion' (Sir Paul Harvey). Being integral to the geometry of a planned landscape, they should not be regarded as FOLLIES. 'When a wide heath, a dreary moor, or a continued plain is in prospect, objects which catch the eye supply the want of variety; none are so effectual for this purpose as buildings. The Mind must not be allowed to hesitate; it must be hurried away from examining into the reality by the exactness and the force of the resemblance' (*Observations on Modern Gardening*, Whately, 1770). The illusion was often enhanced by 'an intermixture of a vigorous vegetation' which 'intimates a settled despair of their restoration' (*ibid.*) and served as a reminder of man's mortality and the transience even of his most noble creations. *See also* OBELISKS *and* TEMPLES

ASH A common tree especially in limestone and chalk country. Like the OAK it attracts lightning and for this reason the ash was anciently endowed with magical and medicinal properties of great power. Its timber is strong and smooth and unlikely to splinter and was ideally suited to handles of tools and weapons needing tensile strength. Naturally curved ash wood was reserved for special purposes and when coppiced it was used for stakes, poles, cart shafts, chairs and hoops.

ASHLAR Masonry constructed of square-hewn freestone. Also thin slabs of dressed stone used for facing walls over RUBBLE. Ashlar is a characteristic of many sophisticated buildings, those of the Cotswolds from the sixteenth century, for example.

ASP A winged, two-legged snake, often with its tail thrust into its ear, may be found in the fabric of churches where it symbolizes disbelief (*see* Psalm 58).

ASSART An area of WOODLAND which has been cleared, enclosed and cultivated. The term is derived from the French *essarter*, meaning 'to clear', and is to be found in early forest laws where payment of a fine was required, together with the consent of the Crown, before woodland could be cleared and cultivated. Assart names include *reading*, *ridding*, *royd*, *sarch*, *stubbing*, *stubbs*.
See also NEWLAND

ASSIZE Until 1972, a periodical county session for the administration of civil and criminal justice (*see* QUARTER SESSIONS). Assize courts were established in the early thirteenth century, their initial function being to weld together different local customs to form a consistent body of LAW. Two or more judges from the High Court in London travelled on a circuit from one major town to the next, visiting each three times a year. There were seven circuits and the system made it possible for local people to have their cases determined locally rather than in London. In more recent times, the assize courts heard criminal cases referred to them from magistrates' courts and civil cases from county courts. Six calendars of assize records have been published (1975) by the Public Record Office.

ASSIZE OF ARMS *see* LAW AND ORDER

ASSIZE OF MORT D'ANCESTOR Established in 1176, a court concerned with determining a plaintiff's claim to an inheritance. An aggrieved claimant could obtain a writ requiring a sheriff to empanel a local jury, the members of which would be familiar with the circumstances of the case. Most common were instances of manorial lords who repossessed property following a tenant's death. The procedure was abolished in 1833.

ASSIZE OF NOVEL DISSEISIN ('recent dispossession') A procedure established in 1166 to decide whether a tenant had been wrongly removed from his holding. An aggrieved tenant could obtain a writ requiring a sheriff to empanel a jury to determine his case. Although the procedure was originally intended to effect a speedy resolution of such disputes, it came to be abused as a means of establishing a title through the filing of a fictional claim. It was abolished in 1833.

ASYLUMS 'There they stand: isolated, majestic, imperious, brooded over by the gigantic water-tower and chimney combined, rising, unmistakable and daunting, out of the countryside: the asylums which our forefathers built with such immense solidity' (Enoch Powell, Minister of Health, 1961).

Enoch Powell's speech signified his government's acceptance of the widely held view that the current framework of provision for the mentally ill was no longer appropriate. From that time, psychiatric care has aimed at integration of patients within the community and the systematic replacement of mental hospitals by small-scale clinics and rehabilitation units.

From 1815, parish overseers were required to provide lists of pauper lunatics for presentation at QUARTER SESSIONS by Clerks of the Peace, and from 1832 private asylums were licensed and inspected by Justices of the Peace. The Victorian era witnessed the unprecedented provision of civic amenities and institutions: schools, libraries, workers' institutes, hospitals, prisons, workhouses for the destitute and asylums for the insane. For over a century the great Gothic Revival water-towers of the Victorian lunatic asylums symbolized the stigma of institutionalized isolation. Even their names became synonymous with madness: on the Isle of Wight, where the Whitecroft asylum's tower was disguised as a clock, those who had been treated were described as having been 'under the clock'. The water-towers were built to provide a substantial head of water in the event of a fire – a constant hazard in such volatile communities. A typical asylum of the late Victorian period housed 3,000 inmates: schizophrenics, anorexics, the deaf and dumb, depressives, women suffering from birth traumas and workers with lead poisoning, Down's Syndrome children, the syphilitic, the senile and the inadequate. Unlike the Victorian penal institutions, from which the prisoners were not permitted to view the outside world, asylums were located on high ground at the edge of towns where 'the air is drier . . .' for 'low spirits are synonymous with moisture, the nerves become flaccid and unbraced, like stringed instruments out of tune. Moist air carries off the electricity from the body, dry air does not . . .' (*Westminster Review*, 1847). The inmates of asylums often enjoyed extensive views as they shuffled in endless circles in the exercise yards or 'airing courts', supervised by an inadequate and often harassed staff. In some instances, asylums were built near railway lines or main roads so that the view was animated and provided entertainment, and therefore a speedier recovery, for the souls within. Many sites exceeded 80 acres and their walls contained small towns, often with their own farms and orchards. The Middlesex County Pauper Asylum, better known as Colney Hatch and later euphemistically called the Friern Barnet Hospital, was designed by Samuel Whitfield Daukes to resemble an Italian monastery. Built in 1849, it was Europe's largest institution for the mentally ill and had its own cemetery, gasworks, bakery, brewery, farm, shoemaker's and upholsterer's shops, a chapel (where men and women were strictly segregated), and what is reputed to have been the longest corridor in Europe. The former Essex County Pauper Lunatic Asylum (now Warley Hospital near Brentford) was described as 'medieval, of the Tudor period, cheerful' when it opened in 1853. Constructed in 87 acres of the former Brentwood Hall estate, it has gardens which were designed in a formal mock-Jacobean style and included two 'pepper-pot' buildings, each with a conical stone roof, which were originally latrines for male and female inmates. There is also a former brew-house where, in 1863, a patient fell into a brewery copper and was certified as having 'died of lock-jaw'! Many asylum buildings are of considerable architectural merit and include designs by Sir Gilbert Scott, Alfred Waterhouse and W.H. Crossland. Crossland's Royal Holloway Sanatorium at Virginia Water in Surrey (built 1884) contains magnificent frescoed interiors and once boasted its own cricket ground. In the 1960s few recognized the potential of such buildings and many were demolished. Today, those that remain are revered for their architectural magnificence and provide a focus for conservationist and developer alike.

See also SOCIAL WELFARE

ATTAINDER Made after a judgement of death or outlawry on a capital charge, a declaration of attainder by act of parliament resulted in the absolute forfeiture of all civil rights and privileges. Acts of attainder were frequently applied during the Middle Ages in association with charges of treason, when a declaration of attainder implied also a 'corruption of the blood'. In these cases, goods, lands, titles and armorial bearings of an attainted person could not be inherited by his heirs until the attainder had been revoked, also by act of parliament. Lands, and any rights in them, reverted to a superior lord subject to the Crown's rights of forfeiture. During the Wars of the Roses, acts of attainder were regularly used by one side to liquidate the other. But it is interesting to note that during the period 1453 to 1504, of 397 attainders, no fewer than 256 were reversed. Attainder was abolished as recently as 1870.

ATTRIBUTED ARMS The heralds of the medieval and post-medieval periods determined that, because all persons of consequence in their society were ARMIGEROUS, so too were the characters of their religion and the heroes of legend and history. Armorial bearings were therefore devised and attributed not only to the saints and martyrs, the apostles and disciples and the Old Testament prophets and kings, but also to concepts and abstractions. Banners of the Trinity, Christ's Passion and the Blessed Virgin Mary accompanied the medieval army into battle and many a warrior emblazoned the *inside* of his shield with religious emblems. To the Archangel Michael was attributed a red cross on a silver field and, not to be outdone, Satan himself bore arms (as a former seraph he was assumed to be armigerous) and to him was attributed a red shield charged with a gold *fess* (horizontal band) between three frogs, a reference from the Book of Revelation. The post-medieval heralds were particularly systematic, beginning with Adam (a plain red shield) and Eve (plain silver). To King David they attributed a gold harp on blue and to Joseph, not a multi-coloured coat as one might expect, but one of black and white chequers. Devices from the attributed arms of historical and legendary characters, and of ancient kingdoms, are much in evidence in the heraldry of civic and corporate bodies: the three *seaxes* (notched swords) of the kingdoms of the East and Middle Saxons and the gold *martlets* (swallows) of the South Saxons, for example. Identification of attributed arms can be great sport – but beware! Many instances are known of medieval tombs on which attributed arms are emblazoned, often those of a patron saint or a religious concept, together with inherited quarterings.

AUGMENTATION OF HONOUR Augmentations are 'additions' to coats of arms, usually awarded in recognition of signal service to the crown. They are of two kinds: the first, now rare, being awarded 'by mere grace'; the second being won by merit. In the first category are augmentations such as those granted by Richard II to his kinsmen Surrey, Exeter and Norfolk, who were permitted to add the attributed arms of Edward the Confessor to their own. In the second category there are many instances of augmentations granted as rewards for acts of valour or outstanding service. Such augmentations seem to have existed since the earliest days of ARMORY, and may appear to 'break the rules' in order to draw attention to the distinction.

AUGUSTINIANS (*also* **AUSTIN** *or* **REGULAR CANONS**) Communities of clerics who, from the mid-eleventh century in Italy and France, adopted the Rule of St Augustine of Hippo (AD 354–430) which required strict personal poverty, celibacy and obedience. Their ethos was formally approved at Lateran synods in 1059 and 1063, and by the early twelfth century members of these communities, which had spread throughout western Europe, came to be known as *Regular Canons*. The term *Austin* is an early English form of Augustine. Independent Augustinian congregations include the Premonstratensians or 'White Canons', who adopted a particularly austere way of life.

AUMBRY *or* **AMBRY** A secure place in which sacred items and relics were stored. Usually a rectangular recess in a wall near the altar, and sometimes retaining the original oak door.
See also PISCINA

AUSTIN *see* AUGUSTINIANS *and* FRIARS

AVENUES From the French verb *avenir*, meaning 'to approach' or 'to arrive', formal avenues of trees became fashionable in the early seventeenth century when they were intended to emphasize the dignity of approach to the imposing residences of the new gentility. Favourite species were the quick-growing Elm and Lime, the latter imported from the Low Countries. Sycamore and Beech were also popular, especially in the West Country, as were avenues of Horse Chestnut. The eighteenth century witnessed the planting of avenues by several civic authorities:

the town council of Dorchester in Dorset, for example, reduced the Roman walls which surround the town on three sides, and created tree-lined promenades, known as the Walks. Such avenues of Chestnuts, Elms, Sycamores and Limes, together with the ubiquitous Plane tree, were to dominate the new public parks of the Victorian age, the 'model villages' of the late nineteenth century, such as Bournville in the West Midlands, and the 'Garden Cities' of the early twentieth century. One of the finest avenues, planted in 1835 at Kingston Lacey in Dorset, has 365 beaches on either side over a distance of 3.5 km (2.2 miles).

AVON Derived from the British *abona*, the word means simply 'river'. The modern Welsh equivalent is the prefix *afon*.

B

BACCHUS *see* ROMAN VILLAS

BACK LANE In villages and small towns, a peripheral lane running parallel to the main street and forming the termination of TOFTS (*see* OUTGANG).

BADGERS *see* PACK-HORSE ROADS

BAILEY *see* CASTLES (MEDIEVAL)

BAILIFF (i) A court official appointed to execute writs and to distrain goods.
(ii) An estate manager, subordinate to a STEWARD (especially in the context of a manorial estate).

BALE TOMBS *see* TABLE TOMBS

BALK 'Sidebalks' were narrow, unploughed strips used for access or as boundaries between cultivated strips in an OPEN FIELD. 'Waybalks' (or HEAD-LANDS) were those which ran at right angles to the ploughed strips. Broader 'common balks' or 'town balks' sometimes served as grass roads. The term is occasionally found as an element in FIELD NAMES.

BALLADS *see* MINSTRELS

BALLISTA *see* SIEGES

BALLY- From the Gaelic *baile*, meaning a hamlet or cluster of dwellings, Bally- is a common place-name element in Ireland and Scotland, the English equivalent being *-ton*, the Welsh *Tref-* and the Cornish *Tre-*.

BALUSTER *see* BALUSTRADE *and* STAIR-CASES

BALUSTRADE A series of short pillars or posts (*balusters*) supporting a handrail and standing on a base (*string*) as a parapet or in staircase construction (*see* STAIRCASES).

BANISTER *see* STAIRCASES

BANNERET The rank of nobility between knight bachelor and baron. Originally a chief feudal tenant (or lesser baron) as distinct from the knight bachelor. In the Middle Ages a knight banneret was permitted to lead troops in battle under his own banneret or small banner.

BAPTIST The Baptists are one of the largest Protestant bodies, tracing their origin from John Smythe (1554–1612), a SEPARATIST exile in Amsterdam who, in 1609, reinstituted the 'Baptism of conscious [adult] believers' and thereby reaffirmed his belief in the individual's responsibility to work for the salvation of his soul. The first Baptist church in England (in Newgate Street, London) consisted of the members of Smythe's church who returned in 1612 under the leadership of Thomas Helwys (1550–1616). From this derived a number of other churches, known as General Baptists, and in 1633 a group of Calvinistic London Separatists established the Particular Baptist churches, whose members believed in predestination and individual redemption. During the seventeenth century, many Baptists were associated with radical spiritual and political movements and were persecuted until the Toleration Act of 1698. With the formation of the New Connexion in 1770, the General Baptists divided, the Old Connexion becoming the *Unitarians*. In 1813 the Baptist Union encouraged greater co-operation among the various branches, and in 1891 the Particular Baptists and the New Connexion formed the Baptist Union of Great Britain and Ireland. Old Baptist registers are kept at the Public Record Office, and most Baptist records are retained at the Baptist Union Library, together with those of the Baptist Historical Society (*see* APPENDIX I).

BARBICAN A fortified outwork of a medieval walled town or CASTLE, usually separated from the gatehouse by means of a drawbridge or defensive causeway traversing a moat (as at Bodiam Castle in Sussex). Usually dating from the thirteenth and fourteenth centuries, a barbican was designed to keep an enemy at his distance or, by dictating his approach, to expose him to attack from archers within the castle walls. The barbican was both a preliminary 'check-point' (credentials would also be inspected at the gatehouse) and, more importantly, a first line of defence before the gatehouse was reached. Consequently, few barbicans have survived intact. One of the most impressive exceptions is that at Lewes Castle in Sussex. Built on three storeys, it guards the road bridge into the castle and is heavily defended with two portcullises and machicolations between twin towers. In most instances, however, little remains to suggest the massive strength of these structures. The fourteenth-century barbican at Goodrich Castle in Herefordshire retains only the lower section of wall; however, its semi-circular (or 'half-moon') ground plan and spur-moat illustrate clearly how an attacker would have been compelled to capture and pass over two drawbridges, set at right angles to each other above steep-sided dry moats, in addition to negotiating a confined gates passage containing a series of gates, portcullises and lateral arrow slits, before reaching the gatehouse. The barbican drawbridge pit is set within the outer part of the gates passage and a small porter's lodge commands a view of the gate on the south side by means of a narrow, angled slit in the outer wall. From the barbican the gatehouse is reached by a sloping causeway over the moat, with a bridge of two spans separated by a deep drawbridge pit. The barbican at Newcastle-upon-Tyne, known as the Black Gate, was constructed by Henry III in 1247. It consists of two D-shaped towers set back to back on each side of an entrance passage defended by a drawbridge over an outer ditch, a portcullis, folding gates and a murder hole in the vault. Set at right angles to the gatehouse, its position enabled archers to cover the entire length of the moat and, as at Goodrich, provided a right-angled passage to impede assailants should they succeed in taking the barbican gate.

BARGE-BOARDS Possibly originating in the medieval *bargus*, meaning 'gallows', a barge-board is hung from the roof projection (the 'barge') on the gable end of a building in order to protect the otherwise exposed ends of roof timbers. Medieval and Tudor barge-boards were often elaborately carved, though few originals remain, and similar ornamentation became a feature of the Gothic Revival of the mid-eighteenth and nineteenth centuries.

BARK HOUSE A building for storing oak bark, which was one constituent of a preservative with which newly manufactured sailcloth and netting were impregnated. The attractive and characteristic tan colour of the materials was attributable to the use of bark in this process.

BARMKIN *see* PELE TOWER

BARMOTE COURT Courts in the Peak District mining areas of Derbyshire where the Crown has mineral rights.

BARNS A word derived from the Old English *bereærn*, meaning 'barley house', for barley was the chief crop of the Anglo-Saxon farmer. Barns must once have existed in their thousands: constructed in a variety of sizes, styles and materials and dating through prehistoric and historic times to the present day. Barns are often difficult to date and may have other buildings added to them. Though intended primarily to store crops, they were used for a multiplicity of purposes and enabled farmhands to carry out many essential tasks under cover in inclement weather. They were used as *shippens* (for milking), for sheltering calves or for protecting ewes at lambing time. Others were provided with first-floor hay lofts and pigeon lofts, constructed within the roof gable, and some were even provided with separate domestic quarters, complete with a hearth and chimney, as in the late medieval barn at Hales Hall, Hales, Norfolk. Not every barn was built for that purpose: many were formed by adapting groups of earlier buildings to provide a single enclosed

The great fourteenth-century tithe barn at Bradford-on-Avon in Wiltshire. Once a granary for Shaftesbury Abbey, it measures 51 metres by 9 metres (167 × 30 feet).

space. Following the DISSOLUTION, many monastic buildings were converted to agrarian use, such as the 'priory barn' at Latton, Essex, which was created out of the ruins of the early fourteenth-century crossing of the priory church, abandoned in 1534. There was a remarkable continuity, both in the construction of the wood framed and thatched barn (reminiscent of the Anglo-Saxon wooden hall), and in its use for the storage of grain, hay, straw, etc., through to the nineteenth century. In the south and east of England, most medieval barns were of timber construction but elsewhere those that have survived are, for the most part, built of stone beneath a timber-framed roof with thatch or stone tiling and with small windows for ventilation. The most impressive barns are those which were constructed as a means of protecting substantial long-term investments. They were either abbey barns, in which the produce of a monastery was stored, or *tithe barns*, which were built to store the community's tithes – a form of tax set at one-tenth of a man's income and paid to the incumbent of the parish. (This was not as straightforward as may first appear – *see* TITHES.) The larger barns were in plan similar to churches: containing a lofty 'nave', with massive lateral tie beams in the roof and heavily buttressed walls, aisles and a pair (or pairs) of *midstrays* ('transepts') in the gable ends of which were tall double doors giving access for wagons to the threshing floor. This was usually constructed of closely fitted 2 inch planks of oak or elm, and the draught between the pairs of doors served to reduce the dust during threshing and to separate the heavier grain from the chaff. The fourteenth-century tithe barn at Bradford-on-Avon in Wiltshire has two pairs of double doors and the CRUCK FRAME abbey barn at Glastonbury in Somerset forms the nucleus of the Rural Life Centre. There are two notable fourteenth-century tithe barns in Oxfordshire, at Church Enstone and Swalcliffe, and examples from the fifteenth century may be seen at Abbotsbury in Dorset and Ashleworth in Gloucestershire. Long open-sided barns, often with magnificent thatched roofs and supported on STADDLE STONES, originated in the sixteenth century and were popular throughout southern England during the eighteenth century when they were used for storing straw after threshing. The Gothic Revival of the late eighteenth and nineteenth centuries inspired the construction of a number of 'tithe barns', the best known of which is Augustus Pugin's remarkable 'medieval' barn at Milford in Surrey. Recently, many barns have been converted to domestic use – often with a conspicuous absence of architectural or historical sensitivity.

BARON The word itself is of uncertain origin: it was introduced into England following the Anglo-Norman Conquest of 1066 to identify the 'man' (vassal) of a great lord, or of the Conqueror himself, though prior to the Conquest a *barony* was simply a chief's domain. In Ireland, a *barony* was a medieval division of a county, corresponding to the English 'hundred'. Following the Conquest, tenants-in-chief of the king below the rank of earl were often referred to as barons. From the thirteenth century the title appears to have been reserved for those magnates summoned by writ to Parliament: greater barons being those who were summoned by direct writ to the King's Council and lesser barons summoned through the county sheriffs. The style itself was introduced by Richard II in 1387. It is now the fifth and lowest rank of the British peerage and the Life Peerage Act of 1958 enabled the Crown to create non-hereditary peerages with the rank and style of baron.

BARONAGE OF SCOTLAND A feudal institution entirely different from the English baronage. The Scottish equivalent of an English baron is a Lord in Parliament. A Scottish baron is similar to an English lord of the manor with additional nobiliary and armorial rights.

BARON COURT (SCOTLAND) In Scotland, the holder of a feudal barony is entitled to hold a Baron Court, similar in authority to that of an English lord of the manor. The president of such a court is a Baron-Baillie and the chief officer a Baron-Serjeant.

BARONET An hereditary rank of the British peerage created by James I in 1611 with the objective of raising money to support his troops in Ulster. The first recipients paid £1,095 for the style Sir and Lady (or Dame) and precedence above knights. In 1625 a baronetage of Scotland was established to provide funds for the colonization of Nova Scotia. Both creations lasted until 1707, when they were replaced by the baronetage of Great Britain which lasted until 1800. In 1619 the baronetage of Ireland was created. On 1 January 1801 both the baronetage of Great Britain and that of Ireland were replaced by the baronetage of the United Kingdom which continues to the present time.

Baronets of England, Ireland, Great Britain and the United Kingdom have as their badge 'the bloody hand of Ulster' – a red hand on a white shield which is borne as an augmentation in their arms. By a grant of Charles I, Baronets of Scotland were assigned a badge comprising the shield of arms of Nova Scotia (on a silver field a blue *saltire* charged at the centre with a shield of the royal arms of Scotland) within a blue circlet and this is depicted, suspended from a tawny coloured ribbon, beneath the shield in the arms of a Scottish baronet.

BAROQUE A classical form of architecture originating in Italy and prevalent in southern Europe in the seventeenth and eighteenth centuries. Originally, the term was applied in a derogatory sense to the often bizarre and bulbous shapes that characterize this singularly vigorous and dynamic style of architecture. It was paralleled by a departure in art, music and literature from the humanism of the Renaissance and a return to the spiritual values of the Roman Church – 'evidence of man's need for belief in something greater than himself' (Yarwood). In Britain, the essentially CLASSICAL ARCHITECTURE of the period succumbed to Baroque influences for a relatively brief period between *c.* 1690 and 1730 before turning to the greater order and discipline of Palladianism. Baroque influences are evident in the later work of Christopher Wren (1632–1723) and in that of his pupil and friend Nicholas Hawksmoor (1661–1736), Sir John Vanbrugh (1664–1726) and Thomas Archer (1668–1743). In the domes and colonnades of Greenwich and, to a lesser extent, in the west towers of St Paul's Cathedral, Wren adopted a restrained Baroque, unlike the massive grandeur and exuberance of Vanbrugh's Blenheim in Oxfordshire and Castle Howard, North Yorkshire (in both of which he was assisted by Hawksmoor), and Hawksmoor's own uncompromising Christ Church, Spitalfields.

BAROUCHE A late eighteenth-century coachman-driven vehicle which originated in France but was popular in Britain. It could be drawn by two or four horses, though six were sometimes used on formal occasions. A semi-open carriage, its hood could be raised from the rear half only, a windscreen immediately behind the box providing protection for the two passengers.

BARREL VAULT *see* VAULTING

BARROWS Earth or stone mounds covering ancient burial sites, or constructed as monuments to the dead, are a familiar sight throughout Britain, particularly in the upland regions of the southern and western counties and in Wales and Scotland, where they are known as cairns. Numerous though they are,

the ravages of the weather and the plough and centuries of looting, for both archaeological 'treasures' and building materials, have taken their toll and the barrows that remain represent but a small proportion of the accumulated burial places of 5,000 years: from the Neolithic barrows of the late fifth and fourth millenniums BC to the last true barrows of *c.* AD 700. Aerial photography can reveal the sites of former barrows, and clues may be obtained through place-name elements. From the Old English *beorg* (meaning 'hillock' or 'mound', especially a grave mound) derive such elements as -bury, -borough, and -bergh. *Hlaw*, usually -law or -low, can also mean 'burial mound' when the first element of the name is a personal one, as in Winterslow. The Norse *haugre* (-howe) and the Welsh *bryn* or *carn* imply barrow names. On the Ordnance Survey maps most barrows are marked simply as *tumulus* – a description which belies the variety of constructional techniques and burial practices adopted by peoples of different periods and locations.

Long Barrows
The first barrows of *c.* 3000–2000 BC were constructed by immigrants, from what is now northern France, on the chalk uplands of southern and north-eastern England. These were simply elongated earthen mounds piled over the bodies or accumulated bones of the dead. Numerous examples on the Dorset downs include barrows at Ridgeway, Pimperne, Kingston Russell and along the Dorset *cursus*, an extraordinary 9.5 km (6 mile) length of twin banks and ditches on the southern edge of Cranborne Chase. Other immigrants, from western France, settled along the sea routes from Cornwall to Scotland, from Ireland to Orkney, and along the estuary of the River Severn and introduced a variety of CHAMBER TOMBS, parabolic or elliptical, which were reopened whenever a family interment was required. These *long* barrows (or, more correctly, *long cairns*) were typically 30 to 90 metres long (100 to 300 feet), 9 to 30 metres wide (30 to 100 feet) and 3 to 6 metres in height (10 to 20 feet), and contained chambers and passages, with walls and roofs constructed of massive stones or sometimes of drystone walling, and with provision for access from the exterior. Within these mortuary enclosures (which are usually located at the broad end of the barrow) were interred the remains of tribal chiefs, their families and other selected members of the community, usually six or eight persons together and between four and twenty-six in total, most of whom were male. There is evidence to

21

suggest that many barrows were remodelled or extended and this, together with the fact that some remained in use until *c.* 2000 BC or later, emphasises both their importance as burial (and, possibly, cult) centres and also the stability of the communities with which they were associated. It is now recognized that many DOLMENS are simply megalithic burial chambers of this type from which the mound of earth has been removed. One of the most important concentrations of Neolithic monuments in Britain is the Cotswold group of eighty-five barrows, of which Belas Knap near Winchcombe and Hetty Pegler's Tump near Uley (both in Gloucestershire) are probably the best known. In Wiltshire, Wayland Smith's Cave near Swindon and the West Kennet long barrow near Avebury have been splendidly restored.

Round Barrows

The most common type of barrow, the round barrow, first appeared in Britain during the BRONZE AGE (*c.* 2500–*c.* 800 BC). The structure and size of these barrows varies according to the period and district, though most commonly they are 4 to 30 metres in diameter (13 to 100 feet), and up to 6 metres high (20 feet). In shape they vary, from that of an inverted saucer to an inverted bowl (the most common) or bell. Burial practices also varied: sometimes the body was laid on a platform at the centre of a ceremonial circle, where it was later buried beneath a circular barrow; crude coffins, fashioned from the hollowed trunks of trees, were sometimes used, as were chests of stone slabs in which skeletal or cremated remains were placed. Graves were sometimes protected by wooden casings ('death houses'), and ashes by upturned earthenware urns. Food vessels, weapons and tools were often placed in the tomb, though jewellery and other precious objects were, at this time, mostly confined to burials of the advanced Wessex culture on Salisbury Plain. Many barrows were encircled with banks, ditches or *a berm* – a level space between the ditch and bank – and are often flat-topped, the depression having been caused by the collapse of the 'death house' or the activities of our antiquarian forebears.

At this time, ritual burial on such a scale appears to have been confined to tribal chieftains and their families; however, the late Bronze Age saw the development of universal cremation and urn burial in cemeteries. Even so, round barrows continued to be raised over the remains of the rich and influential well into the first century AD when, under the influence of Christianity, the custom was abandoned. There is little evidence for a formal burial rite during

the IRON AGE (*c.* 800 BC to AD 43), indeed a large proportion of the population may not have received burial at all. However, in the Yorkshire Wolds a significant group of square barrows dating from this period were found to contain numerous weapons and ornaments. The lofty Bartlow barrows of the Cambridgeshire and Essex border contain the cremated remains of Romano-British magnates, their ashes in bottles surrounded by magnificent bronze artefacts: status symbols for the afterlife. At Rougham, Suffolk, a Romano-British barrow with a gabled 'death house' of brick with a tiled roof contained a wooden, lead-lined coffin, and excavation of seventh-century barrows at Sutton Hoo, on the Suffolk coast, has revealed a magnificent ship burial – possibly that of the East Anglian King Raedwald (d.625).

Square Barrows

Usually only visible in aerial photographs, clusters of small square barrows on the Yorkshire Wolds are probably of Celtic origin. Several have been found to cover chariot burials in which the corpse was accompanied by a dismantled chariot.

Barrows are invariably located on elevated sites, often on or near ancient RIDGEWAYS. Local custom and superstition surround them, and many have proved ideally suited to the erection of GIBBETS or BEACONS. Eighteenth-century landowners, who followed a fashion for tree-planting on ancient barrows, have created considerable problems for today's archaeologists. Prominent clumps of trees look wonderful in a wind-swept, upland landscape, but serious archaeological damage can be caused when trees mature and fall or are brought down in gales.

BARTON A place-name element from Old English *bere* or *bær-*, meaning 'barley', to *beretun* or *bærtun*, meaning 'granary farm'. The term was widely applied to a demesne farm and, in particular, to an outlying GRANGE.

BASILICAN When applied to churches, the term implies a simple rectangular plan with a nave that is both higher and wider than the aisles, from which it is usually divided by COLONNADES, and with an APSE at the East end (or sometimes at both ends). In the early Church, the apse usually contained the ALTAR. In a true basilica, walls are not reinforced and are therefore unable to bear a stone vault. The original Basilica was one of the principal judicial and commercial buildings of ancient Rome and, consequently, basilica occupied a central position in all Roman cities.

BASTARD FEUDALISM The term given by historians to the tie that bound late medieval retainers to their lords, and allowed those lords in turn to wield the political power appropriate to their rank. Without it, the late medieval aristocracy would not have been able to rule their localities or to fight the wars that were such a prominent feature of the fourteenth and fifteenth centuries.

BASTARDY Vestry minutes often contain records of proceedings against fathers for the maintenance of illegitimate children, as do the records of QUARTER SESSIONS from 1844 when mothers were permitted to apply to the courts for maintenance orders. Care should be exercised regarding the historical concept of bastardy and the use of special devices to denote illegitimacy in coats of arms (*see* MARKS OF DISTINCTION).

BASTIDE *see* CASTLES (MEDIEVAL) *and* TOWNS

BASTION An angled projection of a fortification from which defenders may observe the otherwise concealed area at the foot of the ramparts. Also a triangular projection of masonry and rubble at the foot of a tower, constructed both as a buttress and to deter mining beneath the walls. The DRUM TOWERS of some medieval castles appear to be protected by bastions but are actually constructed on a square base, the triangular 'spurs' of which have a similar appearance.

BASTIONED TRACE *see* TUDOR COASTAL FORTS

BASTLES Warfare and an absence of central authority were endemic on the Scottish borders until the end of the seventeenth century. Many sixteenth- and seventeenth-century border FARMSTEADS, especially those of north Northumberland, adopted a unique *bastle* design which afforded rapid protection to both stock and the inhabitants. Black Middens bastle at Tarset in Northumberland is constructed of stone on two storeys. Cattle entered the ground floor through a door in the east gable while the upper room, which had a wooden floor and a fireplace at the west end, was illuminated by two small windows and was reached by means of an outside stair on the south wall.
See also PELE TOWERS

BATH STONE Oolitic limestone quarried in northern Wiltshire, where it occurs in beds of up to 10 metres (30 feet). When quarried it is damp (with 'quarry-sap') and is easily cut and carved before being seasoned. *Aquæ Sulis*, the Roman city of Bath, was constructed of this pale golden stone, and it was used widely throughout the Middle Ages and the fifteenth and sixteenth centuries. It was in great demand during the eighteenth century when Bath was remodelled as a fashionable neo-Roman city.

BATTLEFIELDS Before the Norman Conquest, battles were generally fought on high ground, often near well-established route-ways and fortified hilltop settlements. Much of our understanding of these early battles is derived from ninth-century chronicles which can be tantalizingly ambiguous so that many Anglo-Saxon sites have yet to be identified accurately. Most major battles of the Barons' Wars, the WARS OF THE ROSES and the Civil War of the seventeenth century took place on the lowland plains to the west of the oolitic escarpment that runs from the Devon coast to Humberside. Documentary sources are usually confused, and there is often conflicting evidence of what actually took place, much of it clouded by a variety of political perceptions.

With few exceptions medieval battles were fought during the campaigning season between May and October because of the logistical problems created by mud-churned tracks and swollen rivers. Generally, the advantage lay with a commander who was able to choose his site. Ideally, this would present a variety of hazards to the oncoming enemy, who would be forced into a restricted space in which there would be little opportunity for manoeuvre, and an easily defended position, secure to the rear but providing a means of retreat if required. Senior commanders, magnates whose retinues were led by BANNERETS in their service, took up elevated positions from which they could direct the course of the battle. Each would have responsibility for a particular battalion: usually the *avant-guard*, the *bataille* or the *arriere-guard*. Baggage trains, of supply wagons with equipment and stores, were kept in the rear. Troops of hobelars, pikemen, archers and crossbow-men mustered beneath their lord's STANDARD (the *ancient*) and followed his GUIDONS into battle. Field commanders, the bannerets who actually led these contingents into battle, were accompanied by a lieutenant whose responsibility it was to carry and maintain his master's personal BANNER. This flag (also called the LIEUTENANT) represented the physical presence of a knight in the field and could never be relinquished without shame: '*The Lieutenant is to be saved before the Ancient . . .*' (Shakespeare's *Othello*). Cavalry comprised mounted knights and was considered to be the élite corps of a medieval army. In the early Middle Ages, especially in France, archers and foot-soldiers simply prepared the way for the cavalry to participate in a knightly engagement not far removed from the ritual of the *tourné*. In the fourteenth century, the efficiency of the longbow against the French cavalry was to have a lasting effect on military strategy. Nevertheless, the medieval chivalric tradition of a mounted élite lasted into the present century, and even now survives in the ceremonial pageantry of the Household Cavalry.

Medieval military campaigns were primarily concerned with attrition: destructive marches (*chevauchées*), raids and SIEGES. Full-scale battles were the exception and rarely decisive. It has been calculated that during the WARS OF THE ROSES, the thirty-two year period of dynastic turbulence from the St Alban's incident in 1455 to the battle of Stoke in 1487, actual conflict occupied no more than thirteen weeks, the longest campaign (that of 1471, from Edward IV's landing to the battle of Tewkesbury) lasting only seven and a half weeks. In Britain, there have been comparatively few battles but innumerable skirmishes. It is the sites of these minor engagements that are often overlooked and yet there exists a wealth of documentary evidence, particularly from the Civil Wars of 1638–51, which would enable the researcher not only to identify these lesser battlefields in the context of his own studies, but also to add further to the accumulated evidence of major campaigns.

The last true battle took place not on British soil, but in the skies above southern England. The Battle of Britain (1940) secured command of the English Channel and the abandonment of Hitler's invasion plans. To the historian, the accurate recording of a pillbox is of equal significance as a thesis on Bosworth Field.

Any study must begin with the purchase of a large-scale map of the area and a visit. Many battlefields remain evocative of the distant past, especially when visited in the same month and at the same time of day as that of the battle. Ancient churches in the vicinity of the battlefield should also be visited, for it was there that the vanquished nobility were often laid to rest. Some battlefields, such as Bosworth Field (1485) near Market Bosworth in Leicestershire and Battle Abbey (1066) near Hastings in East Sussex, have official 'battle

trails' with information boards and visitors' centres. Nearly all battlefields are located on private land but remain accessible through the network of footpaths and bridle-ways which may be identified from the Ordnance Survey 1:25000 *Explorer* maps, as may contours and other natural features which may otherwise be obscured by subsequent development.

BATTLEMENT A crenellated parapet at the top of a wall, the indentations being *crenels* and the raised sections MERLONS. Both were originally finished with a coping, though these are now almost invariably missing. Battlements are most frequently found on fortified medieval buildings where they served a military purpose. From the fifteenth century they are found as decorative features on the walls of churches and domestic buildings.

BAULK A strip of earth or turf separating areas of cultivation, or retained between different parts of an archaeological excavation to facilitate the study of vertical sections.

BAWN In Ireland, a walled enclosure or fortified farm, often dating from the early seventeenth century when lands in Ulster were granted to English and Scottish PLANTERS. For example, Salters' Castle at Salterstown, County Derry, built by the Salters' Company of London in *c.* 1619, is a fortified enclosure consisting of a house, high walls and flanking towers all liberally provided with firing loops.

BAY (i) A section of wall between columns or buttresses or a division of a vaulted or timber roof (*see illustration* opposite).
(ii) A recess in a room, especially one formed by a projecting window (*see* WINDOWS).

BEACONS Before the technological revolution of the present century, the most efficient system of rapid communication was by means of beacons located on prominent hilltop sites at intervals of 8 to 16 km (5 to 10 miles). There is biblical evidence for the early use of beacons (e.g. Isaiah Ch. 30, v. 17) and it must surely be assumed that local systems of beacon fires were used by prehistoric hilltop tribes to warn of approaching danger. The Romans developed a sophisticated system of SIGNAL STATIONS and LIGHTHOUSES, and in the Anglo-Saxon period the activities of Viking raiders were communicated by means of beacons at lookout posts where observers 'toted' for danger (from Old English *totaern*). Many hill names retain this Tot-, Tout- or Toot- element: Tothill in Lincolnshire,

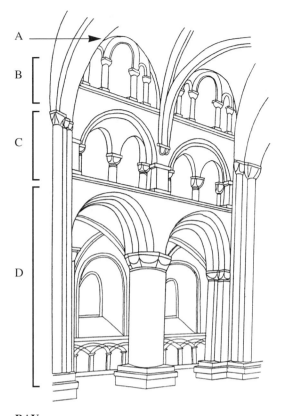

BAY

*A Nave vault; **B** Clerestory; **C** Tribune or
triforium; **D** Nave arcade*

Tottenhill in Norfolk, Nettlecombe Tout and
Worbarrow Tout in Dorset and the Toot Hills of
Essex, Hampshire, Staffordshire and Yorkshire, for
example. A network of beacons is believed to have
developed in the twelfth century, and during the
fourteenth century two major systems were
established to combat French raids off the south
coast and to warn of impending incursions from
Scotland. Beacon systems were revived and
amended to meet successive threats of invasion. In
most counties, a command beacon was maintained at
the most widely visible point and this would be the
'hub' of other chains. A complex network of
beacons, along the south coast and the Severn
Estuary, formed part of the Tudor coastal defences, a
chain of artillery forts guarding against invasion
from the English Channel. Complex signal systems
were devised to indicate, for example, the first
sighting of the enemy and its disembarkation. There
were also special signals for the mustering of troops.
The beacons were fired in 1588 when the Spanish
Armada was sighted, though it seems that the signal

codes were not entirely successful and a simplified
system was used to summon the trained bands to
their parish churches. During the Napoleonic Wars,
the volunteer companies and militia of the southern
counties were on constant alert and beacons were
regularly maintained against the possibility of
invasion – with many false alarms!

Many prominent hills retain their identity as
former beacons, among them Cothelstone Beacon on
the Quantock hills in Somerset, Painswick Beacon
high on the Cotswolds above the Vale of Gloucester,
and the Herefordshire Beacon on the Malvern hills
from where it is said the beacon could be seen in
nine counties. Beacons were not simply large
bonfires: many were carried in stone-built turrets or
metal fire-baskets (*cressets*) on tall poles, reached by
ladders, and (in level landscapes) some may even
have been carried in braziers on church towers, as at
Blakeney in Norfolk. Faggots of brushwood or furze
were maintained at a beacon site for fuel and at
various times a tax (*Beaconage*) was collected for
the maintenance of the local beacon. Beacon fires
were lit to celebrate Queen Victoria's jubilees of
1887 and 1897, Elizabeth II's coronation in 1953
and her jubilee in 1977, and the quatercentenary of
the defeat of the Spanish Armada in 1988.
See also SIGNAL STATIONS, TELEGRAPH *and*
TOOT-HILLS

BEADLE A parish officer whose responsibilities
varied from one area to another. His original
function was probably to supervise attendance at a
manorial court and to serve writs (*see* MANOR),
though in some areas his office was synonymous
with that of the CONSTABLE while in others he
was the constable's assistant.

BEAKER A somewhat controversial cultural
designation applied by some authorities to migrants
from the Rhine basin who settled in the south-east of
Britain during the late NEOLITHIC and early
BRONZE AGE periods and who brought with them
wide-mouthed pottery drinking vessels, in a variety
of distinctive (regional ?) styles, together with
woven cloth and copper implements. It seems
unlikely that there was any large-scale 'invasion'
and settlement, rather a prolonged exposure to
Beaker culture resulting in a drastic reassessment of
native religious beliefs and practices. Beaker burials,
in round BARROWS on elevated sites, differ from
those in long barrows in that they are usually single,
articulated and crouched inhumations, accompanied
by grave goods (the richness of which may have
been indicative of status) which almost invariably

Bronze Age artefacts recovered from a burial site at Dorchester, Oxon, including a beaker, an archer's wristguard and a bronze dagger.

included a beaker, placed with the body. However, it seems likely that these practices may be accounted for by prevailing fashion, and the distribution of beakers by trade and exchange. The 'Beaker Folk' (as they are sometimes called) were farmers and were associated with the first exploitation of copper and tin ores in Britain (bronze is an alloy of copper and tin). The Beaker phase is generally dated 2600–1800 BC and is particularly associated with the development of ritual sites, notably STONE CIRCLES, though Beaker occupation sites are rare.

BEAK HEAD MOULDING *see* ROMANESQUE

BEASTGATES *see* COMMONS

BEASTS (HERALDIC) *see illustration* opposite of the chimerical beasts most often found in coats of arms and armorial decoration.

BEATIFICATION *see* SAINTS

BEATING THE BOUNDS *see* GOSPEL OAK *and* PERAMBULATION

BEAUFORTS *see* WARS OF THE ROSES

BECK From Norse *bekkr*, meaning 'stream', this place-name is common in Danelaw areas of the north-east.

BEDD- Welsh place-name element meaning 'grave', as in Beddgelert, Gwynedd, though in this instance the 'Grave of Gelert' is of eighteenth-century origin

and the 'legend' from which it derives of doubtful provenance!

BEDE HOUSE *see* ALMSHOUSES

BEECH Contrary to popular belief, Caesar's assertion (in *De Bello Gallico*) that the beech is not a British native tree is entirely without foundation, as is the claim that it was introduced into Britain by the Romans. The beech is to be found principally on the dry chalk and limestone hills of southern England. When new, the white wood of the beech cuts like cheese and was favoured for kitchen and dairy ware and, when specially seasoned in cold brine, for churns (though butter tubs were made of LIME wood). Some beech was used for medieval pattens and clog bottoms.

BEEHIVE HUTS Circular, dry-walled buildings with stone-paved floors, stone lintels and corbelled roofs found principally at Skellig Michael, a sixth- or seventh-century monastery on a rocky island of the Kerry coast in Northern Ireland. They probably provided accommodation for one or two monks and are known as *clocháns*. Similar structures, sometimes square or oblong as well as circular, are to be found in other areas where stone was plentiful. The earliest of those recorded in Ireland, Wales, the south-west peninsular of England, the north of Scotland and the Hebrides and Orkneys may date from Neolithic times, although such structures are common to most centuries up to the present and are generally associated with agricultural buildings.

BELFRIES *see* CHURCH TOWERS *and* SIEGES

BELGAE Celtic immigrants from what are now Belgium and northern France who settled the Kent-Hertforshire-Essex area in the late IRON AGE, *c.* 100 BC. Noted for the rich grave goods associated with cremation burials and for the introduction of the potter's wheel and rotary quern for grinding corn, their influence extended to the Sussex-Hampshire-Berkshire area. The Belgae constructed semi-urban settlements, protected by complex earthworks, in preference to contemporary hill forts.

BELL PIT Medieval or seventeenth-century workings from which iron ore or coal was extracted. A circular shaft was dug vertically until a seam was reached; excavation then proceeded horizontally to form a bell-shaped pit. Abandoned pits soon collapsed and are often difficult to identify. The original shafts were at least 2 metres in diameter

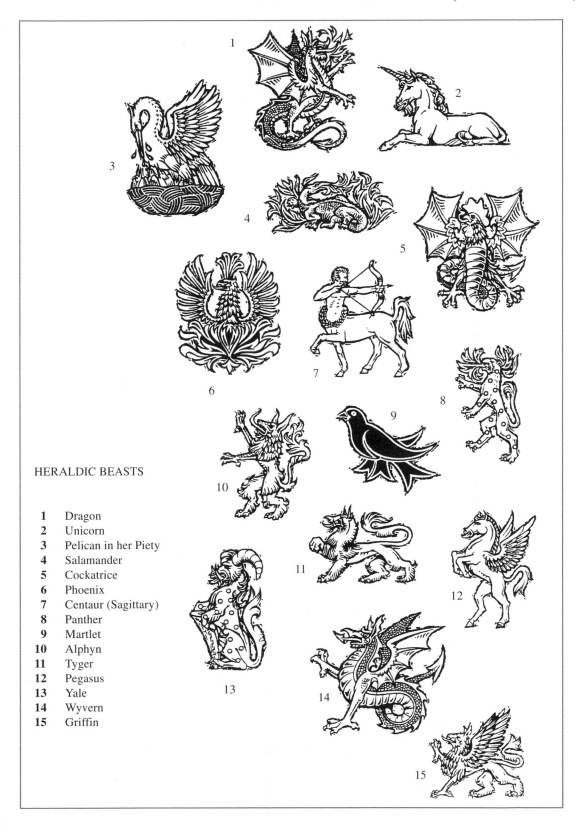

HERALDIC BEASTS

1	Dragon
2	Unicorn
3	Pelican in her Piety
4	Salamander
5	Cockatrice
6	Phoenix
7	Centaur (Sagittary)
8	Panther
9	Martlet
10	Alphyn
11	Tyger
12	Pegasus
13	Yale
14	Wyvern
15	Griffin

(6 to 7 feet), and are now often found in clusters of circular indentations, particularly in areas where there is evidence of former medieval woodland.

BELVEDERE A glazed lantern or turret-shaped room added to the top of a building or constructed on a mound to provide a vantage point over the surrounding countryside. Especially to be found on late eighteenth-century and early nineteenth-century houses and constructed at a time of increasing environmental awareness and romanticism. The Maldon area of Essex is noted for several fine examples. Derived from the Italian *bello* (pleasant) and *vedere* (view), though the medieval *bevoir* will also be found (from the Old French *bel* and *vedeir*, meaning 'beautiful prospect').
See also ARTIFICIAL RUINS, FOLLIES, GAZEBO *and* PROSPECT TOWER

BEN From the Gaelic *beinn*, meaning 'mountain' or 'peak'.

BENCH-END Medieval congregations were rarely provided with seating but as sermons became more popular towards the end of the fifteenth century and an English liturgy was introduced following the Reformation, so listening became fashionable and benches were introduced. At first these were simply boards supported by trestles. Later benches incorporated bench-ends which were often carved in a variety of sophisticated or vernacular styles, often with allegorical or heraldic subjects (*see* CHRISTIAN SYMBOLS). West Country bench-ends tend to have square tops, whereas those in East Anglia often have 'poppy head' finials and are more elaborate.
See also BOX PEW *and* POPPY HEAD

BENCHMARK Found cut into trigonometrical pillars, milestones and the stone fabric of permanent buildings such as church towers, benchmarks were intended to assist the surveyor in determining altitude using an angle iron which is positioned on the horizontal notch of the mark to provide a 'bench' or support for his levelling staff. Benchmarks indicate both a specific point in a sequence of levels and an established height above mean sea level (now given in metres). All ORDNANCE SURVEY maps

Bench ends at (left) Lansallos, Cornwall, and (right) Brent Knoll in Somerset. The mitred pig is probably an unflattering reference to the Bishop of Rome.

show selected spot heights at benchmarks, though only the larger scale maps show them all. The lower half of the mark is the broad arrow-head *sigillum* used to mark the property of the sovereign since the Middle Ages. A list of benchmarks for each area is available from the Ordnance Survey (*see* APPENDIX I).

BENEDICTINES (The Black Monks) The Rule of St Benedict of Nursia (*c.* 480–*c.* 550) provided a cohesive, inclusive and individual code by which monastic life, both spiritual and administrative, could be ordered. Originally, there was no *order* of St Benedict: for two centuries following his death, the Benedictine Rule was simply one of several from which an abbot selected the observances by which his community lived. Successive medieval Popes attempted to bring the Benedictine abbeys under a centralized constitution but the Benedictines themselves preferred to exercise reform through independent local congregations. During the so-called Dark Ages, following the fall of the Roman Empire, the considerable influence of the Benedictine communities successfully maintained the ideals and practice of scholarship and liturgical worship. In tenth-century England, cleric Ethelwold reintroduced large-scale monasticism after a century of decline. With the support of the Anglo-Saxon monarchy, he introduced the strict Benedictine rule and established a series of monasteries 'correcting the foolish with rods' and so antagonizing the 'evil-living clerics', with their 'illegal wives' and partiality for gluttony and drunkenness, that there was an unsuccessful attempt to poison him in his hall at Winchester. The introduction into England of the Black Monks, and the similarly enclosed orders of Benedictine nuns, profoundly affected the subsequent nature of medieval society.

BENEFICE An ecclesiastical office such as a rectory or vicarage.

BENEFIT OF CLERGY Exemption from trial by a secular court accorded to the medieval clergy. In England, this provision was extended to all those whose literacy theoretically qualified them for holy orders. Prisoners were often encouraged to read from the Scriptures in order to avoid a capital sentence for a minor offence. The test was abolished in 1706 and the procedure in 1827 (*see* CANON LAW).

BEREWICKE A dependent village or hamlet within a manor.

BESTIARY A medieval treatise on beasts, both real and imagined. Many of the creatures were imbued with medicinal and spiritual powers or endowed with allegorical significance. The reader was often exhorted to emulate the qualities of certain beasts and to shun others.

BETWS- A place-name element found in Wales and the Welsh border often signifying the site of a former chantry chapel, e.g. Betws-y-Coed, Gwynedd (chapel of the woods). In the Welsh, it can also mean 'birch grove'.

BEVOIR *see* BELVEDERE

BIER *see* LICH-GATE

BILL OF RIGHTS *see* GLORIOUS REVOLUTION, THE

BIRCH A mountain tree with a multiplicity of uses: in the north of Britain, the aromatic birch ensured quality in the distilling of Scotch whisky and the curing of haddies and herrings. Birch twigs were placed at the bottom of cooking pots to prevent the meat from sticking or burning and were used in the making of brooms. At school, a 'birching' was considered to be marginally less welcome than a 'switching'.

BISHOP *see* CLERGY (CHURCH OF ENGLAND), DIOCESE *and* SIGNATURES, ARCHBISHOPS AND BISHOPS

BIVALLATE *see* MULTIVALLATE

BLACK AND WHITE HOUSES *see* TIMBER-FRAMED BUILDINGS

BLACK BOOK OF THE EXCHEQUER, THE *see* PIPE ROLLS

BLACK DEATH *see* PLAGUE

BLACKSMITH *see* FORGE

BLADES *see* TIMBER-FRAMED BUILDINGS

BLAZON To describe a coat of arms using the conventions and terminology of ARMORY. Such a description is itself termed a *blazon*. Familiarity with blazon facilitates the rapid and accurate recording of heraldic devices and enables the historian to make effective use of reference works such as ordinaries,

armories, peerages, etc., and to communicate with armorists, of whom there is a growing number. An accurate blazon is concise and unambiguous and from it heraldic devices may be painted (*emblazoned*) or researched. The conventions of blazon are well established and logical. Relatively few terms are met with regularly, and are learned best through practice. Blazons of arms may be obtained from works such as *The General Armory of England, Scotland, Ireland and Wales* by Sir Bernard Burke, published in 1842 and reprinted by Heraldry Today in 1984. This is essentially a list of armorial references, arranged alphabetically by surname, with blazons of arms for each, together with crests, supporters and mottoes where known.
See also ORINARY

BLEMYA Apparently derived from the Blemmyae of Pliny's *Natural History*, these strange headless creatures, of human form but with eyes and mouth below their shoulders, are to be found in medieval carvings where they represent gluttony.

BLIND ARCADE *see* ARCADE

BLIND HOUSE *see* LOCK-UP

BLOOMERY A forge for producing slag-free bars of iron, known as 'blooms'. In traditional iron-producing areas, such as the Weald of Kent and the Forest of Dean in Gloucestershire, bloomeries were active from the Iron Age through to the nineteenth century. Newly melted iron inevitably contained slag from the layers of ore and charcoal with which furnaces were charged. The metal was re-heated and subjected to incessant hammering (forging) in a bloomery in order to remove the slag. Sites have been identified within the ramparts of Iron Age camps, such as that at Saxonbury near Rotherfield in Sussex; and post-medieval hammer ponds, constructed to impound water to drive the hammers and bellows, are a feature of south-eastern counties. Evidence of a former bloomery is not hard to find: ploughed land usually contains brown lumps of iron-cinder or slag, and place-names such as Cinder Hill, Furnace Wood and Cinderford (all in the Forest of Dean) are indicative of the presence of forges. Such names have a nineteenth-century ring to them but Cinderford, for example, is first recorded as Sinderford in 887 and is derived from the Old English *sinder*, meaning 'dross'.
See also MINERALS

BLOWING HOUSE Known as 'Jews' houses' by nineteenth-century Cornish tin workers, the granite ruins of blowing houses are still to be found on Dartmoor and the Cornish moors. They accommodated smelting works: the mills and furnaces of a traditional tin industry dating from the thirteenth century to the eighteenth. Both the bellows of the charcoal furnace and the 'stamps', which reduced the 'stream tin' ore to powder, were driven by water-power from an overshot wheel in a pit adjacent to the blowing house.

BOARD OF GOVERNORS In England and Wales, the governing body of a school. In documents relating to primary schools, it may be described as a Board of Managers (*see* EDUCATION).

BOARD OF GUARDIANS The governing body of a local workhouse or 'union' (*see* POOR LAW *and* WORKHOUSES).

BOG OAK *see* OAK

BOLDON BOOK *see* PALATINATE

BOLESTID From the Old English *bolla*, a bowl. The term is applied to shallow, saucer-shaped indentations in the ground in which ore and wood were placed and then covered with turf to form a primitive furnace for the smelting of lead. Characteristic of the Peak District, Derbyshire, former sites can often be identified as areas of bare ground poisoned by lead.

BONDING The arrangement of bricks in a wall for structural and decorative purposes. There are essentially two structural principles: continuous vertical joints are structurally unsound and walls of more than 23 cm (9 inches) thickness require bonding by means of HEADERS (bricks laid at right angles to the face of the wall). Early brickwork was haphazard but from end of the thirteenth century, English bond was widely used (*see illustration* opposite) and from the mid-seventeenth century, *Flemish bond* became popular. Many other types and combinations of bonding will be found, the most common of which are illustrated.
See also BRICK

BOOK OF FEES, THE The Book of Fees consists of a number of manuscripts, known as the *Testa de Nevill*, which contain returns relating to land holdings and feudal tenancies dating from 1198 to 1293. Compiled *c.* 1307, the Book has been published in two volumes by HMSO in 1921 and 1923, with an Index in 1931.

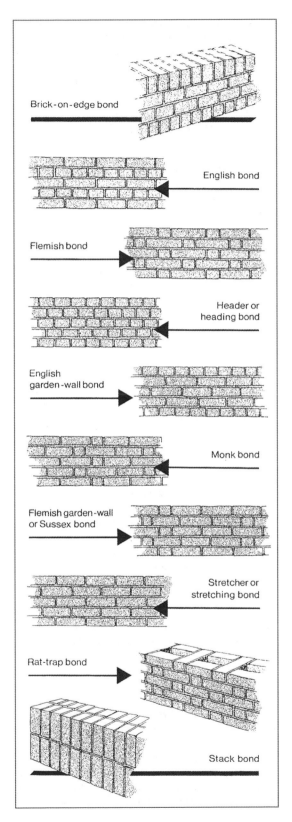

Brick-on-edge bond

English bond

Flemish bond

Header or heading bond

English garden-wall bond

Monk bond

Flemish garden-wall or Sussex bond

Stretcher or stretching bond

Rat-trap bond

Stack bond

BOOK OF HOURS Often the most impressive of all medieval written documents, Books of Hours were personal devotional books widely used by the devout laity from the thirteenth century. Most were embellished more or less elaborately according to the taste and pocket of the patron for whom they were prepared. Some were presented as gifts by calligraphers and illuminators in hope of patronage. Books of Hours provided a series of prayers appropriate to the eight canonical hours into which the day was divided, together with a calendar and various extracts from the Divine Office and Psalms. They were invariably exceedingly beautiful, the illustrations providing also a wealth of information on contemporary social life.
See also MANUSCRIPT ILLUMINATION

BOOKPLATES A decorative label pasted inside the front cover of a book for *ex libris* identification. Bookplates may be dated by their decorative style and often include valuable heraldic and genealogical information.
Further information: The Bookplate Society (*see* APPENDIX I)

BOOK STAMPS The book stamp, with a coat of arms, crest, cypher or other device impressed and often gilded on the vellum or leather bindings of books in private or corporate collections, was in Britain the precursor of the BOOKPLATE and its use continues to the present day.

BOOLEY HOUSE From Irish *buaile*, meaning 'milking place', a summer dairy settlement located in sheltered mountain pastures, to which a tribe or family would move with their cattle during the summer months. Constructed of stones or sods of earth with roofing of heather, Irish booley houses have their Welsh equivalent in the HAFOD and in Scotland the SHIELING.
See also CLACHAN

BOONMASTER see HIGHWAY

BOOTHHALL or **BOOTH-HALL** A name given to a town hall, as in the City of Gloucester. A reference in Atkyn's *Gloucestershire* of 1712 suggests that 'The Booth-hall or Town-hall is subject . . . to the Jurisdiction both of the Out-county and of the City.'

BORDERS (OF SCOTLAND) *see* MARCH

BORE *see* EAGRE

BOROUGH A town administered by a corporation and having privileges confirmed by royal charter or defined by statute. Ancient boroughs often enjoyed rights conferred by charters emanating from the medieval nobility. The Town Council of Sherborne in Dorset, for example, enjoys its mayoral and armigerous status on the strength of a charter from Bishop Le Poore of Salisbury, granted in 1228 to the former borough of Newland, now a suburb of the town. Anglo-Saxon boroughs had a military and defensive function as well as a mercantile one and by the tenth century were independent of the HUNDREDS, some having their own courts (*see* BURH). A feature of the Norman invasion which began in 1066 was the creation of boroughs in association with motte and bailey castles at strategic locations. Grants of exclusive rights to milling, brewing and to hold markets made boroughs an important tool of conquest ensuring that surrounding districts became dependent upon them as their sole commercial focus. The importance of the 'planted' borough was recognized by Edward I in his Welsh campaigns, establishing settlements in association with a network of formidable fortifications, notably the castles and town walls of Caernarfon, Conwy and Denbigh. Many of the characteristics of a medieval borough may still be traced in these towns: the geometric street pattern and broad market streets, for example. Before 1835, many boroughs had the right to levy tolls at the town market, to hear certain civil and criminal cases, and to return a member to the House of Commons. Public elections were rarely held and borough administration was effectively self-perpetuating. By the 1835 Municipal Corporations Act councillors in the 178 boroughs were required to stand for re-election after three years and aldermen after six, and franchise was extended to rate-payers with a residential qualification of three years or more. The Municipal Corporations Act of 1882 consolidated this legislation.
See also MARKETS

BOROUGH ENGLISH The custom whereby the youngest son was considered to be the legal heir. Were a man to die without issue, his youngest brother would inherit. The custom was abolished in 1922–5 (*see* LAW).

BOSSES A boss is a projecting keystone at the intersection of ribs in a stone vault (*see* VAULTING) or of beams in a timber roof. In the magnificent vault of Sherborne Abbey in Dorset there are no fewer than 800 stone bosses, all elaborately carved, painted and gilded with heraldic designs, rebuses and vernacular motifs, some of those in the north transept weighing more than half a ton.

BOTE The right of commoners to remove material from the common for their personal use.
See also COMMONS, FIREBOTE, FOLDBOTE, HEYBOTE, HUSBOTE *and* PLOUGHBOTE

BOTHY *see* SHIELING

BOTTLE SEALS From the middle of the seventeenth century, wealthy wine-drinkers had their specially made bottles embellished with a blob of glass, attached to the body of the bottle, into which was impressed a 'seal'. This would be initials, arms, crest or other device, the finished effect being similar to a wax impression. Tavern keepers also began to personalize their bottles, often with their initials and a representation of their tavern sign and a date. The date probably indicated when the bottle was made rather than when the wine was bottled or laid down, for at that time wine bottles were intended for repeated use. By 1730 the sealing of tavern bottles had virtually ceased, but the tradition was carried on by private individuals well into the nineteenth century. The Oxford colleges began using sealed bottles around the middle of the seventeenth century, and the names of wine merchants began to appear on bottles from the late eighteenth. Seventeenth-century wine bottles were dumpy with a short neck and wide base. In the eighteenth century, these were succeeded by taller cylindrical bottles which more suitable for binning. Both types are found with seals, though these would sometimes become detached and lost. Seals bearing brand names are of a much later date: usually late nineteenth or twentieth century.

BOUNDARIES The Anglo-Saxon colonization of new land and its demarcation into private estates resulted in the creation of thousands of miles of boundaries, some of which corresponded with those of earlier Roman or even Iron Age estates while others followed established trackways and natural features such as streams or were formed by the construction of linear embankments and lanes or 'meres', from the Old English *mǣre*, meaning 'boundary' (*see* GREEN LANES *and* MERE LANE). The practice was not universally welcomed, however, and according to Giraldus Cambrensis, writing in the twelfth century, the Welsh were particularly 'given to digging up boundary ditches, removing limits, disregarding land-marks and extending their property in every possible way'.

Some major boundaries had a lasting effect on the political landscape. In the thirteenth century, for example, Gilbert de Clare, Earl of Gloucester (1243–95), constructed the Shire Ditch on the crest of the Malvern Hills to mark the boundary between his hunting grounds to the east and those of the Bishop of Hereford to the west and for seven centuries the 'Red Earl's' ditch separated the counties of Hereford and Worcester.

The boundaries of a modern civil PARISH rarely conform with those of an ecclesiastical parish or with earlier manorial estates. In many instances, nineteenth-century legislation resulted in the rationalization of parishes, particularly those that consisted of two (or occasionally more) separate parts, and in such cases these 'islands' were absorbed into the parishes within which they were located and the ancient boundaries were modified accordingly. Similarly, the reorganization of local government in 1972–4 resulted in numerous adjustments being made to the administrative boundaries of civil parishes, districts, counties and parliamentary constituencies and these have been incorporated into the 1:25000 *Explorer* Ordnance Survey maps. Nevertheless, numerous ancient boundaries have survived, not only in the delineation of many ecclesiastical parishes, but in the 'boundary markers', sunken lanes, earthworks and other topographical features of the traditional English landscape.

By far the most satisfactory sources of information are the original land *charters*, the earliest dating from the seventh century, which refer to grants of estates to various men and to institutions such as monastic foundations; and major documents, such as the Forest Charter, granted in 1299/1300 by Edward I, which contain records of PERAMBULATIONS. Many of these documents have been published in printed form by local history or record societies but where charters have not been published, the amateur researcher will need guidance from county record offices both to locate the originals and to translate them. References to boundaries in the earliest charters are often frustratingly vague but many later grants describe the limitations of an estate in extraordinary detail, by (often obscure) reference to topographical features and place-names and to adjacent demesne lands. These 'boundary markers', which may include even single trees and stones, are usually (though not invariably) described in clockwise order:

First into *Merecumb*, then into the green pit, then on to the tor at *Merecumbes* spring, then to Denewald's stone, then to the ditch where Esne dug across the road . . . from the stream down where the vixen's ditch meets the brook . . . thence on the old way towards the white stone, thence to the hill which is called 'at the holly', thence to the hoary stone . . . thence eastward into the fort . . . thence to the paved road, thence below the wood straight out to the reed pool, then up the Avon until the old swine-enclosure runs out to the Avon . . . thence along the 'wall-way' to the stone at the stream, from the stone on along the highway to the ditch, thence down to *Wealdenesford*, thence on to the hollow way, thence down the brook to *Hunburgefleot*, and there to the sea.*

* From a grant of twenty hides of land in the South Hams of Devon dated 846: *see* W.G. Hoskin's *Fieldwork in Local History*, Faber and Faber, 1982.

Of course, most areas have since been subject to intermittent manorial and parochial surveys and perambulations, some of which have been conducted in comparatively recent times. By correlating the information from these and earlier documents, and by studying available MAPS, an ancient boundary may be defined. The Royal Commission on Historical Manuscripts maintains a register of relevant documents (*see* APPENDIX I), and most county record offices have collections of nineteenth-century tithe maps and of estate maps, usually dating from the seventeenth and eighteenth centuries, or are able to provide details of where they may be located. Large-scale ORDNANCE SURVEY sheets are essential – 1:25000 is the most useful scale to begin with (the 1:50000 is of little use) – and any research must culminate in field-work. Boundary banks (not to be confused with PARK PALES or WOODBANKS), ditches, green lanes, footpaths, tumuli, standing stones, ponds and even surviving field boundaries suddenly acquire an entirely new significance, and with perseverance obscure documentary references to boundary markers may be identified. A typical perambulation may be 16 or 19 km (10 or 12 miles) in length and can often reveal factors which are not evident from documentary sources, the 'dovetailing' of field boundaries following the division of a single estate into two parishes, for example.

BOUNDS *see* GOSPEL OAK *and* PERAMBULATION

BOVATE *see* OPEN FIELDS

The elevated and curtained 'Squire's Pew' at Croft Spa church, Yorkshire

BOW-FRONTED WINDOW *see* REGENCY ARCHITECTURE *and* WINDOWS

BOWHEREEN *or* **BOREEN** From Irish *bóthairín*, meaning 'cow track', bowhereens are narrow, dry-walled lanes for facilitating the movement of cattle.

BOW STREET RUNNERS *see* LAW AND ORDER

BOX-FRAMING (i) A form of construction using concrete 'boxes' with loads carried on cross walls. Commonly used in structures such as high-rise flats and office blocks.
(ii) The term is also applied to more traditional forms of TIMBER-FRAMED BUILDINGS.

BOX PEW Seventeenth- and eighteenth-century box pews were wainscotted and provided with doors to protect the congregation from drafts. After the Reformation, the ALTAR was no longer the focus of attention but the prayer-desk and PULPIT, and it was to these that the congregation was directed when box pews were installed. Certain 'square pews' were reserved for specific families and were upholstered and often curtained. Others were even more lavishly equipped and furnished, often with a fireplace and private doorway from the churchyard. Such 'parlour pews' were sometimes converted CHANTRY chapels, such as that of the Long family in Draycot Cerne church near Chippenham in Wiltshire and the Hungerford chantry in Salisbury Cathedral which was 'appropriated as a seat for mayor and bishop in sermon time' (Hutchins).

BRACED COLLAR *see* ROOFS

BRANDAE *see* SHRINES

BRANDING Vagrants who refused to work were branded from at least 1547 (*see* POOR LAW), and from 1650 bawds and brothel-keepers could be branded on the forehead with a letter 'B'. By an Act of 1699 prostitutes could also be branded on the cheek, presumably to deter clients as well as a punishment.

BRASS An alloy of copper and zinc, sometimes including minor constituents such as tin. In the Industrial Revolution it was fundamental to the extensive hardware-manufacturing industry of the English midlands, to the engineering trade and, in its purest form, for coinage and to sheathe the bottom of ships.
See also MINERALS

BRASSES (MONUMENTAL) A monumental brass is a flat metal plate engraved with a figure and inscription and affixed as a memorial to the floor or wall of a church or to a tomb. Medieval brasses were, in fact, made of an alloy of copper (75 to 80 per cent), with 15 to 20 per cent zinc and small elements of lead and tin. In the Middle Ages this material was known as *latten*, and later *cuivre blanc* (white copper). Those who worked on monumental brasses were described as 'marblers', a possible reference to the craft of engraving INCISED SLABS from which the monumental brass developed. Indeed, it seems likely that workshops which had traditionally produced lavishly expensive effigies and tombs turned also to the production of brasses as an alternative form of memorial which could be afforded by the average cleric, merchant or gentleman. There are some 7,500 brasses in England, more than any other European country. Brasses originated in the Low Countries in the thirteenth century: the earliest surviving figure brass being that of Bishop Yso von Wilpe (d.1231) at Verden in West Germany. Flemish brasses were imported into England, no doubt at considerable expense, the most important of the fourteenth-century manufacturing centres being at Tournai on the river Scheldt. These brasses were large rectangular sheets of metal set into a slab, the background between the figures being engraved with diaper-work, heraldic devices or other smaller figures. Typical of these large, elaborate imported brasses is that of Abbot Thomas de la Mare at St Albans, Hertfordshire, which measures 2.8 × 1.5 metres (9 feet 3 inches × 4 feet 4 inches).

The majority of surviving English brasses originated from workshops, established in the early fourteenth century at Norwich, York and (particularly) London, which may be identified by comparing the different styles of design and manufacture. Each workshop developed a series of standard templates from which the client would select the most appropriate 'off the peg' design to which personal devices and inscriptions were added. Others were specially commissioned and engraved to a client's specification. It is possible to identify the different 'schools' from the characteristics of a particular brass but, as with EFFIGIES, brasses of this period portray only a stylized representation of a deceased person, not an accurate portrait.

These English brasses comprised a number of separate pieces, cut from a single sheet of metal, each of which was engraved and set within an indentation (matrix) carved out of the stone slab so that the brass was flush with the surface. Each section was secured within its matrix in a bed of black pitch which also protected the metal from corrosion, though later brasses were often fixed by means of brass rivets driven into lead plugs which were compressed within holes in the slab. In many instances, coloured enamels were let into the concave surfaces of the brass to provide heraldic decoration, and this practice continued well into the sixteenth century. Slabs were generally of local stone or Purbeck marble. The earliest figures were usually life-size or slightly smaller but there are examples of demi-figures and miniatures, such as an early sixteenth-century brass at Chinnor in Oxfordshire which is only 19 cm high (7½ inches). Figures are generally accompanied by an inscription, CHRISTIAN SYMBOLS and heraldic devices, all set within a decorative engraved canopy. The segmented nature of medieval brasses made them particularly vulnerable to vandalism and effacement and today, few complete brasses have survived.

The first English brasses are those of bishops or abbots, the earliest of which date from the late thirteenth century. By far the most interesting category is the 'military brass', so called because figures are depicted in armour. Invariably, these brasses contain heraldic devices which facilitate dating and identification and often provide genealogical and personal information not included in the inscription. Indeed, it was for this reason that ARMORY was considered to be such a necessary component in memorials: and of course it also declared the authority and status of the deceased.

The earliest military brass, now only a collection of gaping matrices, is at Aston Rowan in Oxfordshire and dates from *c.* 1314. A series of military brasses, now dated from between 1320 and 1330, illustrates the early use of armorial devices on memorials. The brass of Sir John d'Abernon at Stoke d'Abernon in Surrey shows a knight bearing a shield and pennon on which there are traces of blue enamel from his arms *Azure* (blue) *a Chevron Or* (gold). This was once considered to be the oldest English military brass but has recently been re-dated to 1327. Three other splendid figures of this period are those of Roger de Trumpington at Trumpington

Brasses of Robert Ingleton and his three wives at Thornton, Buckinghamshire (1472). The numerous offspring of each marriage also appear as 'weepers' at the foot of the brass.

all nine enamelled shields which were once set into Lady Margaret's gown are now missing.) Most of these early fourteenth-century military brasses depict figures wearing long heraldic surcoats but these were succeeded by the shorter, tight-fitting jupon during the Camail Period, defined as such from the introduction into England of the *camail*, a form of mail cape suspended from beneath the helmet, from *c.* 1360. The majority of brasses of this period depict armorial devices not on the jupon, which is plain, but on separate shields above or surrounding the figure. It is strange that contemporary workshops should have continued to produce these designs when clients clearly weren't interested in using the jupon for heraldic display. Perhaps the cost of enamelling was excessive or it may be that the jupons were emblazoned in a medium of which no trace remains, though this seems unlikely. This fashion, if such it was, anticipated that of the following century when many figures, both in brasses and effigies, were depicted wearing the plate armour of the period, uncovered and without embellishment. This reflected the current popularity (among the nobility at least) of the magnificent and expensive products of German and Italian armourers. Between 1360 and 1460 only one-tenth of military brasses have figures wearing heraldic garments. However, from the 1460s an increasing number of brasses and effigies show figures dressed in heraldic tabards and these continued well into the sixteenth century, the complexity of quarterings increasing significantly in the Tudor period when descent from (or association with) an 'ancient' family (i.e. pre-Bosworth) was highly prized by the newly created Tudor aristocracy.

Crests and helmets are also represented in military brasses, particularly in those of the fifteenth and sixteenth centuries, when the helm is usually placed beneath or near the head of the figure, though there are examples from the late fourteenth century, such as the hunting horn crest of Sir William de Bryene at Seal in Kent (1385) and the panache of feathers in the crest of Sir John Harsyck at Southacre, Norfolk (1384).

There are also numerous examples of female figures in armorial *kirtles* and *mantles* throughout the medieval and Tudor periods, notably the brasses of Joyce, Lady Tiptoft at Enfield, Middlesex (d.1446, engraved 1470), and Lady Katherine Howard at Stoke by Nayland, Suffolk (d.1452, engraved 1535). Both are examples of retrospective memorials, that of Lady Howard being laid down during the reign of Henry VIII to commemorate descent from a singularly distinguished medieval

in Cambridgeshire, Sir William de Setvans at Chartham, Kent, and Sir Robert de Bures at Acton, Suffolk. All three hold shields of their arms which are repeated on their *surcoats and ailettes* (shoulder-guards): trumpets for De Trumpington and seven winnowing fans (*sept vans*) for De Setvans. (With the revised dating of these brasses, the earliest heraldic example may be that of Margaret, Lady Camoys (*c.* 1310) at Trotton in Sussex. Regrettably, family. (*See* EFFIGIES for the treatment of female armorial dress in memorials.) Those who wish to trace the development of armour or costume through the study of monuments should be aware that many brasses (and effigies) are not contemporary with the death of those they commemorate. Some were retrospective, others were prepared in anticipation of death and the erection of others may have been delayed because of unreliable executors or contested wills. Conversely, the dating of brasses by reference to costume and armour is equally complex. For example, the famous Trumpington brass (*see above*) was for many years attributed to the first Roger de Trumpington (d.1289). However, it was later noted that the small shields on the sword scabbard, and the arms on the ailettes, were crudely engraved with a five-pointed LABEL. These, it was concluded, had been added after the original brass had been engraved and the question of dating was re-examined. It is now believed that the brass was commissioned in anticipation of death by the son of Roger I, Sir Giles de Trumpington (d.1332), and that it was appropriated, and the arms hastily changed, for the tomb of *his* son, Roger II, who predeceased his father in *c*. 1326 and whose arms were distinguished by the addition of a silver label. Brasses do not always mark the place of interment: at Felbrigg in Norfolk the brass of Sir Simon Felbrigg (1416) was engraved in anticipation of his death and placed over the tomb of his first wife Margaret. But when Sir Simon died in 1442 he was buried at Norwich!

Insignia of office are also found in monumental brasses, together with Lancastrian COLLARS of SS and Yorkist collars of suns and roses. The brass of Thomas, Lord Berkeley at Wotton-under-Edge in Gloucestershire shows him in armour decorated with mermaids, the family badge. Occasionally, badges may be incorporated in the overall design of the brass, as at Wollaton, Northamptonshire, where the slab of Richard Willoughby (1471) is inset with small brass whelk shells. There are numerous Garter brasses in which the figure is either robed in the mantle of the Order or wears the Garter on his left leg. The brass of Thomas Boleyn (father of Anne Boleyn) at Hever in Kent shows him in his full Garter robes.

From about 1570 the use of figures declined in popularity and designs were generally armorial: a central, multi-quartered coat of arms surrounded by separate shields representing hereditary and marital connections.

In the sixteenth century, brass plates were incorporated into WALL MONUMENTS and these were usually single sheets engraved with figures, inscriptions and other devices including shields of arms.

The monumental brass declined in popularity from the mid-seventeenth century until the Gothic Revival of the nineteenth, when the brass figure, set into a slab, and the brass wall monument with ornate Gothic inscriptions and elaborate heraldry of the period enjoyed a revival.

See also MONUMENTS, PETRA SANCTA *and* TOMB CHESTS

For the Monumental Brass Society *see* APPENDIX I

BREAD OVEN *see* OVENS

BRECK (*also* **BRAKE** *and* **BROCK**) Wasteland or WASTE that has been cultivated (*see* INTAKE).

BRESSUMER (*also* **BREASTSUMMER**) A horizontal beam, often carved ornamentally, which carries the superstructure in TIMBER-FRAMED BUILDINGS and into which the first-floor joists are tenoned. The term is also used to describe a heavy beam spanning a fireplace or other opening.

BRETATSCHES Medieval hurdles used to form palisades.

BREVIARY A book containing the daily office of the Roman Catholic Church.
See also PSALTERY

BREWERY *see* MALTHOUSE

BREWSTER SESSIONS Annual sessions to license victuallers held during the first fortnight of February.

BRICK Since Roman times, the process of brick-making has consisted of obtaining clay from the ground, preparing and moulding it into shape and burning it. The methods used in this process changed little until the mid-nineteenth century: after excavation, the clay was 'puddled' to remove unwanted material and to provide an even consistency; the brick was then moulded to the required form, using a wooden mould, and dried to reduce shrinkage; final burning was carried out in a clamp, in which the bricks were stacked together with faggots of brushwood as fuel. Clamp firing produced unevenness in size and colour (evident in the attractive variety of medieval and Tudor brickwork) and the system was eventually replaced by burning in kilns, in which the bricks were stacked to allow the passage of hot air between them. Firing took about 48 hours, coal replacing wood as the principal fuel from *c.* 1700. A seventeenth-century innovation was the pug-mill, a mechanical device for puddling which until then had been done (literally) by foot. Pug-mills were at first horse- (or donkey-) powered but later water-power and steam were used.

Roman bricks, used for bonding courses in walling and as facing to a concrete core, had the appearance of tiles: square or oblong, the latter approximately 30 to 45 cm long (12 to 18 inches), 15 to 30 cm wide (6 to 12 inches) and about 2.5 to 4 cm thick (1 to 1½ inches), with mortar courses often as thick as the bricks themselves. Bricks used for flooring were rectangular and thicker, though smaller; and those used to construct *pilae*, the piers of underfloor heating systems, were square. Roman bricks are to be found in the excavated remains of villas and fortifications, but most were 'quarried' from the ruins and re-used in Saxon and medieval buildings, being both durable and freely available. Roman bricks from Caerleon were used in the construction of the eleventh-century hall-keep at Chepstow Castle, Monmouthshire, and misled eighteenth-century antiquaries into thinking it a Roman building. There is little evidence of brick-making following the Roman withdrawal until the earliest known English bricks appeared in the eastern counties in the mid-twelfth century, at Polstead church in Suffolk and Little Coggeshall in Essex, for example. Indeed, contrary to practice in Europe, there was no real brick-building tradition in Britain until the seventeenth century. Little Wenham Hall in Suffolk (*c.* 1275) and the fourteenth-century Holy Trinity church at Kingston-upon-Hull, Humberside, are two of only a small number of notable medieval exceptions. It is surprising that the English for so long failed to recognize the obvious advantages of brick for domestic buildings: baking bricks on site or using local kilns was considerably quicker and cheaper than quarrying, dressing and transporting stone. Eventually, it was the inexorable depredation of the forests for building timber, combined with the immigration of Flemish weavers into East Anglia during the fourteenth century, that encouraged a quickening appreciation of the brick architecture of the Low Countries and the development of a brick-making industry along the east coast in the fifteenth century. Some of the finest late medieval brick buildings date from this transitional period: Hurstmonceux Castle in Sussex (1440) and the gatehouse of Oxburgh Hall in Suffolk (1482), for example. The dimensions of bricks were first standardized in 1477 to conform to the grasp of the brick-layer's fingers and thumb.

During the reign of Henry VIII both the manufacture of bricks and their architectural use became more skilful and imaginative (*see* TUDOR ARCHITECTURE). Chimney-stacks and other architectural features were constructed of ornate brickwork, as at Compton Wynyates in Warwickshire, sometimes under the direction of Italian craftsmen. From the second half of the sixteenth century, many large buildings were constructed chiefly or entirely of brick, such as Hatfield House in Hertfordshire and Charlton House at Greenwich. Building regulations following the Great Fire of London of 1666 encouraged the rapid expansion of the brick manufacturing industry which, together with the gradual acceptance of classical architecture during the seventeenth century and the consequential development of a variety of new bonds (*see* BONDING), presaged the great age of English brick building. A Brick Tax of 1784 to 1850 reduced the popularity of brick in some rural areas, where there was a return to timber for smaller buildings; and a fashion for *stucco*, painted to imitate stone, is evident during the period 1780 to 1830. By the end of the eighteenth century the brick-making industry was perfecting techniques of mass-production in response to the demands of the Industrial Revolution and a rapidly increasing urban population. The Victorian appetite for civic pride and corporate rivalry satiated itself in a welter of architectural activity, and civic, domestic, industrial and ecclesiastical buildings and structures were erected on a vast scale. The predominant material was brick which was available in an extraordinary range of qualities and colours: from extra hard 'engineering bricks' for use in viaducts, tunnels and factories to hand-made, textured bricks for architects such as R.N. Shaw (1831–1912) and Sir Edwin Lutyens (1869–1944). *See also* BRICK NOGGING, TILES *and* SLATES

BRICK NOGGING Late seventeenth- or eighteenth-century patterned brickwork placed between the vertical timbers (*studs*) of a TIMBER-FRAMED BUILDINGS to replace earlier lath and plaster or wattle and daub.

BRIDEWELL *see* PRISONS

BRIDGE-BOTE *see* TRINODA NECESSITAS

BRIDGES Bridges are architectural structures and may be dated accordingly, though vernacular styles of construction can be deceptive: the famous CLAPPER BRIDGES of Dartmoor, for example, have a megalithic appearance but have been built in the same way from the thirteenth century to as late as the nineteenth century.

The Romans built many bridges and CAUSEWAYS to carry their roads. The more important of these were constructed with stone piers and a wooden superstructure. Others were entirely of timber with piles driven into the river-bed.

The medieval attitude towards the provision of bridges was ambivalent: while many local notables and parochial authorities were reluctant to bear the (considerable) costs of bridge-building and maintenance, elsewhere construction was on an impressive scale and reflected not only the demands of trade and commerce for improved communications, but also an awareness by many of the benefits of philanthropy. Numerous individuals and corporations, such as guilds and fraternities, subscribed to the construction and maintenance of bridges at difficult fords and ferry passages, particularly in the hinterland of market towns and ports. Many bridges were associated with religious foundations or chantries, and chapels dedicated to the observance of requiems for the soul of a benefactor or patron saint may sometimes be found near by. A small number of bridges were provided with a bridge chapel: that at Bradford-on-Avon in Wiltshire was

later used as a LOCK-UP. Other urban bridges were fortified, though of these only the gatehouse on the Monnow Bridge at Monmouth remains.

In many instances, tolls were collected and used both to finance the maintenance of the bridge and to swell the coffers of the patron, often a monastic or collegiate foundation or trade guild. Early medieval bridges were simple stone structures, sufficiently wide to accommodate pack-horses with their loads. Some replaced earlier (sometimes Roman) bridges or fords, while others had fords alongside them for use by wagons. Later medieval bridges usually have a roadway width of about 4 metres (12½ feet) and are supported by piers with arches, the undersides vaulted or ribbed and in-filled with rubble for economy (*see* ARCH for dating). Cutwaters were often built into the bases of piers, sometimes only on the upstream side of the bridge. These triangular wedges of masonry were intended to reduce erosion and protect the piers from flotsam by dividing the current. On later medieval and Tudor bridges the parapets are often continued over the cutwaters to provide V-shaped jetties (*abutments*) in the *refuges* of which travellers could seek protection from passing vehicles. Recent repairs to the fourteenth-century White Mill Bridge at Sturminster Marshall

Pack-horse bridge and ford on the Develish at Fifehead Neville, Dorset.

in Dorset revealed foundations consisting of oak piles driven into the river bed, each supporting a flat 'raft' of oak beams. This bridge, the original foundation of which may date from *c*. 1175, spans 61 metres (200 feet) of the river Stour, carrying a 3.6 metre (12 feet) roadway on eight ribbed arches of superb masonry. The engineering skill and financial resources required for its construction suggest that the route was once of major importance, and yet today the bridge carries only a minor road. Indeed, many medieval bridges now service no more than a bridle-way or footpath, such as that on the Caundle Brook at Holwell (also in Dorset), but their existence is clearly indicative of previous route-ways of local, if not regional, importance. Many medieval bridges have subsequently been widened and there are several examples where one side of the bridge is medieval and the other side is of a later date.

In 1285 the Statute of Westminster established that it was the responsibility of the manors to maintain the king's highway outside the towns, but it was not until 1530 that a county rate was permitted to finance the repair of those bridges for which there was no acknowledged responsibility.

Before the end of the seventeenth century, there was little vehicular traffic other than farm wagons and carts. By far the most common means of transporting goods was by pack-horse and numerous PACK-HORSE BRIDGES remain, dating from the medieval and Tudor periods as well as the seventeenth and eighteenth centuries. The development of TURNPIKE ROADS from the late seventeenth century encouraged a parallel period of bridge-building, usually in the architectural style of the period, but with the addition of tollbooths or cottages, as on the Wye Bridge near Whitney in Herefordshire. The Industrial Revolution of the eighteenth and nineteenth centuries, and in particular the creation of canal and railway networks, generated an unprecedented period of bridge-building using new technology and materials. In the early nineteenth century, responsibility for the maintenance of bridges passed to county authorities who served dreadful notice of the penalties awaiting those who defaced their property. Many Dorset bridges, for example, still carry the following notice, dating from the reign of George IV (1820–30):

Any person wilfully INJURING any part of this COUNTY BRIDGE will be guilty of FELONY and upon conviction liable to be TRANSPORTED FOR LIFE by the COURT.

Transportation to Australia ceased in 1867.

BRIDLE-WAYS *and* **BRIDLE-PATHS** Highways over which the public have the following, but no other, rights of way: on foot and on horseback or leading a horse, and possibly with a right to drive animals. A *bridle-path* is a trackway which is (or was) regularly used for riding on horseback but the term implies no statutory right of way. Bridle-ways are clearly marked on Ordnance Survey *Explorer* maps (1:25000) and often follow the routes of ancient trackways or defunct ROADS.
See also ENCLOSURE ROADS *and* HIGHWAYS

BRISURE *see* CADENCY

BRITAIN The island containing England, Scotland and Wales together with other small adjacent islands. The name possibly evolved from the Celtic *Pritani*, meaning 'painted ones', through the Latin *Britannia*, the 'land of the Britanni'. Throughout the Middle Ages the term was used only in an historical context until the reign of Henry VIII (1491–1547) when it entered practical politics relating to the possible unification of England and Scotland. In 1604 James I was proclaimed 'King of Great Britain' and this term was adopted for the United Kingdom in 1707. After this date the terms North Britain (for Scotland) and South Britain (for England) are frequently found in parliamentary legislation.

The term *Great Britain* is now applied to England, Wales and Scotland when considered as a unit. Wales was politically incorporated with England in the sixteenth century and in 1707 the Act of Union formally united Scotland with England.

The *United Kingdom* is the kingdom of Great Britain and (since 1922) Northern Ireland. The term implied Great Britain together with the *whole* of Ireland from 1801 (when the two countries were united by act of parliament) until 1920 (when Ireland was partitioned).

BRITANNIA PRIMA *and* **BRITANNIA SECUNDA** *see* ROMAN ADMINISTRATION

BRITISH SCHOOLS *see* EDUCATION

BROACH SPIRE *see* CHURCH TOWERS

BROADS Large areas of open fresh water in East Anglia. Records in the archives of the Benedictine priory of Ely in Cambridgeshire (now the cathedral) show that the Broads, for so long believed to be an entirely natural landscape, were produced by medieval peat-cutting and subsequent flooding, and at one time were very much more extensive than they are today.

BROADSIDE Ballads, political and religious tracts, etc. published in printed form, on one side only of single sheets of paper, and intended for mass circulation.
See also CHAPBOOK

BROCH Defensive drystone towers found mainly in the coastal areas of the north-east of Scotland and the Northern Isles. The origins of the brochs are still uncertain but the earliest examples are believed to have been constructed as refuges more than 2,000 years ago. Later brochs were fewer in number but very much more sophisticated, both in design and function. They became the focal points of tribal groupings and symbolized the growing authority of Scottish Iron Age chieftains which was to result in the amalgamation of the tribes into small states and, ultimately, in the creation of the Pictish kingdom. Originally 9 to 15 metres high (30 to 50 feet), with hollow walls containing stairways, galleries and narrow chambers, brochs have an interior diameter of up to 12 metres (40 feet), no windows and a single door, which was secured by a bar. Walls could be up to 4.5 metres thick (15 feet), were fireproof and too steep to scale, making a broch almost impregnable. In succeeding centuries brochs were often occupied by peoples of cultures that had nothing to do with the original builders, indeed many were used for agricultural purposes even into the twentieth century.

BROCK see BRECK and INTAKE

BROGGERS see PACK-HORSE ROADS

BRONZE see MINERALS

BRONZE AGE The early and middle Bronze Ages are now dated between *c.* 2500 and 1600 BC and the late Bronze Age between 1600 and 800 BC, though this includes a transitional period during which Bronze Age influences declined as new IRON AGE techniques and cultures were communicated and assimilated.

Similarly, flint and stone implements and weapons, associated with the late Neolithic (*see* STONE AGE), continued to be used during the early Bronze Age which is usually taken to begin with the appearance of artefacts characteristic of the so-called BEAKER people, who were involved in the first exploitation of copper and tin ores of Britain (bronze is an alloy of copper and tin). There is evidence to suggest that by the late Bronze Age a 'fire setting' technique was used to obtain ores in

Irish Bronze Age swords.

comparatively large quantities. Fires were set against a rock face and allowed to burn for many hours so that the heated rock would cool rapidly and crack when doused with water. Radio-carbon dating of charcoal remains of these fires suggests that mines in north and mid-Wales were being worked by this method, and with stone hammers, at some time during the period 1800 to 1000 BC. One mine, at Great Orme's Head in Conwy, had three large galleries, each so far below ground that it would have been necessary to overcome serious drainage and ventilation problems (*see* MINERALS). Throughout the Bronze Age, local and regional agricultural specialization continued to develop, with pastoral farming predominating in some areas and arable in others. A typical small farmstead of this period would have consisted of an enclosure, ditched and banked or palisaded, containing a yard and a cluster of conical huts with thatched roofs and wattle and daub walls. Beyond this, characteristically small, rectangular fields (erroneously known as 'Celtic fields') were cultivated by means of cross-ploughing. Little evidence remains of the agricultural practices of the WESSEX CULTURE of the early Bronze Age, except perhaps in the once extensive areas of heathland in central-southern England which may have originated in widespread forest clearance and eventual soil starvation through over-grazing and excessive cultivation. Agricultural and metallurgical development was accompanied by a gradual increase in population until *c*. 1600 BC when there began an extraordinary population explosion which, within a few centuries, rose to as many as 1 million people. The reasons for this remain obscure, but its effect was the creation of thousands of new settlements and the first major transformation of the landscape. Most of these settlements are now evident only through CROP MARKS and excavation, though there are more tangible remains on the marginal uplands of the north and west where stone was used in the construction of buildings and enclosures (*see* HUT CIRCLES). Many of the trackways which linked these settlements are also evident from the air and may even be preserved within our present network of footpaths and bridle-ways (a further reason why proposals for extinguishment and diversion should be resisted). With a rapidly growing population, competition for land and resources resulted in a significant increase in the construction of defensive HILL FORTS, and archaeological evidence suggests that armed conflict was becoming endemic. Of equal importance was the emergence of planned agricultural landscapes of immense field systems, often of several thousand acres, with regular patterns of fields and boundaries (which sometimes appear to disregard topographical features) and with integrated settlements and trackways, indicative of a total remodelling of vast areas of the landscape during a comparatively short period of time and, therefore, of cohesive and enforceable economic, social and political strategies. The source of these strategies remains obscure, as does the power base from which they emanated. But there can be little doubt that there already existed a degree of hierarchical tribal and territorial authority which was galvanized by the population explosion of the late Bronze Age. The earlier development of BARROWS and numerous ritual sites, in particular the construction of the HENGE monuments and STONE CIRCLES of the late Neolithic and early Bronze Age, could only have been accomplished through the commitment of organized and consolidated societies. Stonehenge in Wiltshire demonstrates also a singular continuity of development, originating as a late Neolithic henge monument, passing through an early Bronze Age phase, during which the great bluestones were transported from Mynydd Preseli in Pembrokeshire, and progressing to a series of phases during which the immense sarsen stones were assembled, dressed and erected, possibly under the auspice of chieftains of the Wessex culture. Abandonment of many of these ancient ritual sites occurred at a time when the effects of the population explosion were becoming apparent. Self-preservation appears to have been a stronger driving force even than primitive religion, and many communities redirected their energies into the construction of defensive settlement sites and the widespread remodelling of the agricultural landscape in order to safeguard livestock and food supplies. It seems likely that this in turn led to a realignment of tribal and community allegiances to the detriment of established inter-tribal religious practices. Elsewhere, however, there was remarkable religious continuity, as in the Neolithic practice of casting precious sacrificial offerings into rivers and meres which, in some cultures, was maintained well into the Iron Age. At Fengate near Peterborough in Cambridgeshire, for example, the remains of an 823 metre (900 yard) sacred avenue and artificial island have recently been excavated. The avenue and island, consisting of about 4 million upright and horizontal timbers, are surrounded by the remains of ritually deposited swords (many deliberately broken in two), jewellery and the corpses of human and animal sacrificial victims mostly dating from the late Bronze Age. The island itself is 137 metres (150 yards) wide, and contained a number of rectangular wooden buildings. This was presumably a religious complex for there is no evidence to suggest that the avenue was used as a settlement causeway.

Bronze Age leather shield from Clonbrin, Ireland.

BROUGHAM Named after the first Lord Brougham, for whom it was built, a small, coachman-driven carriage of the late 1830s originally designed to carry two inside passengers facing forwards and driven from the box to a single horse. A later version, the *bow-fronted brougham* of the 1880s, had a curved glass windscreen directly behind the box.

BUAILE *see* BOOLEY HOUSE *and* SHIELING

BULLA *see* SEALS

BULLAUN From Irish *ballain*, meaning 'cup', bullauns are artificial basins in stones and small boulders and were probably used as mortars. Generally associated with Celtic monastic sites.

BULL'S EYE (or BULLION) *see* GLASS

BURGAGE Tenure in an ancient borough held of the Crown, or of the lords of the borough, and subject to customary rents or services. In the Saxon period burgage rents were called *landgable* or *hawgable*.

BURGESS (i) A citizen of a borough enjoying full municipal rights.
(ii) A member of parliament representing a borough.

BURGH (i) Used by some historians as an alternative spelling of BURH.
(ii) The Scottish equivalent of the English BOROUGH, though before 1832 only royal burghs could return a member of parliament.
See also SCOTLAND

BURGH-BOTE *see* TRINODA NECESSITAS

BURH An Old English term for a fortified town or dwelling. The Anglo-Saxons themselves used the word *burh* when referring to prehistoric or Roman fortifications and applied it to their own fortified towns: refuges constructed in response to the Danish incursions of the ninth and tenth centuries and the first major settlements to be created since the Roman occupation. The *Burghal Hidage*, a remarkable Anglo-Saxon document, lists thirty *burhs* established in Wessex as an integrated defensive system by Alfred before his death in 899. Several were former Roman towns where the defences were utilized

An aerial view of Portchester, Hampshire, a Roman fort adopted as a burh *stronghold.*

(*ceasters*), at Winchester (Hampshire), Dorchester (Dorset) and Bath (Somerset), for example; while others were newly created. Saxon burhs were strategically important settlements, located to take advantage of natural defensive features such as rivers, constructed or redeveloped to a regular street-plan, and surrounded by earthwork defences, apparently requiring four men to defend 5 metres (17 feet) of rampart. A network of roads and trackways also developed, linking *burhs* with each other and with the scattered settlements between.

Perhaps the best example of a newly created *burh* is Wareham in Dorset. Located at the edge of Poole Harbour between the rivers Frome and Piddle, it is defended on three sides by earthworks dating from the late ninth century and on the fourth by the River Frome and its marshes. It was captured in 876 by the Vikings, who overwintered there, and thereafter developed as a port until the fourteenth century. The defences were strengthened in the early twelfth century and again during the Second World War. Other good examples of Saxon burhs at which some evidence remains of their original fortification and street-plan are Wallingford in Oxfordshire, Cricklade in Wiltshire and Lydford in Devon. The subsequent success of a *burh* depended on whether it was able to sustain its function as a trade centre and market: some prospered and became important route-centres, others declined. Former strongholds can often be identified in place-name elements such as '-burgh' or '-bury', though these usually relate to fortified buildings rather than settlements. The English term 'borough' and the Scottish 'burgh' probably originated in the *burh*, though the place-name element '-borough' may also be derived from Old English *beorg*, meaning 'hill'.

BURIAL, RIGHTS OF *see* PARISH

BURIALS *see* BARROWS *and* CEMETERIES

BURY (*also* **BERRY**) A moated farmstead or fort.

BUTT The place-name is commonly associated with what are believed to have been the sites of medieval archery butts. Butt Green, a lane on the edge of the village of Painswick in Gloucestershire, may at one time have been the community's archery field, but regrettably such an assumption is in most instances untenable. Butts certainly existed at the time of the Hundred Years War in the fourteenth and early fifteenth centuries when practice with the longbow was a statutory requirement in every town and village. With rapid advances in the use of firearms,

the longbow ceased to be strategically effective after Flodden Field in 1513 and yet, with the threat of a French invasion, the statute was revived in 1543 and obligatory practice at the butts on Sundays and holidays continued well into the next century. Archery butts usually comprised low mounds against which the targets were placed and although similar mounds may still be found in fields or closes on the periphery of many villages, the only surviving earthworks of certain provenance are those at Wold Newton in Yorkshire, where they seem to have provided protection from stray arrows rather than targets. In almost every case, the place-name relates to the butts or HEADLANDS of medieval open field systems, which often formed winding routes between fields and, being held in common, were gradually established as rights of way.

BUTTER CROSS *see* MARKET CROSS

BUTTERY *see* LARDER

BUTTRESS A projecting support constructed against a wall to counteract the weight of roofs and towers and to compensate for the structurally weakening effects of window openings. The walls of Saxon and Norman stone buildings were invariably of considerable thickness, with small windows and comparatively light timber roofs supported by tie and collar beams. Consequently, they required little reinforcement, and buttresses of this period are generally wide but of low projection. The thinner walls, larger windows and heavy stone vaults of GOTHIC ARCHITECTURE required substantial buttressing with projections of greater depth at the base, reducing in upward stages to the roof level. During the thirteenth century, *angle buttresses* were used at the corners of buildings where they met at 90 degrees (*see illustration*). *Setback buttresses* are similar but are set back slightly to expose the corner of the building. Less common are the large, square *clasping buttresses* which enclose the corners of a tower or porch. In the fourteenth century, *diagonal buttresses* were widely used. These are set diagonally at right angles to the corners of a tower or building. The *flying buttress* (or *arch buttress*) is one by which the thrust of a vault is carried from a wall to an outer buttress by means of an arch or series of arches. The lofty stone vaults, vast windows and slender walls (often little more than cages of stone ribs) that characterize the Perpendicular style of Gothic architecture of the late fourteenth and fifteenth centuries demanded extraordinary ingenuity in order that the downward

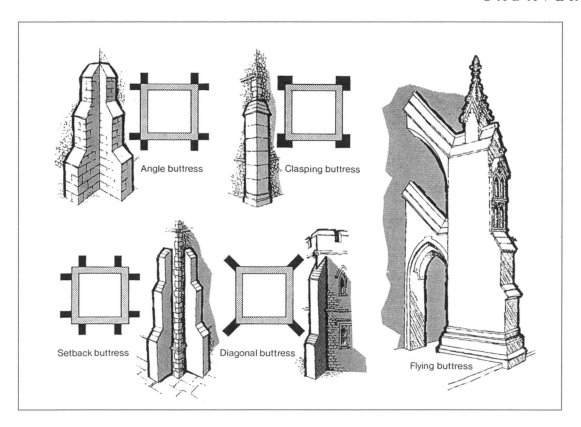

Angle buttress

Clasping buttress

Setback buttress

Diagonal buttress

Flying buttress

and outward thrust of roof, tower and (sometimes) spire should be evenly distributed and counteracted. Mainly through trial and error, the abutment system developed by which arches, placed at the point of greatest thrust (found to be immediately below the springing line of a vault on an internal wall), transferred the pressure through buttresses to ground level and, by means of heavy pinnacles on the buttresses themselves, successfully offset the effect of the thrust. Buttresses were sometimes incorporated into the structure of larger buildings, and may be visible from the interior, as at Gloucester Cathedral where massive 'flying' buttresses, constructed <u>within</u> the transept walls, transfer the outward thrust of the tower to ground level. Buttresses are not confined to medieval churches: the flying buttresses of Wren's St Paul's Cathedral, London (1675–1711), are concealed behind high screen walls which themselves serve as buttresses.

BWLCH A Welsh word meaning 'gap', 'pass' or 'notch', as in Bwlch Efengyl in Powys – the Gospel Pass.

-BY A place-name second element from the Old Norse *byr* and *boær* and Old Danish and Swedish *by*, meaning 'homestead' or 'village' and as such generally found in the North Midlands and north-west of England.

BY APPOINTMENT *see* ROYAL WARRANTS

CADAVER From the Latin *cadaver*, meaning 'corpse', the name is applied to EFFIGIES of the dead when represented in emaciated form and on the verge of decay. Death, and the imagery of decay, haunted the medieval mind, especially following the plagues and pestilences of the early fifteenth

century. Death was personified as a grasping skeleton, often as the 'Grim Reaper' with scythe and timeglass, and decay as worms: *humiliatus sum vermis* – 'by worms I am abused'. Examples of cadavers may be found at Fyfield church in Berkshire (Sir John Golafre, d.1442) and at Tewkesbury Abbey, Gloucestershire, where writhing worms and various snails, toads and mice feast on the corpse of a fifteenth-century abbot.
See also INTRANSI TOMBS

CADENCY (MARKS OF DIFFERENCE) The medieval tenet 'one man one coat' often necessitated the 'differencing' of coats of arms in order that each male member of a family, and of its cadet branches, should possess distinctive arms, a practice known as cadency. Originally, this was achieved by making minor alterations to the design: by varying the colours (*tinctures*) or charges, for example. Since the Middle Ages the three-pointed *label* has been borne by an eldest son during the lifetime of his father. But since the fifteenth century a system of symbols (*brisures*) has been used, each appropriate to a particular male member of a family. In practice (and with the exception of the label), this system has been

Brisures used by the eldest son (label, top), fifth son (annulet, centre) and third son (mullet, bottom). A crescent was used by a second son, a martlet by a fourth and a fleur-de-lis by a sixth.

found to be singularly unsatisfactory and has generally been more honoured in the breach than the observance. In Scotland, a series of borders (*bordures*) is used by succeeding generations which allows the degree of kinship to the main branch of the family to be shown. During the Middle Ages cadency marks were also used to signify feudal tenure and even political allegiance, elements of one coat being transferred to another for this purpose.
See also MARKS OF DISTINCTION

CADET The younger son of an armiger who is the progenitor of a subsidiary branch of a family.

CAIR-, CAER- or CAR- A place-name element meaning 'fortified place', commonly found in Wales and the Marches, Cornwall and the north-west of England. In Ireland, it appears as *Caher-*.
See also -CHESTER

CAIRN *or* CARN A mound of stones constructed either as a waymark, a memorial or over a Neolithic or Bronze Age burial site (*see* CHAMBERED TOMBS). As a place-name, either word may refer to a natural accumulation of boulders or rocky outcrop at a hilltop. Clearance cairns are piles of stones accumulated during the clearance of land for cultivation or pasture, particularly during the Bronze Age. These are usually found in groups, known as cairnfields, such as that containing around 2,500 clearance cairns at Iron Howe in the North York Moors. Accurate identification of the different types of cairn can be difficult for they are often of similar appearance and may be associated with other ruins – of stone circles and collapsed sections of walling of a similar age, for example.

CALDICOTE *see* COLDHARBOUR

CALVINISTIC METHODIST *see* METHODIST

CAMAIL *and* **CAMAIL PERIOD** *see* BRASSES (MONUMENTAL)

CAMPANILE A bell tower, usually detached from other buildings.

CANALS Canals are channels carrying water for inland navigation, though several started life as irrigation systems such as the Roman Car Dyke, which runs from the river Nene at Peterborough in Cambridgeshire to the Witham at Lincoln, and the Fossdyke, which connects the Witham with the river

Trent and is still navigable. Canals are effectively artificial rivers which simply extended an ancient system of natural waterways. England's rivers have, from the Neolithic period, provided immigration routes from the sea to the interior, and in the Middle Ages were often an essential means of communication. The Thames, in particular, provided a convenient and more reliable means of passage than the filthy and often dangerous streets of the metropolis, and barges of all sizes plied the river then just as the familiar taxi cabs navigate the streets today. It was not by chance that the medieval and Tudor royal palaces – centres of government and administration – were sited at the river's edge. Water navigation, using rivers and coastal waters, was also the most effective means of transporting goods and materials. During the fifteenth century, for example, limestone was carried by sea and river from Devon, or even from Caen in Normandy, to the south-east of England because it was considered cheaper and

quicker to do so than to risk the hazards of an overland journey from local quarries. Several rivers were made navigable by the provision of LOCKS during the sixteenth and seventeenth centuries but, with the advent of the Industrial Revolution, rapidly increasing demands for the efficient transportation of manufactured goods and materials between centres of industry were clearly incompatible with an inadequate road system and the unpredictable nature of most natural waterways. Being at first dependent on power from fast-flowing streams, many manufacturing centres were located in upland areas of Britain, far removed from navigable rivers.

The canals of the eighteenth and early nineteenth centuries were the arteries of the Industrial Revolution before their decline in the 1830s with the development of steam traction and the railway system. The great advantage of canal transport is its economy. Water offers minimal resistance to movement and the level nature of routes meant that a

Near Leys Junction on the Stourbridge Canal, West Midlands.

single horse, following tow paths, could haul loads which would otherwise have to be transported by several teams of wagons using roads that were soon transformed into quagmires. Observing the sedate passage of today's pleasure boats, it is difficult to appreciate the impact of canals on commercial and social life in the late eighteenth century. The country must have been in turmoil as tunnels were blasted, embankments thrown up and AQUEDUCTS built. There was work for all during the boom which lasted nearly a century and effectively transformed Britain from an agricultural to an industrial country. Clerks and accountants, surveyors and engineers, blacksmiths and *navvies* – the 'navigators' who worked with pick and shovel on the canal or navigation – all found employment. James Brindley (1716–72) and Thomas Telford (1757–1834) were chiefly responsible for the construction of 6,800 km (4,250 miles) of canals between 1760 and 1840. Brindley began the Bridgewater Canal in 1760 to transport coal from the Duke of Bridgewater's mines at Worsley to Manchester. His great aqueduct over the river Irwell at Barton was considered to be a wonder of the age. Brindley's canal system was intended to connect the major navigable rivers of industrial England: the Thames and Severn, the Mersey and Trent. His policy was to construct canals with a minimum of locks, embankments, cuttings and tunnels. These are known as contour canals and although they were inevitably of greater length, it is significant that the canals built with numerous locks were the first to be abandoned. Telford, 'the Colossus of Roads' (Southey), was the greatest British canal-builder, bridge-builder and road-builder, and the son of a Scottish shepherd. His canals included the great Caledonian Canal which crossed Scotland.

As well as moving raw materials and industrial products, the canals provided the first means of mass transport. It took two days, travelling at 12 miles per hour, to travel from Liverpool to London. The new waterways operated tight schedules with 24-hour fast delivery services, fly boats and passenger and market boats all subject to strict timetables. Cargo occupied most of the space in a 21 metre (70 feet) narrow boat, the bargee and his family occupying dark, cramped quarters in the stern. All members of the family were expected, literally, to 'pull their weight' at locks and in tunnels where narrow boats often had to be 'legged' through, the bargee lying on his back and propelling the boat by pushing on the tunnel walls with his legs.
See also INCLINED PLANES, LOCKS *and* RAILWAYS

For dates of completion of the more important canals *see* Richardson, J., *The Local Historian's Encyclopedia*, Phillimore, 1986.
For the National Waterways Museum *and the* Railway and Canal History Society *see* APPENDIX I

CANDLE AUCTION *see* MEADS

CANDLE-BEAM *see* ROOD LOFT

CANDLEMAS The Feast of the Purification of the Virgin Mary held on 2 February. Old Candlemas Day was 14 February: '. . . the day which was of great import to agriculturalists – the day of the Candlemas Fair. It was at this fair that new engagements were entered into for the twelve months following the ensuing Lady Day, and those of the farming population who thought of changing their places duly attended at the county town where the [hiring] fair was held.' (Thomas Hardy)
See also FAIRS *and* LADY DAY

CANES *see* WINDOWS

CANON *see* CATHEDRALS *and* CLERGY (CHURCH OF ENGLAND)

CANONICAL HOURS *see* MONASTERIES *and* SUNDIALS

CANONICORUM Latinized place-name element indicating that the manor was once owned by a medieval community of canons, as at Whitchurch Canonicorum in Dorset. *See* LATIN

CANONIZATION *see* SAINTS

CANON LAW Ecclesiastical law based on New Testament precepts. A digest of the formal decrees of various councils of the Church (*canons*) and patriarchal decisions (*decretals*) relating to doctrine and discipline. Before the Norman Conquest, the courts heard all suits, both lay and ecclesiastical, with bishops and ealdormen sitting as joint judges. Such courts were disliked by the Papacy, and William of Normandy was able to obtain Papal approval for his conquest of Britain by promising to establish separate ecclesiastical courts to consider those matters which 'belong to the government of souls'. These courts dealt not only with offences against morality and the doctrines of the Church, but also with secular matters such as legitimacy and matrimonial causes. Unlike common law (*see* LAW), much of Canon Law derived from the precepts of

Roman Law. The English Church consisted of the two provinces of Canterbury and York, each divided into dioceses with diocesan or consistory courts, each presided over by a chancellor. Appeals from the consistory courts were brought before the *Court of Arches* (in the Province of Canterbury) or the *Court of Chancery* (in the Province of York), the former presided over by the *Dean of Arches* and the latter by the *Official Principal*. Appeal from the provincial courts to the Pope in Rome was abolished in 1532, and was thereafter a function of the *ad hoc* Court of Delegates which consisted of three judges and three Doctors of Civil Law. Several aspects of Canon Law were transferred to the civil courts during the nineteenth century: since 1833 appeals on matters of conduct have been brought before the Judicial Committee of the Privy Council; in 1857 matrimonial causes were transferred to the new *Divorce Courts* and matters concerning wills and probate to the new *Probate Courts*, both of which were incorporated into the *Supreme Court of Judicature* in 1873 and finally into the Family Division of the High Court in 1970. But the Church Courts remain to deal with disciplinary and moral matters within the Church of England, including those relating to the conduct of priests and certain lay people, such as churchwardens and parish clerks, and with matters concerning the demolition or alteration of church premises. Such courts are not courts of common law.

CANONS REGULAR *see* CATHEDRALS

CANOPY A roof-like projection over a tomb or memorial, usually of stone but also of wood or metal. A canopy is only one part of a MONUMENT: it may surmount a free-standing or recessed TOMB CHEST or a hanging WALL MONUMENT. Canopies developed in the thirteenth century, possibly from the structures placed over the shrines of saints, and are mostly found above the tomb chests of high-ranking clerics of the period. The overall design of a canopy usually followed contemporary architectural style and decoration. Interiors were often vaulted with floreated and heraldic painting and gilding, though much of this original work has been lost through neglect or vandalism. Initially, heraldic work comprised shields of arms indicative of marital or seignoral alliances, but from the second half of the fifteenth century BADGES and CYPHERS were also widely used. There are examples of free-standing tomb canopies having been expanded to form small CHANTRY CHAPELS. Canopies over recessed tombs in church walls were usually less elaborate, though some have ogee and/or cupped arches, and shields of arms will be found on spandrels and on friezes of the Perpendicular period. With the Renaissance, Gothic pillars and arches were superseded by Roman columns and classical pediments which provided the 'new gentility' of the post-medieval period with an eminently suitable vehicle by which to display their heraldry. Invariably, every available surface was utilized for this purpose and where these highly emblazoned canopies surmounted tomb chests the overall effect was even more splendid, for the chest itself would also be decorated with shields and might be surrounded by ironwork which included gilded pennants and scrollwork. Good examples are the tombs of Elizabeth, Lady Hoby (d.1609) at Bisham, Berkshire, which is set against a wall, and that of Bishop Montague (d.1618) at Bath Abbey. From the mid-seventeenth century there was an increasing tendency towards a purer classical treatment with less decoration, and during the eighteenth century the canopy became an architectural feature rather than a structure, eventually to be replaced by the wall monument, and re-appearing only briefly during the Gothic Revival.

CANTREF *or* **CANTRED** In medieval Wales, the land lying between the rivers Conwy and Dee comprised the Four Cantreds, or hundreds, of Rhos, Rhufoniog, Dyffryn Clwyd and Tegeingl (Welsh *cant* = 'hundred', *tref* = 'town').

CAPONIER *see* MARTELLO TOWERS AND COMMISSION FORTS

CAPUT *see* MULTIPLE ESTATE

CARMELITES *see* FRIARS

CAROLINGIAN Of the Frankish dynasty founded by Charlemagne (r. AD 768–814).

CARRELS *see* CLOISTER

CARRIAGE DRIVES In the late eighteenth and nineteenth centuries, many owners of stately homes constructed driveways across the surrounding countryside so that their guests could enjoy the scenery from the comfort of a carriage. These carriage drives were usually of moderate length and gradient, and formed a circuit from the lodge gates of a great house. They were designed to take advantage of broad vistas and spectacular scenery, and were sometimes enhanced by follies, artificial ruins and picturesque stopping places where picnics were taken. Doctor Blackall's carriage drive on Dartmoor, for example, was 9.5 km (6 miles) in length and was constructed in 1869 by Dr Thomas Blackall, who also restored the ruinous manor-house of Spitchwick. Also in Devon is the Revelstoke Nine Mile Drive, built by the first Baron Revelstoke, formerly Edward Baring, head of the Baring Bank, who entertained the rich and famous (including the Prince of Wales) before the collapse of his financial empire in 1890. The 6.3 km (4 mile) Earl's Drive in Cornwall was begun in 1740 by Richard, Baron Mount Edgcumbe, as part of a plan to replace the formal gardens of his house with a 'natural' landscape. This was later extended by the third baron to include the lovely coves of Kingsand, Cawsand and Penlee Point, and acquired its name when the baron was elevated to an earldom. Most carriage drives are in the West Country and Wales, though there is a good example at Studley Royal near Ripon, Yorkshire.

See also FOLLIES *and* CLAIRE VOIE

CARRIAGEWAY A route-way over which there is a public right of way on foot, on horseback and by means of a vehicle, including a car or motorcycle.

See also HIGHWAY

CARRIER Throughout most of the nineteenth century, trains and horse-drawn transport co-existed. Numerous carriers' vans provided regular passenger and delivery services essential to the survival of the rural population. Nearly every village either had its own carrier or one who passed through regularly. The carriers' vans connected villages with the railways and with each other and were in particular demand on market days and Saturdays. They were similar to farmers' wagons, but less robust and with narrower wheels, and were fitted with a canvas awning or 'tilt' supported by wooden hoops. They travelled at about 3 or 4 miles an hour, little more than a good walking speed, and covered comparatively short distances. As well as passengers, carriers conveyed goods in to the towns to be sold, and brought purchases back. Sometimes a selection of goods was delivered to a village 'on approval'. Thomas Hardy, in *A Few Crusted Characters*, described the carriers' vans as 'a respectable, if somewhat lumbering class of convenience, much resorted to by decent travellers not overstocked with money.' During the 1920s they were superseded by motorized coaches or lorries.

See also WAGONS

CARTHUSIANS The Poor Brothers of God of the Charterhouse (originally the *Grande Chartreuse* in Grenoble) was a strictly contemplative order, founded by St Bruno in 1084, with a Rule dating from 1130 that required of them vows of austerity, humility and silence. Like the desert hermits of the past, each monk lived in his own cell, with its garden and patch of cultivated land, working and devoting several hours each day to mental prayer. His clothing was coarse and undyed, and for three days a week he lived on bread and water. On other days he ate scanty rations of fish, eggs and vegetables: no meat was taken. The monks came together for the offices of Mattins, Lauds and Vespers, the other Hours being recited in their cells, and for meals only on feast-days, when conversation was permitted. In order that their priories should not become too large or well endowed, numbers were restricted to a prior and twelve monks, with eighteen lay brothers who had cells and an oratory of their own and were responsible for maintaining the meagre arable holdings, flocks and herds. The first Carthusian priory (or *Charterhouse*) in England was founded by Henry II in 1178 as part of his penance for the murder of Thomas à Becket in 1170. The chosen site was then a remote and inhospitable one at Witham in Selwood Forest on the Somerset-Wiltshire border. Two further Charterhouses were established at Hinton near Bath in 1226 and Beauvale near Nottingham in 1320. Following the onset of the Black Death in 1348–50, at a time when the endowment of monastic communities was otherwise in decline, the Carthusians enjoyed both the respect and the financial support of the nobility. Several priories were endowed by members of the medieval court circle, including the London Charterhouse in 1370. The latest (and largest) Carthusian foundation in England, the House of Jesus in Bethlehem at Sheen on the Surrey bank of the Thames, was founded by Henry V (1413–22), the most puritanical of the medieval English kings. Alone among the English monastic orders, the Carthusians may be distinguished by that integrity and courage of soul which compelled them to stand against Henry VIII at the Dissolution in 1536.

CARTOON *see* STAINED GLASS

CARTSHEDS Unlike cowhouses, which are similar in appearance but face into a farmyard, cartsheds are usually open on the long side *away* from the yard so that stray animals could not wander among vehicles and machinery. 'Parking spaces' were separated by brick piers or wooden posts which supported the roof. The area above was often used as a granary. Encouraged by government grants, many such cartsheds and cowhouses have, in recent years, been converted to other uses, such as self-catering holiday accommodation.

CARTULARY A monastic or estate register-book containing details of deeds, charters, grants, property and other possessions. Also, one who keeps the register and the place in which it is stored.

CARUCADE *see* HIDE

CARUCAGE A land-tax levied from 1194 to 1224 based on the number of carucates (*see* HIDE) recorded in Domesday Book. In areas where land was measured in hides, the term *hideage* or *hidegeld* was used.

CARYATID A female figure used as a column to support an entablature in classical architecture. Male figures are *Antlantes* (plural of *Atlas*), female figures carrying baskets on their heads are *Canophorae* and demi-figures which appear to emerge from the pedestal are either *Herms* (humans) or *Terms* (animals or mythical creatures).

CASEMATE A bomb-proof vaulted chamber used either as a gun emplacement or as quarters for a garrison. Originally, the term was applied to a loopholed gallery from which the defenders of a fortification could command a moat or ditch.

CASHEL From the Irish *caiseal*, a strongly fortified dwelling, often constructed within drystone ramparts and dating from the sixth to the twelfth centuries.

CASTELLAN The governor or captain of a castle.

CASTER *see* -CHESTER

CASTLERY Territory within the administrative jurisdiction of the constable of a castle. *See also* RAPES and LATHES

CASTLES (MEDIEVAL) '. . . they filled the land full of castles. They cruelly oppressed the wretched men of the land with castle works and when the castles were made they filled them with devils and evil men . . .'
The Anglo-Saxon Chronicles 1137

Over 1,000 castles were built in the century following the Norman Conquest. Some were *adulterine* castles, built without authority during the anarchic reign of Stephen (1135–54), but most were constructed in the wake of the Conquest itself by the Norman lords and their allies as they took possession of their lands. These conquerors in a hostile land numbered only a few thousand and their castles became both symbols of subjugation and bastions of paranoia. Before the Conquest, HILL FORTS, Roman *castelli* and Anglo-Saxon BURHS were constructed for communal defence but, with the exception of a very small number of castles built by Anglo-Norman favourites of Edward the Confessor (such as Richard FitzCrob's stronghold at Richard's Castle in Herefordshire, erected in 1032), the concept of the private fortified residence was new in England.

The *motte* fortification depicted in the Bayeux Tapestry (*c.* 1080) originated in the Rhineland and France some two decades before the Conquest. It consisted of a flat-topped, conical mound of earth and rubble, excavated from a surrounding ditch, on top of which was erected a timber palisade enclosing a rectangular wooden tower – the *keep*. The sides of the earthwork may have been coated with a slippery layer of clay and occasionally a stream or lake was diverted to fill the ditch or *fosse* with water. It is unlikely that the motte itself was occupied. It provided a last line of defence and may have been surrounded at its base by a further palisaded bank and ditch. Such strongholds could be constructed very quickly: one was built immediately the invasion army disembarked at Hastings in 1066, and mottes at Warwick, Nottingham, York, Lincoln, Huntingdon and Cambridge were constructed during a single campaign. The largest known motte, at Thetford in Norfolk, had a height of 24 metres (80 feet) and a base diameter of 110 metres (360 feet); however, most were considerably smaller. Many mottes were built within a *bailey*, or fortified enclosure, in which thatched domestic and agrarian buildings were constructed, together with gates and fortified bridges over the surrounding ditches (*see also* 'RINGWORK'). In the Welsh Marches, mottes are known as *tumps*, and in Wales as *tomen*, which can also mean 'heap' or 'dunghill'. Remaining earthworks can be singularly disappointing and suggest that many *motte and bailey* castles were modest indeed by comparison with later medieval fortifications. Few of the earliest Norman keeps were built of stone: the White Tower at the Tower of London (1077–80) and the great keep at Colchester in Essex, the largest in England (*c.* 1085), are of stone construction as is the magnificent hall of Chepstow Castle in Monmouthshire. Built by

The motte and bailey Rayleigh Mount, Essex, c. 1172. (Alan Sorrell)

William fitz Osbern, palatine Earl of Hereford, shortly before his death in 1071, Chepstow was modelled on similar eleventh-century hall-keeps in the Loire Valley and in Normandy and is the earliest dateable secular stone building in Britain (*see also* HALL). Several timber keeps were rebuilt in stone but mottes were often found to be unstable and were abandoned in favour of more suitable natural sites. In Scotland, fortified ramparts, usually enclosing a keep and constructed on a naturally defensive site, date from the eleventh and twelfth centuries.

A prolonged period of internal peace during the reign of Henry I (1100–35) provided an opportunity for remodelling many of the earlier castles, particularly those associated with administrative or strategic centres and royal strongholds. Many twelfth-century magnates constructed magnificent fortified towers or *donjons*, which included both military and domestic quarters: William d'Albini's keep at Castle Rising in Norfolk (1138) and that of Geoffrey de Clinton at Kenilworth in Warwickshire

(1180), for example. Another type of fortification was the circular or polygonal *shell* keep – a misleading term, for these were not towers but stone enclosures, built to replace wooden palisades at the top of mottes. They contained domestic apartments of stone or timber ranged against the stone and rubble wall or 'shell' which was some 2.5 to 3 metres thick (8 to 10 feet) and 6 to 7.5 metres high (20 to 25 feet), the enclosure having a diameter of 12 to 30 metres (40 to 100 feet). Often the bailey palisade was also rebuilt in stone and carried up both side of the motte to join the shell keep, as at Cardiff and Carisbrooke on the Isle of Wight (1136).

The massive square keeps of the late twelfth and thirteenth centuries were virtually impregnable (*see* SIEGES). At ground level, walls were 6 metres thick (20 feet) and they rose to 25 metres (80 feet) or more with splayed buttresses at the corners and at the centre of each face. Corner turrets carried stone spiral staircases to each of four or five floors, and within the thickness of the walls were passages, chambers and GARDEROBES (latrines) which vented to a cesspool or pit below or onto the outside of the walls. Because of the enormous weight of masonry, such keeps had to be constructed on solid ground, usually on a natural eminence, either within an earlier bailey or on an entirely new site. The need for a solid foundation often conflicted with the other essential requirement: a reliable water supply within the walls of the castle. It was often necessary to excavate deep well-shafts in order to reach water, though such measures helped to prevent pollution during periods of siege. Typically, a stone vaulted *undercroft* or basement was used for storage and above this the ground floor would house the garrison with the great hall taking up the entire first floor. Some of the larger halls measured up to 13.5 metres square (45 feet square) and 10 metres high (30 feet), and were often divided by a stone wall, pierced with arches, to support the timber baulks of the ceiling. Fireplaces were set into the thickness of the outer walls, with tapering flues rising diagonally to vent at the outer face. On the second floor were the principal private chambers which, in the larger castles, sometimes

included a chapel, and above was a battlemented platform. Access would normally be at first-floor level by means of a flight of steps passing through a heavily defended forework of two or more towers, each containing massive gates with draw-bars and PORTCULLIS and with a DRAWBRIDGE spanning the gap between the towers. Such an arrangement may be seen at Newcastle-upon-Tyne, Tyne and Wear (1177), though this enters the keep on the second floor. Other examples of square keeps are Dover (1188) and Rochester (1139) in Kent and Goodrich, Herefordshire (*c.* 1160). In Ireland, some rectangular keeps also had distinctive cylindrical turrets (called *flankers*) at each corner, at Carlow Castle in County Carlow, for example.

So successful were these massive donjons that the civil war during the reign of Stephen (1135–54) was essentially a succession of sieges, resolved as often by starvation or treachery as by the use of projectile machines such as the *mangonel* and *trebuchet*. These strongholds had been designed primarily for defensive purposes, but military architects, no doubt influenced by experiences in the Holy Land,

Goodrich Castle, Herefordshire, c. 1425. Built on a rocky outcrop overlooking the river Wye, the massive gatehouse, buttressed drum-towers and curtain walls were constructed c. 1300 around an inner courtyard and twelfth-century keep. A series of garderobes project from the wall to the right of the nearest (south-east) tower. The barbican was added in the fourteenth century. (Alan Sorrell)

perceived a need to provide a besieged garrison with a means of retaliation. Rows of *putlog holes*, still visible just below the *crenels* (openings) of battlements, once supported timber *hourds* (projecting galleries) and larger *pentices* or 'penthouses' (projecting wooden turrets) which were built over battlements both for added protection and so that projectiles could be dropped into the vulnerable area at the foot of a wall. (These timber structures were later superseded by *machicolations* – permanent projecting stone parapets carried forward on corbels between which the offensive material could be thrown). 'Blind spots' on bailey walls were similarly covered by the provision of *flanking towers* (or *mural towers*) from which archers and crossbow-men could command the outer face of the wall while themselves remaining protected (*see* ARROW SLITS). These measures proved so successful that by the end of the thirteenth century, castles were being built or modified to provide fortified enclosures with outer *curtain walls* and circular flanking towers (known as *drum towers* because of their cylindrical shape) which were less susceptible to mining than square towers, the corners of which were structurally vulnerable. Indeed, on a number of castles (particularly in South Wales and the Marches) massive pyramidal buttresses of masonry were built against the exterior walls of drum towers as added protection against undermining. (*Petards*, earthenware pots containing 'Greek Fire' made of sulphur and saltpetre and with cotton thread fuses, were used by Edward I at the siege of Brechin in 1303. This was probably the first time that gunpowder had been used in a siege in Britain, though as yet its potential for mining was unrealized. The substance was singularly unstable and no doubt many an Edwardian soldier was 'hoisted with his own petard'.) Gatehouses were provided to protect the entrance, inevitably the weakest point of any fortification. These consisted of twin towers, usually D-shaped, linked above an entrance passage (the *gates passage*) by a chamber in which were the mechanisms for the portcullises, and *murder holes* through which projectiles could be discharged into the passage or 'killing ground' below and fires extinguished at the base of the raised wooden drawbridge. On either side of the gates passage were guard-chambers and a porter's lodge, with fireplaces and garderobes, entered only from within the gatehouse and containing the draw-bars which secured a series of stout double doors and the drawbridge movement. For many years vestiges of the donjon lingered on in these massive gatehouses, which often contained the principal chambers of the

castle. Of course, treachery from *within* was always a possibility and most castles were built with internal refuges that could be isolated in the event of a rebellion. Harlech in Gwynedd is one of the finest of these 'gatehouse castles', and is also constructed on the concentric principle (*see below*).

In Wales, the most prolific builders of castles were the princes of Gwynedd in the twelfth and thirteenth centuries, but it is the strongholds of Llywelyn ab Iorwerth ('The Great', 1173–1240) and Llywelyn ap Gruffudd ('The Last', d.1282) that are particularly distinctive. Sited in naturally strong, isolated positions they were built to command the route-ways into Snowdonia and round the borders of Gwynedd. Their most characteristic feature is an apsidal or rectangular tower, often joined to an insubstantial and irregular curtain wall, without flanking towers or significant gatehouse, and enclosing a single ward, as at Dolwyddelan (*c.* 1200). Collectively, the castles constructed by Edward I of England (1271–1307) during his subjugation of North Wales (1276–96) represent one of the greatest achievements of medieval military architecture. The disposition and design of each was dictated both by its site, which was chosen to take advantage of natural features and its suitability for provisioning by sea, and its function. Conwy (1282) and Caernarfon (1283–92; Gwynedd) were citadels, integrated within the defensive walls (*bastides*) of the TOWNS they protected, rectangular and elongated, with adjacent lower and upper wards or courtyards and great flanking towers (*see also* BOROUGH). At Conwy, entry was by means of gates passages protected by BARBICANS at the east and west ends. At Caernarfon, the King's Gate (had it been completed) would have contained five doors, six portcullises and numerous murder holes and arrow slits. Harlech, also in Gwynedd (1283), is a combination of gatehouse and *concentric* castle. It stands on a rocky outcrop 61 metres (200 feet) above the former sea level and has a formidable gatehouse, four huge corner towers and walls enclosing a single inner ward. There is also an outer ward protected by a low curtain wall which encircles the castle and its precipitous access from the sea. Beaumaris, on Anglesey, is the epitome of concentric castles. Begun in 1295 but never completed, it was constructed on a level site that provided none of the advantageous natural features enjoyed by other castles. Because of this, Edward's architect, a Savoyard, Master James of St George, 'perfected the ultimate in symmetrical concentric design'. There is no reliance on a central strongpoint and the castle consists of concentric rings of walls, each higher than that outside it so that both inner and outer wards could be defended simultaneously, and with flanking towers located to eliminate 'blind spots'. There is a 5.5 metre (18 feet) wet moat with a fortified dock and two substantial gatehouses to the north and south of the inner ward. Beaumaris was probably modelled on the superb magnatial castle at Caerphilly in South Wales. Begun in 1268, and covering 30 acres, it had concentric walls with corner towers, east and west gatehouses and incorporated a complex system of water defences, fortified dams and islands called *hornworks* (*see* MOATS).

The late thirteenth century saw the development of the characteristic *tower house* stronghold that dominated private fortifications in Scotland late into the sixteenth century. Scottish tower houses were square or rectangular buildings with thick walls, five or six storeys, crenellated walls and turrets, as at Borthwick (*c.* 1430; Midlothian) and Elphinstone (1440; East Lothian). In the fourteenth century, the threat of a French invasion inspired royal support for the building of a number of castles in the southern counties of England, notably Bodiam, East Sussex (1386–8); this is a quadrangular fortification with round towers at each corner, a rectangular tower at the centre of three flanks and in the fourth a gatehouse approached through a barbican and octagonal outwork from wooden bridges set at right angles over a large moat. At Bodiam, the walls *are* the castle: all the domestic buildings and privy chambers, including the chapel and great hall, are constructed within the outer walls rather than erected against them as in earlier castles. Charles Coulson rightly described Bodiam as 'an enigma – outward military ostentation which is so deliberately contradicted by the domesticity of all the features of detail'. There was a revival of the donjon castle in the late fourteenth century, particularly on the Scottish border (*see also* PELE TOWERS), and castles such as Nunney in Somerset (1373) and Wardour in Wiltshire (1393) are tower houses, the latter with an enclosed courtyard, constructed in the French manner for lavish entertainment and domestic comfort but at the same time designed and equipped for defensive purposes. In 1429 Henry VI promised a £10 grant to anyone who would build a castle to his specifications in order to defend the borders of the English Pale in Ireland. These simple three-storey towers, 6 metres long (20 feet), 5 metres wide (16 feet) and 12 metres high (40 feet), became the model for the tower houses of Irish chieftains, such as the fifteenth-century Roodstown Castle, County Louth, and these continued to be built well into the seventeenth century, often within a walled courtyard or BAWN.

Was it the development of GUNPOWDER in the fourteenth century that made the castle redundant, or had they simply become truly impregnable? With a few notable exceptions (e.g. Harlech), fifteenth-century military campaigns were no longer determined by protracted and expensive sieges but by attrition in the field. Whether the commodious fifteenth-century keeps erected by a few members of the English aristocracy were indicative of genuine insecurity or ostentation is open to question: Tattershall in Lincolnshire (1430–50) is constructed of brick! The 'new aristocracy' of the Tudor period had no martial tradition and as the military importance of the castle declined so a desire for domestic comfort and spaciousness increased. In Scotland, the tower house tradition was revived in the late sixteenth century when two or three towers were often constructed to form a single building, with conical-roofed turrets and roof balustrades indicative of domestic rather than military considerations. Perhaps the best example is Craigievar Castle in Aberdeenshire, completed in 1626. Naturally, the romantic Victorian Gothick period produced a number of castles, such as Castell Coch near Cardiff in South Wales (1875–9), but the most theatrical of 'modern' castles must be the extraordinary Castle Drogo in Devon, built (though not completed) by Edwin Lutyens in 1910–13 for Sir Julius Drewe, founder of the Home and Colonial Stores.

When studying a castle two points should be considered:

First, they served a variety of purposes: as residences for magnates and their retinues; as administrative centres and meeting-places for councils and courts; and, above all, as symbols of power and authority. Many castles were isolated outposts in hostile territory; or, as part of a wider defensive system, they may have controlled routeways, bridgeheads, fords and mountain passes, or protected ports and urban centres of trade and commerce.

Second, few castles remain unaltered from when they were first built, and none fits neatly into any particular category. For many, there is evidence of continuous occupation from the twelfth century: some have been entirely rebuilt but most have been remodelled many times, according to the current military and architectural fashion. Many were slighted following civil wars, while others have been successfully adapted for domestic purposes.

Before visiting a castle, study its site on maps of various scales: in relation to other castles, to route-ways and to physical features. Attempt to determine the function and type of the original fortification. When you arrive, always walk round the exterior first and study the defences (ignoring modern additions such as wooden catwalks, bridges and flights of steps which are almost invariably in the wrong place!). Note each line of defence as you enter across the moat, through the gates passage and into the middle or upper ward and the final refuge. Not all defences are as obvious as the drawbridge or portcullises: observe the relative angles of surrounding walls and flanking towers and the open 'killing grounds' between. Look for 'layers' of development: how various parts of the castle have been adapted and remodelled to match the political circumstances of a particular age and the development of siege technology. Only then should you buy the guide book.

CATHEDRA *see* CATHEDRALS *and* CLERGY (CHURCH OF ENGLAND)

CATHEDRAL A church which contains the *cathedra* or throne of the bishop of a DIOCESE.

English dioceses have always been large and her cathedrals, therefore, few in number. Consequently, the medieval cathedrals were able to exercise considerable regional influence and enjoyed patronage of such munificence that the scale and splendour of their architecture greatly exceeds that of most parish churches. This is particularly evident in the development of cathedrals to the east of the crossing, where magnificent provision was made not only for considerable numbers of clergy, but also for the shrines of saints, reliquaries, CHANTRY CHAPELS and royal and magnatial tombs. CHAPELS were often added to the ambulatory for these purposes and many cathedrals built *lady chapels* to the east of the high altar in response to the popularity of the cult of the Virgin during the fourteenth century. With the obvious exception of St Paul's in London (rebuilt by Sir Christopher Wren 1675–1710), no major English cathedral is of a single, unified architectural style. Even at Salisbury, which was constructed within a period of sixty-four years (1220–84), the tower and spire were not completed until *c*. 1380. (For church design and structure *see* CHURCHES.)

Of the seventeen medieval cathedral churches at the DISSOLUTION OF THE MONASTERIES, seven were BENEDICTINE monastic foundations: Canterbury, Durham, Ely, Norwich, Rochester,

Winchester and Worcester, as was Bath which replaced Wells as a cathedral between 1090 and 1218 when the joint diocese was established. In these monastic cathedrals, the bishop was also the titular abbot, though in practice responsibility for the monastic establishment rested with the prior and that for the cathedral with a CHAPTER, so that they were known as cathedral priories. The remaining ten cathedrals were served by canons who were responsible (as they are today) for the maintenance of cathedral services. The *Canons Regular* lived in accordance with a fixed code (Latin *regula*, meaning 'rule') and were, in England, AUGUSTINIAN (or Austin) Canons whose rule was monastic, for which reason their cathedral church at Carlisle was classified as a monastic foundation at the Dissolution. The other nine cathedrals were administered by *Secular Canons* who followed no rule and were free to live where they chose. Of these cathedrals of the 'Old Foundation', five are of pre-Conquest foundation: Exeter, Hereford, Lichfield, London and York; and three date from the reign of William I (1066–87): Chichester, Sarum and Lincoln. The fourth, Wells, regained its former cathedral status from Bath in 1218 and in 1228 a new building at Salisbury replaced the old cathedral at Sarum – now Old Sarum – some 3.2 km (2 miles) away. Secular Canons lived by means of *prebends* or benefices of income from endowed land, manors or even churches. Membership of a non-monastic cathedral chapter was restricted to prebendaries – holders of prebends – and each had his prebendal stall in the cathedral. In some cathedrals, the ancient territorial titles of prebends have been retained, though not the endowments. At the Dissolution, the monastic foundations were reconstituted to become cathedrals of the 'New Foundation' and in the 1540s Henry VIII created six additional sees. Former Augustinian churches at Oxford and Bristol and the great Benedictine churches at Chester, Gloucester, Peterborough and Westminster all became cathedrals, though Westminster was 'demoted' again in 1550. No further sees were established until 1836, and of the twenty new Anglican cathedrals created since then only five are of medieval foundation: St Albans was a Benedictine abbey; Southwark an Augustinian priory; and Manchester, Ripon and Southwell were collegiate churches of secular canons.

Today, English cathedrals are normally administered by a chapter of residentiary canons presided over by a dean or, in recent foundations, by a provost, as at the Cathedral Church of St Philip in Birmingham which became a cathedral in 1905.

There are also non-residentiary or honorary canons, who may have certain responsibilities and privileges, and minor canons, who are responsible for assisting at musical services but are not members of a chapter. In cathedrals of the 'Old Foundation', the *precentor* (who is responsible for the direction of the choral services) is a member of the chapter, while elsewhere he is a minor canon as is his deputy, the *succentor*.

CATHOLIC CHURCH *see* ROMAN CATHOLIC CHURCH

CATHOLIC Literally, 'general' or 'universal', the term may imply the universality of the Church in contradistinction to local Christian communities; it is used to imply orthodoxy as distinct from the 'heretical' or 'schismatical' and it may be used to describe the undivided Church before the schism of East and West in 1054, following which the Western Church referred to itself as 'catholic' and the Eastern Church as 'orthodox'. Since the Reformation, Roman Catholics have come to use it exclusively of themselves, and it is used by those who claim to possess a historical and continuous tradition of faith as opposed to those who are Protestants.
See also ROMAN CATHOLIC CHURCH

CATTLEGATES *see* COMMONS

CAUSEWAYED ENCLOSURE *or* **SEGMENTAL ENCLOSURE** Causewayed enclosures (sometimes, and erroneously, called causeway camps) date from 4300 to 3300 BC. They consist of two to four concentric ramparts and ditches, arranged with considerable precision round a large circular or elliptical central space, and broken with wide, radial causeways. It is the function of these causeways that has yet to be determined and which sets the causewayed enclosure apart from other fortified and inhabited earthworks. As simple entrances to the enclosed space the causeways are excessive, both in width and number, and for this reason the once massive ramparts and ditches through which they pass could not have been defended, neither could the enclosures have been effective corrals. They differ from later HILL FORTS in that they do not appear to have been constructed for domestic or defensive purposes, though there is evidence that some were, on occasions, both occupied and defended. Neither were they confined to the uplands (several have been identified in the Thames valley, for example), though a significant number were located on sites that were later to be used as hill forts, as at Hambledon Hill near Blandford in Dorset. Thomas Hardy's description (in chapter 50 of *Far from the Madding Crowd*) of the ancient sheep fair at Woodbury Hill, Dorset, as 'the Nijni Novgorod of South Wessex' provides a clue to the controversial nature and function of causewayed enclosures. The fair, held within the ramparts of an Iron Age earthwork, was held from the early Middle Ages to the 1950s. Like the great agricultural shows of the twentieth century, it was a place of commerce and communication, of festivity and ritual, and of cultural continuity. Could the causewayed enclosures also have been constructed as focuses of native identity: market, circus, court and ceremonial arena? They were certainly endowed with considerable significance: that at Windmill Hill near Avebury in Wiltshire, with its three concentric ramparts and a diameter of 365 metres (1,200 feet) would have taken 100 men six months to construct, a considerable commitment of resources indicative of a well-organized and highly motivated society. There is also evidence that ditches were renovated periodically, indeed excavations of the ditches at Hambledon suggest that they were still being repaired 1,000 years after the enclosure was built. It has been established that ramparts were often 2 metres high (6½ feet) and ditches 3 metres deep (10 feet), and yet little remains of these massive earthworks other than crop-marks and depressions in the ground.
See also HENGE

CAUSEWAYS *or* **CAUSEYS** A raised footpath, often paved, to assist pedestrians and horses when crossing marshy or flooded land. A medieval causeway at Folke, Dorset, which linked the rectory with the parish church, has recently been restored.

CAVES Caves in Britain have been occupied from the Upper Palæolithic period to the present day, either for shelter or for industrial purposes, and have consistently been associated with superstition and folklore, much of it ARTHURIAN. Caves are most numerous in limestone country, particularly in North Yorkshire and Derbyshire where cave-names containing an Old English *thyrs* or Old Norse *thurs* element were believed to have been the dwelling-places of *thirsts* – demonic giants of Scandinavian mythology, or their marginally less savage relations the *hobythrysts* or *hobthrushes*. Major archaeological finds at Goat's Hole on the Gower Peninsula (1823) and at Kent's Cavern near Torquay in Devon (1825) provided evidence of the extreme antiquity of man and thereby challenged contemporary perceptions of creation. During the Iron Age and Roman occupation, caves from which materials had been quarried to exhaustion were often re-opened and adapted for industrial processes: for the smelting of iron-ore, for example, as in the Forest of Dean, Gloucestershire.

CEASTER *see* -CHESTER *and* TOWNS

CEFN Welsh place-name meaning 'back' or 'a ridge shaped like a back', thus Cefn-crin in Powys is 'the withered back'.

CEILINGS *see* CLASSICAL ARCHITECTURE, ELIZABETHAN AND JACOBEAN ARCHITECTURE, PLASTERWORK, ROOFS, TUDOR ARCHITECTURE *and* VAULTING

CELLARER *see* LARDER *and* MONASTERIES

CELT A member of one of several western European peoples: ancient Gauls and Britons and modern Bretons, Cornish, Gaels, Irish, Manx and Welsh.

During the Iron Age, the Celts occupied a large area of Europe. Although they did not comprise one race or ethnological group of tribes, they shared a common form of speech and an artistic tradition which can be traced to the upper Danube region of the thirteenth century BC and which spread throughout central and western Europe from about the ninth century BC. The Celts of the fifth to the first centuries BC (known as the *La Tène* period) were renowned for their horsemanship, ferocity in battle and the savagery of their Druidical rites. Their way of life was essentially agrarian: their fields were cultivated at regular intervals by means of ox-drawn ploughs and their methods were to influence significantly future agricultural practice. But there was little political cohesion among the tribes so that they were ultimately subjugated by Rome or assimilated by the migratory Germans. Celtic was the tongue spoken throughout England, Wales and southern Scotland before the coming of the Anglo-Saxons in the fifth century AD, and is today spoken in some areas of the British Isles and Brittany and consists of *Goidelic* (Irish, Scots, Gaelic and Manx) and *Brythonic* (Welsh, Cornish and Breton).

CELTIC CROSS The Celtic heritage persists most visibly in art and architecture and especially in numerous stone WHEEL-HEAD CROSSES carved with magnificent interlaced patterns. In Wales, the best examples are to be found in Anglesey, south and south-west Wales, such as the massive eleventh-century cross at Carew in Pembrokeshire which is 4 metres high (13 feet) and is carved with an intricate fretted and interlaced pattern, 50 metres (164 feet) in length. Of the magnificent IRISH HIGH CROSSES, the best examples are at Castledermot, County Kildare, Monasterboice in County Louth and Kilfenora in County Clare. Cornish crosses are generally smaller and of granite so that it was impossible to pierce the space between the limbs of the cross and the encircling annulet. Since 1956 the traditional Celtic cross has also found its way into the official terminology of ARMORY (*see* CHRISTIAN SYMBOLS).

CELTIC FIELDS *see* BRONZE AGE *and* FARMING

CEMETERIES Before the Burial Acts of 1852 (London) and 1853, most people were buried in their parish CHURCHYARDS or in the cemeteries of non-conformist chapels. But by the mid-nineteenth century, overcrowded churchyards were becoming a health hazard and the Burial Acts enabled local authorities to acquire land for the purpose. The many municipal cemeteries which were created at that time were managed by burial boards, elected by vestries. These responsibilities were transferred to district and parish authorities by the Local Government Act of 1894. Burial registers and lists of grave-lots are normally kept in a superintendent's office at the larger public and privately owned cemeteries. The registers for cemeteries which were established before 1837 are kept at the Public Record Office. *See also* BARROWS, CHAMBERED TOMBS *and* PLAGUE

CENSUS The first population census of England and Wales, the Channel Islands and the Isle of Man was taken in 1801. Since then a census has been taken every ten years, except in 1941 when the country was at war. Initially, the purpose of the census was to provide population statistics so that most of the records from 1801 to 1831 do not provide details of individuals. From 1841 an increasing amount of information was gathered and this is available through the FAMILY RECORD CENTRE, the returns for each census becoming available for public inspection after a period of one hundred years. Census information relating to post-1901 returns is available from the National Statistics Office at Fareham, Hampshire. Microfilm copies of the records are widely available at local record offices. *For* addresses *see* APPENDIX I

CENSUS OF RELIGIOUS WORSHIP 1851
Compiled in conjunction with the 1851 population CENSUS, the Census of Religious Worship is an indisputable source of information for the local historian. Returns were made from almost every place of worship (of all denominations) in each parish. The originals are maintained at the Public Record Office (*see* APPENDIX I), while copies are sometimes available at libraries and record offices. The Census provides details of accommodation, pew-renting, average attendances (for the previous twelve months), endowments and the number present at services on 30 March of that year. It also records the foundation of non-conformist chapels built (or adapted) after 1800.

CENTAUR *see* BEASTS (HERALDIC)

CENTERING *see* VAULTING

CENTURION *see* ROMAN FORTS AND CAMPS

CEONOBITE A religious recluse or member of a small community observing the severe rule of St Pachomius (*c.* 290–346). Ceonobites dwelt on remote islands and in the sequestered corners of Dark Age and medieval Britain, living solitary lives of silence, prayer and mortification. They are often incorrectly referred to as ANCHORITES or HERMITS.

-CESTER *see* -CHESTER

CHAIN A ploughman with a team of horses was expected to plough an acre a day – 4,840 square yards. To help him to measure this, a chain 22 yards long (20 metres) was laid along the headland of the field and this indicated the width of the area to be ploughed. From the headland he would plough *furlongs* ('furrow long') of 10 chains or 220 yards (200 metres). When he had completed ploughing this area, his day's work was finished – except for grooming and feeding his horses. On Sundays, he would borrow the farmer's chain to mark out the village cricket pitch – exactly 22 yards long. There are, of course, 80 chains and 8 furlongs to the 1,760 yards of a mile (1.61 km). Gunter's Chain, used for surveying land and named after its inventor, Edmund Gunter (1581–1626), was subdivided into 100 links, 25 of which comprised one *rod*, *pole* or *perch*. Each link was a short piece of wire connected to the next link by a loop.
See also ACRE and FURLONG

CHAINED LIBRARY *see* LIBRARIES

CHAISE The *continental chaise* was a comparatively light-weight privately driven carriage introduced between 1760 and 1780 and popular in Britain until the end of that century. A (usually) single seat and wooden dash-board were suspended above a wooden underframe by strong leather braces, and some versions were hooded.

CHALK WELL *see* MARL-PIT

CHAMBERED TOMBS Neolithic tombs dating from the period *c.* 4100–*c.* 3000 BC. In Britain, their distribution complements that of long barrows (*see* BARROWS) and was determined by the availability of supplies of tough, flat stone. The chronology of chambered tombs remains obscure, and variations of construction often occur within a single region. As the name suggests, these tombs contained one or more stone-built burial chambers and an entrance which, unlike the long barrows, could be sealed and re-opened to accept further interments. There are several distinct types of chambered tombs, all of which were contained within substantial mounds of earth and rubble. The *portal dolmen* tombs (known as *quoits* in Cornwall and *cromlechs* in Wales) are simple structures with a large capstone supported (generally in an inclined position) by upright slabs, two of which serve as portals to the tomb entrance. It has been suggested that, before a new tomb was covered, the corpse was placed on the sloping capstone and allowed to decompose, a ritual known as *excarnation*. Later *gallery graves* of the Cotswold-Severn Group, which have the external appearance of long barrows, usually contain a series of chambers flanking a central passage. Some of

Arthur's Stone on Merbach Hill near Dorstone in Herefordshire, a Neolithic tomb used for collective burial.

these tombs, such as Wayland's Smithy in Oxfordshire, were also provided with façades of standing stones which sometimes extend forward like horns to enclose a ritual forecourt. These are known as *court tombs* and there are several notable Irish examples. Superbly constructed *passage graves*, such as Newgrange in County Meath and Maes Howe in Orkney, appear to represent the culmination of the megalithic tomb-building tradition. These have single burial chambers at the termination of impressive entrance passages and were covered by massive dome-shaped mounds. A variation of this type is the *stalled cairn* of northern Scotland in which upright flagstones divide burial chambers on either side of the passage. There are twenty-four such chambers in the Midhowe tomb on Rousay Island, for example. In the Inverness region, *clava cairns* consist of rubble rings with stone-slab revetments to the inner and outer faces. Some of these tombs, which are often found within STONE CIRCLES, were roofed with overlapping slabs, while others were open. Small Bronze Age *entrance graves*, a simple type of passage grave, are commonly found in West Cornwall and the Isles of Scilly. As with the long barrows, chambered tombs were memorials to a community's élite and as such were constructed in prominent positions where they were impressive symbols of territorial supremacy.

CHAMPERTY The unlawful medieval practice of supporting a plaintiff in the courts in return for a share of the profits of successful litigation.

CHAMPION COUNTRYSIDE *see* COUNTRY-SIDE

CHAMPION *see* APPROVER

CHANCEL Originally that eastern part of a church surrounding the ALTAR and now called the *sanctuary*. The medieval chancel was separated from the gaze of the congregation in the NAVE by the CHANCEL SCREEN or ROOD SCREEN, and it was here that the priest performed the Office and preserved the mystery of the eucharist. The term came to be applied to the entire area between the high altar and the nave when, in CATHEDRALS and CHURCHES with monastic, collegiate or secular foundations, room was required to the west of the high altar to accommodate clergy and choir. Following the Reformation of the sixteenth century, the laity was brought into the chancel for the celebration of the eucharist.
See also AMPLIFIERS, CHOIR *and* MISERICORDS

CHANCELLOR Literally, 'a secretary', chancellors have been known in England since Edward the Confessor introduced the office of the King's Secretary. The office grew in importance until the Chancellor of England (Lord Chancellor) became the highest judicial functionary, ranking in precedence after the royal princes and the Archbishop of Canterbury. The Chancellor is the keeper of the Great Seal and prolocutor of the House of Lords.

CHANCEL SCREEN A carved stone, wood or ironwork screen separating the chancel of a church from the NAVE. Typically, chancel screens are supported on a plinth with a chamfered top edge and are divided into bays, pierced by an opening which may have a gate. Each bay is usually panelled to a third of its height, above which lights (openings), sometimes divided by delicate vertical *muntins*, terminate in pierced tracery within a pointed arch or arches. Such bays have vertical outer frame members called *styles* which are held within horizontal rails at the top and bottom of the screen. A chancel screen may carry a heavy overhanging cornice and if it supports a ROOD it is known as a ROOD SCREEN. Most large monastic and collegiate churches had both a rood screen and a PULPITUM, though in many instances the latter has subsequently been replaced by a chancel screen and no cathedral rood screens survived the Reformation. The thirteenth-century screen at Stanton Harcourt, Oxfordshire, is believed to be the earliest in England. Medieval screens were generally coloured and gilded but regrettably in most areas little remains of their former glory. Many Devon churches contain magnificent examples of fifteenth-century wooden screens, and several retain their original colouring: at Wolborough, for example. The lower panels are often crowded with painted figures and the tracery is bold and the cornice ornately carved. Such screens may stretch from one side of the church to the other in a single, unbroken line. Many excellent Devonshire examples remain, such as those at Ashton, Bovey Tracey, Cullompton and Lapford, and in Somerset at Dunster, Minehead and Banwell. The fourteenth- and fifteenth-century wooden screens of East Anglian churches are somewhat different: they are lighter, higher and generally more finely executed than those in West Country churches. Tracery is not so conspicuous and sometimes there is no tracery at all, particularly when a screen is vaulted, as at Attleborough in Norfolk and Bramfield in Suffolk. Base panels are almost invariably painted and gilded: the Twelve

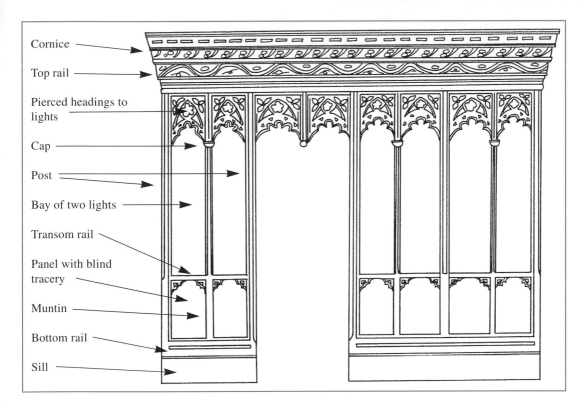

Cornice

Top rail

Pierced headings to lights

Cap

Post

Bay of two lights

Transom rail

Panel with blind tracery

Muntin

Bottom rail

Sill

Apostles is a favoured subject, as are obscure saints and martyrs, angels, prophets and kings. Often the backgrounds are alternately red and green or of rich *gesso* work (gold). There are fine screens at Barton Turf, Ludham, Hunstanton and Ranworth in Norfolk and at Eye, Westhall and Somerleyton in Suffolk. Medieval stone screens are comparatively rare and in parish churches they are generally of similar design to contemporary wooden screens: that at Totnes in Devon is one of the finest, and there are several in Wiltshire (Hilmarton and Compton Bassett, for example) and two interesting examples at Stebbing and Great Bardfield in Essex, both of which combine a rood. Late sixteenth- and early seventeenth-century wooden screens are usually ornamented with round-arched arcading, geometrical patterns of interlaced 'straps' (called *strapwork*) and *S* scrolls, often with obelisks set on the cornice. Most Jacobean examples are screens to collegiate ante-chapels and halls, though there are chancel screens of this period, as at Croscombe and Rodney Stoke in Somerset and at Folke in Dorset, which was rebuilt in 1628 on the site of a former medieval church and contains a magnificent pair of Jacobean screens: the larger being a chancel screen and the smaller separating the north aisle from the nave, together with contemporary communion rails, table, pulpit reading desk and bench-ends. A common feature of this period was the inclusion in the design of the Royal Arms which surmount the centre of the screen, flanked by the arms of a patron or benefactor and those of a bishop impaling the arms of his diocese. A good example is the screen at Abbey Dore, Herefordshire. Larger churches and cathedrals often have several screens (*see also* PARCLOSE *and* TOWER SCREEN) and these, whether in wood or stone, invariably reflect the architectural style of the period in which they were erected. Metal screens, often cast in bronze, are comparatively rare and usually of Victorian or Edwardian origin.
See also PULPITS

CHANCEL VENTILATOR A small opening in the south wall of the chancel of a parish church, originally provided with a grille and shutters which could be opened to admit fresh air when the accumulated smoke of candles and censers became overpowering. Sometimes a seat was also provided on which the priest could recuperate. Occasionally, ventilators may be found on both sides of the chancel, though many have been glazed or blocked.

CHANCERY DECREE *see* ENCLOSURE

CHANCERY Following the Conquest, the office of Chancellor combined all the duties of the present-day secretaries of state. The Chancery is the Lord Chancellor's division of the High Court of Justice. It originated in the governmental structure of the early medieval kings and was the department responsible for issuing charters and letters under the great seal: transmitting royal instructions to the sovereign's subjects. During the reign of Edward I (1272–1307), for example, when the king required letters (in Latin) to be issued by the Chancery under the great seal, he would provide relatively informal instructions (in French) to his chancellor under the privy seal, and these warrants would then be implemented on his behalf. The Chancery Rolls record its activities from 1199 to 1937 and in particular royal grants of titles, privileges and land, and details of *Inquisitions Ad Quod Damnum* – details of commissions convened to investigate such matters as title deeds and the protection of existing rights prior to the granting of fairs and markets.
See also HOUSEHOLD *and* WARDROBE.
The archives of the Court of Chancery are kept in the Public Record Office (*see* APPENDIX I).

CHANNEL DEFENCES *see* MARTELLO TOWERS AND COMMISSION FORTS, PILLBOXES, ROMAN FORTS AND CAMPS *and* TUDOR COASTAL FORTS

CHANTRY A private mass, celebrated regularly for the repose of the soul of a testator and others nominated by him in his will. It was the conviction that a regular offering of the eucharist was the most effective means of redemption that encouraged medieval man to make financial provision in his will for a chantry or chantries. This was particularly so during the fourteenth and fifteenth centuries when the liturgy of the Catholic Church increasingly emphasized the importance of the Mass. Some chantries were endowed during the lifetime of the founder, and the Mass-priest would be obliged to celebrate Masses for his well-being on earth and his soul after death. Chantries were also endowed by guilds and fraternities for the benefit of their members. They were, in fact, a very cheap form of endowment, for even the most humble testator could arrange for one or two masses to be said for his soul. However, it was those with the largest purses (or the heaviest consciences) who were responsible for the erection of the magnificent late medieval CHANTRY CHAPELS and for the endowment of

numerous charitable institutions such as the Hospital of All Saints (now known as Brown's Hospital) at Stamford in Lincolnshire, built in the reign of Henry VII to accommodate ten poor men, together with two poor women who were to be 'attentive and useful to the poor men in their necessities'. The residents of the Hospital of All Saints were required to recite three psalms a day for the soul of the home's founder, Thomas Brown, a prominent wool merchant, and it was a condition of admission that a candidate should not only be 'lowly, devout and poor', but also fluent in chanting 'the Lord's Prayer, the Angelic Salutation and the Apostles' Creed'. Men such as Thomas Brown were prepared to make considerable and often posthumous investments to ensure that their souls did not remain too long in the dreadful limbo-land of purgatory, a concept which was popularly established in the twelfth century and which motivated the building of numerous social institutions as well as chantry chapels and other memorials. In the Suffolk town of Lavenham, Thomas Spring III (known as The Great Clothier) left money to build the superb tower of Lavenham's parish church, and in many of England's great cathedrals there were entire choirs whose tasks included praying for the souls of the departed: at York Minster, for example, where the choristers were known as the College of the Vicars Choral.

CHANTRY CHAPELS The essential difference between an ornate, canopied MONUMENT and a chantry chapel is the presence in the latter of an altar at which masses were celebrated. Cardinal Beaufort (d.1447) provided for 3,000 masses to be said at the altar of his magnificent chapel at Winchester. Some were additional chapels, built on to the main body of the church such as those at Ely and the glorious Beauchamp chapel at St Mary's church, Warwick (*c.* 1450). The majority are very much smaller, and usually comprise a gilded and painted rectangular 'cage' of ornate stone or metal and a delicately vaulted CANOPY. It is significant that the chantry chapels of the high Middle Ages should coincide with the flowering of the perpendicular style of architecture in England. Heraldic embellishment is often sumptuous and will invariably include badges, CYPHERS and REBUSES, as well as arms and crests, incorporated into mouldings, bosses and panels. Such chapels are generally found bridging the piers of the chancel arcade or adjacent to the presbytery. At several churches an additional aisle was constructed to accommodate chantry chapels, for example those at Devizes in Wiltshire and Tiverton in Devon. With the dissolution of chantries

in 1547, many chantry chapels were used for other purposes: the superb Hungerford chantry at Salisbury Cathedral, for example, was converted into an exceptionally ornate mayoral pew.
See also SQUINT *and* STAINED GLASS

CHAPBOOK Printed books (usually of ballads and traditional tales) produced in octavo or duodecimo format designed specifically for sale by chapmen at fairs and markets or, when travelling, from pack-horses and costing 1*d* or 2*d* a copy.

CHAPEL OF EASE *see* CHAPELS

CHAPEL ROYAL *see* CHAPELS

CHAPELRY A term usually applied to the daughter church of a MINSTER but also used to describe a church serving a section of a large PARISH, sometimes with a resident priest who would be subordinate to the incumbent.

CHAPELS Derived from the Latin *cappella*, diminutive of *cappa*, meaning 'little cape', the term refers to the cloak of St Martin which was preserved as a sacred relic by the Frankish kings. In time, the term was applied to sanctuaries where holy relics were preserved and prayers were said. The word is now used to describe sacred buildings which are less than churches:
(i) Chapels in private residences, known as *proprietary chapels*.
(ii) Chapels of private institutions, e.g. colleges, schools and hospitals.
(iii) Part of a large church and having a separate altar.
(iv) Dissenting places of worship, including Roman Catholic, in contradistinction to churches of the Church of England.

Many medieval residences, castles and monasteries contained private chapels, licensed for divine worship by a bishop. In the fourteenth and fifteenth centuries, possession of a private chapel was considered a mark of distinction: some were built within the walls of a house or castle, others adjacent to it. Collegiate, hospice and guild foundations often had chapels, as did later schools, prisons, garrisons and other institutions. Medieval CHURCHES and CATHEDRALS invariably contain one or more chapels dedicated to saints or provided for specific purposes. Of these, the LADY CHAPEL, dedicated to the Blessed Virgin Mary and located at the east end behind the high altar, is usually the largest.

Others are built into the aisles or ambulatory and may be CHANTRY CHAPELS. A *Chapel of Ease* was one which was provided for the ease of those living at some distance from a parish church, and was subordinate to it. Others were built at the roadside, often near river crossings, for the convenience of travellers. In several Welsh churchyards may be found *eglwysau-y-bedd*, 'churches of the grave'. These tiny mortuary chapels are usually located many yards from their parish churches and provide evidence of the Celtic church's practice of building separate chapels for specific purposes. *Chapels Royal* are private chapels attached to the royal court and subject not to the jurisdiction of a diocesan bishop, but to the Dean of the Chapels Royal. Other royal chapels are those in which sovereigns have been buried and were often constructed for that purpose during their lifetimes. Perhaps the most magnificent of these is Henry VII's chapel at Westminster Abbey. Chapels were suppressed by the Chantry Act of 1547 and were closed for public worship, though several more remote examples fortunately escaped the attentions of the reformers.
See also CHAPELRIES, CHURCHES *and* DISSENTING CHAPELS.
For Chapels Society *see* APPENDIX I

CHAPLAIN *see* CLERGY (CHURCH OF ENGLAND)

CHAPMAN A pedlar, from the Old English *cēap*, meaning 'barter' (-man).

CHAPTER (i) A section of a monastic rule and the members of a religious house when assembled to hear a section read or for other purposes.
(ii) The body corporate of a religious house or other ecclesiastical institution, e.g. the canons of a cathedral.

CHAPTER HOUSE A building used for meetings of a CHAPTER. The daily meeting of a monastic chapter commenced with the reading of a *chapter* from the rule of the order, or from the Scriptures, followed by public confession of sins and the remembrance of benefactors. Then followed the business of the day – reports from officers on various aspects of worship and domestic administration – and the management of the monastic estates, for the great foundations were endowed with considerable resources and property. The chapters of secular CATHEDRALS likewise met as a governing body in the chapter house, which was always adjacent to the cathedral or abbey church and usually approached from the eastern alley of the CLOISTER.

The earliest chapter houses were rectangular, as at Bristol and Ely, though that at Worcester was circular, and is still so within. From the early thirteenth century, most medieval chapter houses were polygonal (probably because the acoustics were infinitely superior to those of the earlier rectangular buildings), though the Cistercians continued to build in rectangular form (as at Fountains Abbey in Yorkshire) because their rule demanded austerity. The first of the polygonal chapter houses was at Lincoln, and this established an architectural fashion peculiar to England. Most were octagonal, though Lincoln's was decagonal with a diameter of 18 metres (59 feet). Exterior roofs were usually pointed and the walls buttressed at each corner. As at Lincoln, most chapter houses had wooden roofs which were replaced with stone in the mid-thirteenth century. The chapter house at Wells in Somerset (*c.* 1319) is the finest in England, though by no means the largest. Below the windows is an arcade of fifty-one stalls with beautifully carved canopies and above, springing from a single, slender column, is a superb vault, quite unsurpassed in its architectural exuberance. The chapter house at Westminster Abbey was used by the early house of commons as its meeting-place and it remains under the jurisdiction of Parliament.
See also MONASTERIES

CHAR-A-BANC Introduced in the 1840s, the char-a-banc was a version of the *wagonette*, which carried a number of passengers and a quantity of hand-luggage with inward-facing seats and a raised box-seat for the driver. The char-a-banc, which had cross-seats for seven (including the driver) with a groom's seat in the rear, was generally used for attending sporting events and shooting parties and was usually driven by a four-in-hand. Sometimes, it also had a slatted under-compartment for sporting dogs. Although the char-a-banc was originally used by large households it was later fitted with additional seating for school parties and works outings.

CHARCOAL Charcoal is the black carbonized residue of partially burned wood, produced under conditions which prevent it bursting into flame. The main uses for charcoal were in metal smelting, as a constituent in the production of gunpowder and on ships as a preservative for food and water. In some areas, notably in East Anglia, many houses were heated by charcoal braziers, similar to those once commonly used in France and Flanders. Today, charcoal is still used as a filtering material, and for drawing. Charcoal burning has been a skilled craft for over a thousand years and the characteristic domed kilns of charcoal burners were, until comparatively recently, a common site in many WOODLAND areas. There were, of course, regional variations both in technique and design but most kilns consisted of layers of thin COPPICE wood (alder was considered to be the best) which formed a 'hearth' beneath a heavy covering of turfs. Once ignited, the draught to the hearth was carefully controlled through gaps in the turfs to ensure that there was no flame. Charcoal kilns would smoulder for many days while moisture was removed from the wood and combustible gases extracted through a small hole in the top of the dome. The charcoal burner lived by his hearth, tending it night and day until the turfs could be removed and the brittle, iridescent charcoal cooled ready for packing. When used as fuel charcoal will glow red-hot and burn with very little flame and in a forge or furnace it will become white-hot as the heat intensifies. By the Roman period, charcoal was used for smelting iron ore and forging iron into tools and weapons. The commercial importance of charcoal in the medieval and Tudor periods equalled that of coal in the Industrial Revolution, and manufacturing centres developed in areas such as the Forest of Dean in Gloucestershire and the Weald of Kent where both iron ore and charcoal were readily available.

CHARGE In ARMORY, a pictorial representation or geometrical figure depicted in relief on a shield of arms. Something is 'charged' when it has a charge placed upon it.

CHARITIES From 1786 Clerks of the Peace received copies of accounts etc. from charitable organizations within their jurisdictions and forwarded returns to Parliament. These are now held by local record offices in the records of QUARTER SESSIONS. The Charity Commission for England and Wales, established in 1853, supervises the accounts and activities of registered charities and holds records of these (*see* APPENDIX I). Many charities have maintained their own archives or have deposited them in local record offices.

CHARNELS *see* OSSUARIES

CHARTER A document conferring rights on a body corporate or on an individual. A royal charter was a formal instrument by which a sovereign granted or confirmed lands, liberties, titles or immunities on his subjects in perpetuity. There are two types of *Charter Roll*, the first recording grants and the second confirmations. Both relate to the period 1199 to 1516, after which charters were succeeded by letters patent (*see* PATENT). For land charters *see* BOUNDARIES.

CHARTERHOUSE *see* CARTHUSIANS

CHASE A hunting ground, the administration of which was subject to Common Law, rather than Forest Law. The rules that governed a chase were as rigorous in their protection of *vert* and *venison* as were those of a FOREST, but the application of legal sanctions through the chase courts was limited, more serious prosecutions being remitted to the civil courts. The forest courts exercised an independence which could be despotic, for ultimately it was the sovereign or his representative who was both prosecution and judge. The legal status of a chase was not affected by the rank of its owner, even when it was the monarch himself. There were, of course, exceptions to the general rule: chases belonging to the earls of Lancaster were subject to Forest Law, for example. Medieval chases were less numerous than royal forests, some twenty-six having been identified.

CHEAP Usually found as a street name, from Old English *chepe*, meaning 'market'.
See also CHIPPING

-CHESTER and -CASTER Borrowed from the Latin *castra*, the Old English word *ceaster* means a city or walled town, originally one which had been a Roman station, e.g. Dorchester. But in many instances the meaning seems to have indicated a prehistoric fort generally: all *-chester* names in Northumbria cannot have been Roman stations, for example. The name is also found as *Caster-* and *-caster*, and corrupted to *castle* as in Castleford and Horncastle. In other instances, former Roman towns were renamed, possibly after the Anglo-Saxon chieftain whose people occupied them: Chichester in Sussex is 'Cissi's ceaster', for example, and Rudchester in Northumberland is 'Rudda's ceaster'. Few Roman names for rural settlements remain, and the use of this element in place-names suggests Anglo-Saxon recognition of a Roman or pre-Roman settlement or fort. Under Norman influence several *-chester* names became *-cester*, as in Gloucester and Cirencester, and even *-(c)eter* as in Wroxeter.

Ceaster is one of the three classifications of Anglo-Saxon settlement, the others being the BURH and the PORT.
See also CAIR-

CHESTNUT *see* HORSE CHESTNUT *and* SWEET CHESTNUT

CHEST TOMBS *see* TABLE TOMBS

CHEVAUCHÉE An armed raid, usually into enemy territory, with the aim of inflicting as much damage as possible on the towns, villages, countryside and on the inhabitants. Used most effectively by Edward, the Black Prince, during his expeditions to France in 1355/6.

CHEVET A polygonal APSE surrounded by an AMBULATORY from which radiate a number of chapels. The chevet at Hailes Abbey, Gloucestershire, is a rare English example.

CHIMNEYS Strictly speaking, a chimney (from the Latin *caminus* via Middle English *chimenee*) is a fireplace used both for providing warmth to a room and for cooking. Only in the sixteenth century was the term applied to what is more correctly a *chimney flue* and roof-top *chimney shaft*, capped with a *chimney pot* (*chimney-stacks* contain several flues). The structure within which the flue is constructed is the *chimney breast* and the lintel above the fireplace opening is the *chimney bar*. The *chimney-piece* (or *mantelpiece*) is the decorative structure which surrounds the fireplace. This often incorporates a *mantelshelf* and may extend above the fireplace opening to the ceiling as an ornamental framework. An *angle-chimney* is a fireplace that is constructed in the corner of a room.

Prior to the fourteenth century, heating was provided by an open fire of logs stacked against FIREDOGS set in a hearth at the centre of a room, the smoke escaping by means of an opening or louvre in the roof immediately above the fireplace. In more important buildings (such as Westminster Hall), a louvred lantern structure was often constructed on the roof for this purpose; a device later adapted as a means of venting a number of angle-chimneys and flues (as in the late fourteenth-century abbot's kitchen at Glastonbury Abbey in Somerset).

From the late thirteenth century, fireplaces were sometimes placed against the outside walls of rooms within stone buildings (notably CASTLES), though the earliest of these were vented through the walls at a point immediately above the hearth and, consequently, must have been singularly noisome. By the early fourteenth century, stone hoods were provided to direct the smoke into long, vertical flues, set within the thickness of the walls, with round or octagonal chimney shafts on gable peaks or projecting through the hoardings of castle towers and walkways. The development of the chimney flue was, perhaps, to have a greater effect on the social history of western Europe than any other factor. It resulted in a previously unknown luxury: privacy. Domestic rooms became smaller and, therefore, greater in number, and allowed for a variety of functions which the old communal hall had not. Excessive draughts were no longer necessary to sustain a large central fire and, consequently, corridors and stairways were enclosed, external doors provided with porches and windows more extensively glazed. No doubt, the health of the occupants improved significantly as a result, as did the efficiency of the kitchens.

During the fourteenth century, fireplaces located on different storeys of new buildings were often connected to common chimney flues set within the walls. Fifteenth-century fireplaces had larger hearths and were usually constructed of brick or stone, with wide, four-centre arches (*see* ARCH). With the rapid development of purely domestic architecture in the final decades of the century, chimney shafts, singly or in clusters and usually of stone, were for the first time utilized as decorative features, and by the mid-sixteenth century ornate shafts or stacks had become a characteristic feature of the domestic architecture of the period (*see* TUDOR ARCHITECTURE). These were usually cylindrical or octagonal, constructed of decorative brickwork and terracotta, with ornamental crossed beading, zig-zag and honeycomb patterns, scrolls and fluting, and supported on octagonal or square-shaped fluted and moulded bases.

The highly decorative chimney-pieces of wood, marble and stone which dominated the apartments of the Elizabethan and Jacobean nobility and gentry continued, in a variety of forms, throughout the seventeenth and eighteenth centuries. Intricately carved Elizabethan designs with flanking pilasters, columns or caryatid figures supporting ornate mantelshelves and over-mantels demonstrate strong Flemish influences, or (most often in yeomen's or merchants' houses) were robustly vernacular (*see* ELIZABETHAN AND JACOBEAN ARCHITECTURE). Fireplaces were invariably the focal point of any room and heraldry was the dominant theme in the decoration of medieval and Tudor chimney-pieces. Regrettably few medieval examples remain but those of later times are legion, many of them splendidly flamboyant.

From the second half of the seventeenth century, the design of chimney-stacks and chimney-pieces reflect the evolution of English classicism (*see* CLASSICAL ARCHITECTURE). The former were tall and rectangular with moulded tops, while chimney-pieces were in the classical style, often with over-mantels containing a mirror or painting. Chimney-pieces in the 1670s and '80s were characterized by a profusion of carved and gilded fruit, flowers and birds, but early eighteenth-century examples were comparatively plain, with moulded wooden surrounds (which rarely had a mantelshelf) and a rectangular mirror or picture above. Eighteenth-century chimney-pieces were usually incorporated within the overall design of a room, the classical ornamentation of which often reflected its function: Bacchus for the dining-room and musical motifs in the music room, for example. From about 1720, chimney-pieces were richly carved in marble or wood or decorated in painted and gilded stucco and usually incorporated mirrors and candle-holders above the mantelshelf. From the mid-century, rococo carved and gilded pinewood frames predominated but from 1765 these were replaced by more architectural chimney-pieces, usually with a heavily framed painting or mirror above the mantelshelf. The Adam style, with flanking classical columns or caryatid figures supporting a mantelshelf and entablature, was particularly popular until the 1790s. Carved and inlaid marbles, ormolu, bronze or brass were used for ornamentation with low sculptured relief, especially of classical figures and compositions, on the frieze and side panels of the chimney-piece.

Until the sixteenth century, wood had been the main source of fuel. Logs were burned across a pair of firedogs, or in a shallow fire-basket, in a large *grate* and with a separate fireback to reflect the heat. Indeed, throughout the medieval and early Tudor periods, the primitive central hearth and roof louvre was to be found in many vernacular buildings. But as timber became increasingly scarce, especially in the south-east of England, coal was imported as a substitute. Burning coal produced appalling pollution, particularly in urban areas. This was partly because of the inefficiency of fireplaces with wide chimney openings and strong updraughts which caused the coal to burn rapidly and unevenly, sending considerable amounts of soot (and heat) into the atmosphere. Wood-burning grates were usually made of lower grade metals (sometimes embellished with silver or brass) and these gradually 'burnt out' as a result of the higher temperatures produced by burning coal. Consequently, fireplace openings became smaller and the old iron firedogs were replaced by smaller, free-standing cast-iron baskets (*dog baskets*), which had integral firebacks and were better able to accommodate the new fuel.

From these developed the elegant steel and iron basket grates, enriched by classical ornamentation and urn filials, associated with the 'Adam' style. Regency *sarcophagus* grates were also free-standing on paw feet and were decorated with Egyptian motifs. In the mid-eighteenth century the cast-iron *hob grate* was introduced. This fitted within the fireplace and was designed both to restrict the flow of air through the grate and to concentrated the fire in a small area. Such cast-iron grates were usually painted or black-leaded. (A Scottish firm, Carron & Co., engaged Robert Adam to design classical facia panels for a range of hob grates, and the original moulds were available until as recently as 1939.) The hob grate was not entirely satisfactory, however, and was itself replaced by the *register grate* which had a narrower flue and a trap door (*register plate*) fitted to the back of the grate by which the flow of air could be regulated. The enormous growth in house building in the late nineteenth century resulted in many improvements. Double ('return') flues were incorporated into many chimney systems to ensure a balanced flow of air and from 1880 the cast-iron chimney-piece appeared, together with the integral surround and grate. In many smaller houses, iron cooking ranges were combined with parlour grates.

From the mid-nineteenth century, chimney-pieces became excessively ornate: constructed of brass, marble or stone or of painted iron or wood, with velvet-draped mantelshelves, over-mantels and niches providing accommodation for a profusion of Victorian ornaments. In larger houses, the Gothic Revival inspired numerous fine heraldic chimney-pieces and stimulated a ready market for mass-produced 'medieval' glazed tiles. There was a brief return to classicism in the 1890s and by the turn of the century plain rectangular chimney-pieces with glazed tile surrounds were fashionable.

CHINE From Old English *cinu*, meaning 'cleft'.

CHIPPING From Old English *cēping*, meaning 'market-place' and found as a place-name element at, e.g. Chipping Campden in Gloucestershire and Chipping Norton in Oxfordshire. A market trader was a *cēap-mann* – hence Chapman.
See also MARKETS

CHIROGRAPH *see* INDENTURE

CHIVALRY Both the code of courage and courtesy which were the ideals of medieval knighthood in western Europe, and the system of knighthood itself. The terms 'chivalry' and 'cavalry' share the same linguistic root, confirming that knighthood was the prerogative of the mounted warrior. His effectiveness in battle (and, thereby, his reputation) was greatly enhanced by the introduction of the stirrup and the saddle-bow which provided both manoeuvrability and stability. But the cost of maintaining a horse and equipment was considerable, and membership of such an élite presupposed a man of some position and estate. This exclusive class adopted a code of conduct which aspired to the highest ideals though, as history has shown, few of its members succeeded in attaining them. That none could emulate the perfection of Galahad or Percival did not diminish the code itself which comprised three elements:

1. Belief in the Church and its defence, especially against the heathen as manifested in the Crusades.
2. Courage, and loyalty towards a knight's companions, his feudal lord and sovereign.
3. Respect, pity and generosity in the defence of the weak, the poor and women.

To these was added the notion of romantic love which was to inspire much of the literature of chivalry: Roland in France, Arthur in Britain, El Cid in Spain and the Minnesänger in Germany.

CHIVALRY (HIGH COURT OF) Established in the early fourteenth century as the Court of the Constable and Marshal, the Court of Chivalry is now located in the College of Arms and exercises jurisdiction over matters armorial within England, Wales and Northern Ireland.

CHOIR (*also* **QUOIR**) In the worship of the early Church, all music was rendered by the clergy and congregation. From the fourth century, bodies of singers, comprising clerics in minor orders and boys, assisted in the music of divine services. A *schola cantorum* was established in Rome by Pope Gregory the Great (d.604) and the custom spread through western Christendom so that the medieval cathedrals and monasteries became centres of musical excellence and almost the only places at which a musical education could be obtained. It was not until the fifteenth century that lay singers augmented these choirs.

In architectural terms, the *choir* is that part of a cathedral or monastic or collegiate church between the high altar and the *PULPITUM*, occupied by the stalls of members of the body corporate. As such the term is not applicable to the CHANCEL of a lesser church, indeed it was the Victorian clergy who first introduced stalls for singers into the chancels of their parish churches. It is almost invariably in the choirs of the great cathedrals that medieval architecture enjoys its most glorious manifestation: at Gloucester for example. The *retrochoir* is the area behind (and to the east of) the high altar, often constructed to accommodate both a notable shrine and the multitude of worshippers attracted to it.

See also AMPLIFIERS *and* MONASTERIES

CHOIR SCREEN *see* CHANCEL SCREEN

CHRISM (*also* **CHRISOM**) A mixture of olive oil and balsam used in baptism, confirmation and the consecration of churches, altars and sacred vessels. Chrism may only be consecrated by a bishop and, according to present Latin usage, only on Maundy Thursday: since 1955 at a special mass of the Chrism.

The term is also applied to the images of infants on TOMBS to indicate death in infancy. Chrism children are depicted swathed in their white chrism cloths which were worn for a month following baptism as a token of innocence. Such images are commonly found in BRASSES of the Tudor period.

See also CONSECRATION CROSSES

Effigy of Robert Clayton – who 'died within a few howres after his birth' – at Ickenham, Middlesex.

CHRISTIAN SYMBOLS

The Angels

In the Middle Ages nine Orders of Angels were identified in three hierarchical 'choirs':

1	2	3
Seraphim	Dominations	Principalities
Cherubim	Virtues	Archangels
Thrones	Powers	Angels

Seraphim and cherubim are often represented crowned with fire and with six wings, which may be strewn with eyes. Thrones are sometimes depicted as winged scarlet wheels, often with eyes, and all three principal orders may be depicted as warriors or judges. Angels usually have a pair of wings and a nimbus, and may hold scrolls, instruments of the Passion or musical instruments. Cherubim survived the Reformation but are depicted as having just two wings and a head, for they were distinguished as having perfect knowledge.

Christian Concepts

It was considered blasphemous to represent God in pictorial form and a variety of symbols was adopted, the most common of which are:

The Ray of Light
The Father supporting the Crucifix
A hand encompassed by a nimbus
Three crowned figures
A Trinity
Three interlaced fishes

The *Agnus Dei* or Lamb of God represents Christ. It is usually depicted holding a banner of victory and has a halo charged with a cross.

A dove is frequently found on fonts, where it represents the Holy Spirit at baptism. Seven doves represent the Seven Gifts of the Holy Spirit.

Colours used in vestments and to mark liturgical seasons:

White: Christmas, Easter, Corpus Christi, the Feast of St Mary and feasts of saints who were not martyrs
Red: Pentecost, Palm Sunday, Holy Cross Day and feasts of saints who were martyrs
Green: the periods following Trinity and Epiphany

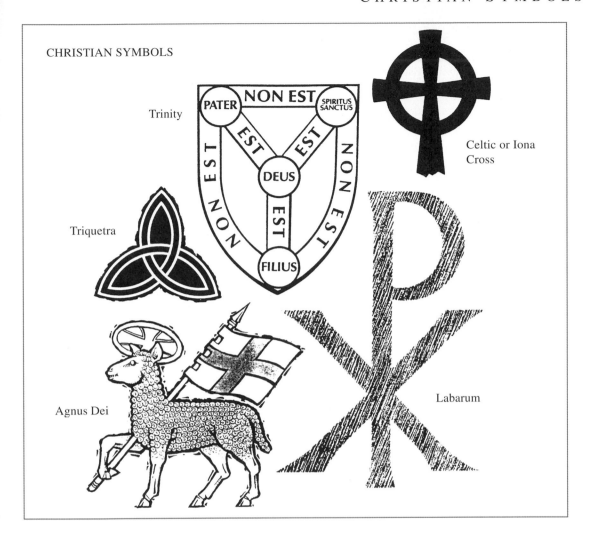

CHRISTIAN SYMBOLS

Trinity

Celtic or Iona Cross

Triquetra

Agnus Dei

Labarum

Purple: Advent and Lent (in some churches unbleached linen is used during Lent to represent penitence)
Black: funerals and requiems

Crosses
The cross is the universal Christian symbol and is widely used in ARMORY, where it has been estimated there are to be found over 400 different forms, though of these only twenty or so are in regular use.

In churches, the most common forms are:

The Christus Rex shows Christ on the Cross, crowned and robed
The *Rood*, a large crucifix suspended or fixed beneath the chancel arch together with the figures of the Virgin Mary and John

The *Latin* or *Passion* cross, which has an elongated upright
The *Greek* cross, which has arms of equal length
The *Calvary* cross, which is a Latin cross mounted on three steps, symbolizing Faith (the uppermost), Hope and Charity
The *Celtic* or *Iona* cross in which the circle symbolizes Eternity.

Devils
The antithesis of good and the enemy of God, the devil in his many forms is prominent in the decoration of early churches: a constant reminder of medieval man's preoccupation with the daily struggle between damnation and salvation. Just as God was depicted in symbolic form, so too the devil assumes the guise of a multitude of beasts and

serpents culled from the imagery of the Old Testament and the medieval bestiaries. Many are depicted being trampled beneath the feet of Christian saints, notably St Michael and St George.

See also AMPHISBAENA, APES, ASP *and* DOOM

Geometrical Symbolism

To the medieval mind every number had a mystic significance and was easily translated into a geometrical shape:

Equilateral triangle represents the Trinity

Two interwoven triangles form the six-pointed Star of David or Creator's Star, each point representing one day of Creation

The Triquetra is an ancient symbol whose three equal arcs represent the Trinity and its continuous form, Eternity.

Baptismal fonts are often octagonal, the number eight representing resurrection and new life.

Monograms

These consist of two or more letters interwoven to form a symbol:

The *Labarum* comprises the first two letters of the Greek word for Christ *Chi* and *Rho*; *IHS* the first three letters for *Jesus*; *MR* was a popular medieval monogram for *Maria Regina*, as was the crowned *M* and the letters *MARIA*; *Alpha* and *Omega*, the first and last letters of the Greek alphabet, signify that Christ is both the beginning and the end.

The Passion

The Instruments of the Passion include:

The Title (*INRI*)
The Crown of Thorns and Nails
The Dice
The Seamless Robe
The Scourges
The Cross and Sheet
The Ladder and Sponge
The Lantern of Gethsemane
THE FIVE WOUNDS OF CHRIST
The Cockerel of Peter's Denial
The Thirty Pieces of Silver
The Hammer and Pincers

Seven

Seven was a holy number: there were seven days in creation; seven phases of the moon; seven spirits before the throne of God (Michael, Gabriel, Lamael, Raphael, Zachariel, Anael and Oriphel); seven Joys of the Virgin (the Annunciation, Visitation, Nativity, Adoration of the Magi, Presentation in the Temple, Finding Christ amongst the Doctors and the Assumption); seven Virtues (faith, hope, charity, prudence, justice, fortitude and temperance); and seven Spirits of God (wisdom, understanding, counsel, power, knowledge, righteousness and divine awfulness). The Seven Deadly Sins, the Seven Sacraments and the Seven Works of Mercy are often depicted in the stained glass and decorative carving of medieval churches. The Deadly Sins are pride, wrath, envy, lust, gluttony, avarice and sloth. The Sacraments are baptism, confirmation, mass, penance, extreme unction, ordination and matrimony. The Seven Works of Mercy are feeding the hungry, giving drink to the thirsty, hospitality to the stranger, clothes to the naked, visiting the sick and those in prison, and burying the dead.

The Seven Champions of Christendom were devised by Richard Johnson who lived in the late sixteenth/early seventeenth centuries. These are: St George of England, who was seven years imprisoned by the Almi'dor, the black king of Morocco; St Denys of France, who lived seven years in the form of a hart; St James of Spain, who was dumb for seven years because of his love for a fair Jewess; St Anthony of Italy, who (with the other champions) was enchanted into a deep sleep in the Black Castle and was released by St George's three sons; St Andrew of Scotland, who delivered six ladies who had lived for seven years in the form of white swans; St Patrick of Ireland, who was immured in a cell where he excavated his own grave with his nails; and St David of Wales, who slept seven years in the enchanted garden of Ormandine.

Symbols and Attributes

The Tree of Jesse (*see* JESSE WINDOW) is usually found in stained glass and is intended to depict Christ's descent from Jesse, the father of King David. The Tree of Life is often found on Romanesque fonts or on a tympanum above a church door and recalls the sentence in Revelation: 'Blessed are they that doeth his commandments, that they may have right to the tree of life, and may enter in through the gates into the city.' The fish was used by early Christians as a secret sign, the letters of the Greek word for 'fish' being the initial letters of 'Jesus Christ, Son of God, Saviour'. Martyrs usually hold a palm, hermits a T-shaped staff and rosary, pilgrims wear a hat with a shell and carry a staff and wallet. Founders usually hold models of the buildings they founded, bishops or abbots hold a crozier or pastoral staff, and popes wear the triple tiara, cope and pallium and carry a triple cross.

anchor	Clement
anvil	Adrian
apple	the fall of man
arrow (piercing breast or hand)	Giles
arrows(s) enfiling crown	Edmund
arrow(s) piercing body	Sebastian
axe	Matthias
balls (3)	Nicholas
banner with red cross	Ursula
basket of fruit or flowers	Dorothea
basket of loaves	Philip
bedstead	Faith
beehive	Ambrose
beggar or cripple (offering cloak)	Martin
bell	Anthony
birds	Francis of Assisi
boat	Jude
bones	Ambrose
book and crook	Chad
bottle	James the Great
box of alabaster	Mary of Magdela
breasts (on a plate)	Agatha
builder's square	Thomas
bundle of rods	Faith
candle and devil	Genevieve
cauldron of oil	Vitus
chains (held by)	Leonard
chalice containing dragon	John the Apostle
children (two carried by)	Eustace
children (three in a tub)	Nicholas
cloak (half)	Martin
cock	Peter and Vitus
comb (iron)	Blaise
cow	Bridget
cross (red on white)	George
cross (saltire)	Andrew
cross (inverted)	Peter
cross - T (carried)	Anthony
cross - T	Philip
devil with bellows	Genevieve
devil underfoot	Michael
distaff	Eve's expulsion
dog with wounded leg	Roch
dogs with torches in mouths	Dominic
doorpost and lintel	Passover
dove	Pope Gregory
dove on sceptre	King Edmund
dove on shoulder	David of Wales

doves in cage	Joseph
dragon	George, Archangel Michael, Martha, Satan and sin
dragon and cross	Margaret of Antioch
dragon led by chain	Juliana
dragon under foot	victory over evil
eagle with nimbus	John the evangelist
eyes in a dish	Lucy
fleur-de-lis	Virgin Mary
gridiron	Laurence
halberd	Jude
head (crowned)	Cuthbert or Dennis
head (man's, at feet of)	Catherine of Alexandra
head carried before altar	Winifred
heart (flaming/transfixed by sword)	Augustine or Mary
hermit	Anthony
hog	Anthony
hook (iron)	Faith or Vincent
horseshoe	Eloy
idols (broken)	Wilfred
keys	Peter
knife and skin	Bartholomew
lamb	Agnes, Francis and John the Baptist
Lamb (Paschal)	Passover
lion	Adrian or Jerome
lion (winged) with nimbus	Mark the evangelist
lion and raven	Vincent
loaves and fishes	disciples
man (winged) with nimbus	Matthew the evangelist
manacles	Leonard
money bag	Matthew
mule (kneeling)	Anthony of Padua
musical instruments	Cecilia
olive branch	Agnes
organ (portable)	Cecilia
otter	Cuthbert
ox (winged) with nimbus	Luke the evangelist
palm	Agnes
pagans being baptized	Wilfred
partridge	Jerome
pelican	Sacrifice of the Cross
pen, ink and scroll	Mark or Matthew
phoenix	resurrection
pincers	Agatha or Dunstan
pincers and tooth	Apollonia
pomegranate	Resurrection and unity
pot and ladle	Martha
roses (crown of)	Cecilia, Dorothy or Teresa

saw	Simon
scallop shell	James the Great
scourge	Ambrose
scroll	the Five Books of Moses
serpent	Satan
shears	Agatha
sheep	Genevieve
sieve (broken)	Benedict
stag	Adrian, Eustace or Hubert
stone(s)	Stephen
swan and flowers	Hugh of Lincoln
sword	Paul or Barbara
sword (flaming)	Adam's expulsion
sword through breast	Euphemia
sword through neck	Lucy
tower	Barbara
tree (beneath foot of)	Boniface
tree (sleeping beneath)	Etheldreda
unicorn	Virgin Mary
weighing souls	Michael
wheel (spiked)	Catherine
windlass	Erasmus
wolf	King Edmund
Wounds of Christ	Francis of Assisi

See also AGNUS DEI (PASCHAL LAMB), CELTIC CROSS, CROSSES, EAGLE, ELEPHANTS, FIVE WOUNDS OF CHRIST, INSTRUMENTS OF THE PASSION, JESSE WINDOW, LABARUM, LION, PELICAN, SCALLOP SHELLS, TREE OF LIFE, TRINITY, TRIQUETRA and WHEEL-HEAD CROSS

CHURCH ALES Major community festivities by which funds were raised for the parish church.
See also CHURCH HOUSES

CHURCH DEDICATIONS see CHURCH SITES

CHURCHES The church will normally be the oldest building in a village and the obvious starting point for any historical investigation, for it is likely to embody the entire development of a community, often from the Anglo-Saxon period to the present day. The omission of a church in *Domesday Book* does not necessarily mean that no eleventh-century church existed (*see* CHURCH SITES). Through the architectural development of a parish church the fluctuating fortunes of a community may be assessed. Indeed, we are as much indebted to those parishes whose comparative poverty has ensured the survival of our oldest Saxon and Romanesque

buildings as we are to those whose prosperity inspired the endowment of our great medieval churches. Contraction, perhaps in the form of blocked aisles and doorways, is usually indicative of economic decline; whereas expansion, epitomized by ornamentation and the addition of chantry chapels, aisles, transepts and ornate towers, indicates the patronage of a prosperous society. Such periods of contraction and expansion may be dated from architectural and documentary evidence.

The Roman Emperor Constantine's acceptance of Christianity in AD 312 was to have important consequences for the development of the Church in Britain. It ensured that Roman Britain was in part Christian before the end of Imperial rule in 410; Ireland was converted by Roman missionaries in the fifth century and Irish monks were instrumental in the later Pictish and Anglo-Saxon conversions. The fifth and sixth centuries saw successive waves of migration to Britain from north Germany and Scandinavia, and the ascendancy of paganism. A papal mission from Gregory I landed in Kent in 597 led by Augustine (d.604/5), who was destined to become the first Archbishop of Canterbury. Within a few months, Christianity was adopted by Ethelbert (d.616), King of Kent, whose wife, Bertha, daughter of the Frankish King Charibert, was already a Christian. Christianity had managed to survive in those areas of sub-Roman Britain where Saxon culture had not penetrated, though the administration and customs of this Celtic Church differed fundamentally from the Augustinian model. Its priests operated among isolated tribal communities, often in a wild and inhospitable landscape, far removed from the influence of Rome. It was of necessity a Church of scattered MONASTERIES and itinerant missions in which the hieratic organization of the Roman Church, with its bishops and dioceses, had little relevance.

In *c*. 603 Augustine attempted to reach agreement with representatives of the Celtic Church on differences in discipline and practice, but without success. Nevertheless, by 627 Christianity had reached Northumbria, and in 633 Celtic monks settled at Lindisfarne (Holy Island) and much of the north was converted. Such 'conversion' was rarely universal, however, for while the aristocracy may have adopted Christianity as its 'official' religion, a formidable element of paganism survived in the customs and practices of the peasantry for many generations. In 664 the *Synod of Whitby* resolved the differences between the two traditions and established an administrative structure which is essentially that of the Church today. Significantly, the Synod created a 'national' Church long before the political unification of the country.

Many monasteries were plundered during the Danish incursions of the ninth century and it was not until the reign of Alfred (King of Wessex 849–99) that the Church enjoyed a period of comparative security. There were three types of Anglo-Saxon church. *Headminsters* were great abbeys: centres of diocesan administration, culture and commerce. Many MINSTERS were the traditional religious centres of the remoter areas where the process of conversion was not complete and where subsidiary churches were established in scattered settlements, each served by a single priest. Others were little more than small communities, founded by a nobleman on his estate, governed by his relatives and staffed by his dependants. By the Norman Conquest, the influence of the 'old minsters' had been superseded by that of the churches they had created and the parish was established as a unit of ecclesiastical administration. *Thegns' churches* were PROPRIETARY CHAPELS built to serve the needs of a lord's estate. The priest was also the lord's chaplain and the lord took the church's tithes. During the twelfth century many proprietary chapels were transferred to monastic control and new parishes created to meet the spiritual needs of a rapidly growing population. Most of the minor ANGLO-SAXON churches were built of timber and only one survives, though much restored, at Greensted-juxta-Onger in Essex. Many churches contain Saxon work, however, and a number of seventh- and eighth-century stone churches survive, including Escomb, County Durham (the earliest complete church in England *c.* AD 680, Brixworth in Northamptonshire and Jarrow, also in County Durham.

The scale and complexity of church building in the century following the Norman Conquest of 1066 was extraordinary. Clearly the Normans considered the simple Anglo-Saxon churches to be inadequate to the needs of a reformed Church and, consequently, they rebuilt nearly every cathedral and constructed hundreds of new monasteries and thousands of parish churches. Most NORMAN (ROMANESQUE) churches, though built of stone, were fairly modest and served by English priests whose education and status were often little better than that of the peasantry. Most were constructed on a simple BASILICAN plan, though a small number followed the Rotunda of Constantine's Church of the Holy Sepulchre in Jerusalem, notably those of the Knights Templar and Knights Hospitaller. The Temple Church in London (1185) and the Holy

The parish church of St Andrew at Evesbatch, Herefordshire.

Sepulchre Church at Cambridge (*c.* 1130, restored 1840), for example, are circular with an inner ring of arcaded columns, a central conical roof and a lower roof above the circular, outer aisle.

From the eleventh century onwards many larger churches were constructed or remodelled to a *cruciform* plan with the lower, elongated limb of a *Latin Cross* forming the NAVE, the upper limb the CHANCEL and the lateral limbs the north and south TRANSEPTS. (In parts of Europe the *Greek Cross* plan was adopted: this has limbs of equal length and, consequently, the naves of many European churches are considerably shorter than their English counterparts.) Churches are generally oriented with the ALTAR at the eastern end of the building. The PRESBYTERY (originally the *sanctuary*) around the altar was usually apsidal but many were rebuilt after *c.* 1150 to provide a square termination, and in larger churches a RETRO-CHOIR or AMBULATORY was added with radiating CHAPELS and a LADY CHAPEL behind the high altar. Before the

Reformation, the chancel was the *sanctum sanctorum* of the clergy, and in CATHEDRALS, monasteries and collegiate churches the stalls of the body corporate lined the walls of the lower chancel or CHOIR, separated from the nave by a massive PULPITUM, which, in many churches, is now used to support an organ. One bay west of this was the ROOD SCREEN and in front of that, the nave altar, at which the laity participated in the Eucharist. In smaller churches a CHANCEL SCREEN effectively performed the same function and may also have supported a rood. Towers were sometimes constructed above the central space or *crossing* where the four limbs of the cross met: an extraordinarily daring architectural innovation, though many Norman towers subsequently collapsed or had to be demolished. On smaller churches a tower was usually erected as a belfry to the west of the nave or in the south-west corner between the nave and south porch (*see* CHURCH TOWERS).

Most medieval churches were entered by the south door, sometimes with a corresponding north door for processional purposes and, in grander churches, an imposing west door beneath the tower. Where a fairly modest church is entered from the north or west there is usually an historical reason, such as the re-siting of an adjacent settlement, as at Marston Magna in Somerset. Business was often enacted outside the south doorway and many porches contain an altar where contracts were signed, as at South Poole in Devon. From the fourteenth century, several porches were constructed with an upper storey so that business could be conducted more conveniently. There is an impressive three-storey porch at the church of St John the Baptist at Cirencester in Gloucestershire. The BAPTISTRY, with its FONT and STOUP, was usually located at the west end of the nave, though these have sometimes been removed to the space beneath the tower.

During the twelfth and thirteenth centuries many timber roofs were replaced with stone vaults (*see* VAULTING), aisles, transepts and porches added and nave walls heightened to support aisle roofs and to provide additional windows. All this, and the construction of new stone towers above the crossing, required considerable structural support and the provision of BUTTRESSES, both at ground level and within the buildings themselves. The naves and chancels of most large medieval churches consist of three storeys: an *arcade* of pillars separating the nave or chancel from the aisles; a *triforium* or *tribune*; and a *clerestory*, which forms the upper level and consists of windows, clear of the roofs of the aisles. A triforium is an arcaded wall passage or area of blank arcading below the *clerestory*. In many smaller churches (and in some larger ones of late-Gothic date) this middle level is omitted. A tribune is an arcaded gallery which extends above the stone vault of the aisle and is generally found, in place of the triforium, in larger churches where the nave was constructed before the end of the thirteenth century. (Many books erroneously refer to the triforium and tribune as though they are synonymous.)

Such ubiquitous and innovative activity reflects the prosperity of the period, which was coincidental with the first flowering of English GOTHIC ARCHITECTURE. Medieval churches were not only places of worship: they were also community centres where commercial, social and even judicial activities took place. Many were the chapels of trade guilds, fraternities and hospices, or the mausolea of the nobility. The great cathedrals exercised considerable regional influence, both ceremonial and commercial. Most were prosperous cult centres, with saints' shrines and reliquaries attracting pilgrims and thereby stimulating local economies. However, it was the corporate ownership of property, and particularly the endowment of land, which ensured the continuing affluence of the cathedrals and monasteries. The fourteenth and fifteenth centuries witnessed a gradual decline in this support and a corresponding increase in the building or remodelling of parish churches. In part, this was attributable to the piety of individual parishioners, anxious to secure eternal rest by their good deeds. It was also inspired by rivalry, both individual and corporate, as in the wool and cloth producing communities of Cullompton and Tiverton in Devon where architectural emulation reached ostentatious proportions, or at Swaffham Priory, Cambridgeshire, where the rival manorial churches of St Mary and Saints Gyriac and Julia stand within each other's shadow. Inevitably, civic pride reflected that of the individual and *vice versa*: the magnificent churches of East Anglia and the Cotswolds are indicative not only of the prosperity of local industry, but also of the pre-eminence of the merchants and manufacturers whose MONUMENTS and CHANTRY CHAPELS rivalled those of the nobility. HERALDRY in EFFIGIES, BRASSES, and in the fabric of the churches they endowed, advertised the pervasive authority of the medieval magnates, even in death. Some endowed not only churches, but also colleges, hospices, almshouses and schools. These are most often found in the vicinity of the parish church, and their founders may usually be identified by an heraldic tablet or inscription.

English medieval architecture reached its apogee in the PERPENDICULAR style of the late fourteenth and fifteenth centuries. Considerable remodelling of earlier buildings had taken place in the mid-fourteenth century, as in the magnificent choir of Gloucester Cathedral (1337–57) where a delicate cage of stonework was introduced, masking the Norman arcade and triforium and extending upwards to embrace an entirely new clerestory of startling dimensions. Gloucester may be considered the archetype of the perpendicular style but it is in the chapel of King's College, Cambridge (1446–1515), that it is most exquisitely expressed. The building of Henry VII's chapel at Westminster (1503–19) and the rebuilding of Bath Abbey (1501–39) continued the perpendicular tradition into the sixteenth century but church building effectively ceased following the DISSOLUTION OF THE MONASTERIES in 1536–9. The few ecclesiastical buildings completed during the next century were built in a Gothic style and even the rebuilding, between 1698 and 1704, of the tower, nave, aisles and transepts of St Mary's, Warwick, owed more to the fifteenth century than to the seventeenth.

The Reformation, completed in 1560, had brought about fundamental doctrinal and liturgical changes, but a great deal of ceremonial was retained, particularly in the cathedrals. The administration of the Church was virtually unchanged, with power vested in the bishops, who were now responsible to the sovereign and not to the Pope. All this was anathema to the PURITANS, who wished for a more radical Reformation, but in the 1630s the bishops, led by Archbishop Laud and enjoying the support of Charles I, ordered an improvement in the standards of ceremonial and a return to more traditional forms of worship (*see* ALTARS). This conflict is often evident in the architecture and furnishings of contemporary, neighbouring churches: in Yorkshire, for example, St John's church, Leeds (1634), has the elaborate woodcarving, canopied pulpit and screens of the Laudian tradition and nearby Bramhope Chapel (1649) an unadorned, rectangular building, simple box pews and three-decker pulpit.

St Swithin, Worcester, described by Betjeman as 'A perfectly preserved example of an eighteenth-century church with all its furnishings intact'.

In Scotland, the Reformation was far more violent and resulted in the establishment of a PRESBYTERIAN administration in the 1560s. Following the Union of the English and Scottish crowns in 1603, an attempt was made to impose English practices on the Scottish Church and there is evidence of this in the interior arrangement of a small number of late seventeenth-century churches. For the most part, however, Scottish churches were dominated by the pulpit, in front of which was the communion table and seating for the elders. In many cases, medieval churches were adapted for this purpose, the larger ones sometimes being divided into two or even three separate preaching houses, though many earlier churches were to be pulled down and replaced during a period of frenetic religious building in the eighteenth century.

Except in Ireland, the seventeenth century saw a complete break with Rome. Those who continued to cling to 'the old religion' did so in a political climate which was at best prejudiced and at worst hysterical. The Great Fire of London in 1666 stimulated a massive rebuilding programme and a revival of the CLASSICAL style of architecture in buildings such as the London churches of Sir Christopher Wren and his contemporaries. These churches were essentially buildings intended for protestant worship. Gone was the medieval sense of mystery and the barrier between priest and people. The new conception of a church was that of a large room in which as many people as possible could hear the preacher in comfort. Churches were rectangular or basilican in plan, frequently galleried and with prominent pulpits and simple table altars, often set within the body of the church rather than at the east end. Triforium and clerestory were replaced by classical colonnades and large, round-headed windows containing clear glass. Interiors were light and often richly decorated. Towers were plain but adorned with an exuberance of steeples '. . . all bright and glittering in the smokeless air'. (Wordsworth, 1802). Some churches of the period have domes, notably St Paul's Cathedral, which was begun in 1675 and completed in 1711. Wren initially proposed a centrally planned church with a large dome 36 metres in diameter (120 feet). This was rejected by the commissioners who considered it to be too far removed from the English tradition. Wren was forced to compromise, so that beneath its dome and classical shell, St Paul's is a conventional, cruciform church with many of the attributes of its medieval predecessor.

Many of the Anglican churches of eighteenth-century England were built to accommodate a rapidly increasing urban population and there are few towns where there is not a large, classical church dating from this period, with box pews, lofty pulpits and elaborate altar-pieces. Most were built by private subscription, the incumbent receiving rents from private pews. Unfortunately, these churches were often built in areas that have long since lost their residential character and many have consequently become redundant. A notable exception is the magnificent BAROQUE church of St Philip, Birmingham, designed by Thomas Archer. Completed in 1725, a rectangular chancel was added *c.* 1803 and in 1905 the church became the city's cathedral. Another of Archer's churches, St John's in Smith Square, Westminster, was restored in the 1960s and is now a concert hall.

The Georgian aristocracy provided us with a wonderful legacy of classical or romantic GOTHICK chapels which, although technically parish churches, were built on country estates as 'private' chapels for the benefit of the owner and his employees. The church of St Michael and All Saints at Witley Court, Herefordshire, continues as a parish church even though the great house to which it was attached has long been a gaunt ruin with trees growing inside its walls. Nearby Shobdon church, built in the mid-eighteenth-century Gothick style, has carpeted and cushioned pews, a three-decker pulpit with canopied sounding board, and elaborately plastered ceilings. Many of these chapels were provided with fireplaces in the family pews, and private access from the adjacent house. Indeed, several were actually incorporated within the fabric of the house itself, though these should not be confused with the many fine private Roman Catholic chapels of the period, such as that at Wardour New Castle, in Wiltshire. Many ancient churches were enlarged and remodelled in the eighteenth century, sometimes with startling effect, as at Whitby in Yorkshire where the medieval church of St Mary was extended to accommodate a growing population and provided with a elegant Georgian pulpit, box pews and gallery. (When two Whitby whaling ships were lost in 1826, a congregation of 3,000 people attended the memorial service there.) Unfortunately, many of these re-modelled churches suffered from later restorations, though several (mostly rural) remain intact, as at Minstead in Hampshire.

The eighteenth century also saw the expansion of nonconformity and the building of Unitarian and Independent chapels: precursors of the ubiquitous Methodist chapels of the next century (*see* DISSENTING CHAPELS).

The nineteenth century witnessed a period of church building unparalleled since that which followed the Norman Conquest. By 1858, over 3,000 new churches had been built in fifty years, during which the population of England had doubled. (In 1851 the Church of England received a devastating blow: statistics relating to church attendance had been obtained from the 1851 census and these revealed that on Sunday, 30 March only 7,261,032 out of a total population of 17,927,609 had attended any form of religious service and of these, only 52 per cent had been to an Anglican church.) But church building was also a reaction against what the Victorians, in particular, perceived to be eighteenth-century vulgarity, both liturgical and architectural. The classical style was denounced as 'pagan' and, therefore, decadent and the Gothick ridiculous. Instead, there was a return to the 'true architecture of Christianity' – that of the thirteenth and fourteenth centuries. (Twelfth-century Romanesque was considered to be crude and fifteenth-century Perpendicular excessive, though both will be found in a few Victorian churches, e.g. the Italian Romanesque church at Wilton in Wiltshire.) The GOTHIC REVIVAL was stimulated by a corresponding theological movement aimed at raising the standards of public worship within the Anglican Church. This emanated from Oxford in the 1820s and was later adopted by members of the Camden Society at Cambridge, who saw the restoration of liturgical ritual and Gothic architecture as being necessary adjuncts to the concept of an historic church. By the 1860s, the embellishments of the Anglo-Catholic 'High Church' had become fashionable, especially in London and the south-east, and many of the new churches were suitably imposing. However, nineteenth-century ecclesiastical architecture was invariably imitative and two-dimensional. Only in a few buildings, such as Augustus Pugin's Roman Catholic cathedral at Birmingham (1839), and in the craftsmanship of individual features, such as G.F. Bodley's rood screen at the Church of the Holy Angels, Hoar Cross, Staffordshire, can the Victorians compare with their medieval predecessors.

Many churches were demolished and rebuilt in a more fashionable style. Even more were heavily 'restored' in a wave of unparalleled architectural vandalism. The Classical style persisted in the great Welsh non-conformist chapels and those of nineteenth-century Yorkshire, though one of several notable exceptions, the Mill Hill Unitarian Chapel in Leeds, was built in the grand Perpendicular style in 1847. In Scotland many new but undistinguished Presbyterian churches were built and a number of Episcopalian churches, such as the Cathedral of St Mary at Edinburgh which, with its three spires, is clearly modelled on the medieval cathedral at Lichfield, Staffordshire. By the mid-nineteenth century, only half the population were regular church-goers, a decline which continued into the twentieth century, particularly in urban areas where many monolithic Victorian churches were so expensive to maintain that they have subsequently become redundant.

Almost without exception, mid-twentieth-century Anglican churches are of conventional design, though constructed with modern materials and using contemporary technology: Guildford Cathedral (designed by Sir Edward Maufe and consecrated 1961) is a cruciform church in the medieval monastic tradition; at Coventry (designed by Sir Basil Spence and consecrated 1962) the nave arcade and vault, chancel and Lady chapel are simply a twentieth-century interpretation of a Gothic theme. The most innovative ecclesiastical building, other than a converted semi-detached house on a suburban Gloucester estate in the seventies, is the Roman Catholic Metropolitan Cathedral of Christ the King at Liverpool (designed by Sir Frederick Gibberd and consecrated in 1967).

Future historians will be able to identify divergent elements in the Anglican Church at the end of the twentieth century. They will note a return to the medieval concept of the church as a community centre; the rejection of 'anachronistic' ritual and 'irrelevant' tradition; the introduction of a new liturgy (the banal *Alternative Service Book* of 1980); the ordination of women and the creation of team ministries and group parishes. They will also be aware of a rapid degeneration in the relationship of Church and State; of a continuing decline in attendance at services and of interminable conflict between the traditional and progressive wings of the Church. There will be a plethora of documentary evidence available: from parochial church council minutes to the transcripts of synodical debates. And there will be the churches themselves, many of which will have been remodelled to meet the requirements of the new liturgy: the lectern, pulpit and stalls dispensed with, pews removed to allow for 'multiple use' and the communion table moved forward into the congregation. Many others will have been renovated, both Anglican and non-conformist, to provide exclusive domestic accommodation for families with a taste for the ecclesiastical.

CHURCH HOUSES Pre-Reformation forerunners of the church hall, several sixteenth-century church houses may still be found adjacent to a church or within a churchyard. They were maintained by the churchwardens for parish festivities, especially 'church ales' at which home-brewed ale was sold for the financial benefit of the church and the local poor. So unbridled were these activities at times that they were roundly condemned by the Puritans and the magistracy, and many church houses had disappeared by the mid-seventeenth century, though some became independent taverns.

CHURCH RATE *see* TAXATION

CHURCH SITES Many ancient churches were built on Anglo-Saxon estates, or by Norman lords of the manor, as proprietary (private) churches, often in the vicinity of a manor-house or occasionally attached to it (*see* CHURCHES). In dispersed communities of hamlets and farmsteads, churches were often built in apparent isolation: at the intersection of route-ways, at river crossings or in the vicinity of a holy well or spring. The omission of a church in *Domesday Book* does not necessarily mean that no eleventh-century church existed. Many were originally chapelries of MINSTERS and evolved as parish churches from the end of the eleventh century.

A large number of churches are located on sites for which there is no apparent rationale. At Knowlton in Dorset the lonely ruins of a twelfth-century church stand at the centre of a circular Neolithic embankment and ditch. The large-scale map reveals that the earthwork is the last surviving of a series, known locally as Knowlton Rings, and that the church, abandoned in the eighteenth century when its roof fell in, was once the parish church of a medieval deserted villages located in a river valley a mile to the south-west. Whatever its original purpose, the earthwork was almost certainly used in successive centuries for ceremonial purposes, and its religious associations perpetuated in the founding of an early church on the site. In AD 601 Pope Gregory instructed Abbot Mellitus (later Bishop of London) that such sacred places should not be destroyed but rather that they should be sanctified and Christian altars set up in the place of pagan ones, thereby ensuring that the powerful religious associations of a site were sustained in the minds of the people and a continuum of worship guaranteed. Throughout Britain (and especially in the West of England) there are numerous instances of pagan sites being adopted as places of Christian worship and these are often located within circular churchyard enclosures. Inevitably, many others await identification (*see also* HOLY WELLS and PAGAN SYMBOLS).

Such sites may sometimes be suggested through a *church dedication*: the hilltop church at Oldbury-on-Severn in Gloucestershire is dedicated to a Saxon saint, Arilda, and stands within a circular earthwork high above the village. Dedications to St Lawrence, who died on a gridiron, are common to many churches with pre-Christian associations, suggestive perhaps of pagan sacrificial flames; and churches dedicated to the saints Catherine, Edward and Michael are frequently sited on eminences and in high places. There are over 600 English churches dedicated to St Michael, and seventy in Wales, of which a considerable proportion are on hilltop sites. It may be that many of these sites are of pagan origin and that the warrior-Archangel Michael was considered an appropriate saint to stand guard over ancestral remains, pagan and Christian alike. But dedications can be deceptive. Different dedications were fashionable at different times and many old dedications have been forgotten, corrupted or changed where no official record has survived. Sometimes the parochial festival (or feast-day) has remained unaltered, and reference to the Roman calendar may assist in discovering both the original dedication and when the church was first constructed on the site.

Some dedications are unique, such as that to St Eata (d.685) at Atcham in Shropshire, and suggest that these churches may have been founded by the saints themselves. This is particularly so in Wales and the Marches, where many churches may be found which possess both a unique or rare dedication and a site for which there is no apparent explanation. Elsewhere, Celtic dedications are usually indicative of a foundation which pre-dates the Synod of Whitby in 664 at which the Celtic tradition was forced to concede to that of Rome. Nevertheless, it is often difficult to differentiate between myth and reality, and in the Celtic Church the term 'saint' was applied to all who were by vocation religious. Neither should the proposition that such dedications trace the journeys of Celtic missionaries and evangelists be given credence. When the provenance of an original dedication can be substantiated it may serve to link clusters of churches with similar dedications to a mother church and, thereby, identify early parishes which have subsequently been fragmented. There are many instances of church dedications being used as place-name elements to differentiate between villages with otherwise identical names: Donhead St Andrew and Donhead St Mary in Wiltshire, for example. But even here dedications can be deceptive: in Essex, the village of Belchamp St Paul has a church dedicated to St Andrew!

So many ancient churches occupy apparently illogical, inconvenient sites that it is not unreasonable to conclude that they were left in splendid isolation following the re-settlement of communities on more favourable sites, or as the result of 'emparking' in the seventeenth and eighteenth centuries (*see* DESERTED VILLAGES). The prospect of 'removing' a village's most substantial stone building must have been daunting indeed, and there must also have been a natural reluctance among a superstitious people to disturb the sanctity of hallowed ground and its ancestral associations. Other churches were late arrivals and sited on the periphery of a village, as at Long Stanton in Shropshire, or occupy a clearly defined croft within a regular village plan, suggesting either that an earlier church was moved to accommodate the new plan or even that it was the first church to have been provided for the community.

The siting of 'modern' churches, that is those that have been built since the seventeenth century, is usually indicative either of the demolition and rebuilding of a church on an earlier site or of a gift of land by a local benefactor. Many Victorian churches were provided in urban areas by *nouveau riche* industrialists, anxious to secure a place in civic history, if not in the Gothick heaven of their assumed forefathers.

CHURCH TOWERS Church towers originated in ninth-century Italy and first appeared in Britain a century later. Most Anglo-Saxon churches were constructed of timber but there were exceptions and it is these stone buildings which have survived. Saxon towers may be recognised by LONG AND SHORT WORK, twin round-headed or triangular belfry openings and shallow piers attached to the wall *lesenes* which were sometimes arranged in an ornamental pattern as at St Peter's, Barton-upon-Humber, North Lincolnshire. The great eleventh-century tower at Sompting, Sussex, has a magnificent oak-shingle Rhenish *helm roof* with four diamond-shaped sloping faces, each descending to a gable. In some instances, an existing church would be heightened at the west end to form a tower and extended to the east in a new nave, as at Barnack church in Cambridgeshire. It seems likely that most church towers were intended simply to accommodate a raised belfry, and where financial constraints precluded the construction of a tower, a bell-cote or bell-gable was built on the western gable instead, sometimes with a second above the altar at the east for a *sanctus* bell.

It is equally true that many communities came to appreciate the defensive advantages of having a tower in their midst, indeed the term *belfry* is of

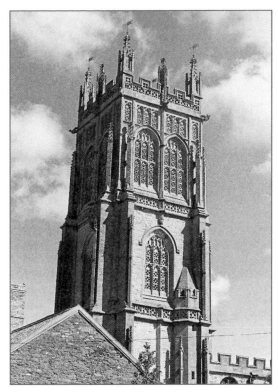

Magnificent mid-fifteenth-century tower of the church of St John the Baptist, Glastonbury, Somerset. The elaborate parapet and panelled middle stage are reminiscent of those at Gloucester Cathedral.

Teutonic origin and means 'a place of safety'. The name was given to the movable tower used in sieges, and came to mean a watch-tower, beacon-tower or alarm bell-tower. In the Welsh Marches, for example, where raids and border disputes were a way of life, massive square towers such as that at Clun in Shropshire provided refuges for the entire community. There are fifty detached church towers (correctly *detached belfries*) in England, of which several are close to the Welsh border and were clearly built for defensive purposes: that at Bosbury, Herefordshire, for example, is nearly 9 metres square (29 feet) and heavily built of stone. The thirteenth-century belfry at Ledbury, Herefordshire, was built next to the church because the task of reconstructing the original building and foundations to accommodate the weight of a tower was considered excessive. It was built in three stages, a fourth being added (or possibly rebuilt) in 1733 when a spire was added by the well-known spire-builder Wilkinson of Worcester. At St Feve, and elsewhere in Cornwall, a detached belfry was built on a nearby eminence because the church itself was hidden in a deep valley. Other detached belfries were sited so that they would not threaten the defences of adjacent castles, as at Berkeley in Gloucestershire (rebuilt 1750). Ironically, it was from this tower that parliamentary artillery terminated the three-year siege of Berkeley Castle in 1645.

Round towers are a feature of East Anglian churches: there are 130 in Norfolk, 40 in Suffolk and 7 in Essex. Of these, some 20 are of Saxon origin and were probably constructed as refuges from Viking incursions. They may be recognized by the location of a single doorway several metres above ground level, a ladder being required to obtain access. Those which date from the twelfth and succeeding centuries were built as simple belfries in a country where suitable stone for constructing square-cornered towers was scarce.

From the eleventh century, the great Romanesque and Gothic churches were built to a cruciform plan, with additional transept walls at right angles to those of the nave and choir to counteract the outward thrust of massive central towers, daringly constructed above the void of the crossing, and sometimes supporting spires. The most magnificent spire, at Salisbury Cathedral, was completed in 1380 and, at 121 metres (404 feet), is by far the tallest in England, though that of Old St Paul's (destroyed by fire in 1561) was nearly 28 metres taller (93 feet).

Most spires are octagonal so that the corner pinnacles of the tower may be accommodated and the spire's weight evenly distributed. On lesser churches, where there are no such pinnacles, a *broach* spire was usually constructed with sloping, triangular splays of masonry buttressing the spire at each corner of the tower. Some cathedrals have three towers, two at the west end and a larger one at the centre. The central tower of Lincoln Cathedral is 81 metres tall (271 feet) and was once crowned with a lead-covered timber spire which, at 157 metres (524 feet), is believed to have been the tallest in Europe but was destroyed in a storm in 1548. Many Norman towers collapsed: of the few that survive, that at Norwich Cathedral (1145) is the tallest and finest, with a graceful spire added in 1490.

Most parish churches have towers at the west end of the nave, and these generally reflect both the architectural style of the period in which they were built and the affluence of the communities who erected them. The magnificent fifteenth-century towers of Somerset, Devon and East Anglian, as well as those of the famous Cotswold wool churches, celebrate in architectural splendour both God's glory and that of their builders.

See also ROUND TOWERS

CHURCHWARDENS *see* PARISH

CHURCHYARD CROSS *see* CHURCHYARDS

CHURCHYARDS It is often the case that a churchyard is older than the church buildings it contains. Oval or circular churchyards are almost invariably Celtic in origin, and often associated with the cemeteries of early monastic foundations. There are also many instances of even earlier sites, often encompassed by ancient earthworks with pagan associations, being used for Christian burial (*see* CHURCH SITES). A raised churchyard may be a further indication of antiquity, for repeated burials will have increased substantially the level of earth above that of adjacent land. There are several instances of an ancient churchyard which was shared by neighbouring parishes and a small number may even contain two churches, as at Swaffham Priory in Cambridgeshire. From the Saxon period, churchyards have generally been of rectangular shape and may conform to the crofts of a regular village plan. In the Middle Ages the churchyard was often the venue for village festivities and social gatherings, for games and commercial transactions: much to the annoyance of the ecclesiastical hierarchy.

Burial in the churchyard is the right of every parishioner irrespective of his beliefs or station in life. The freehold of both the church and the churchyard are the prerogative of the incumbent, in joint possession with the parochial church council: the churchyard is maintained by the council and its use controlled by the parish priest. Gravestones were a seventeenth-century innovation, but most date from the eighteenth century or later. Each gravestone or memorial is owned by the person who erected it, or by his successors, and anyone who removes or defaces a memorial trespasses thereby. Although by custom all the grass contained within a churchyard belongs to the incumbent as part of his endowment, they were frequently grazed by the sexton's animals, the graves being protected with a trellis of osier and bramble. Although the entire churchyard is consecrated ground, there persisted into the last century the practice whereby the virtuous received burial on the salubrious south side of the church and felons and outcasts were consigned to perpetual shadow on the north.

Some churchyards contain ancient free-standing crosses or fragments of crosses, usually located to the south of the church or occasionally found incorporated within the fabric of the building itself, following rebuilding. *Preaching crosses* were probably erected at venues for services conducted by peripatetic preachers from the MINSTERS, and usually pre-date the foundation of a church on the same site. So-called *churchyard crosses* are generally of medieval origin, though some are former preaching crosses. They were intended to sanctify the churchyard and were used for liturgical purposes, the churchyard cross being the second of the processional Stations of the Cross on Palm Sunday and the one at which the Mass was celebrated. After the celebration, the cross itself was wreathed in 'palms', which were usually branches of yew (*see below*). Many survive only as a shaft and stepped base, the tabernacle, with its niches containing 'Papist' images of Christ and the Virgin or the Saints, having been removed by Tudor or Cromwellian iconoclasts. A vacant niche was usually provided for the pyx (vessel), in which the Host was reserved in the Palm Sunday mass. In the Middle Ages, tabernacles were more common than cross-heads, though many Celtic wheel-head crosses have survived and several early Anglian crosses, often with vine-scroll decoration on the shaft, are to be found in the north of England. Secular crosses may also be found in churchyards and a community's former prosperity may be measured by their size and ornamentation. Modern 'reproduction' crosses of all types have been erected in many churchyards, often as war memorials or to commemorate benefactors.

The practice of planting YEW TREES in churchyards probably dates from a pre-Christian belief in the tree's divine status and protective qualities. It was a life-symbol and sprigs of yew were placed in the grave at burial. Although legend relates how yew trees provided shelter for the first Christian missionaries, there is evidence to suggest that in England and the southern Marches of Wales the Norman clergy planted churchyard yews as they had in Normandy before the Conquest. In Ireland, yew trees have been grown in churchyards since the eighth century. The proposition that church precincts were commonly used for archery practice (*see* BUTTS) and that the churchyard yews provided raw material for the famous English longbow is fallacious: bowyers much preferred Spanish wood, which was less knotty, and the trunk of a mature tree would, at best, provide five or six good bows. Only at times of emergency, such as the invasion scares of

the sixteenth century, would the churchyard yews be lopped to provide makeshift weapons. Of course, the leaves and fruit of the yew are poisonous and the prevalence of yew trees in old churchyards may be accounted for in the rebuke of a medieval Norfolk labourer: 'For, as often falls, broken were the churchyard walls. And the knight's herdsman often let his beasts into the churchyard get . . .'. Cattle, ponies and sheep graze safely in the company of yews in the New Forest and on the South Downs, and yet farm stock has often been poisoned by eating yew clippings. It may be that animals recognize the growing tree as poisonous but will eat its foliage if it is found in an unaccustomed place. Ancient yews become extremely stout but the heartwood usually decays and it is often difficult to determine a tree's precise age. The ancient yew (now a relic) in Fortingall churchyard, Perth and Kinross, had a girth of 15 metres (50 feet) and may well be nearly 2,000 years old. The churchyard of St Mary's, Painswick, in Gloucestershire contains a magnificent collection of neatly clipped yews dating from *c.* 1779 – 'just under or just over, but never, reputedly, exactly 100 in number . . .' (Rudder).

See also GRAVESTONES *and* LICH-GATE

CHURL *see* CEORL

CIDER MILLS Prehistoric man is known to have produced a primitive type of cider from wild apples. The word 'cider' comes from the French *sidre* and it is likely that the tall stone wheels (millstones) and circular troughs which comprise a cider mill were also introduced into the south and west of England from twelfth-century Normandy. Cider is the fermented juice of apples. When crushed, the numerous invisible yeast plants present on the skin of a mature apple ferment, turning the apple's sugar into alcohol. Both millstone and trough are usually of granite, the vertical millstone revolving within the horizontal circular trough by means of an axle projecting from a central spindle. The millstone was slowly drawn round by a harnessed donkey, horse or ox as apples were loaded into the trough. The purpose of the mill was to crush the apples before they were placed in a press and the cider extracted. Both millstone edge and trough were grooved so that the apples should be broken rather than pressed. The mill was usually accommodated within a rectangular *poundhouse* or cider-house together with the presses and fermenting-room, where the juice from the pressing was poured into barrels to ferment. The art of cider-making lies in the blending of different types of apple when they are added to the mill. Until comparatively recently, cider was produced and sold locally by farmers using their own apples, or by itinerant cider-makers:

> . . . in the heart of the apple-country nearly every farmer kept a cider-making apparatus and wring-house for his own use, building up the pomace in great straw 'cheeses' as they were called; but here . . . the apple produce was hardly sufficient to warrant each proprietor in keeping a mill of his own. This was the field of the travelling cider-maker. His press and mill were fixed to wheels instead of being set up in a cider-house; and with a couple of horses, buckets, tubs, strainers, and an assistant or two, he wandered from place to place, deriving very satisfactory returns for his trouble. . . .
>
> The outskirts of the town were just now abounding with apple-gatherings. They stood in the yards in carts, baskets and loose heaps; and the blue stagnant air of autumn which hung over everything was heavy with a sweet cidery smell. Cakes of pomace lay against the walls in the yellow sun, where they were drying to be used as fuel. Yet it was not the great make of the year as yet; before the standard crop came in there accumulated, in abundant times like this, a large superfluity of early apples, and windfalls from the trees of later harvest which would not keep long. Thus in the baskets, and quivering in the hopper of the mill, she saw specimens of mixed dates, including the mellow countenances of streaked jacks, codlins, costards, stubbards, ratheripes, and other well-known friends of her ravenous youth.'
>
> (Thomas Hardy, *The Woodlanders*)

Today more than eighty varieties are still grown, some with attractive names such as Cap of Liberty and Slack-ma-Girdle. But the large-scale production of cider is confined to the commercial cider-apple orchards of Devon, Hereford and Somerset.
See also ORCHARDS

CINQUE PORTS A group of medieval ports in south-east England: originally Dover, Hastings, Hythe, Romney and Sandwich, to which Rye and Winchelsea were later added. The Cinque Ports enjoyed certain trading privileges in return for providing naval defence, and this 'arrangement' is known to have existed long before they received their first charter from Edward I. Most of the ancient privileges were abolished in the

nineteenth century, though the Wardenship of the Cinque Ports remains, as a purely honorary office.

CISTERCIANS The Cistercian Order (the White Monks) was founded in 1098 at Châteaux (in Latin *Cistercium*) in Burgundy by Robert of Molesme who, with others, sought to establish a strict form of Benedictinism (*see* BENEDICTINES). After a precarious start, the order spread rapidly during the first decades of the twelfth century, inspired by the energy and personality of St Bernard of Châteaux (1090–1153), so that by 1200 some 500 houses had been established throughout Europe.

The Cistercian life was one of simple communal worship, private devotion, study and meditation; and asceticism in sequestered surroundings, far from the distractions of the outside world. There were strict rules of silence and diet, worship included none of the liturgical intricacies associated with that of the Cluniacs, and the Cistercian rule prescribed manual labour. Churches were to be devoid of all ornament, and the monks wore habits of undyed wool: hence they became known as the 'white monks'. The order's constitution, the *Carta Caritatis*, provided for self-regulation subject to the ordinances of the annual General Chapter of Châteaux, at which each community was represented. Supervision was by means of a mutual system of *visitations* among the 'mother' and 'daughter' houses. The constitution also laid down strict rules for the formation and location of new houses. They were to be founded in places 'remote from the habitations of men', as colonies, or 'daughters', of existing houses, each with an abbot and at least twelve *choir* monks (those in full monastic orders).

Unlike the Benedictine rule, that of the Cistercians forbade receipt of the customary revenues in cash or kind (such as tithes, rents and fees) drawn from the society they had renounced, but gifts of hitherto uncultivated 'desert' land were acceptable: indeed, an effective agriculture was an economic necessity if a community was to survive. Although the choir monks were obliged by their rule to undertake some manual work, a substantial labour force was required to work a community's often extensive arable and grazing lands and to maintain its buildings. The illiterate lay brothers, or *conversi*, whose religious commitment was manifested through their labours, often outnumbered the choir monks by three to one. They would work either in the vicinity of the abbey or on outlying *granges*, which were (in theory) located within a day's journey of the abbey, though some were more distant. These granges were not individual cells (as in the Benedictine model) but agrarian estates, each with a farmstead and oratory, and were staffed only by lay brothers. The *conversi* lived as part of the full community, though their rule was less severe, and the domestic arrangements provided for the two divisions of a Cistercian community are evident in the architecture of their abbeys. Enthusiasm for the Cistercians caused some benefactors to endow lands which were hardly 'desert places' and the monks were often obliged to depopulate such areas, and to degrade villages into granges, by evicting tenants and demolishing their houses and even parish churches.

Cistercian abbeys, which were always dedicated to the Virgin, are architecturally severe by comparison with those of other orders: presbytery, transepts, etc., are usually square-ended, chapter houses are rectangular rather than polygonal, windows contained plain glass, and ornamentation of all kinds was minimal. Despite this austerity, provision was always made for a 'warming house' in the vicinity of the refectory so that the brethren could dry their clothes and warm themselves. The first Cistercian house in England was founded at Waverley in Surrey in 1128 but it was the foundation in 1132 of Rievaulx in the Rye Valley of Yorkshire which aroused the enthusiasm of the English for the Cistercian combination of compassion and asceticism. By the fourteenth century, the prohibition on learning was relaxed and the architectural influences of the Gothic age become more apparent. It was also becoming difficult to recruit sufficient men who were prepared to enter into a life of such austerity as that endured by the lay brothers. Hired labour was increasingly used and there was a move from arable farming (which was labour-intensive) to sheep breeding on a sometimes vast scale. In the seventeenth century, the General Chapter was replaced by national congregations and there was a return to a more strict observance of the order's rule.
See also MONASTERIES

CIVITAS *see* ROMAN ADMINISTRATION *and* TOWNS

CIVITATES PEREGRINAE *see* ROMAN ADMINISTRATION

CLACHAN The traditional settlement of Celtic areas. These varied considerably in size and were sometimes occupied exclusively by a community of a particular class or occupation within a hierarchical society. Clachans usually comprised clusters of stone and rubble dwellings and outbuildings arranged haphazardly amongst associated yards and paddocks. In the highland areas of Scotland, settlements of this type persisted until the traumatic CLEARANCES of the eighteenth and nineteenth centuries. Many clachans were occupied only during the winter months, a large proportion of the community migrating with their livestock to upland settlements during the summer (*see also* BOOLEY HOUSE, HAFOD *and* SHIELING). In Lowland Scots the Gaelic clachan was known as a *fermtoun* ('farm-town'), *kirktoun* if they possessed a church, or *milltoun* if they had a mill.

CLAIRE VOIE A gap in a wall to provide an unimpeded view of a building, landscape feature or vista. Often located beside carriage drives, as at Sherborne, Dorset, where the carriage drive from Sherborne New Castle was diverted through a dry moat to a stopping place from which the medieval bishop's palace could be seen to best advantage through the railings of a claire voie.
See also CARRIAGE DRIVES

CLAM STAFF *see* MUD AND STUD

CLAPBOARD *see* WEATHERBOARD

CLAPPER BRIDGE Narrow bridges or causeways constructed of large horizontal slabs of stone supported by rough stone piers or boulders. They are found mainly in upland areas of south-west England

Tarr Steps on Exmoor in Somerset.

and the Pennines, where suitable materials were readily available. Though of primitive appearance, and almost certainly of prehistoric provenance, many clapper bridges date from comparatively recent times and have undergone constant rebuilding following flood damage. The best known example is Tarr Steps, a low causeway of seventeen substantial stone flags carried on boulder piers over the river Barle in Somerset. Together with a paved approach, it is 55 metres long (180 feet) and was once part of an ancient pack-horse road across Exmoor. It is likely that the causeway dates from the thirteenth century, though some expert opinion suggests an earlier Iron Age origin. Tarr Steps is essentially a causeway: Postbridge on Dartmoor in Devon is in every respect a substantial bridge. Also dating from the thirteenth century, it is constructed of three spans of immense moorstone slabs supported by two large rectangular-shaped stone piers and abutments some 2 metres (7 feet) above the river. Not all clapper bridges are associated with route-ways, neither are they necessarily ancient. Many small primitive causeways were constructed purely for local purposes: to assist in the delivery of the Royal Mail in the nineteenth century, and more recently as part of the leisure footpath network, for example.

See also CAUSEWAYS *and* PACK-HORSE ROADS

CLARENCE Introduced in 1842, the clarence was a modest family vehicle drawn by a single horse driven from the box. Slightly larger than the BROUGHAM, it could seat four passengers and sometimes had a luggage rack on the roof.

CLASSICAL ARCHITECTURE AND CLASSI-CISM The classical Orders were introduced by the Greeks, and later adopted by the Romans, as a set of architectural standards for the design of temples and public buildings. The Orders regulated the proportions and relationships of the three principal elements of their buildings: the *stylobate* (the base); the *column* (the structural pillar); and the *architrave* (the beam carried by the columns). The first three Orders devised by the Greeks were the *Doric* (the simplest and most widely used), *Ionic* (rather more elegant) and *Corinthian* (the most florid and least used). The Romans adapted these Orders to their own, less restrained, taste and added the *Tuscan* (a clumsy version of the Greek Doric) and the *Composite* (an extravagant and unsatisfactory version of the Greek Ionic and Corinthian).

There have been successive revivals of classical architecture from the Renaissance to the present day. By the early seventeenth century, the term 'classic'

was applied to exemplary literature and drama, especially that of ancient Greece and Rome. But the Greek and Roman architectural Orders were not at that time fully understood and it was believed that Rome was the fount of classical architecture and Italy its natural successor. Indeed, the term 'Renaissance' implied a re-birth of the classical culture of ancient Rome and architectural Classicism was to remain Roman until the so-called Greek Revival of the late eighteenth century.

At the beginning of the seventeenth century little was known of classical harmony and proportions. Much of ELIZABETHAN AND JACOBEAN ARCHITECTURE was influenced by various classical sources but these were essentially third-hand and, consequently, buildings were robust, lively and well crafted but demonstrated little evidence of 'the subtle and detailed attention to proportion and line' (Yarwood) of true classical architecture. In Britain, the religious and social upheavals of the first three-quarters of the seventeenth century mitigated against the construction of very large buildings. Nevertheless, it was during this period that the rôle of the individual architect developed: buildings were designed not by anonymous ecclesiastical or military craftsmen, but by intellectually motivated men such as Inigo Jones (1573–1652) and Christopher Wren (1632–1723). In 1570 Andrea Palladio (1508–80) published his *I Quattro Libri dell'Architettura*, a philosophical and visual analysis of his architectural work in Italy, and this was to become the main source of inspiration for the English *PALLADIAN* movement. Inigo Jones had studied in Italy (*c*. 1600) and was responsible for the introduction of the pure Italian Renaissance style into England. He became Surveyor-General of the Works in 1614 and thereby chief architect to the Crown. His buildings were very un-English: pure Italian with as few modifications as possible. His two most revolutionary designs were for the Queen's House at Greenwich (1616–35) and the banqueting hall in Whitehall (1619–21). The former was essentially a design for an Italian villa, though in England it was daringly innovative both for its plan and conception, which were to have a profound influence on subsequent domestic architecture. It was rectangular and symmetrical, without gables or projections, and all the principal rooms were located on the first floor. An apparently solid ground floor supported the main floor above with its lofty ceilings, large windows and splendid central staircase, thereby adding both height and grandeur to the building. This device of raising an entire house onto a 'plinth' to emphasise its magnificence became so popular that it was to last to the end of the nineteenth century, though by that time the original conception had degenerated into the 'half basement' with its token flight of steps to the front door. Inigo Jones was, of course, working to a strict set of architectural conventions and his drawings had to be interpreted accurately by masons who had previously enjoyed considerable latitude in the application of their craft. Houses continued to be built in the Jacobean style, and it was not until after his death that Inigo Jones's conception of classical design was to influence profoundly the development of architecture.

It is from this transitional period that many 'unsatisfactory' classical buildings date. The English climate was not conducive to the development of classical architecture: steep roofs for the clearance of snow and rainwater, massive chimneys venting numerous fireplaces and large windows, needed to maximize the fitful sunlight of an English winter, were all basic requirements that sat unhappily with the concept of classical dignity. It was Christopher Wren who, to a great extent, resolved the conflict between the Italian and native idioms. By a combination of extraordinary inventiveness, mathematical expertise and the use of traditional English building materials (mixing brick, Portland stone and ordinary roofing tiles, for example), Wren created buildings of considerable elegance, dignity and originality. He too was appointed Surveyor-General to the Crown and was charged with the rebuilding of London's churches following the Great Fire of 1666. Despite the constraints of confined sites, Wren's galleried interiors are light and beautifully proportioned with a wonderful feeling of spaciousness and tranquillity, enhanced by large, pale windows and gold and white plasterwork. Exteriors too are of simple design and usually crowned with those ingeniously constructed spires or towers with which Wren's churches are most readily associated (*see* CHURCHES). It should be noted, however, that beyond the City, most new church building was confined to the expanding suburbs, and the predominant building type remained the private house and numerous public and commercial buildings such as hospitals, pump-rooms, customs houses, etc. It was under Wren's influence that the characteristic *Queen Anne* house evolved at the beginning of the eighteenth century. This was essentially a gentleman's residence: a home, dignified and classical, and unpretentious. Outwardly symmetrical and rectangular, they followed the Queen's House at Greenwich, but only in the more pretentious houses were the principal

rooms located on the first floor (*see above*). Hipped roofs were used instead of gables, thus preserving the horizontal line of the eaves which was treated like a cornice. If an additional floor was required, this was provided in the roof space, with windows projecting through as dormers, thereby conserving the heavy horizontal line of the cornice beneath. These dormers often had their own miniature roofs and triangular or curved pediments. Built in local materials, either stone or brick, these charming houses were ideally suited to the English countryside. Exterior angles were often treated with QUOINS and windows (often SASH WINDOWS) had heavy wood or stone frames, substantial glazing bars, surrounding decorative brickwork with stone or brick keystones above, and occasional 'Cupid's bow' scroll-work in a flat arch. Queen Anne doorways are usually canopied, with stone or wooden pediments carried on brackets or (if of brick) on half columns. Such canopies lent themselves to a wonderful variety of decorative treatment: one popular device was to make them so deep and round that it was possible to create a shell motif within. Interiors were dignified and solid with panelled walls; heavily plastered ceilings with ponderous 'still life' motifs and geometrical patterns; heavily framed doors and marble fireplaces with deeply carved mouldings and (often) pediments.

With the deaths of Sir Christopher Wren, his assistant Nicholas Hawksmoor (1661–1736) and the flamboyant Sir John Vanbrugh (1664–1726), the spirit of inventiveness also departed (*see* BAROQUE) and there was a return to the architectural understatement favoured by English society and exemplified in the Palladian principles introduced by Inigo Jones in the previous century.

Eighteenth-century architecture reflected a highly civilized age, characterized by refinement and an accepted standard of architectural good taste. Both the emparked baroque mansion and the *Georgian* terraced town house flourished in a society that believed in the philosophy of materialism and reason. It was a time when the prodigious wealth of the aristocracy and gentry contributed to unprecedented architectural activity, not only in the creation of country houses and mansions with their ornamental parks, classical monuments, temples, OBELISKS, MAUSOLEUMS and GROTTOES, but in the provision of numerous public buildings and urban housing schemes at fashionable spa-towns such as Bath (Somerset) and prosperous trading centres like Norwich (Norfolk) and Bristol. By providing an integrated architectural unit of identical houses, each comparatively modest dwelling could be endowed with the dignity of a large classical building while economizing on valuable urban space. Eighteenth-century terraces were generally of brick or stone with stone topped parapets which concealed sloping slate roofs. Separating the houses were substantial walls designed to carry unobtrusive chimney-stacks and to prevent the spread of fire from one house to the next. These houses were usually of four storeys with a basement beneath street level and the principal rooms on the first floor approached by means of a short flight of steps to the front door. Georgian sash windows have delicate glazing bars and are so precisely proportioned that they provide a wonderful sense of harmony to the façade of a terrace. Ground-floor windows are short and solid, those of the first floor tall and elegant; on the second they are slightly shorter and those at the top of the house are square to arrest the eye. Front doors are generous, panelled and with semi-circular fan-lights. Both door and window openings have plastered and painted surrounds, and inside the front door is a finely crafted rectangular or oval staircase. Many terraces were laid out in broad straight streets, spacious squares, crescents and circuses, one opening out from the next, converging geometrical lines providing vistas punctuated with trees: the converse of contemporary rural landscaping in which avenues of trees focus on distant buildings. Georgian Bath was the (incomplete) creation of John Wood (1704–54) and of his son, also John (1728–81), whose Royal Crescent (1767–75) was the apotheosis of the classical terrace. The provision on such a scale of symmetrical avenues and vistas, which originated in the *piazzas*, circuses and forums of ancient Rome, was innovative in England and yet nowhere else in the world can such a large proportion of the community have enjoyed such dignity. Such enlightened planning was not entirely altruistic: landowners and speculative architects and 'developers' were attracted to the notion of providing elegant surroundings for wealthy tenants, often as second homes for the landed gentry or as residences for the new urban merchant classes. Towards the end of the century, the design of terraced housing became standardized to such a degree that it is only in detail and ornamentation that changing styles may be identified.

From the mid-eighteenth century, there was a drastic re-appraisal of the origins of classical architecture, inspired by wider travel and a growing appreciation of the Greek Doric Order based on first-hand experience of the temples of Paestum and Sicily and of the *Parthenon* itself. This horrified the Palladian movement, who thought the style barbaric and primitive. Renewed interest in the antique, together with a reaction to the excesses of the late baroque and rococo styles, resulted in Neo-Classicism or the Classic Revival of the second half of the eighteenth century. At the same time, a Greek Revival school developed and many of the simple, functional often severe classical buildings of the late eighteenth century are attributable to its increasing influence.
See also REGENCY ARCHITECTURE
For The Georgian Group *see* APPENDIX I

CLASSIS BRITANNICA *see* ROMAN FORTS AND CAMPS

CLAVA CAIRN *see* CHAMBERED TOMBS

CLAYHANGER *see* CLINGER *and* HANGER

CLAY LUMP A traditional East Anglian building material consisting of large rectangular blocks of compressed straw and clay, hardened naturally in sunlight.
See also COB

CLAY PIPES Clay pipes are rarely found intact; however, the bowls alone may be used for dating purposes. The earliest 'fairy' pipes of *c.* 1580–1640 had very small bowls, hardly thicker than the stem, probably because the tobacco smoked by Drake and Raleigh was both exceedingly strong and very expensive. The leathery *Nicotiana rustica* had ten times the strength of today's *Nicotiana tabacum*, though street traders usually adulterated it with blacking, soot, hops, oak leaves and even rhubarb and gunpowder! Adulteration continued until the 1840s when chemical analysis enabled scientists to define 'pure tobacco' and legislation was introduced. Originally, a pipe of tobacco was shared (in the Red Indian manner) but *c.* 1640 bowls became larger and individuals smoked their own pipes. These often had an incised rim and nearly always a spur or step beneath the bowl on which the pipe was rested. Up to the end of the seventeenth century, the top of the bowl sloped away from the stem but, during the eighteenth and nineteenth centuries, was parallel to it. Victorian clay pipes sometimes have the shape of a briar pipe, with or without a spur beneath the bowl. Long-stemmed pipes were known as 'yards of clay' and a smoker would often break off a section of the stem so that the weight and balance of the pipe suited his particular requirements. Clay pipes may be marked with the maker's name, initials, personal device or (occasionally) the date of manufacture and are often

highly decorative, though popular heraldic devices such as Tudor roses, fleurs-de-lis, crowned roses, trefoils and buglehorns may be mistaken for makers' marks. Some bowls may still contain a 'dottle' or lump of partially burned tobacco, especially if they have been plugged by solidified mud.
Further information: The Society for Clay Pipes Research (*see* APPENDIX I)

CLEARANCES From the Middle Ages to the mid-eighteenth century, the ancient clan system of the Scottish Highlands had encouraged over-population, deforestation and environmental abuse on an extraordinary scale: poverty, injustice and disease were endemic. In a climate of perpetual feuding among rival clans, magnatial power was equated with the size of a chieftain's army. The clan system was based upon theoretical kinship and allegiance which bound a chief to his tenant clansmen, and they to him, through a hierarchical system of sub-tenancies and reciprocal military service. With the collapse of the Jacobite rebellion and the rout of the clan armies at Culloden in 1746, the clansmen were disarmed and their Highland territories systematically exploited by those who sought to emulate the English landed gentry. The traditional Highland economy was entirely unprepared for the onset of the Industrial Revolution; however, in response to an apparently insatiable demand for wool to feed the mills and mutton to feed the *nouveaux riches* of the south, Linton sheep were successfully introduced into the Highlands in the 1770s. Immediately, an already impoverished peasantry, with their primitive CLACHANS and cattle and potato economy, became an impediment to progress. The resulting evictions were often ruthless, though some landowners (both native lairds and English newcomers) attempted to provide alternative housing and employment (usually sea-fishing) and others actively encouraged emigration. Most of the clearances were effected during the late eighteenth and early nineteenth centuries, though between 1840 and 1880 some 40,000 people were evicted from estates on the Isle of Skye and this pattern was reflected elsewhere in the Highlands. Despite the Crofters' Holdings [Scotland] Act of 1886, which provided some security for the remaining crofters, clearances continued into the twentieth century, substantial areas being depopulated to provide 'sporting facilities' for those who enjoy stalking the red deer and shooting grouse. Even today, access is denied those who would enter many of the vast grouse moors of the Highlands.
See also SCOTTISH HIGHLAND FORTS

CLEARANCE CAIRNS Similar in appearance to Bronze Age burial cairns, clearance cairns are mounds of stones accumulated during the preparation of land for farming. Although dating from all periods of agricultural activity, many are prehistoric, particularly the extensive *cairnfields* of Bronze Age origin, such as that of Iron Howe in the North York Moors which contains 2,500 cairns.

CLERESTORY *see* CHURCHES *and* MONASTERIES

CLERGY (CHURCH OF ENGLAND) An *archbishop* is responsible for a province of the Church of England: either Canterbury, which covers the dioceses south of the river Trent, or York, which includes those to the north. The Archbishopric of Wales was established in 1920 but before that time Wales fell within the province of Canterbury. The Archbishops of Canterbury and York (Primate of All England and Primate of England and Metropolitan respectively) are privy councillors and have seats in the House of Lords with precedence over dukes. Before the Reformation, archbishops of Canterbury were frequently appointed cardinals by the Pope.
Bishops, whose appointment is vested in the Crown, have jurisdiction over dioceses. A bishop's throne (*cathedra*) is located in the cathedral of his diocese and before the Reformation bishops were appointed by a council of canons (*see* CATHEDRALS). The Bishop of London is also a privy councillor and, with the bishops of Durham and Winchester, sits in the House of Lords with precedence over all other bishops who, until 1841, also had seats (with the exception of the Bishop of Sodor and Man). Since then, only twenty-one sit in the Lords, vacancies being filled by the most senior diocesan bishop without a seat. All Anglican bishops have precedence above barons but below viscounts. In each diocese, one or more *suffragan bishops* may be appointed by the diocesan bishop and are styled by the name of a town in the diocese. They do not sit in the Lords and are not styled 'Lord Bishop'.
A vicar-general is a deputy of an archbishop or bishop. A *dean* (or in recent foundations, a *provost*) presides over the chapter of a cathedral or collegiate church. An *archdeacon* is a senior clergyman having administrative authority delegated by a bishop. He is responsible for the parishes within his archdeaconry, which may itself be sub-divided into rural deaneries, each the responsibility of a *rural dean*. In monastic Britain, *canons* were clerks in holy orders who lived according to a rule; a monk, on the other hand, was simply someone who vowed to follow a life of

austerity, meditation and prayer. Today, a canon is either residentiary with cathedral duties, or has been appointed as a non-residentiary honorary canon in recognition of service to a diocese. (A minor canon is a clergyman attached to a cathedral or collegiate church to assist in services and is not a canon.) In certain cathedrals (such as Wells in Somerset) prebendal stalls are reserved for *prebendaries*. In the Middle Ages the endowment of most non-monastic cathedrals was divided into prebends, each intended to support a single member of the chapter. Holders of prebends became known as prebendaries and in some English cathedrals the territorial titles have been retained, but not their incomes.

A *rector* was originally an incumbent who received the 'Great Tithes': all the customary offerings and dues of his PARISH. He was responsible for the chancel and the rectory and for providing service books and vestments. In many instances, benefices were annexed by corporate bodies such as monastic or collegiate foundations who then received the Great (or Rectorial) Tithes, the Lesser (or Vicarial) Tithes going to a *vicar* who was appointed by them to administer the parish. Following the Dissolution of the Monasteries, many monastic estates became the property of laymen, who also acquired the right to nominate vicars (subject to a bishop's approval), together with responsibility for maintaining the chancel and vicarage. Tithes were virtually abolished in 1936 and a vicar is now appointed to all new livings, the designation 'rector' being applied to an incumbent who was formerly in receipt of great and lesser tithes. A *parson* was originally a rector, though the term is now applied also to a vicar. *Chaplains* were priests without benefices who ministered to private families or to private bodies such as hospitals and nunneries. Today, they perform a similar function in relation to the armed forces and prisons or are the private secretaries of bishops. Before the seventeenth century, a *curate* was an incumbent of a parish but since then the term has come to mean an assistant to the incumbent. A perpetual curate was the incumbent of a parish in which the great tithes had been annexed by an ecclesiastical body or lay person.

CLERK OF THE MARKET *see* MARKETS *and* VERGE

CLERK OF THE PEACE An office established by 1380 to maintain the records of QUARTER SESSIONS, to frame indictments and presentments and (more recently) to advise Justices of the Peace in the performance of their duties.

CLIENT KINGDOM *see* KINGDOMS, ANCIENT *and* ROMAN ADMINISTRATION

CLIFF CASTLE *see* HILL FORTS

CLIMATE Rainfall, temperature and air pressure have been recorded at the Royal Observatory, Greenwich, since 1840. To chart climatic changes before that time, climatologists have developed a variety of techniques including the study of pollen in peat bogs, growth rings in trees and the distribution of plants and animals. They have also analysed personal diaries, military reports, crop records and letters to Crown officials explaining such matters as the non-payment of taxes because of crop failures.

There has been a series of distinct climatic phases since the end of the last Ice Age some 10,000 years ago. A warm epoch, following the Ice Age, peaked between 5,000 and 7,000 years ago, when sea levels rose as the ice sheets melted. Average European temperatures were then 2°C to 3°C warmer than they are today. This was followed by a cold phase during the Iron Age, after which a period of gradual warming continued well into the medieval period. During the Dark Ages summer temperatures were about 1°C warmer than they are now, and in the twelfth century VINEYARDS flourished three to five degrees of latitude further north and between 100 and 200 metres higher above sea level than is possible today. A colder phase lasting from *c.* 1210 to *c.* 1320 was accompanied by violent storms in the North Sea and a reduction in average temperatures of almost 1.5°C. Norse colonies in Greenland struggled for survival and there was famine in Scotland.

The Thames is believed to have frozen only once in each century during the first millenium AD, but from the beginning of the thirteenth century the pattern changed. In 1209 the building of the (old) London bridge altered the flow of water and encouraged the formation of ice which was sometimes several feet thick so that by the winter of 1270 goods which were normally transported by river had to be hauled across land. There was a period of warming from *c.* 1320, but this was followed by a severe phase known as the 'Little Ice Age' which lasted from the end of the fifteenth century until the beginning of the eighteenth. The worst conditions were in the seventeenth century when snow cover in the southern counties of England often lasted for more than one hundred days. The first 'frost fair' was held on the Thames in 1607, while repeated crop failures and starvation were the principal causes of the Scottish

PLANTATIONS in Ulster and the depopulation of East Anglia. But despite its name, the Little Ice Age was not a period of continuous cold: summers towards the end of the seventeenth century were often sultry and the plague and the Great Fire of London in 1666 were in part attributable to drought. The Thames froze for the last time in 1814, and from 1850 to 1950 temperatures in central England rose consistently, particularly in the 1930s and 1940s when a drier climate encouraged a fashion for buildings with flat roofs.

CLINGER A corruption of *Clayhanger*, meaning 'clayey slope' and consequently often associated with a spring-line site (*see* SPRINGS).
See also HANGER

CLIPPING (i) A festive ceremony, probably of pagan origin, in which parishioners form an unbroken human chain round their church to protect it against the power of the Devil (from the Old English *ycleping*, meaning 'embracing'). Clipping often took place on Shrove Tuesday, though the ceremony at Painswick, Gloucestershire, is still held annually on the Sunday following 19 September.
(ii) *See also* COINAGE

CLOAM OVEN *see* OVENS

CLOCHERIUM A detached belfry.

CLOIGTHEACH *see* ROUND TOWERS

CLOISTER From the Latin *claustrum*, meaning 'enclosed place' (hence claustrophobia). In monastic buildings, an enclosed rectangular court surrounded by a covered and colonnaded passageway, the outer elevation of which is formed by the walls of surrounding buildings. The length of passageway on each side of the quadrangle is known as an *alley*, and the open area contained within is the *cloister garth*. This usually incorporates a well and would have been laid out with vegetable beds and herb gardens (the Carthusians used the cloister garth as a burial ground). The cloister was usually on the salubrious south side of the monastic church (though not invariably – see Gloucester below). It was covered with a lean-to roof set against the south aisle of the church and surrounding cloistral buildings. In some instances, the upper storeys of these buildings project over the cloister to form the roof. Early Cistercian cloisters were built of wood, later to be replaced with stone. The arched openings in the colonnade were filled with a combination of glass

Carrels in the fan-vaulted cloister of Gloucester Cathedral.

and wooden shutters, and the northern side, with its abundance of natural light, was often provided with *carrels* for individual study and the writing and illumination of manuscripts. Carrels were usually wooden cubicles, often made draft-free by the provision of doors and canopies, each containing a desk and bench and a clear or unglazed south-facing window by which to work. At monasteries with strong academic traditions, additional carrels were sometimes provided in the eastern or western alleys of the cloister, and a recessed *armarium* for the storage of books.

One of the finest cloisters in England is that at the former Benedictine monastery of St Peter (now the Cathedral) at Gloucester. Built to the north of the abbey church in 1375–1410 (because the town cemetery lay to the south), the cloister has what is possibly the first fan-vault in England. In the south alley are twenty recessed stone carrels of the *scriptorium* and along the western half of the north alley is a superb *lavatorium*, with its own miniature fan-vault, a stone trough for the washing of hands before meals (taken in the adjacent FRATER) and a nearby *aumbry* (recessed cupboard) which contained a supply of dry towels.
See also MONASTERIES

CLON- From the Irish *cluain*, a place-name element meaning 'meadow' or 'pasture'.

CLOSE (i) An enclosure within a settlement, often containing or associated with a dwelling or other building (*see* CURTILAGE). The former closes of a DESERTED VILLAGES may be apparent in boundary banks and ditches, which sometimes also contain evidence of former dwellings. An ancient settlement site may also be suggested by a cluster of small closes within an otherwise open landscape of large fields or in a concentration of field names where 'close' is a common element. *See also* TOFT
(ii) A rectangular hedged paddock or small field at the periphery of a settlement. These were often created, during the partition of an ancient open field in the sixteenth or seventeenth centuries, in order that livestock could be reared close to a village farmstead. They are especially common in central and southern England.
(iii) An enclosed area containing monastic buildings and subsequently the precinct of a cathedral.
(iv) A narrow street-passage.

CLOSED STRING *see* STAIRCASES

CLOSE PANELLING *see* TIMBER-FRAMED BUILDINGS

CLOSE ROLLS These contain registered copies of private letters and documents of the royal Court of Chancery, such as conveyances, writs of summons to Parliament and orders to royal officers. Letters Close were 'closed' (folded and secured with a seal) unlike Letters Patent, which were 'open' and addressed 'To all and singular . . .'. Copies of these documents were made on parchment sheets which were stitched together and stored in rolls, one or more for each regnal year. They are housed at the Public Record Office (*see* APPENDIX I).

CLOSE STUDDING *see* TIMBER-FRAMED BUILDINGS

CLOUGH (*also* **CLEUGH**) A steep-sided valley.

CLUB MEN (*also* **CLUB RISERS**) Associations of countrymen formed during the Civil War (1642–9) to protect their stock and crops against looting by the military, especially during the years of parliamentary supremacy 1644–5. The Club Men were particularly strong in the county of Dorset where, in 1645, they made their last stand on the ancient ramparts of Hambledon Hill. Armed only with clubs (hence their name) and with banners inscribed 'If you offer to plunder or take our cattle, be assured we will bid you battle', between 2, 000 and 4,000 Club Men were routed by the parliamentary army, the 400 who refused to surrender being released and dubbed 'poor silly creatures' by Cromwell. It has been suggested that the celebrated (and virile) Cerne Giant was fashioned by the Club Men as a warning to the marauding soldiery (*see* HILL FIGURES).

CLUNCH Chalk for building, quarried from the hard, grey-coloured beds of the Lower Chalk, sawn into blocks and dried. It is often found used in conjunction with brick dressings or on a footing of SARSEN STONES in buildings dating from the Middle Ages to the nineteenth century.

CLUNIACS Founded by William of Aquitaine in 910, the monastery of Cluny in Burgundy was that most venerated by the Norman kings. Cluniac monasticism of the late eleventh century was marked by a preoccupation with the liturgical: effectively to the exclusion of all intellectual, artistic or educational aspirations. The abbey was described as 'a world in itself, given wholly to the worship of God in a setting of incomparable splendour and untouched by secular intrigue'. The first Cluniac priory in England was founded in 1077 by William de Warenne at Lewes in East Sussex. Thereafter, a further thirty-five houses were founded, many as cells of Norman priories; but none, other than that at Burmondsey (1087), was to rival Lewes, and when King Stephen was buried in his Cluniac abbey at Faversham, Kent, in 1154, the order's influence in England went into decline. No doubt Stephen had in mind the Cluniacs' reputation as 'ferrymen of departing souls': it was they who instituted All Souls' Day (2 November) as an appropriate sequel to All Saints' Day (1 November). The importance of the Cluniacs in England lay not in the size or number of their houses, but in the prominence and influence attained by so many of their brethren.

COAL *see* MINERALS

COASTAL DEFENCES *see* MARTELLO TOWERS AND COMMISSION FORTS, PILL-BOXES, ROMAN FORTS AND CAMPS *and* TUDOR COASTAL FORTS

COAT OF ARMS Correctly, this term should be applied only to the shield of arms, the design of which was often repeated on the surcoat or jupon of the medieval armiger: hence 'coat' of arms (*see* ARMORY).

COB An ancient building material, formed of mud, marl, chalk or gravel with dung and some form of binding material such as hair or chopped straw, used in the construction of domestic and agricultural buildings and walls from the Dark Ages to the present century. Cob walls were built in 'wet' layers of about 0.6 metre (2 feet) on a foundation of moorstone or boulders, each layer being allowed to set for at least seven days before the next was applied. Cob was often strengthened by the addition of horsehair or cowhair, and the walls limewashed for protection and provided with a water-repellent 'skirt' of tar at the base. A sound roof of thatch or tile is necessary to prevent a cob wall washing away into the earth from whence it came, and eaves protrude to ensure that rainwater from the roof is projected away from the surface of the wall and does not accumulate at the base. Thick cob walls keep a house warm in winter and cool in summer. Cob buildings are particularly common in Cornwall, Devon and Dorset where local chalk, pebbles or flint are often included to add substance to the cob. Most surviving cob buildings date from the seventeenth to the early nineteenth centuries and are fairly modest farmhouses, cottages and an occasional parsonage. In the Middle Ages cob was widely used: not only for the 'mud-wall'd tenements' of the poor but also for relatively important buildings such as the fifteenth-century manor-house at Trelawse in Cornwall. In Buckinghamshire, the *wichert* variety of cob consists of local, unbaked, chalky clay.

COCKATRICE *see* BEASTS (HERALDIC)

COCKET A customs seal.

COCKPIT Cock-fighting pits are circular hollows in the ground, usually within a low bank and ditch. Medieval cockpits were often of considerable size: up to 30 metres (100 feet) in diameter. From the seventeenth century, the 'sport' attracted a more genteel clientele and so it moved indoors, necessitating the use of smaller pits. These were often contained in specially constructed or converted buildings. Although cock-fighting is now illegal, regrettably it is far from dead.

COCKSHOOT The trapping of woodcock or other game by the provision of an elongated woodland clearing through which the birds would pass on their evening passage to the wetlands. Nets were strung across one end of the clearing in order to trap the birds in their low flight. The term is found as a place-name element in a variety of forms, e.g. Cockglade, Cockshot, Cockroad, etc., and the method was employed from as early as the twelfth century to the eighteenth.

CODICOLOGY The study of the materials, techniques and personnel in manuscript and book production.

COENOBITE A religious recluse or member of a small community observing the severe rule of St Pachomius (*c.* 290–346). Coenobites dwelt on remote islands and in the sequestered corners of Dark Age and medieval Britain, living solitary lives of silence, prayer and mortification. They are often incorrectly referred to as ANCHORITES or HERMITS.

COERL (CHURL) An Old English term for a free peasant, superior to a serf, who was obliged to do military service. Following the Norman Conquest, his status declined to that of VILLEIN.

COFFIN PATHS *see* CORPSE ROADS

COFFIN STONE, COFFIN STOOL *and* **COFFIN TABLE** *see* LICH-GATE

COINAGE (*Decimal values are indicated in brackets*) In 1897 an immense hoard of 16,000 Roman coins was discovered at Carrawburgh in Northumberland near Hadrian's Wall. They belonged to the years AD 100 to 300 and had been thrown as offerings into a well dedicated to the water nymph Corentina. Most were *denarii*, silver coins which were first minted in 269 BC and continued in use throughout the Roman Empire until the end of the Republic in AD 476. On the reverse of the *denarius* was an image of the twin gods Castor and Pollux riding on horseback to the aid of Rome. The appearance of Julius Caesar's portrait on the obverse contributed to his downfall in 44 BC, for it was perceived by many to confirm his monarchic aspirations. Despite his uncle's untimely end, Caesar Augustus (63 BC to AD 14) and all succeeding emperors continued the practice. They also used the coinage as political propaganda, with their victories, conquests and social reforms depicted on the reverse. The Emperor Vespasian (AD 9–79), for example, issued a coin in AD 70 to commemorate his capture and destruction of the Temple in Jerusalem.

English Gold Coins
 1 Henry III half-penny
 2 Edward III noble
 3 Henry VI half angel
 4 Henry VII sovereign
 5 Charles II guinea

It is likely that the first non-Roman coinage to circulate in Britain was that made by a Belgic tribe during the Roman occupation (*see* BELGAE). Thereafter, it was not until *c*. AD 600 that a mint was established at Canterbury in Kent and gold coins called *thrysma* produced. These remained in circulation until *c*. 775, when they were superseded by silver *sceats*, which were more easily minted. It is difficult to assess the value of a sceat, except that it is known that in Wessex the fine for killing a Saxon was 1,200 sceats, and half that amount for killing a native Briton. We still describe one who has escaped punishment as 'going "scot" (sceat) free'. The silver *penny* was first minted at Canterbury, probably in 760 for King Offa of Mercia, who by that time included Kent in his territories (*see* KINGDOMS (ANCIENT)). It was then known as the *denier* after the Roman *denarius*, and for nearly five hundred years was the only coin struck in England. The penny weighed 22½ grains and there were 240 to the Saxon pound weight of silver. In the tenth century, a cross was stamped on the reverse so that the coin

could be broken accurately into 'broke money', *half-pennies* and quarter pennies (*farthings*), a practice which continued until 1279. (Hence the use of the word 'broke' in relation to money problems.) The designs for Anglo-Saxon coins were not engraved on the dies as they were for Greek and Roman coins but were cut with punches which produced short lines, straight or curved, from which the craftsmen attempted to make up both letters and likenesses. These images of crowned kings, sometimes holding sceptres as symbols of royal authority, were by no means portraits.

From the time of Alfred the Great (871–900), London became the principal mint, though there were several other smaller ones, and his coinage had the London monogram on the reverse. Following his death, the Danes occupied London for a time and issued coins similar in design to those of Alfred. A hoard of 5,000 Danish coins was discovered in 1840 at Cuerdale Hall farm on the banks of the Ribble in Lancashire. These had been buried in *c*. 900, together with over a thousand other coins from continental European and the native Saxon kingdoms. Alfred's grandson, Athelstan (895–939), became the first ruler of all England in 926 and attempted to impose a single coinage. Ethelred II (978–1016) minted considerable quantities of silver coinage in order to pay DANEGELD, and large numbers of pennies from this period have been discovered in Scandinavia. The *mark* and *ora* were not coins but were used as units of accountancy, notably in the DANELAW counties. The mark was a weight of metal initially valued at 128 silver pennies (53.3p) and later revalued (66.6p). The ora was valued at 16 pennies (6.6p).

The Saxon coinage had such a good reputation that, following the Conquest, William I (1066–87) ordered his coinage to be issued in the same way and from the same mints, though the number of local mints was reduced. In the early medieval period, there was approximately £1m of currency in circulation. More than 95 per cent of the coinage consisted of silver pennies and the remainder of half-pennies. In 1180 new pennies were minted, known from the reverse design as the *Shortcross* series. In 1247, during the reign of Henry III (1216–72), the number of mints was further reduced to two, at London and Canterbury, both working under the direction of a single official (*moneyer*). In the same year a new type of silver penny was introduced. This was called the *Longcross* and was intended to discourage the illegal practice of cutting pieces from the coinage ('clipping', which was at times a capital offence) by extending the arms of the cross to the edge on the reverse. This type of coin continued to be minted until 1278 when Henry's son Edward I (1272–1307) added silver *groats* (1½p), *half-pennies* and *farthings* to the coinage. In 1344 Edward III (1327–77) introduced three gold coins – the *florin* (30p), *half-florin* (or *leopard*) and *quarter-florin* (or *helm*) – in addition to the silver coinage. The florin, based on a Florentine gold coin which circulated throughout Europe, was not a success and was withdrawn. It was reintroduced as a silver coin in 1849 and was translated into the *2s* piece and, more recently, the 10p coin. Also in 1344 the Royal Mint issued further gold coins: the *noble* (33.3p), *half-noble* and *quarter-noble*. The noble was a fine coin with the king, standing crowned and armed in the midst of a ship, on the obverse and a biblical text inscribed on the edge to discourage clipping. The noble was replaced in 1464 by a gold coin known as the *angel* (33.3p), which had the Archangel Michael depicted on its obverse. The angel was pierced by a hole and was widely used as a 'touch-piece' to induce good health, and there was also a half-angel called an *angelet*. Gold coins called the *ryal* (50p) and *half-ryal* were also introduced by Edward IV (1461–83) in 1464. Gold coins continued to be minted until the First World War (1914–18), and one of the most splendid of these was the *sovereign* of Henry VII (1485–1509). It weighed 240 grains, was valued at 20*s* and was a large thin coin with a MAJESTY on the obverse and a Tudor Rose and royal arms on the reverse. By the reign of Elizabeth I, the sovereign was valued at 30*s*. It was discontinued by James I in favour of the *unite*, which was of similar value, but was reintroduced from 1817 to 1917 when it was again valued at 20*s*.

The Renaissance clearly influenced the design of coins from that time, the portrait of Henry VII on the famous *testoon* (5p) coin of 1504 (later called the *shilling*), designed by a German die-sinker called Alexander Bruchsal, being one of the finest royal portraits ever to appear on British coinage. Some of Henry VIII's coins were minted of an inferior alloy of silver and copper, and the silver on the tip of the nose on the king's portrait wore thin so that he thereby acquired the appellation 'Old Coppernose'. Gold *crowns* (22½p) and *half-crowns* were issued from 1526 and those of Henry's son, Edward VI (1547–53), show him mounted on horseback, a rarity in British coins, though in 1953 Elizabeth II was portrayed as an equestrian figure in the first crowns of her reign. Later crowns and half-crowns, minted after 1551, were of silver and reduced value (25p/12½p) and were discontinued during the Victorian period except for commemorative

English Silver Coins
  1 *William I penny*
  2 *Henry I penny*
  3 *Edward I penny*
  4 *Henry VI groat*
  5 *Henry VII shilling*
  6 *Elizabeth I sixpence*
  7 *Charles I half-crown*

purposes. A silver *sixpence* (2½p) was introduced in 1551, a coin which survived (in debased metal and, from 1947, in cupro-nickel) until decimalization. A silver *threepenny piece* was also introduced in 1551. This was particularly popular during the Victorian period and was replaced, in 1937, by a twelve-sided nickel-brass coin which was discontinued in 1967. The shillings of Edward VI were inscribed with the date of minting, but in Roman numerals (MDXLIX), the dates beneath his equestrian portrait on the crowns and half-crowns of 1551 being in Arabic numerals. From this time, coins frequently bore their minting dates but the practice of dating all coins by year did not begin until the reign of Charles II (1685–8). Edward VI's half-sister, Mary (1553–8), was married to Philip of Spain and both their heads appeared in profile and facing one another on the obverse of shillings: 'Still amorous and fond of billing / Like Philip and Mary on a shilling.' In 1649, after the execution of Charles I, Parliament ordered gold and silver coins to be struck with

English inscriptions instead of Latin and no portraits. On the obverse was a shield of the cross of St George and the words *The Commonwealth of England*. On the reverse was the date, the motto *God With Us* and the shields of St George and the harp of Ireland. Lord Protector Cromwell intended to mint a very fine set of coins but few seem to have been circulated. In retrospect, the design was significant for it incorporated both a royal crown and a coat of arms in which the royal helm, crest and supporters had been retained suggesting that Cromwell either shared Julius Caesar's monarchal aspirations or that he believed that he held the monarchy in trust.

A number of new coins were introduced following the Restoration in 1660. Among these was the *guinea*, valued at that time at 20s and named after the Guinea Coast of west Africa from where the Africa Company imported gold for the new coinage. There were also 5 and 4 guinea pieces and a half-guinea. It became fashionable for professional fees to be reckoned in guineas, which later were valued at 21s (105p). Silver 4d (old pence), 3d and 2d coins were also issued for general circulation and these, with the penny, became the traditional coins of the MAUNDY ceremonies. Copper farthings and half-pennies were minted in 1672 and from 1860 they were made of bronze. (Farthings were discontinued in 1956 and half-pennies with the introduction of decimalization in 1972.) Queen Mary, daughter of James I, and her husband William of Orange (1689–1702) both appear in a double portrait on coins from 1688 but were replaced by a single portrait of William after the Queen's death in 1694. *Pound notes* (100p) were first issued in 1797 and were recently superseded by decimalized pound coins. *Twopenny pieces* were issued between 1797 and 1799. These were known affectionately as 'cartwheels' because of their size and weight. On the first day of January, 1877 Queen Victoria (1837–1901) was proclaimed Empress of India and the letters IND IMP (*Indiae Imperatrix*) added to her other titles on coinage. These remained (as *Indiae Imperator*) until 1947 when India and Pakistan gained their independence.

Mint marks were often depicted on English coins to show where a legend began and to identify where a particular coin was minted. As medieval coins were not dated, the mint mark also had a periodic significance. Other marks may indicate the workshop in which a coin was made or even a particular craftsman.

COKINI Unmounted couriers: unretained messengers working in the English medieval court.

COLDHARBOUR *and* **CALDECOTE** Originating in the medieval forms of *harbour and cote*, meaning places of shelter and refuge, Coldharbour and Caldecote are common place-names, especially in the Midlands of England. Bestowed as an ironical name on a cold and unpleasant place, they are to be discovered both in maps and itineraries and in the names of former hostelries, wayside inns and farmsteads. Although such names often appear to be of fairly recent origin, there is evidence to suggest an earlier link with unsuccessful attempts at cultivation or ancient route systems and the shelters provided for travellers in inhospitable landscapes (the place-name *Folly* has a similar implication). The term *harbour* (a refuge) may derive from the Old English *here*, meaning an army, and the places where troops were quartered on a HEREPAETH.

COLLAR BEAM A horizontal beam spanning a roof and tying the principal RAFTERS together (*see* ROOFS).

COLLAR PURLIN A horizontal timber running the length of the centre of a roof beneath the COLLAR BEAMS.
See also PURLIN *and* ROOFS

COLLARS During the fourteenth and fifteenth centuries, collars composed of armorial devices were worn as an indication of adherence to a royal house. Some were later adopted by the Sovereign as insignia of office, indeed the collar of SS is still worn by certain officers of the Crown. This famous collar is of obscure origin. It is composed of, or studded with, esses and was probably worn by Lancastrian knights and esquires prior to its adoption as a royal device by Henry IV, sometimes with the swan of De Bohun as a pendant. The Tudors adapted the device, alternating the Lancastrian SS with Beaufort portcullises, and with a Tudor Rose or portcullis as a pendant. The corresponding Yorkist collars were composed of alternate suns and roses, with a white lion pendant (for Mortimer); and, under Richard III, a white boar pendant. These, and the insignia of the various orders of chivalry, may be found on EFFIGIES and monumental BRASSES throughout Britain.
See also SUMPTUARY LAWS

COLLEGE OF ARMS The Corporation of the Officers of Arms in Ordinary, comprising the thirteen kings, heralds and pursuivants of arms, is part of the Royal Household and exercises authority in England, Wales and Northern Ireland for matters

Yorkist collar on effigy of Lord Saye and Sele (d.1471) at Broughton, Oxfordshire.

Lancastrian collar on effigy of Elizabeth Wykham, Broughton, Oxfordshire.

armorial. Royal officers of arms have acted as a corporate body since the early fifteenth century, but did not receive a charter until 1483/4. The College was reincorporated in 1555 at Derby House, near St Paul's Cathedral, and maintains a magnificent collection of heraldic and genealogical records and documents. There is no public access to these, however, and enquiries should be addressed to the Officer-in-Waiting. *See also* CHIVALRY, HIGH COURT OF

COLLET A ring or collar, especially in architectural decoration, metalwork, etc.

COLONIÆ In contrast to native TOWNS, the Roman *coloniæ* were populated with those who enjoyed full rights of Roman citizenship. In the province of Britain, only four *coloniæ* were established: *Colonia Eburacensium* (at *Eburacum* = York); *Colonia Victricensis* (at *Camulodunum* = Colchester); *Lindum Colonia* (at *Lindum* = Lincoln); and *Colonia Nervia Glevensis* (at *Glevum* = Gloucester). Of these, the last three were settlements

for time-expired military men and their families, who lived in a town and benefited from the cultural and institutional benefits of urban life but also held allotments outside it and therefore enjoyed the status and security of independent farmers (*see* ROMAN ADMINISTRATION).

COLONNADE A row of columns supporting arches or ENTABLATURE.

COLOPHON A brief passage at the conclusion of a handwritten document, usually giving the name of the scribe and sometimes including an expression of relief and thanks that the task has been concluded.

COLUMNS *see* OBELISKS

COMB, COMBE, COOMB *and* **COOMBE** *see* CWYM

COMBERS *see* DRYSTONE WALLS

COMMANDERY A manorial estate and hospice belonging to the military order of the Knights Hospitaller of St John of Jerusalem, usually staffed by a small complement of knights with a chaplain and servants. Such manors enjoyed certain privileges: the parish of the commandery at Dinmore, Herefordshire, is entirely free of tithe, the owners of the estate benefiting from immunities granted to the Hospitallers by Pope Paschal II in 1113. Dinmore is known as an ex-parochial or *peculiar* parish for, although it possesses a parish church (one of only four dedicated to St John of Jerusalem), it forms no part of a diocese neither do the bishop nor the ecclesiastical authorities have any jurisdiction there; indeed, until the mid-nineteenth century the parishioners were exempted from paying local rates.

The commandery at Dinmore ranked as third or fourth in importance among the fifty or so similar Hospitaller commanderies established in England and Wales during the twelfth and thirteenth centuries. Each was in the charge of a knight of the Order, the gift of a commandery being the usual reward for outstanding service in the Crusades. In addition to providing income for the Order by the management of the estates, commanderies were regional military training centres and *hospices*, or places of rest for those who returned injured or invalided from the Holy Land. They also afforded shelter and refreshment to travellers and sustenance to the sick and needy. Commanderies accumulated extensive tracts of land, acquired both from the

Templars following their suppression in 1310 and from the endowments of *corrodians*: those who were not members of the Order but enjoyed residential benefits in return for their generosity. At Dinmore, as at other commanderies, local field-names evoke its past in Friars' Grove, Great St John's Meadow, etc.

The parallel order of the Knights Templar possessed similar establishments called *preceptories* though, following the suppression of the Templars in 1312, these were transferred to the Knights Hospitaller, who also adopted the term to describe some of their later commanderies. Typically, the Hospitaller preceptory at Chibburn in Northumberland was built around a central courtyard approached through an arched gateway in a northern two-storey range of domestic buildings, and with a chapel to the south and dwelling-house to the west.
See also ST JOHN OF JERUSALEM, ORDER OF *and* TEMPLAR, KNIGHTS

COMMISSARY COURT A diocesan court concerned with matters of PROBATE which fell entirely within the diocese.

COMMISSION FORTS *see* MARTELLO TOWERS AND COMMISSION FORTS

COMMISSION OF ARRAY *see* MILITIA

COMMONER (i) One who enjoys rights over common land (*see* COMMONS).
(ii) A member of the commonalty: below the rank of peer.
(iii) A student without financial support from a college.

COMMON IN SHACK The right of those tenants who were responsible for the production of the annual crop to release their beasts into a field following harvesting.

COMMON IN THE SOIL *see* COMMONS

COMMON LAW *see* LAW

COMMON OF PASTURE *see* COMMONS

COMMON OF VICINAGE *see* COMMONS

COMMON PLEAS (COURT OF) *see* LAW

COMMONS Collectively, today's commons are the ancient remnants of that vast area of open land, or 'waste', associated with (though pre-dating) the MANORIAL SYSTEM, which was the basis of medieval economic life. A manor was essentially self-sufficient: crops were grown on the best arable land while the poorer soils formed the open waste for grazing and the provision of fuel. In the Middle Ages most villages comprised a cluster of dwellings, with their associated CLOSES, beside or surrounded by OPEN FIELDS, beyond which were sometimes areas of privately tenanted pasture-land, and finally the open expanses and woodland *denns* (clearings) of the common. Common land was not always adjacent to a settlement: as recently as the nineteenth century, some fifty parishes in Cornwall and Devon sent their flocks to summer pastures on Exmoor. Commons varied considerably both in ecology and terrain. Some were vast tracts of moorland and fell; others encompassed the margins of streams (*low commons*) or formed broad, green ribbons of waste between settlements, as in parts of Norfolk. The land itself was vested in the Lord of the Manor, but the various rights enjoyed by the commoners were accorded legal recognition and protected by the courts. Only by the authority of Parliament could the waste or 'common' land be enclosed and the commoners thereby prevented from exercising these rights.

Many commons deteriorated rapidly through over-grazing, resulting in impoverishment of the pasture, and by the thirteenth century the practice of *stinting* or restrictive grazing was increasing. On *stinted commons*, grazing was reserved for farmers, or 'gate-holders', whose rights were limited and the number of beasts released onto the common regulated by the allocation of *gates*: *cattlegates*, *sheepgates* and *beastgates*. The number of animals in a *gate* was determined by seasonal and regional factors. In some upland areas, pastures would be *firthed* (cleared of stock) for a month in the early spring to encourage a strong re-growth of grass before a carefully calculated number of cattle was admitted. At Michaelmas or Martinmas unrestricted numbers of sheep would be brought in from the hills to graze the pastures through to the following spring, while the cattle were fed on hay and straw in the lower enclosures. Stinting continued to be practised through to the nineteenth century, when a *gate* was often calculated by reference to the amount of Land tax paid by each farmer.

Areas of waste began to contract during the Middle Ages as the result of unlawful enclosures and encroachment by those living on the margins of the common land (*see* INTAKES) and by SQUATTERS. In the eighteenth century, advances in agricultural technology made possible (and profitable) the cultivation of land hitherto regarded as waste, and this led to numerous private and local inclosure acts culminating in the Inclosure Act of 1845 (*see* ENCLOSURE). It is estimated that in the early eighteenth century there were between 7 and 10 million acres of common land in England. In Norfolk alone, following eighteenth-century enclosures, there were still nearly 145,000 acres of common, of which only 8,340 acres remain today.

In some parts of the country, common rights still exist (especially those of pasture), but elsewhere the traditional rights of common have fallen into disuse and the main value of common land is recreational. The Law of Property Act of 1925 (Section 193) provided the public with a legal right of access to common land within (former) boroughs and urban districts '. . . for air and exercise'. But the public do not have a legal right of access to all common land, neither do they own it. Under English Law a common, like any other land, must be owned by some 'legal person'. In the Middle Ages this was the Lord of the Manor and may still be so today, though many commons have been sold away from the manor: often to a commercial company, or to a statutory or Crown body. In towns, most commons are owned by the local authority and are used for public recreation. Of course, the owner of a common cannot undertake any activity that is likely to prejudice or interfere with the rights of commoners.

The form of rights enjoyed could also depend on whether a man's dwelling was adjacent to the common or at some distance from it. Full common rights might only be allowed if a man dwelt within a specified area: those from without being *out-commoners*, who enjoyed fewer privileges and suffered greater restrictions. Such out-commoners often travelled to the commons by *outracks* or *straker ways*, which are sometimes evident today in deeply cut HOLLOW WAYS. *Intercommoning*, the sharing of common land (usually a substantial tract of moorland or woodland) by a number of surrounding settlements, is likely to pre-date the manorial system (and, therefore, the Norman Conquest) and may indicate the fragmentation of a former Anglo-Saxon or MULTIPLE ESTATE.

A right of common has been defined as '. . . a right, which one or more persons may have, to take or use some portion of that which another man's soil naturally produces' (Halsbury, *Laws of England*). On most commons, the owner of the soil is entitled to what is left of the produce once the commoners' rights are exercised. The owner is not himself a commoner, for he is legally incapable of enjoying a commoner's rights 'over another man's soil', which is, in fact, his own. His rights are derived from ownership and are, therefore, not common rights.

Of the many rights of common, the following are to be met with most frequently:

(i) *Common of pasture* is the right to graze stock on the common. This may be *agistment*, which is a right to summer grazing, or a *right appendant*, which is applicable only to commoners who occupy land and may graze beasts of the plough, such as horses or oxen, and those that manure the ground, such as cattle or sheep. A *right appurtenant* is similar but requires only that a commoner should possess (not necessarily occupy) land or buildings. It applies only to goats, geese and other livestock which have by tradition grazed a particular common but would not normally be permitted to do so. More rarely, a *right in gross* may be exercised by a commoner who does not occupy land, the right being attached to the man's person. In some areas of FOREST, such as Dartmoor and the Forest of Dean, *venville rights*, which permitted grazing of a common or forest by day, could be purchased from the Crown, an additional charge being levied by which the right was extended to the period between sunset and sunrise. Originally, a right of common of pasture enabled a commoner to graze animals *sans nombre*, but since the Commons Registration Act of 1965 the number of animals must be specified: i.e. by creating *cattlegates* and *beastgates*. These differ from the usual rights of common in that they permit the commoner to benefit from the produce of the common to the exclusion of the owner of the soil. In many upland areas of Britain, rights of common of pasture are essential to the viability of an isolated hill farm.

(ii) *Pannage* is a right 'granted to an owner of pigs to go into a wood of the grantor and to allow the pigs to eat the acorns or beech mast which *fall to the ground*' (Chilton v. London Corporation 1878).

(iii) *Estovers* is the right to remove timber, including *firebote* ('underwood') for fuel and *heybote* for repairing fences or buildings, and the right to collect bracken, etc., as litter for a commoner's animals. *Husbote* is a right to obtain more substantial wood for house-building, and *ploughbote* the right to use wood for making or repairing ploughs.

(iv) *Turbary* is a right to dig peat or turf for use as fuel in a commoner's dwelling.

(v) *Piscary* is a right to fish in lakes, ponds and streams (though not in the sea or in tidal rivers, where there exists a public right of fishing). Fish may only be removed in 'reasonable quantities', sufficient to provide for the domestic needs of the commoner.

(vi) *Common in the soil* is the right to take sand and gravel, stone or minerals for use on the commoner's holding. Rarely, this may also include coal and, although all major coal assets were vested in the Coal Board in 1946, an exception was made with regard to coal dug other than in the course of normal colliery activities.

(vii) *Common of vicinage* permits a man's cattle to stray onto the adjoining common land of a neighbouring manor without molestation.

Information regarding the ownership of lordships of the manor may be obtained from The Royal Commission on Historical Manuscripts, *see* APPENDIX I

COMMUNION RAILS *see* ALTARS

COMPARTMENT In a coat of arms, the base on which the SUPPORTERS are depicted.

COMPLINE *see* MONASTERIES

COMPOSITE ORDER *see* CLASSICAL ARCHITECTURE

COMPTOR *see* PRISONS

COMPURGATION A system by which an accused person might call upon twelve 'oath helpers' to vouch (on oath) for his innocence or good character. In practice, such oaths were measured by the WERGILDS of the oath helpers.
See also SHIRE COURTS

CONCENTRIC CASTLE *see* CASTLES (MEDIEVAL)

CONDUIT A trough or pipe for conveying water. The well-known 'conduit' in the market-place at Sherborne in Dorset was built as a LAVATORIUM in the cloister of the nearby abbey in the early sixteenth century and was moved following the Dissolution in 1539 to form a small market house in Cheap Street.
See also AQUEDUCTS

CONFESSOR *see* SHRINES

CONGREGATIONALIST A member of a church which originated in an early Puritan sect established by Robert Browne in 1580. Browne denounced the

established Church and suffered imprisonment before accompanying his followers to the Netherlands. He later returned to accept a benefice in the Church of England. The *Brownists* (or *Independents*) opposed state intervention in religious matters and maintained the autonomy of each local church. As early as 1550, groups of Independents began meeting together as SEPARATISTS. They formed the backbone of Oliver Cromwell's model army and were forced into non-conformity at the Restoration. They expanded in the nineteenth century and, in 1831, established the Congregationalist Union of England and Wales. In 1972 they joined with the PRESBYTERIANS to form the United Reform Church. Congregationalist registers are now at the Public Record Office, and the central repository for their records is the Congregational Church of England and Wales in London (*see* APPENDIX I). Both the Congregational Historical Society and the United Reform Church History Society maintain records and publish historical material.

CONJUROR One who was reputedly a 'white witch'. This probably meant that he was skilled in treating sick animals – and sometimes people – using methods which may have been considered unconventional at the time. Inevitably, an aura of superstition surrounded such people: Conjuror Minterne, a seventeenth-century squire of Batcombe in Dorset, is said to have leapt on his horse from the surrounding downs and, in so doing, removed one of the pinnacles of the church tower. When he died, he left instructions for his burial half in and half out of the church, the problem being solved by placing him beneath a wall. The truth is more likely that he was merely a homely quack called in by farmers when their beasts were ill.
See also WITCHCRAFT

CONSECRATION CROSS In this context, the term *consecration* implies the dedication of a newly founded church to the exclusive service of God. Consecration crosses were, in the Middle Ages, a visible declaration of this dedication, symbolizing the victory of Christ through the Passion and providing a defence against demoniacal powers. A full set of consecration crosses numbers twenty-four: three on each of the interior walls and a further twelve outside. These small red-painted crosses, each depicted within a circle, were usually incised in stone or cast in metal and affixed to the walls at a height of about 2.4 metres (8 feet), safe from defilement. When a bishop consecrated the church, he would ascend to each cross in turn and anoint it with CHRISM: *Sanctifecetur hoc templum* – 'blessed be this church'. Each cross was provided with a candle bracket: twelve crosses with lighted candles symbolizing the world's enlightenment through the twelve apostles. Some churches still possess one or two consecration crosses and at Edington in Wiltshire there are twenty-one: eleven inside and ten outside. Crosses on door-jambs are not consecration crosses, though these were also intended to ward off the devil.

CONSISTORY COURT A bishop's court concerned with diocesan ecclesiastical administration.

CONSTABLE The constable was originally an officer appointed by a COURT LEET with responsibility for a wide range of duties which have, from time to time, included the collection of rates and special taxes; supervision of WATCH AND WARD; the maintenance of stocks, pillories, lock-ups, etc.; the inspection of alehouses; the supervision of jury service; the apprenticing of pauper children; poor relief and the supervision of itinerants and beggars; the collection of maintenance from the fathers of illegitimate children; the training of local militia and the suppression of riot and unlawful assembly; the apprehension of escaped prisoners or suspected criminals; the organization of rescue and relief at times of shipwreck; the convening of parish meetings and the supervision of church attendance. The ubiquitous constable was even required to impound stray animals and care for the parish bull! As parochial authority grew and that of the manor diminished, the VESTRY assumed many of the duties previously associated with the constable; indeed, it was not unknown for both bodies to appoint constables within the same parish. It was not until 1842 that such parochial responsibilities were legally conferred on vestries, subject to the approval of the justices. Constables were also referred to as borsholder (*or* bozzler), headborough, thirdborough, tithingman or VERDERER (*see also* LAW AND ORDER).

The Constable of England, known as the Lord Chief Constable from the reign of Stephen, was, until the sixteenth century, one of the great officers of state. Originally the Quartermaster of the sovereign's army and Master of the Horse, the Constable presided over the High Court of Chivalry, together with the Earl Marshal. Following the execution in 1521 of Edward Stafford, Duke of Buckingham, the office has remained vacant except for temporary appointments for special occasions such as coronations (*see* CHIVALRY, HIGH COURT OF).

CONSTABLEWICK The jurisdiction of a CONSTABLE.

CONSUMPTION DYKES *see* DRYSTONE WALLS

CONTOUR FORTS *see* HILL FORTS

CONTUBERNIA *see* ROMAN FORTS AND CAMPS

CONVENT A religious community or the building in which it lives. Historically, the term may be applied to communities of either sex, though current usage generally implies a house of nuns.

CONYGER *see* WARRENS

COOPERAGE Barrel- and cask-making probably started with hollowed-out logs, the wooden barrels of the cooper's craft being a much later alternative to the ancient skin and earthenware containers used for water and wine. Most towns and industrial centres had at least one cooperage, where containers were made in which virtually any commodity could be stored and transported. Pails, buckets, milk-tubs, churns, pickling tubs, drinking tankards, *hoggins* (small barrels) for wagoners, light-weight barrels for shepherds, water carts, storage barrels, butter casks, herring barrels and great 'two-man' bathing tubs (known as *cowstalls*) were bound together with withy or metal hoops in a variety of shapes and sizes. For making tubs or barrels, wood has to be specially seasoned (usually in cold brine) before it can be used. White woods such as beech were preferred for dairy ware and churns, and lime wood was considered especially suitable for butter tubs.

COPING A protective capping intended to disperse rainwater from the top of a wall.

COPPER *see* MINERALS

COPPICE (COPSE) The word 'coppice' is a variant of 'copse', from the French *couper*, meaning 'to cut'. But whereas the latter is now used generically to describe any small area of WOODLAND, coppicing is a technical term applied to a special type of tree cultivation.

It has been known for centuries that many deciduous tree species, when cut to ground level, produce a mass of shoots which grow into straight stems, increasing annually in height and thickness. These may be harvested at regular intervals, according to the size required, and the 'crown' or 'stool' of the alder, ash, birch, hazel and sallow will continue to produce such growth after successive coppicing. Other trees, such as the cherry, regenerate by the production of sucker growths from the root system. Such apparently harsh treatment actually invigorates the tree and most ancient woodlands contain the descendants of trees which were first coppiced before the Conquest. When coppicing has been discontinued, such trees often develop strange, convoluted crowns or a number of mature trunks tightly clustered about a common bowl.

Coppicing is an ancient craft dating from the Neolithic period, when considerable supplies of ash, elm, hazel, lime and oak poles were required in the construction of timber CAUSEWAYS in the Somerset Levels. There is also evidence of coppicing during the Roman occupation, and medieval woodlands reverberated with the sounds of a major industry that represented a significant element in a regional economy and supplied all the essential items of a community's life. These included fuel and building materials; besoms, hurdles, handles and hayrakes; wattles, laths and thatching spars; cogwheels and spindles; coracles and lobster pots and all the necessities of the kitchen, bakehouse and brewhouse, as at Ulverscroft Priory in Leicestershire where, in the sixteenth century, seven men were employed in Charnwood Forest to provide between four and eight cart-loads of coppice-work a day.

Most woods were coppiced by rotation, each section being delineated by banks which, with the addition of a fence, served to protect young growths from browsing animals in the critical decade following coppicing. Felling would, of course, depend both on the species of tree and the purpose for which the coppiced wood was intended. Seven-year wood was suitable for wattle- and hurdle-making, twelve-year wood for 'turned-work' and heavier, twenty-year timber for scaffolds, winches and other 'machines'. (More substantial timber for use in building construction and for planks and boards was obtained from standard trees, usually oaks, which grew to maturity above the coppiced 'understorey'.) The sale and felling of 'stands' of coppice timber were closely regulated as was the maintenance of protective hedges and fences. The efficient management of woodland was essential to the economy of a local community and was therefore subject to protection through the courts. Hazel is still coppiced for thatching spars and hurdles, and willows are pollarded for basket-making. But the widespread adoption of fossil fuels, changing building practices, the availability of factory-manufactured goods and the rapid expansion of softwood forests have effectively destroyed the traditional woodland economy and most coppices are now badly neglected.
See also CHARCOAL, POLLARD *and* WOODBANK

COPSE *see* COPPICE

COPYHOLD Villein (unfree) tenure of land was subject to manorial custom and an obligation to undertake certain services for the lord of the manor. The scarcity of labour following the Black Death in the fourteenth century effected the commutation of these feudal obligations to money payments and the creation of copyhold tenancies. Copyhold tenants held their land by right of a title entered in the manor court rolls, a copy of which was given to them: hence *copyholder*. When transferring copyhold property, the tenant was required to surrender it to the lord from whom a new tenant received it by payment of a fine. Copyhold tenure was abolished in 1922.
See also LIFEHOLD *and* VILLEIN

CORACLE A small boat used for river and coastal transport by the ancient Britons and still used by fishermen on the rivers and lakes of west Wales and Ireland. Sometimes circular, but more often rectangular with rounded corners, coracles were constructed of wickerwork and made watertight by animal hides or, more recently, with pitch.

CORBEL A projection of stone, wood or brick supporting an arch, beam, parapet or moulding. *Corbelling* refers to receding courses of stone, brick, etc., supporting a projection such as a chimney-stack or oriel window.

CORINTHIAN ORDER *see* CLASSICAL ARCHITECTURE

CORN DOLLY (*also* **HAG, KIRN BABY, MARE** *and* **NECK**) The traditional corn dolly of rural Britain is almost certainly a fertility symbol: a debased remnant of the ancient Middle-Eastern belief that cereal plants were possessed of a goddess whose survival through the trauma of harvest and the infertility of winter was dependent on man's protection. Prior to the mechanization of agriculture during the nineteenth century, many rural communities maintained the belief that the Spirit of Harvest dwelt in the fields and that, as the reapers cut the corn, the spirit was forced to retreat into the last remaining stems of harvest. On most farms these were plaited, as they stood in the field, into a figure or 'dolly'. Because no man wished to be the one who destroyed the goddess's refuge, the reapers took turns to throw their sickles at the dolly until it was finally severed. It was then carried round the fields in celebration, set in a place of honour at the harvest supper and kept on the farm until the following spring when it was affixed to the harness of the plough-horse or ox and finally trampled into the earth whence it came. Corn dollies varied both in appearance and name from one region to another: typical are the Suffolk Horn, the Cornucopia, the Norfolk Lantern, the Durham Chandelier, the Vale of Pickering Chalice, the Cambridge Bell, Mother Earth, Horn and Whip and the Essex Teret.

CORN DRYING KILNS see FARMSTEADS

CORN EXCHANGE An exchange devoted to the corn trade. Many nineteenth-century corn exchanges have survived and been adapted for other purposes, though the name has often been retained. They originated in the medieval practice which required all purveyors of corn in a particular district to bring their wares for sale on a prescribed market day. By the late eighteenth century, the stalls on which merchants displayed their samples were often brought together in a single building, which came to be known as a corn exchange.

CORNICE A moulded projection surmounting a wall, arch or building. A plaster moulding round a ceiling (see PLASTERWORK).

CORN KILN In the Highlands and Western Isles of Scotland, a circular, stone-lined pit with a thatched conical roof in which grain was dried by hot air drawn through a flue from a turf fire beneath. In some parts of Ireland, similar clay-lined kilns for drying barley were constructed as recesses beneath large boulders. Being naturally unobtrusive, such kilns were often used in the distilling of unlicensed whiskey (potheen).

CORN LAWS see FARMING

CORN RENTS Variable payments made in lieu of tithes following the Tithe Commutation Act of 1836. Assessed by reference to the average price of corn, the rents were reviewed every seventh year.

CORONER An ancient office, dating from before the twelfth century, with a number of responsibilities including the conducting of inquests and determining TREASURE TROVE and DEODANDS. Originally, coroners were Crown officers but they are now appointed by county councils.
See also SHERIFF

CORPSE ROADS (also **COFFIN PATHS, CORPSEWAYS, LICKWAYS** or **LYCHWAYS**) Trackways, often DROVE ROADS or PACK-HORSE ROADS, in remote upland areas along which corpses were borne for burial at a distant churchyard. Medieval parishes in such districts were usually large and composed of widely scattered settlements. These sometimes had subsidiary CHAPELS OF EASE, but the right of burial was often reserved for the mother church and, as a result, bereaved families from remote farmsteads were obliged to arrange for bearers to carry a corpse many miles for interment: an arduous and sometimes hazardous commission, especially in the depths of winter. Journeys of up to 25 km (15 miles) and lasting for two days were recorded in the Yorkshire Dales as recently as the eighteenth century. A corpse road to Lydford, on the edge of Dartmoor, crosses the river Tavey by means of a series of large STEPPING STONES, each of sufficient size to accommodate two pairs of bearers and their uncomplaining companion. In some areas rough-hewn *coffin stones* were provided along the route, on which the corpse or coffin was laid while the bearers rested (see LICH-GATE). It was not until the eighteenth century that coffins were available to any but the more affluent members of society.
See also WAYSIDE CROSSES

CORPSE TABLE see LICH-GATE

CORRODIANS see COMMANDERY and MONASTERIES

CORRODIES The traditional right of medieval kings to demand allowances of food and clothing from monasteries, particularly those of royal foundation.

COSTER-MONGER see ORCHARDS

COTE (also **COT**) A cottage.

COTE-HARDIE see EFFIGIES

COTSWOLD The band of oolite that runs from the Humber to the Dorset coast is at its widest and reaches its greatest elevation in the Cotswolds, a range of limestone hills, largely in Gloucestershire but extending east into Oxfordshire and south-west into Wiltshire. Noted for sheep pastures and formerly a centre of the woollen industry, the wide Cotswold landscape is complemented by its buildings as in no other area of Britain. Manor-houses, churches, farmsteads, cottages and entire villages are constructed of oolitic limestone or 'Cotswold Stone', the colour of which varies from the richest orange-brown in the east to pale creamy greys in the south and west. This wonderful material, which was first used in the construction of Neolithic chambered tombs, has subsequently created the finest vernacular building in Britain, the 'Cotswold style' being a unique variation of the building fashions of the late sixteenth century, characterized by magnificent, steeply pitched, stone-slated roofs and dormers (*see* SLATES), prominent gables, stone mullioned windows and moulded doorcases and dripstones. High quality freestone (*see* ASHLAR) is to be found in deep strata which

are accessible only in the steep north-western escarpment. The inferior material of DRYSTONE WALLS has for centuries been extracted from the upper layers of the oolite in surface pits which are to be found on nearly every upland farm. 'Cotswold' derives from *Cōd's wald* or forest (*see* WOLD).

COTTAGE ORNÉE Cottages, often lodges or entire estate villages, built in the 'picturesque' manner, influenced by early nineteenth-century romanticism rather than domestic convenience. Others were built as romantic country or seaside retreats for the prosperous middle class, especially in the south-western counties (e.g. at Sidmouth in Devon) and the Isle of Wight. English vernacular traditions were plundered and reproduced in extravagant and often incongruous forms: pointed French windows and Elizabethan chimneys, artificial half-timbering and 'eyebrow' dormers set beneath steeply pitched thatch, long ornamental verandas and elaborate 'Gothic' detail. Such cottages for estate workers were often positioned in picturesque

A cottage ornée at Stanbridge, Dorset.

clusters, as 'eye-catchers' to impress visitors as they approached a mansion through its landscaped park. Perhaps the most exuberant example of the *cottage ornée* style (and one of the earliest) is that of Blaise Hamlet on the outskirts of Bristol. Built in 1811 by John Harford, a banker and Quaker, this extraordinary group of nine outrageously picturesque cottages, set round a miniature village green, was designed by John Nash to house Harford's retired retainers from Blaise Castle House.

COUNCIL HOUSING (SOCIAL HOUSING)
Liverpool was the first local authority to build council housing in 1869 and, following the Housing Act of 1890 which enabled local authority housing to be provided by means of public subsidy, several other councils followed suit, including London County Council in 1892 and Manchester in 1896. The Housing Act of 1980 gave council tenants the right to buy their houses from local authorities, often at advantageous prices. As a consequence, the local authority housing stock has diminished rapidly, and rented or 'affordable' housing in many parts of Britain is now provided by charitable housing trusts.

COUNCIL OF TRENT *see* RELICS

COUNTERSCARP The side of a ditch nearest to the besiegers of a fortification and opposite the scarp.

COUNTESS The wife of an earl, or a lady who holds an earldom in her own right.

COUNTESS OF HUNTINGDON'S CONNEXION A Methodist sect of Calvinistic persuasion founded in the eighteenth century by Selina Hastings, Countess of Huntingdon. The noted Methodist preacher George Whitfield was appointed as her chaplain in 1751, and his popularity led to the establishment of several Connexion chapels which attracted the socially better-off. The Connexion registers, for various counties and for the period 1781–1822, are housed at the Public Record Office (*see* APPENDIX I).

COUNTIES Derived from the French *comté*, the county superseded the Anglo-Saxon SHIRE following the Norman Conquest. Many shires conformed with earlier territorial BOUNDARIES: in the eighth and ninth centuries the kingdom of Wessex was divided into Berkshire, Dorset, Hampshire, Somerset and Wiltshire; and in the tenth century the kingdom of Mercia was divided into

Derbyshire, Gloucestershire, Leicestershire, Northamptonshire, Nottinghamshire, Rutland, Staffordshire, Warwickshire, Worcestershire and parts of Bedfordshire, Buckinghamshire and Oxfordshire. Norfolk and Suffolk were shire divisions of the old East Anglian kingdoms, while the counties of Essex, Kent, Middlesex and Sussex were formed out of Saxon territories. In the north, Yorkshire approximated to the Danish kingdom of York, Cumberland was the land of the Cumbras (from *Cymry*, meaning 'the Welsh') and Northumberland was part of the ancient kingdom of Northumbria. The County Palatine of Durham was first granted to Cuthbert in 685 and held by the bishops of Durham thereafter until 1836 (*see* PALATINATE). Cheshire, which had been a Roman province, also became a county palatine under William I, and Lancashire was originally the Honor of Lancaster, the northern part of which extended into Yorkshire. Westmorland was two baronies under the Normans, and Rutland was originally a SOKE in Northamptonshire.

When the Local Government Act of 1888 created county councils, the Isle of Ely, the Soke of Peterborough, East and West Suffolk, East and West Sussex, the Ridings of Yorkshire and the Isle of Wight all became autonomous administrative divisions while remaining, nominally, part of their original counties. The county of Middlesex disappeared in 1964 when, with parts of Essex, Surrey, Hertfordshire and Kent, it was absorbed into Greater London. The Welsh counties were formed after the Act of Union of 1536, Monmouthshire remaining the subject of dispute until its incorporation into the new Welsh county of Gwent in 1974. In Scotland, the Lowland counties were established by Malcolm II in the eleventh century, those in the Highlands dating from the sixteenth and seventeenth centuries. Major revisions of administrative boundaries were effected throughout Britain in 1974, as a result of which several new counties were created while others were lost. At the same time, the charming but anachronistic vestiges of earlier manorial estates, the isolated 'islands' of one county within another (such as the parish of Holwell in Dorset, which was formerly described on maps as 'Somerset Pars'), were absorbed into the new administrative divisions which surrounded them.

COUNT OF THE SAXON SHORE *see* ROMAN FORTS AND CAMPS

COUNT PALATINE *see* PALATINATE

COUNTRY HOUSE *see* CLASSICAL ARCHI-
TECTURE, DEER PARKS, ELIZABETHAN AND
JACOBEAN ARCHITECTURE, ESTATE, LODGE,
MANOR-HOUSE, PALLADIAN *and* TUDOR
ARCHITECTURE

COUNTRYSIDE Lowland England contains two
distinctive types of countryside: the *ancient* and the
planned. Medieval writers distinguished between
fielden and *arden* (field and woodland), and in the
sixteenth century the terms *several* and *champion*
were coined to describe land held 'in severalty' by a
number of small farmers and areas where OPEN
FIELDS still predominated. The term *woodland* was
also used to describe *several* countryside with its
abundance of hedgerow trees:

'It is so, that our soile being divided into
champaine ground and woodland, the houses
of the first lie uniformelie builded in everie
town together, with streets and lanes; whereas
in woodland countries . . . they stand scattered
abroad, each one dwelling in the midst of his
owne occupieng.'
(William Harrison (1535–93))

Ancient countryside is that which has evolved
gradually, whereas planned countryside has the
appearance of having been superimposed on the
landscape. Typical of the latter are the large,
geometrical fields created by parliamentary
enclosures (*see* ENCLOSURE *and* ENCLOSURE
ROADS).

Each type of countryside has its own
characteristics, which have usually developed as a
result of historical rather than geographical factors:

Ancient Countryside:
  Small, irregular fields
  Multi-species hedgerows
  Small hamlets
  Dispersed, ancient farmsteads
  Hollow, winding lanes
  Complex footpath networks
  Numerous copses

Planned (Champion) Countryside:
  Large, regular fields
  Single-species hedgerows
  Large, nucleated villages
  Dispersed 18th/19th century farmsteads
  Straight, regular roads
  Rationalized footpath networks
  Large (commercial) woodlands

COUNTY COURT *see* SHIRE (COUNTY)
COURT

COUNTY NAMES *see* SHIRE

COUPLED ROOF *see* ROOFS

COURT When used as a place-name element (e.g.
Court Farm, Wake Court, etc.) it is likely that the
site (if not the building) was at one time the venue of
a manorial court (*see* COURT BARON *and* COURT
LEET). Some sites may even commemorate the
ancient meeting-place of a former HUNDRED court.

COURT BARON A manorial court which, unlike
the COURT LEET, was a private jurisdiction and
effectively the property of the Lord of the Manor.
The main function of the court was to determine
ESCHEATS and transfers of land, to enforce
manorial custom, and the management of commons
and wastes. Among several officers appointed by the
court was the REEVE, who represented the parish
and collected manorial dues. In some places Courts
Baron and Leet are still convened: at the following
meeting of the Courts of the Manor of Sherborne the
twelve jurors, all freehold tenants of the estate,
appointed a new *hayward* to manage the town
common:

The Manor of Sherborne in the County of Dorset
Notice is hereby given that a Court Leet or Law
Day and View of Frankpledge and a Court Baron of
Kenelm Simon Digby Wingfield Digby, Esq, Lord of
the said Manor, will be holden for the said Manor on
Monday the 23rd day of May, 1988 at 6.00 pm. at
the Council Office, Manor House, Newland in
Sherborne in the said County of Dorset, when and
where all the Residents and Freehold Tenants of the
said Manor and all Public Officers of the said Leet
and Manor, and others concerned in the business of
such Courts respectively are required to attend.

G D Bevir   Steward
Dated 26th April 1988

COURT LEET A manorial court of record and
public jurisdiction responsible for dealing with
minor offences and matters, such as the repair and
maintenance of highways and ditches and the View
of FRANKPLEDGE. Presided over by the Lord of
the Manor or his representative, attendance was
obligatory for all males over a certain age (in some
areas this was as young as twelve). The Court met at
least twice a year and appointed officers such as an

ale-taster, constable and pinder, who was responsible for the *pinfold* in which stray animals were impounded. Courts Leet are still held in many places, often combined with a COURT BARON.

COURT OF SURVEY *see* MANOR

COURT OF WARDS AND LIVERIES *see* WARDSHIP

COURT ROLLS *see* MANOR

COURTS OF LAW
For Common Pleas (Court of), Curia Regis, General Eyre, Gaol Delivery, Exchequer (Court of), King's [Queen's] Bench (Court of) *and* Oyer and Terminer *see* LAW
For Arches (Court and Dean of), Chancery (Court and Official Principal of), Delegates (Court of), Divorce Court, Probate Court *and* Supreme Court of Judicature *see* CANON LAW
For The Staple (courts of) *see* MERCANTILE LAW *and for* 'Pie Powder' (courts of) *see* MARKETS *and* MERCANTILE LAW
For Crown Court *see* QUARTER SESSIONS
For individual entries *see*:
ASSIZE, ASSIZE OF MORT D'ANCESTOR, ASSIZE OF NOVEL DISSEISIN, BARMOTE COURT, BREWSTER SESSIONS, CHIVALRY (HIGH COURT OF), COURT BARON, COURT LEET, EYRE (IN), FOLK MOOT, GRAND ASSIZE, HUNDRED COURT, MAGISTRATE, PETTY SESSIONS, QUARTER SESSIONS, REQUESTS (COURT OF), SHERIFF'S TOURN, SHIRE (COUNTY) COURT, STANNARIES, STAR CHAMBER, VERDERERS *and* WERGILD
See also JURY, JUSTICE OF THE PEACE, LAW AND ORDER, LEGISLATION *and* WARDSHIP

COURT TOMBS *see* CHAMBERED TOMBS

COURTYARD FARM A traditional quadrangular plan, evident in many deserted medieval FARMSTEADS and subsequently adopted in the design of farm complexes through to the nineteenth century. Originally, the quadrangle, with its 'blind' outer walls and doorways opening into the courtyard, provided both shelter and a means of defence, particularly in remote areas such as the Welsh Marches. In many instances, the farmhouse formed one side of the courtyard, which was sheltered from the north by a substantial barn. Stables on the west side faced east into the courtyard so that early morning preparations were illuminated by the rising sun, and timber vehicles in the open-fronted cartsheds to the south were protected from exposure to rain carried by the prevailing westerly winds. Granaries, reached from the courtyard by exterior flights of stone steps, often formed the second storeys of such buildings. There are also many instances of farmhouses being built away from the courtyard and farm buildings, usually to the south. Such 'detached' dwellings are often of a later date than the original farm complex and may reflect both the increasing prosperity and corresponding social aspirations of a gentleman farmer. Sometimes the original farmhouse was plundered for building materials – thereby removing one side of the quadrangle – or was subsequently adapted for other purposes.

COURTYARD HOUSES Cornish settlements or farmsteads dating from *c.* 50 BC to *c.* AD 350, each consisting of a massive wall of boulders surrounding an open courtyard which was accessible from the exterior by means of a single, confined passage. Contained within the thickness of the outer wall was a series of individual roofed chambers, each of which opened on to the courtyard. At Carn Euny, in the west of Cornwall, there is evidence of an earlier timber construction and a *fogou*, or underground passage, used for storage or ritual purposes.
See also SOUTERRAIN

COW LEAZE (i) Meadow land for cows.
(ii) The right to pasture cattle on common land.

CRANNOGS From the Irish *crann*, meaning 'tree', these lake dwellings, which stood on artificial islands constructed by accumulating brushwood, peat and stones within a ring of timber piles or boulders, were numerous in Scottish and Irish lakes for an extraordinarily long period of time. The earliest crannogs were built in the Bronze Age and a few (in Ireland) were occupied during the Middle Ages. Most date from the Iron Age or the Viking incursions of the eighth and ninth centuries, and clearly indicate that a small but significant element of the population was at those times obsessed with its vulnerability to armed attack. Clusters of crannogs have been discovered in the marshy fringes of lakes or remain as platforms in the shallow water, linked by timber causeways just below the surface. There is a reconstructed crannog settlement at Craggaunowen in County Clare.

CRAPPING STONE *see* SLATES

CREDENCE A small table, niche or shelf, sometimes within a FENESTELLA, on which the elements of the Eucharist are placed before consecration.

CRENEL *see* BATTLEMENTS

CRESSET (i) In ARMORY, a fire-basket, usually depicted at the top of a pole.
(ii) The carved holes in *cresset stones* into which cooking fat or grease and floating wicks were placed to provide multiple lamps. Some cresset stones were portable and contained three or four such holes; larger ones were too heavy to move and had perhaps twelve or more cressets. Cresset stones are often found in monastic precincts or preserved in churches.

CRESSET STONES *see* CRESSET

CREST A three-dimensional device affixed to a helmet and so depicted in a coat of arms. During the Middle Ages, crests were considered to be the perquisites of the knightly class: those who possessed both the rank and the resources which enabled them to participate in tournaments where crests were used. Crests were made of light materials (paste board, cloth or waxed leather over a basketwork frame) and were fastened to the helm by means of laces or rivets, the unsightly join concealed beneath a wreath of twisted silk (*torse*) or a coronet. To this was attached a decorative mantling (*lambrequin*) which covered the back and sides of the helm. Crests of the post-Tudor period were often ridiculously complex and few could have been affixed to a real helm: *A Ship in distress on a Rock proper* (Pellew), for example.
See also ARMORY

CROFT (i) An enclosed area of land adjacent to a dwelling.
(ii) A smallholding farmed by tenants in the Highlands and Islands of Scotland: typically, a modest homestead standing in a cluster of small, enclosed fields. Crofting developed following the CLEARANCES of the late eighteenth and nineteenth centuries which compelled surviving clan families to abandon both their homes and their traditional methods of husbandry and adopt a subsistence lifestyle as crofters, often in the new townships of the barren coastal fringe. Each Highlander was allotted an individual croft, or arable smallholding, and limited grazing rights on a common pasture. His meagre income could be

Crest depicting a freeminer of the Forest of Dean in the brass of Robert Greymdour in Newland church, Gloucestershire.

supplemented by small-scale activities such as fishing, weaving and kelp-burning (a large brown seaweed from which substances such as iodine and chemicals for the glass industry are obtained). Exploitation continued throughout the nineteenth century, and many crofters, who had been encouraged to improve their holdings, suddenly found themselves dispossessed and their crofts incorporated into large estates. The Crofters Act of 1886 succeeded in providing much-needed security of tenure for the crofters and, following the Great War, crofting land was transferred to state ownership and the administration of the Crofters Commission.

CROMLECH *see* CHAMBER TOMBS *and* DOLMEN

CROP MARKS It was William Camden (1551–1623) who observed of Richborough, the Fort of the Saxon Shore in Kent: 'Age has erased the very tracks of it . . . it is at this day a cornfield, wherein,

The Roman town of Venta (Caister) near Norwich in Norfolk.

when the corn is grown up, one may observe the draughts of streets crossing one another (for where they have gone, the corn is thinner). . . .'

Such crop marks are produced by variations in the quality of plant growth caused by differences in the soil and subsoil. The presence of buried walls and foundations just beneath the soil's surface will produce weak plants which are vulnerable to dry conditions, while deeper pits and silt-filled trenches retain moisture and allow for the development of a substantial root structure and more luxuriant growth. From the air, such variations of vegetation (usually in a cereal crop) become more evident and may delineate the former walls and buildings of archaeological sites, such as deserted medieval villages or Iron Age fields, or mark the course of a Roman road or Neolithic CURSUS. Aerial photography of crop marks is particularly effective when a low sun shines across a field, the different levels of vegetation casting shadows which clearly trace the structures beneath.

CROSS DYKE *see* DYKES

CROSSES The use of a cross device for decorative purposes pre-dates Christianity by many centuries, but it was to become the universal symbol of the Christian Church. The preponderance of crosses in ARMORY reflects both the influence of the Crusades on the knightly classes and medieval man's preoccupation with his religion.

See also CELTIC CROSS, CHRISTIAN SYMBOLS, CHURCHYARD CROSS, CONSECRATION CROSS, CROSS SLAB, ELEANOR CROSSES, IRISH HIGH CROSS, MARKET CROSS, PENITENTIAL CROSS, PREACHING CROSS, WAYSIDE CROSS *and* WHEEL-HEAD CROSS

CROSSING *see* CHURCHES *and* MONASTERIES

CROSS RAIL *see* TIMBER-FRAMED BUILD-INGS

CROSS SLAB Irish tomb slabs and Pictish SYMBOL STONES, engraved on one or both faces with Celtic Christian crosses, dating from the seventh to the ninth centuries. Despite their function as grave-covers, many tomb slabs are now found in an upright position and have been removed from their original sites.

CROWN *see* COINAGE

CROWN GLASS *see* GLASS

CROWN POST A vertical post at the centre of a TIE BEAM to support a COLLAR BEAM or COLLAR PURLIN, to which it is usually connected by means of diagonal braces (*see* ROOF *and* KING POST).

CRUCIFORM Shaped in the form of a cross (*see* CHURCHES).

CRUCK FRAME *see* TIMBER-FRAMED BUILD-INGS

CRUSADES The Wars of the Cross, to free the Holy Land from the Saracens, began with much optimism and high ideals. They occupied the best of Western Christendom's military, religious and chivalric fervour for three centuries. Yet they achieved virtually nothing, largely because of lack of organization arising from jealousies among the leaders, and failure to come to terms with the terrain, the climate and the need for hygiene.

First Crusade	1096–9
Second Crusade	1147–9
Third Crusade	1189–92
Fourth Crusade	1202–04
Children's Crusade	1212
Fifth Crusade	1218–21

Sixth Crusade	1228–9
Seventh Crusade	1248–54
Eighth Crusade	1270

See also ST JOHN OF JERUSALEM, ORDER OF *and* TEMPLAR, KNIGHTS

CRYPT A vaulted underground chamber, usually constructed beneath the chancel of a church to accommodate tombs and the relics of saints. Some larger crypts (particularly those of the great abbeys and cathedrals) also contain altars for the benefit of pilgrims who wished to pay homage at an adjacent shrine. An *undercroft* is a similar chamber beneath a church, castle or domestic building, wholly or partially underground and originally used for storage, though often (in the present century) adapted for administrative and commercial purposes.

CUCKING STOOL A primitive commode on which the (usually female) victim was ignominiously displayed and subjected to public abuse and well-aimed missiles. The name suggests that it was reserved as a punishment for adultery.
See also SKIMMITY-RIDE

CULTURAL CHRONOLOGY It is now generally recognized that the traditional chronology of pre-history (*see* STONE AGE, BRONZE AGE *and* IRON AGE) is inappropriate to modern archaeology. Dating by 'periods' has always been imprecise. 'Invasion', for example, was rarely a sudden event but more often a lengthy, complex and sporadic process. Communication and assimilation of cultural ideas and innovative agricultural and manufacturing techniques extended over many centuries and were subject to considerable regional variation. Indeed, many technological advances were the result not of 'invasion', but of development through necessity and in response to changing circumstances, such as climate. Likewise, cultural and conceptual evolution was effected by the blending or suppression of traditions, local and immigrant, neither of which were themselves static. Archaeologists are therefore more concerned with specific communities whose way of life may be glimpsed through a variety of material remains, recurring in comparatively limited areas and dated by means of highly sophisticated techniques. These cultural 'nebulae' are used as points of reference in the vastness of prehistoric mutability. The Arras Culture, for example, has been identified as that of a group of immigrants from eastern France, probably refugees from the Galic wars, who settled in what is now North Yorkshire

from about 400 BC. They are known to have buried their dead in large cemeteries of small circular barrows within square ditches, the graves of chieftains and their women containing their chariots and personal possessions. To apply the generic term 'Middle Iron Age' to such a distinctive people would be fallacious.
See also BEAKER *and* WESSEX CULTURE

CULVERIN *see* TUDOR COASTAL FORTS

CULVERY *see* DOVECOTES

CUM Latinized place-name element meaning 'with' (*see* LATIN).

CUP AND RING MARKS Carved patterns consisting of small depressions encircled with rings, often in concentric series and with lines cutting across the rings linking the 'cups'. With no apparent rationale and of uncertain date, they are found on isolated boulders, standing stones and rock outcrops in the remote uplands of Scotland, Ireland and Northumberland and on some Irish chambered tombs. These enigmatic symbols have generally been ascribed to the Iron Age but are more likely to be of Neolithic origin, a stone slab of this type having been discovered in the mound of a Neolithic long barrow at Dalladies near Aberdeen.

CURATE *see* CLERGY (CHURCH OF ENGLAND)

CURIA PRIMA *see* MANOR

A cup-marked recumbent stone at Rothiemay, Aberdeenshire (photo: James Ritchie, 1905)

CURIA REGIS *see* LAW

CURRICLE A privately driven two-wheeled carriage, popular in England during the nineteenth century. It was hooded and low-slung with a rear seat for a diminutive groom or 'tiger'. Driven by a pair of horses, the curricle was reputed to be smart and fast, yet easy to handle.

CURSIVE Handwriting executed without raising the pen so that characters are rapidly formed with a running hand.

CURSUS Once-imposing late Neolithic earthworks comprising parallel embankments about 60 to 185 metres (200 to 600 feet) apart and often of considerable length. Most are now evident only as CROP MARKS in aerial photographs. It has been estimated that some 200,000 cubic metres of earth (260,000 cubic yards) were moved to create the twin banks and ditches of the Dorset Cursus, which ran for 10 km (6 miles) across the ancient landscape of Cranborne Chase. Such an enormous undertaking is indicative of a highly organized and sophisticated society: but what was its function? That the cursus was some sort of prehistoric race-track (as has been suggested) seems highly unlikely, unless such

The Dorset Cursus on Gussage Cow Down with ploughed-out barrows in the foreground.

activities were of a ritualistic nature. Corporate commitment of this magnitude could be inspired only by self-preservation or religious fervour and it seems likely that the Dorset Cursus was constructed as a processional avenue, associated with ceremonial centres and adjacent ancestral cemeteries. But it has also been suggested that (like the Bronze-Age REAVES of Dartmoor) it may have been raised as a physical barrier to delineate tribal territory on its vulnerable south-eastern flank, that nearest to the Hampshire Avon, the principal inland route-way from the Channel coast. It may be that to each cursus may be ascribed an entirely different function and that generic definitions are inappropriate.
See also DYKES

CURTAIL STEP *see* STAIRCASES

CURTAIN WALL *see* CASTLE (MEDIEVAL)

CURTILAGE (*sometimes* COURTLEDGE) (i) In an historical sense, the court and outbuildings attached to a dwelling-house.
(ii) In law, the land in which a dwelling-house and its outbuildings are contained. An area of land cannot properly be described as a 'curtilage' unless it forms part and parcel of the house or building which it contains or to which it is attached.
(iii) The monastic department responsible for the production of vegetables.

CUSTOM *see* LAW

CUSTUMAL *see* MANOR

CUTS *see* RECLAMATION

CUT STRING *see* STAIRCASES

CWM A Welsh word meaning 'valley', with the same derivation as the Old English *comb*, *combe* and *coombe*. Glascwm in Powys is 'the blue valley', Templecombe in Somerset was the site of a Templar preceptory before *c.* 1185 and the neighbouring manor of Abbas Combe was held by the Abbess of Shaftesbury in 1086.
See also DALE

CYCLAS A surcoat cut short at the front and long at the back.

CYCLOPEAN MASONRY Structures constructed of exceptionally large stones which were held in position by their own weight, the interstices being filled with smaller stones.

CYPHER A monogram, sometimes ensigned with a coronet to indicate rank and used as a personal or household device. Particularly popular during the eighteenth and nineteenth centuries, when the use of armorial badges was in decline and the new rich of the Industrial Revolution perceived a need for some means of personal identity.

DALE (i) From the Old Norse *dalr*, meaning 'valley', the term is common in those counties of northern England that were settled by the Scandinavians.
See also CWYM
(ii) *See* OPEN FIELDS

DÄL RIADA *see* SCOTLAND

DAME SCHOOLS *see* EDUCATION

DAMS *see* AQUEDUCTS *and* WEIRS

DANEGELD A *geld* or land-tax raised in Anglo-Saxon England and paid as tribute to the Dane in order to ward off invasion. Such payments were

made throughout the ninth and tenth centuries but, following the catastrophic (though heroic) defeat of the ealdorman Brihtnoth and his local levies at the battle of Maldon (Essex) in 991, the collection and administration of Danegeld was formalized and refined in response to increasing Danish pressure. Immense sums were raised for this purpose during the later years of Aethelred's reign (978–1016), and Cnut (1016–35) levied a similar tax, known as *heregeld*, in order to finance national defence. This was discontinued in 1051 but was revived by William I as a means of raising personal revenues. The term Danegeld persisted in use until its final abolition in 1162.
See also TAXATION *and* VIKINGS

DANELAW The north-eastern area of Britain occupied by the Danes in the ninth and tenth centuries comprising the kingdoms of Bernicia, York and East Anglia and the federation of the *Five Boroughs* of Derby, Lincoln, Nottingham, Leicester and Stamford. It was in the Five Boroughs that the Danes established their administrative and military headquarters. Following the Conquest, the NORMANS attempted to rationalize the often disparate practices of the Danelaw and Saxon administrations. In the Danelaw, divisions had been created out of the former VIKING military districts, each with its central borough, wapentake sub-divisions and a Danish lord (*jarl*) responsible directly to the English king. But in the Saxon shires, administrative and judicial practices, which originated in the laws of Ine, King of Wessex (688–726) and his successors, were effected through shires and hundreds with an ealdorman and shire-reeve representing the king and people.
See also KINGDOMS (ANCIENT) *and* LAW

DARK AGES, THE A simplistic term denoting the apparent obscurity or barbarity of the period following the withdrawal of Rome from Britain at the beginning of the fifth century to the advent of the MIDDLE AGES. Originally, the term was coined by pre-nineteenth-century historians, who tended to disregard everything that was achieved between the fall of the Roman Empire and the Renaissance. It has acquired a more recent significance because of the paucity of contemporary historical information. Despite the absence of documentary records, archaeological, topographical and other sources (such as place-names) have nevertheless provided us with insights into a period of history in which new elements and new patterns emerged which were to influence the development of medieval and modern

Britain. Not least was the introduction of Germanic languages which, with the recedence of the native Celtic tongue, were the ancestral version of modern English.

The Emperor Constantine's conversion to Christianity (in AD 312) led to the partial conversion of the Romano-British nobility before Roman rule came to an end in AD 410, and although Rome had never succeeded in conquering the Irish or the Picts in Scotland, Ireland was converted by Roman missionaries in the fifth century and Irish monks later played a leading rôle in the conversion of the Picts and Anglo-Saxons in Britain. Two major migrations of Germanic-speaking peoples from northern Germany and Scandinavia occurred during this period. The first ANGLO-SAXON settlers were mercenaries who overthrew their British masters and founded their own independent states. During the fifth and sixth centuries further settlers arrived and by the end of the seventh century three major political and military powers had emerged: Northumbria (in north-east England and the south of Scotland), Mercia (in the midlands) and Wessex (in the south and south-west).* The annexation of western Britain was a slow process: Cornwall retained its independence until the ninth century and Wales was never subdued.

The second migration, of VIKINGS from Denmark and Norway, began with sporadic incursions in the late eighth century followed by systematic plundering and colonization from *c*. 850. The English kingdoms of East Anglia, Northumbria and Mercia were eventually subjugated but during the tenth century the West Saxon kings retaliated and briefly created an English kingdom, theoretically unified but in practice divided into regions approximating to the old kingdoms and ruled by powerful earls. In 1016 this passed to the Danish King Cnut, but after 1042 England was again ruled by a West Saxon, Edward the Confessor, until his death in 1065. To the north, the kingdoms of the Picts had been replaced in the ninth century by a new kingdom of Scots, and the Vikings in Ireland were finally defeated at the battle of Clontarf in 1014.

It is inevitable that centuries of conquest should acquire the epithet 'barbarous'. The sixth-century British cleric Gildas described the destruction of his country by the German barbarians: 'Swords glinted all around, and the flames crackled. Foundation stones of high walls that had been torn from their lofty base, holy altars, fragments of corpses, covered as it were with a purple crust of congealed blood, looked as though they had been mixed up in some dreadful wine press.' But this is the obverse side of the sun and, obscure though our vision of the Dark Ages may be, that which has been revealed to us is of a brilliant intensity. The ancient kingdom of Northumbria was 'a land of art and culture, a haven of learning and skill' which in the seventh century became the force that first united England into a single realm. Most of this cultural creativity emanated from the Anglo-Saxon Church and from the monastic foundations in particular. The monasteries of Northumberland and Kent produced the finest illuminated manuscripts, using pigments imported from as far afield as the Himalayas. In churches, Anglo-Saxon artists established a unique and highly influential school of sculpture while England's first poets created epic poetry that marked the beginnings of English literature. This was the age of the *Codex Amiatinus*, the world's oldest surviving Latin bible. Weighing 75 lb and requiring the skins of 500 calves for its vellum pages, it was (probably) made at the monastery of Monk-wearmouth (Tyne and Wear) as a gift for the Pope in AD 716. This was the age of England's first major historian, the Venerable Bede, who produced his *History of the English Church and People* in AD 731; of the magnificent illuminated *Lindisfarne Gospels*; and of the mystical St Cuthbert, whose beautifully carved wooden coffin may still be seen at Durham Cathedral together with an array of superb Anglo-Saxon treasures: the products, not of obscurity and barbarity, but of a highly sophisticated and cultured people.

See also TOWNS

* This is clearly an over-simplification of a complex process: for the political geography of the Dark Ages *see* KINGDOMS (ANCIENT)

DARROCKS *see* OPEN FIELDS

DATE STONES Carved commemorative stones, bearing a yeoman's initials and the date on which his new farmhouse was built, may be found set in walls, above doorways and at the base of chimney-stacks of many late sixteenth- and early seventeenth-century dwellings. This was a time of increasing rural prosperity for a new class of 'yeoman farmer', and the chimney-stack itself became a symbol of this success: the majority of the rural population was still living in medieval hovels ventilated by means of primitive roof holes. Yeomen's houses were designed for greater comfort and convenience but were otherwise comparatively modest dwellings. Many were later absorbed into estates and survive today as cottages, distinguished only by their date stones.

DAUB AND WATTLE see WATTLE AND DAUB

DAY STAIR see DORTER

DE A topographical preposition meaning 'of' or 'from', e.g. Robert de Mowbray. In the barons' letter to the Pope of 1301, the surnames of forty-one knights are prefixed with 'de'. According to Cokayne (*The Complete Peerage*), the prefix was often adopted 'to give an air of antiquity to new creations. The practice was based on ignorance of the nomenclature of the Middle Ages, and has defeated its object, for the prefix *de* in a title is almost always a sign that the dignity, if not the man, is new.'
See also PLACE NAMES

DEAN see CLERGY (CHURCH OF ENGLAND)

DEATH'S HEAD In memorials, a sculptured or engraved skull symbolizing death and, by implication, both its commonality and ultimate victory through resurrection. Most death's heads date from the late fifteenth century to the eighteenth, during which period there was a preoccupation with the inevitability of death and an almost culpable desire to acknowledge, *in memoriam*, the transient nature of privilege and wealth. Many variations are to be found: some have bats' wings and others are carried by figures of children to indicate infant mortality.

DEBATABLE LAND A tract of land between the rivers Esk and Sark claimed by both England and Scotland. The term is sometimes applied to other areas of land, ownership of which was disputed. In the absence of any clear authority, debatable lands often became the haunt of thieves and vagabonds.
See also MARCH *and* OUTLAWS

DECORATED see GOTHIC ARCHITECTURE

DECOY An often remote area of a medieval FOREST or CHASE into which game would be enticed. Such areas were subject to rigorous legal protection and punishment of those who trespassed therein was often severe. In DEER PARKS, game was sometimes lured or driven into a 'funnel' of camouflaged hurdles before being released into open countryside for the chase, and from the Tudor period similar decoys were constructed, at the end of which were 'baiting grounds' in which the kill was effected. Duck decoys were funnel-like enclosures for trapping wildfowl. In the Middle Ages these

were located at the sides of lakes where a tapering arm of water was enclosed in netting and the birds gently driven towards it. By the eighteenth century, duck decoys had become singularly ingenious. Steep-sided artificial lakes were created, each with a number of curving arms (called *pipes*) radiating from the centre like the limbs of a star-fish. The decoy at Morden, near Wimborne in Dorset, was a pool covering just over one acre and with five such pipes. Constructed in 1724 in a remote and densely planted enclosure located in a swampy valley surrounded by heath, it continued in use until 1856, with an annual catch rarely exceeding 500 birds. Wildfowl were attracted to the area by a larger open lake, known as the 'outside decoy pond', which was populated by 'tame' ducks, reared by the Decoy-Keeper whose cottage was nearby. Elsewhere we read that 'the mesmerized wildfowl were enticed into the tapering netted pipes of the decoy by the antics of a dog, trained to meander through a series of hurdles placed on the banks' (*see* COCKSHOOT).

DECURIONES see ROMAN ADMINISTRATION

DEEPING see RECLAMATION

DEER LEAP see DEER PARKS

DEER PARKS Clues to the location of former deer parks are legion, both in documentary and cartographical form and in the landscape: in the survival of great perimeter walls or embankments (not to be confused with WOODBANKS), and in place-names such as Parkend, East Park Farm, North Pale Copse and Park Pale Lodge (all to be found within 1 square mile of the Dorset countryside) and the even older Dyrham in Gloucestershire, *dēor hamm* being an Anglo-Saxon 'deer enclosure'. A medieval deer park was a venison farm of some considerable size, enclosed by a substantial earth bank and deer-proof *palisade* – a ring fence of vertical stakes or *pales*. Hunting was an important, but nevertheless ancillary activity which generally took place in the FOREST and CHASE, the confines of a park being considered too restricted for good sport. Deer for hunting were therefore maintained within the park and released into the surrounding countryside for the chase, much to the inconvenience of the local populace. Deer parks undoubtedly existed in late Saxon England but it was the Normans who were the real innovators: by 1086, about forty deer parks had been established and by 1300 this number had increased to 3,200, covering an estimated 2 per cent of the landscape. Most magnatial and monastic estates included a deer park and therefore enjoyed a reliable supply of fresh venison throughout the winter. These parks varied in size but were of at least 30 acres (12 hectares) and normally between 100 and 200 acres (40 and 80 hectares), though some were very much larger.

Deer parks were almost invariably in WOODLAND country, the trees within the park being pollarded to encourage growth above the reach of browsing animals (*see* POLLARD). Emparkment required a (costly) royal licence and this occasionally included a right to construct a *deer leap*, a complex system of banks and ditches which permitted the egress of wild deer (which were owned by the Crown) but prevented their escape. On occasions, a herd was established through a gift of breeding stock from the Crown. Inevitably, such high concentrations of captive deer were vulnerable to poaching, though it seems that the king's deer were also lured *into* the parks by means of illegal deer leaps and DECOYS. The creation and extension of deer parks by the forfeiture of tenanted and common land caused considerable resentment and hardship among the peasantry, further aggravated by the damage caused to crops and livestock by the bloodsports themselves. Parks were sometimes divided into open *launds* (lawns) for grazing and protected areas of young COPPICE.

Before the Conquest (1066) Britain contained only Red and Roe deer. The Romans may have attempted to introduce Fallow deer to Britain but there is little evidence of their survival and it was the Normans who successfully stocked their parks with Fallow deer in the decades following the Conquest. Fallow deer were notoriously difficult to contain and, despite the construction of high stone walls in place of palisades, many escaped from parks to establish wild herds in the open countryside. By the thirteenth and early fourteenth centuries, ownership of a deer park had become a significant status symbol: the acquisition of a royal licence and possession of the resources necessary to maintain a park were considered to be indicative of considerable influence and privilege, as well as wealth.

With the decimation of the working population caused by the fourteenth-century plagues (*see* BLACK DEATH) labour became an expensive commodity and, consequently, disparking took place on a wide scale during the fifteenth, sixteenth and seventeenth centuries. Only the wealthiest of the nobility managed to retain their parks, in some cases extending them into land which had been taken out of cultivation following the plagues. Such parks are delineated in the MAPS of Christopher Saxton (*c.* 1542–1606) and subsequent seventeenth-century cartographers. Some continued as deer parks, others became stud farms or were cultivated. But many were retained to enhance the environment of a great house and it is ironic that out of the misery and squaller of the Black Death was born the great tradition of English landscaped parks. Former deer parks in which deer still browsed were often retained and 'improved' as symbols of eighteenth-century gentility and good taste by men such as William Kent and Capability Brown, and provided elegant back-drops for the portraits of Reynolds and Gainsborough. Today, commercial herds of deer are still confined within palisaded parks and some of these are of undoubted medieval origin.

On current Ordnance Survey maps, the perimeter embankment of a former deer park may be marked as a '*Park Pale*', though such information should be regarded as a clue requiring further substantiation (*see also* WOODBANKS). Britain's herds of wild deer are now significantly larger than they were during the Middle Ages. No doubt they include many animals of ancient lineage: noble fugitives from England's derelict deer parks.

DEER ROASTS From the Irish *fulacht fiadh* (deer roast), these early meat- processing sites are to be found on the banks of streams especially in Ireland and south and west Wales. Probably of Iron-Age design, they comprised a stone hearth set within a horseshoe-shaped bank of charcoal and stones, with an adjacent shelter and a timber-lined trough between the open end of the hearth and the stream. Water in the trough (sometimes as much as 100 gallons) was taken from the stream and boiled by means of heated stones ('pot-boilers') from the hearth. Carcasses (not just of deer) were scraped and shaved using boiling water, and salted by immersion in warm brine. Loins, hams, etc., would then be smoked inside the shelter. Deer roasts more or less conforming to this basic design were in use for many centuries. They may be discovered singly or in clusters and are now little more than horseshoe-shaped mounds. Though deer roasts were constructed at the water's edge, a stream's course is likely to have altered and the mounds may now be some distance from it.

DEHEUBARTH *see* WALES

DEMESNE From *dominicus* 'belonging to the lord', a lord's demesne consisted of those manorial lands which were reserved for his personal benefit and on which tenants gave free service or *famuli* were employed. The royal demesne comprised those manors held directly by the sovereign and from which Crown revenues were extracted. Similarly, magnates who held several manors would enjoy the revenues of those demesne manors which were not subinfeudated to vassals. A 'home farm' is effectively a demesne farm in that it is worked by, or on behalf of, the owner of an estate containing other farms. Ancient Demesne, defined in Domesday as *terrae regis (Eduardi)*, was land held by the Crown during the reigns of Edward the Confessor and William I. Tenure of Ancient Demesne lands was subject to numerous benefits and exemptions, and was abolished as recently as 1925.

See also MANOR *and* OPEN FIELDS

DEMON NAMES Spectral memories of superstition and folklore are perpetuated in many of the names given by our ancestors to the contorted remnants of wasteland, wooded combs, lonely meres and remote earthworks. To such places, possessed (even today) of a sense of mystery, and to artificial edifices to which man in his ignorance could ascribe no rational explanation, were attributed demonic associations. Dangerous Norse *thyrs* inhabit fords and limestone caves of the North Country; in the south, *pūca* or Puck is ubiquitous, as is the demon known as *scucca*, who is to be found as Shack-, Shock- and Shuck- elements in the names of numerous barrows, hills and streams.

DENARIUS *see* COINAGE

DENDROCHRONOLOGY *see* TREE-RING DATING

DENE-HOLE *see* MARL-PIT

DENN *see* COMMONS

DESERTED GARDENS *see* VEGETATION

DESERTED VILLAGES Thousands of deserted villages (or, more correctly, *abandoned settlements*) have been identified: many more await discovery. Not all are as manifest as Tyneham in Dorset, reluctantly surrendered to the army in 1943 as part of the Lulworth artillery range 'for the duration of the hostilities', or the drowned farmsteads of Elan and Clywedog in mid-Wales.

Before the end of the eighth century, many rural settlements were used for seasonal or migratory occupation or as refuges, inhabited only in times of

danger. Other sites have revealed evidence to suggest a continuity of occupation, particularly of Iron Age communities which survived unaltered into the Roman occupation. It also seems likely that there were groups of peasant dwellings associated with many ROMAN VILLAS. But most of these rural settlements represent intermittent re-occupations, or occupation of a preferred *area* rather than a specific site. Following the withdrawal of Rome in AD 410, Romano-British settlements, and those of immigrant Saxons, tended to be scattered hamlets or farmsteads. A small number of early Saxon 'villages' developed but these generally occupied poor sites and appear to have been abandoned by the mid-seventh century. The development of OPEN FIELDS in the eighth and ninth centuries, and the building of parish CHURCHES to serve a rapidly expanding rural population, provided the stimulus for the creation of what we today perceive as a village: a permanent cluster of dwellings with an identifiable nucleus, providing the focal point for outlying hamlets and farmsteads, many of which pre-date the village itself (*see* VILLAGE). But how permanent were these villages? Some expanded to become towns and even cities: many others declined and were eventually abandoned.

Documentary evidence of deserted villages is meagre before the compilation of Domesday Book in 1086. The destructive Norman *chevauchées* of 1069–71 in the north of England (the 'Harrying of the North') inevitably caused the disintegration of numerous rural communities, but little is known of these. The CISTERCIAN clearances of the twelfth and thirteenth centuries are well documented, however, and resulted in the effective depopulation of those areas identified by the Order as being sufficiently sequestered to meet the stringent requirements of its rule. By 1152, there were fifty-one Cistercian foundations in England, and dozens of rural communities had been dispersed, especially in northern England, in order to satisfy the Cistercians' demand for solitude and exclusiveness and to accommodate the expansion of their estates (*see* GRANGE).

Deteriorating climatic conditions, particularly severe in the fourteenth century, resulted in the gradual abandonment of many of the subsistence communities, created out of the rural population explosion of the previous century, on the margins of the heaths and moors. Such starveacre places were subject to recurring soil exhaustion and severe over-grazing and simply could not survive the changing climatic régime.

Undoubtedly the most popular reason given for the abandonment of a village, and that which persists most strongly in the received traditions of many communities, is the fourteenth-century pestilence known as the Black Death (*see* PLAGUE). There is no doubting the virulence of this terrifying disease and the debilitating effect it could have on a small, rural community. But documentary and archaeological evidence strongly suggest that very few settlements were abandoned *permanently* and, as in the case of villages decimated by civil war, most were re-colonized or replaced by planned villages on adjacent sites. Of course, some villages were lost entirely (such as Tusmore in Oxfordshire which in 1357 was '. . . void of inhabitance since their death in the pestilence'), but of the 2,000 deserted villages that have been recorded, mostly in the Midland counties and eastern parts of England, final abandonment was the result of gradual decline over many decades. Of eighty deserted medieval villages identified in Northamptonshire, for example, only two (Hale and Elkington) are true 'plague villages'. The real effect of the Black Death, and of subsequent recurrences of the plague which lasted into the seventeenth century, was to accelerate a decline in the rural population which was already evident by the middle of the thirteenth century. It was this decline, and the consequential reduction in the availability of peasant labour, which was to result in the eventual abandonment of many medieval rural settlements. Undeterred by legislation intended to curtail their new-found bargaining power, labourers repeatedly demanded more favourable conditions of service, wages rose substantially and landlords sought means by which they could reduce their labour force and more profitably exploit their lands. Inevitably, in a flourishing wool market, they turned to sheep and during the late fifteenth and early sixteenth centuries open fields were enclosed (*see* ENCLOSURE), estates cleared and villagers evicted on an unprecedented scale, creating appalling poverty and almost universal resentment. Hardest hit were the East Midland counties, Norfolk, the Lincolnshire Wolds and the former East and North Ridings of Yorkshire. In the 1480s the priest and antiquarian John Rous noted fifty-eight depopulated villages within 19 km (12 miles) of his native Warwick.

Amazingly, many medieval village sites have escaped the plough and are still evident in apparently haphazard areas of humps and hollows often covering several acres. Upon closer inspection, former streets and BACK LANES may be identified as HOLLOW WAYS of varying width, with adjacent HOUSE PLATFORMS surrounded by low banks and ditches marking the boundaries of CLOSES or TOFTS. There may be evidence of former PONDS or MOATS, or the artificial mound of a MOTTE AND BAILEY castle or WINDMILL; and at the village edge, the RIDGE AND FURROW pattern of ancient open fields is often discernible. Medieval sites in areas of arable cultivation are usually visible only from the air as CROP MARKS. Parish churches were almost invariably plundered for building materials, except those that occupied ancient, venerated sites (often of pagan origin) or were themselves built of freely available materials, such as the flint churches of Norfolk. In such cases the church, or its dilapidated shell, may remain in splendid isolation (*see* CHURCH SITES).

The late Tudor and Elizabethan periods witnessed the dismantling of the last remnants of the feudal system. Magnatial and dynastic strongholds were adapted or replaced by fashionable country mansions, and medieval DEER PARKS extended to incorporate open fields and common waste in vast areas of empty but equally fashionable parkland. Villages were generally considered to be obtrusive in such sylvan settings and were removed, sometimes to be rebuilt outside the park for the benefit of estate tenants. In other cases, the unfortunate peasantry was abandoned together with its villages. The little market town of Milton Abbas in Dorset developed in the shadow of its tenth-century abbey until 1780, when its proximity to the new mansion so offended the sensibilities of Joseph Damer (later the first Earl of Dorchester) that he demolished the entire town, save for one thatched cottage, and removed those inhabitants he was unable to drive away to a new '*model village*' in a deep combe half a mile to the south. The earthworks and hollow ways that mark the crofts and streets of the former town are still evident in the fields to the south of the abbey church. Unlike most medieval desertions, many 'emparked' villages retained their parish churches which, although isolated from the congregations they were built to serve, remain in defiant juxtaposition to the splendid mansions that caused their decline.

From the mid-nineteenth century, relatively few villages were abandoned; where it did happen, it was usually the result of industrial decline (the closure of a colliery for example) or to create reservoirs or military training areas, such as those on Salisbury Plain in Wiltshire.

Clues to the identity of a deserted village may be evident in the double-barrelled names of some civil parishes, such as Knayton-with-Brawith in Yorkshire (Brawith is a deserted village), or in an unusual configuration of parish boundaries, particularly those with a 'dumb-bell' shape, indicative perhaps of the annexation of a former parish by its neighbour.

See also HAMLET

DETACHED BELFRIES *see* CHURCH TOWERS

DEVILS *see* DOOM *and* WALL PAINTINGS

DEW POND Common on the porous chalk uplands of southern England, dew ponds are natural hollows at the lowest point of which a saucer-shaped sump was excavated and carefully lined with impermeable clay and straw and a protective layer of flint. Providing the clay did not dry and crack, such basins would provide small reservoirs of rainwater for grazing animals. It is likely that the earliest prehistoric dew ponds were hollowed out in naturally impervious pockets of clay and that the craft of pond construction developed through the Anglo-Saxon and medieval periods. Despite the mystique that is associated with dew ponds, most date from the seventeenth to the early twentieth centuries, and the notion that they were intended to collect dew probably originated in the romantic antiquarianism of the early Victorians. Today, most dew ponds are no longer functional and appear as circular grassy declivities on the downs.

DEXTER In ARMORY, the left-hand side of a shield of arms when viewed from the front, the right-hand side being the *sinister*.

DIAPER A decorative pattern applied to the surface of a SEAL or heraldic shield but of no armorial significance.

DIKES *see* DYKES *and* RECLAMATION

DIMIDIATION *see* IMPALEMENT

DIOCESE A diocese is an ecclesiastical administrative territory comprising archdeaconries, rural deaneries and parishes, all subject to the jurisdiction (*bishopric*) of a bishop. In the Church of England, the Crown gives a dean and chapter leave to elect a bishop, and nominates the person to be elected. A *see* is the official 'seat' of a bishop and normally stands in the CATHEDRAL (*cathedra* = 'throne') of the diocese.

By the beginning of the ninth century, episcopal sees had been established at Iona, Abercorn, Whithorn, Lindisfarne, Hexham, York, Sidnacester, Lichfield, Hereford, Leicester, Elmham, Worcester,

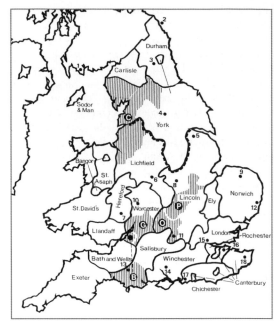

THE ENGLISH DIOCESES OF 1291 AND 1545

The dioceses of 1291, together with those created in 1541–5 (shaded):

C	Chester	B	Bristol
P	Peterborough	O	Oxford
G	Gloucester		

Anglo-Saxon Episcopal Sees:

1	Whithorn	10	Worcester
2	Lindisfarne	11	Dorchester (Oxon)
3	Hexham	12	Dunwich
4	York	13	Sherborne
5	Sidnacester	14	Winchester
6	Lichfield	15	London
7	Hereford	16	Rochester
8	Leicester	17	Selsey
9	Elmham	18	Canterbury

Dorchester (Oxfordshire), Dunwich, Sherborne, Winchester, London, Rochester, Selsey and Canterbury.

At the end of the thirteenth century, the English dioceses comprised: Canterbury (founded in AD 597), London (604), Rochester (604), York (625), Winchester (662), Lichfield (669), Hereford (676), Worcester (*c.* 680), Bath and Wells (909), Durham (995), Exeter (1050), Lincoln (1072), Chichester (1075), Salisbury (1078), Norwich (1091), Ely (1109) and Carlisle (1133); and in Wales: Bangor, St Asaph, St David's and Llandaff (all *c.* 550).

Following the DISSOLUTION OF THE MONASTERIES, a number of the English dioceses were sub-divided to create a further five: Chester (1541), Peterborough (1541), Gloucester (1541), Bristol (1542) and Oxford (1545). Of these, Chester encompassed the western third of the dioceses of York and Lichfield; the creation of Peterborough and Oxford in a narrow, diagonal band across the vast diocese of Lincoln effectively divided it in two, much of the southern half being incorporated in the later diocese of St Alban's (1877). Gloucester was created out of the southern half of the diocese of Worcester, and the new diocese of Bristol comprised a small area north of the city together with a large detached 'island' to the south, transferred from the diocese of Salisbury, and corresponding almost exactly to the old county of Dorset. A sixth diocese, with the Abbey of Westminster as its cathedral, lasted for only a decade from 1540–50.

No further sees were established between 1546 and 1836 but since then twenty new dioceses have been created in response to the rapid expansion of the urban population during the Industrial Revolution and the proliferation of suburban conurbations in the twentieth century.

An association of dioceses is a *province* over which one of the diocesan bishops presides as archbishop. There are two English provinces: that of Canterbury, consisting of all the dioceses south of the river Trent, and that of York, which includes the remaining dioceses to the north. The Province of Wales was created out of the Province of Canterbury in 1920 and two new dioceses formed.

DIOCESAN RECORDS Diocesan records, deposited in the archives of diocesan registries, have mostly been transferred to county record offices. These may include the *Compton Census* returns of 1676 which record the numbers of souls in each parish and details of those who regularly absented themselves from worship.

DIPLOMATIC The study of the form, content and production of documents and records.

DIPTYCH (i) A folding pair of pictures or tablets depicting religious themes or containing genealogical and armorial information. *See also* TRIPTYCH
(ii) Lists of names of living and departed Christians for whom prayers are offered. At one time, these were recited publicly and the inclusion or otherwise of a name was considered to be indicative of communion or excommunication.
(iii) A double-folding writing table.

DIRECTORIES From the mid-eighteenth century until the 1930s, numerous local directories were published providing commercial, mercantile and political information, details of local offices and of the personages who held them, and of the occupants of major residences in towns and rural areas. The best known of these were the Kelly's Directories, published in county or city volumes between 1799 and 1939. Copies of Kelly's and other directories relating to a particular area are generally available at libraries and record offices. There are also extensive collections at the Guildhall Library and the Society of Genealogists, and back copies are held by Kelly's Directories Limited. An almost complete collection of *telephone directories* is maintained by the British Telecom Museum and there are collections at the Guildhall Library and the Historical Telephone Directory Library in London and at the Bodleian Library in Oxford. *For* addresses *see* APPENDIX I
See also POSTAL SERVICES *and* TELECOM-MUNICATIONS

DISPENSARIES Dispensaries, where the poor could obtain medical advice and treatment as well as medicines, were established in many towns in the eighteenth and nineteenth centuries (*see illustration* overleaf). They were financed by philanthropists who nominated a number of patients according to the size of their subscriptions. Details of dispensaries, including lists of subscribers, are held by local record offices.

DISSEISIN The unlawful removal of a freeholder from his property.

DISSENTING CHAPELS Built for 'hymn and sermon' rather than architectural grandeur, 'meeting houses' of the non-conformist congregations are to be found in most villages and nearly every town. The thatched meeting house at Horningsham, Wiltshire, provided in 1566 for the Scottish Presbyterian workforce engaged in the building of nearby Longleat House, is said to be the oldest free church in England. A small number of early Quaker meeting houses remain from the late seventeenth century, when they were first licensed (in 1688 – by application to an Anglican bishop), but most were built for the Methodist congregations of the late eighteenth and early nineteenth centuries and especially, from 1810, for the new Primitive Methodist movement. A typical eighteenth-century urban meeting house was rectangular, often of greater width than depth, and with separate doorways for men and women, who sat apart.

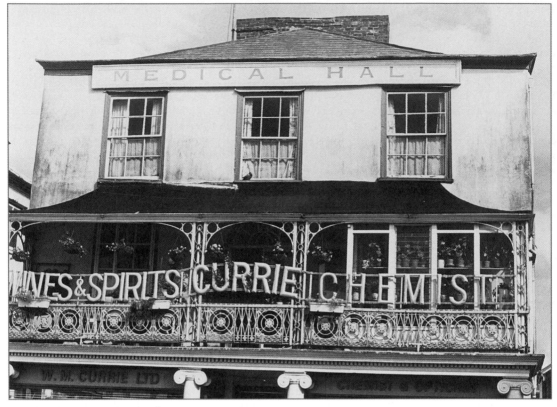

The former medical hall at South Molton, Devon.

Chapels in rural communities were usually simple rectangular buildings, erected on waste ground or squeezed onto an unclaimed length of road verge. Congregations were usually poor and most early chapels were constructed of the cheapest available materials and in the simplest architectural style, with round-topped windows and clear glass. Larger meeting houses were galleried with a prominent central pulpit, from which the preacher was visible (and, more importantly, audible) to the entire congregation. In front of the pulpit was a simple communion table enclosed within low communion rails. As congregations grew, so many rural chapels were replaced by larger, often rather pompous, Victorian buildings, most of which date from the mid-nineteenth century. As a result, village chapels may often be found in pairs.

For Chapels Society *see* APPENDIX I
See also CHURCHES

DISSOLUTION OF THE MONASTERIES

Monastic communities were by no means immune to criticism in the late Middle Ages, but it was in order to appropriate their considerable wealth and to facilitate the establishment of the royal supremacy that Henry VIII demolished the entire system. In 1536 the Act for the Dissolution of the Smaller Monasteries required the suppression of all religious houses with fewer than twelve monks or nuns and an annual value of less than £200, so that 'His Majesty should have and enjoy . . .' all their possessions. GILBERTINE Houses were specifically exempted from this legislation and others (over seventy) were allowed to purchase exemptions at some considerable cost: in both instances, the reprieve was short-lived. Government policy was not necessarily one of outright confiscation: commissioners deliberately sought out vulnerability and exploited it so that monastic communities were steadily persuaded to surrender. Confessions of sinful conduct and incompetent management were the usual instruments by which this induced surrender was effected and should not be taken at face value. The commissioners themselves were often under considerable pressure from members of the nobility and gentry who happened to covet a particular monastic estate and who were known to enjoy royal patronage. At the same time, the often rich and famous shrines were being dismantled: that of St Thomas à Becket at Canterbury was stripped of its encrusted gold, silver and jewels which were carried away in wagon-loads.

The Act for the Dissolution of the Greater Monasteries (of 1539) vested in the Crown all the properties so far surrendered and all remaining eligible monasteries and their vast estates. The Act did not in fact sanction dissolution *per se*, but rather safeguarded the Crown's title to the proceeds. Those who would not comply soon found themselves isolated and facing expulsion, attainder and even execution. Many were themselves tried and convicted of stealing from their own abbeys. On 15 November 1539, Richard Whyting, abbot of the most venerable monastic foundation in England, was hanged, drawn and quartered on the summit of Glastonbury Tor for refusing to release the abbey plate. After a short and often brutal finale, the process of dispossession and dispersal was completed in 1540 and most of the religious brethren pensioned off (though the FRIARS were not) or provided with licences to become incumbents of parish benefices. Perhaps the most significant aspect of the Dissolution was that it was effected with so little opposition (the principal exception being the northern rebellion of 1536–7, known as the 'Pilgrimage of Grace', which was chiefly concerned with the conduct and policies of the government of which the suppression of the lesser monasteries was but one element). No doubt the fact that the breach with Rome was essentially unopposed by the monastic orders in England facilitated the process: the dispersed brethren were not perceived as loyal adherents to the Papacy and the laity readily accepted the Dissolution. It is also significant that, although there was nothing to prevent the re-formation of a conventual community, no existing foundation managed to survive after 1540.

By 1539, explicit orders had been given for the total destruction of all newly surrendered monastic buildings and for the systematic removal of all lead and other materials. Total demolition (an expensive operation) was not always achieved: comprehensive ruination invariably was. Many dilapidated buildings provided accessible supplies of ashlar and rubble for local builders, particularly in those areas (such as East Anglia) where supplies of building stone were scarce. Because of their inherent remoteness, many of the great CISTERCIAN abbeys, such as Tintern in Monmouthshire and Fountains in North Yorkshire, were less vulnerable to plundering and remain as gaunt, skeletal memorials to monastic

exclusiveness. The twelve pre-Norman monastic cathedrals retained both their diocesan status and their lands, which were administered by a dean and chapter. Westminster Abbey became a collegiate royal PECULIAR with a dean and secular canons, and from 1540 to 1550 a diocesan cathedral. The new dioceses created out of the Dissolution ensured the survival as CATHEDRALS of the great medieval abbey churches of Bristol, Chester, Gloucester, Oxford and Peterborough (*see* DIOCESE). Nearly a hundred monastic churches, whose naves had long been parish churches, were retained while others, such as Tewkesbury in Gloucestershire and Sherborne in Dorset, were purchased by local benefactors or acquired for parochial use through diocesan intervention. But such churches were invariably deprived of their cloistral and domestic buildings and at some transepts, chapels and even choirs were demolished. When monastic buildings were sold into private hands, the great church was often the first component to be demolished.

Only rarely was a church small enough to provide comfortable domestic accommodation, as at Buckland in Devon. Elsewhere, the Tudor gentry, attracted as their monastic predecessors had been to fertile, sheltered and beautiful locations, adapted former abbots' lodgings and gatehouses as family residences and retained the monastery kitchens, cellars, barns and outhouses, as at Beaulieu in Hampshire and Forde Abbey in Dorset. The buildings of Malmesbury Abbey in Wiltshire were acquired by a clothier and converted into a factory! Despite the declared intention of the 1536 Act of Suppression that the wealth acquired by the monasteries 'for the maintenance of sin' should be 'converted to better uses', the policy of retaining monastic holdings to provide a reliable source of income for the Crown was never maintained. The only real beneficiaries were the 'new' Tudor gentry – the post-medieval class of ambitious and successful men who through the acquisition of monastic estates were able more quickly to establish their credentials. Estates were valued at twenty times the assessed value of the lands, properties and tithes to be sold, and were transferred to their new owners with comparative ease. Most were already organized in manors administered by professional bailiffs who were unaffected by the change: few were demesne lands. When Elizabeth I ascended the throne in 1558, only a quarter of the estimated £150,000 income once available annually to the religious foundations remained in Crown hands.

See also ECCLESIASTICAL TAXATION RECORDS *and* TUDOR ARCHITECTURE

DISTRAINT The seizure of possessions (usually livestock) in compensation for an alleged breach of feudal obligations or, more recently, of goods in lieu of unpaid rent.

DIVINE OFFICE *see* MONASTERIES

DOCUMENTARY SOURCES *see* ANCIENT DEEDS, ASSIZE (Records), BOOK OF FEES, CENSUS, CENSUS OF RELIGIOUS WORSHIP 1851, CHANCERY (Records), CHARTER (Rolls), CLOSE ROLLS, COUNTESS OF HUNTING-DON'S CONNEXION, CURIA REGIS, DOMESDAY, ECCLESIASTICAL TAXATION RECORDS, EXCHEQUER (Rolls), FEET OF FINES, FEUDAL AIDS, FINE ROLLS, HUNDRED ROLLS, INQUISITIONS POST MORTEM, INQUISITIONS AD QUOD DAMNUM, ISSUE ROLLS, LIBERATE ROLLS, MEMORANDA ROLLS, NATIONAL MONUMENTS RECORD, ORIGINALIA ROLLS, PATENT (Rolls), PIPE ROLLS, PROBATE, STATE PAPERS, TRAILBASTON *and* TREASURY (Records).

Many of the foregoing records are held in the archives of the PUBLIC RECORD OFFICE and the FAMILY RECORD CENTRE, while many are also available in published form.
See APPENDIX I for the House of Lords Record Office, the British Library and the Bodleian Library and for the Royal Commission on Historical Manuscripts, the Early English Text Society, the Harleian Society, the List and Index Society and the Pipe Roll Society.
See also GENEALOGY *and* VICTORIA COUNTY HISTORY

DOG-CART Introduced in the nineteenth century, this two or four-wheeled vehicle was used initially for carrying gun-dogs on shooting parties and was provided with a large under-boot with slatted side-vents for this purpose. The popular two-wheeled version was driven by a single horse and had a double driving seat with two backward-facing seats in the rear, raised footboard and shared back-rest. The four-wheeled type could be driven by a pair and seated either four or six passengers including the driver, though six-seaters were rare and of lower construction with back-to-back seating in the rear. All versions had elliptical springs.

DOG-LEG STAIR *see* STAIRCASES

DOLE (*also* **DALE, DALT** *and* **DOTE**) Area of common MEADOW, and the hay contained therein,

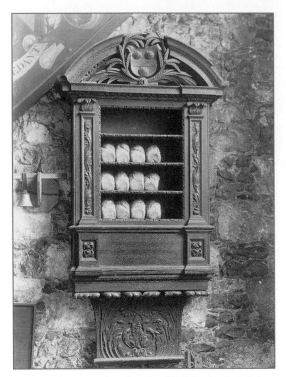

Dole cupboard in the church of St Martin, Ruislip.

allocated to tenants of related OPEN FIELDS. The portions were sometimes allocated by rotation or by lot, hence the colloquial phrases 'to dole out . . .' and 'on the dole', both of which imply a *sparing* distribution of resources. The term is also applied specifically to DEMESNE strips in an open field system.

DOLE CUPBOARDS *and* **DOLE TABLES** A cupboard which was used to contain bread and other food for distribution to the poor. Dole cupboards may be found in many churches and usually date from the sixteenth century or later. Pre-Reformation *dole tables* are singularly rare: that in the churchyard at Powerstock in Dorset dates from the thirteenth century when charitable doles of bread were distributed to the poor.

DOLMEN Seventeenth- and eighteenth-century antiquaries believed that the exposed, table-like stones of Neolithic burial chambers were Druidical sacrificial altars. Originally, a megalith or *capstone* and its supporting 'pillars' would have encased the burial chamber within a BARROW, the earth covering of which was then eroded, exposing the stones. Known as *cromlechs* in Wales, these gaunt

Cromleac (Dolmen) at Ballymascanlon, Co. Louth.

and lonely structures have inevitably found their way into local superstition and folklore. Both terms are now out of favour with archaeologists (*see* CHAMBERED TOMBS).

DOMESDAY Following the Conquest of England in 1066, Duke William of Normandy was crowned king, and most of the lands of the native nobility were granted to his followers. In 1085 '. . . at Gloucester in midwinter . . . the King had thorough and deep discussion with his counsellors about this country, how it was occupied and with what sort of people' and he sent his men '. . . all over England into every shire . . . to find out . . . what or how much each landholder held . . . in land and livestock, and what it was worth' (*Anglo-Saxon Chronicle*). The Commissioners were instructed to ascertain and record all taxable holdings and anything which added to the annual value of a manorial estate (*manerium*), TITHING or TOWNSHIP, including disputed lands. The entire realm, which did not then include Cumberland and Westmorland (present-day Cumbria), was divided into seven circuits and visited county by county, hundred by hundred and township by township. Evidence was taken on oath '. . . from the Sheriff; from all the barons and their

Frenchmen; and from the whole hundred, the priests, the reeves and six villagers from each village.' The *Inquisitio Eliensis* (the Ely volume of returns) also tells us that the Commissioners were required to establish:

The name of the place.

The names of those by whom it was held, before 1066 and since.

The extent of taxable ploughland (expressed as HIDES, CARUCATES or other local units of land measurement), and the number of ploughs, before and after 1066.

The number of villagers, cottagers, slaves and freemen (but not details of their families).

The number of mills and fish-ponds and the extent of meadow, pasture and woodland (it is unclear whether this was coppiced woodland or open wood pasture).

The extent to which fiscal potential had been reduced or increased since 1066.

The value of holdings enjoyed by each freeman.

Details were verified by four Frenchmen and four Englishmen from each HUNDRED, whose names were also recorded, and yet many details were omitted, including several churches and an occasional castle! Because the survey was essentially a means by which feudal law and tenure could be maintained, lands that were exempt from taxation were generally excluded: in particular, those owned by religious houses. But it was not exclusively a tax assessment: its purpose was that every man '. . . should know his right and not usurp another's'. A second group of commissioners was charged with the task of checking their predecessors' returns in '. . . shires they did not know' and 'where they were themselves unknown'. The survey was completed within a year and so pervasive and authoritative was its ambit, establishing every landholder's inescapable liability, that its consequences were likened to those of Domesday itself – the Last Judgement. At Winchester, the returns (written in a form of Latin shorthand) were corrected, abridged and catalogued by reference to landowners, before being copied by a scribe into a single volume. The surveys of Essex, Norfolk and Suffolk were also collated and copied, unabridged, into a further volume dated 1086, but those of Durham and Northumberland and of several towns (notably, London and Winchester) were not transcribed.

Domesday Book – *Liber de Wintonia* – describes, in minute detail, England 'under new management':

LAND OF WALSCIN OF DOUAI

Walscin of Douai holds WINTERBORNE from the King, and Walkhere from him.
Alward and Alwin held it before 1066 as two manors. It paid tax for 6 hides. Land for 4 ploughs. In lordship 2 ploughs; 3 slaves.
5 villagers and 3 smallholders with ½ plough.
Meadow, 12 acres; woodland, 8 acres; pasture 4 furlongs long and 3 furlongs wide.
The value was £6; now £4.

Wimer holds CAUNDLE from William. Alsi held it before 1066. It paid tax for 3 hides. Land for 3 ploughs. In lordship 2 ploughs; 2 slaves.
2 villagers and 2 smallholders with 1 plough.
A mill which pays 3s; meadow, 10 acres; underwood, 3 acres.
The value was and is 40s.*

The Domesday survey was the product of an experienced and sophisticated administration and was undoubtedly unique in early medieval Europe, both in its scope and execution. However, it was the advanced machinery of government inherited from the displaced Anglo-Saxon monarchy that enabled the Normans to complete the survey so quickly and so thoroughly. Inevitably, problems and anomalies exist, especially for the novice who is unaccustomed to interpreting such information and may be unnerved by the complexities of the terminology and format. For example, the listings by landowner often result in references to a single parish being found under a number of owners, and a Domesday reference to a present-day village does not necessarily imply its existence as a *village* in 1086; only the names of manorial estates, tithings and townships were recorded and even these may be concealed in a single entry. The original survey (which has recently been rebound) is at the Public Record Office (*see* APPENDIX I).

* Thorn, C. and F. (eds), *Domesday Book: Dorset* (Phillimore, 1983)

DOMINICANS Known also as the Black Friars from the black mantle worn over their white habit, members of the mendicant Dominican Order, established by St Dominic in 1220/21, are devoted to preaching and study and, like the FRANCISCANS, practised individual and corporate poverty and lived by begging. In the fourteenth and fifteenth centuries, the Order was disrupted by controversy and there was a relaxation of discipline leading to a papal revocation of the law of corporate poverty in 1475, which allowed the Order to hold property. Prior to their decline during the Counter-Reformation, from the mid-sixteenth century, the Dominicans enjoyed academic and intellectual prowess (St Thomas Aquinas is probably the most notable Dominican academic) and were used by successive Popes for preaching crusades and staffing the Inquisition. The Dominicans were also known as 'Friars Preacher', the Franciscans being 'Friars Minor'.
See also FRIARS

-DON and **-DUN** An Old English *-dūn* was a hill, varying in size from humble Hambledon in Dorset to the mighty Snowdon or 'Snow Mountain' of Conwy. The medieval *doun*, while still meaning 'hill', was also applied to open calcareous upland or 'downland' sheep pasture. 'Down' as a distinguishing element preceding a name generally means 'lower', from the Old English *dūne*, e.g. Down Ampney in Gloucestershire. In Scotland the Dun- element implies a defensive site (from Gaelic *dùn, dùin*), as does the Irish *dùn*, as in Downpatrick, meaning 'St Patrick's Fort'.
See also DUNS

DONATIVE PARISH *see* PARISH

DONJON *see* CASTLE

DONOR WINDOW *see* STAINED GLASS

DOOM In most medieval parish churches the CHANCEL and NAVE were separated by a screen supporting the figure of Christ Crucified (the ROOD). The rood screen also separated the clergy from the laity – medieval sanctity from pagan superstition – and in order to concentrate the minds of the latter, the wall above the chancel arch, or a wooden tympanum fixed above the rood screen, was often painted with a lurid representation of The Doom. Typically, this depicted Christ presiding in majesty over the Last Judgement, in which the naked souls of the dead rose from their graves to be weighed by St Michael and received by the angels into eternal paradise or forked by devils into the gaping and fiery mouth of *Hades*. Such a *Hell Mouth* was often depicted as the open jaws of a gigantic whale – the great *Leviathan* of the Book of Job – or the mythical sea-tortoise of the bestiaries, *Aspido Chelone*, who enticed the wicked into his mouth in the midst of their depravity, as at Wiggenhall St German in Norfolk. Such creatures symbolized the devil himself and served to stimulate the medieval

A painting of the Last Judgement on the chancel arch of the church of St Thomas of Canterbury, Salisbury.

preoccupation with salvation and eternal damnation. Usually, only the mouth is depicted in Doom paintings, though in a fifteenth-century window at Fairford Church, Gloucestershire, the whole terrifying creature is shown.

Satan, as one might expect, is prominent, as are his riotous crew of horned and hairy demons. The damned are confined in chains, suspended in gibbets, boiled in caldrons and transported to hell in wheelbarrows and farmstead carts. All levels of medieval society are represented: from popes and kings to peasants and poachers. Most are shown stumbling beneath the burden of their sins: the greedy merchant with his money bags, the malingerer on her knee pads and hand stools, feigning crippledom (as at Hornton in Oxfordshire) and the dishonest ale-wife with her pitcher of watered-down ale and seductive bodice. Most of these murals were painted by local jobbing artists and are singularly vernacular both in style and execution. Medieval pigments of mud, rock and ochre were applied straight on to limewash with brushes of squirrel or hog hair. The wonderful simplicity of line which characterizes the earliest paintings was achieved simply because the artist had no second chance once the pigment was applied. There is evidence to suggest that many were routinely repainted every fifty years or so. When, at the Reformation, the laity was permitted into the chancel for the Eucharist, many Doom paintings were removed or painted over. Victorian 'restorations' also took their toll: rood screens were often dismantled and most surviving Doom paintings destroyed. Nevertheless, some sixty medieval examples have survived, among them murals at Lower Oddington, Gloucestershire, and Clayton, Sussex (twelfth century); Pickworth, Lincolnshire, and North Cove, Suffolk (fourteenth century); Chesterton, Cambridgeshire, and Salisbury (St Thomas's), Wiltshire (fifteenth century); Wenhaston, Suffolk, and Dauntsey, Wiltshire (early sixteenth century). The transitional state of Pergatory, where souls reconciled to God suffered for an indeterminate period, was of little interest to medieval artists: probably because a speedy passage could be guaranteed by indulgences, such as endowing a church or chantry chapel, joining a crusade or pilgrimage or by making a cash donation.
See also WALL PAINTINGS

DOORS Saxon doorways were small with heavy triangular or round heads and wooden doors. Romanesque doorways were often the most richly ornamental feature of a building (especially

Tudor doorway (c. 1500) in the timber-framed Pitchmarket at Cerne Abbas, Dorset.

churches) and were deeply recessed and moulded, the space between the usually square-topped door and the round arch above (the *tympanum*) being vigorously carved in high relief. Medieval doors were usually made of interlinked planks bound with horizontal ledges and with prominent, often decorated, hinges. These panels were sometimes carved with Gothic tracery. Throughout the period, the Gothic pointed arch predominated and in large buildings these were moulded and carved in the contemporary ornamental style. The arch was 'supported' on either side of the doorway by pillars (*jambs*), and the shape and proportion of the arch itself became flatter and wider culminating in the four-centre style of the late fifteenth century (*see* ARCH). These later Perpendicular and Tudor doorways had a square hood-mould above the arch, and spandrels filled with carved ornamentation. The second half of the sixteenth century saw the introduction of the classical rectangular doorway with a moulded surround (*door-case* or *architrave*) and single or double wood-panelled door. Many doorways were flanked by columns or pilasters supporting an entablature and sometimes a pediment.

The earliest classical doors comprised two or three square or rectangular panels, then eight or ten and (by the eighteenth century) six. The heavy main front door to a late seventeenth-century house was still constructed of long planks held together with horizontal wooden straps (*ledges*), the six-panelled door with prominent mouldings and elaborately carved hood dating from the early eighteenth century. These were usually at least 1.8 metre high (6 feet) and a minimum of 0.9 metre wide (3 feet) with the top two panels smaller and rectangular (not square, as in many sham-Georgian examples). Often, the bottom two panels were combined and increased in thickness to save that part of the door from wear and tear. In London the excessive use of timber on the frontages of houses was considered a fire risk and was restricted by the 1709 London Building Act so that designs became more restrained and Palladian in style.

Early eighteenth-century doorcases incorporated columns or pilasters supporting flat cornices or elaborate hoods or canopies. From *c*. 1720, glass FANLIGHTS were introduced into these 'temple' Palladian doorcases and by the end of the century fanlights had become complex, with Robert Adam and others using profuse delicate tracery. At this time, and in more fashionable areas, the familiar Georgian doorway and six-panelled door was superseded by wide double doors at the main entrance, surmounted by a florid fanlight. Between 1800 and 1820, the bottom panels were made flush with the framework leaving four raised panels above. From 1832 (when Continental 'plate' glass was introduced by Lucas Chance), decorative and colourful stained glass panels became popular and by 1840 fanlights were no longer fashionable. (Glazed door panels were used in Georgian town houses, but only in doors leading to rear gardens.)

Early eighteenth-century interior doors (always lighter in construction than exterior doors) had obvious and visible fittings (*door furniture*). Hinges and rim locks were fitted to the surface of the door and, because brass fittings were very expensive until the mid-nineteenth century, these and other items of door furniture were usually of black sheet-iron. By 1750, hinges were concealed and mortise locks set into the body of the door, which had to be particularly thick and heavy to accommodate them. The door handles and knockers of exterior doors were considerably smaller than modern 'brass' reproductions and were made of sheet-iron, painted

Eighteenth-century doorcase with shell canopy at Cerne Abbas, Dorset.

black or lead-colour and positioned at the centre of the door. The knocker was of great importance, most bell-pulls dating from the late nineteenth century and electric bells from *c*. 1900. Postmen always knocked twice and other callers had distinctive knocks which must have been familiar to the servants. Letter-boxes and house number first appeared following the introduction of the penny post in *c*. 1840. Early number plates were often oval china plaques on which the figures were painted in black. Locks remained primitive until the mid-nineteenth century, when the rotating Yale lock was introduced. Doors on old houses were always painted except for veneered interior doors. Some eighteenth-century front doors were made from seasoned oak or imported mahogany and waxed but most exterior doors were of close-grained pine, painted in dark colours, 'graining' being introduced in the early nineteenth century. The inter-war period was the last great age of front door design, when 'Sunburst' and other heavily stylized Art Deco motifs were incorporated into glazed panels and the floor-tiling of porches.

DORIC ORDER *see* CLASSICAL ARCHITECTURE

DORMER WINDOW A projecting upright window in a sloping roof, and having its own independent roof.

DORTER In the cloistral buildings of a monastery, the dorter was the first-floor monks' dormitory, usually situated on the south side of the cloister, from which it was reached by means of a *day stair*. A *night stair* lead from the dorter to the transept of the abbey church and it was by this that the monks descended to attend the early offices. The dorter was a long open room, with a series of low windows, probably one for each bed-stead. The concept of privacy (*see* CHIMNEYS) was considered to be an unnecessary luxury in many orders, as was any form of heating in the dormer, but several monastic houses eventually divided the dormitories to form cubicles, and warming houses were sometimes provided in the vicinity of the stair so that the rising heat would give some relief from damp in the dorter above. Adjacent to the dorter, and usually at right-angles to it, was the *reredorter* or 'house of easement' (otherwise known as the *necessarium* or 'necessary house'). This was the monks' privy, usually a long, narrow room furnished with divisions and wooden seats, venting into a channel beneath which was cleansed by flowing water. The lay brothers' dormitory was often located at the opposite side of the cloister or in an entirely separate building. Regrettably, the second storeys of most cloistral buildings were demolished at the Dissolution and few dorters or reredorters have survived.

See also LAVATORIUM *and* MONASTERIES

DOUBLE MONASTERY A religious house for both men and women and having a common superior. The two sexes lived in separate but contiguous establishments and worshipped in distinct parts of the common church.

DOVECOTES (*also* **CULVERY** *and* **DOVECOT**) There is evidence that the Romans obtained fresh protein from birds which nested in tower-like dovecotes similar to those that were introduced into England from Normandy in the eleventh century. Medieval dovecotes are usually square or rectangular free-standing buildings of stone or brick or, from the thirteenth century, cylindrical with a conical roof and 'lantern', through which the pigeons (domesticated rock-doves with an instinct for nesting on cliff faces)

Unusual fourteenth-century domed dovecot at Cotehele, Cornwall.

could come and go as they pleased. The cylindrical shape accommodated a ladder (or pair of ladders) which revolved on central pivots to provide access to the rows of nesting holes that lined the walls. This mechanism, or *potence* (from OE *potent*, meaning 'crutch'), was often so well balanced that it could be turned at the touch of a finger and enabled the culverer to remove the *squabs* (young birds not fully fledged) with a minimum of fuss. The general impression inside a dovecot was of a circular brick wall with alternate bricks removed from floor to roof level. In fact, each hole was larger than two bricks and was several feet deep to provide ample space for roosting and nesting accommodation for the succession of two-egg clutches produced through most of the year. Many cotes contained more than 1,000 nesting holes and with two pigeons and two young to each there could be up to 4,000 birds feeding freely on the tenants' crops! This no doubt accounts for the fact that dovecotes in the medieval period were restricted to DEMESNE and monastic lands, where they represented a significant element in the domestic economy by providing fresh meat and eggs during the winter and a constant supply of droppings (*guano*) which was used as fertilizer.

Later dovecotes were more varied: sometimes octagonal or rectangular with lectern-shaped vents above the roof, as at Willington in Bedfordshire (1538), or simple box-like structures of brick, stone or timber-framing with polygonal roofs and an attractive variety of vented cupolas (*glovers*). At the close of the seventeenth century, there were over 25,000 dovecotes in England and an act of 1761 enabled freeholders and landlords to erect dovecotes and to license their use by tenants. Church towers were occasionally used as pigeon-houses, and many large farms continued to use dovecotes until the introduction of the new turnip husbandry of the eighteenth century provided for the overwintering of cattle. Smaller pigeon-lofts may also be found in the gable ends of domestic and agricultural buildings attached to country houses dating from the eighteenth and nineteenth centuries.

See also FISH-PONDS *and* WARRENS

DOWAGER A woman with property or a title derived from her late husband.

DOWER Originally, a gift from a husband to his bride on the morning of their marriage (*dowry*), but from the twelfth century the term came to mean a portion of an estate (generally one-third) claimed by a widow in her lifetime or until she remarried. Similarly, a residence (often a subsidiary of a larger house) assigned from an estate to a widow for life is a *Dower House*.

See also GAVELKIND

DOWN *see* -DON

DRAGON *see* BEASTS (HERALDIC)

DRAGON BEAM *see* TIMBER-FRAMED BUILDINGS

DRAIN *see* RECLAMATION

DRAINS Today, average water consumption is 227 litres (50 gallons) per person per day, and yet in the last century it was not unusual for children from even the most prosperous families to die of typhoid ('*bowel-fever*') because of the absence of proper water-borne sewage systems. From 1830, various royal commissions and numerous health board inquiries considered the subject but it was not until the 1890s that effective sewage systems and filtration and treatment plants first appeared in urban areas. The Victorians believed that 'filth diseases' were caused by 'drain air' and developed what is known as the 'two-pipe' system to prevent the inhalation of these 'pestilent vapours' via waste

pipes from sinks, wash-basins and baths. Lavatories and slop-sinks were located outside a house or in a separate, well-ventilated compartment well away from any living-room, bedroom or kitchen. These were connected directly to the drain with a vent above the roof-line, but sinks, baths and wash-basins discharged into an open gully (usually located at the rear of the house and known as a *yard gully*) before entering the drain. Before the end of the Second World War, most houses possessed only a kitchen sink and an outside lavatory and the two-pipe system worked with reasonable efficiency. But an increasing demand for upstairs bathrooms required the provision of a *hopperhead* (an open, tapering container), affixed to an outside wall at first-floor level, through which bath and wash-basin water was discharged and piped to the yard gully beneath. The hopperhead was invariably located near a bathroom or bedroom window and therefore produced the very insanitary effect the two-pipe system had been designed to prevent. As a result, a 'single-stack' drainage system was developed in the mid-1940s and, although originally intended for multi-storey buildings, its use is now almost universal. This consists of a single vertical pipe (*stack*) into which all appliances discharge. The system is dependent on effective seals and traps and incorporates a venting mechanism through which accumulated sewer gases may be released. It was not until the 1960s that public health regulations recognized the distinction between 'waste appliances' (baths, etc.) and 'soil appliances' (lavatories, etc.).

See also WATER-CLOSET

DRASHEL *see* THRESHING

DRAWBRIDGE Medieval CASTLES were almost invariably surrounded by a water-filled moat or dry ditch which was spanned by a drawbridge or series of drawbridges. Some of the larger fortifications also included BARBICANS and other outworks (*hornworks*), and these were similarly defended. A variety of mechanisms was used to raise bridges, the least sophisticated comprising a pair of barrel capstans, located in a room above the gates passage, the chains from which passed through slits in the wall to where they were attached to the bridge below. Such a drawbridge pivoted on its inner edge and could be raised slowly to an almost vertical position, thereby providing additional protection to the portal. Another type of drawbridge, a *turning bridge*, pivoted at some distance from its inner edge, the counterpoised rear section revolving into a pit within the floor of the gates passage. The movement, which was finely balanced, was usually controlled from a porter's lodge, constructed within the wall of the gates passage, from which the lowered bridge would be visible through an arrow slit in the outer wall. The mid-fifteenth-century drawbridges in the Yellow Tower of Gwent (the Great Tower of Raglan Castle, now in Monmouthshire) were of a complex type more commonly found in European castles, though simplified versions were in use in Britain in the previous century. This type of bridge was counterpoised at an upper level, with the deck of the bridge suspended by chains from long wooden shafts attached to the counterpoise and projecting horizontally above the bridge when it was lowered. When raised, the beams themselves would be drawn upward through 90° into vertical grooves in the face of the tower and the deck of the bridge seated in a rectangular housing containing the gate arch, thereby ensuring that it was flush with the wall. At Raglan there were two such drawbridges side by side, the larger one for ceremonial occasions and the smaller (raised by a single beam) for daily domestic use.

Many drawbridges were replaced by permanent structures from the late fifteenth century.
See also MOATS

DRAW PIT *see* MARL-PIT

DRIFTWAY *or* **DRIFT** *see* DROVE ROADS

DRINKING FOUNTAINS The Metropolitan Free Drinking Association, founded in 1859 by Samuel Gurney MP, did much to persuade local authorities that they had a duty to provide water at a time when it was considered less hazardous for the working man to drink beer or gin! Even those houses which were supplied by the private companies could expect only an hour's water 'on tap' each day and there was growing public disquiet with regard to the quality of drinking water, which was often polluted and was inevitably blamed for the spread of cholera and typhoid. Commenting on the Great Exhibition of 1851, *Punch* said: 'Whoever can produce in London a glass of water fit to drink will contribute the rarest and most universally useful article in the whole exhibition.' As part of its campaign, the Association erected *public drinking fountains* and granite *water troughs* for livestock, its constitution stipulating that 'no fountain be erected . . . which shall not be constructed as to ensure by filters, or other suitable means, the perfect purity and coldness of the water'. The first of these formidable monuments of Victorian gothic was the fountain set against the wall of St Sepulchre-without-Newgate near the Old

Bailey in London, the commissioning of which attracted huge crowds in 1859. In 1867 the Association became the Metropolitan Drinking Fountain and Cattle Trough Association and is today the Drinking Fountain Association (*see* APPENDIX I), its legacy the thousands of drinking fountains and water troughs throughout Britain, many of which are still in use.
See also PUBLIC UTILITIES

DRIPSTONE *see* HOOD-MOULDING

DRIVING The annual right of a lord of the manor to examine animals pastured on common land to ascertain whether the owners possessed commoners' rights.

DROM-, DROOM- *and* **DRUM-** Place-name element from the Irish and Gaelic *druim* (Welsh *trum*), meaning 'ridge'.
See also DRUMLIN

DRONG A narrow lane or passage between walls or hedges.

DROVE Farm 'droves', identified only on large-scale maps and often prefixed by a personal name (e.g. Cockeram's Drove, Gile's Drove, Ryall's Drove, etc.), have the appearance of narrow, elongated enclosures. On the ground their function may not be immediately apparent, but the map will probably reveal that they provide radial access to a cluster of fields and their purpose was to facilitate the movement of stock. Droves may be wrongly identified as moribund ENCLOSURE ROADS or as MERE LANES.

DROVE ROADS It seems reasonable to assume that nomadic prehistoric communities drove their herds of livestock from one grazing area to another and, in so doing, established a tradition of route-ways, many of which are now somewhat tentatively delineated on Ordnance Survey maps as 'British trackways'. Because of their suitability for the movement of livestock, many of these route-ways enjoyed a singular continuity of use culminating in the first half of the nineteenth century when widespread ENCLOSURES and the advent of a national railway network made long-distance drove roads obsolete. Droving became important during the Middle Ages when flocks were driven long distances from remote monastic granges and the vast sheep pastures created as a consequence of manorial diversification following the BLACK DEATH (*see* DESERTED VILLAGES).

But it was the sixteenth century that witnessed the greatest increase in traffic: rapidly expanding towns and cities, no longer able to depend on their hinterlands for supplies of fresh meat, effectively created a new generation of strategically positioned livestock markets (sometimes rejuvenating otherwise moribund medieval settlements) where drovers sold on their herds for fattening in the surrounding countryside before re-sale to urban slaughter-houses. It was at this time that many of the more isolated areas of upland Britain began to specialize in the commercial production of beef and, to a lesser degree, mutton which necessitated driving animals long distances over difficult terrain to the livestock markets of the north of England and the Welsh Marches. There was also a rapidly developing Scottish trade (some of it of unlawful origin!) well before the accession of James I (VI of Scotland) to the English throne in 1603.

Drove roads became an integral part of the road network and so numerous were drovers in Tudor England that, from 1552, 'badgers of corn, kidders [of goats] and drovers of cattle' were registered and licensed annually by QUARTER SESSIONS: stability and maturity were essential qualifications, for a drover had to be a married householder and at least thirty years of age. (Registration remained obligatory until 1772.) As a result of this legislation, the licensed drover came to enjoy a professional reputation for integrity which often enabled him to assume the rôle of travelling banker. Cattle worth £500 'on the hoof' was universally recognized as an extremely effective (and secure) method of transferring money. Drovers and their clients often dealt in promissory notes or bills of exchange which were circulated as bank notes are today but, because they were accepted only from reliable clients or their accredited agents, were worthless if they were stolen or fell into the wrong hands. The Black Ox Bank of Llandovery was founded in this way by a Welsh drover, David Jones, whose promissory notes were engraved with a black ox. (The bank became a subsidiary of Lloyd's in 1909, in whose famous black horse device the drovers' 'banks' are commemorated.) Not all drovers were as reliable as David Jones, however, and legislation, introduced at the beginning of the eighteenth century, prevented a drover from declaring himself bankrupt in order to avoid his financial obligations.

Drovers often worked in teams, dividing herds of up to 200 cattle or flocks of 2,000 sheep into smaller units of 50 cattle or 500 sheep, each the responsibility of a single drover and his dogs. The beasts were driven in long columns (cattle from the Scottish islands had to swim to the mainland), travelling about 19 km (12 miles) a day to pre-arranged grazing areas, often inns with adjacent pasture. In the early nineteenth century, drovers received between 3s and 4s a day, which was about twice the wage of a farm labourer, and 10s for the return journey. From this, expenses had to be paid including 9d for winter lodgings, 5d in summer. Cattle had to be shod at a cost of 1s for a complete set of eight *cues* (crescent-shaped shoes): each cloven hoof required two. Sheep were not shod but geese (driven from East Anglia to London for the Christmas markets) had to endure the indignity of a coating of sawdust, sand and tar known as 'stick-a-sole'.

A drove of 200 cattle would raise between 2s and 5s per head in the early years of the nineteenth century, depending on the state of the market and the condition of the beasts. Like other networks, the drove roads comprised a complex system of short-, medium- and long-distance routes which developed and were adapted in response to local and national circumstances appertaining at a particular time. It is estimated that at the height of this trade, at the beginning of the nineteenth century, more than 100,000 cattle were driven south from Scotland in a single year. Highland herds were brought in to *trysts* or gathering grounds in the Lowlands from where they were driven across the border and down the Pennines to centres such as Malham or Hawes in Yorkshire. Here they were bought for fattening by English graziers and driven south once more to the markets of the Midlands and the Home Counties. Similarly, Welsh cattle were driven to markets on the English border, such as Shrewsbury and Craven Arms in Shropshire (the latter still a major livestock market), or further into England to the markets at crossing places on the River Severn, such as Bewdley in Worcestershire and Tewkesbury in Gloucestershire, and even as far as the great cattle fair at Barnet, on the northern periphery of London. Despite the proliferation of the railways, the Scottish trade continued well into the 1880s, and the famous October cattle fair at Bullock Hill, Horsham St Faith in Norfolk survived until 1778.

Drovers were such a familiar element of rural life that their activities and routes are largely unrecorded, and there is a surprising paucity of documentation relating to financial transactions other than those of the drovers' 'banks'. Today, former drove roads are often difficult to recognize in the confusion of bridle-paths and green lanes that lattice the countryside. In some areas, such roads (known as *drifts* or *driftways* in the eastern counties of England) may appear to run contrary to local patterns: on the Pennines, for example, the old drove roads run from north to south while the local market routes cut diagonally across the hills. Many upland drove roads were delineated by ENCLOSURE walls constructed in the eighteenth and nineteenth centuries, and in the lowlands similar hedge-lined roads with wide grazing verges *may* have been drove roads, but not necessarily so. Others may be identified from the Ordnance Survey map, where name elements such as 'drift', 'drove', 'ox' and 'sheep' are usually reliable indicators; and on the Cotswolds, the Welsh Way threads its unerring course from the Severn to the south-east. Sewstern Lane (known locally as the 'Drift') was a celebrated drove road, used predominantly by Scottish drovers, which followed the Leicestershire-Lincolnshire border south into the Midlands. Not all routes identified as drove roads on maps were of the long-distance variety: many were used by local shepherds or herdsmen when driving their livestock to regional fairs or markets (*see also* DROVE).

From the seventeenth century, West Country ports were used increasingly for the import of cattle and sheep both from Ireland and Wales, and towards the end of the century the Old Passage crossing of the river Severn (between Beachley and Aust and now in the shadow of the Severn Bridge) was revived: 8*d* being charged for a horse, 4*d* for a man, woman, child or beast, and 2*s* a score (20) for sheep. A bold inscription on the wall of the seventeenth-century 'Drover's House' on the west bank of the river Test near Stockbridge in Hampshire still announces: *Gwair tymherus porfa flasus cwrw da a gwal cysurus.* To the Welsh drover, *en route* to the Home Counties, the prospect of 'Fine hay, sweet pasture, good ale and a comfortable bed' must have been welcome indeed! The names of other (usually remote) wayside inns, such as 'The Scotsman's Pack' and 'The Eight Shoes', suggest that they were formerly drovers' inns. Invariably, the drovers preferred the ancient ridgeways and upland routes that were free of settlements, tolls, vehicles, crops and other constrictions. Such routes were sometimes waymarked by small clumps of trees, especially Scots pines, and their local names often remain even after the trees have gone. Because of the nature of their traffic, drove roads are usually very much wider than contemporary PACK-HORSE ROADS.

DRUIDISM An esoteric Celtic priesthood in Gaul, Britain and Ireland. Current perceptions of the Druids are based almost entirely on a brief canon of classical literature comprising no more than twenty references, chiefly in the *De Bello Gallico* of Julius Caesar (100–44 BC) and the equally hostile *Annals* of the Roman historian Tacitus (*b.* AD 56). Caesar states that the Druids originated in Britain and that they combined judicial and priestly functions, enjoyed a reputation for natural philosophy and astronomy and were charged with the education of young Gaulish noblemen, which they achieved by means of oral poetry. We are told that they propounded the transmigration of souls, sacrificed murderers, worshipped in forest clearings (*groves*) and believed in the sanctity of MISTLETOE which was removed with a golden sickle when discovered (as it rarely is) growing from an OAK, which they also sanctified. Tacitus records the slaughter of the Druids of Anglesey in AD 60 and the symbolic clearance of their ancient groves. Indeed, Roman suppression of Druidism was ferocious and unrelenting and clearly suggests that it was perceived as a potential focus for opposition to Roman rule. Druidism is evident in the pre-Christian Irish sagas and even then appears to have contained elements of older, pagan faiths. By the end of the seventeenth century, Druidism had become synonymous with DOLMENS, STANDING STONES and HENGES. If a site was clearly of ancient origin and possessed of no apparent rationale, the Druids provided the answer. Contemporary antiquaries considered Stonehenge and Avebury in Wiltshire to have been Druidical temples and all CROMLECHS sacrificial altars. Such notions of 'Druidical remains' linger even today – despite the fact that the Druids belonged to the Celtic period and antedate by many centuries the megaliths with which they were erroneously associated.

DRUM TOWER *see* CASTLES (MEDIEVAL)

DRYSTONE WALLS The craft of drystone walling (in which no mortar is used) is both ancient and unchanging. On the stone-littered hillsides of upland Britain, drystone walls provided convenient repositories for debris as it was cleared to facilitate grazing. Many early 'walls' were little more than heaped accumulations of stones known as *consumption dykes* (*see also* CLEARANCE CAIRNS *and* REAVES) but many were constructed according to principles which were as valid in the Neolithic period as they are today.

The first principle of drystone walling is that each stone 'does its duty by its neighbour': it should be placed in exactly the right position so that it secures adjacent stones and is secured by them. The waller (or, in Scotland, *dyker*) was established as a skilled profession as a consequence of the early eighteenth-century Enclosure Acts (*see* ENCLOSURES) and most of the stone walls of the north of England, Wales and Scotland date from this period. In mountainous areas and hill country thin soils, often severe climatic conditions and an abundance of freely available building materials dictated the construction of walled enclosures, whereas in the lowlands hedgerows predominate (though there are notable exceptions, as in Northamptonshire where there is a reliable source of local stone). Enclosure walls of this period are almost invariably straight whereas those of earlier enclosures tend to be less regular.

The form and dimensions of drystone walls are subject to periodic and regional variation but the method of construction has hardly changed over the centuries. Most are '*battered*' so that, by selecting slightly smaller stones as the height of the wall increases, they are significantly broader at the base than at the top, and conform to the traditional wooden 'A' frame used as a sectional template by some builders who are able to construct 6 metres (20 feet) of wall in a day. The intended path of the wall is first delineated with pegs and lines and the stones deposited on either side to assist selection. A foundation trench is dug, usually about 15 cm in depth (6 inches), and this is filled and compacted with small stones. A double row of *foundation* stones is then laid, each with its long face at right angles to the line of the trench, giving a thickness at the base of about 0.6 metres (2 feet). The cavity is filled with small, carefully arranged 'heart stones', and layers of building and heart stones are then added to a height of about 0.6 metres (2 feet) at which point a 'through band' of long stones is inserted, each spanning the cavity and locking the wall together. Above this, the wall is built to the required height, often with additional 'through bands' if the wall is particularly tall. The top of the wall, which is usually 30 to 38 cm wide (12 to 15 inches), is secured with a 'cover band', similar to the 'through band', on top of which vertical interlocking coping stones (*combers* or *copestones*) are set at right angles to the line of the wall. These provide the downward thrust necessary to secure the effective geometry of the wall and on steep hillsides the work of a skilled waller will be evident in the way in which both horizontal building stones and vertical coping stones are set to compensate for the gradient rather than running with it.

In Scotland, a device known as a 'sunk fence' or 'Galloway hedge' was used to deter the agile Highland sheep from jumping over a wall. Lengths of thorn, inserted horizontally into a wall about 30 cm (1 foot) above the base, were covered with earth on the upper side of the wall and encouraged to take root, thereby providing an impenetrable barrier of thorn on the lower side. The 'Galloway dyke' was a similar means of deterring sheep who were (apparently) disconcerted by the unstable appearance of a 20-metre high wall (6½ feet), the upper portion of which was deliberately constructed with large gaps between lateral securing stones.

Each region of Britain has its own tradition of drystone walling: COTSWOLD walls are precise and uniform because of the remarkable regularity of the easily split oolitic limestone, and the walls of Snowdonia hill farms are invariably constructed of Welsh slate. With the exception of several eighteenth-century Enclosure walls, the dimensions of which were specified in legislation, drystone walls are notoriously difficult to date and may have been repaired or plundered over many centuries.

See also ORTHOSTAT WALLS *and* RING GARTH
For Dry Stone Walling Association of Great Britain *see* APPENDIX I

DUCIS Latinized place-name element meaning 'of the duke', usually indicative that a manor was once ducal property, as at Collingbourne Ducis in Wiltshire (*see* LATIN).

DUCKING STOOL A punishment, usually reserved for scolding women and dishonest tradespeople, by which the victim was harnessed in a makeshift seat at the end of a pole and immersed several times in a convenient pond or river. The last recorded use of a ducking stool in England was at Leominster in 1809 when one Jenny Pipes was paraded through the town and ducked in the river near Kenwater Bridge. The Leominster ducking stool was provided with wheels and was so large that it had to be kept in the priory church, where it may still be seen today.

DUELLING From the archaic Latin *duellum*, meaning 'war', single one-to-one combat was a generally accepted legal means of settling disputes throughout medieval Europe. Culturally, the nobility claimed the right to defend their honour by means of a duel. A knight could throw down his gage (a personal item such as a glove or hat) as a token of defiance and demand combat with an accuser. The challenge was accepted when the gage was picked up. The medieval and Tudor tournament was effectively a duel but without the judicial element.

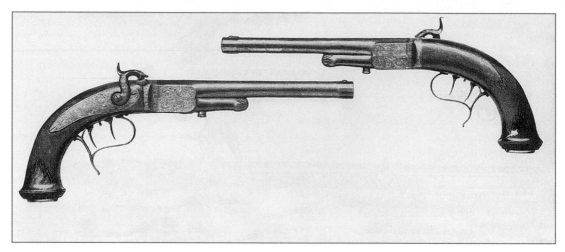

Viennese duelling pistols, 1800.

Although duelling remained the traditional means of defending one's honour (especially among military men), by the eighteenth century it had become an essentially private affair, usually conducted at dawn in the presence of no more than two witnesses ('seconds'). Duelling with deadly weapons became a criminal offence in 1818.

DUKE The most senior rank of the British peerage. Derived from the Latin *dux*, meaning 'leader'. The rank was introduced in England in 1337 although the style had been known before that date, the Conqueror being referred to as *Ducis Normannorum et Regis Anglorum*, for example.

DUN- *see* **DON-**

DUNS In Scotland, fortified homesteads dating from *c.* 600 BC but frequently occupied (and possibly modified) until a much later date. Circular or elliptical, with a diameter of 12 to 15 metres (40 to 50 feet), duns were constructed with immensely thick drystone walls, which were sometimes galleried, and were entered by means of a heavily defended doorway. Lean-to timber buildings were erected against the inner face of the wall. Duns were usually located on easily defended prominences or headlands, especially on the western coast.

DURHAM (COUNTY) *see* PALATINATE

DUX BRITANNIARUM *see* ROMAN FORTS AND CAMPS

DYKES A dyke (*or* dike) is a linear earthwork comprising at least one complementary ditch and bank. Short sections of dyke are indicated by the term *Cross Dyke* on Ordnance Survey maps: otherwise, a local name is usually given. There are comparatively few dykes dating from the Neolithic period. These are usually evident as CROP MARKS in aerial photographs and their function has remained singularly obscure. Others date from the late Bronze and Iron Ages, notably those on the chalk downlands of Wessex, and from the centuries of the Roman occupation through the so-called Dark Ages to the Norman period. Inevitably, in many areas these earthworks present a confusing lattice-work of varying dates and functions, both on the map and in the field, often compounded by a corresponding ubiquity of hill forts, barrows, tumuli, Roman AGGERS and derelict CAUSEWAYS.

On the south-eastern fringe of Cranborne Chase on the Dorset-Wiltshire-Hampshire borders, for example, a number of lengths of dyke known as Grim's Ditch intersect other more substantial dykes known locally as the Dorset Cursus, Bokerley Ditch and Ackling Dyke. The 10 km (6 miles) Dorset Cursus is of Neolithic origin, of unknown function and identified only as crop marks (*see* CURSUS), while the numerous sections of Grim's Ditch date from the late Bronze Age and were probably extensive livestock enclosures (known as 'ranch boundaries') which may also have served as territorial boundaries (*see* GRIM). These enclosure dykes were originally about 3 metres wide (10 feet) and 1.8 metre deep (6 feet) but many have been ploughed out leaving only segmented remains. Ackling Dyke is the impressive Roman agger of the road that once drove straight across the downs south-west from Sorviodunum (Old Sarum) to Durnovaria (Dorchester), while cutting across it, and completely blocking both the road and the miles of open downland on either side, is the 9.6 km (6 miles) length of Bokerley Ditch, a massive defensive dyke, built in *c.* 367 by the Romano-Britons in anticipation of almost inevitable incursions from the east. Bokerley was subsequently dismantled and the Roman road re-opened, but it was later refurbished and for nearly two centuries remained the main line of defence against Saxon invasion. Of far greater sophistication are Roman military structures such as Hadrian's Wall and the Antonine Wall (*see* ROMAN FORTS AND CAMPS).

The finest post-Roman linear earthwork is Offa's Dyke, constructed during the reign of Offa of Mercia (AD 757–96) to mark the 195 km (122 miles) frontier established by his wars with the Welsh. Like many of these later dykes, Offa's was an intermittent earthwork, relying on the terrain to provide a natural boundary for much of its length, with substantial segments of dyke filling the 'gaps'. Shorter, but visually more impressive, are the 11 km (7 miles) length of Devil's Dyke on Newmarket Heath in Cambridgeshire, which has a height of 9 metres (30 feet), and the parallel Fleam Dyke, south-east of Cambridge. Although of uncertain date, it seems likely that both dykes were constructed as part of a defensive system designed to prevent Mercian incursions along the Icknield Way, which they cross at right angles. The 11 km (7 miles) West Wansdyke (from *Wodnes dic* = 'dyke of the god Woden') in Somerset and the 24 km (15 miles) East Wansdyke in Wiltshire are believed to date from the same Dark Age period as the Cambridgeshire dykes and probably served a similar territorial function, the West Dyke being built across the Fosse Way.

What all these dykes appear to have in common is a territorial function that is evident even in the apparently agrarian Bronze Age ranch boundaries. In all cases, the ditch is on the *outside* of the embankment: that of the Antonine Wall was 12 metres wide (40 feet) and 3.6 metres deep (12 feet) and was clearly intended for defensive purposes. However, as even the Romans discovered, such immense earthworks could not be defended throughout their entire length and they were probably intended as 'passive' or symbolic defences, the ditch being an unambiguous declaration of territorial demarcation: anyone crossing the dyke from 'outside' did so knowingly and would be expected to face the consequences of his trespass. Of course, short sections of dyke could be defended, especially against cavalry, and they also prevented (or at least deterred) the wholesale rustling of livestock. Dating and function may be difficult to determine, but the immense achievement of the men who built these ancient dykes cannot be denied. They represent an extraordinary degree of organizational skill and corporate energy: and a singular commitment to a fiercely territorial society.
For irrigation dikes *see* RECLAMATION

E

EAGLE The eagle was the standard of the Roman legion. In ARMORY it is considered to be pre-eminent among the birds, and Charlemagne is said to have adopted an eagle as his device when he was crowned Holy Roman Emperor in AD 800. In the Christian Church, the four beasts 'round about the throne' (Revelation Ch. 4, vv. 6–7) represent the four evangelists and of these the fourth, 'like a flying eagle', symbolizes St John the Evangelist. Until recently, lecterns in the form of eagles were to be found in nearly every church: with wings open as in flight they carried forth the Word and the Light of the Gospel. The eagle's suitability for such a task is explained in the medieval *Book of Beasts*: 'When the eagle grows old and his wings become heavy and his eyes become darkened with a mist, then he goes in search of a fountain, and, over against it, he flies up to the height of heaven, even into the circle of the sun [symbolizing Christ], and there he singes his wings and at the same time evaporates the fog of his eyes in a ray of the sun. Then at length taking a header down into the fountain, he dips himself three times in it, and instantly he is renewed with a great vigour of plumage and splendour of vision.' (Trans. T.H. White, London, 1954)
See also CHRISTIAN SYMBOLS *and* LION

EAGRE *or* **BORE** From the Old English *āegor*, meaning 'flood tide' ('bore' derives from the Scandinavian *bara*, meaning 'billow'), eagres are a phenomenon of several British rivers and have inevitably influenced settlement patterns on their banks. An eagre is a high, steep-fronted wave that occurs when two tides meet or when a spring flood tide rushes up a narrowing estuary. The best known is that of the river Severn, which occurs on about twenty-five days of the year, impelled by the high equinoctial tides. Settlements on the flood plains of such rivers are invariably located on slight eminences, as are farmsteads, which may be surrounded by earthen embankments as an additional precaution against the highest eagres, which occur perhaps once or twice a year.

EALDORMAN Prior to the Conquest, a high-ranking royal official responsible for civil matters at shire courts and the king's chief representative in a county. After the Conquest, the duties and responsibilities of the ealdorman were transferred to the office of SHERIFF. *See also* ALDERMAN, EARL *and* KINGDOMS (ANCIENT)

EARL The third rank in the British peerage, the title 'earl' (which is quite different from the Saxon *ealdorman*) originated in Scandinavia and appeared in England in the time of Canute as an English form of *jarl*. It is the oldest English title and rank, and was the highest until 1337 when the Black Prince was created a duke. The earliest know charter creating an hereditary earl is that of *c*. 1140, by which King Stephen created Geoffrey de Mandeville Earl of Essex.

EARL MARSHAL The great officer of state responsible for state ceremonies (though not 'royal' occasions such as weddings) and hereditary judge of the Court of Chivalry (*see* CHIVALRY, HIGH COURT OF). He has jurisdiction over the officers of arms and matters of heraldry, honour and precedence. The title was originally *Marshal* but is now Earl Marshal and Hereditary Marshal of England, and is vested in the Duke of Norfolk.

EARLY ENGLISH *see* GOTHIC ARCHITECTURE

EARTH HOUSE *see* SOUTERRAIN

EARTHQUAKE Most British earthquakes are caused by movements along geological faults, and are far more frequent than is often imagined: some 1,500 have been recorded since the tenth century. The *Anglo Saxon Chronicles* make mention of a number of 'earthquakes', including one at Michaelmas in 1119 'at some places here in this land, though greatest in Gloucestershire and Herefordshire . . .', presumably along the Malvern

Fault. In 1185 Lincoln Cathedral was damaged by an earth tremor and in 1248 part of the vault was brought down at Wells Cathedral. The most severe British earthquake on record was in the vicinity of Colchester in 1884 when more than 1,200 buildings were damaged, including twenty churches. In 1896 a tremor in the Hereford area was felt over 150 miles away. Other than possible structural damage, which is generally confined to the epicentre, the usual effect of an earthquake is similar to that of an aeroplane breaking the sound barrier, and this may be accompanied by shock waves lasting between 4 and 7 seconds.

EAST ANGLIA *see* KINGDOMS (ANCIENT)

EASTER DUES Cash collected at Easter services for the benefit of an incumbent.

EASTER SEPULCHRE In a number of churches, evidence remains of an Easter sepulchre which was located on the north side of the altar, usually in the sanctuary. It was here that the Blessed Sacrament was kept from Good Friday to early on Easter Sunday when it was returned to the altar with considerable ceremony. The sepulchre at St Mary Redcliffe, Bristol, is said to have included a representation of Heaven '. . . made of Stained clothes' and of Hell '. . . made of timber and ironwork thereto, with Divels to the number of 13.' At the parish church of All Hallows at Sherborne, Dorset (which was dismantled when the town acquired the adjoining abbey church), watchmen were employed to guard the Easter Sepulchre and were provided with ale and a brazier to keep them warm. Most sepulchres were temporary structures, though several richly carved examples in stone have survived (mostly from the fourteenth century), notably those at Hawton, Nottinghamshire; Ledbury, Herefordshire; Northwold, Norfolk; Patrington, Yorkshire; and Heckington and Navenby in Lincolnshire. Carving usually depicts the Resurrection and, above, the Ascension. The lovely early sixteenth-century Easter Sepulchre at Tarrant Hinton, Dorset, is enscribed with the words *Venire et Videte Locum Ubi Positus erat Dominus* ('come and see the place where the Lord lay').

EAU *see* RECLAMATION

ECCLESIASTICAL BUILDINGS *see* CATHEDRALS, CHURCHES, DISSENTING CHAPELS *and* MONASTERIES

ECCLESIASTICAL TAXATION RECORDS
Many ecclesiastical taxation records in the Public Record Office have been published, notably those for the thirteenth, fourteenth and sixteenth centuries. These include *Taxatio Ecclesiastica Angliae at Walliae, auctoritate Papae Nicholai V* of *c.* 1291, a comprehensive record of medieval benefices (published 1802); *Nonarum Inquisitions in Curia Scaccarii*, which relates to a tax of 1341 (published in 1807); and the *Valor Ecclesiasticus, temp Henrici VIII, auctoritate regia institatus* of 1534, which was a survey of all ecclesiastical property in England immediately before the Reformation (published in six volumes from 1810 to 1834) (*see* DOCUMENTARY RECORDS).

EDDISH (*also* **ETCH**) An enclosure.

EDUCATION The ancient medieval universities of Oxford, Cambridge, St Andrews, Glasgow and Aberdeen (King's College) were ecclesiastical establishments subject to international papal authority. The early universities were not a perquisite of the medieval establishment, indeed a university education was one of the few means by which the sons of commoners, or even of aspiring peasants, could rise to eminence. Most students were aged between fifteen and nineteen and few teachers were over thirty. Today's gowns and hoods originated in the academic dress of the medieval universities where students were considered to be clerics and had their heads shaved in the style of a monk. Oxford, the earliest university, is first mentioned in 1184, though it is likely that its foundation dates from the period 1164–9 when access to the university in Paris was disrupted during Henry II's conflict with Becket. It was enlarged by the FRIARS in the 1220s (with the support of Parisian students), and the first colleges (Balliol, Merton and University) were founded in the second half of the century. The curriculum was based on the *Quadrivium* (arithmetic, geometry, astronomy and music) which, together with the lesser *Trivium* (rhetoric, grammar and logic), formed the 'seven liberal arts', all of which were taught in Latin. Medieval scholastic life was dominated by three apparently contradictory features: academic commitment and creativity, bureaucratic repression and sporadic lawlessness.

'Moral Order' – marching into assembly at Thomas Street School, Limehouse, in 1908.

The intellectual achievement of such Oxford scholars as Robert Grosseteste (b. *c.* 1175), Roger Bacon (1214–92) and John Wycliffe (*c.* 1330–84) was considerable, but all five universities earned a certain notoriety for petty regulation and were often viciously repressive. In the early fifteenth century, a master of St Andrews, who rejoiced in the office of Inquisitor of Heretical Depravity, ordered one of his scholars to be burned alive for his heretical views. At Aberdeen, women were not admitted to the university precincts, the students themselves were not permitted to leave without permission and all conversation had to be conducted in Latin. At Cambridge, students were forbidden from visiting the town's alehouses (and were so until 1940) and the university's regulations were enforced by Proctors' Constables who, in the Middle Ages, were armed with pikes (*halberds*),which still feature in university ceremonial. It is hardly surprising that such repressive measures provoked an excessive response from the students. In 1445 Godstow Nunnery near Oxford was apparently a favourite student brothel, and rioting, usually between 'town and gown', was endemic throughout the Middle Ages.

Following the DISSOLUTION OF THE MONASTERIES in 1536–9, monastic grammar and song schools were displaced, together with the small schools that were sometimes attached to medieval CHANTRIES. Their purpose had been the training of priests, and rote learning, particularly of Latin, grammar and music, predominated. The grammar schools by which they were replaced continued to teach in Latin, but there was a greater emphasis on analysis and on an understanding of Classical literature, science and theology, which were at that time considered to be the fount of learning. The contemporary development of printing meant that books were more readily available, though usually only for the preceptor's use, and paper also, so that the boys were able to keep journals or 'common place books' in which extracts from the texts were carefully copied and indexed. The purpose of the 'new' secular grammar schools was to provide the sons of the emerging middle class with a suitable career.

With the decline of the Church, the governance of late Tudor and Stuart England was increasingly the concern of secular administrators, drawn from the swelling ranks of well-educated young men. Latin not only continued as a necessary adjunct to the study of mathematics, medicine and the law, but was also the European language of diplomacy and trade, and Classical literature provided many of the precepts for political life. Nevertheless, stimulated by the introduction of an English bible and prayer book, the use of the English language, both in administration and in business, was increasing rapidly. Many of these sixteenth-century educational foundations remain today and are often known as the King's or Queen's school – Henry VIII's School, King Edward's School and so on. Such appellations do not necessarily imply that they were founded by the sovereign whose name they bear or, indeed, during that sovereign's reign. Many, including the majority of cathedral schools, were re-foundations of earlier monastic or chantry schools: King's School at Sherborne in Dorset, for example, was reputedly founded by St Aldhelm, the first Bishop of Sherborne (d.709), and reconstituted in 1550 during the reign of Edward VI. The royal assent was sometimes required in order that the original foundation should be reconstituted, but in the majority of cases schools were re-established through public subscription or the commitment of a local benefactor. In order to maintain an orthodoxy of religious instruction, all teachers were required to be registered through the established Church. Nevertheless, there were undoubtedly numerous small local schools in which boys learned the basics of reading, writing and numeracy and for which few records remain. The Society for the Propagation of Christian Knowledge (SPCK) was founded in 1698 to provide for the spiritual and educational needs of industrial communities, and by 1750 there were some 1,500 schools for the poor, precursors of the Victorian charity schools, supported through voluntary subscriptions. But education was not compulsory and was certainly not considered to be necessary for girls or for the sons of the lower orders of society. Despite its limitations, the system clearly provided for the needs of an increasingly complex society and continued to do so until the end of the nineteenth century.

The growth of secular education following the Reformation was reflected, briefly, in the creation of several new colleges at Oxford and Cambridge and in Scotland; however, the ancient English universities were generally perceived as Anglican institutions, especially following the Acts of Uniformity in 1559 and 1662, and, consequently, declined in popularity. Teaching was stereotyped and traditional, and collegiate life more social than academic. Several medical colleges were established in London and a number of 'dissenting academies', but serious scholars turned to the European and Scottish universities, which benefited from the English malaise, and to the new university foundation of Trinity College in Dublin (1591). Despite a significant increase in population during the late sixteenth and early seventeenth centuries, there were only seven major universities in the British Isles: four in Scotland, two in England and one in Ireland.

Universal education slowly evolved during the Victorian era (1837–1901). In the mid-nineteenth century the sons of the upper classes usually received private tuition or attended one of the old public schools which had originally been founded to provide educational opportunities for the poor. The girls were often sent to small private schools or were taught at home by governesses. Most public and grammar schools of the period were even then considered to be archaic, both in their ethos and their methods, and singularly out of tune with the general tenor of Victorian philanthropy. Nevertheless, a few notable headmasters, such as Thomas Arnold at Rugby School, both propounded and practised an educational philosophy which was emulated by his more enlightened colleagues and was to serve as a model for the later grammar schools. Smaller residential private schools, the bedrock of the Victorian middle classes, were both ubiquitous and variable, the worst being soulless institutions in which children were condemned to a life of misery and degradation. There were also numerous private *common day schools* which provided low-fee elementary education for poor children. These included the *dame schools*, elementary schools run by women, at which the fees were 3*d* or 4*d* a day. An act of 1833 required that children in employment should also receive a basic education and several factory schools were established for this purpose. From 1844, the Poor Law Commissioners were empowered to send WORKHOUSE children to district schools, which were sufficiently large to meet the educational needs of a group of workhouses. Many schools were provided by charitable organizations such as the nonconformist British and Foreign School Society (founded 1808) which adopted a *monitorial system* by which older children (who were themselves sometimes as young as eleven) taught groups of younger ones, supervised by paid teachers. By 1851, the National Society for the Education of the Poor in the Principles of the Established Church (founded 1811) controlled over 17,000 'national schools'. From 1824, both the *British Schools* (non-conformist) and the *National Schools* (conformist) received substantial government aid. Some of the best 'charity schools' were to be found in rural areas, endowed by local congregations or benevolent landowners.

Education was not compulsory, however, and there was as yet no requirement that teachers should be trained or registered. In the heavily populated urban areas, where poverty and squalor were endemic, educational provision remained sadly neglected, though the Quakers established schools (for children and adults) in some industrial areas. From 1833, state grants for school building were available through the churches but were ineffective, principally because of inter-denominational intolerance. Consequently, educational opportunity in Britain was singularly inferior to that of mid-nineteenth-century France, Holland or Germany, despite the entreaties of many enlightened educationists and a significant body of scientists and industrialists who realized that, despite the euphoria of the new Victorian age, Britain's prosperity could not be maintained if the majority of the populace remained illiterate and uneducated. Some advances in the training of teachers and the building of

The gatehouse at Sherborne School, Dorset. Known locally as the 'King's School', Sherborne was re-founded in 1550 when, after the Reformation, the Government was looking for new schools to teach Protestantism and loyalty to the Crown, replacing the education system which had previously been provided by the monks of Sherborne Abbey.

schools were made in the 1860s, though the Revised Code of 1862 was attacked (by Matthew Arnold among others) for weakening the tenure and status of pupil teachers who were now employed and paid by school managers instead of being apprenticed. Consequently, many young girls, for whom a career in teaching was the only alternative to domestic service, faced both arbitrary dismissal and the ruination of their careers for trivial causes. At this time, a three-year period as a pupil teacher, together with an 'unblemished' character and success in an entrance examination, were necessary qualifications for admission to a two-year course at a teacher training college. For those who could survive the harsh disciplinary regimes of such colleges, the future was bright. A newly qualified teacher in the 1860s could earn as much as £100 a year or more – sufficient to lift the sons and daughters of labouring families into an entirely different social bracket from that of their parents. Advancement was dependent both on the support of patrons and managers and on the recommendations of HM Inspectorate of Schools, whose ubiquitous delvings into log books, punishment books and registers and relentless testing of rote learning must have been a mortifying experience for many young teachers.

It was not until W.E. Forster's Act of 1870 that educational opportunities became freely available. Forster was a Quaker and an enthusiastic educationist who became Vice-President of the Education Department in 1868. As a result of the Act, church schools continued to receive state funding and throughout the country district boards of education were established to provide *elementary schools* and free education for those children whose parents were unable to pay. These *board schools* were secular and undenominational, and were often resented by the voluntary schools which were obliged to provide adequate schooling or face being taken over by a local board. In consequence, the number of church schools built in the six months following the Act was enormous. In 1876 legislation established the principle that all children should receive elementary education and the 1880 Education Act required attendance at school between the ages of five and ten. At that age, a child could obtain a certificate which enabled him to leave school – but only if his attendance had been satisfactory. Legislation of 1891 provided for free elementary education and by the turn of the century the school-leaving age had been raised to twelve. Secondary and higher education were not provided for, however, until the Balfour Education Act of 1902 abolished the school boards and conveyed

responsibility for both phases of elementary education to county and borough councils through the provision of *council schools*. Later, the 1918 Education Act raised the school-leaving age to fourteen and replaced the elementary schools, which provided for children between the ages of seven and fourteen, with separate junior schools (7 to 11) and senior schools (11 to 14), though these were not common until after 1926. All elementary schools, whether primary, senior or all-age, had boards of managers, while grammar schools had governors. (This distinction survived until the 1980 Education Act: all English and Welsh schools now have governors which include a number of elected parents.)

The industrial and economic prosperity of late Victorian and Edwardian Britain, and her growing status as an international power, are reflected in the founding of a large number of new universities and colleges, particularly at the turn of the century when many 'red brick' universities were established in industrial cities such as Manchester (1895), Birmingham (1900), Leeds (1904) and Sheffield (1905).

Educational provision in the nineteenth century may indeed have been inequitable and diverse, but the system by which it was succeeded was to establish standards by which others were assessed. In the decades following the 1944 Butler Education Act, English primary education became pre-eminent, though the selective secondary system of separate grammar, technical and modern schools was less successful. Efforts to replace these with comprehensive schools, which provided educational opportunities for children of varying aptitudes and abilities, often foundered on the rocks of political intolerance. Consequently, comprehensive education was never adequately funded and schools were too often styled not on the highly successful primary model, but on the conventional secondary school which they were intended to displace. From 1944, there developed, in different local education authorities (LEAs), a bewildering mixture of infant (5 to 7), junior (7 to 11) or primary schools (5 to 11) and senior schools (11 to 16 comprehensives, sometimes with a sixth form, secondary modern, bi-lateral, technical or grammar schools), together with sixth-form colleges, community and tertiary colleges, colleges of further education, polytechnics and (particularly in the 1960s) a number of new universities such as Essex (1963), Newcastle (1963), Surrey (1966) and York (1963). In addition, a number of LEAs reorganized their schools following the 1964 Education Act into what is known as the tripartite system of first (5 to 8/9), middle (8/9 to 12/13) and high schools (12/13 to 16, sometimes with a sixth form).

Terminology is equally complex. *Maintained schools* are those which are maintained by LEAs and include both county and voluntary schools. *County schools* are provided by the LEA and *voluntary schools* by a voluntary body which may be a religious denomination or educational trust. *Aided schools* are voluntary schools in which the majority of the governing body comprises foundation governors whose particular duty is to ensure that the school is conducted according to the terms of the trust deed. Aided school governors employ the teachers and ancillary staff (though they are paid by the LEA) and are responsible for the exterior maintenance and repair of the school buildings. *Controlled schools* are voluntary schools in which the governing body has been unable (or unwilling) to accept the financial responsibilities of aided status.

The 1988 Education Reform Act purported to improve educational standards by the introduction of a prescriptive national curriculum and assessment, and by increasing significantly the powers and responsibilities of governing bodies. It also allowed schools the opportunity to 'opt out' of local education authority control (to become Direct Grant schools) and transferred responsibility for a school's finances and the appointment or dismissal of teachers to its governors.

The records of the charitable organizations mentioned above (many of which still function) provide an extraordinarily detailed source of information, as do the statutory log books, punishment books and governors' minute books which are held by all schools. Log books, compiled by head teachers, include inspectors' reports and details of day-to-day occurrences: absences for 'getting in the potato harvest' or 'the School closed for Pack Monday Fair at Sherborne . . .', sad tales of war-time evacuees and orphans, and visits by the 'nits nurse' to check for head-lice (still a recurring problem in many schools). The maintenance of a punishment book was compulsory until the abolition of corporal punishment in 1988. Therein are the harsh realities of school life:

> 1913 April 28th: Mafeking and Sebastopol Cawley ages 10 and 12: Making great noise in the Boys' Lobby during dinner hour of a wet day. These boys were leaning against the door and when teacher opened the door they both fell down and evidently seemed to think it fine amusement. The teacher was not going to countenance this kind of behaviour. 3 stripes each on the hand and 1 on the back. . . . Cawley was cheeky.

See also SUNDAY SCHOOLS
For the History of Education Society *see* APPENDIX I

EFFIGIES Figures representing a deceased person have been incorporated in church MONUMENTS since the twelfth century. Like monumental BRASSES, effigies were generally stylized representations of a deceased person, portraits being rare before the Restoration period. Heraldry announced identity, lineage and status. The earliest effigies were almost invariably of ecclesiastics, carved in low relief and depicted in a standing position. In the thirteenth century, lay figures were also represented, usually recumbent and three-dimensional, though two-dimensional figures continued in the form of INCISED SLABS and

Alabaster effigies of Nicholas Fitzherbert (d.1473) and Ralph Fitzherbert (d.1483) and his wife Elizabeth Marshall at Norbury in Derbyshire where the family held lands from 1125.

monumental brasses. Among the earliest lay effigies were those of King John (d.1216, monument dated 1230) at Worcester Cathedral and William Longespée, Earl of Salisbury (d.1226), at Salisbury Cathedral. Through the thirteenth to the fifteenth century, most monuments were carved in stone, often Caen stone or ALABASTER; however, there were some notable exceptions, including the late twelfth-century oak effigy of Robert, Duke of Normandy (d.1134) at Gloucester Cathedral. The effigy of Henry III (d.1272) at Westminster Abbey was the first of a series of gilt bronze effigies created for members of the English royal family, a fashion later emulated by the nobility, including Richard Beauchamp (d.1439) in his effigy at the collegiate church of St Mary's, Warwick. This magnificent tomb still retains its gilded *hearse* or barrel-shaped metal cage, originally intended to support a pall cover which was removed only on special occasions.

The medieval practice of HEART BURIAL is evident in a number of *miniature effigies*, each erected over the place at which a heart was interred. Such a miniature recumbent knight, complete with hauberk, surcoat, sword and heater-shaped shield, set within a recess of an aisle wall at Mappowder church in Dorset, is just 45 cm long (18 inches) and clasps what appears to be a casket, presumably that in which his heart was buried. Such effigies are usually of thirteenth-century origin and many show signs of having been richly painted and gilded.

Medieval effigies provide invaluable evidence for the development of costume and armour, though it should be remembered that effigies and brasses were often commissioned in anticipation of death or erected some considerable time after interment and therefore reflect the fashion of the time in which they were made rather than that of the person they commemorate.

Armorial display was particularly important (*see* ARMORY) and until the middle of the fourteenth century a knight's effigy usually bore a shield and was clothed in an embroidered SURCOAT, CYCLAS or JUPON, on which the arms were carved and often painted. The detail of arms carved on shield and tunic may still be visible, depending on the depth of the original carving and the effects of defacement and erosion. Effigies were often painted but surviving contemporary medieval paintwork and gilding is rare, many having been refurbished at a later date. The early wooden effigy of Robert of Normandy (*see above*) is coloured, but examination of the shields on the sides of the TOMB CHEST reveals that the heraldry post-dates both Robert's death and the tomb's erection by several

centuries, and the paintwork cannot be original therefore. (The tomb chest was replaced and the effigy refurbished in the fifteenth century, and again following the Civil War.)

From the mid-fourteenth century, shields of arms are more often incorporated into the fabric of the tomb chest or CANOPY, and often display multiple QUARTERINGS. The importation into Britain of magnificent German and Italian armour during the fifteenth century encouraged a fashion among the nobility for discarding any form of heraldic over-mantle, and effigies of the period often reflect this. There was a brief period during the late fifteenth and early sixteenth century when the TABARD became popular. This garment was emblazoned on sleeves and body and will be found in some contemporary effigies. The use of heraldry in medieval and Tudor effigies was not merely decorative: armorial devices were outward and visible symbols of authority and power, and accumulated quarterings and badges conveyed details of ancestry more proudly than any inscription.

Women too bore their marital arms on a *kirtle* (gown or outer petticoat) or *mantle* (cloak) and these appear in effigies as they would have been worn in life. The earliest example is the effigy of Matilda, Countess of Salisbury (d.1281), in Worcester Cathedral. She was daughter and heiress of Walter de Clifford and her cloak is powdered with small shields bearing her paternal arms. Between 1280 and 1330, it was usual for women to display their arms on a mantle which was worn on ceremonial occasions. In effigies (and brasses) the sides of the garment fall forward from the shoulders and the quartered or impaled arms are emblazoned on these: the husband's arms on the dexter (the left when viewed from the front) and the woman's paternal arms on the sinister (the right) – the reverse of when the garment was actually worn for it was intended to be viewed from the back. Sometimes there are 'missing' quarterings and one may reasonably assume that these are simply not visible. Thereafter, for the remainder of the fourteenth century, a close-fitting kirtle was worn beneath a sleeveless *cote-hardie*, the female equivalent of the jupon, and this was often emblazoned with the impaled marital arms. There are also instances of both mantle and kirtle being used for armorial display and in such cases it is always the mantle which bears the husband's arms 'in dominion' over the woman's paternal arms which were embroidered on her kirtle. During the Tudor period, heraldic kirtles and over-mantles continued to be depicted in monuments, though kirtles were now loose-fitting and without a waist. But it seems unlikely that such garments continued to be worn after the mid-sixteenth century, even for ceremonial purposes, and their use in effigies and brasses is seen to decline rapidly from this time. Of course, it should be remembered that heraldic costume, as depicted in effigies and brasses, was intended primarily as a vehicle for armorial display and does not necessarily illustrate a contemporary fashion.

The shield and heraldic garment were not the only vehicles for armorial display: recumbent effigies, both male and female, often have their heads resting on cushions which may incorporate heraldic devices in the embroidery. From the fourteenth century, a knight's head normally rested on a helm to which was attached his CREST with wreath and mantling. Most effigies are depicted with their feet resting on a beast, usually a lion for a man and a dog for a woman. These figures are more often symbolic than heraldic, although the use of other animals is almost certainly of significance. At Puddletown in Dorset, for example, effigies of the Martin family of Athelhampton rest their feet on an ape which was the family crest. Many effigies also include the insignia of chivalric orders, of which the most common is the Order of the Garter. During the first half of the fifteenth century, the SS collar of the House of Lancaster appears on many figures, and again during the early Tudor period, often with a pendant of the portcullis badge. The collar of suns and roses of the House of York is found on effigies dating from the latter half of the fifteenth century, though many were defaced after Tudor's victory at Bosworth in 1485 (*see* COLLARS).
See also MEMORIALS
For Church Monuments Society *see* APPENDIX I

EGLWYS The Welsh for 'church'. Like the Cornish place-name element *eglos*, it is derived through the Romano-Britons from the Latin *ecclesia*.

ELEANOR CROSSES Wayside memorial crosses constructed to mark the progress of the body of Queen Eleanor of Castile, first wife of Edward I, who died at Harby in Nottinghamshire on 29 November 1290 and was buried at Westminster Abbey (though her bowels were first removed and interred at Lincoln Cathedral). From 1292–4, in accordance with her will, a series of elaborate crosses was erected by the king's masons at resting places along the route to Westminster, the best known being Charing Cross in London. Only three crosses survive of the original twelve: at Geddington and Hardingstone in Northamptonshire and at Waltham Cross in Hertfordshire.

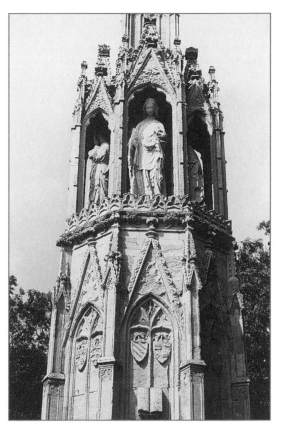

Eleanor Cross at Hardingstone, Northamptonshire.

ELECTRICITY SUPPLY *see* PUBLIC UTILITIES

ELEMENTARY SCHOOLS *see* EDUCATION

ELEPHANTS When found in the fabric of churches, elephants are most likely intended to represent Adam and Eve, with whom (according to the medieval bestiaries) they shared a carnal naïvety and mated only once during a lifetime. Elephants are also found in ARMORY, notably in the punning arms of the Elphinston family and in the civic arms of the city of Coventry, where a single elephant with a castle on its back symbolizes strength and sagacity. *See also* CHRISTIAN SYMBOLS

ELIZABETHAN AND JACOBEAN ARCHITECTURE The reign of Elizabeth I (1558–1603) was a time of transition from the architectural tradition of the late English GOTHIC period to that of the European Renaissance. It was also a time when the religious turmoil of previous reigns was largely quelled and the country's prosperity began to revive. Although the wool trade was in decline, a consequential increase in arable farming led to both a repopulation of the countryside by agricultural labourers and the creation of a substantial middle class of yeoman farmers and owners of small estates. Vernacular building, mostly in stone or brick or using TIMBER FRAME construction, increased rapidly and was characterized by asymmetry of design, modest rectangular windows and sloping, gabled roofs. Smaller homes continued to be constructed in the early Tudor tradition (*see* TUDOR ARCHITECTURE), but with the addition of fireplaces, chimney-stacks and a more substantial staircase. Timber buildings were built more efficiently: constructional timbers were spaced more widely and the central hall provided with an upper floor. In larger houses, interiors were often decorated with plasterwork ceilings, carved chimney-pieces and wall panelling.

Wary of emulating Italian architectural classicism with its papal associations, they relied heavily on French, German and (especially) Flemish books of designs and ornamentation, the illustrations of which provided a rich source of inspiration. Consequently, the so-called 'classical' buildings of the period remained essentially medieval but were clad in a veneer of classical ornamentation, derived principally from the Renaissance architecture of the Low Countries. The most innovative feature of many of these houses was the 'E' or 'H'-shaped ground plan, a development of the traditional defensive medieval four-sided court and one which encouraged the construction of symmetrical buildings in the classical style. Indeed, the characteristic feature of these Elizabethan 'great houses' was an effect of symmetry in the façade, together with the provision of a long GALLERY (for 'promenading' and taking exercise during inclement weather), an imposing staircase and formal gardens. The gatehouse, a relic of fortified medieval and early Tudor manor-houses, was sometimes retained (often in stylized form) as a decorative feature, but more often the shorter, central projecting wing of the building contained an entrance porch which lead directly into the SCREENS PASSAGE of a large hall from which a rectangular staircase, usually built of oak and heavily built and carved, rose to the upper floors.

This was the age of hospitality: members of the 'new gentility' vied with one another to provide accommodation worthy of a perambulating sovereign – often with disastrous financial consequences. Entrance porches (*frontpieces*) were singularly ostentatious with semi-circular arches flanked by 'classical' columns and surmounted by

extraordinary piles of ornate, carved stonework incorporating heraldic devices (not always entirely authentic), elaborate pinnacles and statues of classical deities. The traditional 'hall', once the centre of domestic life, became an imposing reception hall, while the long gallery appears to have been the one architectural feature that no self-respecting gentleman could do without. At Montacute in Somerset (built 1588–1601), the immense long gallery is located at the top of the house, but elsewhere such a room is more likely to be the principal feature of the first floor.

Usually built of stone, with a balustraded parapet, curved Dutch gables and elaborate cartouches, strap-work and other ornamentation, the mansions of the new Elizabethan Age must have impressed the populace just as the great medieval abbeys and castles had confounded their ancestors. Chimney-stacks were usually constructed in pairs or triples, their square, classical appearance contrasting with the corkscrew eccentricities of their early Tudor predecessors. Windows were large and consisted of lozenge or square-shaped leaded panes set within a rectangular grid of vertical stone mullions and horizontal transoms. The most characteristic detail of the period is the lavish use of *strap-work* ornamentation in ceilings, friezes and panelling. Of Flemish origin, this usually takes the form of bas-relief geometrical patterns of interlacing straps or bands, incorporated into fret-work or translated into classical foliage and almost invariably interspersed with a variety of small shapes such as ovals and lozenges. Decorative plaster ceilings were particularly fashionable, their designs derived from late Gothic fan VAULTING.

Typical Elizabethan great houses are Montacute House in Somerset and Hardwick Hall, Derbyshire (1590–7). Burghley House in Northamptonshire represents the transition from an earlier courtyard plan (begun in the 1550s during the reign of Mary I) to an extraordinarily ornate Elizabethan great house (completed in 1587). Not all Elizabethan mansions were built in the classical style or, indeed, of stone. Of the same period, but of entirely different character, are numerous, heavily timber-framed and (often) moated houses, such as Speke Hall, Merseyside (completed 1598), and Little Moreton Hall in Cheshire (completed 1580). Such houses exemplify not a single architectural period, but the culmination of centuries of remodelling and refurbishment.

Legislation in the Jacobean period (James I of England, 1603–25) prohibited the construction of jettied (overhanging) buildings which were such a characteristic feature of urban areas and particularly conducive to the spread of fire. Thereafter, smaller houses were built on a single frame from ground level to eaves. The construction of country mansions continued, but on an even more sumptuous scale, with large windows, decorative (often Dutch) gables, two-storeyed entrance porches and massive open-well staircases leading to the ubiquitous long gallery. The importance of scale and proportion was better understood and interiors were endowed with a classical uniformity which was often missing in earlier Elizabethan interiors. The walls of principal rooms were panelled in oak or decorated with plaster mouldings and divided by classical pilasters or columns into bays containing doorways, windows and two-stage chimney-piece. Further horizontal mouldings provided entablature support, and base or pedestal and plaster ceilings were richly ornamented over the entire surface. Imported coloured marbles for decorative fireplaces were fashionable, as were 'chessboard' floors of black and white marble. Ornamentation was often wildly flamboyant, with classical features inextricably mixed with Teutonic motifs, formalized foliage, well-endowed female *caryatids* and Gothic heraldry. Nevertheless, the Jacobean architectural style remained that of 'Flemish mannerism imposed upon a medieval base' (Yarwood).

It was Inigo Jones (1573–1652) who finally succeeded in bringing Italian Renaissance architecture to Britain (*see* CLASSICAL ARCHITECTURE). Notable Jacobean great houses are Hatfield House in Hertfordshire (1607–12), Knole House in Kent (from *c*. 1605) and Chastleton House in Oxfordshire (1603–12).

ELM The once ubiquitous elm is now a rarity. The Dutch Elm Disease of the 1970s removed all but a few isolated specimens and changed forever the face of the landscape, particularly in the Midlands of England where the species was once known as the 'Warwickshire Weed'. The magnificent elm is essentially a hedgerow tree: today, its suckers may still be found but these will last no more than twenty years if not lopped regularly at about 3.5 metres (4 feet) within the hedge. The elm has a curious wood which is particularly effective against damp and was widely used as 'the poor man's oak' for a variety of purposes. It was especially suitable for the piles of bridges and quays, for sluices, troughs, and, in more recent times, coffins. Because elm wood turns very smoothly, it was also used for rollers, fish-net bobbins and implement handles. In many towns, underground water mains made of hollowed elm trunks were in use until the nineteenth century.

Interestingly (in the light of what we now know of the disease) in timber yards, elm trees had their bark removed for their better preservation.

EMBER DAYS A group of three days in each season which in some churches are observed as days of fasting and prayer. Their original purpose is obscure and at one time there may have been only three such groups, possibly derived from pagan religious observances at seed-time, harvest and autumn vintage.
See also SAINTS' DAYS AND FEAST-DAYS

EMBLAZON To depict armorial bearings in colour. Not to be confused with the term *blazon*, which is to describe heraldic devices using the terminology of ARMORY.

EMBRASURE The recess in a wall behind an arrow loop or window.

ENCAUSTIC TILES Decorated floor tiles dating from the thirteenth to the sixteenth centuries may be found in many medieval churches. These should not be confused with nineteenth-century Victorian reproduction tiles, manufactured in large numbers for church restorations or rebuildings, and often based on medieval designs but of uniform appearance and texture. Victorian tiles will also be

Chapter House tile (c. 1256) at Westminster Abbey.

found throughout a church, while medieval examples are usually confined to the chancel.

During the thirteenth century, several methods were developed for the decoration of plain clay tiles. The pattern could be engraved in outline on the surface of the tile or the design could be carved in relief or counter-relief on a wood-block which was then pressed into the tile. In both instances, the tile was then glazed and fired to produce a patterned tile of one colour. A third method was to fill the matrix of a stamped tile with white pipeclay before it was glazed and fired. This produced the familiar brown and yellow encaustic tile. (Occasionally the design was reversed with a dark pattern set into a light coloured tile.) Early encaustic tiles are usually 12.5 to 15 cm square (5 to 6 inches) and as much as 2.5 cm thick (1 inch) with a 2 mm inlay (⅒ inch).

By the mid-fourteenth century, a flourishing English tile manufacturing industry had been established in the Chilterns, with its centre at Penn in Buckinghamshire. 'Penn' tiles were smaller, only 11.5 cm square (4½ inches) and 2 cm thick (¾ inch). It seems likely that by this time the various stages of manufacture were combined in a single process, the stamp being dipped into the white slip clay before it was pushed into the malleable tile so that the slip remained in the impression when the stamp was removed. This would explain why the slip is very thin and some edges of the inlay may be smudged or missing. The inlay was usually flush with the surface of the tile but a later development in technique resulted in the pattern being slightly concave. Early tiles were produced to decorate royal and magnatial palaces and important religious houses. During the fourteenth century, their use spread to smaller churches and domestic buildings, though in many instances a commonality of design suggests that batches of tiles were 'left-overs' from large monastic commissions and had been donated by a religious house to one or more of its subsidiary churches. Most designs required four tiles to complete a pattern (some required as many as sixteen) and it is often possible to identify individual tiles from a major monastery which have been laid down inaccurately in a parish church – possibly because insufficient tiles of each type were provided to complete a pattern or the workmen were not familiar with the original. It may be that tilers carried out smaller commissions *in situ*, constructing temporary kilns and carrying a selection of wood-blocks with them. This would explain the occurrence of identical tiles in churches many miles apart.

Many designs were used in encaustic relief and counter-relief tiles, including CHRISTIAN SYMBOLS, REBUSES and armorial devices associated with royal or monastic foundations or

Encaustic floor tiles of the thirteenth and fourteenth centuries, each approximately 15 cm square and 2.5 cm thick. Such tiles were produced by 'stamping' into the malleable tile and filling the impression with white clay before glazing and firing. Very often, an armorial design was carved correctly on the stamp but the resultant impression was back to front, as in the arms of Fitzpayne Gules three Lions passant guardant Argent over all a Bend Azure *and the lions of Eleanor of Castile (Queen of Edward I)* Quarterly Castile and Leon. *The unidentified griffin segreant is depicted correctly.*

with the benefactors of a particular church or chantry (*see* ARMORY). Armorial tiles are a considerable aid to research, but not all lions and fleurs-de-lis are of heraldic significance. Confusingly, it is not unusual to find that an armorial design has been carved correctly on the wood-block but the resultant impression is back to front.
See also TILES

ENCLOSURES The appropriation to private ownership of land held in common was itself contingent on the development of the system of open field farming which had been established in many areas of England by the ninth century (*see* OPEN FIELDS). Today's COMMONS are the remnants of the so-called 'manorial system', which became the basis of medieval economic life. Arable crops were grown on the most productive land, while the poorer soils (known as WASTE) were used for grazing and the exercising of other manorial rights such as gathering fuel. The land was vested in the LORD OF THE MANOR but the rights enjoyed by the commoners were accorded legal recognition in the courts so that a lord could not enclose the waste or 'common' land, for in so doing he would be depriving others of their rights. Nevertheless, there was sporadic enclosure of areas of waste which were considered to be superfluous to the needs of a community, or of neighbouring parcels of land which were enclosed by common consent. Despite the apparently phlegmatic attitude of the manorial authorities, many early enclosures were undoubtedly unlawful and must have caused considerable controversy and resentment among the peasantry whose influence in such matters was minimal (*see* ASSART *and* INTAKE).

It was not until the enactment of the Statutes of Merton in 1235 and 1285 that manorial lords were empowered to enclose areas which were not being used by their free tenants. In the thirteenth and fourteenth centuries, STRIPS were often rationalized and redistributed, the DEMESNE strips (*doles*) being brought together in one area to provide more compact and efficient demesne lands which were often separated from the open fields by means of enclosure. Consolidation of land through the exchange of strips was also attempted by the commoners themselves; indeed, there are instances of entire communities agreeing to rationalize and enclose holdings. Most of our ancient HEDGEROWS and field walls date from these early enclosures, their characteristic curving indentations delineating the original parcel of field strips before enclosure.

Enclosure of the open fields, which had begun in the fifteenth century, often gave rise to disputes among the parties so that it became necessary to provide such actions with a legal basis. This was often effected by the manufacture of a fictitious dispute which was taken to court where a *Chancery Decree* would be awarded, thereby validating the enclosure. (The Chancery Decree remained the most effective means of obtaining legal enclosure until it was superseded by the parliamentary acts of the eighteenth century.)

The widespread enclosure of sheep ranges during the Tudor period often resulted in the eviction of whole communities and the disintegration of the open field system in many parts of England, causing appalling deprivation and suffering (*see* DESERTED VILLAGES). Despite a Royal Commission in 1517, the continuing alienation of common land was to be one of the principal causes of popular rebellion in 1536 and 1549: 'Let them not take in their common neither make park nor pasture, for God gave the earth unto men to inhabit and not to sheep and wild deer . . .' (William Tyndale, 1525).

Enclosure by emparkment (*see* DEER PARKS) and by local agreement continued beyond the advent of the parliamentary enclosures in the seventeenth century. The first act of 1604 affected only one parish (that of Radipole in Dorset) and, although other acts followed, it was not until the reign of George II (1727–60) that the movement gained momentum. Encouraged by a Parliament largely composed of country gentlemen and inspired by improvements in agricultural techniques that made it possible (and profitable) to cultivate land previously regarded only as grazing or waste, the period 1750 to 1845 was one of unparalleled activity. The areas affected were generally CHAMPION COUNTRYSIDE where much of the land remained in open field cultivation. Parliamentary enclosure was a statutory procedure, administered by commissioners, and intended both to formalize and to accelerate existing informal practices (which undoubtedly included coercion). The principle of enclosure legislation was that a lord and commoners would each receive an allocation of freehold land in exchange for the legal extinguishment of their former rights:

> Thus, if a former common of 1000 acres was enclosed, the Lord would be allotted, say, 900 acres and the 20 commoners four acres each. The remaining 20 acres may have been allotted for varying public functions, such as a gravel pit for road making, a site for a poorhouse or a field for fuel and also . . . two or three acres 'for the exercise and recreation of the inhabitants'.
> (Ian Campbell)

Having determined that the principal landowners of a parish were committed to the enclosure of common land by the submission of a memorial or petition, Parliament would enact the necessary legislation for the appointment of commissioners. (The General Act of 1836 permitted enclosure without specific parliamentary sanction where two-thirds of those affected by the proposals were in agreement.) Commissioners were usually three in number, typically selected from the ranks of the nobility, the Church and the minor gentry or farming community. A surveyor and valuer would also be appointed by the parish and they would assist the commissioners in determining the enclosure awards. Following a survey, valuation and public consultation (which was often acrimonious), the commissioners would re-allocate the land in compact holdings, each of which was notionally equivalent to the combined portions of common land held by a particular claimant. Following confirmation of the awards, each holding would be enclosed in accordance with the terms of the appropriate act: usually by means of fences, which protected the new hawthorn hedges, and a ditch. Once the boundary fence was completed, internal field divisions could be effected as they were required and in many cases large 50 acre fields (20 hectares) were sub-divided into more manageable units of 5 to 10 acres (2 to 4 hectares).

The cost of administrating the system, and of fencing and planting hedgerows or constructing walls, fell on the recipients of the enclosure awards so that it was not unusual for the smaller landholders to relinquish their holdings as an alternative to penury. The loss of common land, on which many cottagers were dependent, caused widespread destitution and contributed significantly to rural depopulation. It has been calculated (by W.E. Tate) that 7 million acres of common land and common field were enclosed as a result of 5,400 acts passed between 1700 and 1914, though there was a rapid decline in the second half of the nineteenth century despite a major Act of 1845 which was intended to facilitate the enclosure of common land. The reason for this is to be found in the sudden and massive importation of foodstuffs into the United Kingdom from the American mid-west following the end of the Civil War in 1865. This effectively removed the incentive to enclose common land for arable farming and coincided with an increasing demand for open spaces for the 'health and exercise' of a rapidly expanding urban populace.

In large areas of England, parliamentary enclosures transformed the landscape creating large, rectilinear fields and broad, undeviating ENCLOSURE ROADS. Over 322,000 km of hedgerow were planted (200,000 miles): at Oakhill in Somerset 1½ million hawthorn seedlings were required to enclose fields in a single parish. Nevertheless, it has been estimated that only one-fifth of England was affected by enclosure legislation which was (with some exceptions) confined to a wedge-shaped area covering central England from the east coast to Dorset and Hampshire in the south-west. Many regions, and numerous isolated 'islands' of ancient countryside, remain entirely unaffected by parliamentary enclosures, the latter often contained within the boundaries of parishes which somehow managed to resist the pressures for change.

ENCLOSURE AWARD MAPS *see* MAPS

ENCLOSURE ROADS Local roads with an apparent excess of right-angled bends may date from sixteenth- and seventeenth-century field ENCLOSURES. Straight lengths of road, when not of Roman origin, are almost invariably enclosure roads, most of which were established during the period 1750 to 1850 as a consequence of the Parliamentary Inclosure Acts which transformed much of the English countryside, especially in those areas where there had been little previous field enclosure. They were intended to replace an intricate system of tracks and paths, which for centuries had linked settlements and farmsteads with each other and with ancient route-ways, and still exists as a statutory network of BRIDLE-WAYS and FOOTPATHS.

The enclosure process was usually a piecemeal parochial affair, affecting neighbouring parishes at different times, so that there is often an abrupt change of alignment as lengths of enclosure road cross parish boundaries or revert to earlier road patterns. Often, lengths of ancient HOLLOW WAYS may be identified alongside enclosure roads, especially in the vicinity of bridges and fords where old and new routes converge. In parishes where enclosure was not co-ordinated, a moribund enclosure road may end suddenly at a parish boundary and can easily be mistaken for a DROVE (the Ordnance Survey map may resolve this problem).

Where integrated enclosure was possible, and new roads were constructed through a number of parishes, a slight modification of alignment may be discernible as the road crosses each boundary. Most enclosure roads were built with a standard width between hedges or walls of 9.1 to 12.2 metres (30 to 40 feet), though widths of up to 18.3 metres may occasionally be found (60 feet). This allowed sufficient width for traffic to negotiate the waterlogging and deep ruts of winter. Since many of these roads were first metalled, the broad grass verges have sometimes been enclosed by neigh-bouring farmers or by squatters who have built cottages and cultivated long, narrow slings of land.

ENCROACHMENT *see* INTAKE

ENDORSEMENT Something written on the back (*dorse*) of a document, usually an archival reference or related notes.

ENDS Hamlets located within a settlement pattern of larger villages. Particularly common in the East Midlands (and in East Anglia where they are known as GREENS), these hamlets are either remnants of ancient fragmented settlement patterns or the subsidiary settlements of an expanding primary village.

ENFEOFFMENT *see* PROBATE

ENGLISH *see* OLD ENGLISH

ENGLISHRY, THE (i) That area of south-west Wales which, in the Middle Ages, was subject to the authority of the Marcher lords. *See also* MARCH. (ii) *See* MURDER FINE.

ENGROSS (i) To copy a document in a formal hand or in distinct characters.
(ii) To write out a document in legal form for signature.
(iii) To name in a legal list or document.

ENGROSSMENT The combining of two or more holdings.

ENTABLATURE In classical architecture, the combined ARCHITRAVE, FRIEZE and CORNICE, supported by pillars.

ENTAIL To bequeath an estate inalienably to a specified succession of beneficiaries. Although the making of conditional family settlements of freehold property (*entails*) was common practice in the Middle Ages, it was not until 1285 that legislation was enacted which provided a legal basis for such transactions (Statute of Westminster II). Writs, known as *Formedon in Descender*, were made available to enable a donor to recover his lands where the conditions were not kept, though in practice this often led to fictitious legal actions so that the property could be sold.

ENTRANCE GRAVES *see* CHAMBERED TOMBS

EORL An Anglo-Saxon magnate, often also an EALDORMAN.

EPHEMERA Handwritten and printed bits of paper: letters, labels, handbills, posters, tickets, menus, invitations, invoices, etc., intended for short-term use and eventual disposal but now an invaluable primary historical source.
For the Ephemera Society *see* APPENDIX I

EPIGRAPHY The study of inscriptions.

EPIPHANY *see* SAINTS' DAYS AND FEAST-DAYS

EPISCOPI Latinized place-name element applied to a manor that was once held by a bishop. Bishops Caundle in Dorset, until recently Caundle Bishop (the last road sign was removed in 1989) and before that Caundle Episcopi, was once held by the Bishop of Sarum. *See* LATIN *and* MONASTIC PLACE-NAMES

EPITAPHS

> Famed little John a terror was to many a boxing blade,
> But now alas an insult brooks from sexton's dirty spade;
> For coward Death waiting the time till Jack was weak and low
> The moment seized and spite of art put in his favourite blow.

Epitaph to John Marsh, the pugnacious landlord of the Red Lion at Madley in Herefordshire (1793).

The foregoing is typical of many amusing epitaphs which may be found in parish churches and churchyards – though John Marsh's memorial seems to have disappeared from Madley churchyard since the epitaph was first recorded.

From the Greek *epitaphion* (*epi* 'upon' and *taphos* 'a tomb'), epitaphs are commemorative inscriptions on GRAVESTONES and MONUMENTS and are of interest not only for the genealogical information they contain, but also because they epitomize contemporary social and religious attitudes.

Medieval tombs were themselves indicative of a man's status and dignity: the heraldry on EFFIGIES and BRASSES declaring his identity, lineage and authority more effectively than any epitaph. Inscriptions were usually in Latin (though some early brasses are inscribed in Norman French) and contained the briefest of details – name, dates and a religious aphorism – all modestly contained within the overall design of the monument. Those who were not armigerous sometimes included personal devices such as MERCHANTS' MARKS or the symbols of favourite saints (*see* CHRISTIAN SYMBOLS). Medieval man acknowledged the commonality of death and was preoccupied with salvation. This is reflected in the monuments of the period, which are often rich but rarely ostentatious, and in simple expressions of piety and humility.

The materialism of late Tudor society is evident in many sixteenth-century monuments which became increasingly elaborate with exaggerated heraldic display and lengthy florid epitaphs, often written in verse. Implicit in many of these memorials is an assumption that earthly gentility would find its reward in heaven. Some of the verse was of the highest quality (Shakespeare himself is said to have composed the epitaph on the tomb of Sir Thomas Stanley (d.1576) in Tong church, Shropshire) and many early seventeenth-century monuments, though architecturally insensitive, contain epitaphs which accurately reflect the lyricism of contemporary poetry.

While many eighteenth-century monuments are singularly ostentatious, some are also exceedingly graceful, though all too often out of keeping with their medieval surroundings. But the epitaphs inscribed thereon frequently make the most preposterous claims for the self-righteous dead in doggerel which was unlikely to enhance a poet's reputation. Biographical detail was sometimes of a singularly intimate nature, as in Bridget Applewhaite's lengthy epitaph at Bramfield in Suffolk which recalls the 'Fatigues' of her first marriage ('Born by her with incredible Patience / For Four Years and three Quarters, barring three weeks), the 'glorious Freedom' of her widowhood and her decision to 'run the Risk of a Second Marriage-Bed' as well as the full medical details of the 'Apoplectick Dart' which after 'Terrible Convulsions, Plaintive Groans or Stupefying Sleep' eventually dispatched her, at the age of 43, on 12 September 1773. Not all epitaphs would have been welcomed by the churchwardens: at Burford in Oxfordshire, a monument to Lord Chief Justice Tanfield, erected by his widow, complains bitterly of the inconvenience caused by having to bury him in such a backwater.

The religious upheaval of the late eighteenth and early nineteenth centuries resulted in a reaction against such commemorative excesses. Memorials, and the inscriptions they bore, became stylised and bland just as religious observance declined into social convention. In 1843, the Rev. F.E. Paget, Rector of Elfield in Staffordshire, published his *Tract Upon Tombstones* in which he stated that the erection of a tombstone should be 'a Christian act and one that shall benefit the living. The tombstones in the churchyard are, as it were, a book, from whence [visitors] draw their reflections on man's mortality and in which every new inscription is a fresh page.' A proper epitaph, he continued, 'should be characterised by Christian humility, kindness, and by a disposition to say too little rather than too much.'

In the present century there is evidence of increasing conflict between those who oppose the clichÈ and the banal and others who consider epitaphs to be a reflection of personal taste and,

therefore, of contemporary society. In 1994, a Consistory Court ruled that colloquial references to 'dad', 'nanna' and 'grandad' were undignified and inappropriate, a judgment supported by the *Churchyards Handbook** which suggests that gravestones should be raised for the benefit of posterity rather than the transient gratification of a bereaved family. Censorship of inscriptions is nothing new. In 1797 at the church of St Anthony-in-Meneage, Cornwall, the widow of Richard Roskruge suggested an epitaph for her murdered husband 'Doomed by a cruel ruffian's hand to die!' The vicar was not impressed and substituted '. . . a neighbour's erring hand' as 'breathing more of Christian charity'. Certainly, there is little to recommend the ubiquitous 'in loving memory of . . .' and 'RIP' (*Requiescat in Pace* – 'may he rest in peace'). Infinitely preferable is the dignified epitaph 'Here to the earthy part of . . .', inscribed on a seventeenth-century memorial at Folke in Dorset.

Epitaphs are collected and recorded by many of the family history societies whose addresses may be obtained from county record offices.

See also CHURCHYARDS, MEMORIALS *and* WALL MONUMENTS

* Stapleton, H., and Burman, P. (eds), *The Churchyards Handbook* (London, 1988)

EQUILATERAL ARCH *see* ARCH

EQUITY *see* LAW

ERMINE STREET *see* ROMAN ROADS

ESCALADE *see* SIEGES

ESCHEAT Escheated estates were those which reverted to a lord when a tenant died without heirs, or an heir had not attained his majority. Estates could also be escheated when a tenant committed a felony which incurred the forfeiture of his estate. From 1195, Escheators were appointed by the Crown to oversee the collection of revenues from escheated property in a particular county or group of counties. Escheats were abolished as recently as 1925.

See also COURT BARON *and* GAVELKIND

ESCUTCHEON OF PRETENCE *see* HEIRESS, IMPALEMENT *and* MARSHALLING

ESQUIRE In the Middle ages, an attendant (*escutifer* = shield bearer) to a knight. An esquire's feudal service required him to maintain his master's shield and armour, though his responsibilities and duties were considerably wider than this and were, in part, intended to train him in the martial and courtly arts and chivalric code. Many esquires were themselves of noble birth, and in practice pages tended to perform the more menial duties. By 1400, sons of peers and the eldest sons of knights were deemed to be esquires, and in the sixteenth century the title was applied to officers of the Crown. It was thereby considered superior to that of Gentleman, though only by association with a royal office which provided added distinction. The rural '*Squire*' is generally a lord of the manor or major landowner, and the term is entirely colloquial.

See also YEOMAN

ESSEX *see* KINGDOMS (ANCIENT)

ESSOINS *see* LAW

ESTATE, COUNTRY A medieval estate comprised DEMESNE lands together with wide areas of general jurisdiction: an assemblage of customary manorial rights and revenues rather than a physical unit. During the fourteenth century, demesne farming was replaced by an economy based on the payment of rents in lieu of free service and from this evolved the great country estate of the nineteenth century. Typically, such estates may be identified by straight, wide-verged ENCLOSURE ROADS; 'model' villages with an elementary school, restored church, a neat row of alms houses and often a 'Landowner's Arms' public house. Such countryside is invariably that of ENCLOSURE, with substantial farmhouses and quadrangles of outbuildings, all constructed in the same architectural style and of similar materials, set amid large rectilinear fields and mixed plantations, shelter belts and game coverts.

Some estates covered vast areas and included properties in small towns as well as agricultural holdings. Properties owned by a major estate in Dorset and Somerset are still identified by enamelled plaques, each bearing an ostrich crest and an estate number, affixed to their doors, while the field gates of a neighbouring estate are fashioned from the initial letter of the landowner's name.

At the centre of the estate is a substantial area of landscaped parkland, often an enclosed DEER PARK, with LODGES, ornamental lakes and classical temples all visible from a sweeping entrance drive. Finally, the mansion itself, set amidst its stables, walled kitchen gardens, greenhouses, orangery, ornamental dairy, croquet lawns, fountains, terraces and all the appendages of gracious living: manifestations of the wealth,

authority and patronage upon which the estate community depended. But the rationale of such a community was essentially *inter* dependence: the influence of the 'big house' indeed resembled that of a pebble thrown into a pond, but for such an estate to be successful it also needed to be self-supporting. The more progressive estates were (and are) dynamic, enterprising businesses in which there existed a genuine commitment to success from which all members of the estate community would benefit. Perhaps it is for this reason that some 1,500 large privately owned estates remain intact today. Many estate papers (including maps) are now lodged with county or local record offices, though some remain in the archives of the major landowners or their representatives. The Royal Commission on Historic Manuscripts and the National Register of Archives (*see* APPENDIX I) collate and publish information from a variety of sources.

See also COUNTRY HOUSE

ESTATE MAPS *see* MAPS

ESTOVERS *see* COMMONS

EXCARNATION *see* CHAMBERED TOMBS

EX CATHEDRA Literally 'from the chair', in this case that of the teacher, and therefore applicable to any pronouncement made with authority. When the Pope speaks *ex cathedra*, the 'chair' is the papal throne and he is therefore considered to speak infallibly.

EXCHEQUER The Norman kings created two departments to deal with financial matters: the TREASURY and the Exchequer, which was itself divided into the lower Exchequer and upper Exchequer. The lower Exchequer was responsible for receiving moneys and was connected to the Treasury; the upper Exchequer was a court of law which dealt exclusively with fiscal matters until it was merged with the High Court of Justice in 1880. The sheriffs were required to attend the twice-yearly meetings of the upper Exchequer at Easter and Michaelmas in order to pay the income (*farms*) due from their shires. The office of Chancellor of the Exchequer was created in the reign of Henry III (1207–72) and was originally that of assistant to the treasurer of the Exchequer. By the end of the thirteenth century, the PRIVY SEAL was used to transmit orders from the sovereign to the Exchequer. The term Exchequer now denotes the account at the Bank of England into which public revenues are paid. The word is believed to derive via Old French from the Latin *scaccarium* = 'chess board', a reference to the practice of keeping accounts on a chequered table-cloth, the ranks and files of which served in the manner of an abacus. Many of the numerous Exchequer records, which are maintained in the Public Record Office, have been published: notably by the Stationery Office.

EXCHEQUER (COURT OF) *see* LAW

EXPLORATORES *see* ROMAN FORTS AND CAMPS

EXTENT *see* MANOR

EXTRINSECA *see* LATIN

-EY, -EA, -Y A place-name element derived from the Old English *ēg* or *īeg,* or from the Norse *ey,* signifying an island eg. Sheppey = island of the sheep.
See also HOLME *and* YNYS

EYE-CATCHER *see* ARTIFICIAL RUINS *and* FOLLIES

EYRE, IN From the Latin *itinere*, meaning 'on a journey', eyres were judicial circuits undertaken by the king's justices who sat (somewhat infrequently) at sessions of county courts in order to hear Crown pleas and to standardize the administration of justice which, in the Middle Ages, tended to be localized. They were also responsible for auditing royal revenues and inspecting county administration. The system of justices in eyre was introduced in 1166 but was effectively abandoned in 1294 when QUO WARRANTO proceedings and general eyres were replaced by judicial commissions.
See also LAW

FACULTY A licence, issued on behalf of a bishop, permitting alterations or additions to be made to church buildings or churchyards.

FAIR HOUSE *see* FAIRS *and* MARKET HALL

FAIRS The earliest 'fairs' may have been held in CAUSEWAYED ENCLOSURES and at other prehistoric sites. Medieval fairs were generally annual occasions and of greater significance to a local populace than MARKETS. They usually took place (or commenced) on the *feriae*, the feast or holy days of the local church to whose patronal saint the fair was often dedicated. On such days men were freed from labour (holy day became holiday) to engage in both the business and sociability of the fair. Most fairs originated in the thirteenth and fourteenth centuries in the new towns and seigniorial boroughs, and were concerned not only with trade and commerce, but with entertainment and the propagation of news and ideas. Many fairs grew to national, even international importance, lasting for several days and sometimes weeks and, because they were held regularly at a fixed time and fixed place, many became centres of banking and commerce and contributed to the intellectual and cultural development of medieval Europe.

The exclusive right to hold a fair was established through a royal or magnatial charter which specified the day or days on which it was to be held, though some smaller fairs possibly originated in village WAKES. Enterprising manorial lords or burgesses who obtained charters profited from the revenues which could be raised through farming out stalls or 'pitches' to lessees. Often, booths, utensils, etc., were provided and these were stored in a 'Fair House' when not required (*see* MARKET HALL). Fairs inevitably attracted merchants who were able to offer exotic and high quality goods not normally available at markets, and for this reason many continued to be held until the distribution of merchandise was transformed by the advent of the railway age and an efficient postal service in the nineteenth century.

Several fairs outgrew their market squares and were removed to a more suitable site on the periphery of the town, sometimes within the ramparts of an ancient earthwork, such as that on the summit of Woodbury Hill near Bere Regis in Dorset, which was in constant use as a fairground from the early Middle Ages to the 1950s. (*See* Thomas Hardy, *Far From the Madding Crowd*, chapter 50, for a vivid description of the annual fair at Woodbury.) But the anticipated profits which encouraged many medieval magnates to apply for charters did not always materialize: establishing a fair was a speculative business and while many fairs flourished or specialized others became moribund.

A sheep fair, c. *1900.*

Sheep fairs (such as Tan Hill Fair on the Marlborough Downs in Wiltshire) and others of medieval origin, at which goods and beasts were sold, were known as charter fairs. Statute fairs derived from legislation enacted during the reign of Elizabeth I (1533–1603) which required district or HUNDRED meetings to be convened annually for the appointment of employees and the settlement of wages and contractual disputes. These 'hiring fairs' were often held in anticipation of CANDLEMASS DAY (2 February) and those wishing to find new employment would carry symbols of their trade: shepherds their crooks, maids their mops and so on. Indeed, many statute fairs survive today as 'mop fairs' or 'pack [pact?] fairs'. Woodbury Fair lasted for five days: the first was called 'Wholesale Day', the second 'Gentlefolks' Day', the third 'Allfolks' Day', the fourth was the sheep fair and the Friday was 'Pack and Penny Day', when remaining goods were sold off cheaply. *See also* VILLAGE GREENS

FAMILY RECORD CENTRE The Family Record Centre in London houses numerous documents of a personal nature, notably the CENSUS returns from 1841 to 2001, certificates of birth, marriage, death and adoption from 1837, and wills proved in the Prerogative Court of Canterbury from 1383 to 1858. For public documents *see* PUBLIC RECORD OFFICE (PRO).
For addresses *see* APPENDIX I

FAMILY HISTORY *see* GENEALOGY

FAMULI Paid estate workers, as opposed to manorial tenants whose labours formed part of their service.

FANLIGHT A window above a door which, in the eighteenth century, was usually semi-circular with radiating glazing bars in the form of a fan.

FAN VAULT *see* VAULTING

FARM A comparatively recent term derived from the Latin *firma*; a fixed money rent applicable to a consolidated holding (Middle English *ferme*) created by means of sixteenth-century piecemeal ENCLOSURE of OPEN FIELDS. The nearest medieval equivalent was MESSUAGE but there was no medieval 'farmer': the terms YEOMAN, ACREMAN, HUSBANDMAN, etc., being applied at different times to a variety of circumstances.

FARMHOUSES *see* FARMSTEADS

FARMING Little landscape evidence of agricultural activity survives from the early millennia, though a number of important communal sites of fourth-millennium BC farming communities are known (*see* CAUSEWAY ENCLOSURE). After *c.* 2000 BC, there is more substantial evidence: tracts of Bodmin Moor in Cornwall, for example, contain the remains of field boundaries, clusters of buildings, trackways and even planned enclosures which appear to have been used for agricultural purposes. From *c.* 1600 BC there was a significant increase in population and, in many areas of Britain, the development of planned agricultural landscapes covering thousands of acres and with settlements and trackways integrated into large field systems (*see* BRONZE AGE). As the climate deteriorated in the centuries around *c.* 1000 BC, upland farmland declined, but elsewhere activity increased so that during later prehistoric times, and throughout the Roman occupation, farming communities expanded rapidly (*see* INFIELD-OUTFIELD CULTIVATION).

The erroneously named *'Celtic' fields*, dating variously from the Bronze and Iron Ages and the Romano-British period, consisted of clusters of small rectilinear enclosures bounded by *lynchet banks* or field walls, constructed of stone as it was cleared from the fields. It may be that many lynchet banks, formed from the accumulated debris of ploughing, originally carried hedgerows. Early 'Celtic' fields were probably cultivated by means of the primitive *ard* plough which consisted of little more than a carefully selected branch that was well balanced and sufficiently pointed to break the surface but did not possess a mould-board to turn a furrow. In those areas where ancient field patterns have survived, many 'Celtic' fields are still cultivated within their original enclosures: in parts of Cornwall, for example. 'Celtic' fields often extended outwards in a radial pattern from a central farmstead or were arranged in a tessellated pattern similar to the bonding of a brick wall. Large-scale planning may be evident in great clusters of fields which share a common orientation and are bounded by ancient DROVES.

During the eighth and ninth centuries a system of OPEN FIELD cultivation developed in many areas of England. In some places, this system was to last for a thousand years but elsewhere the ancient COUNTRYSIDE remained, characterized by the sporadic enclosure of land and the consolidation of dispersed FARMSTEADS.

Agriculture dominated the economy of England throughout the Middle Ages, though for many production was often barely above subsistence level. Life was not only hard but precarious: for most peasants a staple diet of bread and beer depended on a successful harvest and, therefore, on the vagaries of the weather. The advent of the BLACK DEATH in the mid-fourteenth century accelerated a decline in the rural population which had been evident since the previous century. The consequential reduction in the availability of peasant labour resulted in a significant increase in sheep farming which was less labour-intensive and, with a rising wool market, more profitable.

During the late fifteenth and early sixteenth centuries, many open fields were enclosed, estates cleared and villagers evicted on an unprecedented scale (*see* DESERTED VILLAGES). Nevertheless, at the turn of the century approximately 90 per cent of the population of 2 million still lived in the villages, hamlets and isolated farmsteads of an essentially rural England and worked the land in familial or other units of five or six people. During the Tudor and Stuart periods, agricultural production increased significantly. So too did the population, which by 1714 (when the last of the Stuarts died) had increased by 150 per cent. Despite unprecedented urban growth, by the end of the seventeenth century there was a substantial grain surplus and a flourishing export trade. This was due in part to the sporadic reorganization of open field strips into compact, enclosed holdings (especially in the Midland counties) and a trend towards the amalgamation of small holdings to form larger, more coherent farms. Many areas of marsh and fen had been brought into production (*see* RECLAMATION), as had hitherto unproductive land, often by means of UP AND DOWN HUSBANDRY. By the end of the seventeenth century, new techniques, such as the creation of WATER MEADOWS, and the introduction of field crops such as carrots, potatoes, turnips, red clover and ryegrass (which improved the fertility of light soils) ensured the final exorcism of the spectre of famine which had haunted the medieval peasant.

A number of contemporary antiquarians and cartographers have left us with a vivid impression of the landscapes of sixteenth- and seventeenth-century Britain, notably in the *Itinerary* of Leland (1506–52), Camden's *Brittania* (1561–1623) and Defoe's *Tour of Britain* (1659–1731). Gregory King, writing at the end of the seventeenth century, suggested that approximately half of England and Wales was under cultivation as pasture and meadow (valued by King at an annual rent of 8*s* 8*d* an acre) and arable (5*s* 6*d*). Despite the wholesale felling of

Working in the fields before mechanization took over.

timber for fuel and building materials during the sixteenth century, King also estimated that there remained 3 million acres of managed woodland and coppice (5*s*), together with 3 million acres of forests, parks and commons (3*s* 8*d*), and a further 10 million acres of 'heaths, moors, mountains and barren land' (valued at 1*s* for sheep feed).

By the early nineteenth century, the translation of the open field system to one of small compact farms, worked for the most part by tenant farmers, was completed. But high taxation, the continuation of TITHES (until 1836) and the imposition of the Corn Laws caused considerable unrest within the farming community.

First introduced in 1815, the *Corn Laws* were an attempt to maintain the prosperity enjoyed by British agriculture during the Napoleonic Wars and originally allowed the importation of foreign grain only after the price of home-grown wheat had risen above 80*s* a quarter. The intention was to maintain a balance between the price of grain and the cost of production so that the poor could afford to buy while the farmer continued to make a reasonable living. Unfortunately, the legislation had precisely the opposite effect: the mechanism was unable to cope with climatic variations, or with a rapid growth of

the urban population, and the price of bread rose dramatically so that both producers and consumers suffered. (Between 1801 and 1851, the population of England and Wales doubled to nearly 18 million.) In 1828 a sliding scale of import duties was introduced but opposition to the Corn Laws continued, and they were eventually repealed in 1846, splitting Peel's Conservative Party in the process. Large quantities of wheat had been imported during the first half of the nineteenth century, mostly from Russia and north-west Europe, in order to feed the expanding towns of the Industrial Revolution but from *c*. 1850 the USA (and later Canada) became the main source. The abolition of the Corn Laws persuaded many farmers to turn from arable to pasture: from corn production to beef and dairy produce, for which there was a ready market.

Until recently the term '*Agrarian Revolution*' has been applied to what was perceived as a relatively rapid transformation of British agriculture during the eighteenth century, particularly associated with contemporary innovators such as Jethro Tull and 'Turnip' Townsend, and aristocratic landowners such as Coke of Holkham (in Norfolk) and the Duke of Bedford. Tull's seed drill of 1701, which facilitated the sowing of seeds at a controlled rate in

The International Harvester Titan, *an early internal combustion paraffin engine, was one of the popular American machines imported during the Great War.*

accurately spaced rows (and thereby made possible the control of weeds by horse-drawn hoe), did indeed have a significant impact both on agricultural practice and rural employment, but analysis of farming business records and crop and stock inventories has resulted in a reassessment of the 'Agrarian Revolution' and its extension back to the end of the sixteenth century and forward to the beginning of the twentieth. It is now acknowledged that the 'revolution' took place on individual farms rather than among an élite of innovative 'improvers', and it was the accumulative effect of farmers' inventiveness, over a lengthy period of time, which resulted in agricultural advancement. Of greatest significance were the rationalization of scattered, inefficient holdings and their transfer as compact, commercially viable units to farmers with capital, expertise and a commitment to an expanding market economy (*see* ENCLOSURE); the rapid conversion of previously uncultivated land

into arable after 1750; the introduction of new crops and the application of scientific principles to many agricultural operations.

Nevertheless, a rapid increase in the urban population and a corresponding demand for food failed to stimulate technical innovation: before 1850 a reliable supply of cheap labour was not conducive to mechanization. Most mechanical and biological innovation has taken place since 1880 and the 'improvement' of agriculture since the beginning of the seventeenth century should therefore be regarded as evolutionary rather than revolutionary. From the mid-nineteenth century, however, an acceleration in the movement of population from rural to urban areas resulted in a significant reduction in the agricultural labour force and the introduction of limited mechanization. From 1840, THRESHING by steam gradually replaced other methods and from 1851 horse-drawn reaping machines were introduced, followed by reaper-binders in the 1870s (*see also* TRACTION ENGINES). Although by 1914 nearly all the corn harvest was brought in mechanically, there was little evidence of change in beef and dairy farming. Milking machines were available from the 1880s and the Lawrence refrigerator enabled cooled milk to be transported to the urban markets by rail, but the emphasis on the production of liquid milk did little to encourage the mechanization of cheese- and butter-making.

The Victorian preoccupation with steam power inspired the introduction of a variety of ingenious, but rarely effective machines, some of which drew implements across the fields by means of winches and cables. Only in the farmyard was steam power a success, particularly in threshing and similar tasks. By the end of the nineteenth century, a number of engineering firms, such as Ransomes of Ipswich, were producing a variety of light-weight, all metal 'cultivators'. Drawn by pairs of horses, many of these implements continued in use until the 1940s and may still be found in sequestered farmyard corners and abandoned field barns. The first oil-driven tractor was introduced in 1899, and by 1914 a number of British firms were producing machines with internal combustion engines, though few were intended for commercial use (*see also* WAGONS).

Of far greater significance were the advances made in the application of scientific principles to agriculture. In particular, the German scientist Liebig established the relationship between plant nutrition and the composition of the soil which lead, through the analysis of manure, to a greater understanding of nitrogenous and non-nitrogenous elements. Guano had been used as fertilizer since 1804, but in the 1850s vast quantities were imported by commercial companies, especially from Peru. The widespread use of fertilizer, together with a significant increase in land drainage, brought many marginal areas into production, and by 1875 British agriculture was flourishing. However, this was shortly followed by a period of depression. Refrigeration was introduced in the 1880s and encouraged a gradual increase in the importation of meat, especially from Argentina, Australia and New Zealand. Canadian wheat began to flood the market at a time of exceptionally bad harvests in Britain (especially that of 1879), and by 1900 there had developed a critical imbalance in the food supply: the industrial/urban conurbations effectively controlled the market while the agricultural/rural communities were in serious decline.

In Ireland, there had been a similar increase in population but little corresponding industrial growth or urban development. Much of the grain production was exported to Britain and it has been estimated that over half the population of 8 million existed on a diet of potatoes. A partial failure of the potato crop in 1845 was followed by complete failure in 1846 and 1847. A marginally better crop in 1848 failed to stem the tide of starvation or emigration, and in four years the population fell by 1 million, with a further 3 million suffering destitution. As a result of wholesale evictions following the Potato Famine and a massive programme of emigration (particularly to the USA) the population of Ireland was reduced to 5½ million by 1871.

For the British Agricultural History Society *and* the Institute of Agricultural History *see* APPENDIX I

FARM RENT Rent paid, or service undertaken, in return for a landholding.

FARMSTEADS A farmstead is the dwelling and associated operational buildings of a farmer (*see* FARM *and* FARMING). Contrary to popular belief, much of the Romano-British countryside was well populated, with farmsteads and hamlets distributed at intervals of 0.8 to 1.6 km (½ to 1 mile). The seventh-century settlement at Chalton in Hampshire consisted of a series of adjacent farmsteads each with a rectangular wooden dwelling surrounded by a square or rectangular fenced enclosure. The enclosure contained two or three further buildings and possibly incorporated a farmyard. That none of the buildings had a byre attached suggests a greater reliance on sheep rather than cattle. At other settlements, such as West Stow in Suffolk, the sunken-hut type of building predominates. This structure consisted of a rectangular hollow (which may have been boarded over) enclosed by a simple roof supported by upright wooden posts carrying a ridge pole. Isolated, self-contained farmsteads, surrounded by their own fields, may have had a similar appearance.

The late Saxon period witnessed the creation of champion COUNTRYSIDE in which OPEN FIELDS encompassed the richest land and farmsteads were located together within villages. But in many areas the ancient countryside remained, together with numerous dispersed farmsteads, the sites of which often represent a continuity of occupation through to the present day. Place-names composed of a personal name combined with the ending -*ingas* (e.g. *Haestingas* = Hastings) may be indicative of an Anglo-Saxon farmstead, ownership of which had become sufficiently consolidated for it to be associated with a particular family. Many early farmsteads are recorded in DOMESDAY Book

An 'open-yarded homestead': an early Victorian design by J.L. Morton.

(1086) but there is usually insufficient detail to identify the locations precisely. In some cases, farmsteads were removed to more favourable sites while retaining their names, and in others entire hamlets subsequently contracted leaving only a solitary farmstead.

During the medieval period, many farmsteads developed from monastic GRANGES or were created when ASSARTS were brought into use. Some ancient farmsteads were contained within a medieval moat which may still be evident in the field or on the Ordnance Survey map (later examples were often built as status symbols rather than for defensive purposes), while others still retain the names of their medieval owners or builders. In moorland areas and fen country, attempted cultivation was often short-lived, the remains of farmsteads surviving in names which evoke the despair of their medieval builders, such as Starveacre, Breakall and COLDHARBOUR, and in

numerous isolated ruins. The remaining farmsteads which characterize the nucleated villages of champion countryside almost invariably occupy sites which have been in constant use since the open fields were first established. But even in champion countryside isolated farmsteads are to be found outside the villages. These were usually built in outlying areas of reclaimed WASTE or occasionally in parcels of land which were enclosed by agreement to provide blocks of strips, within the open field, of sufficient size to support a farmstead.

Although some farmsteads have survived (in part, at least) from the fourteenth and even the thirteenth centuries, most post-date the sixteenth century and of these the majority were built following parliamentary enclosures in the eighteenth and nineteenth centuries. The redistribution of land through ENCLOSURE did not always result in the immediate removal of farmsteads to the 'new lands', however. In many cases, removal from the village was delayed for some considerable time while the necessary and expensive hedgerows and ditches were provided following enclosure; indeed, village farmsteads continue in use today, even though their enclosure award fields may be located in the outer regions of the parish.

Numerous new farmsteads were built during the period of greatest enclosure activity (1750–1850), particularly those provided for tenant farmers on large estates. Many major landowners even employed teams of architects and builders to develop their *model farms*, each located conveniently at the centre of a newly acquired block of land, using local building materials and constructed in a uniform vernacular architectural style round a regular courtyard plan. At worst, these model farms demonstrated little more than an uninspiring functionalism or eccentric ostentation (*see* FERME ORNÉE); at best, they were splendid examples of architectural style combined with agricultural efficiency. Some were provided with impressive (and pretentious) features such as arched and crenellated gateways (farmers usually found other uses for them: as pigeon lofts, for example) but more importantly, the model farms of the first half of the nineteenth century were singularly innovative in such matters as the removal of effluent and the provision of adequate water pumping and distribution systems (usually referred to locally as *rams*). These not only pumped water to the steam ploughs and traction engines in the fields, but could also benefit the tenants of an entire estate whose cottages were connected with the rams (*see also* MODEL VILLAGES). On some cattle farms, traditional shippens (milking shed) were replaced by purpose-built dairies which incorporated complex water and drainage systems.

Traditionally, *farmhouses* needed large hall-kitchens in which to accommodate the farmhands but, as wage-labour became more common, and social distinctions more apparent, so the service rooms and offices were removed to the rear of the house (often adjacent to the yard), and by the mid-eighteenth century most new farmhouses were designed as residences which would not have appeared out of place in the high street of the local market town. By the mid-nineteenth century, farmhouses had become almost standardized in appearance: often constructed of red brick on three storeys, they formed the centre-piece of the model farm complex.

The existence or otherwise of a farmstead today is not necessarily a reliable indication of long-term occupancy of a particular site: many new farmsteads are built each year (often to replace older complexes inconveniently located within villages), while other sites may have been in continuous occupation since the Iron Age. There are also considerable regional archaeological variations. In the far north of England, for example, the dominance of pastoral farming in hill-country is suggested by the linear arrangement of dwelling/barn/shippen in a single range of buildings constructed along a hillside or 'stepped' into a slope. The transhumance practised (until quite recently) in the Cumbrian fells is evident in numerous abandoned SHIELINGS, and the insecurity of the Scottish borders is reflected in the defensive BASTLES of Northumberland. The thatched timber farmsteads of southern England originated in the large roundhouses of the first millennium, some of which were nearly 18 metres in diameter (60 feet); and many ROMAN VILLAS were the farmsteads of great estates, often occupying well-established sites.

Most *farmyards* changed little, either in appearance or function, from the Middle Ages to the First World War. They are the working centres of farms and are especially interesting and varied, both in the design of individual buildings and in the materials used in their construction (*see* COURTYARD FARMS). Yards were often enclosed on three sides within a range of buildings including a barn, an upper storey granary (entered by external stone steps), stables, wagon sheds, pigsties and, on dairy or mixed farms, a shippen, sometimes with a *tallet* (an open-fronted hay loft) above. On the open side would stand the rickyard or pond. A sure indication of the efficiency of a farmyard was the presence of a substantial *midden*, from which the farmyard manure was removed to the fields. Particularly distinguished are the great BARNS which represent considerable long-term capital investment. Although primarily used to process and store the cereal harvest, barns were constructed as multi-purpose buildings, places of work (and sometimes play) which could also be used for housing livestock and for carrying out a multiplicity of daily tasks, especially in inclement weather. Those which have survived are usually constructed in the very best vernacular style, using materials characteristic of a particular area, but the majority of storage and crop-processing buildings did not always achieve such architectural distinction or permanence. COB was frequently used, as were WATTLE AND DORB, to fill the upright spaces of TIMBER-FRAMED BUILDINGS, and later these were often replaced by BRICK NOGGING.

The *shippen* (*also* shippon, byre, milking shed or cow-house) was as essential to the pastoral or mixed farm as the barn was to the arable farm. At least one row of wooden stalls would be provided, each for one or two beasts, a drainage system and access to a midden. The door was usually of sufficient width for a single cow to pass through and there was sometimes a separate loose-box provided for sick or pregnant cows. Stables were the equivalent of the modern garage, and indispensable to the life of the farmstead. They were invariably cobbled, with a central drain, stalls or loose-boxes with troughs for water and fodder, hayracks and, traditionally, a HAG STONE. Often there was an adjacent 'tack room', with rows of wooden pegs on which harnesses were hung and maintained, and sometimes a small fireplace.

In the vicinity of the farmstead may be found a variety of other buildings (or their remains): many large estates had their own FORGE and DOVECOTE, and some farms had their own CIDER MILLS. Other buildings were connected with crop production and the needs of livestock. Whereas grasses and other cattle food were stored 'green' to make better silage, cereals had to be dried before they were stored, and the remains of *corn drying kilns*, some dating from the Middle Ages, may still be found, often as hollowed mounds in the fields. The OAST-HOUSES of Kent, Sussex and Herefordshire were kilns for drying hops. Corn mills were once ubiquitous in the agrarian landscape, access to a mill being essential if a farmer was to convert his cereal crop into a marketable commodity (*see* WATER-MILLS *and* WINDMILLS). But not all machinery was wind- or water-powered. In the late eighteenth and early nineteenth centuries, a number of polygonal or circular *wheelhouses* were constructed to provide covered, ventilated accommodation for a horse which, by walking in circles around a mechanism to which it was attached, would provide power to a variety of grinding and threshing machines in an adjacent barn by means of a series of shafts and gears. These wheelhouses were often endowed with local names, such as gin-gang, gin-house, horse-gear, track-shed and wheel-rig.

European agricultural policies of the late twentieth century have resulted in a decline in the fortunes of the small farmer and a corresponding growth in corporate holdings. Numerous farmsteads have been sold off as private dwellings, to be replaced by modern complexes of buildings more suited to the needs of large-scale agriculture and a rapidly changing technology.

FARMYARDS *see* FARMSTEADS

FARROW A path.

FARTHING *see* COINAGE

FEALTY An oath of allegiance made by a VASSAL in recognition of obligation and fidelity to a feudal lord.

FEAST-DAYS (FIXED AND MOVABLE) *see* SAINTS' DAYS AND FEAST-DAYS

FEE Freehold property which could be inherited.

FEET OF FINES From the Latin *finis*, meaning 'conclusion', a fine in this context was a formal conveyance of land. Such an agreement was itself legal but the 'dispute' which it determined was fictitious, so a fine was essentially a means of ensuring that all such transactions should be registered in the courts. The practice dates from the reign of Henry II (1154–89) and originally each party received a copy of the agreement; however, from 1195 a third copy, the 'foot of the fine', was filed by the Treasury. Such documents, which are maintained by the Public Record Office, provide a wealth of local detail and many have been published.

FELL A place-name element, commonly found in the north-western counties of England, from the Old Norse *fjall*, meaning 'mountain', e.g. Scafell in Cumbria and Mickle Fell in North Yorkshire.

FELONY A generic term formerly applied to a class of crimes which were regarded by the law as being of greater severity than those described as misdemeanours. The class (which included murder, wounding, rape, arson and robbery) comprised those offences for which the penalties formerly included forfeiture of land and goods. Forfeiture was abolished in 1870 but in English Law procedural differences were maintained until the distinction between felonies and misdemeanours was abandoned in 1967. No such distinction ever existed in Scotland.

FENESTELLA A canopied niche in the south wall of a presbytery containing a PISCINA and often an AUMBRY or CREDENCE or SEDILIA.

FENS *see* RECLAMATION

FERME ORNÉE In the late 1730s Philip Southcote created his whimsically picturesque Woburn Farm in

150 acres of Thames meadowland near Chertsey and in so doing established a model for numerous imitations. Intended to blend 'the useful with the agreeable', Southcote's ferme ornée consisted of a mock-Gothic house set in the midst of a working farm but with carefully planted trees, winding walks and cunningly arranged vistas so that 'the beauties which enliven a garden are everywhere intermixed with the properties of a farm'. Initial enthusiasm for Southcote's ferme ornée produced a rash of extravagant imitations such that by the end of the century many eminent landscape gardeners, such as Humphry Repton, had entirely rejected the concept – despite the attentions of William Kent, who had designed a castellated cow-shed for Rousham in Oxfordshire in 1738. Several 'rustic' Gothic farmhouses, often with verandas, barge-boarding and thatch, were built in the early nineteenth century, especially in Kent, Surrey and the Isle of Wight. These often had separate driveways leading to the house and farm 'offices', with 'wild and irregular' hedges bordered by broad, green drives and gravel walks. The ferme ornée enjoyed a revival during the Victorian period when several splendid Gothic farm buildings were constructed, almost invariably as fanciful appendages to large mansions, such as the Royal Dairy of the home farm in Windsor Great Park, built in 1858. *See also* COTTAGE ORNÉE

FERMTOUN *see* CLACHAN

FERRIES With some notable exceptions, few ferries have survived the age of motorways and tunnels. Those that remain are for the most part located in remote areas of scattered islands and indented coastlines such as the west coast of Scotland, or in major conurbations such as Liverpool where, despite a road tunnel, ferries across the Mersey continue to provide a valuable commuter link with Birkenhead. There is evidence to suggest that ferries formed part of the Roman road network. The most obvious example is where the Humber (*Abus flumen*) bisects Ermine Street, on its northerly course from Lincoln (*Lindum*) to York (*Eburacum*), between Winteringham Haven and Brough (*Petvaria*). Another ancient ferry (possibly also Roman) is evident in the eleventh-century place-names of North and South Ferriby, villages located on either bank of the Humber a few miles east of Ermine Street and west of the twentieth-century Humber road bridge. These and other similar 'ferry' place-name elements derive from *ferja*, which is Old Norse and therefore more commonly found in the northern counties of England than in the south,

where *pass*, *passage* and *lode* have the same meaning. Other elements include *hythe* and *staithe* (commonly -*stather*), both indicative of a landing place or wharf, the latter being of Norse origin.

Ferry boats carried iron ore across the Severn Estuary (*Sabrina flumen*) from Roman workings near Lydney in the Forest of Dean to the Fosse Way on the Gloucestershire Cotswolds. This route, the Arlingham Passage, was in continuous use until the last century, as was the medieval ferry from Aust to Beachley, Gloucestershire, which was abandoned with the opening of the Severn road bridge in 1966. Constructed on a rocky outcrop near Beachley is the chapel of St Twrog, once the cell of hermits who maintained the ferry (*see also* HERMITAGE). At another Severn crossing, up stream near Stourport, Worcestershire, the medieval hermits of Redstone Rock operated a ferry on an important SALTWAY from Droitwich, and in Devon the Starcross ferry across the Exe was maintained by monks from the Benedictine abbey of Sherborne in Dorset. By the thirteenth century, the ownership of such a ferry had become an exclusive privilege or 'liberty' granted by the Crown – and a singularly profitable one. The mechanics of ferries have changed little: most were flat-bottomed wooden barges, hauled from one bank to the other by means of a continuous rope or chain, and capable of carrying pack-horses and light vehicles as well as pedestrians.

FEUDAL AFFIX *see* PLACE-NAMES

FEUDAL AIDS Medieval lords enjoyed an entitlement (set out in *Magna Carta*) to financial aid which could be exacted from their free tenants for ransoming the lord's person, for knighting his eldest son and for the marriage of his eldest daughter. Such were the abuses of the system that in 1275 minimum ages were specified: fifteen for the eldest son and seven for the eldest daughter! Kings often exercised this right (which was not abolished until 1660) and in addition, they might obtain aid for other purposes, usually when a state of necessity existed and funds were required 'for the common good'. Initially, such taxation, known as '*gracious aids*', was authorized on an individual basis and limited to 20*s* for a KNIGHT'S FEE or 20*s* for rented land with an annual value of £20. But during the thirteenth century, a formula evolved which enabled the Crown to raise taxes (or enact other legislation) by means of the concept of *plena potestas* ('full power') derived from Roman law. This was based on the need to obtain a full measure of consent for taxes which were to be paid by all subjects, irrespective of tenurial status. From 1268, representatives – knights, burgesses and citizens – were summoned to (some) parliaments on the basis of *plena potestas* and had to bring with them letters of authority giving them 'full power' to act on behalf of the communities they represented. Records are maintained at the Public Record Office and six volumes, entitled *Feudal Aids* and containing details of assessments and inquisitions during the period 1284 to 1431, were published between 1899 and 1921.

FEUDAL SYSTEM A medieval European political-economic system based on the relationship of vassal and superior: the former holding land of the latter on condition of homage and military service or labour. The nobility held land of the Crown in return for specified military service, and the peasantry lived on their lord's land and were obliged to provide labour or a share of their produce in return for his protection. In England, the feudal system began to break down during the thirteenth century, though FEUDAL TENURE was not abolished until 1666.

FEUDAL TENURE Tenure of land in return for military service. Almost invariably, such tenure was eventually commuted to money payments.

FFYNNON From the Latin *Fontana*, a Welsh place-name indicative of a spring, well or natural 'fountain' (*see* HOLYWELLS).

FIEF An area of land held by means of a grant of a superior: in fee or on condition of military service.

FIELD (i) The correct term for an enclosed 'field' is CLOSE, a true field being a large area of arable land divided into STRIPS.
(ii) In ARMORY the surface of a shield or flag on which charges are placed.
(iii) Used to describe the site of a battle, e.g. Bosworth Field in Leicestershire (1485).

'FIELDEN' COUNTRYSIDE *see* COUNTRY-SIDE

FIELD NAMES Rapid technological innovation in late twentieth-century agriculture has not diminished the need for field names. Adam's Bounty, Wimberry Slade, Gallows Jack, Galloping Meadow and Partridge Place are precise locations whose characteristics are as familiar to today's solitary tractor driver as they were to his more numerous predecessors, though perhaps less intimately so. Remnants of medieval OPEN FIELDS may still be evident in names such as Great Field and West Field, and the sub-divisions (*see also* FURLONG) were also identified by names, some of which survived ENCLOSURE: Upper Tomshot (*shott* = furlong), for example. The component STRIPS (*selions*), on the other hand, passed from one tenant to another and although they may have been identified by names, these would have been as transient as those who tilled them. Many post-medieval fields were endowed with names which are of considerable interest to the local historian, though it should be remembered that field boundaries have often been re-defined or removed to amalgamate fields, and their names may have changed or been lost with them. Fields may also have acquired new characteristics or functions. An ancient enclosure at Glanvilles Wootton in Dorset, once recorded as Jerusalem Mead (because, like the real Jerusalem, it was some considerable distance from the original village farmstead), became Newlands Mead following an eighteenth-century enclosure award and the building of a farmstead on the farmer's new land. In the same parish, another Newland field-name records the creation of a medieval ASSART on the periphery of a former open field, subsequently enclosed but retaining in one particularly large field the original name – Great Field.

Field names can be remarkably enduring (some may be dated from the early thirteenth century), while others evolve with confusing rapidity or have become corrupted and contain archaic elements the origins of which are not always immediately apparent. Thus Warren Knap, an east Somerset field containing a hilltop warren, became the tautologous Warnop Top, and the Middle English *pightel* (a small enclosure) was confusingly corrupted to Pig Hill by generations of farmers, ignorant of the word's original meaning. Following the parliamentary enclosures of the eighteenth and nineteenth centuries, many fields were either created or re-defined and re-named, often to commemorate contemporary events or personalities such as Waterloo and Sebastopol, Wellington and Raglan.

John Field, in his book *English Field Names* (David & Charles, 1972), identifies twenty-six categories of field name:

Size of field, e.g. Fifacre
Distance from village farmstead, e.g.
   Jerusalem Mead, Antioch, etc.
Direction, e.g. East Field
Order, e.g. Middle Leys
Shape, e.g. Shakefork and Scutcheon
Nature of soil, e.g. Clinger ('Clayhanger')

Fertility, e.g. Starveacre Piece

Topographic features, e.g. Knapfield (*knap* = hillock)

Type of cultivation, e.g. Outroyd (*royd* = an assart)

Crops, e.g. Averhill (*aver* = oats)

Flora, e.g. Eldersfield

Domestic/farm animals, e.g. Oxmead

Fauna, e.g. Brockholes (badgers' setts)

Buildings, e.g. Millfield

Other man-made features, e.g. Updyke Field

Identity of owner/ tenant, e.g. Talbot's Land

Occupation of owner/tenant, e.g. Fowler's Piece

Identity of beneficiary of income from land, e.g. Priest Acre

Value of land, e.g. Far Angelet (*angelet* = a half ANGEL)

Archaeological features, e.g. Roundbarrows, Martyr Bones and Battle Acre

Folklore associations, e.g. Gandlins (Gandelyn's) Field

Arbitrary names, e.g. Balaclava and Plutarch

Boundary references, e.g. Gospel Field (*see* GOSPEL OAK)

Legal references, e.g. Copyhold

Industrial references, e.g. Upper Scowles (*scowles* = iron workings)

Recreational references, e.g. Little Plaster (*plaistow* = playing field)

Generally, field names are more interesting (and informative) in those areas which have remained unaffected by parliamentary enclosures. Even so, some of the names chosen in the eighteenth and nineteenth centuries may still provide clues to the past: barrows that have been lost to the plough, demolished buildings, half-forgotten religious sites or the lingering spectres of demons and hobgoblins in some sequestered corner of a farm. Personal names of all periods are common, though many are satirical (ribald, even!) and may allude to personal characteristics or nick-names.

When researching field names one should always begin with those who have actually worked the land and are able to recall workaday names from memory. These should then be compared with the field names recorded in tithe maps, drawn as a result of the granting of tithe awards in many parishes following the Tithe Commutation Act of 1836. Numerous estate and other maps, on which field boundaries are delineated and names given, may be found in the archives of county record offices. Many estate maps are still held in private ownership and, again, a county record office should be able to assist with information and guidance.
See also PLACE-NAMES

FIELD SYSTEM 'Field System' references on an Ordnance Survey map are usually indicative of prehistoric or medieval archaeological sites identified as having been cultivated and/or enclosed. *See also* FARMING, FARMSTEADS, ENCLOSURE, HEDGEROWS, LYNCHETS, OPEN FIELDS, RIDGE AND FURROW *and* STRIP LYNCHETS

FIELD WALKING *see* ARCHAEOLOGY

FILLET In architecture, a narrow, flat band between mouldings.

FINE ROLLS From the Latin *finis* meaning 'conclusion', the Fine Rolls record payments for writs, grants and licences made under the Great Seal. These include payments for licences to marry, for the acquisition of wardships, for entering into livery, for obtaining release from custody, for the granting of tolls and customs, markets and fairs and for permission to trade in wine, cloth and corn and for extracting minerals. Fine Rolls are maintained at the Public Record Office and a *Calendar of Fine Rolls*, covering the period 1272–1509, was published by HMSO from 1911 to 1963.

FINGERPOSTS *see* SIGNPOSTS

FIREBACKS The gradual introduction of the enclosed chimney flue and fireplace from the late thirteenth century resulted in a number of innovations, including the cast-iron fireback which both protected the stone wall at the back of the hearth and reflected heat into the room. It was also found that because the metal absorbed and conserved heat (effectively an early storage radiator) the up-draught in the chimney flue could be maintained, thereby improving the efficiency of the grate. Many firebacks incorporated traditional designs such as religious symbols, floral motifs and scroll-work; others bear the royal arms, though these are not always contemporary and usually have no particular significance. Other firebacks were made for specific fireplaces and included armorial devices appropriate to the family who commissioned them. Care should be exercised, however, for it may not be assumed that a fireback has remained in its original location and the HERALDRY may not relate to the house in which it is found. There are also many modern (usually inferior) imitations.
See also CHIMNEYS

FIREBOTE The right to remove wood from common land for fuel.

FIREDOGS A firedog or *andiron* is a metal stand (usually one of a pair) used for supporting logs in a fireplace. This ancient method was intended to raise the burning logs above the hearth-bed so that an up-draught of air was maintained. From the late thirteenth century, when enclosed chimney flues and fireplaces began to replace the central open hearths of earlier communal halls, shallow fire-baskets were sometimes slung between the andirons. With the importation of coal in the seventeenth century, these baskets were adapted to accommodate the new fuel but firedogs continued in use and were later incorporated into the design of free-standing grates (*see* CHIMNEYS). Because wood burns at a lower temperature than coal, many pre-seventeenth-century firedogs were embellished with intricate silver or brass filials. In many vernacular buildings, firedogs were used for wood-burning until the late nineteenth century.

FIRE INSURANCE MARKS (FIREMARKS) The idea of insurance against fire damage originated in sixteenth- and seventeenth-century advances in house-building (*see* ELIZABETHAN AND JACOBEAN ARCHITECTURE) and accelerated after the horrors of the Great Fire of London in 1666. Timber-framed houses were particularly vulnerable and their owners were expected to pay the highest premiums. Some Fire Offices even established their own fire brigades to minimize losses, and during the eighteenth and nineteenth centuries insured properties were identified by distinctive firemarks (known as *plates* or *plaques*), affixed to the house wall and bearing the company's device and (on early examples) a policy number. Plates were originally of lead but in the early 1800s

Firemark of the Bath Sun Fire Company.

copper was used, to be superseded by iron or tin in the 1820s. They served not only as identification marks, but also as effective advertisements for the insurance companies and it is not unusual to find entire streets of houses all bearing the same firemark.

Fire marks can sometimes be helpful in tracing the history of a building, for each mark had a policy number and the records of the insurance company (or its successor) are often still in existence. Such records can provide a description of the property when it was first insured together with any subsequent alterations, and sometimes even the contents of the house. The Chartered Insurance Institute has two major collections of British plates in its museum (*see* APPENDIX I). Many of the devices used are of armorial origin, such as the three silver leopard's faces on blue of the Salop Company, taken from the arms of both Shropshire and Shrewsbury (the county town). Heraldic beasts were particularly popular: the salamander of the Commercial Union Company, for example, and the singularly appropriate phoenix of the Phoenix Fire Office (founded 1682), a device which in 1936 was incorporated in the Phoenix Assurance Company's new coat of arms.

FIREPLACES *see* CHIMNEYS

FIRE SERVICE There is evidence that the Romans operated a fire-fighting corps (*vigiles*) during the occupation of Britain, but for many centuries thereafter there was no organized service and fire-fighting relied on local volunteers using primitive equipment such as leather buckets, hooks and grappling irons. William the Conqueror (1066–87) ordered that all household fires should be extinguished at sunset by means of a metal cover and, consequently, the evening bell came to be known as the *couvre feu* ('curfew') bell. Church bells were also used to raise the alarm, by ringing reverse peels, and this method of summoning volunteer firemen persisted into the twentieth century in some rural areas. Medieval administrators attempted to reduce the risk of fire in London and other cities by controlling the building materials used in the construction of new houses, and throughout the country supplies of buckets, ladders and hooks were maintained in churches (the canvas buckets which served the Puddletown community in Dorset are still kept in the church).

Organized fire brigades originated in the private brigades of the fire insurance offices which were established in London after the Great Fire of 1666 and responded only to the needs of their fully paid-up clients. Before the urban expansion of the Victorian era, therefore, most large towns relied either on the haphazard voluntary provisions of the old corporations or the self-interest of the insurance companies. In rural areas, the larger estates often had their own horse-drawn pumps, manned by estate workers, while some communities arranged corporate policies with the insurance companies whose FIRE INSURANCE MARKS may still be seen above cottage doorways in many villages.

In 1833 the insurance company brigades amalgamated to form the London Fire Engine Establishment. The new brigade was primarily concerned with saving property and with just seventy-six fire officers under a Scot, James Braidwood, was responsible for the entire London area. Braidwood was killed at the Tooley Street fire of 1861 and was succeeded by an Irishman, Captain Shaw, who quickly recognized the impossible demands required of his tiny brigade by a rapidly expanding metropolis. Partly as a result of Shaw's perseverance, the Metropolitan Fire Brigade Act was passed in 1865 and for the first time responsibility for the extinguishing of fires was placed on a public authority. In the following year the London Fire Engine Establishment was taken over by the Metropolitan Board of Works (later the London County Council and the Greater London Council) and became the London Fire Brigade. By the time of his resignation in 1891, Shaw had succeeded in creating the best trained and equipped fire service in the world. In the 1870s there were 500 firemen and 150 engines, with steam pumps and specially trained horses, operating from 159 stations and with an annual budget of £100,000.

But the statutory fire protection enjoyed by the people of London was not universally available. Local authorities were empowered to meet the expenditure from their rates and some larger towns had already established municipal brigades (Edinburgh in 1824 and Manchester in 1828, for example), but for the most part the service was dependent either on wealthy benefactors (such as the Prince of Wales' Brigade at Sandhurst and that of Lord Leconfield at Petworth in Sussex) or on volunteer crews of local worthies.

Until the mid-nineteenth century, all fire-engines were hand pumped and were largely inadequate for the task. In the 1850s steam-driven engines began to replace the old hand pumps, and the early years of the twentieth century saw the introduction of the motor engine: at Tottenham in 1903 and Finchley in 1904. By 1920, the London Fire Brigade was fully motorized. Sprinkler systems were first incorporated into buildings in 1812, portable fire extinguishers in 1816, street fire escapes in 1819 and the electric telegraph for fire alarms in 1861. Breathing apparatus (using oxygen) and the turntable ladder were first used in 1904.

It was not until the Fire Brigades Act of 1938 that Fire Authorities were established throughout Britain and local municipal authorities were, for the first time, required to provide a free fire-fighting service. At the outbreak of the Second World War in September 1939, there were some 1,400 local authority brigades in England and Wales and a further 185 in Scotland. During the 'Blitz', from September to December 1940, there were 34,000 fire calls in London alone and the heavy air-raids on London and other cities during 1940–1 proved the need for a unified command with standard operational procedures. As a result, in August 1941 all brigades were formed into the National Fire Service. After the war, the Fire Services Act of 1947 restored responsibility for the provision of a fire-fighting service to local government, though with fewer authorities and with a greater degree of central control. Following the Local Government Act of 1972 the number of local authority fire brigades was reduced to 55 in England and Wales and to 12 in Scotland.

FIRESTONE *see* FLINT

FISH-PONDS The medieval method of preserving meat in brine was so unreliable (and the results so unpalatable) that many manors and most religious houses possessed their own sources of fresh protein, notably DOVECOTES, WARRENS and fish-ponds. Of these, the fish-pond was of singular importance for it provided a reliable source of food on the numerous 'fish days' that were observed throughout the year and on which no 'flesh' (i.e. red-blooded meat) could be eaten. Abstinence was particularly important in religious communities whose rules determined that the forgiveness of sins and the attainment of everlasting life were contingent on austerity and self-denial. Consequently, even the most insignificant of religious houses possessed its own fish-pond and many of these were retained when monastic buildings were converted to private homes following the DISSOLUTION OF THE MONASTERIES. Today, most medieval fish-ponds are dry, their leats silted and their sluices long abandoned. Typically, they are rectangular and flat-bottomed with retaining embankments raised 1 metre (3 feet) above ground level and with two or three adjacent *stew ponds* where young fish were raised. The main pond sometimes contained an artificial island for wildfowl. Another type of pond, similar to those created for fish farming and angling today, was the *scoop pond*, which was formed by digging out or damming a small coomb just below the spring line on a scarp face.

Carp were the most popular fish, though pike, perch, bream, roach, tench, trout and elvers were also farmed. Poaching was a constant problem and the earthworks of decayed fish-ponds are most often found in the vicinity of domestic buildings where they could more easily be observed and protected. They were also incorporated in the water defences of some medieval castles and moated homesteads (*see* MOATS).

FITZ- Surname element meaning 'son of', often applied in the Middle Ages to illegitimate children.

FIVE BOROUGHS *see* DANELAW, KINGDOMS (ANCIENT), TOWNS *and* VIKINGS

FIVE WOUNDS OF CHRIST The expletive 'Zounds!' (God's wounds), in common usage for at least two centuries after the Reformation, reflected an earlier medieval obsession with the notion that contemplation of Christ's wounds (Isaiah: 'the wells of salvation') would provide protection against sudden unconfessed and unabsolved death. This was of particular significance during the second half of the thirteenth century when the BLACK DEATH decimated the population. Consequently, representations of the Five Wounds of Christ are ubiquitous in the fabric of late medieval churches, depicted in stained glass, stone and wood. There are numerous variations, but most show five disembodied wounds or Christ's heart, hands and feet pierced and imbrued with blood. They are sometimes crowned or contained within shields and may be mistaken for heraldic devices.
See also CHRISTIAN SYMBOLS *and* INSTRUMENTS OF THE PASSION

FLANKERS *see* CASTLES (MEDIEVAL)

FLANKING TOWERS *see* CASTLES (MEDIEVAL)

FLASHING *see* STAINED GLASS

FLAT *see* FURLONG

FLAVIA CAESARIENSIS *see* ROMAN ADMINISTRATION

FLEET From the Old English *flēot*, meaning 'sea inlet' or 'stream'. The Dorset village of Fleet lies between East and West Fleet, which together form a narrow channel of brackish water separated from the English Channel by the 16 km (10 mile) length of the Chesil Beach. Several other 'Fleet' names are to be found along the Essex coast.

FLINT A variety of quartz consisting of irregular nodules of nearly pure silica, dark grey or black in colour, and occurring in association with chalk which provides it with its white coating. Despite its apparent ordinariness, this extremely hard and fissile mineral was of singular importance in the development of civilization: it provided Neolithic man with implements (axes) and, when struck, it would produce fire. The Anglo-Saxons knew it as *firestone*. There is evidence to suggest that before *c.* 3000 BC the population of southern Britain was dependent on imported implements from the STONE AXE FACTORIES of the north and west. Thereafter, they tended to exploit local sources of flint, either in open-cast workings or by quarrying through several strata to reach the best beds. At Grimes Grave in Norfolk, pits 6 to 12 metres deep (20 to 40 feet) were sunk through substrata of inferior material to the 'floorstone' level where galleries, radiating from the base of each pit, were excavated using red deer antlers and the shoulder blades of oxen and illuminated by lamps of animal fat. The Grimes Grave area was mined continuously until *c.* 2100 BC, some 800 shafts being dug during that period. The black flint nodules extracted from these mines were rough-dressed into axes on the knapping floors before being exported over a wide area as *rough-outs*, to be finished and polished by those who acquired them. Most of the twenty or so sites identified as Neolithic flint mines are located on the chalk uplands of southern Britain. No doubt many others have been erased by ploughing, but in the field they have the appearance of broken ground, covering several acres, with clusters of shallow circular depressions.

Because of its strength and durability, flint is frequently found as a building material in chalk districts of south and east England and has continued in use for this purpose from the Iron Age to the present day. The Romans used it, in conjunction with brick and mortar, in the construction of the walls of Silchester (near Reading in Berkshire) and the forts of the SAXON SHORE. Before the fourteenth century, whole flints were embedded in the mortar of walls, which were further strengthened with stone and flint rubble and lacing courses of stone or brick.

But from the late thirteenth-century split and shaped (*knapped*) flints, with their dark facets outwards, were often used in conjunction with brick or stone to form chequer-work and other geometrically patterned surfaces. A special decorative technique called *flushwork* also developed at this time. Knapped flint, set in mortar within the matrices of intricately carved freestone facings, was a feature of many East Anglian churches and continued, there and elsewhere, into the sixteenth century, by which time a high standard of craftsmanship had evolved. Walls of knapped flint (usually with brick or stone quoins) are commonly found in domestic and agricultural buildings in the southern counties of England and in some areas flint courses may alternate with similar horizontal bands of brick or stone.

FLOAT Introduced towards the end of the nineteenth century, the float was a utilitarian two-wheeled vehicle driven by a single pony, and used by farmers for market and dairymen for their milk-rounds. It was low at the back, entered by a rear door and usually had 'splashers' or mudguards. In towns, floats were usually driven from a standing position to afford a better view of traffic and in some urban areas they continued in use as milk-delivery vehicles until the 1950s.

FLORIN see COINAGE

FLUSHWORK see FLINT

FLY (*also* **LANDAULET**) The fly of the mid-nineteenth century was a small coachman-driven vehicle for two passengers drawn by a single horse and widely used as a station cab in rural districts. *See also* LANDAU

FLYING BUTTRESS see BUTTRESS

FOGOU see COURTYARD HOUSE and SOUTERRAIN

FOLDBOTE The right to remove wood from common land to make hurdles for sheep-folds.

FOLKLORE AND LEGEND Just as an oyster will form a pearl round an irritating particle of sand, so our ancestors created a rich legacy of folklore and legend out of the frustrations of their limited understanding. Although we now dismiss many traditions as mere superstition, it should not be assumed that our forebears were any more credulous

than ourselves: we too are sensitive to the uncertainties of our time and create our own mythologies to deal with them. Collectively, the myths, customs and legends of Britain provide a unique 'memory bank', not only of long-abandoned religious, cultural and social observances but also of the aspirations and fears, experiences and perceptions of countless generations of our ancestors. Just as our language (and, indeed, our blood) contains elements acquired from a variety of racial sources, constantly suppressed and revived, modified and corrupted, grafted on to one another or superimposed on earlier usage, so too has folklore come through to us as a hybrid echo of the past. Out of this complexity there emerged a tradition which even Christianity could not erase: in times of adversity, the old gods are invoked and the former holy place re-visited. The significance of folklore, and particularly of local traditions, should not be dismissed by the historian: it may provide clues to the origins of FIELD NAMES, for example, or facilitate the identification of vernacular architectural carvings.

Local tradition has often been dovetailed with more substantial legend. There are, for example, numerous 'Arthurian' sites which, although not identified in the canon of Arthurian literature, have acquired legendary associations because of distinctive topographical features or corrupted traditions which recommend them as mythological locations (*see* ARTHURIAN BRITAIN). Folk-etymology is readily incorporated into local 'tradition'. The hamlet of Kingstag in Dorset has long been associated with the legend of the White Hart of Blackmoor Vale, the beauty of which so enchanted Henry III that he gave orders that the beast should be neither hunted nor killed. Local tradition has it that, despite the king's orders, the white hart was slaughtered on the bank of the river Lydden at Kingstag by one Sir Thomas de la Lynde and that the king was so enraged that he imprisoned Sir Thomas and imposed a tax called 'White Hart Silver' on the Vale. In fact, the name originally meant 'kinges stake' and referred to a boundary post within the ancient royal Forest of Blackmoor which, nevertheless, is also known as the Forest of the White Hart. More recently, the 'half real, half imagined country' of Thomas Hardy's *Wessex* has created its own mythology, complete with numerous local traditions associating real locations with those of Hardy's novels and poetry. Perhaps the strongest traditions are those associated with domestic entertainment prior to the advent of mass communication in the twentieth century. The oral traditions of heroic sagas and legends, embellished no doubt with references to familiar landmarks, were communicated by MINSTRELS throughout the medieval and Tudor periods as 'talkyngs' and ballads, often to large, aristocratic audiences which included also retainers and dependants who, in turn, conveyed them to the yeomanry and peasantry. Thus, folklore and legend were woven into the warp and weft of the fabric of English society.

For Folklore Society *see* APPENDIX I

FOLK MOOT A community assembly, usually of a town or shire.

See also LAW

FOLLIES True follies are man-made structures which have no apparent rationale other than to pronounce the eccentricity of the builder. A folly is a conceit: a self-indulgent creation, often indicative of profligacy or obsession verging on madness. Of course, there are exceptions: McCaig's Tower, for example, a gigantic two-storeyed Gothic coliseum at Oban, Scotland, was built in 1900 by the eponymous 'art critic and philosophical essayist and banker' with the intention of relieving local unemployment. The underwater billiard room, built in the 1920s at the Surrey home of the financier Whittaker Wright shortly before he committed suicide, and the nineteenth-century replica of Dallington church steeple (Sussex), erected by 'Mad' Jack Fuller who swore that he could see the original from his home and found that he could not, are just two examples of true follies.

ARTIFICIAL RUINS and constructions such as the BELVEDERE, GAZEBO, GROTTO, MAUSOLEUM, OBELISK, PAVILION, PROSPECT TOWER and TEMPLE have distinctive functions and are not really follies, though they are often described as such. Many of these so-called follies were built as romantic elements within landscaped parks, sited as EYE-CATCHERS to enhance perspective and focus attention or as vantage points from which the best views might be enjoyed. Many were erected as melancholy MEMORIALS to a family's greatness, while others marked the boundaries of estates or were intended to endorse a horticultural theme: a Chinese pagoda in an Oriental garden, for example. Even Sir Thomas Tresham's Lyveden New Bield in Northamptonshire, described as 'the grand-daddy of the English folly', was originally intended as a garden house and banqueting hall. Built in the 1590s, this gaunt, roofless building is of cruciform plan which, with its numerous religious panels and inscriptions, provides an unambiguous architectural reference to Tresham's conversion to Roman Catholicism. Tresham's religious obsession is also reflected in his triangular Trinitarian Lodge, a true folly of 1593, the three-gabled walls of which are divided into three panels each decorated with trefoils and other symbols of the Trinity.

There are numerous similar early examples but most architectural 'follies' date from the eighteenth century and the great period of landscaping associated with William Kent (1685–1748) and Lancelot ('Capability') Brown (1716–83) and the later 'picturesque' romanticism of Humphry Repton (1752–1818) (*see* GARDENS). *Chinoiserie* was rampant in the mid-eighteenth century, exemplified by the Chinese House at Harristown, County Kildare, which was originally designed as a pavilion for the gardens at Stow in Buckinghamshire. It has deep eaves, latticed windows and is painted in Chinese red, ochre yellow and soft grey-blue. Several of Britain's follies have been converted to dwellings, notably many of those in the ownership of the Landmark Trust (*see* APPENDIX I) such as the extraordinary giant Pineapple at Dunmore Castle in Scotland.

See also HERMITAGES

For the Folly Society *see* APPENDIX I

FOLLY (place-name) *see* COLDHARBOUR

FONT- *and* **-FONT** *see* SPRINGS

FONTS A font is a receptacle, normally made of stone, for baptismal water. In the early Church, these were large basins set below ground level in which the candidate was immersed or submersed in baptismal water, and it was not until the early Middle Ages, when infant baptism and affusion (the pouring of water over the head) became the general practice, that fonts were raised above floor level. In the Christian Church the Mass and baptism are considered to be pre-eminent among the seven sacraments, baptism emphasizing entry into the Christian life and the purging of sin. Consequently, every medieval church possessed its font, which was symbolically located near the entrance. A number of early fonts, little more than stone tubs, large enough to accommodate a standing adult and hardly raised above floor level, demonstrate the transition from the practice of immersion to that of affusion. But most surviving fonts were intended for infant baptism and are shallow and raised on pedestals or plinths to a convenient height.

Many Saxon fonts resemble an upturned drum and for that reason are known as *drum fonts*. They are usually lined with lead, stepped at the base and decorated with crude but vigorous motifs, arcading and cable mouldings. Twelfth-century ROMANESQUE fonts, constructed at a time of ubiquitous church building, may be elaborately carved with CHRISTIAN SYMBOLS and biblical scenes such as the Baptism of Christ and the Crucifixion. Norman *pedestal fonts* are often square and set within the carved capital of a short octagonal stem and drum-shaped pedestal. Another type of font of the same period has a large *cup bowl* supported on a substantial cylindrical stem and four angle shafts, all rising from a square plinth and having the appearance of an orchestral *timpano*. In some instances, the font seems almost to have been built upon representations of the devil, often in the form of strange and mythical creatures which are 'oppressed' both by the weight of the masonry and by the sacrament of baptism itself.

In order to avoid the lengthy process of sanctification before each christening, a supply of baptismal water was retained in the font, the lead lining of which prevented seepage through the porous stone. The practice of removing holy water for 'medical' and other, more sinister, purposes was so commonplace by the thirteenth century that an ecclesiastical statute required that lids should be fitted to fonts, secured by means of iron bars and padlocks. The remains of the staples, by which the bars were held in place, may still be found on many fonts, leaded into the stonework on either side of the bowl.

Twelfth-century font at the church of St Peter and St Paul at Mappowder, Dorset.

Twelfth-century Romanesque font and 'oppressed' devil-creature at St Michael's church, Castle Frome in Herefordshire.

By the fifteenth century, a number of font covers had been replaced by magnificent elongated canopies (*see* TABERNACLE), carved and fashioned in the intricate architectural forms of the late Middle Ages, the PELICAN being a particularly popular motif. Some canopies were so heavy that they had to be raised by means of a mechanism known as a *font crane*. Others were permanent stone structures erected above and around the font. These elaborate canopies often surmounted late fourteenth- and fifteenth-century fonts, commissioned as part of the re-modelling of many churches. Typically, they were octagonal or hexagonal in shape with sophisticated but subdued ornamentation which sometimes included the armorial devices of a patron or benefactor. Following the Reformation, the dome or cupola shaped canopy was introduced and, in newly built churches, the baptistry was almost invariably located at the west end, usually beneath the tower.
See also CHURCHES

FOOTPATHS Highways over which the public has a right of passage on foot only. Footpaths are clearly marked on Ordnance Survey *Explorer* maps (1:25000) and often follow the routes of ancient trackways or defunct ROADS. More can be learned of the historical development of a locality from its network of ancient paths and BRIDLE-WAYS than from any other feature.

Some paths may be the remnants of prehistoric route-ways while others once linked the settlements of Celtic and Anglo-Saxon Britain. Some were long-distance routes, used by medieval pack-horse trains and generations of drovers; others form radial networks of paths linking outlying farmsteads with a village nucleus (often with the tower of the parish church at its hub) and with each other. Many converge on fords, ferries and bridges or were adopted to delineate the boundaries of demesne lands or ecclesiastical and civil parishes. More recently, others have been created out of the diversions of perambulating postmen where they were obliged to abandon the highway in order to service outlying farms and country houses (*see* ROYAL MAIL). The provision of STILES in field boundaries along the course of a footpath is a comparatively recent innovation: our ancestors would have been accustomed to following familiar, well-beaten tracks along the headlands of fields and through open countryside.

Many rights of way have been extinguished or diverted in recent years, and a (significantly smaller) number created. This practice is generally intended to 'rationalize' the local footpath network (invariably for the benefit of the landowner), usually by redirecting paths round field boundaries. It should be remembered that the majority of paths and bridle-ways are considerably older than most enclosures and the researcher should always be suspicious of routes which follow a zig-zag course along field edges and appear deliberately to avoid crossing fields. A recent 'rationalization' scheme may have replaced a network of considerable antiquity. All such extinguishments, diversions and creations of public rights of way are recorded by the highway authorities and these records are available at county council offices, together with copies of definitive maps for each parish. Footpaths may still be established by twenty years' uninterrupted use, though the owner of a private path may safeguard against this by displaying a notice indicating that the path is private. A footpath remains a highway even when a farmer fails to reinstate it after ploughing (which is his statutory responsibility) or if he allows it to be obstructed by growing crops or erecting barbed wire. Walkers should always follow the line of a path even when it is obstructed: to do otherwise (by a diversion round the field's edge, for example) is to trespass.

See also ENCLOSURE ROADS, GREEN LANES *and* HIGHWAYS

FORCE A tenth-century place-name element from the Old Norse *fors*, meaning 'waterfall', generally confined to the north-west of England.

FORDS Crossing places of rivers and streams, which were known to provide firm and reliable passages throughout the year, almost invariably became focal points of converging route-ways and, consequently, many developed into commercial settlements. The ubiquity of *ford* place-name elements (and regional variations: *rhyd* in Wales; *red*, *ret* or *rit* in Cornwall and -*wath*, from the Old Norse *vath,* in the north-west of England) is indicative of the numerous river crossings which existed before the advent of bridge-building in the Middle Ages. The approaches to a former ford may still be discernible in the vicinity of a more recent bridge, or apparent in the (often dramatic) diversion of an ancient road from its original course to cross a river by a bridge before returning to its earlier route on the opposite bank. But the provision of a bridge did not necessarily render an earlier ford redundant. In many instances, mostly on WINTERBORNES, fords are found alongside narrow PACK-HORSE BRIDGES which were necessary when a stream was in flood. In Ceredigion, the place-name Pont-rhyd-y-groes means 'Bridge of the Ford of the Cross' and a number of notorious fords (such as that at Christian Malford on the Avon in Wiltshire) were marked by a *cristelmæl* or crucifix, intended both to commemorate those who had drowned in their inconstant waters and to protect future travellers from a similar fate.
See also BRIDGES *and* FERRIES

FORESHORE In law, the foreshore is that part of a beach between the medium low-tide mark and the medium high-tide mark: that which is 'subject to the flux and reflux of the sea'. The foreshore belongs 'to the Sovereign by virtue of his prerogative' unless it has been granted elsewhere, which is often the case. It is unlawful to remove sand or shingle or goods cast upon the foreshore from a wreck. Since the reign of Elizabeth I, such goods are the property of the person or persons who have 'franchise of the wreck': in other words, those with authority to exercise a royal prerogative (*see* TREASURE TROVE). But 'when a dog or cat escapes alive out of a ship, that said ship shall not be adjudged a wreck; the goods shall be kept by the King's Bailiff, so that if any sue within a year and a day the goods shall be restored to him.' (The King's Bailiff is now the Receiver of Wrecks.)

FORESTALLER *see* MARKETS

FOREST MARBLE A limestone ideally suited to the manufacture of stone roofing slates.

FORESTS The popular perception of a forest is of 'a large tract covered with trees and undergrowth' (*Oxford Dictionary*). This is far removed from the medieval definition which was strictly a legal one, concerned with the protection of vert and venison and the administration of Forest Law. Hunting forests encompassed a wide variety of countryside: woodland, moor and heath, wastes and even cultivated land. One of the most satisfactory definitions of a forest is that of an eighteenth-century writer James Lee, quoted in Thomas Hearne's *Curious Discourses on English Antiquities:*

> The word *forest* . . . doth signify . . . all things that are abroad, and neither domestical nor demean [demesne]: wherefore *foresta* in old time did extend into woods, wastes and waters, and did contain not only *vert* and venison, but also minerals and maritimal revenues. But when *forests* were first used in England I find no certain time of the beginning thereof; and, although that ever since the Conquest it hath been lawful for the King to make any man's land (whom it pleased him) to be *forest*, yet there are certain rules and circumstances appointed for the doing thereof. For, first, there must issue out of Chancery a writ of *perambulation*, directed unto certain discreet men, commanding them to call before them XXiiij Knights and principal freeholders, and to cause them, in the presence of the officers of the forests, to walk or perambulate so much ground as they shall think to be fit or convenient for the breeding, feeding and succouring of the King's deer, and to put the same in writing, and to certify the same under the seals of the same Commissioners and Jurors unto the Chancery.

It is clear that forest territory was originally that vast 'no man's land' which extended beyond those areas which had been cleared, enclosed, cultivated or grazed. These wildernesses were possessed by (or of) the Crown and several were used by the late Saxon kings for hunting (notably the New Forest). But it was the Normans who recognized the advantages of combining sport with exploitation and it was they who created the bureaucratic framework within which the forests were defined, extended and protected by law. Where definition of a forest was considered necessary a formal procedure of perambulation and registration was used. There can be little doubt that an inherent love of the chase stimulated the creation of vast hunting forests under the Norman kings. But this should not conceal the fact that a regular and substantial supply of fresh protein was also an essential requirement of a numerous and often itinerant court and, because hunting was enjoyed by a privileged few, membership of that élite could be manipulated as a form of patronage at minimal cost to the Crown. The distribution of forests corresponded closely with that of royal manors so that the king could progress from one estate to another, assured of a constant supply of meat for his legion companions and retainers as well as a day's sport (bucks were hunted in summer and autumn, and does from early September to the beginning of February, after the breeding season).

The forests also provided *largesse* in the form of gifts of beasts for the stocking of magnatial DEER PARKS and income could be derived from the imposition of fines, from the granting of ASSARTS and from the sale of privileges and exemptions from the Forest Law. In 1204, for example, the people of Devon paid 5,000 marks so that the Forest Law (which at that time applied to the entire county) should be limited to the forests of Exmoor and Dartmoor.

WOODLAND within the forests was managed commercially and special enterprises were sometimes permitted, such as cattle farms (*vaccaries*), mining and quarrying – always providing that such activities were not detrimental to the vert and venison. 'The breeding, feeding and succouring of the King's deer' had precedence over every other consideration and from this principle developed a system of regulation known as Forest Law, applicable to the royal forests and those chases held by the earls of Lancaster (*see* CHASE). Not only were the beasts (known generically as *venison*) protected but so was their habitat and any form of vegetation which could be serviceable to the deer (the *vert*). Nevertheless, there existed certain rights which could be acquired (such as those of HEYBOTE, PANNAGE and TURBARY) and which could be exercised without detriment to the deer. Each 'right' was defined with great precision, often as a consequence of protracted negotiation, and could be suspended under certain specific circumstances: in a hard winter, for example, when a period of *heyning* would be declared during which the grazing of domestic animals would be curtailed to the benefit of the deer.

Forest Law was undoubtedly effective in the context from which it evolved, but inevitably it became oppressive and ultimately the cause of almost universal resentment. In particular, the special authority of the courts which administered the Forest Law outside the Common Law, the arbitrary (and often unlawful) extension of forest limits and the frustration caused by constant disputes and bureaucratic procrastination over individual rights, led to organized resistance and ultimately contributed to *Magna Carta* in 1215 and the Charter of the Forest two years later. This effectively brought to an end the institution of new forests, which had grown in number from about 25 at the time of Domesday Book in 1086 to almost 150 in 1217.

At the heart of each forest was a refuge in which the deer (fallow, red and roe) lived and bred. This was surrounded by an area of marginal land, often cultivated or grazed and containing farmsteads and settlements (Colchester was within the bounds of Essex Forest), in which the deer were protected and over which hunting might take place. Although technically within the forest 'bounds' (and therefore subject to Forest Law), marginal land was not necessarily in the ownership of the Crown. But the game within the forest was, and landholders were powerless to control the depredations of browsing deer or the ravages of the huntsmen and their followers.

Contrary to popular belief, *poaching* or the unlawful removal of timber was punishable by fine (or imprisonment for habitual offenders) and not by mutilation. Dogs could be 'lawed' (mutilated) to prevent their use for hunting, or 'humbled' (their claws were clipped) so that they should not harm the deer, but even this could be avoided by payment of a fine. Deer were permitted free access to land and enclosure fences had to be low enough to allow for this or provided with leap-gates (*see* LYPIATT). Only foresters had the authority to drive deer from land, even when herds were discovered grazing in growing crops. The forests were administered by two justices, responsible for the forests to the north or to the south of the River Trent, and each forest had its warden who controlled a large contingent of foresters (*free-foresters*), the more senior of whom were often from well-to-do local families, and woodmen (*woodwards*). Several hereditary offices were established: in 1148 the Earl of Oxford was the Hereditary Steward of the Royal Forests in Essex and in *c.* 1270 the Earl of Norfolk and Suffolk, as well as being Hereditary Marshal of England, Hereditary Steward of the Household and Hereditary Bearer of the Banner of St Edmund, was also Hereditary Warden of Romford Forest and Hereditary Forester of Farnedale

During the thirteenth and fourteenth centuries, assarting had reduced significantly the peripheral areas of forests and the authority of the Forest Law, which had been strictly enforced during the twelfth century, was similarly eroded. By the Tudor period, the forest institutions and courts were preoccupied, not with the maintenance of diminishing royal prerogatives, but with the commercial exploitation of remaining assets for the benefit of landowners and commoners. Charles I attempted to reconstitute Forest Law, but the anticipated revenues from grants of exemption failed to materialize, the legislation being overtaken by the onset of civil war.

Widespread disafforestation from the sixteenth and seventeenth centuries, a rapidly increasing demand for mature timber (particularly during the Napoleonic Wars), and the parliamentary enclosures of the eighteenth and nineteenth centuries have reduced the former forests and chases of medieval England to spectral remnants, for the most part commemorated in forest place-name elements. *Purlieu* was marginal land, once unlawfully taken into a forest, and *-lee*, *-ley* or *-leigh* (from the Old English *lēah*) was a clearing in woodland, for example (*see* -LEE). 'Lodge' names are common and originate in the lodges at which hunting parties were lodged or those occupied by foresters, each responsible for a *walk* or division of the forest. In the present century, vast forests of conifers have been planted to satisfy an ever-increasing demand for paper and (at the time of writing) 'community forests' are being proposed for industrial hinterlands to provide attractive landscapes which will support wildlife and help local employment.
See also CHASE *and* VERDERERS

FORFANG A reward for recovering stolen property.

FORGE Once the nucleus of every rural community, the village smithy is now almost invariably a private dwelling, though the name 'forge' often remains as a reminder of its former function. The smith himself was both a farrier (from the Latin *ferrum* = iron), who specialized in shoeing horses, and a blacksmith, who was able to turn his hand to a multiplicity of other tasks associated with the working of blackmetal (iron). As a farrier, he was expected to be an equinal expert (even a horse-doctor) as well as a shoeing smith and, consequently, he became a key figure in rural life. In remote areas (and *in extremis*), he even extracted teeth. By the end of the nineteenth century, he was required to

General odd-job 'smithy' at Grundisburgh, Suffolk, in the early 1900s.

maintain farm machinery and vehicles, to repair and manufacture a variety of tools and implements and to provide ironwork for other crafts: new links for broken chains, replacement 'antique' hinges for ancient doors and ornamental curlicues for gates, for example. In matters mechanical, it was to the smith that the community would turn for advice and it was therefore inevitable that by 1900 he was becoming a motor mechanic. Before 1914, most villages had managed to retain their economic self-sufficiency and in this the smith played an essential rôle. Large estates also had their own workshops and forge which serviced the needs, both agricultural and domestic, of the household, the home farm and the tenanted holdings.

The term *forge* is often used synonymously for the actual workshop or smithy. Correctly, it is an open hearth, raised to a convenient height with a canopied chimney flue and a means of creating a forced but controlled draught to raise the temperature of the fire above that of ordinary combustion. This is usually achieved by hand- or water-operated bellows. The familiar *anvil* (correctly, the *London anvil*) was in general use by the nineteenth century and is a development of earlier and less sophisticated devices on which the iron could be hammered into the

required shape. It weighs from 50 to 150 kg (111 to 333 lb) and each part has a specific function. The *face*, or flat upper part, is that on which most of the work is carried out. It is of hardened steel and produces a vigorous recoil of the hammer, thereby requiring less energy to raise it after each blow. Next to the face is the *table*, a narrow strip of softer mild steel or iron on which is placed metal which is to be cut with a cold chisel. This ensures that the edge of the chisel will not be turned should it cut through to the surface below. The conical projection is the *beak* (or *bick*) on which curved objects (such as horseshoes) are shaped. At the opposite end of the beak is the *punch hole*, over which hot metal is placed when holes are punched (e.g. the nail-holes in horseshoes).

Most of the numerous tools used by a smith have evolved through constant use, refinement and adaptation. A farrier uses a *catshead* and a shoeing hammer which has a claw for removing nails from old shoes. For general ironwork, a blacksmith has a 1 kg (2.2 lb) *ball peen hammer*, with a head slightly rounded on one side, and a *sledge hammer* weighing up to 9 kg (20 lb). This may be used by an assistant who, in the noise and heat of the forge, will respond to visual signals from the smith as he manipulates

the forging on the anvil with his tongues. The forging is taken from the forge when it is evident from its colour that it has reached the required temperature and is therefore malleable, and as much work as possible must be completed before the iron cools.
See also HARNESS, HORSESHOE *and* WAGONS

FORMEDON IN DESCENDER In the thirteenth century, when land was granted to a son or daughter (particularly when they married) the donor would often attempt to ensure that the land remained in his family and would revert to him should the donee's line of descent fail. In practice, it was impossible to create ENTAILS in this way so, from 1285, a statute required that writs, known as Formedon in Descender (from the Latin *forma doni*, meaning 'form of gift'), should be available to enable a donor to recover lands lost when conditions were not observed. This statute effectively created secure entails and its later interpretation was to bring about major changes in the landholding structure of England.

FORTIFICATIONS *see* CASTLES (MEDIEVAL), HILL FORTS, MARTELLO TOWERS AND COMMISSION FORTS, ROMAN FORTS AND CAMPS, SCOTTISH HIGHLAND FORTS, SIEGES, TUDOR COASTAL FORTS *and* PILLBOXES

FORTS OF THE SAXON SHORE *see* ROMAN FORTS AND CAMPS

FORUM *see* MARKETS *and* TOWNS

FOSS(E) From the Latin *fossa*, meaning 'long ditch' or 'trench', especially one associated with a fortification (*see also* CASTLE). The Fosse Way, so called from the fosse or ditch on each side, ran for 300 km (200 miles) from Axminster (Somerset) to Lincoln via Bath (Somerset) and Leicester, and marked the limit of the first stage of Roman occupation in the mid-first century AD.
See also ROMAN ROADS

FOUNDLINGS Foundlings, the abandoned infants of unknown parents, were usually a charge on the poor rate (*see* POOR LAW), details of which were recorded in vestry minutes, now held by local record offices. Foundlings also appear as such in parish registers.

FOUR-CENTRE ARCH *see* ARCH

FOURGON A large nineteenth-century four-wheeled composite carriage used for carrying luggage and with an enlarged box-seat for personal and domestic servants. It was sent ahead of a travelling carriage (*chariot*) when touring abroad and was the responsibility of a courier escorted by an armed guard. The fourgon arrived in advance of the main party so that rooms could be prepared and luggage unpacked.

FOUR-WHEEL CAB ('GROWLER') This cab replaced the HACKNEY CAB and was similar to the privately-owned CLARENCE. Widely used in towns from the 1840s, some 'four-wheelers' continued in operation until the 1930s, when they were sometimes fitted with taxi-metres. During the second half of the nineteenth century, growlers acquired a reputation for being dirty and their drivers abusive. The majority of cabs were either hired out to their drivers or driven by employees, and the horses, tended by a staff of grooms and 'strappers' (who were responsible for the harness), were invariably overloaded and overworked, unlike the younger and smarter horses which drew HANSOM CABS.

FRANCHISE A liberty, privilege or exemption by grant or prescription.

FRANCISCANS The mendicant Order of Friars Minor (or 'Grey Friars' as they were known from the colour of their habits) was founded by St Francis of Assisi in 1209. The distinguishing feature of the order's rule (which was finally confirmed in 1223) was an insistence on absolute poverty both severally and corporately. In practice, difficulties inevitably arose but they were overcome by means of a legal fiction of vesting ownership of the order's property in the Pope. By 1317–18, a more moderate view prevailed and the order was permitted to hold property corporately. Laxity increased during the fourteenth century and throughout the following centuries the order's integrity was frequently threatened by 'reforming' factions. Nevertheless, the Franciscans were the most successful of the orders of friars to settle in England and they attracted to their ranks some of the most brilliant men of their time. The Franciscans were also known as 'Friars Minor', the DOMINICANS being 'Friars Preacher'.
See also FRIARS

FRANKALMOIGN Land granted by a lay person for the benefit of an ecclesiastical body, usually conditional upon the provision of a CHANTRY.

FRANK FEE Tenure which required no obligatory service.

FRANKLIN A free tenant or farmer, usually enjoying reasonable prosperity and often a manorial steward or bailiff.
See also MANOR *and* YEOMAN

FRANKPLEDGE In many areas of Anglo-Saxon England, each VILL was sub-divided into *tithings* of ten households. Each tithing was charged with a corporate responsibility for the conduct of its members and for ensuring that anyone accused of an offence was available to answer the charge at the COURT LEET. The system was known as frankpledge and was administered in each tithing by a *tithingman* (*also* borsholder, headborough *and* thirdborough). Some classes of society (e.g. knights and clerks) were exempt.
See also LAW AND ORDER

FRASS Decomposing timber.

FRATER Correctly a refectory but, because of the term's Latin derivation (*frater* = 'brother') it is sometimes applied in error to a monastic 'common room'. Clearly, to the medieval monk the fraternal breaking of bread must have been of the utmost significance – hence its use in the context of the refectory (*see* MONASTERIES).

FRATRUM *see* LATIN

FREEHOLD (*also* **FRANK TENEMENT** *and* **FREELAND**) The holding of property in absolute possession. Freehold property was not subject to manorial custom and could be disposed of without restriction. A *flying freehold* is that part of a building which extends over another building to which it is attached.
See also RELIEF

FREEMAN (i) A tenant who held land at a fixed rent and free of feudal service.
(ii) A man who has served his apprenticeship and is free to conduct his trade in his own right.
(iii) Prior to the Municipal Corporations Act of 1835, a freeman was a citizen who was entitled to claim exemption from tolls and a share of the profits of his city of borough. The Act franchised non-freemen in positions of local government, and the term is now occasionally conferred as an honorary title by a city or corporation.
   The origins of freemen are to be found in the medieval merchants and craftsmen whose influence helped to found and stabilize urban communities. Townspeople have enjoyed certain privileges for centuries: in 1071 William I confirmed the 'laws' of London which were claimed from the time of the Roman occupation. The Assize of Arms of 1181 refers to 'all Burgesses and the whole community of freemen', King John's charter to Nottingham of 1200 speaks of 'our free burgesses of the Merchant Guild' and a similar charter of 1201 refers to a grant to the men of Hartlepool that they should be free burgesses.
   Freemen were not men who had been freed from serfdom: they were subject only to their own corporate authority and to that of their king. Every man who entered to the Freedom of the City of York was required to pledge himself on oath to the preservation of City and Sovereign by all means at his disposal. In York, such privileges existed well before 1100. Admission was either by *patrimony* or by *servitude* to a master craftsman who was himself a freeman. Only freemen could trade within the city, participate in its governance or hold the office of mayor. Each freeman was required to serve the mayor in any way that was necessary: by maintaining the fabric of the city or by taking up arms on the citizens' behalf. From the beginning of the twelfth century (and possibly before) York was self-governing. Not only did the freemen influence the development of trade and industry, but as the mayor and council they also controlled the administration (and political allegiance) of the city.
   The rights and privileges enjoyed by these ancient boroughs and corporations were specified and confirmed from time to time by means of royal charters. In one of the earliest York charters, dated from Westminster between 1155–62, Henry II confirms to the freemen all their 'liberties, laws and customs in England and Normandy and throughout the Coasts of the Sea'. York continues to admit freemen, as do nearly fifty other towns and cities (there were at least 155 in 1840). Many of these maintain archival material including freemen's rolls from which may be extracted details of a city's trade and manufactures, the extent of its population and the social conditions of its inhabitants since the Middle Ages.
See also GUILDS

FREEMINER The origins of freemining in the Forest of Dean, Gloucestershire, are lost in antiquity, though the earliest records date from the thirteenth century. A freeminer is one who is born in the Hundred of St Briavels (an area bounded by the estuaries of the Severn and Wye and a line from Gloucester to Ross-on-Wye) and who, attaining the age of twenty-one, has worked one year and a day in a coal or iron mine in the Hundred and has been registered in the Books of the Gaveller, the official who administers the miners' rights. As a freeminer, he is then entitled to own up to three mines (*gales*) and to work them 'without let or hindrance'. Freeminers' rights were recognized in the Dean Forest Mines Act of 1838.

FREESTONE Easily sawn stone.

FREE WARREN A franchise, obtained from the Crown, granting rights to kill or keep beasts and game, and of particularly significance in the context of Forest Law (*see* FOREST).

FRIARS The two great orders of friars, the FRANCISCANS (the Grey Friars or Friars Minor) and the DOMINICANS (the Black Friars or Friars Preacher) originated in the thirteenth century as adherents to the precepts of St Francis of Assisi (1181/2–1226) and St Dominic (1170–1221). A Spaniard by birth, Dominic's objective was to prepare a team of preachers capable of counteracting the spread of heresy in southern France and he took the institutions of the AUGUSTINIAN canons as his model. In 1220 he is said to have met with Francis, whose influence persuaded him to adopt the Franciscan ideal of absolute poverty, both several and corporate, which had been adopted by the early Franciscans as the *Regula Bullata* (the First Rule) in 1209. The Dominican Order was established at two general chapters at Bologna in 1220 and 1221, while the Franciscans recast their First Rule in 1221 and brought it into its final form in 1223.

The Franciscans and Dominicans, unlike the monastic orders, were international brotherhoods of individuals whose members were itinerant preachers, ministering to the needs, and dependent on the charity, of those who employed them or from whom they begged. Both were MENDICANT orders (Latin *mendicare* = 'to beg'), whose members did not belong to a particular religious house or community, as did the monks, the properties needed for the administration of the orders being held on their behalf by the Pope or some other patron. The Dominicans divided Europe into a number of provinces, each under the jurisdiction of a prior. A provincial chapter, comprising representatives of the constituent houses, met annually to elect a *diffinitor*, by whom they would be represented at a general chapter (which also met annually), and four *diffinitores* responsible for the administration of the chapter.

For two years of a three-year cycle the general chapter was attended by the *diffinitores* and for the third by the provincial priors. A master-general of the Order was elected (for life) by an *ad hoc* general chapter. By the 1240s, the Franciscans had adopted a constitutional organization very similar to that of the Dominicans.

The Dominicans arrived in England in 1221 and within fifty years had established some forty-six houses. The Franciscans followed in 1224 and by 1255 had forty-nine houses, more widely dispersed than those of the Dominicans who had preferred to concentrate their activities around the universities. Ironically, the Franciscans attracted to their number many of the most brilliant men of the age and this resulted in the effective usurpation of the Dominicans' rôle as intellectuals and scholars and the diminution of Franciscan principles.

Other orders included the Order of the Hermits of St Augustine – the *Austin Friars* – (an order distinct from the Austin Canons) who, as their name suggests, began as communities of hermits (in the mountains of Italy) dedicated to the Augustinian rule. Like the Dominicans, they became scholars and preachers but the order grew slowly in England starting in small country towns and eventually moving into the larger urban centres with some thirty-four houses. The *Carmelites* (or White Friars) also originated as a hermit community located on Mount Carmel in Palestine. They were the most contemplative of all the friars with thirty-seven English houses, some of which were remote from towns. Like the Carmelites, the smaller orders of Friars of the Holy Cross (the Crutched Friars), the Friars of the Penitential Sack and the Pied Friars were all under Dominican influence and their function was to teach and preach as priests and instructors among the urban laity.

The popularity of the friars in thirteenth-century England was in part attributable to their preference for going into the world instead of withdrawing from it, and partly because their poverty contrasted with the rapidly increasing wealth of the monastic foundations. But of even greater significance was the concentration of pastoral work in the towns, where the friars must have been a familiar and reassuring sight and where enormous crowds were attracted to their preaching. (The sermon was the principal medieval means of mass-communication and several urban churches, with long hall-like naves, were constructed by the Dominicans to accommodate congregations.)

It was this popularity which bred increasing resentment and hostility among the lay clergy and the monasteries. Parish priests, for the most part poorly trained and held in low regard by their parishioners, were unable to compete with the sermons of the mendicants or with their competence in hearing confessions. They were also losing valuable revenues from burial fees as people opted in increasing numbers for burial in the friars' churchyards rather than those of their parishes. The poverty and humility of the friars were characteristics with which the populace readily identified, while the unremitting acquisition of wealth which typified many of the monastic foundations was thrown into sharp relief by the comparison. The response of the late medieval 'establishment' was predictable. Misinformation found its way into the works of Chaucer and Langland and even influenced the redoubtable Wycliffe. There can be little doubt that there was some justification for criticism of the friars during the fourteenth and fifteenth centuries: observation of the First Rule had become lax and many friars employed decidedly dubious devices to extract money from patrons or to persuade young people to join their orders. Nevertheless, such criticism was by no means universal, indeed there is considerable evidence to suggest that there was no significant decline in the number or quality of bequests and benefactions to the mendicant orders until the Reformation.

FRIEZE In classical architecture, a horizontal band of sculpture filling the space between the ARCHITRAVE and the CORNICE (*see* ENTABLATURE). A horizontal band of decoration along a wall near the ceiling.

FRONTPIECE The principal façade or entrance of a building.

FROSTERLEY MARBLE *see* PURBECK MARBLE

FULLING *see* WOOL

FUMAGE A Saxon form of taxation based on the number of chimneys on a house.

FUNERARY HERALDRY Funerals of the late medieval and Tudor nobility were often magnificent spectacles, not least the processions which preceded the committal in which the deceased's 'achievements' were paraded. These included his spurs, gauntlets, crested helm, shield, sword, tabard and banner, which was retained for display in the church, the best-known example being those of Edward, the Black Prince

(d.1376), at Canterbury Cathedral. Several less grandiose examples of funeral achievements have survived in parish churches, mostly from the sixteenth century, and from these may be traced the gradual evolution of funeral heraldry from the practical equipment of medieval warfare and tournament through the stylized, artificial helms, crests and tabards of the Tudor period to the heraldic substitute, the funeral HATCHMENT of the seventeenth, eighteenth and nineteenth centuries.

Banners of members of the various orders of chivalry will also be found in many British churches. These are invariably 1.5 metres square (5 feet), embroidered with the knight's arms and fringed in two or more colours. The banner of a deceased knight is the perquisite of the king of arms of the order to which he belonged but, in practice, it is normally conveyed to the family and displayed in their parish church.

FURLONG (*also* **FLAT** *and* **SHOTT**) Originally, the term meant the length of the furrow in the common field which was theoretically considered to be a square of 10 acres. The furlong as a unit of measurement was therefore dependent on the definition of an acre and this varied considerably according both to time and place. Nevertheless, from the ninth century, when it was considered to be the equivalent of the Roman *stadium* or one-eighth of a Roman mile, the term *furlong* has always been used to describe an eighth part (220 yards) of an English mile irrespective of its agricultural definition. (*See also* ACRE *and* CHAIN.)

The term was also applied to a (roughly) rectangular block of parallel strips within an open field, each block identified by name (*see* STRIP). This suggests the possibility of an earlier system of small field divisions pre-dating the creation of the open field, though it seems more likely that most medieval furlong divisions were, in fact, sub-divisions of previous 'long furlongs' composed of 'long strips'. There is also evidence to suggest that in some areas crop rotation was practised on the basis of furlongs rather than OPEN FIELDS.

FURMITY (*also* **FRUMENTY** *and* **FURMENTY**) A concoction of hulled (de-husked) wheat, raisins, etc., boiled in milk.

FURNACE POND *see* HAMMER POND

FYRD *and* **FYRD-BOTE** *see* MILITIA *and* TRINODA NECESSITAS

GALANAS In medieval Wales, sums of money paid as recompense for murder.

GALE *see* FREEMINER

GALETTING *see* SLATES

GALILEE A vestibule reserved as a chapel for penitents at the western end of a church in the early Middle Ages. Derived from the NARTHEX of Byzantine churches, the term was sometimes extended to include the western section of the nave which was considered to be less sacred than the remainder of the church. The term may have originated in the 'Galilee of the Gentiles' of Matthew (Ch. 4, v. 15). Galilees were not a feature of English medieval parish churches (entry was normally through a southern porch) but there are examples at some cathedrals, notably Ely and at Durham, where a line across the floor marks the limit beyond which women could not pass. The term was later applied to the vestibules of Stuart and Georgian churches of the seventeenth and eighteenth centuries.

GALLAUNS Irish standing stones.
See also MONOLITH, OGHAM STONES, STONE CIRCLES *and* STONE ROWS

GALLERY (i) In churches and chapels (mostly those dating from the seventeenth and eighteenth centuries) a tiered upper storey constructed to provide additional seating. Following an act of 1644, which banned organs from churches, west galleries were often added to medieval churches to accommodate 'choirs' of village musicians playing traditional instruments such as viols, hautboys, flutes and serpents. These choirs compiled 'psalm books' of music, much of which was composed by members of the community, and established a tradition of instrumental playing and part-singing which continued from one generation to the next until the second half of the nineteenth century. John Foster, a renowned eighteenth-century musician from Ecclesfield in Yorkshire, attracted over 5,000 mourners to his funeral; and a Shropshire blacksmith is reputed to have built his own iron cello so that he could join his village choir. But the Victorian clergy, always enthusiastic in their search for greater respectability, drove out many west gallery choirs: that at Puddletown in Dorset was replaced by a barrel organ in 1845, for example. The devastating effect on a choir of the introduction of an organ or harmonium is described vividly in Thomas Hardy's *Under the Greenwood Tree* (*see* ORGANS).
(ii) A minstrels' gallery was often constructed above the SCREENS PASSAGE in late medieval halls (*see* MINSTRELS).
(iii) A characteristic of many large Elizabethan and seventeenth-century houses was the long-gallery, an elongated apartment running the full length of the building, usually on the first or second floor, with windows on three sides and fireplaces on the fourth (*see* ELIZABETHAN AND JACOBEAN ARCHITECTURE).
(iv) *For the* triforium gallery *see* CHURCHES

GALLERY GRAVES *see* CHAMBERED TOMBS

GALLETING Pebbles (French *galet* = a pebble) or stone chips applied to mortar for decorative purposes or to reduce the amount of mortar required and increase durability. A common technique found in buildings in south-east Norfolk and parts of Kent, Surrey and Sussex.

GALLOWS A gallows was a scaffold for the hanging ('turning off') of criminals. Usually consisting of two upright posts and a cross-piece, the scaffold was of sufficient width to allow a two-wheeled cart to pass between the uprights: the cart which bore the victim and his (or her) coffin. Up to the eighteenth century, gallows were usually erected at prominent crossroads on the outskirts of towns, partly as a warning to potential law-breakers and partly because of the superstitions which often surrounded such places: suicides and criminals were also buried there. In larger towns, multiple hangings and other, more barbarous, forms of execution required triangular gallows or 'triple trees' of three posts and cross-pieces, the best-known example being that at Tyburn on the main west road out of London. Not surprisingly, few gallows have been preserved, though their sites may often be ascertained from local place-names and from the archaeological records of parishes maintained by county record offices, though in rural areas these should more correctly be referred to as GIBBETS rather than gallows.

By 1840, the 'Bloody Code' with its innumerable capital offences (theft of goods worth 5*s* in value, for example) had been abolished, as had the STOCKS and PILLORY and roadside gibbet (*see also* LARCENY). Although capital punishment was restricted to crimes of murder and treason, public executions, known as 'hanging matches', remained well-attended spectacles until the passing of the Capital Punishment Amendment Act of 1868. Such gatherings must have resembled fairs or race-meetings, attracting numerous purveyors of pies, furmity and ginger beer, and itinerant hawkers of ballads, 'lamentations' (faked confessions) and grotesque mementos. On 17 April 1840 the Cornish *West Briton* reported:

The execution of the brothers Lightfoot who murdered Mr. Nevill Norway took place at Bodmin on Monday last in front of the County Gaol . . . the town of Bodmin on the Sunday evening presented the appearance of a fair . . . thousands of persons traversed the high roads during the night . . . and by twelve o'clock, the hour of the execution, there could not have been less than twenty to twenty-five thousand persons present. The brothers were launched into eternity together and died almost immediately. After hanging for an hour the bodies were cut down and put into a couple of black coffins . . . they were then buried in a hole in the coal yard in front of the prison.

At some gaols in Assize towns, the temporary gallows was little more than a hinged flap set against the prison wall with a beam above to carry a rope. At Newgate, the gallows (first used in 1783) was a more elaborate structure consisting of a substantial black-covered platform surmounted by the stout uprights and cross-beam of the scaffold from the middle of which hung a short chain. Below the cross-beam was the trap, worked by a lever like a pump handle which released a draw bar beneath. Executions at Newgate usually took place on Mondays. The gallows having been assembled in the early hours, spectators would begin to arrive at about 4.00 a.m. and between 6.00 and 7.00 the rope, 'coiled up like a serpent', was laid on the platform. As the church bells began to strike the hour, 'a murmurous roar' of anticipation, 'awful, bizarre and indescribable', signalled the arrival of the condemned man, his wrists pinioned by a leather strap, preceded by the chaplain and followed by the public executioner. With cries of 'Hats off!' and 'Down in front!' from the crowd, the chaplain would read aloud while the executioner strapped the man's legs together, pulled a nightcap over his face and

adjusted the rope through the chain and around his neck. Returning down the steps, he would pull the lever that released the trap. If the neck was not broken by the fall (as was often the case) an assistant would heave at the man's legs until strangulation was complete. The body remained suspended for an hour before being lowered into a coffin and buried beneath Newgate's Birdcage Walk.

From 1868, executions were carried out privately within the prison and capital punishment for murder was finally abolished in Britain in 1965.
See also PUNISHMENT

GAMBREL ROOF *see* ROOFS

GAOL DELIVERY *see* LAW

GARDEN CITIES *see* TOWNS

GARDEN MOUNTS The forerunner of the GAZEBO, a garden mount or mound was sometimes raised in an enclosed medieval or Tudor garden to afford a prospect beyond the enclosing walls or hedges. Mounts were sometimes planted with fruit trees or provided with a summer house or arbour. They were also known as toots or TOOT-HILLS.
See also PROSPECT TOWER *and* TEMPLES

GARDENS In its earliest form, a garden was an enclosure of thorn or scrub intended to keep domestic animals in and wild ones out. More substantial ramparts of dried mud, earth or stone were constructed for defensive purposes and when nomadic communities settled, these enclosures became places for cultivation. The earliest recorded gardens in Egypt, *c.* 3000 BC, were rectangular and surrounded by mud walls to absorb the sun's heat. They contained a dwelling-house and irrigation channels which divided the garden into geometric areas where onions (part of the Egyptian staple diet) and other vegetables were grown, together with herbs for medicinal use. Inevitably, in the gardens of the rich and influential, the irrigation channels and enclosure walls became stylized to provide formal pools and arbours, overhung with vines for shade and relaxation.

This style of garden characterized those of the Islamic world for several thousand years and from it derived the gardens of Roman town houses with their central courtyards and colonnaded peristyles (the forerunners of the monastic cloister GARTH), flower-beds and paths, pergolas and statuary, fountains and formal pools. The Roman conquerors of Europe brought with them numerous plants, vegetables and fruits as well as their knowledge of agriculture and horticulture. The kitchen garden of a Roman VILLA was the woman's responsibility, and she was judged by how well it was run. The market gardens of Roman estates were essential to the rural economy of occupied territories and of Britain in particular.

Horticultural practice declined following the withdrawal of Rome from Britain in the late fourth century AD, though it is known that leeks, cabbages and dried peas and beans formed some sort of subsistence diet during the so-called Dark Ages that followed. In the sixth century, St Benedict decreed that all Benedictine monasteries should become self-sufficient. The domestic buildings of monasteries were laid out on the Roman court and cloister plan, and within the cloister garth the monks cultivated medicinal plants, herbs and vegetables, sometimes in a series of raised, rectangular beds (*see also* VINEYARDS). Plans exist, from the early twelfth century, of the monastery gardens at Canterbury which included a *herbarium* (herb garden) orchards

and vineyards, all watered by an elaborate irrigation system. It is generally assumed that British medieval gardens remained essentially utilitarian until the early sixteenth century. This was certainly true of the average villager, whose natural preoccupation with the production of food was to be subject to the vestigial obligations of the Norman feudal system for several centuries.

From the late fifteenth century, as the residences of the nobility became less defensive, so areas of cultivation began to extend outwards to provide orchards and vegetable gardens and the formal pleasure gardens illustrated in contemporary HERBALS and books of poetry such as the *Romance of the Rose*. Typically, these show a series of walled and trellised gardens, connected by arched openings, with close-clipped hedges, turf seats, mulberry bushes and water-fountains. From these evolved the *knot garden* of flower-beds and gravel pathways. Beds were small, usually raised and laid out in intricate geometric patterns with dwarf shrubs such as box or thrift or herbs like rosemary forming

The deserted King's Knot Garden at Stirling Castle.

low, neatly clipped edges. Spaces were filled with washed or coloured gravel or earth, and beds planted with flowers such as lilies, lavender, marigolds, roses, primroses and gillyflowers.

During the sixteenth and seventeenth centuries, English garden design followed that of Renaissance Italy and France, with stone staircases, terraces and elaborate water features, fountains and cascades. But the English horticultural Renaissance was less rigorously formal: the climate was more conducive to mixed planting and the style more whimsical than grand. The garden at Hampton Court Palace was to provide a model for the gardens of the Tudor nobility. MAZES, labyrinths, pavilions, arbours, sundials, GARDEN MOUNTS and elegant topiary characterized the gardens of the period which remained formal and geometric in character with separate (usually walled) areas designated for growing fruit and vegetables, including many introduced by adventurers returning from the New World (notably the potato and maize). Pleasure gardens, which flourished under the Tudors and Stuarts, went unattended during the Commonwealth (1649–60), when utilitarian vegetable and fruit gardens were temporarily *de rigueur*.

Following the Restoration, there was in England a developing interest in horticulture and a new emphasis on plants grown for their appearance rather than for their culinary or medicinal attributes. The seventeenth century witnessed the opening of the first British botanic gardens and an increasing use of orangeries and conservatories to protect vulnerable plants. From the second half of the seventeenth century (inspired by a Frenchman, André le Nôtre), European gardens became even more elaborate, with long, magnificent vistas, rectangular canals and *parterres* (arrangements of flower-beds) which were both larger in scale and more intricate than earlier knot gardens. Le Nôtre also introduced the *pattes d'oie* ('goose feet'): hedge-lined avenues which radiated through the surrounding woodland and forest of a great estate. Spectacular though these gardens may have been, they were still not places for colourful floral display and their scale was incompatible with the requirements of the average English manor-house or small country estate.

During the eighteenth century, there was a reaction in England against the artificiality of formal gardens and from this emerged the landscaped gardens and PARKS inspired by the patron/architect Lord Burlington (1694–1753) and created with aesthetic determination by William Kent (1685–1748), 'Capability' Brown (1716–83), Humphry Repton (1752–1818) and others. Formal gardens were everywhere erased to be replaced by landscaped parklands in which all things natural were accentuated and enhanced with cloud-reflecting lakes, classical TEMPLES, OBELISKS, bridges, GAZEBOS and GROTTOES. But opinion was divided as to the appropriateness of classical ornamentation in the English landscape. To many, the Gothic 'ruin' had a prescriptive right to its place in what had once been medieval countryside, while the classical obelisk, temple or triumphal arch were considered to be alien and intrusive. Differences were reconciled by allowing that Gothic ruins were appropriate to Gothic mansions and classical structures to classical ones – providing that they should always appear to be 'modern contemporaries . . . the idea of a Greek ruin in England being a contradiction both to history and experience' (Burgh, 1783). Few of these landscaped gardens remain, largely because of a revulsion of taste in the early nineteenth century directed at the notion of 'improving' nature, which was by then considered to be artificial and even blasphemous. Perhaps the best preserved landscaped garden is that created by the architect Henry Flitcroft (1697–1769) at Stourhead in Wiltshire. Begun in 1741, the meres in a bleak valley were dammed to form a series of lakes and the banks decorated with architectural ornaments amid ornamental trees and flowering shrubs.

The landscaped park, on the other hand, was to have a lasting effect on the British countryside. The already extensive grounds and DEER PARKS of numerous country mansions were enlarged, contours altered, artificial hills created and valleys excavated, canals converted to serpentine lakes and straight lines of avenues and paths abandoned. Everywhere 'Nature was triumphant' (though contrived) and a sense of space prevailed with broad vistas and artificial perspectives created through careful tree-planting and the judicious provision of 'eye-catchers' and ARTIFICIAL RUINS. Walls and hedgerows, which otherwise would have intruded on the landscape, were rendered unnecessary by the introduction of the HA-HA, a sunken ditch with a vertical outer side which prevented animals from escaping. The boundaries of estates were obscured by further tree planting, providing cover for game, while beyond the confines of the park, parliamentary ENCLOSURE of the commons and open fields proceeded apace. In a letter of 1805, the poet Wordsworth (1770–1850) expressed a commonly held objection to changing 'a whole country into a nobleman's livery'. But like many a latter-day conservationist, Wordsworth failed to recognize that what he described as the 'holiness of nature' was as much man's creation as it was the Almighty's. Throughout the eighteenth and nineteenth centuries, the day-to-day culinary and horticultural requirements of the great aristocratic households were provided for by complexes of kitchen gardens, cold-frames, orangeries, conservatories, carnation houses and GREENHOUSES, all linked to increasingly sophisticated irrigation, heating and ventilation systems and staffed by a hierarchy of ill-paid gardeners and labourers.

The Victorian Age saw a return to geometric gardens characterized by cluttered ornamentation, the brightly coloured and over-patterned flower-beds of civic parks and suburban villas exemplifying the tastes of an emergent middle class. Victorian travellers and explorers returned from far-flung corners of the British Empire with a bewildering variety of new and exotic species. An unsurpassed interest in plants was reflected in numerous gardening publications, notably *The Gardener's Magazine* (first published in 1826) and *The Suburban Gardener and Villa Companion* (1838). But all this activity resulted in gardens which were out of tune with their English setting: rockeries, aviaries, ferny grottos and palm houses packed with exotic plants proliferated. Fortunately, two eminent Victorians, Gertrude Jekyll and William Robinson, proposed an alternative 'English' style, and such was the success of their advocacy that it was they who were chiefly responsible for the English garden as we know it today. Their writings coincided with the restoration of many long-neglected smaller country houses and cottages, and their ideas appealed especially to a new breed of gardeners, exponents of the joys of a rural utopia and the first commuters of the railway age. Jekyll, who had a wonderful sense of colour and texture, effectively invented the herbaceous border, and Robinson, in his book *The Wild Garden*, proposed the planting of 'natural' gardens with shrubs and trees from other countries which would then be left to their own devices. Throughout this period, a growing urban preoccupation with an apparently idyllic English countryside resulted in an Edwardian perception of the 'cottage garden' far removed from the stark realities of rural life at the turn of the century.

In the late twentieth century, the garden is again an extension of the home as it was in ancient Rome. Garden cities have been conceived and built, each house having its own garden. Large gardens have become uneconomic and, with an almost universal increase in leisure time, small ones have multiplied.
See also ALLOTMENTS *and* ROCOCO
For the Garden History Society *see* APPENDIX I

GARDEROBE In medieval castles and houses the garderobe was a latrine or privy, usually a single cell at the end of a short, crooked passage within the thickness of a wall from which a shaft vented to a cesspool beneath. Others consisted of stone benches in cubicles (*gongs*) which jettied out on corbels high above a moat. Most latrines were little more than chutes in an outer wall and must have been exceedingly draughty. Those of the private chambers were marginally more sophisticated with provision for braziers to heat water for washing and a degree of privacy. The largest of the three town gates at Conwy was fitted out as an office for Edward I's private secretariat who benefited from the last word in thirteenth-century lavatories: twelve separate cubicles project from the walls, discharging into the stream below. It was believed that fumes from a privy assisted in the preservation of fabrics and clothing was often stored in the immediate vicinity of a garderobe. Indeed, in the Middle Ages the term 'garderobe' was used to describe both a bathroom and a dressing-room or ante-chamber where clothes were kept: a *wardrobe*. Being located in the outer walls, latrine chutes were considered to be a vulnerable area of a castle's defences and were often designed so that they could not be used to gain access during a siege.
See also CASTLES (MEDIEVAL) *and* WATER-CLOSET

GARGOYLE From the Old French *gargouille*, meaning 'throat', a gargoyle is a projecting gutterstone, sometimes (though not necessarily)

Gargoyle at Mappowder church, Dorset.

incorporating a lead water-spout and often carved to depict a grotesque visage, beast or figure (*see also* PAGAN SYMBOLS). Its function was to traject rainwater away from the walls and footings of a building. This was particularly necessary when, in the fourteenth century, ornamental traceried parapets were developed as a means of finishing off a wall. With no eaves to carry rainwater away from the building, it was necessary to provide lead bow-gutters behind the parapets and gargoyles to discharge the rainwater at regular intervals.

GARLAND (i) In ARMORY, a circular wreath of leaves. A *chaplet* is a similar wreath with a flower (usually a rose) depicted at each quarter.
(ii) An anthology, usually of medieval or Tudor origin.

GARTH Derived from the Old Norse *garðr*, meaning 'enclosed ground used as a yard or paddock', the term continues to be used in that sense in the northern counties of England where it is applied specifically to a small grassy enclosure. Elsewhere, it describes an enclosed space or 'yard' with a hard surface, as in courtyard and farmyard. But this is a recent interpretation and the words 'garth' and 'yard' were originally applied to any small enclosed space as in churchyard/ churchgarth, stackyard/stackgarth, appleyard/ applegarth, etc.

An applegarth was an apple orchard and a stackgarth an area in which hayricks were kept. A fishgarth was an enclosed space for the taking of fish on the seashore or in river shallows. A cloister garth was the area enclosed within the CLOISTER of a monastery, generally used as a vegetable and herb garden or (by the Carthusians) as a burial ground (*see* MONASTERIES).

GARTHENDS *see* TOFT

GASCONY *see* AQUITAINE

GAS SUPPLY *see* PUBLIC UTILITIES

GATE *and* **YAT** Place-name elements derived from the Old English *geat* or *gæt*, meaning 'gate' or 'pass' and evident in such names as Gatehampton, Oxfordshire; Claygate and Reigate, Surrey; Yately, Hampshire; and Donyatt, Somerset. Such a 'gate' is often a natural opening in cliffs, as at Margate, Kent, or a gap in a range of hills, as at Symonds Yat, Herefordshire, a settlement located in a deep ravine cut by the river Wye. Sometimes the name is specifically associated with access to a forest, as at

Woodyates in Cranborne Chase, Dorset, and Symonds Yat, which is on the northern fringe of the Forest of Dean. Some 'gate' names in the north of England and in the Scandinavian midlands are derived from the Old Norse *gata*, meaning 'road', as in Clappersgate, Cumbria, and Harrogate, Yorkshire.

GATEHOUSES The entrance to any fortification is likely to be its weakest point of defence. For this reason, the builders of HILL FORTS constructed overlapping ramparts to protect entrances, the Romans erected defensive towers wherever a wall was pierced by gates, and the medieval builders of CASTLES and fortified TOWNS contrived massive gatehouses, typically rectangular in plan with flanking drum towers and first-floor chamber (often a chapel) above a central GATES PASSAGE protected by a series of DRAWBRIDGES, PORTCULLISES and stout double doors secured by iron draw-bars. Many monastic and ecclesiastical buildings were likewise protected by gatehouses, some of which (e.g. the moated Bishop's Palace at Wells in Somerset) have defensive devices comparable with those of contemporary castles.

Although by the end of the fifteenth century such formidable structures were no longer considered necessary, there remained (especially in more remote areas) a constant threat of pillage from brigands and TRAIN BANDS and many mansions and manor-houses retained or constructed some means of defence, a moat or enclosure wall and fortified gatehouse being the most common. Like their medieval predecessors, these Tudor and Jacobean gatehouses provided both secure accommodation and a port of entry at which visitors could be interrogated by a gatekeeper or porter (*portarius*) before entering or leaving the courtyard. They also provided an ostentatious manifestation of the status and wealth of the owner, a rôle later adopted by the lodges of country houses (*see* LODGE).

Gatehouses (with porters' lodges) were also incorporated in the quadrangles of Oxford and Cambridge colleges. Several date from the early sixteenth century and are lofty, elegant structures magnificently embellished with decorative architectural features and the emblazoned heraldic devices of their founders and patrons. Architectural vestiges of gatehouses and enclosure walls are to be found in the ornamental pavilions and balustrades which surround the forecourts of several late sixteenth-century houses, such as Montacute in Somerset.
See also MONASTERIES

Early seventeenth-century timber-framed gatehouse to the thirteenth-century Stokesay Castle, Shropshire.

GATES PASSAGE In the GATEHOUSE of a medieval CASTLE or fortified town, the principal entrance passage through which entry and egress are controlled.

GAVELKIND An ancient custom by which, in the event of intestacy, the estate of a tenant was divided equally among his sons or (if he had no sons) among his daughters. For this purpose, a tenant was considered to be of age at fifteen and the estate could only be escheated when there were no heirs (*see* ESCHEATS). The estate so divided did not include that portion which comprised the widow's DOWER (which could be up to half). Gavelkind was abolished as recently as 1925.
See also WARDSHIP

GAZEBO A small pavilion or summerhouse set on an eminence so as to command a view that would otherwise be obscured by a garden wall.
See also BELVEDERE, FOLLIES, GARDEN MOUNT *and* PROSPECT TOWER

GELD (i) An Old English term denoting an extraordinary tax calculated on land holdings. *See also* DANEGELD *and* TAXATION
(ii) A Saxon term for tribute paid in compensation for a crime.

GENEALOGY The history of families (not necessarily one's own) is inextricably linked with the history of a location. Civil registration, CENSUS returns, parish and non-conformist registers, wills and parish records are the usual starting points for research, but there are numerous other sources of information, many of which are often overlooked. In the local record office will be discovered judicial records, many dating from the sixteenth and seventeenth centuries. It is likely that some members of a family will be found therein, either answering for their misdemeanours or summoned in some other capacity.

Among these records, which include those of QUARTER SESSIONS in the custody of the

CLERK OF THE PEACE, will be found depositions, indictments, presentments, order books, rolls of the sessions, coroners' records, licences to trade, rolls of papists, removals of paupers and so on. Cases which were sent from quarter sessions to the ASSIZES are kept at the Public Record Office, as are some prison and criminal records. From 1536, deeds and sales had to be enrolled with the clerk of the peace for a county (or at Westminster), while other similar leases and deeds are deposited in county record offices.

Land Tax Assessments, dating from 1780 to 1832, are also held in county record offices. An act of 1779/80 required that assessment of land tax on freehold property should determine electoral qualification. Owners of freehold property assessed at 40s a year were entitled to vote. The assessors were required to compile three duplicate lists of those who qualified, one of which was deposited with the clerk of the peace. From 1832, the Representation of the People Act abolished assessment as a means of enfranchisement and required instead the compilation of an annual register. Records of other taxes may be found in the archives of the county record offices, for example, the HEARTH TAX, assessed at 2s a year for every hearth and collected from 1662–88, and the extraordinary Hairpowder Tax of 1794.

Also in the records of the clerks of the peace are Convictions of Felons, which date from the period 1699–1827. Certificates, known as 'Tyburn Tickets', were issued to anyone apprehending a felon (see FELONY), providing that guilt was proven. These exempted the holder from holding parochial office in the parish where the crime was committed. Parishioners were delighted to be relieved of such unrewarding offices and, although certificates were supposed to be assigned to a specific person and one other, they became extremely marketable commodities. Copies of these certificated were enrolled with clerks of the peace.

Most county record offices also act as official diocesan registries. These include the records of bishops and archdeacons as well as numerous documents relating to other officials and jurisdictions. Some bishops' registers may date from the thirteenth century, but the most useful archives are those of the ecclesiastical or church correctional courts, which deal with adultery, fornication, bastardy, defamation of character, blasphemy and other similar offences. Wrong-doers were first 'presented' by churchwardens before facing a church court which dispensed penances and excommunications. Diocesan records also contain

documents relating to disputes and probates of will as well as licences for clergy, schoolmasters, midwives, physicians and surgeons to practice. Non-conformists may be traced through Meeting House certificates, which were required by law during the period 1688 to 1852 by all those who wished to hold congregational meetings. These were obtained by application from an Anglican bishop and they contain the names, addresses and denominations of dissenters.

Research beyond the introduction of parish registers in 1538 is often difficult, but manorial documents contain the activities of medieval COURTS BARON and COURTS LEET, and tenants appear in court rolls. Manorial surveys provide a wealth of information regarding tenancies, changes of occupation and disputes relating to manorial custom. Modern departmental records, including those of the armed forces, are available at the Public Record Office at Kew. The College of Arms in London, Lord Lyon King of Arms and the Court of Lord Lyon in Edinburgh and the Chief Herald of Ireland's Office (Genealogical Office) in Dublin all possess substantial collections of pedigrees and ordinaries (lists of coats of arms) and the Harleian Society publishes pedigrees and other genealogical information based on the HERALDIC VISITATIONS. Other sources are the *Inquisitions Post Mortem*, a type of medieval estate duty, and the wills and administrations of the Prerogative Court of Canterbury and the Prerogative Court of York dating from the fourteenth century, especially those dating from 1653–60 when all wills and administrations were, without exception, proved in the Prerogative Court of Canterbury during the Commonwealth period. Details of property disputes were recorded at the Court of Chancery and are available through the Public Record Office.

See APPENDIX I for the above organizations and for the Society of Genealogists and the Federation of Family History Societies

GENERAL GAOL DELIVERY *see* LAW

GENTLEMAN In the Middle Ages the word *gentil* meant 'noble'. A statute of Henry V required that in certain legal documents the 'estate, degree or mystery' of a defendant must be stated, and the style 'gentleman' came into use to signify a condition between ESQUIRE and YEOMAN. The term *les gentiles* was used in an act of parliament of 1429 to describe men holding freehold property of 40s a year or more. From the sixteenth century, the term seems to have been applied to all those who were not required to labour and therefore employed servants. Members of professions, military and naval officers, barristers, etc., were considered to be gentlemen, some of them being entitled to the designation 'esquire'.

GEOMETRICAL STAIRS *see* STAIRCASES

GEORGIAN (i) Possessing architectural characteristics associated with the reigns of the first four kings George (1714–1830) (*see* CLASSICAL ARCHITECTURE).
For the Georgian Group *see* APPENDIX I
(ii) In other contexts (especially literature), also applicable to the reigns of kings George V and VI (1910–52).

GESITH *see* THANE

GESSO SOTTILE *see* MANUSCRIPT ILLUMINATION

GIBBET A post with an arm from which an executed criminal (or a severed torso or limb) was hung, usually in chains or contained within a metal cage, as an example to passers-by. Following the Bloody Assize of 1685, the notorious Judge Jeffreys ordered that the bodies of those who were hanged for their complicity in the Monmouth Rebellion should be dismembered and distributed throughout the countryside to hang on gibbets as a grim deterrent to those who would take up arms against their king. The sites of former gibbets may sometimes be identified from local place-names or from the records of archaeological sites of parishes held by county record offices. Few have survived, though the post of a sundial in West Parley churchyard in Dorset once supported the gibbet on Parley common. Gibbets were intended both to humiliate the deceased and to strike fear into the hearts of would-be transgressors, and were usually located at prominent crossroads, which rapidly became associated with local superstition. Gibbets ceased to be used towards the end of the eighteenth century.
See also GALLOWS *and* PUNISHMENT

GIG The early type of gig was essentially a sporting vehicle but the name was later applied to any light or cheap two-wheeled carriage, often driven by those who could afford nothing better. If a gig cost less than £12 to build it was taxed at only a few shillings but had to be painted with the words 'Tax Cart'. Gigs dating from the second decade of the

nineteenth century were of better design and construction. The *whiskey*, for example, was similar in appearance to the earlier CURRICLE but was drawn by a single horse or pony, its body attached directly to the shafts and decorated with woven cane-work. The whiskey was used for short, high-speed journeys and was popular from about 1812, while the *dennet gig*, which was introduced *c.* 1814, was suitable for town or country use and was named after a fashionable actress.

GILBERTINE Founded by Gilbert of Sempringham (*c.* 1089–1189) in 1131, the religious communities of nuns of the Gilbertine Order (the only truly English monastic order) initially followed a simplified version of the Benedictine Rule but as their numbers grew, and lay brothers and sisters joined them, their direction was entrusted to Canons Regular following the Augustinian Rule. The communities then took the form of DOUBLE MONASTERIES.

GILL (i) A wooded ravine, usually containing a stream.
(ii) A mountain torrent.
(iii) A unit of liquid measurement equal to ¼ pint. In some areas this is called a *jack*, the ½ pint being a gill.

GINS *see* MAN-TRAPS

GLASS The earliest known application of a fusion of sand and soda (glass) is the decorative green glaze found on Middle Eastern domestic and personal items from *c.* 4000 BC. Pure glass objects were manufactured in Mesopotamia from *c.* 2500 BC; glass vessels were used from *c.* 1500 BC and moulded glass from *c.* 1200 BC. The most significant innovation was the use of the blowpipe, possibly in Syria during the first century BC. This was a hollow iron tube, similar to those used today, some 1.25 metres to 1.5 metres in length (4 to 5 feet) with a mouthpiece at one end and a knob at the other.

The ingredients required for glass-making were then, as now, soda ash, pure silica sand and lime. The presence of a minute quantity of an impurity will affect the transparency, consistency and colour of the glass. Today, a variety of ingredients is added to produce glass of differing quality and for specific purposes: borax for heat-resistant glass, for example. Producing and sustaining the extremely high temperatures required for the successful fusion of the ingredients must have been a formidable problem and melting was generally carried out in two or more stages in stone or brick furnaces.

Glass for WINDOWS was manufactured throughout the Roman Empire and many Romano-British houses had glazed windows, though after the withdrawal of Rome (AD 410) domestic window glass was a rare and costly luxury enjoyed only by the most affluent and influential members of society right through to the fifteenth century. Ingenious substitutes were often used to fill small medieval window openings: thin sheets of alabaster or horn; oiled linen, paper or parchment treated with gum arabic and pieces of mica. But in many churches, STAINED GLASS was used at least from the twelfth century. By the sixteenth century, window glass was more widely used but was still an expensive commodity which had to be protected by wooden lattices and sometimes even removed when the occupants were away from home.

The small quantities of glass made in Britain at this time were generally of inferior quality to that which could be obtained from Europe, especially from northern France (*Normandy Glass*), north-west Germany (*Rhenish Glass*) and Flanders, where quantities of pure white sand were readily available. Contemporary British glass was usually manufactured locally using immediately available materials and producing glass of a grey or green-brown colour, mostly for bottles and inferior glazing.

Glasshouse place-names are generally indicative of sites where glass was once made, usually in areas of former forest or woodland where sand (or crushed flint for bottles), lime and potash were freely available, together with charcoal for the furnaces.

Prior to the eighteenth century, *cylinder glass* (also known as *broad glass*, *green glass* and *muff glass*) was hand-blown by the cylinder method. The molten glass (called *metal*) was gathered onto the blowpipe and blown into a sphere. Then, by swinging and twisting it in the air, the craftsman would blow the sphere into a hollow cylindrical 'sack' which was then cut open (with the 'ends' removed) and flattened and cooled into a rectangular panel. Cooling took place in an *annealing oven* which permitted the glass to cool gradually, thereby avoiding unnecessary stresses which would make the finished glass brittle. Medieval panels of cylinder glass were small: generally 63 cm × 38 cm (25 inches × 15 inches).

In the early seventeenth century, a rapidly increasing demand for window glass, combined with legislation forbidding the use of England's diminishing supplies of timber for fuel in certain industries, resulted in the concentration of glass workshops in areas where furnaces could be fired with coal. The cost of transporting coal was prohibitive, and numerous small workshops, all producing indifferent quality glass, were forced to close, while major centres were established in Tyneside and south Lancashire where (fortuitously) the Lancashire coast provided copious quantities of high-grade sand. It was in response to these new circumstances that the British evolved a new, and highly successful, type of coal-fired furnace, though the industry continued to rely on European (mostly French) expertise.

An improved method of making cylinder glass was developed in Europe during the eighteenth century. This produced *sheet glass* in large panes which were ideally suited to window glazing but at a time when the effects of the WINDOW TAX constrained its manufacture in Britain. Nevertheless, 83,610 square metres (900,000 square feet) of sheet glass were used in the construction of the Crystal Palace in Hyde Park in 1851.

Normandy or *crown glass* was manufactured in northern France during the Middle Ages and in England from the sixteenth century, but only in limited quantities. It was not until the later eighteenth century that crown glass replaced cylinder glass in Britain because of its suitability for the larger panes of Georgian windows and its natural and lustrous fire finish. A pear-shaped blob of molten glass (*metal*) was blown into a bubble or *globe*, the blowpipe broken off and the globe transferred to an iron rod called a *pontil* or *ponty*. The glass was then reheated and the ponty spun rapidly until, through centrifugal force and with a loud 'pop', the glass flattened out into a disc of glass (the *table* or *crown*) some 1.2 to 1.8 metres in diameter (4 to 6 feet). The table was then removed from the rod and, after cooling in an annealing oven, cut into pieces of the required size, and the thicker *bullion* or 'bull's-eye', formed where the rod had joined the glass, returned to the furnace. Contrary to popular belief (and modern practice), these 'bull's-eyes' were never used in shop or street windows, but occasionally in places where a translucent effect was required. Crown glass has a slightly uneven surface but a brilliant fire polish due to the flattening process. Eighteenth-century hand-blown crown glass animates a building in a way which modern glass cannot, though reproduction 'Georgian' crown glass may be found in more recent buildings.

Plate glass was introduced into England in *c.* 1620 by Sir Robert Mansell, who engaged Italian craftsmen to manufacture mirrors using high quality materials. Plate glass was made to a greater thickness than crown glass, using the cylinder method but with materials which were as pure as possible and a lengthy process of grinding with sand to remove flaws and polishing with rouge to produce a lustrous finish. So costly was this process that in seventeenth-century England plate glass was used exclusively for MIRRORS and coach windows. For most of the eighteenth century, plate glass for glazing windows had to be imported from the French who enjoyed a near-monopoly in the production of glass by a method of casting. Molten glass was poured directly on to a flat surface on which it was rolled out. But contact with the surface and the roller inevitably meant that both sides of the glass sheet lost their transparency and considerable grinding and polishing was required. The cost of establishing such a process was prohibitive and it was not until 1776 that the first British factory capable of producing cast plate glass was constructed at St Helens (Merseyside), where its immense casting-hall was immediately nicknamed the 'Cathedral'. This was the first of several such factories to be established during the late eighteenth and nineteenth centuries, and the industry responded to an increasing demand for large-size panes by developing improved grinding and polishing techniques and innovative mechanical handling processes. Even so, plate glass was not widely used for domestic glazing until 1838 and this had an irregular surface which is easily distinguished from modern products.

GLASSHOUSE (place-name) *see* GLASS

GLAZING BARS *see* WINDOWS

GLEBE From the Latin *glæba*, meaning 'soil', glebe land was that which was anciently set aside for the maintenance of the parish priest. The income of most medieval priests was dependent on the receipt of TITHES, which included payments made by parishioners on important occasions (*altarage*), the receipt of the second-best beast of a deceased person (*mortuaries*) and the produce of glebe land. Glebe land varied considerably in quality, acreage and location. In some parishes, the glebe was sufficiently profitable or extensive for the priest to sub-let part of it, and former parsonage buildings may still be found to include a barn and yard which once serviced the glebe lands. But in most cases, the parson's labours would of necessity equal those of his parishioners. Clues to former glebe land may be found in place-names and FIELD NAMES, and in enclosure patterns of strip-shaped fields which, because of the special status of glebe land, survived the informal re-allocation of land in the period before parliamentary enclosures. Unlike other holdings, glebe land was rarely sold or exchanged so that post-medieval maps in which glebe land is shown may also provide clues to the distribution of strips in the former OPEN FIELDS. Glebe lands were also known by the Latin term *sanctuarium*, from which has derived the entirely spurious notion that a parish church enjoyed special rights of SANCTUARY.
See also PARISH

GLEN From British *glenno*, meaning 'valley': in Welsh *glyn* and in Gaelic *glean*.

GLORIOUS REVOLUTION, THE The events leading to the deposition of James II from the English throne and the accession of his daughter Mary and her husband William of Orange in 1688. This was confirmed by the *Bill of Rights* in October 1689, which also guaranteed the Protestant succession and set out the principles of parliamentary supremacy.

GLOSS A commentary on a text, usually added in the margin or between the lines of text.

GLYWYSING *see* WALES

GNOMON *see* SUNDIALS

GOBLIN NAMES *see* DEMON NAMES

GOLD *see* MINERALS

GOLD BEATERS SKIN An animal membrane used to separate leaves of gold foil during beating and, in the eighteenth and nineteenth centuries, as sticking plaster.

GORE (*Scottish* = **GAIR**) A small triangular or irregularly shaped piece of land at the junction of two furlongs.

GOSPEL OAK A place-name associated with parish boundaries and the medieval festival of Rogation (or Cross Days), held on the three days preceding Ascension Day. Introduced into England during the eighth century, this festival combined pagan tradition with religious observance and practical necessity. Rogation days were prescribed days of prayer and fasting associated especially with prayers for a bounteous harvest. The Major Rogation (25 April) was a Christianized version of the pagan observance *Robigalia*, which was a procession through the cornfields to pray for the preservation of the crops, especially from mildew. Minor Rogations originated in fifth-century Gaul, where processional litanies were observed to protect the land against earthquakes and other perils. The festival itself consisted of a perambulation during which crosses and green boughs were carried, divine blessings invoked on the land and the crops and the boundaries of the village confirmed by tracing crosses in the ground. At traditional stopping places the priest would read from the scriptures, the 'stations' being marked by an oak tree or other familiar feature. Place-names such as Gospel Oak, Gospel Thorn and Amen Corner are the relics of this ancient festival and are invariably located on contemporary ecclesiastical parish boundaries (though these may subsequently have been altered). The attendant festivities were sometimes excessive and were (rightly) considered to have pagan associations so that, following the Reformation, the 1662 Book of Common Prayer ordered the observance of the three Minor Rogations as 'Days of Fasting and Abstinence' and the procession was reduced to the *'beating of the bounds'* with willow wands, a tradition which later became the formal PERAMBULATION of a parish VESTRY.

GOTHIC ARCHITECTURE The architectural style current in medieval Europe from the late twelfth century to the mid-sixteenth. Although the term is widely used in the context of church architecture, it is equally applicable to medieval domestic buildings of stone construction.

The term 'Gothic' was first used by the sixteenth-century painter, architect and historian Giorgio Vasari (1511–74) to imply disapprobation of all things medieval. To the post-Renaissance mind, Gothic architecture symbolized barbarism and that of the Renaissance intellect: the verticality of faith versus the horizontality of enlightenment.

There were four phases of the Gothic style, each dependent on that which preceded it and fashioning that which followed. Each phase grew further away from the solidity which characterized ROMANESQUE architecture and closer to the 'seemingly ethereal fragility' (Yarwood) of the late fifteenth century. Above all, the medieval architect was attempting to achieve an appearance of lightness and elegance in direct contrast to the heavy sturdiness of the Romanesque and, unlike Classical and Renaissance buildings, the great medieval cathedrals were therefore conceived from the inside outwards. How he would have rejoiced in the Victorian Crystal Palace of 1851! Larger than

Wren's St Paul's, the luminescence of its 83,610 square metres (900,000 square feet) of glass and the pure functionalism of its construction were precisely the architectural objectives which motivated medieval church builders for four centuries. It was this relentless quest for unattainable perfection (equated in the medieval mind with the greater glorification of God) which inspired architecture of the most extraordinary ingenuity and audacity and, in particular, the development of the stone vault and abutment (*see* VAULTING). The 'heavenward thrust' of glass and stone created that feeling of ascension which is the essence of Gothic architecture. And yet these great medieval buildings are essentially functional: every piece of stone is critical to the equilibrium of the building and (as at Richard Roger's twentieth-century Lloyd's building in London) no part of the structure is deliberately concealed. Like a house of cards, weight is distributed, and structural stability maintained, by translating the outward thrust of an ARCH into the downward thrust of a corresponding pier or buttress. Nothing is superfluous: even a pinnacle is part of the structural equation, adding its weight to a buttress or corner tower. As the Middle Ages progressed, so too did man's understanding of structure and his ability to apply new engineering techniques. Buildings became larger, higher, lighter and the geometry ever more complex.

The familiar Gothic classification of *Norman, Early English, Decorated* and *Perpendicular* was devised by Thomas Rickman (1776–1841) and first published in his book, *An Attempt to Discriminate the Styles of English Architecture from the Conquest to the Reformation*. Other forms of classification have been advocated but those which attempt to apply specific dates to what was essentially an evolutionary process ignore both transitional elements, which are present in the gradual movement of one architectural phase to the next, and significant regional variations. Furthermore, architectural features were often added to those of an earlier period: at Gloucester Cathedral, for example, a fourteenth-century remodelling of the eleventh-century choir resulted in the construction of a spectacular perpendicular stone-ribbed 'cage' which masked the original Romanesque arcade and was extended upward into a magnificent new clerestory and vault.

Rickman's *Norman* period is that which is now described as English *ROMANESQUE* and is easily recognized through the builders' preoccupation with solidity, exemplified by massively thick walling, small window openings and arcades of immense pillars supporting 'rounded' (semi-circular) arches (though experimentation with the pointed arch and ribbed vault began in *c.* 1130).

The *Early English* period (also *First Pointed* or *Lancet* from the characteristic narrow, pointed *lancet window*) is endowed with a certain austerity of form and a beauty of proportion best seen (in its most developed form) at Salisbury Cathedral in Wiltshire, built between 1200 and 1275. Typically, the vaulting has plain quadripartite ribbing; tiers of lancet WINDOWS pierce the walls of the aisles, clerestory and transepts in pairs and threes; and the tall piers of the nave have clustered shafts (of black Purbeck marble) and simple moulded capitals in a characteristic inverted bell form. The Early English period established the form of Gothic architecture. Later periods expanded on it: in particular, through the development of complex vaulting and buttressing which enabled larger areas of wall space to be devoted to glass.

The need for *tracery* (ornamental stone mouldings within a window) arose from the Early English practice of grouping two or more lancet windows beneath a single arch head (*hood-mould* or *dripstone*) which was intended to direct rainwater away from the openings. This created an awkward space (*spandrel*) between the window openings and the arch head, which at first was carved and pierced to provide the earliest form of tracery (*plate tracery*). From this simple device developed a variety of forms by which the Gothic phases are most readily identified. From the mid-thirteenth century, single windows were divided by slender stone 'bars' (*bar tracery*) to provide larger areas of glass, one of the earliest forms being *Y-tracery* in which a Y-shaped mullion divided the window into two narrow vertical lights and a smaller top light. This later developed into *intersecting tracery* in which two or more mullions intersect each other in curves at the head of the arch.

The *Decorated* period (also *Curvilinear, Flamboyant* or *Geometric*) refers to the *middle pointed* style of window tracery, which lasted from *c.* 1275 to *c.* 1375. The increased width of buildings, achieved through advances in vaulting, had created a need for greater internal illumination: windows became larger and wider and clerestories higher. This in turn increased the height of the nave and resulted in the development of the *arch buttress* (or *flying buttress*) which conveys the thrust of the vault and main roof over and beyond the aisles (*see* BUTTRESS). The increase in window size was accommodated by an equilateral arch and several mullions giving three, five, seven and even nine lights and ever more complex tracery. At first, this was essentially geometrical with circles, quatrefoils and trefoils, but in the fourteenth century *flowing* or *curvilinear tracery* evolved, based on the OGEE form of double-curving lines producing flowing flame-like shapes. *Reticulated tracery* was a development of this, circles forming a lattice of ogee shapes. Decoration also became more elaborate in the form of stone carving, coloured window glass and painted and gilded stonework. The nave of Exeter Cathedral in Devon (1275–1369) is a superb example of this period.

The final, and by far the longest, of Rickman's periods was the *Perpendicular*, which lasted from the late fourteenth century to the end of the fifteenth (when it became *Tudor Gothic*). Characteristic of the period is the delicate vertical tracery of windows and stone panelling (from which the term 'perpendicular' is derived), with regular horizontal divisions and slender fluted pillars leading upward into an exuberance of intricate fan-shaped vaulting (known as *fan vaulting*) exemplified in the magnificent Chapel of King's College, Cambridge (1446–1515) and Henry VI's Chapel in Westminster Abbey (1503–19). Windows of the period are significantly wider and the arches flatter, those of the late Perpendicular and Tudor Gothic periods being of the *four-centre* type (*see* ARCH). *Reticulated* or *panel tracery* features both in windows and in wall panels and is characteristic of British architecture of the period. This form of tracery incorporates both mullions and transoms, thereby creating rows of small glass 'panels' with more complex tracery confined to the upper tiers within the arch. Many earlier buildings were remodelled at this time (*see* Gloucester *above*), including both Winchester and Canterbury Cathedrals, where the naves were rebuilt. These late Gothic builders very nearly achieved the perfection sought by their thirteenth-century predecessors. Their buildings are lofty, spacious and brilliant, with a minimum of masonry supporting a maximum of glass. But in the over-elaboration of detail they fall short of that ideal.

See also CHURCHES, MONASTERIES *and* TUDOR ARCHITECTURE

GOTHICK A derogatory term used to describe the excesses of romantic medievalism in late eighteenth- and nineteenth-century literature, architecture, etc.

GOTHIC REVIVAL Gothic influences have always been present in British architecture. Although subdued by classicism during most of the

GOTHIC WINDOW TRACERY

1 Y-tracery (13th century)
2 Intersecting tracery (13th century)
3 Geometrical tracery (early 14th century)

4 Reticulated tracery (14th century)
5 Panel tracery (late 14th century)
6 Panel tracery (late 15th and early 16th centuries)

seventeenth and eighteenth centuries (*see* CLASSICAL ARCHITECTURE), Gothic buildings continued to be constructed, usually to complement or complete earlier medieval structures such as Christ Church College, Oxford, where Christopher Wren added the famous Tom Tower in 1681, and Westminster Abbey, the western towers of which were designed by Nicholas Hawksmoor just before his death in 1736.

During the second half of the eighteenth century, romantic medievalism (*see* GOTHICK) became fashionable as an alternative to Palladian formality. In 1750 Sir Horace Walpole created a Gothic country villa at Strawberry Hill, Twickenham, and thereby fashioned also an epithet 'Strawberry Hill Gothic', which was to become synonymous with charm, elegance and superficial medievalism. Thereafter, a number of architects designed 'Gothic' buildings which were essentially dramatic and picturesque and full of personalized detail. Perhaps the most successful of these was James Wyatt (1746–1813), who for many years experimented with romantic Gothic styles and whose most spectacular creation, Fonthill Abbey in Wiltshire, was likened to a medieval cathedral: 91 metres in length (300 feet) and with an 85 metre tower (278 feet) above the crossing. The omission of support arches beneath the tower (specified by Wyatt but ignored by the builder) resulted in its collapse in 1825.

At the turn of the century, medievalism was still not taken seriously: decorative Gothic features were incorporated into buildings but proportions, structure and materials were ignored. During the early nineteenth century, slender iron-work pillars supported vaulting covered with plaster panels and rib-like moulding. At that time, the Gothic style was considered to be appropriate only to ecclesiastical and collegiate buildings but from *c.* 1840 the Gothic Revival began in earnest. The real turning point was the rebuilding after the fire of the Palace of Westminster in 1834. The architects, Sir Charles Barry (1795–1860) and Augustus Pugin (1812–52), created a neo-Gothic masterpiece of immense authority and containing ornamentation and craftsmanship of the highest quality.

But the Gothic Revival was not simply an architectural movement; it was inspired by idealists who believed that only those who lived a good and moral life could create anything truly worthwhile. They revered all things medieval, espousing the art and architecture of that time as the epitome of human endeavour. They abhorred the artificial, especially the sham-gothic work of preceding generations with its cast iron and plaster. Rigid guidelines for Gothic design were set out in *The Ecclesiologist*, the journal of the ecclesiological movement which promoted the 'Middle Pointed' period of the late thirteenth and early fourteenth centuries as the only pure architectural style (*see* GOTHIC ARCHITECTURE). Despite this preoccupation with authenticity, most Gothic Revival buildings are immediately recognizable and do not possess the vitality of their prototypes. Gothic architecture took over 400 years to evolve: the setting in place of every stone was innovative and dependent on the cumulative experience of generations of skilled craftsmen. The Gothic Revival

took place at a time when there was an unprecedented demand for urban housing and for cheap, mass-produced materials. The skills of Pugin's specially trained craftsmen who worked on the Palace of Westminster were of little relevance in such a market.

The *High Victorian Gothic* period, from 1855 to 1885, was a time of ubiquitous architectural activity. Eminent architects of the time include George Gilbert Scott (1811–78), William Butterfield (1814–1900) and Alfred Waterhouse (1830–1905) but, with some notable exceptions, the precepts of the Ecclesiological Society inevitably gave way to pragmatism, and throughout the land town halls, universities, churches and railway stations, public baths and reading-rooms, hotels and country houses were constructed in a pastiche of Romanesque and Gothic styles.

See also VICTORIAN ARCHITECTURE
For the Victorian Society *see* APPENDIX I

GRACIOUS AIDS *see* FEUDAL AIDS

GRANARY Most free-standing granaries date from the late eighteenth and nineteenth centuries. The platform (or *staddle*) was raised above ground level on brick arches or *staddle stones* so that air could circulate beneath the grain. Staddle stones (which were also known as *stack-stools* and used to support the staddles of ricks) were mushroom-shaped and designed (somewhat optimistically) to discourage rats and mice from ascending and entering the building. A cat-flap was often let into the door of the granary for the same purpose. Most free-standing granaries were square with brick or weatherboarded walls and a tiled roof. Other granaries, incorporated into farm buildings, are invariably found on an upper floor, above a stable or cart shed, for example.
See also RICKYARD

GRAND ASSIZE This court developed during the twelfth century as part of the system of General Eyres (*see* EYRE *and* LAW). Aggrieved tenants who wished to establish their right to land could obtain a *writ of peace* issued by a sheriff who also nominated four knights of the shire to elect twelve further knights to determine the case. Their decision was then communicated to the Justices in Eyre. The procedure was abolished in 1833.

GRANGE The Cistercian monasteries of the twelfth and early thirteenth centuries accumulated vast endowments of land from Norman magnates whose admiration of Cistercian piety conveniently matched their own preoccupation with salvation. Many of these lands were so remote and fragmented that it was impossible for them to be worked directly from the abbey itself and a system of outlying farms (*grangia*) and subordinate lodges developed, staffed by lay brethren and administered centrally by the abbey cellarer (*see* MONASTERIES). Furness Abbey in Cumbria, for example, had eighteen granges located at strategic sites throughout its estates, and at Kilnsey in Wharfedale (one of the granges of Fountains Abbey in Yorkshire) there were seven subordinate lodges, each manned by one or two lay brothers together with a cowman or shepherd. So successful was the system in its early days that other monastic orders adopted it for their own estates.

During the thirteenth century, however, endowments of land to monastic foundations declined. There was also a significant reduction in the recruitment of lay brothers, aggravated in the fourteenth century by the Black Death and a more competitive labour market. The monastic foundations were increasingly perceived as being avaricious and corrupt and, although the Cistercian rule required that monasteries should be detached from the evils of everyday life, the occupants of the granges inevitably experienced daily contact with local communities and were ill-equipped to cope with the numerous conflicts of interest that ensued. Difficulties in recruiting sufficient lay brothers lead to the employment of local peasant labour and granges were increasingly leased to laymen with a consequential weakening of the monastic system.

Granges varied considerably: some were substantial complexes of purpose-built agricultural and domestic buildings with a barn and chapel. Others were small farmsteads, adapted to accommodate two or three staff. Several developed as settlements or were converted to domestic use following the Dissolution, though not all 'Grange' place-names are genuine.

See also BARTON

GRATES *see* CHIMNEYS

GRAVESTONES

The nobility and gentry have almost invariably been commemorated, and frequently interred, inside their parish churches. Inspired by the grandeur, both of execution and sentiment, of these MONUMENTS, the new breed of self-conscious yeoman farmers, tradesmen and master-craftsmen of late seventeenth-century England commissioned memorial headstones to be erected over the churchyard graves of those whose

lives, aspirations and achievements they wished to commemorate (*see also* TABLE TOMBS). The oldest churchyard memorials are from this time, and though a small number of gravestones may appear to be of an earlier date it is likely that these were raised retrospectively in the following century. In many parishes, the earliest concentration of gravestones will often coincide with the parliamentary ENCLOSURE of land from which many of the wealthier parishioners benefited both economically and socially.

Churchyard headstones tended to imitate the style of earlier memorials found within the church and these in turn reflect contemporary religious and architectural fashion. Significant regional variations also occur, the eighteenth-century headstones of slate and freestone areas being particularly suited to the carving of classical forms, for example. Frederick Burgess (*see below*) identified four phases in the development of gravestone design. Still in evidence in the late seventeenth and early eighteenth centuries was the medieval and Tudor preoccupation with mortality and corruption exemplified by such devices as the Death's Head, Hourglass and Reaping Hook. This was followed, in the later eighteenth century, by symbols of the Resurrection and, influenced by the spread of Methodism, a concern with a means of salvation expressed through allegorical figures such as Faith, Hope and Charity. Early nineteenth-century gravestones returned to the image of the Cross (which previously had been considered Popish) before being overtaken by a welter of mass-produced sentimentality and neo-Gothic symbolism in the Victorian era.

Churchyard inscriptions (*see* EPITAPHS) are collected and recorded by many of the family history societies whose addresses may be obtained from county record offices.

GREAT BRITAIN *see* BRITAIN

GREAT ROOD *see* ROOD (ii)

GREAT SEAL

The first 'great' seal of England was probably that of Edward the Confessor (1003–66), but it is more practicable to trace the development of the Great Seal from the reign of William I (1066–87) who used a seal with the *majesty* copied from that of Henri II of France (a depiction of the king seated in state) and on the obverse an equestrian figure, also of the king. Subsequently, the faces were reversed, the majesty becoming the obverse and the equestrian the reverse. The Great Seal is used to authenticate important documents issued in the name of the sovereign, and the matrix is held by the Lord Chancellor, who was sometimes also referred to as the Lord Keeper (of the Seal).

See also CHANCERY, PRIVY SEAL *and* SEALS

GREEK FIRE *see* SIEGES

GREEN *see* VILLAGE GREEN

GREEN HOUSE *see* MARKET HALL

GREENHOUSES Pliny records that the Emperor Tiberius (42 BC–AD 37) had his favourite cucumbers grown in 'raised beds made in frames upon wheels' which 'were moved and exposed to the full heat of the sun; while in winter they were . . . placed under the protection of frames glazed with Lapis secularia.' It may be that the Romans brought their methods with them to Britain but it was not until the thirteenth century that the practice of forcing was developed in Europe. (The theologian and herbalist Albertus Magnus (1193–1280) was apparently accused of witchcraft because of his skill in growing fruit and flowers out of season.) The real pioneers were the Dutch and French, and in England, at the end of the sixteenth century, hotbeds were used only to raise the seedlings of melons, cucumbers and cauliflowers. By the seventeenth century, forced plants were matured in earth placed on deep hotbeds of fresh horse manure which generated considerable heat through bacterial activity. The plants were protected from above by a covering of straw mats or painted cloth supported by poles arched over the bed or placed at the corners. This rudimentary protection was still being used in England fifty years after glass frames and cloches had been introduced from France.

By the mid-eighteenth century, the great market gardens, which stretched from Westminster to Chelsea and Fulham, were adopting the 'new' methods with great success and systems of intensive intercropping were proving exceedingly profitable. Nevertheless, the rapid expansion of the suburbs in the mid-nineteenth century forced many commercial producers further away from their London markets and it was not until the 1930s, stimulated by new import duties, that English growers could again compete with the French. This was achieved by the use of Dutch lights, continuous cloches and a significant increase in the number of heated greenhouses for commercial crops.

The heated greenhouse developed alongside the frame and the hotbed. The first European greenhouses were constructed in the late sixteenth and early seventeenth centuries as orangeries which, in England, were often substantial stone buildings in the grand style with large windows in the south wall and a stove or open fire to maintain air temperatures. Towards the end of the seventeenth century (following the Restoration in 1660), many orangeries were adapted to accommodate the collections of exotic plants which were then fashionable. But there was little understanding of the problems involved: there was insufficient glass in the walls (and none in the roof until the early eighteenth century), heating systems remained crude and inefficient and greenhouses were often poorly sited and unable to take advantage of the precious winter sun. Circulating hot-water systems were introduced in *c.* 1816 (some forty years after the French had first used them) and the production of sheet GLASS in the 1830s resulted in greatly increased areas of glazing (following the abolition of tax on glass in 1845) and encouraged the development of complex ventilation and irrigation systems.

Most greenhouses were used for forcing flowers or 'exotic' fruit and it was not until late in the eighteenth century that vegetables were being grown in English greenhouses. Blooms for cutting, which required straight-stems, were grown in 'Carnation houses', located in the open to ensure upright growth (unlike other greenhouses which at this time were usually constructed against a northerly wall). These were usually square buildings with high glass walls to accommodate the blooms. But the cost of heating and maintenance proved increasingly prohibitive, as did the notion of providing for the needs of an immense household. The decaying skeletons of an estate's greenhouses and frames may still be found within the walls of many former Victorian and Edwardian kitchen gardens but in Britain the late twentieth century is the age of the 'compact' garden, the small greenhouse and the conservatory.

GREEN LANES A green lane is a term with no legal meaning. It is a physical description of an unsurfaced track, often hedged and usually of some antiquity. It may be a FOOTPATH, BRIDLE-WAY or CARRIAGEWAY, or may not be a right of way at all. Many green lanes originated as *meres*, double-banked ditches excavated to define the BOUNDARIES of Saxon estates. These were considerably deeper than normal drainage ditches and, unlike green ways which are portions of ancient route-ways, they usually run for only a few miles before petering out.

See also DROVE, MERE LANE *and* PACK-HORSE ROADS

GREEN MEN Pagan symbols commonly found in the foliated stonework and ornamental wood carving of medieval churches. These male heads or masks, wreathed in foliage, which is often depicted growing from their mouths, eyes, ears and nostrils, are ideally suited to the ornamentation of capitals, corbels, bosses, misericords, etc. The Green Man is a creature of folklore, very ancient, who, as the Green Knight of Arthurian connotation, is a superhuman being of strange powers and deemed to be the incarnation of Spring who must be slain in Winter to renew life for the next year. He is a symbol of fertility, the May King (Green Man, Man-in-the-Oak or Jack-in-the-Green) of May Day ceremonies who, wreathed in garlands of oak and hawthorn (may tree), feigned death and then came to life to comfort and dance with his disconsolate May Queen. In Christian imagery, the Green Man became a symbol of Easter, of resurrection and the continuity of life in some form. Green Men of the ecclesiastical variety wear decidedly mournful expressions: those depicted on innumerable inn signs are infinitely more cheerful and possibly commemorate the sites of former May Day festivities (*see* PAGAN SYMBOLS, SHEELA-NA-GIG *and* WODEHOUSE).

GREENS Hamlets located within a settlement pattern of larger villages. Particularly common in East Anglia (and in the East Midlands where they are known as ENDS), these hamlets are either remnants of ancient fragmented settlement patterns or the subsidiary settlements of an expanding primary village.

GREGORIAN CALENDAR The 'New Style' calendar was introduced by Pope Gregory XIII who, in 1582, declared that 5 October should be 15 October. This was generally adopted in Catholic countries but in England the calendar was not changed until 1752 when 3 September became 14 September. Eleven days were thereby lost from the fiscal year, the beginning of which was moved from 25 March to 6 April to compensate, and New Year's Day changed from 25 March to 1 January. Correctly, reference to dates falling between 1 January and 25 March prior to 1753 should be referred to as, for example, 28 January, 1748/9. Pope Gregory also decreed that of the centesimal years only those exactly divisible by 400 should be counted as leap years.
See also JULIAN CALENDAR

GRIFFIN *see* BEASTS (HERALDIC)

GRIM A name commonly associated with various longitudinal earthworks, mostly in the south of England (e.g. Grim's Dyke in Wiltshire and Grims Ditch on the Dorset-Wiltshire border). Believed to derive from *Grim* (meaning 'masked one'), it was one of many names for the Anglo-Saxon god Woden, the god of victory and death and of magical power. Because of this last attribute, Woden was often invoked to account for the construction of otherwise inexplicable earthworks: Wansdyke (*Wōdnes dyke*) in Wiltshire, for example. In other instances, Woden place-name elements may suggest religious sites which pre-date the Anglo-Saxons' seventh-century conversion to Christianity. Woden's Norse counterpart Odin was also called *Grimr* by the Scandinavians.
See also DYKES

GRISAILLE Thirteenth- and fourteenth-century window glass to which a delicate silvery-grey coating of paint was applied, often with lightly painted leaf and stem patterns on a background of cross-hatching and interlaced strapwork. Such glass remains translucent and enhances the coolness and tranquillity of an interior. In the fourteenth century, colourful painted and STAINED GLASS motifs, including human figures and armorial devices, were often inserted in the grisaille.

GROAT *see* COINAGE

GROG *see* TERRACOTTA

GROINED VAULT *see* VAULTING

GROTTO Grottoes originated in the formal gardens of Renaissance Italy as classical temples and fountains dedicated to water nymphs and dryads. In eighteenth-century England they were enclosed water features, decorated with rococo shells, spars, minerals, etc. But with the development of the landscape garden, grottoes were created which imitated the natural water-filled caves of limestone districts. There were localized 'schools' of grotto-makers, such as that of Joshua Lane, of Tisbury in Wiltshire, whose masterpiece may still be seen beside the lake in the gardens of Stourhead.
See also FOLLIES

GROVE Place-name element from Old English *grā fe*, meaning 'woodland thicket'.
See also HOLT

'GROWLER' *see* FOUR-WHEEL CAB

GROZING IRON *see* STAINED GLASS

GUIDON A small version of the medieval STANDARD, carried before a troop of retained men and essential as a rallying point in battle. The modern cavalry standard is a direct descendant of the guidon and is often described as such.

GUILDHALL Not all guildhalls are associated with the medieval guilds. Many are simply town halls: local authority offices, sometimes constructed on the site of a former guildhall, but more often housed in the Gothic Revival chambers of Victorian romantics. In small towns and villages, the presence of a guildhall may indicate the failure of a medieval town to expand, as at Thaxted in Essex, where a magnificent guildhall was built for the town's Guild of Cutlers in *c.* 1420. In other cases, the term 'guild' may refer to chambers of trade or local friendly societies (*see* GUILDS).

GUILDS (*also* **GILDS**) Guilds derive their twelfth-century origins from the religious fraternities which evolved round a church, monastery or hospice to

Interior of the fourteenth-century Guildhall at Leicester.

which they attached themselves and whose saint they adopted as their patron. Members of those fraternities who lived together often worked together in a common trade or craft, and they developed into mutual protection societies making provision for the poor, sick and needy in their communities and promoting the interests of their crafts including apprenticeship and the power of search which gave each company the right to inspect all goods handled by its members. This gave guilds an effective weapon against competition from strangers to their city and a constructive measure to keep their own members in line, to maintain high standards of work and so make the guild stronger.

A guild's authority was (and is) obtained through royal charter and since 1560 the *livery companies of the City of London* have also been required to apply for a grant of livery from the Court of Aldermen, who have to be satisfied that 'a number of men of good repute from some trade or mystery not already represented by an existing guild have joined together for a time sufficiently long to justify the belief that they will continue to hold together and are not likely to fall apart from lack of interest or support'. A *liveryman* is both a FREEMAN of the City of London and a senior freeman of his guild who is entitled to wear the uniform (*livery*) of his company and to exercise other privileges. In due course, by seniority, he becomes eligible for membership of a guild's governing body (*Court of Assistants*) and, thereafter, he may advance through the various degrees of Warden and Master.

Many phrases in common usage have originated from the livery companies: 'on tenterhooks', from the double-ended hooks in the Clothworkers' arms; 'baker's dozen', from the efforts of the Bakers' provision of the *vantage loaf* to avoid all risks of incurring a fine for short weight; 'at sixes and sevens' originated in the struggle of the Merchant Taylors and the Skinners companies for sixth and seventh place in the table of precedence; 'hallmarking', from the marking of precious metals at Goldsmiths Hall; and, at the completion of his apprenticeship, the submission by an aspiring smith of his first piece of craftsmanship – his 'masterpiece' – to the Master and Wardens of the Company of Goldsmiths.
See also CHANTRY *and* TOWNS

GUINEA *see* COINAGE

GUNPORTS With the introduction of artillery in the late fourteenth century, embrasures and arrow slits within the walls of medieval castles were modified to accept the new technology. The small circular openings, originally added to an arrow loop to accommodate the crossbow, were enlarged to accept the barrels of primitive cannon, and the sloping embrasures levelled to form 'decks' on which the cannon would stand. The first gunports of the 1360s were of this type, for example, those in the refashioned defences of Southampton. Occasionally, embrasures were extended downwards within the walls and a separate gunport inserted below an existing arrow slit. By 1380, gunports with diameters of up to 25 cm (10 inches) were being incorporated in defences, as in the West Gate at Canterbury in Kent, and within a short time gunports were simply round holes widening within the walls to provide a level deck on which the cannon was mounted. By 1500, gunports were large with square embrasures, for example, those of the Tudor forts of Devon and Cornwall.

See also ARROW SLITS *and* GUNPOWDER

GUNPOWDER An explosive mixture of potassium nitrate, charcoal and sulphur, 'villainous salt petre' is generally believed to have been introduced into English warfare in the first half of the fourteenth century by Edward III against the Scots but may have been used even earlier at the siege of Stirling in 1297 by Edward I. The primitive hand-held weapons of the late medieval period were small, slow and discharged only bolts and garrots, while early cannon were significantly inferior in every respect to siege-weapons such as the *mangonel* from which the word 'gun' is probably derived (*see* SIEGES). In order that the barrels of these guns should not burst, the ballistic force of the powder used was deliberately low; even so, early cannon were probably as dangerous to their users as they were to the enemy. The only effect they had on castle design in the fourteenth and fifteenth centuries was the introduction of GUNPORTS, suggesting that they were used more often in defence than attack.

In the late fifteenth century, the development of guns and cannon was rapid. The 'great iron murderer Muckle Meg' (now at Edinburgh Castle) dates from 1450, though she blew up in 1680 and was later restored. Such cannon were undoubtedly effective as bombards but they were extremely expensive, notoriously slow and difficult to move and rarely available when and where they were needed. With the exception of a small number of well-documented occasions, cannon had hardly any part to play in medieval siege warfare and were not a determining factor in the decline of the medieval castle. Only by the mid-sixteenth century had guns become generally effective and extensively employed.

See also CASTLES (MEDIEVAL)

GUYENNE *see* AQUITAINE

GWYNEDD *see* WALES

GYPSIES The first gypsies (or gipsies) reached England in the beginning of the sixteenth century when they were known as 'Gypcians' or 'Gipsons' because it was believed that they had originated in Egypt. Although the gypsies themselves had no tradition of asiatic origin, it was eventually demonstrated that their language (*Romany*) shared common features with Sanskrit and the later Indian languages to which were added loan-words, including elements of Persian, Slavonic and Byzantine Greek, and other local linguistic features acquired as the gypsies migrated across late medieval Europe from the south-east. It would appear, therefore, that they were originally a nomadic Indian people of low caste who lived by seasonal work, itinerant trade and providing entertainment (e.g. fortune-telling). Justices of the Peace (*pokonyos* in Romany) invariably moved them on; indeed, one of the earliest references to 'Egyptians' (meaning gypsies) is in a handbook for magistrates published in 1514. In 1530 it became a criminal offence merely to be a gypsy and many were executed before the law was changed in 1784. With intermarriage and gradual cultural assimilation, the Romany language has effectively become a jargon, the nomad's tent and cart exchanged for a caravan (now motorized) and the hawker's trade expanded to wholesaling. In Scotland and Ireland, gypsies are often known as *tinkers*, a term which is more correctly applied to any itinerant repairer of kettles, pans, etc.

GYPSUM *see* ALABASTER *and* PLASTERWORK

HABEAS CORPUS A writ requiring a person under arrest to be brought before a court especially to establish the lawfulness of his arrest, thereby ensuring that imprisonment cannot take place without a legal hearing. The right to sue for a writ of *Habeas Corpus* is an ancient common law right pre-

dating *Magna Carta*, though it was not formally recognized by Parliament until an act of 1679 and was often disregarded before this date.
See also LAW

HACKNEY CAB Hackney coaches began to operate in London in 1625. Initially, there were only twenty but within a decade Charles I was forced to issue an order restricting them, and by the reign of George III (1760–1820) the number had increased to 1,000, operating by licence and paying a duty of 5*s* a week to the Crown. Drivers of hackney cabs were required to give way to gentlemen's coaches and 'persons of quality'.

HADRIAN'S WALL *see* ROMAN FORTS AND CAMPS

HAFOD In Wales, a summer settlement located on upland pastures. In Snowdonia, transhumance persisted until the nineteenth century. The *meifod* was a 'middle' or 'May' settlement: effectively, a staging-post *en route* to the summer *hafod* (*see* BOOLEY HOUSE, CLACHAN *and* SHIELING).

HAGIOSCOPE *see* SQUINT

HAGODAY *see* SANCTUARY

HAG STONE
> To hinder the Night Mare they hang on a String a Flint with a hole in it by the manger. . . . It is to prevent the Night Mare *viz.* the Hag from riding the Horses who will sometimes sweat at Night. The Flint thus hung does hinder it.
> John Aubrey

The flint, with the natural hole representing the 'All-Seeing Eye', was intended to ward off the ghostly Hag, whose nocturnal visitation to a stable caused the horses to sweat and presaged death. The phrases 'nightmare', 'hag-ridden' and 'all of a sweat' originated in this rural tradition.

HA-HA A combined wall and outward-sloping ditch constructed at the perimeter of a garden to prevent livestock from entering. The top of the wall is at ground level so that from within the garden, and from the windows of the house, the view into the surrounding park or countryside is unimpeded. The ha-ha dates from the eighteenth century and is associated with the great age of landscaped PARKS and GARDENS. The term itself probably originated in the Old English *haya*, meaning 'hedge', though it

has been suggested that it is derived from an eighteenth-century French interjection intended to deter adventurous ruminants. Many ha-has have been filled and levelled but may still be evident in long arc-like depressions in fields near a country house.
See also HEUGH

HALE (*also* **HALL**) A small portion of land.

HALF-TIMBERED HOUSES *see* TIMBER-FRAMED BUILDINGS

HALL The humble 'hall' or entrance lobby of a modern house is all that remains of what was once the most important room in a dwelling-house, if not the *only* room. In hovel and castle alike, the hall was the administrative, social and domestic centre of life. The great barn-like halls of the Saxon nobility were rectangular or circular, with thatched roofs supported by timbers and walls constructed of stone rubble, cob or wattle and daub. Smoke from central hearths drifted upwards to a hole in the roof and the main hall was surrounded by ancillary buildings and a palisade. Such halls were centres of community activity as well as being the focus of a magnatial court (*see* MULTIPLE ESTATE).

The Norman William fitz Osbern's castle at Chepstow (Monmouthshire), completed in 1071, comprised an immense rectangular two-storeyed hall-keep within a stone-walled bailey containing wooden garrison buildings, granaries and stables. Such halls, uncommon in Britain, were, by *c.* 1000, being constructed in many parts of western Europe both as symbols of magnatial prestige and as defences against internecine aggression.

In most early medieval CASTLES, the hall was usually built within the keep, above ground-floor level where it could be defended and, if necessary, isolated. As fortifications became more sophisticated so great halls were constructed at ground level within the protecting walls of the inner bailey, the keep (or gatehouse) being reserved as a final refuge for use *in extremis*, as at Goodrich, Herefordshire, constructed *c.* 1300. (There are several exceptions to this: at Wardour in Wiltshire, for example, an impressive hall was provided above the gates passage when the castle was built in 1390.) In their domestic buildings, the Normans raised timber-framed halls (*see* TIMBER-FRAMED BUILDINGS) to first-floor level above stone-vaulted undercrofts which were used for storage and as stables. The halls themselves, approached by means of external stone stairs, were used for domestic and business purposes and for receiving guests, and often had a small private parlour (*solar*) at one end. A number of the few surviving medieval halls are those of trade guilds and fraternities associated with churches or hospices (*see* GUILDS). A variety of hall known as the *aisled hall* was constructed with pierced walls, the posts and horizontal beams (*wallplates*) of which carried the roof trusses over flanking aisles in the manner of a church, thereby creating greater internal space. At this time the open hall was the principal component of a dwelling, aisled halls being particularly associated with twelfth-century nobility, though by the fourteenth century this method of construction was widely used in more modest dwelling-houses. Though much altered, about 100 examples are known to have survived. Throughout the Middle Ages, halls retained their public as well as their domestic function. Many estates were rarely visited by their owners and the hall was used for periodic festivities as well as being the administrative and business centre of a manor and, often, its courtroom. Many manor-houses, therefore, consisted of a hall and little else.

The development of the CHIMNEY encouraged the creation of small, private chambers as bedrooms and parlours. These, together with specialized rooms for food preparation and storage (and, in larger households, accommodation for servants who had previously occupied the hall), were obtained by lengthening the house and constructing cross-wings at right angles to the original hall. Many medieval buildings acquired both domestic and defensive characteristics. The magnificent and evocative Great Hall at Stokesay Castle, Shropshire, built in *c.* 1285 to replace an earlier wooden hall, was provided with a solar at its southern end and private chambers above an earlier tower (*c.* 1240) to the north. It was essentially the hall of a prosperous wool-merchant who, in 1291, obtained from Edward I a licence to fortify and crenellate his home, adding a substantial keep-like tower (*c.* 1291–1350), linked to the solar by a fortified passage-way.

The fourteenth-century *Wealden House* design (which, despite its name, is not confined to the Kentish Weald) evolved from the earlier aisled hall, and consisted of an open hall flanked at each end by two-storey bays containing service rooms at one end and accommodation at the other. The upper stories projected outwards (*jettied*) from the front of the house beneath a single roof-span. Such houses continued to be built in the fifteenth and sixteenth centuries but the ratio of public space (the hall) to private space (chambers) steadily decreased, reflecting a desire for greater personal comfort and

convenience and an increased appreciation of the concept of private family life.
See also SCREENS PASSAGE

HALLMARK A mark used at Goldsmiths Hall (*see* GUILDS) and by assay offices in the United Kingdom to indicate the standard of gold, silver and (since 1975) platinum, to secure a uniform quality and to prevent fraud.

Hallmarking dates from a statute of 1300, which required the Goldsmiths Guild to use the leopard's head hallmark (the *King's Mark*) as an indication of quality. (As an important customer of the London goldsmiths, Edward I had a strong interest in maintaining the standard of their products.) The Worshipful Company of Goldsmiths (established in 1150 as a fraternity of gold and silversmiths) has been responsible for the assaying and marking of plate since receiving its royal charter of incorporation in 1327, together with various provincial assay offices, notably at Edinburgh, Birmingham and Sheffield (all still functioning); Norwich (closed in 1702), York (1856), Exeter (1883), Newcastle (1884), Chester (1962) and Glasgow (1964). With certain exceptions (such as Royal Plate), all gold, silver and platinum articles are required to be hallmarked before being offered for sale. The death penalty for counterfeiting the British hallmark was reduced to fourteen years' transportation as recently as 1773. The marks impressed in the metal include symbols indicating the maker, standard, assay office and date.

Since 1363 it has been compulsory for the maker to stamp his mark on a piece of silver plate before sending it to the assay office. At first, marks were devices such as a bird, a hart, a cross, etc., many of which were armorial or alluded to the maker's name. Towards the end of the sixteenth century, makers began using cyphers and monograms and, from 1739, they were required by law to use the initial letters of their Christian and surnames. It was in response to this regulation that many silversmiths began to re-register their marks: Paul de Lamerie (the finest of the London smiths) incorporated a crown to indicate royal patronage, for example. The practice continues today, though most marks are those of firms rather than individual craftsmen.

The standard mark follows that of the maker. The lion device indicates that the metal has been passed as sterling silver (i.e. 92.5% pure silver). The earliest mark was a *lion passant guardant* (from the English royal arms) with its face looking outward. Since 1822, it has been a *lion passant* (i.e. looking straight ahead in the direction in which it is going). From

1697 to 1720, the lion was replaced by the image of Britannia and the silver standard raised to 95.84 per cent. On sterling silver assayed at Sheffield and Chester, the lion has always been *passant reguardant* (i.e. looking over his left shoulder). The Irish office used a crowned harp. At Edinburgh a thistle was used prior to 1975, when the *lion rampant* (i.e. a lion rearing on his hind legs) of the former Glasgow office was adopted.

Town marks indicate the assay office responsible for testing the article. Most English-made silver is sent to London for hallmarking which complicates the identification of provincial silver. The leopard's head continues to be the London mark, though from 1478 to 1821 it was crowned and the *lion's head erased* (i.e. cut off at the neck) appears on Britannia standard silver from 1697 to 1720 (and remained valid for fine silver until 1975). A crown was used by Sheffield from 1773 to 1975, the Tudor Rose gold mark now being used also on silver and platinum. The Birmingham office has used an anchor since 1773: in the upright position for silver and on its side for gold. Edinburgh uses a castle on both gold and silver items. All the important former offices used devices based on their civic arms: a ship sailing from the port of a castellated town for Bristol; a castle above a lion for Norwich; five lions on a cross for York; a triple-towered castle for Exeter; three castles for Newcastle; a sword between three wheat-sheaves (the arms of the county of Cheshire) for Chester; and for Glasgow (somewhat optimistically) '. . . on a Mount an Oak Tree surmounted by a Salmon with a Signet Ring in its mouth, on top of the tree a Redbreast and in the sinister an Ancient Handbell . . .'.

The date letter indicates the date on which the object was assayed (which is almost invariably the date when it was made). Date stamps on London-made silver, indicating the day to the nearest twelve-month, have been used for over four hundred years without repetition. For twenty consecutive years, the twenty letters from A to U (excluding J) are used with the same style of shield and letter throughout. After U has been reached, the styles of both shield and letter are changed. The Birmingham and Edinburgh offices also use all the letters excepting J, but Sheffield adopted a different cycle and the former assay offices used less regular systems of date-marking.

See also PEWTER *for* touch marks.

-HAM (i) Old English *hām*, meaning 'homestead, manor, estate, village'. The most usual application is probably 'village' but the clear implication is 'home' – that which is secure and familiar. It is never used alone and rarely as a first element. When a further element *-ing-* is added, it is likely that the name will be that of a man's tribal *hām*, dating from the early period of settlement: Rockingham, Northampton-shire, is 'the home of Hrōca's people' and Winter-ingham, Lincolnshire, 'the *hām* of Wintra's people', for example.

See also -TON

(ii) Old English element *ham(m)* or *hom(m)* is also common and may mean either 'meadow' (especially the flood plain of a stream or river) or 'close' (an enclosed plot of land). Often used alone (e.g. East and West Ham in Essex) or as a first or second element, as in Dyrham, Gloucestershire (meaning 'enclosure for deer'), and Otterham, Cornwall (meaning 'meadow frequented by otters'). Most *hams* are on low-lying land and almost invariably located in the south of England.

HAMLET A hamlet is a cluster of residential, agricultural and ancillary buildings, larger than a FARMSTEAD but of insufficient size to maintain the range of public buildings, services and facilities associated with a VILLAGE. The popular definition of a hamlet as 'not having a church' is patently unsound: there are numerous examples of hamlets consisting of a church, former rectory, farmstead, two or three cottages and little else. Many villages have developed from the amalgamation of adjacent minor settlements which, had they retained their integrity, would now be defined as hamlets. In other areas, the hamlet continues to represent the principal component of an ancient rural settlement pattern. It was only towards the end of the Saxon period that larger villages began to develop where now they predominate: particularly in the English midlands and other areas where OPEN FIELDS were introduced. It is undoubtedly true that a number of hamlets developed as secondary settlements (often enlarged farmsteads) as a result of the rapid expansion of villages in the early Middle Ages. But it is equally true that most hamlets were already established by the twelfth and thirteenth centuries, and that their pedigrees may extend back to the Roman period and beyond. The term itself implies a place of permanence and security for an extended family group: as in Arlingham, Gloucestershire, derived from *erlingeham* – 'the *hām* of the people of the earl' (*see* -HAM). Many hamlets merged or expanded to become villages and even towns: Gillingham in Dorset, for example – 'the *hām* of Gylla's people'. Others declined to become solitary farmsteads (*see* HENDREF) or were abandoned entirely (*see* DESERTED VILLAGES). But in many areas, the ubiquity and stability of these ancient hamlets remain characteristic features of the countryside. Most have altered little in size or form since they were first established some sixteen centuries ago.

See also -TON *and* TOWNSHIP

HAMMER BEAM *see* ROOFS

HAMMER POND A type of millpond associated with the production of iron, specifically in the Weald of Kent but also in other areas such as the Forest of Dean in Gloucestershire. In order to maintain and control a reliable supply of water to drive the trip-hammers of forges, a string of hammer ponds was created by constructing dams (*bays*) of clay (or sometimes of stone or brick) at intervals along the bottom of a valley. *Furnace ponds* were similarly provided to ensure a head of water to drive blast furnace bellows (blast furnaces were introduced at the end of the fifteenth century). Industrial ponds of this type may date from the sixteenth, seventeenth or eighteenth centuries and many were adapted for other uses during the Industrial Revolution.

HAMMER POST *see* ROOFS

HAMPTON (*also* -**HAMPTON**) A common place-name element, but a complex one:
(i) Old English *Hāmtūn*, meaning the 'principal settlement' or 'chief farmstead' of a neighbourhood.
(ii) Old English *Hēa-tūn*, meaning 'high *tūn*', an elevated farmstead or settlement.
(iii) Old English *Hamm-tūn*, meaning '*tūn* in a hamm', a farmstead in a close or meadow.
(iv) Old English *Hæmetūn*, derived from *hām tūn*, meaning 'the dwellers at the home . . .', usually accompanied by a further description, e.g. Ditchampton in Wiltshire – 'the dwellers at the home by the dyke' (Grims Ditch) (*see* -HAM).

HANGER Old English *hangra* is a derivative of the verb *hang* and originally denoted a slope. The place-name element *hanger* now means 'wood on the side of a steep slope', though the earlier meaning is evident in names such as Clayhanger, meaning 'clayey slope' (*see also* CLINGER). As with HOLT, the first element is often the name of a tree, e.g. Oakhanger.

HANGING *see* GALLOWS *and* LARCENY

HANSOM CAB Named after an architect, Joseph Hansom, the early hansom cabs of the 1830s were rather clumsy vehicles, designed with particularly large wheels so that they were difficult to overturn. Later hansoms were much lighter, with the driving seat at the rear of the passenger compartment, providing both a clear view of the traffic for the driver and privacy for the passengers. Most hansoms were used as public conveyances for one or two passengers, though a large number were privately owned and driven by coachmen. The passenger compartment was entered by means of flap doors at the front, though a later enclosed version (the *brougham-hansom* or *bow-fronted hansom*) was entered by a carriage door on the near-side of the vehicle.

HARD LABOUR *see* PRISONS

HARNESS (HORSE) Like the blacksmith's FORGE, a harness-maker's shop was once found in almost every village and may still be commemorated in the names of cottages such as 'Saddlers'. In rural communities dependent on horses (and, in earlier times, oxen) for transport and motive power, the making and repairing of harnesses was an essential industry. In particular, the harnessing of draught animals was a craft which had developed by trial and error over thousands of years, the earliest VEHICLES (*c*. 1500 BC) being drawn by means of a single pole to which a pair of horses was harnessed. The central pole remained in use for vehicles drawn by more than one horse, culminating in the highly developed stagecoach, while a pair of shafts was used when single-horse vehicles became practicable.

For heavy draught work, the ox or bullock was almost universally used for ploughing and hauling wagons throughout the Middle Ages and oxen were still to be found working on some farms in the 1860s. Ox harness was simple and cheap and could be constructed easily enough from wood and leather thongs by the medieval peasant. Harness-making developed as a craft precisely because the horse was a very different animal, both physically and temperamentally, from the ox. Horses were relatively fast-moving, sensitive and easily injured, and they were most effectively controlled by the use of bridle and bit. Of course, a saddle and stirrups were also required for riding, and pack-horses were provided with pack-saddles in which commercial goods were carried.

It was the Romans who developed the *collar* as a means of attaching a horse to a vehicle. Before this, the breast harness had been used: a broad strap across the animal's chest to which the traces were attached. In most parts of the world the breast harness is still used, but in Britain the more efficient and (for the harness-maker) technically more demanding Roman collar was adopted. Breast harness is adjustable and will usually fit any size of horse. The collar will not, and for this reason individually fitted collars were commissioned by well-run farms and these would be altered if they had to pass from one horse to another. On the highways, each member of the best coaching teams had its own harness. Collars are roughly egg-shaped with the upper (narrow) end fitting over a horse's neck and the lower (broader) end butting against its shoulders and chest. (The collar is placed over a horse's head with the wider part uppermost and then turned into its correct position.) The *body* of the collar was tightly packed with straw, tailored to conform to the animal's contours, and faced with serge where contact was made with the neck and shoulders. Firmly secured between the front leather section (*wale*) and the body are two curved wrought-iron or brass sections (*hames*) which form a clasp running round the collar, joined by a hinge or short chain at the base and drawn together by straps (*hame straps*) at the top. These carry the *tug hooks* to which the chains or straps (*traces*) are affixed and the rings through which the reins are passed. The forward thrust of the horse is thereby transferred through the collar and the strong metal tug hooks without the horse's body coming into contact with a rigid surface.

A full set of draught harness consisted of some twenty different straps, all of which had to be produced from sheets of inflexible leather. This was usually obtained from a local tannery and, although cow hides were used, most harness-makers preferred horse hides which, with a working population of many million horses, were in plentiful supply. The stiff sheets of leather were made pliable by the repeated application of tallow and mutton fat. Leather for a draught harness was died black and that for riding brown. Each piece of harness had a specific function and, therefore, had to be of the appropriate strength and flexibility, easily adjustable and correctly sewn. The *bridle* consisted of a *headpiece*, *cheekpiece*, *blinkers*, *browband* and *noseband*. The *saddlepad* at the centre of a horse's back was held in place by the *girth* and by the *fillet strap* (or *meeter strap*), which led back to the tail piece (*crupper*). Over the saddlepad was the *backband*, on which the shafts were supported. The *breeching* comprised a number of long straps which allowed the horse to exert a braking effect when going downhill and facilitated reversing.

Saddles were originally soft pads of material held in place by a girth and without stirrups, which are

believed to have been used first by Mongol horsemen and introduced into Britain by the Normans (*see* CHIVALRY). The foundation of the saddle (*tree*) is made of beechwood, curved to fit over the horse's back, and to the underside of this are attached two pads resting on either side of the spine. These (like collars and saddlepads) are usually lined with serge, though linen or even calfskin is used for high quality saddles. The harness-maker has never made his own saddle trees, a singularly specialized and localized craft which was concentrated in the Walsall district of the West Midlands where most saddlers' tools and equipment were also made. On top of the saddle tree are the *flap* and *skirt* (usually of calfskin) and the *seat* which should be of pigskin.

Metal *pendants* for enhancing horse harness appear to have been used since the late Bronze Age. Most early examples are extremely plain but medieval pendants were cast to a high quality and richly decorated using heraldic devices in coloured enamels. By the eighteenth century, it was the fashion to decorate carriage-horse harness with finely wrought precious metal crests and other armorial devices on the brow bands, blinkers, side-straps, martingales and saddles. In imitation of these, nineteenth-century harness ornaments (*horse brasses*) were bought in large numbers to embellish the harness of plough and wagon teams, dray horses and carriers' and roundsmens' cobs in an age when the appearance of a team reflected the status of the owner as well as the self-esteem of the employee. Such ornaments were not purely decorative: like the ancient protective amulets from which they derived, they were considered to bring good luck and to safeguard a horse from evil.

Early nineteenth-century brasses were manufactured from sheets of *latten* (an alloy of copper, zinc, lead and tin) with a hammer and punch, and are of simple design and inferior quality. But from the mid-nineteenth century, when the prosperity of a farm or estate was invariably equated with the number of working horses it employed, the production of harness ornaments increased significantly. Victorian brasses, although mass-produced by casting and lacquered to reduce corrosion, were often superbly designed and executed. Designs (usually pseudo-heraldic beasts, eagles, crosses, crescents, etc.) were skilfully carved in a close-grained wood (usually pear) which was applied to a mould of damp sand. These traditional horse brasses are known as 'Walsalls' because of a near-monopoly of manufacture in that area in the nineteenth century. In the early years of the twentieth century, ceramic enamels were applied to provide areas of solid colour in horse brasses, many of which were made by hand using a repoussée technique rather than by sand casting.

One of the first representations of a *horse bell* is in Caxton's *Game and Playe of Chesse* (1476), in which an illustration of a mounted knight shows a large bell on his horse's crupper. By the early seventeenth century, horse bells were offered as prizes at the races: in 1610 a magnificent set of three engraved silver gilt bells was presented by the Sheriff of Chester. The intention of horse bells was clearly to warn fellow travellers of an approaching rider or vehicle:

> The horses wore their bells that day. There were sixteen to the team [of four horses harnessed to a heavy timber carriage], carried on a frame above each animal's shoulders, and tuned to scale, so as to form two octaves, running from the highest note on the right or offside of the leader to the lowest on the left or nearside of the shaft horse. Melbury was among the last to retain horse bells in that neighbourhood; for living . . . where the lanes yet remained as narrow as before the days of turnpike roads, these sound-signals were still as useful to him and his neighbours as they had ever been in former times. Much backing was saved in the course of a year by the warning notes they cast ahead; moreover, the tones of all the teams in the district being known to the carters of each, they could tell a long way off on a dark night whether they were about to encounter friends or strangers.
> (Thomas Hardy, *The Woodlanders*)

For the National Horse Brass Society *see* APPENDIX I

HART The ubiquitous hart or stag is to be found depicted in churches and on inn signs and emblazoned in heraldry. In the fabric of churches a hart may be represented in its old age fighting a snake or dragon whose flesh, when devoured, will restore the hart to health and vigour: a thirteenth-century allegory of Christ destroying the devil. Numerous inns dedicated to the 'White Hart' often refer to the favourite device of Richard II, inherited from his mother Joan of Kent and worn as an indication of royal preferment by countless of the king's sycophantic courtiers. Legendary white harts, often marked out for royal protection by a golden collar, once haunted the forests and chases of

England – Blackmoor Vale in Dorset is still known as the Vale of the White Hart (*see* FOLKLORE *and* LEGEND).

HATCH A fenced enclosure.

HATCHING To represent colours in ARMORY (*see* TINCTURES).

HATCHMENT A diamond-shaped heraldic panel, of wood or of canvas within a wooden frame, usually found in a church, where it may be affixed to a wall or removed to a ringing chamber, vestry or some other equally inaccessible quarter. The word itself is a corruption of 'achievement' and suggests that hatchments originated in the FUNERAL HERALDRY of the medieval nobility and were therefore erected in churches following interment. Practice varied, but in some areas a hatchment was hung above the door of the deceased's house, during a period of mourning, before being returned to the church. In Scotland, two hatchments were painted, one for the house and the other for the church, and in England there are several examples of hatchments for the same individual being erected simultaneously in the churches of his various estates.

The earliest diamond-shaped hatchments date from *c.* 1627, though the rectangular MEMORIAL BOARD, erected to the memory of an individual and bearing both his arms and (unlike hatchments) an inscription, are usually of sixteenth-century origin. Early hatchments are generally small, 1 metre square

Punning arms of Rabbet in a hatchment at Bramfield, Suffolk. The widow's arms are depicted on a white background, though the crest is clearly that of her late husband.

Funeral Hatchments

1 Husband (wife surviving)
2 Wife (husband surviving)
3 Bachelor
4 Widow
5 Widower
6 Spinster

7, 8, 9 & 10 Husband
(second wife surviving)

Funeral hatchment above the door of Horsington House, Somerset, c. 1900.

(3 feet), with narrow frames decorated with symbols of mortality such as hourglasses, mortheads and crossbones. They were painted in a vigorous style, unlike those of the nineteenth century which, for the most part, are of poor artistic quality. Late eighteenth- and nineteenth-century hatchments are larger, their wider frames often covered with black cloth and decorated in the corners with rosettes. The use of hatchments was at its peak in the mid-nineteenth century, but declined rapidly during Victoria's reign.

It is the treatment of the background which makes the hatchment unique, the arrangement of black and white divisions in relation to the various elements of the shield-of-arms being indicative of the identity and status of the deceased person (*see illustration*). Care should be exercised, however, for coats of arms in hatchments do not necessarily conform to the conventions of *marshalling* which govern the arrangement of heraldic quarterings elsewhere (*see* ARMORY).

Non-armorial devices appear in hatchments of all periods. Cherubs' heads are frequently found above the diamond-shaped 'shields' in women's hatchments; skulls fill the vacant corners beneath motto scrolls while flags, sometimes bearing battle honours, embellish the hatchments of many military or naval men.

Mottoes in hatchments are most unreliable. Many refer to mortality (e.g. *Resurgam* or *In Coela Quies*) and should not be confused with family mottoes which may also appear in a hatchment, though rarely so.

Eighteenth- and nineteenth-century illustrations and engravings and the records of antiquarian county histories indicate that there were once many more hatchments in our parish churches than there are today. Canvas and wood are unlikely to survive centuries of damp and neglect or the over-enthusiastic 'restorations' of the nineteenth century. At Shrewsbury in Shropshire two churches contain twenty and twenty-one hatchments respectively, although in Britain this is exceptional. Most churches, if they have any, have one or two. In Scotland, there are few hatchments remaining and these tend to follow the European practice of surrounding the central coat of arms with small shields representing probative branches of the deceased. Royal hatchments are rare and may easily be mistaken for the ubiquitous armorial boards, emblazoned with the royal arms and hung in churches since 1534 (*see* ROYAL ARMS IN CHURCHES).

HAUGH (*also* **HERNE**) An area of level land contained within the loop of a river.

HAVOD In the Welsh, a summer dwelling or farmstead.

HAWGABLE *see* BURGAGE

HAWTHORN A thorn bush which produces red haws or 'hags' (Old English *haga*) and the evocative white May Flower of English folklore. Hawthorn was commonly found in medieval woodland and waste and was later the shrub most often used in the ENCLOSURE hedgerows of the eighteenth and nineteenth centuries. The hawthorn blooms in May – the month between spring and summer – and sprays of May flowers were 'brought in' on May Day (but never before) and hung about the doors and windows of houses and in the byres and stables to drive away the devil at a time of natural growth. No doubt because of this association, it became a symbol of youthful aspiration and during the fourteenth and seventeenth centuries hawthorn blossom was revered as a symbol both of love and of the pastoral pleasures of the countryside. The revised calendar of 1732 brought the first day of May forward by thirteen days (and into a colder season) so that the hawthorn now blossoms two weeks late for the traditional festivities.

HAY A fence or hedge. Also an enclosure, particularly one within a park (*see* DEER PARKS).

HAYBOTE *see* HEYBOTE

HAYWARD One who had charge of fences and enclosures. Often, the hayward was a manorial official, responsible for ensuring that cattle did not stray from a town common (*see* COURT BARON *and* MANOR).

HEAD DYKE *see* RING GARTH

HEADER The narrow face of a BRICK. A *bull header* is made specially for circular work and has one end thicker than the other.

HEADLAND A small area of untilled land at the end of a strip in an open (medieval) field where the plough was lifted and turned. Ancient headlands may still be identified by accumulations of soil, carried forward and deposited by the plough, which now appear as smooth earthworks in the uncultivated angles at the edge of a field. Sometimes a series of headlands provided a route between fields and these may later have become lanes.
See also BALK, BUTT *and* RIDGE AND FURROW

HEADMINSTER *see* CHURCHES

HEARSE *see* EFFIGIES

HEART BURIAL The medieval practice of interring a man's heart, the seat of love and piety, in a place other than that in which his body was buried was particularly common during the thirteenth and fourteenth centuries. Frequently, such heart burials took place in monastic churches, notably the sequestered abbeys of the Cistercian order such as Sweetheart Abbey (*Dulce Cor*) in the county of Dumfries and Galloway, where the heart of its founder John Baliol was buried. Similarly, the heart of a thirteenth-century Bishop of Hereford was interred at the Cistercian Abbey Dore, Herefordshire, the spot being marked with a miniature effigy of the bishop. In many localities, tradition links these miniature effigies with the heart burial of a local crusading knight: a not unreasonable assumption when the difficulties of transporting a rapidly deteriorating corpse from the Holy Land are considered. There are good examples at Mappowder in Dorset (*see* EFFIGY) and Horsted Keynes in Sussex (probably the work of the same artist) and at Bottesford, Leicestershire and Halesowen Abbey, Worcestershire. At Tenbury, in the same county, a half-size effigy is depicted clasping a heart in his hands.

Perhaps the most controversial heart burial was that of the Dorset poet and novelist Thomas Hardy (1840–1928). Hardy had specifically willed that he should be buried at Stinsford, Dorset, 'out there' with his parents, sister and his first wife. Despite this, a Westminster Abbey funeral was arranged and

A miniature effigy commemorating a thirteenth-century heart burial at the church of St Peter and St Paul, Mappowder in Dorset.

only after the local vicar interceded was it decided that Hardy's ashes should be buried in the Abbey and his heart at Stinsford. It was a final irony that would have been appreciated by Hardy but which was met with local cynicism and even ribaldry: 'Almighty, 'e'll say, " 'ere be 'eart, but where be rest of 'e?"'

HEARTH TAX 'Hearth money', a tax on the number of hearths within a building, was levied from 1662 to 1689 (1690 in Scotland). The tax (2s for each hearth or stove) was collected from the occupier of premises in two instalments, on Lady Day and at Michaelmas. There were many exemptions: those who were in receipt of poor relief; those inhabiting properties worth less than 20s a year and not required to pay parish rates; charitable institutions (e.g. almshouses) and 'industrial hearths', though smiths' forges and bakers' ovens were taxed. An act of 1663 required that all hearths were to be included in the returns, including those that were exempt from tax, and from 1664 all who had more than two chimneys were obliged to pay the tax (if stopped-up chimneys were discovered, the tax was doubled!). Hearth Tax records provide an indication of the size of houses during this period, and lists of returns and many original documents are held by the Public Record Office (*see* APPENDIX I). Many have been published, especially the most informative returns for the periods 1662–6 and 1669–74.
See also TAXATION

HEATER SHIELD *see* SHIELDS

HECTARE A metric unit of square measure equivalent to 2.471 acres.

HEDGEBOTE *see* HEYBOTE

HEDGEROWS Hedgerows are a characteristic but rapidly diminishing feature of the lowland landscape of Britain. In England and Wales, 175,418 km (109,000 miles) of hedgerow were lost during the period 1947 to 1985, representing 22 per cent of the 1947 total of 796,623 km (495,000 miles). Moreover, the rate of loss has accelerated from an average of 4,667 km (2,900 miles) per annum in 1970–9 to 6,437 km (4,000 miles) per annum in 1980–5 and 8,127 km (5,050 miles) in 1985–98. The farmers' rationale, that most hedgerows are comparatively recent additions to the countryside, is clearly untrue for in those parts of lowland Britain not seriously affected by parliamentary enclosures,

the present landscape was in most essentials already in existence by the mid-fourteenth century.

Historically, hedges served to delineate a territorial boundary and to provide a barrier which both contained and protected the animals within. It is likely that some lynchet banks of so-called 'Celtic' fields carried hedges and that thorn barriers, both 'quick' and 'dead', were used during the Iron Age and Roman occupation. 'Dead hedges' (of stakes, brushwood and stones) persisted as the main hedge type until well into the Middle Ages and may still be seen surrounding ancient fields in Cornwall. Late Saxon and medieval OPEN FIELDS were often surrounded by a perimeter hedge as were assarts, closes and the early enclosures of the thirteenth century (*see* ASSART *and* CLOSE). It is quite possible that the forest shrubs and trees at the edge of an assart were managed to produce a stock-proof barrier and hence a hedge. There are numerous references to hedgerows in medieval documents, many relating to enclosure in contravention of the Forest Laws (*see* FOREST). In the ancient COUNTRYSIDE, where open fields had not been established, the serpentine hedgerows and small irregular paddocks must have created an impression of an apparently haphazard and thickly wooded landscape. Young hedging plants, saplings and seedlings, described by John Fitzherbert as 'quicksettes' in his *Boke of Husbandry* (1534), were obtained from wastes and woodland: 'whyte thorn [hawthorn] and crabtree for they be beste, holye and hasell be good' (*see* HEYBOTE). These early hedgerows originally contained a variety of species, therefore, but in many instances geological or microclimatological factors will have encouraged the dominance of a particularly invasive shrub and the number of species will have declined. For this reason alone, the proposition that the age of a hedgerow may be calculated by multiplying by 100 the number of species growing in a 27-metre length of hedge (30 yards) is of doubtful validity. It is often the case, though not invariably so, that ancient hedgerows will contain a greater variety of species than an eighteenth- or nineteenth-century enclosure hedge, but cartographical and documentary evidence is far more reliable than 'species counting', especially when there appears to be little agreement with regard to which 'species' should be counted. It is the form and function of a hedge which is important and the field pattern of which it is a part.

It has been estimated that some 32,187 km (20,000 miles) of new hedges were planted during the parliamentary enclosures of the eighteenth and nineteenth centuries (*see* ENCLOSURE). The enclosure awards required recipients of new holdings to delineate and secure their boundaries and this was usually achieved by means of a ditch and double fence within which a new hedgerow was planted. A typical enclosure award stated that '. . . plots of land allotted by virtue of this Act shall be inclosed and fenced round with ditches and quickset hedges with proper posts, rails and other guard fences to such quickset hedges – and the said quickset hedges, ditches and fences when properly made shall thereafter be properly kept up, maintained, scoured and supported by the person or persons whom the same plot shall be allotted.' Most (though not all) parliamentary enclosure hedges are of 'quickthorn' (hawthorn), which was usually stipulated in an award and supplied in bulk by commercial nurseries. Many of the large, regular fields were later subdivided, again with straight hedgerows, to form smaller and more convenient units. A small number of hedges were not planted but developed 'spontaneously' where the condition and composition of neglected land has encouraged colonization by a particular species, following the line of a former wall or fence, for example.

Various hedgerow types predominate in different parts of the country and reflect both the purpose for which they were created and the availability of materials and plants. In parts of Cornwall, a 'hedge' is a low stone wall encircling an irregularly shaped field, while in Devon and parts of Wales it is a high turfed bank (*hedgebank*) surmounted by a line of living shrubs. Fuchsia hedges are still found in parts of south-west Ireland; holly hedges are common in Staffordshire and in the Somerset levels hedges of osiers mark the boundaries of submerged fields in winter. The hop fields of Kent and Herefordshire are protected by tall, dense shelter hedges sometimes more than 6 metres high (20 feet). But for most people, the typical hedge is that of the Georgian enclosure landscape of the East Midlands: a line of low shrubs (predominantly hawthorn), up to 2 metres wide (6½ feet) and maintained at between 1.2 and 1.8 metre in height (4 and 6 feet), forming the boundary of a field or garden. This is the standard 'Midlands bullock hedge' which is normally flanked by a ditch but has no hedgebank. Sheep hedges are generally low and impenetrable, to prevent the animals from scrabbling through the base of the hedge, while the Leicestershire bull fence (known as the *bullfinch*) is an especially tall, robust version of the Midlands bullock hedge, intended to withstand heavy shoving and leaning. Left to their own devices, hedges quickly become overgrown and can eventually form long, narrow strips of woodland such as the 'shaws' which border fields in parts of the Weald of Kent.

Early management was probably by COPPICING every twelve to fifteen years, adjacent fields being put to arable until the hedge had grown sufficiently to provide an effective stock-proof barrier and the fields returned to pasture. The traditional cut and laid hedge was probably not widely established until the eighteenth century when management conditions were included in enclosure awards and tenancy agreements. Each area has its own distinctive style of management and even the design of the ubiquitous billhook (which, with the slasher, is the basic tool of the hedge-layer) varies from one county to another. Hedges are 'laid' every fifteen to thirty years depending on their condition: a 'thin' or poorly maintained hedge may need to be re-laid after only eight. Weak and misaligned growth is first removed, together with unwanted shrubs such as elder, leaving a number of tall, vigorous stems which are partly cut through with a billhook to leave a 'hinge' of live wood at the base. The stems are then bent over (*laid*) so that they lie flat or diagonally upwards with the lowest stems as close to the ground as possible. The bushy tips of the stems (*pleachers*) are laid so that they face into the field and each section is restrained by ash or hazel poles, hammered vertically into the line of the hedge (on the ditch side) at intervals of between 46 cm (18 inches) and 91 cm (3 feet), depending on local custom (in many areas of Wales, the poles are set diagonally within the hedge). Pliable lengths of hazel or willow are then pleated round the tops of the posts and pleachers to form a binding (*hethering*). In Wales, the sheep hedge varies considerably in detail from one area to another. All are low and often 'double brushed', the pleachers being laid in from both sides of the hedge so that the bushy ends project alternately on one side and the other to ensure dense growth. In some areas of Wales, neither hethers nor stakes are used and dead wood is often packed into the hedge to provide a temporary barrier while the hedge matures. The characteristic turf banks and hedges of Devon and Cornwall require specialized tools: the mattock and the Devon shovel. Laying rejuvenates a hedge and encourages vigorous growth. Trimming by machine results in the formation of an outer 'crust' of twigs, to the detriment of the interior of the hedge which can become hollow, and encourages the growth of hedgerow weeds which may retard the regrowth of the young woody shoots.

HEIR One who has inherited, and enjoys possession of, a title, property or arms. The term is often mistakenly used to mean an *heir apparent* who is one whose right of succession is inalienable. An *heir presumptive* is one whose right of succession is dependent on the absence of an heir apparent.

HEIRESS (HERALDIC) An heraldic heiress is a daughter who has inherited arms from her deceased father, there being no brothers or surviving issue of brothers. The arms of an heraldic heiress are shown on an *escutcheon of pretence*, a small shield at the centre of her husband's shield. Both her arms and those of her husband are transmitted to their children as QUARTERINGS, her husband's arms being in the first quarter. When there is more than one daughter, all are co-heiresses and all transmit their father's arms on equal terms. An *heiress in her issue* is one through whose issue arms descend when all male lines of her father have failed. In this way, it is possible for descendants of the daughter of an armiger to inherit his arms several generations after her death.
See also MARSHALLING

HELL *and* **HELL MOUTH** *see* DOOM

HELM ROOF *see* CHURCH TOWERS

HENDREF In Welsh, 'a winter dwelling' but also indicative of a former settlement which has declined to a single farmstead.

HENGE The term 'henge' is derived from the Old English *hengen*, meaning 'hanging', and was applied specifically to the lintels and trilithons of Stonehenge. Its use (from *c.* 1926) as a generic term for circular Neolithic monuments is erroneous and misleading, nevertheless it is now in common usage.

A henge has the appearance of a circular or oval embanked enclosure breached by a single causewayed entrance or by a pair of opposing entrances with interlocking embankments. Unlike HILL FORTS, henge embankments are generally *outside* the quarry ditches which provided the material for their construction. These ditches, now often filled with silt and eroded by ploughing, were originally very deep and were sometimes excavated in concentric pairs or threes, as at Maxey Quarry near Peterborough in Cambridgeshire, where a circular cluster of small pits containing ritual offerings was also discovered. The major henges date from *c.* 3500 to *c.* 2500 BC and vary enormously in size: at Avebury in Wiltshire the ditch, which was once 9 metres deep (30 feet) and tapered to a flat floor 4.6 metres wide (15 feet),

Hilltop enclosure at Carrownrush/Carrowmalby, Co. Sligo.

encloses an area of nearly 29 acres. The much smaller Maumbury Rings, on the outskirts of Dorchester in Dorset, was adapted by the Roman inhabitants of *Durnovaria* as an amphitheatre and was later used as a fort in the Civil War and as a place of public execution in the eighteenth century. Several henges were developed by the erection of STONE CIRCLES and avenues of standing stones, and at a number of sites excavation has revealed evidence of concentric circular arrangements of huge post holes which have been interpreted as roofed buildings, 30 metres in diameter (98 feet).

The question which has consistently exercised archaeologists concerns the precise function of henge monuments. It seems likely that they gradually superseded earlier CAUSEWAYED ENCLOSURES and were therefore centres of commerce and communication, of festivity, ceremonial and ritual. The construction of such massive earthworks would have required a considerable commitment of resources indicative of a well-organized and highly motivated society. There can be little doubt that their principal function was a religious one, for no other motive could possibly have inspired such commitment (other than self-preservation, as in the case of hill forts). It is likely that the major henges also came to represent a sense of cultural continuity and a focus of territorial identity, functions which, since the Middle Ages, have been associated with the great cathedrals. Why then, at Priddy Circles in Somerset, are there no fewer than four great henges in close proximity, and three at Thornborough Circles near Ripon in Yorkshire? There are also numerous lesser-known sites where clusters of small henges (*minor henges*) may be found, at Knowlton in Dorset, for example. These tend to date from the late Neolithic and early Bronze Age, are much more widely distributed than the major henges and often contain settings of posts, stones, pits and burials.

HENGIST *and* **HORSA** *see* JUTE

HEPTARCHY A misleading term often applied to the seven kingdoms of Anglo-Saxon England: Wessex, Sussex, Kent, Essex, East Anglia, Mercia and Northumbria. Its use in this context erroneously implies the existence of a unified system of government (*see* KINGDOMS (ANCIENT)).

HERALD OF ARMS An officer of arms of the middle rank between kings of arms and pursuivants of arms. Generally used as a generic term for all officers of arms.

HERALDRY All matters relating to the duties and responsibilities of the kings, heralds and pursuivants of arms. The term is frequently and erroneously used as a synonym for ARMORY, that aspect of a herald's work which is concerned with the marshalling and regulation of coats of arms and other devices and insignia.
For heraldry societies *see* APPENDIX I

HERALDS' COLLEGE *see* COLLEGE OF ARMS

HERALDS' VISITATIONS By the fifteenth century, the use and abuse of coats of arms was becoming widespread. At that time, the English kings of arms were required to survey and record the devices and pedigrees of those using arms and to correct any irregularities. Occasional tours of inquiry were held but it was not until the sixteenth century that heralds' visitations were undertaken in a regular and systematic way. In England, major visitations took place throughout the country in (*c.*) 1580, 1620 and 1666, minor visitations being conducted at other times. The practice was discontinued at the accession of William of Orange when it was considered inadvisable to draw attention to those who remained loyal to 'the old ways'. The original heralds' notebooks were used as a basis for manuscript copies, most of which have been published. These are a very useful source of early pedigrees, though it

should be borne in mind that they may occasionally contain unauthorized additions or alterations which may not be immediately apparent. Many of these volumes have been published by the Harleian Society (*see* APPENDIX I) and others by county record societies. Many of the manuscripts on which the printed versions are based are held in the British Library in London. There are also good collections of printed visitation records at the Guildhall Library, London; the Society of Genealogists and the Institute of Heraldic and Genealogical Studies (*see* APPENDIX I).

In Ireland, the social upheavals which followed the plantation schemes of the sixteenth and seventeenth centuries produced many changes in Irish society, not least of which was an influx of English and Scottish families many of whom were armigerous. The first Irish visitation took place in 1568 and was conducted by Ulster King of Arms whose office had been created just sixteen years earlier. Not only did the Irish visitations record and confirm arms and titles, they also served to establish the claims of gentry families previously unknown to the Ulster office. However, the total number of entries of the combined Irish visitations from 1568 to 1649 is less than 300. Of greater value to historians is the series of (*c.* 3000) funeral certificates dating from the 1560s to the 1690s. At that time, heirs or executors were legally obliged to provide the Ulster office with a certificate on which were recorded the arms and pedigree of a deceased armiger. The original Visitation and Funeral Certificate manuscripts are held by the Chief Herald of Ireland (*see* APPENDIX I) and copies of both are deposited with the College of Arms in London.

In Scotland, Lord Lyon King of Arms has always enjoyed a greater degree of legal authority over matters armorial than his brother kings of arms in England and Ireland and for this reason visitations are undertaken for specific purposes and in pursuit of his statutory duties as head of the heraldic executive in Scotland.

HERBALS 'There is no herbe or weede but God hath gyven vertue them to helpe man.' In the Middle Ages the culinary uses of herbs were so taken for granted that they were hardly ever mentioned in herbals, treatises which were almost entirely devoted to the medicinal properties of herbs and SPICES. Many of the herbs we know today were introduced into England by the Romans, and particular areas of the country gradually established reputations for growing specific herbs: mint at Mitcham in Surrey; saffron at Saffron Walden, Essex; and lavender at

Market Deeping in Lincolnshire, for example. Many of London's streets still bear the names of their medieval and Tudor herb markets: Camomile Street, for example, was once a market for the surplus produce of the great houses in the St Paul's area. In the last decades of the fourteenth century Richard II established a fashion in the experimental use of herbs for culinary purposes. He employed innovative cooks and encouraged them to catalogue successful dishes in 'herballs'. The herbs used at that time were stronger in flavour than those used today as they had to temper the pungent taste of salted meats and game. One consequence of the Dissolution of the Monasteries (1536–9) was to transfer many monastic gardens into the hands of private owners. The monasteries had previously been the chief source of horticultural innovation but from that time the initiative was taken up by the nobility and gentry.

The sixteenth century was an exciting time not only for gardening, but for producing books about it. The rapid development of printing techniques in the previous century encouraged the production of numerous herbals in Germany, the Low Countries, Italy and England. These were still largely concerned with the medicinal qualities of plants but are of interest to anyone concerned with the history of herb and vegetable growing, and are often beautifully illustrated with woodcuts and engravings. John Gerard's *Herbal* of 1597 is one of the best known, though it was reproduced from a Belgian work and is flawed in the translation. It was corrected, enlarged and improved by Thomas Johnson in 1633 and it is on this edition that Gerard's undeserved reputation rests. Perhaps the most familiar name is that of Nicholas Culpeper (1616–54) whose obsession was botany 'explained in terms of astrology'.
See also GARDENS *and* WORT

HEREDITARY OFFICES A characteristic of feudalism was the creation of numerous hereditary (or heritable) offices by which service to the nobility or to the Crown was rewarded. Such offices were by no means sinecures, however, and were concerned with the administration of those aspects of society which appertained directly to the Crown or to the running of magnatial estates. The earliest recorded offices date from the eleventh and twelfth centuries: in 1119, for example, Robert, Earl of Gloucester was Hereditary Governor of Caen and Hereditary Banner-bearer of Bayeux Cathedral, and in the 1190s the Earl of Arundel was Hereditary Chief Butler of England and Hereditary Patron of Wymundham Abbey. Several hereditary offices were often the

prerogative of one man: in 1270, for example, the Earl of Norfolk and Suffolk was Hereditary Marshal of England, Hereditary Steward of the Household, Hereditary Bearer of the Banner of St Edmund, Hereditary Forester of Farnedale and Hereditary Warden of Romford Forest. Such offices are legion and were by no means confined to the upper echelons of society. Numerous hereditary foresters, falconers and farriers; stewards, sewers and sheriffs; constables and chamberlains; warders and keepers of castles, almoners and patrons of religious houses embellish the pedigrees of prince and yeoman alike. Many hereditary offices have been extinguished and others are now held for purely ceremonial purposes.

HEREGELD *see* DANEGELD

HEREPAETHS *or* **HEREPATHS** Several Saxon land charters refer to *wegs* or trackways along territorial boundaries of which the most common road name is *herepaeth*, probably meaning a trackway used for military and administrative purposes – for border patrols, for government officials and their armed escorts and for the rapid movement of troops (Old English *here* meaning 'army'). No doubt they were also used by the populace for journeys beyond their immediate locality. Perhaps the best-known *herepaeth*, on the Marlborough Downs, runs for 11 km (7 miles) between Avebury and Marlborough on the line of a prehistoric trackway and is still known as 'Herepath' or 'Green Street'. A similar *herepaeth* in the Vale of Pewsey, also in Wiltshire, is commemorated in Harepath Farm near Bishops Cannings. The city of Hereford was a place on a *herepaeth* where armies were quartered before fording the river Wye and proceeding into Wales.
See also COLDHARBOUR *and* MILITARY ROADS

HERIOT An obligation incumbent on an heir to return to the lord the military apparel and equipment of a deceased tenant which, it was assumed, had originally been supplied by the lord. The obligation, which originated in the Saxon period, could include a horse, harness and weapons, depending on the status of the tenant, and applied equally to freemen and villeins. The custom was superseded in the second half of the eleventh century by the gift of the best beast by the heir, and this was later commuted to a money payment – effectively a fee to enter the land. Heriot was abolished as recently as 1922.

HERMIT From the Old French *ermite*, the popular perception of the medieval hermit is one of a solitary, religious recluse. But unlike an

ANCHORITE or COENOBITE, a hermit was committed to public service as a guide, ferryman or river pilot, providing frugal hospitality and shelter to travellers. For this reason a hermit's dwelling was usually located at the intersection of route-ways, often in difficult terrain (*see* HERMITAGE).

HERMITAGE Many of the sites to which the term 'hermitage' is traditionally ascribed were, in fact, ANCHORAGES or the cells of solitary CEONOBITES and religious mystics. Because of the nature of the hermits' calling, most hermitages were located in the vicinity of route-ways: at bridges, fords, ferries and causeways, and where tracks entered inhospitable country. The buildings themselves were not necessarily insubstantial, indeed some were subsidiary houses of monastic foundations. Many hermitages were created within rock piles or out of natural caves, such as the twelfth-century chambers of Blackstone Rock above the river Severn at Bewdley, Worcestershire. Some hermitages incorporated a small chapel and accommodation for travellers. Perhaps the best example is the fourteenth-century two-storey hermitage of the Holy Trinity, cut into a sandstone cliff above the river Coquet at Warkworth in Northumberland. This comprises a sacristy and small chapel within the rock to which a hall, kitchen and solar were added in masonry. There is evidence that the hermit kept a small farm and orchard above the cliff. But for many hermits, a temporary shelter sufficed and of these little remains except, perhaps, a place-name such as Hermitage in Dorset and Armitage in Staffordshire.

During the eighteenth and nineteenth centuries, neo-Gothic 'hermitages' added to the romanticism of several landscaped parks, perhaps the best example being that at Fonthill Park in Wiltshire. The 'Hermit's Sanctuary' in the woods of Burley House in Leicestershire was the home of a nineteenth-century hermit, employed by the Earl of Nottingham for the delectation of his guests. At Longleet in Wiltshire, a hermit was dismissed when he failed to make his customary appearance before Lord Bath's house-party and was later found to be drunk at the local inn.

HEUGH (*also* **HOE** *and* **HOO**) From the Old English *hōh*, meaning a 'ridge' or 'spur' of land. Also used to mean a 'bank' or 'steep slope', from which the term HA-HA may have derived.

HEYBOTE (*also* **HAYBOTE** *and* **HEDGEBOTE**) The right to remove wood from common land and to erect and maintain fences.
See also COMMONS

HEYNING *see* FOREST

HIDE This term originally signified the amount of land which could be ploughed annually by a team of eight-oxen. Clearly, this varied according to the quality of the land but was usually between 160 and 180 acres. The hide was used as a unit of tax assessment in the DOMESDAY survey of 1086 and may have been the basis of the HUNDRED, an administrative division of a shire dating from the tenth century. Alternative terms are *carucate*, *husbandland*, *ploughland* and *sulung* (*see* CARUCAGE). The term is also found in place-names, such as Piddletrenthide in Dorset, meaning 'place of thirty hides by the [river] Piddle'.

HIDEGILD The commutation of a sentence of flogging to payment of a fine.

HIGHWAY A way over which the public has a right to pass and repass. A *right of way* is a legal concept and a highway the strip of land to which it is applied. The nature of the right is dependent on the type of way which, under common law, may be a FOOTPATH, BRIDLE-WAY or CARRIAGEWAY. The term *public right of way* is generally applied only to unsurfaced tracks and not to roads normally used by motor vehicles. GREEN LANES are not necessarily public rights of way. The term 'Queen's [or King's] Highway' refers to the notion of royal protection enjoyed by all travellers on a public road.

In 1555 the Highways Act required that a 'Surveyor of the Highways' should be appointed (usually in Easter week) by the churchwardens, constable and representatives of each parish. (The surveyor was alternatively known as *boonmaster*, *stonewarden*, *waymaker*, *wayman* and *waywarden*). In 1662 the law was amended so that the surveyor was elected by a majority of parishioners, and from 1691 he was appointed by the justices from a list of eligible landholders in a parish. The office was unpaid and, from 1691, usually filled by rotation. The Surveyor was obliged to inspect the roads at least three times a year and to organize the statute labour or arrange commutations. Each able-bodied householder or tenant was obliged to provide four days 'statute' labour a year (from 1691 this was increased to six), to provide a substitute or pay a fine. Certain other parishioners were required to provide a cart for road repairs.

Before 1835, therefore, the upkeep of roads was generally the responsibility of manors, parishes or turnpike trusts (*see* TURNPIKES). But in that year, an act empowered QUARTER SESSIONS to appoint paid district surveyors, to bring together groups of parishes 'for the better maintenance of the highway' and for a highway rate to be levied. The Highway Act of 1862 extended this authority and highway boards, charged with the responsibility of administering the highways within these groups of parishes, were established. (These were abolished in 1894 but their records remain with county record offices.) The Local Government Act of 1888 transferred responsibility for the maintenance of highways to the newly established county councils, and the Local Government Act of 1894 brought minor roads within the jurisdiction of local authorities. A further Highway Act of 1959 established that it was the duty of county councils 'to assert and protect the rights of the public to the use and enjoyment of all highways in their district and to prevent as far as possible the stopping up or obstruction of these highways'.

HILARY The education and law term beginning in January near the feast-day of St Hilary on 13 January (14 January in the Roman Catholic calendar). St Hilary (*c.* 315–*c.* 367) was Bishop of Poitiers and the leading Latin theologian of his age.
See also MICHAELMAS *and* TRINITY

HILL FIGURES Large, eye-catching figures are easily created on the steep slopes of calcareous downland by removing the top layer of turf and thin subsoil to expose the white chalk beneath or by excavating trenches and packing them with chalk rubble, as at Uffington in Oxfordshire (*see below*). Because of their startling and often primitive appearance, many figures of comparatively recent date are endowed with an illusion of antiquity, enhanced by the proximity of prehistoric earthworks and encouraged by local 'tradition'. In reality, the majority of hill figures belongs to a species of folly, dating from the eighteenth, nineteenth and twentieth centuries and for which there is reliable documentary evidence. Of the ten white horses of Wiltshire, for example, all but one (that at Westbury) date from between 1778 and 1937. Most were cut by eccentrics, particularly during the period 1788 to 1863, and were probably inspired by the earlier

The Cerne Giant at Cerne Abbas, Dorset. The earthwork above the Giant's head is almost certainly a prehistoric enclosure and is known locally as the Trendle.

Westbury Horse which was itself remodelled in 1788. Those at Devizes, Ham Hill and Pewsey have become obliterated through neglect, though a new Pewsey horse was cut in 1936. On the slopes above Osmington, near Weymouth in Dorset, the mounted figure of George III is depicted riding *away* from his favourite resort (much to the annoyance of the local populace in 1815). Blériot's first cross-Channel flight is commemorated in a chalk aeroplane cut above Dover in 1909 and there are numerous military emblems, notably a series of regimental badges, at Fovant Down above the Nadder Valley in Wiltshire, carved during the First World War.

The celebrated naked giant at Cerne Abbas in Dorset typifies the controversy surrounding many hill figures. The 55 metre (180 feet) figure is explicitly virile and wields a primitive club in his right hand and is believed once to have carried a cloak over his outstretched left arm. He has therefore been identified with the god Hercules, and until recently was believed to date from the Romano-British period, though Saxon, Iron Age and Bronze Age origins have also been proposed. However, there is no mention of him in the extensive medieval documents for Cerne, or indeed until 1742, and it seems extraordinary that generations of local people should have been prepared to undertake the regular scouring necessary to conserve the figure without any reference remaining to what must have been (as elsewhere) singularly festive and noteworthy occasions. At Plymouth in Devon, for example, Tudor audit books record payments made 'for ye renewing of ye pyctur of Gogmagog a pon ye howe', and the scouring of the Uffington White Horse in Oxfordshire became an annual event, accompanied by races, competitions and festivities. It is hard to believe that the Benedictines of Cerne would have selected such an outrageously pagan site for their monastery in 987 or that they would have tolerated the giant's defiant presence throughout succeeding centuries. Even if their intention was deliberately to challenge paganism, there is no record. Neither is there any place-name evidence to suggest that the giant is of genuine antiquity. Many eighteenth- and nineteenth-century illustrations of the Cerne Giant omit his most prominent attribute, which is 9 metres (30 feet) in length, and the local clergy opposed the scouring of 1868 because they believed it would corrupt local morals. The equally famous Long Man of Wilmington in Sussex, a symmetrical figure holding a staff in each hand, does not appear in records until 1779, though by this time he was of sufficient antiquity for him to be in a poor state of repair. Similarly, the Whiteleaf and Bledlow crosses

in the Chilterns are first mentioned in 1742 and 1827 but it has been suggested that they may be of medieval origin and, until the eighteenth century, neglected and obscured. Certainly, the Whiteleaf Cross is in a prominent position above the ancient Icknield Way.

Of the many hill figures to have exercised generations of romantic antiquaries, few appear to be of certain antiquity. The (former) Plymouth Gogmadog Giant is known to have been maintained during the Middle Ages and may have been older, while the stylized Uffington Horse is mentioned in documents relating to a monk named Godrick who held the manor of Spersholt 'near the place which is commonly called White Horse Hill' in the eleventh century. Recent excavations have revealed that there may have been a series of Uffington horses buried beneath the present figure, each of a slightly different design. Many archaeologists suspect that the horse was originally created in the first century BC as a giant totemic symbol associated with a nearby Celtic hill fort, while others believe it to be of Anglo-Saxon origin. Regular scouring is essential if chalk figures are to be preserved and there can be little doubt that many have been lost through neglect, including the intriguing Plymouth Gogmadog. Others, such as the Wilmington Long Man, have been modified by over-enthusiastic (or mischievous) scouring.

Not all hill figures are cut into chalk, however. At Tysoe in Warwickshire there was, until the eighteenth century, a red horse cut into the ironstone scarp overlooking the Vale of the Red Horse (the place-name suggests antiquity). The Kilburn Horse in the North York Moors, formed of clay and grey rubble in 1857, requires a regular application of whitewash, and near Peterhead, in Aberdeenshire, the Mormond Stag of *c.* 1870 is composed of blocks of limestone and quartz.

HILL FORTS There are an estimated 2,520 hill forts in Britain, of which some 1,420 are south of Hadrian's Wall. The function of each evolved over a considerable period of time, as did the structures themselves. The popular perception of hill forts is that they date from the IRON AGE and were constructed in response to a prolonged series of incursions of warlike Celts, from the Rhineland and Saxony, armed with a new technology that included formidable iron weapons. In fact, defensive hilltop earthworks were constructed during the NEOLITHIC period and the BRONZE AGE, long before the introduction of iron. One of the earliest known examples, at Hambledon Hill in Dorset, is from *c.* 3500 BC and consists of some 3 km (2 miles) of complex earthworks enclosing an area of more than 160 acres. Neither does the archaeological evidence suggest large-scale invasion before the Belgaeic settlement of south-eastern Britain in the late Iron Age. Indeed, the internecine attentions of a neighbouring tribe, covetous of land and livestock, posed a far greater threat than invasion. Even the term 'fort' is often of doubtful validity: in many instances these hilltop enclosures, accurately described elsewhere as *rampart farmsteads*, were simply stockades occupied by small communities of (occasionally belligerent) farmers and herdsmen. Palisaded hilltop enclosures were constructed through the late Neolithic period and the early Bronze Age. From the mid Bronze Age a number of 'compact' hill forts were constructed with small enclosures surrounded by ramparts and ditches, together with several large forts such as that at Rams Hill on the Berkshire Downs. An increasing preoccupation with defence, which accelerated during the late Bronze Age, is indicative of increased competition for productive land, caused by climatic deterioration from *c* 1300 BC. Not all defensive sites were on hill tops, however: an immense artificial fortified island, constructed on a timber 'raft' some 100 metres (100 yards) in diameter and a similar distance from the shore or a shallow lake, was discovered near Peterborough in Cambridgeshire and is believed to date from *c.* 800 BC.

Iron Age hill forts were, for the most part, constructed and adapted in response to local circumstances and incorporate important regional variations. A few major sites were directly integrated within a network of territorial boundaries, while others seem to have enclosed granaries and storehouses for surplus food. As with earlier HENGES and CAUSEWAYED ENCLOSURES, their construction represented a considerable commitment of resources indicative of a well-organized and highly motivated society. The embankments of the immense Stanwick fort in North Yorkshire enclose an area of 750 acres, for example.

The structure of a hill fort was dependent on the chosen site and, in particular, the bedrock. The ubiquitous *contour forts* of the calcareous Wessex uplands were sited on open prominences, easily defended and commanding wide views over the surrounding vales. They were usually accessible from ancient ridgeway routes and the construction of earthworks was facilitated by the comparatively easily worked chalk and the natural contours of the hill (similar defensive earthworks in low-lying landscapes are called *plateau forts*). Ditches could

Maiden Castle near Dorchester, Dorset. The earlier enclosure, and the foundations of a small Roman temple, can be seen in the lower half of the photograph.

be excavated to a depth of 6 metres (20 feet) and the ramparts strengthened with timber revetments. Palisades and walkways were added, together with overlapping embankments at vulnerable entrances which were further protected by timber gatehouses.

Many hill forts were occupied intermittently for several centuries. The celebrated Maiden Castle near Dorchester in Dorset, for example, began as a Neolithic causewayed enclosure dating from before 3000 BC. After the ditches of the enclosure had been levelled, an enormous earthwork was constructed measuring 546 metres (1,790 feet) in length. (This was probably a bank barrow, the largest recorded Neolithic 'barrow'.) After sporadic occupation, the area was deserted in the Bronze Age, though there are numerous contemporary barrows both on the ridge to the south and one in the south-west quarter of the enclosure itself. The Iron Age hill fort began with a small enclosure of 14 acres on the eastern knoll, approximating with the former Neolithic causewayed enclosure. This had a single rampart (which is still visible, running across the interior) but later the defences were extended to enclose the entire hilltop with an area of 47 acres. An independent community (possibly of several thousand inhabitants) developed within the enclosure, living in clusters of circular thatched dwellings which were later reorganized into regular 'streets' with ancillary barns and granaries. Two further ramparts were added and the two entrances heavily defended with complex interlocking and revetted embankments, bastions and narrow elevated causeways, bridges and entrance passages intersecting the ditches and ramparts. Such planned settlements could have lasted for many centuries, but at Maiden Castle excavations have revealed a war cemetery containing the remains of thirty-four people buried with their grave goods, many mutilated by sword cuts and one with a Roman iron arrow-head embedded in his spine. These must have been the last defenders of the hill fort, defeated by Vespasian's Second Legion in AD 43 or 44. It is possible that occupation continued for some years after the conquest while the Roman *Durnovaria* (Dorchester) was being established. There is, however, archaeological evidence to suggest that the site was used as a fort by the Roman army and, in the second half of the fourth century, a Roman temple was built inside the ramparts. Sporadic burials and finds indicate that there was at least discontinuous occupation of the hill in the Saxon and medieval periods.

Hill forts were constructed and modified for a variety of functions depending, for the most part, on local circumstances. Many were farmstead enclosures in which livestock was kept and surplus food stored; others were occupied as refuges in times of danger, and several became the fortified 'proto towns' of large communities, sometimes (as at Hod Hill in Dorset) containing the residence of a Celtic chieftain and his extended family, acquiring thereby additional territorial and political significance as a tribal capital. By the first century BC, many smaller hill forts had been abandoned but the major sites could be regularly spaced across the landscape and no doubt served as centres of regional administration and trade as well as controlling river crossings and coastal harbours (*see* KINGDOMS (ANCIENT)).

No less numerous, but not always so readily identifiable in the landscape, are the defended sites built on rock outcrops in the mountainous regions of the north and west of Britain where bedrock was tough and unyielding. Shallow ditches had to be cut from the underlying rock and ramparts constructed of boulders, often supported by a timber framework (*see also* BROCH, DUN *and* RATH).

The so-called *Cliff Castles* of the south-west of England were built on precipitous coastal headlands, defended by natural cliffs and ramparts and ditches constructed across the landward side. Elsewhere, similar *promontory forts* occupy spurs of land with steep natural slopes and earthworks raised across the neck of the promontory: at Symonds Yat Rock in Herefordshire, for example. These defended sites varied considerably in size and function and generally date from the period *c.* 1500 to 150 BC, though at many occupation (and adaptation)

continued well into the Roman period. Many were little more than *rampart settlements*, fortified farmsteads containing a cluster of dwellings and ancillary buildings, while others were of considerable size. One of the largest, and perhaps the best preserved, is that of Tre'r Ceiri in Gwynedd, a fortified 'town' which contains traces of at least 150 stone dwellings and was occupied throughout the Roman period.

During the so-called Dark Ages, a number of hill forts were re-occupied and their defences remodelled to provide strongholds for the Romano-British and Celtic nobility. Excavations of the hill fort at South Cadbury in Somerset have revealed evidence of Neolithic occupation, multi-vallate Iron-Age defences and indications of a temple, built late in the Roman period. A defensive revetted drystone wall of *c.* AD 500 was further strengthened in the late Saxon period, and there are traces of what may be an early cruciform Christian church (*see* ARTHURIAN BRITAIN). In Cornwall, the hill fort of Castle Dore is reputed to have become the territorial capital of the chieftain Cynfawr who constructed a great hall within the Iron Age ramparts.

See also BLOOMERY *and* SOUTERRAIN *and for place-names* BURH, CAIR- *and* -DON

HIPPED ROOF *see* ROOFS

HIPPINGS *see* STEPPING STONES

HISTORIATED INITIAL In documents, an initial capital letter within which is an illustration associated with the text.

HOBELAR Effectively 'mounted infantry' – lightly armed medieval troops who travelled on horseback but fought on foot.

HOE From the Old English *hōh*, meaning a 'heel' or projecting ridge of land, as in Ivinghoe in Buckinghamshire and the celebrated Plymouth Hoe in Devon.

HOLLINS Woodland in which holly was grown.

HOLLOW TURNERY The making of hollow wooden utensils such as bowls.

HOLLOW WAY Lengths of sunken track, usually on sloping ground, worn into soft rock such as chalk or limestone by the constant passage of cattle and traffic such as pack-horses and tranters' wagons. Many hollow ways are still used for driving farm

animals and by ramblers and local pedestrians, while others have been abandoned following the creation of an improved alternative route such as a TURNPIKE or ENCLOSURE road or the re-siting of a bridge. They are also a feature of DESERTED VILLAGES, where former streets may be identified as hollow ways running between HOUSE PLATFORMS and CROFTS. Many of our traditional sunken lanes were hollow ways until repeated applications of tarmac arrested their erosion. Some hollow ways are prehistoric: those running down to water from an Iron Age HILL FORT, for example. Many others are of comparatively recent date and have may been formed or enlarged by the movement of farm vehicles and machinery. Place names such as Holloway in Middlesex and Holway in Somerset mean a 'hollow or sunken road'.
See also MULTIPLE TRACKS *and* PACK-HORSE ROADS

HOLLY An ancient tree common to the FOREST and CHASE where it provided winter forage. The white wood is tough, lacks resilience and cannot easily be split or broken. Because of its bludgeoning qualities it was widely used for tools such as wedges and flails but never for driving animals. To thc holly are ascribed protective characteristics: it is abhorred by witches and legend associates its blood-red berries and spiky leaves with Christ's Passion. It is likely that holly has been used for its decorative qualities since pre-Christian times, its shining green leaves and brilliant red berries providing welcome colour in the dead of winter.

-HOLME (i) Place-name element from Norse *holmr* signifying an island, e.g. Steep Holme and Flat Holme in the Bristol Channel and Axholme in Lincolnshire.
See also EY- *and* YNYS
(ii) In other contexts, a water meadow or low land standing just above flood level.

HOLOGRAPH A manuscript written entirely in its author's own handwriting.

-HOLT From the Old English *holt*, meaning 'wood', this place-name element is often combined with a tree name, e.g. Bircholt, Buckholt (beech wood), etc.

HOLY WELLS Places where water wells from the ground have always been venerated as sources of life: hence their almost invariable female dedication. The Neolithic practice of casting precious and sacrificial offerings into rivers and meres was, in some cultures, maintained well into the Iron Age and is even echoed in the Arthurian legends. In Celtic society, the afterlife was often portrayed as being beneath or beyond the water, and islands were regarded as the last refuges of the dead. SPRINGS were identified with Iron Age deities who possessed powers of healing and could foretell the future. At Carrawburgh, a fort on Hadrian's Wall, an extraordinary variety of offerings has been discovered at the well of the Roman goddess *Coventina*, the lady of the sacred spring, including some 16,000 coins which show that her cult lasted to the end of the Roman occupation.

With the gradual introduction of Christianity into Britain, the worshipping of pagan water gods was repeatedly forbidden, but pragmatism prevailed and numerous sacred wells were re-dedicated to Christian saints so that the populace could continue to benefit from their supposed restorative properties. Particularly popular were the saints Agnes, Anne and Helen, the last two probably substituted for the Celtic goddesses Annis and Elen, and in Cornwall alone there are more than 100 holy wells, many of them bearing the names of local missionary-saints.

Medieval holy wells often provided a source of revenue for local religious and monastic foundations. Some were consecrated for baptismal purposes while others established reputations for healing specific ailments: St Cynhafel's well near Denbigh was believed to cure warts, for example. Many were established as curative centres, complete with reservoirs, well-houses and ancillary chapels, and attracted pilgrims who lodged at their hospices. With the Reformation holy wells were deprived of their saintly attributes but continued to attract those who wished to 'take the waters'. The curative properties of natural springs were first investigated scientifically during the seventeenth and eighteenth centries and this led to the discovery of several new wells or 'spas', a term suitably devoid of religious connotations, derived from the sulphur springs at Spa near Liège (*see* SPAS).

Several holy wells continue to be 'venerated'. At Bisley in the Gloucestershire Cotswolds, for example, and at Tissington, one of several villages in the Derbyshire Peak District where the wells are 'dressed' each year with religious pictures composed of natural objects impressed into clay panels, a tradition dating from the eighteenth century but probably of pagan origin. St Winefride's Well, at Holywell near Flint, is still the site of an annual open-air celebration of the Mass and has been a place of pilgrimage since the Middle Ages. It is but one of an estimated 1,000 sacred wells in Wales and there are probably a further 1,000 in England and Scotland, though many are little more than nettle-covered holes in the ground with little sign of the stone structures which often surrounded them.

The Old English *well*, *wiell* or *wæll*, meaning 'well', 'spring' or 'stream', is commonly found in place-names, often as a second element to variants of 'Holy-', suggesting the site of a holy well. But the cult of the water gods was not a prominent one during the Saxon period and many 'holywells' have a different meaning or date from a later time. In Lincolnshire, the first element of Holywell is the Old English *hǽl*, meaning 'omen', so that the name translates as 'wishing well'; and whereas Holwell near Weymouth in Dorset means 'holy spring or stream' another Holwell, near Sherborne in the same county, is said to derive its name from the Old English *holh*, meaning 'hollow', and *walu*, meaning 'a ridge of earth or stone', which accurately describes the topography of the original settlement. Nevertheless, there is a 'well of unknown period' recorded in the county listings of archaeological sites and this, with its flight of steps, is still in evidence at Holwell today.

See also KEEIL, PAGAN SYMBOLS *and* SHRINES

HOME FARM *see* DEMESNE

HOMESTEAD A dwelling-house, occasionally moated, with its adjoining land and outbuildings.

HONOR A collection of estates, often distributed over a large area, owned by a TENANT-IN-CHIEF of the Crown.

HONORIAL COURT A court concerned primarily with landholdings appertaining to an HONOR.

HONOUR A group of KNIGHT'S FEES or manors administered by a superior and an honorial court comprising honorial barons as principal under-tenants. Such groupings were often (though by no means invariably) regional and based on a particular magnatial castle.

HOOD-MOULD A projecting moulding constructed above an arch to divert rainwater from the opening. Known also as a *dripstone*. A rectangular hood-mould is sometimes termed a *label*.

HOP ACRE *see* OAST-HOUSE

HOP KILN *see* OAST-HOUSE

HOPPERHEAD *see* DRAINS

HORNWORK *see* CASTLES (MEDIEVAL)

HORSA AND HENGIST *see* JUTE

HORSE-BLOCKS, HORSE-STEPS *and* **HORSE-STONES** *see* UPPING STOCKS

HORSE BELLS, BRASSES *and* **PENDANTS** *see* HARNESS (HORSE)

HORSE CHESTNUT Introduced into England in *c.* 1630, principally for planting in avenues and walks, the horse chestnut is not related to the SWEET CHESTNUT but originated in the Balkan mountains. In the eighteenth century, its pyramidical shape was considered to be more appropriate to the (then despised) formal garden, but it enjoyed increasing popularity in the Victorian period.

HORSESHOE The shoeing of horses and working oxen by nailing protective iron soles to the hoof was practised in Britain by the tenth century, and the farriery of the blacksmith had developed into an important craft in the medieval manor by the thirteenth (*see also* FORGE). Although the basic shape of a horseshoe has remained unaltered, in detail it has varied from county to county and from age to age. In shoeing, the smith begins with one of the horse's forefeet so that the animal can be reassured. The old shoe is removed by drawing the nails and the hoof (which is effectively an enormous toenail which continues to grow when protected from abrasion) is trimmed with a special knife. The shoe is first fitted cold and then heated, modified on the anvil and fitted again when it is 'black hot' (not quite glowing). Although this produced clouds of acrid smoke, a horse rarely reacts when familiar with the process. When the shoe fits it is cooled in a nearby water trough and secured by seven or eight nails (according to the type of shoe), countersunk on the underside and clenched where they protrude from the upper surface of the hoof. Contrary to superstition, horseshoes in ARMORY are always depicted with the points downwards.

HORSE STEPS A type of stepped CAUSEWAY, usually medieval, constructed to assist trains of pack-horses over steep and difficult terrain. In Wales, where there are several examples, such a route-way is called *sarn*, meaning 'causeway', though the term is also applied to Roman roads. For this reason the ancient pack-horse route through the

Rhinogs, by the pass of Bwlch Tyddiad, from Harlech (where there was a medieval port) to Bala is known in English as the Roman Steps, though it is almost certainly of medieval origin.

HOSPICE A lodging for travellers, especially one maintained by a religious order.

HOSPITALLER, KNIGHTS *see* ST JOHN OF JERUSALEM, ORDER OF *and* COMMANDERY

HOSPITALS Medieval hospices were charitable institutions, founded by livery companies, guilds and private individuals or groups of benefactors, and concerned as much with housing the elderly and infirm as tending to the sick (*see* ALMSHOUSES). The majority of hospices were established as a form of CHANTRY where the residents were required to pray for the souls of those on whose charity they depended. Some served the needs of specific groups of people such as pilgrims and lepers. Typically, the Leper Hospital of St Margaret and St Antony at Wimborne in Dorset was founded in the thirteenth century, encouraged by the Pope who granted an indulgence of a year to anyone who contributed to its building or to its maintenance. Christ's Hospital in London was founded by Edward VI (1547–53) on the site of Grey Friars Monastery, originally as a foundling hospital (for deserted and illegitimate children) though it soon became the famous Blue Coat School. There were also monastic hospices, but most of these were destroyed following the Dissolution of the Monasteries in 1536–9: St Bartholomew's ('Bart's'), St Thomas's and the Bethlehem hospital for the insane ('Bedlam') are notable exceptions, all of which were re-founded under lay control.

G.M. Trevelyan, in his *English Social History* (1944), describes the eighteenth century as 'the age of hospitals'. It was a century when the population of England and Wales increased from 5½ million to nearly 9 million, the result of an increased birth rate and a very much reduced death rate, attributable to improved medical services and, in the cities, to a decline in the consumption of cheap gin. Despite a proliferation of private 'mad-houses', to which were committed those whose behaviour was an embarrassment to fashionable society, this was indeed the 'Age of Enlightenment' and nowhere was its spirit more apparent than in the medical profession's commitment to science and philanthropy. The trade of 'barber-surgeon' was transformed into a specialist science; the practice of midwifery was revolutionized and military hygiene

reformed on scientific principles which were to influence the treatment of civilian patients.

Advances in professional skills were supported by the foundation of hospitals: lying-in hospitals were established in many towns and county hospitals for a variety of patients. The famous hospitals of Guy's, St George's, Westminster, London and Middlesex were all founded between 1720 and 1745, while the medieval St Thomas's had been remodelled at the beginning of the century. The Foundling Hospital was opened in 1745, its supporters including Handel (who gave an organ) and Hogarth (who painted a picture). Between 1700 and 1825 no fewer than 154 new hospitals and dispensaries were opened as the result of co-ordinated voluntary effort and subscription, and the majority of these were taken into the National Health Service following its inception in 1948. The records of several of these hospitals are held at the Public Record Office and there are archives and a library devoted to the history of asylums and hospitals at the Bethlehem Royal Hospital, Beckenham, Kent.
See also ASYLUMS *and* SOCIAL WELFARE

HOSTELLER *see* MONASTERIES

HOURDS *see* CASTLES (MEDIEVAL)

HOURGLASS *see* PULPITS

HOUSEHOLD The structure of the medieval magnatial *familia* or household was usually modelled on that of the sovereign's. Not only were members of the household collectively and individually responsible for the personal needs of the noble and his numerous relations and guests, they were also charged with the administration of his estates or, in the case of the sovereign, with his realm. They were also expected to take up arms on their lord's behalf, both in times of war and in defence of his territories and rights. In return, they received LIVERY AND MAINTENANCE and enjoyed his patronage. The sons of noble and knightly families were expected to serve in the households of superiors where they received academic as well as military and courtly training. Even the younger brothers of kings were not exempt: in 1461, for example, the young Richard, Duke of Gloucester (the future Richard III) joined the household of Richard Neville, Earl of Warwick, at Middleham in Yorkshire.

In government, the administration was essentially that created by the Norman kings. The office of the Exchequer oversaw the finances of the realm following long established bureaucratic procedures, and the CHANCERY issued charters and letters under the GREAT SEAL, thereby transmitting instructions to the king's subjects. But at the heart of the governmental system was the household: a flexible, personal instrument consisting at one level of the sovereign's domestic entourage or *domus* (with departments such as the kitchen, the saucery, the pantry and the scullery) and at another, the *Wardrobe*. This was a central department which, from the mid-thirteenth century, effectively annexed the responsibilities formerly associated with another department, the Chamber. During the reign of Edward I (1272–1307), the Wardrobe enjoyed increasing financial autonomy and, unlike the Exchequer, was capable of expanding to meet changing national demands, such as war. It became the chief spending department of central government, indeed the PRIVY SEAL was retained by the Controller of the Wardrobe so that letters of instruction, authenticated by this seal (*warrants*), could be sent to the Exchequer and the Chancery and to royal officials throughout the realm. The officials of the household, and especially those of the Wardrobe, were essential to the effective government of the country both in peace and war. It also provided the core of the royal army (the corps of royal household knights and esquires) which could be expanded rapidly in time of war and was retained through the Wardrobe. In the mid-1280s, lists of those receiving the royal livery include some 570 names, ranging from high-ranking officials to scullery boys.

Many of the great English offices of state originated in the households of the dukes of Normandy well before the Conquest and there is little doubt that the ducal establishment itself was modelled on that of the kings of France. The *Constitutio Domus Regis*, compiled for King Stephen in *c*. 1136, indicates that at that time there were four principal ranks of household officer:

First: Chancellor, Steward, Master Butler, Master Chamberlain and Constable.

Second: Master Dispenser of the Bread, Master Dispenser of the Larder, Master Dispenser of the Buttery, Master of the Writing Desk, Clerk of the Spence of the Bread and Wine and Duty Chamberlain (deputy to the Master Chamberlain).

Third: Deputy Constables, Master Marshal and Chamberlain of the Privy Purse.

Fourth: Dispenser of the Pannetry, Dispenser of the Larder, Keeper of the Butts,

Chamberlain of the Candle and four Marshals of the Household.

The stewards were responsible for the hall and those departments connected with food over which the butler had no jurisdiction (*see* LARDER). In England, the butler was responsible for the butlery, wine selection, the dispensers, etc. (in France, the office was of far greater importance, controlling the royal vineyards, collecting taxes from certain abbeys and sitting as a judge in the scourt). The chamberlain was in charge of the royal Bed-chamber (and, immediately after the Conquest, was also the royal Treasurer). Towards the end of the Norman period, a separate office of Treasurer was created, and by 1135 this was considered to be as important as that of Chancellor and other offices of the first rank. The constables initially controlled the stables (from which their title derives), the kennels, the mews and anything relating to the king's sporting activities. They were also quartermasters, responsible for the payment of the king's soldiers. Initially, the marshal's duties included supervision of the royal stables, though by 1385 the office had attained considerable military and judicial importance comparable with that of the constable.

From these household offices evolved the eight great officers of medieval government, each responsible for his own department: Lord High Steward, Lord High Chancellor, Lord High Treasurer, Lord President of the Council, Lord Keeper of the Great Seal, Lord Great Chamberlain, Lord High Constable and Earl Marshal. (As the influence of the Wardrobe grew during the thirteenth century so too did that of its controller so that a further office, Lord Privy Seal, was eventually established.) In time, many of the lesser household offices became sinecures, granted as royal patronage and perceived by recipients as a means of advancement. As the functions of monarchy and government diverged, so many of the major offices became offices of state while others remained as offices of the royal household. Most still exist, though in much modified and often ceremonial form.

HOUSE OF CORRECTION *see* PRISONS

HOUSE PLATFORM The final visible remains of a decayed dwelling, a house platform usually has the appearance of a level, rectangular 'dais' around the edge of which the outlines of walls may be discernible, breached by the openings of former doorways. Series of platforms, often adjacent to a HOLLOW WAY, are a feature of many DESERTED

VILLAGES. Single platforms (sometimes surrounded by evidence of ancillary buildings) usually denote former farmsteads or single cottages. Many house platforms have been obliterated by ploughing, while others have been reduced by quarrying for building materials followed by natural erosion. Even so, they may still be evident as CROP MARKS or identified by the presence of nettles which flourish in the phosphate-rich soils of former habitations.

HOVEL *see* MUD AND STUD

HOW(E) A burial mound or natural hillock.

HUE AND CRY The pursuit of a felon was the responsibility of the parish in which he was discovered or to which he was known to have fled. Parishioners were obliged to 'raise the hue and cry' by shouting and the blowing of horns.
See also LAW AND ORDER

HUGUENOT A member of the Calvinistic French Protestants who were in constant conflict with the Roman Catholic majority throughout the latter part of the sixteenth century. Of disputed origin, the term was in popular use by 1560 and came to include also Protestant refugees from Spanish persecution in the Low Countries. Calvinistic French communities increased rapidly following a synod held in 1559 but a series of internal religious wars, culminating in the Massacre of Bartholomew in 1572, caused many Huguenots to flee to Protestant countries, including England. The *Edict of Nantes* of 1598 provided for religious and political freedom, but the Catholic Church in France maintained its pressure against the Huguenots and in 1685 Louis XIV revoked the *Edict*, forcing many to apostatize or flee from France. Those who came to England were required to apply for either naturalization or denization. Most became members of the numerous Huguenot churches in England and subsequently many French surnames have become anglicized or even translated.
For the Huguenot Society *see* APPENDIX I

HULKS *see* TRANSPORTATION (PENAL)

HUNDRED A tenth-century administrative division of a SHIRE, administered by a reeve, who served writs on behalf of the sheriff of the shire, and later by a constable, who was responsible for the apprehension of criminals. These administrative divisions may have originated as units of a hundred taxable hides, each HIDE being the amount of land required to maintain an extended free family, or else as units of ten tithings (*see* FRANKPLEDGE). New hundreds were still being created in the seventeenth century by Justices of the Peace at QUARTER SESSIONS, but by the nineteenth century they had ceased to have any significant function having been superseded by a variety of manorial, parochial and judicial authorities. In 1894 the Local Government Act established the district councils which were effectively the successors to the HUNDRED COURT. In Kent, hundreds were known as *lathes* (the sub-divisions of which were hundreds), in Surrey *rapes*, in East Anglia *leets*, in the Isle of Wight *liberties* and in Cumberland, Durham, Northumberland and Westmorland *wards*. In the Danelaw counties (principally Derbyshire, Leicestershire, Lincolnshire, Nottinghamshire and parts of Yorkshire) they were known as *wapentakes* (Old Norse for 'weapon-taking'), each sub-division being a hundred.

HUNDRED COURT The hundred court, attended by the freemen of the hundred, was presided over by the Hundred Reeve, a bailiff of the SHERIFF to whose shire court there was a right of appeal. The hundred court was convened once a month at an open place, which was usually distinguished by some landmark or feature such as a barrow or crossroads. The court was particularly concerned with criminal offences and private pleas, though it also levied taxes and could consider minor ecclesiastical matters. The jury of a hundred could also be empanelled by the Crown to provide local information. From 1217, two further annual meetings of the court were added. These were called the Sheriff's Tourn and were held at Easter and Michaelmas with the sheriff or his deputy presiding. Hundred names and boundaries are listed in most county histories and in the *Victoria County History* series, while on the Ordnance Survey map there may be evidence of former court sites in the convergence of ancient trackways at prominent places or in place-names such as the common Moot Hill or names such as Motcombe in Dorset (from the Old English *gemō t-cumb*, meaning 'valley where moots were held') and Skirmett in Buckinghamshire (*scīrgemōt*, meaning 'shire moot'). It should be remembered, however, that a MOOT (or *mote*) could be convened for purposes other than those of a hundred court.
See also LAW AND ORDER

HUNDRED HOUSE A workhouse provided and maintained by a group of parishes within a HUNDRED.

HUNDRED ROLLS Corruption in local administration, particularly the usurpation of liberties, was endemic in the second half of the thirteenth century. The Hundred Rolls record the findings of an investigation into local government conducted in 1274/5 on the direct instruction of Edward I. In 1278 the Statutes of Gloucester required all holders of franchises to prove their titles through QUO WARRANTO proceedings. Both sets of records are maintained by the Public Record Office and contain invaluable details of thirteenth-century local administration. Two volumes of *Rotuli Hundredorum* were published in 1812 and 1818, together with an *Index*. *Placita de Quo Warranto* was also published in 1818 and this contains transcripts of many of the proceedings which followed the survey of the hundreds.

HUNTING LODGE Medieval forests were vast, and long distances were covered by a hunting party and its attendant officials and servants in the course of a day. Hunting lodges, strategically distributed throughout a FOREST or CHASE, were necessary both as places of refuge during and after a long day's sport and as centres of operation for the various foresters and woodmen who were responsible for the maintenance of the vert and venison. Lodges and keepers' dwellings were also provided in many of the larger DEER PARKS and often occupied vantage points on high ground from which spectators might observe a ceremonial hunt. Regrettably, hardly any ancient hunting lodges remain, though the decaying earthworks of their former moats and fish-ponds may still be discernible. These suggest that a typical medieval lodge was a castle in miniature: a square, central tower containing a hall and kitchens (and sometimes a chapel) set within a rectangular moated enclosure entered by means of a bridge and gatehouse. Perhaps the best example is the Barden Tower, one of six lodges constructed in the Clifford hunting grounds in Wharfedale, Yorkshire. The original tower was enlarged in 1485 and remodelled in 1658.
See also LODGES

-HURST A place-name element from the Old English *hyrst* with a variety of interpretations including 'hillock', 'sandy knoll', 'copse', 'wood' and 'wooded eminence'. The original meaning was probably 'brushwood' and the usual interpretation is 'wood', e.g. Crowhurst in Sussex meaning 'a wooded coomb' and Brockhurst in Warwickshire meaning 'badger wood'.

HUSBANDLAND *see* HIDE

HUSBANDMAN A tenant farmer.

HUSBOTE *see* COMMONS

HUT CIRCLES Surprisingly numerous in those areas of upland Britain which have escaped the plough, these relics of prehistoric dwellings consist, for the most part, of slightly raised saucer-shaped platforms delineated either by a ring of moss or heather or by the remnants of a drystone wall. Occasionally, the upright slabs of the entrance portal may also be found. Depending on the period of construction and the availability of materials, the low 1.5 metre (5 feet) walls were built using small boulders of surface granite (*moorstone*) or timber posts and wattle and daub. Both types of hut were provided with a conical thatched roof carried on rafters which, in larger buildings, were supported by an inner ring of upright poles. The huts varied in size from 2.7 to 9 metres in diameter (9 to 30 feet) and contained sleeping platforms and hearths from which the smoke rose to a hole in the apex of the roof. Many hut circles date from the early IRON AGE but the majority are from the early and middle BRONZE AGE, following which deteriorating climatic conditions and land exhaustion resulted in the abandonment of many exposed upland areas. Some hut circles are remarkably old: excavations near Holyhead in Anglesey revealed that similar dwellings were occupied in the late Neolithic period. Hut circles may be found singly, in small clusters or in 'village' groupings, often within oval-shaped compounds of several acres and peripheral areas of cultivation. The stone or earth ramparts of these enclosures often exceeded 1.8 metre in height (6 feet) and many contained a stream or spring, as at Riders Rings on Dartmoor near Buckfastleigh in Devon where two enclosures, one of 7 acres and the other of 3, each contain twenty hut circles.

HYPOCAUST A term derived from two Greek words meaning 'the place heated from below' and applied to the Roman system of heating domestic buildings by circulating hot air beneath the floors and within the walls. The hot air was conveyed from a basement wood-burning furnace to chambers created beneath floors, which were supported on low pillars of rectangular bricks, and to wall flues of hollow box tiles. Hypocaust systems were particularly effective in heating bathhouses and may still be seen at many villas such as that at Chedworth in Gloucestershire (*see* ROMAN VILLAS).

HYTHE *see* FERRIES

I

Impalement   Escutcheon of Pretence

Dimidiation

ICE HOUSE A type of cold store (*glaciére*) introduced from France during the seventeenth century, though primitive ice houses were constructed in Britain before that time. At Ludlow Castle in Shropshire, for example, an underground chamber was created in the outer wall of the dry moat. In winter, ice blocks, packed in straw, were transported on horse-drawn carts from the Welsh mountains and set against the walls of the chamber in which perishable foodstuffs were stored. Seventeenth-, eighteenth- and early nineteenth-century ice houses were much more sophisticated. They were usually located in the parks of great houses and provided ice for the preparation of sweets and iced drinks. Today, the artificial mound concealing a domed or barrel-vaulted roof is often the only clue to a stone or brick-walled chamber beneath, with its egg-shaped ice-well, narrow, geniculated entrance tunnel and doors designed to maintain a constant temperature within. Melting ice discharged by means of a drain at the base of the ice-well in which a grill, covered with reeds or straw, protected an air trap (like an S-bend in a lavatory). A distinctive type of ice-house was 'bottle'-shaped with an upper opening large enough to admit a man. The entire contents of an ice-house could be ruined by damp and consequently an impervious clay capping was provided beneath a covering of soil or turf. Most are located in open, elevated positions, to encourage the rapid evaporation and dispersal of rain water, and many will be found near lakes from which the winter ice was removed, crushed and compressed in the ice-well to form a solid mass. Vegetables were sometimes stored in niches in the chamber walls.

ILLEGITIMACY *see* BASTARDY

ILLUMINATION *see* MANUSCRIPT ILLUMINATION

IMBREX *see* TILES

IMMEMORIAL EXISTENCE *see* LAW

IMPALEMENT In ARMORY, the vertical division of a shield to incorporate two different coats of arms side-by-side. A husband may impale his wife's arms to the sinister of his own, unless she is an heraldic heiress in which case they are placed on an *escutcheon of pretence*, a small shield at the centre of the larger one, which is said to be *in pretence*. Holders of certain offices which carry with them armorial bearings may impale their personal coats with those of their office, the latter being placed in the dexter. These are known as arms of office. An early form of impalement was *dimidiation*, by which the dexter half of one shield of arms was combined with the sinister half of another, often with quite extraordinary artistic results!
See also MARSHALLING *and* QUARTERING

IMPROPRIATE Benefices, and the associated greater tithes, which passed to lay rectors following the Reformation.

IMPROVEMENTS (SCOTTISH) By comparison with the harsh CLEARANCES of the Scottish Highlands, the eighteenth-century agricultural 'revolution' in the Lowlands and north-east was almost humanitarian. Unlike their English counterparts (*see* ENCLOSURE), Scottish landowners were able to enclose common moors and

RUNRIG ploughlands without first obtaining parliamentary sanction. But in most parts of Scotland, the potential advantages of agricultural improvement and innovation were restricted by adverse climatic conditions, poor soils and a tradition of settlement which tended to support an excess of workpeople. Nevertheless, in many areas the runrig system was replaced by new or revised tenancy agreements and holdings of regular enclosures bounded by hedgerows or CONSUMPTION DYKES. Enclosure was accompanied by a rationalization of holdings which favoured a minority of fermtoun landworkers (*see* CLACHAN) who were offered new farms and farmsteads on long leases (*tacks*) and encouraged (or required) to improve their lands by drainage operations, the planting of shelter belts and the introduction of rootcrops. The quality of livestock was also improved through the development of the Aberdeen Angus and Ayrshire strains. Agricultural innovation in England was communicated by numerous absentee landlords, through their estate managers (*factors*), to the tenant farmers who collectively transformed vast areas of the Scottish Lowlands from bleak runrig cultivation to verdant (and profitable) landscape. Disintegration of the old settlement patterns inevitably created a surplus of labour and, in many instances, eviction. This was by no means as severe as in the Highlands, however, and many landowners succeeded in creating new villages and work opportunities in fishing or manufacturing. An estimated 150 planned settlements were established between 1745 and 1845, few of which have subsequently prospered. Such villages may be often be identified by a uniformity of architectural style, a 'grid-iron' or linear plan and no apparent rationale for their existence.

IN Latinized place-name element meaning 'among' (*see* LATIN).

INCISED SLABS Among the earliest examples in Britain of these engraved stone MEMORIALS is a collection of over 200, dating from the eighth to the tenth centuries, at Clonmacnois in Ireland. But it was during the period from the eleventh century to the mid-fourteenth that coffin-shaped slabs, usually incised with a simple cross, became numerous. These were usually of hard sandstone, though there were regional variations: Purbeck and other marbles in the south of England, gritstone in Derbyshire and Northumberland, and Bath and Ham stone in the south-west, for example. In the western Highlands of

Ledger stone in All Saints' church, Swanton Morley, Norfolk.

Scotland, a vigorous Celtic school developed using mica-schist, and by the Reformation alabaster was widely used in the English midlands.

Human figures first appeared in the twelfth century. These were often of priests though there were also early military figures, such as that of a knight at Sollers Hope, Herefordshire. Unlike BRASSES and EFFIGIES, British incised slabs rarely depict heraldic figures, most armorial display being confined to coats of arms on small shields. One of the earliest armorial slabs, at Gilling-on-Rydale in Yorkshire, is incised with a cross, gauntlets and a shield of arms. There are occasional examples of heraldic figures, such as those of Sir Johan de Botiler (*c.* 1285) at St Brides Major in the Vale of Glamorgan and of John Foljambe (d.1499, monument *c.* 1515) at Sutton Scarsdale, Derbyshire, in which he is depicted in full armour and emblazoned tabard, with his head resting on a crested helmet and his feet on a chatloup, a chimerical creature granted to the Foljambe family as a BADGE in 1513.

Such slabs, which were almost invariably laid in the church floor, were clearly liable to excessive wear and many were eventually lifted and set upright against a wall or raised onto a plinth. An even greater number have been lost or their detail defaced. Some incised slabs may have been embellished with inlaid materials, especially those imported from the Low Countries. Regrettably, little remains of the pitch and painted lead (and occasionally copper or enamel) with which the figures were coloured.

During the seventeenth century, incised slabs depicting full-length figures were replaced by *ledger stones*. These were usually of black marble (*see* TOUCH) or local stone such as slate and bore a simple inscription and a deeply incised roundel containing a coat of arms or other device. Ledger stones, which remained popular to the nineteenth century, were usually set in the floor above an interment (especially in the chancel) though a few have been found on TOMB CHESTS and TABLE TOMBS. Many East Anglian churches contain particularly good examples of finely executed and engraved ledger stones.

INCLINED PLANE An ingenious means of raising tub-boats from one level of a CANAL to another, thereby obviating the need to construct expensive flights of LOCKS. Tub-boats were lighter and smaller than conventional narrow boats and their use was, for the most part, restricted to the minor canals of the west of England. The boats were lifted or lowered inside a timber 'cage' which was pulled hydraulically, or by steam, up and down the incline on two sets of grooved runners. On some canals, the tub-boats themselves were fitted with wheels and were hauled from one level to another, often counterpoised with boats travelling in the opposite direction. The Bude Canal in Cornwall (completed in 1826) had five inclined planes, each operated by a waterwheel, with gradients of between one in four and one in seven. On the Tavistock Canal (1817) in Devon, an inclined plane lowered boats, loaded with copper ore, 73 metres (240 feet) from the canal terminal to Morwhellam Quay on the river Tamar.

INCLOSURE ACTS *see* ENCLOSURES

INCUMBENT A rector, vicar or perpetual curate in charge of a parish.

INCUNABULUM An early printed book, especially dating from before 1501, often with handworked painting and illumination.

INDENTURE A formal inventory or agreement: that binding an apprentice to a master, for example. The term derives from the practice of repeating the text of an agreement on a single sheet of paper or vellum and separating the two identical texts by cutting in an irregular manner so that the indentations of each party's document complement those of the other, thereby making it impossible to substitute a forged agreement or to alter the original. Medieval indentures were often prepared for a number of parties to an agreement and sometimes the word *chirograph* was written across the indented line to show that there were several copies of the same text.

INDENTURE OF FEOFFMENT *see* RELIEF

INDULGENCES *see* SHRINES

INDUSTRIAL REVOLUTION The transformation of British society, during the second half of the eighteenth century and the first half of the nineteenth, in which the majority of the working population shifted from agricultural to industrial occupations. The Industrial Revolution was preceded by the AGRARIAN REVOLUTION, which effected a drastic reduction in the agricultural labour force and a corresponding increase in the urban population. This in turn stimulated an enormous demand for cheap, mass-produced goods and provided a substantial supply of manual labour for the new mills and factories. The two 'revolutions' may indeed be regarded as a single force by which society was reconstructed in order to feed and employ a population that was increasing with prodigious rapidity.

The Industrial Revolution was caused by unprecedented scientific and technological innovation and in particular by the application of steam power. Industry itself created a demand for machines and for the tools to manufacture and maintain them, thereby stimulating further mechanization. The transportation of raw materials and coal to manufacturing centres and the distribution of finished goods to markets, both at home and abroad, required a massive investment in road improvements and in the construction of CANALS, RAILWAYS and steamships, and a substantial labour force. The skills acquired through this process became marketable commodities in their own right and were exported to developing countries, together with the necessary machinery and services. Britain became the most powerful industrial country in the world but the profound social and economic problems which resulted from such a fundamental transformation of society were to dominate domestic politics for over a century.
See also MINERALS and STEEL

INFANGENTHEOF The right of a manorial lord to try and punish a thief arrested in his manor. *See also* OUTFANGENTHEOF

INFANTRY VOLUNTEERS Known in several counties as 'The Bang-up Locals', the local Infantry Volunteers were recruited in the early nineteenth century to assist in the defence of the country against threatened French invasion. Like the Home Guard of the Second World War, they were part-time soldiers who remained at home as civilians, carrying on their peacetime occupations. The Volunteers attended periodic drills and had to be ready to be called out in an emergency, when they would be treated as Regular soldiers, liable to normal military discipline and rates of pay. Formed originally in 1794, the Volunteer Infantry was disbanded when the Peace of Amiens was signed in 1802, but reconstituted in 1803 when war broke out again. Inevitably, it was in the coastal counties of southern England where the threat of invasion was most keenly felt. Typically, at that time, the Dorset Volunteers consisted of 28 companies, totalling 2,000 men, with most towns and larger villages recruiting at least one company.

Weapons were not always available and many volunteers were obliged to use pikes, which were considered to be obsolete and an affront to a Volunteer's dignity and self-esteem – just as they were in 1942 when the War Office decided to issue them to certain units of the Home Guard. Indeed, some Volunteers actually resigned when they were issued with pikes, which were intended for use by those able-bodied men who had not volunteered but who, in the event of an invasion, were expected to collect a pike from the local church. A 'return of Arms', dated 3 September 1803, reveals that in the County of Dorset there were 3,000 pikes in Dorchester, 900 in Wareham, 1,000 in Bridport and 100 at Lulworth Castle – the 1,000 which had been stored at Weymouth had been destroyed by fire at the barracks!

While the once-weekly drill was necessary, it was invariably boring and repetitive, with the same movements being practised week after week. A young lady visiting a Hampshire village one evening found '. . . the men exercising in their surock frocks – the poor creatures both tired and awkward and not inspired by martial ardour. However, everybody is a soldier here, whether they like it or not.' Occasionally, a Field Day was held when Volunteers were able to train with men of other companies. *See also* MILITIA

INFEUDATION The granting of land to a VASSAL.

INFIELD-OUTFIELD CULTIVATION An ancient form of cultivation based on the maintenance in constant production of an 'infield', which relied for its fertility on constant applications of manure, together with 'outfields' of poorer quality land, sections of which were periodically ploughed and cropped to exhaustion before being returned to pasture. The combined outfields were substantially larger than the infield (which was usually about one-fifth of their size), and beyond them an extensive area of WASTE provided rough grazing in the summer months. With regional variations, the system appears to have been developed in prehistoric Britain and in some areas it persisted beyond the introduction of OPEN FIELDS in the late Saxon period. In Scotland, it was widely used until the CLEARANCES and IMPROVEMENTS of the eighteenth and nineteenth centuries (*see* MULTIPLE ESTATE *and* RUNRIG).

INFIRMARY *and* **INFIRMARIAN** *see* MONASTERIES

-ING *and* **-ING-** A common place-name element with a number of derivations, the most common of which are:
(i) As a suffix (meaning 'place of') to Old English names of, for example, streams (as in Guiting in Gloucestershire: *gyte* meaning 'flood') and of habitations (as in Clavering in Essex: *clæfre* meaning 'clover').
(ii) From the Old English -*ingas*, derivatives of personal nouns implying 'the descendants of –' or 'the dependants of –' (as in Barking in Essex: *Berecingas* meaning '*Berica's* people') or of topographical features (as in Avening in Gloucestershire: *Æfeningas* meaning 'the dwellers by the river called Avon').
(iii) -*ing*- is very common in combination with elements such as -*hām* (as in Birmingham in the West Midlands, meaning 'the *hām* or homestead of *Beornmund's* people'); -*tūn* (as in Withington in Gloucestershire, meaning '*Widia's dūn* or hill'); -*feld* (as in Bedingfield in Suffolk, meaning 'the field of *Bēda's* people') and -*leah* (as in Madingley in Cambridgeshire, meaning 'the *lēah* or glade of *Māda's* people).

INGLE-NOOK From the Gaelic *ingle* meaning 'hearth', a seat within a recessed fireplace (*see* CHIMNEY).

INGS Common meadows, or pasture on the banks of a stream.

INHUMATION In this context, the burial of a corpse rather than the interment of cremated remains.

INJUNCTION *see* LAW

INK Most medieval and early modern texts were written in inks made from a mixture of oak-galls, iron sulphate and gum Arabic, though a darker but less stable ink was also produced from carbon, gum and water.

INLAND Land located close to a farmstead.

INN SIGNS The names of Britain's 60,000 inns range from the eccentric *Cow and Snuffers* in Glamorgan, *The Rorty Crankle* in Kent and the *Bull and Spectacles* in Staffordshire, to those which are of considerable antiquity, as are the symbols by which they are recognized. Regrettably, there is an increasing tendency to change the names of inns without regard to their historical significance. At Lydlinch in Dorset, for example, the local inn was re-named the *Deer Park* in 1988, after a deer park at Stock Gaylard some 2 km (1.2 miles) distant. The owner's intention was to provide his establishment with a more 'relevant' name. What he apparently failed to appreciate was that the original *Three Boars* were the arms of the lords of the manor who lived at Stock Gaylard. In the past, there were usually sound political reasons for such changes. Following the Battle of Bosworth in 1485, for example, many *White Boar* taverns were hastily re-named and their signs modified to show the blue boar device of the victorious Earl of Oxford instead of the white boar of the ignominious Richard of Gloucester. Similarly, numerous *King's Arms* have been repainted, reflecting changing dynastic fortunes, often by artists whose understanding of heraldry was minimal.

Traditional names, such as the *Green Man*, often indicate the sites of former festivals or holy days (*wakes*) (*see* GREEN MAN), while many others are corruptions of religious concepts or names: *Peter's Finger*, for example, being a rustic version of St Peter ad Vincula – St Peter in Chains – and the *Goat and Compass* which is a corruption of 'God Encompasseth Us'. Names with religious associations are often of medieval origin: *The Lamb*, *The Anchor* and *The Cross Keys*, for example, may commemorate inns which were provided by monastic and collegiate establishments to accommodate pilgrims (*see* SHRINES) or teams of itinerant craftsmen.

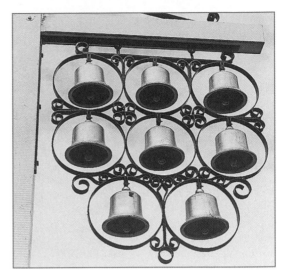

The 'Eight Bells' at Dover, Kent.

The *Pig and Whistle* is derived from the Saxon custom of drinking *ewassaili*, a spiced beer, from a communal *piggen* or pail. The pail was marked on the inside with ivory pegs to indicate the allowance for each drinker: hence the expression 'taking him down a peg' when a man's companions deprived him of his fair share. Many pub names recall former heroes: there are eighteen generals and nearly fifty admirals commemorated in inn names, Lord Nelson being by far the most popular.

That such sources of local history should be lost through ignorance of their origins is most regrettable. The process began in the nineteenth century when brewers took advantage of the growth in literacy to plaster their pub walls with beer advertisements and to replace many signs with lanterns bearing only the brewer's name. In the 1930s *The Times* ran a campaign to restore traditional pub signs, an editorial rightly proclaiming that 'Inn signs are the story-boards of English history!' Today, the tendency is to replace them with outlandish, meaningless names such as *Slug and Lettuce*, *Fig and Furkin* and the *Apothecary's Spectacles*.

Inn signs originated in the medieval practice by which tradespeople declared their function to an illiterate populace. The butcher, the baker and the candlestick-maker each had his own symbol, as did the taverner and maltster. Other twentieth-century survivors are the bloody, bandaged pole of the barber-surgeon and the pawnbrokers' gold discs which originated in the *bezants*, or gold coins of Byzantium. By the end of the fourteenth century, the provision of a prominent and distinctive sign outside taverns and alehouses was a legal requirement, at least in London. Wishing to make it easier for government officials to check the quality of beer sold, Richard II decreed (in 1393) that 'Whosoever shall brew ale with the intention of selling it must hang out a sign or forfeit his ale.' In many cases, these must have been very much larger than they are today: in 1419 the encroachment of signs above the highway was restricted by statute to just over 2 metres (7 feet).

The origins of many inn names are often obscure. The Romans often hung a bush of vine leaves outside their taverns (*tabernae*) to show that wine was for sale, hence the popular name *The Bush*. This was sometimes reduced to a garland of evergreens, and the hoop in names such as *Eagle and Hoop* is probably derived from this. (It seems likely that the expression 'a good wine needs no bush' has a Roman origin.) The *Bag of Nails* is probably a corruption of Bacchanales, the fesival held in honour of the Roman god of wine. Many inn names have an obvious armorial origin: they are simply called the *So-and-So Arms*, though all too often the heraldry of the signs is inaccurate or (perversely) has been replaced by lettering. Such names usually refer to the family arms of a past or present lord of the manor (as at Lydlinch above) or to a guild or other institution which at one time was associated with the area: as rector or patron of a parish, for example. Even more common are badges and crests taken from the arms of local families such as the *Bear and Ragged Staff* of the earls of Warwick, the *Eagle and Child* badge of the Stanley earls of Derby and the punning *Talbot* badge of the Talbot earls of Shrewsbury. Many of these inns are of medieval origin or occupy sites of former ancient hostelries provided by magnates for their retainers and manorial tenants. In such cases, a lord's badge (which was worn by his retainers) would have been a familiar symbol of corporate identity and affiliation – far more so than the coat of arms which was personal to the lord and his family. Inns with *So-and-So Arms* names are almost invariably more recent than those named after single devices, usually dating from the eighteenth and nineteenth centuries. The *Pembroke Arms* and the *Green Dragon* at Wilton in Wiltshire, for example, both refer to the heraldry of the Herbert earls of Pembroke (of Wilton House), but while the former is of comparatively recent origin the latter name is derived from 'the dragon grene' badge used by the medieval earls of Pembroke and the site is probably of some antiquity.

Common signs such as the *White Lion* and the *Chequers* are almost certainly of armorial origin but are less distinctive and therefore more difficult to identify. The white lion may be that of the former Mowbray dukes of Norfolk or of the Mortimer earls of March, or indeed of several other families who used the same device, just as the chequers may be those of the De Warenne family whose arms were *Chequy Or and Azure* (gold and blue) or may have originated in the arms of an entirely different family. A further possibility (and an increasingly common one) is that the sign has been repainted incorrectly, by a sign-writer unaware of its heraldic derivation. To determine the correct origin of an inn sign may require research into the heraldry of many local families and lords of the manor over several centuries, and the name itself will often have survived long after the estate has changed hands or the family died out. The *Hind's Head* at Aldermaston in Berkshire, for example, is the crest of the Forster family, lords of the manor before 1711. Conversely, the name of a local inn may provide a clue to a former lordship of the manor.

Inn signs may not portray exactly the pub's name: the *Prince of Wales* may have a sign of three ostrich feathers (the badge of the Heir Apparent to the English throne), for example, while at Sonning in Berkshire the sign of *The Bull* shows the coat of arms of the Marquis of Abergavenny, the name of the inn being derived from the bull supporters and crest.

Inns called the *King's Arms*, *Queen's Arms*, *Duke of York*, *Duke of Cambridge*, etc., are ubiquitous. Most royal arms are those of the Tudors or the present Queen, though Stuart and Hanoverian examples are also to be found. Although only reigning for seven years, William IV succeeded in creating more inns (and is commemorated in more inn signs) than any other monarch. The 1830 Beerhouse Act permitted any householder to open a beerhouse on payment of 2 guineas. Consequently, 24,000 new pubs opened, many of them gratefully named after the king. At Winchester, the sign of the *King's Arms* has the earliest royal arms of England (*Gules three Lions passant guardant Or*) and claims to date from the reign of Henry III (1216–72). Royal heraldry should *not* be taken to date an inn, however, for signs are regularly repainted and the owner or painter may choose to 'update' the arms: the 'modern' royal arms from 1837, for example, are much simpler and easier to paint anew than to repaint a complicated Hanoverian coat. Queen Victoria decreed that no inn sign should depict a likeness of any member of the royal family – a law which remains of the statute books today. Royal or dynastic allegiance is indicated in many signs by the use of royal badges such as the *White Hart* of Richard II and Edward IV, the *Sun in Splendour* of the Yorkist kings and the *Antelope* and *White Swan* of the Lancastrians which were inherited through marriage from the De Bohun earls of Hereford (in such cases, the antelope should not be represented as the natural but as the heraldic antelope: a deer-like creature with a horn on the nose and serrated antlers). These last examples demonstrate the need for vigilance, for badges were transferred both by inheritance and through the acquisition of seigniories and were frequently translated into crests and supporters.

INNS OF CHANCERY Colleges of law students affiliated to the INNS OF COURT: New Inn (1485) to the Middle Temple; Barnard's (1454) and Staple (1378) to Gray's Inn; Furnival's (1383) and Thavie's (1348) to Lincoln's Inn; Clement's (1480), Clifford's (1345) and Lyon's (1413) to the Inner Temple.

INNS OF COURT The collegiate houses of the four London law societies which exercise the exclusive right of calling to the English bar and thereby of conferring the rank of barrister-at-law. Of several early inns of court, there remain only Gray's Inn, Lincoln's Inn, the Inner and the Middle Temple. The subsidiary INNS OF CHANCERY no longer exist.

IN PRETENCE *see* IMPALEMENT

INQUISITIONS AD QUOD DAMNUM *see* CHANCERY

INQUISITIONS POST MORTEM An inquest held on the death of one of the Crown's TENANTS-IN-CHIEF to determine the date of death and the lands held at that time and to confirm the identity and age of the heir. The process was conducted by the official *Escheator* who was responsible for deciding how much tax (known as *relief*) should be paid by the heir on entering his estate. If the heir was a minor, the estate reverted to the Crown until he came of age. Records began in the reign of Henry III (1216–72), and many are indexed at the Public Record Office (*see* APPENDIX I).

INQUISITION, THE An ecclesiastical court established for the detection and punishment of heretics in *c.* 1232. The officials of the Inquisition were chiefly Dominicans and Franciscans whose notorious methods of interrogation included torture (though this was accepted practice in judicial procedures of the time). Those accused of heresy who refused to confess were tried before an inquisitor assisted by a jury of clerics and laymen. Penalties for heresy included confiscation of goods, imprisonment and surrender to the secular authorities which invariably meant death by burning at the stake. In 1542 the Inquisition was assigned by Pope Paul III to a church department, known as the *Holy Office* or *Congregation of the Inquisition*. This became the final court of appeal in trials for heresy and ultimately an organ of papal government.

INSTRUMENTS OF THE PASSION In Christian symbolism, the Instruments of the Passion include: The Title (*INRI*, the Latin initials for Jesus of Nazareth King of the Jews), The Crown of Thorns and Nails, The Dice, The Seamless Robe, The Scourges, The Cross and Sheet, The Ladder and Sponge, The Lantern of Gethsemane, The FIVE WOUNDS OF CHRIST, The Cockerel of Peter's Denial, The Thirty Pieces of Silver, and The Hammer and Pincers.
See also CHRISTIAN SYMBOLS

INTAKE The encroachment of peripheral areas of common, usually without authority or consent. ENCLOSURE of this kind was common practice in the Middle Ages when the outlying margins of common land were taken in to cultivation, often temporarily as part of an INFIELD-OUTFIELD system. These early intakes may often be identified in field-name elements such as *breck* and *brock*. In more recent centuries, miners in parts of the Pennines were permitted to construct cottages and enclose smallholdings on the edges of commons in order to supplement their incomes and to provide pasture for pit-ponies and pack-horses.
See also ASSART *and* SQUATTER

INTERCOMMONING *see* COMMONS

INTRANSI TOMBS Medieval double-decker tombs with two effigies of the same person: splendour and piety above and pathetic cadaverous mortality beneath.
See also CADAVER *and* TOMBS

INTRINSECA *see* LATIN

IONIC ORDER *see* CLASSICAL ARCHITECTURE

IRELAND Following Celtic settlement, Ireland developed as independent tribal territories over

Ulster

Belfast

Connaught

Meath

Tara

Dublin

Leinster

Munster

16c English Pale

IRELAND

From 800 to 1100, the political and economic life of the Irish Sea coast was dominated by Scandinavian military activity and trade. A VIKING stronghold was established at Dublin in 841 which, by the 850s, had become the home of a dynasty of kings descended from the ancient Norwegian house of Vestfold and the administrative centre of Norse colonization on the eastern coast. The Dublin kingdom remained aggressively pagan until the pilgrimage in AD 980 of King Olaf Cuaran to Iona. By the mid-eleventh century, Dublin had acquired its own Norse bishop and diocese and it retained its Scandinavian independence and culture until it was finally suppressed by Anglo-Norman invaders in 1169.

Christianity reached Ireland by the fourth century and was consolidated by St Patrick (*c.* AD 390–*c.* 460). Born in Britain, he was captured at the age of sixteen by Irish pirates and spent six years as a herdsman in County Mayo. Having escaped and returned to Britain, he underwent training for the Christian ministry and was sent as 'bishop in Ireland' to spend the remainder of his life establishing the Irish Church and conciliating Irish chieftains. Inspired by the missionary commitment and academic achievements of the early monastic foundations, the country became a leading cultural centre in the period following the decline of the Roman Empire. English invasion began in the twelfth century under Henry II but his initial authority was never adequately secured, and by the sixteenth century was confined to the English Pale, an area round Dublin.

which the lords of Tara exercised nominal suzerainty. The Irish royal houses are probably the oldest traceable dynasties in Europe, descending from kings who were regnant before the conversion of Constantine the Great in AD 311. Prior to the Norman invasion of Ireland in the late twelfth century, the island was divided into a number of provincial kingdoms all of which (in theory) were subject to the High King who ruled from Tara. Although the number of provincial kingships varied, five came to have a permanent existence: Ulster, Munster, Leinster, Connaught and Meath, the last being the appanage of the High King and included his seat of Tara. For several centuries the High Kingship was disputed between the kings of the *Ui Niall* (Ulster) and those of the *Eoghanaghta* dynasty (Munster) before the former succeeded in securing the title. Following the arrival of Henry II in Ireland, the dynasties continued to rule as independent princes under the lordship of the kings of England for several centuries. But following the Reformation, and the determined process of anglicization in the later fifteenth and early sixteenth centuries, the Gaelic principalities finally collapsed, though all but the royal house of Leinster have continued to exist down to the present time.

The Tudors succeeded in extending English rule throughout Ireland, but constant insurrection, particularly against the imposition of protestantism, resulted in the 'plantation' by English and (later) Scottish families who were provided with confiscated land in an attempt both to anglicize the country and to secure its allegiance (*see* PLANTATION). In Ulster, the descendants of these families retained a distinctive identity and, after an unsuccessful rebellion of 1798, the union of Britain and Ireland was formalized in 1802. But the failure of the potato crop in 1840 (Ireland's staple diet at that time) served to emphasize the disparities between the comparatively prosperous, protestant Ulster and the destitution of the remainder of Ireland, which was entirely dependent on a rapidly declining agricultural economy. Thousands died in the famine or were forced to emigrate.

Despite gaining considerable public exposure of Irish grievances and inspired by the parliamentary successes of the nationalist leaders Charles Parnell

(1846–91) and John Redmond (1856–1916), the Home Rule movement failed to achieve its objectives, and implementation of the Home Rule Act of 1914 was suspended by the outbreak of the First World War. Redmond's aim was a free Ireland within the British Empire but, although under his leadership the Irish obtained control of local government, his moderate approach lost him support which then passed to the extreme nationalists under Eamon de Valera (1882–1975). By an act of 1920, the country was divided into Southern Ireland and Northern Ireland. Southern Ireland became the Irish Free State in 1921, Eire in 1937 and the Republic of Ireland in 1949.

IRISH HIGH CROSS There are about 100 known examples of these wheel-head crosses in Ireland, of which a notable minority are exquisitely carved with elaborate, interlaced motifs and depictions of biblical stories. Earliest examples are of the eighth century and are almost invariably associated with Irish-Celtic monastic sites.

Muredath's Cross at Monasterboice, Co. Louth.

IRON *see* MINERALS

IRON AGE The Iron Age in Britain is now dated between *c*. 800 BC and AD 43, though this includes a lengthy transitional period during which BRONZE AGE influences declined as new techniques and cultures were communicated and assimilated. Celtic traders and settlers began to arrive from the European mainland at this time, bringing with them iron tools and weapons and progressive agricultural methods, notably the plough. The *Hallstatt* culture (also known as *Iron Age A*) originated in central Europe and was particularly influential over much of the lowland zone of Britain where there was a gradual proliferation in the use of iron implements (notably, sickles, adzes and ploughshares) and of localized iron working. This was followed (from *c*. 450 BC) by the *La Tène* cultures (known as *Iron Age B*) from central and western Europe, who settled in the south-east, and (from *c*. 100 BC) by the BELGAE.

In many areas, the Bronze Age type of enclosed settlement of circular dwellings and peripheral cultivation continued, but elsewhere (and particularly on the chalk uplands of the south-west) numerous HILL FORTS were constructed and remodelled in response to changing circumstances. New types of crops were introduced, including Celtic beans and winter wheat and barley, grown in arable fields similar to those of the late Bronze Age. Grain was stored in circular granary pits or in raised granaries: covered platforms supported on corner posts. Horses were managed, probably for traction, cattle and pigs were kept and sheep provided wool for weaving on wooden loom-frames. Systems of linear earthworks, or 'ranch boundaries', were probably farmstead enclosures constructed to contain and protect livestock. The La Tène cultures are associated with superb craftsmanship and an extraordinary richness of design which was applied, not only to jewellery and other personal items, but also to everyday domestic artefacts, armour and weapons.

There was also a strengthening of territorial control, with hierarchical structures based on the concentration of resources and manpower around a tribal chieftain and his extended family. Territories were often clearly defined, using natural features such as rivers and by the construction of great linear earthworks. Many hill forts were extended and provided with additional defences and in the mountain regions of the north and west numerous fortified homesteads and settlements were built in stone, often constructed with impressive craftsmanship (*see* BROCH). The widespread remodelling and strengthening of fortified settlements also suggests increased rivalry among the tribes and competition for trade and diminishing

Reconstruction of an Iron Age farmstead at Little Woodbury.

resources. The extraordinary complexity and scale of many of these sites would appear to reflect both their designation as territorial administrative, ceremonial and trading centres and the prestige of particular Celtic chieftains. Their magnitude was unequivocal evidence of a chieftain's ability to command the allegiance of thousands of men and their function was therefore to deter would-be aggressors as much as it was to provide a formidable defence.

The Iron Age climate was cold and excessively wet, which may account for the proximity of water to many ritual and ceremonial sites, though the practice of casting precious and sacrificial offerings into rivers and meres was of Neolithic origin (*see* BRONZE AGE for details of Fengate, Cambridgeshire). In Celtic society, the afterlife was often portrayed as being beyond or beneath water and islands were sometimes regarded as the refuges of the dead. Indeed, there are clear echoes of these prehistoric practices in the medieval Arthurian legends. The general populace does not appear to

have received inhumation burial, though aristocratic burials have been found in very richly furnished graves, some containing the chariots of dead warriors.

In the late Iron Age, a variety of goods was imported from Roman France, Germany, Italy and Spain through ports on the south coast. Although the Roman invasion of AD 43 effectively ended the Iron Age, in most areas the native way of life continued even beyond the conquest of northern Britain in AD 84. The Iron Age was a time of rapid expansion: at its close there were probably 2 million people living in England. The agricultural landscapes created during the late Bronze Age were developed and expanded so that by the end of the prehistoric period England had become a crowded country of isolated farmsteads, hamlets, villages and hilltop fortresses, its primaeval forests replaced by several cycles of regeneration and felling in managed woodlands, and the intensity of agricultural exploitation already causing localized erosion and soil exhaustion. The texture of today's landscape was already established before the first Roman foot stepped onto British soil.

See also CULTURAL CHRONOLOGY *and* KINGDOMS (ANCIENT)

IRONS Prisoners were restrained in a variety of manacles and chains from the twelfth century and were said to be held 'straitly' (*see* PRISONS).

ISSUE ROLLS A series of rolls dating from 1240 to the end of the seventeenth century (but with omissions from 1480 to 1567) recording payments made from Crown revenues. These are maintained at the Public Record Office and a number have been published.

J

JACK (i) A small piece of redundant land.
(ii) A small flag flown at the bows of a ship.
(iii) A colloquial term for a medieval retainer.
(iv) A sleeveless coat worn especially by an archer.
(v) An infantryman's garment of rough canvas strengthened with plates of metal or horn.
(vi) *See also* GILL

JACKS OF THE CLOCK Carved and painted human figures which strike the bell of a clock. In Britain, the earliest example is believed to be the late fourteenth-century jack-clock at Wells Cathedral where two 'quarter jacks' strike the quarter hours and 'Jack Blandifer' the hours.

JACOBEAN ARCHITECTURE *see* ELIZA-BETHAN AND JACOBEAN ARCHITECTURE

JACOBITE An adherent of the deposed King James II of England (1685–8) [also James VII of Scotland (1633–1701)], or of his descendants. Also a supporter of the Stuart claim to the British throne after the Revolution of 1688. The Jacobites enjoyed substantial support from the catholic Highland clans, and from France – when it was politically advantageous. There were three attempts to regain the throne, in 1689–90, 1715 and 1745–6,

culminating in Culloden, the last pitched battle to be fought on British soil, following which the clans were finally suppressed.

JAGGER *see* PACK-HORSE ROADS

JARL *see* DANELAW

JESSE WINDOW Christ's descent from Jesse, the father of King David, depicted in a church window in the form of a *Tree of Jesse*. This springs from the recumbent body of Jesse and terminates in Jesus of the Virgin and Holy Child, with the intermediate descendants represented on foliage scrolls branching out of each other (*see* CHRISTIAN SYMBOLS).

JESUIT A member of the Society of Jesus, an order of priests founded in Paris in 1534 by Ignatius Loyola and others. Although established as a missionary order, the Society became the spearhead of the Counter-Reformation. Members saw themselves as a disciplined force, effective in the defence of the Roman Church, and their success as missionaries, preceptors and scholars was, indeed, formidable. The arrival of the Jesuits in England in *c.* 1580 added impetus to RECUSANCY which contemporary statesmen regarded as insidious and dangerous. Remarkably, tombstones may occasionally be found in Anglican churches marking the graves of Jesuit priests. At Hampreston in Dorset, for example, there are two such memorials, each inscribed with the tell-tale post-nomial initials 'S.J.' and dated 1745 and 1750: a time of intense Catholic persecution.

See also ROMAN CATHOLIC CHURCH

JEWS Large numbers of Jews came to England in the decades following the Norman Conquest but they were not permitted to trade or to practice agriculture and were acceptable only as money-lenders at a time when usury was forbidden to Christians by Canon Law (though it was undoubtedly practised privately). Although of use to the Crown and the nobility, the Jews were singularly unpopular and many were massacred in 1189–90. In the following century, their usefulness declined and they were finally expelled in 1290. In part, medieval anti-semitism was the result of religious prejudice and resentment against the Jewish community, which tended to maintain a separate and distinctive identity. But more particularly, it reflected an almost universal suspicion and jealousy of Jewish commercial success which came to be associated in the common mind with sharp practice; thus the persecution of

Jews was the inevitable reaction to every economic or social crisis. Despite the opposition of the Church, Oliver Cromwell re-admitted the Jews in 1655 but they were not granted political equality until the mid-nineteenth century. Synagogues retain their own records but the Jewish Historical Society publishes historical material and the records of the Anglo-Jewish Association are retained at the Society's address. There are also the Mocatta Library and the Jewish Museum (*see* APPENDIX I).

JOURNEYMAN (i) One who is paid according to the amount of work done or at a rate per piece, i.e. 'piecework'.
(ii) A qualified artisan who is employed by another.
(iii) An itinerant craftsman.

JUDICIAL EYRE *see* EYRE

JULIAN CALENDAR The calendar introduced by Julius Caesar in 46 BC in which the standard year has 365 days and every fourth year is a leap year of 366 days. The GREGORIAN CALENDAR was introduced in 1582 to compensate for the ten days which had accumulated as a result of the Julian calendar being 11 minutes and 10 seconds too long, although the change was not effected in England until 1752.

JUPON The successor to the SURCOAT: a short, sleeveless coat worn over armour and emblazoned with the arms. Popular from the mid-fourteenth to the mid-fifteenth century, at which time plate armour became so highly embellished and valuable that it was fashionable for it to be worn without covering. The later TABARD was worn for purely armorial purposes.

JURY A jury is a body of persons sworn to render a verdict in a court of justice or in a coroner's court. A petty (or trial) jury consists of twelve persons who try the final issue of fact in criminal or civil cases. From 1285, jury service was subject to a property qualification. This was revised in 1664 and again in 1692 when eligibility was extended to those possessed of freehold, copyhold or life-tenure of property with an annual value of at least £10. From 1696, lists of eligible jurors were presented to QUARTER SESSIONS and from 1730 long-term lease-holders occupying property valued at £20 a year or more were also eligible. The Jury Act of 1825 restricted jury service to those between twenty-one years of age and sixty who were possessed of freehold property with an annual value of at least £10 or of leasehold property worth £20, or householders occupying dwellings which were worth £30 a year.

JUSTICE OF THE PEACE In 1277 and 1287 'Keepers of the Peace' were appointed by a commission under the Great Seal to keep the peace within a stated jurisdiction, usually a county. These 'inferior magistrates' acquired the name Justices (*Justicers*), and the power to try minor offences, by a statute of 1361. They gave their services without pay but, in order to exclude from office those who were considered too poor to be suitable, a statute of Henry VI required that a justice should hold lands worth £20 a year. (This was increased to £100 a year in 1744.) In the fourteenth century, there were usually four or five justices appointed to each county but this number was increased to six in 1388 and to eight in 1390. In 1461 cases previously brought before the Sheriff's Tourn were transferred to the QUARTER SESSIONS, and by 1565 there were between thirty and forty magistrates appointed to each county. Parochial officers (such as parish constables) were responsible to the justices of the peace for the satisfactory performance of their duties. The justices tried cases before a jury in quarter sessions and dealt with minor matters in petty sessions. Today, magistrates (both lay and stipendiary) hold preliminary hearings and determine minor cases.
See also MAGISTRATE *and* SHERIFF

JUTE (i) A member of the Low German tribe who invaded southern England during the fifth century and established a kingdom in Kent. According to legend, the invasion was commanded by the brothers Hengist and Horsa. Both words, however, mean 'the stallion' and it is likely that they refer to the emblem (and possibly the nickname) of the invading chieftain who claimed descent from Odin, one of whose attributes was the mythical horse *Sleipner*. The white horse was later adopted as the armorial device of Kent. Both elements may be found in the Somerset villages of Henstridge and Horsington: the former meaning 'the ridge of the stallions' and the latter 'the homestead of the horse-keepers'.
See also ANGLE *and* SAXON
(ii) Fibre from the bark of tropical plants used for making sacking etc.

JUXTA Latinized place-name element meaning 'alongside' or 'by', as in Bradwell-juxta-Mare in Essex ('-by the sea') (*see* LATIN).

K

KEEIL Small stone-built rectangular chapels in the Isle of Man dating from the seventh century into the early Middle Ages. Several are located near HOLY WELLS (*chibbyr*) and most are dedicated to Irish saints.

KEEP *see* CASTLES (MEDIEVAL)

KEL- *and* **-KELD** *see* SPRINGS

KENT *see* KINGDOMS (ANCIENT)
For HENGIST AND HORSA *see* JUTE

KEYSTONE *see* ARCH

KINBOTE Payment of a fine to the family of a murdered person.

KINGDOMS (ANCIENT) It seems likely that some form of prehistoric suzerainty evolved during the late BRONZE AGE in response to a sudden increase in population around 1600 BC. This tendency towards territorial authority was refined and consolidated through the IRON AGE, partly as a result of the pressures of immigration and competition for diminishing resources. These 'kingdoms' were cohesive regional groupings of tribal districts which shared a common name. Each district possessed at least one administrative and ceremonial centre or 'capital' (often a strategically positioned and heavily defended HILL FORT) and was governed through its own hierarchical structure under a chieftain and his extended family.

During the later Iron Age, trade with the continent of Europe developed significantly and by 100 BC increasing (and often violent) political competition among the southern tribes resulted in the formation of larger territorial federations and a further increase in centralized authority. That in the south-west, for example, was focussed on the Durotrigian port at Hengistbury Head, Dorset, where minerals and precious metals from Cornwall, the Mendips and Wales were assembled and distributed through Armorican traders in exchange for high quality pottery, metalware and Italian wines. At this time, many hill forts were abandoned in favour of a select number of conspicuously fortified sites from which

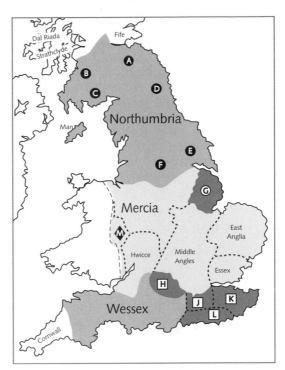

THE ANCIENT KINGDOMS, 597–850

Constituent kingdoms:

Northumbria	*Mercia/Wessex*
A *Gododdin*	**H** *Berkshire*
B *Kyle*	**J** *Surrey*
C *Rheged*	**K** *Kent*
D *Bernicia*	**L** *Sussex*
E *Deira*	
F *Elmet*	*Mercia*
	M *Magonsaete*
Northumbria/Mercia	
G *Lindsey*	

river crossings, major route-ways and harbours could be controlled. Some, such as Maiden Castle and Ham Hill in Dorset, also became major administrative centres.

In the south-east, a flourishing continental trade in raw materials and slaves attracted the ambitious attentions of the Belgic nobility, anxious to acquire land for themselves and their followers. Incursions were aimed at the annexation of established British communities by élite bands of nobles and warriors who at first exercised local rather than territorial authority. Nevertheless, between *c.* 120 and 50 BC there was a rapid expansion of Belgic political influence in the south-east from which evolved a number of tribal kingdoms which were, for a time, to exploit successfully the proximity of south-east Britain to Roman Gaul.

Roman policy during the conquest of Gaul (58–50 BC) was to enter into alliances with tribal rulers (who thereby enjoyed the status of 'client kings') so that during this period a number of dominant kingdoms emerged in the south east of Britain, notably the Trinovantes, the Catuvellauni, the Atrebates and the Kingdoms of Kent (see ROMAN ADMINISTRATION). Peripheral tribes, such as the Coritani and Iceni in the east, the Dobunni in the midlands and the Severn basin, and the Durotriges in the south, engaged in the procurement of raw materials and slaves which were traded on to the stronger kingdoms who in turn supplied the markets in Gaul and the Roman world. In the thriving south-east, society developed round a number of extensive new or enlarged settlements, each contained within complex systems of linear earthworks, constructed to delineate the political, economic and ceremonial *oppida* of kings and district chieftains (*see* OPPIDUM). By contrast, tribal society in the peripheral areas retained its more traditional political structure which, for the Durotriges, remained that of the fortified hilltop settlement. Fierce rivalry for control of the trading ports of the south-east, notably Colchester (*Camulodunum*), culminated in the uniting of the Catuvellauni and Trinovantes under the client king Cunobelinus. Following his death, his vast territories, which included the kingdom of the Atrebates and peripheral encroachments in the midlands and Kent, were divided between Cunobelinus' sons, Togodumnus and Caratacus, both of whom were vehemently anti-Roman. Ensuing political instability, exacerbated by the expulsion of the client king Verica of the Regni (an area around Chichester), actuated the Roman invasion of southern Britain in AD 43 and the establishing of two major client kingdoms ruled by Cogidubnus (Verica's successor) in the south and by Prasutagus in the eastern lands of the Icini. Both kingdoms enjoyed limited autonomy in return for co-operation with Rome but were finally suppressed following the Boudican revolt of AD 60 when Prasutagus' widow refused to honour the treaty by which her late husband's territories were to convert to Rome at his death.

During the Roman occupation, most of Britain was divided into *civitates*, self-governing divisions based on pre-conquest tribal territories and, in the late third century, into provinces.

Bede, writing in the eighth century, described his immigrant ancestors as belonging to one of three groups: the Angles (from Schleswig) of the east and north, the Saxons (from northern Germany) of the south and the Jutes (from Denmark) of east Kent, the Isle of Wight and Hampshire. While there is archaeological evidence to support the generality of Bede's statement, it is of course an over-simplification and in practice the political structure of the fifth and sixth centuries was complex and constantly changing. During these two centuries of ANGLO-SAXON immigration and Romano-British and Celtic resistance, most of what is now England consisted of a multitude of minor territories or *statelands*, each ruled by a chieftain and encompassing no more than 39 to 104 square km (15 to 40 square miles). Inevitably, the more powerful of these absorbed or annexed their weaker neighbours to form unified territories or federations, often of considerable size and influence, from which emerged the seven great Anglo-Saxon kingdoms, sometimes collectively termed the HEPTARCHY. Typical of this process was a sixth-century stateland of some 65 square km (25 square miles), centred at Wootton Wawen in Warwickshire. It was probably established by Stoppa, an Anglian chieftain of a tribe whose ruling élite had migrated from East Anglia where their ancestors had arrived from Denmark a century before. By AD 620, the Stoppingas stateland had been absorbed into the neighbouring kingdom of the Hwicce which was itself to become part of the kingdom of Mercia in the eighth century. (The name 'Mercia', which is not contemporary, derives from the Old English *mierce*, meaning 'boundary people'.) Several statelands have been identified through place-name evidence. Eight parishes in Essex, for example, have 'Roding' place-name elements, derived from the Old English *Hrōþingas* meaning 'Hrōþa's people'. This was a stateland of some 65 square km (25 square miles), probably founded by its chieftain Hrotha in the sixth century and later absorbed into the kingdom of the East Saxons.

A small number of Anglo-Saxon mercenaries had already settled in Britain during the Roman occupation, mostly on the eastern and southern coasts where they were deployed to guard against sporadic raids. A further (and larger) group of mercenaries was engaged by Romano-British chieftains to resist Pictish incursions down the east coast following the withdrawal of Roman forces in AD 408. It is likely that these groups established the first Anglo-Saxon settlements in Kent and Sussex, having rebelled against their British masters, and thereby prepared the way for two centuries of Anglo-Saxon immigration.

The inexorable Saxon conquest and settlement of the south was temporarily checked by a British force in *c*. AD 500, possibly at the battle of Mount Baden (which has been identified by some as Badbury Rings in Dorset), but as the Saxons pushed westward, so the native British submitted or retreated into the fastnesses of Cornwall (to become the 'West Welsh'), the north-west and Wales, leaving behind them the embryo kingdoms of the South, East, West and Middle Saxons and Kent. In the north-east, the kingdoms of Lindsey, Deira and Bernicia were similarly emerging from a complexity of native and Anglian settlements, as were the kingdoms of the East and Middle Angles and Mercia in the east and the midlands.

Three forces are evident in the political dynamics of the period. Firstly, there was the unifying influence of what was effectively a single English Church (though in two provinces) within which a series of kings 'held empire' (Bede) as overlords of all the kingdoms south of the Humber from the late fifth to the late seventh century. Secondly, there remained surprising degree of institutional and administrative continuity from the Roman occupation and thirdly, there was the influence of the warrior nobility. Success in battle and the accumulation of tribute and plunder, so vividly described in the contemporary epic poem *Beowulf*, encouraged patronage and attracted military support. This 'heroic' ethos is reflected in constantly shifting political and military allegiances and in a succession of internecine wars, dynastic feuds and assassinations. In the longer term, it resulted in a gradual absorption of the smaller kingdoms into the greater.

For most of the seventh century, England was dominated by Northumbria and its kings who were overlords of all England except Kent. Northumbria was created in AD 651 out of the annexation of Deira by the kingdom of Bernicia, to which were added the kingdoms of Gododdid in the north, Kyle and Rheged in the north-west and Elmet in the south.

From the end of the seventh century, political power passed to the rival kingdom of Mercia and the subject kingdoms of the Hwicce in the south-west midlands, the Middle Angles, the East Saxons and Magonsaete, a territory in the southern Marches of Wales. These kingdoms had been acquired by the Mercian King Penda (*c*. AD 610–55) during the seventh century, together with Lindsey, which was annexed from Northumbria by King Aethelread of Mercia in AD 679. But it was Offa (AD 757–96) who added the even more significant south-eastern trading territories of Berkshire, Kent and Sussex in AD 779–80 and that of the East Angles in AD 790 (though the last regained its independence in *c*. AD 825 and Kent, Sussex, Surrey and Berkshire reverted

to the kingdom of Wessex following the dynastic feuds of the early ninth century).

It was Offa who was responsible for the building of the unique system of linear earthworks on the western frontier of his territories where they abutted those of the Welsh kingdom of Powys. It now seems possible that the 130 km (81 miles) of Offa's Dyke were constructed in just two weeks by 100,000 conscripts brought together from throughout the kingdoms. The administrative complexities of such a strategy must have been immense but its psychological and military advantages are clear. Sections of dyke connected natural barriers to form a frontier of 193 km (120 miles) from the Dee Estuary in the north to the mouth of the Wye in the south. In its day, the dyke must have been formidable: from the bottom of an immense ditch (on the Welsh side) to the top of the palisaded embankment it presented an almost vertical face 9 metres in height (35 feet). Nevertheless, the strength of resurgent Welsh power was such that within only thirty years of the dyke's construction, the Mercians were forced to build a second and even stronger line of defences, now known as Wat's Dyke, which included twelve forts along its length (four of which have survived). Mercia's supremacy ended abruptly when, at the battle of Ellendun (near Wroughton in Wiltshire) in AD 825, its King Beornulf was defeated by King Egbert of Wessex.

The Danish raids of the first half of the ninth century culminated in the invasion of the Great Army in AD 865 and the reduction of the Anglo-Saxon kingdoms of Northumbria, (eastern) Mercia and East Anglia to Danish military rule and the suppression of the native dynasties under the DANELAW at the centre of which was a group of five fortified towns in the east midlands, known as the *Five Boroughs*: Lincoln, Stamford, Nottingham, Leicester and Derby. Only Wessex survived to become a focus of English resistance and re-conquest under Alfred the Great (AD 849–99) and his successors. Alfred's pragmatic recognition of the Danelaw in AD 886 (which by then comprised Bernicia and York in the north-east, the Five Boroughs and East Anglia) did not deter his son Edward the Elder (AD 899–924) or his daughter, Aethelfled 'Lady of the Mercians' (who ruled English Mercia) from waging a relentless war of attrition against the Danes. This was continued by his grandsons Athelstan (AD 924–39), Edmund (AD 939–46) and Eadred (AD 946–55) so that at Eadred's death the House of Wessex exercised nominal control of a kingdom which extended from the south coast to Lothian in the north.

But this disparate collection of former kingdoms had yet to be brought together as a cohesive political whole, and in this process the Anglo-Saxon EALDORMEN played a vital part. In ninth-century Wessex, each ealdorman had responsibility for a single shire but in the tenth century many were charged with the governance of an entire region – ealdormanries – which perpetuated the political geography of former ancient and independent kingdoms. From such a power base, it was not difficult for many ealdormen to establish positions of authority and influence which often exceeded those of their kingly predecessors. Relatively few nobles (*thegns*) from north of the Trent attended the West Saxon court, for example, and several northern ealdormen were, in practice, treated as hereditary lords or 'half kings' of their territories, beyond the influence of the English court which rarely moved north of the Thames valley. In the tenth century, the West Saxon system of administrative divisions (*shires*) was extended into Mercia. Several shires were administered from an English or Viking BURH and some perpetuated earlier tribal identities. In these early shires may be found the origins of several of the pre-1974 counties of southern and central England, while the shires of Sussex, Essex, Kent, East Anglia and York reflect even earlier divisions. Former Danelaw territorial divisions were generally of less significance than those of the ancient kingdoms, though the boundaries of the county of Yorkshire were, until 1974, essentially those of southern Northumbria and the Danish kingdom of York.
See also IRELAND, SCOTLAND, WALES *and* VIKINGS

KING OF ARMS The senior rank of officers of arms. Only a king of arms has authority to grant armorial bearings, and in England and Wales this is subject to the formal approval of the Earl Marshal in the form of a warrant.

KING POST A central vertical post rising from a tie beam to the ridge piece of a timber roof. A *queen post* consists of two vertical posts instead of one (*see* ROOFS).

KINGS AND QUEENS *see* RULERS OF ENGLAND AND OF THE UNITED KINGDOM

KING'S BENCH (COURT OF) *see* LAW

KING'S PEACE, THE *see* LAW AND ORDER

KING'S WIDOW A widow of a TENANT-IN-CHIEF who was unable to re-marry without the Crown's consent.

KIRKTOUN *see* CLACHAN

KIRTLE *see* EFFIGIES

KISSING GATE *see* STILES

KITCHENER *see* LARDER *and* MONASTERIES

KNAP(P) From Old English *cnæpp*, meaning 'hillock' or 'mountain top'.

KNAPPING *see* FLINT

KNIGHT BACHELOR The lowest degree of knighthood but perhaps the most ancient. Knights were originally required to perform military service in exchange for the lands granted to them (*see* KNIGHT'S FEE) but this duty was gradually commuted to a money payment (*scutage*). In the medieval army, the knight bachelor would command the smallest unit, perhaps consisting of only a few personal retainers. He was not a member of an order of chivalry and displayed his arms on a pennon, the tails of which would be cut off to form the small banner of the BANNERET if he were promoted in the field of battle.

KNIGHT BANNERET *see* BANNERET

KNIGHT SERVICE *see* KNIGHT'S FEE *and* MILITIA

KNIGHT'S FEE (i) Also known as *Knight Service*, a feudal obligation to provide military service to the Crown in the form of a fully armed and equipped knight, together with his retainers, for forty days each year. The system of knight service was introduced by Henry II in 1181 and was intended to provide the king with a readily available military reserve, raised by his TENANTS-IN-CHIEF as part of their feudal obligation. In practice, knight service was often commuted to the payment of a fine (*scutage*) and was abolished in 1660. *See also* MILITIA *and* TRINODA NECESSITAS.
(ii) Territory held by a knight in return for military service to his superior.
(iii) A variable measurement of land, dependent on the quality of the soil, which was considered necessary to maintain a knight and his family for a year.

KNOCK A place-name element from the Old Irish *cnocc* and Gaelic *cnoc*, meaning 'hillock'. Along the east coast of England a knock is a sandbank.

KNOT GARDENS *see* GARDENS

KYLE Scottish place-name element from the Gaelic *caol*, meaning 'narrow' and implying a sound or strait as in the Kyles of Bute. South of the border, it is found as a British river name derived from the Welsh *cul*, which also means 'narrow'.

L

LABARUM A common Christian symbol comprising the first two letters of the Greek word for Christ (*Chi* and *Rho*) and depicted as an X bisected by a P (*see* CHRISTIAN SYMBOLS).

LABEL (i) In architecture, a rectangular-shaped HOOD-MOULD.
(ii) *See* CADENCY

LADY CHAPEL *see* CATHEDRALS, CHURCHES *and* MONASTERIES

LADY DAY The Feast of the Annunciation held on 25 March and, until 1752, New Year's Day (*see* GREGORIAN CALENDAR). In the rural calendar, Lady Day was the day on which yearly contracts, entered into on the preceding CANDLEMAS DAY (2 February), became effective. In many areas, *Old Lady Day* (6 April) was used for this purpose. In Victorian Dorset:

> These annual migrations from farm to farm were on the increase. . . . When Tess's mother was a child the majority of the field-folk . . . remained all their lives on one farm, which had been the home also of their fathers and grandfathers; but latterly the desire for yearly removal had risen to a high pitch. With the younger families it was a pleasant excitement which might possibly be an advantage. The Egypt of one family was the Land of Promise to the family who saw it from a distance, till

by residence there it became in turn their Egypt also; and so they changed and changed.

Thomas Hardy, in *Tess of the D'Urbervilles*, describes in detail the 'house ridding' and the

> preliminaries of the general removal, the passing of the empty waggons and teams to fetch the goods of the migrating families; for it was always by the vehicle of the farmer who required his services that the hired man was conveyed to his destination. That this might be accomplished within the day was the explanation of the reverberation occurring so soon after midnight, the aim of the carters being to reach the door of the outgoing households by six o'clock, when the loading of their movables at once began. A wet Lady Day was a spectre which removing families never forgot; damp furniture, damp bedding, damp clothing accompanied it, and left a train of ills. The day being the sixth of April, the Durbeyfield waggon met many other waggons with families on the summit of the load, which was built on a wellnigh unvarying principle, as peculiar, probably, to the rural labourer as the hexagon to the bee. The groundwork of the arrangement was the family dresser, which, with its shining handles, and finger-marks, and domestic evidences thick upon it, stood importantly in front, over the tails of the shaft-horses, in its erect and natural position, like some Ark of the Covenant that they were bound to carry reverently. Some of the households were lively, some mournful . . .

See also SETTLEMENT AND REMOVAL RECORDS

LAITHE-HOUSE Common in the north and west of Yorkshire, laithe-houses are farmsteads in which the combined byre and barn (the *laithe*) was constructed as an elongated extension of the dwelling with which it shares the same roof. Most laithe-houses are from the late eighteenth and early nineteenth centuries, though the earliest known example dates from *c.* 1650. In larger laithe-houses, a lofty arched opening provided access to the barn for hay-wagons which were unloaded directly onto the upper storey hay-loft, below which were the cattle stalls and stables.
See also LONGHOUSE

LAMBREQUIN *see* CREST

LAMMAS Lammas Day was the first day of August (the *Gule of August*), on which it was customary to consecrate bread made from the first ripe corn of harvest. (In Scotland it is one of the QUARTER DAYS.) Lammas Land (*also* Half Year Land) was common MEADOW on which manorial tenants were allowed to graze their livestock from Lammas Day until the next sowing (*see* SAINTS' DAYS AND FEAST-DAYS).

LAMPYTT *see* MARL-PIT

LANCET *see* ARCH, GOTHIC ARCHITECTURE *and* WINDOWS

LAND *see* OPEN FIELDS *and* STRIP

LANDAU The original landau was introduced from Germany towards the end of the eighteenth century and was a semi-closed carriage with a double hood which could be used in all weathers. On early versions, hoods were of harness-leather, which was so rigid that they opened only 45°. In wet weather the interior was singularly hot and stuffy and the leather, treated with oil and blacking, produced an unpleasant smell. The bodywork of early landaus was square with a low floor but later versions had deeper, curved bodies (*canoe-landaus*) and, during the second half of the nineteenth century, the hoods were improved so that they folded almost flat. Landaus were drawn by two or four horses and held up to four passengers, with room on the box for a coachman and groom.

LANDGABLE *see* BURGAGE

LANDSCAPING *see* GARDENS

LAPIDARY INSCRIPTION An inscription engraved on stone.

LAPS AND ROLLS The usual method of constructing a lead roof is for lengths of lead to be laid with their edges overlapping. The 'laps' are then 'rolled' to make them waterproof.

LARCENY Grand Larceny, the theft from a house of goods worth more than 12*d*, was a capital offence. Petty Larceny, theft of goods worth less than 12*d*, was punishable by WHIPPING or, from 1717, penal TRANSPORTATION.

LARDER A room or cupboard for storing food, also a medieval domestic department. In medieval households and monastic establishments, the Larderer was responsible for the acquisition and storage of provisions including meat which was, of course, cooked in the kitchens. Bread was the province of the *pantry*, and there were also the departments of the *poultry* and the *saucery*. Utensils and equipment were maintained by the *scullery* and table linen by the *napery*. Wine was the concern of the *buttery* and vegetables were provided by the *curtilage*. In the monastic hierarchy, the *Cellarer* was responsible for all these departments, together with the produce of the dairy and the brewhouse, while the *Kitchener* managed the serving of meals in the Abbey refectories, which were the responsibility of the *Refectorian*. Many of these terms have been perpetuated through the great household establishments of recent centuries.
See also HOUSEHOLD *and* MONASTERIES

LARGE FRAMING *see* TIMBER-FRAMED BUILDINGS

LASHER An artificial open drain excavated to divert flood water back to a river, usually in the vicinity of a mill or lock.

LATH AND PLASTER Material used for ceilings, and for the internal walls of TIMBER-FRAMED BUILDINGS, consisting of a framework of interlaced or parallel laths (usually split hazel or willow) covered with layers of plaster which often contained a bonding agent such as horsehair.
See also WATTLE AND DAUB

LATHE *see* HUNDRED
For the Kentish lathes *see* RAPES

LATIN Latin prepositions used as place-name elements probably originated in medieval legal documents which were, of course, written in Latin. Deeds transferring or delineating land often distinguished between settlements which otherwise had no means of individual identity by describing them as Upper and Lower Slaughter, Gloucestershire, Great and Little Tew, Oxfordshire, and so on. Sometime, the Latin original was retained, as with Minterne *Magna* (Greater) and Minterne *Parva* (Lesser), Toller Fratrum (which belonged to the brothers of Forde Abbey) and Toller Porcorum (which was apparently renowned for its pigs), for example. Many Latin names have survived in isolation, though Ryme Intrinseca (Inner Ryme) was so described to distinguish it from the now lost village of Ryme Extrinseca (Outer Ryme). All the

The lavatorium in the cloister of Gloucester Cathedral.

foregoing are in Dorset, a county rich in Latinized place-names.
See also AMBO, CANONICORUM, CUM, DUCIS, EPISCOPI, IN, JUXTA, MONACHORUM, MONASTIC PLACE-NAMES, REGIS, SOROR-UM, SUB *and* SUPER

LATTEN *see* BRASSES (MONUMENTAL)

LAUDS *see* MONASTERIES

LAUNDS *see* DEER PARKS

LAVATORIUM A washing-place, usually in the domestic buildings of a monastery.
See also CLOISTER *and* MONASTERIES

LAW (**COMMON LAW** *and* **EQUITY**) The origins of the rule of law are complex for they are drawn from both Germanic and Romanic roots. The early rulers of post-Roman Britain were Germanic barbarian kings whose perception of justice and the law was radically different from that of Rome. It was based on status, on the *wergild* or 'blood price' and on the feud (or fear of the feud) in a society in which to be worthy of the law was dependent on belonging to a free tribal group.

Only gradually did the concepts of an ordered kingship and social justice based on a *code* of law begin to take shape, encouraged by the *Synod of Whitby* (AD 664), following which the differences between the Celtic and Roman traditions in the British Church were resolved and a cohesive administrative structure established. The influence of a unified Church facilitated the evolution of a judicial system: West Saxon law was codified by the early eighth century, for example. But although many of the principles of the Romanic code were acknowledged, the administration of law remained essentially customary. All laws were administered by local assemblies (*folkmoots*) and by a county sheriff, often sitting with the ealdorman and the bishop, in the hundred and shire courts. Sheriffs administered the laws in their respective areas and determined cases on the basis of local custom. Many local customary rules of law were, by this time, similar to those in other parts of the country, but there were many notable differences. The principle of PRIMOGENITURE, for example, was almost universally acknowledged except in Kent, where GAVELKIND tenure was exercised, and in Suffolk, Nottingham and Bristol where property passed to the youngest son under the custom of *Borough English* (these customs were abolished as recently as 1925).

Remnants of the Germanic code remained, however: *trial by ordeal* in criminal cases (based on the notion of divine intervention) persisted in some areas despite the Church's condemnation. *Ordeal by Fire* required the accused (a freeman) to carry a heated iron for a distance of 2.75 metres (9 feet) during the Mass, after which his hand was bandaged and if, after three days, there were no scars he was declared innocent. In *Ordeal by Water*, the accused was bound and immersed: if he (or she) was innocent he sank and was rescued. (In 1215, the clergy was forbidden to take part in such proceedings which the Church considered to be founded on superstition. Nevertheless, in many remote areas these practices were revived from time to time, especially during the witch-hunts of the mid-seventeenth century.)

The Norman kings did not attempt to change English customary law entirely; indeed, many charters of William I specifically permitted boroughs to hold courts and dispense justice 'according to the laws of Edward the Confessor'. They did, however, seek to establish uniformity in the law and this was achieved through a system known as the *General Eyre*, by which representatives of the Crown were commissioned to inspect local administration in the shires, including the auditing of royal revenues. During these inspections, the commissioners sat in local courts and heard cases, so that gradually they acquired a judicial rather than an administrative function. Judges for the General Eyre were selected from the *Court of Common Pleas* (or Court of the Common Bench), a sub-division of the King's Court at Westminster responsible for hearing civil cases between subjects.

The General Eyre was abandoned in the reign of Richard II (1377–99) but by that time a system of circuit judges of the King's Bench (*see below*) had already been established, the first commission dating from the reign of Edward III (1327–77). These judges, who were also made Justices of the Peace in order to widen their jurisdiction, succeeded in creating a uniform body of 'common' law, applicable throughout the kingdom, by selecting the best of local customary rulings and applying them universally, together with new rulings made by the judges themselves. In order to be recognized by the courts as having the force of law, local custom must have existed continuously and without interruption, 'from the time when the memory of man runneth not to the contrary' (Blackstone). From the sixteenth century, the limit of legal memory (*Immemorial Existence*) was arbitrarily fixed at 1189. Nevertheless, matters relating to the ownership of land were generally considered in the context of the post-Conquest system of feudal tenure rather than ancient custom.

Civil actions were usually heard at Westminster, but when it was necessary to call local witnesses, judges from the King's Bench were authorized (by *Commissions of Assize for Civil Actions*) to try such cases while on circuit, thereby enabling juries to determine a case on matters of fact, legal arguments being heard later at Westminster. *The Court of the King's* [or *Queen's*] *Bench* was senior to the Court of Common Pleas and dealt with criminal and serious civil cases. Prior to *c.* 1400, the court travelled with the king. Thereafter, it remained in London until its jurisdiction was transferred to the Queen's Bench Division of the High Court in 1873. Commissions of Oyer and Terminer, dating from 1329, required judges to 'hear and determine' any complaints of serious crimes alleged to have been committed within their respective circuits. *General Gaol Delivery* was a commission, dating from 1299, which enabled a judge to try all prisoners held in gaols within the jurisdiction of his circuit. (All courts of assize were abolished as recently as 1971.)

Initially, many of these judges were clerics but few exercised their priestly duties. They were chosen principally because they were literate and intelligent and they could be remunerated through a stipend from an affluent Church rather then a salary from an impecunious sovereign. This practice was true of many other Crown servants, though from the mid-thirteenth century the number of lay judges began to increase. When not on circuit the justices sat in the various Royal Courts at Westminster, where the best of customary laws from the various circuits were clarified and assimilated. Common law therefore came to depend on the principle of *stare decisis*, by which a new rule of law was established whenever a judge determined a matter which had not previously been considered. Such decisions were followed by other judges in subsequent cases: a practice which later crystallized into the principle of judicial precedent.

The Royal Courts developed out of the *Curia Regis* (King's Council), which was originally a magnatial body of royal advisers. The first court so established was the *Court of Exchequer*, which originally dealt with disputes arising from the administration of royal revenues but later dealt with a variety common law actions. The *Court of Common Pleas* was established in the reign of Henry II (1154–89) to determine disputes between the king's subjects. The *Court of King's Bench*, which was initially closely associated with the sovereign himself, exercised a supervisory jurisdiction over other courts by the use of prerogative writs. These were available, at the discretion of the Court, to aggrieved subjects who, by petitioning the Crown, could thereby question decisions of the inferior courts or bring an action in one of the king's courts. Common law writs were issued in the king's name by the Royal Chancery (the Chancellor was also the king's Chaplain and Head of Parliament) in the form of sealed letters instructing a named person (a manorial lord, a county sheriff or the defendant, for example) to undertake whatever was specified in the writ.

Equity, the principles of justice as supplementing law, developed out of the shortcomings of early common law and in particular the limitations of the system of writs. Many petitioners were unable to gain access to the King's Courts because of the procedural complexities of the system, the very cost of which must have deprived many of obtaining justice. Defendants could defer consideration of a writ by pleading *essoins*, for example. These were standard defences, such as absence on a crusade or sickness (by which action could be postponed for a year and a day), which were often used to delay what were often sound claims. (Originally, such a defence had to be verified by four knights commissioned for the purpose). Similarly, some common law actions were determined by *wager of law* which was dependent on the degree of influence exerted by a defendant's patrons or those of the plaintiff (*see* LIVERY AND MAINTENANCE). An award of damages (a money payment) was the only common law remedy available in proven cases of civil wrong. This was often inappropriate, for the common law could not require the performance of neglected obligations, the cessation of a wrong or the abatement of a nuisance. Furthermore, the common law did not recognize trusts and there was no means of ensuring that a trustee would not neglect the interests of beneficiaries to his own advantage.

As a consequence of these impediments, many claimants began to address their petitions to the King in Council or sometimes to the sovereign himself. Initially, the Council considered such petitions, including those received by the king in person, but later the function was delegated to the Chancellor who determined them 'in the light of conscience and fair dealing' and was able to provide remedies beyond the limitations of the common law. *Injunctions* were issued to terminate wrongs, for example, and decrees of *specific performance* enforced the performance of obligations. Equity was not confined, as was common law, by the constraints of the writ system, but as the volume of work increased so too did the number of apparently conflicting decisions and it was said, during the fifteenth century, that 'Equity varies with the Chancellor's foot'. As a result, the practice of *stare decisis*, which had so effectively unified the diverse customs of common law (*see above*), began to influence the development of Equity. The appointment of Sir Thomas More (1478–1535) as Chancellor in 1530 precipitated this change for, like his successors of the post-Reformation, he was not a cleric but a common lawyer, well versed in the system of precedent.

There was, however, a period of rivalry between the two systems culminating in the *Earl of Oxford's* case in 1615 when it was determined that where common law and Equity conflicted, the latter should prevail. Thereafter, the two systems operated with mutual tolerance and complementary jurisdictions. Nevertheless, equitable and legal remedies had to be obtained through different courts until as recently as 1873–5 when an amalgamation of the English courts enabled litigants to obtain both under the same action and in the same court.

It was not until 1731 that a statute required that all proceedings in the law courts should be in English: legislation which greatly offended many lawyers.

See also CANON LAW, COURTS OF LAW, HABEAS CORPUS, JURY, LEGISLATION, MERCANTILE LAW, PRISONS *and* PUNISHMENT

LAW AND ORDER Within the numerous communities of the Anglo-Saxon and Danelaw kingdoms, a variety of judicial systems evolved, based on custom and administered through people's courts whose elected officials were responsible for the day-to-day regulation of a community's affairs and for the enforcement of its court's rulings. By the mid-tenth century, the kingdom of Edgar the Peaceful was divided into shires, each with its SHERIFF (shire-reeve) who was responsible through the shire courts for 'keeping the peace' and, in an emergency, could call out the *posse comitatus*: all the available men in the shire. The shires were themselves divided into *hundreds*, each with its own court and consisting of a number of *tithings* of ten households, which stood security for each other and were led by a tithingman in a system known as FRANKPLEDGE. Crime was committed, not against an individual, but against a community: it was a crime against the peace, eventually defined as the *King's Peace*, and it was therefore the responsibility of all male members of the community between the ages of twelve and sixty to bring the offender to justice. If they failed to do so, the tithing could be punished. Minor offences were brought before the local MOOT court. More serious cases were taken to the hundred court, where they were heard by a *reeve*, or to the shire court to be determined by the sheriff.

Few changes were effected by the Norman administration following the Conquest of 1066: shires became counties with Norman sheriffs and officials and the duties of tithingmen were defined in law and made obligatory, but for the most part the system of tithings, hundreds and shires was considered to be effective and was adapted rather than replaced. In 1133 Henry II introduced full-time judges and annual judicial circuits from which evolved the English system of common LAW. Keepers (or Conservators) of the Peace were appointed to each county in 1277 and 1287 and these became JUSTICES OF THE PEACE in 1361: '. . . one Lord and with him three or four of the most worthy in the County with some learned in law.' The Statute of Winchester of 1285 reaffirmed the obligation of a locality to attend to its own law and order with a High Constable in each hundred and under him Petty Constables in each tithing. In TOWNS a system of *Watch and Ward* was introduced which required up to sixteen watchmen to guard a town's walls and gates during the hours of darkness (the *watch*) and to convey all strangers and wrong-doers to the warders at sunrise on the following day (the *ward*). The Statute also revised the Anglo-Saxon system of HUE AND CRY, whereby anyone attempting to make an arrest could summon others of the parish to join him in pursuit. It also established the *Assize of Arms* which required all men between the ages of fifteen and sixty to maintain weapons with which to keep the peace. The system of parochial or borough self-regulation continued, with some modification, through the Tudor period. The vestry of a PARISH appointed a constable or constables who were to assist the Justices in maintaining the King's Peace as well as carrying out numerous other duties (*see* CONSTABLE). Constables were ordinary citizens

who rarely wanted the job which was unpaid and unpopular, and the more prosperous citizens often paid deputies to do the work for them. In 1663 the City of London began to pay night-watchmen to guard the streets at night. These 'Charlies', as they came to be called, carried a bell, a lantern and a rattle and were armed with a staff but were badly paid and were often too decrepit to be effective. It was not until the eighteenth century that other towns promoted their own acts of parliament, enabling them to levy rates for lighting and watching streets, and for many centuries the Justices of the Peace, the constables and the watchmen carried the responsible for maintaining law and order.

In the eighteenth century, the expanding communities of the industrial conurbations were experiencing appalling problems of lawlessness and vice. In London, outside the City itself, over 100 separate parishes were still policed by parish constables, sometimes assisted by watchmen at night. In 1715, as a consequence of widespread disturbances, the Riot Act increased the powers of the magistrates to deal with 'tumults and riotous assemblies'. This usually meant calling in the MILITIA but, in 1756, Henry Fielding the author and Chief Magistrate for Westminster, organized from his offices in Bow Street a paid force of constables, who came to be known as the *Bow Street Runners*. The office also published descriptions of criminals in *The Weekly Pursuit*, which was widely circulated in London and the Home Counties. Following the Gordon Riots of 1780, when only the militia was available to suppress insurrection, a bill, aimed at establishing a police force in London, was withdrawn in 1785 because of adverse public opinion. A Select Committee, appointed to consider the same matter, reported in 1822 that 'It is a practical impossibility to reconcile any effective system of police with that perfect freedom of action and exception from interference which is one of the great privileges and blessings of society in this country.' This was at a time when it was officially estimated that one in twenty of the population of London was a criminal. In 1792 seven new magistrates offices were opened in London, each with six full-time constables. The Bow Street force was increased in 1805 and its Horse Patrol revived, the first uniformed police in the country. This consisted of fifty-four former cavalry troopers whose chief task was to rid the roads round London of highwaymen.

With the defeat of Napoleon in 1815, thousands of soldiers returned home, many of them without jobs or homes, to cities which were already teeming with the homeless and unemployed. Inevitably, magistrates turned to the militia to maintain law and order in the ensuing social unrest which was met with brutality and bloodshed (notably the Peterloo Massacre of 1819). It was hardly surprising, therefore, that the public continued to oppose the formation of a civil police force: most people simply did not believe that the public could be protected and law and order maintained without bloodshed. Nevertheless, Sir Robert Peel (who was to become Home Secretary in 1822) established a system of policing which was to become the model for all future police forces. The Metropolitan Police Act of 1829 authorized the commissioning of a civil force of 3,000 paid constables within central London (but excluding the City) under the jurisdiction of the Home Secretary. Their first objective was to prevent crime and in carrying out their duties they were to be 'civil and obliging to all people'. So effective were Sir Robert's 'peelers' or 'bobbies', with their truncheons, rattles and uniform of blue coats and top hats, that many criminals left London for other towns which were singularly unprepared to deal with them. In 1834, for example, the City of Liverpool had a population of 250,000 and 50 night-watchmen.

Encouraged by the Municipal Corporations Act of 1835, which permitted town councils to appoint Watch Committees and establish police forces, many followed London's example. But at least half the new corporations created by the Act were reluctant to meet the necessary expense. Further legislation, the County Police Act of 1839, enabled Justices of the Peace to establish paid police forces in the rural areas of their counties, but by 1853 thirteen boroughs and half the counties of England and Wales still had no police force. (The Act also extended the Metropolitan Police District to a radius of some 24 km (15 miles) of Charing Cross.) The 1856 County and Borough Police Act finally required all counties to employ their own police forces, both for rural areas and for boroughs which were to be policed by a combined force, and in 1862 the last county (Rutland) qualified for its government grant and the days of the medieval night-watchman were over. The Local Government Act of 1888 (by which the new county councils were created) abolished all police forces in towns with populations of less than 10,000 and established Standing Joint Committees comprising equal numbers of elected representatives and magistrates. There were further amalgamations of forces following the Police Act of 1946, and in 1964 a further Police Act established police authorities, composed of two-thirds councillors and one-third magistrates, and with each force explicitly under the control of its Chief Constable who was given powers of appointment, discipline and promotion over subordinate ranks. The Act also gave the Home Secretary power to amalgamate police areas in the interests of efficiency and a large number of amalgamations have subsequently been effected, particularly following the Local Government Act of 1972.

Policewomen were first introduced during the First World War and a small number were afterwards retained in London as the Women's Police Service. Their uniform included an ankle-length skirt, made to unbutton down the side to facilitate the pursuit of criminals. In 1922 the women's force was reduced to 22 as an economy measure but by 1939 numbers had again increased to the original figure of 100. There was further recruitment during the Second World and the formation of the Women's Auxiliary Police Corps, which undertook the duties of policemen who had joined the armed forces. Numbers continued to increase throughout the fifties and sixties and in 1975 the Women's Branch ceased its separate existence.
See also COURTS OF LAW *and* PUNISHMENT

LAWN An area of pasture in a park or wood (*see* DEER PARKS).

LAY Not ordained into the clergy. Since the eleventh century, lay brothers (or sisters) have been accepted as members of religious orders. They are generally occupied in manual work and are not bound to the recitation of the Divine Office. A lay rector is a layman who is in receipt of the rectorial tithes of a benefice and is legally responsible for the repair of the chancel of the church.
See also PORTIONISTS

LAY BROTHERS *see* LAY *and* MONASTERIES

LAY SUBSIDY A form of lay TAXATION which originated in the so-called 'Saladin Tithe' of 1181 and was levied (for specific purposes such as the financing of foreign wars) throughout the Middle Ages, the last occasion being in 1623. Lay subsidies were taxes originally assessed at one-tenth of the value of a person's movable possessions but were later rendered more equitable by requiring one-tenth of townspeople and one-fifteenth of those living in rural areas – hence the common term *Tenths and Fifteenths*. Records are held at the Public Record Office (*see* APPENDIX I).
See also SUBSIDY ROLLS

LAZY BEDS Cultivation ridges produced by spade cultivation in poor soils, typically the eighteenth-

and nineteenth-century potato beds of Ireland, though other examples may be of considerable antiquity.

LEA (i) (*also* **LEYE, LUYE** *and* **LYE**) A British river name possibly derived from *lug-*, meaning 'light'.
(ii) Place-name element from Old English *lēa*, dative of *lēah*, meaning 'wood' or 'clearing' (*see* -LEE).

LEAD *see* MINERALS

LEADED LIGHTS *see* WINDOWS

LEAH *see* LEE

LEAME *see* RECLAMATION

LEASE (i) (*also* **LEAZE**) Common meadow land.
(ii) A contract by which the owner of a building or land permits another to occupy or use it for a specified period of time, usually in return for payment (*see* LEASEHOLD *and* RELIEF).

LEASEHOLD Tenure held by LEASE: usually for a specific number of years or a number of 'lives' recorded in the original lease. When such a lease expired, new terms or names could be added on payment of a fine, though this arrangement was not always mutually acceptable (*see* LIFEHOLD *and* RELIEF).

LEASOW Pasture, either enclosed or common. The term was also used synonymously with CLOSE in parts of the West Midlands.

LEAT (*also* **LEET**) A trench for directing water to a mill-wheel or for other industrial or domestic purposes.

LEAZE (*also* **LEASE**) Meadow land: often common land on which manorial tenants had rights of pasture.

LECTERN Medieval lecterns were usually (though not invariably) located on the north side of the high altar where they supported the *Gospels* during the Mass. In some churches, early stone lecterns may still be found protruding from the north wall of the chancel (as at Crich in Derbyshire), but following the REFORMATION most were replaced by movable lecterns or reading desks in the nave from which the lessons were read at Matins and Evensong. These desks often formed the middle 'deck' (above the parish clerk's seat) in a 'three-decker' PULPIT, but from the 1840s, many congregations followed the example of the cathedrals and re-introduced separate lecterns, usually on the northern (or 'Gospel') side of the nave in front of the chancel arch. Most lecterns used today reflect the neo-Gothic style of the Victorian period and are of nineteenth- or twentieth-century origin.

There are two basic types of lectern: (i) a revolving two- or four-sided reading desk supported on a pillar, and (ii) an eagle (or, rarely, a pelican) with outstretched wings, usually standing on a sphere supported by a baluster stem and circular moulded base. There are also rare examples of bookplates supported on the wings of an angel, as at High Bray, Devon.

Lecterns are generally made of wood, latten or brass. Several desk lecterns are medieval (particularly those with four-sides, such as the wooden lectern at Detling, Kent) and once supported the large books used for antiphonal singing. (There are good examples in brass at Merton College chapel, Oxford, and in Eton College chapel, Buckinghamshire.) One-sided desk lecterns are usually of nineteenth- or twentieth-century origin.

Medieval eagles are comparatively rare (though Victorian and later versions are legion) and mostly date from the fifteenth and early sixteenth centuries. The eagle's outstretched wings support the book which is often 'protected' by three beasts fashioned at the base of the column. Just over forty medieval brass eagle lecterns remain (as at Wolborough and Bovey Tracey in Devon and Clare in Suffolk) and some twenty carved in wood (at Astbury in Cheshire and Ottery St Mary in Devon, for example). These early eagle lecterns are usually very austere in appearance and brass examples may be composed of several parts slotted together. Many originated in the workshops of a fifteenth-century 'school' of East Anglian craftsmen who exported throughout Europe (including one lectern in St Mark's, Venice). Many post-Reformation eagle lecterns are flanked by single bracket candle holders with glass tulip-shaped shades. The eagle is the symbol of the Apostle St John, whose words (in John's Gospel and Revelation) 'soared up into the presence of Christ' just as the eagle of the medieval bestiaries renewed itself by flying into the sun. The pelican is the mystical emblem of Christ.
See also LITANY DESK

LEDGER STONES *see* INCISED SLABS

Eagle lectern at Fotheringhay, Northamptonshire.

-LEE (*also* **-LEIGH** *and* **-LEY**) A common second element in place-names, derived from the Old English *lēah* (*see* LEA) and corresponding to the Old High German *lōh*, meaning 'grove', the Low German *lōh*, meaning 'thin wood', the Old Norse *ló*, meaning 'low-lying meadow' and the Latin *lūcus*, meaning 'grove'. The most common and original meaning is 'a natural area of open land within a wood' (i.e. a glade), as in Farsley, Yorkshire, which means 'a clearing covered with furze', and numerous Langley ('long *lēah*') names. But variations may be deduced from accompanying elements: the names Lambley, Northumberland, and Calverley, Yorkshire, for example, suggest areas of woodland cleared as pasture for lambs or calves, and clearings at Wheatley, Essex, and Flaxley, Gloucestershire, were probably created for the cultivation of wheat or flax. In other instances, the meaning 'wood' is apparent, as in Oakleigh, Kent, Haseley, Oxfordshire and Ashley Green, Buckinghamshire, and at Yardley, Essex, where *yards* or spars (Old English *gyrd*) were obtained. In several instances, the meaning 'grove' or 'glade'

may also suggest a pagan ceremonial site, as in Thundersley, Essex, dedicated to the god Thor.

Variations such as Lea, Lee, Leigh, Lees and Leese occur alone but rarely as first elements. Abbreviated secondary elements are evident in names such as Marcle, *mearc-lēah*, meaning 'boundary wood', and Ocle, a variant of Oakley, (both Herefordshire); Eagle, Old English *āc-lēah*, meaning 'oak wood' (Lincolnshire); and Barlow, Old English *bār-lēah*, meaning 'clearing of the boars' (Derbyshire). The Scandinavian equivalent -*augh* is found in such names as Healaugh, meaning 'high grove', and Skirlaugh, being 'a clearing where the shire moot met' (both Yorkshire).

LEET *see* HUNDRED *and* LEAT

LEGATE *see* ROMAN FORTS AND CAMPS

LEGENDS *see* FOLKLORE AND LEGENDS

LEGISLATION The earliest legislation dates from *c*. AD 600, though prior to the twelfth century there were few statutes and most law was case law. The earliest Norman legislation was in the form of royal charters, but during the reign of Henry II (1154–89) a profusion of assizes, constitutions, provisions and charters proceeded from the King in Council or from occasional assemblies of nobles and clergy summoned from the shires. Parliamentary legislation became more general during the fourteenth century: at first, this was achieved by means of a request or *prayer* to the sovereign but later Parliament formulated its own bills for presentation. During the Tudor period, the modern practice of carrying a bill through three readings before presenting it for royal assent was established, together with the *Preamble*, an often lengthy exposition of the reasoning and justification for the proposed legislation. Thereafter, Parliament became increasingly independent and the practice of law-making by statute increased accordingly. But it was not until the nineteenth century that statutes became an important source of law and although the bulk of legislation is considerable, common law remains the basis of our legal system, of which statutes are still a comparatively small element. Nevertheless, many complex or novel economic and social matters could never be determined by the submission of cases in the courts, and statute law has developed in order that the enactment of this type of legislation should be facilitated.

A statute is the ultimate source of law and even when it conflicts with common law or equity (*see*

LAW), a statute prevails for no court or institution may question the validity of an act of parliament. Statute law may be used to abolish moribund common law rules or to change the common law in order to reflect more accurately the values of society or prevailing circumstances. Statutes, even those which are clearly obsolete, may be repealed only by Parliament through the Statute Law Repeal Acts. An act of parliament is binding on all those within its jurisdiction, though an act may be repealed by the same or subsequent parliaments for, despite the concept of the absolute sovereignty of Parliament, it cannot bind itself or its successors. Modern legislation is often so complex that the detail of implementation is not normally included in the statute itself but is contained in *statutory regulations* formulated by civil servants under the authority of the appropriate Secretary of State. This form of law, known as *delegated* or *subordinate legislation*, is just as binding as the statute from which it is derived.

-LEIGH *see* FOREST *and* -LEE

LEPER SQUINT *see* SQUINT

LESENE *see* CHURCH TOWERS

LETTERS PATENT *and* **LETTERS CLOSE** *see* PATENT

LEVELS *see* RECLAMATION

-LEY *see* FOREST *and* -LEE

LEY LINES Generations of youngsters have been charmed by Alfred Watkins' notion 'that mounds, moats, beacons and mark stones fall into straight lines throughout Britain, with fragmentary evidence of [prehistoric] trackways on the alignments'. The sixty-five-year-old Watkins 'perceived the existence of a ley system in a single flash' while riding across the hills near Bredwardine on the Welsh border. But when his theory was published, first in *Early British Trackways* (1922) and later in *The Old Straight Track* (1925), it caused violent controversy in archaeological circles. While it remains anathema to the archaeologist and historian, the ley line theory has expanded into a supernatural cult. We are now asked to believe that ley lines form a kind of invisible national grid along which passes a mystical force which may be experienced through the standing stones and other 'markers' along its course.

All of this is most unfortunate, for Watkins'

original idea may contain an element of truth. We know that late Neolithic, Bronze and Iron Age peoples communicated and traded with each other, sometimes travelling considerable distances through inhospitable and unfamiliar terrain to do so. It is not unreasonable to assume that they followed route-ways which were waymarked by cairns and sky-line notches, as they are in mountainous regions today. A society which was capable of constructing the great earthworks and barrows of the period was surely sufficiently advanced to recognize the benefits of waymarking (and, therefore, controlling) the route-ways through its territory. To do so, they may have used the 'smoke signal' method of aligning 'markers' and this would indeed produce multi-point alignments on the map, especially if intermediate waymarks were added later. But this does not imply that the tracks themselves were also straight and invariable. Travellers, then as now, must have selected the most appropriate route between one 'marker' and the next having regard to prevailing conditions and the gradients which lay before them. No doubt many of these prehistoric 'signposts' have survived, but the landscape contains an enormous accumulation of topographical features, many of which lend themselves to such an interpretation. It is little wonder, then, that so many apparent 'alignments' may be identified.

LIBERATE ROLLS Writs under the authority of which royal officers made certain payments on behalf of the Crown. They originated in the CLOSE ROLLS but after 1226 constituted a distinct type of document which remained in use until 1426. They are of particular interest in that many of the earlier documents itemize purchases made in specific localities. Liberate rolls are maintained at the Public Record Office and a *Calendar of Liberate Rolls* in six volumes, covering the period 1226 to 1272, has been published by HMSO from 1917 to 1964.

LIBER NIGER SCACCARII (*The Black Book of the Exchequer*) *see* PIPE ROLLS

LIBERTY (i) A group of manors, to the lord of which were granted certain privileges of the Crown and from which the sheriff's authority was excluded. (ii) An area located outside a borough in which freemen exercised certain rights, e.g. of pasture. (iii) The equivalent of a HUNDRED in the Isle of Wight.

LIBRARIES Medieval books were, of course, extremely rare and usually written on continuous

The chained library at Hereford Cathedral.

rolls of parchment or vellum which only later may have been cut and arranged into folio form (*see* MANUSCRIPT ILLUMINATION). Even in the century after the Mainz-born Gutenberg produced the first printed Bible and Psalter in 1456, significant collections of books were to be found only in the libraries of major religious and academic houses and of the most eminent magnates. Not all these collections were private, however. During the fifteenth century, a number of 'public' libraries were established: Duke Humphrey's at Oxford, the University Library at Cambridge, Whittington's at Grey Friars in London and another at Guildhall, for example. Just as today books are protected from theft by sophisticated electronic devices, so the librarians of the medieval and Tudor periods looked to the security of their extremely valuable collections. The famous chained library at Hereford Cathedral is the largest of its kind to have survived. Each of its 1,500 handwritten and printed books has a chain attached to the front edge of one cover and to a rod on the bookcase. Only by turning a key to

release the rod may a book be removed or added. Wooden desks and benches, placed conveniently between the oak bookcases (installed in 1611), facilitate study without the necessity of releasing the books from their fetters.

One of the many consequences of the Dissolution of the Monasteries (1536–9) was the fragmentation of several monastic libraries and the destruction of many irreplaceable manuscripts. In part, this was the result of contemporary attitudes to the old libraries: most beneficiaries of the Dissolution preferred the *de rigueur* printed folios of Caxton and his successors to the inconvenient and archaic manuscripts of the early Church.

By the seventeenth century, the number of private libraries had increased significantly, though the notion of every fine mansion possessing its own correspondingly fine library had not yet become the fashion. Private libraries varied in size and character, from the substantial collections of Samuel Pepys and of the Cotton family to the modest bookshelf in a yeoman's farmstead. Public libraries were still singularly few in number and difficult of access. Evelyn, writing in his diary in 1684, says:

> Dr. Tenison [later Archbishop of Canterbury] communicated to me his intention of erecting a library in St. Martin's Parish, for the public use, and desired my assistance, with Sir Christopher Wren, about the placing and structure thereof, a worthy and laudable design. He told me there were thirty or forty young men in orders in his parish, either governors to young gentlemen or chaplains to noblemen, who being reproved by him on occasion for frequenting taverns and coffee-houses, told him they would study or employ their time better, if they had books. This put the pious doctor on this design; and indeed a great reproach it is that so great a city as London should not have a public library becoming it.

Tenison's library occupied the upper floor of a large house built in the precincts of St Martin's, the lower floor being used as a workroom for the poor. Although a substantial proportion of the population could now read and write with sufficient proficiency to administer their everyday affairs, printed matter remained inaccessible to all but the educated few.

The eighteenth century was the age of the great country house where large parties of guests were entertained for weeks and even months together. The Hanoverian mansion invariably possessed a library appropriate to its grandeur and to the status of its owner, filled with leather-bound volumes of the classics, illustrated travels, county histories and collections of cartographical plates, engravings and prints, the cover of each book stamped with the family arms or crest and the fly-page embellished with an engraved BOOKPLATE. This too was a time of vigorous literary and scientific activity, stimulated by numerous local publishing houses and the popularity of subscription publishing, particularly among aristocratic private collectors and private book clubs.

But 'circulating libraries' were also to be found, both in London and the provinces (notably Bath and Southampton), the first being established in Edinburgh in 1729, where books were lent out to the citizens for 'an easy price'. The first community or parochial library was founded in 1741 at Leadhills in Lanarkshire, probably at the instigation of James Stirling, general manager of the Scots Mines Company, as part of a package of social reforms. Stirling believed that prosperity was dependent on an orderly and sober community and a disciplined workforce. The Leadhills library was managed by a Reading Society of miners together with the local schoolmaster and minister. At a time when a miner's earnings rarely exceeded 10s (50p) a week, membership fees were 2s 6d (12.5p) and the annual subscription 4s (20p). Attempts at public enlightenment often encountered fierce opposition, however. As late as 1775 the circulating library in Edinburgh was described as an 'evergreen tree of diabolical knowledge.' Such rampant conservatism is hardly surprising for these early libraries, institutes and READING-ROOMS proved to be instruments of considerable social and political change, and the choice of books on their shelves reflects both the social attitudes of a particular community and the way in which those attitudes changed in response to social and economic forces.

In 1850 Parliament authorized the provision of free public libraries but it was not until the 1890s that many local authorities responded. Despite the magnificence of many Victorian civic libraries, the public rarely enjoyed direct access to material: readers were first obliged to search the card indexes before submitting a request and the books were then located and brought from the shelves by the librarian.

LICH-GATE (*also* **LYCHGATE**) Many CHURCHYARDS are entered by means of a roofed structure known as a lich-gate. The term, which was adopted by Victorian ecclesiologists, is derived from the Old English *lich*, meaning 'corpse'. Indeed, 'corpse gate' (*lich-gate*) was in common usage until comparatively recently, though it was applied to any opening or stile by which a cortège might gain access to a churchyard.

Although there were many covered churchyard gateways in the Middle Ages, it was the requirement in the 1549 Prayer Book that the priest, 'metyng the corpse at the church style', should there commence the *Order for the Burial of the Dead* that encouraged the provision of shelters for that purpose. (The 'church style' was later defined in the 1662 Prayer Book as the entrance to the churchyard.) Sometimes the cortège had to wait for the arrival of the parson, and this brief respite must have been welcomed by the bearers who often had to carry a corpse for many miles along rutted tracks from outlying hamlets and farmsteads (*see* CORPSE ROAD). Before the eighteenth century, it was usually the shrouded corpse which was set down on the *corpse table* in the lich-gate (or, sometimes, on an adjacent wall), coffins being available only to the more affluent members of

The four-gabled lich-gate at Monnington-on-Wye, Herefordshire.

society. As roads improved so many parishes acquired a *bier* for shorter journeys and for transferring the coffin to the graveside,where it was 'made readi to be laid into the earth'. This was usually a wheeled contraption of wicker-work within a wooden frame, though later examples (many of which may still be found gathering dust in crypts and redundant farm buildings) were sprung and had solid rubber 'tyres' and rollers on which the coffin was secured.

Corpse tables or *coffin stones* were wooden or stone plinths on which the corpse (or coffin) was placed at the entrance to the churchyard. Regrettably, few have survived: those at Bolney in Sussex, Chiddingford in Surrey and Atherington and Ashprington in Devon are able exceptions. At Maltby in Yorkshire, a fourteenth-century table tomb was removed to the lich-gate for this purpose, while in many parishes a simple three-legged *coffin stool* was used. In some areas, rough-hewn coffin stones may sometimes be found at resting places along the route taken by a cortège from a remote dependent church to a mother church which retained parochial burial rights.

Few medieval gates have survived without structural alteration, particularly to the timber framework, though several fourteenth-century examples still have original barge-boarding characteristically decorated with scrolls and floral motifs. There are fine medieval examples at

Whitbourne, Herefordshire, Anstey and Ashwell in Hertfordshire and Boughton Monchelsea in Kent. Most lich-gates are from the seventeenth and eighteenth centuries, though many appear to be of some antiquity and are often difficult to date. That at Painswick, Gloucestershire, for example, is a substantial plaster and timber-frame building supporting a small gabled 'parish room'. Its timbers, particularly the decorative barge-boards on which are carvings of bells, are clearly very old but it was built as recently as 1901 by local craftsmen using timbers removed from the belfry. Occasionally, early church stiles and seventeenth- or eighteenth-century lich-gates are found side-by-side, as at Llanfaglan, Gwynedd, and some churchyards have two or more lich-gates of different dates, as at Troutbeck, Cumbria, where there are three. Not all parishes could afford a covered entrance, and the provision of a lich-gate is often indicative of the generosity of local benefactors. Many nineteenth-century lich-gates were erected to commemorate local worthies or as the final flourish of a church restoration (or rebuilding), while more recent examples have served as war memorials, paid for by public subscription.

Bearing in mind the rich variety of Britain's vernacular architecture, lich-gates are surprisingly uniform in design and there are few regional variations. They are frequently found constructed of materials which are used neither in the church nor in adjacent walls, indeed many pre-date the walls of which they are now a part. There is clear evidence to show that lich-gates served a purpose entirely distinct from that of a simple gateway (*church hatch*) in a boundary wall and in many cases they were sited in isolation. Most early examples have open timberwork with curved braces and additional wind braces in the roof. These were followed by timber structures, usually supported on masonry footings or in-filled with stone or brick. Footings gradually increased in height to become low walls and these remain the most common form of structure, usually with timber framing supporting the roof. Lich-gates are generally defined by the structure of their roofs, by far the most common types being the longitudinal or 'porch' roof, the ridge of which corresponds to the passageway beneath, and the latitudinal or 'shed' type, in which the ridge is set at right angles to the passageway. Occasional examples may also be found of gates where two roof ridges intersect at right angles in a symbolic cruciform shape with four gables, as at Painswick and Clun, Shropshire (dated 1733). There are also pyramidal roofs as at Pulborough, Sussex, and More, Shropshire. Most are tiled but there are

Nineteenth-century lich-gate at Charlton Horethorne, Somerset.

thatched examples as at Fleet in Lincolnshire. Some lich-gates are built entirely of stone, the unique seventeenth-century gate at Astbury, Cheshire, for example, has battlements and pinnacles in keeping with its fourteenth-century church. Many lich-gates are provided with bench seats for the convenience of bearers and these are usually of stone or slate. At Mylor, Cornwall, a modern (1928) commemorative lich-gate has been erected over an ancient granite coffin stone flanked by stone seats and a Cornish stepping-stone 'style' on either side.

Unlike domestic gatehouses, surprisingly few lich-gates were adapted for other purposes. Nevertheless, there are several unusual exceptions, including the combined lich-gate and belfry erected at Great Bourton in Oxfordshire in 1882 and the medieval gate at Anstey in Hertfordshire, part of which was once used as the village lock-up. At Wykeham in Yorkshire, the tower of a former church was retained as a lich-gate to the new building and at Egham in Buckinghamshire a fifteenth-century porch was similarly preserved.

LICK-WAYS *see* CORPSE ROADS

LIERNE *and* **LIERNE VAULT** *see* VAULTING

LIEUTENANT (i) In the Middle Ages, a military or household officer responsible for the maintenance of a BANNER.
(ii) Since the mid-sixteenth century, a Lord Lieutenant has been appointed as the Crown's representative in each county of the United Kingdom. Before the Tudor period, the office was that of the sovereign's 'lieutenant' who was usually a nobleman and in time came to be known as 'Lord Lieutenant'. A Lord Lieutenant was custodian of the county records (*Custos Rotulorum*) and was charged with the sheriff's former responsibilities for the county militia and defence (e.g. signal beacons). Lords Lieutenant are still appointed by the Crown but their duties, other than overseeing the appointment of magistrates, are essentially ceremonial. There are also Deputy Lieutenants (*abb.* DL) who hold their offices for life.
See also SHERIFF

LIFEHOLD A form of LEASEHOLD tenure dependent on a certain number of 'lives' (usually three) recorded in the original lease. In *Tess of the D'Urbervilles*, Thomas Hardy describes the fate of many Victorian lifeholders:

> A depopulation was . . . going on. The village had formerly contained, side by side with the agricultural labourers, an interesting and better informed class . . . including the carpenter, the smith, the shoemaker, the huckster, together with other nondescript workers other than farm-labourers; a set of people who owed a certain stability of aim and conduct to the fact of their being life-holders . . . or copyholders or, occasionally, small freeholders. But as the long holdings fell in they were seldom again let to similar tenants, and were mostly pulled down, if not absolutely required by the farmer for his hands. Cottagers who were not directly employed on the land were looked upon with disfavour, and the banishment of some starved the trade of others, who were thus obliged to follow. These families, who had formed the backbone of the village life in the past, who were the depositaries of the village traditions, had to seek refuge in the large centres; the process, humorously designated by statisticians as 'the tendency of the rural population towards the large towns', being really the tendency of water to flow uphill when forced by machinery.

See also COPYHOLD

LIGGERS *see* THATCHING

LIGHTHOUSES A royal charter granted to the Brethren of Trinity House in 1514 by Henry VIII conferred on them general powers to regulate

1. *The Emperor Hadrian, who visited Britain in c. AD 122, was an expert in frontier defences having served in the imperial borderlands of Syria and the Balkans. By AD 123 legionaries had begun to lay the foundations of a wall that was to run across the north of Britain from Wallsend in the east to Bowness in the west, a distance of 122 km (76 miles).*

2. *Archbishop Corbeil's keep at Rochester Castle, Kent. With a height of 35 metres (115 feet) to the top of its corner towers it is the tallest Norman keep in Britain. Five storeys high, including a 'double' storey containing the hall and solar, a well shaft rises the full height of the keep so that water could be drawn at each level.*

3. *Windsor is one of Britain's largest castles, enclosing 13 acres within its walls. It has enjoyed favour as a royal residence since William I built a motte and double-bailey fortification on a cliff-top site above the Thames in 1067. Since then, almost every monarch has added to or rebuilt some part of the castle.*

4. Richard of Haldingham's Mappa Mundi *of c. 1290 at Hereford Cathedral. The map, which measures 165 by 135 cm (65 by 53 inches), has been described as a 'fantastic compendium of God's creation' and embodies medieval conceptions of the shape and nature of the world. In such maps, Paradise is depicted at the top and Jerusalem at the centre with Asia filling the upper (eastern) half and Africa and Europe the lower quarters.*

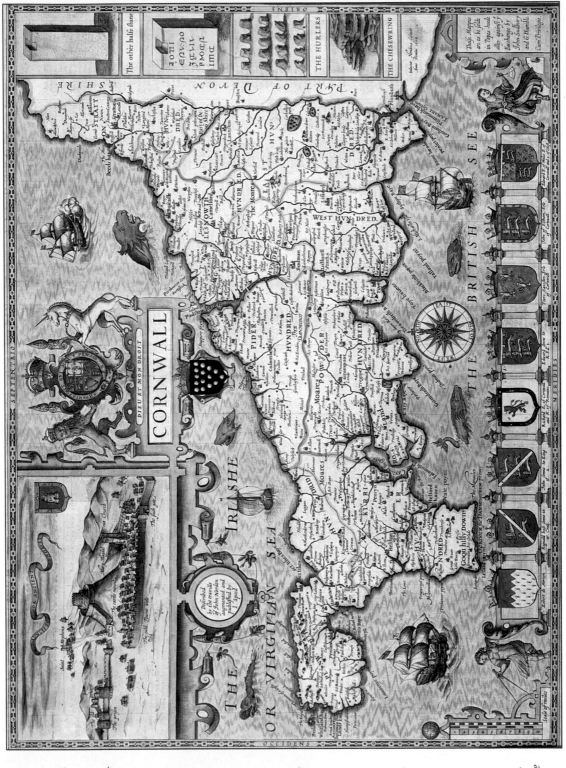

5. Map of Cornwall by John Speed (1542–1629) from the third edition of the Theatre of the Empire of Great Britain, an atlas of the counties of England and Wales, together with general maps of England, Scotland, Ireland and Wales. These were based on the work of Christopher Saxton (1542–1611) but included much new material, notably plans or views of principal towns and heraldic embellishment. Speed's maps were generally uncoloured, though hand-coloured versions were sometimes commissioned while others were coloured at a later date, notably in the Victorian period.

6. Medieval stained glass in the south chancel window of St Peter's church, Broughton, Staffordshire. St Mary and St Francis are depicted in the upper (fourteenth-century) lights while the kneeling figures are those of Sir John Delves and his wife, Ellen. Sir John and his son were killed at Tewkesbury in 1471 and the fifteenth-century memorial glass is believed to have come from the Delves family home at Doddington.

7. Highly dramatic stained glass by Morris and Company, designed by Sir Edward Burne-Jones (1833–98), in the east windows and west tower window of Birmingham Cathedral includes a depiction the Ascension (illustrated) of 1884–5.

8. Roman and medieval Gloucester was served by waterborne transport and in 1580 the City was granted the status of a port by Elizabeth I. However, the River Severn was not easily navigable and from 1793 the Gloucester and Berkeley Canal was constructed so that the river could be by-passed. In 1820 the canal was linked to the network which served London, thereby making Gloucester an important trade link with the industrial Midlands. By 1827 the canal was fully operational and at that time was the longest and widest ship canal in Britain. By the mid-1860s larger ocean-going vessels could no longer navigate the canal and much of the trade was diverted to the Avonmouth Docks, Bristol, leaving a rich legacy of warehouse buildings.

9. Ironbridge, Shropshire: the birthplace of the Industrial Revolution. The bridge over the River Severn, from which the town takes its name, was the first cast-iron bridge to be constructed in England. Designed by Abraham Darby or Thomas Pritchard, the bridge was erected by Darby in 1777–9 with iron from the nearby Coalbrookdale foundry. The delicate, cast-iron structure is 61 metres long (200 feet), nearly 14 metres high (45 feet) and its semi-circular arch spans 30.6 metres (100½ feet).

10. The massive 43 metre tower (141 feet) of Lavenham church, Suffolk, dominates the surrounding countryside and the market village which lies in its shadow. Lavenham's church was rebuilt in the late fifteenth century by the de Vere earls of Oxford and a consortium of local clothier families to celebrate the Tudor triumph at Bosworth in 1485. It is one of the grandest of all perpendicular churches, though the gloomy chancel had not been replaced when the Reformation brought work to a close.

11. Fotheringhay church, Northamptonshire, described by Simon Jenkins as 'a galleon of perpendicular on a sea of corn'. Built on a hill beside the River Nene, Fotheringhay was a collegiate foundation. Its patron, Edward, Duke of York, died at Agincourt in 1415 before his college was completed. Richard of Gloucester (later Richard III) was born in the nearby castle (now only an earthwork) in 1452 and in recent years the church has become a shrine to the Yorkist dynasty. The choir and collegiate buildings were demolished following the dissolution of the chantries in 1547 leaving only the nave and splendid octagonal tower on its square base as the parish church.

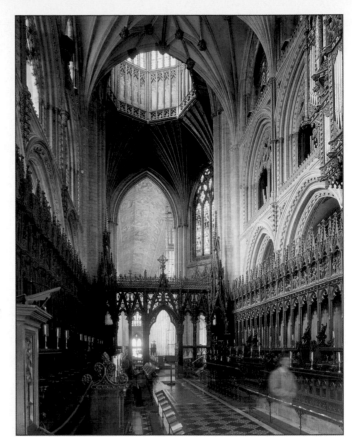

12. Bishop John Hotham's choir and Octagon at Ely Cathedral, rebuilt in the 1330s after the Norman crossing tower had collapsed: '. . . behold! Suddenly and swiftly the bell tower crashed down upon the choir with such a thunderous noise that one might think an earthquake had occurred.' In both conception and execution, Ely's Octagon, with its unique lantern soaring above, represents the highest genius of medieval craftsmen.

13. In 1340, for 'the security and quiet of the canons and ministers resident there', Bishop Ralph of Bath and Wells (1329–63) secured a royal licence 'to build a wall round the precinct of the houses of him and the canons and to crenellate and make towers in such a wall'. At this time many religious houses were accused by their burgesses of avarice and sharp practice and this friction often turned to violence. The walls, moat and gatehouse which guard the Bishop's Palace at Wells comprise one of the most formidable episcopal defensive systems ever built.

14. *The little market town of Milton Abbas, Dorset, developed in the shadow of its tenth-century abbey until 1780 when its proximity to his new mansion so offended the sensibilities of Joseph Damer (later the first Earl of Dorchester) that he demolished the entire town, save for one thatched cottage, and removed those inhabitants he was unable to drive away to a new 'model village' in a deep combe half a mile to the south.*

15. *The village green, rest house and school (with its famous carillon) at Bournville, Birmingham. In the early decades of the twentieth century a number of philanthropic employers provided model villages for their workpeople. Bournville was built by the Quaker Cadbury family complete with an adult education college, schools, concert hall, recreation grounds, public baths and many other facilities – but no public houses.*

pilotage. In 1604 James I confirmed further rights concerning the compulsory pilotage of shipping and the exclusive right to license pilots on the river Thames. Legislation of 1566 enabled the corporation to erect seamarks, and in 1685 its constitution was defined in law. During the seventeenth century, the Corporation of Trinity House erected beacons, laid buoys, granted certificates to pilots, examined and recommended masters for the Navy, appointed British consuls in foreign ports and on occasions even acted as an auxiliary press-gang. Trinity House is one of the three lighthouse authorities in the United Kingdom and Ireland, the others being the Northern Lighthouse Board (responsible for the waters of Scotland and the Isle of Man) and the Commissioners of Irish Lights (responsible for the waters of both Northern Ireland and the Republic of Ireland). Trinity House derives its authority for the provision and maintenance of lighthouses around the coasts of England, Wales and the Channel Islands, and for wreck marking and dispersal, from the Merchant Shipping Act of 1894.

The histories of individual lighthouses vary considerably. Many occupy sites where beacons have for centuries warned of submerged rocks and perilous currents. Most were originally erected by corporations and shipowners, often through public subscription. In 1669, for example, Sir John Clayton was granted a patent to erect a lighthouse at Portland in Dorset. But his scheme failed and it was not until the early eighteenth century that Captain William Holman, supported by the shipowners and corporation of Weymouth, petitioned Trinity House for the building of a lighthouse on Portland Bill. But the proposal was resisted by Trinity House who stated that they did not believe that the lights were necessary and that shipowners would not be able to afford to maintain them. To their eternal credit, the people of Weymouth persisted in their petition and in 1716 Trinity House obtained a patent from George I and issued a sixty-one year lease to a private consortium who built two lighthouses with enclosed lanterns and coal fires. But the lights were badly maintained and in 1752 inspectors reported that they had approached by sea to find that 'it was nigh two hours after sunset before any light appeared in either of the lighthouses' and with the termination of the lease the lights reverted to Trinity House. In 1789 a Weymouth builder, under contract from Trinity House, demolished one of the towers and erected a new one at a cost of £2,000. It was sited so that it served as a marker by day or night to direct ships moving up and down channel or into Portland Roads clear of the notorious Race and the Shambles sand-

bank. Above the doorway was a marble tablet bearing the inscription:

For the Direction and Comfort of Navigators; For the Benefit and Security of Commerce and for a lasting Memorial of British Hospitality to All Nations This Lighthouse was erected by the Worshipful Brethren of Trinity House of Deptford Strond. Anno 1789

In 1788 Portland became the first lighthouse in England in which Argand lamps were installed. These were lighted with oil and furnished with highly polished reflectors and lenses. (In 1798, when Napoleon threatened invasion, two cannon were also installed.) New high and low lighthouses were built in 1869 but these were later replaced by the present building.

LIGNUM UNDULATUM *see* PANELLING

LIME and LIMEWASH Quicklime is difficult to handle and can burn the skin. When used as a fertilizer, lime was spread with great care, a particularly still day being chosen for the purpose. On these occasions, butter was often applied round the eyes of beasts and men as protection. Quicklime boils with intense heat when water is added and *limewash* was for centuries made by packing course waste fat in a tub of quicklime and adding water, the effect of which was to heat and distribute the fat. When used as an external wall-covering to a building, the fat content of limewash did not dissolve in the wet thereby making the coating waterproof. Limewash was also used for preserving food, especially on long sea voyages, and was found to be more reliable than salt. It was customary to limewash dried hams, for example. Lime was also used for cleaning wooden utensils such as churns. *See also* LIMEKILNS

LIMEKILNS The decaying remains of limekilns are numerous features of the countryside, particularly in chalk and limestone areas, and are included (by parishes) in county archaeological listings. Other, usually commercial, kilns may be found in coastal areas and on the banks of tidal rivers. Most date from the eighteenth and nineteenth centuries when they were used to burn limestone to produce lime both for mortar and, more particularly, for fertilizing acid land. Many were operated by the landowners themselves though larger kilns were managed commercially, especially during the period of the Napoleonic Wars when extensive areas of new

land were brought into production as a consequence of rapidly increasing corn prices. Where possible, kilns were located close to easily quarried sources of lime or chalk, but in many cases the raw materials had to be acquired from commercial quarries and transported to local kilns by barge and pack-horse or donkey. A typical kiln consisted of a circular or square structure, 3 to 4 metres in height (10 to 15 feet), containing one or more sandstone-lined crucibles (known as *bodies*) each some 2.7 metres in diameter (9 feet) and 2.1 metres deep (7 feet), at the base of which was a grate. Alternate layers of limestone and fuel (usually a low quality coal called *culm*) were fed into the kiln from above onto a bed of brushwood which was ignited through kindling holes. After burning, the lime and ash were raked out from the grate through an arched tunnel in the side of the kiln. Kilns of similar design are known to have been used during the Middle Ages though very few remain. Compacted lime ash was often used as flooring material in tenants' cottages.
See also LIME AND LIMEWASH

LIMES *see* DYKES

LIME TREES Several varieties of lime were imported in large numbers from the Low Countries during the seventeenth century to create avenues and arbours in the parks and gardens of country houses. These were mostly the Common Lime, a hybrid much favoured by John Evelyn (1620–1706), the gardener and diarist.

LINEAR EARTHWORKS *see* DYKES

LINENFOLD *see* PANELLING

LINHAY A West Country term for a two-storey 'lean-to' structure, the upper floor (*tallet*) being an open-fronted hay barn with an animal shelter beneath. Some examples incorporate nesting niches for doves in a side wall of the upper storey.

LINTEL A horizontal stone or beam spanning an opening and supporting the wall above.
See also ARCH

LION The lion is ubiquitous, both in ARMORY and in the imagery of the Church. In the Middle Ages he was considered to be the embodiment of courage, strength and nobleness, the King of Beasts and a fitting symbol of kings and kingdoms and of the great magnates. One of the earliest examples of hereditary arms is that of William Longespée,

natural son of King Henry II, who bore six gold lions on a blue shield, as did his grandfather, Geoffrey of Anjou. The lions of mythology have magic in their tails: by sweeping them over their tracks they obliterate their paw-marks and make their ways unknown; by swinging them over their bodies they render themselves invisible. Thus, the longer the tail, the greater the magic. The lion is always alert and sleeps with his eyes open. He is of such a noble and compassionate nature that he will not attack a stricken man and is angered only when wounded. He fears nothing except a white cockerel and if he is sick he is cured by eating a monkey. According to the bestiaries, lion cubs were born dead and remained so for three days whereupon their father breathed into their faces and gave them life. For this reason, the lion is associated with Christ risen from the dead and is often depicted in church carvings as fighting with the devil in a dragon's form. Confusingly, the lion may also be found as a symbol of evil, trodden underfoot like the dragon and the serpent of the Psalms. The winged lion represents St Mark the Evangelist, being one of the four beasts around the throne 'which rested not day and night' (Revelation).
See also CHRISTIAN SYMBOLS

LIPGATE *and* **LIPPET** *see* **LYPIATT**

LISTED BUILDINGS *see* NATIONAL MONU-MENTS RECORD

LITUS SAXONICI (Saxon Shore) *see* ROMAN FORTS AND CAMPS

LIVERY Derived through the French *livrée* from the Latin *liberare*, meaning 'to liberate or bestow', and originally meaning the dispensing of food, provisions, clothing, etc., to retainers and domestic servants. In the Middle Ages the term was applied to the uniforms, badges and other indications of patronage and partisanship of those who accepted the privileges and obligations of LIVERY AND MAINTENANCE. *Liveries* were the distinctive colours used for this purpose.
See also GUILD

LIVERY AND MAINTENANCE The practice of maintaining and protecting large numbers of retainers in return for domestic and military services. Maintenance was common throughout Europe in the Middle Ages and particularly so in England during the fourteenth and fifteenth centuries, when a magnate's influence was judged by the number of men wearing his badge and liveries and his ability to protect them when necessary in the courts of law. The ability of a magnate to summon to the field of battle large retinues of men whose allegiance was bought through the practice of livery and maintenance was a characteristic of the Middle Ages and a major factor during the civil wars of the period. This was recognized by successive sovereigns who attempted to legislate against abuses of the system, thereby reducing the effectiveness of the nobles' private armies. It was not until 1540 that the practice was finally suppressed, the private army effectively abolished and the Middle Ages brought to a close.

LIVERY COMPANY *see* GUILD

LIVERY OF SEISIN *see* RELIEF

LLAN- *and* **LAN-** Place-name elements *llan-* in the Welsh and *lan-* in Cornish, meaning 'church', are usually followed by the name of the founder. In Celtic areas, churches are almost invariably dedicated to the saints who actually founded them, usually between the fifth and seventh centuries. *Llan-* place-names are not confined to Wales: there are numerous examples in the border counties of England, such as Llanwarne in Herefordshire, which means 'Church by the swamp or alders'.

LLYN In the Welsh, 'lake' or 'pool'.

LLYS-, LIS-, LES- *and* **LISS-** A Celtic place-name element, *llys-* in the Welsh, *lis-* or *les-* in Cornish and *lis-* or *liss-* in Gaelic, meaning 'court' or 'hall', probably a territorial capital. Liscard in Cheshire, for example, means 'hall on a cliff'.

LOAM A rich soil of sand, clay and decayed vegetable matter.
See also MARL-PIT

LOB'S POUND *see* LOCK-UP

LOCAL HISTORIAN, THE *The Amateur Historian*, founded in 1952, became the official journal of the British Association for Local History in 1961 (*see* APPENDIX I). In 1968 its name was changed to *The Local Historian*, a reflection of its increasingly academic readership.

LOCAL HISTORY PRESS LTD The Local History Press aims to promote local history in all its forms among as many people as possible, and to encourage local historians to communicate with each other and with the widest possible public, so that the relevance of local history to all sections of the community can generally be appreciated.
For address *see* Appendix I

LOCH In Scotland, a lake or land-locked sea inlet.

LOCK The earliest river locks were barriers or weirs, known also as 'stanches' or 'stanks', the purpose of which was to retain levels of water sufficient to supply mill leats and to allow for navigation by means of a 'gate' in the weir through which boats could be hauled. When river levels were low, the gate could be opened to allow a 'flash' of water to carry a boat through – hence the alternative term *flash lock*.

Pound locks were first used in Germany, Italy and the Low Countries in the late Middle Ages in order to overcome gradients where tunnelling or the construction of aqueducts were not practicable. Pound locks 'impound' water in short sections of river or canal, the levels of which can be raised or lowered by means of sluice-gates located at either end of narrow, masonry-lined basins. Boats are carried from one level to another as the water level rises or falls within the lock. When the operation is complete, one pair of gates remains closed to retain the required water level and the other opened to allow egress. The earliest pound locks were very cumbersome devices with single gates opening vertically. The twin double gates of the modern lock were invented by Leonardo da Vinci (1452–1519). These open and close horizontally by means of balance beams and were first introduced into Britain on the pound locks of the Exeter Ship Canal in 1563.

The flight of thirty locks on the Worcester and Birmingham Canal (opened 1815) at Tardebigge, Worcestershire, is the longest continuous flight in Britain, exceeding by one the equally famous flight on the Kennet and Avon Canal at Devizes in Wiltshire. No fewer than fifty-eight locks, including 'The Thirty' at Tardebigge, carry the Worcester and Birmingham Canal from the River Severn over the Lickey Hills, an apparently innocuous barrier which also boasts the steepest railway incline in Britain. To an engineer, a range of minor hills such as Lickey was more problematic than mountainous terrain where there was effectively only one alternative: tunnel or go round. The construction of sophisticated lock systems such as Tardebigge enabled bulk cargoes to be transported cheaply to and from the industrial heartlands of the English Midlands and the North, and expedited the Industrial Revolution.
See also CANAL, INCLINED PLANE *and* WEIR

LOCK-UP Before the formation of the police forces, each parish elected a constable whose responsibilities included the supervision of watch and ward (*see* LAW AND ORDER), the apprehension and detention of suspected criminals and the maintenance of the village STOCKS and lock-up. The lock-up was a gaol where felons were detained pending their removal to court, and drunks and trouble-makers were locked up for the night. Most were little more than a secure shed made available for the purpose by a local farmer, and performing other functions when not required by the constable, or squeezed into an unwanted space between two other buildings, as at Filkins in Gloucestershire. As such, many of those that remain are difficult to identify, though an unusually stout door, sturdy bolts and an absence of windows may provide a clue.

However, in some places more substantial buildings were used. At Stratton in Cornwall, for example, the solid timber door to the south porch of the parish church retains to this day 240 nails spelling out the colloquialism 'CLINK', and at Bradford-on-Avon in Wiltshire the ancient oratory on the river bridge was commandeered as a gaol, as was part of the medieval lich-gate at Anstey in Hertfordshire. In larger villages and towns, lock-ups known as Lob's Pounds or *blind houses* (because of the absence of windows) were sometimes provided. Many early examples were constructed of timber, while others were little more than brick or stone block-houses with heavily bolted doors and a barred window. Several were replaced in the eighteenth century by octagonal or circular *roundhouses* with thick walls and domed roofs in the 'classical' style.

A few purpose-built lock-ups have survived. The best known of a small number of more sophisticated 'classical' examples, at Bruton in Somerset, is a cylindrical structure, built in 1779 and containing a cell just 2 metres (7 feet) in diameter (*see* MARKET HALL *and* PRISONS).

For the Village Lock-up Association *see* APPENDIX I

The Town Bridge at Bradford-on-Avon, Wiltshire. Of medieval origin, it was modified in the seventeenth century and its tiny chapel pressed into service as a lock-up.

LODES In East Anglia, artificial navigation channels linking the peripheral communities of the southern Fens with the main Fenland waterways and the North Sea. At least three lodes are of Roman origin and many date from the medieval period. The remains of wharfs (*hythes*) and canal basins at several former inland ports provide evidence of a once-thriving trade which, at Reach in Cambridgeshire, was sustained from the Roman occupation to the coming of the railway in 1884.
See also FERRIES *and* RECLAMATION

LODGE Eighteenth- and nineteenth-century lodges are the direct descendants of the medieval and Tudor GATEHOUSE within which a lodge-keeper would control entrance and egress to a castle or walled town, college or cathedral precinct. A lodge, or pair of lodges sometimes linked by a masonry arch, was often built in a similar style to that of the great country house to which it was a kind of architectural *hors d'oevre*. While lodges often housed gatekeepers, responsible for security and for containing deer within the park, they were also intended to impress the visitor and to remind the estate community of its position in life. Within the fabric of such buildings the coat of arms or other devices of the original owner may be discovered, carved in stone and intended to declare both his prosperity and gentility, and his authority. Large country houses, surrounded by parkland, invariably possessed a number of entrances and at each would be a lodge or gateway. Today, many of these entrances are no longer in use though, somewhat incongruously, the ostentation of their lodges and ornamental gates often remains.
See also COTTAGE ORNÉE, FOREST, GRANGE *and* HUNTING LODGE

LOLLARD A term of contempt, of Dutch origin, meaning 'mutterer' or 'mumbler', conferred on those who professed to follow John Wycliffe (*c.* 1330–84) in his opposition to the established order within the English Church. They rejected priestly authority and advocated evangelical poverty in imitation of Christ and the studying of the scriptures in the vernacular. Official attitudes to the Lollards varied considerably, but they were generally considered to be heretics and were often violently suppressed.

LOMBARD (*LANGOBARD*) Lombards were a small but well-organized Germanic people from the Lower Elbe who invaded Italy in AD 568 and founded a kingdom in the valley of the Po.

Universally recognized as a Christian kingdom by the mid-eighth century, Lombardy represented a serious political threat to the Papacy but was defeated in AD 774 by Charlemagne. Throughout the Middle Ages, Lombardy financiers and bankers exercised considerable influence in the commercial affairs of Europe.

LOMBARDY POPLAR Although it originated in central Asia, the Lombardy Poplar was introduced from Italy by the Earl of Rochford in 1758 and planted in his landscaped gardens at St Osyth Priory in Essex. It was much favoured as an adjunct to the neo-classic architecture of the Regency period, though was much despised by champions of the picturesque.

LONG AND SHORT WORK Typical of Anglo-Saxon structures, alternate long vertical and short horizontal stones set in the termination of a wall to provide additional strength: to the corners of a tower or a doorway jamb, for example.
See also QUOIN

LONG BARROW *see* BARROWS

LONGHOUSE The term refers specifically to the distinctive type of long, low dwelling introduced into northern Britain from Scandinavia in the ninth century. It is also applied generically to dwellings in which accommodation for family and livestock is provided beneath the same roof, a practice first evident in several excavated Bronze Age roundhouses. The boat-shaped longhouses of ninth-century Scotland, Orkney and Shetland were constructed of stone blocks infilled with turf and with timber-framed roofs covered with thatch or heather weighted down with stones.

From the tenth century, longhouses were usually rectangular with low, windowless walls and thatched roofs. The living area and byre were separated by little more than a timber or rubble partition and a low doorway pierced the long front wall. Longhouses were roughly constructed of whatever materials were immediately available, usually turf, stone or WATTLE AND DAUB. Consequently, they were in need of constant repair and were often rebuilt, usually on or near the original site. Early Medieval longhouses were of similar external appearance but often with a second doorway in the rear wall. Inside, the two doorways were linked by a cross-passage (used by man and beast) from which further internal doors led to the byre on one side (usually at a lower level) and the living quarters on the other. With the development of a substantial internal partition, the original open hearth was set against it and eventually provided with a chimney flue within the thickness of the wall.

There were, of course, considerable regional and chronological variations in the development of longhouses. In the north-east, primitive types of longhouse continued in use well into the Middle Ages, while in the south-west, separate accommodation was often provided for livestock and the original byre incorporated into the domestic quarters. In the north-west, farming families sometimes built LAITHE-HOUSES and retained their longhouses as outbuildings. In other areas (such as Herefordshire and Cumbria), a number of substantial timber-framed longhouses were built during the sixteenth and seventeenth centuries. At the same time, and continuing into the eighteenth century, many 'classic' stone and thatch longhouses were constructed, notably in Devon and Dorset. Typically, these were built round a substantial central chimney flue and partition wall with a spacious cross-passage and an attic floor inserted above the domestic quarters which now included both a living-room (*hall*) and a parlour or dairy.

LONNING An ancient route-way in the north of England.

LORD (i) The abbreviated style of a peer below the rank of duke.
(ii) An honorary prefix used by the younger sons of dukes and marquesses.
(iii) The style of Scottish Lords of Sessions.

LORD LIEUTENANT *see* LIEUTENANT

LORD OF THE MANOR Following the Conquest of 1066, England was divided among the followers of William I who remained, in theory, the owner of the kingdom. The smallest holding within these granted estates has subsequently become known as the 'manor'. The highest level of tenancy, held of the king, was the tenancy-in-chief (*lordship in fee*). Magnates in this category sometimes let to lesser lords (*mesne tenants*) who, on occasion, let to *their* followers, who thereby became *tenants-in-demesne*. The 'lord of the manor' could belong to any of these categories but was always the tenant on whom the actual feudal obligation rested. Thereafter, overlordships of manors tended to become forgotten and after 1290, when the statute of *Quia Emptores* forbad further subinfeudation, qualifying clauses

were inserted in conveyances to prevent future claims of overlordship. The term itself means 'landlord' and a lord of the manor was not necessarily titled or even armigerous.

The identity of lords of manors and the service (*fees*) by which the manors were held may be obtained from the *Book of Fees* (or *Feudal Aids*) and *inquisitions post mortem*. Since 1926, all matters relating to the ownership of manors and the location of manorial records have to reported to the Master of the Rolls and this information may be obtained from the National Register of Archives (*see* APPENDIX I). In the late twentieth century, lordships of manors have become marketable commodities despite the fact that they bring with them little more than an archaic title.
See also MANOR
For the Manorial Society *see* APPENDIX I

LOST VILLAGES *see* DESERTED VILLAGES

LOUGH In Ireland, a lake or sea inlet.

LOW SOUTH WINDOW *see* CHANCEL VENTILATOR

LUGG Place-name element derived from the base *leuk-* or *louk-* of the Welsh *llug*, meaning 'bright'. In Wales, the Llugwy and Lligwy are 'bright streams'.

LUNETTES *see* TUDOR COASTAL FORTS

LYCHGATE *see* LICH-GATE

LYCHWAYS *see* CORPSE ROADS

LYNCHET BANKS *see* FARMING

LYNCHETS A series of low ridges or 'ledges' of earth formed by the continuous ploughing of a hillside and the gradual movement and accumulation of soil on the downward slope. Most lynchets are of Iron Age or Roman origin, though some may date from the Middle Bronze Age. Often (and erroneously) referred to as 'Celtic fields' on Ordnance Survey maps.
See also STRIP LYNCHET

LYPIATT (*also* **LIPGATE** *and* **LIPPET**) A place-name meaning 'leapgate': a low section of fence which may be leaped by a deer but which prevents livestock from straying.
See also FOREST

M

MACHICOLATIONS see CASTLES (MEDIEVAL)

MAGISTRATE A civil officer responsible for the administration of the law who, in the Middle Ages, was often also a member of the executive government.
See also JUSTICE OF THE PEACE

MAGNA A place-name element meaning 'greater', as in Minterne Magna in Dorset. Minterne Parva, or 'lesser Minterne', is located half a mile to the south.
See also LATIN

MAGPIE HOUSE *see* TIMBER-FRAMED BUILDINGS

MAIL-COACH The once familiar mail-coach, designed by John Palmer of Bath in 1784, was a four-wheeled covered vehicle adapted to carry the Royal Mail (*see* POSTAL SERVICE). Mail-coaches were drawn by teams of four horses in stages of 11 to 16 km (7 to 10 miles) according to gradients and the condition of roads. The first service ran between London and Bristol, and by 1807 had extended west to Penzance in Cornwall, east to Great Yarmouth in Norfolk and north to Berwick-on-Tweed on the Scottish border in Northumberland. All routes radiated from London with junctions at important centres such as Canterbury in Kent, Exeter in Devon, Shrewsbury in Shropshire, Oxford and York. In Wales, the mail-coaches connected with the Irish mail-packets at Holyhead in Anglesey and Milford Haven in Pembrokeshire. The fastest mail-coaches ran at speeds of up to 16.5 km per hour (10¼ miles per hour). The *Quicksilver*, for example, which ran between London and Falmouth in Cornwall, covered the 283 km (176 miles) to Exeter in Devon in sixteen hours, and it is said that time-keeping was so accurate that those who lived along the route would set their clocks by the passing of the mail.

The coaches, which were built by the firm of John Vidler and Company of Millbank in London and hired to the government, were painted in the royal livery of scarlet, maroon and black and distinguished by the royal arms which were painted on door panels. The guard-in-charge wore a scarlet uniform and sat with the mail-bags in a locker at his feet. He carried a blunderbuss and pistols for protection and a metre-long horn (the 'yard of tin') for sounding warnings (many guards provided their own horns of silver or brass). In appearance, the first mail-coaches were high-slung with elbow springs at the front and C springs at the rear. Both the box seat and the bodywork were mounted on a heavy framework (*perch*) and there were no outside seats for passengers, the guard sharing the box with the driver and luggage stowed on the roof. The later version, which was balanced on semi-elliptical springs, had a padded seat for three passengers on the roof of the central passenger compartment and directly behind the box, which was shared by the driver and fourth passenger. There was a rear seat for the guard, and pairs of driving and side lamps together with a triple-aspect lamp on the driver's footboard. The suspension of later mail-coaches and STAGE-COACHES was of the 'telegraph' type, which comprised four semi-elliptical springs at the front and rear of the underbody together with pairs of longitudinal and transverse springs.

MAINPERNOR A guarantor who provided sureties against a defendant's failing to appear in court. In the late thirteenth and early fourteenth centuries, a mainpernor or guarantor was also required to ensure that selected magnates, knights and free tenants attended councils or Parliament when summoned. Writs, asking for representatives to attend, were sent to the sheriffs who then had to arrange for men to be selected, probably by election.

MAINPRISE A writ to a sheriff requiring him to obtain sureties for a defendant's appearance in court.

MAISONS DIEU *see* ALMSHOUSES

MAJESTY *see* GREAT SEAL *and* SEAL

MAJUSCULE Handwriting in which the letters are written large. Usually used to describe capitals, but not necessarily so.
See also MINUSCULE *and* UNCIAL

MALTHOUSE Like food processing, the production of alcoholic beverages began as domestic crafts: brewing, fermenting and distilling from a wide range of vegetable substances. Stimulated by inadequate and polluted water supplies and rapid urban growth, some of these processes had developed into important local industries by the advent of the Industrial Revolution. The production of beer (including ale, porter, stout, etc.) by brewing

Stacking barrels with pulleys at Trafford Park, Manchester, in the early 1900s.

a *mash* of fermenting *wort*, a liquid obtained from treated barley (*malt*), and adding hops or other flavouring, became a significant industry in London, Dublin and other large towns in the eighteenth century. Ironically, many of those who at first exploited this expanding market were philanthropic non-conformists, anxious to provide a wholesome alternative to the consumption of gin which, at that time, was a serious social problem. Breweries burgeoned in every large town where there was a good supply of water and ready access to urban markets, notably at Burton-on-Trent.

Malting is the process of allowing the grains of barley to begin germination in controlled conditions of humidity and temperature and then arresting the conversion of starch to sugar by drying the grain in a kiln. This is achieved by first soaking the grains and then leaving them to germinate on large floors over which warm air circulates freely. The specialized nature of the process resulted in the development of independent *maltings*, usually small local firms whose premises were characterized by pyramidal roofs with capped vents. There were also numerous smaller malthouses in rural areas, producing malt on a comparatively modest scale and often completing the brewing and fermenting processes to provide for

the needs of the local populace. Wort, a mixture of malt and water, was boiled and hops and yeast added. Fermentation then took place in large wooden vats from which the beer was eventually drawn to be kegged or bottled. The strength of beer was reckoned by the quantity of malt to the barrel, 'twelve bushel strength' being the strongest. The larger brewers usually retained their own coopers to make the oak barrels, which were delivered to local public houses by fleets of horse-drawn drays. It was not until the beginning of the twentieth century that steam wagons replaced the drays, and brewing remained an essentially localized industry until the post-war development of road transport and the proliferation of regional 'chains' of public houses.
See also OAST-HOUSE
For the Brewery History Society *see* APPENDIX I

MALTOLT Taxation derived from customs duties on exported goods such as wool (*see* TAXATION).

MANGONEL *see* SIEGES

MANOR A feudal estate (from the Latin *mansus*) and, for five hundred years after the Conquest, the essential unit of local government, though it is likely that several important elements of the 'manorial system' had been established long before 1066. A fundamental of the *land law*, introduced, applied and expanded by successive Norman kings, was 'no land without a lord and no lord without land'. A manor was held of the king by a LORD OF THE MANOR (literally, 'landlord') either directly or through one or more *mesne lords* (*see* SUBINFEUDATION). Many held several, often widely dispersed, manors, the day-to-day management of each being entrusted to an elected officer known as a reeve and the administration of a manorial court (or group of courts) to a steward (*see below*).

In practice, the term '*manorial system*' is fallacious, for there was no such thing as a 'typical' manor. Generalizations are inevitably misleading, therefore, and historians prefer to study individual manors, recognizing that each was possessed of characteristics and customs which rarely conformed to a 'system' and were often unique. A manor itself might encompass a number of TOWNSHIPS and FARMSTEADS; it may have been reorganized around a new and more substantial VILLAGE; or it may have retained the boundaries of an earlier Saxon (or even Roman) estate. A manor could be part of a PARISH, contiguous with its boundaries, or it could be spread over a number of parishes. It would usually comprise the lord's DEMESNE lands and the common ploughland, meadowland and WASTE. Over much of England, the arable land of a manor consisted of three or more large OPEN FIELDS in which the inhabitants held scattered strips according to their relative TENEMENTS. The lord's demesne land might similarly be distributed within the open fields or contained in a consolidated block of the most fertile strips. From the produce of these demesne lands was derived the wealth of the manor, together with a variety of feudal dues, rents and fines exacted by the manorial court. The earliest manors were worked by VILLEINS, who laboured on the demesne lands in return for their tenements (known as *villein tenure*), together with one or more FRANKLINS who were free tenants. As the feudal system decayed, villein tenure increasingly became commuted to money payments, a form of tenure known as COPYHOLD.

The manor was governed by a manor court, a periodic meeting of tenants convened and presided over by the lord of the manor or his steward, who was usually a man of some substance and often trained in law. Manorial custom determined both the frequency and the conduct of these meetings which were usually held at intervals of between six weeks and six months. Though the procedure was judicial, the manorial courts considered both judicial and administrative matters, such as the transfer of property (*alienationes*), sitting either as COURTS BARON or COURTS LEET. The over-riding principle was that of custom by which the rights and responsibilities both of the lord and the tenantry were determined: 'Justice shall be done by the lord's court, not by the lord.' Many customs were already of 'ancient foundation' at the time of the Conquest and were to form the basis of Common Law (*see* LAW). The manor court was not entirely autonomous, however, for it was subject to the authority of the royal courts in certain areas such as the rights of free tenants. All tenants were obliged to attend manorial courts and were eligible for election as jurors. Defaulters who failed to attend or refused to serve as jurors were fined, unless they were able to demonstrate 'good cause' to the satisfaction of the court. Manorial officers (other than the bailiff who was appointed by the steward as his manager) were elected at an annual meeting of the court. These included the REEVE, the BEADLE, CONSTABLE, HAYWARD, ALE-TASTER and two AFFEERORS. When the lordship of a manor changed hands a special Court of Recognition (*Curia Prima*) was held, at which the new lord was formally 'seized' of his tenants' service and received their renewed oaths of fealty. A *Court of Survey* was also convened, at

which were recorded all the manorial lands and the customary dues by which they were held.

The records of manorial courts are an invaluable source of information to the local historian. Of these, the most significant are the *Court Rolls*, which were compiled by the steward's clerk as minutes of proceedings, including disputes and changes in the occupancy of holdings. The customary rights and responsibilities of a lord and his tenants were set out in the *Custumal* and details of the location and size of the various holdings were recorded in the *Terrier*. *Jury Verdicts* were retained in a separate record and details of rents due and paid were kept in the *Rental*. In the *Valor* were recorded the financial value of holdings and the *Extent* was a document in which were summarized the customs, valuation and tenancies of a manor at a given time. Since 1926, all manorial records and changes of ownership of lordships of manors have to be reported to the Master of the Rolls. The Royal Commission on Historical Manuscripts (*see* APPENDIX I) maintains a *Manorial Documents Register* from which may be ascertained the names of the manor or manors in each parish and the last-known location of manorial records. In many cases, these are held by the solicitors of families holding lordships of manors but many have been deposited at county record offices. There are also notable collections of manorial records at the Public Record Office, the British Library and Birmingham Reference Library (*see* APPENDIX I).

MANOR-HOUSE Many 'manor-houses' are not what they seem, having acquired the name to accommodate the social aspirations of a previous owner, no doubt enhanced by the acquisition of a lordship of a manor. Some occupy sites of former manor-houses and many are indeed the ancient dwellings of feudal manorial lords or their stewards. The term is sometimes applied erroneously to the principal house of an estate or village but is mainly found as an architectural term for a late medieval country house.

The traditional perception of the fifteenth century as a time of political instability and internecine warfare (*see* WARS OF THE ROSES) is in sharp contrast to the self-assurance and optimism evident in the architectural activity of the period. Numerous castles and fortified houses were remodelled and new houses built to provide greatly improved standards of domestic comfort and convenience so that by the beginning of the fifteenth century the practice of fortifying country houses had been largely abandoned. Drawbridges and portcullises were replaced by permanent bridges and ornate gatehouses, often with chapels on the first floor. Buildings were raised from one to three storeys and provided with tall chimney stacks and gables. Former curtain walls were dismantled and replaced by new ranges of buildings containing private apartments and improved domestic arrangements. Outer defensive walls were pierced with windows and doorways in the contemporary GOTHIC style and new fireplaces and flues set within the walls. Nevertheless, features such as gatehouses and moats were not always abandoned, for by their 'antiquity' they declared both the owner's prosperity and his lineage. The Great Hall too was retained as the social and administrative centre of the manor and the venue for the manor court. Good examples of late medieval manor-houses are those at Great Chalfield in Wiltshire (*c*. 1480), Lytes Carey in Somerset (1450), Cotehele in Cornwall (1485) and Mannington Hall in Norfolk (1460) (*see* LORD OF THE MANOR *and* MANOR).

MANORIAL SYSTEM *see* MANOR

MANSARD ROOF *see* ROOFS

MANSE An ecclesiastical residence, especially that of a Scottish Presbyterian minister.

MANTLING *see* CREST

MAN-TRAPS Several varieties of man-trap were used, in rural districts especially, to catch and maim poachers, trespassers and others who were not welcome in the coverts and parklands of Merry England. There was the toothless variety, 'the jaws of which resembled the jaws of an old woman to whom time has left nothing but gums'; there were the half-toothed *gins*:

> two inches of mercy, two inches of cruelty, two inches of mere nip, two inches of probe, and so on, through the whole extent of the jaws. There were also, a class apart, the bruisers, which did not lacerate the flesh, but only crushed the bone. . . . The sight of one of these gins, when set, produced a vivid impression that it was endowed with life. . . . Each tooth was in the form of a tapering spine two and a quarter inches long [6 cm], which, when the jaws were closed, stood in alternation from this side and from that. When they were open the two jaws formed a complete circle between two and three feet in

diameter [.6 to .9 metres], the plate or treading place in the midst being about a foot square [.3 metres], while from beneath extended in opposite directions the soul of the apparatus, the pair of springs, each one having been in its prime of stiffness to render necessary a lever or the whole weight of the body when forcing it down . . .
(Thomas Hardy, *The Woodlanders*)

Such traps were made illegal in the 1830s, though in several areas they continued in use for some time thereafter.

MANUSCRIPT ILLUMINATION Although paper-making was known in Spain and Italy by the twelfth century, PARCHMENT and VELLUM were the chief materials used for writing throughout medieval Europe until the development of PRINTING in the late fifteenth century. Parchment was ideally suited to ornamentation as well as writing, and some of the finest artistic works of the Middle Ages are the illuminated manuscripts produced in the *scriptoria* of monastic houses. A manuscript which is described as illuminated is one which is decorated in colours and gold. When the page is bent, and the gold is caught by the light, it appears to possess a lustrous quality unequalled by other forms of decoration. The gold is applied either in the form of a powder mixed with a suitable water-based medium and used as a pigment or in the form of leaf, either directly to the working surface or on a plaster ground of *Gesso Sottile* (deactivated calcium sulphate, lead carbonate, an animal glue and sugar). This plaster ground is either applied with a quill pen or painted on and dries hard, flexible and raised. The leaf is then applied and polished or burnished with an agate burnisher.

In Britain, the early medieval schools of Ireland and Northumbria produced manuscripts of extraordinary skill and originality in the interlacing and counterpointing of geometrical and animal patterns and subtle variations of colour. The best known of these Celtic manuscripts are the *Lindisfarne Gospels* and the *Book of Kells*. In Europe, the Byzantine tradition, with its florid use of gold and vermilion, continued into the Carolingian period to produce works in which the emphasis was on illuminated ornamental motifs. In England, the (incomplete) twelfth-century *Winchester Bible* contains the work of five different artists and, in its obvious Byzantine influences and its emphasis on naturalistic elements, is one of the finest and most innovative products of the illuminator's art. From

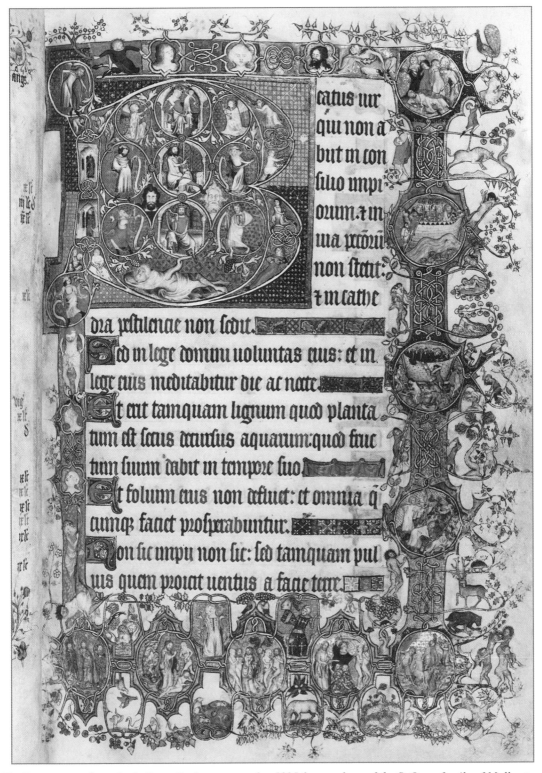

The Beatus page from the St Omer Psalter, executed c. 1325 for members of the St Omer family of Mulbarton in Norfolk, whose portraits appear in medallions beneath the text.

the end of the twelfth century, the art of the miniaturist flourished, notably in the production of the great bibles. (The work of the *miniaturist* is not concerned with that which is small but with the use of red lead for colouring, the latin verb *minire* meaning 'to colour with red lead'.) In the later Middle Ages, increasing use was made of enlarged and ornamented initial letters in which illustrations of biblical and naturalistic scenes were inserted.

Beautifully illuminated breviaries, psalters, missals and books of hours were commissioned by medieval magnatial families as gifts to superiors and as benefactions to religious houses. These contained exquisitely executed illustrations of the agrarian year, biblical scenes, devotional texts and the lives of saints and martyrs, often identified as the patron saints of recipients. Heraldry was eminently suited to illumination. An illuminated book of hours commissioned by John, Duke of Bedford, brother of Henry V, as a wedding present for his bride, Anne of Burgundy, was executed in 1423 by a team of artists under Pol de Mimbourg, one of three brothers who were the finest illuminators of their day. The Bedford arms and badges, the silver eagle, the black antelope and the golden tree stump of Woodstock appear as decorative motifs throughout, as do the arms and devices of Burgundy.

Not all illumination was confined to religious manuscripts: genealogies, romances and many official documents were also illuminated (as they are today) and almost invariably embellished with heraldry. An illuminated book of French romances presented by John Talbot, Earl of Shrewsbury, to Henry VI's bride, Margaret of Anjou, in 1445 contains a magnificent genealogical table showing the French and English royal descents from St Louis. It is filled with heraldic devices, all glittering in burnished gold.

MAPS The term 'map' is derived from the Latin *mappa*, meaning 'napkin'. Fascinating though Hereford Cathedral's *Mappamundi* (Richard of Haldingham, *c.* 1290) may be, such early maps are of little direct relevance to the local historian other than to facilitate one's understanding of the medieval mind. At that time, there were three entirely dissimilar images of the world, each with its own origin and serving different sections of medieval society.

The first, the humanist *Ptolemaic* maps of the twelfth century, exemplified the world view of ancient Greece based on geographical data gathered by the second-century astronomer and geographer Ptolemy of Alexandria. These maps were drawn according to Ptolemy's perception of a world 'held together by an astronomically determined mathematical grid' which was to become the standard reference of the Renaissance. (Unfortunately, Ptolemy's calculations were so inaccurate that Columbus mistook eastern America for Japan!) The second, the *mappaemundi*, were fantastic compendia of God's creation, sanctioned by the Church and constructed round the symbolic core of a T (life) within an O (eternity), the latter representing the hemisphere and the T the Mediterranean with the rivers Dom and Nile forming the cross-piece. In such maps, Paradise is depicted at the top and Jerusalem at the centre, with Asia filling the upper (eastern) half and Africa and Europe the lower quarters. The third category consisted of the mariners' or *portolan* charts which were devised from first-hand experience to aid navigation in the Mediterranean and Black seas in the thirteenth century and gradually expanded so that by the sixteenth century all the coastlines of the known world were delineated. It is interesting to note that a belief in a 'flat earth' is evident in none of these early maps, not even in the *mappaemundi*. In 1569 Garardus Mercator devised a projection which both presented a curved surface in two dimensions and endeavoured to satisfy the requirement of navigators for a chart on which a compass course could be laid down as a straight line.

The earliest maps of Britain are also of little value to the local historian: the Matthew Paris map of 1250, for example, is intrinsically interesting but contains little accurate information. The finest examples from the sixteenth century are brilliant works of art, 'gifts fit for a prince'. These delineate coastlines, as accurately as knowledge allowed, the blank spaces 'blossoming into a pictorial and heraldic geography', full of fantasy and legend. (R.V. Tooley). The first county maps appeared in the late sixteenth century, the oldest known series being that of Laurence Nowell (1559–76), though these remained unprinted. Christopher Saxton (1542–1611), the 'father of English cartographers', produced an entire series of English and Welsh counties during the period 1574–9, These were published as *An Atlas of England and Wales* in 1579, but the most notable of his later works was a magnificent large-scale map of England and Wales on twenty-one sheets and with a scale of 8 miles to the inch. The maps of John Norden (1548–1626) were of a better quality and (unusually for the period) not only showed roads and distances but also included a grid system. Regrettably, only the Middlesex and Hertfordshire maps were completed before his death, those for Cornwall, Essex, Hampshire, Surrey and Sussex being printed much later.

William Camden (1551–1623) published his *Britannia* in 1607 with a Latin text and a series of county maps. This was reissued in 1610 and 1637 with an English text and the same maps engraved by William Kip and William Hole from Saxton's maps of 1579, though reduced in size to 35 × 28 cm (14 × 11 inches). In 1611 John Speed (1542–1629) produced *The Theatre of the Empire of Great Britain*, an atlas of maps for the counties of England and Wales, together with general maps of England, Scotland, Ireland and Wales. These were also based on Saxton's work but included much new material, notably plans or views of principal towns and heraldic embellishment. This was followed by a 'pocket' atlas which, because of its reduced size, was less elaborate. Both were particularly popular and ran to many editions. Speed's maps were generally uncoloured, though some contemporary owners commissioned hand-coloured versions.

J. Bleau published his first atlas of the counties of England and Wales in 1645 as part IV of *Theatrum Orbis Terrarum*. His maps included the arms of the principal nobility and gentry of each county, though there are often blank shields, indicative, perhaps, of 'vanity' publishing, the cost of producing the atlas being met in part by the financial contributions of those whose arms appeared in the maps.

The name of the cartographer (who surveyed and drew the map) is often found inscribed on copies of his maps, together with the word or abbreviation *auctore, de., delt., delineavit* or *descispit*; the name of an engraver may similarly be denoted by *caelvit, engr., fecit, incidente, sc., sculp* and *sculpsit*. These early maps are singularly attractive but unfortunately they contain insufficient detail to be of much assistance to the local historian. Hills, forests, rivers and deer parks are shown pictorially, and towns and villages are marked with standard symbols. But roads are rarely shown and while the heraldry and town plans are informative, these too may be depicted inaccurately.

Cartography improved significantly towards the end of the seventeenth century, notably in the work of the prolific Robert Morden (d.1703) and of John Ogilby (1600–76). Ogilby's *Britannia* (1675) contained 100 plates of road maps, each printed to look like a series of six or seven vertical strips of parchment on which a main road was depicted together with towns, villages, junctions and roadside features, familiar to the seventeenth-century traveller, such as inns, churches, bridges, windmills, beacons and even gallows. Although of a small scale, these maps are of great interest, especially when compared with later ORDNANCE SURVEY maps. Ogilby invented a 'wheel dimensurator' with which he measured each statute mile. These measurements were used after 1740 to locate MILESTONES on main roads. The *Britannia Depicta or Ogilby Improv'd* (1720) of Emmanuel Bowen (d.1767) consisted of 270 plates of road and county maps and John Cary (1754–1835), in his *New and Correct English Atlas* (1787), produced a series of maps notable for its accurate depiction of roads.

Many localized maps were produced for specific purposes and these can be of inestimable value to the researcher.

Estate maps usually encompass a manor, park or farm or sometimes just a group of fields or the grounds of a country house. Although late sixteenth- and seventeenth-century estate maps are known, most date from the eighteenth century or later. They are usually very detailed, and may even delineate precisely every feature of a formal garden or park. Many are retained in the archives of large landowners, while others have been transferred to county record offices. Indexes of estate papers are maintained by the Royal Commission on Historical Manuscripts (*see* APPENDIX I).

Enclosure Award maps show only those parts of a parish which were subject to reorganization as the result of parliamentary ENCLOSURE in the late eighteenth and early nineteenth centuries. In those areas of late enclosure (such as the Midlands), the old strips and areas of land described as 'ancient enclosures' are also shown. Of particular interest are field names (and acreages) which may be identified from numbers on the map and the corresponding entries in the award. The Enclosure Acts provided that copies of the award should be deposited with the Clerk of the Peace for the county and the archives of the parish concerned. If extant, these, together with accompanying maps, will be found in the local or county record offices.

Tithe maps for England and Wales were produced between 1838 and 1854 as a result of the Tithe Commutation Act of 1836 by which payments in kind and MODUS were commuted to money settlements based on the ownership of property (*see* TITHES). Detailed parish maps, accompanied by registers (*terriers*) of land-holdings, were deposited with the Tithe Redemption Commission (whose archives are now with the Public Record Office at Kew – see APPENDIX I) and the appropriate diocesan and parochial authorities. Unlike enclosure maps, tithe maps cover an entire parish and are often very large. In most maps, all properties are shown, including houses (which are numbered) and gardens as well as larger land-holdings and remaining areas of common. In many cases, the tithe map may be the earliest complete cartographical record of the parish since enclosure maps were often limited to those areas still in common. It will also delineate the boundary of the 'ancient' (ecclesiastical) parish which may differ from that of the civil parish. The commutation awards provide details of landowners (in alphabetical order) and tenants, types of dwelling, FIELD NAMES and land use. Most tithe maps are now held by county record offices.

For geological and historical maps *see* ORDNANCE SURVEY

For the Close Society *see* APPENDIX I

MARCH From the Old English *mearc*, meaning 'boundary', from which are derived place-name elements such as Marcle (Herefordshire) meaning 'boundary wood'. Historically, a march is a tract of land on the borders of two territories, such as the medieval Calais March and the marches of Wales and Scotland.

Following the Conquest, most of King William's followers received dispersed estates, thereby avoiding a potentially dangerous concentration of magnatial power, but on the remote borders of Wales and Scotland he created counties palatinate whose overlords were charged with the defence of the realm. In the north, a Prince Bishop ruled over the vast territories of his PALATINATE of Durham while in the marches of Wales the king created the earldoms of Hereford, Shrewsbury and Chester.

William also selected the most rapacious and unruly of his followers, who might otherwise have threatened his authority, and gave them licence to annex any lands they could wrest from the Welsh. In time, these Norman 'adventurers' (*see* ADVENAE) were to overrun nearly half of Wales, taking advantage of the disunity of the Welsh princes and minimal interference from their sovereign (*see* WALES). They mounted expeditions to seize the territories of any native ruler too weak to resist them and what they gained 'by the power of their swords and of fortune' they passed on to their descendants as Marcher lordships, private kingdoms in all but name. William II (r.1087–1100) also encouraged the Marcher Lords to conquer what they could, and in the Welsh borderlands they planned their strategy

with care: each castle serving to protect its neighbour, and the whole system forming a network that guarded every important river and gap in the hills.

By the mid-twelfth century, this fiercely independent warrior aristocracy occupied much of eastern Wales together with the south coast from Chepstow to St David's and had established a triple line of defences along the border. In the Marcher zone, some 48 to 80 km deep (30 to 50 miles), the Normans introduced their own laws and culture (though in some areas Welsh communities which had submitted to Norman overlordship were allowed to live by their ancient laws and customs) and exercised the power life or death over the population for whom access to the Crown courts was effectively denied. No real attempt was made to restrict the power of the Lords Marcher, whose lands had become a refuge for fugitives and dissidents, until in 1471 Edward IV instituted the Council of the Marches of Wales which was maintained as an administrative authority until its abolition in 1689. The Marcher lordships themselves were finally abolished in 1536 when the five new counties of Denbigh, Montgomery, Radnor, Brecon and Monmouth were created. The political pattern of the Welsh Marches was constantly changing throughout the Middle Ages as families failed in the male line, heiresses married into other families (sometimes forming alliances with the Welsh nobility) or lands were confiscated by the English kings. Of the 136 Marcher lordships mentioned in the Act of Union in 1536, 41 had reverted to the Crown either through forfeiture, conquest or marriage.

The Scottish *Borders*, although not named as such until the thirteenth century, were from the earliest times the disputed territory of contending races or nations (*see* SCOTLAND). The exigencies occasioned by the constantly recurring Border wars and incursions of the thirteenth to the sixteenth centuries resulted in the building of numerous castles and PEEL TOWERS, each strategically placed to control route-ways and river crossings and almost invariably in sight of one another to facilitate the rapid communication of signals of invasion or alarm. In 1460 Northumberland alone possessed 37 castles and 78 towers, and the Scottish side was equally well defended.

By the fifteenth century, the Borders had effectively become ungovernable and the two kingdoms agreed that an element of control should be exercised through the creation, on both sides of the border, of divisions known as the East, West and

Middle Marches. Salaried officials (*Wardens*) were appointed by their respective sovereigns to each division and endowed with considerable administrative and judicial authority. The wardens represented their sovereign in their respective divisions and the office was at one time hereditary, being the prerogative of a few of the senior magnates who held estates on the Borders. At certain times, a day of truce was held when the English and Scottish wardens met, examined each other's credentials, and attempted to settle any matters that might be in dispute among their followers. As may be imagined, not all such meetings ended amicably! One district which was the cause of considerable trouble to the wardens of the West March was that known as the *Debatable Land* which lay partly in England and partly in Scotland. First mentioned in 1449 as 'the lands called Batable or Threep lands', its chief families were the Grahams and the Armstrongs, clans of 'desperate thieves and freebooters', whose constant antagonism was finally concluded in the seventeenth century when the Grahams were transported to Ireland and forbidden to return on pain of death. Other districts of the Borders periodically required the armed intervention of the Scottish commissioners, and as late as 1606 the Earl of Dunbar seized and hanged 140 brigands.

The character and way of life of Borderers were similar both on the Scottish and English side. The magnates lived in large, heavily fortified castles while the lesser nobles and gentry occupied peel towers and fortified farmsteads. The feudal bond between chiefs and the principal men of their clans was that implied in the term 'kindly tenant': a tenant being of the chieftain's family or having held his lands in succession for several generations. This tie was not dependent on the payment of rent, either in money or in kind, but on kinship, and bound the leading members of the clan to corporate self-interest and self-defence.

The union of the crowns removed some obvious grounds of contention between the Border clans and from the middle of the seventeenth century the Borders gradually subsided into a more stable and peaceful condition.

MARCHER LORD *see* MARCH

MARCHIONESS The wife of a marquess or a woman who holds a marquisate in her own right.

MARCLE *see* MARCH

MARK *see* COINAGE

MARKET CROSS It has been suggested that market crosses were intended to sanctify commercial transactions or were erected to commemorate the granting of a market's charter. In effect, they declared the authority of the market and, in their size and elaboration, its status (indeed, many markets had more than one cross). But like the CHURCHYARD CROSS, which is of similar design, they were probably possessed of a variety of functions not least of which was to provide a focal point from which the assembled traders and townspeople could be addressed by corporation or market officials and itinerant preachers. Most are of medieval origin, though of many only the stepped base and a broken shaft remain to tell of a community's former aspirations. In several of the more successful commercial centres, late medieval and Tudor benefactors provided for the construction of polygonal roofed shelters, or *butter crosses*, their walls pierced by arches and with a lantern or cross crowning the canopy. John Leland (*c.* 1505–52) described the late fifteenth-century cross at Malmesbury in Wiltshire as 'a right fair and costely peace of worke in the market-place made al of stone & curiusly voultid for poore market folkes to stande dry when rayne cummith.' In some less prosperous towns, such as Castle Combe in Wiltshire, the original cross had a shelter constructed around it, while at Sherborne in Dorset the former lavatorium was removed from the abbey to the market-place where it served both as a conduit and market shelter. *See also* MARKET HALL *and* MARKETS

MARKET HALL Early market halls (also known as *market house*, *green house* and *fair house*) of the late fourteenth and fifteenth centuries were erected on the greens or in open spaces where MARKETS and FAIRS were held. Others date from the late sixteenth and early seventeenth centuries when expanding trade encouraged competition among many smaller market towns. Several of the market halls of this later period were supported on pillars with space beneath for stalls. A singularly beautiful example is the small stone-built Jacobean market hall at Chipping Campden in the Gloucestershire Cotswolds, while at Wymondham in Norfolk an octagonal timber-framed market hall was erected above the MARKET CROSS. The upper storeys often accommodated the *Court of 'Pie Powder'* (*see* MARKETS) which was responsible for the administration of the market including the collection of rents, tolls and fines, all of which provided revenues to the feudal sponsor of the market. Others had enclosed lower storeys in which the market

Bristol's fourteenth-century market cross, removed to the landscaped gardens of Stourhead, Wiltshire, in 1733.

booths, hurdles and other equipment were stored. Many market halls were abandoned or adapted for a variety of other purposes such as guildhalls, chapels and schools. Others were in turn replaced in the nineteenth century by larger covered markets with classical facades. Almost invariably, a town's STOCKS and LOCK-UP were conveniently located in the vicinity of the market cross or hall.

MARKET HOUSE *see* MARKET HALL

MARKETS It is possible that the earliest 'markets' and 'fairs' in Britain were held within the concentric earthworks of Neolithic CAUSEWAYED ENCLOSURES. Certainly, increasing trade throughout the Bronze and Iron Ages must have been contingent on the development of strategically located sites for barter and exchange: at crossing places on the great ridgeways, for example, defined perhaps by STONE CIRCLES and HENGES within which negotiations were conducted and agreements sanctified.

During the Roman occupation (AD 43–410), a central *forum* or market-place was incorporated into every Roman town. Not unlike a modern shopping precinct, the *forum* was a large, paved open space with public services (such as water conduits and aqualis) and access to colonnades of shops. The *forum* was both the centre of a region's trade and commerce and the focal point of its community. With the withdrawal of Rome, the structured commercial system on which these markets depended began to disintegrate, though it seems likely that in some instances the old meeting-places continued in use.

In the centuries that followed, Saxon chieftains built their strongholds and the monks their abbeys and such places inevitably attracted a scattered but increasingly gregarious populace, anxious to join with others in the celebration of saints' days and holy days or to witness the administration of justice and the settlement of disputes in the lord's courts. For itinerant merchants, travel was both slow and dangerous, so that these large gatherings of people, enjoying the security of monastic or magnatial patronage, provided ideal opportunities for trade. Edward the Elder (AD 900–25) decreed that all buying and selling should take place openly in a market-place and within the jurisdiction of a town-reeve. As permanent communities developed round many abbeys and castles so markets and fairs flourished and by the late tenth century tolls were being exacted, both by the Saxon kings and by the nobles and clerics who organized and controlled the movement of goods between their estates.

In the early Middle Ages, 'markets' and 'fairs' were similar occasions and quite distinct from the religious feast-days and holy days which had their own traditions and ceremonies. Gradually, FAIRS emerged as more seasonal gatherings, often on the periphery of towns or at prominent sites in the surrounding countryside, whereas markets were held weekly and always in towns or villages. Royal mints were also established at various centres to provide an authoritative and standardized COINAGE for a rapidly expanding commerce.

After the Conquest, many of these customary markets and fairs were recorded in DOMESDAY Book and eventually regularized under the Norman kings by the granting of charters which permitted the receipt of revenues. The acquisition of a market charter was obviously of great financial advantage, to both a manorial lord (who would receive the tolls and taxes levied on his markets and fairs and the fines exacted for breaches of trading regulations) and to the Crown (from whom the privilege was almost invariably purchased). Many charters were granted by sovereigns to their own estates in anticipation of future prosperity and others were granted as gifts in recognition of signal service to the Crown.

As commercial expertise increased so foreign merchants were attracted to the larger English markets, bringing with them oriental spices, wines from Bordeaux and pottery, silks and glass from the Mediterranean. Restrictions, aimed at alleviating the problems of inequitable competition, included the staggering of market days throughout a week in a particular area; the prosecution of *forestallers* (or *regrators*), merchants who traded before reaching a market and sold on at a profit; and the imposition of limits on the proximity of markets. (A reasonable day's journey for an unmounted man was considered to be 32 km (20 miles) which, when allowing time to walk to market, time to do business and time to walk home again, was divided by three to give 11 km (6⅔ miles), the statutory distance between markets in the fourteenth century. 'And all these things it will be necessary to do by day and not by night on account of the snares and attacks of robbers.')

While many markets have been held on the same weekday for 500 or 600 years, the aspirations of numerous medieval entrepreneurs exceeded the commercial potential of their markets, which eventually foundered, usually because they were geographically unsustainable or as a result of intense competition or the ravages of plague. Consequently, there are numerous tiny boroughs whose medieval charters have guaranteed continuing political and legal privileges not enjoyed by larger and more prosperous communities. Bishops Castle in Shropshire, for example, was the smallest borough in England until 1967 when it lost that distinction but none of its quaintness. Many market charters were granted by the Norman kings, but the greatest proliferation took place during the thirteenth century, when some 3,300 markets were authorized, with a further 1,560 grants in the fourteenth century before the advent of economic decline. A fair or market usually fell within the jurisdiction of a lord of the manor whose steward presided over the *Court of 'Pie Powder'* (a corruption of *pieds poudreux*, meaning 'dusty footed' travellers). This court met in a building called a *tolbooth* or *tolsey* and was responsible for both the general administration of the market and the maintenance of law and order for the duration of the market. Local traders often traded first, outsiders (known variously as *stallingers*, *censers* or *chensers*) either waiting their turn or paying a supplementary fee in order to jump the queue.

At first, parish churches were often used as repositories for documents and valuables, trading taking place in the porch and precincts. In 1285, however, a statute was passed forbidding the holding of fairs in churchyards and by 1448 the clergy was so incensed by 'the abominable injuries and offenses done to Almighty God because of fairs and markets upon their high and principal feasts' that trading was finally removed into the space beyond the churchyard wall, and fairs prohibited on Good Friday, Ascension Day, Corpus Christi, the Assumption of the Virgin Mary, All Saints and on any Sunday except the four at harvest time.

As England prospered, rows of semi-permanent stalls were erected in the larger markets and may be evident in street names today: the *Shambles*, for example, being the area of a market where fish and flesh were sold. Names such as Cheap Street and Sheep Street are also indicative of early markets. So too is Chipping in place-names, derived from the Old English *cēping* or *cıeping* meaning 'market' or 'market town', as in Chipping Norton in Oxfordshire. Any dwelling beside a market square could buy a licence to serve ale on market day. Official MARKET HALLS were erected as administrative offices in which goods were weighed by the Ponderator, and scrutinized and stored by the Overseers of the Market and other officials. From 1640, the senior official was the Clerk of the Market, appointed by the lord of the manor or town mayor. On market days the Clerk announced the commencement of trading at ten and its cessation at sunset. (The Clerk of the Market was originally a Crown official, responsible within the VERGE for supplying market goods to the royal household and for the examination of weights and measures.)

A market's success depended on its accessibility: roads to and from markets had to be maintained and, in several instances, special roads or *portways* were built. Portway is a term derived from the Latin *porta*, the port or gate of a market town at which borough officials scrutinized traders' credentials and collected tolls and rents. In some cases, the word *port* became synonymous with 'market', as at Langport in Somerset.

In response to the rapid growth of the urban population in the industrial nineteenth century, corn halls and permanent cattle markets were established at county towns and other major trading centres, together with extensive covered market-places, often with grand porticoes in the classical style. In the twentieth century, the development of motorized road transport resulted in a rationalization of markets during both wars (to save energy and fuel), and a drastic reduction in the number of livestock markets. Initially, many small rural markets foundered but elsewhere the separation of livestock from general trading has provided both additional space and the impetus for the restoration of street markets which are increasingly popular, particularly in those ancient towns where pedestrian precincts have been created.

See also MARKET CROSS

MARK OF DIFFERENCE see CADENCY

MARK OF DISTINCTION In ARMORY, a charge added to a coat of arms to indicate BASTARDY. Contrary to popular belief, it is not the *bend sinister* which denotes illegitimacy but the *bordure wavy*, which has been in use since the eighteenth century, and in Scotland the *bordure compony*. The *baton sinister* (erroneously called a 'bar sinister' by fiction writers) has almost invariably been used for this purpose in the English royal family, though there

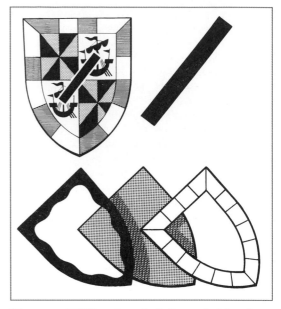

The arms of William Campbell, Bastard of Argyll, with a bordure compony denoting illegitimacy. Top right: a baton sinister. Below: a bordure wavy and a bordure compony.

have been notable variations, particularly during the Middle Ages when there were few established armorial conventions relating to bastardy. The Beauforts, for example, the illegitimate line of John of Gaunt and Katherine Swinford, following their legitimation in 1397, adopted the royal arms within a border of the Beaufort colours, silver and blue. Care should be exercised regarding the concept of bastardy itself: frequently, marks of distinction were intended to indicate that the armiger was not in legitimate line of succession, not that he was personally illegitimate.

MARL-PIT (*also* **DENE-HOLE, DRAW-PIT** *and* **CHALK WELL**) The practice of spreading marl and manure on fields is undoubtedly of prehistoric origin. Marl, a mixture of clay and lime, is known to have been used by the Romans to improve the fertility of acid soil and Saxon charters refer both to *lampytts* (loam-pits) and to marl-pits. In those areas where chalk occurs near the surface, it could be dug easily, leaving a pock-marked surface of shallow marl-pits. Elsewhere, extraction was more difficult and deep shafts had to be sunk, most of which have subsequently collapsed forming water-filled hollows. The digging of marl-pits continued from the medieval period through to the end of the nineteenth century. Field names and trackways with

'marl' or 'chalk' elements are usually indicative of areas in which former marl-pits may be found. The Old English *calc* ('chalk') is of greater antiquity than the Old French *marle* ('marl'). 'Chalk' place-name elements, such as Broad Chalke in Wiltshire, are therefore likely to be older than those containing 'marl', as in Marlingpit, Hampshire, which is probably of medieval origin.
See also LIMEKILNS

MARQUESS *or* **MARQUIS** The second rank of the British peerage, introduced in 1385. The term was introduced from Europe, though from an early date it was sometimes applied to lords of the Welsh and Scottish marches. The wife of a marquess is a marchioness.

MARSHAL *see* MARSHALSEA

MARSHALLING In ARMORY, the correct ordering of heraldic devices in a coat of arms to signify marriage, inheritance or office.
See also IMPALEMENT *and* QUARTERING

MARSHALSEA In the thirteenth century, the department responsible for the royal horses: not only those actually with the household, but also the numerous studs and farms where they were bred and kept. The senior officer of the Marshalsea was the *Marshal*. In 1385, the office, which by that time had assumed considerably greater significance, was granted to Thomas Mowbray, Earl of Nottingham, who a year later was given the title of *Earl Marshal*. In the late Middle Ages, the Marshal was, with the Lord High Constable, the first in military rank beneath the sovereign, and it was his responsibility to marshal the various contingents of troops and retainers in battle, to organize state ceremonies and to judge matters armorial brought before the Court of Chivalry. In the performance of his various duties he would undoubtedly have depended on the advice of the heralds and today the Earl Marshal continues to exercise jurisdiction over the officers of arms as hereditary judge in the High Court of Chivalry.

MARTELLO TOWERS AND COMMISSION FORTS Martello towers are forts built on the English coast from Sussex to Suffolk against invasion during the French Wars. Successors to the Forts of the Saxon Shore (*see* ROMAN FORTS AND CAMPS) and the TUDOR COASTAL FORTS, they were themselves superseded by the shore batteries and mid-channel forts of the 1860s and the concrete PILLBOXES of the Second World War.

Martello tower on the coast at Seaford, West Sussex.

Martello towers are named after Torre della Mortella ('Tower of the Myrtle'), a fortification commanding the Gulf of San Fiorenzo north of Corsica, the impregnability of which so impressed the English that they copied its simple but effective design for the coastal defences of the south-east. One hundred and three oval-shaped Martello towers were constructed between 1804 and 1812 from Seaford, East Sussex, to Aldeburgh, Suffolk, the first seventy-four guarding the vulnerable 80-km (50-mile) coast between Eastbourne, Sussex, and Folkestone, Kent. Each tower was constructed of brick with a thicker 4 metre wall (13 feet) to seaward and a rotating platform carrying a 24-pounder cannon on a 3 metre (10 feet) thick 'bomb-proof' roof. Beneath this, garrison quarters for twenty-four men were reached by a ladder or drawbridge through a doorway 6 metres (20 feet) above the ground. Forty-three Martello towers have survived, including that at Dymchurch in Kent which has been restored to its original form.

Within fifty years of Napoleon's final defeat at Waterloo, the development of the French 'Ironclad' battleship and the innovative rifled gun, with its greatly increased range and accuracy, rendered the Martello towers ineffective. With Anglo-French relations at a low ebb, a Royal Commission was established to 'consider the defences of the United Kingdom' and, realizing that re-fortification of the entire coast was out of the question, the Commissioners decided that resources should be concentrated on protecting the Navy's Channel bases against bombardment. During the 1860s, seventy-six *Commission forts* were built around Chatham in Kent, Portsmouth in Hampshire, Plymouth in Devon and Milford Haven in Pembrokeshire at a cost of £10 million. Most were shore batteries, curved ramparts of casement embrasures, designed to block seaward approaches to the vital naval establishments. The best examples are Hubberstone Fort at Milford Haven, Hurst Castle on the Solent in Hampshire and Fort Bovisand near Plymouth.

Where harbour approaches were too wide to be protected by land batteries, circular towers with tiers of guns were constructed on the seabed. All six have survived: four between Portsmouth and the Isle of Wight, where they guard the Spithead naval anchorage, and off Plymouth and Portland in Dorset. Portsmouth and Plymouth were also protected from a landward bombardment by the construction of massive series of mutually supporting forts to the rear. The best surviving example, fort Brockhurst at Portsmouth (1858–62), was designed to direct up to seventy guns on enemy batteries from a gun-mounting keep and polygonal ramparts of casemates approached by ramps from an inner ward (*parade*) and protected from close-range attack by a detached outwork (*ravelin*) and galleries (*caponiers*) which projected into the surrounding dry moat. The Commission forts were originally to be built in granite and brick but armoured shields, of alternate layers of wrought iron and teak up to 60 cm (2 feet) thick, were fitted to protect the casemates of shore batteries, while the seabed forts were constructed entirely of iron and concrete.

By the end of the century, defence policy had changed significantly and the Channel forts were superseded by the building of 'the greatest navy the world has ever seen'.

MARTLET *see* BEASTS (HERALDIC)

MASONS' MARKS Devices used by stone masons to mark their work. Each mason had his distinctive mark which could be passed from father to son. They were usually hastily and shallowly incised and measure about 5 cm (2 inches) in height. The marks were numerous and varied and include simple cyphers, geometrical patterns and runic-type symbols. Registers of marks were maintained by the medieval masons' guilds both to avoid duplication and to ensure that bad workmanship could be traced. Most medieval masons were peripatetic craftsmen who often worked in teams. It is therefore possible to trace the movements of a particular mason or group of masons from one commission to the next through the identification of their marks. Glaziers and wood carvers used a similar system: several of

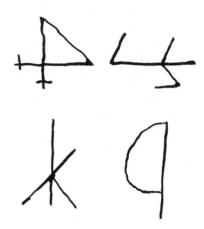

the misericords at Ludlow church in Shropshire are distinguished by a carver's mark of an uprooted plant, for example.

See also MERCHANTS' MARKS

MASS-DIALS *see* SUNDIALS

MATRICULATION OF ARMS In Scotland, it is an offence to bear arms unless they have been matriculated with Lord Lyon King of Arms and entered into the *Public Register of All Arms and Bearings in Scotland*. Matriculation is not simply registration: the process requires the correct marshalling of the arms, together with the appropriate marks of difference indicating relationships within an armigerous family.

MATTINS *or* **MATINS** Originally the Breviary Office for the night (*see* MONASTERIES) but now more commonly used for the service of Morning Prayer in the Church of England. The office in the *Book of Common Prayer* was based on the medieval Mattins with supplements from Prime.

MAUNDY The Maundy ceremony of washing the feet of the poor commemorates Christ's washing of the Apostles' feet at the Last Supper (John 13). The ceremony was performed by royal or other eminent persons or ecclesiastics, on the Thursday before Easter (*Maundy Thursday*) and was commonly followed by the distribution of clothing, food or money. Except in the Roman Catholic Church, all that remains in Britain of this ceremony is the distribution of specially minted silver *Maundy Money* by the sovereign. From the time of Henry IV (r.1399–1413) the number of recipients has corresponded to the number of years of the sovereign's age (*see* COINAGE *and* SAINTS' DAYS AND FEAST-DAYS)

MAUSOLEUM A large and magnificent tomb or monument. The term was derived from the marble tomb of Mausolus, a fourth-century King of Caria in Asia Minor, which was accounted one of the Seven Wonders of the World. The mausoleum designed by Nicholas Hawksmoor (1661–1736) at Castle Howard in North Yorkshire took more than ten years to build (it was begun in 1731) and is probably the earliest of many such classical structures to be erected in the landscaped parklands of the eighteenth- and early nineteenth-century aristocracy. It was described by Horace Walpole as 'a mausoleum that would tempt one to be buried alive'. Many mausoleums were intended as memorials rather than tombs, but the aristocratic perception of death as a dignified withdrawal from the plebeian gaze is evident in the cool classicism and romantic isolation of most of the mausoleums of this period. But the distinction between several later mausoleums and follies is often difficult to detect. The nineteenth-century Petersons' Tower in the New Forest, Hampshire, built by a retired judge from India, was both a folly and a mausoleum. Having completed the building of his house, Thomas Peterson was reluctant to put his labour-force out of work so he devised a work-creation scheme for the construction of a thirteen-storey 'campanile' which was to be the tallest concrete tower in the world. Inspired by a local spiritualist group (the New Forest Shakers), he is said to have been supported in his scheme by the posthumous attentions of Sir Christopher Wren, and the tower was eventually completed in 1885. When Peterson died twenty-one years later, at the age of ninety-three, his ashes were placed in a crypt beneath his folly. The building was deconsecrated in 1968 and sold for £100.
See also FOLLY

MAXIMA CAESARIENSIS *see* ROMAN ADMINISTRATION

MAYOR The head of the municipal corporation of a city or borough. Also the head of a district council with the status of a borough and, since 1972, of a town (parish) council which has been granted mayoral status. The earliest mayoralty (London) probably dates from 1191, but by the mid-thirteenth century most boroughs were appointing mayors whose authority was determined by their borough charters. Legislation of 1835 and 1882 relieved mayors of many of their executive responsibilities. The *Mayor's Brethren* was a body of twenty-four aldermen, responsible for the administration of a town, together with forty-eight other residents who comprised the Common Council.

MAYPOLE A stripped tree erected on a village green as the focal point of May Day dancing and celebrations. The pole is often painted with stripes and decorated with foliage to represents the tree (usually a white hawthorn) which was selected by the young people of a village for particular homage as a symbol of fertility. The May Day festival was superimposed on the Celtic ceremony of *Beltane* which celebrated the beginning of summer with great bonfires in honour of the sun. Until comparatively recently, young people decorated their homes with greenery and flowers collected from the woods and fields as a means of ritually conveying the fertilizing powers of nature into the community. May Day rites, which were revived in the Victorian period by the writer John Ruskin, include the crowning of the May Queen (usually accompanied by Jack o' the Green or a similar male figure), Morris Dancing and dancing round the maypole.

MAZES The name derives from the archaic term *mazed*, meaning 'baffled' or 'amazed'. In Britain, there are two types of maze: the turf maze and the puzzle hedge maze.

The turf maze, with gullies cut between grass paths, is distinctive to England, though they were also known in medieval Germany, and the Roman Pliny (AD 23–79) wrote of 'mazes made in the fields to entertain the children'. Only eight turf mazes have survived, but a further sixty sites have been identified, all in the lowland regions of northern, central and southern England. The maze at Alkborough in South Humberside is known as 'Julian's Bower', a name which may derive from Iulus, the son of Aeneas, the hero of Virgil's classic poem. Iulus is said to have taken part in the labyrinthine games of Troy, so it is not unreasonable to suggest that the Romans also created Cretan-type mazes during the occupation; indeed, many turf mazes were situated in or near Roman settlements. There are also examples of mazes known as 'Maiden's Bower' which may have originated in ancient fertility rites, introduced by Dark Age immigrant settlers as part of their culture. The 'Game of Troy' (*Lusus Troiae*) was widely enjoyed on medieval GREENS and PLAISTOWS, and the *troy* appellation in place-names is often indicative of a former turf maze, though this is thought by some to be a Tudor conceit, since classical allusions were fashionable at that time. Perhaps the finest turf maze is the spade-shaped Troy maze at Somerton in Oxfordshire, measuring 17 × 15 metres (57 × 50 feet) and with a path 402 metres long (440 yards).

Peculiar to southern England is the name *Mizmaze*, as at Breamore in Hampshire, which consists of eleven rings round a circular mound. The county historian Hutchins recorded that the Miz Maze at Leigh in Dorset was neglected by the 1770s but prior to that it was the custom for the young men of the village to scour the trenches and repair the banks once every six or seven years. Regrettably, only the enclosing earthwork survives of the hexagonal maze which is located on a hillock at the highest point in the parish. Literary and antiquarian references to turf mazes indicate that they were used for games, particularly at festivals and fairs, though their origins may have been religious. The similarity in design between the cruciform Christian labyrinth in the floor of Chartres cathedral and several English turf mazes suggests that they may have been re-cut on the French model during the Middle Ages.

The Renaissance puzzle hedge maze was essentially a *divertissement*, set within the formal gardens of a cultured society. The hedge maze at Hampton Court Palace is the earliest in England and was probably created by Cardinal Wolsey (*c*. 1475–1530), though it was replanted in 1690. While many turf mazes were abandoned following the Reformation, hedge mazes flourished until the eighteenth century when 'natural' landscaping was introduced and many formal gardens abandoned. They were revived by the Victorians and there are notable mazes from that period at Chevening in Kent (1820), Glendurgan in Cornwall (1833), Somerleyton Hall in Suffolk (1846) and Hatfield House in Hertfordshire (1840, though this probably replaced an earlier maze).

MEAD (i) An alcoholic drink made from fermented honey and water.
(ii) A meadow.
(iii) Lands vested in a parish for the upkeep of the poorhouse. The *aftergrass* of a mead is that which grows after the first crop has been mown for hay. At Leigh in Dorset 9 acres of aftergrass at Alton Mead and Beer Mill Mead are sold annually by means of a *candle auction*, a custom dating from at least 1732. Bids are made as a candle slowly burns down, the successful bid being the final one made before the flame dies. The purchaser is entitled to graze his cattle on the aftergrass from Lammas to Lady Day (12 August to 11 February in the following year), though as a result of modern farming practices aftergrass is no longer available and other benefits have been substituted. The proceeds of the Leigh Candle Auction are now used for charitable purposes within the parish.

MEADOW It has been estimated that 95 per cent of Britain's traditional meadowlands have been lost since 1947, and the practice of mowing and drying hay in June to provide feed for livestock during the following winter has largely been superseded by the early cutting of silage, green fodder which is stored and fermented in silos. The common meadows of the manorial system (*dole meadows*) were usually situated on low-lying ground near a stream or river and were divided among the tenants into strips (*doles* or *dales*), each demarcated by boundary stones (*merestones*) and temporary hurdle fences. In some manors, doles were reallocated each year by rotation or by drawing lots (*lot meadows*). Demesne meadow was generally separate from the common meadow and was usually mown by the tenants in return for customary privileges: a gift of cheese and mutton and as much hay as each could lift on his scythe, for example. The hay harvest traditionally began on 24 June (the Feast of St John) and once the hay crop was mown, dried and gathered the meadow would be grazed by the commoners' livestock for the remainder of the season. *Lammas meadows* were grazed from Lammas (Old English *hlaf-mass*, meaning 'loaf mass') on 1 August, when the villagers' attentions turned to the grain harvest, to Candlemas on 2 February when re-growth began in the meadow.
See also WATER MEADOW

MEDIEVAL ROADS Most ROMAN ROADS were strategically planned and brilliantly engineered and, following the Norman Conquest of 1066, they formed the foundation of a communications network which again radiated from an administrative base at London. But while the Roman Fosse Way, Watling Street and Ermine Street, together with the earlier Icknield Way, were given royal protection, and in the mid-fourteenth century some 40 per cent of routes were of Roman origin, most medieval roads 'made and maintained themselves' (C.T. Flower) and were essentially ancient trackways which developed in response to changing circumstances while others regressed.

So-called DROVE ROADS and PACK-HORSE ROADS were used by a variety of travellers and acquired their designations only because they functioned primarily (though by no means exclusively) as routes for the movement of livestock or for pack-horse trains. At this time, most bulky goods were transported by means of a comparatively efficient water-borne trading system, the hinterland of each coastal or river port serviced by roads, the standard and reliability of which improved as they converged on their destination. Similarly, FAIRS and MARKETS depended for their commercial success on the safe arrival of customers from surrounding settlements and on the ability of merchants and traders to travel conveniently from one engagement to the next. Pilgrims and magnatial retinues also travelled by road, both on foot and on horseback, and many wayside inns were established at this time to accommodate them, particularly along the more popular pilgrimage routes (*see* SHRINES). But travel could be dangerous: in 1285 a statute of Edward I required that where a road passed through woodland an area extending to 18 metres (60 feet) on either side of the highway should be cleared of vegetation in order that robbers and outlaws should not find concealment there. Few medieval roads were actually created, other than Fenland causeways around Ely and a number of Edwardian military roads in North Wales.

The repair and maintenance of roads, BRIDGES and CAUSEWAYS was largely in the hands of monastic houses and borough authorities, anxious to attract commercial investment and trade. Medieval legislation was principally concerned not with the fabric of a road or track, but with its legal status as the King's Highway, a right of way, established by custom, over which the traveller was at liberty to 'pass and repass' (*see* HIGHWAY). As is the case today, this right of way was variable: obstructions could be circumnavigated by entering onto neighbouring land. Manorial courts were obliged to attend to matters which might impede or cause annoyance to 'the passers-by in the King's Way', but it was not until 1555 that parishes were obliged to appoint an unpaid officer, the *Surveyor of the Highways*, who was required to inspect roads and bridges in the parish three times a year and to organize the statute labour to repair them.
See also ROADS

MEDIEVAL TILES *see* ENCAUSTIC TILES

MEER *see* MERE

MEIFOD *see* HAFOD

MEMORANDA ROLLS These rolls were kept by the King's Remembrancer and the Lord Treasurer's Remembrancer and are concerned with EXCHEQUER business, particularly monies owing to the Crown. They supplement the PIPE ROLLS and contain many items of local interest. Memoranda Rolls are maintained at the Public Record Office and several have been published.

MEMORIAL BOARD (i) An inexpensive form of heraldic WALL MONUMENT painted on wood or canvas and mostly dating from the seventeenth century. Usually square or oblong and between 0.6 and 2 metres in diameter (2 and 6 feet), there are also diamond-shaped examples which may easily be confused with HATCHMENTS. As the name suggests, memorial boards are commemorative and usually have a text which includes such phrases as 'In Loving Memory of . . .' and 'Near Here Lies Buried . . .' together with biographical details and a biblical quotation or even a verse praising the character of the departed. Symbols of mortality such as death's heads (*mortheads*), crossbones and hourglasses were also popular as decoration.
(ii) *See* WAR MEMORIALS

MEMORIALS *For* memorials in CHURCHES *see* BRASSES, EFFIGIES, EPITAPHS, GRAVE-STONES, HATCHMENTS, INCISED SLABS, MEMORIAL BOARDS, MONUMENTS, TABLE TOMBS, TOMB CHESTS *and* WAR MEMORIALS

Many FOLLIES and classical eighteenth-century structures were erected as memorials in the emparked grounds of country houses: *see* GARDENS, MAUSOLEUM, OBELISK *and* TEMPLE

MENDICANT Mendicant FRIARS were members of those orders which were forbidden to hold property. Consequently, they worked or begged for a living and were not bound to a particular religious house (Latin *mendicare* = 'to beg'). In the Middle Ages they worked mainly in towns and enjoyed extensive privileges, including exemption from episcopal jurisdiction and faculties for preaching and hearing confession, which caused considerable hostility.
See also FRANCISCANS *and* DOMINICANS

MENHIR *see* MONOLITH

MERCANTILE LAW *Lex Mercatoria* or the Law Merchant is based on mercantile customs and usages. The Common Law of England (*see* LAW), which in the Middle Ages was primarily concerned with rights over land, was often unable to cope with the numerous and varied disputes resulting from the rapid development of foreign trade. Merchants generally determined such disputes according to the trading customs of their own countries and as many of them came from the Mediterranean and western Europe, it was inevitably that a significant element of Roman Law should eventually find its way into English common law. The Courts of Pie Powder dealt with mercantile law as it applied to trade within the jurisdiction of a particular market and also assumed parochial responsibilities for the maintenance of law and order while the market was in session (*see* MARKETS). Edward III (1327–77) gave foreign merchants the right to trade in specific English towns known as *Staple Towns*, which were required to convene *Courts of the Staple* to resolve trading disputes. Since the Common Law was then deficient in commercial rulings, these mercantile courts again looked to the customs of foreign merchants when determining disputes, and even when a common law solution was available, the procedures of the mercantile courts almost invariably facilitated a more rapid decision and were consequently more popular. Nevertheless, from the seventeenth century, many rules of the Law Merchant were incorporated into the common law which increasingly came to consider commercial matters. Perhaps the most important mercantile custom to be recognized was that of the negotiability of a bill of exchange: a principle which brought the sale of goods within the common law.

MERCHANTS' MARKS In the broadly illiterate society of medieval England, the ownership of trade goods was ascertained by reference to identification marks which were stamped on bales, casks and other containers or on the goods themselves. For safety reasons, a consignment of items for dispatch by sea was often dispersed among a number of vessels. In such circumstances it was essential that the cargo should be properly marked to avoid confusion, and within the Hanseatic League merchants' marks on trade items were regarded as proof of legal ownership.

The nature of a merchant's mark was threefold: it had to be recognizable, unambiguous and capable of being drawn, painted or scratched quickly. The majority of marks were built on the foundation of a single vertical 'stem': some combined a merchant's initials in an elementary form of cypher, while others were runic in appearance.

Merchants' marks came to be used by non-armigerous men in much the same way as coats of arms were used by gentlemen. Members of the same family could sometimes be distinguished one from another by the adoption of small but distinctive variations in the family merchant mark, just as the cadet branches of armigerous families may be identified by the cadency marks added to their arms. With increasing prosperity, merchants proudly

displayed their marks in the fabric and artefacts of their homes and in the window glass, tombs and memorials of the churches which benefited from their patronage. They were often displayed within a shield for this purpose; indeed, there are several examples of non-armigerous merchants who, having married heraldic heiresses, impaled their merchant marks with their wives' arms. The merchants who attained armigerous status invariably continued to use their familiar and respected merchant marks alongside their newly-acquired (and less familiar) arms. On the magnificent Canynge tomb at St Mary's Redcliffe, Bristol, for example, the family arms are flanked on each side by their merchant marks. Although there were related classes of marks, indicating places of origin and craftsmanship (such marks were made on furniture and pottery, for example) there is as yet no evidence to suggest that the marks of merchants from the same guild, town or trade contained any common elements or were subject to any form of systematic registration or control, unlike those used by goldsmiths, masons and armourers.

See also MASONS' MARKS

MERCHET *also* **MARCHET** A payment from a tenant on the occasion of the marriage of his son or daughter.

MERCIA *see* KINGDOMS (ANCIENT)

MERE From the Old English *mære*, meaning 'boundary land'. A strip of land, a bank or ditch between furlongs or fields. A *merestake* or *merestone* is a boundary marker; in this context, it is also spelt *meer* and *mear*. Some *mere* place-names have this derivation, such as Merridge in Somerset, meaning 'boundary ridge', but *see also* -MERE.

-MERE A common place-name element from the Old English *mere*, meaning 'lake' or 'pool'. Many locations with -mere and -more names are of considerable antiquity and may still possess a pond, as at Ashmore (Old English *æscmere*, meaning 'pool where ash trees grew'), an isolated village high on the chalk hills of Cranborne Chase in Dorset.
See also -MORE

MERE (*or* **MEARE**) **LANE** Wide grass strips which once served to divide the open fields of adjacent estates or parishes (from the Old English *mære*, meaning 'a boundary'). Unlike drifts (which are similar in appearance), mere lanes tend to follow parish BOUNDARIES, though modern civil and ecclesiastical parishes do not necessarily conform with their medieval predecessors.
See also DRIFT *and* GREEN LANES

MERLON (*also* **COP**) The solid part of a battlement between two crenels.

MESNALTY An estate held directly of the Crown by a mesne lord.

MESOLITHIC *see* STONE AGE

MESSUAGE (*also* **MESE**) A dwelling and the land surrounding it.

METAL DETECTORS *see* TREASURE TROVE

METALS (i) In ARMORY, the TINCTURES *Or* (gold) and *Argent* (silver), often represented by yellow and white.
(ii) *For* bronze, copper, gold, iron, lead, silver *and* tin *see* MINERALS

METHODIST A member of a protestant denomination which originated in an eighteenth-century evangelistic movement inspired by John Wesley (1703–91) and Charles Wesley (1707–88) who, in 1738, began a ministry which propounded individual communion with God without the need for the intervention of a priest. Although within the Church of England, the movement was denied the use of Anglican churches and was forced to hold meetings out of doors. The Methodist Society (known as the 'Holy Club') was established in 1740

and, later, a governing body, the Methodist Conference.

The movement formally separated from the Church of England in 1791, but there were several secessions. The first of these was the Methodist New Connexion which broke away in 1797 and joined with the United Methodist Free Churches in 1907 to form the United Methodist Church. The Independent Methodists were formed in 1805 and the Primitive Methodists in 1808. The Bible Christians (*Bryanites*) seceded in 1815 and joined the United Methodist Church in 1907. It was not until 1932 that most of the methodist groups were united, together with the original or 'Wesleyan' Methodist Church, to form the Methodist Church in Great Britain.

The supreme authority of the Methodist Church is the Conference which comprises equal numbers of ministers and laymen. Peculiar to Methodism is the class-meeting by which 'All members shall have their names entered on a Class Book, shall be placed under the pastoral care of a Class Leader, and shall receive a Quarterly Ticket of Membership.' At the weekly class-meeting for 'fellowship in Christian experience' enquiry is made into the conduct and spiritual progress of individual members. Early Methodist registers are housed at the Public Record Office, records are kept at the Methodist Archives and Research Centre, and the Methodist Missionary Society has deposited its archives with the School of Oriental and African Studies at the University of London. Each Methodist area also has its own archivist, details of whom may be obtained from the Connexional Archivist (*see* APPENDIX I).

In Wales, a Calvinistic form of Methodism was established by Howell Harris (1714–73) and others, who formed their first Association in 1743. Although they wished to remain within the Church of England, they were obliged to seek the protection of the *Toleration Act* and to register their meeting houses as DISSENTING CHAPELS.
See also COUNTESS OF HUNTINGDON'S CONNEXION

MEZZANINE In a building an additional storey between two others, usually entered from a half-landing.

MICHAELMAS (i) A quarter day: the Feast of St Michael and All Angels on 29 September (*see* QUARTER DAYS AND RENT DAYS *and* SAINTS' DAYS AND FEAST-DAYS).
(ii) The academic and law term beginning near Michaelmas. *See also* HILARY *and* TRINITY

MIDDEN *see* FARMSTEADS

MIDDLE AGES, THE For the purposes of this book, the medieval period is taken to begin with Duke William of Normandy's victory at Senlac Hill in 1066 and to end with the Dissolution of the Greater Monasteries in 1539. But 'Unlike dates, historical periods are not facts. They are retrospective conceptions that we form about past events, useful to focus discussion, but very often leading historical thought astray.' (G.M. Trevelyan). Traditionally, the Norman Conquest of 1066 is taken to be the 'beginning' of the Middle Ages in England and the defeat of Richard III at Bosworth in 1485 to be the 'end'. But H.R. Loyn, editor of *The Middle Ages: A Concise Encyclopaedia* (1989), considers the eleven centuries from *c.* 400 to *c.* 1500, while the *Oxford Reference Dictionary* defines the Middle Ages as being 'the period in Europe after the Dark Ages (*c.* 1000–1400) or in a wider sense *c.* 600–1500.' Robert Fossier, in his *Illustrated History of the Middle Ages* (1986), considers medievalism in a European context and defines the period as beginning in 1250 and lasting until 1520.

It is undoubtedly true that medieval society (or that of any historical 'period') may only be studied fruitfully if it is considered not as a static order, but as a complexity of continuous and evolving processes and relationships without any definable beginning or end. Nevertheless, our common perception of medievalism would lead many to agree with Fossier when he suggests: 'We . . . should tread carefully; Henry V was medieval, Henry VIII was not: these are our limits.' Our response to the term is almost invariably intuitive rather than intellectual. Providing we acknowledge the limitations of our perception, no harm will be done.
For another view, see LIVERY AND MAINTENANCE

MIDDLESEX *see* KINGDOMS (ANCIENT)

MIDSTRAYS *see* BARNS

MILECASTLE *see* ROMAN FORTS AND CAMPS

MILESTONES (*also* **MILEPOSTS**) Nearly 100 Roman milestones have now been located in Britain, though very few remain *in situ*, the majority having been re-located to accommodate road improvements or removed to museums. Some informed travellers of distances to nearby towns but most simply marked off the miles and were inscribed only with the name of the ruling emperor. Extraordinary as it may seem, no further milestones were erected until 1728 when a series, each bearing the arms of Trinity Hall, was provided by the college on the A10 road near Cambridge. In 1697 direction posts or stones at 'cross highways' were required by law (*see* SIGNPOSTS) but it was not until the Turnpike Acts of 1744 and 1766 and the General Turnpike Act of 1773 that statutory provision was made for the erection of mileposts along the turnpike roads (*see* TURNPIKES). Many of these are still in place, some of them in stone, some cast in iron and others engraved in the walls of buildings. Each Turnpike Trust vied with the next in the provision of attractive and distinctive markers. Local craftsmen were often commissioned for this purpose and their use of vernacular names such as Shaston for Shaftesbury, Dorset, cannot have been appreciated by many long-distance travellers. Some bear instructions, such as 'Take-off', inscribed on a stone near Callington in Cornwall. This marked the spot, at the summit of an incline, where any additional horses were to be unharnessed and returned to the toll-house at the foot of the hill from where they had been hired.

MILITARY ROADS The ROMAN ROADS were, of course, constructed principally to facilitate the rapid and efficient deployment of large numbers of men and equipment throughout the province as well as to encourage commerce and trade (*see also* ROMAN FORTS AND CAMPS). These old roads continued to be used for military purposes in the Saxon and medieval periods and often influenced the site of a battle. In 1066 Harold moved south towards Hastings by the Roman road from London to Rochester and Maidstone, while roads from Castleford and York, which intersected at Tadcaster, brought together the Yorkist and Lancastrian armies at Towton in 1461. In 1485 the decisive battle of Bosworth was fought on a Roman road out of Leicester where it crossed the angle of the Fosse Way and Watling Street. The Anglo-Saxon HEREPAETHS were trackways used for military and administrative purposes as well as by ordinary travellers.

In Scotland, following the uprisings of 1715 and 1719, a network of military roads was constructed by the British authorities in an attempt to subjugate the Highland clans. Begun in 1725, road-building continued intermittently into the 1740s under the direction of General George Wade who had been appointed Commander-in-Chief of the British forces in the Highlands in 1724. At his instigation, military strongholds at Fort Augustus and Fort George were built and from these, together with Fort William and the new roads, Wade effectively controlled the Highlands. Several of Wade's roads have been adapted for modern use, though elsewhere impressive lengths have long been abandoned, perhaps the finest (and certainly the most spectacular) being that which ran from Laggan Bridge to Fort Augustus across the Corrieyairack Pass (*see also* SCOTTISH HIGHLAND FORTS).

During the late eighteenth and nineteenth centuries, an almost paranoiac fear of invasion across the Channel resulted in the construction of several military roads along the south coast, especially during the 1860s when fears that Napoleon III would attack England were at their height. Among these, the military road from St Catherine's Point to Freshwater Bay on the Isle of Wight is a notable example.

MILITIA A military force, usually raised from the civil population to supplement regular troops in an emergency.

The *Fyrd* of the Anglo-Saxon period was a force comprising thegns who owed *fyrd-bote* or military service as one of their obligations under the TRINODA NECESSITAS. King Alfred divided the Fyrd so that one half was resting while the other was on duty. From 1070, a system (now known as *Knight Service*) was introduced whereby the king's tenants-in-chief agreed to provide a number of knights equipped and available for service for a specified period. In peacetime, this was usually an annual commitment of forty days. By 1100, tenants were able to commute their military service by payment of 'shield-money' (*scutage*) which was fixed at 20s per knight's fee and was recouped by the tenant-in-chief from his tenants. (Scutage was last levied in 1327.) In 1181 Henry II issued an *Assize of Arms* which determined the weapons and equipment required of each knight, freeman and burgess. Juries from each town or hundred were charged with assessing the degree of military obligation. Each possessor of a knight's fee and each free layman owning effects or receiving rents in excess of 16 marks was required to provide a coat of mail, a helmet, shield and lance. Likewise, a free layman whose property did not exceed 10 marks was obliged to provide a mail jacket (*haubergeon*), an iron skull-cap (*chapelet*) and a lance. Justices were sent out to enforce the assize, and sheriffs were responsible for raising the levy.

By the thirteenth century, the unfree peasantry was also liable for military service, an obligation which was confirmed in 1285 and not repealed until 1558. *Commissions of Array* were appointed by the Crown to compile *Muster Rolls* which listed, by counties, all those who were available for military service. In the Tudor period a LORD LIEUTENANT was nominally responsible for the *posse comitatus*, or county militia, though in practice it was usually the Deputy Lieutenant who ensured that parish constables raised the required levies. All able-bodied men between sixteen and sixty were liable for service, and formal inspections (*general musters*) were held in each shire at least once every three years. The Tudor militia was divided into ten classes, the equipment for each being prescribed by law: some were required to keep only a longbow, helmet and JACK while, at the other extreme, others had to provide 16 horses, 80 suits of light armour, 30 longbows and 40 pikes. It was at this time that *Trained Bands* were established, forces who were liable for specialist military training and acquired a justifiable reputation for public indiscipline and lawlessness.

Before 1660, there was no standing army and the county militias represented the principal means of defending the kingdom. But the system was essentially feudal, both in the way in which troops were levied and in the way the militias were financed. Its deficiencies became even more apparent during the Civil War of the 1640s when many militia troops refused to serve beyond their county borders. Volunteer companies (the first of which was formed in 1537 as the Guild of St George) were far more flexible and were, by definition, disciplined mercenaries.

Following the Restoration, the Militia Act of 1672 established a system of military service based not on a feudal obligation, but on a statutory one. Fears of a French invasion during the 1750s resulted in the Militia Act of 1757 and with it the effective creation of a territorial army which, at that time, numbered some 32,000 men. This was followed, in 1758 and 1759, by legislation permitting the raising of volunteer companies. These tended to comprise men of more independent means than those who served in the compulsory militia. They also preferred to train separately and to maintain their own headquarters, and an Act of 1782 formalized this distinction. But the volunteer companies were required only during wartime or when the peace was threatened. They were therefore disbanded in 1783, reformed in the 1790s and disbanded again after the Peace of Amiens in 1802, only to be reformed in the following year after which their popularity declined until the late 1850s when relations with France were once more becoming strained. In 1807, the Local Militia Act raised battalions of Local Militia within each county but, unlike the county militias, they were not required to serve beyond their own or adjacent counties and they were disbanded at the conclusion of the Napoleonic Wars in 1816. Annual militia returns were submitted to QUARTER SESSIONS by the Lords Lieutenant.

See also INFANTRY VOLUNTEERS *and* LAW AND ORDER

For the Military History Society *and the* Society for Army Historical Research *see* APPENDIX I

MILLING SOKE *see* WATER-MILLS

MILLPOND Many millponds, or their silted remains, are of considerable antiquity and may be of medieval or even Roman origin. But most date from the eighteenth century, when a reliable and easily regulated head of water was an essential requirement of industry. Not only did the availability of water-power determine the location of numerous small mills and workshops, it also prescribed those areas of Britain which were to lead the way in the early decades of the Industrial Revolution. Millponds were constructed by damming a stream, thereby creating a roughly triangular pond from which water was released through hatches and conducted to the mill-wheel by means of leats. As the mills proliferated, so the systems of sluices and leats became more complex. In many instances, pools ran dry and supplementary leats had to be provided to carry water from hill-side reservoirs on spring-lines. By 1786 industrialists were becoming 'steam-mill mad', and at the end of the eighteenth century many millponds were providing water not for motive power, but to service the steam engines of the Industrial Revolution.

MILLS *For* breastshot mill, click mill, fulling mill, horizontal mill, overshot mill, tidemill *and* undershot mill *see* WATER-MILLS

For post mill, smock mill, tower mill *and* windpump (marsh mill) *see* WINDMILLS

MILLTOUN *see* CLACHAN

MINERALS The earliest metal ore mine as yet identified in Britain is a copper mine on the Great Orme peninsula near Llandudno in Conwy. Radio-carbon testing indicates that the mine was in production by 1700 BC and was probably in continuous use for more than two centuries. It contains more than 275 metres (300 yards) of galleries, some of them more than 46 metres

(50 yards) below the original ground level. Stone hammers, chisels and gouges have been discovered and it is likely that fire was used to fracture the rock. After extraction, the copper ore was smelted into copper which was then mixed with Cornish tin to produce bronze. It has been estimated that the copper mined at Great Orme was sufficient to produce up to 100 bronze axes in a single year. Slave labour may have been used, or the mine may have been worked seasonally by a group of families.

Until recently, most archaeologists were agreed that bronze-making technology was introduced into Britain from the continent during the BRONZE AGE. It has also been suggested that there was little exploitation of Britain's not inconsiderable mineral resources prior to the Roman occupation and that ores were generally imported at that time. But many now believe that bronze-making techniques were developed independently, probably in the Wicklow Mountains of Ireland around 2100 BC, and that pre-bronze copper smelting was introduced into the British Isles around 2500 BC, possibly from the Iberian peninsula.

During the Roman occupation mineral deposits were second only to agriculture as a source of wealth; indeed, they probably prompted the Claudian invasion and the creation of a Roman Province of Britain in AD 43. Within a decade, the Romans had begun to exploit the silver-bearing lead of the Mendips in Somerset; they mined for gold in West Wales; for iron in the Weald of Kent and the Forest of Dean in Gloucestershire; and, in the third century, they revived the Cornish tin mines.

It was a general principal of Roman provincial government that mines and quarries were the property of the state (though there were some exceptions), and these were administered on the state's behalf by procurators, the military or (rarely in Britain) lessees (*conductores*). At many mines, the workforce (usually slaves, condemned criminals, prisoners and forced labour) appear to have been subjected to intolerable conditions and there is evidence to suggest that at some mines they may even have been fettered in underground caves where they both worked and slept. Conditions varied, however: the Mendip lead miners of Charterhouse seem to have lived in a comparatively civilized settlement, and the gold miners of Dolaucothy in Carmarthenshire may even have been provided with a pit-head bathhouse. The Romans were extremely efficient engineers: their workings were well designed, drained and ventilated and under their control the mineral output of the British Isles increased significantly. Coal was much valued by the

Romans both for smelting and for domestic heating and was mined extensively, usually at outcrops but also by shafts and galleries, in all the coalfields of England, South Wales and southern Scotland. The widespread use of coal, even in peasant villages, suggests that it was readily available and that the problems of transportation (often over considerable distances) were by no means insurmountable.

The principal copper-mining areas were in Shropshire, North Wales and Anglesey. The mines at Great Orme (*see above*) continued in use and may have been leased to private companies, and at Llanymynech in Shropshire excavations and debris have provided evidence of second- and fourth-century occupation. The ore was smelted in hut villages: ordinary native settlements distinguished only by their singularly un-Celtic straight rows of dwellings and small, coal-fired furnaces. Once firing and smelting was completed and the slag removed, a circular *bun-ingot* of copper remained at the base of each furnace.

Lead, in particular, was required in enormous quantities both for water-pipes and for silver. As with most ores, the lead was separated from waste rock by crushing and washing: the heavier lead sinking to the bottom. Silver was extracted by heating the lead in a strong current of air on a bed of bone-ash, which absorbed the lead leaving pellets of pure silver. The saturated bone-ash (*cupel*) was then re-smelted to recover the lead which was cast into pigs marked *ex arg[entariis]* to indicate that they had been processed in the silver-works. The pigs were also marked with an imperial inscription, to show that they were state property, and often with that of the military authority responsible for the mine and silver-works. The principal lead-workings were in Somerset and Derbyshire, though there were also mines in the Shropshire, Flintshire, Yorkshire and Northumberland hills. Many pigs from the Mendips in Somerset were exported by way of Southampton to Gaul.

There appears to have been an attempt to revive the tin mines of the Cornish STANNARIES during the late first and early second centuries. But Roman interest was not maintained and it seems that tin mining was generally left in native hands until the mid-third century when the provincial authorities, fearing the exhaustion of its mineral deposits, re-directed its attentions to the extraction of tin and to Cornwall in particular. This resulted in a substantial increase both in output and in the number of tin and PEWTER vessels in domestic use throughout Britain during the fourth century. Bronze working was widely diffused, though there may have been centres of manufacturing excellence, notably in the north and west where there is archaeological evidence of the concentrated and large-scale production of high quality bronze artefacts. Native and Roman silversmiths and goldsmiths prospered during the occupation and a great deal of finely wrought native jewellery has come down to us from that time.

The Weald of Kent was a significant centre of IRON AGE activity before the Roman conquest and was further developed during the first decades of occupation. The Forest of Dean in Gloucestershire was also extensively mined for iron ore from the first century, and these two areas remained the chief sources of iron, though there was no significant area of Roman Britain in which iron ore of some kind was not available. In Britain, the ore was usually smelted in a primitive *bowl-furnace*: a clay-lined hole in the ground to which the blast was introduced over the edge of the bowl. The purpose of smelting was not to bring the ore to melting point, and therefore to liquefy the metal, but to produce *blooms* of impure iron which were then purified by heating and hammering (*see* BLOOMERY). The Romans had not invented the water-powered trip-hammer, and the size of blooms was therefore restricted by the weight of a hand-held hammer. Consequently, iron could be produced only in small quantities and blooms had to be re-heated and welded together when larger items were required. Ironwork of excellent quality was already being produced by the Celts, particularly that of the *La Tène* period, and it seems unlikely that the Romans introduced any new technical processes to Britain, though the industry expanded rapidly under their control. Iron goods were manufactured throughout the province: every town had its blacksmith, every regiment its smithy and every villa its forge.

In the Middle Ages the miner enjoyed rights and privileges derived from ancient usage and he was, therefore, a freeman, unlike the feudal peasant. Wage-labour was common and most miners were probably poor; but, except in some of the Crown mines, where a system of impressment was used, miners generally enjoyed free tenure of their small mining properties and in some areas (such as the south-west), they were exempt from tallages, tolls and subsidies. In the Cornish Stannaries of the fourteenth century, more than 1,000 men were entitled to the rank of tinner – freemen with extensive rights of prospecting, with their own courts and in most civil matters answerable only to the warden. The freeminers of the Forest of Dean in Gloucestershire continue to enjoy certain rights of ancient usage to this day.

Tin, lead and coal were the principal commodities mined in late medieval England and investment in mining supplemented the incomes of men of all classes. When control of the Stannaries was vested in the Duchy of Cornwall in 1338, the annual output of tin had reached 700 tons and Crown revenues exceeded £2,000. Despite the debilitating effects of the Black Death, one Abraham the tinner was said to have employed 300 in 1357. Lead was mined chiefly for its silver, principally in the neighbourhood of Bere Alston in Devon and in the Mendips in Somerset, where the mines were leased to the Bishop of Bath and Wells. By 1340 the Devonshire mines were in decline, and by the end of the century it was the mines of Derbyshire, Nottinghamshire and Yorkshire that were contracted to provide lead for the repair of the Great Hall at Westminster. The Forest of Dean continued to be the most important iron-producing area, though London was again turning to the Weald of Kent for its supplies. Most of the English coalfields were already being worked to some extent, though open-cast extraction continued until the mid-fourteenth century when the first vertical shafts were sunk. Coal (*secole* because it was usually transported by sea) was used mainly for smelting and working metals, but with the increase in chimney flues towards the end of the fourteenth century it was beginning to be used for domestic purposes also.

The late Tudor period was a time of expansion in lead, copper and tin mining. The Mendips continued to yield large quantities of lead for export through the nearby port of Bristol, innumerable small tin mines flourished in Cornwall and Devon and untapped supplies of copper in the remoter parts of the north-west attracted miners from Germany. In particular, English iron was acknowledged to be of the finest quality. In 1543 an iron cannon was cast in Buxted in Surrey. This was the first casting in Britain and was effectively the first tentative step towards the Industrial Revolution. It was significant because it represented an entirely new way of making iron. Instead of the ancient, low-temperature method of producing blooms which had to be worked into wrought iron, the high temperatures of the new 'blast' furnace actually melted the iron, thereby enabling it to be cast as finished objects. If a more flexible iron was required, the cast iron was run into 'pigs' which were re-heated in a hearth (*finery*) to remove most of the carbon thereby converting it to wrought iron. The development of the blast furnace meant that considerable quantities of iron could be produced as a continuous process: iron ore and charcoal were added at the top and the molten iron tapped from the bottom.

The need for a constant supply of timber for charcoal and the availability of fast-flowing water to provide motive power inevitably determined the location of iron works. There were, of course, substantial supplies of coal available, but at this time coal produced iron that was 'red-short' and brittle, and of little use to a rapidly expanding market for iron goods. In 1709 Abraham Darby (1678–1717) manufactured the first high-grade iron in a coke-fuel furnace at Coalbrookdale in Shropshire. Darby was indeed fortunate in his location. Not only did coal and iron outcrop together in Coalbrookdale, they were also of the right type for making cast iron and to provide coke, which was Darby's method for removing the gases in coal which produced 'red-short'. Limestone, which was required as 'flux', was also available and the navigable river Severn provided both power and access to markets. In 1779 Darby's grandson erected the first iron bridge (at Ironbridge in Shropshire) which, at that time, was also the largest iron structure in the world. Although Darby's company prospered, his methods were not an immediate success, probably because his product did not convert into good quality wrought iron, the greater tensile strength of which made it particularly suitable for the moving parts of machinery. In 1784 Henry Cort adapted the reverberatory furnace (in which heat reverberates from the roof of the furnace onto the metal) so that pig iron could be melted and the excess carbon burned out to convert the cast iron to wrought iron. In this type of furnace (which had previously been used for non-ferrous metals), fuel and metal are held in separate containers and coal could therefore be substituted for the more expensive charcoal without contaminating the iron. The *pudding process*, as it was called, facilitated the production of large quantities of wrought iron, the basic engineering material of the INDUSTRIAL REVOLUTION. *See also* BRASS *and* STEEL.

The market for lead continued to expand and the Mendip mines predominated until the end of the seventeenth century when other centres developed in the north Pennines, Durham, Northumberland and the Peak district of Derbyshire. But compared with the large copper and tin mines, lead-mining operations in the mid-eighteenth century were often small in scale, though the accumulated output of a great number of such mines exceeded that of copper and tin. As late as 1872, there were in Derbyshire 200 separate mines, most of which were producing less than 5 tons of ore a year. Cornish copper mines dominated production throughout the eighteenth and early nineteenth centuries, and from the mid-nineteenth century the Devon Great Consols mine (close to the Cornish border) was for a time the most important copper mine in the world. Indeed, this was a time of massive expansion in the mines of the West Country: in 1838 no fewer than 27,208 workers (including women and children) were employed in 160 Cornish mines, and by 1851 the total labour force numbered 30,284 males and 5,922 females. (Unlike their sisters in the coalfields, Cornish women were not required to work below ground.) The mining industry was of considerable strategic importance for the Industrial Revolution but it could not have expanded as it did without technological and engineering innovation: the introduction of James Watt's steam-ngine which made possible the pumping of deep levels, for example. But the importation of cheaper, more accessible ores presaged the demise of British metal mining in the late nineteenth century and large numbers of West Country miners emigrated, taking with them the accumulated skills and knowledge of many generations.

For the National Association of Mining History Organizations *see* APPENDIX I

MINIATURIST *see* MANUSCRIPT ILLUMINATION

MINSTER Anglo-Saxon minsters were religious communities, usually comprising a priest and a group of monastic or secular assistants (collectively known as a *familia*), which served as centres of conversion and administration from the seventh century prior to the development of a system of ecclesiastical parishes. (In Wales, *clasau* performed a similar function, though these were usually staffed by an abbot and hereditary canons.)

A minster settlement usually consisted of a church and thatched outbuildings surrounded by a wooden palisade or wall of turf and stone. They were almost invariably established on Saxon royal estates and served vast territories, their missionaries protected by royal or thegnal patronage in recognition of the administrative and cultural services provided by the minster staff (*see* MULTIPLE ESTATES).

Gradually, the peripatetic clergy of the minsters were replaced by priests attached to proprietorial CHAPELS or churches subordinate to the minsters themselves, and by the late Saxon period many minsters had either decayed or been incorporated into the parochial system.

Evidence of former minsters remains, not only in well-known churches such as York Minster and Wimborne Minster in Dorset, but also in place-name elements such as the *eccles-* of Ecclesfield in West Yorkshire and Eccleston in Cheshire, derived from the Latin *ecclesia*, or 'church' (Welsh: *eglwys*). Kidderminster, Worcestershire, was 'Cydda's minster' and at Sturminster Newton in Dorset was 'the minster by the river Stour'. Many others are as yet unidentified, though it is reasonable to assume that as stone was used only in the more important Saxon churches, those that have survived as fragments of later buildings are likely to have been of minster status. In other cases, even when no Saxon work remains, the historical relationship of a group of churches may indicate that one was traditionally superior to the others and this may well have been a Saxon minster. Some historians use the term 'minster' in its vernacular sense when describing 'family monasteries', small communities established by noblemen on their estates, governed by relatives and administered by dependants.

See also CHURCHES, PARISH *and* TOWNS

MINSTRELS The minstrels of medieval and Tudor society provided a service equal in importance to that which is available through television today: music, drama and entertainment; the dissemination of news and information; political comment; popular songs and ballads – the 'soap operas' of medieval England, lengthy tales of familiar personalities (such as the ubiquitous Robin Hood) on to which were grafted fresh sub-plots and characters as they passed from one generation to the next. The minstrels made up a diverse profession. Many were permanent members of royal or magnatial households, established men of substance with rich patrons and the status of esquire, while others were independent, itinerant professionals or casual entertainers who counted minstrelsy as an occasional service among many. Some were accomplished musicians, singers and players of the harp, vielle or psaltery; others were acrobats, jugglers or magicians; actors, storytellers (*fabulators*) and declaimers of momentous events and stirring deeds: 'Sitteth alle stille ant herketh to me . . .'. In an ordnance of 1315 it was maintained that 'indolent persons, pretending minstrelsy' were seeking payment and hospitality, and rules were set out for the proper conduct of the profession. Nevertheless, in 1469 Edward IV incorporated the royal minstrels as a guild, declaring that

> no minstrel of our kingdom . . . shall in any way exercise this art or occupation within our kingdom henceforth unless he be a member of the guild . . . [for] rough peasants and craftsmen of various mysteries . . . have

pretended to be our own minstrels . . . and although they are not intelligent or expert in that art or occupation, and are occupied in various activities on week-days . . . on feast-days they travel from place to place, and take all the profits on which our aforesaid minstrels . . . ought to live.

(A. Myers, *English Historical Documents*, 1969)

But the legislation proved ineffectual and many a 'rough peasant', who had built up a repertoire and could attract an audience, continued to supplement his meagre income by entertaining the local populace on feast-days.

Many minstrels belonged to companies who toured the great magnatial and monastic households. The bursar's account for Fountain's Abbey, Yorkshire, in the 1450s records payments to (among others) the minstrels of Beverley (16*d*), the players of the Earl of Westmorland (2*d*) and the minstrels of Lord Arundel (16*d*) as well as to a story-teller 'whose name was unknown' (6*d*), the Boy Bishop of

Elizabethan minstrels were classed as vagabonds unless they obtained a licence to travel from place to place.

Ripon (3*s*) and a fool called Solomon ('who came again') (4*d*).

During the reign of Elizabeth I (1558–1603), the already stringent laws against vagabonds were extended to include itinerant musicians who, unless vouched for by noblemen by whom they were regularly employed, were ostracized by the musical establishment and could be severely punished.

One of the earliest bodies of musicians not directly subsidized by royal or magnatial patronage were the town or city *waits*, a word of Nordic derivation meaning 'watcher' or 'guard'. These were members of the watch and ward (*see* LAW AND ORDER) who formed themselves into bands of instrumentalists both to entertain the local populace and to perform at civic functions. Proud of their municipal or guild livery, these groups claimed a musical monopoly in their neighbourhood and jealously urged the authorities to outlaw wandering buskers and entertainers. In sixteenth-century York, for example, a strict apprenticeship was required under the jurisdiction of the fellowship of musicians and a 'searcher of the waits' appointed to enforce their monopoly. In time, the terms 'minstrel' and 'musician' were used to differentiate between vagabond entertainers and those entitled to perform music exclusively with a royal, magnatial or civic warrant.

See also GALLERY *and* SCREENS PASSAGE

MINT MARK *see* COINAGE

MINUSCULE In handwriting, a small letter as opposed to a capital or UNCIAL. Also various types of small CURSIVE script.
See also MAJUSCULE

MISERICORDE A thrusting dagger, especially for the *coup de grace*.

MISERICORDS A misericord is a hinged wooden seat which, when tipped up, presents a ledge for the user to rest on when in a standing position. Usually found in the chancel stalls of cathedrals and former monastic and collegiate churches and in chantry chapels, most date from the mid-thirteenth century to the late fifteenth. Their function was to provide support and relief for clergy and choir who were able to rest without sitting as they stood through interminable daily offices (*miserere* = 'have pity'). Where misericords have survived, every stall seems originally to have been provided with one, suggesting that it was not only the elderly and infirm who had need of them.

Being the most sacred part of the pre-Reformation church, the CHANCEL was lavishly decorated and yet would have been seen by only the privileged few. Among the most enigmatic decorative imagery was that of the carved misericord which, by the mid-fifteenth century, had acquired a tradition of its own. Many designs are unique but others, or variations of them, were widely used by carvers who appear to have worked from design books. These would be submitted to the patron or vestry who would then select those designs which were considered appropriate to a particular church, at the same time commissioning others which were entirely new. Each collection therefore has its own unique flavour and reflects the tastes of a period as well as local influences and contemporary political allegiances. Fifteenth-century Ludlow in Shropshire, for example, was thrust into the forefront of national politics, being one of the principal strongholds of Richard, Duke of York. In Ludlow church, Yorkist badges are much in evidence both in the misericords and in the splendid bosses of the chancel roof immediately above the stalls. Heraldic symbolism was ideally suited to such carvings, as were images culled from the medieval bestiaries and from folklore and legend, moral allegories and cautionary tales. There is evidence to suggest that in some instances both stalls and misericords may once have been painted and gilded.

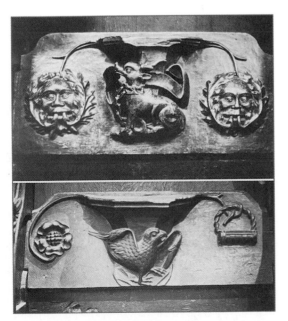

Misericords in stalls from Fotheringhay church, now at Tansor, Northamptonshire.

Misericords have often been removed from their original stalls and rearranged during restoration. In some instances, they have been moved elsewhere, as at Tansor in Northamptonshire, for example, where the mid-fifteenth-century misericords originated in the collegiate chancel at nearby Fotheringhay. There can be little doubt that following the Reformation many sets of monastic stalls provided fuel to melt the roofing lead salvaged for Henry VIII's war-effort, though fortunately others were retrieved for use in parish churches.

MISSAL A liturgical book containing the words and ceremonial directions for the celebration of the Mass and, from the tenth century, combining in one book the devotions which had previously appeared in several. Their development was encouraged by the medieval practice of saying private masses and many missals are exquisitely illuminated.

MISTLETOE With its Druidical associations (mostly dating from the eighteenth century!) mistletoe is still revered for its magical qualities and its powers of inducing fertility. In the counties of the lower Severn, where mistletoe is more common than elsewhere, decorated boughs were taken into the house at Christmas-time where they remained for the ensuing year to ward off evil spirits. Norse mythology tells us that mistletoe provided a refuge for woodland spirits until other trees regained their leaves and that it was so sacred that it could only be cut by a priest using a golden sickle.

MITRE ARCH *see* ARCH

MIZMAZE *see* MAZES

MOAT-, MOD-, MOT- *and* **MUD-** Place-name elements which may indicate the meeting-place of a former HUNDRED COURT or MOOT, e.g. Mottistone in the Isle of Wight, from the Old English *mō tera stān*, meaning 'the stone of the speakers'. Such elements may not be immediately apparent, as in Mobberley in Cheshire, meaning 'glade' (*lēah*) with an 'assembly mound' (*gemōtbeorg*).

MOATS Most medieval CASTLES were constructed within a moat or ditch, though not all moats were filled with water. The moat's function was clearly a defensive one, but water-filled moats also provided a means of waste disposal for castle refuse and sewage and (ironically) could be stocked with fish. Moated castles were entered by a series of hornworks, BARBICANS and DRAWBRIDGES, the most formidable being those of Caerphilly Castle in South Wales. Built between 1268 and 1326, Caerphilly was provided with seemingly impregnable concentric stone and water defences radiating, in a succession of increasingly larger circles, from a central inner ward. The principal (eastern) line of outer defences consists of a moat spanned by two drawbridges and backed by a huge curtain wall (*bastion*) and gatehouse. Within this, and surrounding the other three sides of the fortress, nearly 30 acres of lakes and moats discouraged the use of contemporary siege instruments, which could not be brought within range of the walls, and made tunnelling beneath the lakes to undermine the walls impossible.

But not all moats were built on such a grand scale: at least 5,000 moated homesteads were constructed in England and lowland Wales between *c.* 1150 and *c.* 1350, and are a particular feature of East Anglia, Essex and the South and East Midlands. Some were simply platforms on which wooden halls and outbuildings were erected, an encircling moat and palisade providing a comparatively inexpensive means of protection from man and beast. Others were walled enclosures, containing a substantial stone-built dwelling and ancillary buildings, entered by means of a bridge (or bridges) and often a GATEHOUSE. There can be little doubt that in the more remote, unruly areas of the kingdom these moats were intended primarily to provide security for the household, but the fact that in many instances the bridge was immobile and the moat extended round only three sides of the enclosure confirms that the possession of a semi-fortified house and moat (even a token one) was also a matter of status at a time when rights and obligations were determined by class.

There are many instances, notably from the fourteenth century, of former castles being re-modelled to provide more convenient residential accommodation. But while drawbridges were often replaced by permanent structures of brick and stone, and towers and curtain walls demolished or reduced, gatehouses and moats were nearly always retained to provide a degree of security. So too with many new buildings of the fifteenth century: Oxburgh Hall in Suffolk, for example, was provided in the 1480s with a moat and substantial gatehouse at a time of agricultural unrest and scavenging by bands of unemployed soldiers. From the fifteenth century, many moated homesteads were abandoned in favour of more extensive and salubrious sites, leaving their wooden buildings to rot and disappear without trace. Similarly, a number of medieval castles and fortified homesteads were demolished and new Tudor buildings constructed within their moated enclosures. Many moats were incorporated into the pleasure gardens of Elizabethan and Jacobean country houses where they added a hint of romantic antiquity both to the silvan setting and to the social aspirations of the new gentility.

MODEL FARMS *see* FARMSTEADS

MODEL VILLAGES *see* DESERTED VILLAGES *and* TOWNS

MODUS A private arrangement agreed between a vicar and a parishioner for the commutation of tithes paid in kind to a cash payment.

MOEL In the Welsh, *moel* means 'bare' or 'bald' and is often found in the names of hills and mountains which appear so, for example, Moel Lefn, meaning 'smooth hill', and Moel Hebog, the precipitous 'hill of the hawks' above Beddgelert in Gwynedd. Of an even earlier but common derivation are the Malverns, the 'bald hills' which divide Here-fordshire and Worcestershire.

MOIETY Generally, a half-portion of an estate.

MONACHORUM Latinized place-name element meaning 'of the monks', indicative that a manor was once possessed by a monastic foundation (*see* LATIN *and* MONASTIC PLACE-NAMES).

MONASTERIES For the MONASTIC ORDERS *see* individual entries.

Monasticism
Monks vowed to follow an ascetic, disciplined life devoted to prayer and humility. They were not required to become priests and only the clerical order could administer the SACRAMENTS. Like the ordained clerks, monks received the *tonsure*, the circular shaved patch on the crown of the head which signified commitment to the Church (though not necessarily to ordination). But from the sixth century, as a result of papal influence, a distinction was made between the clerical order, which served the spiritual needs of lay people under the authority of a diocesan bishop and his household of clerks (*familia*), and the monastic order, which was devoted to a cloistered existence. In practice, however, the distinction was frequently blurred: many monks who were also priests (or even bishops) were, by 600, exercising significant influence beyond the precincts of their monasteries.

The Cistercian Melrose Abbey in the fifteenth century. (Alan Sorrell)

Monastic expansion in England lasted from the Conquest to *c.* 1220. Thereafter, the monastic houses remained numerous but as their prosperity increased so their popular credibility declined in an age of famine and uncertainty culminating in the Black Death of the mid-fourteenth century. During the thirteenth century, one-third of a typical monastic community consisted of monks and two-thirds of paying guests (*corrodians*), visitors and servants. The largest community in England was that of the Benedictine abbey of St Alban's in Hertfordshire, where there were 100 monks. But elsewhere, at the great Cistercian and Benedictine houses, establishments usually numbered between 60 and 70 and, in the houses of other orders, perhaps no more than 30. Of a population in thirteenth-century England of about 3 million, 1 out of every 150 persons was a monk, canon or nun. There were some 4,000 Benedictines, 3,000 Cistercians, 500 Cluniacs and 200 Carthusians: monks who were not clerics but men who had vowed to pursue a life of austerity, contemplation and prayer 'outside the gates of the world'. Of canons, who were clerks in holy orders and lived according to a rule, there were some 3,000

Augustinians, 1,000 Gilbertines and 800 Premonstratensians. In addition, there were about 7,000 nuns of the various orders and 500 knights Templar or Hospitaller.

Lay brothers (and, in Gilbertine houses, lay sisters) were an important element of the monastic population. They were not bound to the recitation of the Divine Office and were generally occupied in manual and domestic work. In the mid-twelfth century lay brothers had outnumbered the monks in Cistercian houses by 3 to 1, and the Carthusians, Austin Canons and Benedictines had also recruited them in large numbers. But during the thirteenth century, their numbers steadily declined so that by 1350 few remained in the monastic communities. In part, this was the result of 'market forces', but in many monasteries the often tense relationship between monks and lay brethren had proved to be incompatible with the objectives of monastic life. As the numbers of lay brethren decreased, so a veritable army of wage-earning servants moved in. It is estimated that in the thirteenth century there were 40,000 monastic servants (twice the number of monks, canons and nuns), many of whom lived with their families in the monastery precincts. Their tasks ranged from curers of herrings to keepers of the wax and cressets (lamps) and Worcester Priory even maintained a crew of five boatmen on the river Severn.

Of course, domestic help was needed not only to free the monks of routine chores, but also to provide for the numerous guests who comprised about one-sixth of a monastery's population. Many temporary guests were accommodated without charge but others generated a substantial income through *corroderies* – annuities of land or money made over to a monastic foundation in return for guaranteeing the comfort and security of the benefactor (and sometimes his family) in old age. Ironically, it was the possession of vast tracts of land (obtained through corroderies and endowments) and numerous manorial estates and GRANGES which eventually diverted monastic energy away from quiet contemplation and prayer to the administration and commercial exploitation of property and promoted many an abbot to the dual status of spiritual leader and magnate, responsible to the brethren by whom he was elected, to the tenants of his estates and (if he was called upon to hold office) to the Crown. His instructions came as from God and in his monastery or priory he was both good shepherd and autocrat, elected for life. But in practice, many abbots lived as ecclesiastical magnates with their own households and retinues, dispensing patronage and exercising political and judicial authority. In such cases, responsibility for the day-to-day life of a monastery and the welfare and conduct of the monks was delegated to an abbot's deputy-general, the *prior* (*see also* PRIORIES).

The *obedientiaries*, or monastic officials, usually numbered between fifteen and twenty depending on the size of the monastery, though Cistercian houses were not organized on hierarchical principles. The senior obedientiaries were the prior and sub-prior(s); the *sacristan*, who, with the sub-sacristan, was responsible for the abbey church; and the *cellarer*, who, with the sub-cellarer(s), was responsible for the properties of the monastery, including all revenues, rents and patronage. The cellarer also exercised supervision over the various domestic departments and was responsible for the maintenance of the monastery buildings; for the acquisition of food, drink, clothing, fuel and livestock; and for tenants, lay brethren and servants. Responsible to the cellarer were the *kitchener*, who ensured that meals were of a suitable quality and served on time; the *refectorian*, who organized the refectory; the *hosteller*, who ran the guests' house; and the *infirmarian*, who had

charge of the infirmary. The *almoner* provided for the needs of the poor and infirm who could not leave their homes, and gave food, clothing and money to pilgrims, beggars and lepers who called at the monastery gate. The *novice-master* instructed the novices in the Rule and prepared them for the demands of monastic life. He also gave lessons in reading, singing and comportment. By 1200 the practice of offering children in infancy to be educated as *oblates* in religious communities had been abandoned and thereafter the age at which a *postulant* could make application for admission to a monastery or nunnery was generally between seventeen and nineteen. Once admitted, a postulant became a *novice* and was required to give all his possessions to the monastery or to the poor, though his clothing was kept so that he could re-enter the world if he so wished or if he was required to leave. The noviciate lasted for a year, at the end of which time the novice (if accepted) made his vows and swore obedience to the Rule. The *precentor* maintained the monastery library and was responsible for its music.

Spared the necessity of domestic chores, a monk's life was nevertheless one of discipline and routine. The primary responsibility of a monastic community was to recite the *Divine Office*, the eight *canonical Hours* or services of the liturgy, and each day's pattern was determined by the hours of daylight. At the March and September equinoxes, for example, when night and day each last twelve hours, the brethren rose from a seven-hour sleep at two o'clock to attend the 'night watch' meditation of *Nocturn* and *Mattins*. The Day Hours began with Lauds ('praises'), which was recited at first light, and *Prime* at sunrise. Then followed *Terce* (third hour), *Sext* (sixth hour), *None* (ninth hour), *Vespers* (at sunset) and *Compline* (sung to 'complete' the hours before retiring at dusk). All eight hours consisted of Psalms, hymns, lessons, antiphons, versicles, responses and prayers, led by the *precentor* and his deputy, the *succentor*, and were sung in plainsong or Gregorian chant. The Hours did not include confession, which was made in chapter before the abbot and brethren, and Mass was celebrated each Sunday. During services, the choir monks occupied the stalls and the lay brothers the nave and each had their own entrance to the church. The intervals between the Hours were devoted to work, with a two-hour rest period following None and the (only) daily meal taken after Vespers.

The Buildings
By the thirteenth century there were over 1,000 English monasteries, the richest being early English

foundations which had acquired undeveloped land before the twelfth century, and those of the Cistercians, which were invariably situated in remote areas where there were fewer constraints on development. The monasteries varied considerably, both in resources and structure. Many monastic churches were less than 30 metres in length (100 feet) while others, such as Winchester and St Albans, were five times that size. A site had to be comparatively level with a reliable water supply not only for drinking, but also for cooking, washing and drainage, building works and FISH-PONDS. At many urban monasteries, such as London Charterhouse, conduits were built for this purpose and the Franciscan friars were acknowledged experts in the use of lead piping. As monastic sites became permanent, complex systems of conduits and stone-clad drains and sewers were constructed, many of which are still in evidence, as at the Cistercian abbey of Tintern in Monmouthshire. Space for expansion and quietude was also necessary: at Thetford in Norfolk the Cluniac priory became so beleaguered by urban housing that it had to be moved to a new site outside the town. The availability of substantial quantities of firewood was also an important consideration: Byland Abbey in North Yorkshire was moved four times in fifty years before a satisfactory site was found.

The enclosed monastic precincts were entered by means of a *gatehouse*, at which visitors could be identified and their credentials checked before being admitted. Many gatehouses had separate side entrances for pedestrians while a central vaulted gates passage was of sufficient height to allow for the movement of heavily laden wagons. Chambers above the gatehouse were often used as a courtroom or schoolroom and occasionally a small prison was incorporated into the building, as at the Benedictine priory at Ely in Cambridgeshire. Some gatehouses were crenellated, while others (notably those of the Cistercians) included a chapel for the use of lay brothers. At Westminster, a parish church (St Margaret's) was built outside the Abbey gatehouse for the benefit of the lay community. Beyond the gatehouse would be the buildings of a self-sufficient and self-contained community: a great barn (often of considerable size), granary, bolting-house (where corn was sieved), bakery, malthouse, brewery, smithy and stables, together with a house and dining hall for monastic servants and the cloistral buildings.

The monastic CLOISTER was a covered passageway constructed around a rectangular open space or GARTH and sometimes containing the monks' washing facilities and the SCRIPTORIUM.

Adjacent to this court, and above the passageway, were the most important buildings of the monastery: the chapter house, dormitory, refectory, the abbot's lodgings, the infirmary and, of course, the abbey church itself.

The cruciform-shaped church usually stood on the north side of the cloister (though not invariably so), the longer (western) arm of the NAVE providing shelter to the cloistral buildings without cutting off the sunlight. Although the interiors of ANGLO-SAXON and ROMANESQUE churches were often dark, later Gothic buildings were constructed to admit as much natural light as possible (*see* GOTHIC ARCHITECTURE). The principal door was at the west end, facing the gatehouse, and was often set within an imposing façade and sometimes flanked by twin towers, as at Durham. Eastward was the nave, in larger churches flanked by aisles to the north and south and separated from them by arcades of massive pillars above which rose the triforium and clerestory (*see* CHURCHES). Some naves were of extraordinary length: that at Norwich, for example, is 76 metres long (250 feet). At the eastern end of the nave, were the ROOD SCREEN (none survived the DISSOLUTION OF THE MONASTERIES), the crossing and PULPITUM, and above the crossing the tower (*see* CHURCH TOWERS). East of the pulpitum, and at a higher level than the nave, was the CHANCEL or CHOIR with its wooden stalls, each provided with a MISERICORD and a desk for service books and raised on a stone base as a protection against damp, possibly above an acoustic chamber (*see* AMPLIFIER). At the west end of the choir were the LECTERN and abbot's stall, which was usually on the south side, and to the east were the PRESBYTERY and the raised SANCTUARY in which was the high ALTAR.

In larger churches, chapels to the east of the sanctuary were linked by an apsidal aisle or *ambulatory*, as at Tewkesbury Abbey in Gloucestershire, or *retro-choir* (*see* CHOIR), screened from the high altar by a REREDOS. Of these chapels, the most important is often a *lady chapel*, usually of late medieval date, its size and architectural splendour reflecting a contemporary cult-like veneration of the Blessed Virgin Mary. English monasteries were rich in relics, particularly of native saints, and these were often retained in ornate canopied SHRINES, few of which survived the Dissolution. Kings, princes and magnates sought burial in or near the sanctuaries of the great abbeys and numerous CHANTRY CHAPELS were erected in the fourteenth and fifteenth centuries. Many shrines and royal tombs became so popular that additional accommodation had to be provided for the thousands of pilgrims who travelled from all over Britain and Europe to offer prayers and supplications and to swell monastic coffers.

In the *transept*, the northern and southern arms of the cruciform building, were side chapels and subsidiary altars. A door in the north wall of the northern transept led to the community's burial ground, and from the southern transept a door opened on to the *night stairs* by which the monks descended from their first-floor dormitory to attend the night office (*see below*). A further door led from the transept to the cloister and was used as a processional entrance before High Mass on Sundays and feast-days. While eminent members of the monastic community might be buried beneath INCISED SLABS in the chapter house or cloister (or, from the fifteenth century, in the abbey church itself), most brethren shared a common grave in the monastery's cemetery, which was approached by means of the *slype*, a wide covered passageway from the cloister. The slype was generally used for conversation, which was forbidden in the cloister itself, and in some monasteries it developed into a library, though books were generally stored where they were needed: in the sacristy, the choir, the cloister or the frater.

The CHAPTER HOUSE was normally within, or connected to, the eastern range of cloistral buildings in the upper storey of which was the DORTER or monks' dormitory with the latrines or *rere-dorter* on the same floor and, in many Benedictine monasteries, a warming-house below. (This was usually the only room in a monastery, other than the kitchens and infirmary, where a fire was permitted.) The refectory or FRATER was usually on the south side of the cloister, again on the upper storey though in a few houses it was on the ground floor, and in several (such as Rievaulx in Yorkshire) it was set at right angles to, and south of, the cloister alley. In several cloisters, at the foot of the frater stairs, was the LAVATORIUM where the monks washed after rising and before meals. The monastery's *kitchens* were also near the frater, either in the adjacent western range of the cloister or in a separate building to reduce the risk of fire. Chimney flues and ovens were set within the thickness of walls (though there may also have been a central hearth) and around the kitchens ancillary buildings housed the pantry, buttery, bakery and other domestic offices.

The guests' chambers and *abbot's* (or Prior's) *lodgings* were usually in the western range of the cloistral buildings. The lodgings would normally

The late fourteenth-century Abbot's Kitchen at Glastonbury Abbey, Somerset.

include a parlour, dining-room, bedchamber and chapel, but as many abbots rose to positions of political influence, so their responsibilities for entertaining eminent guests (and their households) increased. Separate dining halls were provided at many monasteries, adjacent to the abbot's chambers and with suites of guests' rooms beneath. From the thirteenth century, many abbots had three-storeyed houses built, with dining halls on the middle floor and a parlour and bed-chamber above. Some even had their own kitchens, the most splendid of which was the Abbot's Kitchen at Glastonbury Abbey in Somerset. Such opulence was not always of the abbot's choosing but was expected of him by the magnates and prelates who relied on the monasteries for hospitality. In Cistercian monasteries, however, the western range of cloistral buildings was originally used to accommodate lay brothers who were provided with a common room and refectory on the ground floor and a dorter above. As the numbers of lay brothers declined in the fourteenth century, their quarters were often adapted for use as accommodation for guests and for administrative purposes.

The *infirmary* was usually built to the east of the eastern cloistral range and was intended both for the sick and infirm and for those who were too old or too deranged to cope with the astringent demands of monastic life. Dietary rules were relaxed for those in the infirmary and as these often included guests, food was usually obtained from the abbot's kitchen. The great hall of an infirmary contained at least one large fireplace and its own lavatorium and latrines. The beds were arranged between pairs of high windows in the side walls and faced a central space, as in a modern hospital ward. Many infirmaries were of considerable size, indicative of the practice of *phlebotomy* or blood-letting, which was considered to be a medical necessity. Following phlebotomy, a monk was required to rest for three days during which time he could enjoy rich food and relaxation in the monastery gardens, could rise late and was excused choir. Consequently, the frequency of blood-letting was, in most orders, restricted: four times a year for Cistercians, five times for Carthusians and eight for the Austin canons.

MONASTIC PLACE-NAMES The extraordinary number and diversity of monastic place-names bear witness to the prosperity of the medieval church. Most names originated in endowments of lands, for the benefit both of a religious order and the soul of the benefactor, or were granted in return for CORRODORIES. Some recall the sites of minor religious houses, usually dependencies or GRANGES, and a small number commemorate former abbeys, as at Cerne Abbas in Dorset where only the ornate gatehouse remains (*abbas*, from the Latin for abbot). Typical are names such as Abbotsbury ('the manor of the abbot'), Friar Waddon ('the hill of the friars where woad grew'), Whitchurch Canonicorum ('the stone church of the canons'), Toller Fratrum ('land by the Toller stream belonging to the brethren') and Maiden Newton ('the new homestead of the sisters'), all in Dorset; White Ladies Aston ('the eastern homestead of the Premonstratensian Canonesses') in Worcestershire; Newton Abbot ('the new homestead of the Abbot') and Monkton ('the homestead of the monks') in Devon; two villages of Stoke Prior, one in Herefordshire and the other in Worcestershire ('place of the Priors' or possibly 'cell of the Priors'); and Fryerning ('the place of the brothers') in Essex. Not all are strictly monastic: the 'brothers' who dwelt at Fryerning were knights Hospitaller and canons could be either priests in canonical orders or the secular canons of a cathedral.
See also EPISCOPI, LATIN, MONACHORUM, PLACE-NAMES *and* SORORUM

MONKEY PUZZLE TREES The 'Chile Pine' was introduced into Britain in 1795, though most Victorian specimens originated in a batch of seeds which were imported in 1844. The name is said to have been coined by one Charles Austin who, while attending a ceremonial planting in 1834, grasped one of the leaves, pricked himself and declared 'it would be a puzzle for a monkey!' By the 1860s the tree was commonly called the Monkey Puzzle Pine and there was widespread enthusiasm for planting single specimens in the front lawns of Victorian villas where they were supposed to complement the contemporary architectural style.

MONOGRAM Two or more letters interwoven to form a symbol.

MONOLITH (*also* **MENHIR** *and* **STANDING STONE**) Most standing stones are impossible to date and because their original function is usually unclear they have inevitably attracted a variety of local myths and traditions. The solitary King's Stone on the Oxfordshire-Warwickshire border, for example, is 2.5 metres high (8 feet) and is clearly associated with a circle of stones (the 'Whispering Knights') which stands beside a ridgeway some 91 metres (100 yards) to the south. These are reputed to be the fossilized figures of a royal army which conquered all of southern England before reaching Little Rollright where disaster struck. Climbing the hill on which the village stands, the victorious king was met by a witch who told him 'Seven long strides though shalt take! If Long Compton canst thou see, King of England thou shalt be.' Knowing that Long Compton was just beyond the brow of the hill the king stepped forward but a mound obscured his view and the witch cackled 'As Long Compton thou canst not see, thou and thy men hoar stones shall be!' And stones they remain to this day. This is typical of the legends surrounding such isolated and apparently inexplicable stones and STONE CIRCLES.

Most are undoubtedly prehistoric and were erected by Neolithic or Bronze Age peoples for ritualistic or ceremonial purposes, over burial sites, as route-markers or at important meeting-places, strategically located on ridgeways and prominent hill tops. Others, of more recent date, may have delineated the boundaries of manors or parishes or simply been rubbing posts on which livestock could rid themselves of fleas. There can be little doubt that down the centuries such stones have served a variety of purposes: Saxon MOOTS may well have met at a standing stone which, in prehistoric times, had been a familiar trading location at the intersection of route-ways. The same stone could later have been used to define the limits of a medieval manorial or monastic estate, the boundaries of which may be evident today in those of ecclesiastical or civil parishes, districts or (as at Rollright) counties.

Some stones are of immense size: the tallest, at Rudston, East Riding of Yorkshire, is 8 metres high (26 feet) and consists of a 26-ton slab which was transported some 16 km (10 miles) to its present site beside the church. The fact that so many of these often enormous stones were hauled over such distances suggests that, to prehistoric man, what they represented and where they were placed were of considerable significance.

See also OGHAM STONES

MONUMENTS Memorials in churches, erected to perpetuate the memory of an individual, developed from the practice of carving designs on stone coffin lids and on slabs which were exposed in a church floor. The earliest surviving lids are from the eleventh century and are carved in shallow relief with simple decorative designs, usually foliage or Christian symbols.

It is likely that depiction of the human form was reserved, in the twelfth century, for eminent ecclesiastics, the earliest known example in England being that of Abbot Gilbert Crispin (d.1117) at Westminster Abbey. In these early monuments the image was recessed into the slab, but from the beginning of the thirteenth century it gradually assumed a more three-dimensional effigial form. One of the earliest knightly EFFIGIES is that of William Longespée, Earl of Salisbury (d.1226), in Salisbury Cathedral. This effigy provides evidence of the early systematic use of hereditary armorial devices (*see* ARMORY).

During the Middle Ages the three-dimensional effigy was widely used by the nobility and by eminent knights and clerics and was normally placed on a TOMB CHEST. Two-dimensional figures were also depicted on INCISED SLABS and in monumental BRASSES. Tomb chests with effigies (and, occasionally, brasses) could be free-standing or placed against a wall and were sometimes surmounted by a CANOPY. (Free-standing canopied tomb chests were the precursors of CHANTRY CHAPELS.) The development of armour and costume may be traced through such figures, though it should be remembered that memorials are not necessarily contemporary with the death of those they commemorate, for many were prepared years (or even decades) beforehand while others were commissioned retrospectively and may be in a later

Eighteenth-century monument to Lord Wyndham, by Rysbrack, at Salisbury Cathedral.

style. The figures in effigies and brasses are stylized: it was the accompanying heraldry which announced the identity, lineage and status of the deceased. It became the practice to place man and wife (or wives) side by side but children were not usually represented, except as WEEPERS around the base of the tomb or by shields, illustrative of marital alliances.

From the Renaissance, standing, kneeling or reclining figures are in evidence, as are WALL MONUMENTS which have no tomb chest. Two distinctive types of memorial, which date from the late sixteenth and early seventeenth centuries, are the TRIPTYCH, which consists of a hinged set of three painted panels and originated in the portable altars of the medieval nobility, and the *obelisk*, a tall, four-sided tapering pillar, usually placed on a plinth. During the seventeenth century, the effigy was often omitted from the wall monument to produce the *wall tablet* and its cheap and simple precursor, the MEMORIAL BOARD. During the late sixteenth and early seventeenth centuries, heraldry proliferated, often ostentatiously so, reflecting the changing nature of armory from the practical to the ceremonial and symbolic. It was now necessary to provide artificial helms, gauntlets, tabards and other items of FUNERAL HERALDRY which, in the previous century, would have been readily available. It was at this time that the funeral HATCHMENT was introduced as an inexpensive substitute for the elaborate trappings of the heraldic funerals of the nobility and gentry. The seventeenth century also saw the development of CLASSICAL ARCHITECTURE which influenced the design of church monuments. Tomb chests became unfashionable, columns and pediments predominated and, while kneeling effigies remained in hanging monuments, most figures were depicted in more natural poses and the grief of a surviving spouse was often shown. This culminated in the BAROQUE period when imposing figures were often modelled to capture a significant moment in the deceased's life, and ornate carved fruits, garlands and cherubs' heads were incorporated into designs, particularly in wall monuments.

But there was a reaction against the excesses of the Baroque during the early eighteenth century and a reversion to the more classical styles; indeed, figures were often depicted in classical costume, surrounded by images of ancient Rome. The two-dimensional pyramid was a common motif, particularly in wall monuments, and the earlier tomb chest was reintroduced as the *sarcophagus*, which often had figures of the deceased, his family or allegorical characters sitting or leaning against it. The area at the base of the monument was often devoted to biographical or genealogical details or incorporated a frieze depicting a scene from the deceased's life, particularly of those who had enjoyed successful military or naval careers.

In the nineteenth century, the classical Roman style was replaced by that of Greece, usually in black and white marble, and the two-dimensional pyramid motif was replaced by the *stele*, a rectangular slab surmounted by a low, triangular pediment. The size of these monuments varied from small inscribed tablets to large hanging monuments with an inscription in the base and a sculpted relief figure, usually an angel or the deceased, in classical Greek dress, resting against an urn or sarcophagus. The Greek revival continued into the second half of the century when it was overtaken by the GOTHIC REVIVAL. Naturally, there was a return to the 'medieval' tomb chest and effigy, sometimes surmounted by a canopy, and to the figured monumental brass. But most Victorian effigies combine a variety of medieval influences and rarely reproduce accurately the style of a particular period. Brass wall monuments and plaques were also popular, with their now familiar 'Gothic' lettering

and decorative capital letters. From the end of the nineteenth century, large funeral monuments became unfashionable and, in most cases, impracticable. Memorials took the form of commemorative wall tablets and window glass, or the provision of church furniture and fittings as bequests 'in memoriam'.
See also CADAVER, INTRANSI TOMBS, STAINED GLASS *and* TOMBS
For The Church Monuments Society, The Royal Commission for Historic Monuments *and the* Monumental Brass Society *see* APPENDIX I

MOOR From the Old English *mōr*, a moor is a stretch of open uncultivated land and may be applied to marshland and fen as well as upland landscapes. Found as a place-name element, as in Exmoor in Somerset and Devon, Ot Moor in Oxfordshire and Morcott in Leicestershire, meaning 'cottage on the moor'.

MOOT (*also* **MOTE**) A legislative assembly of people, of particular importance during the Saxon period. Moot courts (*gemotes*) were convened for a variety of purposes including HUNDRED COURTS (*hundred-motes*) and town courts (*burgmotes*). The *witan* were members of the *witenagemot*, the supreme council of Anglo-Saxon England, composed of the bishops, the ealdormen of the shires and several of the king's friends and dependants (from the Old English *wita*, meaning 'a man of knowledge').

-MORE A place-name element derived either from the Old English *mōr*, meaning 'moor' or 'fen' (*see* MOOR), or from the Old English *mere*, meaning 'lake' or 'pool' (*see* -MERE).

MORFA In the Welsh, a moor, fen or marsh.

MORGANNWG *see* WALES

MORTHEAD *see* MEMORIAL BOARD

MORTMAIN Mortmain means, literally, 'dead hand' and in this context it is the hand of the Church. Land which was granted by laymen to ecclesiastical bodies became free of escheats and reliefs, thereby reducing the revenues of the manorial lord. Various medieval Statutes of Mortmain prohibited the transfer of land without a lord's consent and restricted the ability of the Church to acquire property in this way. Current practice relies on the Mortmain and Charitable Uses Act of 1888 and subsequent amendments.

MORTUARY A customary levy received by a parish priest from the estate of a deceased parishioner.

MOSSEYING *see* SLATES

MOTTE AND BAILEY *see* CASTLES (MEDIEVAL)

MOTTO An aphorism, the interpretation of which is often obscure. A motto is usually, though not necessarily, included in a coat of arms where it is depicted below the shield or (as in Scotland) above the crest. Historians should beware of mottoes when attempting to identify a coat of arms, for they may be changed at will and are, therefore, singularly unreliable clues.

MOULDING A modelled surface of a building. Many mouldings are decorative while others project from vertical surfaces to protect them from rain and snow. The form and ornamentation of mouldings are characteristic of certain periods of building and often facilitate the identification of architectural styles.

MOUNTING BLOCKS *and* **MOUNTING STONES** *see* UPPING STOCKS

MOUSESTEAD *see* THRESHING

MUD AND STUD An inferior but common method of timber-frame construction used in many rural hovels through to the end of the eighteenth century. Timber posts (*clam staffs*) were driven into the ground and linked at the top by horizontal beams to form the framework of walls. The spaces between the posts were then filled with vertical staves and coated with a clay daub. No sill beam or stone footing was used and, because the clam staffs were set directly in the soil, they decayed rapidly. *See also* TIMBER-FRAMED BUILDINGS *and* WATTLE AND DAUB

MULLION A vertical bar dividing the lights of a window. *See also* TRANSOM

MULTIPLE ESTATE Extensive Dark Age territories comprising a head manor (*caput*) and subordinate settlements and land units, each responsible for the provision of specialized goods and services to the caput. The caput itself generally occupied the best lands in the estate and was where the lord had his HALL and court. It may have been a substantial settlement or merely a large farmstead, and usually the caput and estate were known by the same name. Both the tenants of the caput and the bondsmen of subordinate territories would operate an INFIELD-OUTFIELD system of farming and certain resources of the estate, such as areas of upland grazing, might be shared (*intercommoning see* COMMONS). Some multiple estates may have originated as Iron Age territories, administered through networks of central and dependent HILL FORTS, while others may have been established during the Roman occupation. It would appear that the early Church developed through the multiple estate system: MINSTERS were established at several major (notably royal) head manors and in due course numerous daughter churches were provided in outlying settlements. In the late Saxon period, many multiple estates became fragmented as lands were granted to monastic foundations or redistributed as a result of inheritance or royal patronage. The system was finally reduced by the widespread redistribution of landholdings following the Norman Conquest of 1066.

MULTIPLE TRACKS A fan-like complex of minor trackways usually diverging from a point at which travellers would normally leave an enclosed lowland landscape before ascending onto the open hills. At such a point, a number of options would be available depending on the time of year and the condition of the ground. Tracks which were worn and difficult would be abandoned for new ones and eventually the more popular routes might be eroded to form HOLLOW WAYS, many of which have been in continuous use from prehistoric times to the present day. Another form, the *parallel track*, is a common though often transient feature of the countryside. This is formed where travellers have forsaken a muddy and rutted trackway for a new but parallel course.

MULTIVALLATE An earthwork having more than two encircling ramparts. Those which had two are *bivallate*, and one *univallate*.

MULTURE *see* WATER-MILLS

MUNICIPIA *see* ROMAN ADMINISTRATION

MUNTIN A vertical framing piece between door panels, openings (*lights*) in screens, etc (*see* CHANCEL SCREEN).

MURAL TOWERS *see* CASTLES (MEDIEVAL)

MURDER FINE (*also* **ENGLISHRY**) A fine imposed on a HUNDRED in which a Danish or Norman victim was murdered. No fine was extracted if the victim was English.

MURDER HOLES *see* CASTLES (MEDIEVAL)

MUSTER ROLL *see* MILITIA

MYND *see* MYNYDD

MYNYDD In the Welsh, 'a mountain' (adopted in Old English as *myned*) and evident not only in Mynydd Preseli (Pembrokeshire), Mynydd Eppynt (Powys) and numerous other Welsh mountain names, but in the English Minton and Longmynd in Shropshire, and Minehead and Mendip, Somerset.

NAILBOURNE *see* WINTERBORNE

NANT In the Welsh, *nant* means 'valley', as in Nant Ffrancon, Gwynedd, and Pennant ('head of the valley'), Ceredigion. Also found in Cornish place-names, such as Nantstallon.

NAPERY *see* LARDER

NARTHEX In early Christian churches, a vestibule which extended transversely across the western end of the building, separated from the nave by a screen or wall. Also known as a *galilee* or *antenave*, it was often set aside for the exclusive use of women and penitents.

NATIONAL MONUMENTS RECORD (NMR) Previously part of the Royal Commission on the Historical Monuments of England, the National Monuments Record is now run by English Heritage. It is England's national archive of heritage information and contains over 12 million items covering architecture, archaeology, aerial photographs and maritime sites in England. The NMR collections include 3 million photographs of buildings; almost total coverage of the country in aerial photographs; data on most known archaeological sites; textual records for buildings included the Listed Buildings Information service; 50,000 measured drawings; and an extensive reference library. The NMR offers a wide range of services which are freely accessible to the public. There are research rooms and other facilities at Swindon, Wiltshire and London (*see* APPENDIX I).

NATIONAL SCHOOLS *see* EDUCATION

NAVE From the Latin *navis*, meaning 'ship', the nave is the main body of a church, originally separated from the CHANCEL by a ROOD SCREEN or CHANCEL SCREEN and, in the great monastic churches and cathedrals, by a rood screen and PULPITUM.

In the medieval church, the Divine Office was observed in the *sanctum* sanctorum to the east of these screens but sermons were preached in the nave, where parishioners gathered in large numbers for worship, assisted in their supplications by the terrifying images of the DOOM and other salutary WALL PAINTINGS. The majority of the congregation would stand in the body of the nave, though a stone ledge was sometimes provided so that the elderly and infirm could 'go to the wall' to rest. But the nave of the parish church also performed a variety of other functions: it was a venue for guild plays and processions, for parochial assemblies and the church ales, which the Puritans found so distasteful (*see* CHURCH HOUSES).

Many naves were extended sideways by the addition of side aisles, the nave walls and roof supported by arcades of pillars. At Milton Abbey in Dorset, the nave was never built and the great fourteenth- and fifteenth-century church consists of choir, transept and tower; while at nearby Sherborne, a second nave was added at the west end of the abbey nave to provide a chapel-of-ease for the townspeople. Many naves failed to survive the Dissolution of the Monasteries: at Abbey Dore in Herefordshire, nothing remains of the once magnificent early thirteenth-century nave which fell into disrepair following the abbey's suppression in 1536, though the choir and transept were restored in the early seventeenth century.

The naves of many of the great cathedrals are enormously long: 76 metres (250 feet) at Norwich in Norfolk, for example, and 87 metres (285 feet) at St Albans in Hertfordshire. They are also very tall and constructed in three stages (the arcade, the tribune or triforium, and the clerestory – *see* CHURCHES) in order that the weight of the vault, roof and tower

Milton Abbey, Dorset, where the building of the nave was abandoned, possibly as a consequence of the Black Death.

should be distributed outwards and as much light as possible admitted to the interior (*see* VAULTING). The nave at Westminster Abbey (begun by Henry III in the thirteenth century but not completed until after 1375) is 31.4 metres high (103 feet) and 11.75 metres wide (38½ feet). It is the tallest vault in Britain and its extraordinary French Gothic proportions inspire that feeling of ascension which is the essence of GOTHIC ARCHITECTURE.

NAVVIES *see* CANALS *and* RAILWAYS

NAZE *see* NESS

NEATHERD *see* VILLAGE GREENS

NEOLITHIC *see* STONE AGE

NESS A place-name element from the Old Norse *nes* and the Old English *ness* and *næss*, meaning 'promontory', as in Bowness ('bull's headland') in Cumbria and The Naze and Foulness ('cape frequented by birds') in Essex. In the English form it may also mean 'projecting ridge', as in Shropshire

where both Great and Little Ness occupy elevated sites. Not all *ness* names are immediately apparent: Claines in Worcestershire, for example, is derived from the Old English *clæg-næss*, meaning 'a clayey point of land'.

NEWEL *and* **NEWEL POST** *see* STAIRCASES

NEWLAND *and* **NEWLANDS** A common place-name meaning 'newly cleared land' or 'newly acquired land'. Many Newland names can be traced from the thirteenth and fourteenth centuries, and almost certainly refer to ASSARTS or to the creation of new suburbs in TOWNS, while later examples probably originate in various types of ENCLOSURE.

NIGHT STAIR *see* DORTER *and* MONASTERIES

NOBLE *see* COINAGE

NOCTURN *see* MONASTERIES

NOGGIN A small drinking vessel having a capacity of about 1 gill (¼ of a pint).

NOGGING *see* BRICK NOGGING *and* TIMBER-FRAMED BUILDINGS

NONE *see* MONASTERIES

NORMAN ARCHITECTURE *see* ROMAN-ESQUE

NORMANS The great conquering people from Normandy in northern France who, from 1050 to 1100, subjugated England, southern Italy and Sicily. The Duchy of Normandy evolved from territory around Rouen granted to the Viking chieftain Rollo in 911 which, despite its origins and continuing Scandinavian immigration during the first half of the tenth century, developed in the eleventh century as a characteristic French territorial principality.

Norman warriors seem to have been present wherever warfare was taking place but there does not appear to have been a coherent policy of conquest: England, for example, was the victim of the political opportunism of a reigning duke. From *c.* 1025 Normandy had been convulsed by internecine warfare and Duke William's eventual pacification of the duchy after 1050 appears to have been achieved principally through a strategy of diverting aggression against neighbouring states. The childless King Edward ('the Confessor') of

England (r.1042–66) nominated Duke William as his successor and in 1064 Earl Harold, who had effectively dominated Edward's court during the last years of his reign, reluctantly swore homage to William and promised to support his claim to the English throne. But on Edward's death in January 1066, Harold was elected king, thereby precipitating two invasions within months of his accession. He defeated his half-brother Tostig and the Norse King Harald Hardrada at Stamford Bridge but was himself slain by the Conqueror's army at Senlac ('the lake of blood') in Sussex.

William retired to nearby Hastings, to the motte and bailey castle he had already constructed there, and waited for the English capitulation. But, 'when he saw that no-one would come, he went up with all the army . . . and ravaged all the parts he went over' (*Anglo-Saxon Chronicle*). Hundreds of villages appear to have been ransacked as William rapidly established control over southern England before being crowned at Westminster on Christmas Day 1066. But northern England proved more recalcitrant and Norman rule only became effective there following the ruthless suppression of a major rebellion in 1070. The invasion had been carried out with the Pope's blessing, and many of the native English believed that the 'lake of blood' at Senlac was evidence of God's displeasure. The great men of the realm 'from necessity submitted when the greatest harm had been done; and it was very imprudent that it had not been done earlier, as God would not better it for our sins' (*ibid*).

No doubt Harold's duplicity incurred William's indignation, but the duke must also have recognized that invasion, and the prospect of territorial conquest, would serve to concentrate the energies of his rancorous aristocracy. In the event, '1066 was an opportunity which was ably taken'. The conquest of England offered unlimited scope for the personal aggrandizement of ambitious warriors through service to the Norman kings and magnates and through the acquisition of new lands from bases securely under Norman control (*see* MARCHES) or through marriage to Anglo-Saxon heiresses. The Norman system of lordship provided cohesion to these often disparate groups of warriors, who were not exclusively Norman but included large numbers of Flemings, Bretons, Poitevins and other Frankish mercenaries. The acquisition of land by a lord was invariably followed by the granting of constituent estates to vassals: thereby men from Montgomery in Normandy are named in DOMESDAY as holding land in Shropshire of their lord, Roger de Montgomery, for example.

Old Sarum, 3 km (2 miles) to the north of Salisbury, Wiltshire, where a Norman castle, cathedral and town were built within the ramparts of an Iron Age camp. Old Sarum was abandoned in 1220 when a new cathedral was built at New Sarum, now Salisbury. Nevertheless, until 1832 the ten voters of Old Sarum continued to return two members to Parliament, including Pitt the Elder.

During the decade of Norman settlement following the Conquest, the native English aristocracy was almost entirely replaced in positions of secular and ecclesiastical authority by a new ruling class which established and maintained control through the sword, the stirrup and the keep. All land belonged to the Conqueror, whose followers held their estates by his pleasure and in return for specified services. Estates were confiscated and redistributed to the Norman lords and their dependants, many of whom already held lands in Normandy, so that by 1080 only 8 per cent of estates held directly of the king remained in native hands. Latin replaced English as the language of administration and French became the language of the aristocracy. An archaic English Church was also reformed and by the time of William's death in 1087 only one English bishop, Oswald of Worcester, remained, the rest having been replaced by foreigners. In the parishes, English priests continued to preach in the vernacular in churches built by native craftsmen, but the larger churches, abbeys and cathedrals, built in stone and in the alien ROMANESQUE style, were almost exclusively staffed by foreign clergy. The highly developed and distinctive Wessex and DANELAW systems of administration and justice were rationalized, exploited and centralized by the new management.

Norman England was essentially a colonial society, with the immense new cathedrals and castles symbolizing the invaders' power and the *Domesday Book* his ruthless efficiency. But *Domesday* also reveals that the Norman Conquest had little real effect on the peasantry; indeed, some actually enjoyed greater freedom, for slavery, a common phenomenon in Anglo-Saxon society, was abolished under the Norman rule. While most peasants continued to cultivate their holdings and to provide service on their lord's demesne, the new aristocracy consolidated their estates and constructed their CASTLES. Some endowed MONASTERIES, which at first tended to be English dependencies of Norman foundations, but in the twelfth century were more often new CISTERCIAN houses.

At this time, there was a significant increase in population and commercial and economic expansion which led both to the development of new towns as regional centres of administrative, political and mercantile activity and to the colonization of many of the more remote regions by individuals and communities. But perhaps the most significant change was a cultural one: England now looked towards France and no longer to Scandinavia. Amalgamation of the two territories was never on the political agenda, however: under the Normans, England had its own institutions and government as did Normandy. Henry II (1133–89) ruled from the Scottish border to the Pyrenees but the Angevin 'empire' remained essentially a confederation in which England and Normandy were linked more closely to each other than they were to Anjou, Maine, Touraine, Aquitaine, Poitou or Auvergne.

The independent existence of the Duchy of Normandy ended when, in 1204, it was conquered by the Capetian kings of France, though successive English dynasties continued to press claims to the ducal territories and exercised limited military and political authority in the duchy, notably during the so-called 'Hundred Years War' of the late Middle Ages (1340s–1450s).

NORTHUMBRIA *see* KINGDOMS (ANCIENT)

NOTARY A professional scribe. Each notary authenticated the documents for which he was responsible by drawing a distinctive notarial symbol at the foot.

NOVEL DISSEISIN A common form of medieval legal action intended to provide a swift and effective method of recovery for someone ejected from lands he occupied (*disseisin*). A jury would be asked if the plaintiff had been disseised unjustly, and if they agreed that he had lost his lands without judgement, they would be restored to him by the sheriff. The action related to occupation (*seisin*) and not to the question of ultimate right. It was originally intended to apply only to recent (*novel*) acts, though in 1275 a legal limit of 1,242 was applied to retrospective actions.

NOVICE and **NOVICE-MASTER** *see* **MONAS-TERIES**

OAK A native forest tree and that which is most often associated with England. There are two native species: the common or *pedunculate* oak (which has stalked acorns and short-stalked leaves) and the *durmast* oak (with stalkless acorns and long-stalked leaves). Both vary in quality according to soil; clay soil makes a particularly tough wood, for example. Remnants of ancient oak forests may be seen not only in mature hedgerow trees, but also in the rapid colonization by oak saplings of cleared woodland, neglected commons and pastures, and even roadside wastes. Oak wood is renowned for its strength and durability.

So common was the oak, and so ready to hand, that it provided all the basic materials for house-building, furniture-making, boat-building, fencing, and the smelting of ores. Oaken beams were not sawn and they invariably show the marks of adze and cloven work. Evenness and symmetry are obtained by pairing the split halves of the same tree or branch (hence, a person is 'the splitting image' of another when possessed of an exact likeness). Most oak timbers in buildings are pegged together because the wood was too difficult to nail. Numbers were scratched on a beam at each joint so that the builders should be able to piece them together. Oak floorboards may be recognized by the wavy surface left by adzes when they were smoothed. Oaken posts and pillars in buildings are always positioned with the root-end uppermost to prevent damp rising.

Wall panelling, stair-timbers, church pews, screens and pulpits are invariably of oak. Root stumps of the oak were used by blacksmiths as bases for their anvils; York hams were smoked over smouldering oak sawdust; ink was made from oak galls; and, in the west of England, oaks were coppiced to provide bark for tanning hides. The spokes of cartwheels were fashioned from oak and were sometimes adapted to make rungs for ladders. Oak is impervious to alcohol and is therefore used for wine casks and beer barrels. In the medieval woods, corns and beechmast were beaten down in the autumn to provide for the annual fattening of pigs (and, incidentally, produced very hard bacon!).

The keel, frame and ribs of every great wooden ship from the Viking period to the present day have been of oak. The timber of over 3,000 trees was required to construct Nelson's *Victory*, and the destruction of the forests dates from the wholesale felling of oaks for ship-building in the seventeenth and eighteenth centuries.

From pre-history, oaks have been associated with divine power, possibly because they were observed to attract lightning from the heavens and were thereby the instruments of the sky-gods: the Roman *Jupiter*, the Anglo-Saxon *Thunor* and the Scandinavian *Thor*. During the Bronze Age, oak wood was burned for cremation and was used for coffin burial. Charles II commemorated his escape from the battle of Worcester (1651), and his concealment in the famous Boscobel Oak, by adopting a crowned oak tree as his emblem on his restoration. The famous Major Oak in Sherwood Forest, Nottinghamshire, is reputed to be over 800 years old, though the average life span of an oak is 250 years.

Bog oak is that which has been protected from decay by the acid peat in which it has lain for many centuries. It is singularly dark in colour and is used for ornamental work.

OAKUM PICKING The undoing of old tarred rope to make caulking for ships' timbers. Required of prisoners who were not on hard labour and of some residents of workhouses, oakum picking frequently disabled the fingers.

OAST-HOUSE (*also* **HOP-KILN**) *Oast* means 'kiln' which, in this context, was used for drying hops before they were sent to market. Although a native of England, the hop plant was not grown for

Kentish oast-houses, c. *1900.*

brewing before the fifteenth century and then only to meet the domestic requirements of a farmstead. Flemish kiln designs were introduced into England in the early sixteenth century and hop-growing expanded rapidly, particularly in Kent and Sussex, parts of Surrey and Hampshire and west of the river Severn from northern Gloucestershire through Herefordshire to southern Shropshire. On the hop farms, with their characteristic rich soils, high hedges (wind-breaks) and rows of tall, latticed hop frames, a *hop acre* was reckoned to be the area occupied by 1,000 plants, usually about half an acre.

Most surviving oast-houses date from the nineteenth century, when a rapid increase in the urban population stimulated a demand for beer (*for* the brewing process *see* MALTHOUSE). In a typical design, a slatted drying floor was constructed 3 metres (10 feet) above the firebox of the kiln. Hot air circulated through this floor and through the covering of horsehair cloths on which the hops were spread. Smoke was released, and the draft controlled, by means of an adjustable, revolving cowl at the apex of a characteristic pyramidal or conical roof. The kiln was usually attached to a two-storey building, the lower floor of which was used for servicing the kiln and the upper floor for cooling and packing the hops after they had been removed from the adjacent drying floor. Long sacks (*pockets*) were suspended through 'treading holes' in the cooling floor and packed tightly from above by the feet of the farm-worker. Pyramidal chimneys mostly date from the eighteenth century, while conical designs were first used in Kent in the early nineteenth century and elsewhere from the 1830s. Several technically advanced pyramidal chimneys were constructed in Herefordshire in the 1870s and in the south-eastern counties from about 1910. In recent years numerous oast-houses have been converted for residential purposes.

OATH HELPER A witness called by a defendant to swear to his innocence. The credence given by a medieval court to the oath helper's testament depended on his WERGILD, the monetary value of his life.

OBEDIENTIARIES *see* MONASTERIES

OBELISK A tapering, usually four-sided stone pillar, named *obeliskos* ('little spit') by the Greeks after the copper-capped pyramidions of Egyptian pillars. These belonged to the Sun God and were placed before Egyptian temples where they reflected the rays of the sun. Many were carried off as trophies and inspired a variety of similar forms throughout the ancient world, eventually arriving in Britain in the CLASSICAL ARCHITECTURE, GARDENS and church MONUMENTS of the eighteenth century. In parkland, obelisks were intended as 'eye-catchers', focal points in an otherwise 'natural' landscape, in keeping with the classical spirit expressed in the Palladian mansion and sometimes marking the limits of an estate, as at Barwick in Somerset. Others were erected as melancholy memorials to a family's greatness. (These larger obelisks are marked as such on Ordnance Survey maps.) Unlike the original *obeliskos*, which was fashioned from a single piece of granite, most eighteenth-century obelisks are constructed with a brick core and freestone facing.
See also FOLLIES

OBLATE *see* MONASTERIES

OBTUSE ARCH *see* ARCH

OGEE A double continuous curve (like an S). An *ogee arch* has two ogee curves meeting at the apex.

OGHAM STONES *Ogham* is an ancient British and Irish alphabet of twenty characters formed by parallel strokes and notches on either side of, or across, a continuous line. It seems to have originated in the south-west of Ireland in the fourth century and is traditionally ascribed to one Ogma, though its original purpose remains unclear. Standing stones inscribed with *ogham* script are found not only in Ireland, where there are more than 300, but also in the Isle of Man, Cornwall, Scotland and Wales (notably in West Wales), where they commemorate the chieftains of minor principalities or kingdoms established by migrating Irish following the Roman occupation. The inscriptions are usually repeated in the native language and Ogham and, in some instances, in Latin.
See also PICTISH STONES

OLD ENGLISH 'English' was originally the dialect of the Angles but the term has subsequently been extended to include all the dialects of the vernacular, whether Anglian or Saxon. Old English (or Anglo-Saxon) is the language which developed from the composite dialects of Germanic-speaking tribes of Angles, Saxons and Jutes who settled in Britain from the mid-fifth century. It was an inflected language, though these endings gradually decayed until most of them had been lost by the fifteenth century. It was also essentially a spoken language, although by the time of Alfred the Great (AD 849–99) a standard literary version was emerging. In addition to native Celtic elements and words surviving from the Roman occupation, vocabulary expanded through the spread of Christian culture and the influence of Scandinavian invaders in the ninth and tenth centuries. By the late tenth century the Wessex dialect had become dominant.

Following the Norman Conquest of 1066, Anglo-Norman was quickly established as the language of the aristocracy and Latin that of the administration. It has been estimated that some 33,000 Old French words were absorbed into the English language in the centuries following the Conquest, but from the fourteenth century English was again the standard and, despite the influence of French, the Germanic *nature* of the language has been maintained, even though the original native English element is probably now a minor one. By the sixteenth century most vowels were pronounced as they are today.

The traditional historical phases of linguistic development are *Old English* (up to *c.* 1150), *Middle English* (*c.* 1150 to *c.* 1500) and *Modern English* (from *c.* 1500), which derives from the East Midland dialect and that of London. But in practice the language evolved gradually and with considerable regional variations.
See also ANGLE *and* SAXON

OLD LADY DAY *see* LADY DAY

OLD-STYLE Usually a reference to the calendar prior to its reform in 1752, by which New Year was defined as 1 January and the English calendar was brought into line with those of European countries by the omission of the days from 2 to 14 September 1752.

OMNIBUS Omnibuses were introduced from Paris to London by George Shillibeer in 1829 as a cheaper and more comfortable alternative to the HACKNEY CAB and short-distance STAGECOACH. The service began with two four-wheeled single-deck vehicles drawn by bay horses harnessed three abreast. There was comfortable accommodation for twenty-two passengers who were seated inside on cushions, provided with newspapers and charged no more than one-third of the fares paid by outside passengers on stagecoaches. Unlike the drivers of hackney cabs, the conductors and drivers of omnibuses were civil, clean and sober.

The *Shillibeers*, as they were called, were an immediate success, making over £100 a week from twelve daily return journeys between the Bank of England and Paddington, but were later banned by the Metropolitan Police who considered that three-horse 'buses were a traffic hazard. Shillibeer then introduced a number of two-horse vehicles carrying up to sixteen passengers, with longitudinal seating and a rear entrance and step. The *knifeboard omnibus* was a double-deck vehicle introduced in the 1850s. This had low back-to-back seating on the roof, which was reached by means of a ladder, and travelled at about 13 km per hour (8 miles per hour). The later *garden-seat 'bus* of 1881–1914 had double rows of forward-facing seats on the upper deck, and safe outside steps with a handrail and 'decency board' which enabled ladies to ascend without immodestly revealing their petticoats. The driver was perched on a box at the front of the upper deck and the conductor travelled on steps at the rear which, by 1880, had been replaced by a platform.

OPEN FIELDS In many parts of lowland England, open field farming was practised for nearly 1,000 years. Even today, it may be found in a modified form (*see below*), though in most parishes the open fields had disappeared by the mid-nineteenth century. The origins of the system remain obscure but it is likely that it was introduced during the eighth and ninth centuries as a means of controlling the balance between grazed and cultivated land and of ensuring an equitable distribution of holdings among the various members of an estate community. The open fields contained no walls, hedges or permanent fences and were subdivided into FURLONGS, compact units of between 5 and 10 acres, orientated according to the contours of the land and often producing herring-bone or chequered patterns in the landscape (*see* RIDGE AND FURROW). One tenant might hold an entire furlong, but more often it was divided into STRIPS (*lands* or *selions*), held of a manorial lord in return for work on a set number of days annually on his DEMESNE land. Often described as the 'Three Field System', each village probably had from three to five fields of between 100 and 350 acres, depending on the size of the community.

Although there is little evidence of how open field systems were introduction, such an exercise must have required considerable reorganization, both of existing farming practices and of a community's social structures and attitudes. Changes of such magnitude could not have been implemented without a lord's commitment to the system or his determination that they should be imposed, arbitrarily if necessary, on an unwilling tenancy. Many dispersed farmsteads and hamlets were abandoned and new VILLAGES created. The open fields may themselves have been superimposed on earlier INFIELD-OUTFIELD systems or the enclosures of so-called Celtic fields.

On all estates, the community enjoyed customary rights of grazing on the common pasture and WASTE, on the fallow field (*see below*) and on the stubble after harvesting. There were considerable regional variations in the management of the open fields, however. In 'common' systems, for example, ploughing and harvesting were administered by the COURT LEET and undertaken communally, while in 'open' systems there was no central organization, though regulation was effected through the manor court and its elected officer, the reeve. The complexities of the system, and the numerous obligations of an individual tenant both to his lord and to his neighbours, required a considerable degree of co-operation and team work. Few peasants owned sufficient oxen or horses for a ploughing team and most covenanted to share resources with a neighbour, breaches of faith resulting in fines and payment of damages. A typical peasant holding consisted of a *virgate* or *yardland* (in the north of England, an *oxgang* or *bovate*). This could vary from 15 to 40 acres, depending on local custom and the quality of the land, and was made up of strips distributed throughout the open fields.

The essence of the open field system was crop rotation, a practice which may have been introduced to Britain on the agricultural estates of the Roman occupation. Most villages having three fields, the sequence was fallow – wheat – legumes (pease and beans), though oats, barley and rye were sometimes grown instead of wheat. Some villages had only two fields, one of which would lie fallow each year, while elsewhere additional fields may have been created by assarting (*see* ASSART), particularly as the medieval population increased, or by the division of a larger field.

Many of the former farmsteads of 'new' medieval villages survive today and there is considerable documentary and cartographic evidence of open field systems as they were in the seventeenth, eighteenth and nineteenth centuries. Of the few which survived ENCLOSURE, the best examples are at Laxton in Nottinghamshire, Braunton in Devon and Gamelsby in Cumbria. At Braunton Great Field there are about 140 sections, some as small as half an acre, divided by turf baulks. The strips once numbered 400 but have been consolidated as adjacent plots were acquired by the same farmer. Nevertheless, the names of the furlongs are precisely those of a survey dated 1324. Oulton

Open fields at Laxton, Nottinghamshire.

Broad Dales is a 56-acre field close to the village of Gamelsby in Cumbria. It is divided into strips or blocks known locally as *darrocks* or *dales*, which are divided not by baulks, but by marker stones. Local farmers own one or more darrocks, which they cultivate as they please during the winter and graze communally in the summer, the number of animals being regulated by the number of darrocks owned. As in all open field systems, holdings have been consolidated to form more convenient units. Former open fields may be marked *Field System* on Ordnance Survey maps.

See also GLEBE *and* MANOR

OPEN STRING *see* STAIRCASES

OPPIDUM A Latin word meaning 'town', and applied during the Roman occupation of Britain to native fortress-towns, notably the major HILL FORTS. In Suetonius' account of the life of Vespasian (one of the Roman commanders of the invasion in AD 43, and later Emperor) we are told that, in the south, Vespasian captured more than twenty *oppida*, among them Maiden Castle in Dorset which was, at that time, a territorial capital with a substantial population and sophisticated fortifications. In more recent usage, an *oppidan* is a townsman and, in university towns, one who is not a

member of the university or is a student who is not resident in a college.
See also KINGDOMS (ANCIENT) *and* TOWNS

OPUS RETICULATUM *see* RUBBLE

ORATORY A chapel licensed for private use.

ORCHARDS While prehistoric peoples were gatherers of wild fruits and may have used apples to make a primitive form of cider, there is no evidence of planned cultivation before the Roman occupation of Britain from AD 43. The Romans were expert in fruit-growing, and orchards no doubt formed a significant part of their agricultural estates (*see* ROMAN VILLA). They introduced many distinct varieties of dessert apple into Britain, including the Court Pendu Plat which is still used in breeding programmes.

From the late seventh century until *c.* 1100 apple cultivation was largely a monastic occupation, notably at the Benedictine houses of Evesham and Pershore in Worcestershire. Orchards were a common feature of the medieval estate where apples were cultivated both for cider-making and for cooking. Legal documents distinguished between the garden (*gardinum*) and orchard (*artus*), and a deed of 1205 specified that 200 Pearmains should be supplied annually to the Crown by Robert de Evermere as part payment for the lordship of Runham in Norfolk.

The Pearmain and the Costard varieties were widely grown in the thirteenth century, costards being hawked by London costard mongers (later, *coster-mongers*) in the late fifteenth century at about 4*d* per hundred. Pippins (trees grown from pips) were widely acclaimed in Tudor and Elizabethan England, where they were known as Queenings, Russetings, Leathercoats and Apple-johns (because they ripened near St John's Day). In the sixteenth century, Codlings, which were 'coddled' or partially boiled, were favoured for cooking. The eighteenth and nineteenth centuries were the great age of apple cultivation, during which numerous new varieties were developed, including the famous Cox's Orange Pippin.

There are numerous FIELD NAMES and PLACE-NAMES, such as Orchardleigh in Somerset and Appledore in Devon, though some apparent 'apple' names in fact derive from the Welsh *aber*, meaning 'river-mouth', and 'orchard' similarly may mean 'wood', from the Welsh *argoed*.

Regrettably, most of England's orchards have been grubbed out, often leaving field surfaces which

are similar in appearance to RIDGE AND FURROW, the hollows having been formed between the rows of trees.
See also CIDER MILLS

ORDEAL BY FIRE *and* **ORDEAL BY WATER** *see* LAW

ORDINAL A medieval manual intended to acquaint a priest with the offices to be recited in accordance with the variations of the ecclesiastical year.

ORDINARY i) In ARMORY, an ordinary is one of a number of bold rectilinear charges also known as the Honourable Ordinaries.
ii) An ordinary of arms is a reference book which lists the heraldic descriptions (*blazons*) of shields of arms alphabetically by the charges they contain. Proficiency in the use of blazon is essential if an ordinary is to be used to identify arms. The best known ordinary is J.W. Papworth's *Ordinary of British Armorials*, first published in 1874 and reprinted in 1977 (pub. Five Barrows).
iii) An ecclesiastical superior.

ORDNANCE OF LABOURERS *see* PEASANTS' REVOLT

ORDNANCE SURVEY Ordnance Survey maps are the essential tools of the local historian and always a joy to possess.

During the second half of the eighteenth century, when Britain was faced with the threat of invasion from France, accurate maps of the south coast of England were needed by the British Army. A survey was carried out by the Board of Ordnance, a Crown organization mainly responsible for artillery, with offices in the Tower of London. The Board's work followed the example of a pioneering Scottish cartographer, General William Roy, who had produced military maps at the time of the Scottish rebellion in 1745. Once the survey of the south coast had been completed at a scale of 1 inch to 1 mile, the new style of map-making was in considerable demand, the Industrial Revolution in particular creating a need for good quality mapping so that major engineering and constructional projects could be defined and demographic and social changes recorded.

The first edition or *Old Series* of one-inch maps is an interesting though perplexing historical instrument because of the complexity of its development. The Trigonometrical Survey of England and Wales was founded in 1791 and the first regular sheet (Essex) published in 1805. But the national one-inch map was not completed until the publication of the last sheet (the Isle of Man) in 1873. After this date, *Old Series* maps remained in print and were not universally superseded by the *New Series* sheets until the early 1890s, a century after the original conception of the scheme, during which time numerous modifications were made progressively, not only to newly published sheets but also to existing copper plates. *Old Series* maps are therefore subject to considerable variation and the delay between survey and publication varies from a few years to twenty.

After 1847, railway revisions were effected and special map series produced such as the *Index to the Tithe Survey* and the *Geological Survey*. Dating the content of these early maps is often difficult; nevertheless, the facsimile series of post-1860 *Old Series* one-inch sheets (published by David and Charles) provides a fascinating view of the late nineteenth-century landscape and, with its copious notes, enables the historian to trace the complex development of a particular map. The third edition was published by the beginning of the twentieth century and the seventh edition by 1961.

Since the original Trigonometrical Survey, maps at a variety of scales have been produced using a network of over 20,000 *trigonometrical stations* ('trig points'), triangulation pillars set in elevated positions in open countryside or on tall buildings such as church towers. Triangulation pillars are shown on maps as small triangles, each containing a spot-height (*see below*). Surveyors measured the angle and distances between these points to provide a base from which shorter distances could be measured and locations plotted accurately. Today, aerial and satellite photography are used in map revision, and gradually the familiar old trig points are disappearing one by one – often to the consternation of local people who, in several cases, have fought successfully for their retention. Height was measured against (Cornish) sea level and BENCHMARKS (a horizontal line above an arrow) may still be seen carved on milestones, buildings, etc., at regular intervals along many roads. These are shown, with the height at a particular point (*spot height*), on large scale maps. Today, all information is stored in digital form on computer and may be used to draw out any part of a map required by a customer. Large-scale mapping is available at over forty Ordnance Survey agents throughout the United Kingdom, in both digital form (*Superplan Data*) and paper (*Superplan Plots*).

The following map series and services are of particular interest to the local historian:

Urban areas are surveyed at 1:1250 scale (50 inches to 1 mile) and detail includes information such as house numbers and names, while rural areas are surveyed at 1:2500 scale (25 inches to 1 mile). Mountain and moorland areas are shown in maps at the scale 1:10000 (6 inches to 1 mile), as are several towns and cities.

The *Landranger* series covers the whole country in 204 maps at a scale of 1:50000 (2 cm to 1 km or 1 ¼ inches to 1 mile).

The excellent *Explorer* series at 1:25000 (4 cm to 1 km or 2½ inches to 1 mile) gives more detailed information such as field boundaries, footpaths and rights of way in England and Wales.

Historical maps at 1:625000 scale (1 cm to 6.25 km or 1 inch to 10 miles) include *Roman Britain*, which shows known military sites, roads and place-names against a background of modern Britain; and *Ancient Britain* (up to AD 1000) which shows the geographical distribution of some of the most important visible ancient monuments.

Superplan is the Ordnance Survey's 'tailor-made', large-scale, site-centred mapping system. Each *Superplan* plot is individually produced to order which means that plots can be up to A0 size or even larger, and at any scale from 1:200 to 1:10,000. Every plot includes all the latest available surveyed information and can include ground areas and parcel numbers. *Superplan Data* provides similar information in a form which is specially designed for computer-aided design (CAD) in DXF format on a standard floppy disc, CD-ROM or via e-mail.

A *Siteplan* pack provides six copies of a project site and may be precisely centred on any property address in the country.

Landplan is the first graphic product to be digitally derived from a variety of thematic and topographical databases. It is a 'plot on demand' service on paper or film at 1:5000 or 1:10 000 scales.

The *Historical Data* service is available in a range of formats. Map data is scanned from Ordnance Survey's historical archive of County Series and superseded National Grid mapping back to the mid-nineteenth century.

The *Geological Series* of maps, based on Ordnance Survey maps, is published by the British Geological Survey, while *Soil Survey* maps are available from the Soil Survey and Land Research Centre. *For* addresses *see* APPENDIX I
See also MAPS

ORDO *see* ROMAN ADMINISTRATION

ORGANS The Puritans considered that instrumental music distracted the mind and soul from divine worship and in 1644 an act of parliament required the removal of organs from churches. In many areas, implementation of the act was rigorous: organs were smashed and the pipes carried off to be used for more mundane purposes. Congregations, especially in rural areas, reacted by erecting west galleries in their churches to accommodate 'choirs' of instrumentalists to lead the singing (*see* GALLERY). These in turn were replaced by harmoniums and organs in the second half of the nineteenth century, when the old 'psalm books' were burned and galleries demolished by reforming clergymen who, accustomed to the surpliced choirs of their Oxford and Cambridge colleges, sought to impose their own brand of respectability on their rural congregations. Most organs in parish churches date from this time and some still have the handle by which air was pumped into the bellows, usually by a 'poor boy of the parish'. They were invariably played by an 'outsider' (such as the vicar's wife or the schoolteacher) and, with the introduction of *Hymns Ancient and Modern* in 1861, served to divide congregations and, indeed, communities. In *Under the Greenwood Tree*, Thomas Hardy describes vividly the effect on the Mellstock string choir of the arrival of an organ, acquired by the progressive Parson Maybold to impress the comely Miss Fancy Day.

The traditional music of the west gallery became that of the non-conformist chapel and of the village 'band' which continued to celebrate Christmas, Easter and Harvest by performing musical perambulations round the parish. Many organs were squeezed into side chapels or aisles and are often singularly obtrusive and ugly. There are older examples, however, other than those in the cathedrals and collegiate chapels: the church at Old Radnor in Powys has an early sixteenth-century panelled organ case, and at Stanford-on-Avon in Northamptonshire there is a fine organ case dating from the mid-seventeenth century.

ORIEL *see* WINDOWS

ORIENTATION Tradition has it that medieval CHURCHES were invariably constructed with the chancel to the east for symbolic reasons: that Jerusalem is in the east and that the rising sun represents Christ, the Sun of Righteousness. The fallacy was inevitably compounded by Victorian ecclesiologists, many of whom were obsessed with symbolism. But the simple truth is that, in these northern climes, natural early morning light was needed for the celebration of Divine Office which was, of course, celebrated in the chancel or adjacent chapels.
For the medieval builders' preoccupation with luminescence *see* GOTHIC ARCHITECTURE

ORIGINALIA ROLLS These contain copies of charters and grants to civic and other corporate bodies, together with information concerning estates, manorial surveys and other related matters. Originalia Rolls are maintained at the Public Record Office and several have been published.

ORMOLU Gilded bronze or brass used in architectural decoration.

ORTHOSTAT WALLS Large irregular boulders interspersed with smaller stones in field walls of the western uplands of Britain and parts of Ireland. Many orthostat walls may be of considerable antiquity and were probably constructed from boulders cleared during the first cultivation of adjacent land. Excavations at Shaugh on Dartmoor have revealed that such a wall was built *c*. 1500 BC, but most are difficult to date and may be of comparatively recent construction.
See also DRYSTONE WALLS

OSSUARIES Charnel houses associated with churches where graveyards were inadequate to provide for the needs of an urban community. In some instances, endowed charnel-chapels were also provided in which prayers were offered for the souls of the dismembered dead. The medieval ossuary and chapel in the churchyard of Old St Pauls, London, were revered by the populace as exemplifications of immortality. Crypts were often used as ossuaries and most were hygienically cleared in the nineteenth century. At Micheldean church, Gloucestershire, the rood loft stair continues downwards into a vaulted ossuary complete with a chute for the bones.

OUBLIETTE *see* PRISONS

OUT-COMMONERS *see* COMMONS

Ossuary at Mere, Wiltshire.

OUTFANGENTHEOF The right of a manorial lord to apprehend a thief beyond the boundaries of his estate and to return him for trial in his own court.
See also INFANGETHEOF

OUTGANG A perimeter lane separating the TOFTS of a village nucleus from the surrounding fields. In more recent times, called a BACK LANE.

OUTLAWS Those who were literally 'outside the law' were usually men or women who had either absconded or escaped from custody before being brought to court in order to answer criminal charges. If thereafter they failed to appear before a court, having been summoned to do so on four occasions, they were declared outlaws, their goods forfeited and, denied the protection of the realm, they could be killed on sight. With nothing to lose, most fugitives joined with others to form outlaw bands living by petty crime in remote areas where they were effectively beyond the law. Of course, the archetypal outlaw was Robin Hood, but in answer to the question 'Who was he?' the answer must be 'There were more than one'. This still allows for an original, but his identity is lost in the 'obscurity created by his own fame. Real people move in the shadows, their crimes revealed before the courts, but by borrowing [Robin Hood's] reputation they dissolved his identity.' (Holt, 1989)

From 1547, many vagrants turned to outlawry as an alternative to branding and servitude (*see* POOR LAW). Outlawry was abolished as recently as 1879.

OVENS Before the seventeenth century, home-baking was carried out in a flat-lidded earthenware or iron baking-pot placed within the ashes of an open hearth. Ovens were incorporated into the walls of many cottages from the seventeenth century, usually to one side of the main chimney flue; the familiar bulging semi-cylindrical exterior projection, with its masonry walls and sloping tile or slate roof, traditionally referred to as a '*bread oven*'. Inside, the domed lining was usually beautifully constructed of close-fitting stones or bricks, sometimes with an additional lining of clay. The oven door was generally to one side of the open hearth, which continued in use until superseded by a coal range in the nineteenth century. Before baking, the oven was pre-heated by a small fire, of faggot-wood or furze, lit in the base of the oven. When this had died down, the ashes were hastily removed and the door shut on the dough, pies, etc., which gently baked in the diminishing heat, supplemented by latent heat from the adjacent chimney flue. *Cloam* ovens of Devon and Cornwall were made of earthenware and set into the otherwise unsuitable cob walls of cottages.

OX DROVES *see* DROVE ROADS

OXGANG *see* OPEN FIELDS

OYER AND TERMINER Commissions of Oyer and Terminer were royal commissions of *ad hoc* appointees charged with authority to 'hear and determine' specific cases of treason, insurrection, murder, coining and other serious crimes within a particular county. The records were kept by Clerks of the Peace.
See also LAW

P

PACK-HORSE BRIDGE *see* PACK-HORSE ROADS

PACK-HORSE ROADS For over four millennia, from the late Neolithic period to the end of the nineteenth century, goods for barter and trade were transported on the backs of ponies by merchants and journeymen using an increasingly complex network of route-ways, many of which were to form the basis of our modern road system. There could have been few discernible differences in the appearance of the itinerant Iron Age smith, the medieval market trader and the nineteenth-century tinker. Each had his pack-horse, or pair of horses, with panniers of varying size and construction slung across the animal's back to distribute the weight of the load,

which could be as much as 100 kg (220 lb). The advantage of the pack-horse was its ability to traverse terrain which would otherwise be inaccessible to wheeled vehicles. Before the introduction of turnpikes in the eighteenth century, roads throughout Britain were generally little better than quagmires and the use of pack-horses was universal, carts and wagons being entirely unsuitable for transporting goods over long distances.

With the proliferation of monastic estates and the expansion of medieval MARKETS, FAIRS and overseas trade, teams of pack-horses, following a lead pony in single file and sometimes numbering two dozen or more, carried an enormous variety of goods, depending on the commerce of a particular region. Some teams belonged to monastic houses, merchant companies and guilds, while others were available for hire, carriers being employed by the owner on a casual basis. The lead horse of a team always had bells attached to its harness, so that other travellers would be alerted to the team's approach. Such bells were recalled as recently as 1897: 'When the pack-horse traffic ceased hundreds of those sonorous bells were sold for old metal, and the brokers' shops were for a time full of them.' (G.N. Wright, 1985). In the north country of the nineteenth century, coal and iron ore were transported in by pack-horse, as were building materials and household goods, at a rate of 1s (5 pence) per ton per mile. In that part of England, the train-master was known as a *Jagger* after the sturdy German ponies which, with Scottish Galloways, were bred for the purpose.

As they converged on a market or port, the pack-horse trains inevitably shared the highway with all manner of travellers, but in open country they tended to follow more remote routes, avoiding wherever possible natural hazards and towns and, from the eighteenth century, toll-gates. For this reason, many pack-horse roads are today little more than bridle-paths, their continuing status as highways confirmed as legal rights of way on the Ordnance Survey maps.

There is one feature which in particular marks out a former pack-horse road from other trackways: the *pack-horse bridge*. Wherever possible, pack-horse teams crossed rivers by existing fords or bridges, but in many instances their routes were so far removed from conventional highways that special bridges had to be built, usually by manorial or monastic landlords, who in the Middle Ages were responsible for the maintenance of bridges. However, most pack-horse bridges date from the period 1650 to 1800, and were provided either by public levy or by local benefactors (such as merchants of the Wool Staple)

A pack-horse train, after an original drawing by Louis Huard.

who had a vested interest in facilitating trade. In upland regions, such as the Pennines and the Lake District of Cumbria, these bridges usually consist of a single, steeply arched span high above the waters of a mountain torrent. Pack-horse bridges were usually of sufficient width to allow for the passage of a single animal and were rarely provided with parapets, which would have obstructed the panniers. (Where parapets are found, they are almost invariably a later addition.) They were also paved with cobbles or stone flags which extended on either side of the bridge.

Elsewhere, many narrow stone pack-horse bridges were built: sometimes alongside fords so that streams could be crossed even when in full spate, and sometimes more impressive structures, incorporating two or more arches. Such bridges, often approached by sunken HOLLOW WAYS and now serving only a footpath or bridle-way, are generally indicative of the course of former pack-horse roads. Many of these roads were constructed as elevated CAUSEWAYS, raised above marshy

ground and just wide enough to accommodate a pony and its panniers, while others were flights of rough-hewn stone 'steps', such as the so-called Roman Steps in the Rhinog mountains of Gwynedd.

Like the drove roads, the major pack-horse routes attracted wayside inns whose names often commemorate their origins; local names such as 'Jagger Lane', 'Badger Gate' and 'Brogger's Path' recall the days of the jaggers, of the *badgers* or licensed corn-carriers, and of the itinerant *broggers*, who traded in small quantities of wool. In Dorset, Packers Hill is located on a former pack-horse road near Sherborne.

The proliferation of turnpike trusts in the eighteenth century did little to diminish the efficacy or popularity of the pack-horse system; indeed, most gangs of carriers studiously avoided having to pay tolls and when necessary sought out alternative ancient GREEN LANES and DROVE ROADS (which are wider than pack-horse roads) to bypass the TURNPIKES. In Cumbria at this time, there were no fewer than 354 pack-horses in Kendal alone. It was the massive expansion of trade during the Industrial Revolution which finally destroyed the pack-horse system, notably the construction of the canal and rail networks by which huge quantities of goods and materials could be transported cheaply and efficiently. The pack-horse simply could not compete.

See also BRIDGES, CLAPPER BRIDGES *and* MEDIEVAL ROADS

PADSTONES *see* TIMBER-FRAMED BUILD-INGS

PAGAN SYMBOLS In AD 601, just four years after the arrival of St Augustine in Canterbury, Pope Gregory the Great wrote to Abbot Mellitus, a missionary-priest, advising him that pagan shrines should not be destroyed but purified with holy water so that in time they would 'become temples of the true God'. The early missionaries took great care not to alienate the native population by attempting to impose a raw Christian ideology on an already diverse and complex religious culture. Elements of pagan worship were adapted or incorporated into the practices of the early Church: Christian altars and relics replaced pagan idols and native festivals were assimilated into the great feast-days of the Church, notably Christmas and Easter. Many early churches were built within or adjoining pagan religious sites (*see* CHURCH SITES) and the wells and springs of native water gods were re-dedicated to missionary saints (*see* HOLY WELLS). This policy of gradual religious substitution was effective but it created an enduring cultural ambivalence. At Codford St Peter in Wiltshire, a fragment of a ninth-century cross shaft is carved with the vigorous image of the pagan 'mallet god' *Sucellos*, bringer of happiness. Pagan gods are commemorated in the days of the week and in innumerable field and place-names and a formidable sub-culture of pagan belief persisted throughout the Middle Ages.

There is a fallacious tradition that carvings of pagan symbols, and of the grotesques and monsters of the medieval bestiaries, were confined to the exterior fabric of churches in order that a sinful peasantry should be alerted to the need to seek redemption. But this was also the function of the DOOM and other WALL PAINTINGS which are found *inside* churches and which depict images of eternal damnation no less horrific than the iconography of the pagan imagination. The fusion of pagan and Christian imagery is particularly evident in the decorative work of the ROMANESQUE period but later medieval masons also delighted in the carving of pagan symbols, notably in GARGOYLES, roof-bosses, corbels and in the capitals of pillars, even in the most sophisticated of urban churches. These carvings included fertility-cult symbols as well as mythical creatures and humorous and obscene images of medieval life. How, despite prohibition by the Church, such a tradition was sustained throughout the Middle Ages remains a mystery, but there is no doubting the extraordinary tenacity with which paganism maintained its hold on the medieval mind. Many of these carvings have been destroyed in successive restorations, particularly during the nineteenth century when pre-Christian fertility symbols were considered to be improper. But many examples have survived, notably the hideous SHEELA-NA-GIG and the ubiquitous GREEN MAN images.

See also CHRISTIAN SYMBOLS

PAGI *see* ROMAN ADMINISTRATION

PALAEOGRAPHY The reading, dating and localization of handwriting. Palaeography is more than the study of how to read old documents. An understanding of scribal rules and conventions and of the peculiarities associated with particular places and periods can facilitate the identification of specific writers and assist in ascertaining the provenance of a document from the evidence of the script. The amateur local historian will rarely have recourse to an original document and, in any event, will require expert advice both in its interpretation and in determining its provenance and, indeed, its authenticity. Most important historical documents have been transcribed and are available, often with explanatory notes, through libraries and record offices or by appointment with the archivists of specialist collections. But for the most part, the interpretation of handwriting in more mundane documents and maps (such as those which accompany tithe and enclosure awards) is a matter of patience and common sense. It is at the parochial level that most local historians will at some time experience difficulties, for there is little one can do to remedy retrospectively the calligraphic idiosyncrasies of a Georgian rector or a semi-literate parish clerk.

PALAEOLITHIC *see* STONE AGE

PALATINATE The word *palatine* means 'pertaining to a palace' and the Palatine Counties were those over which Norman magnates and their successors exercised royal jurisdiction. The original counties were those of the Welsh MARCH (ruled by the earls of Chester, Shrewsbury and Hereford) and the Scottish borders (ruled by the Prince Bishop of Durham). The palatinates were necessary for the defence of the Conqueror's new realm but elsewhere holdings were dispersed to prevent the concentration of magnatial power.

The *prince bishops* of Durham are unique in the history of England. They were appointed by the king as *counts palatine*, head of church and state in a vast territory which included all the lands between the rivers Tyne and Tees, land around Crayke and Northallerton in Yorkshire and an area along the river Tweed in Northumberland known as 'North Durham': Norhamshire, Islandshire, including Holy Island, and Bedlingtonshire. This was St Cuthbert's diocese, the seventh-century bishopric of Lindisfarne which, from 995, was administered from Durham. The customary dues of its vast estates are recorded in 1183 in what is now called the *Boldon Book*. The Palatinate was effectively a kingdom within a kingdom and, as defenders of the realm in the north, the prince bishops were charged with the defence of the Scottish border. By the fourteenth century, the Palatinate was at the height of its military power, its warrior-bishops uniquely commemorated in the ducally-crowned mitre and sword in the coats-of-arms of all subsequent bishops of Durham. They had their own chancellors, Exchequer and mint; they administered the civil and criminal law; granted charters for markets and fairs and exercised rights of forfeiture. Inevitably, the bishops' authority was reduced under the Tudor kings; nevertheless, in 1585 the Bishop of Durham was the largest landholder in the country with eighty manors worth £2,500 annually. The failure of the Northern Rising in 1569 succeeded in suppressing local opposition to the bishops' traditional domination of local affairs and single-faction politics continued in County Durham until the mid-nineteenth century. The bishops' powers were finally vested in the Crown in 1836 and the palatinate courts abolished by the Courts Act of 1971.

PALE (i) A stake used in a fence (*see* PALISADE).
(ii) A boundary.
(iii) A district or territory subject to a particular jurisdiction or confined within agreed boundaries (*see* MARCH). The *English Pale* was the hinterland of Calais, the only part of France to remain in English possession at the end of the Hundred Years War in 1453. The *Pale* comprises those parts of Ireland over which England has exercised jurisdiction: these have varied in extent at different times.

(iv) In ARMORY, an ORDINARY consisting of a broad vertical stripe.

PALIMPSEST A manuscript on which the original writing has been effaced to make room for new material. Also a monumental brass which has been turned and re-engraved on the reverse.
See also BRASSES (MONUMENTAL)

PALISADE Strictly a fence of PALES, but in modern usage also of iron railings. A verb meaning to enclose with a palisade.
See also DEER PARKS

PALLADIAN A neo-classical style of architecture based on the concepts of the Italian Andrea Palladio (1508–80), whose buildings exercised considerable influence on the architecture of western and northern Europe in the seventeenth and eighteenth centuries. Palladio followed Renaissance practice by addressing the architectural traditions of ancient Rome, and in particular of the temples. He adapted what he knew of Roman building to the needs of the sixteenth century, innovating where necessary but always maintaining both symmetry and effect. In England the first exponent of Palladian design was Inigo Jones (1573–1652). His was essentially an English interpretation of the style rather than a copy of Palladio's designs. The Banqueting House in London (1619–22) is Jones' masterpiece, but his first Italian Renaissance design was the Queen's House in Greenwich, begun in 1616.

A Dutch Palladian style was introduced into English domestic buildings in the second half of the seventeenth century. The chief revival of Palladianism occurred between 1720 and 1760, inspired by Lord Burlington (1694–1753), Colen Campbell (1676–1729) and William Kent (1685–1748), notably in the great houses of the period such as Chiswick House in London (1725–9) and in public buildings such as the Assembly Rooms in York (1731–2). Numerous country houses were also built in the Palladian style, as at Stourhead in Wiltshire (completed in 1724) and Mereworth Castle in Kent (1723), both of which were designed by Colen Campbell, and William Kent's magnificent Holkham Hall in Norfolk (1734). Many Palladian terraces and smaller houses were also constructed, often by builders working from books of architectural drawings.
See also CLASSICAL ARCHITECTURE

PANDY A Welsh place-name denoting the site of a former fulling mill.

PANELLING From the thirteenth century, the interior walls of larger houses and public buildings were often lined with wooden boards (*wainscoting*) which were placed vertically and overlapped one another as in a clinker-built ship. (Wainscot was usually oak imported from the Baltic coast and used also for wagons or 'wains'.) During the fifteenth century, panel and frame construction (*joined woodwork*) was introduced from Flanders. The panels, thin sheets of wood, were tapered on all four sides and fitted into grooves within a framework of thicker wood. The horizontal and vertical strips of the frame (*rails* and *stiles*) were united by mortise and tenon joints and fastened by square oak pegs inserted into round holes. This type of panelling was used for centuries on walls and ceilings and in doors and furniture.

Early panelling was rarely carved but was sometimes painted in coloured designs. From the late fifteenth century until about 1550, *lignum undulatum* ('wavy woodwork') decoration was popular, each panel being carved with a representation of a piece of material folded vertically. (From the nineteenth century, this style of decoration has been described as *linenfold*). Later examples may have a decorative 'punched' border to represent embroidery and a further variation of the design, known as *parchemin*, resembles a curled piece of parchment. Early sixteenth-century panels were often decorated with a central roundel, incorporating heraldic and other devices, and from about 1550 a profusion of English Renaissance motifs appeared. At this time, inlays (usually of bog oak, holly and laburnum) and painted and gilded ornamentation were also used.

From the 1630s, entire walls, together with window and door openings and chimney-pieces, were incorporated into classical designs comprising entablature, pilasters and plinth. During the seventeenth and eighteenth centuries, panels were often plain or raised at the centre (*fielded*) and by the eighteenth century pine or deal had replaced oak and this was painted in a light colour with ornamentation picked out in gilt or ormolu.

PANNAGE *see* COMMONS *and* FOREST

PANTHER *see* BEASTS (HERALDIC)

PANTILES *see* TILES

PANTRY *see* LARDER

PAPAL BULL *see* SEALS

PAPER Paper was first used in England as a writing surface from the fourteenth century but it was not manufactured here until the late fifteenth century, and even then only in small quantities. In the late seventeenth century, Huguenot immigrants specialized in its production.

PARALLEL TRACK *see* MULTIPLE TRACKS

PARCHEMIN *see* PANELLING

PARCHMENT A writing surface made from the treated skins of sheep or goats. The lighter 'flesh' side was preferred for formal documents but both sides were used in the writing of rolls and books. *See also* VELLUM

PARCLOSE A stone or timber screen separating one part of a church from another (*see* ALTARS *and* CHANTRY CHAPELS).

PARDONER *see* SHRINES

PARGETING Decorative PLASTERWORK (*pargeting*) was popular in the sixteenth and seventeenth centuries, particularly on the exterior walls and gable-ends of smaller timber-framed town houses in Essex and Suffolk and in parts of Cambridgeshire and Kent. Some pargeting was incised but most remaining examples comprise panels of high relief ornamentation: usually foliage, flowers and geometrical and heraldic designs. These were made by applying moulds to the wet plaster and finishing by hand. The term may derive from the practice of throwing plaster on to the façade, hence '*pour jeter*'.

PARISH Dating from the ninth and tenth centuries, when parish churches superseded the MINSTER system, the parish remains the smallest unit of ecclesiastical administration, having its own church or churches (*see* CHAPELRY) and served by an incumbent to whom parishioners originally paid ecclesiastical dues and tithes and to whose religious ministrations all inhabitants of a parish are entitled. Most early parish churches were provided by Saxon lords, the boundaries of whose estates almost certainly corresponded with those of the parishes. Many parishes are therefore of considerable antiquity, while others may have been merged following the extinction of a neighbouring settlement (*see* DESERTED VILLAGES) or 'rationalized' as the result of legislation. A parish may also once have contained one or more medieval

MANORS, while sometimes a single manor may have encompassed several parishes. A *donative parish* is one which is exempt from diocesan jurisdiction, also known as a PECULIAR.

An incumbent is nominated by the patron of the benefice (with, in modern times, certain rights of preference being available to the parochial church council) and may be removed only in exceptional circumstances. The incumbent is a *rector* or *vicar*, the distinction being of an historical nature. If, formerly, all the tithes were attached to the benefice for the maintenance of the incumbent it is a rectory; otherwise it is a vicarage (*see* CLERGY *and* GLEBE). (Team rectors and vicars are different and were created by the Pastoral Measure 1968.)

At one time, the *churchwardens* were responsible for presenting offenders against ecclesiastical law and they still have power to remove a person's hat during divine service. Their other duties have, from time to time, included the management of parish property and finances and the upkeep of the fabric of the church; the provision of facilities for worship (including the allocation of pews); with the Overseers, supervision of the education and relief of the poor; the maintenance of parish arms and the payment of members of the militia; and the extermination of vermin. The churchwardens also represented the views of parishioners, both corporately and severally, in parochial matters and were responsible for encouraging church attendance and ensuring that the young were baptised. In many large parishes there were often three or four churchwardens appointed to represent different *townships*, administrative divisions of a parish which levied a separate poor rate and appointed their own constables. Until recently, the churchwardens were known as the 'Vicar's Warden' and 'People's Warden', their staffs of office bearing a mitre and crown respectively. They are now chosen (traditionally on Easter Tuesday) by the joint consent of the incumbent, those who are on the Church Electoral Role and the local government electors who reside in the parish.

Persons dying in a parish or resident there before death or having a close relative buried in the churchyard have a legal right to burial there. But if they are unbaptised, suicides in their right mind or excommunicated, there can be no service from the Book of Common Prayer. The freehold of the churchyard is vested in the incumbent, who enjoys the rights of herbage, but its maintenance is the responsibility of the parochial church council and may be paid for out of the rates by the (civil) parish council. It is a criminal offence to strike anyone in a church or churchyard. The registers of baptisms, marriages and burials are in the custody of the incumbent but modern regulations for their preservation usually cause those not in current use to be deposited, frequently in county archives.

Successive acts of parliament, particularly in the sixteenth and seventeenth centuries, encouraged the development of secular parochial authority administered through *vestries*. Early parishes levied a church rate, but legislation enabled them to levy rates for poor relief (*see* POOR LAW) and for the maintenance of the highway. At this time also, the manor courts were in decline and for a while there was an overlapping of manorial and vestral interests. Most were *open vestries* at which any male ratepayer could attend and vote, but in populous areas where the open vestry system could become unmanageable many parishes succeeded in establishing *select vestries* which, although self-perpetuating and undemocratic, were often more effective. A vestry was responsible for appointing the churchwardens, sexton, Overseer of the Poor, Surveyor of Highways and constables, and for the annual PERAMBULATION of the parish boundary.

The civil and ecclesiastical components of vestral authority were finally separated by the Municipal Corporations Act of 1835, which consolidated urban parishes into boroughs, and the Local Government Act of 1894, which established (civil) parish councils of elected members in rural areas with a parochial population exceeding 300 (or between 200 and 300 if agreed by a parish meeting). Since 1919 the administration of ecclesiastical parishes is vested in parochial church councils. One consequence of these changes is that the boundaries of ecclesiastical and civil parishes may not always coincide.

PARISH CHEST A term used by local historians to denote the wealth of information relating to individual communities, much of which originated in Thomas Cromwell's directive of September 1538 which required that a 'sure coffer' should be kept in every church as a repository for parish registers.

PARISH CLERK A layman who assisted the parish priest in the administration of the church and in the performance of minor duties during services such as leading the singing, reading the gospel or epistle and making the responses.

PARK PALE *see* DEER PARKS

PARKS Of the numerous medieval DEER PARKS, very few survived to the end of the seventeenth

The parish chest at Bradford Abbas, Dorset. There are three padlocks, each with a different key, so that the incumbent and the two church wardens must be present at the same time in order to open the chest.

century. Thereafter, the fashion was for domestic opulence surrounded by contrived countryside. Some ancient deer parks became landscaped parks and many contained deer, though these were usually kept as ornamentation; indeed, some later parks were stocked with deer for this purpose. Vast acres of uncultivated parkland were intended to emphasise the status, wealth and privilege of the owner. The approach to a country house, through ornate lodge gates, along sweeping sun-dappled driveways past tumbling cascades and dark copses, with vistas of distant woods and hills and serpentine lakes, provided a gradual intensification of emotional experience culminating in a visitor's first glimpse of the mansion itself, a moment as contrived as the landscape through which he had passed. Add to this a suggestion of ancient and noble ancestory, hinted at by the armorial devices on the lodge gates and herds of grazing deer, and the picture was complete.

In the late seventeenth century, the French fashion for formal parks reached England. Formality, which had previously been confined to GARDENS in the immediate vicinity of a house, spread beyond the HA-HA and into the surrounding parkland with geometrical avenues and plantations, eye-catchers and strategically positioned Italianate buildings. But few of these formal parks remain, for by the mid-eighteenth century Romanticism had become fashionable and artificial landscape was endowed with a natural appearance, enhanced by ARTIFICIAL RUINS, water features and grottoes. In the nineteenth century, large numbers of exotic plants were introduced into Britain and many parks were modified to accommodate substantial collections of alien trees and shrubs. Many parks have subsequently been surrendered to commercial uses, but ironically it is often their artificiality which marks them out from other agricultural land. In the avenues of fine trees, open vistas and planned woodlands one may still appreciate their former glories.

PARLIAMENTARY ENCLOSURES (INCLOSURES) *see* ENCLOSURES

PARSON *see* CLERGY (CHURCH OF ENGLAND)

PARTERRE *see* GARDENS

PARVA *see* LATIN *and* MAGNA

PASSAGE *see* FERRIES

PASSAGE GRAVES *see* CHAMBERED TOMBS

PATCH *see* PIGHTLE

PATENT In 1516 letters patent replaced CHARTERS as the form in which royal grants are made. They are 'open' documents intended for public consumption (Latin *patere* = to open), often addressed 'To All and Singular to whom these Presents shall Comeb . . .'. Armorial bearings, for example, are granted by means of signed letters patent to which the seals of the granting kings of arms are appended. *Patent Rolls*, which contain copies of letters patent, were begun in 1201 and are still maintained today. Private documents may be described as *letters close* and, unlike letters patent, may only be opened by the breaking of a seal.

PATRON *see* ADVOWSON

PATTENS Wooden over-shoes.

PATTES D'OIE *see* GARDENS

PAVILION (i) A projecting part of a façade of a building.
(ii) Peripheral buildings attached by side wings to a principal central building but forming part of the architectural whole.
(iii) A small ornamental structure or summer house in a garden or park. *See also* FOLLIES.
(iv) In ARMORY, a medieval tent or a canopy-like structure within which a coat of arms is occasionally displayed.

PEASANTS' REVOLT The 'Great Revolt' of English artisans and yeomen, notably from the counties of Kent and Essex, caused by poor economic conditions, unpopular TAXATION and repressive legislation. In 1381 the rebels marched on London, killing several unpopular ministers and occupying the city. After the death of their leader, Wat Tyler, the young Richard II acceded to a number of the rebels' demands and they were persuaded to disperse. However, the government immediately revoked the concessions and re-established its authority.

The principal cause of unrest, which was to re-emerge throughout the following century, was the *Ordnance of Labourers*, a series of reactionary labour laws which sought to reverse the improved conditions enjoyed by labourers as a consequence of depopulation following the Black Death (*see* PLAGUE). Although the Peasants' Revolt failed to attain its immediate objectives it stimulated an almost universal resistance to serfdom which ultimately rendered it uneconomic.

PECULIAR A place exempt from the jurisdiction of a bishop in whose diocese it is situated. Peculiars usually derived from the possession of land in one diocese by a senior church dignitary who held office in another. The *Royal Peculiars* are churches connected with royal palaces or castles: St George's Chapel at Windsor Castle and Westminster Abbey, for example, which are exempt from any jurisdiction other than that of the sovereign.
See also PARISH

PEDDARS WAY *see* ROMAN ROADS

PEDIGREE A genealogical table illustrating descent through the male line. The term is said to have originated in the practice of writing the names of forebears in groups of circles which, when joined by curved lines, were thought to resemble the imprint of a crane's foot, a *pied de gru* in French. A chart which records all direct line ancestors, both male and female, is termed a Birth Brief, Blood Descent or Total Descent.

PEDIMENT In classical architecture, the triangular gable above the ENTABLATURE often used as a decorative feature above doors, windows and niches. The horizontal base moulding may be incomplete (*broken* pediment), the apex of the triangle may be omitted (*open*) or the top members may be curved and scrolled (*segmental*).
See also TYMPANUM

PEEP *see* PRIESTS' HOLES

PEGASUS *see* BEASTS (HERALDIC)

PELE TOWERS A type of tower keep dating from the mid-fourteenth century to the seventeenth,

Pele tower at Corbridge, Northumberland.

characteristic of the marches on both sides of the Scottish border (*see* MARCH). In England, they were built as fortified homesteads by the lesser nobility as protection against Scottish incursions across the border in the centuries before the Act of Union in 1707. A typical stronghold, such as the Vicar's Pele at Corbridge in Northumberland (*c.* 1300), consisted of a rectangular tower with immensely thick stone walls pierced by small window-openings and entered at first-floor level by means of a stone flight of steps or (in early examples) by a ladder which would be hauled inside whenever danger threatened. The ground floor usually contained store-rooms, and in most towers these would originally have been accessible only from the floor above, thereby reducing the risk of attack by fire or explosion from beneath. On the first floor was the hall and above that a further floor of chambers and an upper platform with a parapet and sometimes a corner observation tower which may also contain the chimney flues. Some had a tent-like hoarding within the upper platform and, in most examples, a walled courtyard (*barmkin*) protected livestock and crops from marauders. Others were more sophisticated; the imposing fourteenth-century Chipchase and Belsay towers in Northumberland, for example, had crenellated and machicolated parapets

and projecting wings containing the staircase, entrance and small chambers.

There are ninety pele towers in Cumbria alone, of which Sizergh Castle is perhaps the best example. Several were extended and remodelled to provide substantial dwellings: Nappia Hall in Wensleydale (Yorkshire), for example, has an additional west tower linked to the original pele tower by a mid-fifteenth-century great hall. The term *pele* originated in the palisaded enclosure (hence 'paling' and 'beyond the pale') and was probably introduced in the present context by nineteenth-century antiquarians.
See also BASTLES *and* CASTLES (MEDIEVAL)

PELICAN Traditionally, the pelican is devoted to her young and is depicted piercing her breast ('vulning herself') in order that they should be revived by her blood. Thus the 'pelican in her piety' became a mystic emblem of Christ whose blood was shed for mankind.
See also BEASTS (HERALDIC) *and* CHRISTIAN SYMBOLS

PEN A place-name element which, in the Welsh, means 'end' or 'summit', as it does in many Cornish and British names such as Penyghent in Yorkshire ('hill of the border country') and Penselwood in Somerset ('sallow wood on an eminence'). In Old English, *pen* or *penn* means 'pen' or 'enclosure', but in this form it is usually found as a second element, as in Owlpen in Gloucestershire ('*Olla's* enclosure') and Ipplepen in Devon ('*Ipela's* fold'), though Inkpen in Berkshire probably contains the British word for 'hill' and is a reference to Inkpen Beacon. The name *Pennines* is an eighteenth-century figment extracted from the works of the literary forger Charles Bertram (1723–65).

PENDLE *see* SLATES

PENITENTIAL CROSS Unusual crosses of which few examples have survived. A penitential cross is distinguished by the grooves worn into its base by the knees of penitents as they knelt in supplication. The best example is in the churchyard at Ripley in Yorkshire.

PENNINES *see* PEN

PENNY *see* COINAGE

PENS Before the eleventh century, pens were made from dried reeds. Thereafter, until the nineteenth century, the quill pen was used. This was formed from a goose feather (though feathers of swans, ravens, crows and even turkeys were also used), the hollow quill of which retained a small quantity of INK which was released by gentle downward pressure on the nib while writing. When used as pens, feathers were always stripped down to the quill, the larger end of which was carefully shaped and split with a pen-knife to form the nib. Metal nibs date from the mid-nineteenth century and fountain pens from the end of that century. The pens used for producing the magnificent illuminated manuscripts were themselves kept in superb pen-cases: one mid-eleventh-century example at the British Museum is made from walrus ivory, obtained from Lapland through Viking traders and carved with mounted warriors in combat with a dragon, two lions and a pair of archers in the act of shooting birds from a tree.

PENTHOUSE *see* SIEGES

PENTICE *see* CASTLES (MEDIEVAL)

PENTRE A place-name element from the Welsh *pentref*, meaning 'village' or 'homestead'.

PEPPERCORN RENT A nominal or very low rent. A pepper-berry is of no appreciable value and given as rent is a simple acknowledgement that the tenement is to continue in the ownership of the person to whom the peppercorn is paid. Peppercorn rent does not have the same meaning as QUIT RENT.

PERAMBULATION Perambulation, or 'beating the bounds', of a PARISH is still practised in some places, though as a custom rather than of necessity. Until well into the second half of the nineteenth century, vestries were charged with the responsibility of investigating the boundaries of their parishes to ensure that boundary stones and other markers had not been removed and that no new (and unrated) buildings had been erected without their knowledge. The perambulation included the incumbent and officers of the VESTRY, together with various schoolchildren and village notables, all armed with wands of office, usually willow rods, which were used to 'beat the bounds'. This annual procession replaced the ancient Rogation ceremonies, which were of eighth-century origin but contained elements of paganism and were banned following the Reformation. The willow wands are a clear remnant of these festivals (*see* GOSPEL OAK), and on occasions boys were also beaten or bumped on the ground so that they would '. . . well remember the bounds of the parish within which they dwell', though the original intention was that their protestations should drive away evil spirits, presumably into the neighbouring parish.

The medieval royal FORESTS were also perambulated by Crown officials in order that there should be no ambiguity with regard to the extent of forest jurisdiction. Not only were there special laws protecting game within the forests, but also many which restricted the exploitation of land, with prohibitions on grazing livestock and on clearing areas for cultivation.

PERCH A variable measure of between 9 and 26 feet (2.7 and 7.9 metres), but eventually standardized at 16½ feet (5 metres).
See also CHAIN

PERPENDICULAR *see* GOTHIC ARCHITECTURE

PERPETUAL CURATE A priest nominated by a lay rector to serve a parish in which there was no regular endowed vicarage. As the name suggests, perpetual curates were appointed in perpetuity and once licensed by a bishop could not be removed.

PETER'S FINGER Once a popular inn-name, a corrupted form of St Peter ad Vincula.
See also INN SIGNS

PETER'S PENCE *see* ST PETER'S PENCE

PETRARIA *see* SIEGES

PETRA SANCTA *see* TINCTURES

PETTY SESSIONS Meetings of local justices, held since the Tudor period, and more recently a minor court presided over by two or more magistrates for the summary trial of certain offences. Petty sessional records are usually retained by clerks of the peace.

PEW RENTING (CONDUCTIO SEDILIUM) Writing in the late eighteenth century, Gilbert White, the naturalist and antiquarian, described his church at Selborne, Hampshire, '. . . nothing can be more irregular than the pews of this church which are of all dimensions and heights, being patched up according to the fancy of the owners.' White's experience was not unusual, for in the seventeenth and eighteenth centuries the order of seating in parish churches reflected a rigid social structure and was regarded as a matter of the utmost importance by those concerned. Rented accommodation varied from elaborate and often ostentatious family pews to rectangular high-sided box pews, which provided comparative privacy and comfort, and benches, which were reserved for particular farmsteads and tenements. Of course, additional rented accommodation resulted in additional income for the churchwardens, often to the exclusion of those who could not afford to pay for their seats and were crowded together on makeshift forms in the aisles and galleries. It is little wonder, therefore, that so many turned to the nonconformist chapels, which were relatively free from social snobbery.

PEWTER From the Old French *peutre*, a grey alloy: usually twenty parts of tin to three of lead and one of brass. Widely used from the Roman period to the nineteenth century for drinking vessels, plates, etc. In 1348 a number of reputable pewter-makers, anxious to maintain the standards of their craft, formed themselves into a guild which for one and a half centuries regulated the lead content in pewter. Later legislation required that each pewterer should have his own mark which was to be recorded on a *touch-plate* at the Pewterers' Hall. The original plates were lost in the Great Fire of London in 1666, but a new series was struck in 1668 and this included the marks of many of the established pewter-makers. A *touch mark* is not the same as a HALLMARK stamped on items made of precious metals such as silver and gold. It usually consists of the maker's name and place of manufacture and some form of pictorial device (*see* MINERALS).

PHAETON Early phaetons were light, four-wheeled open sporting vehicles, usually drawn by a pair of horses, and popular from the 1770s to the mid-nineteenth century. They were usually privately owned and driven at a time when improvements in the maintenance of roads encouraged driving as a fashionable pastime. Drivers of phaetons were considered to possess a devil-may-care attitude comparable with that of *Phaethon*, son of the Greek sun-god *Helios*, whose attempts to handle his father's sun chariot ended in disaster. Typical was the *crane-necked phaeton* of the 1780s and 1790s, which had a double seat suspended high above the ground and was driven by a pair of horses or four-in-hand. The curved irons or 'cranes' beneath which the forewheels could turn a full lock made it a singularly unstable vehicle. Front wheels were often as much as 1.5 metres in diameter (5 feet), while rear wheels could be between 2 and 2.5 metres high

George IV driving his phaeton: he is known to have driven 22 miles in two hours. (Engraving: J. Dickinson)

(6 and 8 feet). Later phaetons were often much heavier, indeed the *mail phaeton* of the late 1820s was a huge vehicle similar to a coach with a solid undercarriage and driven by a pair of horses harnessed to a coach pole with chains rather than leather traces. It had a raised seat and hood at the front and a low seat behind, and accommodated three passengers and a driver.

PHILOLOGY The historical and comparative study of languages.

PHLEBOTOMY Blood-letting (*see* MONASTERIES).

PHOENIX *see* BEASTS (HERALDIC)

PHOTOGRAPHY The world's first photograph was taken in 1826 by a Frenchman, J.N. Niepce. It resulted from an exposure which lasted several hours and was a picture of barn roofs produced on a pewter plate using a substance which hardened under the influence of light. This was followed by the *daguerrotype* of *c*. 1838, taken on a silver-coated copper plate and developed by exposure to mercury vapour giving a positive image of white on silver.

In 1841 the English amateur scientist W.H. Fox Talbot patented the *calotype*, a negative process by which an unlimited number of prints could be produced from a paper negative and reduced exposure time to a matter of minutes. This removed the necessity for the head-clamps and arm props, which had made studio portraiture such an ordeal, but speed was gained at the cost of richness of shadow detail and subtlety of tone and it was not until the 1850s, and the development of the collodian wet plate, that the great age of Victorian photography began. This process required an impeccably clean glass plate, coated with collodian (formed by dissolving gun-cotton in ether or alcohol mixed with silver and iron iodides), to be treated uniformly and rapidly with a further coating of a light-sensitive emulsion of silver nitrates. The entire process had to be carried out in total darkness and in a dust-free atmosphere. The plate had then to be exposed while the emulsion was still wet and then developed and fixed. The photographic process itself took no more than a few seconds but the preparation was a lengthy and complex business. As may be imagined, the equipment necessary to produce and develop a single glass plate was extraordinarily cumbersome and the early photographers took with them wagons or baggage trains loaded with test tubes, pans, basins, chemicals, thermometers, portable dark rooms, a variety of glass plates, water and the means of heating or cooling it.

In 1856 a flexible film was first used instead of a glass plate and colour photography developed from the work of Clerk Maxwell in 1861. By the 1860s smaller hand-held cameras were also available, which were lighter and considerably easier to use. One, the *Pistolgraph* had a spring shutter released by a trigger from which the word 'snap-shot' was coined. But the greatest advance, and that which enabled photographers to record life as it happened, was the development of the dry plate in the 1870s. This made possible the production of a light-sensitive surface well in advance of being used and which could be stored until needed. No longer was a portable dark-room a necessity and, with hand-held cameras and exposure times of less than one second, the age of documentary photography had begun.

Photographs are, of course, an essential source of information for the local historian but it should be remembered that the apparent pomposity of Victorian life as we now observe it in many early photographs is more the result of the way in which the images were recorded than of the attitudes of the subjects themselves. Until about 1860, life in photographs always had to be arranged and organized: it was rarely spontaneous. The arrival of a photographer's van was an event of considerable significance in a small community, with everyone making a point of passing that way at least once in order to watch the goings-on or even to be persuaded to pose for posterity. Many of the subjects in the earliest photographs were born well before the invention of photography. Some may have been veterans of Waterloo or were octogenarians, born when many of the states of America were still British colonies. As documentary evidence photographs have much to say of England's social history and landscape but, particularly in the nineteenth century, there is also much that is contrived. Just as today, we are presented with that which the photographer wishes to communicate, so the Victorian or Edwardian camera-man selected his subjects with care, a selection which may tell us as much about contemporary attitudes as the photographs themselves. Whether the subjects appear happier or wiser than their successors is debatable, but what is certain is that they lived very different lives: an ordered and comparatively peaceful existence that was to change forever in August 1914.

There are numerous collections, mostly dating from the first decades of the present century, both in private archives and in those of county museums and record offices. Many are of villages, including innumerable churches, while others boast of Edwardian civic pride and architectural achievement. Undoubtedly the most interesting photographs of this period are those of former rural landscapes which are now buried beneath suburbia.

There is a major collection of early photographs at the Museum of English Rural Life at the University of Reading and the Fox Talbot collection is now housed at the Science Museum, London (*see* APPENDIX I).

PICKLE *see* PIGHTLE

PICT A member of an ancient people whose origins and ethnological affinities remain a matter of dispute but who appear to have been formed out of a fusion of IRON AGE tribes in northern Britain. In *c.* AD 300 the *Picti* were referred to by the Romans as hostile tribes occupying territory to the north of the Antonine Wall (*see* ROMAN FORTS AND CAMPS). This territory was apparently divided into northern and southern 'kingdoms' which were themselves sub-divided into provinces. The Pictish culture was regarded as somewhat bizarre by contemporaries and contained features which were of BRONZE AGE rather than Celtic origin. According to the chroniclers, the Picts were assimilated with the Scots following occupation under Kenneth MacAlpine in *c.* 843.

PICTISH STONES Mysterious remnants of Pictish culture (*see* PICT), these remarkable granite or sandstone symbol stones are believed to be of seventh-century origin and are divided into two categories: Class I stones, unshaped slabs engraved with pagan symbols; and Class II stones, early Christian crosses which, presumably, reflect Pictish

A Class II Pictish cross at Glamis, Tayside.

the term is synonymous with *pillar*, which may be of square or multi-sided section and sometimes encircled by attached or detached shafts (a *compound* or *clustered pier*). In CLASSICAL ARCHITECTURE a pier is not the same as a *column* or *pilaster*, both of which are characterized by the capital and base of a classical order.

PIERS *see* RESORTS

PIGHTLE (*also* **PATCH, PICKLE** *and* **PINGLE**) A small enclosure.

PIKE A pointed mountain or hill, as in Grisedale Pike, Cumbria, derived from the Norse *pök*, meaning 'dagger', or *päk*, meaning 'cudgel', and cognate with the Old English *pēac*, meaning 'hill' or 'peak'.

PILASTER A rectangular classical column partly built into, partly projecting from, a wall.

PILGRIMS *and* **PILGRIMS' WAY** *see* SHRINES

PILL A term applied to tidal creeks in the south-west of England and Wales, derived from the Welsh *pwll* and Old English *pyll*, meaning 'pool', such as Pont Pill off the Fowey Estuary, Cornwall, Garron Pill off Milford Haven, Pembrokeshire, and Bullo Pill off the Severn Estuary in Gloucestershire.

PILLAR *see* PIER

PILLBOXES The German *Zeppelins* and Gotha bombers of the First World War (1914–18) were terrifying manifestations of an entirely new type of warfare, and thereafter the British regarded bomber attack as the main threat to national security. Consequently, after 1918 the government concentrated on establishing an effective air force and on maintaining naval superiority, while coastal and land defences were virtually ignored. With the fall of France in May 1940 Britain was therefore unprepared to meet the threat of German invasion across the English Channel. While the service chiefs believed that invasion would be delayed until Hitler had gained superiority in the air, they urged that Britain should 'be organized as a fortress'.

There followed the most rapidly executed (and often makeshift) programme of defensive building in the country's history. Within a fortnight of the evacuation of the British Expeditionary Force from Dunkirk, completed on 2 June 1940, 'emergency batteries' of long-range guns in quick-setting concrete casements had been established around

conversion to Christianity and are carved in a decorative style similar to that of Christian Northumbria. The symbols on the Class I stones represent animals, both real and mythical; real objects (such as mirrors, combs and caldrons) and complicated abstract devices. The stones may have been erected as memorials to the dead but they could also have had tribal or territorial associations. The significance of the symbols themselves, which have also been found on Pictish metalwork and cave carvings, remains a mystery. To the Romans, *Picti* meant 'painted ones', and the symbols may have been tattooed on bodies as a primitive form of tribal heraldry. There are about fifty distinctive symbols and several hundred stones, many of which remain in isolated splendour in the Scottish landscape.

PICTISH CROSSES *see* PICTISH STONES

'PIE POWDER', COURT OF *see* MARKETS

PIER A solid support of brick or masonry carrying a lintel or the thrust of a *pier arch*. In ROMANESQUE and GOTHIC ARCHITECTURE

Dover and other major ports, and the system was extended rapidly along the coast from Cornwall to Lincolnshire. Likely landing-beaches were liberally covered with obstacles: rows of concrete block 'tank traps', barbed wire and scaffolding 'spikes'. The strategically placed defences of nineteen centuries of threatened invasion were again pressed into service. MARTELLO TOWERS, TUDOR FORTS, medieval CASTLES and even prehistoric earthworks provided cover for artillery emplacements, and to these were added the most numerous of Britain's fortifications: 200,000 concrete mini-forts or 'pillboxes'. These were nearly all built to standard designs, by local builders, with walls varying in thickness from 15 cm to 84 cm (6 inches to 2 feet 9 inches). When the fall of France became inevitable, General Ironside (Commander-in-Chief of the Home Forces) ordered the strengthening of the 'coastal crust' and the construction of a series of inland 'stop-lines' which would prevent German columns breaking through from the coast. During the summer of 1940, thousands of pillboxes were built in a defensive ring extending southwards from Scotland down the east coast, along the south coast and up the west coast as far as the Solway Firth.

Most pillboxes were of the common hexagonal type, with a loophole for a Bren light machine-gun in each of five walls, and an entrance flanked by loopholes in the sixth. The small 'Tett Turret' was a concrete one-man emplacement sunk into the ground with a rotating turret above ground level, while the larger Pickett-Hamilton fort, designed for five men, could be raised or lowered by means of a hydraulic mechanism in about ten seconds. Many pillboxes were ingeniously disguised – as beach kiosks, haystacks, gravestones, piles of logs, summer houses and even a fairground carousel – or concealed within the ruins of ancient fortifications such as Pevensey Castle in Sussex. Conversely, many apparent pillboxes were little more than canvas mock-ups armed with painted telegraph poles.

However, it was acknowledged that these measures would do little more than delay the anticipated invasion force and, to prevent a German breakthrough 'tearing the guts out of the country', stop-lines of anti-tank obstacles and pillboxes were erected along a General Headquarters Line (also known as the Ironside Line) which was intended to protect London and the industrial Midlands. It ran from Burnham-on-Sea in Somerset to the north of Glastonbury and across the Mendip Hills near Dinder. From Midsomer Norton it continued to Bradford-on-Avon where it followed the Kennet and Avon Canal to Reading in Berkshire and south to Farnham in Surrey before

Camouflaged pillbox at Beaulieu, Hampshire.

continuing in an easterly direction to Guildford, Reigate, Tonbridge and Maidstone, ending at Chatham on the river Medway. In the east, the line ran from the Thames Estuary at South Benfleet north to Chelmsford, Cambridge and nearly to Peterborough. There were other stop-lines: the Taunton Line, for example, which ran south from Pawlett in Somerset via Bridgwater, Taunton, Ilminster, Chard and Axminster to the Devon coast at Seaton. Other lines divided the country into defensive squares, with pillboxes at strategic positions such as river crossings and railway bridges. When Ironside was succeeded by General Alan Brooke the defence policy was also changed. Many lines were left unfinished, while defensive 'islands' were established round major ports and manufacturing cities.

In the event, the fate of Britain was determined not on the beaches or at the stop-lines, but in the skies above southern England and, with the postponement of the German *Operation Sealion* in October 1940, the invasion threat receded and on 31 December 1956 the coastal defences of Britain officially ceased to exist.

PILLORY (*collistrigium*) A wooden frame, supported by an upright pillar or post, with holes through which the head and hands were secured as a punishment. To be 'pilloried' was to be humiliated in public just as confinement in the STOCKS resulted in one becoming a 'laughing stock'. Pillories, in which offenders were forced to stand, were most often found in towns whereas stocks were universal. Both were usually located in or near the market-place (*see* MARKETS) where the day's vegetable and animal refuse was invariably thrown at the unfortunate miscreants.
See also PUNISHMENT

PILLOW MOUND *see* WARREN

PINDER *see* PINFOLD

PINEAPPLES The pineapple-shaped finials of seventeenth- and eighteenth-century stone gate pillars are indeed intended to represent the apples (cones) of pine trees. The term 'pineapple' was applied to the fruit *ananas* when it was introduced to English hot-houses from central and south America in the early eighteenth century.

PINFOLD A pound for stray animals maintained by a manor or vestry and the responsibility of a minor officer known as a *pinder*. Pounds were essential adjuncts to OPEN FIELDS which were, by definition, unenclosed and in which stray livestock could cause considerable damage to growing crops. Grazing was confined to the common, to the village CLOSES and to whichever of the open fields was fallow or had just been harvested. All beasts were the responsibility of their owners and were released from the pound only on payment of a fine. On occasions, it would be necessary for an unclaimed beast to be 'cried' (announced) at the local market in the hope that the owner would come forward. Most medieval pounds were small fenced or hedged enclosures though later stone or brick pounds were often constructed on the sites of former medieval ones. Some of these have survived, such as the open crenelated polygonal structure at Raskelf, Yorkshire with its arched and barred door and window openings. Others are commemorated in local place-names such as The Pound House, Pound Lane, etc. The feudal office of pinder (also *pound-keeper* or *punder*) was a necessary but unpopular one: there can have been few volunteers for a post which was often subject to abuse and occasionally to assault (*see* COURT LEET).

PINNACLE A miniature spire constructed both as a decorative termination to a parapet or BUTTRESS and (essentially) to provide additional weight in order to counteract the outward thrust of a vault.

PIPE ROLLS The Great Rolls of the Exchequer which, from 1120, were compiled annually from the accounts of Crown revenues rendered by sheriffs. The series ended in 1834 when the EXCHEQUER systems were revised. The term probably originated in the 'pipes' or rods around which the documents were rolled and their appearance when stored. The earliest extant roll is that for 1130/31 (Henry I) and they include the *Liber Niger Scaccarii*, *The Black Book of the Exchequer*, a survey of England compiled in 1166. The Pipe Rolls are maintained at the Public Record Office and the Pipe Roll Society has published many early rolls which are of particular value to the local historian (*see* APPENDIX I).

PISCARY *see* COMMONS

PISCINA A stone basin in which a priest rinsed the chalice and paten after Mass. Having been in contact with the Elements (the Host and the wine, which were believed to have been transubstantiated into the body and blood of Christ), and with the sacred vessels in which they were contained, he would also wash his hands. From the piscina, which was usually set within an arched niche to the south of an altar, a drain conveyed the water (itself sanctified through contact with the Elements) to the consecrated ground of the churchyard. Some late thirteenth- and early fourteenth-century piscinas have two basins: one for the vessels and the other for the hands. In some churches the piscina is free-standing on a pillar and is then termed a *pillar piscine*.
See also AUMBRY, FENESTELLA *and* SEDILIA

PISTYLL In the Welsh, a water spout or cataract, as in Pistyll Gwyn, the White Cataract near Llanymawddwy, Gwynedd.
See also RHAEADR

PIT ALIGNMENTS Evident only as CROP MARKS in aerial photographs, the original function of these long chains of Neolithic or Bronze Age pits remains a mystery.

PLACE-NAMES Place-names and FIELD NAMES provide an invaluable source of information for the local historian. They can provide clues to features of the landscape which are no longer apparent; they afford a glimpse of the people who once lived in a place (Gylla's people, who occupied a Dark Age homestead (*hām*) at Gillingham in Dorset, for example); or they can tell us who held manorial lands at Okeford Fitpaine during the Middle Ages. However, most names were not originally given to VILLAGES, of which there were very few before the eighth century, but rather to earlier TOWNSHIPS and locations in which villages were later established and from which the names were devolved.

The superficial interpretation of modern forms of place-names can be extremely misleading, for names which appear to be derived from the same source may have originated in entirely different etymons: Highlow in Derbyshire, Highnam in Gloucestershire and Highway in Wiltshire, for example, seem to possess a common element. But Highlow is derived from the Old English *hēah hlāw*, meaning 'high hill'; Highnam from *hīwan hamm*, meaning 'the monks' meadow'; and Highway from the West Saxon *hīeg* and the Old English *weg*, together meaning 'a track along which hay is carried'. Thus, place-names may contain linguistic elements culled from Anglo-Norman, British, East Frisian, East Saxon, Flemish, Frisian, German, Gaelic, Gaulish, Greek, Gothic, Indo-Germanic, Irish, Latin, Low German, Middle Welsh, Norwegian, Old Breton, Old British, Old Cornish, Old Danish, Old Dutch, Old English (or Anglo-Saxon), Old East Scandinavian and West Saxon sources. Add to this the distinct possibility of corruption through illiteracy, dialectal modification and selective pronunciation and one will begin to appreciate the complexity of accurate interpretation.

With the diversity of meanings which may be derived from a single element, experts will normally turn to documentary evidence in order to establish the earliest recorded form of a name and may also consider the topography of a particular area before selecting that interpretation which they believe to be most appropriate. It should be borne in mind, however, that the names recorded in the *Domesday* survey refer to estates and not necessarily to villages.

Dr Margaret Gelling (*see* APPENDIX II) proposes six successive linguistic 'layers' which may be present as elements in English place-names. The first of these is a pre-Celtic tongue evident, for example, in those RIVER NAMES which contain elements which cannot otherwise be accounted for in Celtic or Germanic. The second is a form of Celtic (British), found in river names such as Avon, Axe, Bollin, Derwent, Rodin, Ure, Thames and Tyne and

in place-names containing British, Welsh and Cornish elements. The third but comparatively attenuated layer is LATIN, and the fourth is OLD ENGLISH (Anglo-Saxon), from which is derived the majority of place-names now in use. The fifth layer, Scandinavian, and especially Old Norse, is commonly found in place-names in the DANELAW of eastern England, and the sixth layer, Norman-French, was introduced into England following the Conquest of 1066.

Feudal place-names are those which include a *feudal affix*, the name of a family who held the manor during the centuries of feudal service. Such families descended from the Norman, Flemish and Breton followers of the Conqueror and their names indicated their places of origin, such as De Turberville and D'Abitot. It probably took several generations of occupation by the same family before an affix became established and most date from the thirteenth and fourteenth centuries. Since then, they have clung like 'burrs of the past' to the names of many villages, despite subsequent changes in ownership and the division of estates. Other feudal affixes have royal or ecclesiastical origins: in Somerset, for example, the manor of Templecombe was held by the Knights Templar and the present parish incorporates the former manor of Abbas Combe which was held by the Abbess of Shaftesbury. *See also* MONASTIC PLACE-NAMES.

The Caundle villages of Dorset provide a lively illustration of how place-names have evolved. The etymology of Caundle itself is obscure but it is believed to have been either a Celtic river name meaning 'division' or 'boundary' or the British name for a minor range of hills, shaped like an upturned saucer, at the periphery of which the five villages are situated. It is variously spelt as *Candel*, *Candele* and *Caundel* and it has been suggested (by Ekwall – *see* APPENDIX II) that it is associated with *Cantmæl* (now Camel in Somerset) which may be identical with the Welsh *cant*, meaning 'rim', and *moel*, meaning 'a conical bare hill'. Certainly, the geographical reference is an accurate one, though the hills are now thickly wooded, and several of the indigenous population still pronounce the name 'cändle'.

The medieval Caundle Episcopi, once held by the bishops of Sarum, became Caundle Bishop and remained so until recently when (regrettably) it was changed to Bishops Caundle (*see* EPISCOPI). Stourton Caundle was, from the thirteenth century, Caundel Haddone (later Caundle Haddon), a manor held by the descendants of Henry de Haddone from

1202. Occasional use of this early name persisted into the late sixteenth century despite the fact that the manor was held by the lords Stourton from 1461 and eventually became Stourton Caundle (pronounced 'Sturton'). In the same group of villages Purse Caundle is believed to have derived from the Old English *prëost*, meaning 'priest', for it was a manor of Athelney Abbey; but there is also evidence of a thirteenth-century armigerous Purse family whose Dorset ancestors are said to have held a manor of that name from 1055. Caundle Marsh (once Candelemers) occupies an area of low-lying land near the Caundle Brook; and Caundle Wake, now a subsidiary hamlet of Bishops Caundle, was a manor held by Ralph Wake in the late thirteenth century.

Although many of the more common place-name elements are included as entries in this book, the researcher should always consult a number of reliable reference books, notably the excellent county series published by the English Place-Name Society, remembering that in many instances even expert opinion may be divided.

For the English Place-Name Society *see* APPENDIX I

PLAGUE During the first decades of the fourteenth century, climatic changes resulted in a series of poor harvests causing starvation and malnutrition which, by the 1330s, had debilitated the peasant population of Europe. Recent evidence has shown that by 1341, eight years before the arrival of the *Black Death* in England, many villages were already depopulated and their lands left uncultivated. It is now clear, therefore, that climatic change, famine and depopulation preceded the plague and, by reducing immunity to disease, contributed to its virulence.

The Black Death of 1349/50 first arrived in Britain through ports in the West Country (traditionally Melcombe Regis in Dorset) and is generally believed to have been a form of bubonic plague, though some scholars have suggested that it was anthrax. The initial symptoms, a blackish often gangrenous pustule at the point of a flea bite, was followed by an enlargement of the lymph nodes in the armpits, groin or neck. Haemorrhaging occurred beneath the skin causing the purplish blotches called *buboes*, from which the bubonic plague is named. Cells died in the nervous system, which may explain the *danse macabre* ritual which often accompanied the Black Death, and between 50 and 60 per cent of victims died. The disease was carried by fleas living in the fur of black rats (*Rattus rattus*) and would have passed to humans only when so many rats had

died that the fleas were forced to adopt unfamiliar human hosts. (Female black rats were capable of producing two hundred offspring a year. In Britain the species is believed to have become extinct in the wild in 1988.)

The fourteenth-century pandemic probably originated in Mongolia in the 1320s and reached Europe by *c.* 1347. Amazingly, there was no attempt to prevent its spreading across the English Channel or even to discourage contact with the stricken Continent. Indeed, two weeks before the plague's arrival the Archbishop of York was warning of its inevitability, and of 'the sins of men, whose prosperity has made them complacent and who have forgotten the generosity of God'. Presumably, he was not referring to the emaciated peasantry. When the disease finally struck, the only provision made by the establishment was the excavation of mass grave-pits. At Clerkenwell, outside the walls of London, 50,000 corpses were buried in a 13-acre cemetery established by Walter de Manny, who later founded a Carthusian monastery on the site as a memorial to the dead. This later became the Charterhouse, the cloister, chapel and gatehouse of which have survived, as have the foundations of the original cemetery chapel in which penitential services were held during the Black Death. At Clerkenwell a small lead cross was placed on the chest of each victim before burial. Estimates of the numbers who died during the Black Death vary enormously but at least 20 per cent of the population must have perished in this way, and some historians have proposed figures of 40 or even 50 per cent. A fourteenth-century monk, of Rochester in Kent, wrote:

> To our great grief the plague carried off so vast a multitude of people that it was not possible to find anybody to carry the corpses to the cemetery . . . mothers and fathers carried their own children on their shoulders to the church and dropped them in the common pit . . . such a terrible stench came from these pits that hardly anyone dared to walk near the cemeteries.

The nobility and gentry, with a more reliable diet and a marginally greater perception of hygiene, fared somewhat better, though neither rank nor privilege brought immunity: at Crich in Derbyshire a local knight, William de Wakebridge, erected a tiny CHANTRY CHAPEL to the memory of his wife, father, two sisters and three brothers, all of whom had been cut down by the plague in the summer of

1349. At Gloucester, the terrified inhabitants barred the city gates to refugees fleeing from plague-stricken Bristol, while at Winchester the populace was urged to parade barefoot round the market-place and to recite the seven penitential psalms three times a week – but to no avail, for well over half the population perished.

The effects of depopulation are evident in the commercial and agricultural decline of many communities and in a deterioration in craftsmanship. At Ledbury church in Herefordshire, for example, the mid-fifteenth-century decorative capitals of the north arcade are of significantly inferior workmanship to those of the south arcade, which were carved in *c.* 1340. Many settlements became moribund, though (contrary to popular belief) only a small number of villages were abandoned as a direct result of the plague (*see* DESERTED VILLAGES).

Further outbreaks of bubonic and (possibly) pneumonic plague occurred until the eighteenth century, notably a virulent epidemic in London vividly described in 1665 by the diaryist, John Evelyn:

Came home, there perishing near 10,000 poor creatures weekly; however I went all along the city and suburbs from Kent Street to St James's, a dismal passage, and dangerous to see so many coffins exposed in the streets, now thin of people, the shops shut up, and all in mournful silence, not knowing whose turn it might be next.

It was the Great Fire of September 1666 which destroyed some 13,000 rat-infested houses and finally relieved London of the 'accursed pestilence'. The name Black Death dates from 1833 and is a translation from the German.

PLAISTOW (*also* **PLASTOW** *and* **PLASTER**) Derived from the Old English *pleg-stow*, meaning 'a place for sport', plaistows were medieval playing fields where a community enjoyed its recreation. Some plaistow sites may also have been meeting-places of manorial and hundred courts. Many occupied ancient earthworks, others comprised an enclosure adjacent to a church or an open space defined by a road junction at the centre of a village (*see* VILLAGE GREENS). Some are recalled in turf MAZES and in field and place-names such as Plestor at Selborne, Hampshire. This was the '*locus ludorum*, or play space . . . a level area near the church of about forty-four yards by thirty-six' in which 'a vast oak, with a short, squat body, and huge

horizontal arms extending almost to the extremity of the area . . . surrounded with stone steps, and seats above them . . . the delight of old and young, and a place of much resort in summer evenings.' (Gilbert White, 1789). The Selborne plaistow also served as a market-place and, possibly, as a meeting-place for the village assembly (MOOT). In Cornwall, such a 'place of play' was called a *plan-an-guare*, of which there are notable circular examples at St Just-in-Penwith, Perranzabuloe and within the Perran Round (*see* ROUND).

Some *camp-* place-names may indicate an enclosure (Latin *campus*) where camp-ball, a primitive version of football, was played. Names such as Follifoot (Yorkshire) and Hesket (Cumberland) have equestrian connotations: the former is derived from the Old English *fola* (or Old Norse *foli*), meaning 'foal', and *gefeoht*, meaning 'fight' (*folgefeoht* would therefore mean 'horse-fight'), and the latter is from the Old Scandinavian *hestaskeið*, meaning 'race-course'.
See also WAKE

PLAN-AN-GUARE *see* PLAISTOW

PLANK *see* SLATES

PLANNED COUNTRYSIDE *see* COUNTRYSIDE

PLANTATION Colonization of a new or conquered country. For example, the Plantation of IRELAND was a government-sponsored settlement of British families and institutions (such as the livery companies of the City of London) on confiscated land during the sixteenth and seventeenth centuries.

PLANTER A pioneer colonist, a settler.

PLASH (*also* **PLASHET** *and* **SLOUGH**) An area of waterlogged ground.

PLASTERWORK Medieval plaster, for both interior and outdoor use, was made from lime, sand and water, together with various other materials which were added to prevent cracking and to encourage binding. These included straw and hay, animal hair, feathers, dung and blood. Plaster of Paris was introduced into England in *c.* 1255. This was made by burning calcium sulphate (*gypsum*, obtained from the Montmartre area of Paris), which was mixed with water to produce a hard, high quality plaster. Initially, Plaster of Paris was expensive and was used only in important buildings, but when gypsum deposits were discovered in

England (notably on the Isle of Purbeck in Dorset and in the Trent and Nidd valleys) its application became more widespread (see also ALABASTER).

The ornate and decorative plaster CEILINGS of sixteenth-, seventeenth- and eighteenth-century buildings were clearly influenced by fifteenth-century Italian Renaissance work in *stucco duro*, a malleable plaster of lime, gypsum and powdered marble which set gradually, allowing time for the design to be executed, and produced a very hard, fine finish. To this the Elizabethans added a variety of ingredients including ale, beeswax and eggs. Plasterwork in the sixteenth and early seventeenth centuries was usually confined to ceilings, the walls of rooms being encased in wooden PANELLING. Plaster decoration was modelled by hand and in the great country houses of the eighteenth century, such as Houghton Hall in Norfolk, Italian plasterers (*stuccadori*) were often employed for this purpose, the accounts for Houghton detailing a significant increase in the consumption of red wine during four months of 1726.

During the 1760s, neo-classical styles became fashionable and architects such as Robert Adam (1728–92) incorporated the elegant motifs of classical Rome into the plasterwork of ceilings and walls. His designs were adaptable and could be made in a studio before being assembled on site. By the end of the century there were few houses which did not possess at least a decorative plaster *cornice* in their principal rooms, for 'Without a cornice, no room can have a finished appearance' (Louden). Cornicing was usually made by applying a layer of plaster to the angle between a wall and ceiling and scraping a shaped template (*horse*) along its length to produce a 'run' cornice.

At this time, a number of patent stucco products were available which (it was claimed) facilitated modelling and were of superior consistency and hardness. John Nash (1725–1835) also developed a plaster of sand, brick-dust, lead oxide and powdered limestone which had the appearance of stone and was intended for exterior use. Later, cement was added for this purpose, and by 1840 a number of patent gypsum plasters were available, such as Keene's Cement. In 1856 the introduction of fibrous plaster, reinforced with a layer of hessian, enabled large sections of plasterwork to be pre-cast. A characteristic feature of the 1850s was the plaster ceiling rose from which hung a gas chandelier. The 'vitiated air' of burning gas lamps was removed by means of pipes, inserted in the ceiling rose, and venting to air-bricks in an outside wall. Most large houses built before 1914 had some decorative plasterwork and this will sometimes show the original function of a room: intertwined grapes and foliage suggest a dining-room, for example.

Plasterboard was introduced in *c.* 1920 when there was a shortage of skilled plasterers after the First World War. This consisted of a layer of gypsum plaster sandwiched between sheets of cardboard. *See also* PARGETING

PLATEAU FORTS *see* HILL FORTS

PLATE GLASS *see* GLASS

PLEACHING The traditional craft of trimming and interlacing branches to form a stock-proof hedge (*see* HEDGEROWS).

PLEDGE HOUSE *see* PRISONS

PLENA POTESTAS *see* FEUDAL AIDS

PLINTH The extended base of a tower or column. Also a base supporting a statue, vase, etc.

PLOUGHBOTE The right to remove wood from common land in order to make or repair a plough. *See also* COMMONS

PLOUGHLAND *see* HIDE

PLURALIST One who believes in a form of society (*pluralism*) in which members of minority groups maintain independent traditions.

PLURALITY A benefice or office held with another, or the simultaneous holding of two or more benefices by a single clergyman.

POACHING *see* FORESTS, MAN-TRAPS *and* SWINGEL

POLE *see* ROD

POLICE *see* LAW AND ORDER

POLISSOIR Stones in which grooves have been made by the sharpening of tools and weapons. Some of the stones in the Avenue at Avebury in Wiltshire were scoured in this way by flint and stone axes. They are usually found as series of straight, parallel grooves and have the appearance of being highly polished, quite unlike the smoothest natural rock surface. Early examples are rare in Britain, but medieval polissoirs may sometimes be found in the stonework of church porches and in castle masonry where they were made by the sharpening of swords and arrow-heads.

POLLARD From the Norman-French *poll*, meaning 'head', pollarded trees (usually oak, beech, elm or hornbeam), grown to produce a regular crop of poles, were once a common feature of the countryside. If a young broad-leaf tree is cut across about 2.5 metres from the ground (8 feet), it will send out fresh shoots to form a bushy crown which, after some ten to twenty years, may be cut for poles or 'loppings' and the cycle begun again. Repeated pollarding produces successive crops of small poles suitable for fencing and basketry. Pollarding was preferable to the alternative COPPICE method which, because the trees were lopped near the ground, produced young shoots which were susceptible to damage by browsing animals during the first decade of growth. The trunk of a pollarded tree is known as the *bolling*. Riverside willows and some town trees such as limes are occasionally pollarded but the practice of producing timber poles in this way has, in most places, been abandoned. Nevertheless, old pollarded trees are numerous and even though they may not have been pollarded for over a century they are easily recognized by the 'crown' of branches springing from one level.
See also WOODLAND

POLL TAX A form of individual direct TAXATION introduced in the late fourteenth century as a result of dissatisfaction with the system of LAY SUBSIDIES (*see also* SUBSIDY ROLLS). Three poll taxes were levied in 1377, 1379 and 1380 and were singularly unpopular, only paupers being exempt (*see* PEASANTS' REVOLT). The tax was revived in 1513, and again in 1990 when it caused civil unrest and was rapidly replaced. Surviving records, up to its abolition in 1698, are at the Public Record Office (*see* APPENDIX I).

POMACE Pulped apples used for cider-making.

PONDS *see* ARMED POND, DEW POND, FISH-POND, HAMMER POND, -MERE *and* MILLPOND. *For* FURNACE POND *see* HAMMER POND

PONT The Latin word *pons*, meaning 'bridge', adopted by the British and now commonly found in Welsh and Cornish place-names.

POORHOUSE Before the WORKHOUSES were built every parish owned a few cottages which were used to accommodate the poor. For the most part, these were little better than hovels, damp and insanitary, with just one room and a ladder giving access to the roof space. Parishes also provided clothing, fuel and relief in cash. In 1715 Widow Fudge of Yetminster in Dorset was given 5*s* to buy fuel for the winter, while at neighbouring Batcombe (where the former poorhouse is now an attractive cottage) the poor were permitted to remove fuel (usually furze) from a field which is still known as the Poor Lot.

The parish also made provision for medical care and for burial. The Yetminster Vestry accounts record that 'Mr. Meech, apothecary of Cerne, to be paid five guineas per annum for physick and surgery except lying-in women and compound fractures'. In 1762 a grant of 7*s* and 10*d* provided for a child's 'coffin, bell, grave, shroud and a drink'. Apprenticeships were also arranged for the sons of poor families, though these were not always in the immediate area and it was not uncommon for boys to be sent to London or to sea. In 1744 one James Eyles of Sherborne was indentured to Nathanial Brooks of Newfoundland, mariner, to 'learn the art and mystery of catching, curing and preserving fish'. One wonders whether he ever saw Dorset again.

POOR LAW Vagrancy was a perennial problem throughout the medieval period. From 1388, a labourer was prevented from leaving his parish without a testimonial from the local Justices, and any beggar who was unable to work could be returned to his place of birth. The *Statute of Mortmain* of 1391 required that in parishes where the rectorial tithes were held by an ecclesiastical or monastic foundation a proportion of that income was to be reserved for the relief of the poor. From 1494, able-bodied vagrants could be punished by whipping, the loss of an ear or even by hanging, and from 1530 those who were incapable of working were required to obtain a begging licence from the magistrates. Following the Dissolution of the Monasteries in 1536–9, responsibility for the maintenance of the impotent poor passed to the parishes. To discourage vagrancy, able-bodied vagrants were required to work, and private alms-giving was made an offence, the penalty being a fine of ten times the amount given (though charitable donations could be solicited on Sundays by a parish priest and his wardens). In 1547 these measures were further modified so that a vagrant who refused to work could be branded with a V (for vagabond) and condemned to servitude for a period of two years. If he absconded during that time, he was adjudged a slave for life and branded with an S on his cheek. As a result, many turned to outlawry (*see* OUTLAWS).

The Poor Law of 1563 required that 'two able persons or more shall be appointed gatherers and collectors of the charitable alms of all the residue of people inhabiting in the parish' and in 1572 the office of Overseer of the Poor was created, an elected parish official responsible for supervising endowments and charitable funds. From 1597, parishes were able to levy a poor rate: paupers were to be provided with work, and supplies of materials were kept for this purpose. In some areas, the first POORHOUSES were built as a result of this legislation. But it was the Poor Law Act which followed in 1601 which established the administrative pattern of relief for the next two centuries. Relief was to be available to three categories of person: the able-bodied (who were to be provided with work), the impotent poor and those who were unwilling to work. The churchwardens of each parish, together with two or more substantial landowners, were to act as Overseers of the Poor responsible for collecting the poor rate, which was to be used

> . . . for setting to work the children of all such whose parents shall not be thought able to maintain them . . . for setting to work all such persons, married or unmarried, having no means to maintain them, and who use no ordinary or daily trade of life to get their living by . . . for providing a convenient stock of flax, hemp, wood, thread, iron and other ware and stuff to set the poor on work . . . [and] . . . for the necessary relief of the lame, impotent, old, blind, and such other among them being poor and not able to work.

The Law of Settlement Act of 1662 enabled Overseers to remove from their parishes any stranger who was unable to persuade them of his ability to obtain work within forty days or who did not rent property worth £10 a year. A stranger could claim settlement in his adopted parish after forty days, and many parishes (known as *close parishes*) became adept at denying itinerant strangers *settlement certificates* which, once granted, entitled the holder to claim poor relief. Workers could obtain temporary employment in other parishes (at harvest time, for example) by means of certificates issued by the Overseers of their home parishes which guaranteed that they would be taken back. Registers of those receiving poor relief were kept from 1691 and by the

Settlement Act of 1697 paupers were required to wear a large letter P on their clothing together with the initials of their parish. The same Act enabled strangers to settle in a new parish if they could obtain a certificate from their home parish agreeing to take them back should they ever have need of poor relief.

Knatchbull's General Workhouse Act of 1723 empowered parishes, or groups of smaller parishes (*unions*), to build workhouses and by 1776 there were some 2,000 in England. At this time, all paupers were generally confined to the precincts of the workhouse but Gilbert's Act of 1782 provided for the able-bodied to obtain work outside, indoor relief being available to the impotent poor. The SPEENHAMLAND SYSTEM of the late eighteenth century encouraged employers to reduce wages in the knowledge that the parish would make up the difference. This resulted in a significant increase in claims for poor relief and eventually to the Poor Law Amendment Act of 1834. This reduced greatly the provision of outdoor relief and encouraged administrators to make conditions in the workhouses as unpleasant as possible so that they should be perceived as a place of last resort (*for further detail, see* WORKHOUSES).

The 1834 Act required that the Poor Law should be administered by three Commissioners, inspection being delegated to Assistant Commissioners to whom Boards of Guardians were responsible for the day-to-day management of parochial poor relief, though the vestries continued to levy the poor rate (*see* PARISH). These Boards of Guardians were elected locally, though the franchise was restricted to landowners and rate-payers whose incomes were assessed for the purpose, the wealthiest being allowed six votes. From 1847, the Poor Law Board was responsible for the administration of the Poor Law, though its work was carried out through civil servants, and in 1871 its duties were transferred to the newly established Local Government Board which was also responsible (among a variety of matters) for public health. Workhouses were re-named Poor Law Institutions in 1913, and in 1919 the Ministry of Health was made responsible for the Poor Law until the Local Government Act of 1929, by which the term 'pauper' was officially abolished, together with Boards of Guardians, and local authorities were encouraged to convert workhouses to infirmaries. The modern system of social security and other benefits was established in 1946.

The records of the Overseers of the Poor before 1834 were kept in vestry minutes which are now retained in the archives of county record offices where the later records of the Guardians of the Poor for individual parishes or unions may also be found (*see* SOCIAL WELFARE).

POPPY HEADS Ornamental finials at the tops of bench-ends. Common from the fifteenth century, in form they usually resemble a three-dimensional fleur-de-lis.

Poppy head finial.

PORCORUM *see* LATIN

PORT From the Latin *porta*, meaning 'gate', and *portus*, meaning 'harbour: port of entry', a place-name element which, in Old English, could mean 'harbour', 'town' or 'gate'. Porchester, Hampshire, was 'the Roman fort by the harbour', while the name Langport, Somerset, means 'long-town' or, more precisely, 'long market-place'. At Portgate, Northumberland, there was a 'gateway' in the Roman wall, the Old English element *-geat* (also 'gate') being added to the name for emphasis (*see also* YAT).

The term *port* suggests that some form of control was exercised over those who wished to enter the harbour or market for commercial purposes (*see* TOWNS). In the Welsh, *porth* has the same meaning. A port is one of three categories of Saxon settlement defined as *ceasters* (towns on well-established Roman sites), *ports* (commercial market centres) and *burhs* (fortified settlements). In common usage, a port is a mercantile harbour, though these are not necessarily coastal or even estuarine: from prehistory, navigable rivers have functioned as highways to the sea and many became important commercial arteries for inland towns such as York, Gloucester, Norwich, Oxford and Cambridge.

PORTAL DOLMEN *see* CHAMBERED TOMBS

PORTCULLIS A heavy iron grating (or wood reinforced with iron), raised and lowered to block the entrance passage of a fortress etc. Few working portcullises remain, but there is ample evidence of their former use in most medieval castles, the gates of walled towns and fortified manor-houses, and in several ecclesiastical establishments, such as the fourteenth-century gatehouse of the Bishop's Palace at Wells in Somerset: a stern reminder of the political power of the magnates of the medieval Church. Look for vertical grooves in the walls on either side of a gate passage, together with horizontal slits in the vault through which the portcullises were raised and lowered by means of geared windlass mechanisms in the rooms above the passage. Had it been completed, the great King's Gate (built 1296–1323) at Caernarfon Castle in Gwynedd would have contained five sets of doors and six portcullises in the gate passage alone. Portcullises were also installed in BARBICANS and used in SALLY-PORTS and POSTERNS, such as the fine 'miniature' postern portcullis (*c.* 1300) in the north wall of Goodrich Castle, in Herefordshire. (*See also* CASTLES (MEDIEVAL) *and* GATEHOUSES.)

In ARMORY the portcullis was originally a badge of the Beaufort descendants of John of Gaunt and Katherine Swynford. The portcullis may have been chosen to indicate that, prior to their legitimation in 1397, the Beauforts were debarred from the English throne because of their illegitimacy. It was a favourite device of Henry VII, whose mother was Lady Margaret Beaufort. A crowned portcullis is still one of the royal badges and is used specifically in connection with the Palace of Westminster.

PORTIONISTS Persons (usually diocesan dignitaries) appointed to sinecures and granted residences near a parish church together with a right to appropriate its revenues and to appoint a vicar. Following the Reformation, portionists usually became lay rectors, though in practice they were frequently in holy orders.

PORTLAND STONE The Isle of Portland, the 'Gibraltar of Wessex', was described by Thomas Hardy as a 'huge lump of freestone' jutting into the Channel from the Dorset coast: strange, bleak, almost treeless and with cliffs on every side. Its fine, hard oolitic limestone was first introduced to London by Inigo Jones in 1619 in the King's Banqueting House in Whitehall, and Christopher Wren chose Portland stone for the rebuilding of London after the Great Fire of 1666, notably in the new St Paul's Cathedral and numerous City churches. The stone was quarried in immense blocks, trolleyed down short slipways and winched by 'slingers' onto barges to be transported along the south coast and up the River Thames. Wren's wineglass device may still be discovered on huge discarded blocks of stone in the quarries of east Portland, a few of which are still worked today. Portland stone is not confined to Portland, however. Further east, the Tilly Whim Caves near Durlston were once quarried (a *whim* is a stone miner's windlass) and the stone extracted from quarries at Chilmark in Wiltshire for the construction of Salisbury Cathedral in the thirteenth century also belongs to the Portland series. *Portland Cement*, manufactured from chalk and clay, was patented in 1824 by a Leeds brick-layer Joseph Aspdin, who fancied that it bore some resemblance to the white Portland limestone.

PORTWAY *see* MARKET

POSSE COMITATUS *see* LAW AND ORDER

POSTAL SERVICE In medieval England, royal messengers carried government documents and retainers conveyed those of their magnatial masters. By the beginning of the sixteenth century, the term 'post' was applied to men with horses strategically stationed along the principal roads from London. Each was responsible for carrying 'at alle speed' the sovereign's 'packet' or mail to the next relay station and for providing suitable horses for this purpose. The term corresponds to the *equites dispositi* ('posted horsemen') of classical and later times. The office of Postmaster of England was established in the reign of James I (1603–25), with responsibility for 'the sole taking up, sending and conveying of all packets and letters concerning our service or business to be despatched to foreign parts'. From 1609, all post for destinations in this country *had* to be carried by the Royal Mail.

The first regular delivery service between London and Edinburgh began in 1635, and by 1644 one Edward Prideaux had established a weekly distribution of post to various parts of the country. An Act of 1656 created 'one general post-office and one officer stiled the Postmaster-General of England and Comptroller of the Post Office'. A private Penny Post service operated in London in 1680 but this, together with a number of other private schemes, was incorporated in a general Post Office for the three kingdoms in 1710. MAIL-COACHES first ran from Bristol to London in 1784 and within twenty years there were more than 200 coaches in service with the title 'Royal Mail' painted on their sides. They were a prominent feature of the roads during the TURNPIKE era: toll-gates opened at the sound of a horn and each coach carried an armed guard.

Mail was first carried by rail on the Liverpool–Manchester line in 1830. Initially, letters were charged by weight and distance, but in 1840 a Warwickshire schoolmaster, Roland Hill, supported by popular demand in the face of an obdurate Post Office and political indifference, finally persuaded Parliament to introduce the standard Penny Post. Hill's plan for a postal delivery, pre-paid by means of a self-adhesive stamp, was to improve the quality of life of every member of society. In particular, and for the first time in the nation's history, it enabled the poor to communicate directly with the loved ones from whom they were separated, an innovation which must have contributed significantly to the popularity of elementary education. With the opportunities offered by the railways, increasing literacy and the massive movements of population in Victorian England, the use of the postal service increased some twenty-four fold to 1,800 million letters and 400 million packets a year. The business world also benefited from cheap postage and the system was an enormous financial success, one which was imitated by every civilized country in the world and which, in 1874, led to the founding of the Postal Union and the development of international mail services.

In the countryside of the late nineteenth century, the postal service was a highly efficient and comparatively inexpensive means of communication. Many were attracted to the security and respectability of the postman's job, symbolized by his uniform and the epithet 'Royal' which established his credentials as being above those of other men. But discipline was strict, the hours long

In the 1890s a rural postman often walked over 20 miles a day and was paid 30s (£1.50) a week.

and wages low. In the 1890s a postman earned about 30s a week (£1.50), which was less than a skilled craftsman. In his novel *Desperate Remedies* (1871), Thomas Hardy describes the daily round of a rural postman:

> . . . the clock struck five . . . the postman for the Tolchurch beat . . . reached the bottom of the street, gave his bags a final hitch-up, stepped off the pavement, and struck out for the country with a brisk shuffle. [He] was a short, stooping individual . . . laden on both sides with leather bags large and small, and carrying a little lantern strapped to his breast, which cast a tiny patch of light upon the road ahead. 'Yes, a long walk – for though the distance is only sixteen miles on the straight – that is, eight to the furthest place and eight back, what with the ins and outs to the gentlemen's houses, it makes two-and-twenty for my legs. Two-and-twenty miles a day, how many a year?' Besides the small private bags of the country families, which were all locked, the postman bore the large general budget for the remaining inhabitants along his beat. At each village or hamlet [he] came to, the postman searched for the packet of letters destined for that place, and thrust it into an ordinary letter-hole cut in the

door of the receiver's cottage – the village post offices being mostly kept by old women who had not yet risen. . . . It frequently happened that the houses of farmers, clergymen, &c., lay a short distance up or down a lane or path branching from the direct track of the postman's journey. To save time and distance, at the point of junction with some of these paths with the main road, the gatepost was hollowed out to form a letter-box, in which the postman deposited his missives in the morning, looking in the box again in the evening to collect those placed there for the return post.

Postcards were available from *c.* 1870, and postal orders, by which money could be transferred by post, from 1881. The oldest post-box still in use in Britain is at Holwell in Dorset. It was cast in metal

The oldest post-box in Britain at Holwell, Dorset.

by John N. Butt and Co., Gloucester, between 1853 and 1856 and is octagonal with the words 'Post Office Letterbox' above Queen Victoria's cypher and the maker's name. The red-painted box is about 1.5 metres high (5 feet) and each angle of the eight sides is fluted. The vertical slot for letters, which is less than 2.5 cm wide (1 inch) × 14 cm deep (5½ inches), has a hinged flap on the inside to keep out the rain.

Roland Hill, who was secretary to the Postmaster-General from 1846–64, also presided over the development of the *electric telegraph*, a system which had been pioneered by private enterprise. The first transatlantic telegraph cable was laid in 1858, though it did not function properly until 1866, and the expansion of the system enabled governments to influence world affairs (such as the conduct of the Boer War) with a rapidity which had previously been impossible. The first air-mail service, from London to Paris, was introduced in 1919.

See also DIRECTORIES *and* TELECOMMUNICATIONS

For the Postal History Society *and* Post Office Heritage Services *see* APPENDIX I

POSTERN A small private entrance in the wall of a castle, fortified town, monastery etc. The term SALLY-PORT is also used, though this has a more specific architectural meaning.

POSTILION From the mid-eighteenth century, many fast carriages on good European roads were driven by postilions, outriders who sat on the near-side horse of a pair and drove its partner. In England, very few private coaches were postilion-driven, though post boys could be hired with their teams at inns, known as *posting-houses* and located at intervals of 16 to 19 km (10 to 12 miles) along the major roads. But the post-chaise was always considered little better than an expensive alternative to the STAGECOACH.

POSTING-HOUSES *see* POSTILION

POSTULANT *see* MONASTERIES

POT METALS *see* STAINED GLASS

POTSHERD *see* SHERD

POULTRY (THE) *see* LARDER

POUNDHOUSES *see* CIDER MILLS

POUNDS *see* PINFOLD

POWYS *see* WALES

PRAEMUNIENTES A clause contained in a parliamentary summons requiring bishops to arrange for a specified number of other clergy (notably abbots) to attend at a particular session of Parliament. In 1295, for example, thirty-seven Benedictine and sixty-two Cistercian abbots were summoned, though this number was exceptional and in the Parliament of 1302 the numbers were reduced to twenty-three and twenty-one respectively.

PRAETORIUM *see* ROMAN FORTS AND CAMPS

PREACHING CROSS *see* CHURCHYARDS

PREBENDARY *see* CATHEDRALS *and* CLERGY

PRECENTOR *see* CATHEDRALS *and* MONASTERIES

PRECEPTORY *see* COMMANDERY

PREDELLA A platform or uppermost step on which an ALTAR stands or a shelf on which a REREDOS is supported.

PREMONSTRATENSIAN CANONS The 'White Canons' belonged to an order founded in 1120 by St Norbert at Prémontré near Laon. Their rule was that of St Augustine with additional austerities.

PREROGATIVE COURTS OF CANTERBURY AND YORK *see* PROBATE

PRESBYTERIAN The earliest organization of the Christian churches in Palestine resembled that of the Jewish synagogues, each administered by a board of 'elders'. Similarly, Presbyterianism incorporated the principle of government by committees of presbyters or 'overseers', which its sixteenth- and seventeenth-century proponents regarded not as innovative but as a restoration of the New Testament model. Presbyterian churches are normally governed by a hierarchy of courts: the Kirk-Session, Presbytery, Synod and General Assembly, all of which are representative bodies of ministers and elders whose authority is based ultimately on election. Ministers are elected by the people but ordained by a presbytery which has jurisdiction over a particular area. The doctrine of Presbyterian churches is therefore essentially Calvinistic.

The Presbyterian Church in Scotland was founded in 1560 and became the official national church in 1647. In seventeenth-century England, the Presbyterian Church was unpopular and was overthrown following the Restoration of 1660. Re-established in 1876, the Presbyterian Church of England united with the greater part of the Congregational Church of England and Wales to form the United Reform Church in 1972.

The archives of the Presbyterian Church of England are maintained in the library of the United Reform Church History Society. Other material is kept at the School of Oriental and African Studies at the University of London and also at the Dr William's Library in London (*see* APPENDIX I).

PRESBYTERY (i) The eastern part of a church beyond the choir.
(ii) The residence of a Roman Catholic priest.
(iii) The court of the Presbyterian Church which exercises jurisdiction over a particular area.

PRESENTMENT (i) A jury's statement to a court on matters within its knowledge, or of a manorial court concerning alienations of land.
(ii) A statement made on oath in an ecclesiastical court or by a churchwarden during a VISITATION.

PRESENTS 'By these presents . . .' or (as in a patent of arms) 'To All and Singular to whom these Presents shall come . . .' is a legal term meaning 'by this document . . .'.

PRESS-GANG A military or naval detachment employed for recruiting purposes. Press-money was made available for an initial payment, and once the recruit had accepted the 'King's shilling' he was thereafter obliged to be ready for service whenever his attendance was required. Press-men were those who had been so impressed. In practice, the press-gangs were often coercive and even brutal, and many good men were taken from their families by the application of force or excessive alcohol.

PRESS YARD The courtyard of a penal or other institution in which belligerent inmates were forcibly restrained.

PREST A payment or service required in advance by custom or promise.

PRETENCE, IN *see* IMPALEMENT

PRICKING Small holes pricked in parchment to serve as a guide for RULING, as for the staves in 'prick song books' of clerks.

PRIEST Early English versions of the New Testament distinguished between *presbyter* and *sacerdos*, but by the eleventh century the word 'priest', which is an etymological contraction of *presbyter*, was ambiguously used for both. With the spread of Christianity, the presbyters adopted more fully the functions of priests and as the parish priest became the normal celebrant of the Eucharist, and customarily exercised the power of absolution, his supernatural functions and powers were emphasized and he acquired a position outside the feudal hierarchy while remaining subordinate to his bishop, the validity of his position being dependent on ordination. The medieval perception of the priesthood was therefore almost exclusively concerned with the Mass. This was later rejected by the Reformers, though the term 'priest' was retained in the Book of Common Prayer apparently to ensure that deacons would not celebrate the Holy Communion. Members of religious communities were not necessarily priests, but only ordained clerks were permitted to administer the *sacraments*: baptism, absolution, confirmation (the prerogative of the bishop), ordination of clerks, matrimony, communion, unction for the sick and dying, and the casting out of evil spirits.

PRIESTS' HOLES Secret hiding-places incorporated into the houses of Roman Catholic families in anticipation of religious persecution. No county is richer than Worcestershire in such hiding-places. Most are connected with Catholic persecution, and in particular with the Gunpowder Plot of 1605, though in some cases the reason for their construction and use is obscure. The manor-house at Cleeve Prior, for example, contains such a hide and yet it was occupied throughout the seventeenth century by a staunchly protestant family, the Bushells. Nevertheless, the byways of this remote countryside must have witnessed many secretive comings and goings among the great recusant houses of Grafton Manor, Huddington Court, Coughton Court (in neighbouring Warwickshire) and Hindlip, the headquarters of the Jesuit mission led by Father Garnet.

Huddington Court contains two wonderful priests' holes, constructed by the legendary 'Little John' Owen, master-builder of hides and Garnet's servant who died on the rack in 1606. One hide opens into an upper storey room which was probably once the

The medieval Priest's House at Muchelney in Somerset.

chapel. The entrance is concealed by a detachable wainscote panel and the beams of the timber framing round the entrance are chamfered to afford easier access. Typical of Owen's designs, there is also an inner hide and bolt-hole by which the priest could make his escape. Entrance to the other hide is so cunningly concealed that it was only discovered by chance in the 1940s. In the corner of an attic bedroom part of an apparently solid timber and plaster wall swings open on hidden pivots to reveal a secret chamber. The 'door' includes a substantial timber upright which appears to support an even heavier rafter. Regrettably, of Hindlip nothing remains. Drawings show that it was an extraordinary rambling agglomeration of gables, turrets and towering chimneys, while a writer, who visited the house shortly before its destruction in the early nineteenth century, stated that:

> Its every room had a recess, a passage, a trap door, or secret stairs, the walls were in many

places hollow, the ceilings false, several chimneys had double flues, one for passage of the smoke the second for concealment of a priest, no one – except those immediately concerned – having key or clue to the whole maze of secrets.

It is hardly surprising that Father Garnet eluded the most rigorous searches for eight days and was captured only when privation forced him to give himself up.

With the destruction of Hindlip, Harvington Hall, also in Worcestershire, contains the finest extant collection of priests' holes in England. Extended by the (Protestant) Pakington family in *c*. 1578, Harvington passed to the (Catholic) Yate family in 1631. The seven priests' holes were probably incorporated into the house at about this time and were no doubt in regular use during the fresh wave of Catholic persecution which followed Titus Oates's 'Popish Plot' of 1678. All are ingenious, three particularly so. The first of these is entered by lifting a stair in a flight of five between the second-floor landing and the head of the great staircase. The hide itself is behind the wall of the dining hall and was contrived by lowering the ceiling of the adjacent pantry. Another, entered through a trap in the floor of a latrine, is concealed beside the chimney of the kitchen below and has a small bolt-hole opening into a shaft which extends the full height of the building and contains a pulley which once drove the kitchen spit. A third hide, discovered in 1897, is in the room known as Dr Dodd's library, where one of the seemingly substantial vertical beams in the brick and timber wall swings outwards on concealed pivots when pressed near the top to reveal the narrow entrance to the hide.

Some priests' holes were provided with a means of observing the comings and goings of a search party, but most viewing holes (*peeps*) are not associated with hiding-places and were provided simply to enable a host to keep an eye on his guests in the hall below his chamber. Some peeps are ingeniously disguised: there are several examples of 'glass eyes' in portraits and hinged 'knots' in wainscoting.

PRIME *see* MONASTERIES

PRIME MINISTERS OF GREAT BRITAIN AND OF THE UNITED KINGDOM

Sir Robert Walpole	Whig	[1721]–1742
Earl of Wilmington	Whig	1742–1743
Henry Pelham	Whig	1743–1754
Duke of Newcastle	Whig	1754–1756
Duke of Devonshire	Whig	1756–1757
Duke of Newcastle	Whig	1757–1762
Earl of Bute	Tory	1762–1763
George Grenville	Whig	1763–1765
Marquis of Rockingham	Whig	1765–1766
Earl of Chatham	Whig	1766–1768
Duke of Grafton	Whig	1768–1770
Lord North	Tory	1770–1782
Marquis of Rockingham	Whig	1782
Earl of Shelburne	Whig	1782–1783
Duke of Portland	coalition	1783
William Pitt	Tory	1783–1801
Henry Addington	Tory	1801–1804
William Pitt	Tory	1804–1806
Lord William Grenville	Whig	1806–1807
Duke of Portland	Tory	1807–1809
Spencer Perceval	Tory	1809–1812
Earl of Liverpool	Tory	1812–1827
George Canning	Tory	1827
Viscount Goderich	Tory	1827–1828
Duke of Wellington	Tory	1828–1830
Earl Grey	Whig	1830–1834
Viscount Melbourne	Whig	1834
Duke of Wellington	Tory	1834
Sir Robert Peel	Conservative	1834–1835
Viscount Melbourne	Whig	1835–1841
Sir Robert Peel	Conservative	1841–1846
Lord John Russell	Whig	1846–1852
Earl of Derby	Conservative	1852
Earl of Aberdeen	coalition	1852–1855
Viscount Palmerston	Liberal	1855–1858
Earl of Derby	Conservative	1858–1859
Viscount Palmerston	Liberal	1859–1865
Earl Russell	Liberal	1865–1866
Earl of Derby	Conservative	1866–1868
Benjamin Disraeli	Conservative	1868
William Ewart Gladstone	Liberal	1868–1874
Benjamin Disraeli	Conservative	1874–1880
William Ewart Gladstone	Liberal	1880–1885
Marquis of Salisbury	Conservative	1885–1886
William Ewart Gladstone	Liberal	1886
Marquis of Salisbury	Conservative	1886–1892
William Ewart Gladstone	Liberal	1892–1894
Earl of Rosebery	Liberal	1894–1895
Marquis of Salisbury	Conservative	1895–1902
Arthur James Balfour	Conservative	1902–1905
Sir Henry Campbell-Bannerman	Liberal	1905–1908
Herbert Henry Asquith	Liberal	1908–1916
David Lloyd George	coalition	1916–1922
Andrew Bonar Law	Conservative	1922–1923
Stanley Baldwin	Conservative	1923–1924
James Ramsay MacDonald	Labour	1924
Stanley Baldwin	Conservative	1924–1929
James Ramsay MacDonald	coalition	1929–1935
Stanley Baldwin	coalition	1935–1937
Neville Chamberlain	coalition	1937–1940
Winston Spencer Churchill	coalition	1940–1945
Clement Richard Attlee	Labour	1945–1951
Sir Winston Spencer Churchill	Conservative	1951–1955
Sir Anthony Eden	Conservative	1955–1957
Harold Macmillan	Conservative	1957–1963
Sir Alexander Douglas-Home	Conservative	1963–1964
Harold Wilson	Labour	1964–1970
Edward Heath	Conservative	1970–1974
Harold Wilson	Labour	1974–1976
James Callaghan	Labour	1976–1979
Margaret Thatcher	Conservative	1979–1990
John Major	Conservative	1990–1997
Tony Blair	Labour	1997–

PRIMOGENITURE The state or fact of being first-born. The custom or right of succession and inheritance by a first-born child. *Male primogeniture* further restricted inheritance to a first-born son. Primogeniture was abolished in 1925. *Ultimogeniture* was inheritance by the youngest son.

PRINCE BISHOP *see* PALATINATE

'PRINCE OF WALES' FEATHERS' *see* ROYAL ARMS IN CHURCHES

PRINTING Although printing was known in China it probably developed independently in western Europe and emerged late in the medieval period, stimulated by an increased demand for books and a corresponding increase in manuscript production. The mechanical problems of producing 'artificial' script were resolved by the Mainz-born goldsmith Johann Gutenberg (*c.* 1400–68), whose method of printing was to remain the standard for three and a half centuries. In 1455 he completed the first printed book, the *Gutenberg Bible*, in an edition of 200 copies printed with hand-cut lead type-fonts on paper and vellum in the German Gothic script of contemporary manuscripts. By 1500 some sixty printing centres had developed in Germany, while in England the first press was established in the precincts of Westminster Abbey in 1476 by William Caxton (*c.* 1422–91), who had learned his trade at Bruges. The first dated printed English book, *The Dictes or Sayengis of the Philosophres*, was produced in the following year. Caxton went on to produce more than eighty texts, including the works of Malory, Gower and Chaucer as well as translations of Virgil's *Aeneid* and the French romances. From 1799 until 1869 there was a statutory requirement that all printing presses should be licensed by magistrates.

PRIOR *see* MONASTERIES *and* PRIORY

PRIORY A religious house presided over by a prior or prioress. The head of a monastic house was either an abbot (abbess) or prior (prioress) and it is not always possible to draw a clear distinction between the two titles. Under the Benedictine influence, the term came to denote a monk who ranked next to the abbot and acted as his deputy. Later, it was applied also to the heads of mendicant houses and of small houses which were dependencies of abbeys. All Cistercian, Premonstratensian and Victorine houses were abbeys and all Carthusian and Cluniac houses were priories, being daughter houses of the Grand Chartreuse and Cluny (though anomalously the Cluniac house of Bermondsey was an abbey). The

great Benedictine foundations were abbeys, as were some Augustinian houses, but the majority of houses of both these orders, and those of the Gilbertines, were priories. The Benedictines distinguished between *conventual priories*, which were self-governing houses, and *obedientiary priories*, which were dependencies of abbeys.
See also MONASTERIES

PRISE The compulsory purchase of provisions and the requisitioning of transport for the purpose of maintaining a peripatetic royal household. Cash transactions were rare: most goods were obtained in return for wardrobe bills or *tallies* which promised future payment but frequently remained unfulfilled. From the late thirteenth century, this royal *right of prise* was gradually extended to include the provisioning of armies in the field against the Scots and Welsh. Attempts were made to remedy this abuse through a number of statutes in which 'torteous' (unlawful) prises were condemned and the Crown's rights and responsibilities more clearly defined. In particular, the Statute of Purveyors of 1362 provided a definitive statement which was to serve for the remainder of the medieval period. It required that no goods should be taken without consent; that they should be paid for; and that they should be used to maintain the royal household, not the army. Nevertheless, goods were frequently purchased at a rate below their market value and it was often financially advantageous for merchants to purchase exemptions from the parish constables who were responsible for arranging the transactions. The term does not have the same meaning as *purveyance*, which was the legitimate purchase of provisions in time of emergency.

PRISONS The concept of imprisonment as a punishment is a comparatively recent one. In the medieval period, cells in castles and within the fortifications of walled towns were generally used to confine those awaiting trial, sentence or execution, or 'strangers' apprehended by the watch and held pending investigation by the constables of the ward on the following day (*see* WATCH AND WARD). Nevertheless, underground cells beneath a castle tower or gatehouse often included a 'bottle-neck' dungeon, or *oubliette* (from the French *oublier*, meaning 'to forget'), and there can be little doubt that many a condemned man or habitual trouble-maker was incarcerated in such places. In the thirteenth and fourteenth centuries, the Crown granted franchises to lords for the maintenance of prisons. But neither the owner nor the Crown undertook to maintain the prisoners themselves, and expenses and profits were exacted from the relatives of the inmates (the last franchise prisons were abolished in 1858).

Debtors comprised one of the largest categories of prisoner. Those who owed money were confined, often in comparative comfort, until their debts (which included the accumulated fees for accommodation and 'comforts') had been paid by their families or friends. Accusations of debt were themselves often fraudulent and in some areas (notably in London) special debtors' prisons (*comptors*) were established under the jurisdiction of the sheriffs. The earliest purpose-built prison was probably that at Hexham in Northumberland (1330), while, more typically medieval, the castle of the Constable of St Briavels in Gloucestershire (*c.* 1275) contains both a debtors' prison (*pledgehouse*) and an *oubliette*.

Most boroughs had a LOCK-UP, and temporary *cages* were often provided at markets and fairs in which offenders were confined before being transferred to a more secure gaol. Imprisonment as a punishment, or as a means of protecting society, was not established until the end of the fifteenth century and even then freedom could usually be purchased. Before the nineteenth century, it was generally believed that death or transportation provided protection enough and the number of offences which nominally incurred the death penalty increased from about 50 to 160 during the period 1688 to 1765 and exceeded 200 by the early nineteenth century.

The modern perception of imprisonment as a mode of punishment grew from the *'house of correction'*, a place which, in the sixteenth century, was used for housing beggars and vagrants (and unmarried mothers) who 'threatened the peace of the community', and in which prisoners were set to hard labour (*see* POOR LAW). By the mid-sixteenth century, every county possessed such a prison, modelled on (and named after) the *Bridewell* at Blackfriars in London and administered by the local justices. Parishes were obliged to provide *Rogue Money* for the relief of poor prisoners in the county jails.

The Bridewells' original function was gradually superseded by that of imprisoning petty offenders, and overcrowded and insanitary conditions, together with oppressive and often brutal supervision, led to a vigorous crusade for prison reform. In 1729 a parliamentary inquiry investigated conditions at the Fleet and Marshalsea prisons, where gaolers were known to have tortured debtors to death while attempting to extract fees from men who, by definition, had no money. But English prisons remained a national disgrace for the remainder of the century, local authorities preferring to delegate their responsibilities to gangs of disreputable free-lance 'turn-keys' rather than to paid public officials.

Towards the end of the eighteenth century, John Howard (*c.* 1726–90) travelled throughout Britain exposing abuses and scandals in the prison system. His work, *State Prisons in England and Wales* (1777), provided the impetus for improvements in the building and management of prisons, but it was not until 1865 that a fully effective beginning was made in securing uniform standards of treatment. In part, this was a consequence of a significant decline in penal TRANSPORTATION in the early 1850s and a corresponding increase in custodial sentences which placed a further strain on the prisons. It was also coincidental with improvements in policing and the passing of the County and Borough Police Act of 1856 (*see* LAW AND ORDER).

The change to more effective administration and supervision resulted in more rigorous conditions: 'In place of filth, gaol-fever and corruption came the treadmill, the crank and strict regimentation.' There was widespread concern that the old-style prisons,

Wormwood Scrubs Prison, 1903.

with their haphazard arrangements and endemic corruption, were little better than 'academies of crime'. The new regime was therefore intended to reduce communication among prisoners to a minimum by keeping them so well occupied that they would have little opportunity (or energy) for corrupting one another. In some prisons, the inmates were even required to wear masks so that nothing could be conveyed by their features. In the mid-nineteenth century there were two types of prison: local houses of correction for those serving short sentences and for prisoners awaiting trial or sentence; and the long-term convict prisons, which also provided an alternative to penal transportation. These were usually specialized institutions but initially they included both purpose-built prisons and the old filthy hulks moored in the lower reaches of the Thames. One effect of the new penal system was to reduce the physical and mental health of the inmates and, therefore, their ability to commit crime. At the dreaded 'Steel' (Bastille) House of Correction in Coldbath Fields, London, the treadmills were operated from a series of compartments in which the prisoners were confined for fifteen minutes at a time treading down wheels of twenty-four steps at a regulated, agonizing rate:

> . . . the men can get no firm tread . . . from the steps always sinking away from under their feet and that makes it very tiring. Again the compartments are small, and the air becomes very hot, so that the heat at the end of a quarter of an hour renders it difficult to breathe.

Another exercise was 'shot-drill' which '. . . none but the strongest could endure'. For this, the prisoners were marshalled in rows round a hollow square at intervals of 3 metres (9 feet). At a warder's command, each picked up a 24-pound cannon ball, carried it to his neighbour's position and dumped it before returning to his own station where a fresh ball awaited him. This drill continued for 75 minutes. The 'crank' was an engine consisting of a sand-filled drum with a spindle running through it which was turned by a crank-handle. Revolutions were recorded on a dial and no immediate supervision was necessary. At the Steel, the crank was so dreaded that it was employed as a punishment for recalcitrant prisoners who could also be birched or flogged.

Ironically, prisoners in the long-term jails were less tormented and spent most of their working hours in the open air and enjoyed better rations. There were considerable discrepancies in the treatment of prisoners in different institutions and sentences varied enormously. It was therefore possible to find young boys imprisoned for causing a public nuisance, alongside criminals serving sentences for a brutal assault. In 1850 there were some 17,025 men, women and children in criminal prisons in England and Wales, the majority being short-term offenders. *Tickets of leave* were available to some who were nearing the end of a satisfactory sentence and were released on parole subject to supervision.

It was not until 1877 that what may be called a coherent national penal system emerged, and responsibility for the provision of prisons was finally transferred from the county authorities to the Home Office. Records of the administration of prisons prior to that date should have been transferred to national archives but some remain in county record offices where details of prisoners in gaols and houses of correction may also be found.

Records of prisoners from 1770–1894 and Prison registers for the Fleet and King's Bench prisons in London are at the Public Record Office, Kew. An index of persons held for debt in London's prisons from 1775 is held by the Corporation of London Record Office and the archives of the Howard League for Penal Reform are held at the Modern Records Centre at the University of Warwick (*see* APPENDIX 1).

In several county towns the cells beneath former county courts have been retained and are open to the public. At Dorchester in Dorset, for example, both the original courtroom in which the Tolpuddle Martyrs were tried and the subterranean cells in which they were held serve as grim reminders of the severity of nineteenth-century justice.

See also COURTS OF LAW *and* PUNISHMENT

PRIVATUM SIGILLUM *see* PRIVY SEAL *and* SEALS

PRIVY *see* WATER-CLOSET

PRIVY SEAL The *privatum sigillum* was, in England, a twelfth-century innovation and was held by the clerks of the king's chamber. It was attached to documents that were afterwards to pass the GREAT SEAL, particularly instructions to the Exchequer or CHANCERY. It was also appended to lesser documents which nevertheless required royal approval. By the fourteenth century, the authority of the privy seal rivalled that of the GREAT SEAL and in the reign of Edward II (1307–27) a *secretum* was introduced for the sovereign's personal use.

See also HOUSEHOLD

PROBATE The official proving of a will and testament. Originally wills and testaments were separate legal documents, written in Latin and subject to CANON LAW. A will (*voluntas*) was a statement by which a person (the testator) regulated the disposal of his land and property. A testament was concerned with debts and the disposal of personal goods. Both were documents of binding force, revocable ('ambulatory') until the testator's death but irrevocable thereafter. Following the death of the testator, the executors appointed in the will were required to 'prove' the will before the appropriate ecclesiastical court which exercised jurisdiction over probate matters. If the testator left goods worth more than £5 (*bona notabilia*) this was usually the archdeacon's court, though if he had estate in more than one archdeaconry jurisdiction reverted to the diocesan bishop, either through the CONSISTORY COURT or a COMMISSARY COURT. Where an estate extended over more than one diocese, then probate would be granted to either the Prerogative Court of Canterbury or the Prerogative Court of York. (It has been estimated that some 36,000 wills exist for the period 1383 to 1528 in the Prerogative Court of Canterbury.) Records of the Prerogative Court of Canterbury are available at the PUBLIC RECORD OFFICE and the FAMILY RECORD CENTRE. Peculiars exercised their own jurisdiction, known as testamentary peculiar (see PECULIAR). The executors (who usually included the wife, if she survived, or a son) had to satisfy the court that the will was an accurate expression of the last wishes of the testator. They then carried out its provisions under the court's supervision. Most wills were proved quickly and administered within a year or so, but a deathbed will disposing of large amounts of property could produce long years of litigation and its original provisions could be considerably modified.

Probate records of judgements relating to contested wills usually include the words 'by decree' or 'int. dec.' (interlocutory decree). Once the will was proved, the original copy was filed and a probate copy given to the executors which noted where and when probate was approved and to whom probate was given. If someone died intestate (without making a valid will), a letter of administration had to be obtained and administrators appointed by the court. In such cases, the personal estate usually went to the widow and children or, in the absence of children, to other relatives.

To make a will or testament, boys had to be over fourteen and girls over twelve. Married women could make a will only with their husband's consent (this was not revoked until 1882). A wife's property belonged to her husband – though she could leave a list of 'supplications' for his consideration. Widows and spinsters could make wills but inevitably the majority of surviving medieval wills were made by men. At that time, it was generally only the wealthy who made wills, though there are exceptions; felons, outlaws and traitors were unable to make wills because their property was forfeit to the Crown.

Property was classified as personal or real. Personal property (personalty) consisted of movable goods and chattels both animate and inanimate, also the remaining years on a leasehold. Real property (realty) consisted of freehold land, the disposal of which was subject to manorial custom and regulation. The Heir at Law received all the land except a small portion which belonged to the deceased's wife by dower right. This often meant that a daughter might receive nothing if the heir was a male cousin, though it was possible to effect a legal solution to this problem. This was known as *enfeoffment* by which the testator enfeoffed (surrendered) his land to feoffees who were entrusted to use the lands according to the testator's wishes. Common law regarded the feoffees as the beneficial owners but they were unable to use the land for their own purposes.

The personal estate had to be divided into three: one third for the widow, one third for the children and the remaining third to be disposed of according to the testator's wishes. If there were no children then it would be divided in two, and if the testator made no provision for the disposition of the remaining part then it went automatically to the Church.

A will was also a religious document intended to ease the testator's soul of any earthly burdens and to prepare him for the hereafter. Wills were usually made close to death and followed a standard format, opening with the testator committing his soul to God and affirming that he is 'of sound mind'; various saints would then be invoked and orders given for prayers and masses which, it was hoped, would expedite the soul through Purgatory. After this, the testator would dispose of ('devise') his worldly goods and lands, making arrangements for the payment of any debts, especially those to the Church, and for bequests of money 'to pious uses'. Such bequests were intended to ensure that prayers would be said for the soul of the testator and masses celebrated in his memory (see CHANTRY). The rich endowed CHANTRY CHAPELS or even chantry colleges where prayers were offered in perpetuity by chantry priests, while others (of more modest means) were commemorated in the chapels of their GUILDS. Probate was essentially an ecclesiastical matter and it is hardly surprising, therefore, that the majority of wills were written in an incumbent's hand, or witnessed by him, and that they were so carefully scrutinized by the ecclesiastical courts.

Of course, we cannot be certain from a person's will if they really were as pious during their lifetime as the will may suggest, for a will was often made in anticipation of death and the life hereafter. It may also be difficult to ascertain whether the terms of the will were carried out precisely as the testator wished, though there is often visible evidence in his parish church, for example, or in benefactions to a religious community or the endowment of an almshouse, hospice or similar charitable institution. When considered from the opposite perspective, wills and (from 1529) the accompanying probate inventories (*see below*) are invaluable sources of information concerning the condition and appearance of a church at a particular time, of its furnishings and possessions (such as books, plate and vestments) and of altars, aisles, chapels, clerestories, porches, towers and other additions and alterations which were effected through endowments and bequests of money, goods or land. They can provide evidence of early dedications and of parochial customs and ceremonies: at Thelnetham in Suffolk, for example, where one John Cole (d.1527) ordered that 'a new crosse to be made and sette upp where the gospell is saide upon Ascension Even'. He also left 3 acres of land to provide for the distribution of bread and ale at the cross during the Ascension procession.

Wills also provide evidence of changing religious attitudes, especially following the REFORMATION. At the beginning of the sixteenth century, for example, most (Catholic) testators bequeathed their souls to God and '. . . to the blessed Virgin Mary and the whole Company of Heaven'. Thereafter, a gradual change of emphasis is evident so that, by the 1560s, most (Protestant) testators dedicated themselves '. . . to Almighty God and his only son our Lord Jesus Christ, by whose precious death and passion I hope to be saved'.

The ecclesiastical courts continued to exercise jurisdiction over wills and testamentary matters until 1858. When attempting to trace an early will, the researcher should first ascertain the name of the testator's parish. From this it will be possible to establish in which of the various courts the will was proved. (There is a simplified guide to the probate courts in J. Richardson's *The Local Historian's Encyclopedia.**) The archives of pre-1858 wills are usually to be found in county record offices. They may include inventories of effects (probate inventories) which date from the period 1529 to 1750 and were compiled, on behalf of the executors, by two disinterested parties. Since 1858 all copies of wills and letters of administration have been deposited at the Principal Registry of the Family Division though local record offices usually have copies of the indexes.

* Richardson, J., *The Local Historian's Encyclopedia* (Phillimore, 1986).

PROMONTORY FORTS *see* HILL FORTS

PROPRIETARY CHAPEL *see* CHAPELS

PROSPECT TOWER

> Heav'ns, what a goodly prospect spreads around,
> Of hills, and dales, and woods, and lawns, and spires!
> James Thomson (1700–48)

Prospect towers are probably the most worthwhile and enjoyable of that group of buildings to which has been ascribed the generic term 'folly'. In fact, they are not FOLLIES at all for they have a very obvious function. Most were constructed in the eighteenth or nineteenth centuries in order to 'command the prospect' or distant view of a romantic landscape. They were intended to enhance man's appreciation of nature and they reflect the spirit of the age of pastoral romanticism as clearly as the paintings of the English landscape school and the poetry of Coleridge and Wordsworth.

Prospect towers were built in a variety of shapes and architectural styles, medieval Gothic being particularly favoured for its intrinsic romanticism, and they often contained a well-appointed upper room in which visitors to a great house could be entertained with tea and poetry while meditating on the beauties of nature through telescopes ('prospect glasses'). Several towers commemorate past events or historical characters such as Edgehill Tower (1747) above the battlefield of Edgehill in Warwickshire, and King Alfred's Tower (1772) at Stourhead in Wiltshire. Perhaps the most impressive of all is the Beacon Tower, high on the Cotswold scarp near Broadway in the south-eastern corner of Worcestershire. Built in 1796 for Lady Coventry, it commands a magnificent view over several counties and was once the home of Dante Gabriel Rossetti. In his *Encyclopaedia of Gardening* (1828), Loudon wrote:

> The prospect tower is a noble object to look at, and a gratifying and instructive position to look from. It should be placed on the highest grounds of a residence, in order to command as wide a prospect as possible, to serve as a fixed recognized point to strangers, in making a tour of the grounds. It may properly be accompanied by a cottage; or the lower part of it may be occupied by the family of a forester, gamekeeper, or any rural pensioner, to keep it in order.

PROTECTORATE, THE Oliver Cromwell was appointed Lord Protector at the behest of the army in December 1653 and held the office until his death in September 1658. The Protectorate achieved considerable success in foreign wars but the uneasy relationship between Protector, Parliament and army caused difficulties at home which were only alleviated by the influence of Cromwell's personality. After Oliver Cromwell's death, his son Richard proved incapable of maintaining the regime and its subsequent collapse resulted in the RESTORATION of Charles II in 1660.

PROVINCE *see* DIOCESE

PROVOST (i) A manorial official responsible for the husbandry of the commons and for the maintenance of ditches, hedges and the security of stock.
(ii) The chief magistrate of a Scottish burgh.
(iii) *See also* CLERGY (CHURCH OF ENGLAND)

PSALTER A book containing the Psalms.
See also PSALTERY

PSALTERY (i) An ancient and medieval stringed instrument.
(ii) A book containing the Psalms and other matter for recitation at the Divine Office. Psalteries were superseded by *breviaries*, liturgical books containing not only the psalms but also the hymns, lessons, responsories, canticles, etc., used in the Divine Office. Like breviaries, medieval psalteries are often beautifully illuminated.

PUBLIC RECORD OFFICE (PRO) Established in 1838 under the control of the Master of the Rolls, the Public Record Office is an essential source of information for the local historian. All records 'of a public nature' were brought together at that time, and to these were added the contents of the State Paper Office (from 1854) and the records of all government departments (except the India Office) when they were no longer required for administrative purposes. The collection is in two principal divisions comprising judicial and state records with additional material obtained from a variety of other sources. The PRO building at Kew, which was completed in 1977, contains 150 km (93 miles) of shelving to which is added a further 1.6 km (1 mile) every year (which, incidentally, represents only 5 per cent of the documentation created by government!). The accommodation includes a document reading-room, microfilm reading-room, research enquiries room, and a map and large documents room. You may make notes with pencil, typewriter, laptop or Dictaphone and there is a sensible ordering procedure so that you can order a document and then wait over a coffee, in the shop or at the lake-side until your bleeper tells you that the document has arrived. Alternatively, you may order up to three documents before you arrive using the PRO on-line catalogue. The PRO publishes an excellent guide to its services and facilities: *New to Kew*. Census returns (from 1841) and records of births, marriages and deaths (from 1837) are held at the Family Record Centre, London.
See also DOCUMENTARY SOURCES
For addresses *see* APPENDIX I

PUBLIC UTILITIES A dependable *water* supply was a prerequisite of every settlement and invariably determined both its location and its development. Farmsteads and villages were dependent on water obtained from SPRINGS or from *wells* which were excavated to the summer water-table. A Saxon well at Odell in Bedfordshire consisted of a pit from which water was drawn in a wicker basket. Medieval wells were often bottle-shaped with stone-faced shafts (*see also* HOLY WELLS). Water was conveyed in lead or earthenware pipes or stone conduits to several Roman towns in occupied Britain, and in the medieval and early Tudor periods the towns of Southampton (1420), Hull (1447), Bath (1500) and Gloucester (1542) obtained charters enabling them to construct piped water systems. In the late sixteenth and early seventeenth centuries, a number of AQUEDUCTS were constructed to provide supplies of fresh water to towns such as Plymouth and Cambridge, and between 1609 and 1614 the New River Company laid a pipeline from Hertfordshire to London using wooden pipes which proved to be singularly unreliable. Cast-iron piping became available in the 1790s and the Metropolitan Paving Act of 1817 required that all new pipes (which, in urban areas, could only be laid beneath the main streets) were to be of iron.

In practice, a Royal Commission of 1845 reported on the unhygienic nature of urban water supplies and in towns private companies made large profits selling dangerously impure water which, in London, was even distributed in untreated form direct from the Thames. Even those houses which were supplied by the private companies could expect only an hour's water 'on tap' each day and there was growing public disquiet with regard to the quality of drinking water, which was often polluted and was inevitably blamed for the spread of cholera.

In the countryside, most villages and settlements continued to rely upon wells and springs until the mid-nineteenth century. The Public Health Act of 1848 enabled local authorities to provide water supplies at public expense, but in rural areas the cost of such undertakings was usually prohibitive. In 1878 the Public Health (Water) Act required that all new rural housing had to be built within reasonable distance of a water supply (many village pumps date from that time), while the rapid expansion of the urban population had outpaced the ability of private companies to provide adequate water supplies and many cities established their own municipal water authorities with parliamentary consent to impede and extract water. With typical Victorian ingenuity, cities like Manchester, Liverpool and Birmingham, which did not have sufficient local supplies, constructed dams, formed artificial lakes and pumped water great distances along aqueducts into filter beds and distribution systems which are for the most part still in use today. *See also* DRINKING FOUNTAINS

Disposal of *sewage* and refuse were the responsibility of the PARISH, but as the industrial conurbations grew it became impossible for individual urban parishes to deal with the problem. London's solution had always been to use the Thames as an immense drain, the inadequacy of which was to impress itself on the sensibilities of the country's legislators when they were driven by the 'Great Stink' of 1851 from the newly built Houses of Parliament. As a result, a young engineer, Joseph Bazalgette, was commissioned to construct a major drainage system converging on two large trunk sewers which discharged London's effluent from north and south into the Thames through a pair of great Gothic PUMPING HOUSES at Abbey Mills and Crossness, down-river from the City. The scheme was completed in 1865 but it was soon discovered that, instead of being washed out to sea,

the effluent was carried back into London on the tides and equipment had to be provided to treat the sewage before it was pumped into the river. London's example was followed in towns and cities throughout the country but even today the treatment and disposal of sewage and refuse is, in many parts of Britain, a national embarrassment.

Gas, derived from coal by distillation, was first used in Britain in 1792 to light the office of the Scottish steam engineer William Murdock, who first developed the process. In 1805 gas lighting was used in a Manchester factory and two years later Pall Mall in London became the first public thoroughfare in the world to be lit by gas. The Chartered Gas Light and Coke Company, founded at Westminster in 1812, was the first of several private companies to produce and supply gas. By 1820 there were seven gasworks in London and the number of gaslights in the capital's streets had increased from 4,000 to 51,000 in only five years. Many of the major towns and cities had gas lighting by 1819, and by the 1840s gaslights were to be found in the streets, shops and residences of even the smallest rural towns.

It was not unusual at that time for a single street to be supplied by more than one company, and soon after 1850 'zoning' arrangements were agreed so that a single company was responsible for supplying the needs of a specific district. These arrangements were incorporated in the Metropolis Gas Act of 1860, which also set standards for illumination. Gas lighting was followed in the 1860s by the use of gas for cooking and for heating water. By the end of the century, most of the smaller gas-producing companies had amalgamated, but by this time they were beginning to compete with electricity.

Faraday's early experiments with *electricity* in the 1830s resulted in the use of powerful arc lamps in LIGHTHOUSES in the 1860s and electric lighting in some important streets (such as the Thames Embankment in London) and public buildings (such as the reading-room at the British Museum) in the 1870s. But it was not until Edison and Swan developed a basic light-bulb in the 1880s that domestic lighting became feasible. The town of Godalming, Surrey, was the first in the world to have electricity supplied for public and private use in a three-year experiment from 1881. The supply was generated at first by water-power and then by a steam engine, but following the experiment the town reverted to gas lighting.

Unlike gas, the supply of electricity was in the hands of local authorities. Bradford, Yorkshire, had

Lamp standards awaiting removal to the scrap yard, Hyde Park, London, 1958.

Latin Church: St Augustine of Hippo, St Gregory, St Ambrose and St Jerome. There are good fifteenth-century examples of the latter at Trull in Somerset and Castle Acre in Norfolk.

Liturgical changes effected by the Reformation resulted in a greater emphasis on direct communication between the priest and his congregation, and the pulpit acquired a more central rôle in worship, as did the reading desk (or reading pew) from which the priest read the prayers, lessons and litany. In the seventeenth and eighteenth centuries, these were often combined in 'double-decker' pulpits, each tier having its own means of access, and, in some churches, also incorporating the parish clerk's desk (or clerk's pew) from which the clerk led the responses. The upper preaching tier of these great 'three-decker' pulpits towered above even the tallest BOX PEWS in the nave.

Victorian ecclesiologists, fired with an enthusiasm for all things medieval, destroyed many triple- and

the first municipal power station in 1889, and the first London station was opened at St Pancras in the following year. The Electric Lighting Act of 1872 enabled the Board of Trade to grant seven-year licences to private generating and distribution companies. These licences were renewable but local authorities were able to buy back an enterprise after twenty-one years if they so wished (this was increased to forty-two years in 1888). But the use of electrical power in homes and factories was uncommon before the 1920s.

PUISNE JUDGE A junior judge in the common law courts.

PULPITS In medieval churches the CHANCEL was a mysterious *inner sanctum* in which the Mass was celebrated and from which the congregation in the nave was separated by a CHANCEL SCREEN. But the popularity of itinerant preachers in the fourteenth century (notably the Franciscan friars) is reflected in the number of pulpits erected in that period, usually set against the wall of the nave or against a pier. The earliest example dates from *c.* 1340, though most surviving pre-Reformation pulpits are from the fifteenth and early sixteenth centuries. From the Latin *pulpitum*, meaning 'platform', they were constructed of stone or of oak with traceried panels which sometimes contained carved or painted motifs depicting the likenesses of the Four Evangelists or familiar preceptors such as the Four Doctors of the

Fifteenth-century pulpit at Fotheringhay, Northamptonshire: a gift of Edward IV.

double-decker pulpits though some escaped, notably the seventeenth-century three-tiered pulpit at Kedington, Suffolk, which has retained its *tester*, or overhead sounding-board which amplified and directed the voice of the preacher, together with the iron stand for an hourglass and even a stand for the parson's wig. There are other fine examples at St Mary's church, Whitby, Yorkshire, and Old Ditton near Westbury, Wiltshire, where the original box pews and galleries have also survived. Jacobean *hourglasses* may still be found in many churches, or the wrought-iron supports in which they once stood. Church attendance being compulsory, preachers addressed captive audiences for at least an hour. If at the end of that time the parson turned the hourglass over, the congregation knew they were in for a further hour of preaching!

PULPITUM All English cathedrals and major abbeys once had a pulpitum: a massive transverse stone screen and platform separating the NAVE from the CHANCEL and pierced by a central opening with doors. The primary purpose of the pulpitum was to segregate the CHOIR and to provide a backing for the stalls, thereby securing for the monks or canons both privacy and protection from draughts. Possibly, as the word implies, the forerunner of the PULPIT and also used as a gallery for singers, many have been removed and others used to support an organ. Not to be confused with the CHANCEL SCREEN or ROOD SCREEN.
See also MONASTERIES

PUMPING HOUSES *and* **WATER-TOWERS** For the new Victorian water and waste-disposal authorities (*see* PUBLIC UTILITIES) it was not enough that their buildings and equipment should function efficiently. Precisely because they were entrusted with providing clean water and treating sewage, they wanted buildings which inspired public confidence in their work and which compared favourably with those of other corporations. As a result, they constructed cathedral-like pumping stations and water-towers disguised as castles and campaniles, immense dams and serpentine AQUEDUCTS, many of which remain in use today. One of the most magnificent is the Abbey Mills pumping station, which discharges sewage from Bazalgette's great north London sewer into the Thames at Bromley-by-Bow. Built in 1865–8, it has the appearance of an Orthodox church complete with a spiky central dome surrounded by smaller cupolas and is built on a Greek cross plan. Regrettably, its two minaret-like chimneys were demolished during the last war when it was found that they were being used for navigational purposes by the *Luftwaffe*. Within the perimeter walls, formal gardens and avenues of plane trees and black poplars lead to the superintendent's residence and to the pumping station with its four deep, hooded stone porches, each with a pair of immense copper and bronze doors. The architectural detail is extraordinarily ornate, with striped window heads, rich foliated corbels, barley-twist rainwater pipes and polychrome tiles. The eight massive beam engines were removed in the 1930s but the station's exotic cast-iron interior has survived. Its focal point is an octagonal arcade of pillars, open to a dome above and surrounding a well, two storeys beneath the entrance level, in which an amazing 'lobster-backed' joint links the three great sewers constructed of sections curving in three dimensions in the bowels of the building. More numerous are water pumping stations such as those at Kew in Surrey, Ryhope in Tyne and Wear, Portsmouth in Hampshire and Papplewick in Nottinghamshire. Built between 1883–5 to pump water from underlying Bunter sandstone beds to the rapidly expanding Nottingham conurbation, Papplewick, with its inlaid Renaissance pilasters and capitals adorned with life-size pelicans, is reminiscent of the original wing of the Victoria and Albert Museum.

The construction of water-towers was an opportunity to design eye-catchers which were taller than any of the follies erected by the great eighteenth-century landowners. Water-towers must, of course, be higher than any of the properties they serve and they were therefore erected in commanding positions and dominated the surrounding landscape. The most eccentric is the 'House in the Clouds' at Thorpness in Suffolk, which looks like an illustration for the 'Old Woman Who Lives in a Shoe'. Built in 1923, it has a five-storey house serving as a pedestal for a 30,000 gallon water tank, itself disguised as a weatherboarded 'house' complete with steeply gabled roof, chimney stack and windows. The soaring dock tower at Grimsby in Humberside is 91 metres high (303 feet), some 5 metres (16 feet) higher than the *Torre del Mangia* in Siena on which it was modelled in 1851. Its function (until it was replaced in 1892) was to provide pressure for the hydraulic system of lock gates, sluices and cranes on the docks, its 33,000 gallon water tank producing an operative pressure of 90 lb per square inch.

Unique triple expansion pumping engines at Kempton Park Pumping Station.

PUNISHMENT *see* ATTAINDER, BRANDING, COURTS OF LAW, CUCKING STOOL, DISTRAINT, DUCKING STOOL, GALLOWS, GIBBET, HARD LABOUR, HIDEGILD, IRONS, KINEBOTE, LARCENY, LAW AND ORDER, LOCK-UP, MURDER FINE, OUTLAWS, PILLORY, POOR LAW, PRISONS, SCOLDING, STOCKS, TORTURE, TRANSPORTATION (PENAL), TRIAL BY BATTLE, TRIAL BY ORDEAL, WERGILD *and* WHIPPING

PURBECK MARBLE Used by the Romans in Britain and much favoured by the church-builders and monumental masons of thirteenth- and fourteenth-century England and Normandy, Purbeck marble is a not marble at all but a dark, fossiliferous limestone which occurs in two narrow strata in the Isle of Purbeck in Dorset. Its northern equivalent is *Frosterley marble*, a black or dark grey limestone extracted from quarries at Frosterley in County Durham.
See also TOUCH

PURITANS Members of a reforming protestant movement dating from the reign of Henry VIII (1509–47) who, dissatisfied with the Elizabethan religious settlement, sought a further purification of the Church of England. They were particularly influential among the merchant classes and at first attacked 'unscriptural forms of worship', ornamentation, vestments and other 'trappings of the corrupted Church'. But from 1570 the more extreme members began to attack the institution of the episcopacy itself. The Civil War of 1642–9 led to the temporary triumph of Puritanism but also to its proliferation into sects so that the term ceased to be appropriate after 1660.

PURLIEU (i) Disafforested land on the periphery of a forest.
(ii) Land added to an ancient forest without authority.
See FORESTS

PURLIN A horizontal beam running parallel to the ridge of a roof and carrying the common rafters (*see* ROOFS).

PURSUIVANT OF ARMS An officer of arms of junior rank.

PURVEYANCE *see* PRISE

PUTLOG HOLES *see* CASTLES (MEDIEVAL)

PYX-SHRINE *see* TABERNACLE

Q

QUADRIVIUM *see* EDUCATION

QUAKERS The Society of Friends originated in the activities of George Fox (1624–91), the son of a Leicestershire weaver who began preaching in 1647 and whose precept was that 'truth is the inner voice of God speaking to the soul'. The term Quaker is derived from the spiritual 'trembling' manifested at early meetings. The Society was established in 1668 and its library in 1673. They rejected the sacraments and were opposed to formal services and to paid ministers. They refused to take oaths or to enter into military service. Before the Toleration Act of 1689, they were subjected to much persecution, refusing to meet secretly and stressing the importance of outward observances in speech and plain living. Quakers have a strong commitment to pacifism and their devotion to social and educational work has earned them almost universal respect. All known Quaker registers were copied in 1837 and the originals sent to the Registrar General in 1840. These are now housed in the Public Record Office. A central repository of records is maintained in the Society of Friends Library, though many are retained locally (*see* APPENDIX I).

QUAR, QUARL, QUARR *and* **QUARREL** Place-name elements derived from the medieval *quarrere* and *quarelle*, meaning 'quarry'. More rarely, the name may suggest the site of a medieval forge where crossbow bolts (*quarrels*) were manufactured, or a workshop where small glass panels were made (*quarries* or *quarrels*).

QUARREL *see* QUAR *and* STAINED GLASS

QUARRIES Quarries were once numerous in the countryside. At a time when transportation of materials was both difficult and expensive, the more fortunate medieval communities usually enjoyed a right to extract their own building stone, chalk or lime (*see* LIMEKILNS), while quarries such as those at Purbeck and Portland in Dorset, Barnack in Cambridgeshire and Ketton in Leicestershire were of an entirely different scale, exporting rare and high quality stone for prestigious building works, and supplying areas such as East Anglia, where chalk and flint were the only freely available local materials. Old quarries may sometimes be mistaken for other types of earthwork but their overgrown pits and spoil-heaps usually lack the regularity of form which is associated with abandoned settlements and deserted farmsteads. Many may be identified from early estate and other maps or from place-name elements such as QUAR *and* STĀN. Of course, there may have been intermittent quarrying of a particular site during several centuries and dating may be difficult.
See also MINERALS

QUARRY *see* QUAR *and* STAINED GLASS

QUARTER DAYS and RENT DAYS

Lady Day	25 March
Annunciation of the Blessed Virgin	
Michaelmas	29 September
Feast of St Michael and All Angels	
Christmas	25 December
Feast of the Nativity	
Midsummer	
Up to and including 1752	6 July
Thereafter	24 June

See also LADY DAY, LAMMAS, MICHAELMAS *and* SAINTS' DAYS AND FEAST-DAYS

QUARTERING In ARMORY, the method (known as *marshalling*) whereby the shield of arms is divided to display both the paternal arms and those acquired through marriage with heraldic heiresses.

QUARTER SESSIONS The quarterly meetings of the justices of a county, riding or county town which originated in 1361 when Keepers of the Peace became Justices of the Peace with authority to determine cases. From 1363, they began to meet four times a year at Easter, Midsummer, Michaelmas and Epiphany. In 1461 indictments which had previously been heard by the Sheriff's Tourn (*see* HUNDRED COURT) were transferred to quarter sessions. These were criminal cases such as riot, murder, assault and poaching and the quarter sessions were not concerned with civil matters or with cases of treason or forgery. The Tudors gave the justices wide-ranging new powers and responsibilities, and in carrying out these duties they gradually replaced the sheriffs in the administration of local affairs. From 1531, they dealt with the administration of the POOR LAW, and from 1601 were responsible for the appointment of parochial Overseers of the Poor. The Clerk of the Peace advised the court in matters of law and sessions were usually attended by the High Sheriff or his deputy and high and petty constables.

In the eighteenth century, increases in the urban population resulted in the creation of administrative divisions in several counties, and quarter sessions were held more frequently in some towns than in others. Sessions were of two types: county quarter sessions (which were presided over by a group of magistrates) and borough quarter sessions (presided over by a practising barrister of at least five years' standing who was known as a *Recorder*). Less administrative business was undertaken in sessions, and standing committees of justices were appointed for dealing with particular problems, assisted by permanent officials such as the County Treasurer, Inspector of Weights and Measures and Surveyor (Bridgemaster). In 1819 justices were permitted to divide their number so that separate courts could sit simultaneously, and from 1834 their work was reduced by the creation of a number of *ad hoc* bodies such as boards of Poor Law guardians. In 1888 the Local Government Act transferred most of the non-judicial functions of quarter sessions (and most of their paid officials) to the new county councils. In criminal matters ASSIZE courts overlapped with quarter sessions, assizes dealing with the gravest offences. Quarter sessions and assizes were replaced by the Crown Court in 1972. This hears criminal cases in continuous sessions in the main towns and cities while the High Court determines civil cases.

Quarter session records, dating from the Tudor period (and sometimes before) to 1889, are an invaluable source of local historical material for they concern not only crime and punishment but also land, enclosure awards, licensing, charities, the MILITIA, rates and taxes, roads and bridges,

religion, social welfare, the Poor Law, lunatics and a variety of other subjects. Initially, they were the nominal responsibility of a private individual (often a senior justice) called the Keeper of the Rolls (*Custos Rotulorum*) but from the Tudor period most records were deposited with clerks of the peace. Quarter session records are now maintained in county record offices.

QUEEN ANNE HOUSE *see* CLASSICAL ARCHITECTURE

QUEEN ANNE'S BOUNTY *see* TITHES

QUEEN POST *see* KING POST *and* ROOFS

QUERNS A stone device for milling by hand. The earliest *saddle stones* consisted of two stones between which the corn was ground by a lateral motion of the upper stone across the lower. These were superseded in the late Iron Age by the *rotary quern*, two round stones of similar diameter, the upper one of which was rotated on the lower grinding surface by means of a wooden handle. Medieval querns comprised a thin, round upper stone which was turned on an iron spindle within a flat-bottomed 'bowl' carved out of a circular or octagonal base stone some 9 cm deep (3½ inches) and between 23 and 38 cm across (9 and 15 inches). The meal or flour was removed from between the two grinding surfaces by means of an angled hole which pierced the side of the base. Some bases were decoratively carved, the opening in the side terminating in the mouth of a human head, for example. Such bases were more durable than the thinner top stones and several have found their way into churches in the belief that they were primitive fonts.

The Old English *cweorn* is found as a place-name element and may indicate the site of a former quarry from which querns were obtained. It is evident in such names as Quarley, Hampshire ('glade where millstones were found'), Quarndon, Derbyshire ('hill where millstones were quarried') and, less obviously, Whernside, Yorkshire, which has the same meaning.

QUIRE (i) Four sheets of parchment folded together in eight leaves, a number of which were bound together to make a book.
(ii) An alternative spelling of CHOIR. A *quirister* is a chorister.

QUIRISTER *see* QUIRE

QUIT RENT A fixed annual rent which released a tenant from manorial service. Abolished as recently as 1922, quit rent is not the same as PEPPERCORN RENT.

QUOIN From the French *coin*, meaning 'corner' or 'angle', a quoin is the external angle of a building and *quoins* or *quoin stones* are the dressed stones forming the angle. In Anglo-Saxon buildings, *long and short work* comprises quoins laid so that long vertical slabs alternate with short horizontal ones.

QUOITS *see* CHAMBERED TOMBS

QUO WARRANTO From 1278 a claim that franchisal rights were exercised by ancestral precedent could be inquired into by a writ of *Quo Warranto*. This was intended to ascertain by what warrant the original jurisdiction was exercised. In 1290 the Statute of Quo Warranto enabled anyone who could prove continuous use of a franchise by himself and his ancestors since 1189 to have his position confirmed by means of letters patent. The system was abandoned, along with EYRES, in 1294. *See also* HUNDRED ROLLS

RACK RENT The maximum rent that a tenement may fetch in a year.

RAFTER Any of the sloping beams within the framework of a roof. *Principal rafters* are those which carry the PURLINS (*see* ROOFS).

RAG *and* **RAGSTONE** A hard, course stone which is not FREESTONE.

RAGWORK *see* RUBBLE

RAILINGS Railings on houses built before the First World War have almost entirely disappeared, as have those which once surrounded the elegant eighteenth-century squares and gardens of many large towns. Most were requisitioned by the government in 1941–2, during the Second World War, to make

Ornamental railings at Hampton Court Palace.

tanks and munitions, each householder being provided with a receipt guaranteeing compensation of between 2*s* 6*d* (12½p) and 5*s* (25p). But some railings did survive, notably those which were erected around the basement areas of terraced houses and were intended to prevent pedestrians falling from the pavement into the well below.

All railings were made either of wrought or cast iron. Wrought iron is much more malleable than cast iron and can be beaten into shapes to produce remarkably ornate gates and decorative panels. But whereas wrought iron is unsuitable for mass-production, cast iron is ideally suited to bulk manufacture and the difference between wrought- and cast-iron railings is not always immediately apparent, though broken ironwork is most likely to be cast iron as it is much more brittle.

One of the most effective uses of wrought iron is in *overthrows*, wishbone-shaped pieces of ironwork which may be seen above the gates of many early eighteenth-century houses and from which was hung a lantern to illuminate the pathway or front door steps. During the later decades of the century, first-floor balconies with cast-iron railings and verandas became fashionable in Regency towns such as Leamington in Warwickshire and Cheltenham in Gloucestershire and these proliferated during the 1820s and 1830s when designs from *The Smith and Founder's Directory* of 1824 were popular (*see* REGENCY ARCHITECTURE). A further development in the 1840s was the window guard: low horizontal railings or a single *anthemion* (a decorative foliated panel) fitted to wide stone sills to retain the substantial window-boxes of the period. The usual method of fitting decorative railings was to drill a socket in the stonework base, insert the ironwork and fix it by pouring in molten lead.

RAILWAYS By the time that a workable steam locomotive first evolved, the practice of transporting materials by means of horse-drawn 'trains' of wagons, running on a fixed track of wooden planks or iron rails, was well established. In this way, substantial loads could be moved with considerably less effort than that required to haul a similar load on a rough-surfaced road. The earliest medieval 'tracks' were parallel rows of stones with grooves, to guide the wooden wheels of carts, cut into their surfaces. Wooden 'wagonways' had been used at quarries and collieries since the early sixteenth century, and by the end of the eighteenth century many wagons were provided with flanged iron wheels and ran on iron rails. The Surrey Iron Railway of 1803 was the first public railway and, like the first passenger-carrying Oystermouth Railway of 1807 (at Swansea in South Wales), its trains were drawn by horses.

It was inevitable that STEAM POWER should be exploited as a means of traction in the collieries of the Industrial Revolution and at first it was used to haul wagons by cable. It was on the coal truck plateway of Pen-y-Darn colliery in South Wales that Richard Trevithick's (1771–1833) steam locomotive first ran in 1804, though it was not until the introduction of Blenkinsop's rack-rail system on the Middleton railway in 1812 (at Leeds in Yorkshire) that initial problems of adhesion were overcome. A year later, Hedley's *Puffing Billy* proved that sufficient natural adhesion could be obtained on a normal track without recourse to the cumbersome rack.

Transportation of goods and materials by canal, though comparatively cheap and reliable, was also extremely slow and industrial activity expanded so rapidly that the canal system was unable to keep pace. In particular, it had become essential that coal should be moved efficiently and cheaply from the pit-heads to the ports and manufacturing centres.

It was Robert Stephenson (1803–59) who first exploited the potential of the railway as a country-wide transportation system for raw materials, finished goods and passengers. His father, George Stephenson (1781–1848), is traditionally credited with many of Robert's achievements (including the building of the *Rocket*), but the records of the House of Lords select committee on the development of the London–Brighton line (1836) indicate that grave doubts were expressed concerning the elder

Stephenson's engineering ability and credibility. George Stephenson was a colliery engineman who in 1825 engineered the Stockton and Darlington Railway, the world's first public steam railway. But while this was a commercial success, it was not until the opening of the Liverpool and Manchester line of 1830 that the Railway Age really began. The line was developed by a group of entrepreneurs whose objective was to break the monopoly of the north-country waterways. The Stephensons were able for the first time to combine steam traction for both goods and passenger trains, using a double track with a favourable gradient, sophisticated engineering works and a basic signalling system. In 1829 the directors of the Liverpool and Manchester Company offered a £500 prize to the designer of a steam locomotive which was capable of matching a stringent set of criteria. In winning the Rainhill trials, Robert Stephenson's *Rocket* finally confirmed the superiority of steam over horse traction and, before long, corporations throughout the country were clamouring for their own railway connections – though others remained equally obstinate in their opposition to the 'diabolical iron roads'.

Development was rapid, though opposed by many private landowners (who often demanded exorbitant compensation for routes across their land) and by the canal companies (who resented the loss of business). Encouraged by manufacturers and traders, who enthusiastically welcomed this new form of quick and reliable transport, there were two periods of intense railway investment: during the years 1836 to 1837 and between 1844 and 1848. By 1840, 2,414 km of track (1,500 miles) had been laid and services established connecting London with the industrial conurbations of the Midlands and north-west. The 'railway mania' of the mid-1840s, during which over 4827 km of line (3,000 miles) were laid, culminated in a spectacular financial crash in 1847. But by that time the great companies of the Railway Age had been established. The success of the new railways, and in particular the speed with which they were constructed, was effected by the availability of a substantial workforce of skilled *navvies* ('navigators') and experienced engineers who had learned their trade on the cuttings, embankments, aqueducts and tunnels of the canal system which the railway network now superseded. By comparison with the construction of the present motorway system, the achievement of the pick-and-shovel Irish navvies is monumental. High standards are workmanship were required and the companies competed with one another in the architectural magnificence of their buildings, some of which have

Navvies at work on the Saunderton Cutting near High Wycombe, Buckinghamshire, in 1905.

rightly been described as the cathedrals of the Victorian age. A direct route from London to Glasgow was completed in 1848 and, during the second half of the nineteenth century, the railway networks expanded rapidly, promoted and funded by the industries which they had helped to create.

This was a time of bitter commercial rivalry and of great engineers. In 1833, Isambard Kingdom Brunel (1806–59) became Chief Engineer of the Great Western Railway before turning to steamship construction with the *Great Western* in 1837. Brunel chose a gauge of 7 feet ¼ inches (2.14 metres) for his superbly engineered London to Bristol Great Western Railway but this brought his company into conflict with other railways, all of which had adopted Stephenson's standard gauge of 4 feet 8½ inches (1.435 metres). The standard gauge eventually carried the day but Brunel's broad gauge was retained on the Great Western until 1892.

By the end of the century, many small lines had been amalgamated to form the great companies which were to dominate the railways until the grouping of 1923. (At this time the 'Premier Line' – the London and North Western Railway – was the largest joint-stock corporation in the world.) There was intense and often acrimonious rivalry among the large companies, exemplified in 1895 by races from London to Aberdeen on the east and west coast routes. Goods traffic grew rapidly, though such was the demand for cheap transportation that the railway companies were forced to buy out the canal companies who continued to offer stubborn resistance.

The Duke of Wellington had opposed the railways because he believed that they would 'encourage the lower classes to move about'. This they certainly did, and the availability of cheap rail travel contributed to profound social and demographic change. Mail-coaches were gradually withdrawn from service and the great highways of the eighteenth century became deserted, their posting inns falling on hard times and their toll-gates left unattended. Elsewhere, the arrival of a railway stimulated urban growth and often revived the commercial activity of moribund medieval market towns and inland river ports such as Gloucester and Chester. New 'railway towns', such as Crewe in Cheshire and Swindon in Wiltshire, were created to service the companies' immense engineering requirements, 'commuter' towns began to expand on the periphery of London and other cities, and even the remotest of rural communities might suddenly find its fortunes transformed by the proximity of a rail junction, as at Templecombe in Somerset. Similarly, numerous minor coastal settlements grew around rail-heads, such as Blackpool in Lancashire, Bournemouth in Dorset and Scarborough in Yorkshire, all of which developed as major seaside resorts in the nineteenth century following the arrival of the railways and encouraged by the popularity of excursion trains from inland industrial conurbations. Elsewhere, many coastal termini expanded as ports: Folkstone in Kent, Southampton in Hampshire and Middlesbrough in Cleveland, for example.

The earliest passenger compartments were of a similar design to the stagecoaches which they replaced. They had facing seats and there was no means of communication from one to another until through-corridor trains were introduced in the 1890s, together with bogie-coaches, restaurant and sleeping cars and lavatory facilities. Third-class accommodation was cramped and uncomfortable and persisted until the 1870s when the Midland Railway introduced two-class travel.

The world's first underground railway was the 6-km (3¾-mile) Metropolitan Railway, which opened in 1863 between Paddington and Farringdon Street in London using steam locomotives with condensers. (It is now part of the Circle Line in London's Underground system.)

In the early years of the twentieth century, the railway monopoly remained unchallenged. Nevertheless, there was widespread dissatisfaction with the standard of service and particularly with the rates charged for conveying goods. The success of electric tram-cars in several urban areas provided the impetus for the electrification of lines in Newcastle and Liverpool and the creation in 1909 of the London, Brighton and South Coast's South London Line which was to lead to the eventual electrification of much of the new Southern Railway after 1923. During the First World War (1914–18), the entire network was brought under the control of a central committee and by the Railways Act of 1921 a total of 120 companies, covering 36,800 km of track

(23,000 miles), were brought together in four large undertakings which, from January 1923, comprised the London, Midland and Scottish; the London and North Eastern; the Southern; and the Great Western – the only company to retain its identity and most of its former territory. Inevitably, rivalries remained but the re-constituted railways were better able to meet the challenge of a rapidly expanding road transport system and electric trams. The Second World War effectively bankrupted the railways and they were nationalized on 1 January, 1948. Following the appointment in 1962 of an industrialist, Dr Richard Beeching, as head of the new British Railways Board, over 8,000 km of track (5,000 miles) and 2,000 stations were closed and the rolling stock fleet cut by half.

For comprehensive details of railway formations *see* Richardson, J., *The Local Historian's Encyclopedia*, Phillimore,1993.

Bradshaw's Railway Guides contain a wealth of historical information, notably annual timetables. They are available in original and reprinted form.

For the National Railway Museum, the Railway and Canal Historical Society *and the* Tramway Museum Society *see* APPENDIX I

RAMPART A broad-topped defensive wall of masonry or earth surrounding a settlement, castle or other fortified site.

RAMPART SETTLEMENTS *see* HILL FORTS

RAMS (WATER) *see* FARMSTEADS

RANCH BOUNDARIES *see* DYKES

RAPES *and* **LATHES** Rapes in Sussex and lathes in Kent are ancient divisions each comprising several HUNDREDS. It is likely that they originated in tribal territories and therefore pre-date shires. William I reorganized the six Sussex rapes as *castleries*, each area maintaining one of the castles which guarded against incursions from the south coast: Chichester, Arundel, Bramber, Lewes, Pevensey and Hastings. Kent was also divided into six lathes which were later redefined as Sutton-at-Hone, Sheppey, Scray and Aylesford, together with St Augustine and Hedeling which were later combined to form a single lathe.

RATH From the Gaelic *ràth*, meaning 'circular fort', a defended Irish farmstead usually contained within a circular rampart and ditch. Examples date from the Bronze Age to the early medieval period.

Some 35,000 sites have been identified though many are recognizable only from the air or from the common *rath* place-name element.

RAVELIN A defensive detached outwork of a fortification with two embankments raised before the counterscarp (*see* MARTELLO TOWERS AND COMMISSION FORTS).

READING (*also* **RIDDING**) *see* ASSART

READING-ROOM Reading-rooms burgeoned in the mid-nineteenth century, particularly in those areas where the Liberal and Chapel movements were strong. People from the local community came to the reading-rooms to read books, journals and papers which they could not afford to buy themselves. Soft drinks were often available and reading-rooms became alternative meeting-places at a time when excessive drinking in public houses was causing increased concern in Victorian society. Few reading-rooms remain intact today and many have been converted to domestic accommodation. Several of the larger 'Institutes', which also provided recreational facilities and opportunities for educational advancement, still function as centres of community life in many larger rural villages and small towns.
See also LIBRARIES

REANS (*also* **REINS**) Boundary land.

REBECCA RIOTS Riots which spread from the Preseli Hills of Pembrokeshire in South Wales in 1839 and 1844 as the result of a series of bad harvests. Anger and frustration were directed at the turnpike trusts who, it was claimed, were exploiting an impoverished farming community by erecting an excessive number of TURNPIKES. Toll-gates were attacked and destroyed and violence proliferated until a parliamentary commission acknowledged the extortionate nature of the tolls. The Welsh drew inspiration from the Bible: '. . . they blessed Rebekah, and said to her, may your descendants possess the gates of those who hate them' and the saboteurs wore womens' clothing as befitted the 'children of Rebekah'.

REBUS (*non verbis sed rebus*) A pictorial pun on a name. Rebuses were especially popular in medieval ecclesiastical circles and were widely used as personal devices and to decorate the fabric of buildings, chapels and tombs. At Milton Abbey in Dorset, for example, a stone corbel has been carved

and painted in the form of a windmill on top of a wine barrel (*tun*), the rebus of a former abbot of Milton.

RECLAMATION A thousand years ago, vast stretches of coastal Britain consisted of waterlogged fens (from the Old English *fen* and East Saxon *fæn*, meaning 'marsh') characterized by reed beds and expanses of brackish water broken by isolated 'islands' of impervious rock. Little original fenland remains in Britain: the waterlogged nature reserves of Wicken, Holme and Woodwalton fens in Norfolk serve to illustrate what vast areas of lowland eastern England must have looked like 1,000 years ago. From the eleventh to the end of the thirteenth century, the population of Britain increased dramatically as did the demand for productive land. Forests and waste were cleared (*see* ASSART), marshes drained and the frontiers of arable land extended, often beyond the margins of cultivable soil. Existing settlements expanded into the 'newlands', while many new hamlets were established in areas of reclamation. In order to encourage agrarian expansion, peasants were often offered reclaimed land at low rents by feudal lords and by the monastic foundations who possessed the financial resources for such undertakings. The Benedictine abbey of Glastonbury, for example, was largely responsible for the drainage of the Somerset levels and Christ Church Priory at Canterbury in Kent (now the cathedral) reclaimed much of Romney Marsh in the late thirteenth and early fourteenth centuries. In the Fens (the low-lying districts of Lincolnshire, Cambridgeshire and Norfolk), the Priory of Peterborough created the new parish of Market Deeping (Norfolk), an extension on reclaimed land of the older settlement of Deeping St James (from the Old English *dēoping*, meaning 'deep fen').

Drainage of the Fens began in the Anglo-Saxon period and continued through the Middle Ages. But the process was inevitably a lengthy and laborious one which demanded either the substantial resources of a great monastery or the commitment of an entire community, each villager accepting responsibility for an area of fen which corresponded, proportionally, to his holding of arable land. Local communities were also required to maintain and repair the dikes and sea walls which not only conserved reclaimed land but also guarded against recession: no trace now remains of the east coast villages of Wilsthorp, Hartburn, Hyde, Old Aldeburgh, Ravenspur, Snitterley, Overstand, Whimpwell and Old Dunwich, all of which disappeared beneath the waves of the North Sea long ago. Erosion on such a scale is invariably matched elsewhere by massive deposition and much of the coast is fringed with mud flats which have evolved through salt marsh into fresh water marsh and eventually grassland: a natural cycle of a hundred years or more which can be accelerated by the provision of artificial embankments. Around the Wash, in Lincolnshire and Norfolk, settlements with names such as Fleet Haven, Holbeach, Moulton Seas End and Seadyke, now some 24 km (15 miles) from the coast, tell of successive enclosures by dike and embankment and of a continuous process of land reclamation from the Roman occupation to the present day.

Medieval records tell of attempts to drain the fenlands round Boston in Lincolnshire: at Saturday Dike in 1160, at Hassock Dike in 1190 and at Common Dike in 1241, while in 1286 the people of Holbeach and Whaplode, to the south of the Wash, were constructing great dikes to keep back the sea.

In the sixteenth and seventeenth centuries, major reclamation work was undertaken along the north-western coast of the Wash from Holbeach to Wainfleet while inland, in the fens between Wisbech, Peterborough and Cambridge, some 3,368 square km (1,300 square miles) were reclaimed by the Earl of Bedford and others (including the Dutch engineer, Vermuyden) in a scheme conceived in 1630. Extensive new drainage channels and sluices were cut, notably the remarkable Old Bedford River, which was 21 metres wide (70 feet) and 34 km in length (21 miles). The project was interrupted by the Civil War but was resumed in 1651 with the cutting of the New Bedford River (or Hundred Foot River) followed by the Forty Foot Drain, the Twenty Foot River and the Sixteen Foot Drain. At first, the scheme appeared to be successful but the engineers had not realized that the rapid drying-out of the peat soils would lead to shrinkage and erosion. Gradually, the peat level dropped below that of the drainage channels and wind-operated pumps had to be installed in order to drain the land. By the end of the eighteenth century, differences in level of up to 3 metres (10 feet) were common. Further wastage was averted by the introduction of the steam pump at the beginning of the nineteenth century and the electric pump in the twentieth.

Reclamation has endowed us with two very distinctive types of countryside. Large-scale, corporate undertakings have created a geometrical landscape of long, straight drainage channels, wide open rectangular fields and nucleated settlements connected by straight roads. In contrast, small-scale, individual schemes have provided irregular landscapes of ditches, banks, fields and lanes with dispersed farmsteads and settlements.

There remains a rich variety of regional terms for the artificial drainage ditches of these mysterious landscapes: the *rhines* of Sedgemoor in Somerset and of the marshes along the Severn Estuary (from the Old English *ryne*, meaning 'water channel') and the *sewers* of Romney Marsh in Kent and of the eastern fens where drainage is controlled by a Session of Sewers (a term derived from the Anglo-French *sewer*, meaning 'overflow channel' and originally applied to fish-ponds). In the Fen-country itself there are *dykes*, *lodes* and *eaus* (from the Old English *ēa*, meaning 'stream') and medieval *leams* and *cuts* (*see* LODE). Many names commemorate the men who sponsored them: Morton's Leam, cut in 1478–90 for Bishop Morton of Ely, and Popham's Eau, which linked the rivers Nene and Ouse in 1605, for example. The term *drain* first appeared in the Tudor period and *level*, which commonly describes an extensive tract of marshland, originated in the reclamations of the seventeenth century.

See also BROADS *and* FARMING

RECOGNIZANCE A pledge, made before a court or magistrate, to observe a condition, e.g. to appear when summoned, to keep the peace, etc. Recognizances were bonds, held by the Clerk of the Peace, which assured the appearance of defendants, witnesses and prosecutors at QUARTER SESSIONS.

RECORDER *see* QUARTER SESSIONS

RECTOR *see* CLERGY (CHURCH OF ENGLAND), PARISH *and* TITHES

RECUSANCY Refusal to attend the services of the Church of England. In Elizabethan and Jacobean England, strict penalties were imposed by various statutes and it was not until the Catholic Relief Act of 1791 that recusancy ceased to be a crime.

REDDLE (*also* **RADDLE, REDDING** *and* **RUDDLE**) Reddle was red ochre, a greasy pigment composed of fine clay and an iron oxide (haematite), used for marking sheep. At 'tupping time', reddle was painted on the underside of the rams and, in due course, a large red-brown mark would appear above the tail of the ewes which had mated. The shepherd could then calculate when these ewes were likely to lamb. In *The Return of the Native*, Thomas Hardy describes vividly a travelling reddleman of the 1840s:

> When he drew near he perceived it to be a spring van, ordinary in shape but singular in colour, being a lurid red. The driver walked beside it; and, like his van, he was completely red. One dye of that tincture covered his clothes, the cap upon his head, his boots, his face, and his hands. He was not temporarily overlaid with the colour: it permeated him. The traveller with the cart was a reddleman – a person whose vocation it was to supply farmers with redding for their sheep. He was one of a class rapidly becoming extinct in Wessex . . .

RED POSTS *see* SIGNPOSTS

REEVE A man of villein status elected or nominated by his fellow tenants to arrange the day-to-day business of a MANOR and to undertake other duties which varied according to the customs of a particular manor or area. In return he received special grazing rights together with a payment from the tenants and sometimes a remission of rent and feudal dues. Because of his position, the reeve usually represented the tenants in negotiations with the lord of the manor or his steward and, in the absence of specially appointed officers, he was also responsible for the general agricultural policy of the manor and for its livestock. (*See also* COURT BARON, LAW AND ORDER *and* SHERIFF.)

REFECTORIAN *see* LARDER *and* MONASTER- IES

REFECTORY *see* FRATER *and* MONASTERIES

REFORMATION This somewhat imprecise term covers a complex series of changes which took place in the Western Church between the fourteenth and seventeenth centuries. Protestants rejected the authority of the Papacy, both religious and political, and sought authority in the original text of the Scriptures through vernacular translations. The English Reformation was an insular process responsive to particular social and political forces which themselves arose from a long-standing monarchical policy of extending the sovereignty of central government. The term is usually applied specifically to Henry VIII's successful repudiation of Papal authority in England and to a series of acts of parliament in 1534 which severed financial, judicial and administrative links with Rome. But it was not until after his death in 1547 that doctrinal Protestantism became official policy. In retrospect, the most regrettable manifestation of the English Reformation was the wanton destruction of medieval statues, wall paintings, stained glass, rood screens and altars, culminating in the ravages of Cromwell's iconoclasts who destroyed anything of beauty they could find. Before the Reformation, nearly every parish church possessed a representation of the Madonna and Child, usually in a hooded niche in the outside wall of a tower. These were particularly detested by the reformers and surviving examples, such as that at Cerne Abbas, Dorset, are extremely rare.

See also DISSOLUTION OF THE MONASTERIES

REGENCY ARCHITECTURE Strictly speaking, the term Regency refers to the years 1811 to 1820 when George, Prince of Wales (later George IV) acted as regent during his father's final bout of insanity. In practice, the term is applied to the transitional period in architecture and the arts from *c.* 1790 to 1830, during which Georgian Britain moved inexorably towards the Victorian Age.

From the mid-eighteenth century, there was a drastic re-appraisal of the origins of CLASSICAL ARCHITECTURE, inspired by wider travel and a growing appreciation of the Greek Doric Order. Renewed interest in the antique, together with a reaction to the excesses of the late baroque and rococo styles, resulted in the Classic Revival of the second half of the eighteenth century. Regency architecture belongs in character to this period but not slavishly so. It is well proportioned and detailed, with minimal decoration and is often light-hearted and romantic, far removed from the turmoil of the Industrial Revolution. But Regency architects worked empirically and as a result their buildings reflect a readiness to experiment with a variety of stylistic sources.

The typical Regency house is built of brick and is covered in *stucco* or painted plaster. The fashion for stucco was imported from Italy, where it was intended to imitate stone (*see* PLASTERWORK). In England, it was used as an inexpensive facing material which could easily be moulded and painted to produce all the richness and refinement of Greek carving, fluted columns and complicated cornices at a fraction of the cost of worked stone. Terraces were still laid out in the grand Roman manner as in Regent's Park, London (John Nash 1752–1835), which was begun in 1812, and Lansdown Crescent in Bath (John Palmer 1738–1817), built in 1789–93; but more typical of the period are the smaller and less pretentious terraces of towns such as Cheltenham, Gloucestershire, and Brighton, Sussex. They have about them the slightest suggestion of decadence and insubstantiality. First-floor windows are tall and narrow, with minutely small glazing bars, and open onto delicate ironwork balconies roofed in curving metal. Decoration is minimal, the terraces relying for their effect on pleasing proportions and painted walls. In the later and simpler terraces, front doors and ground-floor windows are usually round-headed. The detached houses and small villas of the period are similarly well proportioned, with fine ironwork verandas and garden windows which rise from ground level. Curved *bow-fronted windows* were also fashionable with numerous local variations, as were painted shutters, low-pitched slate roofs and wide projecting eaves.

See also RAILINGS

REGENT A person appointed to administer a state during the minority, absence or incapacity of a reigning monarch.

REGIS Latinized place-name element meaning 'of the king', indicating that a manor was once held by the Crown, as at Lyme Regis in Dorset. Beware the spurious Georgian or Victorian use of the term to suggest royal patronage, usually of a spa or resort (*see* LATIN).

REGNAL YEARS In the Middle Ages it was the custom for documents to be dated by reference to the

year of a monarch's reign: for example, 3 Henry III would indicate a date of 1218/19, the king's third regnal year beginning on 28 October 1218 and ending on the following 27 October. As one would expect, regnal years were not used during the Commonwealth (1649–60), while Charles II calculated his first regnal year from the death of his father to his own succession: 29 May 1660 to 29 January 1661. References to regnal years will be found up to the last century, though by then they were usually accompanied by the *Anno Domini* date.

REGRATOR *see* MARKETS

REGULAR A general name for clergy who are bound by religious vows and live in a community, in contradistinction to secular clergy.

RELEASE and REVERSION *see* RELIEF

RELICS The material remains of a saint after his death and sacred objects with which he had been in contact. The bodies of martyrs were venerated from the mid-second century and in Rome attracted cults whose members worshipped at the martyrs' tombs. The Second Council of Nicaea in 787 ordered that no church should be consecrated without them and the veneration of relics was approved for the English Church by the Council of Constantinople in 1084. But the cult was never as popular in Britain as it was in continental Europe, where its influence increased significantly during the Crusades. Quantities of relics, invariably spurious, were brought back from the Holy Land to be displayed in richly decorated *reliquaries* and carried before processions at religious festivals. Many gave rise to superstitious practices, vestiges of which are discernible today.

In the Middle Ages the cult acquired a theological foundation. The unique dignity of the bodies of saints as receptacles of the Holy Spirit was emphasized, together with the sanction given by God in making them the occasion of miracles. Such relics attracted innumerable pilgrims to the more famous SHRINES, at which prayers of supplication were offered in the hope of salvation and cures for a multiplicity of ailments. The doctrine was later confirmed by the *Council of Trent*, convened at Trento in northern Italy from 1545 to 1563, which defined the doctrines of the Church in opposition to those of the REFORMATION.

RELIEF (i) A fee paid to a feudal tenant-in-chief by the purchaser of a freehold property. Such properties, which could be disposed of without hindrance, were conveyed by *livery of seisin*, which required the vendor to present a turf from the property being conveyed to the purchaser. This transaction, which symbolized the transfer of ownership, was always performed before witnesses and was usually recorded in a deed of conveyance (*indenture of feoffment*). Relief could be avoided, however, by the freeholder conveying the property to a number of people who held it for the benefit of the original owner. This device (which resulted in a loss of revenue to the Crown) was negated by the Statute of Uses (1535) which determined that the original owner remained the *de jure* owner and therefore liable for the Relief. The Statute of Enrolments of the same year prohibited secret conveyancing and made the enrolment of conveyances obligatory. A freeholder could lease his land to an occupier by means of a deed of grant (*Release*) while retaining a future interest (*Reversion*) which was an incorporeal hereditament and which could be conveyed without livery of seisin. Eventually, a *Lease and Release* procedure permitted a freeholder to sell his reversion without payment of a Relief and this facility remained in general use until 1841.

(ii) A money payment made by an incoming tenant in order that he should succeed to his inheritance. During the Saxon and early Norman periods, the term generally inferred military obligations though these were later commuted to money payments which varied according to the size of the estate. The custom was generally abused both by the Crown and by tenants-in-chief and was eventually regulated by *Magna Carta* in 1215. Reliefs of this type continued to be paid until 1661.

(iii) *For* Parish Relief *see* POOR LAW

RELIEVING OFFICER An official who administered poor relief (*see* POOR LAW).

RELIQUARY *see* RELICS *and* SHRINES

RENAISSANCE Any revival of the arts and learning may be described as a *renaissance*, a French term meaning 're-birth'. It has been applied specifically to the Carolingian Renaissance which began at the court of Charlemagne (r.768–814); to the Northumbrian Renaissance of the late seventh and early eighth centuries; the twelfth-century Renaissance of Western Europe and to the Italian Renaissance, the incomparable flowering of art and learning influenced by classical models which began in fourteenth-century Italy and by the end of the fifteenth century was spreading northwards throughout Europe.

The Italian *rinascimento* began in the world of literature and spread to sculpture and painting. In architecture, the Renaissance ideal (adopted from the ancient Romans) was that all buildings should possess three qualities in equal part: beauty, strength and usefulness. The great age of Renaissance in Italy was the *cinquecento* – the sixteenth century. But even before the Reformation, contacts between sixteenth-century Protestant England and Catholic Italy were limited and its repercussions were mostly intellectual. There were notable (mostly pre-Reformation) exceptions, such as Torrigiano's magnificent tomb for Henry VII in Westminster Abbey (1512–18), but few Italian artists ventured beyond the northern shores of France and when classicism finally arrived during the reign of Elizabeth I (1558–1603) it did so indirectly via Flanders and France. Pure Italianate Renaissance architectural form was eventually introduced into England by Inigo Jones (1573–1652) in the following century (*see* CLASSICAL ARCHITECTURE).

RENTAL *see* MANOR

RENT DAYS *see* QUARTER DAYS AND RENT DAYS

REPUTED MANOR An estate administered on a manorial basis but having no freehold tenants.

REQUESTS (COURT OF) Courts for the recovery of minor debts. Superseded by the county courts and what are now known as the small claims courts.

REREDORTER *see* DORTER *and* MONASTERIES

REREDOS A decorative stone or wood screen, usually supported on a shelf (*predella*) and covering the wall behind and above an altar or filling the space between two piers to the east of a sanctuary. Many late medieval reredoses were richly decorated with painted panels, set together in a wooden frame, or tiers of ornate canopied niches containing sculpted alabaster figures which were originally brightly coloured and gilded. Regrettably, few of these figures escaped the attentions of the Reformation's iconoclasts, and most surviving reredoses contain little more than empty niches – like rows of broken teeth (*see illustration* overleaf). Post-reformation reredoses were more austere, with the Ten Commandments, the Creed and the Lord's Prayer (and the occasional cherubim) painted on

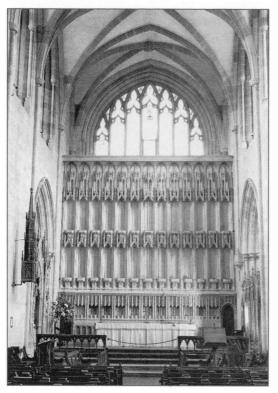

Rows of empty niches in the reredos at Milton Abbey, Dorset.

boards which were often enclosed in classical pilastered frames.

RESORTS The earliest resorts were the inland SPAS: Bath (with its Roman *thermae*), Buxton, Malvern, Tunbridge Wells and many others where eighteenth-century society went to take the waters and to disport itself. The first seaside resorts also developed because of the health-giving properties of bathing and inhaling salt air and, like the spas, they offered a range of fashionable attractions. Scarborough on the Yorkshire coast was probably the first, but from the mid-eighteenth century a number of south-coast resorts developed rapidly following the success of Melcombe Regis (Weymouth) in Dorset, which enjoyed the patronage of George III (1760–1820), and Brightelmstone in Sussex, which became the Prince Regent's Brighton.

Soon the practice spread from fashionable society to the middle class, but it was not until the railway network reached the coastal towns that day excursions to the seaside became a Victorian proletarian institution. The temperance societies were the first to appreciate the benefits of removing working people from the temptations of their traditional wakes and galas to the more salubrious (and sober) resorts. But before long, thousands of day-trippers from London and the northern industrial

Weymouth esplanade and beach in 1898. (F. Frith)

conurbations were flocking to the seaside, not to bathe but in search of amusement, sea air and the token 'paddle'.

Before the Bank Holidays Act of 1871, the half-Saturday was still not universally available and Sunday was the most popular excursion day. The railway companies also provided excursion trains from London to the south coast on summer Mondays, thereby exacerbating the problem of absenteeism in the metropolis. In the Lancashire cotton towns, employers' recognition of the traditional Wakes Weeks led to the spectacular development of Blackpool in the 1850s and '60s, the first town devoted entirely to the holiday industry, and to the popularity of the North Wales resorts, with their long beaches and romantic Snowdonian setting. As wages rose and holiday entitlement increased so the traditional activities and amusements of fairs and wakes were transferred to the seaside. Excursion trains, often of incredible length, carried families and firms on their annual outings to resorts such as Scarborough and Whitby in Yorkshire, Redcar and Saltburn in Cleveland, Aberystwyth in Ceredigion, Yarmouth in Norfolk and Margate and Ramsgate in Kent, where they would parade in their weekend finery on the promenade, listen to the band in the pleasure gardens, eat seafood and drink in the numerous pubs, spend their savings in the burgeoning souvenir shops and seek entertainment on that most characteristic feature of the Victorian resorts – the pier.

The Brighton chain-pier was opened in 1823 as a quay for the Dieppe packet, but its success as a fashionable promenade was later emulated by other resorts, all of which constructed their own piers, each terminating in a pavilion for entertainment and refreshment. With the growth of the 'popular' day-trip resorts, those seeking longer and more restful holidays travelled further along the railway lines to sedate resorts such as Sidmouth, Ilfracombe and Torquay in Devon, Ventnor on the Isle of Wight, Eastbourne in Sussex and Bournemouth in Hampshire (now in Dorset), though Cornwall remained remote until the river Tamar was bridged by the railway in 1895. It was not until 1911, when holidays with pay were secured by the Trades Union Congress, that the modern holiday resort, with its hotels and guest-houses, came into its own.
See also TOWNS

RESTORATION, THE Following the death of Oliver Cromwell in 1658, his son Richard proved incapable of maintaining the PROTECTORATE. With no alternative form of government available, a faction under General Monck arranged for the return of the exiled Charles II in 1660 and the restoration of the (Stuart) monarchy in Britain.

RETABLE *see* ALTARS

RETRO-CHOIR *see* CHOIR

RETTING POND A pond in which flax, hemp or timber was immersed when green to season and dispose it for future use.

RHAEADR In the Welsh, a waterfall or cataract, as in Rhaeadr Ddu (the Black Falls) and Rhaeadr y Wennol (the Fall of the Swallow).
See also PISTYLL

RHAGLAW AND RHINGYLL In medieval Wales, the equivalent of the English steward and bailiff.

RHINES *see* RECLAMATION

RHINGYLL *see* RHAGLAW AND RHINGYLL

RIB AND RIBBED VAULT *see* VAULTING

RICKYARDS While the practice of building ricks or stacks of corn and hay after harvesting (and of straw after threshing) is an ancient one, the provision of a rickyard in the vicinity of a farmstead is a comparatively recent innovation and one which has itself been superseded by bale-stacks in Dutch barns or in the sheltered corners of fields.

The term *rick* is of Anglo-Saxon derivation and *stack* is Old Norse, but there is little evidence to suggest that the varieties of shape and construction may also be traced to particular origins or regions. Round and rectangular ricks were to be found together on the same farms in the midland and southern counties, though smaller round stacks with conical thatched roofs were more commonly found in the wetter north of England than in the south, as were *pikes* which were constructed round a central pole. Ricks were shaped like a small house and had thatched roofs with finials (dozzles), though thatching was in some areas superseded by the use of tarpaulins in the late nineteenth century and, more recently, by plastic sheeting.

To protect them from damp, most stacks and ricks were built on platforms (*staddles*) which were themselves supported on brick arches or mushroom-shaped stone piers (*staddle stones*) which were designed to prevent rats and mice from entering the corn (*see* GRANARY). Before the eighteenth century, corn was cut by hand, stooked to dry, loaded on to hay-wagons and stacked in ricks or stored in BARNS, where it was thrashed by hand throughout the winter. But with improved agrarian methods and rapidly increasing yields, barns could no longer contain the produce of a single harvest and it became necessary to provide a sheltered yard in which large numbers of ricks or stacks could be erected. This was almost invariably located near the farmyard itself, often adjacent to the barns and other outbuildings which provided protection from the elements.

Such an arrangement also facilitated the operation of horse-powered threshing machines, which were introduced in the 1830s. From the 1860s, these were replaced by steam-powered threshers, driven by means of a belt from the flywheel of a traction engine which, with its itinerant engineer, was usually hired by the hour (*see* THRESHING).

RIDDING From the Old English *ryding*, meaning 'clearing', the term is used to describe a GREEN LANE which passes through a wood (*see* ASSART).

RIDGE AND FURROW Ridge and furrow is most noticeable when a low sun casts long shadows across a 'corrugated' field or when in winter strips of melting snow pattern the land with a texture like that of corduroy. Such vestiges of late Saxon and medieval cultivation have survived only where they have been preserved from later deep ploughing, usually in parkland or pasture, and are most commonly found in areas of heavy clay soil.

Plough ridges and their adjacent furrows cut obliquely across the contours of the land to encourage drainage. They are popularly mistaken for the strips of ancient OPEN FIELDS, but these were much wider and usually contained two, three or more adjacent and parallel ridges (*see* STRIP). When fallow fields were ploughed in late spring, topsoil was redistributed from the ridge into the furrow by anti-clockwise ploughing (known as the 'casting of the tilth'). But during two clockwise ploughings later in the season, the mouldboard of the plough would turn the soil back towards the centre of the ridge to create the familiar domed cross-section which could be as much as 1 metre (3 feet) above the adjacent furrow. Teams of six or even eight oxen were used for ploughing, and the turning manoeuvre had to begin well before the HEADLAND was reached at the termination of each furlong, the turn to the left creating the reversed-S shape of a typical ridge.

Most surviving examples are of medieval origin, though the practice probably pre-dates the Anglo-

Saxon period, for traces of ridging have been discovered *beneath* Hadrian's Wall. Dating of ridge and furrow is difficult, though straight ridges may indicate more recent ploughing, possibly originating in the eighteenth and early nineteenth century when a 'narrow rigg' system persisted in some areas. Eighteenth- and nineteenth-century rectilinear enclosure boundaries and roads invariably cut across the gently curving parallels of medieval ridge and furrow; and in former orchards, where apple trees were planted in straight rows, regular undulations caused by root growth may have a similar appearance.

RIDGE PIECE The principal timber running along the apex of a roof (*see* ROOFS).

RIDGEWAYS From the Old English *hrycg weg*, meaning 'a way along a ridge', the ridgeways of the calcareous uplands of southern England have for centuries provided a swift and reliable means of communication. But the popular notion that prehistoric man occupied the uplands and rarely descended into the 'impenetrable forests of the vales' is not supported by archaeological evidence and it is now generally acknowledged that the late prehistoric landscape was intensively settled and farmed, and that there evolved a complex network of tracks of which the ridgeways were but a part. Nevertheless, discoveries of ancient trade goods confirm that many ridgeways, both in southern England and elsewhere, were favoured as trading routes along which early 'markets' may have been established, possibly at prominent and accessible sites such as the mysterious CAUSEWAYED ENCLOSURE at Windmill Hill near Avebury in Wiltshire where even today five bridle-ways converge.

Ridgeways were literally 'highways' which tended to follow watersheds, descending to cross valleys only when there was no practical route round a valley-head. But they were not necessarily long-distance routes and it is unlikely that they were perceived as such by the majority of those who used them. For most people, they were probably little more than a convenient and strictly localized means of travelling from one place to another – between HILL FORTS, for example. They consisted not of a single path, but of broad 'zones' of communication composed of a number of minor tracks, roughly parallel to each other and crossed by lateral routes connecting adjacent settlements. The ridgeway on the Berkshire Downs, for example, passes through the traces of thousands of acres of prehistoric fields and would almost certainly have been one of many lanes traversing an entirely cultivated landscape.

From the Middle Ages, ridgeway routes were used by pack-horse trains and drovers because they tended to be more reliable in bad weather and generally avoided tolls and towns. During the ENCLOSURES of the eighteenth and nineteenth centuries, many ridgeways were provided with low banks and hedges to define the limits of the track and to prevent travellers and livestock from encroaching onto neighbouring land.

Names of the various ridgeways are mostly of recent origin, coined by enthusiastic antiquarians to fit 'the pseudo-history of roads and tracks' (Christopher Taylor), though some appear in medieval and later documents. In the 1950s O.G.S. Crawford identified four principal routes: the so-called Icknield Way, which ran from near the Wash in Norfolk south-west past Stonehenge on Salisbury Plain in Wiltshire to the Channel coast; the ridgeway which followed the South Downs from near Beachy Head in Sussex to Stonehenge where it was joined by the North Downs ridgeway from Canterbury in Kent before continuing into the south-west peninsula; and the ridgeway which followed the chain of limestone hills from the Humber, south-west through Lincolnshire, Northamptonshire and the Gloucestershire Cotswolds and on to the Mendips in Somerset. (It is interesting to note the pivotal rôle of Stonehenge in three of these alleged long-distance routes.) Edith Brill and H.W. Timperley later defined the Great Ridgeway, described by Geoffrey Wright as 'the oldest road in Britain'. This ran south-west from East Anglia, following the Chilterns and crossing the Berkshire and Wiltshire downs before skirting the Vale of Blackmore in Dorset and continuing to the mouth of the Axe in Devon. Such definitions, though attractive, obscure the fact that the function and form of all route-ways are subject to adaptation and even to regression, and that most are segmental and depend for their survival on the ever-changing requirements of the traveller (*see* ROADS). Nevertheless, many ridgeways have become highways, established by custom and recognized by law, with lengths preserved beneath tarmac or designated as footpaths and bridle-ways on Ordnance Survey maps.

RIDING Derived from the Old Swedish *thrithiunger*, meaning 'a third part' and an administrative area of a DANELAW shire. Yorkshire was divided into North, East and West Ridings by the Danes, each with its own court or assembly which came between the Wapentake and Shire

courts. Lindsey, the largest and most northern division of Lincolnshire, was also divided into North, South and West Ridings.

RIGHT APPENDANT, RIGHT APPURTENANT *and* **RIGHT IN GROSS** *see* COMMONS

RIGHT OF PRISE *see* PRISE

RIGHT OF WAY *see* HIGHWAY

RIGHTS OF COMMON *see* COMMONS

RING GARTH (*also* **RING FENCE** *and* **HEAD DYKE**) Dating from the tenth or eleventh centuries, a continuous drystone wall erected to prevent animals from grazing on cultivated land. A particular feature of the Cumbrian Lake District, a ring garth follows the break in the slope of a valley and so separates the fertile bottom land from the course fell-side grazing. Ring garths are continuous and, because they were built first, are not crossed by other walls which always abut them. They were often constructed of large, rounded boulders taken from stream beds, whereas later walls were usually built of rougher stone removed from the fields or hewn from nearby quarries.

RINGWORK A circular embankment constructed of upcast material from a surrounding ditch and originally palisaded to form a fortification. The origins of such earthworks are obscure, although it appears that several were adopted following the Conquest of 1066 as sites for mottes (*see* CASTLES (MEDIEVAL)). Perhaps the best known example is the formidable embankment of uncertain origin surrounding William d'Albini's stone hall-keep (*c.* 1138) at Castle Rising in Norfolk.

*William d'Albini's splendid hall-keep (*c. 1138*) at Castle Rising, Norfolk, is almost dwarfed by the castle's massive ringwork defences.*

RIPARIAN RIGHTS A riparian is an owner of land bordering a river. River water may be impounded and extracted by a riparian who may also fish from his river bank providing he is above the reach of the tide. There is an inalienable public right of passage over navigable water which is subject only to the control of a river authority. Tidal waters are for public enjoyment and navigation, riparian rights existing only above a point which is reached by the tide twice a day.

RIVER NAMES The names of major rivers generally have British (or earlier) derivations, while most minor rivers and streams have names which originated during the Anglo-Saxon and Scandinavian settlements. In many cases, the Old English *ēa*, meaning 'river', was added to names which were even then of considerable antiquity, names which now end in -y, -ye, -ey, -ea.

All immigrants arrived by water and most ventured inland by navigable rivers. Thereafter, the larger rivers continued to impinge on everyday life as major landscape features which could either facilitate or impede travel and which often came to delineate territories. It is little wonder then that the old river names were adopted and perpetuated by the new settlers and that, for the most part, those names should possess the most basic of meanings.

From the British *iscā* are derived Axe, Exe, Esk and Usk, all meaning simply 'water'; and the ubiquitous Avon and Welsh Afon originate in the British *abonā,* meaning 'river'. Names such as Tame, Tamar, Tavy, Teme, Thame and Thames, and the Welsh Taf and Taff, also have a British derivation and mean 'dark river'. Trent, from the British *trisantōn*, describes a river which is liable to flood, and Derwent and Dart mean 'river where oaks grow', from the British *dervā*, meaning 'oak'. Dee (in the Welsh, *Dyfrdwy*) is derived from *Dēvā* and means 'the holy river'.

But the origins of several well-known river names remain obscure, notably the Ribble, Severn and Wye (also numerous Wey names). Ouse may mean 'water'; Stour 'powerful river'; Tees 'surging river'; Test 'running water' and Tyne simply 'river', but such interpretations remain conjectural.

Not all major river names are British: Irwell is derived from the Old English *irre*, meaning 'wandering', and Mersey comes from the Old English *mǣres-ēa*, 'boundary river', for example.

But while the majority of larger rivers have names which are of British (or earlier) derivation, most minor rivers and streams have English names, reflecting the influence of local settlements on minor place-names: the Blackwater ('dark-coloured stream') and Lambourn ('stream where lambs are washed') in Berkshire; the Hamble ('crooked') and Medina ('middle') in Hampshire; the Piddle ('marshy land') in Dorset and the Blythe ('gentle') in Suffolk, for example. There are also concentrations of minor river names in Cumbria and the West Country which are of British derivation: for example, the Calder ('violent water'), Cam ('crooked'), Dacre ('trickling stream') and Lyne ('smooth') in Cumbria; the Divelish ('black stream'), Frome ('brisk'), Lidden ('broad'), Lyme ('flood stream') and Wynford ('white stream') in Dorset; the Brue ('vigorous') and Chew ('river of the chickens') in Somerset; the Leadon ('black stream') and Windrush ('white fen') in Gloucestershire; the Arrow ('silver'), Dulas ('black stream'), Garren ('crane') and Lugg ('bright stream') in Herefordshire and the Dowles ('black stream'), Roden ('swift river') and Tern ('powerful') in Shropshire. Scandinavian origins are evident in such river names as Greta ('stony stream') and Rothay ('trout stream') in Cumbria, Winster ('that to the left') in Lancashire and Skell ('resounding') in Yorkshire.

Rivers have also provided names for settlements: Sherborne in Dorset, for example, is derived from the Old English *scīreburne*, meaning 'bright stream'.

See also PLACE-NAMES

ROADS The word 'road' was first used in 1596 in Ogilby's maps. Prior to that, and for long afterwards, they were known as 'highways' or simply 'ways'. From the trackways of pre-history to the motorway network of the second half of the twentieth century, tracks and roads have developed or regressed in response to the requirements of many different types of traveller. The medieval merchant, whose trains of pack-horses often traversed the entire country, would take a direct route, one which would facilitate the rapid and economic transportation of his goods. The itinerant journeyman would follow a lengthy and tortuous course, criss-crossing the countryside to ensure that every hamlet and farmstead was visited in a strict and predictable rotation. The peasant labourer, who rarely left the confines of a small number of adjacent parishes, would undertake journeys of short duration which would radiate from his home like the spokes of a wheel. At times, their paths would cross and at others they might briefly share the same track and, perhaps, each others' company. Each selected the most appropriate route in a network of trackways which was already

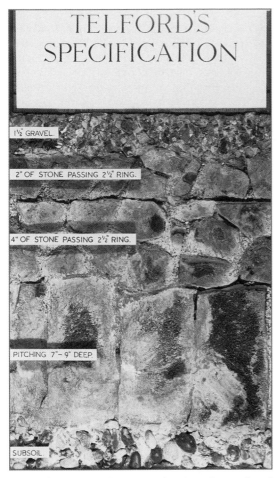

TELFORD'S
SPECIFICATION

1½ GRAVEL.

2" OF STONE PASSING 2½ RING.

4" OF STONE PASSING 2½ RING.

PITCHING 7"- 9" DEEP.

SUBSOIL.

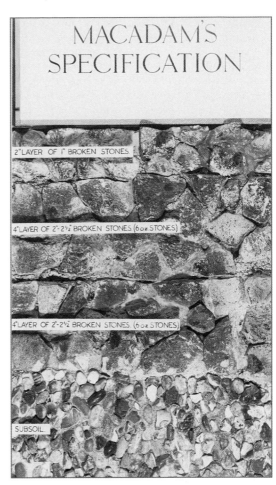

MACADAM'S
SPECIFICATION

2" LAYER OF 1" BROKEN STONES.

4" LAYER OF 2"-2½" BROKEN STONES (6oz STONES)

4" LAYER OF 2"-2½" BROKEN STONES. (6oz STONES)

SUBSOIL.

Telford's and Macadam's specifications for road surfaces

established by the eleventh century and may be identified today as footpaths, bridle-ways and carriageways on the 1:25000 maps of the Ordnance Survey.

Historical and archaeological evidence suggests that today's road pattern is of considerable antiquity, possibly originating in the communications system of an intensively settled late prehistoric landscape. Therefore, with the exception of the major Roman roads, limited lengths of eighteenth- and nineteenth-century turnpikes and enclosure roads, and twentieth-century motorways and bypasses, there can be no sure way of dating a highway. The 'pseudo-history of roads and tracks' (Christopher Taylor) which continues to preoccupy many local historians has tended to obscure this perception. The conventional chronology of prehistoric ridgeway, Roman military road, Anglo-Saxon track, medieval

highway and nineteenth-century turnpike is convenient but flawed and simplistic, and in order to understand roads we need to take their antiquity for granted and study instead their changing function and form as succeeding generations of our ancestors adopted them to their requirements.

There are, of course, clues to be found in the characteristics of a particular length of road: even the Romans were unable to construct all their roads so that they invariably connected two points in a straight line. Obstacles had to be avoided, which may subsequently have been removed or overcome, and many of the factors which determined the sites of river crossings and fords have since been superseded by advancing technology. Series of abrupt right-angled diversions remain a distinctive feature of many landscapes. These may have been caused by a variety of regional factors usually associated with settlement and the enclosure of land. Such lanes may be found running tortuously between the walls of small fields created out of peripheral WASTE and medieval ASSARTS or follow the zigzag HEADLANDS of former open fields. Many abrupt diversions resulted from the emparkment of country estates in the seventeenth and eighteenth centuries. These often occur at lodge gates or where park walls have been built across the line of a road which may be picked up again on the other side of the park. The enclosure commissions of the eighteenth and early nineteenth centuries often disregarded the past completely and laid out straight sections of wide new road which often deviate slightly at a parish boundary in order to enter an adjacent parish which may not have been enclosed at the same time.

It should be borne in mind that before the late seventeenth century, traffic consisted almost entirely of pedestrians or beasts of burden. From 1700, carriage, cart and wagon traffic increased significantly: on many hillsides new diagonal routes replaced ancient hollow-ways which were too steep and narrow for wheeled traffic, and there was a widespread demand for the improvement of road surfaces. From 1555, parishes were responsible for the maintenance of the highways but their neglect led to the recognition in law of Turnpike Trusts and to the construction or repair of 35,400 km of road (22,000 miles) between 1700 and 1840. Many turnpikes were surfaced with compacted layers of broken stones, a method devised by J.L. Macadam (1755–1836) whose ingenuity is commemorated in *tar macadam*, a smooth dust-free crust which was first applied as a road surface in 1907 after motor cars with pneumatic tyres had been admitted to the public roads for the first time in 1896.

See also BRIDGES, BRIDLE-WAYS, CARRIAGEWAY, CAUSEWAYS, DROVE ROADS, ENCLOSURE ROADS, FOOTPATHS, FERRIES, FORDS, HIGHWAY, HOLLOW-WAYS, GREEN LANES, MEDIEVAL ROADS, MILITARY ROADS, MULTIPLE TRACKS, PACK-HORSE ROADS, PORTWAY (*see* MARKETS), RIDGE-WAYS, ROMAN ROADS, SALTWAYS *and* TURNPIKES

ROCOCO The final phase of the BAROQUE style of architecture and decoration. In Britain, the mid-eighteenth-century rococo style is primarily a decorative one, found mainly in interiors, its delicacy and playfulness contrasting with the subdued exteriors of contemporary classical buildings. It is manifested mainly in the treatment of stucco wall decoration, doorway surrounds, chimney-pieces and monuments. Rococo work is generally in low relief and composed of ribbons, scrolls, floral wreaths, seaweed, shells, birds and animals in white and pastel tones and with only light gilding. The illuminative effect is often enhanced by the use of wall mirrors. A brief Rococo period of garden design occurred during the transition from the formal style of the seventeenth century to the more natural flowing shapes of the eighteenth. The 6-acre Rococo garden of Painswick House, Gloucestershire, is possibly the only complete survivor from this period and is being restored to its original form, as depicted in a Thomas Robins painting dated 1748.

ROD (*also* **POLE**) A measure of 16½ feet (5 metres) (*see* CHAIN *and* ROOD).

ROE A small portion of land.

ROGATION *see* GOSPEL OAK, PERAMBU-LATION *and* SAINTS' DAYS AND FEAST-DAYS

ROLLS OF ARMS Any collection of coats of arms, whether written in the language of ARMORY (*blazon*), painted or tricked on drawings, listings or even carvings of shields (as in the cloister vault of Canterbury Cathedral) constitutes a roll of arms. But the term is generally applied to strips of vellum or parchment, sewn together and rolled up or bound into books, on which rows of shields have been painted and identified. Most of these manuscripts are of medieval or early Tudor origin and illustrate the mobility of the knightly classes throughout Europe and the development of armorial devices. They are classified as *Occasional Rolls*, which relate to an event such as an expedition, tournament or siege; *Institutional Rolls*, associated with foundations and religious and chivalric orders; *Regional Rolls*, which list the arms of armigers in a particular administrative area such as a county; *Illustrative Rolls*, which illustrate stories or chronicles and may therefore contain imaginary arms such as those of the Knights of the Round Table; and *General Rolls*, which are combinations of other types.

ROMAN ADMINISTRATION From the time of its incorporation into the Roman Empire, Britain was designated as a consular province with a governor appointed as the Emperor's deputy responsible for both military and civil affairs. Such men were experienced and able administrators: senators who had held the consulship and had served in other frontier provinces of the Empire.

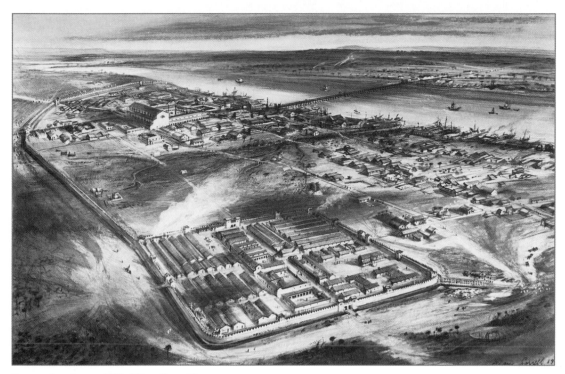

Roman London, c. 200. (Alan Sorrell)

As commander of the four (later three) legions and numerous auxiliary regiments, the governor of Britain was required to maintain the peace of the conquered territories and to defend and extend the boundaries of the Empire. He was also responsible for military recruitment, for supervising the civil communities and for the construction and maintenance of roads. Although in criminal matters citizens could appeal direct to Rome, a provincial governor was otherwise responsible for determining appeals from the courts, where he exercised legal jurisdiction over Roman citizens and in cases concerning capital punishment or penal service in the mines. (Financial and fiscal matters were the responsibility of the *Procurator Augusti Britanniae* who was answerable not to the governor, but to the Emperor in Rome on whose behalf he collected taxes and received the revenues of imperial estates and paid the administration and army.)

In the British province, the governor was also concerned with the politically sensitive affairs of the *client kingdoms* which had been established as a consequence of Julius Caesar's negotiations of *c.* 55–54 BC. Under treaty arrangements, which lasted well into the first century, these kingdoms retained a degree of autonomy during the lifetime of a ruler, on

whose death they acceded to the authority of Rome. As the client kingdoms were incorporated into the province and the garrisons moved north and west to the frontier zone, so local self-governing communities were established among the native Britons (*civitates peregrinae*) together with self-governing towns of Latin or Roman citizens (*municipia* and *coloniae*) which were intended to effect a civilizing influence on the indigenous population and to provide a military reserve. During the first century, *coloniae* were established by imperial charter first at Colchester (*Camulodunum*) in AD 49, and later at the former legionary fortresses of Lincoln (*Lindum*) and Gloucester (*Glevum*) and at York (*Eburacum*), and a *municipium* at St Albans (*Verulamium*). Each was surrounded by its own territory (*territorium*) which was administered by the town's ruling body, a council (*ordo*) of up to 100 members (*decuriones*) together with two or three pairs of executive officers. The senior of these were the *duoviri iuridicundo*, who were responsible for the administration of the law courts and meetings of the *ordo*. Next, the *aediles* were responsible for the maintenance of public buildings and utilities such as roads, aqueducts and sewers; and in some towns a third pair, the *quaestores*, attended to financial

ROMAN CATHOLIC CHURCH

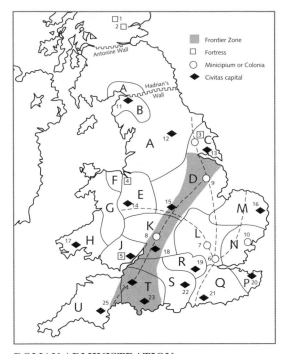

ROMAN ADMINISTRATION

Civitas
A Brigantes
B Carvetii
C Parisi
D Coritani
E Cornovii
F Deceangli
G Ordovices
H Demetae
J Silures
K Dobunni
L Catuvellauni
M Iceni
N Trinovantes
P Canti
Q Regnenses
R Atrebates
S Belgae
T Durotriges
U Dumnonii

Fortresses
1 Pinnata Castra (Inchtuthil)
2 Horrea Castra (Carpow)
3 Eburacum (York)
4 Deva (Chester)
5 Isca (Caerleon)

Municipia or Colonia
6 Londinium (London)
7 Verulamium (St Albans)
8 Glevum (Gloucester)
9 Lindum (Lincoln)

10 Camulodunum (Colchester)

Civitas Capitals
11 Luguvalium (Carlisle)
12 Isurium Brigantum (Aldborough)
13 Petuaria (Brough on Humber)
14 Viroconium Carnoviorum (Wroxeter)
15 Ratae Coritanorum (Leicester)
16 Venta Icenorum (Caister St Edmunds)
17 Moridunum (Carmarthen)
18 Corinium Dobunnorum (Cirencester)
19 Calleva Atrebatum (Silchester)
20 Durovernum Cantiacorum (Canterbury)
21 Noviomagus Regnensium (Chichester)
22 Venta Belgarum (Winchester)
23 Durnovaria (Dorchester, Dorset)
24 Lindinis (Ilchester)
25 Isca Dumnoniorum (Exeter)

matters under the jurisdiction of the magistracy (*magistratus*).

Most of Britain was divided into areas of local government (*civitates*) which, for the most part, corresponded with former Iron Age tribal territories after which they were named (*see* KINGDOMS, ANCIENT). Each *civitas* was administered from a cantonal capital, probably through an *ordu* and executive similar to those of the *coloniae*. The *civitates* were sub-divided into small administrative units (*pagi*) and each town (*vicus*) enjoyed a degree of self-government, some of the larger ones comprising several *vici* or districts.

In AD 197 the province was divided into Upper (southern) and Lower (northern) Britain and in the early fourth century, at a time of increasing prosperity and almost universal citizenship, Lower Britain was itself divided into *Britannia Secunda*, with an administrative centre at York, and *Flavia Caesariensis*, with a capital (probably) at Lincoln. In the south, Upper Britain was also divided into *Maxima Caesariensis* and *Britannia Prima*, which were administered from London and Cirencester respectively.

See also ROMAN ROADS *and* ROMAN VILLAS

ROMAN CATHOLIC CHURCH That part of the Christian Church which is in communion with the Pope whose office is acknowledged to be in succession to St Peter and the Apostles in whom Christ invested the power of the Holy Spirit. Its doctrine is characterized by a strict adherence to tradition together with a belief in the infallibility of the living voice of the Church. It has a complex hierarchical organization of bishops and priests with the Pope at its head. Supernatural life is mediated to individual Christians by members of the hierarchy in the seven sacraments, and the Mass is at the centre of liturgical life. Communion is required at Easter and attendance at Mass is obligatory on all Sundays and Feasts of Obligation.

Catholicism was the religion of England and Wales prior to the REFORMATION, but following the Acts of Uniformity of 1552 and 1559, which made Catholics liable to fines, the political climate deteriorated and strict anti-Catholic legislation was introduced. Catholics were tolerated during the Protectorate (1653–9) but persecuted following the Restoration (1660). They were prevented from holding civil or military office by the Test Act of 1673 and from Parliament by the Test Act of 1678. In 1778 the Catholic Relief Act enabled Catholics to own land but it was received with hostility, culminating in the Gordon Riots of 1780. The

Catholic Emancipation Act of 1829 removed many constraints, such as discrimination against Catholic teachers and schools, but it was not until 1871 that Catholics were readmitted to the universities.

The *Recusant Rolls*, dating from 1592 to 1691, list many Catholics (as well as non-conformist Protestants) and are held at the Public Record Office. Several have been published by the Catholic Record Society, which also publishes *Recusant History*. Catholics were obliged to register their names and landholdings with clerks of the peace in 1771 and these records should be available in county record offices. Unofficial registers of births, marriages and deaths were maintained but few pre-date 1778 and most remain in the archives of the Church.

See also CATHOLIC, JESUIT *and* RECUSANCY

For the Catholic Archives Society, the Catholic Record Society, the Duke of Norfolk's Library and Archives, the Franciscan Archives (English Province), the Public Record Office *and* the Record Office of the Society of Jesus *see* APPENDIX I

ROMANESQUE A style of art and architecture prevalent in Europe *c.* 1050–1200 which reached its fullest development in central and northern France. In England, architecture of the period is often referred to as Norman.

As the name suggests, Romanesque architecture was inspired by the classical buildings of ancient Rome and the basilican plan with its nave, aisles and apsidal termination which was adopted in Romanesque churches. In central Europe, Romanesque masons developed variations of classical themes, using the semi-circular arch, arcading and tunnel vaults, and their buildings were vigorously decorated with foliated and other motifs. In northern and western Europe, a more austere Romanesque style reflected Carolingian influences rather than those of classical Rome, and from this a distinctive Norman style developed in the tenth century.

Following the Norman conquest of England in 1066, there was a significant cultural decline from the achievements of the Anglo-Saxon period, with the notable exception of architecture. The Anglo-Saxons were not great builders and little remains of their larger churches such as Ripon (of which only the crypt has survived), the minster at York or Bishop Aethelwold's great church, built in the second half of the tenth century when Winchester was England's capital. Edward the Confessor's Abbey of Westminster, of which the Bayeux Tapestry provides but a tantalizing glimpse, was almost certainly the first Romanesque church in England, built to emulate the great churches of Normandy with an arcade of rounded arches, clerestory windows and a lofty tower with corner turrets.

The Normans were the greatest builders of their time and from this later period of Romanesque architecture there are numerous superb examples, though no major church escaped subsequent Gothic alterations and additions. The oldest example is the abbey church of St Alban's in Hertfordshire, which became a cathedral as recently as 1877. Rebuilt between 1077 and 1115, it is one of England's largest cathedrals and internally is a building of austere majesty. It is the only major medieval church not to have been built of dressed stone, local flint being used for the walls and tile-like bricks, plundered from the ruins of nearby Roman *Verulamium*, for the angles of doors and windows. Because of the materials used there is an absence of carved decoration: the huge brick piers were plastered over, whitewashed and painted with geometrical patterns and nowhere was any vaulting attempted. (Following the Reformation, St Alban's was reduced to the status of a parish church and became badly dilapidated before being insensitively restored during the period 1877–94.) Norman work of this period may also be seen at Winchester Cathedral Priory, where the transepts preserve their original character. These were built in the period 1079–93, and being of limestone (from the Isle of Wight) they are in all respects superior to those at St Alban's.

Eleventh-century Romanesque masonry was massive, with walls of up to 7 metres (24 feet) at the base for safety and to compensate for poor quality mortar and wide jointing. Window openings were small, so that the walls should not be weakened, and decoration minimal.

The twelfth century was a period of intense building activity and experimentation: walls became less massive, the masonry more finely jointed and there was an increasing use of carved ornament. Early mouldings had been cut very sparingly with shallow hollows, fillets and chamfers but later Romanesque work was profusely carved, mostly in geometrical forms, the most common of which were the familiar zigzag (*chevron*) decoration used in the deep mouldings of round arches and cylinder-shaped stones (*billets*) which alternated with spaces in hollow moulding. Sculptural decoration in doorway arches, capitals and tympana included floreated and animal forms, human figures, biblical scenes and monsters (none of the carved twelfth-century

Romanesque south door at Kilpeck, Herefordshire.

the twelfth century (*see* GOTHIC ARCHITECTURE) and, despite subsequent alteration and enlargement, many eleventh- and twelfth-century naves, doorways and western façades have survived. The naves of Tewkesbury Abbey in Gloucestershire, Southwell Minster in Nottinghamshire and Gloucester, Ely and Rochester Cathedrals are among the finest, as is the west façade of Southwell. But at Durham 'we reach the incomparable masterpiece of Romanesque architecture' (Alec Clifton-Taylor, *The Cathedrals of England*, 1967). Not only is the Norman building unusually complete but its design is unlike any other. The most startling innovation was the provision of stone-vaulting throughout the entire building during its construction from 1093 to 1133. Prior to this, Romanesque masons were not sufficiently skilled to vault major spans, and most buildings had timber roofs, many of which were later replaced with stone vaulting during the Gothic period. The choir vault at Durham (*c.* 1100) developed cracks and was replaced in the thirteenth century but the transepts have the earliest high-level ribbed vaults in Europe (1120) and in the vault of the magnificent nave, with its arcade of alternating circular and composite pillars, the transverse arches are, for the first time, pointed (*see* VAULTING). It seems that the architect of Durham was the first in Europe to overcome the problems of abutment associated with the erection of a lofty vault. The building even has flying buttresses: concealed within the sloping roofs of the tribune.

ROMAN FORTS AND CAMPS Traces of numerous Roman forts and encampments remain in the landscape, particularly in the frontier zones of the north and west. Unlike the native British defensive enclosure, the shape of which was dictated by its site, a Roman encampment was invariably rectangular with rounded corners.

The Roman army consisted of two elements: legionaries and auxiliaries. Legionaries were recruited from Roman citizens from throughout the Empire. Their equipment consisted of a linen undergarment, a cuirass of metal strips, a bronze helmet with an iron liner and iron-studded sandals. They were armed with two spears and a short stabbing sword and dagger, and carried a rectangular, leather-covered wooden shield, strengthened with metal. A legion was commanded by a *legate* and consisted of some 5,000 men divided into 59 *centuries*, each of about 80 men under a *centurion*. Centuries were further divided into 10 *contubernia* of 8 men who, as the name implies,

capitals in the Crypt of Westminster Abbey has a Christian theme.) Typically English is *beak-head* ornament, in which the heads of birds and beasts were carved in hollow mouldings so that the beaks or tongues overlapped into adjacent round mouldings.

Anglo-Norman sculpture was an extraordinary pot-pourri of influences: from Scandinavian to Levantine and from French to Byzantine. Many of the sinuous and diabolical creatures depicted in Romanesque carvings are of Celtic origin (*see* PAGAN SYMBOLS), while others were introduced through BESTIARIES and the importation of highly decorated eastern silks. This merging of Christian and pagan mythology, which was to continue well beyond the Romanesque period, is best observed in the ornamental carving of smaller churches such as Kilpeck in Herefordshire (*c.* 1140), where a local school of sculpture produced carvings of extraordinary vigour and imagination.

Romanesque design continued in England until the advent of the Gothic style in the last decades of shared one billet. During the Claudian period, the Roman army consisted of twenty-nine legions, of which four took part in the invasion of Britain.

Auxiliaries were not Roman citizens (though they became so when discharged) and were drawn from the frontiers of the Empire. Unlike the legions, the auxiliary forces tended to retain the dress and equipment of their place of origin and they provided the Roman army with light infantry and most of its cavalry. The infantry consisted of *cohorts* and the cavalry of *alae* (wings) of between 500 and 1,000 men. The British garrison originally included auxiliaries from Germany, Holland and Bulgaria, and these were later augmented by units from Syria and Yugoslavia as well as native recruits from the British tribes. Auxiliaries greatly outnumbered legionaries during conquest, and throughout the Roman occupation there were at least as many auxiliaries as there were legionaries in Britain. They were required to man outposts and frontiers, the legions being held in reserve and employed in the construction of roads and fortifications.

The Roman army 'carried a walled town in their packs' so that at the end of a day's march into hostile territory a 'marching camp' would be erected for overnight defence against surprise attack and wild animals. Typically, this consisted of a rectangular enclosure of ramparts 1.5 metres in height (5 feet) with a palisade of pointed stakes (each soldier carried two stakes during the day) and a surrounding ditch. Within this enclosure the soldiers pitched their eight-man tents in rows of ten with a centurion's tent at the end of each row. The ramparts of several marching camps have survived, notably in Wales, Scotland and northern England, their size dependent on the strength of the expeditionary force: that at Rey Cross on the Yorkshire–Cumbria border is the most impressive and was the temporary home of the entire *Legio* IX during its conquest of the Brigantia.

Conquered territories were controlled from permanent forts. These were intended primarily for offensive purposes and their sites were not necessarily easily defensible but rather commanded major routes in mountain passes and river valleys. But on the frontiers and in more remote areas they also formed part of complex defensive systems, linked by roads and SIGNAL STATIONS. These forts usually had two or three lines of V-shaped defensive ditches which sometimes contained sharpened stakes concealed in pits (known as 'lilies') or deep inward-facing revetments within which unsuspecting attackers might be trapped. Initially, compacted turf 'bricks' were used to form

vertical walls some 3 to 5.5 metres thick (10 to 18 feet) with timber footings, platforms and revetments and gates and flanking towers for ballistas. But by the time of Hadrian (AD 117–38), many turf and timber forts were being rebuilt in stone and a number of new stone forts were also constructed. Within the rectangle of walls, a headquarters building (*praetorium*) and commander's lodging were surrounded by store-rooms and stables and regular rows of barrack-blocks, each containing separate quarters for the ten *contubernia* of a century and its centurion. Such buildings were usually built of stone, as was the inevitable bathhouse, which was sometimes located outside the walls.

The smallest forts might house a single century, while others, such as Hardknott, Cumbria, and Bainbridge, Yorkshire, were garrisoned by cohorts of auxiliaries. The great legionary fortresses of York, Chester, Caerleon, Exeter and Lincoln were military towns covering 60 acres or more, with streets, hospitals, amphitheatres, bathhouses and exercise halls and accommodation for over 5,000 men. There were also 'practice camps', such as that near Llandrindod Wells in Powys, where men learned both to construct and to attack fortifications.

The Emperor Hadrian, who visited Britain in AD 121, was an expert on frontier defences having served in the imperial borderlands of Syria and the Balkans. He knew that if the British province were to fall to the barbarians then other provinces across the Channel might follow. By AD 123, legionaries had begun laying the foundations of a wall that was to run across the north of Britain from Newcastle-on-Tyne in the east to Bowness in the west: a distance of 122 km (76 miles). Originally, the eastern section was to be constructed of stone with walls 6 metres high (20 feet) and 2.5 to 3 metres thick (8 to 10 feet) with a western section consisting of a turf rampart, though this was rebuilt in stone within a few decades of the wall's completion in 133. To the north of the wall was a ditch, 12 metres wide (40 feet) and 3 metres deep (10 feet), and at intervals of one (Roman) mile were *milecastles*, or miniature forts, between which were pairs of turrets which were provided with beacons for signalling. A typical milecastle contained accommodation for thirty men and gates to the north and south by which movement across the frontier could be controlled.

Like other permanent forts, the wall was not simply a defensive structure: it was intended to act as a barrier which could be patrolled effectively and along which communications could be maintained. When necessary, a garrison could enter hostile territory to engage the enemy or reinforce a defensive

Turret 51B, Hadrian's Wall.

action by a flanking movement against an adjacent sector of the wall. A strategic reserve was maintained against the possibility of large-scale attack and originally these troops were garrisoned in a chain of forts on the *Stanegate*, a military road built by Agricola from Corbridge to Carlisle several miles behind the wall. But the erection of the wall caused so much unrest, particularly among the Brigantes to the south, that the reserve was brought forward into fifteen new forts built along the wall itself.

At the same time, a military zone (*vallum*) was cleared to the south of the wall. This was 36 metres wide (120 feet) and consisted of a central ditch, a patrol track and lateral embankments together with causeways which crossed the *vallum* opposite each fort. Civilians crossing the *vallum* other than by the causeways were intercepted by patrols. In all, about 12,000 men served on the wall, of whom perhaps one-tenth would be actively engaged in patrolling the border, while the remainder formed the strategic reserve. Both forces were composed entirely of auxiliaries and included cavalry detachments and *exploratores* or frontier scouts.

Within a decade of the completion of Hadrian's Wall, the Emperor Antonius Pius was reappraising the frontier situation in Britain and a new governor, Quintus Lollius Urbicus, was charged with the task of re-occupying southern Scotland and of building a new wall between the Firth of Forth and the Firth of Clyde. Begun in *c.* 140, the Antonine Wall was constructed entirely of turf and was defended by a deep ditch and outposts to the north and a series of forts located along its 60-km length (37 miles). Before work began on the wall, six garrison forts were built at intervals of 13 to 14.5 km (8 to 9 miles) and these were linked by a military road. Between these forts a series of small fortifications, of similar plan and function as the milecastles of Hadrian's Wall, were built at intervals of approximately 1.6 km (1 mile). Later, further forts were added, making nineteen in all, though these were not as large as the original six. The wall itself was 4 metres high (13 feet) and built on a heavy stone base 4.5 metres wide (15 feet). It is unlikely that both walls were occupied simultaneously and the Romans, unable to consolidate the new frontier, finally abandoned it in *c.* 163 in favour of Hadrian's Wall.

From the last decades of the second century, Frankish and Saxon raiders began crossing the North Sea from northern Europe, where Roman defences on the Rhine prevented landward expansion of their territories, to plunder the rich provinces of Gaul and Britain. By the second century, bases had been established for the Channel Fleet (the *Classis Britannica*) at Dover and Boulogne, both of which were provided with immense lighthouses, 24 metres tall (80 feet) and with beacons from which pillars of smoke guided shipping by day and flames by night. But the isolated coastal and estuarine settlements along both sides of the Channel were particularly vulnerable to attack and pirate activity increased significantly after *c*. AD 200 so that the Romans began building coastal forts to defend a number of eastern harbours, notably Brancaster in Norfolk and Reculver on the north coast of Kent. In AD 276 barbarian tribes from beyond the Rhine overran Gaul by land, while their ships established virtual control over the seas around Britain. It is likely that it was in response to this that a great chain of Roman forts was built to guard the *Litus Saxonici*, the *Saxon Shore* of France and Britain.

Of the British forts nothing remains of Walton Castle near Felixstowe in Suffolk or of the fort at Dover (*Dubris*) and there is little left of Brancaster on the Wash (*Branodunum*) or of Reculver (*Regulbium*) in Kent. Near Bradwell in Essex the fort of *Ythancaestir* endures in fragments, as does Stutfall Castle (*Lemanis*) at Lympne in Romney Marsh. But the remains of Burgh Castle (*Gariannonum*) in Suffolk, Richborough (*Rutupiae*) in Kent, Pevensey (*Anterita*) in Sussex and Portchester (*Portus Adurni*) in Hampshire testify to the extraordinary scale of the fortifications. At Richborough, which may have been the operational headquarters of the entire system, the earlier earthworks were replaced by a massive stone fort with turreted walls over 3 metres thick (10 feet) and 7.5 metres high (25 feet) within a deep double ditch. At Portchester, the complete perimeter of Roman walls, with fourteen (of twenty-one) remaining semi-circular towers, enclose the ruins of an early twelfth-century castle and an Augustinian monastery. The forts provided safe anchorages for the squadrons of the Channel fleet and each had its own garrison of auxiliaries. The Saxon Shore forts of Britain and Gaul formed a unified system, designed to discourage landing to the north of the Straits of Dover and to drive raiders into the narrowest part of the Channel where they could be intercepted by the fleet from Dover, Richborough or Boulogne.

In the early fourth century, the frontier defences of the north were rebuilt and recommissioned and command of the northern garrisons was vested in the *Dux Britanniarum*, the commander of the provinces of Britain, with administrative and military headquarters at York. At the same time, the western coast of Britain was provided with defences against Irish incursions, including a fort at Cardiff which, following restoration in the 1860s, affords an impression of how the Saxon Shore forts may have looked with their crenellated walls, external turrets for artillery engines and U-shaped windows through which bolts were propelled from spring guns within the walls.

By 340, the Channel system of defences was commanded by a general called the *Count of the Saxon Shore* and a new fort was built at Pevensey in Sussex to guard the long stretch of coast between Lympne and Portchester. Unlike most roman forts, it was oval in plan and has remained in almost constant service: as a Norman and medieval castle, an Elizabethan gun-emplacement and to conceal PILLBOXES during the Second World War. The 'Barbarian Conspiracy' of 367 resulted in yet another wave of incursions, but this time co-ordinated and therefore more effective. Count Theodosius, who was sent from Gaul with a relieving army, took nearly two years to restore order to the province and then began repairing and strengthening town walls and coastal defences. To these he added a series of fortified signal towers on the Yorkshire coast, each some 30 metres high (100 feet). But within thirty years they had been demolished by those against whom they had been erected.

See also ROMAN ADMINISTRATION, ROMAN ROADS, ROMANS *and* ROMAN VILLAS

For the Roman Military Research Society *see* APPENDIX I

ROMAN ROADS Some 11,900 km (7,400 miles) of Roman road have been identified in Britain, most of which were constructed during the first century as military roads. A complex communications network already existed before the Roman invasion of AD 43, but this consisted for the most part of local trackways, and a system of metalled roads was rapidly superimposed on the landscape to facilitate the deployment of Roman troops and equipment necessary to extend the frontiers of the province and to effect military control over a newly subjugated people.

The importance of the Roman road system cannot be exaggerated. It was the first coherent 'national' transport and communications network and was so well planned and engineered that, despite minimal maintenance, it remained in constant use throughout the Middle Ages (*see* MEDIEVAL ROADS). Indeed, no new roads were constructed until the TURNPIKES and ENCLOSURE ROADS of the eighteenth century. In Britain, as in other provinces, the road network serviced the major cities and military garrisons and provided an efficient, but strictly official, communication and transportation system with post-houses and relay stations located at regular intervals along the principal routes.

A glance at any road atlas will confirm that many of today's roads follow Roman alignments which traverse both map and landscape with mathematical precision. It seems likely that chains of sighting posts (possibly using beacons and 'smoke signals') were erected by the Roman surveyors who preceded the engineers and construction gangs, each section of a route being directed through an intervening sighting post to the one beyond. Such a system would, of course, result in the familiar segmental pattern of straight roads with their abrupt changes of course and adjustments effected where obstacles had to be avoided or where gradients were considered to be too severe.

All military personnel were trained and equipped to construct roads but labour for maintaining them was usually provided by the native population of the *civitas* or tribal division through which a particular section ran. Roads were usually built on a bed (*agger*) formed of material thrown up from flanking drainage ditches. This would be covered with a layer of gravel or sand and rubble to provide drainage and a paved or cobbled surface which could be as much as 13.5 metres wide (45 feet). The celebrated section of road on Blackstone Edge near Littleborough on the North York Moors is typical of this type of construction, though its authenticity as a Roman road has been questioned. Elsewhere, traces of Roman road remain as footpaths and bridle-ways or have been buried beneath cultivated or residential land, their original alignments evident only in a conjectural extension of lines on a map. Others were adopted as convenient and easily recognizable boundaries to Anglo-Saxon estates and have since been perpetuated in parish boundaries. Many sections of eighteenth- and nineteenth-century enclosure roads also have deceptively straight alignments but reference to an Ordnance Survey map will usually show that they are essentially local roads which often revert to a more tortuous course at a parish boundary.

Most of the names by which Roman roads are now known were acquired in the centuries following the occupation, when their original Latin designations were abandoned in favour of native ones: Stanegate on the Scottish border, for example, in which the Scandinavian word for road (*gata*) is combined with *stane* to make 'stony street'; and

Seven miles of Watling Street from West Pennocrucium near Penkridge in Staffordshire.

Peddars Way in East Anglia which was 'the road of the pedlars'. The Fosse Way, which followed the original frontier zone from Humberside to the Channel coast in Devon, was named after its prominent lateral ditches (*see* FOSSE) and both Watling Street and Ermine Street derived their names from the Saxon tribes through whose territories they passed, the *Wæclings* of Hertfordshire and the *Earnings* of Cambridgeshire. Watling Street ran north-west from the Channel coast at Richborough in Kent (*Rutupiæ*), through London (*Londinium*) and St Albans (*Verulamium*) to Wroxeter (*Viroconium*) in Shropshire. Ermine Street ran north from London to Lincoln (*Lindum*) where it joined the Fosse Way. The word 'street', which is applied to several Roman roads, originated in the Latin *via strata*, 'a laid way', thence the Old English *stræt*. Some names can be deceptive: despite a local tradition, the so-called Roman Steps through the Rhinog mountains in Gwynedd are medieval, though the route itself is probably prehistoric.

See also MILESTONES, ROMAN ADMINIS-TRATION, ROMAN FORTS AND CAMPS *and* ROMANS

ROMANS The Roman Empire lasted from 27 BC, when Octavia effectively became a constitutional monarch with the title Augustus, until the Barbarian invasions of the fourth and fifth centuries ended with the deposition of Romulus Augustulus, the last Roman Emperor, in AD 476. At its height, Roman influence extended from Armenia and Mesopotamia in the east to the Iberian peninsula in the west, and from Egypt in the south to the Danube and the Rhine in the north. In AD 395 the Empire was divided into the Western or Latin Empire which, after lapsing in 476, was revived by Charlemagne in 800 and persisted as the Holy Roman Empire until 1806; and the Eastern or Greek Empire which lasted until 1453.

The arrival of the Romans in Britain in 55 BC marks the end of pre-history and the beginning of recorded history. But historical sources have little to tell us of everyday life in the province. The common perception of 'Roman Britain' is one of an orderly and civilized colonial society exemplified by superbly engineered roads, buildings and fortifications, tessellated pavements and sophisticated hypocaust systems. In reality, most of rural England remained unchanged, notwithstanding the presence of foreigners, and the majority of the population continued to live in huts of clay, wood and stone with thatched roofs and floors of compressed earth. But indigenous society was not primitive: Britain possessed a highly developed trading system and social life long before the arrival of Rome; farmsteads and settlements were properly distributed and organized, and in Wales, for example, many agricultural and commercial settlements enjoyed levels of prosperity equal to those of the Roman villas. Roman activity in Ireland was confined to occasional military incursions and trade so that late Iron Age Irish society continued well into the fifth century and evolved through the influence of medieval Christianity rather than that of Rome.

To Julius Caesar, who spent much of his career as commander of the Roman armies in Gaul, Britain was a military inconvenience. Protected by the Channel, the southern tribes provided mercenaries for service with the nobles of Belgic Gaul and a safe haven for dissidents and exiles. Caesar crossed the Channel in 55 BC but was forced to withdraw after only a few days. In the following year, he returned with five legions and, by his own account, subdued the British and brought them within the influence of Rome, though others said that he had 'revealed Britain without conquering it'. After only two months, Caesar was obliged to return with his army to Gaul which was threatened by insurrection. During the century which followed, Britain remained outside the Roman Empire, preserved from further invasion by civil wars in Rome and later by

imperial policy. Nevertheless, in the south-east, where Caesar had been most active, alliances were made and new farming and domestic practices introduced (such as the heavy metal plough and the pottery wheel).

In the following century, the emergence of a vehemently anti-Roman regime in southern Britain provided an opportunity for annexation. The Roman Emperor Claudius had strong personal and political reasons for initiating military action in support of treaties broken by the new regime. He was also aware that the Rhine garrison had grown dangerously large and that the redeployment of surplus manpower to Britain would reduce the possibility of mutiny. The invasion of AD 43 was one of the most carefully planned and skilfully executed operations ever undertaken by the Roman army. In the summer of that year a force of 40,000 to 50,000 men, under the command of Aulus Plautius, embarked from the coast of Gaul. It comprised four legions: Legio II Augusta (under Titus Flavius Vespasianus, who was to become the Emperor Vespasian); Legio XX Valeria; Legio XIV Gemina; and Legio IX Hispana, together with *auxilia* units of lightly armed cavalry and infantry recruited from the frontier provinces. Only one landing place has been identified, at Richborough in Kent, though it is likely that part of the invasion force also landed in west Sussex. The Roman advance was delayed by a fierce, two-day battle at the Medway before the Thames was reached, a passage forced and bases established along the southern bank. The way to the Catuvellaunian OPPIDUM of Colchester (*Camulodunum*) lay open but Aulus Plautius halted, sending to Rome for the Emperor Claudius. In August the Emperor arrived and entered Colchester in triumph, accompanied by ceremonial elephants, to receive the British surrender. Claudius stayed for just sixteen days and did not return.

The conquest then moved into its second phase: Legio XX remained at Colchester while Legio IX and XIV marched into the north and west midlands respectively and Legio II moved against the *Durotriges* in the south-west, meeting fierce resistance. As the conquest advanced, permanent forts were built to control key points in centres of native population and to protect lines of communication. These forts were usually manned by garrisons of 500 auxiliaries, but could also include a legionary component, as at Hod Hill near Stourpaine in Dorset. Legio XX was provided with a permanent fortress at Colchester, while other legions were divided into *vexillations* and based at a number of lesser forts. By AD 47, a broad fortified frontier zone

The Roman Temple within the ramparts of Maiden Castle, Dorset, was built some three centuries after the hillfort fell to the II Augusta legion in c. *AD 44.*

had been established from the Humber to the Devon and Dorset coast, bounded to the north and west by the rivers Trent and Severn which provided both a physical barrier and a clear demarcation of the subjugated territories which rapidly acquired all the legal and administrative machinery of a Roman province. The construction of the Fosse Way, a military road which ran along the entire length of the frontier, facilitated the swift deployment of troops and delineated what was almost certainly intended to be a permanent boundary.

But the late 40s and 50s were dominated by resistance, notably from the Silures under Caratacus who 'crept through the glens and swamps like bandits', and the Brigantes on the northern fringes of the frontier zone. At one stage, in about AD 54, the Emperor Nero even contemplated a complete withdrawal from Britain which he believed had become too troublesome to hold. By AD 58, it was decided (not for the last time) that the only effective policy was to protect the prosperous south by exercising control over the barbaric tribes of the north and west, and the Fosse frontier was to be abandoned. But in AD 60, Roman officials arrived in

East Anglia to claim the lands of the Iceni which were due to pass to Rome on the death of the client king, Prasutagus. The Roman claims were fiercely resisted by Boudica, the late king's widow, and she and her children were molested by the officials. The ensuing revolt threatened the entire south-east which, because of the absence of a large part of the army in Wales, was particularly vulnerable. The unwalled towns of *Camulodunum* (Colchester), *Londinium* (London) and *Verulamium* (St Albans) were destroyed and horrifying atrocities committed. Seventy thousand are said to have perished and momentarily it seemed that the province would be lost. But Roman retribution was swift and thorough: the British were heavily defeated, possibly near Mancetter in Warwickshire, Boudica committed suicide and the Iceni were finally suppressed.

The Emperor Hadrian visited the province in *c.* AD 122 and to him is attributed the decision that Scotland was too inhospitable for Roman administration, though his successor Antoninus Pius continued to push northwards but without lasting success. Each gave his name to a major Roman fortification: Hadrian's Wall, which was constructed shortly after the Emperor's visit, and the turf-built Antonine Wall, which crosses Scotland from the Clyde to the Forth (see ROMAN FORTS AND CAMPS).

From AD259 to 273 affairs in Britain were directed from Cologne, and from 286 the Province was ruled by the self-declared Emperor Carausius, a former commander of the British fleet who was himself deposed and murdered by his assistant Allectus in 293. The Province was recaptured and returned to the Empire by Constantius Chlorus, father of Constantine the Great, in 296. At this time, the northern frontier was being pressed by the Picts, and Wales by Scotti raiders from Ireland, and from the mid-fourth century these attacks increased, as did incursions from the North Sea. In 367 Picts, Scots and Allacotti invaded northern Britain. General confusion and declining morale led to desertions from the army and widespread brigandry and lawlessness. But the Roman general Count Theodosius succeeded in restoring order and archaeological evidence suggests that at this time the towns remained secure.

In 383 another British commander, Magnus Maximus, declared himself Emperor and withdrew a large part of the British army to the Continent. A further serious invasion was averted in 398 with the arrival of the Roman general Stilicho, but this was the last time that the central government was to divert troops for the defence of Britain. In 406 the army in Britain again elected its own Emperor, Marcus, who was deposed in the following year by Gratian. Clearly, the political situation was becoming untenable and when fresh invasions of barbarians from across the Rhine threatened communications with Rome, Gratian was deposed and a senior soldier, Constantine, charged with restoring the situation. This he did by removing the remainder of the British garrison to Gaul. In 408 the defenceless British faced a major barbarian invasion. Realizing that they could expect no help from Rome, the Britons established their own government and prepared to repel the invaders. Finally, in 410 the Emperor Honorius wrote to the cities of Britain telling them to look to their own defences.

See also ROMAN ADMINISTRATION, ROMAN FORTS, ROMAN ROADS and ROMAN VILLAS
For the Society for the Promotion of Roman Studies see APPENDIX I

ROMAN TOWNS see ROMAN ADMINISTRATION and TOWNS

ROMAN VILLAS A villa was the prestigious country residence of a prosperous, and possibly aristocratic, Roman or Romano-Briton. Surrounded by an agricultural estate, of which it was the administrative centre, a villa was the home of an extended family and its numerous servants. Such estates were almost invariably located in the fertile English lowlands. They varied considerably both in size and importance, many being remodelled farmsteads which had acquired the trappings of civilization as a result of the entrepreneurial success or political advancement of their owners. Lands were both cultivated commercially or leased to tenants who lived in traditional native farmsteads and hamlets on the periphery of an estate.

Typically, a villa was constructed of good quality stone with tiled roofs, glazed windows and internal walls rendered with painted plaster. Many were provided with additional refinements such as TESSELLATED PAVEMENTS, HYPOCAUST heating systems and bath complexes. Initially, most would comprise four or five rooms, to which verandas and further suites of rooms would be added to form quadrangular series of buildings surrounding courtyard gardens. Within the curtilage of the villa but a short distance from it were the estate's agricultural buildings and accommodation for the workpeople, usually a native barn-like structure with aisles divided into living quarters.

Some villas were provided with sophisticated series of baths (*thermae*) and incorporated suites of rooms for use in winter (*tepidaria*), heated to a moderate temperature by hypocaust systems. The bathing process began in the *caldarium*, which comprised small compartments with hot baths. Following a scrubbing-down treatment, which included scraping with a *strigil*, the bather would plunge into a cold-water swimming bath (*frigidarium*) and would then be massaged and oiled.

Many villas date from the fourth century, when towns were in decline and rural areas offered greater commercial potential and political stability. In the decades following the withdrawal of Rome (AD 410), many villas seem to have been abandoned and allowed to decay along with the culture by which they were created. But several sites were later re-occupied and their estates translated into Anglo-Saxon and medieval manors, the boundaries of which sometimes delineate more recent parishes: that of Withington in the Gloucestershire Cotswolds, for example.

It is likely that several Roman villas were not prestigious private residences at all but religious centres dedicated to the worship of pre-Christian deities, notably *Bacchus*. Excavations at Littlecote near Hungerford in Berkshire suggest that what was previously believed to have been a villa may, in fact, have been the Bacchic equivalent of a monastery. Chedworth in Gloucestershire, the most celebrated of villas, was probably a pagan healing centre with votive altars, bathing facilities, accommodation for pilgrims and one of Britain's largest Roman temples located on a hillside nearly 1 km (0.6 mile) to the east.

The Bacchic evidence at these and several other 'villas' is particularly important. In the late Roman period, when paganism was competing with Christianity, the Bacchic cult developed into an almost monotheistic paganism in which a rich assortment of deities was absorbed into a supreme deity: the combined god Zagreus-Bacchus, son of the classical god Zeus, who was murdered by his enemies and reborn as Bacchus. The Greek philosopher Plutarch described him as 'the God who is destroyed, who disappears, who relinquishes life and then is born again'. As in Christianity, death and resurrection and the 'oneness' of Father and Son are central to the Bacchic theme and it is hardly surprising, therefore, that a late Roman tessellated pavement, discovered in 1963 at Hinton St Mary in Dorset, should have as its centre-piece the head not of Bacchus, but of Christ.

ROMANY *see* GYPSIES

ROOD (i) A measurement equivalent to 40 square RODS or POLES (i.e. a quarter of an ACRE) but with regional and historical variations.
(ii) A crucifix, from the Old English *rod*, meaning 'cross'. The medieval *Great Rood* was a carved and painted figure of the crucified Christ, supported at the centre of a rood beam which spanned a chancel arch, and usually flanked by the figures of the Blessed Virgin Mary and St John. Most Great Roods were removed at the Reformation (*see also* ROOD LOFT *and* ROOD SCREEN). Other roods may be found carved in wood or stone within the fabric of churches.

ROOD LOFT A projecting gallery which ran beneath the ROOD and above the ROOD SCREEN. It was usually reached by means of a curved flight of steps within an adjacent wall and provided access to the rood, which was covered during Lent, and to the rood beam on which numerous candles were placed (hence the alternative term *candle-beam*). Like the PULPITUM in larger churches, the rood loft was sometimes used by singers and musicians. Most rood lofts were removed at the Reformation leaving only the stone steps, which were usually blocked to provide a convenient cupboard for cleaning materials.

ROOD SCREEN In medieval churches, a decorative stone or wooden screen which separated the chancel from the nave and supported a ROOD LOFT, above which was the Great Rood (*see* ROOD). Most screens were pierced with traceried lights and a central opening which afforded access to the chancel. Both loft and screen were usually richly decorated with coloured and gilded carving, the panels below the tracery of the screen sometimes containing painted figures of the saints. Unlike roods and lofts, many screens survived the Reformation as CHANCEL SCREENS. A small number of remote churches have retained both rood screen and loft, notably at Llanelieu and Partrisho, Powys; St Margaret's, Herefordshire; Llangwm Uchaf, Monmouthshire and Llanrwst, Denbighshire.
See also PULPITUM

ROOFING TILES *see* TILES *and* SLATES

ROOFS The earliest roofs were conical structures consisting of timbers which radiated from a central pole to the ground or to a low circular wall and were covered with turf or thatch. With the development of rectangular buildings, a simple tent-like roof structure was used and from this evolved the open timber-trussed roof which, until the sixteenth century, covered the majority of buildings. The earliest type was of CRUCK FRAME construction but this lacked headroom and more elaborate structures developed.

In its simplest form, the medieval trussed roof consisted of a long beam (*ridge-piece*) which extended horizontally along the length of the apex of the roof and was supported at each end by the gables of the building. From either side of the ridge-piece, parallel timbers (*principal rafters* and less substantial *common rafters*) were carried downward to timbers (*wallplates*) laid along the tops of the side walls of the building and secured by means of stone CORBELS set into the walls. Further horizontal beams (*purlins*) were incorporated at intervals between the ridge-piece and the wallplate and, to counteract the outward thrust of the roof on the wall, massive beams (*tie beams*) spanned the interior space at wallplate level. These were pinned or tenoned to the wallplates and often curve upwards at the centre where a vertical post (*king post*) or pairs of posts (*queen posts*) secured the structure to the ridge-piece. Further tie beams (*collar beams*) were sometimes incorporated above the wallplate level and curved *arch braces* or straight *struts* added for

Late fifteenth-century rood screen and projecting loft at Swimbridge, Devon.

reinforcement. *Coupled roofs* have neither tie beams nor collar beams, and *braced collar* roofs were constructed with collar beams and arch braces but no tie beams. Horizontal rows of wooden *battens* were affixed to the outside surfaces of the rafters from which overlapping or interlocking TILES, SLATES or SHINGLES were hung, or the roof thatched, to provide a weather-proof outer surface (*see also* THATCHING).

The pitch of a roof is determined by the materials used: thatch and pantiles require a steep pitch to throw off rainwater; Cotswold stone needs a pitch of about 45°, whereas sandstone roofs in northern England need only 30° and slates even less. In many cases, the original roof-covering has been changed: a steeply pitched roof with gable ends extended to form a coping above the level of the tiles or slates is usually indicative of earlier thatching, for example.

In the last decades of the fourteenth century, the *hammer-beam* roof evolved. Hammer beams are abbreviated tie beams which project at wallplate level and are supported from corbels by arch-braced *wall posts*. Vertical *hammer posts* rise from the inner ends of the hammer beams and are secured to collar beams and purlins (*collar purlins*). This structure enables the weight of a roof to be carried across a much wider span than would otherwise be possible. At Westminster Hall in London, for example, an immense hammer-beam roof, constructed in 1399 of Sussex oak, spans a floor space measuring 87 metres (290 feet) by 20 metres (68 feet) on walls 28 metres high (92 feet). Hammer-beam roofs and double hammer-beam roofs (those with two tiers of projecting beams) reached decorative perfection in the fifteenth century, particularly in East Anglian churches. The projections often terminate in carved angels,

Braced-collar roof of the fifteenth-century Great Barn at Tisbury in Wiltshire.

The late fourteenth-century roof of Westminster Hall, London, re-built by Richard II 'to create an architectural space which would provide an appropriately magnificent setting for the exercise of his royal authority' and which 'combined the latest technological developments of hammer beams and arched-braced construction'. (Michael Bennett)

sometimes exceeding one hundred in a single roof, and these may bear emblazoned shields or other armorial devices. The wallplate or cornice may also be richly carved with painted and gilded figures. In some medieval halls and churches, the wooden equivalent of the stone vault may also be found: the *wagon roof*, a continuous timber roof of half-cylindrical section.

From *c*. 1470, there was an increasing emphasis on domestic comfort and privacy and the provision of chambers with flat wood or wood and plaster *ceilings*. The first ceiling panels were supported by massive wooden beams, augmented by smaller timbers (*joists*) which spanned the spaces between beam and walls. But gradually the roof structure itself was adapted to form triangular frames of rafters, the horizontals of which served as ceiling joists to the room below. Perhaps the most innovative period in roof design occurred during the rebuilding which followed the destruction of over 13,000 houses in the Great Fire of London (1666). But as Isaac Ware wrote in the eighteenth century (*A Compleat Body of Architecture*), 'The great caution is, that the roof be neither too massy nor too light', for roof design is considerably more complex when larger spaces have to be covered and problems of stability overcome.

Most roofs are of gabled (or *saddleback*) construction, but there are three other types of roof which are commonly found in urban areas dating from the eighteenth and nineteenth centuries. In the M-shaped roof, the centre of the M is supported by a beam which spans the width of the house from front to back and is drained by means of a gutter and lead-lined trunk in the rear roof space and a downpipe at the back of the house. Named after the seventeenth-century architect François Mansard, the *mansard roof* has a double pitch with a steep slope to a height of at least 2.5 metres (8 feet) and a shallow top section to the ridge. The third type is the *valley roof* in which the rafters are set on the party walls of a terrace house forming a 'valley' at the bottom of which a gutter, on a central supporting beam, runs from front to back.

Other types are the *hipped roof*, in which the ends slope outwards to a cornice instead of terminating in gables; the *half-hipped roof*, the ends of which slope immediately beneath the ridge but then finish in a gable; and the *gambrel roof*, one end of which terminates at the ridge in a small gable before sloping to a cornice.

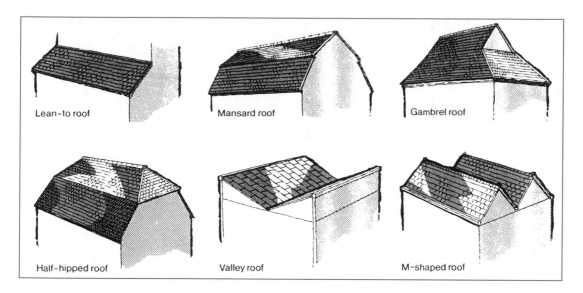

Lean-to roof | Mansard roof | Gambrel roof

Half-hipped roof | Valley roof | M-shaped roof

ROPE-MAKING Roperies generally date from the era of sailing ships in the eighteenth and early nineteenth centuries, though a considerable amount of rope was used in other industries such as mining. The characteristic feature of a ropery was the *rope-walk*, which was a long shed or open path along which men walked backwards while paying out rope fibres from a supply carried round their waists. At the starting end of the rope-walk, a machine was rotated which twisted the various fibres into strands and the strands into rope.

Sail- and net-making are often associated with roperies, as at Bridport in Dorset where a rope-making industry, using locally grown hemp, had been established by the thirteenth century. Twine, yarn and ropes were spun and twisted in the long gardens behind the houses and hung out to dry in the town's remarkably wide streets. According to a local saying, criminals who were condemned to death by hanging were to be 'stabbed with a Bridport dagger'.

During the INDUSTRIAL REVOLUTION, new processes and machinery were introduced which required the construction of mills, and consequently both traditional roperies and rope-walks declined.

ROSES, WARS OF THE *see* WARS OF THE ROSES

ROSE WINDOW A circular window with a complex traceried design. This type of window is often confused with the WHEEL WINDOW, which is also circular but contains a design of 'spokes' radiating from a central hub. Both are commonly found in medieval cathedrals, particularly in the gable walls of nave and transepts.

See also GOTHIC ARCHITECTURE *and* WINDOWS

ROTTEN BOROUGH A borough which was represented by a member in Parliament even though the population had been severely reduced in numbers (*see* TOWNS). Such members were often selected by a single influential person or family. Rotten boroughs were abolished by the Reform Act of 1832.

ROUND A native settlement of the Roman period comprising a cluster of oval stone dwellings within a circular embankment and ditch. Most commonly found in the south-west peninsula.

ROUND BARROWS *see* BARROWS

ROUNDHOUSE *see* LOCK-UP *and* WINDMILLS

ROUND TOWERS Irish campaniles associated with monastic houses dating from the period before the arrival of the Cistercians at the end of the twelfth century. Such towers often exceed 30 metres in height (100 feet) and taper gracefully to a conical top. They have few windows and a doorway which could only be reached by a ladder. The *cloigtheach* or 'bell-house' contained not a fixed bell and bell-rope, but a series of ladders by which a monk would ascend the tower to ring a hand-bell from the top storey.

It seems likely that the towers' primary function was a defensive one and that they served as watch-towers and refuges against tenth-century Viking raids. From the twelfth century, many were superseded by square towers. But several good examples have survived, notably at Coulm Cille's monastery at Kells in County Meath; at the monastery of St Colman, Kilmacduagh, County Galway, where the tower is 34 metres high (112 feet); and at St Mac Cuilinn's monastery at Lusk in County Dublin, where a medieval square tower was built on to the old *cloigtheach*.

ROYAL ARMS IN CHURCHES The royal arms will be found painted, and sometimes gilded, on boards affixed to the interior walls of many churches. They were erected as tokens of loyalty to the Crown and obedience to the sovereign as head of the Church, and consequently all but a very small number date from after 1534 when Henry VIII assumed the title of 'Supreme Head on Earth of the Church of England'. Royal devices from earlier periods will also be found in glass, furnishings, memorials, etc., but their function is mainly commemorative.

Although there is no known statute relating to the practice, churchwardens' accounts suggest that in most churches the royal arms were erected on top of the chancel screen in place of the ROOD, or above the chancel arch, during the reigns of Henry VIII and Edward VI. The initiative may have been taken by zealous churchwardens for, during the reign of Edward VI, the curate and wardens of St Martin's in Ironmonger Lane, London, were instructed to restore the rood and take down the royal arms they had erected. Following the succession of the Catholic Mary I, most royal arms were removed from

churches, notable exceptions being those at Westerham in Kent and Rushbrooke in Suffolk. But the process was again reversed by her successor, Elizabeth I, for whom several examples are to be found, including a faded mural on the nave wall at Puddletown church in Dorset.

The practice was maintained during the early Stuart period, and in 1614 the Archbishop of Canterbury instructed a painter-stainer to 'survey and paynte in all the churches and chappells within the Realme of England, the Kinges Majesties Armes in due form, with helmet, crest, mantell, and supporters as they ought to be, together with the nobel young princes.' This directive, and its reference to the future Charles I, may have encouraged the appearance of boards bearing the 'Prince of Wales' Feathers', though that in Sherborne Abbey, Dorset, is dated 1611 and suggests that the practice existed before the directive was issued. (The so-called *Prince of Wales' Feathers* device is the badge of the heir apparent to the English throne, not all of whom have been invested as princes of Wales.) In 1631 the Archbishop again issued instructions that the royal arms should be painted or repaired, together with the Ten Commandments and '. . . other Holy sentences'.

During the Commonwealth (1649–60), many examples of the royal arms were destroyed or defaced, while others were taken down and hidden or turned round and the Commonwealth arms painted on the reverse! Following the restoration of Charles II in 1660, a statute requiring that the royal arms should be displayed in all churches resulted in many old boards being brought out of hiding and repainted, and new ones made.

Although the composition of the royal arms was to change several times after 1660 (*see illustration*), royal arms in churches were affected only once more by changing dynastic fortunes. So concerned were the early Hanoverians with the claims of Stuart Pretenders that many Stuart arms in churches were repainted with those of Hanover. But the work was not always accurate, with the only the fourth quartering being changed, and in some cases a painted canvas of the Hanoverian arms was hastily stuck over the board, as at Cirencester in Gloucestershire.

Most royal arms were painted on square or oblong boards or canvas, though there are also examples in cast plaster, carved wood and cast iron. All reigns from James I to Victoria are represented, though there are few from the twentieth century, those to Elizabeth II at Remenham, Berkshire, and Shepton Montague in Somerset being exceptional. Many

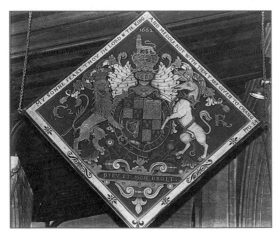

The royal arms of Charles II at Milborne Port, Somerset. Erected in 1662, just two years after the Restoration, the legend is singularly apt.

ROYAL ARMS

Royal Arms: 1 The Norman kings (attributed); 2 1195–1337; 3 1337–1405; 4 1405–1603; 5 1603–88 and 1702–07; 6 1688–1702; 7 1707–14; 8 1714–1801; 9 1801–37; 10 1837–present.

were moved from their original positions by Victorian restorers and dating is often difficult. Most have neither dates nor initials and dating by reference to the marshalling of the various quarterings is not always conclusive: one combination was used by Queen Anne for only seven years and yet, following her death in 1714, the Hanoverian royal arms remained unchanged for eighty-seven years. Even examples with initials or dates must be treated with caution as they may have been altered: J (James) or C (Charles) were often changed to G (George), although their Stuart origins may still be evident in the floreated form of the initials. Similarly, dates may commemorate an alteration rather than the original painting and with careful examination the old date may be found painted out beneath the new.

Churchwardens' accounts often provide invaluable information concerning the construction, repair and repainting of royal arms in churches.
See also COLLARS

ROYAL MAIL *see* POSTAL SERVICE

ROYAL PECULIAR *see* PECULIAR

ROYAL WARRANTS A warrant is a document issued by a sovereign, or on the sovereign's behalf, authorizing a certain course of action to be taken.

The most familiar warrant is that which is issued in respect of personal service to the sovereign or to members of his family or household. Henry II is believed to have granted the first Royal Warrant, and from the mid-twelfth century such charters were granted collectively to trade guilds such as the weavers, drapers and mercers. The practice seems to have been well established during the reign of Elizabeth I and it is likely that the royal arms were first displayed by tradesmen in the eighteenth century. The majority of these were in the cities of London and Westminster and in other towns with royal associations such as Edinburgh and Windsor. In the eighteenth century, the *Royal Kalendar* included such worthies as the Royal Rat-Catcher and the Royal Mole-Taker, though in 1775 a disgruntled Andrew Cooke complained that he had been omitted as Royal Bug-Taker, even though he had 'cured' some 16,000 beds 'with great applause'.

In the late eighteenth century, the use of the royal arms for advertising purposes was discreet, by means of small advertisements in newspapers, in books and on trade cards. As the nineteenth century progressed, warrants were granted for specific products as well as general services to the sovereign and his family. Such warrants were granted under oath and by the Board of the Green Cloth, but the system was revised in Victoria's reign when responsibility passed to the Lord Chamberlain's office and the Royal Household Tradesmen's Warrants Committee. The Royal Warrant Holders' Association received a royal charter in 1907.

A royal warrant lapses at the death of the member of the royal family in whose name it was granted, though the grantee may continue to use the phrase 'By appointment to His (or Her) Late Majesty', but not the coat of arms. Today, about 1,000 firms enjoy the privilege of displaying the royal arms and they are listed in Debrett's *Alphabetical List of Royal Warrant Holders*.

ROYD *see* ASSART

RUBBLE The term *rubble* does not necessarily imply inferior construction: walls built of stones of differing sizes, bound with mortar and sometimes laid in courses, are singularly durable. *Random rubble* is arranged without any particular coursing or design, while *coursed random rubble* consists of stones of various shapes laid in horizontal courses. *Opus reticulatum* is Roman rubble walling consisting of square-shaped stones laid on end to form an interlocking diamond pattern. *Ragwork* is rubble walling, usually a weathering face, composed of polygonal stones. *Square snecked rubble* contains small stone blocks (*snecks*) which are laid to interrupt long vertical joints.

RUBRIC A textual heading, usually in red ink.

RULERS OF ENGLAND AND OF THE UNITED KINGDOM

Saxon

Edwy	955–959
Edgar	959–975
Edward the Martyr	975–978
Ethelred the Unready	978–1016
Edmund Ironside	1016

Danish

Cnut	1017–1035
Harold I	1035–1040
Harthacnut	1040–1042

Saxon

Edward the Confessor	1042–1066
Harold II (Godwinson)	1066

Normandy	
William I	1066–1087
William II	1087–1100
Henry I	1100–1135
Stephen	1135–1154

Plantagenet	
Henry II	1154–1189
Richard I	1189–1199
John	1199–1216
Henry III	1216–1272
Edward I	1272–1307
Edward II	1307–1327
Edward III	1327–1377
Richard II	1377–1399

Lancaster	
Henry IV	1399–1413
Henry V	1413–1422
Henry VI	1422–1461

York	
Edward IV	1461–1483
Edward V	1483
Richard III	1483–1485

Tudor	
Henry VII	1485–1509
Henry VIII	1509–1547
Edward VI	1547–1553
Mary I	1553–1558
Elizabeth I	1558–1603

Stuart	
James I of England and VI of Scotland	1603–1625
Charles I	1625–1649

Commonwealth (declared in 1649)	
Oliver Cromwell (Lord Protector)	1653–1658
Richard Cromwell	1658–1659

Stuart	
Charles II	1660–1685
James II	1685–1688
William III and Mary II	1689–1702
Anne	1702–1714

Hanover	
George I	1714–1727
George II	1727–1760
George III	1760–1820
George IV	1820–1830
William IV	1830–1837
Victoria	1837–1901

Saxe-Coburg-Gotha	
Edward VII	1901–1910

Windsor	
George V	1910–1936
Edward VIII	1936
George VI	1936–1952
Elizabeth II	1952–

RULING Lines which were incised or drawn on a writing surface in order to guide the hand and to delineate the area in which the text was to be written. Before the mid-twelfth century, ruling was effected with the dry point of a sharp implement. Thereafter, until the end of the thirteenth century, lead was used and then ink.
See also PRICKING

RUNES Letters of the earliest Germanic alphabet, used especially by the Scandinavians and Anglo-Saxons from the third century and most frequently found inscribed on memorial stones and crosses or cross fragments, such as the early eighth-century Bewcastle Cross in Cumbria and the Ruthwell Cross in Dumfries and Galloway. The original alphabet, apparently of Etruscan origin, consisted of twenty-four runes to which others were added, mostly derived from carved prehistoric symbols. Runes are narrow, angular figures composed of straight lines and may have been used 'to invoke higher powers, to affect and influence the lives and fortunes of men' (R.W.V. Elliot, *Runes*, A & C Black, 1963). The English increased the alphabet to twenty-eight and the Scandinavians reduced it to sixteen.

Both the Bewcastle and Ruthwell crosses are of English origin, whereas the runic crosses on the Isle of Man have Norse inscriptions dating from the tenth to the twelfth centuries. The most extraordinary collection of Scandinavian runes, carved by a party of Norse crusaders *en route* for the Holy Land in 1152, is to be found on the stones of the Maeshowe chambered tomb on Mainland, Orkney.

By the tenth century, the English had abandoned the practice of carving runic inscriptions on crosses and memorials, though medieval masons and merchants sometimes adopted runes as personal devices (*see* MASONS' MARKS *and* MERCHANTS' MARKS).

RUNRIG A form of INFIELD-OUTFIELD farming operated by the tenants of Scottish communal farms in the centuries preceding the CLEARANCES and IMPROVEMENTS. Infield ('mukked land') was kept in continuous production by regular manuring and was sub-divided into 'breaks' in which barley, oats, peas and rye were grown by rotation. Tenants' holdings were dispersed in strips throughout the field, each comprising an immense ridge of plough-soil which often measured 1.8 metres in height (6 feet), 10 metres broad (30 feet) and up to 0.8 km in length (half a mile). This form of cultivation, which required teams of ten or more oxen to haul the ploughs, was intended to ensure that the crests of the ridges were always well drained and productive even in the wettest summers. Tenancy agreements were complex and removed incentives for long-term improvements so that runrig farming was often synonymous with exploitation and poverty.

RURAL DEAN *see* CLERGY (CHURCH OF ENGLAND)

RUSTICATION Introduced by Inigo Jones (1573–1652) from Renaissance Italy, rustication was employed extensively in eighteenth- and nineteenth-century classical architecture. Rustication was a method of providing contrasting textures in stonework by projecting square ASHLAR or decorative blocks of stone forward from the recessed mortar courses, usually on basement or lower storeys of buildings and on columns. These projecting blocks were usually ornamented: chamfered, diamond pointed, frosted and rock-faced (all of which are easily identified) and vermiculated, carved to represent the random path of worms.

RYAL *see* COINAGE

S

SAC AND SOC Manorial jurisdiction including a right to hold a court and to receive revenues and services.

SACRAMENTS, THE *see* PRIEST

SACRAMENT HOUSE *see* TABERNACLE

SACRISTY *and* **SACRISTAN** *see* MONASTERIES

SADDLEBACK ROOF A gabled roof, usually of a tower.

SADDLE BARS *see* WINDOWS

SAGITTARY *see* BEASTS (HERALDIC)

ST JOHN OF JERUSALEM, ORDER OF Among the many new religious orders which came into being in the eleventh and twelfth centuries were the military-religious orders of the Knights Templar and Knights Hospitaller. Both originated in the decades following the capture of the Holy City by the crusaders in 1099 and the establishing of a Christian Kingdom of Jerusalem which stretched from northern Syria to the Sanai desert (*see* CRUSADES). The Knights of the Hospital of St John of Jerusalem provided shelter and care for the sick, poor and weary pilgrims who visited the holy places, while the Templars guarded the holy places of Jerusalem, protected travellers and lived according to the rule of Bernard of Clairvaux. Both orders were endowed with substantial revenues, property and lands in the new kingdom and throughout Catholic Europe.

Within a few years of the orders' foundation, most of the brethren, while living under vows of religion, were conventual knights (their priests were known as *chaplains*) and the two orders played an increasingly significant rôle in the defence of the Christian settlements in Palestine and Syria and in the administration of the Kingdom of Jerusalem. They constructed and garrisoned castles and fought alongside crusading forces in the perennial wars against the Egyptians and Turks. The convent of each order was situated in the Holy Land, with dependent priories and estates throughout Europe. Each order had about fifty PRECEPTORIES or COMMANDERIES in the British Isles, many commemorated by place-names such as St John's Jerusalem in Kent, St John's Wood in London, Templecombe in Somerset, Temple Guiting in the Gloucestershire Cotswolds and Fryerning in Essex, 'the place of the brothers'.

Driven from Palestine with the rest of the Catholics in 1291, the Hospitallers took over the island of Rhodes, off the coast of Asia Minor, which became their base for naval operations against Muslim shipping. The island was ruled as a semi-independent state until 1522 when it was seized by the Ottoman Turks and the knights removed to the island of Malta which they held as a sovereign power from 1530 until 1798.

Following the persecution and papal suppression of the Templars in 1312 (*see* TEMPLAR, KNIGHTS), most of their properties were transferred to the Hospitallers.

From 1312 to their dissolution by Henry VIII in 1540, the English Knights Hospitaller comprised a minor, though well-endowed, branch of an international order, drawn (as required by its statutes) from the armigerous families of the noblesse. Discipline was firm and a knight's vow of obedience to the rule was strictly observed. Chastity and poverty were also required, though in practice a successful knight could enjoy his possessions until they were claimed by the order at his death. The Hospitallers' headquarters were at St John's Priory, Clerkenwell in London and it was there that an aspiring knight would undertake his novitiate before travelling to Rhodes where several years of military service against the Mohammedans would normally lead to promotion to the rank of commander. As a senior member of the order, he would be responsible for the administration of its estates and finances, serve as a diplomat or be seconded into royal or magnatial service. The arms of the order were a plain white cross on red and its habit black with the badge of a white 'Maltese' cross on the shoulder.

For the Order of St John Library and Museum *see* APPENDIX I

SAINT PETER'S PENCE Annual tribute of one penny from every householder possessed of land of a certain value, paid to the Papal See from *c.* 787 until Henry VIII's break with Rome when it was discontinued by statute in 1534.

SAINTS The practice of invoking and venerating the saints and martyrs has long been an element in Catholic devotion. They are perceived as being accessible as a medium of intercessionary prayer: because of their holiness they are close to God and yet they also remain close to man whose nature they share. From the eighth century, the lives of the saints were read at Mattins but various councils found it necessary to curb the excesses and superstition of popular devotion. In the early Church, bishops controlled the cult of the saints in their diocese, but the veneration of some saints spread beyond regional limits and the resulting problems required papal intervention. The first historically attested canonization is that of Ulrich of Augsburg in 993.

In *c.* 1170 it was asserted that no one should be venerated as a saint without the authority of the Roman Church and this became part of western Canon Law. In the Roman Catholic Church, *canonization* is the definitive sentence by which the Pope declares a dead person to have entered into heavenly glory and ordains that a new saint should be recognized throughout the Church. (*Beatification*

is slightly different in that it permits the public veneration of a faithful Catholic in a particular church, diocese, religious order or country.)

The cult of the saints was repudiated by the reformers, notably the Calvinists who objected that it was not specifically recommended in the Scriptures.

See also CHRISTIAN SYMBOLS, CHURCH SITES, SAINTS' DAYS AND FEAST-DAYS *and* SHRINES

SAINTS' DAYS AND FEAST-DAYS

1 January	Circumcision of Christ
6 January	Epiphany
13 January	St Hilary the Bishop
25 January	Conversion of St Paul
2 February	Purification of the Blessed Virgin Mary and the Presentation of Christ in the Temple (Candlemas)
14 February	St Valentine
24 February	St Matthias
1 March	St David
12 March	St Gregory
17 March	St Patrick
18 March	St Edward, King of the West Saxons
25 March	Annunciation of the Virgin (Lady Day or Ladymas)
4 April	St Ambrose
23 April	St George
25 April	St Mark
1 May	St Philip and St James the Less
26 May	St Augustine, first Archbishop of Canterbury
24 June	Nativity of St John Baptist
29 June	St Peter and St Paul
2 July	Visitation of the Blessed Virgin Mary
22 July	St Mary Magdalene
25 July	St James the Apostle
1 August	Lammas Day or Lammastide (prior to 1753)
6 August	Transfiguration
10 August	St Lawrence
13 August	Lammas Day (from 1753)
24 August	St Bartholomew the Apostle
8 September	Nativity of the Virgin Mary
14 September	Holy Cross Day (Holy Rood Day or Roodmas)
21 September	St Matthew the Apostle
29 September	St Michael and All Angels (Michaelmas)
30 September	St Jerome

18 October	St Luke
25 October	St Crispin
28 October	St Simon and St Jude the Apostles
1 November	All Saints (Hallowmas or All Hallows)
2 November	All Souls
11 November	St Martin (Martinmas)
22 November	St Cecilia
30 November	St Andrew
6 December	St Nicholas
8 December	Conception of the Blessed Virgin Mary
21 December	St Thomas the Apostle
25 December	Christmas
26 December	St Stephen
27 December	St John the Evangelist
28 December	Holy Innocents (Childermas)
29 December	St Thomas à Becket

MOVABLE FEAST DAYS (*see also* individual entries)

Septuagesima	The third Sunday before Lent
Sexagesima	The second Sunday before Lent
Quinquagesima	The Sunday before Ash Wednesday
Shrove Tuesday	The Tuesday before Ash Wednesday
Ash Wednesday	The first day of Lent
Palm Sunday	The Sunday before Easter and the sixth Sunday in Lent
Maundy Thursday	The day before Good Friday (*also* Sheer Thursday)
Good Friday	The Friday before Easter Sunday
Easter Sunday	The first Sunday following the first full moon after the vernal equinox (between 22 March and 25 April)
Rogation	The fifth Sunday after Easter Sunday
Rogation	The Monday, Tuesday and Wednesday preceding Ascension Day
Ascension Day	The Thursday following Rogation Sunday (between 30 April and 3 June)
Whitsunday	Pentecost, the seventh Sunday after Easter
Trinity Sunday	The Sunday following Whit Sunday and the eighth after Easter
Corpus Christi	The Thursday after Trinity Sunday

Advent Sunday	The Sunday nearest to 30 November
Ember Days	The Wednesday, Friday and Saturday following:
	i) the first Sunday in Lent
	ii) the Feast of Pentecost (Whit-sunday)
	iii) 14 September (Holy Cross Day)
	iv) 13 December (St Lucy)

See also EMBER DAYS, GOSPEL OAK, PERAMBULATION *and* QUARTER DAYS AND RENT DAYS

SALAMANDER *see* BEASTS (HERALDIC)

SALLY-PORT A type of POSTERN, usually a passageway from a fortified building, by which troops undertook a 'sally' or sortie against the enemy.

SALOP *see* SHIRE

SALT Until comparatively recent times, vast quantities of salt were required in every household in order to preserve meat and fish throughout the winter, following the slaughter of livestock in the autumn. From the Roman period, if not before, salt was obtained from inland saltfields, such as at Nantwich and Northwich in Cheshire, and coastal saltings and natural brine springs, such as those at Droitwich, Worcestershire, which was called 'Salt Springs' (*Salinae*) by the Romans.

In Leland's day there were three springs at Droitwich, each escaping through a fault in the permian roof of a vast underground reservoir of brine. According to tradition, the Great Spring had once run dry but was caused to flow again by Droitwich's patron saint, Richard, who, until the Dissolution, was commemorated in an annual 'dressing' of the spring and attendant festivities. Around the springs clustered the salt-pans which, in the Middle Ages, were owned by surrounding manors from which fuel was supplied in order to evaporate sufficient salt for their needs. The brine was boiled in the leaden pans, drained in wicker baskets and dried in ovens into salt 'loaves'. But as the number of pans increased during the Tudor period, brine had to be conveyed to them by wooden pipes, and although firing was restricted to the six months from midsummer to Christmas, local supplies of timber became exhausted and fuel had to be brought in from neighbouring districts. The people of Droitwich enjoyed rights over their salt in return for an annual payment of £100 to the Crown, the owner of each pan paying an equal share. Leland, in his itinerary, states that there were 360 pans and that each, therefore, paid 6*s* and 8*d*. Following the Dissolution, there must have occurred a process similar to that of the Tudor ENCLOSURES for Leland says that, whereas 'the comoditie thereof be syngular great, yet the burgesses be poore . . . bycawse gentlemen have for the moste parte the great gayne of it, and the burgesses have all the labowre.'

During the seventeenth and eighteenth centuries, the trade remained in the hands of a small number of producers and the natural springs were supplemented by boreholes which, at the end of the eighteenth century, were encased in wood. In 1805 a tax of £30 a ton was imposed on salt and by the time this was removed in 1825 many small producers had sold out to larger undertakings who were better able to meet the capital investment required. Towards the close of the century, iron piping was introduced which enabled the lower brine levels to be penetrated and prevented the inflow of water from intervening freshwater springs. Great quantities of brine were obtained, with a salt content of 42 per cent as opposed to the 28 to 37 per cent of earlier brine.

At this time, the salt industry had become such an economic battle-ground that in 1888 the manufacturers formed a cartel: the notorious Salt Union Company. But within a year of its formation, the price of salt had doubled and the industry went into decline, along with numerous local tradesmen whose financial stability was dependent on that of the salt trade itself.

SALTERGATE *see* SALTWAYS

SALTWAYS Known in the Danelaw counties as *saltergates* (from the Scandinavian *gata*, meaning 'way' or 'road'), saltways were PACK-HORSE ROADS which, by the Middle Ages, were regularly used for the distribution of salt from inland saltfields, coastal saltings and natural brine springs (*see* SALT). Although such roads were not used exclusively for this purpose, the salt merchants (*salters*) and their trains of pack-horses must have been such a familiar sight that their routes became known as saltways and the places through which they passed, or at which they rested, endowed with names such as Salterhebble, Yorkshire ('the salt-sellers' footbridge'), and Salterford, Nottinghamshire ('salt-sellers' ford'). But such names may have saline rather than commercial

implications: Saltford in Somerset, for example, was once a tidal ford.

SAMPLERS From the Latin *exemplar*; at a time when pattern books were prohibitively expensive, samplers were portable examples of embroidery stitches upon which new patterns and stitches could be worked. Usually of linen with stitching in silk and cotton threads, decoration was often in bands (known as *band samplers*), typically of alphabets, numerals and flowers and with an inscription such as 'Hester Syson is my name and with my needle I wrought the same October 20th in the Year of Our Lord 1659'. In the eighteenth century, samplers became a child's exercise in embroidery, requiring hours of painstaking work. A rapidly expanding collection of samplers is to be found at Montacute House, Somerset (National Trust).

SANCTUARY (i) From the Latin *sanctus*, meaning 'inviolable', is derived the Right of Sanctuary which, in medieval England, was of two kinds: ecclesiastical and secular. Ecclesiastical sanctuary developed through usage from the Saxon period and originally applied only to that area in the immediate vicinity of a bishop's throne (*cathedra*), though this was later extended to the curtilage of a church, from which a criminal could not be removed. Within forty days he was permitted to take an oath before a

Sanctuary knocker on the north door of Durham Cathedral.

coroner by which he confessed his crime, swore to *abjure the realm* and to submit to banishment. Some churches possessed sanctuary knockers (*hagodays*), large brass escutcheons adorned with the head of some monstrous beast. By grasping the ring of the hagoday, a fugitive could claim sanctuary from his pursuers. Contravention of the laws of sanctuary was a serious crime, punishable by excommunication.

Secular sanctuary relied upon a royal grant and in theory might be applied to any franchise where a lord exercised *jura regalia*. For this reason, secular sanctuary is often confused with ecclesiastical sanctuary, for fugitives frequently sought refuge in a church in franchise, especially in ecclesiastical liberties such as Durham. The privileges of sanctuary were restricted to seven cities in 1540. Sanctuary for crime was abolished in 1623 and for civil purposes in 1773.

(ii) That part of a church containing the ALTAR or, if there are several altars, the high altar.

SANCTUARY CROSSES Medieval roadside crosses erected to delineate the boundaries of an ecclesiastical liberty within which certain privileges were enjoyed (*see* FRANCHISE *and* SANCTUARY). There were eight such crosses around Ripon of which only one, the Sharrow cross, survives.

SANCTUS BELL (SACRING BELL) A bell housed in a turret at the junction of the nave and chancel. Also a hand-bell rung at Mass to focus the people's attention.

SARCOPHAGUS A stone coffin (*see* MONU-MENTS).

SARN Welsh place-name meaning 'causeway' and also applied to Roman roads.
See also HORSE STEPS

SARSEN STONES Immense sandstone boulders of the Eocene period which occur in southern England and are a particular feature of the Marlborough Downs in Wiltshire. The term is probably derived from 'Saracen', a convenient aphorism which was often applied prior to the seventeenth century to objects of incongruous appearance for which there was no rational explanation. Many thousands of sarsens were removed for building materials, not least those which were transported to Stonehenge and Avebury circles (also in Wiltshire) and to the sites of Neolithic chamber tombs such as Wayland's Smithy, Berkshire, and the Devil's Bed and Bolster,

Somerset. In the Middle Ages large blocks of undressed sarsen were used as a foundation for church towers and buttresses, and since the seventeenth century many Wiltshire farmers have used it in the construction of farm buildings and for gateposts, bridges, paving and field walls. It is rarely used for domestic buildings, however, for the exceptionally hard silica surface of split stone causes condensation.

SART (*also* **SARCH**) *see* ASSART

SASH WINDOWS *see* WINDOWS

SAUCERY *see* LARDER

SAW PIT A framework, erected over the mouth of a pit, on which timber is placed and sawn with a long two-handled saw by the 'top and bottom sawyers' standing one on a raised platform and the other in the pit beneath.

SAXON A member of a north German tribe originally located in territories round the mouth of the Elbe. Together with the Angles and Jutes, the Saxons conquered and colonized much of southern Britain in the fifth and sixth centuries.
See also ANGLE, ANGLO-SAXON, JUTE *and* OLD ENGLISH

SAXON SHORE *see* ROMAN FORTS AND CAMPS

SCALLOP SHELLS The device of St James the Apostle (*see* CHRISTIAN SYMBOLS). More than 300 medieval English churches are dedicated to St James, and the scallop shell is frequently found depicted in stone, glass and wood in the fabric of these churches. It was also the badge worn by pilgrims returning, usually via Bordeaux, from the saint's shrine at Santiago de Compostela in Spain, which by the twelfth century had become the most important centre of Christian pilgrimage after Jerusalem and Rome. Scallops were sewn on pilgrims' clothing or worn on their hats or shoulder bags (*scrips*) and were sometimes carved in their effigies or engraved on monumental brasses.
See also SHRINES

SCAR In northern Britain, a common place-name element from the Old Norse *sker*, meaning 'rock, crag or reef'.

SCEAT *see* COINAGE

SCHILTROM A defensive military formation consisting of a heavily armoured square or circle of troops.

SCHOOLS *see* EDUCATION

SCLAVEIN *see* SHRINES

SCOLDING A scold was a woman who disturbed the peace. Scolding was usually punishable by means of the DUCKING STOOL.

SCOOP POND *see* FISH-PONDS

SCORE In East Anglia, a cleft similar to a CHINE, and in Cheshire and Lancashire a term meaning 'common pasture'.

SCOT A member of a Gaelic tribe (*Dál Riada*) which migrated from Ireland to northern Britain during the sixth century.

SCOTLAND Early inhabitants of the northern-most area of Britain were Picts and Celtic peoples who arrived from continental Europe during the Bronze Age and early Iron Age (*see* CELT *and* PICT).

The northern boundary of the Roman Empire in Britain was Hadrian's Wall, except for a period of about forty years when the Antonine Wall was built from the Clyde to the Forth, effectively delineating the Pictish territories to the north (*see* ROMAN FORTS AND CAMPS). A series of complex developments, culminating in 1018 with the emergence of a southern Scottish kingdom under Malcolm II, began with invasions of Gaelic-speaking peoples from Antrim in Ireland in the fifth and sixth centuries. These were the *Dál Riada*, the original 'Scots', who gradually forced the indigenous Picts northwards and eastwards out of Argyll, Arran and Bute and established themselves in three tribes (the *Cenél Loairn*; the *Cenél Gabráin*; and the *Cenél n Oengusa*) in the western isles and coastal belt.

In the sixth century, Irish missionaries established monastic houses along the Firth of Lorne and on Rum, Eigg and Tiree and, with the arrival of Columba at Hinba and then Iona in *c.* 563, the early Church became established in Scotland. By the seventh century, Columban Christianity had spread to the Pictish kingdom where, as a result of matrilineal royal succession and the intermarriage of Pictish princesses with Scottish kings, Dál Riada influence gradually increased, resulting ultimately in the absorption of the Pictish kingdom by the Scots in the ninth century. South of the Clyde and Forth, was the British kingdom of Strathclyde, and the territories of the *Goddodin* in Lothian which were overrun by Angles from Northumbria in the late sixth and seventh centuries. To the west, the Angles had advanced to the Solway, capturing the British kingdom of *Rheged*, and in *c.* 720 an English bishopric was established at Withorn in southern Galloway. By the eighth century, a precarious balance existed among the Picts, Scots, Britons and Angles but in the last decades of the century this was seriously threatened by Norse incursions and the establishing of heathen colonies in Orkney and Shetland.

By *c.* 850, the Vikings occupied Sutherland, Caithness and the west coast north of Islay and, following the fall of Iona and the arrival of the Vikings on the shores of Argyll and Kintyre, the Cenél Gabráin, under Kenneth mac Alpine, moved into the central lowlands where they established new bases (such as Scone) from which they dominated the southern Pictish kingdom south of the Mounth. At the same time, the Cenél Loairn moved inland up the Great Glen to overrun the northern Pictish kingdom around the Murray Firth. The tenth-century *Orkneyinga Saga* records the ensuing conflict between the Norse earls of Orkney (who controlled territories as far south as Oykell in Sutherland) and the new northern Scots kingdom of Moray, which retained its autonomy into the eleventh century.

In the tenth century, the Cenél Gabráin pursued a successful policy of expansion into Lothian, Strathclyde and Cumbria which was to secure the dynasty of Kenneth mac Alpine and ultimately the kingdom of modern Scotland. Substantial Norse settlement of Galloway and the Northumbrian territories to the west of the Pennines, and the emergence of the Danish kingdom of York, effectively isolated the northern English and, following a series of wars and diplomatic manoeuvres, they were forced to abandon Edinburgh. In *c.* 973 Kenneth II secured much of Lothian and, following victory over the Northumbrians in 1018, his son Malcolm completed the annexation and established a Scottish border at the Tweed. This was later recognized by the Treaty of Falaise in 1174 and confirmed in 1237 by the Treaty of York.

Scotland remained an independent kingdom for six centuries, despite recurring English attempts to impose political domination, notably by Edward I and Edward III. With the exception of the Wars of Independence and the volatile Borders (*see* MARCH), medieval Scotland was a singularly peaceful country: her only military activity was against England, and that only rarely. But it was a

SCOTLAND 550–1018

kingdom of two very distinctive parts: the Lowlands and the Highlands.

In the twelfth and thirteenth centuries, the Scottish monarchy succeeded in creating manageable administrative units (*sheriffdoms*) in the Lowlands but the Highland clans remained stubbornly resistant, both to political change and to the influence of the Church. Sovereignty of the West was achieved in the thirteenth century but the Macdonald Lordship of the Isles remained beyond effective control even into the fifteenth century. In the Lowlands, a determinedly 'European' society flourished in the new *burghs* at a time of relative economic expansion and administrative development. New cathedrals and monasteries were established, and metropolitan sees created (though somewhat belatedly), in a Church which was now perceived to be part of the Church Universal. But although the Highlanders were considered to be anachronistic by the ambitious Lowland Scots, they represented an impregnable bastion against English imperialism.

Military victories over the Scots were easily achieved, but the problems of annexation and of exercising political control from London of such a remote and alien region were insoluble. Similarly, Scotland did not attract the expansionist attentions of European monarchs for whom the country's relative poverty (even of the Lowlands) and inhospitable terrain were singularly unappealing.

In the Middle Ages Scotland's political strength lay in her potential as an ally against the English and her kings exploited their advantage to the full, particularly in their relationships with the French. Once the administration had abandoned its unrealistic policy of extending its southern border in 1237, the Scottish people were able to enjoy centuries of relative peace, free of the burdens of war-time taxation and military service which alienated succeeding English kings from their subjects. Therein lay the strength of the Scottish monarchy. Local administrative and commercial affairs could be conducted without government intervention; trade with the Low Countries, the Baltic, Spain and even England flourished and Scotland's rôle as a major political power in Europe was confirmed. Academics and churchmen returning from the great European universities disseminated new ideas and stimulated debate and, from 1560, the Kirk was expressing an outward-looking self-assurance which reflected both its own eminent position in the Universal Church and the optimism of contemporary Scottish society. The Crowns of Scotland and England were united in 1603 and the parliaments in 1707.

See also CLEARANCES, KINGDOMS (ANCIENT) *and* SCOTTISH HIGHLAND FORTS

SCOTS PINE Few native pines survived the climatic changes of pre-history, the majority of today's pines being descendants of those introduced in the 'picturesque' planting of the eighteenth century when such trees were used to accentuate natural landscape features.

SCOTTISH BORDERS *see* MARCH

SCOTTISH HIGHLAND FORTS While the GLORIOUS REVOLUTION was accepted with relative equanimity in England, it was fiercely resisted by the Scots. In 1689 John Graham of Claverhouse (known as 'Bonnie Dundee' or 'Bloody Claver's', according to one's political persuasion) raised the Highland clans in the Stuart name and butchered a Williamite army in the pass of Killiecrankie. Although the uprising was broken at Dunkeld, the remote and conservative Highlanders remained loyal to the exiled descendants of King James for the next sixty years and supported the Jacobite risings of 1715, 1719 and 1745.

Following the abortive 'Fifteen', the government embarked on a policy of containment of the Highland clans. The military base at Inverlochy had already been repaired and renamed Fort William following Dundee's revolt, and to this four new fortified barrack blocks were added, the best surviving example being at Ruthven in Badenoch. But these measures proved inadequate during the rising of 1719, and a far more comprehensive programme of 'pacification' was begun by General George Wade in 1724. During the next fifteen years, 420 km (259 miles) of MILITARY ROADS were constructed, together with forty bridges, linking a network of forts on the hitherto inaccessible Highland 'frontier' with each other and with the Lowlands from which they were supplied and reinforced. The most important of these roads followed the Great Glen across the mountains from Inverness in the north-east (where Wade's modernized castle was re-named Fort George), along the shore of Loch Ness to the new outpost of Fort Augustus, and on to Fort William on the south-west coast. While Wade's strategy was admirable, in practice the landing of Prince Charles Edward Stuart in 1745 found most of the forts undermanned or even undefended and the Prince used the new roads to advance on Edinburgh. The Highlanders took Ruthven, Fort George at Inverness and Fort Augustus and laid siege to Fort William (the last siege ever conducted in Britain) before rejoining the Prince's army for the final battle at Culloden Moor.

The horrors of Culloden were followed by a further brutal period of 'pacification' and the extirpation of the Highland way of life, through the notorious CLEARANCES and the construction of new roads and forts, of which the most impressive is Fort George at Ardersier. Begun in 1748 as a replacement for its namesake which had been destroyed in the rising, Fort George remains one of the most complete and formidable military fortifications in Europe. It protrudes like an immense masonry ship into the Moray Firth with a ditch, ravelin and twin bastions protecting its landward side and accommodation for 1,600 men in elegant Georgian barracks or shell-proof rooms within the 21-metre thickness (70 feet) of the ramparts, which were lined with eighty cannon.

SCOWLES In the distinctive vocabulary of the Forest of Dean in Gloucestershire, the word *scowl* means 'debris'. It is applied specifically to the collapsed and overgrown remains of ancient iron-workings and iron-ore pits located along a narrow band of crease limestone which runs for several miles across the Forest. Iron-bearing sandstone is easily identified by its dark red staining and the rusty appearance of water in springs and streams. Workings at Bream and Clearwell were certainly active in the medieval period and may have been exploited by the Romans who are known to have extracted iron ore near Lydney, from where it was carried across the river Severn to the Fosse Way.

SCRATCH-DIALS *see* SUNDIALS

SCREENS PASSAGE A passageway separated from a medieval HALL by a decorative stone or wooden screen (*spere* or *speer*), often with a GALLERY above (*see* MINSTRELS). The front door usually opened into one end of the screens passage with the buttery, kitchen and other domestic offices at the other. The screen was intended to reduce draughts from these doorways and enabled the domestic staff to carry out their duties unobserved by guests in the hall. Although essentially a medieval feature, screens passages were provided in several great houses of the Elizabethan and Jacobean periods. The late sixteenth-century screens passage at Montacute House, Somerset, for example, served as an ante-chamber to the great hall which, by that time, was both a communal living-room and reception area.

SCRIPTORIUM A writing-room, especially in a monastery, where documents were written (often copied), illuminated and painted (*see* MANUSCRIPT ILLUMINATION). The scribes and illuminators who worked in a scriptorium were responsible to a master.
See also MONASTERIES

SCULLERY *see* LARDER

SCUTAGE *see* KNIGHT BACHELOR *and* MILITIA

SEALS A seal (*sigil*) is a piece of wax, lead or paper attached to a document as a guarantee of authenticity, or affixed to an envelope or receptacle to ensure that the contents may not be tampered with other than by breaking the seal. The piece of stone or metal upon which the design is engraved, and from which the impression is taken, is called the *matrix*. The Keeper of the Seal was an official who was responsible for the security of the matrix. Even before the development of ARMORY, seals bore distinctive devices which often alluded to the names of their owners: thus a man called Raven might use a raven on his seal.

From the twelfth century, sigillary devices first appear on shields, the various shapes of which provide clues for the dating of seals (*see* SHIELD). The first occurrence of a shield of arms in the seal of an English monarch is to be found in the second seal of Richard I

Seal of John de la Pole, Earl of Lincoln, who was killed at the battle of Stoke in 1487.

interspersed both in the legend and in the diapered background of the majesty. The legend on the second seal of Richard I (*see above*) refers to the king as *Rex Anglorum*, but thereafter successive English sovereigns were described on their seals as *Rex Anglie* until the legend was changed by James I to *Rex Angliae* in 1603 and by Charles I to *Rex Magnae Britanniae* in 1627.

Henry VIII (1509–47) made use of a golden *bulla* on which was depicted the royal arms within a collar of the Order of the Garter. A bulla was a disc of metal, originally lead, which was attached to documents, particularly those emanating from the Pope. Hence the expression *Papal Bull*, meaning the actual document.

SEAWEED LANES Also known as 'wrack roads', seaweed lanes run direct to the beach from which seaweed was collected and removed by cart or pack-horse for use as fertilizer. The 'wrack harvest' took place after the winter storms, while in some areas of Northern Ireland seaweed was cultivated in submarine wrack-beds from which it was harvested between March and June.

SECRETUM see SEALS

SECULAR In an historical context, secular clergy live in the general community as distinct from the 'regular clergy' who are members of religious orders and usually live a monastic life.

In Canon Law, the term *Secular Arm* is used to describe the State or any lay authority concerned in ecclesiastical cases.

SECULAR CANONS *or* **HONORARY CANONS** *see* CATHEDRALS

SEDILIA Stone seats built within the south wall of a CHANCEL, often with an adjacent PISCINA. Sedilia were usually provided for the priest who celebrated the Mass, and for the deacon and sub-deacon who assisted him. The seats were sometimes stepped and occupied according to rank, the highest (and that nearest the altar) being for the celebrant. In some churches, nineteenth-century remodelling has raised the chancel floor so that the seats of the sedilia appear to be uncomfortably low.

SEE *see* DIOCESE

SEGMENTAL ARCH *see* ARCH

SEGMENTAL ENCLOSURE *see* CAUSEWAYED ENCLOSURE

(*c.* 1195), which shows on the reverse an equestrian figure bearing a pointed shield charged with three lions. From this time also, magnates and knights began using equestrian figures of themselves in armour, with their arms depicted on the shield and horse-cloths (*caparison*). These official seals were large, and sovereigns and magnates generally used a PRIVY SEAL (*privatum sigillum*) to authenticate warrants to their clerks, who would then issue documents on their master's behalf under a GREAT SEAL. A personal seal (*secretum*) was used for private matters.

The continued use of the same seal by succeeding generations of a family contributed to the development of the hereditary nature of armory. Whereas a simple shield was ideally suited to a circular seal, the elongated fourteenth-century coat of arms, with its helm and CREST, created awkward spaces between the motif and the surrounding legend. These were filled with decorative patterns (*diaper*) and the figures of beasts or chimerical creatures, many of which were armorial badges which, from the fifteenth century, were often adopted as SUPPORTERS.

In England, the Great Seal of the realm has always been two-sided, like the coinage, with a different device on each side. Typically, the principal side (*obverse*) depicted the enthroned sovereign (the *majesty*) and the reverse his equestrian figure. The Great Seal of Edward IV (1461–83) shows the quartered arms of France and England with fleurs-de-lis and the Yorkist badges of roses and suns

Fenestella with piscina and sedilia. Here, the sanctuary floor was raised during a nineteenth-century restoration making the seats of the sedilia appear uncomfortably low.

SEIGNIORIAL, SEIGNEURIAL, SEIGNORAL *or* **SEIGNORIAL** Appertaining to the ownership of territory, or to territorial jurisdiction.

SEISIN (*also* **SEIZIN**) Possession, in contradistinction to ownership. Although an incoming tenant was 'seised in law' once his tenancy was agreed, he was unable to take possession of his land until he was 'seised in deed'. This was achieved by the outgoing tenant (or lord of the manor) presenting him with a token gift, such as a turf from the land in question, known as 'livery of seisin'. He was thereby seized of his land and the dispossessed tenant disseized.
See also NOVEL DISSEISIN

SEIZE QUARTIERS Proof of *seize quartiers* (i.e. that all sixteen of an armiger's great-great grandparents were entitled to bear arms in their own right) was sometimes proposed as a means of defining true ancestry, 'true blood' and, therefore, undisputed gentility. In Britain, the proposal has always been regarded with considerable scepticism and has nothing to do with MARSHALLING.

SELION *see* OPEN FIELDS *and* STRIP

SEPARATIST A title applied to those who separated from the Church of England.

SEPTUAGESIMA *see* SAINTS' DAYS AND FEAST-DAYS

SEQUESTRATION A legal procedure by which sequestrators are appointed to administer the emoluments of a vacant benefice for the benefit of the next incumbent.

SERJEANTY *or* **SERGEANTY** In the Middle Ages a serjeant was someone of less than knightly rank in the service of a lord (*Petty Serjeanty*); a knight in attendance on a sovereign (*Grand Serjeanty*); or an officer of Parliament charged with enforcing its dictates. By the twelfth century, garrison knights were invariably outnumbered by what contemporary pipe rolls describe as serjeants whose successors appear in later records as owing forty days' military duty in time of war.

The importance of this class in feudal society must have been considerable for it undoubtedly included many men of substance who were, in arms and equipment, little inferior to knights. But to a considerable degree, they fell outside the process which, in the twelfth century, brought tenure by knight-service under royal control and, for the most part, the sovereign rarely intervened in the relationship between a lord and the man who held lands of him by military serjeanty. In practice, the office of serjeant increasingly came to be associated with the performance of personal rather than military duties, and many serjeants were, for example, gamekeepers or physicians.

SETTLEMENT AND REMOVAL RECORDS
The 1697 Settlement Act prevented strangers from residing in a parish unless they could demonstrate by means of a Settlement Certificate that their home parish would be willing to take them back if they claimed poor relief. When this occurred, Removal Orders were issued, records of which are now maintained in the archives of QUARTER SESSIONS held by local record offices.
See also SOCIAL WELFARE

SETTLEMENT CERTIFICATE *see* POOR LAW *and* SETTLEMENT AND REMOVAL RECORDS

SEVERAL COUNTRYSIDE *see* COUNTRYSIDE

SEVERALS Land held by an individual, as opposed to common land.

SEWERS *see* PUBLIC UTILITIES *and* RECLAMATION

SEXAGESIMA *see* SAINTS' DAYS AND FEAST-DAYS

SEXT *see* MONASTERIES

SEXTON An official responsible for grave-digging, bell-ringing and other jobs in and around a parish church. The sexton was appointed and paid by a parish, incumbent or churchwardens.

SHACK-, SHOCK-, AND SHUCK- *see* DEMON NAMES

SHAMBLES *see* MARKETS

-SHAW A common place-name element from the Old English *scaga*, meaning 'thicket or copse', as in Shawbury, Shropshire, once 'a fortified place [*burg*] and valley by a copse', and Ottershaw, Surrey, meaning 'a copse where otters are found'.

SHEADING An electoral division in the Isle of Man and one of the six medieval districts into which Sir John Stanley divided the island when he became King of Man in 1405.

SHEELA-NA-GIG A grotesque female form particularly associated with ROMANESQUE decoration. Possibly a vestigial pagan fertility symbol or sculpted as a reminder of the fifth of the Seven Deadly Sins (lechery), there are notable examples at Kilpeck, Herefordshire, Whittlesford, Cambridgeshire and Fiddington, Somerset. The name, which derives from the Irish meaning 'Sheila of the paps', was coined by Victorian antiquaries in search of a suitable euphemism. *See also* PAGAN SYMBOLS

SHEEP STELL Stone circles in hill country which provided emergency protection for sheep in bad weather. Most are built on sloping land and have only one entrance. Wooden cribs, attached to the inside of the walls, were filled with hay at the first sign of bad weather. The sheep were herded into the stell where, crowded together, they would retain body heat and would trample falling snow to water which ran off down the slope.

SHELL KEEP *see* CASTLES (MEDIEVAL)

SHELTER BELTS Rows of trees, usually planted during the eighteenth and nineteenth centuries, to protect cultivated land from erosion, orchards and hop-fields from wind damage and livestock from the worst excesses of the elements. Long screens of sheltering beeches, pines or larches mostly date from the nineteenth century when ENCLOSURE spread to the uplands. They were anathema to landscape gardeners such as Humphrey Repton (1752–1818) who valued the 'natural' countryside of the eighteenth century. Orchards and hop-fields are often protected by rows of poplars and tall quickthorn hedges.

SHERD (i) A woodland clearing.
(ii) In archaeology, a broken piece of earthenware (*potsherd*).

SHERIFF A 'shire-reeve' (*scīrgerēfa*). The office of sheriff superseded that of EALDORMAN as the Crown's deputy and consequently the most important member of the executive in a county. Prior to the emergence of the JUSTICES OF THE PEACE in the fourteenth century, the sheriff was the main agent of the courts and was responsible for the Crown revenues of his shire. He was also responsible for the MILITIA until this duty passed to the LIEUTENANT and eventually to the Lord Lieutenant. In 1170 an inquiry considered malpractices by sheriffs and this resulted in the appointment of CORONERS.
See also HUNDRED COURT, LAW AND ORDER *and* REEVE

SHERIFFDOM *see* SCOTLAND

SHERIFF'S TOURN *see* HUNDRED COURT

SHIELDS Effigies, monumental brasses, etc., may be dated with reasonable accuracy by reference to the shield held by a figure or depicted elsewhere on a monument. In the eleventh century, and at the beginning of the twelfth, shields were long, narrow and kite-shaped, covering most of the body. They had rounded tops and were made of wood covered with tough boiled leather. Such shields were in use at Hastings and during the First Crusade, where raised edges, studs and bosses were often picked out in colour. During the twelfth century, the tops of shields became flatter and decoration more personal (*see* ARMORY). By the fourteenth century, the shield used by nobles and knights had become very much smaller and shaped like a flat-iron (called a *heater shield*), being roughly one-third longer than it was broad.

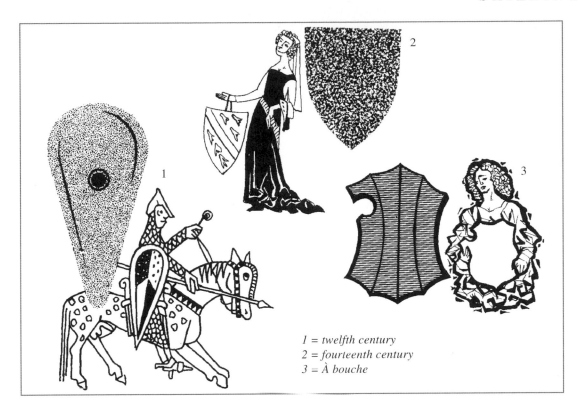

1 = twelfth century
2 = fourteenth century
3 = À bouche

The increasing efficiency of the longbow and crossbow, and the rapid development of plate armour, reduced the effectiveness of the shield as a means of defence and by the fifteenth century it had been abandoned except for heraldic purposes at tournaments, pageants, etc. It was at this time that the *à bouche* shield was most in evidence: this had a small piece cut from the side to allow for the free movement of a lance in the joust. After the sixteenth century, numerous stylized shields found their way into armory, few of which could ever have been used on the battlefield.

The shield is the only essential element in a coat of arms and, with the banner, the principal means of displaying arms.

SHIELING 'Here every way round about in the *wasts* as they tearme them you mey see as it were the ancient *Nomades*, a martiall kinde of men, who from the moneth of Aprill onto August, lye out scattering and summering (as they tearme it) with their cattell in little cottages here and there which they call *Sheales* and *Shealings*' (Camden, 1610).

These summer settlements of transhumaning pastoral farmers were once common on the fells of northern England and in the mountains of Scotland, Ireland and Wales. Many sites must be of considerable antiquity: the annual migration of a Scottish CLACHAN community and its livestock, for example, traditionally coincided with the pagan feast of Beltane (May Day) and only ceased when the system was destroyed by the brutal CLEARANCES of the late eighteenth century. On Lewes, in the Outer Hebrides, the BEEHIVE HUTS of shielings were occupied until 1859. In Wales, transhumance persisted in Snowdonia until the mid-nineteenth century (*see* HAFOD), and in Celtic areas of Ireland the BOOLEY HOUSE (*buaile*) served the same purpose as the shieling.

The huts (*bothies*) of a typical shieling had stone or turf walls and were clustered beside a mountain stream, beyond which small areas of cultivated land provided a crop of oats or rye. In northern England, these upland summer settlements are commemorated in place-name elements such as -erg, -airey and -arrow, derived from the Celtic *airidh* and Old Norse *ærgi*, meaning 'shieling', as in Sizergh, Cumbria, and as a first element in names such as Airyholme, Yorkshire.

Another Scandinavian word for shieling, *sætr*, is also found in -satter, -seat and -sett names, such as Appersett Pasture, Wensleydale, Yorkshire, and as a first element in Satterthwaite, Lancashire. Similarly, the Norse *skáli*, meaning 'hut or temporary shelter', is evident in -scale and scaw- names such as Bowscale and Seascale, Cumbria, and in Scafell, Scawdale and numerous others.

SHILLING *see* COINAGE

SHINGLES Wooden tiles used for covering walls and roofs since the Roman period until the end of the Middle Ages when, because of fire hazard, they were generally replaced by clay tiles, though for structural reasons shingles were retained on a number of church spires. Usually of oak, they measured 12.7 × 25.4 centimetres (5 × 10 inches) and were laid with an overlap, each tile being thicker at the lower edge.
See also ROOFS, SLATES, THATCHING *and* TILES

SHIPPEN (*also* **SHIPPON**) *see* FARMSTEADS *and* BARNS

SHIRE From the Old English *scīr* evolved the word 'shire' which, by the end of the ninth century, was applied to the administrative divisions of Wessex and within a century to those of East Anglia and the Midlands. Each shire comprised a number of smaller administrative units: HUNDREDS in the south and WAPENTAKES in the former Danelaw territories. Some shires retained their tribal identities: Middlesex was the land of the Middle Saxons, Cumberland the land of the Cumbras and Dorset that of the Dornsæte, for example. Others were distinguished by the names of their principal settlements: Hereford-shire, Worcester-shire, York-shire and so on. Not all are quite so obvious today: Wiltshire was named after the town of Wilton (*Wiltunscir*); Hampshire from *Hamtūn*, the old name for Southampton, (*Hamtunscir*); and Shropshire from *Scrobbesbyrigscir*, which meant 'the shire with Shrewsbury at its head'. (In its Norman form, Shropshire was *Salopescira*, hence the alternative name Salop.)

Following the Norman Conquest, the shires were superseded by COUNTIES, though the word

The County Court at Dorchester, Dorset, where the Tolpuddle Martyrs were convicted and sentenced to transportation in 1834. Although no longer in use, the court room and the cells beneath have been preserved and are open to the public.

remained in general use until the late Middle Ages and several counties still refer to their administrative offices as the Shire Hall.

SHIRE (COUNTY) COURT Shire courts in the Saxon and early Norman periods comprised freemen of the SHIRE and were presided over by the EALDORMAN. They met twice a year to determine both civil and criminal cases (*see* MOOT). Defendants were judged by their reputations rather than by evidence so that an understanding of local circumstances was of the utmost importance when reaching a verdict. A defendant was entitled to summon witnesses of good character who would 'join their oaths to his' in order to vindicate his plea of innocence (*see* COMPURGATION). The Normans replaced the ealdorman with the SHERIFF and gradually the shire courts were absorbed into the king's justice and administration.

Prior to the creation of separate ecclesiastical courts in 1072, the bishops also assisted the ealdormen or sheriffs in the shire courts. From 1166, Justices in EYRE dealt with the more important cases in the county courts, and further restrictions were placed on the jurisdiction of sheriffs with the appointment from 1194 of CORONERS. From the thirteenth century, the importance of the shire courts declined as that of the QUARTER SESSIONS increased. County courts now deal with civil matters of a local nature.

SHOCK A group of corn-sheaves propped up together to encourage the drying and ripening of the grain before removal from the field.

SHOTT *see* FURLONG

SHRINES In AD 156, the author of *The Martyrdom of Polycarp* wrote that the martyr's bones had become 'more valuable than refined gold'. However, by that time, the mortal remains of saints and martyrs (*see* RELICS) had already acquired a broader potency that affected all objects which themselves had been in contact with the remains or, indeed, with the tomb in which they were preserved. Christians believed that reliquaries and shrines contained the living presence of the saints and that miracles could be performed through contact with his bones or the cloths (*brandae*) which had been touched by them (*see* Acts Ch. 19, v. 12). Such tombs were therefore places of healing, protection, forgiveness and spiritual guidance.

Palestine itself was perceived as a vast relic: it became the Holy Land of Christian imagination in which certain locations were particularly venerated for their associations with Christ. Thus, pilgrims immersed themselves in the Jordan as Christ had done and plucked leaves from the palm trees of Jericho and wore them in their hats, thereby acquiring the popular name of 'palmers'. Pilgrims to the Holy Land increased in number during the third and fourth centuries, many of them adding their own inventions to 'the steadily burning fire of their devotion'.* Two monks, for example, claimed to have discovered the head of John the Baptist in the ruins of Herod's palace and before long most churches in the Holy Land had acquired a 'relic' of some sort so that, by the beginning of the fifth century, pilgrimage was developing commercially, with the provision of lodgings and guided tours of the sacred sites.

By this time, Europe had also established its own centres of pilgrimage, notably at Rome where the relics of martyrs killed during the persecutions were venerated by thousands of pilgrims, including four Anglo-Saxon kings. Shrines of lesser saints and martyrs burgeoned throughout Europe and every church coveted a holy relic. In the sixth century, Pope Gregory the Great sent to Augustine and the missionaries in England 'all things necessary for the worship of the Church' including 'relics of the holy apostles and martyrs', and the second Council of Nicaea (787) ordered that no church should be consecrated without relics, which were to be placed in or upon an altar in a *reliquary*, or in a crypt beneath.

Throughout Europe the market in relics expanded rapidly: not only those of native saints but of imported items from Rome and Palestine, the majority of which were of extremely dubious provenance. This unsavoury trade flourished for several centuries, partly because it was believed that all relics possessed miraculous powers of self-multiplication. In Britain, Bede (d.735) refers to shrines of native saints such as Alban, Oswald, Chad and Cuthbert which were visited from the fifth century. Not all saints were martyrs; some were *confessors* who had witnessed to the faith through suffering or by the impeccability of their lives. They were judged by the efficacy of their relics to work miracles and many were thereby acclaimed saints. In medieval Norfolk, for example, there were some seventy places of pilgrimage associated with local saints or their relics.

Very few shrines acquired truly international popularity. After Palestine and Rome came the shrine of St James at Santiago de Compostela in northern Spain (*see* SCALLOP SHELLS) and, in France, the shrines of St Martin at Tours and that of the reputed head of John the Baptist at Amiens. In

Germany were the relics of the Three Kings at Cologne and the shrine of the Holy Coat (the seamless robe of Christ) at Trier. Italian shrines included the tomb of St Francis at Portiuncula near Assisi, that of St Anthony at Padua and the Holy House of Loreto, which had miraculously been transported from Nazareth to Italy in 1295. Of contemporary English shrines only those of St Thomas à Becket at Canterbury and Our Lady of Walsingham, Norfolk, belonged to this first order, though Glastonbury in Somerset, with its mythical associations with Joseph of Arimathea and King Arthur, was also popular as were the remote shrines of St Magnus on Orknay and Ynys Enlli (Bardsey), the 'island of innumerable saints', off the Lleyn peninsula in Gwynedd.

The popularity of pilgrimages in the Middle Ages owed much to the practice of prescribing them as penances. Confession was followed by absolution which freed the repentant Christian from guilt but not from the punitive consequences of his sin. These could be commuted by performance of a penance and many of those who were convicted of serious crimes by the ecclesiastical courts undertook long pilgrimages clothed in sackcloth and ashes and with bare feet and fettered limbs. From the twelfth century, relief from purgatorial suffering could also be obtained by means of *indulgences*: certificates which stated that a period of purgatory had been remitted. Announcing the First Crusade at Clermont in 1095, Pope Urban II offered a plenary indulgence to all those who confessed their sins and 'took the cross', and in the thirteenth century the Franciscans claimed a papal plenary indulgence for all pilgrims to their shrine of the Portiuncula. Papal confirmation of this concession in 1294 established a precedent which was followed by the custodians of numerous other shrines who sought partial indulgences from their bishops or

St Alban's shrine and watching loft at St Albans, Hertfordshire.

from the Pope himself. Inevitably, such privileges had to be paid for, but they must have represented a sound investment for the price continued to increase throughout the fourteenth century.

Many shrines acquired the right to offer indulgences associated with more famous shrines, thereby attracting pilgrims who could see little point in exposing themselves to the hazards of a long and expensive journey overseas. The sale of indulgences also enabled those who were too old or infirm to go on crusade to send a substitute and still claim the benefits of a plenary indulgence. Similarly, a substitute pilgrim could be engaged, even by a man's family after his death or as a result of a clause in a will which required prayers to be offered for the soul of the testator at a particular shrine (*see also* CHANTRY). Eventually, indulgences could be commuted to money payments and in the late medieval period *pardoners* competed with each other, and with the local shrines, in the sale of certificates.

Not all those who set out on pilgrimage did so as a means of penance, however. In an age of rudimentary medical practice many travelled to shrines whose relics were associated with miracles of healing and the relief of suffering. The Fourth Lateran Council of 1215 had declared that illness was caused, not by physical ailments, but by sin and it therefore followed that a visit to a shrine was likely to do more good than a visit to a physician. Others perceived the shrines as tangible evidence of the spiritual world of heaven, far removed from their own temporal existence but attainable through physical contact with the relics of saints and martyrs. Such places fed the medieval imagination and brought even the most sceptical of men into contact with the historical Jesus and the characters of a seemingly heroic age.

The acquisition of potent and popular relics was, in medieval terms, a guarantee of financial security if not commercial success for many of the larger monastic foundations (*see also* TOWNS). Hostelries such as the George at Glastonbury and the George Inn at Winchcombe in Gloucestershire were built to accommodate pilgrims in the fifteenth century, as was the New Inn at Gloucester. The body of the murdered Edward II (d.1327) had been received for burial by the Abbot of St Peter's (now Gloucester Cathedral) in the previous century. Denied canonization by the Pope, Edward's remains nevertheless attracted enormous numbers of pilgrims whose patronage financed the rebuilding of the superb perpendicular choir in the abbey church (1337–50). But not all cults were successful; indeed, the majority were surprisingly short-lived. Even at Canterbury, where in 1220 (the year of the

translation of the relics) offerings at Thomas à Becket's tomb had totalled no less than £1,142, annual income from pilgrims to the shrine had declined to £36 by the Dissolution.

Roads were rarely for the exclusive use of pilgrims, though causeways and bridges were often provided for their benefit, particularly where routes converged on a particular shrine. Along the more popular routes, many of which came to be known as *Pilgrims' Ways*, numerous wayside inns, hostels, chapels and hospices developed, such as the infirmary at Castle Acre in Norfolk which was provided for ailing pilgrims on their way to Walsingham (*see also* SLIPPER CHAPEL).

Pilgrimage was essentially a popular and spontaneous expression of emotion, one which was never admitted as an essential of Christian duty but which was generally tolerated and, in many cases, encouraged by the Church. As the cult grew, so it became necessary for the Church to exercise control, and in some cases even to prohibit certain practices such as the veneration of HOLY WELLS, many of which were considered unsuitable for such purposes because of their pagan origins. Despite the continuing success of several major shrines, the numbers of pilgrims on the roads of England declined during the fourteenth and fifteenth centuries and, as Chaucer's *Canterbury Pilgrims* suggests, many took the journey simply for the pleasures of travel and each others' company. For the majority of medieval society, to embark on a pilgrimage must have been the realization of a lifetime's ambition: a unique opportunity to gain experience of the world beyond the confines of their village. Before leaving, it was necessary to obtain a priest's blessing, to make confession and, if the pilgrimage was to be a lengthy one, to make a will. Most pilgrims wore a long, coarse tunic known as the *sclavein* and a broad-brimmed hat turned up at the front. They travelled in bands for mutual protection and usually on foot, though in the later centuries more often on horseback. Before returning, pilgrims purchased the distinctive badge of the shrine they had visited and this was worn on their tunic or hat as proof of their pilgrimage.

In a severely attenuated form, pilgrimage in Britain survived the Reformation and remained a powerful image of the Christian tradition. Indeed, in the nineteenth century it enjoyed a modest revival with the emergence of the Anglo-Catholic wing of the Church of England and today Walsingham and Lourdes are as popular as ever they were in the Middle Ages.

See also MONASTERIES

* Adair, J., *The Pilgrims' Way* (Thames and Hudson, 1978)

SIEGES The primary military function of a medieval castle was an offensive one, as a base for active operations by which surrounding territory could be controlled. But as such it was of considerable value in war and it was the need for impregnability which, above all other requirements, dictated a castle's design and architectural form (*see* CASTLES (MEDIEVAL)).

The early motte and bailey castles of England and Wales were very effective strongholds against the heavy cavalry of mailed knights, which at that time dominated warfare. Inevitably, fire was especially dangerous to timber defences but, at the beginning of the twelfth century, there is little evidence of the use of more advanced techniques of siege-craft which had been practised in the classical world centuries before. The introduction of stone defences was both the result and the cause of advancing methods of attack. These methods were not necessarily innovative in the historical sense, but were techniques of the classical past which were reintroduced and modified in the West in response to the changing nature of warfare. From the twelfth century, the science of siege-craft remained largely unchanged until almost the end of the Middle Ages.

The introduction of GUNPOWDER into warfare in the fourteenth century had surprisingly little immediate effect and throughout the medieval period the castle maintained a supremacy of defence over attack, within the limitations of human endurance and the maintenance of adequate supplies.

Two methods of attack were used against a fortified position: bombardment and close assault. Medieval artillery consisted of the great stone-throwing 'siege-engines' (*petraria*) which battered a breach in the defences through which an assault could be made. There were three main types. The *mangonel* consisted of a long arm, with a cup or sling for the projectile at its free end, which passed through ropes stretched between upright posts. These ropes were twisted by windlasses, the arm pulled down against the torsion, and the projectile hurled towards the target when the arm was released. A more powerful engine was the *trebuchet*, which was introduced in the late twelfth century and worked on the counterweight principle. Like the mangonel, projectiles were directed at a target from a revolving arm pivoting between two uprights, but the motive power was provided by an immense counterweight which could be moved along the shorter end of the arm to obtain the correct range and trajectory. Both machines were used for hurling stone balls but other projectiles could be used such as the dreaded *Greek Fire*, a combustible mixture which was probably introduced by Richard I from Byzantium, and the corpses of dead animals which were intended to spread disease within a castle walls. The third type of engine was the *ballista* or *springald*, which projected iron bolts in the manner of an enormous crossbow. This was used for picking off the enemy and, with its low trajectory, could be aimed with considerable accuracy. There were other devices for breaching defences at close quarters. These included the *battering ram*, usually a large tree-trunk capped with iron, which was swung on ropes from a supporting, protective framework. Battering rams were most often used against gates but against masonry the smaller, iron-pointed *bore* was more effective.

By far the most efficient method of destroying a section of wall was by undermining which, in

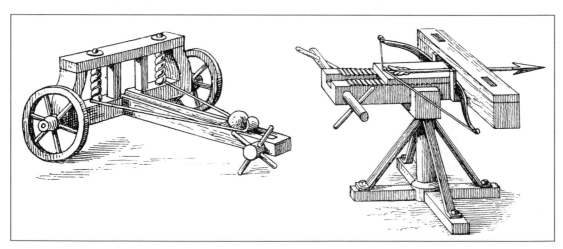

Catapult and espringal.

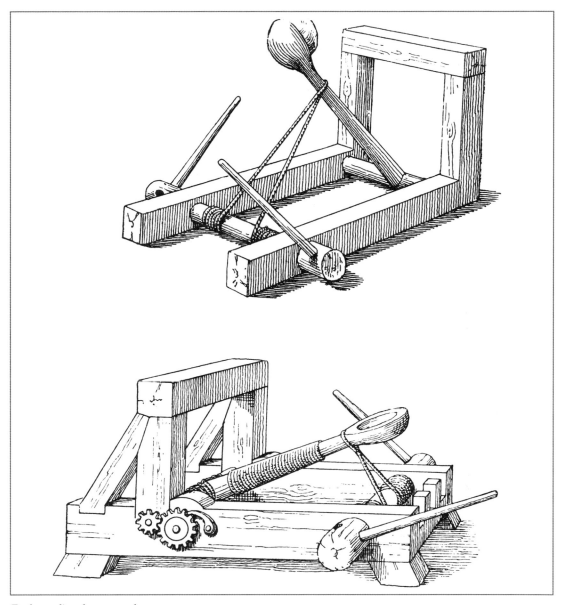

Early medieval mangonel.

England, was first used by William the Conqueror against the walls of Exeter in 1068. Expert miners tunnelled beneath the foundations of the target area of wall and shored them up with timber props. The mine chamber was then filled with combustible material and fired so that when the props burned through the masonry collapsed into the cavity and the wall was breached. Only castles built on rock, such as Goodrich in Herefordshire and Harlech in Gwynedd, could withstand such a form of attack, while elsewhere sophisticated water defences were devised, as at Caerphilly in South Wales. Many of these operations were carried out from beneath a *penthouse*, a large movable wooden 'shed', the reinforced roof of which provided protection from arrows and bolts and from missiles dropped from above.

The most common, though hazardous, means of entry was by the use of scaling ladders (*escalade*), a development of which was the *belfry*, a great movable tower which was trundled across a filled-in moat or ditch and positioned hard against a castle wall. This provided protection for the attackers who were able to concentrate their force on a vulnerable area of the battlements and it also served as a useful observation and shooting platform when not otherwise required. Many of these siege weapons acquired fanciful names such as 'Tortoise' or 'Cat', applied to the penthouse because of its stealth, or 'Mouse' for the bore and 'Malvoisin' ('Bad Neighbour') for the great petraria.

SIGIL *see* SEALS

SIGNAL STATIONS There can be little doubt that prehistoric man communicated over long distances by means of smoke or light signals from hill-top observation posts (*see* TOOT-HILLS). Similarly, during the Roman occupation of Britain, signal stations were incorporated into Hadrian's Wall and were erected as an early-warning system along vulnerable stretches of coast and on the roads which extended beyond the northern and south-western frontiers of the Province, including several to the north of the Antonine Wall (*see* ROMAN FORTS AND CAMPS). On the north Devon coast, signal stations gave warning of raiders from Ireland, and on the East Anglian and Yorkshire coast they guarded against Saxon incursions from the North Sea and were almost certainly augmented by a fleet of scouting ships.

The impressive network of signal stations constructed after AD 369 on headlands between Goldsborough and Filey on the north-east coast provided early warning of Pictish raids to the garrisons at York and Malton. Each consisted of a tall, stone-built watch-tower standing within a walled courtyard with corner towers (that at Scarborough has been reconstructed). These signal stations are only visible one from another in clear weather and the precise method of relaying messages remains a mystery. Elsewhere, Roman signal stations were built in a variety of forms: some consisted of an earthen platform within a rectangular embankment and ditch; others were raised wooden platforms enclosed by ramparts; and some were simply solitary stone towers, those on Hadrian's Wall projecting forward to facilitate communication. *See also* BEACONS *and* TELEGRAPH

SIGNATURES, BISHOPS AND ARCHBISHOPS Archbishops and bishops of the Church of England, the Church of Ireland, the Episcopal Church of Scotland and the Church in Wales, sign, after a representation of the Cross, by their Christian name followed by their province or see. These are spelled normally, with the following exceptions:

Archbishops

Canterbury: Cantuar	Wales: Cambrensis
York: Ebor	

Bishops

Carlisle: Carliol	London: Londin
Chester: Cestr	Norwich: Norvic
Chichester: Cicestr	Oxford: Oxon
Durham: Dunelm	Peterborough: Petriburg
Edinburgh: Edenburgen	Rochester: Roffen
Exeter: Exon	Salisbury: Sarum
Gloucester: Gloucestr	Winchester: Winton

The following will also be found in recent usage

Ely: Elien	Truro: Truron

SIGNPOSTS The first direction stones were erected by public spirited individuals such as one Nathan Izod, whose stone on Broadway Hill in Worcestershire is dated 1669 (*see* MILESTONES). Signposts at 'cross-highways' were originally known as 'direction posts' and were first required by law in 1697 at a time when the number of travellers on England's roads was increasing rapidly. The intrepid Celia Fiennes, writing of Lancashire in 1698, observed that '. . . at all cross wayes there are Posts with Hands pointing to each road with the names of the great town or market towns that it leads to.' But despite legislation, signposting remained sporadic until the General Turnpike Acts of 1766 and 1773 when the provision of direction posts at TURNPIKE crossroads was made compulsory.

Until recently, many eighteenth- and nineteenth-century *finger-posts* survived in rural areas, but regrettably European Community regulations have hastened their replacement with a more prosaic design. Because of their location at crossroads, many finger-posts inevitably acquired sinister or mysterious reputations (*see* GIBBETS *and* SUICIDES) while others were sometimes painted a distinctive colour. In Dorset, for example, there are still five 'Red Posts', the originals of which must have served a particular purpose. It has been suggested that coloured markers once denoted meeting-places on the boundaries of parishes, hundreds or counties, that these were later absorbed into the turnpike system to mark the extent of a trust's responsibilities, and that they were finally replaced by finger-posts which retained the traditional red colouring.

This may be so, but there are sometimes other (more colourful) possibilities. The red post on the A31 near Wimborne points the way to the village of Bloxworth and to Botany Bay Farm where, in the prison-like barn, convicts rested over night on their journey to Portsmouth and transportation to the penal colonies of Australia. The eighteenth-century barn once contained a stout central pole to which prisoners were attached in chains for the night. The Red Post is just a day's walk from Dorchester gaol and may have been painted red so that illiterate guards would not lose their way.

SIKE A riverside meadow and, in the north country, a small stream (from the Old Norse *sik* and the Old English *sic*) which may run dry in summer.

SILL *see* TIMBER-FRAMED BUILDINGS

SILVER *see* MINERALS

SIMONY The buying or selling of ecclesiastical offices.

SINISTER The right-hand side of a shield of arms when viewed from the front. In armory the sinister is considered to be inferior to the DEXTER or right-hand side.

SKIMMITY-RIDE A skimmington ride, also known as 'riding the Stang' (from the Old Scandinavian *nith-stöng*, meaning 'pole of ridicule') was a public demonstration of disapproval with the conduct of a local couple, effigies of whom were tied to a horse and paraded through the streets while the crowd maintained a noisy vigil outside the offenders' houses throughout the night. The ride was particularly aimed at those who had committed adultery.
See also CUCKING STOOL

SLADE (*also* **SITCH**) Land in a valley bottom, from the Old English *slæd*, meaning 'dell'.

SLANG *see* SLING

SLATES The term 'slate' was originally applied to any kind of split stone (from the Old French *esclate*, meaning 'something split'). This included not only slates for roofing, but also *flags* for floors and other uses such as gravestones. Stone slates have been used for roofing since the Roman period and in many areas have remained a feature of vernacular buildings since that time. In the Gloucestershire COTSWOLDS, the

production of stone slates provided income for the Knights Templar at Temple Guiting and there is evidence to suggest that their tile-pits remained in almost continuous production until the beginning of the twentieth century. Since the Roman period such slates have been roughly hexagonal in shape, with a squared 'tail' and narrowing at one end. They were (and are) fastened to the battens with iron nails, though in the medieval period when nails were expensive oak pegs were used on less important buildings. In some districts the slates were bedded on moss (*mosseying*), which provided protection against melting snow and had to be renewed periodically (hay or straw were also used). Not all slates come from specialist quarries: most villages of the limestone belt which runs north-east from the Cotswolds through Oxfordshire and Northamptonshire had their own sources of building stone and, in many cases, tile-pits (*slat quarrs*) nearby.

Stone for slates comes in thin layers which also provide *planks*, fencing slates which are held together by iron clamps. A frosting process was probably first used at Stonesfield quarries in Oxfordshire at the end of the sixteenth century. By this method, *pendles* of fissile limestone are left exposed during the winter so that the moisture in the thin films of clay between the layers freezes and expands causing the pendles to split easily into slates.

Before this, quarries were chosen where stone split naturally so that the slatter's only task was to shape and trim the slates. At Stonesfield, the stone was mined, with shafts descending to 20 metres (65 feet), and the pendles hauled to the surface by a windlass. When frost occurred at night the church bell was rung bringing the villagers from their beds so that the pendles could be uncovered as quickly as possible.

A slatter worked in a shelter of straw-covered hurdles with a *crapping stone* between his knees. This was a narrow stone set edgewise on the ground on which he trimmed three sides of each slate with a slat hammer until it was of the right shape and thickness. The edges were then trimmed by battering along them with the hammerhead, and a peg hole made in the narrow end by tapping lightly with the point of a slat pick. Piled 'ten flat and ten edgeways', 250 slates were considered a good day's work. Roofing slates varied in length and were measured against a slatter's rule or *wippet stick* which, in the Cotswolds, was marked with twenty-seven notches.

Each size of slate had its own name but these varied, not only from one region to another but among individual slatters. At Stonesfield, beginning with the smallest slates at the roof ridge and working down to the largest under the eaves, they were: short, middle and long cocks; short and long cuttings; muffetts; short, middle and long becks; short and long bachelors; short and long nines; short and long wivots; short and long elevens; short and long twelves; short and long thirteens); short and long fourteens; short and long fifteens and short and long sixteens. There were numerous other names and variations such as duchesses and countesses, farwells, chilts, warnetts and wippets.

Workmanship was judged by the quality of swept valleys, which were always the weakest part of a stone-tiled roof. 'Valley stones' had to be cut triangular in shape and arranged so that they left no cracks where the water could enter. Experts at *galetting*, as the craft was called, refused to use lead for this purpose, though modern tilers have no such reservations.

Roofs sometimes appear to have sagged because of the weight of the slates but this is not necessarily so for many were built in a curved fashion so that the slates held each other in place thereby reducing the risk of lifting by wind.

The Cotswold roofs are undoubtedly the finest, but heavy limestone slates from the Isle of Purbeck are found on houses in Dorset and Somerset and various kinds of sandstone provide roofs in many areas from the south-east of England to the Welsh border and the north country. In West Yorkshire, many of the industrial houses built before the 1860s had roofs of heavy stone slates which in time turn almost jet-black on the outer surface.

The term 'slate' is now generally applied to the blue-green metamorphic rocks of Wales, Cornwall and Cumbria which, because of their formation, cleave more precisely than limestone or sandstone to produce thinner slates. This type of slate was used as a roofing material from the early medieval period but only widely so since the nineteenth century. It was cheap to extract and process and a slate roof weighed considerably less than stone, thereby reducing the need for substantial and expensive timber framing. Consequently, millions of slate roofs were constructed during the Victorian Age and the quarries of Blaenau Ffestiniog and Llanberis (Gwynedd) prospered.

See also ROOFS, THATCHING *and* TILES

SLAT QUARR *see* SLATES

SLAUGHTER An unusual place-name element from the Old English *slōhtre*, meaning 'a waterlogged place: a slough', as at the picturesque Upper Slaughter and Lower Slaughter in the Gloucestershire Cotswolds.

SLAVE TRADE The English trade in African slaves, crimped on the shores of Africa and transported to Spanish colonies in America, was begun by John Hawkins (1532–95) in the reign of Elizabeth I, though in so doing he nearly destroyed legitimate trade with the natives who quickly learned to regard the white man as their natural enemy. In the following centuries, the trade became essential to the commercial success of American colonies such as Virginia, where it was encouraged by a tobacco-planter aristocracy whose life differed from that of English country gentlemen only in the possession of slaves. By the mid-eighteenth century, general trade with America was shared by London with Bristol, and with Liverpool where the slave trade was closely connected with the cotton manufacturing industry of Lancashire.

More than half the slaves carried across the Atlantic made the 'middle passage' in the squalid holds of English ships. In 1771 some 50,000 slaves were transported to the Americas in 'slavers' from London (58 ships), from Bristol (23) and from Liverpool (107). The Liverpool 'slavers' carried cargoes of finished Lancashire cotton goods to Africa where they were exchanged for slaves who were then transported across the Atlantic, the ships returning to Britain with cargoes of raw cotton, tobacco and sugar. The planters of the West Indian Islands and American colonies bought Lancashire cotton goods to clothe their slaves and the supply of labour from Africa enabled them to provide the raw material of the Lancashire industry.

In 1750 Horace Walpole wrote '. . . we, the British Senate, that temple of liberty, and bulwark of Protestant Christianity, have this fortnight been pondering methods to make more effectual that horrid traffic of selling negroes. It has appeared to us that six-and-forty thousand of these wretches are sold every year to our plantations alone! It chills one's blood.' Philanthropists such as William Wilberforce (1759–1833) campaigned for the abolition of the slave trade and slavery. As a member of parliament and a close friend of Pitt, who supported his campaigns, Wilberforce devoted his time and considerable eloquence to denouncing the trade and in 1791 introduced a bill for its abolition though, opposed by powerful vested interests, it was not enacted until 1807 and all slaves in British dominions were not freed until 1833. In Britain, slaves officially became freemen in 1772.

SLING (*also* **SLANG**) A narrow strip of land, usually between fields or enclosing a SQUATTER cottage on a broad roadside verge.

SLIP A building in which ships are constructed. The finest series of early slips in Britain is at Chatham Dockyard, Kent. The earliest surviving slip is a huge gabled building constructed of massive timbers in 1838 and erected so that wooden warships could be built under cover. This was followed in 1847–8 by three iron-frame slips (which pre-date the innovative railway train-sheds of the 1850s) and in 1853–5 by the colossal Slip No.7, designed by Colonel Green of the Royal Engineers. Next to the slips a further line of gabled, weatherboarded buildings contains the Mast House and Mould Loft in which full-size templates of the ships were drawn out on a huge floor. These buildings, and the associated Ropery, were built in the eighteenth century, the Commissioner's House of 1703 being the oldest surviving naval building in Britain.

SLIPPER CHAPEL A chapel in which pilgrims removed their shoes before approaching a SHRINE. The fourteenth-century 'Shoe House' or Slipper Chapel at Houghton St Giles, Norfolk, is situated about one 1.6 km (1 mile) from the shrine at Walsingham. Here, the pilgrims would pause and meditate before embarking on the final stage of their journey – barefoot and penitent.

SLOGAN Also known as *slughorn*. The battle cry of the chief of a Scottish clan or house. It may be the same as a MOTTO.

SLOUGH *see* PLASH

SLYPE *see* MONASTERIES

SMALL FRAMING *see* TIMBER-FRAMED BUILDINGS

SMELTING *see* MINERALS

SMITHY *see* FORGE

SMOCKS Until the late nineteenth century, many rural occupations had distinctive clothing. Most workers on the land wore smocks, a term derived from an Old English word meaning a shift, chemise or shirt. These were tunic-like linen garments made in a simple fashion from rectangular pieces of material with the extra fullness gathered in at yoke and cuffs by forming small pleats ('smocking'). They were usually embroidered on the front, and on the cuffs and collar, with traditional devices by which a particular region or trade could be identified: trees and leaves for woodmen; crooks,

hurdles and hearts for shepherds; and wheel-shapes for carters, for example. As a rule the embroidery was executed in a matching thread or one slightly darker than the smock itself.

Smock-frocks were essentially working clothes, best suits being reserved for Sundays and holidays and second-best for visiting relations. In Thomas Hardy's *Far from the Madding Crowd*, Gabriel Oak's visiting clothes are described as 'a degree between fine-market-day and wet-Sunday selection'. Hardy also tells us that by the late nineteenth century 'the genuine white smock-frock of Russia duck [untwilled linen] and the whity-brown one of drabbet [twilled linen]' were 'only seen on the shoulders of old men. Where smocks are worn by the young and middle-aged, they are of blue material . . . a mangy old coat is often preferred.'
(Thomas Hardy, *A Dorsetshire Labourer*, 1883)

SMUGGLING By the end of the sixteenth century, tobacco was being smuggled into Cornwall by French, Flemish and English ships in open (and often armed) defiance of the custom-house officers. During the seventeenth and eighteenth centuries, there was a significant increase in the smuggling of tobacco, proof spirits and sugar, and in 1784 it was calculated that of the almost 6 million kg of tea (13 million lb) which had been consumed in Britain, only 2½ million (5½ million lb) had been imported legally.

Despite often severe penalties, smuggling and poaching were generally regarded as comparatively innocent occupations by most people, ones which added a little excitement to an otherwise mundane existence. Even the eminently respectable Parson Woodforde wrote in 1777: 'Andrews the smuggler brought me this night about 11 o'clock a bagg of Hyson Tea 6 pound weight. He frightened us a little by whistling under the parlour window just as we were going to bed. I gave him some Geneva and paid him for the tea at 10/6 per pound.' During the Napoleonic wars (1800–15), and the years which followed, high import restrictions were placed on wines and spirits, especially on those from France. As a consequence, smuggling flourished.

By the nineteenth century, smuggling networks were already well established in many of the more remote coastal communities. These consisted of the smugglers themselves, who arranged for the safe landing of the merchandise, and local recruits or 'land smugglers' who stored the contraband and assisted in its distribution. When the 'Preventive-men' were known to be about, a ship would be 'burnt off' by means of a warning signal and further 'runs' attempted through different, pre-arranged landing-places on succeeding nights. When all else failed, the tubs were strung to a stray-line and sunk a little way from the shore, bearings taken of the precise location and, when the Revenue Men had finally departed, a grapnel (*creeper*) dragged along the bottom to retrieve the line. A 'run' would always be attempted during a 'dark', the time between moon and moon, and contraband removed from the beach by teams of 'land-carriers', the two 'tubs' slung upon the chest and back of each man often producing a terrible sensation of suffocation.

Many writers have described the extraordinary ingenuity of smugglers and their accomplices in the concealment and distribution of contraband. Thomas Hardy, in his Preface to *Wessex Tales*, for example, tells of '. . . the many devices for concealing smuggled goods . . . that of planting an apple-tree in a tray or box which was placed over the mouth of the pit is, I believe, unique.' Many local place-names hint at these clandestine operations. To the rear of the young Hardy's home at Higher Bockhampton in Dorset, for example, is the notorious 'Snail-Creep', a smugglers' track leading inland from the coast on which the lonely cottage was a regular staging-post. Hardy's grandfather

> sometimes had as many as eight 'tubs' in a dark closet – each tub containing four gallons. The spirit smelt all over the house, being proof, and had to be lowered for drinking. The tubs, or little elongated barrels, were of thin staves with wooden hoops . . . They were brought at night by men on horseback, 'slung', or in carts. A whiplash across the window-pane would wake my grandfather at two or three in the morning, and he would dress and go down. Not a soul was there, but a heap of tubs loomed up in front of the door. He would set to work and stow them away . . . and nothing more would happen till dusk the following evening, when groups of dark long-bearded fellows would arrive, and carry off the tubs in twos and fours slung over their shoulders. Many years later, I think in my mother's time, a large woman used to call and ask if any of 'it' was wanted cheap. Her hugeness was caused by her having bullocks' bladders slung round her hips, in which she carried the spirits.
> (Hardy, *Memoranda I*)

SNECK *see* RUBBLE

SOCAGE (*also* **SOKEMANRY**) Tenure of lands by service of determinate quality: either free socage or the inferior villein socage. Such a holding could be alienated by the tenant and inherited without restriction, subject only to the payment of a fee by the heir. A tenant by socage was a *socman* or *sokeman*. Socage was abolished in 1660.

SOCIAL WELFARE *see* ASYLUMS, BASTARDY, CHARITIES, DISPENSARIES, FOUNDLINGS, HOSPITALS, POOR LAW, SETTLEMENT AND REMOVAL RECORDS *and* WORK HOUSE

SOCIETY OF FRIENDS *see* QUAKERS

SOFFIT *see* ARCH *and* STAIRCASES

SOKE A pre-Conquest DANELAW district or estate within which a lord exercised personal jurisdiction in certain townships. It is likely that these originated in the ninth century as settlements of disbanded Danish soldiers owing common allegiance to a single lord and subject to the jurisdiction of his Soke Court. Tenants were freemen, but because the land within a particular soke might be contained within a number of manors, some townships and farmsteads were subject to divided lordship and custom. Sokes have featured in local administration since Domesday when their authority was recognized by statute. Indeed, charters providing for '. . . soc and sac, toll and theam' (the right to receive manorial profits and services, to hold a court, and to levy dues and determine punishments) date from 1020 onwards. Before the reorganization of local government in 1974, the Soke of Peterborough, which contained thirty-two townships, was a separate county.

SOKEMAN *and* **SOKEMANRY** *see* SOCAGE

SOLAR A private chamber usually located to take advantage of the sunniest aspect of a medieval house or castle and used as a quiet withdrawing-room by a lord, his family and guests. The solar, which was usually on the first or second floor, was generally reached by means of a stair which ascended from the daïs end of the great hall.

SOLSKIFT *see* SUN DIVISION

SORORUM Latinized place-name element meaning 'of the sisters' and indicative that a manor was once held by a monastic foundation of nuns.
See also LATIN *and* MONASTIC PLACE-NAMES

SOUND MIRRORS By the 1920s, aerial bombardment was being taken seriously as a threat to Britain's security. Keen to establish itself, the Royal Air Force began to encourage innovation, including a series of sound mirrors which were constructed along the south and east coasts – the first at Dover in 1917.

Sound mirrors were concrete bowls or lengths of concave wall designed to detect approaching aircraft at about 24 km distance (15 miles) in good climatic conditions. Located on cliff-tops, and facing across the English Channel, the circular mirrors were about 6 to 7½ metres in diameter (20 to 25 feet) with a concave spherical surface. A microphone was moved about in front of the mirror while an observer listened to the sound through headphones. By noting the position of the microphone where the sound was loudest, the direction and height of the approaching aircraft could be calculated. Inevitably, as aircraft speeds increased such primitive devices became redundant and were superseded by Radio Detection and Ranging (radar) stations.

At least seven sound mirrors have survived, four of which are in Kent. Of these, the best examples are at Greatstone-on-Sea, one of which is a 61-metre long (200-foot) concave wall mirror built in a parabolic shape.

A tester, adapted for use as a side table, at Bradford Abbas, Dorset.

SOUNDING BOARD An umbrella-like wooden canopy (*tester*) above a PULPIT which was intended to amplify and direct a preacher's voice for the benefit of his congregation. Most surviving sounding boards arc of Jacobean origin and were often incorporated into double- or three-decker pulpits.

SOUTERRAIN Souterrains are underground passageways associated with Iron Age dwellings in Ireland and Scotland, and in Cornwall where they are known as *fogous*. Souterrains are found in a variety of shapes and can measure up to 60 metres (196 feet) in length. Those in Scotland, where some 200 have been identified, mostly date from the period of Roman occupation. Examples on Orkney and Shetland were roofed with horizontal flag-stones and were entirely subterranean, while many of those in eastern Scotland were partially subterranean and probably had exposed timber roofs covered with stones and turfs. The Cornish fogous are from the Romano-British period and in Ireland souterrains date from the sixth to the twelfth centuries.

Various theories have been proposed with regard to the function of these strange tunnels, which extend outwards from a dwelling and appear to lead nowhere. In Scotland, where they are also known as *weems* or *earth houses*, they were once believed to have been provided as refuges or for ritual or ceremonial purposes. They are certainly well constructed and their curving, zigzag and bottle-like forms must have been created for a specific purpose, but the prevailing view is that they were simply storage chambers.
See also COURTYARD HOUSE

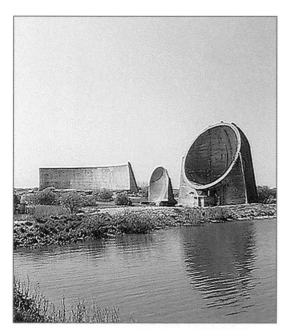

The sound mirrors at Greatstone-on-Sea on the Kent coast.

SOVEREIGN *see* COINAGE

SPANDREL The space between the curve of an arch and the surrounding moulding or framework, also between the curves of adjoining arches and the moulding above.

SPARS Sharpened timber pegs for fastening down thatch (*see* THATCHING).

SPAS The town of Spa in Belgium, celebrated from the medieval period for the curative properties of its mineral springs, gave its name to many British TOWNS which, from the eighteenth century, endeavoured to establish reputations as salubrious and fashionable inland resorts. The Romans encapsulated and controlled a number of mineral springs, notably at *Aquae Sulis* (Bath in Somerset), which was established on the Fosse Way within forty years of the invasion, and at *Aquae Arnemetiae* (Buxton in Derbyshire). From the later Roman period, and throughout the Dark Ages, there occurred a gradual translation of pagan beliefs and practices into those of the early Church, not least the veneration of water gods whose sacred springs were re-dedicated to local saints and often became places of healing and pilgrimage. In the Middle Ages the ecclesiastical authorities attempted to suppress the veneration of HOLY WELLS, which were correctly perceived to have pagan associations, but many continued to attract the lame and sick of medieval society and following the Reformation their popularity as places of curative pilgrimage increased, while that of SHRINES declined.

In the Elizabethan period, Buxton was already established as a fashionable resort for 'great numbers of nobility and gentry' (Camden) who came to drink the waters and were housed in fine lodgings erected by the enterprising Earl of Shrewsbury.

Under the late Stuart kings, spas were much frequented by those who sought both health and fashionable society: the waters of Bath were beginning to attract the aristocracy and Buxton and Harrogate (in Yorkshire) were popular with the northern gentry and their families. By the second half of the eighteenth century, Bath had become so popular that it was decided to rebuild its streets in a style befitting 'the solid splendour and comfort of that age'. (The first census of 1801 shows that, with 30,000 inhabitants, Bath had become ninth in the list of English cities.) In the late eighteenth century, a number of other towns attempted to emulate Bath's commercial success: Royal Leamington Spa in Warwickshire and Cheltenham Spa in Gloucestershire, with their pump rooms, promenades and elegant Regency terraces and town houses, are two notable examples of towns which enjoyed a transitory reputation for the efficacy of their waters. Cheltenham's mineral spring was discovered in 1715 and its first pump room opened in 1738. But it was the visit in 1788 of George III, an inveterate frequenter of spas, which established the town's reputation as a fashionable resort.

This was also a time of rapid imperial expansion and the therapeutic properties of mineral waters attracted large numbers of military officers and colonial administrators to spas such as Cheltenham, Leamington, Buxton and Matlock. In Derbyshire, it was the efforts of the fifth Duke of Devonshire (and of his successors) which, from 1780, established Buxton as a second Bath. Today, the nine springs, which are estimated to reach between 1,000 and 1,500 metres below ground (3,300 and 5,000 feet), produce nearly a quarter of a million gallons of warm water each day. Camden discovered the curative qualities of the mineral springs at Leamington in 1586 but it was not until 1786 that the first pump room was built and the town acquired its royal prefix following Queen Victoria's visit in 1838.

Not all spas were so successful: Tenbury Wells in Worcestershire, for example, attempted to establish itself as a spa in 1839. Towards the end of the nineteenth century, there was a revival of interest in 'balneology', founded on a contemporary fascination of science and a preoccupation with the deteriorating physical condition of the average town-dweller. The old notion of simply wallowing in the waters or drinking it in quarts was superseded by the use of 'atomizers' and 'vapourizers'. The waters were injected into orifices, jetted and sprayed or applied with electric shocks. There were inhalation rooms, humage rooms (for douching eyes, ears and throat 'with or without steam'), Sitz baths and needle baths, atomized spray rooms, the Aix-le-Bains douche and the Turkish system. But the revival was short-lived and the once-fashionable spas were succeeded by the Victorian and Edwardian seaside RESORTS.

SPECIFIC PERFORMANCE *see* LAW

SPEENHAMLAND SYSTEM A system of supplementary poor relief first adopted in the Berkshire village of Speenhamland in *c.* 1795. Parishes attempted to supplement low wages with an allowance related to the cost of bread. But the benefit differed from one parish to the next and was abused by employers who reduced wages knowing that parishes would make up the difference. As a result, the number of people claiming poor relief actually increased (*see* POOR LAW).

SPEER *and* **SPERE** *see* SCREENS PASSAGE

SPICES Most spices are indigenous to the Far East and were introduced to medieval Europe by travellers, notably Crusaders and Venetian merchants. Initially, they were used in the preparation of dyes, perfumes, confections, food preservatives, medicines and for ceremonial and religious purposes. But increasingly, with herbs, they were used to temper or enhance the pungent flavour of salted meat and game and were considered to be an essential luxury by the medieval and Tudor nobility.

Many spices were rare and expensive and consequently formed the basis of a unique currency, stimulating voyages of exploration and influencing trade and commerce. Competition for the control of routes encouraged advances in ship-building, navigation and communication and to the discovery of new lands.

Spices were purchased whole, and ground in a pestle and mortar, often by a specially designated Yeoman Powder Beater. There were three basic types of mixed spices: *whyte pouder* was ginger and mace mixed with confectioners' sugar; *pouder douce* was any blend of sweet spices, anise, fennel and nutmeg; and *pouder fort* was a blend of ginger or galangol, cinnamon and mace.

Interestingly, the convention of raising one's little finger while eating or drinking originates in the practice of keeping this finger free from grease when eating from medieval bowls so that it could be employed for dipping into the selection of spices which was always on the table.
See also HERBALS

SPIGOTS Wooden pegs used as bungs in the vent-holes of barrels and casks.

SPINNING GALLERY In Cumbria, an open-sided gallery for drying fleeces and, in fine weather, for spinning (*see illustration* overleaf).

SPIRES *see* CHURCH TOWERS

SPIRITUALITIES Sources of ecclesiastical income, such as TITHES, which were exempt from secular control. Conversely, *temporalities* were ecclesiastical holdings which were subject to such controls.

SPITAL A place-name element usually indicative of a medieval hospice.

SPOT HEIGHTS *see* BENCHMARKS *and* ORDNANCE SURVEY

SPRINGALD *see* SIEGES

SPRINGERS *and* **SPRINGING LINE** *See* ARCH

SPRINGS Springs emerge on slopes where an impermeable layer of material, such as clay, prevents further downward movement of accumulated rainwater. Or they may be brought to the surface along faults in underlying rock or at a water-table, the plane below which the ground is saturated. As reliable sources of fresh water, springs have determined the location of innumerable farmsteads and settlements from which have developed villages, towns and even cities. Chains of springs (*spring-lines*) often correspond with the contours of a scarp slope, as do the settlements which depend on them, or may be traced along a fault line by means of a geological map (*see* ORDNANCE SURVEY). Many springs became HOLY WELLS with both pagan and Christian associations. Place-name elements such as -well and -wall, derived from variations of the Old English *wella*, meaning 'well, spring or stream', are very common, as are -font and Font- names, from the Old English *funta*, itself derived, via the British *funt[93]n*, from the Latin *fontis*, meaning 'spring.' In the north of England, -keld and Kel- elements have the same meaning, from the Old Scandinavian *kelda*.

SQUARE BARROWS *see* BARROWS

SQUATTER Squatters were landless peasants who settled unlawfully on the margins of COMMONS in the hope of securing grazing and possibly land (*see* INTAKES). Squatters were a perennial problem in most parishes: they were an impediment to those who wished to exercise their customary rights of common but, if they belonged to the parish, they could also be a considerable burden on the poor rate if evicted.

Squatters' hovels often appeared overnight: from which fact is derived the fallacious belief that the

Former spinning gallery at the Farmers' Arms Inn, Lowick in Cumbria.

erection of a chimney somehow bestowed 'squatters' rights'. (In Wales, there existed a tradition known as the *tŷunnos*, the 'house of the night', whereby it was believed that settlement rights could be established if a dwelling were built between sunset and sunrise so that, by morning, smoke could be seen rising from its chimney: hence the alternative name, 'morning surprise'.) Landowners would sometimes offer work in a neighbouring parish so that the squatters' cottages could be demolished in their absence. Some landlords were prepared to compromise, however, accepting meagre rents from intakes rather than paying increased poor relief.

Innumerable squatter cottages were erected during the seventeenth and eighteenth centuries, on peripheral common land and broad road-side verges. Many remain today, characterized by their narrow 'slings' of land, or clustered in small hamlets, often with derogatory names such as Poverty End and Lawless Bottom.

Most squatters lived on the very edge of society, endeavouring to eke out a living from the left-over resources of a village community. The contemporary perception of their way of life as being shiftless and even immoral is apparent in a report to the Board of Agriculture, written in 1794:

> Let those who doubt go round the commons now open, and view the miserable huts and poor ill-cultivated, impoverished spots erected, or rather thrown together . . . which . . . affords them a very trifle towards their maintenance, yet operates upon their minds as a sort of independence; this idea leads the man to lose many days' work, by which he gets a habit of indolence; a daughter kept at home to milk a half starv'd cow, who being open to temptations soon turns harlot, and becomes a distrest mother instead of making a good useful servant.

SQUEEZE-BELLY *see* STILES

SQUINT (HAGIOSCOPE) Squint is a term coined by Victorian ecclesiologists to describe openings cut obliquely through masonry to afford a limited view

Hagioscope or squint at Mappowder, Dorset. As in other churches where the chancel has been extended to the east, the altar is no longer visible through the opening.

of the high altar from subsidiary chapels and side-aisles. Hagioscopes were usually provided for the benefit of CHANTRY priests who were required to interrupt their own proceedings when the parish priest began the High Mass. The notion that *leper squints* were provided for those who, because of their condition, were unable to join the congregation in the nave is almost certainly fallacious. In the medieval period the celebration of the Mass was not normally witnessed by the congregation, the chancel being separated from the nave by a CHANCEL SCREEN. Hermit-priests were sometimes lepers, however, and there are examples of unusual hagioscopes, the position of which suggests that they may have been provided for this purpose.

SQUIRE An entirely colloquial term for a LORD OF THE MANOR or major landowner.
See also ESQUIRE

STADDLES *and* **STADDLE STONES** *see* GRANARY *and* RICKYARD

STAGECOACH The earliest stagecoaches ran between some of the more important towns during the second half of the seventeenth century and were effectively larger versions of the private town coaches of the nobility. A century later, stagecoaches were competing for passengers with the first MAIL-COACHES but, although charging cheaper fares, they were not as comfortable or as fashionable as the rival service and were not so well protected from highway robbery. But on the many routes which were not contested, stagecoaches provided the only means of travel for the majority of the population and by the early nineteenth century, when roads were improving (*see* TURNPIKES), stagecoach travel increased significantly.

In many respects, later versions of the stagecoach bore a superficial resemblance to the mail-coach. But they carried more passengers, often with fourteen riding in the open in addition to the driver and guard and the first-class travellers seated in comparative comfort in the body of the coach. Unlike the sober mail-coaches, stagecoaches were painted in gaudy liveries with fanciful names such as *Tally Ho!*, *Red Rover* and *Esperance* painted on the side and rear panels, together with the coach's destination. Night coaches were cheaper, slower and notoriously unreliable. They were often drawn by teams which were unfit for daytime duties and even included horses which were blind. Passengers were frequently required to disembark before a coach could ascend a steep incline, but with the construction of new roads and the introduction of compacted road surfaces (*see* ROADS), conditions improved and the stagecoach companies prospered.

Most stagecoaches were driven four-in-hand and teams of horses were changed at coaching inns located at regular intervals along a route. Such inns may still be recognized by their wide arched entrances, of sufficient height to admit a crowded stagecoach to the inn yard and with fender stones on either side of the opening to prevent the coach wheels from colliding with the walls. Smaller, short-distance stagecoaches with teams of two horses ran on local and suburban routes (*see* OMNIBUS). By the mid-nineteenth century the use of stagecoaches was declining as they were superseded by the newly developed RAILWAYS.

STAGE-WAGON The stage-wagon (or 'waggon') was the poor man's STAGECOACH. It too plied between the major towns of Britain but carried a significantly larger proportion of merchandize and luggage. They were large panel-sided vehicles, with broad-tread wheels, drawn by teams of ten or twelve

Stagecoach preparing to leave the posting house in Old Road, Guildford, Surrey. (F. Frith)

heavy horses, the drivers walking alongside with cart-whips or directing the team from the back of an agile pony. Passengers were protected from the elements by a heavy canvas cover stretched over a series of hoops (*tilts*). Stage-wagons operated only during the spring and summer months, being entirely unsuited to wintry conditions. Even then, progress was so slow and the ride so uncomfortable that most would prefer to walk beside the wagon for at least part of their journey.

STAINED GLASS The term 'stained glass' is a misnomer: it should be described as 'painted and stained glass'. The earliest record of painted glass in England goes back as far as AD 680 when Bishop Biscop sent to Gaule for 'verrers' (later known as glaziers) to come to Monk Wearmouth in Cumbria, where he was building a church, to paint the glass and fix it in place. Although coloured glass was used in church WINDOWS from the seventh century, the earliest surviving examples in England are from the twelfth. Most medieval coloured glass was manufactured in France and Germany and imported into England where it was made into windows. The

Romans produced slabs of coloured glass, but the idea of holding pieces together within a lead framework to form a patterned window is believed by some to have originated in Byzantium.

Before the sixteenth century, window GLASS was made from a mixture of wood-ash and river sand which was heated into molten form and either spun on the end of a rod into a circular sheet or blown into a long cylinder and cut longitudinally to produce a flat sheet. Coloured glasses (*pot-metals*) were made by adding different metallic oxides to the molten clear glass: cobalt for blue, copper for ruby, manganese for violet, silver salts for yellow, iron for green or yellow, and small quantities of gold for a rose red. The colour produced also depended on the way the furnace was fired and different results were achieved by varying the level of oxidation. The ruby and blue glasses were very dark and a technique called *flashing* was used to make them more transparent.

Using a blowpipe, a bubble of molten coloured glass was dipped into molten white glass and worked into a white glass panel which was coated on one side with a layer of the desired colour. The design

408

(*cartoon*) of the window was drawn on a whitewashed table by draughtsmen (*tracers*) and the pieces of coloured glass cut to the required shape. Before the introduction of the diamond cutter in the sixteenth century, this was done by means of a hot iron which was drawn across the glass and cold water applied, causing the glass to crack along the incision. The pieces were then trimmed with a *grozing iron* to a more precise shape, and details such as faces, hair, limbs, linen folds and foliage were painted in a mixture of metallic oxide (iron or copper), powdered glass and gum. Finally, the glass sections were set out on an iron plate and covered with ash before being fired at a high temperature (using beechwood) in a clay and dung kiln. This fused the paint onto the coloured glass. The pieces were then reassembled and bound together in a lead framework (*armature*) with putty forced into the crevices between the lead and the glass. Lead was a most suitable material for this purpose, for it was malleable when unheated and, having a low melting point, was easily cast into strips with grooves at the sides to accommodate the glass.

As the craft developed, the lines of the lead framework were incorporated into the design itself and, from the fourteenth century, the flashed surface of coloured glass was often removed (*abraided*) to leave a pattern of clear glass which, when repainted with silver oxide and fired, turned to a dark yellow which passed for gold. This was particularly useful in heraldic designs when 'metal' charges (gold or silver) were depicted on a blue or red field, as in the ubiquitous royal arms of England (Gules three Lions passant guardant Gold). Many heraldic devices were not of a convenient shape to be confined within strips of lead and while large charges, such as beasts, could be built up of several pieces of glass leaded together, very small or repetitive charges were often difficult to reproduce. This problem was overcome by using small pieces of coloured glass and painting around the outline of the motif with brown enamel to leave only the shape as the unpainted surface. Alternatively, a whole sheet was painted with brown enamel and the appropriate area scraped away to form the desired shape. This technique may be seen in the equally ubiquitous ancient arms of France (Azure semy of Fleurs-de-lis Gold) in which the small diamond-shaped panels (*quarries* or *quarrels*) bearing fleurs-de-lis alternate with strips of blue glass for the field, producing a pattern of lozenges.

When completed, the window was fitted into the stonework opening by means of lead strips which were attached to iron saddle-bars or, in larger window openings, set within a decorative metal armature. As tracery became more complex in the fourteenth century, so the upper lights of windows were used to accommodate separate sections of an overall design.

Gothic buildings were conceived from the inside, the heavenward thrust of glass and stone culminating in the 'ethereal fragility' (Yarwood) of the perpendicular period (*see* GOTHIC ARCHITECTURE). The 'realm of divine and saintly imagery' which, in the windows of the great abbey churches, seemed to reach almost from earth into heaven, may indeed have educated and informed a largely illiterate Christian population (*see* CHRISTIAN SYMBOLS) but there can be little doubt that its principal function was a spiritual one. Windows of the twelfth and thirteenth centuries (up to *c.* 1260) were predominantly ruby and blue and created a 'homogeneous fabric of light' (Panofsky) which induced a sense of almost mystical contemplation. The 'unearthly glow' of suspended light, which characterized glass of this period, is rarely evident in windows of the fourteenth century, which inclined more to yellows and greens, and is entirely missing from the wide perpendicular windows of the fifteenth century.

Regrettably, little early glass remains intact in England and it is difficult for us to appreciate its magnificence without visiting European cathedrals such as Chartres. From the mid-twelfth century, most windows comprised a central pictorial motif contained within a medallion and a geometrical border. The years 1260 to 1325 are notable for *grisaille glass* (from the French *gris*, meaning 'grey'): large areas of clear quarries surrounded by borders of monochrome foliage decoration and occasional medallions in colour. The best-known example is the Five Sisters window in the north transept of York Minster which has an almost three-dimensional quality. Many later medieval windows were *donor windows*, erected both as memorials and to commemorated the generosity of benefactors. For this reason at least half the surviving medieval church glass contains an element of heraldry: usually that of an armigerous family or group of benefactors. At this time, the practice of endowing chantries was particularly popular. These were bequests which enabled priests to pray for the souls of the departed and of relatives, friends and others, including the king and influential lords (*see* CHANTRY *and* CHANTRY CHAPELS). Shields or other heraldic devices in a chapel window may therefore be those of the people for whom prayers were to be said as well as those of the deceased benefactor.

Throughout the medieval and Tudor periods, senior churchmen, magnates, guilds and fraternities

Fifteenth-century glass commemorating Sir Thomas Clopton and his two wives in Holy Trinity church, Long Melford, Suffolk.

endowed money for the repair of churches and, especially in the fourteenth century, groups of citizens would often combine to pay for the refurbishing of their parish church. At Dorchester Abbey in Oxfordshire, for example, the south window of the chancel contains twenty-one heraldic shields to record those who financed the extension of the sanctuary in *c*. 1340. Perhaps the greatest of all commemorative windows is the magnificent fourteenth-century east window in the choir of Gloucester Cathedral. Constructed between 1347 and 1350, it is 11.6 metres wide (38 feet) and 22 metres high (72 feet): the size of a tennis court and the largest stone traceried window in England. In the lower lights are the shields of the Gloucestershire knights who fought at the battle of Crècy in 1346. In the fifteenth century, donor windows became popular and these often contained full coats of arms or kneeling figures wearing tabards of the benefactor's arms.

Following the Reformation, countless medieval windows were destroyed and replaced with glass in which no religious or allegorical subjects were permitted. The duties of the iconoclast are vividly described by Richard Culmner in *Cathedrall Newes from Canterburie* (1644): '. . . on the top of the citie ladder, near sixty steps high, with a whole pike in the hand, rattling down Becket's glassy bones from the great idolatrous window.' Heraldry was an obvious and politically acceptable alternative and one which particularly appealed to the newly-created Tudor aristocracy. Anxious to prove themselves equal in blood to the old magnatial families, they erected MONUMENTS and commemorative windows which positively radiated heraldic splendour, their arms incorporating numerous acquired (or assumed) ancestral QUARTERINGS. The fashion for Renaissance motifs, landscapes and classical figures continued into the seventeenth, eighteenth and early nineteenth centuries and, from the late sixteenth century, transparent coloured enamels were widely used so that windows were treated as complete pictures and resembled transparent oil paintings.

The Gothic Revival of the nineteenth century encouraged a return to the use of stained glass, notably by artists such as William Morris and Burne-Jones, whose windows in the chancel of Birmingham Cathedral are particularly fine. In parish churches, many new windows containing heraldic glass were erected by lords of the manor and often these contained series of shields showing the arms of predecessors. This practice seems to have been popular with those who acquired manors by purchase rather than by inheritance, as at Puddletown church in Dorset and Aldermaston in Berkshire. Also during the nineteenth and twentieth centuries, glass may have been installed or refurbished as a memorial to an individual or family and small shields, military insignia and school or university arms were often incorporated in a window design or in the tracery lights. Many such memorials commemorate those who lost their lives in the world wars.

At what stage and to what extent secular buildings were glazed is uncertain (*see* GLASS). Chaucer (before 1372) refers to his chamber where 'with glas were al the windows wel y glazed' with scenes from the Trojan wars. Stained glass in domestic buildings was intended to be both decorative and to impress visitors, and the heraldry of the owner and the families with whom he was associated were obvious subjects. At Athelhampton in Dorset there are several superb examples of late fifteenth-century and early sixteenth-century heraldic windows in the Great Hall, though some bays contain Victorian restorations. The importance of heraldic display to the Tudor aristocracy is evident in the magnificent library windows at Montacute House in Somerset and Charlecote Park in Warwickshire.

Glass is particularly vulnerable both to the elements and to vandalism and while some stained glass remains in its original location many fragments (or even entire windows) have been moved several times and may now be combined with glass of an entirely different period. A series of twelfth-century biblical figures at Canterbury Cathedral in Kent are surmounted by heraldic figures of the fourteenth century, while at Salisbury in Wiltshire there are six thirteenth-century shields at the base of the west window which is composed principally of fifteenth-century glass. During the Gothic Revival of the nineteenth century there was a flourishing market in miscellaneous fragments from the windows of 'restored churches', and many of these may still be seen illuminating the stairwells of Victorian houses.

STAIRCASES The earliest staircases were little more than ladders linking two floors. (Stairs of this type were occasionally to be found in miners' cottages of the north-east of England in the early decades of the twentieth century.) In early medieval CASTLES and monastic buildings, solid stone exterior stairs were constructed against courtyard walls, providing access at first-floor level. In turrets, or within the thickness of stone walls, spiral staircases (*turnpike stairs*) were contained within cylindrical shafts and rose in a series of identical stone steps (*winders*), each cut to fit precisely within the shaft and held in place by the interlocking core of the steps immediately above and below. Such stairs invariably ascend in a clockwise direction thereby facilitating the use of a pike when facing down the stair in a defensive position but impairing its use when attempting to ascend by force. By the fifteenth century, wooden 'open tread' ladder-type staircases (without *risers*) provided access within a building, usually by means of a single flight set against a wall or in two flights at right-angles to each other in the corner of a hall. Such staircases were usually built of oak and were supported by a massive pillar (*newel post*). By the late sixteenth century, the *dog-leg* staircase had developed. This was of heavy construction with broad flights rising parallel to each other, connected at each level by landings. Early seventeenth century examples have square oak newel posts at each angle, and thick supports (*balusters*) for the handrail which were often elaborately carved (*turned*) on a lathe. From the dog-leg construction evolved the *open well* which is to be found in many Jacobean buildings of the early seventeenth century. In this type of staircase, the flights ascend the walls of a square stairwell around a central space.

Seventeenth-century oak staircases were particularly heavy and ornate, often with carved heraldic beasts surmounting the newel posts, though from the 1670s they were less ponderous in appearance with shaped and moulded handrails and panelled balustrades and newels, carved with elaborate scrolls and foliage. Eighteenth-century staircases were less massive and often of superb craftsmanship, though work of this quality was found only in the finest houses. (In 1725 wood-carvers who specialized in the manufacture of staircase components could earn 3*s* a day when most domestic servants earned little more than £2 a year.) From 1700, pine was widely used instead of oak which was becoming scarce, especially in the south-eastern counties, and soft-wood balusters were usually painted an off-white (*stone colour*). From the mid-eighteenth century, staircases with wrought iron balusters and mahogany handrails became fashionable and thereafter balusters and handrails (*banisters*) became progressively lighter in construction and of more elegant appearance. Many eighteenth-century and Regency staircases had stone or marble steps and open-string balustrades with slim ornamental balusters in groups of twos or threes. They were often of cantilevered construction, with one end built into the wall, and were of circular or oval design (*geometrical stairs*). Nineteenth-century

Closed-string carved wood staircase, c. 1680.

staircases often reflected Gothic Revival influences with wrought-iron balusters, handrails and newels. But by 1900 the typical staircase of a fashionable residence had a mahogany handrail and pine balusters, usually 'grained' to look like mahogany.

There are two basic methods of stair construction: the *closed string* and the *open string* (or *cut string*) stairs. The *string* is the plank of wood (or panelling) which runs along the side of the stair, and parallel to the wall, by which the horizontal upper surfaces of the steps (*treads*) are supported at the outer edge. The string of a closed stair has a straight edge which conceals the ends of the treads, while that of an open stair is cut in steps on which the treads are seated and on which the balusters stand. Too often in Victorian and Edwardian houses, balusters have been boxed in with hardboard and the decorative carving of newel posts removed. The underside (*soffit*) of a staircase of this period is invariably covered with lath and plaster which provide additional strength to the structure. When the outer edge of the lowest step of a staircase is carried round the newel in a scroll it is known as a *curtail step*.

STAITHE *see* FERRIES

STĀN An Old English place-name element which may appear alone, as in Staines, Surrey, where it means simply 'stone' (perhaps a pronounced landscape feature or even a Roman milestone), and as a second element -*ston(e)*, as in Radstone, Northamptonshire, from *rōde stān*, meaning 'rood stone', in other words a 'stone with a cross'. Folkstone, Kent, probably once possessed a 'meeting-place stone', and Harston, Leicestershire, a 'grey boundary stone'. As a first element, *stān*- may refer to a stone enclosure or building, a quarry or even to the stony nature of the local soil, as at Stanwardine, Shropshire, or to the 'paved [Roman] way' at Stanway, Essex. Many Stow- names are also derived from *stān*, as in Stowell, Somerset, meaning 'stony stream', and Stowford, Devon, a 'stony ford'. *See also* STOW-.

STANDARD (i) In managed deciduous WOODLAND, standard trees are those which are permitted to grow freely without coppicing or pollarding. Understorey timber was harvested on a ten- to twenty-year cycle, but standard trees (mostly oaks) were felled between eighty and a hundred years after planting to provide heavy structural timbers. They were usually replaced with saplings planted at a density of twelve to the acre (*see* COPPICE *and* POLLARD).

(ii) The greatest of the medieval LIVERY flags, the long, tapering standard served as a mustering point for feudal retainers during military campaigns and at tournaments. It carried the household liveries and badges of a particular magnate, and in battle several standards and GUIDONS would be in simultaneous use, but only one BANNER which was essentially a personal flag. Civic standards are sometimes hung in parish churches as at Launceston in Cornwall.

STANDING STONE *see* MONOLITH, OGHAM STONES, STONE CIRCLES *and* STONE ROWS

STANEGATE *see* ROMAN FORTS AND CAMPS *and* ROMAN ROADS

STANNARIES The tin-mining district of Cornwall and Devon, in which mining activities are regulated by the *Stannaries Court*. In 1508 the Stannary tinners were granted exemption from certain forms of taxation by a charter of Henry VII which was ratified by Henry VIII in 1511 (*see* MINERALS).

STAPLE *see* WOOL

STAR CHAMBER (COURT OF) A chamber at the royal palace of Westminster, said to have gilt stars painted on the ceiling, where in the fourteenth and fifteenth centuries the Privy Council met in its judicial capacity to consider both civil and criminal matters affecting the Crown. Revived by Henry VII in 1487, the Court of Star Chamber dealt particularly with the suppression of LIVERY AND MAINTENANCE and with perjury and serious misdemeanours such as riots. Under the Tudors and early Stuarts the court acquired notoriety for its arbitrary and oppressive judgements. It was abolished in 1640.

STARE DECISIS *see* LAW

STATELAND *see* KINGDOMS (ANCIENT)

STATE PAPERS State Papers are the official documents of the departments of secretaries of state from the early sixteenth century. Those in the Public Record Office commence in 1509 and cover a period of two and a half centuries. Indispensable to the local historian are the *Letters and Papers: Foreign and Domestic* which contain a wealth of information. Many State Papers are available in published form are listed in *Government Publications, Sectional List 24: British National Archives* (HMSO).

STATUTE OF MORTMAIN *see* POOR LAW

STEAM POWER The development of the atmospheric engine, and its successor the steam engine, was a technological advance of considerable significance. Not only were they the first 'man-made' sources of power, replacing wind, water and muscle, they were also chiefly responsible for the INDUSTRIAL REVOLUTION and Britain's ascendancy as a major industrial power.

The principles of governing the operation of atmospheric and steams engines were understood by the seventeenth century, but it was not until the second decade of the eighteenth century that effective commercial engines were developed. Thomas Newcomen (1663–1729) erected the first practical working atmospheric engine in 1712. A metal-worker and toolsmith by trade, his 'Fire Engine' was designed with a working knowledge of the resources and materials available. Supported by a brick and wood building, it had a timber engine beam and low pressure boiler. The piston was sealed with leather and the seal made good with water. The only component which required specialist manufacture was the hand-finished brass cylinder, though even this expense was greatly reduced by the development of good quality cast-iron cylinders by Darby and Wilkinson. At the time, Newcomen engines required a considerable capital investment by mine-owners and industrialists but they were the only effective means of removing water from mines and by 1775 there were some sixty engine-driven pumps in the Cornish metal-mines alone.

But the Newcomen engines were not efficient: condensation of steam took place within the cylinder which had to be cooled for each piston stroke. James Watt (1736–1819), a Scottish engineer, overcame the problem of fuel wastage at each cycle of the cylinder by introducing a separate condenser which was cooled while the temperature of the main cylinder was maintained by insulation. Watt was granted his historic patent for 'a new method for lessening the consumption of steam and fuel in fire engines' in 1679 and six years later he went into partnership with the Birmingham industrialist Matthew Boulton (1728–1809). Further innovations included the concept of 'horse power' for the measurement of output; a double-acting engine in which steam expanded and condensed alternately on both sides of the piston; a flying-ball governor which controlled the speed of the engine; and the conversion of the back-and-forth motion of a piston to rotative motion which extended the use of engines from pumping to driving lathes, cable-drums, hoists and textile machinery which had previously been dependent on water-power. Boulton and Watt engines proved so efficient that royalties were calculated by comparing fuel consumption with that of earlier Newcomen engines.

Richard Trevithick (1771–1833) was an English engineer who pioneered the railway locomotive. In order to improve the efficiency of the steam engine to cope with the increasing depth of mines, he developed a double-acting model which worked at considerably higher pressures than the Watt engines. Unlike earlier engines, which had operated on the same principle as that of a kettle over a fire, Trevithick's Cornish boiler consisted of a long horizontal cylinder in which the fire-box, which ran through the centre, was completely surrounded by the boiler. The double-acting closed cylinder, in which the piston was forced both up and down by steam pressure, had been developed by Watt but its efficiency had been impaired by the use of pressures which were little higher than atmospheric pressure. The Cornish boiler was patented in 1802 for stationary and locomotive use and during the next half century, Trevetherick erected fifty stationary engines for mills, ironworks and mines in Cornwall and Wales. His first steam carriage of 1801 was not a success: neither public opinion nor road surfaces favoured it. He then built a steam locomotive for the ironworks at Pen-y-Darn in South Wales which, in 1804, successfully hauled five wagons containing 10 tons of iron and seventy men, though it was found that the cast-iron rails were not adequate (*see* RAILWAYS). Many Boulton and Watt low-pressure engines remained in use, even into the early decades of the twentieth century. But the development of high-pressure double-cylinder (*compound*) and triple-expansion steam engines in a variety of forms made possible the extraordinary industrial and commercial expansion of the Victorian Age.

-STED *and* -STEAD The Old English *stede*, meaning 'place' or 'site of a building', is a common place-name element, particularly in the counties of south-east England and East Anglia. Chipstead, Kent, for example, is derived from *cēapstede*, meaning 'market place', and the various Hempsteads are simply *hāmestedes* or 'homesteads', though Hempstead, Norfolk, is more likely 'the place where hemp (*henep*) was grown'.

STEEL A malleable alloy of iron and carbon. In the eighteenth century, steel for the Sheffield cutlery industry was made by a process called *cementation*. Bars of good quality wrought iron (*see* MINERALS), surrounded by powdered charcoal, were hermetically sealed in a sandstone or clay container and heated for up to ten days. This process produced 'blister bars' which only had carbon diffused into the surface and therefore needed repeated forge-welding to provide a more homogeneous steel. In 1740 Benjamin Huntsman succeeded in producing an exceptionally hard steel by re-melting blister steel in a crucible and skimming off the slag. But it was not possible to produce such good quality steel on a large scale until the 1860s when the Bessemer converter was introduced.

STELE *see* MONUMENTS

STELLAR VAULT *see* VAULTING

STEPPING-STONES It is almost impossible to date stepping-stones, or *hippings* as they are called in parts of the north of England. If they are large and eroded through constant use they may be of early medieval origin, while others may have been provided for local purposes which are not immediately apparent. On Dartmoor, for example, a CORPSE ROAD crosses the river Tavy by means of a series of rectangular granite stepping-stones, each at right angles to the stream and of sufficient length to allow the bearers to cross two by two on their way to Lydford churchyard.

STEWARD The chief agent of a manorial lord with responsibility for the administration of a manor, for maintaining its records and presiding over its courts. *See also* BAILIFF

STEW PONDS *see* FISH-PONDS

STILES From the Old English *stigel*, meaning 'to climb', stiles allow people but not livestock to climb over a fence, hedge or wall. Strictly speaking, many so-called stiles are really gates which allow limited access through an obstruction rather than over it. The *squeeze-belly*, for example, consists of a pair of timber posts set close together in the ground but curving upwards and outwards so that pedestrians may pass through by turning sideways as they do so. A similar arrangement, but of wrought iron, may be found in the ornamental fencing of gardens and park-land, as may the traditional *kissing gate* which, when opened, allows a pedestrian to pass into an intermediate enclosed space from which he may proceed only by closing the same gate behind him. A true stile consists of an arrangement of steps, usually constructed of wood or stone and often incorporated into the structure of the fence or wall itself. At one time, there were numerous attractive regional variations of design and materials but, regrettably, few have survived. In the Lake District the term refers to FOOTPATHS leading on to high ground, as in High Stile.

STILTED ARCH *see* ARCH

STINT The number of cattle a commoner was permitted to pasture on a common. In the north of England, the term *gate* has the same meaning.

STINTED COMMONS *see* COMMONS

STITCH A small portion of land.

STOCKS An act of 1405 required that every community should maintain stocks for the punishment of offenders. These were usually erected in public places such as village greens or market squares so that passers-by could contribute to the severity of the sentence, details of which were sometimes displayed on an adjacent notice board. Most stocks consisted of a pair of 'clamping boards' which closed together like jaws, with a hinge at one end and a padlock at the other. Offenders were secured by their ankles which protruded through apertures cut into the inner edges of the boards. This form of punishment was practised throughout the medieval period and continued to the beginning of the nineteenth century when the

Stocks at Holwell, Dorset.

administration of justice was becoming less parochial and more centralized. The term is derived from the Old English *stocc* meaning 'tree trunk' and relates to the upright posts by which the clamping boards were supported. Stocks provided both a means of confinement and a method of punishment by public humiliation and were sometimes combined with a PILLORY and WHIPPING post.

Unpaid manorial or parish officers (petty constables), who were answerable to the justices of the peace for the maintenance of law and order and for the execution of warrants, could restrain trouble-makers in the stocks pending their appearance before the magistrates. Petty offences such as drunkenness, blasphemy and participating in sports on a Sunday could be punished by confinement *in compedibus* – usually four hours in the stocks. Beggars and vagrants, both male and female, could be whipped bare-back at the whipping post or set in the stocks before being returned to their place of origin (*see* LAW AND ORDER).

A remarkable number of village stocks have survived, indicative perhaps of the fact that every community once possessed its own means of punishment. It is unlikely that they will have retained their original medieval timbers, however, and most have been provided with replacement clamping boards. There are several original metal stocks, mostly dating from the late eighteenth and nineteenth centuries. Those at Painswick in Gloucestershire are constructed of iron and, because of their appearance, are known as 'spectacles stocks'. Elsewhere, there are examples of stocks with accommodation for two, three and even four miscreants and a set at Dorchester in Dorset (now kept in the cells of the former Crown Court) has five apertures, suggesting that on occasions only one leg was restrained. Strangely, some offenders were provided with shelter from the elements, as at Ottery St Mary in Devon where the stocks were constructed beneath a protective canopy. There are examples of whipping posts at Stow in Lincolnshire, Aldbury in Hertfordshire and Meldreth in Cambridgeshire. The location of village stocks may sometimes be ascertained from the summaries of archaeological listings compiled for each parish by county record offices.

See also LOCK-UP, MARKET HALL *and* PUNISHMENT

STONE AGE The first stage of three in the classification of prehistoric periods devised by Christian Thompsen (1788–1865) on the basis of the material used for weapons and tools; the others being the BRONZE AGE and the IRON AGE. This tripartite classification, which was subsequently elaborated and refined, was broadly confirmed in Europe by stratification of archaeological finds. However, it remains little more than a convenient series of benchmarks for the amateur historian, and the majority of archaeologists prefer to work from a CULTURAL CHRONOLOGY which may be more precisely applied to their research.

The Stone Age period is itself sub-divided into the *Palaeolithic* (formerly called the Old Stone Age), the *Mesolithic* (the Middle Stone Age) and the *Neolithic* (the New Stone Age).

The *Palaeolithic* period was by far the longest and is usually sub-divided into Lower (extending from the first known appearance of artefacts 2.5 million years ago), Middle (100,000 to 35,000 years ago) and Upper (35,000 to 11,000) Palaeolithic. Dating is inevitably approximate and has recently been thrown into confusion by the discovery of comparatively sophisticated flint implements at a site at High Lodge, near Mildenhall, Suffolk, which appear to date from 450,000 to 500,000 years ago. Before this discovery the only comparable flints found in Britain and continental Europe were believed to date from 100,000 to 200,000 years ago. Such 'tool kits' of well-shaped flakes, chipped from the sides of flint nodules, and comprising knives, serrated cutting tools, woodworking tools and scrapers for cleaning animal skins, are far removed from the only type of sophisticated implement, the hand axe, previously known from this early period. The evidence of High Lodge '. . . throws conventional ideas about cultural succession in the Stone Age right out of the window' (Dr Jill Cook). The Middle Palaeolithic period was the era of Neanderthal man and the Upper Palaeolithic period saw the emergence of *Homo sapiens*, capable of surviving the tundra conditions of the last glaciation, living in caves and in the open and hunting migratory animals such as the reindeer. It seems likely that a complex system of social interaction and verbal communication had developed, thereby enabling individuals to co-operate in resolving mutual problems: to provide warmth, shelter and protection and to hunt in bands.

Excavations in Gough's Cave at Cheddar Gorge, Somerset, have produced bone, antler and stone implements made by late Ice Age cave-dwellers 11,000 to 10,000 BC, including a rare type of prehistoric tool made of reindeer antler and with deeply incised spiral grooves which would have served to plane the wooden shafts of spears or arrows or to soften leather thongs. The Cheddar excavations also revealed evidence of probable cannibalistic practices. Like other similar sites, the Gorge was probably of great economic (and possibly ritual) significance. It is likely to have provided a natural funnel through which migrating wild horses, red deer and other animals had to pass on their way through the Mendip hills, and the caves would have served as bases from which the passing herds could be ambushed.

The *Mesolithic* period (10,000 to 5,000 BC) falls between the end of the last glacial regime and the advent of agriculture. Separation of what is now Britain from the continent of Europe took place during this period. Mesolithic man enjoyed an alternative diet to that of his predecessors, whose limitless supply of meat from the disappearing tundras was gradually replaced by a diversity of smaller animals, fish, birds and plants. Such resources were both seasonal and variable, depending on habitat, and demanded a nomadic way of life with temporary occupation of domestic sites and hunting/gathering groups of various sizes. Flint tools and weapons of the period reflect this diversity: many are tiny *microliths*, used as barbs and arrow tips designed for specialized purposes. Dug-out boats were made which were used in transport and for fishing, with nets, traps and hooks and lines. Bows were widely used, as were antler or bone harpoons. Mesolithic man may also have cleared small areas of woodland to attract the animals he hunted and to encourage a diversity of edible plant-life.

The *Neolithic* period (5,000 to 2,400 years BC) is characterized by the first domestication of animals, the use of polished or ground stone weapons and implements, the development of pottery and the widespread clearance of the native forest. When the first immigrant farmers arrived from western Europe, some time before 4000 BC, they would have discovered an indigenous population of aboriginal hunter/gatherers and a land clothed with temperate deciduous forest. They brought with them an understanding of basic agriculture and animal husbandry that enabled them to master their environment. Many areas of woodland were cleared, particularly on the lighter soils of river basins, and cultivated to produce primitive wheats and barleys or grazed by pigs, sheep and (especially) cattle. In some areas (notably Ireland and Cumbria), small patches of forest may have been cleared by felling and burning and crops sown. When yields fell the land was grazed and eventually reverted to forest when new areas were cleared. Elsewhere (as on the chalk uplands of Wessex) clearances were on a larger scale and permanent.

One of several Neolithic burial chambers in the Boyne Valley, Co. Meath, dating from c. 3000 BC.

Inevitably, few traces remain of this first 'agricultural revolution', or of the domestic settlements of the Neolithic farmers themselves. It is the burial sites and ceremonial centres of the later Neolithic period that serve to remind us of their success and of the distinctive social organization that resulted from it. With an accumulation of surplus food and wealth in the form of goods for exchange and barter, settled communities developed and there was a rapid growth in population, and a consequential development of trade and industry based on the mining of flints and other stones for the large-scale production of polished axes and other artefacts. These communities generally consisted of dispersed homesteads of small rectangular buildings each occupied by a nuclear family, though towards the end of the Neolithic period larger village communities developed, some of which were defended. There is also apparent in many homesteads of the period a striking similarity of architectural design with contemporary tombs, as though the homes of the living were models for the residences of the dead. The tiny artificial island settlement in Loch Olabhat on the Hebridean isle of North Uist, for example, is roughly circular with a diameter of 22.9 metres (75 feet), a massive stone façade and an in-turned funnel-like entrance. Tombs in the area are of similar design and dimensions. This settlement probably housed an extended family of up to a dozen people while a typical local Neolithic tomb would have accommodated at least a dozen individuals from the same community or family line.

Tombs, of course, were made of stone and designed to last forever whereas dwellings were mainly of wood and were demolished and rebuilt every few decades. They were constructed of thatch and wattle on timber uprights and stonewall footings and appear to have had internal walls, hearths and box-beds and floors covered with straw and heather. The artificial island at Loch Olabhat was constructed of 20,000 cubic feet of stone, was protected by a perimeter post and wattle fence on a stonewall base and was approached by a 12 metre (40 feet) wooden causeway. Built in *c.* 3500 BC it was occupied for at least three centuries during which it was remodelled more than eleven times. Hundreds of similar artificial islands were constructed in Scottish and Irish lakes but Loch Olabhat is by far the earliest of those identified. Food remains suggest that the occupants raised cattle, grew cereals and collected hazel nuts from the woods and winkles from the seashore.

Throughout Britain, the widespread construction, by means of organized communal labour, of structures such as BARROWS, HENGE MONUMENTS, CAUSEWAYS and CAUSE-WAYED ENCLOSURES, suggests the existence of unified and hierarchical societies with tribal and territorial obligations and traditions.

For the Prehistoric Society *see* APPENDIX I

STONE AXE FACTORIES Prehistoric axes were of two types: those for everyday use, and those crafted for ceremonial purposes. They were made from two basic materials: FLINT, which was obtained in large quantities from flint mines, and hard igneous or metamorphic rocks which were obtained from axe factories. This is the name now given to sites which were selected both for the quality of the material extracted and the ease with which it was worked. Some 550 axe factories have been identified in the Lake District of Cumbria where tuff (formed from volcanic ashes) was extracted and roughly shaped on site before being transported to the coast for polishing and grinding. It has been estimated that scree at Pike O'Stickle in the Langdales represents the debris from 45,000 to 75,000 stone axe-heads. Elsewhere, axe factories have been identified in County Antrim in Ireland, the Lleyn peninsula in Wales and in Cornwall. Neolithic and Bronze Age axe-heads have been found at considerable distances from the factories where they originated, suggesting the existence of a systematic trading system.

STONE CIRCLES There are more than 1,000 stone circles in Britain. They were dismissed as primitive by the Romans and condemned as 'the devil's work' by the early Church, despite its policy of adapting pagan sites for its own purposes. In the Middle Ages the ecclesiastical authorities ordered the demolition of many circles, including that at Avebury, Wiltshire, where the stones proved indestructible and had to be toppled over and buried. (Forty such stones were uncovered in 1938, one of which was found to conceal the corpse of a barber, together with coins dated 1307 and scissors still in perfect working order.) Medieval man believed the stones to have been wrought by 'the great skill of Magick' of Saracen giants (hence *sarsens*), or by Merlin or Julius Caesar. But this did not prevent him from plundering the circles and avenues for building materials, a practice which continued until the beginning of the twentieth century. Sir Christopher Wren thought that stone circles had been spewed forth by a volcano, while Samuel Pepys asserted that they were surely 'growing out of the ground'. In the seventeenth century, antiquaries transformed the circles into druidical temples, and by the eighteenth they had become places of bloodcurdling sacrificial rites.

In the first half of the twentieth century, it was generally accepted that the stones had been erected by invading hordes of BEAKER warriors, and in the 1960s they became observatories, designed by astronomer-priests with an understanding of geometry and advanced mathematics. To some, they are mystical generators, pumping out energy along a prehistoric national grid (*see* LEY LINES). Why should Neolithic man have hauled more than 200 4-metre, 35-ton sarsen stones across almost 5 km (3 miles) of the Malborough Downs to Avebury? What was so special about the site at Stonehenge in Wiltshire that it was considered necessary to transport the blue stones all the way from the Preseli Hills of Pembrokeshire? Many archaeologists are now of the opinion that the blue stones were not transported to Stonehenge by man but were moved onto the Wiltshire uplands by glaciers and that concentrations of these 'alien' stones provided the impetus for the erection of the stone circles. The consensus view seems to be that the majority of stone circles, which date from the period *c.* 3200 to *c.* 1800 BC, were erected for religious and ritual purposes and as centres of tribal assembly and commercial activity, many of them within existing henges (*see* HENGE).

But every circle is different, both in design and construction and each may therefore reflect the requirements and religious practices of a particular tribe. Why, for example, was a tiny chambered tomb carefully constructed within the tapering pillars of Callanash in the Hebrides? Why is Stonehenge the only circle in Britain to have lintel-stones spanning its uprights? Why do some circles contain a MONOLITH at their centre and others have avenues of stones leading from them? The most likely explanation is that, because of their location, the sites attracted a concentration of human activity so that, with the passing of the centuries, they acquired an aura of cultural and religious continuity and pre-eminence, just as the great medieval cathedrals represent the genius of our ancestors in our own millennium. Using all their ingenuity, both Neolithic and medieval man attempted to endow such places with suitably impressive structures, using materials and techniques which, for their respective periods, were exciting and innovative. Like the kings and magnates of the Middle Ages, prehistoric chieftains and their families chose to be buried in ground which had been sanctified by successive generations of their forebears, and it seems likely that the authority and status of certain dynasties is reflected in the periodic remodelling and embellishment of the greatest of the stone circles, just as the potency of certain medieval

The Rollright Stones on the Oxfordshire–Warwickshire border near Long Compton.

shrines is evident in the architectural splendour of the great monastic churches.

The proposition that the stone circles were essentially ceremonial and religious centres is supported by the discovery, in 1989, of a unique and vast double-ring timber enclosure located astride the river Kennet 1.6 km (1 mile) south-east of Avebury circle. Dating from *c.* 2500 BC, it was probably but one component in a massive complex of structures which were spread over at least four square miles of countryside and which included the Avebury circle itself. The circular outer wall had a circumference of 700 metres (2,300 feet) and was probably about 7 metres high (23 feet), whils a second inner wall was 540 metres in circumference (1,770 feet) and up to 9 metres high (29.5 feet). It is estimated that at least 3,000 tree trunks were required for the construction of the double enclosure, and its appearance must have been singularly impressive. Archaeological evidence suggests that the structure was used for religious and secular purposes, with perhaps no clear division between the two. Many stone circles and other prehistoric sites are also located in the immediate vicinity of rivers, or are linked to them by 'avenues' of stones or parallel embankments, and water worship of some description may have featured in religious practices, particularly those of the BEAKER period (2700 to 2000 BC), at which time there was a significant increase in the development of henges and circles.

It would appear that stone circles were therefore erected as places of assembly, sanctified by continuity of use and by offerings of human cremated bone, for seasonal gatherings and the performance of rituals, possibly associated with water and with the sun or moon. Each is different both in design and construction and therefore in conception. Many are of sufficient size to accommodate an entire tribe, while others are simply the remains of kerb stones which once enclosed a (now eroded) round barrow and are not stone circles at all.

STONE ROOFS *see* SLATES

STONE ROWS There are seventy known examples of stone rows on Dartmoor in Devon. These alignments of small stones, dating from *c.* 2700 to *c.* 2000 BC, may be found in single or double rows and, occasionally, in threes. Alignments are not always straight, and the double rows are not of sufficient width to have been routeways and are often blocked at each end by larger terminal stones. They are not associated with STONE CIRCLES, or with the later Bronze-Age field-patterns of the Moor, and their original function remains a mystery.

STONEWARDEN *see* HIGHWAY

STOUP A small stone basin, originally containing holy water, set on the right of the main door or porch of medieval churches. Stoups, which have no drain, were replenished regularly with holy water, which was mixed with salt, exorcised and blessed. Before crossing the threshold of the church, a visitor would dip his fingers in the holy water and make the sign of the cross, thereby acknowledging his baptismal promises, the shedding of Christ's blood and the washing away of sins. The word is correctly *stop*, meaning a pail or basin, and the practice was suppressed following the Reformation.

-STOW A place-name element derived from the Old English *stōw*, meaning 'place', as in Chepstow, Monmouthshire, which was a 'place of trade' (*cēap stōw*), and Bristol, a 'place by a bridge' (*brycg stōw*). When used alone, *stōw* probably implies a 'holy place', possibly a monastery or hermitage. Stow-on-the-Wold, on the Gloucestershire Cotswolds, was once *Edwardstowe*, its church dedicated to St Edward the Martyr.
For Stow- *see* STĀN

STRAKER-WAY *see* COMMONS

STRAPWORK Ornamental interlacing of broad bands or 'straps' commonly found in the decoration of late Elizabethan and Jacobean ceilings, friezes, panelling and screens (*see* ELIZABETHAN AND JACOBEAN ARCHITECTURE).

STRAT- (*also* **STREAT-**, **STREET-** *and* **STRET-**) A place-name element from the Old English *strǣt*, derived from the Latin *strata*, meaning 'paved way'. *See also* ROMAN ROADS

STREET *see* ROMAN ROADS *and* STRAT-

STRETCHER A brick or piece of masonry placed lengthwise in the face of a wall.

STRING *see* BALUSTRADE *and* STAIRCASES

STRING-COURSE A raised horizontal band of bricks or masonry on a building.

STRIP (*also* LAND *and* SELION) The strip was the fundamental unit of cultivation and of tenancy in the open-field farming system (*see* OPEN FIELDS). Most holdings consisted of between forty and eighty strips and there was no standardized size, the dimensions of a strip varying significantly from one part of the country to another. In the midland counties of England, strips were usually about 7 metres wide (8 yards) and 200 metres (220 yards) long. Each covered approximately one-third of an acre and a parcel of parallel strips was known as a FURLONG ('furrow's length'). A typical *virgate* (of about 30 acres) could consist of as many as ninety strips scattered

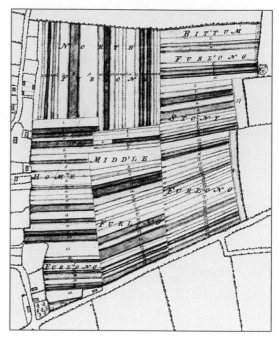

From an eighteenth-century estate map of Strettington, Sussex.

throughout the open fields to ensure an equitable distribution of plough-soil. Each strip consisted of a number of parallel 'plough ridges' (*see* RIDGE AND FURROW) and the furlongs were sometimes separated by marker stones. The open-field system was probably of late Saxon origin and the strips may at first have been considerably larger, sometimes exceeding 1,000 metres in length (1,093 yards) and 9 metres in width (10 yards). These were later subdivided to form the smaller, medieval strips. Strip patterns are shown on many of the MAPS which were prepared for ENCLOSURE and other purposes in the eighteenth and nineteenth centuries, and these often show where adjacent strips have been amalgamated.

STRIP LYNCHET Artificial hillside terraces created by medieval peasant farmers at a time when additional cultivable land was required to provide for the needs of an expanding rural population. It is likely therefore that most strip lynchets were already in existence before the arrival of the Black Death in 1348 (*see* PLAGUE). They were created by repeated ploughing in one direction so that the soil was turned outwards, thereby expanding the level surface of each terrace which was separated from adjacent strips by steep banks, though these may subsequently have lost their impact through erosion and modern ploughing. Strip lynchets are

usually found in those areas where there was insufficient ploughland in the OPEN FIELDS and where level ground was at a premium. They seldom occur singly and usually run parallel to the contours of a hillside, sometimes measuring as much as 230 metres in length (250 yards). Many strip lynchet systems are marked as such on 1:25000 Ordnance Survey maps.
See also LYNCHET

STUBBING (*also* **STUBBS**) *see* ASSART

STUCCO *see* PLASTERWORK *and* REGENCY ARCHITECTURE

STUDS *see* TIMBER-FRAMED BUILDINGS

STYLE *see* CHANCEL SCREEN

STYLOBATE *see* CLASSICAL ARCHITECTURE

SUB Latinized place-name element meaning 'under', as in Aston Subedge and Weston Subedge, Gloucestershire, which are located at the foot of the Cotswold ridge (*see* LATIN).

SUBINFEUDATION The granting of land by a VASSAL to be held of him by his vassal (*see* MANOR).

SUB-ORDINARY In ARMORY, a minor armorial charge of geometrical shape subordinate to the ORDINARY or principal charge.

SUBSIDY ROLLS Lists of tax-payers, arranged by villages and towns, together with the amounts of tax to be paid. The types of assessment vary: some were a tax on land or houses, some related to movable goods and some were *poll taxes*, applicable to all of a certain age. Perhaps the most important series of subsidy rolls to have survived is that of 1327, which is arranged by counties and by towns and villages and comprises the names of the more prosperous members of society who were required to pay. Poll tax returns are even more valuable for they applied to everyone over the age of sixteen and provide information concerning population and, in some cases, details of names and occupations. Unfortunately, very few poll tax returns have been published in printed form.
See also TAXATION

SUCCENTOR *see* CATHEDRALS *and* MONASTERIES

SUFFRAGAN BISHOP *see* CLERGY (CHURCH OF ENGLAND)

SUGAR LOAF A conical hill in the shape of a sugar loaf. Victorian kitchen manuals recommended 'loaf sugar' for preserving. Sugar loaves of various sizes were made by filtering cleaned sugar through charcoal into conical clay moulds. The sugar loaves in their moulds were dried by sugar bakers in large, heated warehouses which were notoriously inclined to catch fire! The last firm to sell sugar loaves in London ceased trading in 1893 when their premises were destroyed by fire. The best-known Sugar Loaf is the mountain (596 metres) to the north-west of Abergavenny in South Wales.

SUICIDES Before its abolition in 1823, the law required that those who took their own lives should not be buried in consecrated ground and it was common practice for anyone who committed suicide to be interred at a crossroads in their PARISH. For this reason, many lonely crossroads still attract tales of superstition and intrigue.
See also WAYSIDE CROSSES

SULUNG *see* HIDE

SUMPTUARY LAWS Medieval laws intended to restrict private expenditure. Charles V of France, for example, forbade the use of long-pointed shoes, a fashion vehemently opposed by the Church. In fourteenth-century England, contemporary writers tell of the extravagance of dress and cuisine of the period, and in 1336 Edward III attempted to legislate against such excesses. In 1363 costume was regulated by law and a further act of 1444 sought to control clothing when it formed part of the wages of servants, specific allowances being permitted to bailiffs and overseers (5s a year), principal (4s) and ordinary servants (3s 4d), for example (*see* LIVERY). A further statute of 1463 (Edward IV) legislated for the control of clothing of persons of all ranks. Indeed, a succession of laws from that year up to 1532 sought to limit excesses by forbidding untitled people to wear such things as purple silk, gold chains and COLLARS, cloth of gold and crimson velvet. Controls were also applied to the use of furs, ermine being reserved for the nobility and, as a token of royal favour, to other magnates close to the Crown. It may be that the extensive use of ermine in the coats of arms of Garter Knights of the period was intended to indicate their privileged position in society.

Similar acts were passed in Scotland: in 1433 (James I) the manner of living of all orders in

Scotland was prescribed, in particular the consumption of pies and baked meats which was forbidden to all below the rank of baron. In 1457 (James II) an act was passed against 'sumptuous cleithing'. The Scottish sumptuary law of 1621 was the last of its kind in Britain.

SUNDAY SCHOOLS Sunday schools first appeared in the mid-eighteenth century, though it was Robert Raikes who in 1780 inspired the Sunday school movement with the foundation of a school in Gloucester. Raikes engaged four women teachers and the pupils were charged 1*d* a week. In 1775 a society was formed for the 'Establishment and Support of Sunday Schools throughout the Kingdom of Great Britain' and in 1803 the Sunday School Union was founded in the London area.
See also EDUCATION

SUNDIALS Before the introduction of clocks into some churches in the fourteenth century, the canonical hours (*see* MONASTERIES) were evinced by means of a *mass-dial* set on the south wall or buttress of a church, usually in the vicinity of the porch and at eye-level. Saxon dials, carved with great precision and sometimes with inscriptions added, usually consist of a double circle divided into four by radial lines, each of which may terminate in a cross. The later, and more numerous, medieval

scratch-dials are rather crudely inscribed with the duodecimal divisions of the day, the radial lines cut at intervals of 15°. In many examples, the line which would have been reached by the shadow of the metal style (*gnomon*) at 9.00 a.m. is more clearly incised, this being the 'mass line' which marked the hour when Mass was said on Sundays and feast-days.

The function of these dials was to ensure that the bell was rung at the correct time to mark the canonical hours and for this reason the clock-faces which superseded them were often visible inside to church to assist the bell-ringer. But they served other purposes: the eleventh-century dial above the south door of Edstone church in Yorkshire bears the inscription *Orlogi Viatorum*: 'hour-teller of wayfarers'. On several churches there are a number of dials, each intended for use during a different season of the year. Ornate seventeenth- and eighteenth-century sundials were usually provided to remind the observer of his mortality and of the need for repentance rather than to inform him of the time.
See also TURF DIALS
For the British Sundials Society *see* APPENDIX I

SUN DIVISION (SOLSKIFT) In the late Saxon and medieval periods, many feudal estates in northern England achieved an equitable distribution of poorer and better quality cultivable STRIPS in the OPEN FIELDS by means of a system of rotation

Saxon dial at the church of St Gregory, Welburn near Kirkby Moorside in Yorkshire.

which is known to have existed in Scandinavia in the Dark Ages. Sun division, which, as the name implies, related to the course of the sun, determined the precise arrangement of holdings within each FURLONG which corresponded with that of the TOFTS in the village itself, so that neighbours at home were also neighbours in the fields. Contemporary documents often refer to the position of lands in relation to the sun: 'towards the sun', for example, which probably meant to the south-west, and 'towards the shade' meaning the north-west.

SUN IN SPLENDOUR *see* ROYAL ARMS AND BADGES

SUPER Latinized place-name element meaning 'on', as in Weston-super-Mare ('- on the sea'), Somerset (*see* LATIN) .

SUPPORTERS Figures, usually beasts, chimerical creatures or of human form, placed on either side of the shield in a coat of arms to 'support' it. Unlike other elements in a coat of arms, supporters have no practical origin and cannot be traced with any certainty before the fifteenth century. Though similar devices may be found in early SEALS, where they occupy the space between the shield and the outer decorative border, their use was almost certainly decorative. With some notable exceptions, the use of supporters is restricted to peers, knights of certain chivalric orders and major corporations. *See also* ARMORY

Lion and dragon supporters in the arms of Edward VI.

SURCOAT A long coat of linen, split at the sides to facilitate movement, especially on horseback, and originally intended to protect mail from heat or rain.

Dating from the Crusades of the twelfth century, the surcoat provided an obvious means of displaying armorial devices – hence 'coat of arms'. By the middle of the fourteenth century, the surcoat had been succeeded by the shorter JUPON and CYCLAS.

SURVEYOR OF THE HIGHWAYS *see* MEDIEVAL ROADS

SUSSEX *see* KINGDOMS (ANCIENT)

SWALING The practice of maintaining moorland grazing by burning off heather to promote new growth. A *swale* is a meadow, especially one in an area of poor drainage.

SWAYS *see* THATCHING

SWEAT-HOUSES Communal sweat-houses were used in Ireland from the Dark Ages until the early years of the twentieth century for the relief of rheumatic aches and pains. A typical *tighthe alluis* consisted of a small, dry-walled building, with a corbelled roof and chimney hole, which was pre-heated for twenty-four hours by a turf fire, the ashes of which were swept out immediately before use. Sweat-houses were usually situated on the banks of streams so that the occupants could bathe or wash themselves in cold water immediately after treatment.

SWEET CHESTNUT A staple ration of the Roman legions was a nutritious flour called *pollenta* made from chestnuts. For this reason, the Romans are credited with introducing the chestnut from Italy *c.* 30 BC. It is particularly common in Nottinghamshire, Norfolk and Gloucestershire, but rare in Scotland and Ireland. Although the chestnut has a 500-year life span and may grow to 37 metres in height (120 feet), it is rarely planted for timber because natural cracks (*shakes*) make it difficult to saw into large planks. Most chestnut is grown as twelve-year COPPICE, a process which may be repeated for one hundred years or more. The coppice wood is used for hop poles and gateposts, and in Kent and neighbouring counties triangular pales are strung together on wires to form cleft-pale fencing which is both durable and difficult to climb.

SWINGEL A poachers' weapon comprising a pair of flails, each reinforced with strips of iron, and united by three or four links of chain.

SYCAMORE The sycamore was introduced into Scotland from France in the late fifteenth century and is so named because it was once believed to be the fig-mulberry of the Bible (*Sycomorus*). In England, it was popular in the late sixteenth century when it was extensively planted in the fashionable shaded walks of country houses. Sycamore wood is pale and strong, though not durable in the open. It is used for furniture, flooring, carved woodware, textile rollers and in violin-making. Being a particularly robust tree, the sycamore is commonly found on exposed northern uplands where copses have been planted as shelter for farmsteads.

SYMBOL STONES *see* OGHAM STONES *and* PICTISH STONES

TABARD A dress coat worn over armour from the late fifteenth century to the mid sixteenth century. Similar to the JUPON but reaching below the thigh and with broad sleeves to the elbow, the tabard was emblazoned front and back and on the sleeves and served a purely armorial purpose. Today, tabards of the royal arms are worn by the heralds on ceremonial occasions.

TABERNACLE (i) A canopied structure used as a portable shrine by the Israelites during their wanderings in the wilderness. It contained the Ark of the Covenant, a wooden chest in which the writings of Jewish law were kept.
(ii) From this, any architectural feature or decorative motif (*tabernacle work*) which resembles a canopied structure: a tower-like font cover, for example.
(iii) Specifically, a hanging *pyx-shrine* or *sacrament house*, shaped like a tapering ornamental tower, in which the Blessed Sacrament was reserved. Very few medieval tabernacles survived the Reformation. A superbly carved, oak tabernacle at Milton Abbey, Dorset, is fixed to the north wall of the presbytery, while that from Hessett, Suffolk, is now at the British Museum. In the Middle Ages tabernacles were suspended in front of the High Altar and were raised and lowered by means of pulleys, as at West Grinstead, Sussex, where the pulley socket has survived.

Medieval tabernacle at Milton Abbey, Dorset.

(iv) From the sixteenth century, the term has been used to describe a box of precious metal in which the Blessed Sacrament is reserved on a communion table.

TABLE TOMBS (CHEST TOMBS) Not to be confused with TOMB CHESTS, table tombs are chest-like MEMORIALS of stone erected in many churchyards over the graves of the more prosperous members of seventeenth- and eighteenth-century society. Many of the Cotswold clothiers' tombs at Painswick in Gloucestershire are elaborately carved in Baroque and later Rococo styles and represent the finest collection of table tombs in Britain. A *bale tomb* is a variety of table tomb on top of which is carved a stone representation of the cylindrical medieval hearse (*see* EFFIGIES). Because of their shape, table tombs are also referred to as *altar tombs*.

TAL- A Welsh place-name element meaning 'end', as in Tal-y-llyn, Gwynedd, which means 'lake end'.

TALLAGE A manorial tax, usually paid at Michaelmas, which was superseded by other forms of local taxation in the fourteenth century. Tallage

Clothiers' tombs in Painswick churchyard, Gloucestershire.

was also exacted by the Crown on boroughs and towns which had belonged to the Crown during the reigns of Edward the Confessor and William I and where the tenants continued to enjoy certain privileges and exemptions. Such lands were known as *terræ Regis* or *ancient demesne* and the tenure was finally abolished in 1925.

TALLET *see* FARMSTEADS

TALLIES *see* PRISE

TARN From the Old Norse *tjorn*, meaning 'small lake', 'black and sullen' tarns of 'not unpleasing sadness' (Wordsworth) are commonly found in the upland regions of northern England.

TAXATION In 1066 William I (1066–87) inherited the revenues of his Anglo-Saxon predecessors, including numerous customary taxes and the *geld* or land tax. Direct taxation in the form of DANEGELD was introduced in the late Saxon period to provide for protection against the Danes. As such it was abolished in 1051, but continued to be levied by William and his successors on various occasions to finance military operations. But its effectiveness was largely undermined by the numerous exemptions granted by Henry I (1100–35), and by the mid-twelfth century the geld was realizing no more than £4,000 annually and from 1162 was allowed to lapse. It was replaced briefly by CARUCAGE, a form of land tax based on information obtained in the

DOMESDAY survey, but this proved ineffectual and both Richard I (1189–99) and John (1199–1216) serviced their rapidly increasing expenditure by the exploitation of feudal and judicial revenues, notably overlordship and the extraction of considerable sums from their tenants-in-chief. Magnatial resentment, and ultimately rebellion, resulted in the Great Charter of 1215 (*Magna Carta*), which severely restricted the king's right to determine these and other 'incidents of feudalism' to which he was entitled.

This form of feudal taxation was perceived as being singularly inequitable by those from who it was exacted: the tenants-in-chief, whose loyalty was essential to the maintenance of government. John, therefore, sought to devise a system which would produce a tax yield sufficient to maintain his government in war-time but which would also satisfy a potentially rebellious establishment. For a precedent, he turned to the so-called 'Saladin Tithe' of 1181, which had raised a subsidy on the value of movables to finance the third crusade, and in 1207 levied a tax of one-thirteenth on movable property, which raised £60,000. Inevitably, the tax caused almost universal hostility, for it affected almost the entire property-owning population. Nevertheless, the system of LAY SUBSIDY was established and remained the principal source of revenue throughout the medieval period and into the sixteenth century.

In one respect, it differed essentially from other forms of taxation: as feudal overlord the king was able to take reliefs and other 'incidents' from his tenants-in-chief, but he was not entitled to impose a national tax on his subjects' property without some form of mandate. Henry III (1216–72) obtained the barons' approval for such taxation, but by the mid-thirteenth century even the members of his council were beginning to express doubts regarding their authority in such matters. In 1254 they required that four knights should be summoned from each county for this purpose and, from 1264, the burgesses of the towns. Together, the knights and burgesses eventually comprised a national assembly or parliament at which the needs of the king were considered against the grievances of his subjects and government demands for taxation determined accordingly. By the mid-fourteenth century, a customary rate of one-tenth and one-fifteenth had been established: one-tenth being exacted in the towns, where there was a greater concentration of wealth, and one- fifteenth in rural areas. Taxers were appointed to each county together with sub-taxers who were responsible for the assessment and collection of taxes. Before 1332 individuals were assessed personally but thereafter a fixed sum was exacted from each village or borough community with an exemption for all those whose movables were valued at less than 10s.

A system of indirect taxation was also attempted in the reign of King John who, in 1202, imposed customs duties of one-fifteenth on all imported and exported goods. Although these duties were suspended in 1206, Edward I (1272–1307) revived the system in 1275 when he imposed the so-called *Ancient Custom* on the exportation of wool. Each 165-kg (364-lb) sack of wool was charged at the rate of half-a-mark, and a consignment of hides (a *last*, weighing approximately 1,818 kg (4,000 lb)) was levied at 300 hides (*wool-fells*) and a mark. In 1294 a *maltolt* of £3.6.8 was also charged on each sack of good wool and £2 for other wool, though this was later standardized at £2 for both. Resentment was widespread and the charge was abolished in 1297, only to be reintroduced for alien merchants in 1303. The maltolt remained the cause of acrimonious dispute between the Crown and Parliament until the mid-fourteenth century when it was finally agreed that the king should retain it at a standard rate of £2.3.4 but that the tax should be granted only by parliamentary approval. In the event, the market could not bear the cost of the tax and wool exports fell from over 40,000 sacks in 1304 to less than 10,000 in the early sixteenth century. (In part, this decline actually contributed to the prosperity of English clothiers who were able to purchase their raw materials more cheaply than their Flemish or Italian competitors and to export broadcloths at advantageous prices because they carried a duty of only 14d each.)

With the decline of the wool trade, and diminishing returns from lay subsidies, *poll taxes* were levied between 1377 and 1381 in an attempt to remodel the taxation system (*see* POLL TAX). But these proved to be so unpopular (*see* PEASANTS' REVOLT) that further experimentation was deferred. During the fifteenth century, a series of income taxes were levied but again these proved to be inequitable in that they tended to fall most heavily on landowners.

Medieval taxation was extraordinarily inefficient. Government statistics were so inaccurate that anticipated revenues invariably failed to materialize, and bribery and corruption were endemic in the administration of the taxation system.

Although exempt from lay subsidy, the clergy were expected to pay other forms of taxation both to the Crown and to the Pope, and the increasing frequency of dual taxation led to the emergence of the convocations of Canterbury and York, autonomous bodies representing the clergy of the two English provinces. The convocations were usually convened to coincide with sessions of Parliament so that fiscal policy could be formulated in direct response to government demands for money. The valuation of benefices of 1291 (known as the *Taxation of Pope Nicholas IV*) provided the basis for clerical grants to the Crown for the remainder of the medieval period. *Church rates*, which were used to defray the expenses of parish churches, were levied on all freehold and leasehold properties until 1868. (*See also* SAINT PETER'S PENCE *and* TITHES.)

The imposition of lay subsidies continued under the Tudors and James I until 1623. All those over the age of sixteen who were liable to taxation were listed in the *Great Subsidy Rolls* of 1524/5, now preserved at the Public Record Office.

At the Restoration of the Stuart monarchy in 1660, the country was close to bankruptcy. The Commonwealth (1649–60) had accumulated debts of at least £2 million pounds in addition to the incalculable cost of two decades of civil war. Parliament responded by curtailing royal expenditure with the introduction of the civil list and by abolishing feudal tenures, an act of 1660 'taking away the court of wards and liveries and tenures held from the Crown and by knight service and purveyance, and for setting a revenue upon His Majesty in lieu thereof'. The Act effectively dismantled the last vestiges of the ancient system of Saxon-Norman tenurial service by declaring 'that it be forever hereafter free to all and every of the subjects of His Majesty to sell, dispose or employ . . . his goods to any other person or persons'. A number of new taxes were also introduced including a poll tax in 1660, which was graded by rank, and a HEARTH TAX (1662–89).

The late seventeenth and eighteenth centuries were a time of frenetic fiscal activity. Innovative taxes including a revised land tax (1692–1832), initially charged at a rate of 4s in the pound, a Registration Tax on baptisms, marriages and burials (1694–1706), a WINDOW TAX (1696–1747) and a duty on printed paper and similar commodities (1711). In 1747 a tax was levied on the possession of carriages and in the same year a new type of window tax was introduced (this was subject to a series of revisions in 1758, 1761 and 1766). Taxes, reminiscent of the medieval SUMPTUARY LAWS, were exacted on items such as silver plate (1756–77), playing cards and dice, and on the employment of male servants (1777–1852). These taxes, which were originally intended to finance the American war (1775–83), were later extended to include the employment of gamekeepers (1784–1807) and female servants (1785–92) and to the possession of horses (1784–1874), coats of arms (1793–1882), hair powder (1795–8), dogs (1796–1882) and clocks and watches (1797–8). Details of these taxes, and of the income generated by them, are contained in *English Historical Documents 10* (*see below*) and in *Statutes at Large* published by the Stationery Office. A revised Land Tax of 1892 continued in modified form until 1949 and the Window Tax was replaced in 1851 by House Duty, which was levied on inhabited houses until 1924. Income tax was introduced in 1799 to finance the war against France, was abolished in 1802 and revived in 1803 at the rate of 2*s* in the pound.

For the Library of HM Customs and Excise *see* APPENDIX I

TEGULA *see* TILES

TELECOMMUNICATIONS One of the most remarkable features of the Victorian Age was the development of a communications system which, at the beginning of the nineteenth century, would have been viewed with incredulity by an essentially parochial society. By the turn of the century, people of all social classes were able to travel and to make direct contact with each other, newspapers and journals were distributed within hours of publication and the delivery of letters and packages through the POSTAL SERVICE was, in many respects, more efficient than it is today.

All this was achieved by means of a rapidly expanding network of RAILWAYS, and it was the directors of the Great Western Railway who first adopted Cooke and Wheatstone's electric telegraph as a method of signalling the movement of traffic. In America, Samuel Morse (1791–1872), the inventor of the Morse code, produced his first working model in 1835, while in England the first practical telegraph of 1837 linked Euston station in London with Camden station a mile away. A few years later, when the railway telegraph facilitated the arrest of a murderer, public interest was stimulated and the telegram established as the standard means of business and social communication until *c.* 1880 when telephones became more generally available. The advent of underseas cables enabled telegraph messages in Morse code to be communicated between continents and contributed significantly to the effective administration of the British Empire.

In 1876 Alexander Graham Bell (1847–1922) patented the first 'Electric Speaking Telephone'. Bell, a Scot who had emigrated to America, brought his invention to Britain, and by 1879 the first telephone exchange was in service. By the end of the century, telephone cables had been laid across the English Channel making possible direct and immediate communication throughout Europe. Extraordinarily, there was no telephone link with the United States of America until 1958, communications during the Second World War being by means of radio-telegraphy (*see below*).

The Post Office acquired the monopoly of telephone and telegraphic communication in 1896 and in the same year, a young Irish-Italian named Guglielmo Marconi (1874–1937) arrived in England with an invention which was to change forever the nature of telecommunications. The telegraph and telephone could only operate when parties were linked by cable: ocean liners, for example, were often completely isolated for weeks on end. Marconi's patented 'wireless telegraph' brought him instant success and he established a manufacturing company in Chelmsford to supply equipment to naval and commercial vessels, his first major client being Lloyd's of London. By 1901, Marconi was able to transmit a signal from Poldhu in Cornwall to St John's in Newfoundland and by 1912 could produce a continuously oscillating wave, essentially for the transmission of sounds other than the Morse code.

See also TELEPHONE BOXES

For the British Telecom Museum *and* Historical Telephone Directory Library *see* APPENDIX I

TELEGRAPH Networks of SIGNAL STATIONS were established in the southern counties of England in the early nineteenth century in anticipation of possible invasion from France. There were two types of signalling system, the semaphore and the shutter, both of which used signal stations located on hill tops within sight of one another at intervals of 13 to 19 km (8 to 12 miles). Signals of the semaphore type incorporated a pair of wooden arms which could be adjusted by means of ropes and pulleys to convey messages in semaphore.

The shutter system, or Murray Telegraph, relied on various configurations of shutters within a frame. The Admiralty Shutter Telegraph conveyed messages from London to Portsmouth and Plymouth from 1796 to 1825. Each signal station comprised six shutters arranged in two vertical rows mounted in a frame which was secured to the roof of a building. Like Venetian blinds, the slats of each shutter could be positioned to present either a solid face or a space. It was, therefore, possible to form up to sixty-three different letters, numerals, commonly used words or pre-determined phrases. The frame stood 6 metres high (20 feet) and each shutter measured about 1 metre (3 feet) square. The first operating system linked London with Deal and Sheerness in 1796, while the extension to Portsmouth was completed in the following year. The link to Plymouth, which branched off the

Portsmouth system at South Harting, Hampshire, was not completed until 1806.

For the most part, the buildings on which the telegraphs were located consisted of two rooms: one for living quarters and the other for operating the shutters by means of ropes and pulleys. Fixed telescopes pointed in each direction enabling the 'glass man' to see the next station – weather permitting! Each station was manned by three men, so that one was always on duty, and the team received an allowance of 6*d* a day for coal and candles. Unbelievably, the records show that a single cipher trial message was sent from London to Plymouth and back again in 3 minutes – a distance by the telegraph's route of 800 km (500 miles)! The eastern section of the system was modified in 1805 to include signal lights so that messages could be sent at night. Several of the more substantial telegraph stations have survived, some of them as rather fine houses with splendid views. Others are recalled in place-names such as Telegraph Hill near Minterne Magna, Dorset.

See also BEACONS *and* TOOT-HILLS

For electric telegraph *see* POSTAL SERVICES *and* TELECOMMUNICATIONS

TELEPHONE BOXES The first public telephone boxes appeared in 1921. Type K1 boxes were made of concrete and had red wooden doors, eight-light windows, projecting eaves, four enamelled 'Telephone' signs and an ornamental finial. Type K2 boxes, which were introduced in 1927, were made of cast iron and painted red overall with dome-shaped roofs ventilated in the top panels by four perforated crowns, each above an illuminated 'Telephone' sign. The doors and sides had long windows of eighteen lights. Type K3, introduced in 1929, was similar but constructed of concrete and without the crown ventilators. It was painted stone colour with window frames in red. Type K4, which dates from 1930, was also in cast iron and painted red but had only three 'crown' ventilators, the fourth side having a light which illuminated stamp-vending machines and posting-box which were incorporated into one side of the box. The short-lived type K5, introduced as an experiment in 1935, was built in concrete and had simple four-panel windows in the upper part of the door and walls. None is known to have survived. The once familiar type K6, which was introduced at the same time as the K5, was constructed of cast iron and painted red overall. Ventilation was by slits beneath the 'Telephone' opals, and in the door and sides eight horizontal window panels were divided at the outer edges by vertical glazing bars. New style 'Telecom' cubicles were introduced in the 1980s.

For the British Telecom Museum *see* APPENDIX I

TEMPLAR, KNIGHTS (THE POOR KNIGHTS OF CHRIST AND OF THE TEMPLE OF SOLOMON)
Together, the Hospitallers, the Teutonic Knights and the Knights Templar formed the three most powerful orders of chivalry to emanate from the CRUSADES. Within a few years of their foundation most of their brethren, while living under vows of religion, were conventual knights (their priests were known as *chaplains*) and the orders played an increasingly significant rôle in the defence of the Christian settlements in Palestine and Syria and in the administration of the Kingdom of Jerusalem. They constructed and garrisoned castles and fought alongside crusading forces in the perennial wars against the Egyptians and Turks.

Founded in 1118/19, by Hugues de Payns and Godeffroi de St Omer, the Order of the Poor Knights of Christ and of the Temple of Solomon was given a convent (headquarters) close to the Temple of Solomon by King Baldwin II of Jerusalem so that they should 'fight with a pure mind for the supreme and true king'. The knights, who lived according to the rule of Bernard of Clairvaux under an elected Master of the Temple, dedicated themselves to the protection of pilgrims in the Holy Land and quickly achieved the sanction of the Church. By the end of the thirteenth century, the Templars had become established in almost every European kingdom and were in receipt of enormous grants of land. But their widespread influence attracted influential enemies. Strange stories circulated about their 'secret rites' and their failure to mobilize their considerable resources in 1291 following the fall of Acre (the last Christian stronghold in the Holy Land) caused universal resentment.

Eventually, in 1308, Philip IV of France moved against them. Having obtained papal support for his campaign, Philip persuaded most European rulers to suppress the Templars. The order's officers were arrested, on the grounds of alleged heresy, sorcery, sodomy and corruption, and in France at least thirty-eight Templars are known to have died during 'examination'. In 1310 sixty-seven Templars were burned at the stake; in 1312 the Pope transferred many of the order's holdings and possessions to the Hospitallers (*see* ST JOHN OF JERUSALEM, ORDER OF); and in 1314 the Grand Master of the order was burnt alive in front of Notre Dame in Paris on the instructions of Philip the Fair. But by then, the Templars had created for themselves what was effectively a

The Arrest of the Templars, 1308, from the fourteenth-century Chronicle of St Denis.

sovereign state in the Greek islands, notably at Rhodes which they eventually lost to the Ottoman Turks in 1522. The order's convent was re-established in Malta, in 1530, where it remained until 1798.

Although in several countries the order survived, in England it was suppressed, though without undue severity. Its headquarters still stand at Temple Church in Fleet Street, London, a building which was based on the Holy Sepulchre at Jerusalem. The habit of the order was white with a red cross of eight points worn on the left shoulder and its badges were the *Agnus Dei* and a strange device consisting of two knights riding on one horse, presumably an allusion to the original poverty of the order. Both the Templars and the Hospitallers had about fifty PRECEPTORIES or COMMANDERIES in the British Isles, many commemorated by place-names such as St John's Jerusalem in Kent, St John's Wood in London, Temple Breuer, Lincolnshire, Templecombe, Somerset and Temple Guiting in the Gloucestershire Cotswolds.

TEMPLE PLACE-NAMES *see* TEMPLAR, KNIGHTS

TEMPLES (GARDEN) Classical eighteenth-century garden temples were both eye-catchers (for looking at) and cool summer pavilions (for looking from). They were created by architects such as Sir John Vanbrugh (1664–1726), inspired by the paintings of Poussin and Clause Lorraine, in the landscaped parklands of William Kent (1685–1748) and his contemporaries, together with artificial lakes, grottoes and cascades. But by the mid-eighteenth century, other temples of Gothic, Muslim and even Chinese derivation were beginning to appear, together with ARTIFICIAL RUINS, none of which pleased the connoisseur. Perhaps the best examples of classical temples are those at Stourhead in Wiltshire dating from 1750 to 1770.
See also FOLLIES *and* MAUSOLEUMS

TEMPORALITIES *see* SPIRITUALITIES

TENANCY AT WILL Tenure which was entirely at the disposal of the lord to whom it was granted as a reward for loyal or signal service to the Crown.

TENANT-IN-CHIEF (TENANT-IN-CAPITE) A tenant who held his lands immediately of the Crown. *See also* WARDSHIP

TENEMENT (i) Land held of a superior. *See also* MANOR
(ii) Any rented land or dwelling.

TENTHS AND FIFTEENTHS *see* LAY SUBSIDY *and* TAXATION

TENURE *see* ACREMAN, ALLOTMENT, ANCIENT DEMESNE, BOROUGH ENGLISH, BURGAGE, COPYHOLD, DEMESNE, DISSEISIN, ENGROSSMENT, FARM, FEE, FEUDAL TENURE, FRANKALMOIGN, FRANK FEE, FREEHOLD, FREE WARREN, GLEBE, KNIGHT'S FEE, LEASEHOLD, LIFEHOLD, MESNALTY, MORTMAIN, QUIT RENT, RACK RENT, SAC AND SOC, SEISIN, SERJEANTY, SOCAGE, TENANCY AT WILL *and* TENANT-IN-CHIEF

TERRACOTTA Unglazed earthenware material, usually brownish-red in colour, containing *grog*, previously fired earthenware which has been ground to a fine powder. Introduced to sixteenth-century Britain from Italy, where the word means 'baked earth', terracotta is harder and less porous than brick and is used as an ornamental building material and in statuary.

TERRÆ REGIS *see* TALLAGE

TERRIER *see* MANOR

TERSE *see* MONASTERIES

TESSELLATED PAVEMENTS Tessellated mosaics consisted of small cubes (*tesserae*) of different materials (glass, marble, coloured limestones, sandstones, etc.) embedded in an impervious material to form a decorative finish to a floor or wall. Although the technique originated in Greece, the first extensive use of mosaic was by the Romans, who developed a durable and waterproof cement in which the fragments were fixed. The classical Roman mosaic tradition was continued in the Christian period, notably in Byzantine buildings, but in western Europe the technique was superseded from the thirteenth century by a more naturalistic form of fresco painting.

In Britain, by far the best examples are to be found in ROMAN VILLAS of the fourth century AD. These appear to have been executed by itinerant mosaic artists, some of them of native origin and some from other parts of the Empire, who worked from cartoons selected from specimen books of patterns and Graeco-Roman mythical scenes. Many mosaics of the period include references to pagan divinities such as Bacchus, while at Hinton St Mary, Dorset, the centrepiece of the mosaic is the head of Christ (now in the British Museum).

TESTER *see* PULPITS *and* SOUNDING BOARD

TESTOON *see* COINAGE

THANE (*also* **THEGN**) One of the Anglo-Saxon military élite and a member of a royal or noble household. Prior to the ninth century, the term *gesith* had the same meaning. The *wergild* or value placed on a thane's life was reckoned to be 1,200*s*.
See also KINGDOMS (ANCIENT)

THANKFUL VILLAGES Coined by Arthur Mee in his *King's England* series of county books, a 'Thankful Village' is one to which all its men returned from the First World War (1914–18). In his *Somerset* volume, Mee describes the village of Woolley, near Bath:

This hamlet of 13 houses sent 13 men to the Great War and every one came back. So it is that Woolley is one of the Thankful Villages. In Somerset there are 8 but in all England there are only 32. We could find no shop in Woolley, no inn, no school, no letter-box, but we found this plain brass tablet: *To the Glory of God and in thankful remembrance of the safe return of all the men connected with this parish who by land and sea served their King and Country in the Great War.* Amazingly, Upper Slaughter, in the Gloucestershire Cotswolds, sent 44 men to war and all returned, while the village of Cayton, Yorkshire, sent 43.

Thankful Villages

Bedfordshire	Stanbridge (33 men)
Cambridgeshire	Knapwell (23)
Derbyshire	Bradbourne (18)
Gloucestershire	Coln Rogers (25)
	Little Sodbury (6)
	Upper Slaughter (44)
Leicestershire	Willesley (3)
Lincolnshire	Bigby (10)
Northamptonshire	Woodend (19)
Nottinghamshire	Maplebeck (2)
	Wigsley (7)
	Wysall (17)
Norfolk	Ovington (14)
Rutland	Teigh (11)
Somerset	Aisholt (8)
	Chelwood (4)
	Rodney Stoke (17)
	Stanton prior (4)
	Stocklinch (19)
	Tellisford (3)
	Woolley (13)
Suffolk	South Elmham (11)
Wiltshire	Littleton Drew (22)
Yorkshire	Catwick (20)
	Cayton (43)
	Cundall (12)
	Norton-le-Clay (16)

See also WAR MEMORIALS.

THATCHING Thatch, from the Old English *thæc*, meaning 'roof covering', is a roofing of straw, reeds, sedge, rush or similar material. Prehistoric buildings were covered in a variety of materials, including turf and heather, and many were thatched. Throughout the post-Roman and medieval periods thatch, usually of straw, reed or fern, was the most common form of roofing because it was both cheap and effective, SLATES, TILES or oak SHINGLES being used only in buildings of some importance or where they were freely available.

It has been calculated that 30 cm (1 foot) of thatch provides insulation equivalent to a tiled roof together with 10 cm (4 inches) of fibreglass. A thatched roof also has a steep pitch (about 50°) so that water is shed quickly, the eaves throwing rainwater clear of the building without recourse to gutters, down-pipes, soakaways or soffit boards. There are many regional variations of design: in East Anglia, for example, the thatching of the roof ridge is raised at the gable ends in order that water should be thrown back onto the main roof and the plaster or daub of the gable walls protected, while in Sussex the thatch of the ridge is often carried round the gable. Most thatched roofs are now made of water reed or wheat straw, the latter being either combed wheat reed or long straw.

The covering of thatch (the *coat*) comprises numerous small bundles of parallel stems (*yelms*) set in horizontal and vertical strips (*courses* and *lanes*). The first yelms are tied to the purlins and laths of the bare roof (*see* ROOFS) and, as the thickness of the thatch increases, additional yelms are tamped home and secured by long hazel wands (*sways*), held by hooks to the roof timbers, and by staples (*spars*) of split hazel or willow driven into the thatch. In a water reed roof, a thin layer of thatch (*backfill*) is used as a base and a *tilting fillet* placed at the eaves to angle the thatch. The finished edge of the thatch where it overhangs the gable is known as the *barge*. Hazel or willow saplings (*liggers*) are used for fixing and decorating the roof ridge which consists of bundles (*ridge rolls*) of reed, straw or sometimes sedge which run along the top of the ridge-piece beneath an additional 10-cm (4-inch) layer of scalloped thatch and interlaced liggers.

Water reed, especially high quality Norfolk reed, can serve for up to eighty years; combed wheat reed lasts from thirty to forty years; and a long straw roof up to twenty-five years. But the efficacy of a thatched roof varies considerably: the steeper the slope of the roof the longer the thatch will survive and much depends on climate, thatched roofs in the wet and warm south-west of England, for example, lasting only half the time of those elsewhere. Generally speaking, the older the roof the darker the colour of its thatch and the more worn and ragged its eaves. Thatch varies in thickness between 22 cm (9 inches) and 41 cm (16 inches), a thicker coat providing greater protection but wearing more quickly. Today, many thatched roofs are covered with wire or plastic netting to protect them from damage caused by birds and rodents. However, this practice impedes the flow of rainwater from the roof, encourages the formation of ice within the thatch and makes it harder to pull burning material away in the event of fire. Many roofs which were formerly thatched have been stripped and covered with slates or tiles. Such a roof usually has a particularly steep pitch and, on larger houses, may have copings above the gables.
For the National Society of Master Thatchers *see* APPENDIX I

THEGN *see* THANE

THEGN'S CHURCHES *see* CHURCHES

THORP(E) A common place-name element derived from the Old Scandinavian *þorp*, meaning 'subsidiary hamlet', and indicative of Danish settlement rather than Norwegian. Danelaw thorps developed round the subsidiary farmsteads of a village, as in Burnham Thorpe, Norfolk, which, although now an independent parish, was once an outlying hamlet of nearby Burnham. Old English *þrop* names, such as Eastrip ('eastern thorp'), Somerset, Southrop ('southern thorp') and Hatherop ('high thorp'), Gloucestershire, and various Thrups and Thrupps, are also indicative of outlying or dependent farmsteads of villages or manors.

THRESHING Flailing was usually done by teams of four to six labourers, beating in rotation to four/four time, each man wielding a traditional flail (*drashel*) with which he beat a layer of cereal 'on the stalk' against the hard threshing floor of the barn (*see* BARNS). The floor was located in the space between the doors on opposite sides of the barn and divided by *mousteads* from the remainder of the building. After threshing, the doors would be opened and the flailed crop separated (*winnowed*) into grain, husks and straw by throwing it into the air, the chaff being carried off by the through-draught from the doors.

Thousands of sheaves had to be hauled to the barn from the fields, but as steam replaced muscle so thatched ricks were often built together in field corners or on staddles in a RICKYARD where they awaited the arrival of the traction engine and threshing-machine. Horse-powered threshing-machines were introduced in the 1830s and from the 1860s these were replaced by steam-powered threshers, driven by means of a belt from the flywheel of a TRACTION ENGINE which, with its itinerant engineer, was usually hired by the hour. In order that the operation should be performed as economically as possible, the threshing-machine was run continuously by night and day until the work was finished:

They were busily 'unhaling' the rick, that is, stripping off the thatch before beginning to throw down the sheaves. . . . Close under the eaves of the stack, and as yet barely visible, was the red tyrant that the women had come to serve – a timber-framed construction, with straps and wheels appertaining – the threshing-machine which, while it was going, kept up a despotic demand upon the endurance of their muscles and nerves. A little way off there was another indistinct figure; this one black, with a sustained hiss that spoke of strength very much in reserve. The long chimney running up beside an ash-tree, and the warmth which radiated from the spot, explained without the

Steam threshing at Smeetham Hall, Sudbury, 1911.

necessity of much daylight that here was the engine which was to act as the *primum mobile* of this little world. The rick was unhaled by daylight; the men took their places, the women mounted and the work began. . . . Tess was placed on the platform of the machine, close to the man who fed it, her business being to untie every sheaf of corn handed on to her by Izz Huett, who stood next, but on the rick; so that the feeder could seize it and spread it over the revolving drum, which whisked out every grain in one moment. A hasty lunch was eaten where they stood . . . the inexorable wheels continued to spin, and the penetrating hum of the thresher to thrill to the very marrow all who were near the revolving wire cage.
(Thomas Hardy, *Tess of the D'Urbervilles*, 1891)

THRYSMA *see* COINAGE

-THWAITE From the Old Norse *thveit*, a common second element in place-names, especially in the counties of Lancashire, Cumbria and North Yorkshire, and with a variety of meanings: usually a woodland or forest clearing or meadow.

TICKET OF LEAVE *see* PRISONS

TIE BEAM Structural timber or timbers extending horizontally from one side of a roof to the other (*see* ROOFS).

TIERCERON RIBS *see* VAULTING

TILES Clay tiles, like bricks, are fired in kilns though they need to be harder and of finer quality. The Romans used baked roof tiles but in this country production ceased in the first century and did not begin again until the Middle Ages when the use of shingles or thatch for the roofs of town houses became a fire hazard. Floor tiles were widely used in the medieval period but tile-hanging or weather-tiling of walls was a late seventeenth-century innovation. The tiles were hung from horizontal wooden battens or pegged or nailed into mortar courses and were intended to provide protection from rain and snow. In the north of England slate-hanging served the same purpose.

Glazed *brick tiles* (also *weather tiles* or *mathematical tiles*) were widely used during the period 1760 to 1830 when they were applied to walls, either on wooden boards or battens as in tile-hanging, or affixed as an outer membrane to timber or brick. They were produced in a variety of colours and, as the name suggests, were the same size as bricks. They were used both as an effective means of weather-proofing and also for decorative purposes, notably in the fashionable terraces of Sussex and Kent.

Roofing tiles varied considerably: the Romans favoured a combination of rounded tile (*imbrex*) and flat tile (*tegula*), the *imbrices* covering the joints between the *tegulae*. *Pantiles* are large S-shaped interlocking roofing tiles which were first imported from Flanders in *c*. 1635 and produced in England from the early eighteenth century.

See also ENCAUSTIC TILES, ROOFS *and* SLATES

TIMBER-FRAMED BUILDINGS Hardwood, notably oak, was a readily available building material in many areas of Britain until the seventeenth century. Unlike buildings constructed of stone, brick or cob, a timber-framed structure consists of a load-bearing framework of timbers with the spaces in the framework filled with other materials such as LATH AND PLASTER, WATTLE AND DAUB, WEATHERBOARD or BRICK (*nogging*). This type of construction is also known as *half-timbering* because the timbers are not complete logs but are cleft longitudinally. Inevitably, there are many variations of timber-frame construction which reflect both the techniques of different regions and periods and the social aspirations of the original owners. There are, however, two basic types of construction: cruck frame and box frame.

Crucks are pairs of massive incurving timbers (*blades*), each pair cut from a single tree, which form a series of arches supporting a ridge beam. Originally, these buildings comprised a simple hall, with pairs of primitive crucks curving inwards from ground level to a roof of interlaced branches covered with thatch, brushwood or turf. Later buildings were constructed in bays, each 3.6 to 4.9 metres wide (12 to 16 feet), separated by crucks and strengthened by purlins and crossing rafters. The simplest dwellings consisted of a single bay with crucks at either end, while larger and more prestigious buildings would contain a number of bays. Cruck timbers are sometimes visible in gable ends, though many are concealed by plaster and in the northern counties the entire framework is usually encased in stone. Cruck buildings could be protected from damp by raising the base of the crucks on a timber sill, on *padstones* or plinths (known as *full cruck*), or given extra height by seating them on a low stone wall (*raised cruck*). By the fourteenth century,

Cruck-frame cottage at Didbrook, Gloucestershire.

the crucks of more distinguished buildings were supported on taller, ground-storey walls (*upper cruck*) so that the cruck frame would effectively form a roof space, enclosing a substantial second storey. (Most surviving 'cruck cottages' are either of full or raised cruck construction but have had improvised first floors added to provide sleeping accommodation.) The roof of the magnificent abbey barn at Glastonbury in Somerset was constructed (in *c*. 1345) on the cruck-frame principle. In order to overcome the problem of spanning the width of the building (10 metres or 33 feet) a system of two-tier cruck-framing was devised: the lower crucks linked by a collar beam on which the upper (smaller) crucks are supported. This massive oak structure, with its traditional joints and wooden pegs, supports 80 tons of stone SLATES (*see also* ROOFS).

The distribution of cruck-frame buildings, confined almost entirely to the midland and western counties of England and to Wales and Scotland, suggests that this method of construction is very old indeed, possibly of British origin and pre-dating the Anglo-Saxon settlements. It was widely adopted for all types of building during the Middle Ages and continued to be used in the dwellings of the poorer rural classes up to the eighteenth century when thousands of cruck-frame hovels were demolished and replaced by stone

The magnificent seventeenth-century Feathers Inn at Ludlow, Shropshire.

cottages. (Clan families evicted during the CLEARANCES are said to have carried their cruck frames away with them!) The best remaining examples of cruck-frame buildings are to be found in the English counties west of the river Severn: notably in the (former) county of Herefordshire.

Far more common are *box-framed* buildings, which are known to have been constructed during the Roman occupation though no pre-medieval example has survived. Most are from the late medieval and Tudor periods and were built for those more affluent members of society who could afford well-constructed and, therefore, more durable dwellings (*see also* HALL). Box-framing, as the name implies, consists of horizontal and vertical timbers with braces and struts added to provide rigidity. The frame was usually erected on a footing of impervious material, often a low wall of stone or brick, on which a horizontal baulk of timber (the *sill* or *plate*) was seated. Strong vertical posts (*studs*) were mortised into the sill and their upper ends tenoned into further horizontal timbers which, in single-storey buildings, either supported the lower ends of the roof rafters (*wallplate*) or linked the back and front of the house (*cross rail*). In two- or three-storey buildings this beam carried the joists of the floor above, in which case it is known as a *bressumer*. *Large framing*, in

which the framework is minimal but substantial and often strengthened with curving braces, usually dates from before the mid-fifteenth century, while *small framing* consists of small square panels within a lighter framework of numerous horizontal and vertical timbers. In the midland and southern counties of England, infill panels are usually square, but in East Anglian buildings dating from the thirteenth to the seventeenth century the frame is often divided into narrow vertical panels by closely spaced studs. *Close studding*, as this technique is called, became popular in other areas from the fifteenth century, particularly in more prestigious buildings where an often excessive use of expensive timber was intended to reflect an owner's affluence. Where an upper storey projects over the ones below, the overhang is described as a *jetty*, and where a building is jettied on two or more sides, additional support is provided by an internal cross-beam (*dragon beam*) running diagonally to the corner post.

Late sixteenth- and seventeenth-century timber-frame buildings are often ornately decorated with carved barge boards and exaggerated small-framing (*close panelling*) containing geometrical motifs. But by the late seventeenth century, such timber-framed buildings had become unfashionable and were superseded by classical houses built of brick or stone. During the eighteenth and early nineteenth centuries, old timber-framing was often concealed beneath layers of plaster, while many inferior timber-framed cottages were constructed using poor quality timbers. The colloquial terms 'black and white' and 'magpie house' refer to the nineteenth-century practice (fortunately no longer fashionable) of treating exposed timbers and decorative carving with black bitumen and the infill with whitewashed plaster.

Timber framed buildings were usually pre-fabricated, the principal timbers cut to size on site and other components obtained from a local workshop. Unseasoned oak was most commonly used in major buildings, with elm for internal work. (It has been calculated that no fewer than 300 oaks and 30 elms would have been required for the construction of a typical West Suffolk farmhouse.) The infilling was added as the framework was erected so that each storey was completed in turn.

TIME IMMEMORIAL *and* **TIME OUT OF MIND** *see* ANCIENT USER *and* LAW

TIN *see* MINERALS

TINCTURES The metals, colours and furs used in ARMORY.

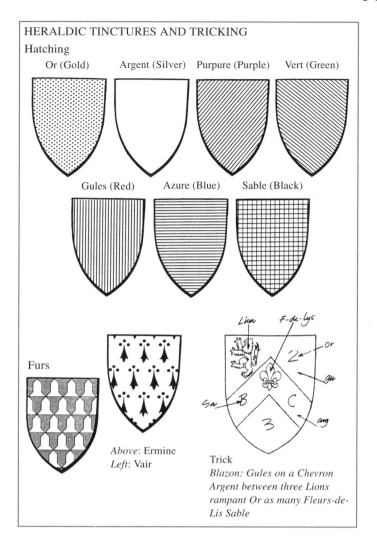

HERALDIC TINCTURES AND TRICKING

Hatching

Or (Gold) Argent (Silver) Purpure (Purple) Vert (Green)

Gules (Red) Azure (Blue) Sable (Black)

Furs

Above: Ermine
Left: Vair

Trick
Blazon: Gules on a Chevron Argent between three Lions rampant Or as many Fleurs-de-Lis Sable

Metals:

Or (Or)	gold, often depicted as yellow
Argent (Arg)	silver, usually depicted as white

Colours:

Gules (Gu)	red
Azure (Az)	blue
Sable (Sa)	black
Vert (Vt)	green

Two further colours are uncommon:

Purpure (Purp)	purple
Murrey (Mu)	mulberry

The so-called 'stains' are rare:

Sanguine	blood-red
Tenné	tawny

Furs:

Ermine (Erm)	white with black 'tails'
Vair	white and blue 'pelts'

each of which is possessed of several variations.

In armory, the *tincture convention* requires that metal shall not lie on metal, nor colour on colour. This convention seems to have been universally accepted from the earliest times and is clearly intended to facilitate the accurate identification of armorial devices.

Since the seventeenth century, the *Petra Sancta* system of hatched lines has often been used to denote tinctures in uncoloured drawings and engravings (*see illustration*). Sketches are often 'tricked', with tinctures indicated by abbreviations (*see above*) and charges, when repeated, represented by numbers or letters.

TINKER *see* GYPSIES

TITHE BARNS *see* BARNS

TITHE MAPS *see* MAPS

TITHES A tax of one-tenth, specifically a tenth part of the annual produce of land or labour, formerly levied to support the clergy and the Church. There were three types of tithe: praedial tithes (calculated on income from produce), mixed tithes (calculated on income from stock and labour combined) and personal tithes (calculated on income derived entirely from labour). Produce raised through tithes was stored in tithe barns (*see* BARNS). Income from customary sources, such as woodland and waste, was exempt. In parishes where the RECTOR was not the incumbent, the tithes were apportioned between the rector (which might be an institution such as a collegiate or monastic foundation) and the vicar (who was appointed to take charge of the parish) and were known respectively as the Great or Rectorial Tithes, and Small or Vicarial Tithes. Vicarial Tithes were generally those raised from labour and minor produce and as such were invariably the most difficult to collect. From 1391, monastic rectors were required to set aside a proportion of their tithes for the benefit of the poor of their parishes. Following the Reformation, many monastic holdings were conveyed by the Crown into private ownership so that a lay person could claim Rectorial Tithes.

The Tithe Commutation Act of 1836 permitted tithes to be commuted to rent charges and commissioners were appointed to negotiate land values in the various parishes. The survey records of the commissioners, and their large-scale maps, were deposited in the Public Record Office, diocesan registries and parochial authorities. Tithe maps (*see* MAPS) are now held by county record offices and the Royal Commission for Historical Manuscripts maintains a register of existing tithe records. The Tithe Act of 1925 transferred tithe rent charges to the *Queen Anne's Bounty* fund which had been established in 1704 to receive and administer for the benefit of the poorer clergy the ecclesiastical revenues annexed by Henry VIII. Tithes were finally extinguished by the Tithe Act of 1936.

Just outside the entrance to Thornford church, Dorset, is the 'tithe tomb' on which the incumbent sat to receive the tithes on St Thomas's day. The tithe money was placed in a hollow carved out of the top of the tombstone.
See also GLEBE *and* TAXATION

TITHING (i) *See* FRANKPLEDGE *and* LAW AND ORDER
(ii) A land division, originally considered to be one-tenth of a HUNDRED.

TITLE DEEDS Some 12 million houses in England and Wales are now recorded in the Land Registry. Once registered, early title deeds, wills, family settlements and other old documents relating the previous conveyances are no longer required. Even when houses are not registered, it is normally only necessary for the deeds to be checked back for fifteen years to prove that the vendor is indeed the owner. Building societies usually ask solicitors to 'weed out' unnecessary documents and as a result a wealth of invaluable historical evidence has been lost. Fortunately, there is a growing tendency for house-owners (or their solicitors) to deposit title deeds and other related papers in local record offices where they are available for public inspection.

TOFT In many medieval villages, dwellings were arranged in rows on either side of a main thoroughfare. Behind the dwellings, and at right angles to the road, elongated and parallel plots of land (*tofts*) extended to a BACK LANE or to the boundary of adjacent closes (*see* CLOSE). Tofts were provided, independently of holdings in the OPEN FIELDS, so that tenants could cultivate vegetables, soft fruit and herbs and perhaps keep a pig and poultry. Although remnants of former tofts are commonly found throughout England, they are a particular feature of many north country villages. Neighbouring tofts were often amalgamated and, in the sixteenth and seventeenth centuries, they were sometimes extended beyond a back lane into adjacent fields to form *garthends*. As a legal term, 'toft and croft' is used to describe the curtilage of a homestead and its adjoining paddock.

TOLBOOTH *see* MARKETS

TOLL-HOUSES AND GATES *see* TURNPIKES

TOLSEY *see* MARKETS

TOMB CHEST The term is misleading for tomb chests do not contain mortal remains but are simply a form of MONUMENT. Not to be confused with TABLE TOMBS (which are also described as chest tombs), tomb chests first appeared in the thirteenth century, inspired by the SHRINES of saints whose bodies were often enclosed in chest-like structures above ground level. Early tomb chests were surmounted by a coped top but these were superseded by INCISED SLABS, BRASSES and EFFIGIES.

Most tomb chests were free-standing but over the centuries many have been moved to a side wall. Where this has occurred, the decorative carving may be seen to continue to what is now the back of the chest. Where tomb chests were originally set against a wall they were usually placed within a low arch, the wall itself providing a canopy above. Alternatively, the tomb chest, its canopy, pillars and arch may be combined to form a screen between two parts of a church: the chancel and an adjacent chapel, for example.

In the thirteenth and fourteenth centuries, the decoration of the sides and ends of a chest reflected contemporary architectural styles: panels containing carved quatrefoils (or, more rarely, trefoils, hexafoils or octofoils), or miniature blind arcading, often with WEEPERS carved within the recesses, for example. From the mid-thirteenth century, painted and gilded shields of arms were added, either within the quatrefoils or in the recesses of the arcading, or on the spandrels on either side of the figures. During the fifteenth century, weepers were superseded by figures of angels, which sometimes carry shields, or the spaces in the arcading were filled entirely with heraldic devices. Following the Reformation, religious motifs were replaced by heraldic ones and Renaissance influences are evident in the gradual introduction of classical forms, both in the decoration and in the structure of the tomb chest itself. The sides of the chests were often divided into panels using balusters, pilasters and colonettes. Figures were rarely used and heraldry, both on the tomb chest and its integral canopy, became increasingly elaborate. From the end of the sixteenth century, many tomb chests were constructed on two levels to accommodate two or even three effigies. From the mid-seventeenth century, the tomb chest was superseded by the hanging WALL MONUMENT and it was not until the GOTHIC REVIVAL of the nineteenth century that tomb chests became fashionable once again.

For the Church Monuments Society *see* APPENDIX I

TOMBS *see* BARROWS, BRASSES, CANOPY, CHAMBERED TOMBS, CEMETERIES, EFFIGIES, GRAVESTONES, INCISED SLABS, MONUMENTS, PLAGUE, SHRINES, TABLE TOMB, TOMB CHEST *and* WALL MONUMENT

TOMEN A Welsh place-name meaning 'mound', and usually a reference to an early fortification, as in Tomen y Mur, 'the mound of the wall', a Norman motte near Trawsfynydd, Gwynedd.

Fifteenth-century tomb chest and effigy attributed to Edward, Prince of Wales, son of Richard III, at Sheriff Hutton, Yorkshire.

-TON From the Old English *tūn*, originally meaning 'enclosure' and thereafter progressing to 'enclosure surrounding a dwelling', 'homestead' and ultimately 'village'. There are numerous etymological variations of *tūn*, but its use generally post-dates that of *hām* (*see* -HAM) and implies a later or subsidiary settlement (*see* HAMLET *and* TOWNSHIP), possibly one within an enclosure of some sort. The meaning is most commonly 'homestead' or 'village', though in many cases villages developed from homesteads and may even have expanded to become medieval TOWNS.

First elements of -ton names are often descriptive of those who occupied them: Orcheston in Wiltshire, for example, was Ordric's *tūn* and Luckington in Somerset was the *tūn* of Luca and his people. Others were associated with royal, magnatial, monastic or episcopal estates: Kingston, Castleton, Monkton and Bishopstone, for example. Tūn is rarely found as a first element, Tunstall in Durham and Tunstead in Derbyshire being two notable exceptions.

TONSURE *see* MONASTERIES

TOOT-HILLS Hill- and cliff-top names such as Nettlecombe Tout, Hounstout and Hambury Tout, Dorset, are derived from the Old English *tōtærn*, an observation post from which men kept watch ('tooted' or 'toted') for Danish raiders (hence the phrase 'touting for business'). Many toot-hills were provided with a shelter and an elevated platform or mound to assist those who kept guard. Tothill, Lincolnshire, derives its name from a nearby toot-hill, and the first element of place-names such as Totternhoe, Bedfordshire ('ridge with a look-out house') and Totterton, Shropshire ('hill with a look-out house') is derived from the Old English *tōtian* meaning 'to observe', and is also evident in Tosson, Northumberland (*tōt-stān*, meaning 'look-out stone') and Tostock, Suffolk (*tōt-stoc*, meaning 'look-out place'). In Shetland and Orkney, 'ward-hills' or 'wart-hills' (from the Old English *weard-setl*, meaning 'watching seat') were also used for this purpose.
See also BEACONS, SIGNAL STATIONS *and* TELEGRAPH

TOR *and* **TORR** The Old English *torr*, meaning 'a rocky peak', is most often found in the dialectal form *tor*, derived from the Cornish *tor*, meaning 'protuberance', and corresponding with the Welsh *tor*, meaning 'bulge', 'belly' or 'boss' and the Gaelic *torr*, meaning simply 'hill'. Tor names are most commonly found in the south-western counties of England but also appear in Derbyshire where they may have been introduced by medieval tin miners from Cornwall.

Glastonbury Tor in Somerset, Sheepstor in Devon and High Tor at Matlock, Derbyshire, are three well-known landmarks; however, *tor* and *torr* elements are also found in place-names such as Torbryan (where the manor was held by Wydo de Brianne in 1242) and Tormoham (a manor held by William de Mohun in the thirteenth century), both in Devon.

TORC An ornate collar or neck-ring, almost certainly worn by Celtic chieftains, often fashioned in gold and among the most magnificent items of IRON AGE craftsmanship.

TORSE *see* CREST

TORTURE Punishment by torture was authorized by royal warrant in 1310 and has been used as a means of extracting 'confessions' from the earliest recorded times.

TOUCH A black marble quarried near Tournai in Belgium (hence 'Tournai Marble') and, from the twelfth century, imported into Britain notably in finished fonts and tomb-slabs (*see* INCISED SLABS) and decorative mouldings of the Tudor and Jacobean periods. Tournai marble is similar in appearance, though by no means identical, to Purbeck and other cheaper 'marbles' by which it was replaced (*see* PURBECK MARBLE). Touchstone was also used for testing alloys by the marks they make on it.

TOUCH MARK *see* PEWTER

TOURNAI MARBLE *see* TOUCH

TOWER HOUSES *see* CASTLES (MEDIEVAL)

TOWERS *see* CASTLES (MEDIEVAL), CHURCH TOWERS, FOLLIES *and* ROUND TOWERS

TOWER SCREEN An ornamental screen, usually of wood, separating the nave of a church from the space beneath a tower at the west end.
See also CHANCEL SCREEN

TOWNS Most towns came into existence as the result of policy decisions made either by individuals or by institutions. While geographical and economic factors undoubtedly influenced those decisions, very few towns simply grew from settlements which happened to be in favourable locations. In the majority of cases, therefore, towns were planned and it is this that distinguished them from other types of settlement. Nevertheless, there is great variation in their origins and development and in their size and morphology. Individual towns may have regionally distinctive characteristics, or characteristics that occur only in towns that perform a particular function. Towns are an important archaeological and historical source as buried remains, buildings, structures and plan characteristics help us to study the past and provide a link to our history.

The major HILL FORTS, such as Hod Hill and Maiden Castle in Dorset, were effectively Iron Age towns: densely populated urban complexes with well-defined 'streets', well-ordered arrangements of dwellings and ancillary buildings and substantial defensive ramparts. Such settlements exercised territorial authority and were centres of commercial, administrative and military activity (*see* OPPIDUM).

To the Roman invader, reared on the classical perception of the city state, such settlements must have seemed primitive indeed. But the Romans themselves never really succeeded in recreating in

Britain the thriving, bustling towns of the Mediterranean with their overcrowded apartment blocks and jostling concourses. Indeed, even the largest Roman towns in Britain were small by comparison: *Londinium* (London) contained only 330 acres within its walls, *Corinium* (Cirencester in Gloucestershire) 240 acres and *Verulamium* (St Albans in Hertfordshire) 200 acres. In the century following the invasion of AD 43, a network of towns developed in southern Britain, each about 96 km (60 miles) from its neighbour and located within a native tribal territory. (*For* the different categories of Roman settlement *see* ROMAN ADMINIS-TRATION). Most of these major towns were fortified with substantial palisaded ramparts, many of which were replaced by stone walls in the third century at a time when the government in Rome was anxiously responding to pressures from outside the Empire. Although Britain seems to have been relatively free from these attacks and to have flourished (*see* ROMAN VILLAS), nevertheless, further defensive measures were considered necessary in the fourth century, notably the addition of towers to town walls (*see* ROMAN FORTS AND CAMPS).

The notion that Roman towns were systematically laid out with streets and public buildings conforming to a geometrical 'grid' is only partially true. Military bases and COLONIÆ such as *Glevum* (Gloucester), which was primarily a town for army veterans, are likely to have been planned in this way from the outset but elsewhere regularity appears to have been the result of remodelling in the late first century. In many instances, the results failed to meet the planners' expectations and the shape of even the larger towns was polygonal rather than rectangular. At *Alauna*, near Alcester in Warwickshire, a 15-acre 'new town' was constructed next to an earlier Roman settlement towards the end of the second century. This had an earthen rampart 1,370 metres (1,500 yards) in circumference and contained more than 100 buildings but the reason for its construction, and for the fortification of twenty other towns at that time, remains a matter of contention among archaeologists.

The walls of a typical Roman town were pierced with gateways through which passed dual carriageways and separate pedestrian walk-ways. In the centre of each *civitas* was a large rectangular complex (*forum*) of administrative offices and law courts and beneath several towns (such as York and Lincoln) stone-built sewers carried away the waste from public baths and lavatories. Water was often conveyed by culvert from outside the town walls, as at *Durnovaria* (Dorchester in Dorset), and most major settlements were provided with a temple and theatre or amphitheatre. Few temples in Roman Britain possess the classical characteristics of those in Italy or France: most are Romano-Celtic with a distinctive ground-plan and, presumably, a distinctive function.

The popular perception of the DARK AGES is one of deserted Roman towns, dilapidated villas and a rapid reversion to barbarism. It is true that there was no discernible revival of urban affairs until the seventh century, when a number of former Roman towns were designated as the administrative centres of dioceses, notably London, Canterbury, Dorchester-on-Thames, Winchester and York. But in the late Saxon period, several new towns were established at proto-urban settlements which, well before the end of the eighth century, had developed characteristics which marked them out from the normal agricultural settlements of the period. For the most part, they were the administrative centres of royal estates and therefore already exercised civil authority within territories which had evolved from earlier minor kingdoms and tribal units. Many possessed a MINSTER and had developed trading functions superior to those of neighbouring settlements. Significantly, most were located at or near former Roman sites, suggesting that such places had regained their status very much earlier than is generally acknowledged and that many had never been entirely deserted.

Indeed, it is highly unlikely that, following the withdrawal of Rome, the entire indigenous population should suddenly abandon the towns and other Roman settlements and the network of metalled roads which radiated from them. No doubt they fell into disrepair, in the absence of a cohesive and skilled workforce, but the pattern was established which was to provide the foundation of many late Saxon towns such as Rochester in Kent, Bradford-on-Avon in Wiltshire and Dorchester in Dorset. These later towns may have been promoted by their royal or ecclesiastical owners or remodelled with regular street patterns and market-places to encourage expansion, but the potential for commercial growth was already there.

Anglo-Saxon sources indicate that there were three types of town, those which developed on former Roman sites being known as *ceasters*. A defensive system of fortified BURHS was also established in southern England during the reigns of Alfred the Great (AD 871–99) and his Saxon successors as a direct response to the threat of Danish invasion. The third and more numerous category of Anglo-Saxon town was the PORT or commercial trading centre. These were not necessarily located on coasts or navigable rivers: many were inland market towns such as Milborne

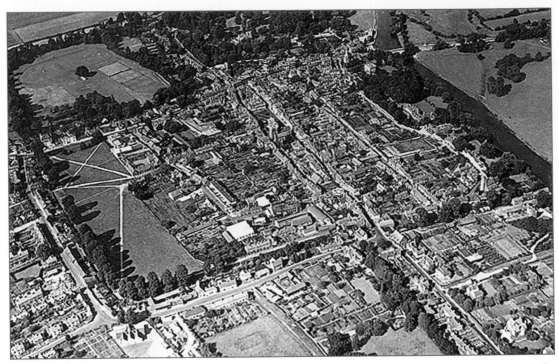

Aerial view of Wallingford, Oxfordshire, showing the rectangular enclosure of the original Saxon fort with the river Thames forming the fourth side.

Port and Langport in Somerset. In the DANELAW, several new towns were created, notably the *Five Boroughs* of Derby, Nottingham, Stamford, Leicester and Lincoln, the last two on former Roman sites.

From the tenth to the thirteenth centuries, numerous planned towns were added to existing villages by their owners in order to encourage trade Professor W.G. Hoskins has identified five such towns in north Oxfordshire alone, four of them (Banbury, Chipping Norton, Deddington and Woodstock) dating from the twelfth century, and the fifth (Bicester) from the thirteenth. Several were castle towns, built outside the gates of late eleventh-century fortresses such as Alnwick in Northumberland, Ludlow in Shropshire and Chepstow in Monmouthshire, while others were entirely new, laid out on 'green-field' sites like that at Salisbury in Wiltshire. The planned origins of such towns are often clearly evident in the regular grid-like pattern of their streets and the rectilinear disposition of ancient boundaries. Kingston-upon-Hull, Humberside (1293), Stratford on Avon in Warwickshire (1196), Liverpool, Merseyside (1207) and Leeds in West Yorkshire (1207) are but four notable examples of early medieval planned towns, three of which developed into major cities. In Wales, King John (1199–1216) and Henry III (1216–72) established

new towns: Montgomery in Powys for example. Henry's son, Edward I (1272–1307), had seen and built new towns on a rectangular grid plan within stone walls during his campaign in Gascony and each of his new Welsh CASTLES (with the exception of Harlech in Gwynedd) was provided with walled towns (*bastides*) and inhabited by colonies of English merchants and tradespeople. The magnificent walls and flanking towers of Caernarfon (Gwynedd) and Conwy (Conwy) survive to this day, as do sections of several baronial bastides such as the late thirteenth-century wall of Tenby in Pembrokeshire.

Medieval magnates, particularly those who owned castles, encouraged communities to develop nearby, both to provide for the needs of their households and to increase revenues from increased trade and commerce (*see* MARKETS). Settlers were attracted by land grants, low rents and other privileges and organized trading monopolies which offered economic security and the right of controlling one's own property within a town. Each freeholder had one or more plots of land with a building abutting the street in which he lived, worked and traded (*see* BURGAGE). More than forty English towns retain sections of their original medieval walls and several their gates which closely resemble castle GATEHOUSES. Although originally constructed for military purposes, town walls facilitated the maintenance of LAW AND ORDER and effectively controlled access to a town's trading facilities which were jealously guarded by the granting of borough charters and other protective franchises and by the formation of GUILDS. But such grants were haphazard: ambitious manorial lords were able to obtain borough status for small communities in anticipation of commercial success and the historical landscape is littered with the relics of failed towns (*see also* ROTTEN BOROUGH). Conversely, several substantial communities such as Ludlow in Shropshire, which possessed all the attributes of towns, were not legally defined as such until the late Middle Ages. From the mid-thirteenth century, there was a decline in the economic conditions which had previously encouraged the building of new towns but many prospered and expanded, either by ribbon development along existing streets or by the addition of new suburbs. Many *Newland* place-names in towns originated at this time.

In the early fourteenth century, London probably had a population of nearly 120,000 and cities such as York, Norwich, Lincoln and Bristol each had about 20,000 inhabitants. Of a total population of 5 million it is now believed that at least 700,000 lived in towns. Urban society was also very well organized with medieval old peoples' homes, orphanages, hospitals, social clubs and hotels. Large numbers of social institutions were provided by wealthy benefactors (*see* CHANTRY), by ecclesiastical foundations (*see* SHRINES) and by fraternities, such as the Guild of Our Lady at Lavenham, Suffolk, whose fifteenth-century meeting-hall was built in part to ensure that Masses were said for the souls of all paid-up members and as a social club for the town's élite, with its own resident cook and musician.

The Black Death of 1348–69 effectively curtailed the creation of new towns, Bewdley, built in 1477 on the banks of the river Severn in Worcestershire, being the last medieval planned town. With the coming of the Tudor dynasty, and the growth of England's material prosperity, there was a revival of urban markets and seaports. But after the sixteenth century, few new towns were established: Whitehaven, Cumbria, was begun in 1660 and developed as a successful coal port and ship-building centre, and the expansion of the Royal Navy resulted in new seventeenth-century towns at Chatham and Devonport, Devon, and at Portsmouth, Hampshire, the suburb of Portsea was added in the early eighteenth century.

In the medieval period, the expansion of an urban population had usually been accommodated by sub-dividing plots and in-filling open spaces, particularly markets which had often outgrown their original sites.

But from the mid-seventeenth century, the formless conglomeration of buildings and social classes which had characterized many medieval towns was superseded by the introduction from Italy of new ideas of urban planning and architectural style which reflected more accurately the growing prosperity of the period. The concept of open circuses and squares with terraces of elegant town houses, such as Bloomsbury Square (1661), St James' Square (1665) and Soho Square (1690), London, was to dominate urban planning for two centuries, reaching its apotheosis in the Georgian city of Bath (*see* CLASSICAL ARCHITECTURE *and* SPAS).

However, there was another side to the coin. The towns of the INDUSTRIAL REVOLUTION also had their terraces, but these were of 'tunnel-back' and 'blind-back' houses, often with inadequate sanitation, small rooms and large families. By contrast, nineteenth-century civic authorities vied with one another in the magnificence of their public buildings, and the 'dark satanic mills' of Victorian industrial magnates loomed above the regimented terraces just as the castles and abbeys of their Norman predecessors had dominated a subjugated people. Indeed, the pattern of earlier medieval fields is sometimes discernible in the disposition of blocks of nineteenth-century terraces.

Several new towns were built to serve both the canal system and the railway network. Goole in Humberside, for example, was a planned canal port founded in 1819 by the Aire and Calder Navigation Company. In Cheshire the town of Crewe was a railway town and Swindon in Wiltshire became a notable engineering centre. The railways also helped to create numerous coastal RESORTS, while fashionable suburbs, such as Edgbaston in Birmingham, developed to accommodate a new and rapidly expanding middle-class. In the early decades of the twentieth century, a number of *garden cities* were built, such as Welwyn Garden City in Hertfordshire, and several philanthropic employers provided *model villages* for their workpeople, such as Bournville on the south-western outskirts of Birmingham, built by the Quaker Cadbury family complete with an adult education college, schools, concert hall, recreation grounds, public baths and many other facilities – but no public houses.

The most successful towns are those whose origins are least apparent. The charm of medieval Lavenham has survived only because it failed to develop after an early period of prosperity, just as Stourport, Worcestershire, has retained its nineteenth-century character because of the failure of the canal system on which it was founded. In contrast, much of medieval Gloucester was destroyed in the 1960s when the developers' bulldozers moved in to reveal ancient TIMBER-FRAMED BUILDINGS behind Victorian façades.

TOWNSHIP (*also* **VILL**) An administrative unit within a PARISH which levied a separate poor rate and may have appointed its own CONSTABLE. The origins of townships are unclear, though most are of undoubted antiquity. When ecclesiastical parishes developed in the late Saxon and medieval periods large numbers of townships were often incorporated within the new boundaries. In the parish of Halifax in Yorkshire, for example, there were no fewer than twenty-two townships. Township communities were often scattered among neighbouring farmsteads and HAMLETS and could be administered corporately by a township assembly. Townships may be identified by Old English *-vill* and *-tūn* place-name elements (*see* -TON).

TRACERS *see* STAINED GLASS

TRACERY *see* GOTHIC ARCHITECTURE *and* WINDOWS

TRACKWAYS *see* HIGHWAY, RIDGEWAYS *and* ROADS

TRACTION ENGINES The age of the steam traction engine lasted from the mid-nineteenth century to the 1930s and during that time developed in a variety of forms from the showman's engine to the THRESHING engine and the ploughing engine. Plough-teams of five men would set out each season, usually just before Easter, with two giant engines and equipment to work as freelance engineers on

Steam ploughing, 1970.

farms throughout lowland Britain. Payment was usually made by the acre ploughed and competition for employment was fierce. The day began at 5.00 a.m. and lasted until sunset, when supper was followed by sleep in a wagon as it was hauled behind an engine to the next farm.

TRADE TOKENS Tradesmen's tokens were widely used during the seventeenth century in place of lawful coinage which, in the smaller values, was frequently in short supply. Trade tokens were an illegal but tolerated system of money-by-necessity, privately issued by merchants particularly during the period 1648 to 1679, when legally minted small change was especially scarce. A very large group was that issued by taverners: in London alone nearly one-third of an estimated 3,000 different tokens in circulation were of this type. Almost every trade issued tokens: barber-surgeons, wool-merchants, apothecaries, mercers, fishmongers and tobacco-sellers whose substitute coins bore designs which were associated with their trades.

TRAILBASTON At the beginning of the fourteenth century, a systematic approach to the widespread problem of lawlessness was required and special 'trailbaston' commissions were established under Edward I (*bastons* being the cudgels carried by members of criminal bands). The earliest appointments of 1304 were justices of general oyer and terminer who were charged to inquire into such offences as extortion and the hiring of men to assault others. By the following year, so many criminals had been taken that it was a matter of some urgency that they should be brought to trial and the Ordinance of Trailbaston was promulgated. This established five judicial circuits, to hear cases which had occurred between the summers of 1297 and 1305. These commissions were renewed in the autumn of 1305 and again in 1307.

The trailbaston inquiries revealed endemic brutality and even murder, particularly at fairs and markets, and corruption was found to be rife among the gentry: many local justices used their position to influence pleas and protection rackets were commonplace. At York, for example, commissioners discovered that a group of wealthy citizens held the city in a stranglehold under the guise of a religious guild, and in Staffordshire alone some 300 men were outlawed as a consequence of the trailbaston hearings. But the hearings were unpopular and often inequitable: anyone who knew how to use a bow and arrow might be accused of belonging to a criminal band and those who had acquired some knowledge of the law might be charged with conspiracy. Although the proceedings were comprehensive and evidently successful, they did not provide the system of local LAW AND ORDER that was so badly needed and many were of the opinion that they had been introduced simply to restore the king's financial fortunes. A *Calendar of London Trailbaston Trials under Commissions of 1305 and 1306* was published by the Public Record Office in 1976.

TRAIN BANDS (*also* **TRAINED BANDS**) Lawless groups of former magnatial retainers whose military services were no longer required following the Wars of the Roses and the suppression of LIVERY AND MAINTENANCE in the early sixteenth century. Often these were synonymous with special forces within the county MILITIA who, in the Tudor period, made themselves available for military training and acquired a justifiable reputation for indiscipline.

TRANSCRIPT A duplicate of entries in parish registers furnished annually to a bishop or archdeacon by churchwardens.

TRANSEPT The transverse portion of a cruciform church, usually referred to as the north and south transept with the *crossing* between.

TRANSHUMANCE *see* BOOLEY HOUSE, HAFOD *and* SHIELING

TRANSOM A vertical bar dividing the lights of a window.
See also MULLION

TRANSPORT *see* CANALS, CARRIER, DROVE ROADS, PACK-HORSE ROADS, RAILWAYS, RIDGEWAYS, ROADS, TURNPIKES *and* VEHICLES (HORSE-DRAWN)

TRANSPORTATION (PENAL) Penal servitude in the American plantations was introduced in 1597 under Elizabeth I, but when these colonies were lost in 1776 following the War of Independence, the hulk system was introduced. *Hulks* were old wooden battleships which were partially dismantled to leave only the rotting body of a ship as a floating prison in which convicts were permanently chained in appalling conditions. In 1770 New South Wales had been annexed for Britain by Captain Cook (1728–79) and needed colonizing, and it was suggested that the severe overcrowding of the hulks could be relieved, and a new colony established, by transporting convicts to New South Wales in Australia. Transportation

Orders were issued by Clerks of the Peace who also arranged contracts for the conveyance of convicts and Botany Bay and Sydney became the first settlements.

The solution was expedient and apparently painless, according to Lord Ellenborough who stated in 1810 that transportation was regarded by its victims 'as a summer airing by an easy migration to a milder climate'. On arrival, a convict became the property of the Governor but was usually 'assigned' – a euphemism for sold – to a free settler. If the convict 'misbehaved' or absconded from the new master, the punishment might be flogging or removal to a chain gang or penal settlements such as Norfolk Island and Port Arthur in Tasmania which acquired a reputation for brutality. At home, legislation of 1816 was singularly harsh: a starving cottager who went out to take a hare or rabbit for his family's pot could be transported for seven years if caught carrying his nets at night.

The most celebrated case of penal transportation was that of the six farm labourers from the village of Tolpuddle in Dorset (the Tolpuddle Martyrs) who in 1833 attempted to form a union to obtain an increase in wages and were sentenced to seven years' transportation on a charge of administering unlawful oaths. George Loveless fell ill after the trial and was separated from his colleagues and sent to Portsmouth where he spent six weeks in the *York* hulk before sailing to Van Dieman's Land (Tasmania) on 25 May 1834 (*see* SIGNPOSTS). The five other men were conveyed to Plymouth where on April 11 they set sail for New South Wales in the convict ship *Surrey*. James Hammett later told how he had been 'sold like a slave for £1. The convicts' names were written on slips of paper, the agents drew lots, each man at £1 per head.' After landing in Sydney, the Standfields, James Loveless, Brine and Hammett were kept in military barracks until they were dispersed to different farms,

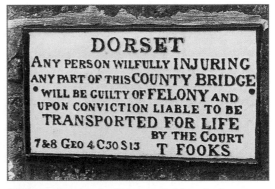

Public notice attached to many bridges in the county of Dorset.

walking hundreds of miles to their destinations. George Loveless arrived at Hobart Town on 4 September and was interviewed by the Governor, Colonel George Arthur. After one week on a chained road gang, he was transferred to the government farm where conditions were better. The Martyrs' harsh sentences caused widespread protests in Britain and two years after their conviction they were pardoned and repatriated.

Transportation records are maintained at the Public Record Office (*see* APPENDIX I) and a list of felons transported to the American colonies from the Home Counties during the period 1719 to 1744 has been published. Censuses of the Australian and Tasmanian penal colonies are also held by the Public Record Office and there is an excellent Martyrs' Museum at Tolpuddle, Dorset.

TRANTER A hawker or occasional CARRIER whose livelihood in the 'haggling business' depended on his horse.

TREASURE TROVE Treasure Trove is a royal prerogative applicable to gold or silver coins, plate or bullion which have been hidden deliberately and are of unknown ownership. The discovery of such a hoard must be reported and ownership determined at a coroner's inquest.

In recent years a trench-war has developed between Britain's 16,000 metal-detector users and the Department of the Environment which wants to make compulsory by law the reporting of finds of 'portable antiquities' by everyone other than professional archaeologists. Scotland, Eire and Northern Ireland already have such legislation but, ironically, Italy, Greece and Turkey, where there are the strictest controls, also have the largest underground trade in smuggled antiquities. Archaeologists are justifiably concerned by incidents such as the looting by trespassers with metal-detectors of a hoard of Roman coins at Wanborough, Surrey, and by the damage which may be caused to archaeological sites by irresponsible treasure-hunters. While few detector-users object in principle to reporting, many are concerned that legislation would result in a time-wasting increase in reports of archaeological trivia by over-conscientious amateurs and an increase in the deliberate concealment of worthwhile finds by those who wish to avoid the often expensive complexities of the process of law.

A particularly grey area is the traditional practice of 'beach-combing', highlighted by the discovery in 1987 of a ninth-century Viking harness-mount on the foreshore at Harkstead, Suffolk. Metal-detecting on the foreshore (the area between low and high water) is not a public privilege and requires specific consent from the landowner or lessee which, in the case of 55 per cent of Britain's foreshore, is the Crown. Although there appears to be no legal precedent establishing the Crown's title to foreshore finds, the Harkstead harness-mount was claimed by the Crown Commissioners.

TREASURY The Norman kings created two departments to deal with financial matters: the EXCHEQUER and the Treasury, which was responsible for receiving and paying out monies on behalf of the sovereign. From the second half of the sixteenth century, the Treasury began to supersede the functions of the Exchequer, and in the eighteenth century the First Lord gradually assumed the rôle of Prime Minister. Subsequently, prime ministers have invariably held the office of First Lord of the Treasury, the functions of the office being carried out by the Chancellor of the Exchequer. *Treasury records*, which contain details of towns, transport, commerce, trade and so on are maintained at the Public Record Office. They comprise the minutes and correspondence of the Treasury Board from 1557 and 1745 and are published in the *Calendar of Treasury Papers* (in six volumes), the *Calendar of Treasury Books* (in thirty-two) and, for the period 1729 to 1745, the *Calendar of Treasury Books and Papers* (five volumes).

TREBUCHET *see* SIEGES

TREE OF JESSE *see* JESSE WINDOW

TREE OF LIFE A decorative motif consisting of a stylized representation of 'the tree of life . . . in the midst of the garden' (Genesis Ch. 2, v. 9). In the Western Church it is a symbol of Salvation and is found, for example, in medieval WALL PAINTINGS. *See also* CHRISTIAN SYMBOLS

TREE RING DATING Dendrochronology is a method of dating timber by studying its annual growth-rings. A tree adds a ring of growth each year: in dry years this is of limited growth, while in wet years more luxuriant growth produces a wider ring. Timber may be dated accurately by matching sequences of rings with those from a living tree of known date. Using tree ring dating, standard growth plots may be compiled for different historical periods, and in Britain the method has been used to date timbers (usually oak) from Roman and medieval structures.

TREF- The Welsh *Tref-* or *Tre-*, meaning 'homestead' or 'hamlet', is a common place-name element in Wales and is also found in Herefordshire and

Lancashire, and in Cornwall, as *Trev-* and *Tre-*. In the modern Welsh, *tref* means both 'home' and 'town'.

TRENDAL A circular candle-holder suspended before a ROOD.

TRENDEL Trendel in street names, and evident in place-names such as Trentishoe in Devon and Trull in Somerset, is derived from the Old English word meaning 'circle'.

TRIAL BY BATTLE *see* APPROVER

TRIAL BY ORDEAL *see* LAW

TRIBUNE *see* CHURCHES

TRICK *see* TINCTURES

TRIFORIUM *see* CHURCHES

TRIGONOMETRICAL STATIONS ('TRIG POINTS') *see* ORDNANCE SURVEY

TRILITHON Two upright stones supporting a third horizontal stone.

TRINITY (i) The academic and law term beginning after Easter.
See also HILARY *and* MICHAELMAS
(ii) A common CHRISTIAN SYMBOL representing the Holy Trinity.

TRINITY HOUSE *see* LIGHTHOUSES

TRINODA NECESSITAS The basic feudal obligations of all villeins consisting of military support (*fyrd-bote*), the repair of fortifications (*burgh-bote*) and the maintenance of roads and bridges (*bridge-bote*).

TRIPTYCH A set of three painted panels hinged together so that they may be folded together. Triptychs probably originated in the portable altars of the medieval nobility and are usually placed against a wall or free-standing. Like the DIPTYCH (which has two panels), a triptych usually depicts religious themes, though a very small number contain genealogical and armorial information such as the St John triptych at Lydiard Tregoze in Wiltshire, which was erected *c.* 1615 for Sir John St John (d.1594) by his son, also Sir John, Bart. The front displays a number of genealogical trees with the arms associated with each generation. When

opened, the panels reveal paintings of Sir John and his wife kneeling on a sarcophagus and flanked by their daughters and their son and daughter-in-law. *See also* MONUMENTS

TRIQUETRA An ancient symbol whose three equal arcs represent the Holy Trinity and its continuous form, Eternity (*see* CHRISTIAN SYMBOLS).

TRIVIUM *see* EDUCATION

TROY TOWNS *see* MAZES

TRUCK From 1830, a series of Truck Acts was directed against the 'truck system' whereby workpeople received their wages, or part of their wages, in the form of vouchers which could only be exchanged at a company shop. The 1831 Act required that wages, other than those of domestic servants, should be paid in cash.

TRUE BILL A bill of indictment which, when presented to a grand jury, was endorsed as a 'true bill' if it was considered that a *prima facie* case had been made.

TUDOR ARCH *see* ARCH

TUDOR ARCHITECTURE Tudor buildings remained essentially Gothic in form (*see* GOTHIC ARCHITECTURE) and, with the exception of the chapel of Henry VII at Westminster (1503–19), are nearly all secular. (The magnificent King's College Chapel at Cambridge (1446–1515) and St George's Chapel, Windsor (1475–1509) were also completed during this period.)

The heavily fortified medieval castle had become an architectural anachronism long before 1485, and by the Reformation there were sufficient churches for everyone. The DISSOLUTION OF THE MONAS-TERIES made available vast tracts of land and created unique opportunities for the building of country houses, farmsteads and estate dwellings which were enthusiastically exploited by the new Tudor establishment. The confiscation of church property also enabled Henry VIII (1509–47) to embark on a programme of large-scale building, intended both to enhance his personal esteem and to increase England's prestige abroad. But even Henry's palaces, and those of his magnates, were characterized by an intimacy of detail which reflected domestic rather than ecclesiastical or military functions. Windows and doors were smaller and buildings often contained numerous chambers, each with its own fireplace and garderobe. But the most characteristic feature of Tudor buildings was the use of BRICK which suddenly acquired an almost universal popularity, inspired by the success of earlier East Anglian buildings.

The Great Houses of Tudor England were singularly beautiful: walls of warm red brick and romantic vestiges of more turbulent days such as elaborate GATEHOUSES, placid water-filled moats and mock crenellations, combined with steeply pitched roofs, clustered gables, turrets and ornate 'cork-screw' chimneys to create buildings of unparalleled eloquence and charm. Lavish heraldic display, both in architectural features and in the fabric and furnishings of interiors, reflected the newly acquired social status of the Tudor nobility and gentry. The chambers of most Tudor mansions were usually panelled from floor almost to ceiling in the characteristic linen-fold pattern of the period (*see* PANELLING).

Fireplaces in the principal rooms were often of considerable size, with four-centred arches and massive carved overmantles. It was from this time that coal was used more widely as domestic fuel but coal smoke was noxious and more efficient chimney flues were developed by which the smoke was removed to a point well above roof-height (*see* CHIMNEYS). With the introduction of chimney flues, the traditional HALL (which had previously been open to the rafters) could be provided with a second storey, thereby doubling the available floor space. At this time, the underside of the new floor, and the beams and joists on which it rested, was usually left bare, plaster ceilings being provided from the Elizabethan period (*see* ELIZABETHAN AND JACOBEAN ARCHITECTURE).

Window openings, usually of stone set into brickwork, were sufficiently small to accommodate an opening casement of iron and glass and were either single or grouped in pairs or threes beneath a stone or brick hood. They have flat arched heads, usually cut from a single piece of stone, and the corners often contain small triangular depressions: the last remnants of Gothic tracery. Larger windows were Perpendicular in style, with tracery and STAINED GLASS, and the oriel window was particularly popular. Tudor arches are invariably four-centred (*see* ARCH) or of a modified form which is flatter and has straight, sloping members rather than curved ones.

Not all Tudor buildings were of brick: stone continued to be used in some districts and in many heavily wooded areas, such as Cheshire and Warwickshire, TIMBER-FRAMED BUILDINGS were more common, the infilling between the oak timbers being of brick laid in a variety of decorative 'herringbone' patterns. Very often the lower storey was built of brick with a top storey and roof of timber.

In rural areas where there was a strong conservative building tradition architectural detail is seldom a true guide to date and this is particularly true of vernacular dwellings which continued to be constructed in the traditional way for many years after the Renaissance.

TUDOR COASTAL FORTS With the re-opening of hostilities with France a number of artillery forts were constructed in the 1520s and 1530s but it was not until 1539 that

> King Henrie the Eight, having shaken off the intolerable yoke of the Popish tyrannie, and espying that the Emperour was offended for the divorce of Queen Katherine his wife, and that the French King had coupled the Dolphine his son to the Pope's niece, and married his daughter to the King of Scots, so that he might more justly suspect them all, than safely trust any one, determined . . . to stand upon his owne gardes and defence: and therefore with all speede, and without sparing any cost, he builded Castles, platfourmes and block-houses, in all needfull places of the Realme. (John Lambarde)

These included the entire coastline from Land's End in Cornwall to Kingston-upon-Hull on Humberside, for Henry recognized that the enmity of the Emperor implied also that of Spain and Flanders as well as France. The resulting scheme of national defences was the most comprehensive since that of the Saxon Shore (*see* ROMAN FORTS AND CAMPS) for, unlike the piecemeal defences of the previous two centuries, it was directly controlled by central government and financed by the substantial revenues obtained from the DISSOLUTION OF THE MONASTERIES.

The forts (there were twenty on the south coast alone) were constructed with low thick walls to resist enemy artillery and their guns, which were at first imported from the Low Countries and later manufactured in Sussex, were cast in one piece rather than barrel-forged and could therefore take a more powerful charge and fire a larger ball over a longer distance. The first series of forts was built to protect the Channel coast between Thanet and Dover in Kent and, because of their shape, they are sometimes referred to as Tudor Rose forts. Deal, the first and most complex of these, consists of a central circular 'keep', from which radiate six semi-circular bastions (*lunettes*), within a 'curtain wall', also with six lunettes, and a broad dry moat and outer wall. Within these walls are 145 embrasures, though not all would be used simultaneously: the guns would be moved from port to port on wheeled carriages, while

The Tudor coastal fort at Deal in Kent.

the heaviest artillery was mounted in three tiers on the reinforced roofs of the curtain wall bastions, on the bastions of the keep and on the roof of the keep itself. These were intended for long-range use against ships, though the fort could also be defended on the landward side, and the moat and inner ward were covered by numerous handgun loops.

By 1540, forts had been constructed at Walmer, Sandown, Dover and Sandgate (near Folkstone), Kent; Camber (near Rye), Sussex; Calshot and Hurst, Hampshire; East and West Cowes on the Isle of Wight, and Portland, Dorset. The chain was then extended to include Harwich, Essex and Kingston-upon-Hull in the north and westward to Portsmouth, Hampshire, Poole and Weymouth, Dorset, and St Mawes and Pendennis, Cornwall. The forts commanded the sea-approaches to important harbours and vulnerable sections of the coast and were essentially medieval-type fortresses, intended primarily for offensive operations against sea-borne incursions. However, artillery such as the mid-sixteenth-century *culverins*, which could fire an 8 kg ball (18 lb) more than 1,600 metres (over a mile), rendered the Tudor forts obsolete almost before they were completed. Because of their design, they presented far

too large a target to an enemy's cannon and the semicircular walls of bastions were impossible to defend with gun-fire at close quarters. Consequently, there emerged the *arrow-head bastion* which presented a minimum target to an enemy and, because of its straight sides, could be defended with a small number of guns.

The first arrow-head bastions were constructed in 1546–7 to guard the Solent at Portsmouth and at Yarmouth on the Isle of Wight. In 1558 the defences of Berwick-upon-Tweed on the Scottish border were reconstructed with five large rectilinear bastions, each completely covering its neighbour and the length of curtain wall between. Like the earlier arrow-head bastions, the walls of Berwick's innovative defences were constructed of compacted earth with masonry facings designed to absorb the impact of heavy artillery fire. Thereafter, this *bastioned trace* structure was to provide the foundation of large-scale British fortresses for over three centuries. Walmer Castle is now the official residence of the Lord Warden of the CINQUE PORTS.

See also CHANNEL DEFENCES, COASTAL DEFENCES, FORTIFICATIONS *and* MARTELLO TOWER

TUMPS *see* CASTLES (MEDIEVAL)

TUMULUS A generic term for ancient burial mounds, BARROWS and CAIRNS.

TUN A measure of capacity: one tun = 250 wine gallons.

TUNNEL VAULT *see* VAULTING

TURBARY *see* COMMONS *and* FOREST

TURBINE *see* WATER-MILLS

TURF DIALS The origin of turf dials is unclear but it has been suggested that they were simply patterns cut in the close grass of upland sheep walks by medieval shepherds and served a similar purpose to scratch-dials (*see* SUNDIALS). They are commemorated in field and hill names such as Dialhill, Dial Bank and Dial Mead.

TURNPIKES Turnpikes were originally the gated entrances of walled towns where travellers' credentials were checked and through which the movement of merchandise was controlled and tolls collected. No doubt the gates passage was of sufficient width for a sentry to 'turn' his pike horizontally in order that each group of market-goers should be scrutinized and admitted in turn. Subsequently, the term was applied not only to the check-points themselves but also to the 'turnpike roads' which passed through them.

The Highway Act of 1555 made parishes responsible for the maintenance of highways within their boundaries but the resources of many parishes were unequal to the task, while others simply chose to ignore the legislation (*see* ROADS). In 1663 an act was passed which was to change forever the financing of highway maintenance. With increasing traffic, the Great North Road was in urgent need of attention, particularly those sections which passed through the East Midlands, and the act enabled justices of the peace in those counties to levy tolls for their repair. The first toll-gate or turnpike was erected at Wadesmill, Hertfordshire, and this consisted of a simple bar which could be opened or closed to control traffic. Although the experiment was not deemed to be a success at the time (the turnpikes were eventually dismantled), further legislation was introduced towards the end of the seventeenth century by which several turnpike trusts were created and these proliferated rapidly in the following century. Groups of trustees, usually local businessmen with a pecuniary interest in transport, raised capital to finance schemes for diversions and road improvements by offering interest rates of 4 or 5 per

Toll-gate and cottage at Shaldon Bridge, Teignmouth, Devon. (F. Frith)

cent against loans which were repaid from the tolls charged to road-users. Initially, the trusts employed their own turnpikemen but later franchises were offered at auction to speculators who anticipated making more from tolls than was paid at auction.

The earliest turnpikes consisted of tapering bars of iron or wood which pivoted and turned on a central pillar. These were later superseded by conventional gates, often in pairs and with a side gate for pedestrians. At each toll-house (*see below*) a board was erected on which was displayed a list of charges and several of these have survived. A typical toll was a farthing a head for cattle and sixpence for a carriage and horse, though the pecuniary interests of members of a trust were sometimes evident in the charges made: at the Craven Cross Bar on the Keighley to Kendal road, for example, a two-horse cart was charged 1*s* 1½*d* but a similar cart carrying coal paid only 3*d*. At some turnpikes, heavily-laden vehicles were weighed in order to determine the toll. Pedestrians were not normally charged, neither were farmers' dung carts, harvest wagons and cattle travelling between farm and field and vehicles on their way to church,. A single ticket provided for any number of return journeys along a particular section of road during the day on which it was issued.

Turnpike roads did not necessarily follow earlier routes: several new roads were constructed and others diverted to avoid HOLLOW WAYS or raised on CAUSEWAYS over badly drained land. Many FORDS were bridged and gradients reduced by cuttings and most roads were straightened and widened and generally improved by ploughing out ruts and compacting the surface with stones. When roads were up-graded, villages often flourished which had previously been backwaters, while others declined when a turnpike road passed them by.

The toll-roads were by no means universally popular: the REBECCA RIOTS of 1839 and 1844 began as a result of the excessive number of toll-gates erected in the impoverished agricultural areas of south-west Wales, and drovers and the masters of pack-horse trains avoided the turnpikes wherever possible (*see* DROVE ROADS *and* PACK-HORSE ROADS). Circumventing a toll-gate was comparatively easy in open countryside but as route-ways converged on towns many turnpike trusts negotiated with landowners to prevent the use of side roads and back lanes by erecting obstacles which may still be evident in local names such as Chain-Bar Lane and the Chainway.

Nearly 2,000 individual turnpike bills were presented to Parliament in the eighteenth century until in 1773 a general Turnpike Act was passed which facilitated the process so that by 1820 some 32,000 km (20,000 miles) of roads had been improved in England and Wales and, although the standard of such roads was variable, the efficiency of road transport was transformed. But as the canal and then the railway networks spread, so capital was transferred from the turnpike trusts into new canal and railway companies and with increased competition the volume of road traffic declined. In particular, the coaching trade, which had enjoyed a period of rapid expansion during the turnpike era, was unable to compete with the railways and the last turnpike ceased to operate in 1895. (*See also* CANALS *and* RAILWAYS.)

A particular feature of turnpike roads, and one which is still evident today, was the *toll-house* in which lived the pikeman or toll collector. A small number are still in use on privately owned stretches of road, such as that at Whitney near Hay-on-Wye in Herefordshire which was exempted from taxation by the Whitney Toll Bridge Act of 1796 (and is so exempt today). But most former toll-houses have now been converted to private roadside dwellings with names that recall their past, such as Farthing Gate on the Dorchester to Sherborne road in Dorset and Max's Gate, after which Thomas Hardy named his newly built house in 1885. Because of their function, toll-houses were always conspicuous and several were located at the centre of particularly busy roads or at road junctions. Most abutted the roadside with a small ticket window facing the traveller as he passed through the gate. Different trusts adopted their own architectural styles (as they did their own fashions in SIGNPOSTS), but the most common type has three sides to the front with the ticket-window at the centre and side windows affording views along the highway so that the gate-keeper could anticipate the arrival of travellers.

TURNPIKE STAIR *see* STAIRCASES

TUSCAN ORDER *see* CLASSICAL ARCHITEC-TURE

TYBURN TICKET *see* GENEALOGY

TYGER *see* BEASTS (HERALDIC)

TYMPANUM The space enclosed within a PEDIMENT, or between a lintel and the arch above. The tympanum above the main entrance to a church is often ornately carved.

TŶUNNOS *see* SQUATTER

ULTIMOGENITURE *see* PRIMOGENITURE

UNCIAL In handwriting, letters having the large rounded forms used in Latin and Greek manuscripts. Unlike CURSIVE scripts, uncial letters were not joined together. The term is also applied to capital and other large letters in documents dating from the fifth to the eighth centuries.

UNDERCROFT *see* CASTLES (MEDIEVAL) *and* CRYPT

UNICORN *see* BEASTS (HERALDIC)

UNITARIAN A sect, dating in England from the mid-seventeenth century, which believes in the unipersonality of God and rejects the doctrines of the Trinity and the Divinity of Christ. Unitarian archives are kept at the Unitarian Headquarters and records are published by the Unitarian Historical Society (*see* APPENDIX I).

UNITE *see* COINAGE

UNITED KINGDOM *see* BRITAIN

UNIVALLATE *see* MULTIVALLATE

UNIVERSITIES *see* EDUCATION

UP-AND-DOWN HUSBANDRY Introduced in the sixteenth century, and popular during the seventeenth, up-and-down husbandry was a system of rotation which began with the cultivation of pasture and the production of cereal crops which continued until a field began to show signs of diminished fertility. It was then allowed to revert to pasture and was manured by grazing livestock. Variations of the system continue today: ley farming, for example, in which a field is sown with selected grasses instead of being left to regenerate naturally. Typically, the leys of grass were left unploughed for six or seven years and cultivated for four, though this could be extended to six years if the ground had been fertilized with marl. By this system, the normal ploughland yield of the OPEN FIELD could be doubled.

UPPING STOCKS As the name suggests, upping stocks were used for mounting a horse and until recently were one of the most common reminders of the equestrian age and also one of the most vulnerable. They were of particular benefit to those who rode pillion and were usually positioned so that the passenger could mount or dismount directly from a garden without stepping into the mire of the road or farmyard. A typical upping stock consists of a low square brick or stone platform with a flight of three or four steps at one side. Many were adapted and enlarged in the present century to facilitate the loading of milk churns onto the backs of lorries before the introduction of tankers.

Although still numerous, countless upping stocks have been destroyed, regardless of their historical associations and quite often in contravention of regulations relating to the conservation of adjacent buildings of which, technically, they formed a part. It is often extremely difficult to date upping stocks: many were built during the eighteenth and nineteenth centuries and are contemporary with the buildings they served. Others may be of considerable antiquity but few, including many of medieval and Tudor origin, are listed or specifically protected. Upping stocks are also known as horse-blocks, horse-steps, horse-stones, mounting-blocks and mounting-stones.

VACCARY Cattle pasture.
See also FOREST

VAGABONDS *see* POOR LAW

VAGRANTS *see* POOR LAW

VALETTI *see* YEOMAN

VALLEY ROOF *see* ROOFS

VALLUM *see* ROMAN FORTS AND CAMPS

VALOR *see* MANOR

VASSAL A person who held land of a lord and owed FEALTY to him.

VAULTING Vaulting is the arched interior of a roof, usually constructed of stone or brick though some eighteenth- and nineteenth-century vaults were built in wood or plaster. Vaulted ceilings are a characteristic of medieval GOTHIC ARCHITECTURE and of the nineteenth-century GOTHIC REVIVAL but are normally only found in CATHEDRALS, major churches and in the smaller components of parish churches such as the ceiling of a porch or tower.

The shape of the vault follows the geometry of the ARCH and the simplest vault is, therefore, that which accompanies the semi-circular ROMANESQUE ('Norman') arch. This is known as the *barrel vault* (also *tunnel vault* and *wagon vault*) and is commonly found in Roman and later Romanesque buildings and is so named because of its semi-circular section and barrel-like appearance. Where two barrel vaults intersect at right angles they form a *groined* or *cross vault*. Because of the enormous thrust exerted on supporting walls, the barrel vault was found to be singularly unsuited to wide spans, particularly in the monastic churches of western Europe, the components of which (nave, choir, transepts and aisles) were invariably of different heights and widths and could not be accommodated within a structure which was constrained by the geometry of the semi-circular arch. In addition, the interior roofs of many early abbey churches were constructed of timber, and were a considerable fire hazard, and it was the need for brick or stone vaulting, combined with the structural limitations of the round arch, which lead to the development in the early medieval period of the *ribbed vault* and pointed arch.

Ribs are raised bands of stone or brick which spring from the wall to support and strengthen the vault. The ribbed vault consisted of a quadripartite framework (bisected by diagonal ribs), supported during construction on a temporary timber structure (*centering*). Once the spaces between the ribs (*webs* or *cells*) had been infilled with cut stone pieces or bricks the vault became self-supporting and the centering was removed. Vaults are divided into bays by *transverse arches* and, while bays created by semi-circular arches were inevitably square, the diagonals of a ribbed vault were longer than the sides and it was therefore impossible for all the ribs to be semi-circular. This problem was overcome by adopting the pointed arch, which originated in the Middle East and, by the twelfth century, had already spread to countries such as Spain and Sicily where

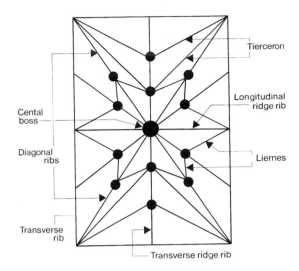

Roof vaulting.

there was a strong north-African influence. The pointed arch was ideally suited to vaulting of various heights and spans and, during the four centuries of the Gothic period, it enabled buildings of increasing complexity and architectural audacity to be constructed throughout western Europe.

The early quadripartite ribbed vault, which consisted of four compartments within each bay, formed the basis for all future designs. Stone BOSSES were added at the intersection of ribs and these were often heavily carved with gilded and painted motifs. In the fourteenth century, intermediate *tierceron ribs* were added which extended from the springing of the vault (the point at which it began to splay upwards) to the *ridge rib* (at the apex of the vault) and from this developed the *lierne vault*, in which additional interlocking ribs (*liernes*) were introduced, forming elaborate patterns within the basic structural framework of ribs. A *stellar vault* is one in which the lierne ribs form a star-shaped pattern.

The final Perpendicular phase of the Gothic period is characterized by *fan vaulting* which, as the name suggests, is an ornamental vaulting of inverted half-conoids (cones with concave sides). Each pair of half-conoids just meet at the centres of their curves, all the ribs are equidistant from each other and in most cases all have the same curvature. In a fan vault, the ribs were carved from a stone slab rather than supporting it, and the joints between the blocks may often be seen passing across the purely decorative tracery of the ribs. Fan vaulting was an English innovation, the earliest known example being in the chantry chapel of Edward, Lord Despenser at Tewkesbury Abbey,

Gothic Vaulting: (top left) quadripartite ribs in the nave vault of Durham Cathedral, c. 1120; (top right) ribbed tierceron vault in the nave of Exeter Cathedral, 1353–69; (bottom left) lierne vault in the presbytery of Gloucester Cathedral, c. 1350; (bottom right) fan vaulting in the chapel of King's College, Cambridge, 1446–1515.

Gloucestershire. Despenser died in 1375 and it is likely that the same mason was responsible for the magnificent fan vaulting in the cloister at nearby Gloucester Cathedral which was completed not later than 1412. Fine examples of fan vaults are those at Sherborne Abbey, Dorset (1475–1500) and King's College Chapel, Cambridge (1446–1515).

In most great medieval churches, with the exception of those of the more austere monastic orders, vaulting would originally have been ablaze with brilliant colour and gilding. Although beyond the range of normal eye-sight, the detail of carving and painting was faultlessly executed and was clearly intended for the greater glorification of God. It is only through the modern camera lens that we are privileged to approach such perfection for the first time.

VEGETATION Deserted cottage gardens and TOFTS may often be identified from the type of vegetation which has become established on the site. Nettles, for example, are a reliable indication of former human activity, as are many 'weeds', such as ground elder, which were once grown for food and other domestic purposes.
See also CROP MARKS *and* DESERTED VILLAGES

VEHICLES (HORSE-DRAWN) *see* BAROUCHE, BROUGHAM, CARRIER, CHAISE, CHAR-A-BANC, CLARENCE, CURRICLE, DOG-CART, FLOAT, FOURGON, FOUR-WHEEL CAB ('GROWLER'), FLY, GIG, HACKNEY-CAB, HANSOM CAB, HARNESS, LANDAU, MAIL-COACH, OMNIBUS, PHAETON, POSTILION, STAGECOACH, STAGE-WAGON, VICTORIA *and* WAGONS

VELLUM A fine form of PARCHMENT prepared by limewashing and burnishing from the skins of calves, kids or lambs.

VENISON *see* FOREST

VENVILLE RIGHTS *see* COMMONS

VERSAL LETTER The initial letter of a verse or paragraph, usually embellished or illuminated.

VERDERER From the early eleventh century, verderers were appointed to administer the 'vert and venison' of a FOREST. In the medieval period, there were four verderers appointed to each forest. They were elected by freeholders in the county court and were required to attend a Court of Attachment which was usually convened at intervals of forty days. In

the Forest of Dean in Gloucestershire, the Verderers' Court still meets (in the court-room of what is now the Speech House Hotel) to determine disputes according to the forest laws and to control freemining and other activities within the court's jurisdiction.

VERGE The medieval court was a peripatetic one and wherever it resided there came into being a territory or 'verge' which extended like an immense nimbus around the king's person. Within the verge, which had a radius of 19 km (12 miles), the court exercised a special jurisdiction particularly with regard to the procurement of goods and services for the royal retinue. This was the responsibility of the Clerk of the Market, an officer of the court who was also concerned with weights and measures. For a time, the Clerk's authority was extended to include all the MARKETS in England, but his duties were invariably conceded to local landowners, and in 1640 legislation required that he should operate only within the verge and that elsewhere the responsibility for the proper administration of markets should be vested in manorial lords or municipal officers.

VERNACULAR (i) The language or dialect of a country or of a particular indigenous class or group.
(ii) Characteristics, such as building styles and materials, appertaining to a particular locality.

VERT (i) In BLAZON, the TINCTURE green.
(ii) Any species of plant or tree that provided food for game, especially deer (*see* FOREST).

VESPERS *see* MONASTERIES

VESTRY *see* PARISH

VICAR *see* CLERGY (CHURCH OF ENGLAND) *and* PARISH

VICTORIA COUNTY HISTORY A series of volumes known collectively as *The Victoria History of the Counties of England*, the compilation of which commenced in 1899 and continues today under the direction of the Institute of Historical Research of the University of London (*see* APPENDIX I). The aim of the project's founders was to research and to record in detail the history of every English county, using original source material. The original intention was that there should be general and topographical volumes for each county, the first describing political, economic, ecclesiastical and social factors, and the second the history of individual parishes arranged in hundreds, wapentakes or wards. But in practice many county series have taken a different form: that for Dorset, for example, includes a volume devoted to Domesday. The *Victoria County History* is an invaluable guide to records and source material, though none of the articles of which each volume is composed should be accepted uncritically for there are inconsistencies and some entries have been superseded by more recent research.

Of equal interest is the vast collection of slip references compiled in the late nineteenth century by a team of ladies who combed manorial and parish records in the Public Record Office for information relevant to the *VCH* project. These slips are now held by the Institute of Historical Research and are available to serious researchers. *The Victoria County History* volumes for each county are necessarily weighty and expensive. The excellent Longman series of regional histories, however, is comparatively inexpensive and includes twenty-one volumes: two for each of ten regions (pre- and post-AD 1000), with an additional volume for the Welsh Borders in the later period.

VICTORIAN ARCHITECTURE The Victorian Age was one of great contrasts: pomp and splendour and appalling squalor; whimsical romanticism and innovative feats of engineering. The romantic movement, which found beauty in rusticity and medievalism, had at first expressed itself in Gothic ruins and fashionable curiosities such as the COTTAGE ORNÉE and the Gothic library and music-room. But the social evils of the INDUSTRIAL REVOLUTION created in many a need to seek out what were perceived to be the more wholesome characteristics of an earlier age. They attempted to encourage the making of artefacts by hand, tried to revive the medieval craft guilds and regarded as worthless all things made by machine. In particular, they admired GOTHIC ARCHITEC-TURE for its structural honesty, but failed to apply that quality imaginatively to contemporary buildings and instead imitated the sombre detail of the Early English style. Nevertheless, it was because of this quality of escapism that architecture of the GOTHIC REVIVAL enjoyed almost universal popularity. Many larger houses, designed for affluent clients by eminent architects and built by the finest craftsmen using traditional skills and materials, may indeed be considered successful. But what was fashionable among the élite of one generation was imitated by the middle classes of the next, and as the budget diminished so the quality of construction and materials deteriorated, leaving the pretentious *bijou* residences of the 1890s.

The medievalists did not have things all their own way, however, and the classicists continued to build in the Renaissance manner. By the second half of the nineteenth century, an architectural compromise appears to have emerged. Buildings of an ecclesiastical or scholastic character were almost invariably Gothic, while civic and commercial buildings were usually designed in a ponderous classical style. There were, of course, exceptions: the hotel fronting St Pancras Station in London, built in 1860 at the height of the Railway Age, is a magnificent example of high Victorian Gothic.

It was the engineers who recognized the potential of the new technology and of materials such as sheet glass, cast iron and (later) steel. Great railway termini such as Paddington in London (1852–4) and immense structures like the Forth Bridge in Scotland (1890) were constructed under the joint direction of a principal architect and a principal engineer. But the benefits of the new technology did were not universally appreciated. Even at the beginning of the nineteenth century, thousands of new working-class homes were needed to accommodate the rapid expansion of population in the industrial conurbations. The seemingly endless, uniform rows of squalid, insanitary slums are the other legacy of the Victorian Age (*see* TOWNS).
For the Victorian Society *see* APPENDIX I

VICTORIA Dating from *c.* 1860, the Victoria was an elegant coachman-driven four-wheel vehicle without doors. It was favoured by the Prince of Wales (afterwards Edward VII) and by Queen Victoria, after whom the English version was named. It remained popular until 1900 as a parade carriage and was driven by a single horse or pair of horses and carried two forward-facing passengers. A later and larger version, which carried four passengers, was known as the *double Victoria*.

VICTORINES An order of canons regular founded by William of Champeaux at the former abbey of St Victor in Paris in 1113. The twelfth-century Victorines included in their number many famous scholars, mystics and poets. In England, the order's first house was at Wigmore, Herefordshire, but of greater influence was the abbey of St Augustine, Bristol, which was to become the cathedral of the new diocese following the Reformation.

VICUS The smallest settlement unit recognized by Rome for administrative purposes: similar in size to a small medieval market town with an established road system, public buildings and an elected magistrate (*see* ROMAN ADMINISTRATION).

VIKINGS A generic term, from the Old Norse word for 'pirate', to describe the Scandinavian traders and marauders who ravaged much of northern Europe, and spread eastwards into Russia and Byzantium, between the eighth and eleventh centuries. Early Viking expeditions were little more than speculative incursions but in later years they tended to end in conquest and colonization. The Vikings travelled in streamlined longships of clinker construction, powered by sail and oars and of shallow draught which made them ideally suited to raiding along the estuarine coasts of Britain.

Norwegian Vikings settled in the Orkney and Shetland islands in the eighth century from where they explored westward to Iceland, Greenland and north America and south to Ireland and western Britain. During the three centuries from c. 800 to 1100, the political and economic life of the Irish Sea was dominated by Scandinavian trade and military activity. By 841 a Viking stronghold had been established at Dublin and this was to become the base from which Norse colonists on the Irish coast were united under Olaf the White, of the Norwegian house of Vestfold. In the 860s Olaf subjugated the Norse settlements of the Hebrides and Galloway while raiding deep into

Scotland and Ireland. Olaf's companion in the kingship of Dublin, Ivar, was joint leader of the Great Army which invaded England in 865 and conquered York and southern Northumbria in 866 (*see below*).

Remarkably, from 850 to 954 a united Viking kingdom, administered from Dublin and York, extended from the coastal settlements of the Irish Sea and across northern England to the east coast. York became a notable North Sea port and trading centre, while Dublin was essentially an armed stronghold providing protection for traders and slave-raiders. The two capitals were linked by a number of routes, the most popular of which was by sea to the Firths of Forth and Clyde and overland *portage* (carrying the longboats) following the Antonine Wall across lowland Scotland.

The Danish Vikings first appeared off the eastern and Channel coasts of Britain in the ninth century. Their strategy was one of mobility, surprise and speed, but when met by superior force they were prepared to avoid battle and to retreat if necessary. Using navigable rivers, they ventured inland and established bases from which raids were conducted on horseback, overwhelming native settlements and carrying off the treasures of defenceless monasteries with impunity. In 865 the Great Army invaded, and under the impact of this massive force the native kingdoms crumbled, with the notable exception of Wessex (*see* KINGDOMS (ANCIENT)).

Alfred the Great, King of Wessex (871–99), together with his son and grandsons, was chiefly responsible for maintaining a focus of English resistance and ultimately for the conquest of the Danes and the unification of England. He established an army which was so organized that sections could be rested while campaigns were sustained; he built a chain of fortified towns on the borders of his kingdom (*see* BURH); and he remodelled his fleet so that it was capable of opposing that of the Danes: 'Then King Alfred ordered warships to be built to meet the Danish ships: they were almost twice as long as the others, some had sixty oars, some more; they were swifter, steadier and with more freeboard; they were built neither after the Fresian design nor after the Danish, but as it seemed to him that they could be most serviceable.' (*Anglo-Saxon Chronicle* 896).

So effective were Alfred's measures that, following the defeat of the Danes at Edington (Wiltshire) in 878, a frontier was agreed which divided the kingdoms of Wessex and Mercia to the west from Norwegian Cumbria in the north and the DANELAW territories of Bernicia, York, the Five Boroughs, East Anglia and (eastern) Kent to the east. This frontier ran diagonally across England

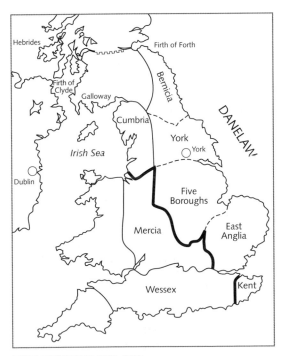

THE VIKINGS 850–955

from Chester to London following, in the Midlands, the Roman Watling Street and, in the south-east, the rivers Great Ouse and Lea. Alfred's policy was to secure his kingdom by the construction of strategically located fortified *burhs*, while maintaining a war of attrition along the frontier zone. A fresh series of Danish attacks began in 892 but were repulsed by Alfred's reorganized forces and in 896 they withdrew: 'Thanks be to God!' exclaimed the author of the *Anglo Saxon Chronicle*.

On his death, Alfred's policy was continued by his son Edward the Elder (899–924) and by his daughter, Aethelfled 'Lady of the Mercians', who ruled that part of Mercia around the Severn basin which had not been surrendered to the Danes in 874. The *Anglo Saxon Chronicle* describes how, from 917 to 920, both the Danes and the West Saxons became entrenched along the frontier from Towcester to Bedford and south of Danish Northampton. But by 924 Edward had captured the Five Boroughs and secured his northern border against invasion from the Norwegian kingdom of Dublin, while the Danes of York desperately struggled to maintain their autonomy.

Despite the formidable opposition of Viking rulers such as Olaf Guthfrithsson and Eric Bloodaxe, Alfred's grandsons, Athelstan (r.924–39), Edmund (r.939–46) and Eadred (r.946–55), finally conquered the Danelaw and by the end of his reign Eadred was king of all England. But their victory was short-lived. The *Anglo Saxon Chronicle*, written during the last years of Aethelred's reign (978–1016), is marked by recriminations of defeat at the hands of the Norsemen for which the king himself is made the scapegoat.

A series of well-organized campaigns in the 980s and the arrival of great armies in the 990s under Olaf, later king of Norway, and Swein, king of Denmark, were met by levies summoned under local ealdormen and by payments of the tribute known as DANEGELD. Further waves of invasion from Scandinavia continued in the first decades of the eleventh century, notably under Swein and Thorkell the Tall, and huge gelds were paid to the victorious Viking armies: £24,000 in 1002, £3,600 in 1007 and £48,000 in 1012. Aethelred's attempts to reorganize resistance and to rebuild his fleet had little effect against Thorkell's campaign of 1009–13, and by the end of 1013 Swein was recognized as king and Aethelred fled to Normandy.

Although recalled after Swein's death in the following year, Aethelred's defence of his kingdom foundered when his eldest son, Edmund Ironside, attempted to usurp his father's throne. Crippled by illness and betrayal, Aethelred died in 1016 and, following stout resistance by his son, England was divided between Edmund, who retained Wessex, and the Danish king Cnut, Swein's successor, who ruled over the North. But following the premature death (murder?) of Edmund in the same year Cnut remained to rule all England (1017–35). Although Edward the Confessor, a descendant of Alfred, became king in 1042 the Viking threat remained. An attempted invasion in 1066 was suppressed by Harold II at Stamford Bridge but even after the Norman conquest, William I was obliged to maintain a standing army in England against the threat of Danish invasion. Ironically, the NORMANS were themselves descended from Frankish and Viking settlers in northern France.

VILL *see* TOWNSHIP

VILLAS *see* ROMAN VILLAS

VILLAGE GREENS Section 22 of the *Commons Registration Act* 1965 defines a green as either 'land set out under any Act or Award for the recreation of the inhabitants' or 'land subject to a customary right of playing lawful sports or pastimes, evidenced by at least 20 years exercise of the right'. From about 1830, at a time when large tracts of common were being enclosed, many small areas were allotted specifically 'for the exercise and recreation of the inhabitants'. An award at Stourpaine in Dorset, for example, allotted: 'unto the Church wardens and Overseers of the Poor of the said Parish . . . all that piece or parcel of land numbered 21 on the said map containing four acres, to be held by them and their successors in trust as a place of exercise and recreation for the inhabitants of the said Parish and neighbourhood . . .'

Nearly all awards made after 1845 included recreational allotments, for the Inclosure Act of that year required the Commissioners to explain their reasons to Parliament when no such provision was made. Recreational allotments were made over either to public officers such as churchwardens and overseers or (until 1876) to private persons. In both cases, they could enjoy or let the herbage but held the land as trustees and could do nothing which was likely to interfere with the rights of the inhabitants. For centuries, the courts have recognized that the people of a locality may acquire a customary right of recreation over a particular piece of land, and once established that right cannot be lost by abandonment. By the Inclosure Act of 1857 and the Commons Act of 1876 it is a criminal offence to damage a village or town green or to encroach upon it.

The emphasis placed on recreational use in recent legislation suggests that village greens invariably evolved as PLAISTOWS. In fact, small areas of common land developed within settlements for a multiplicity of reasons, while others were actually set aside and designated for specific purposes. Perhaps the earliest examples of 'planned' greens are to be found in a small number of villages on the edge of Salisbury Plain in Wiltshire which were laid out during the Roman period. But most greens are of medieval origin and were usually established as a result of the gradual enclosure of common grazing land by sporadic peripheral settlement or as open space provided for a market and fair. Many greens originated in this way during the thirteenth century, and in some cases buildings were demolished in order to accommodate a market. At South Zeals in Devon, for example, where a charter of 1299 granted a weekly market and two fairs annually, the entire village was rebuilt on a regular plan with a broad market-place on the through-road at the centre of the village.

Several greens were created as a result of the expansion of adjacent villages. Great Shelford in Cambridgeshire, for example, once consisted of two hamlets separated by a meadow which survived as a green as the hamlets expanded towards each other and finally amalgamated. Many greens were used to provide over-night grazing for livestock, especially those with ponds (*see* DROVERS). Others may have been used as assembly areas within which the cattle from adjacent dwellings were marshalled each morning by the village cowman (*neatherd*) before being driven to the common grazings.

Many greens were reduced or obliterated by ENCLOSURE and encroachment. This could occur through the gradual constriction of a green by peripheral settlement, by the erection of dwellings on the green itself (*see* SQUATTERS) or by the creation of front gardens for the benefit of houses lining the green, as at Cold Kirby in Yorkshire. It seems likely that numerous villages once possessed greens which have subsequently been lost in this way.

VILLAGES It has been estimated that there are over 10,000 villages in Britain. Definition of the term is difficult for it has no legal or tenurial significance and is derived from the Latin *villaticus*, meaning 'an assemblage of dwellings outside or pertaining to a villa'. Some authorities have defined a village as 'a nucleated rural settlement of twenty or more homesteads', while others apply the term only to those settlements which contain a parish church. Perhaps the most satisfactory definition is one which is arrived at by the consensus of those who live there: if a settlement is perceived to be the focus of parochial activity then it is invariably referred to as a

village. Even in the suburbs, a vestigial nucleated settlement may still be described as 'the village' by older members of the community.

Permanent settlements have existed in Britain since the fifth millennium BC but sophisticated villages such as Rinyo and Skara Brae in Orkney are exceptions in a more typical pattern of dispersed and often transitory HAMLETS and FARMSTEADS which persisted from the Neolithic period through the Bronze and Iron Ages. Many of the early Bronze Age HILL FORTS were constructed as refuges and were therefore occupied only when danger threatened. Several large enclosed compound settlements, such as the celebrated Grimspound on Dartmoor, were innovatory as was the Bronze Age port at Runnymede Bridge on the Thames.

During the Iron Age, a number of major hill forts developed and flourished as local capitals and trading centres in a heavily populated and cultivated countryside. In the Roman period, several settlements grew round local industries, such as those producing pottery in the east midlands, while others developed as minor commercial or administrative centres (*vici*). Several of these Roman 'villages' were planned: at Claydon Pike in Gloucestershire, for example, an Iron Age settlement was remodelled around a straight through-road with a central square and small 'apartment blocks' served by side streets.

During the Roman occupation, the population of Britain had risen to nearly 5 million but by the Domesday survey of 1086 this had fallen to little more than 2 million. During the intervening centuries of economic depression, political insecurity and social regression, the Roman precepts of community life were effectively abandoned. It was an age not of Anglo-Saxon conquest but of assimilation, and immigrant settlements were for the most part piecemeal and sporadic. Contrary to the traditional view, they were also small and often located on the poorest land at the periphery of indigenous communities. Many parishes still reflect this pattern of scattered Saxon farm clusters: Hazelbury Bryan in Dorset, for example, which has no obvious centre or village green and consists of a number of dispersed minor settlements, one of which (Droop) contains the parish church and school, another (Wanston) the former post office and shop, and a third (Pidney) the village pub and playing field.

The development of nucleated villages began in the eighth century partly as a result of the proliferation of parish CHURCHES and, more significantly, as a consequence of the introduction of the OPEN FIELD estate system. It is difficult to ascertain whether the churches were built to serve existing settlements or whether villages grew round their churches. What is more clear, however, is that nucleated villages were created wherever estates were sufficiently large to accommodate the so-called 'manorial system' of open fields, pasture, meadow and commons. Conversely, where the open field model was inappropriate the landscape of dispersed hamlets and farmsteads survived (*see* COUNTRYSIDE).

In the late Saxon period, thousands of new villages were established, a process which continued into the twelfth century. It should be noted, however, that the *Domesday* survey recorded estates rather than villages. A substantial number of *vills* were divided into two or more manors, while many manors occupied more than one location. During the Middle Ages, villages expanded, contracted, were re-sited or disappeared and it was only towards the end of this period that they began to take on a more durable form.

Many villages are *linear settlements* which have rows of house plots strung out along one or both sides of a street or elongated green. Others are *enclosure settlements* in which the house plots and roads are located round the margins of an open space, often a VILLAGE GREEN or market square. An *agglomerated* settlement conforms to no obvious plan and has no apparent nucleus. The plots usually line more than one street and the dwellings are set out at angles to each other. Each of these categories may be divided further into regular or irregular forms and may be found as a component of a more complex settlement pattern. In many cases, the original plan may not be apparent: where the central space of an enclosure settlement has been developed by building, for example.

Many villages were planned as TOWNS, particularly in the early medieval period, and these may be recognized by their regular proportions, straight alignments, geometrical open spaces and house plots of roughly equal size. The acquisition of a market charter often resulted in the building of a new enclosure settlement or the extension of an existing hamlet to incorporate a new market square or green. Many of these planned villages are in fact 'failed' medieval towns where development was either ill-conceived or anticipated commercial success which was never realized.

Polyfocal villages are those which developed from the amalgamation of several independent settlements, some of which may have declined while others prospered. Such villages may be recognized by the existence (either in the field or in documentary sources) of the several churches, manor-houses and greens which were once contained within the various components and by the broken alignment of lanes or streets which mark the division of the earlier hamlets. Shrewton in Wiltshire, for example, comprises the former settlements of Elston, Maddington and Rollestone. Most medieval villages contained only two or three buildings of any permanence: a church, a manor-house and sometimes a tithe barn. Consequently, the form of a village would fluctuate as insubstantial buildings decayed and new areas were developed.

Wholesale migration could result from the need to find more productive land or a more favourable site and in many cases, both in the medieval period and later, entire villages were removed by the owners of 'closed' estates, often for entirely egoistic purposes. Village populations increased rapidly in the late Saxon and early medieval periods but in the fourteenth century, economic decline, a deteriorating climate and the debilitating effects of PLAGUE caused the contraction or abandonment of many settlements, particularly those which, because of earlier land shortages, had been established on uncompromising sites (*see* DESERTED VILLAGES).

The creation of villages continued long after the medieval period. Often these were '*model villages*', built to replace earlier settlements abandoned as the result of emparkment, or provided as accommodation for estate or factory workers.

VILLEIN Following the Norman Conquest of 1066, any unfree tenant who held his land subject to agricultural service and fines was described as a villein. Although of superior status to a slave, a villein was generally annexed to a lord's person and could, therefore, be transferred from one owner to another. He was known as a *villein in gross* and as such neither he nor his daughter could marry without his lord's consent, he was unable to bring a suit in the king's court or to acquire land that would not be taxed. In return, he held land by *villein tenure*, grazed his livestock on the common pasture and removed hay from the common meadow. A *regardant villein* was annexed to a lord's MANOR rather than to his person. Depopulation following the Black Death in the fourteenth century meant that villeins enjoyed greater bargaining power and tenure was gradually converted to COPYHOLD.

VINEYARDS A favourable CLIMATE encouraged viticulture in southern England and the south Midlands from the eleventh century. Writing in *c.* 1123, William of Malmesbury stated that no other English shire had more vineyards than Gloucestershire and that wines from the Vale of Gloucester were hardly inferior to those of France. Most vineyards were on monastic estates, on well-drained south or south-east facing slopes, sheltered from cold north winds and from prevailing south-westerlies. The earliest English vineyards seem to date from a sustained period of clement weather in the eleventh and twelfth centuries and there is little evidence to support the popular notion that the Romans grew grapes during the occupation of Britain. Somerset vineyards were maintained by the Mohuns at Dunster from the twelfth to the fifteenth century, and wine from the vineyards at Claverton, on the sheltered slopes above the Avon near Bath, was still considered to be of excellent quality in the late seventeenth century. Vines were grown further north but for unripe grapes used for culinary purposes (*verjuice*) rather than for wine. In place-names the word 'vine' is probably derived from the British *ffin*, meaning 'boundary', though it has been suggested that some 'winter' names may indicate former vineyards.

VIRGATE *see* OPEN FIELDS *and* STRIP

VISCOUNT The fourth rank of the British peerage, the first creation being in 1440. The title itself is considerably older: in the days of the Carolingian Empire the *vice-comites* were the deputies of the counts and gradually assumed hereditary rights. The wife of a viscount is a viscountess.

VISITATION A periodic inspection of parochial affairs made by a bishop or archdeacon.
See also HERALDS' VISITATIONS

VITRIFICATION A large number of Scottish HILL FORTS include ramparts of rubble and interlaced timbers which were deliberately set on fire in order that the rubble should become vitrified (changed to a glassy substance by intense heat). It is hardly likely that the defensive properties of the rampart were improved thereby and the reasons for the practice remain a mystery.

VOUSSOIRS *see* ARCH

W

WAGER OF LAW *see* LAW

WAGONETTE *see* CHAR-A-BANC

WAGON ROOF *see* ROOFS

WAGONS Until the first decades of the twentieth century, the transport of goods beyond the rail and canal networks depended on the horse-drawn carrier's cart (*see* CARRIER), the delivery van and the four-wheeled wagon. At that time, some of the heavier commercial road traffic was transferred to the early 'steamers' (*see* TRACTION ENGINES) and the motorcar gradually replaced the gig and trap, the carriage and brougham as a means of private transport (*see* VEHICLES (HORSE-DRAWN)). But despite the introduction of the pneumatic tyre in the 1930s, vehicles with wooden wheels continued to be used on many farms until the mid-twentieth century.

The making of bodies and underframes for large four-wheeled wagons was the task of carpenters and joiners, while the manufacture of iron-tyred wooden wheels required the specialist skills of the wheelwright. The design of the large 'harvest' wagons varied in different parts of the country and the regions remained faithful to their distinctive patterns, traditions being maintained even in the colouring and style of lettering on front and tailboard. The Lincolnshire wagon, for example, had a deep narrow body strengthened at the sides with a framework of 'spindles' and based on designs introduced by the Dutch when they drained the Fens. Like the East Anglian wagon, it was expected to work on flat terrain and could therefore accommodate large wheels and a high centre of gravity. In the hills of the West Country and the Cotswolds, however, stability was of greater importance and wheels were smaller. The gauge of wheels also varied from one region to another which was one of the reasons why the long-distance transport of heavy goods failed to expand before the coming of the canals. Most rural roads were unsurfaced so that wagons travelling from another area, and with wheels of a different gauge, would find it impossible to follow the ruts created by local traffic and ran the risk of capsizing.

Although a farm vehicle, the wagon performed a whole range of functions within a community. In so doing, it might travel thousands of miles and outlive several masters yet never leave the confines of a parish. Details of bodywork and dimensions were dictated by local standards. Length varied from 2.4 to 3 metres (8 to 10 feet), and deck-boards were laid according to regional practice. Lincolnshire wagons, for example, are usually cross-boarded, while the Oxfordshire wagon has the boards running lengthways so that loose cargoes could be unloaded from the rear with shovels. The sides of the body were often strengthened with wooden struts or iron *standards*, L-shaped fitting bolted to the deck and sides. In southern and western counties, wagons with low sides sometimes had wheelguards (*hooped raves*) which prevented loads from falling onto the wheels and produced the wonderful ship-like lines of traditional Devon, Dorset, Oxford, Somerset and Wiltshire wagons.

Body timbers were carefully planed and chamfered to reduce weight without affecting the structure, and many wagons were beautifully carved. One Wiltshire farmer stipulated that his new wagon should have no 'postles' on it for he was not going to waste his money on images of the apostles which he could see every Sunday in church. The underframe of the wagon carried the body and into this were inserted the front and rear axles which were coupled by a long timber called the *pole* through which the forward strain was transmitted to the rear wheels. The front wheels were mounted on a *fore-carriage* which swivelled in a horizontal plane, early wagons needing half a field in which to turn,though by 1900 a wagon could turn within its own length.

Wheels, which were often the height of a man, were made from separate pieces of timber assembled so that the rim was a true circle with the hub (*nave*) at its centre. They had to be as light as possible but strong enough to carry loads of up to a ton on a variety of (usually uneven) surfaces. They also had to compensate for the lateral movement of the wagon caused by the rolling motion of a walking horse. This was achieved by constructing a wheel in the shape of a shallow cone (known as a *dish*) with its point nearest to the body of the vehicle and the spokes slanting outwards from the hub to the rim. Wheel-making commenced with the *nave*, shaped from seasoned elm and about 30 cm both in length and in diameter (1 foot). Mortises for the spokes were chiselled out around its circumference, always an even number (usually twelve or fourteen) so that each of the rim segments (*felloes*) could be attached to a pair of spokes. A special gauge was used to ensure that the square holes were precisely spaced and angled to accommodate the spokes. These were of oak, shaped and trimmed with a *spokeshave*, and provided with square tenons (*feet*) so that they would not twist when mortised into the nave. Tenons on the outer ends of the spokes were then inserted into the rim which was built up from curved felloes of ash or beech and shaped from a template of the correct diameter.

The tyres were occasionally applied in strips (*strakes*) but more often a continuous iron circle or *hoop* was used. The wheel was laid flat on a tyring platform and its circumference measured with an instrument called a *traveller*. An iron bar was then cut to the required length, heated, rolled flat into a hoop and the ends welded. It was then re-heated and carried by three men using long-handled tongues

(*dogs*) to the tyring platform where it was laid on the wheel and hammered over the rim and doused. When cold, a hoop would not quite encircle the wheel and, for a rear wheel, the difference between the inside circumference of the tyre when cold and the outer circumference of the rim had to be precisely measured so that after expansion in the forge it would shrink by the correct amount when cooled.
See also FORGE

WAGON VAULT *see* VAULTING

WAIN A horse-drawn wagon: usually a large agricultural vehicle, the design of which may vary from one region to another.

WAINSCOTING *see* PANELLING

WAITS *see* MINSTRELS

WAKE Although shrouded in pagan antiquity, the medieval practice of commencing celebrations on the eve of a patronal festival is not entirely extinct. After the wakeful vigil of the preceding night, the community would assemble in the parish church to celebrate Mass and this would be followed by dancing, drinking and sports on the VILLAGE GREEN or PLAISTOW or even in the churchyard itself. Many FAIRS originated in medieval wakes, and celebrations were usually staggered so that neighbouring parishes could enjoy each others' wakes. As a place-name element, the word usually refers to the family of Wake (as in Caundle Wake, Dorset, where the Wakes were lords of the manor) but in field names the meaning is more likely to refer to the village festivities.

WALES The Roman road between *Deva* (Chester) and *Isca* (Caerleon) marked the first boundary between what we now call England and Wales and separated the Romanized Britons to the east from the semi-independent Britons of the western uplands. Although the Romans subjugated the Deceangli in the north of the country, the Ordovices of mid-Wales and the Silures of the south maintained a stubborn resistance until some time after AD 50 and their leader Caradog (Caractacus) is commemorated in numerous place-names on both sides of the border. Although numbered among the Roman provinces of Britain, apart from the south-east Wales was hardly touched by Roman culture and little affected by the withdrawal of Roman administration in the early fifth century. British resistance to the Saxon invasions inspired the Arthurian legends and the *Historia Regum Britanniae* of Geoffrey of

WALES

Monmouth which placed Arthur and his followers firmly in a Welsh context. The Britons achieved fifty years of comparative peace in the first half of the sixth century, during which time their literature flourished, the Welsh tribal territories emerged as kingdoms and Christianity permeated the Celtic world. This was the 'Age of Saints' when Celtic missionaries founded hundreds of churches, many of which still bear their names. The organization of the Celtic Church was entirely different from that of Rome for its bishops exercised a purely spiritual function with no territorial jurisdiction.

It was during the sixth century that the Britons, who were cut off by the advancing Saxons from their kinsmen in Strathclyde and Cornwall, began to describe themselves as *Cymry*, meaning 'fellow countrymen', though they were known as *Wealas* or 'strangers' to the Saxons. The battles of Chester (615) and Oswestry (641) mark the western limit of the Anglo-Saxon advance in the north and central borderland, with the river Wye delineating the southern boundary of the Kingdom of Mercia. The Saxons never succeeded in penetrating further into Wales and the great eighth-century dyke built by King Offa of Mercia to mark the western boundary of his kingdom was as much a symbol of failure as it was of authority (*see* KINGDOMS (ANCIENT)).

Viking attacks were heavy during the second half of the ninth century, especially around the western peninsulas, and the English King Alfred sent military assistance to Gwynedd anticipating Welsh submission.

Viking incursions continued through much of the tenth and eleventh centuries and, although no permanent Scandinavian influences are apparent (other than in some place-names), it is possible that during the eleventh century parts of Gwynedd were at times under the control of Dublin Vikings.

The often anarchic process of unification of the numerous small Welsh kingdoms which had begun in the seventh century culminated in the emergence of four major kingdoms, each divided into cantrefs or hundreds: *Gwynedd* in the north-west, *Powys* in the north-east, *Deheubarth* (Dyfed) in the south-west and *Glywysing* (later known as *Morgannwg*) in the south. Although the size and influence of these territories fluctuated, their princes remained the chief leaders of Welsh resistance against the English from the time of the Norman Conquest to the Statute of Rhuddlan in 1284. The ninth century was dominated by the expansion of Gwynedd, and the tenth by conflict between Gwynedd and Deheubarth whose kings were dynastically related. Indeed, the great names of early Welsh history, Rhodri Mawr (d.878), Hywel Dda (d.950), Maredudd ab Owain (d.999) and Gruffydd ap Llywelyn (d.1063), were all princes of Gwynedd and Deheubarth who succeeded in extending political conquest beyond the boundaries of their kingdoms.

In the mid-eleventh century, political pre-eminence was contested by Gruffydd ap Rhydderch and Gruffydd ap Llywelyn, each of whom employed Viking and English mercenaries to supplement his forces. In 1055 Gruffydd ap Llywelyn succeeded in becoming the first ruler of all Wales but his rise to power had alerted the English and he was defeated in battle and killed in 1063. The north Welsh kings were then appointed by the English, whose influence was soon overtaken by the Normans, though it is doubtful whether English overlordship was ever precisely defined or, indeed, sustained.

From 1070, the Normans embarked on the conquest of Wales and by 1093 had secured effective control of the south. While the Saxons had exercised only a minimal influence on the Welsh, the Normans created a permanent zone of attrition which extended south from Chester and west into the conquered territories. This was the MARCH in which the most rapacious and unruly of Duke William's followers were granted lands. Bleddyn ap Cynfyn, King of Gwynedd and Powys, died in 1075 and was succeeded not by his young son, but by the self-appointed Gruffydd ap Cynan. At a time of intense Norman military pressure, Gruffydd succeeded in creating a kingdom which extended from Anglesey in the north to the Vale of Clwyd and south to the borders of the kingdom of Deheubarth. When he died in 1137 (at the age of eighty-two), he was succeeded by his eldest son Owain who assumed the name Owain Gwynedd in order that he should be distinguished from his rival Owain ap Gruffydd of Powys who also adopted the name Owain Cyfeiliog. It was at this time that the titles 'king' and 'prince' were abandoned in favour of the less provocative appellation 'lord', though the rulers of Gwynedd retained their princely title, presumably by general consent.

In southern Wales, Rhys ap Tewdwr, the last independent lord of Deheubarth, was killed by the Normans in 1093 and was succeeded by his son Gruffydd who, having eventually made his peace with Henry I of England, died in 1137. The most famous of his four sons was Rhys ap Gruffydd (1153–97), known to history as The Lord Rhys (*Yr Arglwydd Rhys*), who befriended Henry II and was restored to his estates as ruler of Deheubarth until his death in 1197.

The kingdom of Powys, which had achieved prominence under Madog ap Maredudd, passed to his nephew Owain Cyfeiliog who (unlike Owain Gwynedd) maintained an alliance with the English. Under his leadership, Powys continued to prosper but when he died in 1197 he was succeeded by Gwenwynwyn, whose impetuosity resulted in military defeat and eventual subjugation by Llywelyn Fawr (the Great), Prince of Gwynedd. Born in 1173, Llywelyn Fawr (Llywelyn ab Iorwerth) became a leading figure in English politics and ruled over a united Wales until his death in 1240. But his son Dafydd ap Llywelyn failed to consolidate his father's achievements and it was not until the succession in 1246 of Llywelyn Fawr's grandson, Llywelyn ap Gruffydd, that the primacy of the Princes of Gwynedd was re-established. By 1267 Llywelyn ap Gruffydd ruled with greater authority and over wider territories than any Welsh prince since the Norman conquest. He negotiated an alliance with Simon de Montfort and even survived de Montfort's fall to be confirmed by Henry III as Prince and overlord of all Wales in the Treaty of Montgomery in 1267. But in 1276 a dispute between Llywelyn and Edward I resulted in conflict and a drastic reduction in his powers, and his involvement in a further rising in 1282 led to the conquest and subjugation of Gwynedd in 1282-83. Although Llywelyn's political ambitions alienated other Welsh lords and ultimately contributed to his defeat by Edward I, at his death in 1282 he was deeply mourned as the last native prince of Wales: 'Great torrents of wind and rain shake the whole land, the oak trees clash together in a wild fury, the sun is dark in the sky and the stars have fallen from their courses' (bardic elegy).

By the Statute of Wales (1284) the principality of Gwynedd was brought under English rule and divided into three counties: Caernarfon, Merioneth and Anglesey. CASTLES and fortified boroughs were constructed and populated with English merchants and the Marcher lordships consolidated and extended. But increasing prosperity under English rule could not conceal widespread resentment of the commercial privileges enjoyed by the burgesses of the English towns in Wales and of the exclusion of Welshmen from high office in secular and ecclesiastical administration. From 1400, Owain Glyndŵr (1344–1416?), a descendant of Rhys ap Gruffydd, harnessed this resentment in open rebellion and for a while exercised the authority of a native prince. He became a national hero and, despite his disappearance in 1412, sporadic insurrection and disorder persisted until after 1485 when a part-Welshman, Harri Tudur (1457–1509), ascended the English throne as Henry VII.

WALK *see* FOREST

-WALL *and* **-WELL** *see* SPRINGS

WALL MONUMENT A late sixteenth-century development of the canopied TOMB CHEST, the wall monument was either secured to the wall (*hanging wall monument*) or supported at ground level (*standing wall monument*). The style and decoration followed that of the canopied tomb chest with figures shown kneeling or as demi-effigies. Heraldry was usually concentrated in the canopy during the sixteenth and seventeenth centuries, but in the eighteenth century the canopy was abandoned or reduced to an ornamental form rather than an architectural structure. A popular design comprised a figure of the deceased in front of a two-dimensional pyramid embellished, at the apex, with a coat of arms.

Modest versions of the wall monument are often described as *wall tablets*. These were of stone and, in the seventeenth century, usually consisted of a central plaque bearing an inscription within a frame decorated with shields and surmounted by a coat of arms. During the eighteenth century, wall monuments varied considerably both in size and in style, and heraldry remained an important though subdued element of design with a shield or cartouche above or at the base, the arms being the only element of colour in the monument other than coloured marbles. When the deceased had enjoyed a military or naval career, or had been a prominent churchman, the monument was often flanked by guns, flags, a crosier or other appropriate devices.

Elegant neo-classical black-and-white tablets characterized the period 1780 to 1840 and were a

Seventeenth-century monument to members of the Bedingfeld family at Oxburgh, Norfolk.

WALL PAINTINGS In the Middle Ages, the interiors of parish churches would have been very different from the quiet sober places they are today. Then, they were like immense picture books of painted plaster intended for the edification of the illiterate masses and designed to inspire fear and obedience.

The walls of most pre-Reformation churches were covered with murals depicting not only the lives of the saints and scenes from the scriptures, but also terrifying images of the inevitability of death and of divine judgment and retribution. In 604 St Gregory the Great declared that the walls of parish churches were to be the *biblia pauperum*, the bible of the poor, and throughout the Middle Ages murals were considered to be the normal finish for church walls.

Professional painters travelled from church to church working on newly plastered walls, wetted with lime-water and smoothed with lime putty (stiff slaked lime), using inexpensive natural colours ground and tempered with lime-water or skim-milk. Delicate work often required the use of pigments and size. Pigments included iron oxides (which produced reds, browns, yellows and purple), lamp black (candle soot), malachite (the green carbonate of copper), azurite (the blue carbonate of copper) and lime putty for white. Squirrel hair (from the tail) was used for the finer brushes and hog's hair for others, and the pigment was often worked from scallop shells.

About 2,000 British churches retain traces of these murals and though many are fragmentary and faded some 200 are well preserved. At Peakirk, Cambridgeshire, for example, sections of a Life and Death morality painting have survived in which skeletal ghosts are depicted castigating the Three Kings as they enjoy themselves in the hunt – surrounded by the maggots, beetles and flies which will one day devour those of the congregation who persist in denying their own mortality. Such paintings echo a poem written at the court of Margaret II, the thirteenth-century queen of Flanders, in which three corpses warn the Three Kings: 'As you are, so once we were. As we are, so shall ye be'. At Gussage St Andrew, Dorset, a painting of the Passion of Christ uniquely depicts the despairing Judas hanging himself from a tree. A number of paintings illustrate the consequences of working on a Sunday, the implements used by sinners being used to inflict pain on Christ himself. At West Chiltington, Sussex, for example, the wounded Christ is portrayed surrounded by the instruments of a variety of trades and occupations. More than seventy Last Judgement murals survive in Britain (*see* DOOM). Typically, that at Chaldon, Surrey, portrays the naked figures of the damned being thrown into the caldron of Hell by

reaction against the flamboyance of earlier BAROQUE and ROCOCO monuments which recited the virtues of the deceased both in their architectural and sculptural ostentation and in the immense banality of their inscriptions. In these tablets, a panel of white marble, usually a scroll or sarcophagus bearing a dignified inscription, is set against a background of black marble with sculpture in shallow relief. The tablet may be oval, rectangular or shield-shaped and surmounted by a draped urn, a broken column, a tree of life or a figure of grief with a bowed head. During this period, heraldry was often restricted to a CREST or was omitted entirely. Perversely, this coincided with the increasing popularity of funeral HATCHMENTS: at Pangbourne, Berkshire, for example, there are hatchments to seven members of the Breedon family but none of their monumental inscriptions includes heraldry.

Wall tablets of the late nineteenth and twentieth centuries are for the most part unobtrusive and contain carved and painted coats of arms and finely carved inscriptions.

See also MONUMENTS

a gang of dog-headed, pitchfork-wielding demons. The Hell Mouth often features in these paintings, a terrifying device which probably originated in the biblical story of Jonah and the whale.

Medieval imagery is often sexist: gossips are invariably depicted as women, urged on by devils who sit on their shoulders and press their heads together, while symbols of the seven deadly sins are often depicted sprouting from the richly dressed (or naked) body of a woman, herself representing the fundamental evil of pride. The portrayal of the emotions as deadly sins was intended to remind the villeins of their place in feudal society and the total of a man's sins determined whether he would go to Heaven or to Hell. It was St Michael who weighed an individual's deeds and his scales appear in wall paintings such as those at Nassington, Northamptonshire and Barton, Cambridgeshire, where the judgement is depicted as a contest between the Devil, sitting in the left-hand pan of the scales, and the Virgin Mary whose rosary she has placed in the right. The late medieval cult of the Virgin Mary was based on the Virgin's ability, as the Mother of Mercy, to intercede on behalf of even the most wicked of sinners and at Corby Glen, Lincolnshire,

Painting of St Christopher on the north wall of Breage church, Cornwall.

and Broughton, Buckinghamshire, she is depicted as the Virgin of the Mantle, sheltering sinful souls beneath her protective cloak.

The medieval mind was preoccupied with death, and with the appalling possibility of endless expiation in purgatory. Consequently, paintings of St Christopher were particularly popular for it was believed that merely by looking at his image death could be delayed by a day. There are fine paintings of the saint at St Mary's, Hayes in west London and at Albury, Surrey.

Most surviving paintings have been revealed in the past 150 years, though many others were unwittingly destroyed during Victorian 'restorations'. Most lay forgotten beneath layers of whitewash applied after 1547, when the government ordered the 'obliteration' of 'popish and superstitious' images, and in 1644 when, during the Civil War, the parliamentary authorities appointed a Commissioner for the Destruction of Images. Ironically, the coatings of whitewash may have assisted in the paintings' preservation.

WALLPAPER One of the earliest known British wallpapers, dating from 1509, was discovered at Christ's College, Cambridge, on the back of a legal document attributed to Henry VIII. Such early papers were printed from woodblocks and imitated contemporary fabric designs. The influence of blackwork embroidery, for example, is evident in the predominance of black and white patterns.

Wallpaper became fashionable in the late seventeenth century when advertisements for 'paper stainers' and for production patents appear from *c.* 1680. In 1693 the diarist John Evelyn recorded that Queen Mary owned a number of Chinese paper hangings. These hand-painted papers were particularly popular in the eighteenth and nineteenth centuries when they were imported from China by the East India Company (in consequence of which they were known as 'India Papers').

The most significant innovation was the roll of wallpaper 11 metres long (12 yards) and about 66 cm wide (22 inches) formed from a series of large pieces of hand-made 'rag' paper. These dimensions remain virtually unchanged.

Duty was imposed on rolls of wallpaper from 1712 to 1860 and the excise stamp may sometimes be found on the reverse of old paper when it is removed.

Before *c.* 1830, all papers were hand-printed, six or even eight square wooden blocks being required for the different colours. It was essential that the correct amount of colour should be mixed for, once used, it was impossible to mix more of precisely the same shade and an entire series of rolls would be wasted. The colour was poured onto a waterbed and the block, which weighed about 13.5 kg (30 lb), was laid on the bed to ensure an even spread of colour on the raised design. The block was then lowered carefully on to the paper, to which a background colour had already been applied, and the process repeated for the length of the roll using a different block for each colour. The printing of a single roll would often take a week to complete.

The paper was either glued directly to the walls or to lining paper applied to canvas frames (newspapers were sometimes used for this purpose) and the upper edges nailed and covered with an edging strip. Hand-made papers had narrow margins (*selvedges*), one of which was removed and the other made to overlap the adjacent strip when hanging the paper. Although machine printing on continuous rolls of paper was introduced in the 1830s, edge-to-edge joining was not practised until a century later and there are many instances of overlapping disguised by cut-out birds and flowers glued over the joints.

For the WALLPAPER HISTORY SOCIETY *see* APPENDIX I

WALLPLATE A structural timber running horizontally along the top of a wall from one end of a roof to the other (*see* ROOFS *and* TIMBER-FRAMED BUILDINGS).

WALNUT TREES 'Beat stake, wife and walnut tree, the more you beat 'em, better they be'. Walnut trees are said to benefit from a good 'beating' in spring in order that the sap may run freely, thereby attracting insects to 'set' the nuts, and to encourage the growth of short fruiting spurs. Such trees were reputed to produce the hardest wood for crossbows and gun-stocks. Folklore also equates the running sap and well-distributed pollen of a 'beaten' tree with fertility.

It is believed that the Romans first introduced the walnut to Britain and the Saxons knew it as the *welsh nut* (meaning 'foreign'). By the eighteenth century, walnut was generally considered to be the best, and most valuable, wood for cabinet-making and wood carving. Innumerable walnuts were felled during the Napoleonic Wars to provide for the ornamentation of ships and the provision of gun-stocks. Walnut trees have a life span of 200 years.

WAP From the Old English *wapol*, meaning 'pool' or 'mire', the word has for centuries been associated with water rites and may be of pagan origin. At the Randwick Wap in Gloucestershire, held annually at the beginning of April, a 'mayor' is 'chas'd in'

(elected) and enthroned in the waters of the Mayor's Pool. Also found as a place-name element, e.g. Waplington, Yorkshire, which means 'the *tūn* of the people at the pool'.

WAPENTAKE From the Old Norse *vápnatak*, meaning 'flourish of weapons', a wapentake was an administrative district in the former DANELAW shires of Derby, Leicester, Lincoln, Nottingham and parts of Yorkshire. It has been suggested that the word is derived from the Scandinavian practice of raising one's sword to signify assent at a judicial assembly. *See also* HUNDRED

WARD (i) The north country equivalent of a HUNDRED.
(ii) An administrative division, especially for electoral purposes.
(iii) A minor in the care of a guardian or court.
(iv) The notches of a key designed to prevent duplication.
(v) A yard within the walls of a CASTLE.
(vi) The closing of common meadows before the commencement of sowing.

-WARDINE *see* -WORTH

WARDROBE *see* CHANCERY *and* HOUSEHOLD

WARDSHIP With the exception of GAVELKIND tenure, the Crown was entitled to hold and administer the estates of a deceased TENANT-IN-CHIEF pending the coming-of-age of an heir at twenty-one or an heiress at fourteen. During that time, the Crown received the revenues of the estate and was able to determine the marriages of both a ward and a widow. Wardship could be avoided or terminated by marriage and the child of an infirm or elderly father was usually married off at an early age, which could be at twelve for a girl and fourteen for a boy. A ward who refused to enter into an arranged marriage or who married without consent caused a fine on the estate. Wardships were frequently delegated, either as a means of patronage or to the highest bidder, and they became a potent means of magnatial advancement in the medieval period. The *Court of Wards and Liveries* administered the funds received by the Crown from wardships, marriages and the granting of livery (*see* RELIEF). Both the practice and the court were abolished in 1646 but its records are maintained at the Public Record Office.

WAR HEADS *see* CASTLES (MEDIEVAL)

WAR MEMORIALS Many villages possess a wall memorial, usually a stone cross or pillar with a stepped base bearing on each of its sides an engraved list of those who died in the service of their country. Often, especially during the First World War (1914–18), several members of the same family were killed and many small communities were decimated.

Most war memorials were erected by public subscription, usually at a crossroads or sometimes in the vicinity of a churchyard. However, not all memorials were placed out of doors: many were memorial boards which were hung in chapels and schools. It was not unusual for Church and Chapel to disagree on an appropriate location and so identical boards were painted: one for the church school and the other for the chapel. Many memorial boards have survived, often to gather dust in a school stock-cupboard.

One of the finest war memorials is at Briantspuddle, Dorset. Carved by Eric Gill, it consists of a tall cross with a life-size statue of the wounded Christ on the north side and a Madonna and Child beneath a canopy on the south.
See also: THANKFUL VILLAGES

WARRANT A written authorization to receive or supply money, goods or services or to carry out an arrest or search.
See also ROYAL WARRANTS

WARRENS Warrens, known variously as *conygers*, *coningers*, *coneygarths* or *coneries* (from the Old French *coninière*), were areas set aside for the raising of rabbits and, like medieval FISH-PONDS and DOVECOTES, their purpose was to provide a manorial or monastic estate with a regular and fresh supply of meat. The term is derived from the feudal right of 'free warren' which regulated the hunting of all small game. Manorial and monastic warrens were usually established on common grazing lands or in the vicinity of DEER PARKS and were numerous by the thirteenth century.

The rabbit is not native to Britain but was introduced by the Normans towards the end of the twelfth century, possibly from Spain. Originally, adult rabbits were known as *coneys*. When they were first introduced, rabbits were unable to adapt to the harsh British climate, were incapable of burrowing and even had to be fed on hay in winter. They were reared as a culinary delicacy, and to provide a soft fur for lining garments, and were captured by means of ferrets and nets. Contemporary illustrations suggest that in the medieval and Tudor periods this was considered to be predominantly women's sport.

It was not until the mid-fourteenth century that rabbit numbers had increased sufficiently for them to be considered vermin. Even then they were protected within and beyond the limits of a warren and tenants were not free to kill rabbits on their land until the passing of the Ground Game Act in 1880.

Although some warrens were established on islands, most were contained within a rampart and ditch, sometimes with a hedge or fence, to deter predators and poachers. The majority were no larger than a paddock, although some extended over considerable areas: Lakenheath Warren in Suffolk, for example, covered more than 2,200 acres and was enclosed by a 16-km bank and ditch (10 miles). Such warrens brought their owners large profits and poaching was always a serious problem. Many warreners were therefore provided with fortified refuges such as the (surviving) two-storey stone-built lodge on the Prior of Thetford's fifteenth-century warren in the Brecklands of Norfolk.

Some warrens were delineated by marker stones; an old wayside cross (Bennett's Cross) near Postbridge on Dartmoor, for example, was adopted for this purpose and carved with the letters 'W-B' for 'warren boundary'. Series of *pillow mounds*, known locally as 'berries' or 'burys', were usually constructed in post-medieval warrens, and artificial burrows were provided to encourage breeding, the tunnels excavated and lined with stone or dug as boreholes. Tudor documents record payments for the provision of 'a great long auger of iron to make and bore coney holes within the King's beries new made'. As the name suggests, pillow mounds are usually of an oblong configuration, generally some 30 metres long (100 feet) and 10 metres wide (30 feet) and surrounded by shallow ditches. Shapes vary, however, and circular pillow mounds may easily be mistaken for barrows or windmill mounds.

Many warrens were established within the ramparts of ancient HILL FORTS, such as that on Pilsdon Pen in west Dorset, which provided ready-made protection for the breeding grounds. Others are marked on estate maps or are commemorated in *warren* or *coney* field and place-names (not to be confused with earlier place-names derived from the Old English *cyning* or the Old Norse *konungr*, both of which mean 'king').

Many pillow mounds were still in use in the nineteenth century, but by the early decades of the twentieth century, rabbits had become a major threat to agriculture and were decimated by the terrible myxomatosis epidemic of 1953.

WARS OF THE ROSES, THE The period of internecine strife between the houses of York and Lancaster lasting from the St Alban's incident in 1455 to the battle of Stoke in 1487, the last occasion on which a reigning monarch was required to take the field in person against a rival claimant to his throne. During these thirty-two years of dynastic turbulence, actual fighting occupied no more than thirteen weeks, the longest campaign (of 1471), from Edward IV's landing to the battle of Tewkesbury, lasting only seven and a half weeks.

The notion that the two houses adopted their respective roses in the Temple Garden may be attributed to Shakespeare (*Henry VI Part I*) and the term 'Wars of the Roses' originated in Sir Walter Scott's *Anne of Geierstein*, which was written in 1829. In fact, the red rose was a 'cousin' of the golden rose which was introduced as a royal device by Henry III's queen, Eleanor of Provence. It was associated with the title of Lancaster since its adoption by Eleanor's second son, Edmund Crouchback, and descended to John of Gaunt through his marriage to the Lancastrian heiress, Blanche. Thus it became the distinctive device of the Lancastrian kings and of Gaunt's illegitimate Beaufort line. (The Beauforts were later legitimated by act of parliament confirming a patent issued by Richard II, though their half-brother, Henry IV, added the words *excepta dignitate regali* to the patent, thereby debarring them from succession to the throne. But he failed to make the disqualification law by a further act of parliament and it was later argued that a royal patent could not alter one confirmed by Parliament and the Beauforts therefore enjoyed a rightful claim to succession.)

A white rose was the badge of Roger Mortimer, second Earl of March who died in 1360, grandfather of Richard II's heir, also Roger, the fourth Earl of March who was killed in 1398. It was by his Mortimer descent that Richard Plantagenet, Duke of York, could claim the throne, a fact which he emphasized by selecting the white rose from his numerous badges.

The two roses came to represent the principles of parliamentary sanction, by which the Lancastrians held the crown, and 'strict legitimism', which was the foundation of Yorkist rule. More recently, the red rose has been adopted as a symbol of democratic socialism. The proliferation of red and white roses in the armory of the counties of Lancashire and Yorkshire is of doubtful validity for both are essentially dynastic symbols.

WASTE The peripheral land of a manor on which tenants exercised their rights of commonage.
See also COMMONS *and* ENCLOSURE

WATCH AND WARD *see* LAW AND ORDER

WATER MEADOWS (FLOATED MEADOWS)
Many low-lying meadows flood naturally in winter, the percolation of warm, mineral-bearing water keeping the frost out of the ground and stimulating grass into early growth.

From the sixteenth century, winter flooding was often regulated to provide grazing for sheep and lambs in the early spring. The meadows were usually flooded again in April to encourage a June hay crop, and in summer to refresh the land and to hastened a new flush of growth. Complex systems of dikes, leats and hatches developed during the late seventeenth, eighteenth and nineteenth centuries.

George Boswell, in his *Treatise for Watering Meadows* (1742), set out in considerable detail his system for improving grasslands in river valleys. This was dependent on the crucial discovery that water should be kept moving, to prevent it from freezing, to maximize the availability of salts, and also because stagnant water loses its oxygen, which kills the grass underneath.

'Flooding upwards' was achieved by constructing a dam to hold back the waters which would flood the meadows upstream; while 'flooding downwards' involved damming a river and directing the waters by means of a canal (*head-main*) with outlets to a herringbone network of raised channels (*carriers*) from which the meadows were flooded and the water returned to the river by drains. The meadows themselves were divided into parallel beds along the downward slope, each about 10.7 metres wide (35 feet), curved in section, and up to 185 metres long (200 yards). This system ensured that all winter long the meadows were covered by a few inches of moving water.

There was also a West Country system of horizontal leats which ran parallel to the scarp face of hills and collected water below spring lines. When the leats were full, the water would overflow evenly across the meadows to the river. Water meadows were most numerous in the calciferous counties of Wessex but were also found in East Anglia and the East Midlands.

By the mid-nineteenth century, about 6,000 acres of water meadows had been created in Dorset to provide extra grazing for the ever-increasing numbers of sheep that brought the county its prosperity. All the major river valleys were criss-crossed with dikes and ditches and the rivers punctuated with weirs to flood or 'drown' the land. Thomas Hardy described the meadows near his home as 'watered on a plan so rectangular that on a fine day they look like silver gridirons'. No 'drowners' work these water meadows now but the channels and hatches are still a major feature of the Frome valley to the east of Dorchester.

WATER-CLOSET Many ancient civilizations had elaborate drainage systems and lavatories which, in construction and efficiency, surpassed anything of later periods up to the nineteenth century. The Elizabethan Sir John Harrington designed the first water-closet in England. At his home near Bath (Somerset) he installed a cistern from which a flow of water descended through a pipe to flush a lavatory pan. The supply was controlled by a hand-operated tap and released from the pan by means of a valve. Most of Harrington's contemporaries dismissed his invention as a joke, though Elizabeth I is said to have had a model installed at Richmond Palace.

The first patent for a water-closet was taken out in 1755 by a watch-maker, Alexander Cummings, and by the 1870s they had been installed in most middle-class homes. But as there was rarely an adequate water supply or sewage system, most water-closets were poorly cleansed and drained into cesspools. It is hardly surprising that the Victorians remained highly suspicious of the 'noxious gases' created by sewage (*see* DRAINS) and many water-closets were located at some distance from habitable rooms, often in a specially built wing which projected from the back of a house. Improvements included ceramic pans which replaced earlier metal ones, and the introduction of more efficient flushing systems and the S-bend on outlet pipes in which trapped water prevented drain odours from rising. In towns, cesspools were later connected by pipe to sewage systems but in rural areas many remain in use or have been replaced by septic tanks.

Until comparatively recently, most farms, cottages and even village schools were served by privies. A *privy* was a brick shed, located several yards to the rear of a dwelling, in which a simple wooden bench with holes was set above a cesspit. Many privies, sometimes with accommodation for four or more persons and with seats at different levels for adults and children, were still in use until the 1950s.
See also GARDEROBE

WATERMARKS A watermark is a paper manufacturer's symbol visible when the paper is held against the light. Watermarks are useful when attempting to date and locate the manufacture of paper and may assist in the detection of a forged document. At first, the devices found on both European and British papers were simple shapes: a

ram's head on Bordeaux paper of 1330 and a sword in 1351, for example. Armorial watermarks first appeared towards the end of the fifteenth century, and in the seventeenth and eighteenth centuries, when watermarks were also used to denote paper quality and sheet size, heraldic devices often indicated royal, noble or civic patronage. More recently, manufacturers began to use cyphers, trade marks and logotypes to identify their own brands of paper, though grades of paper used exclusively by sovereigns and departments of government have been marked with royal badges and cyphers for centuries.

WATER-MILLS It is likely that water-mills were introduced into Britain by the Romans. They were numerous in the Saxon period and some 6,000 mills were recorded at the time of the DOMESDAY survey, though there were undoubtedly many more.

Milling soke was a feudal monopoly exercised by most (though not all) lords of the manor. In practice, many mills were leased to tenant millers and manorial custom required that the peasants should have their corn ground in the lord's mill on payment of a toll (*multure*), usually one-sixteenth of the grist ground. (From the thirteenth century, the toll was usually commuted to a money payment.) The lord, who was responsible for major repairs, had first claim on his mill for grinding corn from the DEMESNE LANDS, while the peasants could be fined for grinding their corn at home or for patronizing a rival mill. No fewer than eighty QUERNS, confiscated in 1274 from recalcitrant tenants of the Abbot of Cirencester, (Gloucestershire), were later used to pave the abbey floor. The right of a miller to receive a constant and unimpeded supply of water remains today.

Water-mills were of four types, all of which harnessed the power of falling or running water to turn the grind-stones between which the grain was milled. In the *horizontal mill* (or *click mill*), which was of Saxon origin, the wheel was positioned horizontally across a stream from which water was directed to the paddles by means of a chute. There was no gearing and the grinding stone, which was on the floor above, was driven directly by the shaft of the wheel. The *undershot mill* was a Roman innovation and was reintroduced into Britain towards the end of the Saxon period. It consisted of a vertical wheel with flat blades at its circumference, the lower section of which came into contact with the water. The flow of water to the blades could be regulated by means of a weir and sluice-gate set within a leat (*see* WEIRS).

The *overshot mill*, introduced in the Middle Ages, was more efficient and was particularly well-suited to hill country. Again, water was directed and

Overshot mill at Ambleside, Cumbria.

controlled by means of a leat but was supplied, at the top of the wheel's circumference, to a series of buckets which caused the wheel to revolve in a clockwise direction by the downward motion and weight of the water. The *breastshot mill* was similar, but the water was directed into the buckets at a point level with the wheel's axle, causing it to turn in an anti-clockwise direction.

Tidemills, dating from the late fourteenth century, were a type of undershot mill driven by the flow of water from a large but shallow millpond constructed on the landward side of the mill. Water was impounded at high tide by means of sluice-gates and released when the tide had dropped sufficiently to provide an adequate fall of water.

The *mill race* is the often turbulent stretch of water immediately downstream from a mill. In all but the horizontal mill, the millstones were driven (at approximately 150 revolutions per minute) by a series of wooden cogwheel gears. From the thirteenth century, water-power was also used to drive *fulling mills*, in which hammers, fitted to a moving beam, removed the grease and grime from woven cloth by pummelling the fabric under water (*see* WOOL). In the same century, water-powered *forge hammers* were also introduced in the Weald of Kent and other iron-producing areas and, in the fifteenth century, water-wheels were used to drive the bellows of the first blast furnaces (*see* MINERALS). Water-powered paper-mills are known to have operated on the river Lea near Hertford in the late fifteenth century and there were gunpowder mills in south-east England from the seventeenth century.

The *turbine*, a horizontal wheel enclosed in a chamber with controlled inflow and outflow ports, was introduced in the early nineteenth century when the supremacy of the water-mills as the principal source of industrial energy was being challenged by STEAM POWER. It was also a time of migration from the sources of water-power to the coalfields of the INDUSTRIAL REVOLUTION.
See also WINDMILLS

WATER SUPPLY *see* AQUEDUCTS, PUBLIC UTILITIES *and* RAMS

WATER-TOWERS *see* ASYLUMS *and* PUMPING HOUSES

WATER TROUGH *see* DRINKING FOUNTAINS

-WATH A place-name element, from the Old Scandinavian *va*, meaning 'ford', commonly found in Cumbria and north Yorkshire and usually preceded by a descriptive element such as *skirt* ('dung-coloured') as in Skitwath, Cumbria.

WATLING STREET *see* ROMAN ROADS

WATTLE AND DAUB A primitive type of walling in which a row of vertical stakes or branches (*wattles*) were interwoven horizontally by smaller branches or reeds and a coating of mud and dung (*daub*) plastered on to one or both sides. The wattle and daub walls of thatched Anglo-Saxon dwellings were often reinforced by turves and moss, and medieval wattles were usually interwoven with laths rather than branches.

Wattle and daub was the most common method of filling the panels of TIMBER-FRAMED BUILDINGS. The tips of hazel or ash wands were secured in holes drilled in the timber framing and the wands woven to form a basketwork within each panel. The panels were then plastered on both sides with daub and sealed with limewash. Straw or horsehair was usually mixed with the plaster to provide greater strength and durability.

This type of walling is of considerable antiquity (at Fengate in Cambridgeshire, a wooden framed building, dating from *c.* 2500 BC, was found to have wattle and daub walls) and yet was still used in many parts of the country in the construction of low quality rural dwellings as recently as the nineteenth century. There are also many variations: in some instances, vertical oak staves were used instead of wattle and in East Anglian buildings the staves were often set horizontally with wattles tied to them.

From the fifteenth century, decaying wattle and daub panels were often replaced by BRICK NOGGING, particularly in farm buildings, even though the limewashed daub was more effective against water penetration than brick.
See also MUD AND STUD

WAYMAKER, WAYMAN *and* **WAYWARDEN** *see* HIGHWAY

WAYSIDE CROSSES Crosses were erected along tracks and highways for a multiplicity of reasons. Some commemorate events the details of which are long since forgotten. Others mark resting places along CORPSE ROADS or were intended simply to guide travellers through inhospitable terrain. There are concentrations of such crosses on the North York Moors and on Dartmoor in Devon. Most wayside crosses are of medieval origin, are often of crude execution and may be mistaken for monastic boundary markers.

Inevitably, wayside crosses (especially those at crossroads) have attracted the superstitious. Formerly, suicides were not allowed to be buried in consecrated ground and it was the practice to bury them at crossroads. It was also common practice to suspend the corpse of an executed person in a metal cage at a crossroads (*see* GIBBET) so that justice could be seen to have been done and as a deterrent to others. The Cross-and-Hand, an isolated roadside pillar on the downs above Batcombe in Dorset, is mentioned by Thomas Hardy in *Tess of the D'Urbervilles*: ''Tis a thing of ill-omen . . . put up in wild times by the relations of a malefactor who was tortured there by nailing his hand to a post and then hung. The bones lie beneath. They say he sold his soul to the devil, and that he walks at times.' The origins of this 'cross' are unknown but it is possible that it was erected as a boundary marker by monks from the nearby abbey of Cerne.

Late seventeenth-century weathercock at Bradford Abbas, Dorset.

WEALD *see* WOLD

WEALDEN HOUSE *see* HALL

WEATHER *see* CLIMATE

WEATHERBOARD (CLAPBOARD) A timber cladding consisting of lengths of board fixed to the exterior of a building, usually horizontally though sometimes vertically, to provide additional protection and insulation. Weatherboard is usually overlapping, as in a clinker-built boat, but is sometimes tongue and grooved so that it has a flat appearance.

WEATHERCOCKS *and* **WEATHER-VANES** A weathercock is a three-dimensional, hollow metal sculpture mounted on a spire, or above a tower, and revolving easily to indicate the direction of the wind.

Not all weathercocks are cockerels. Some are the emblems of patron saints, such as the gridiron of St Lawrence on the churches of St Lawrence, Jewry in the City of London, Ramsgate in Kent and Tidmarsh, Berkshire. On the church of St Mary-le-Bow, Cheapside, a huge 2.7 metre (9 feet) dragon, weighing over 2 cwt, is probably a representation of the mythical Thames dragon which appears in the coat of arms of the City of London. There are other dragons at Ottery St Mary, Devon, Sittingbourne, Kent, and Upton, Norfolk. A magnificent golden galleon on the tower of Henstridge church, Somerset, was the gift of Royal Navy airmen stationed at the nearby aerodrome during the war.

Without documentary evidence, weathercocks are often very difficult to date. One of the earliest references, a riddle in the *Exeter Book* of about 750, describes a weathercock as a hollow belly pierced by a rod. Many are of medieval appearance but are likely to have been replaced several times, though the original design may have been copied on each occasion. Cockerels symbolize vigilance and, most importantly, have tails which are ideally suited to catch the wind.

Unlike weathercocks, weather-vanes were intended both to show the direction of the wind and to display heraldic devices. They are effectively rigid metal flags and it has been argued (by Col. R. Gayre, *Heraldic Standards and Other Ensigns*, Oliver and Boyd, 1959) that in the medieval period the shape of a vane was dictated by the rank of its owner. The use of vanes, which probably originated in France, is evident in England from the thirteenth century and it is likely that the word is a corruption of *fane*, derived from *fannion*, meaning 'banner'. Heraldic vanes are generally found on the gables and pinnacles of major domestic buildings, particularly those of the Tudor period. Two examples are the banner-shaped vanes of the Lucy family at Charlecote, Warwickshire, and the swallow-tailed pennons of Lambeth Palace in London. Both sets are painted with coats of arms and the borders, decorative fleurs-de-lis and 'tails' are gilded to catch the sun.

Unfortunately, most weather-vanes have lost their original heraldic decoration and Victorian examples are often Gothic Revival imitations and were never painted.

WEBS *see* VAULTING

Monument (1631) to the Savage family at Elmley castle, Worcestershire. At the feet of William Savage, his son Giles and his daughter-in-law (who cradles an infant in her arms) are William's surviving grandchildren. Both the disposition of the 'weepers' and the superb quality of the carving are unusual for this period.

WEEM *see* SOUTERRAIN

WEEPERS Small stone or bronze figures set in the sides of TOMB CHESTS and other MONUMENTS as symbols of perpetual mourning. They first appeared on tombs towards the end of the thirteenth century and remained popular throughout the medieval, Tudor and Jacobean periods. Weepers usually represent a dead man's family and on medieval tombs may include members of eminent and magnatial families with whom the deceased was related by inheritance or marriage. Individuals may sometimes be identified by small shields of arms placed beneath the niches in which they stand. Medieval weepers were finely carved, dignified figures, cloaked and hooded, their heads bowed and their hands clasped in supplication. Elizabethan and Jacobean weepers are often crude by comparison. These usually comprise two graduated groups of kneeling figures, one of sons and the other of daughters, and occasionally a babe in swaddling-clothes bringing up the rear (*see* CHRISOM).

WEGS *see* HEREPAETHS

WEIGH-BRIDGE A platform scale, flush with the road, for weighing vehicles and beasts. The earliest reference to a weigh-bridge is in a report of 1796, *Arts and Manufacturing VI* by Ralph Salmon, in which are described 'weigh-bridges or engines with their apparatus, for the purpose of weighing carriages'. Eighteenth- and nineteenth-century examples are rare: in almost every case, the platforms have been removed, though the attendant scales-house may have survived. At Sherborne, Dorset, a circular red brick building at the roadside (similar in appearance to a large pillar-box) is the only remaining clue to the location of a former public weigh-bridge.

WEIRS A weir is a dam built across a river or canal to raise the water-level upstream and to control its flow. Weirs are particularly associated with WATER-MILLS and were constructed to divert river water, by means of artificial channels (*goits*), to millponds from where the flow to the mill-wheel would be regulated through sluice-gates.

A more ancient type of weir was the *fish-weir* (or *fish-hedge*), a funnel of wattle panels arranged across a river and kept in place by boulders and posts driven into the river bed. Excavations in former meanders of the River Trent in Nottinghamshire have revealed fish-weirs of this type dating from the eighth century BC to the early sixteenth century AD. Saxon fish-weirs were usually set obliquely across a river with baskets near the bank in which the fish, or more usually elvers and lampreys, were collected. On the Tidenham estate in Gloucestershire, there were twenty-one weirs on the Severn and thirty-eight on the Wye in 1060.

Norman weirs usually consisted of chevron-like rows of oak stakes and wattle panels arranged to form a funnel which narrowed downstream. The DOMESDAY survey of 1086 recorded some twenty-one weirs (*piscarae*) in Nottinghamshire and these would have been of both types. There were strict laws relating to the use of weirs for fishing: 'at every weir . . . every alternate fish belongs to the lord of the manor and every rare fish which is of value . . . and no one has the right of selling any fish for money when the lord is on the estate without informing him.' (Tidenham records 1060).

Medieval weirs and dams were constructed with a core of boulders and clay retained behind a timber framework. They required constant maintenance and repair as the result of flooding and intermittent sabotage by disgruntled navigators. In *c.* 1395 the Archbishop of York complained that 'fish garths' were seriously impeding river navigation on the Trent and the enlargement of a weir on the Ouse caused the sinking of two ships and their valuable cargoes.

Mill-weirs also caused problems. When a river was impounded, to raise a head of water for milling, navigation was interrupted both in the vicinity of the weir and downstream. Acts of 1352 and 1399 attempted to regulate the impounding of water so that millers operating downstream of their rivals would not be disadvantaged, but it seems that the legislation was not widely observed and disputes were commonplace.

Weirs were maintained by manorial tenants who may have been responsible for repairing specific sections (*doles*) of the structure. At Otley in Yorkshire, each 3.4-metre dole (11 feet) of a 41-metre mill-dam (45 yards) was the responsibility of a particular tenant, an obligation which remained until the mid-eighteenth century.

No medieval weirs have survived, but there can be little doubt that many water-mills and their associated weirs, millponds and sluices occupy the sites of medieval or even earlier predecessors.
For DAMS *see also* AQUEDUCTS

WELLS *see* HOLY WELLS, PUBLIC UTILITIES *and* SPRINGS

WELSH MARCHES *see* MARCH

WERGILD Compensation payments for death or injury based on the value of a man's life. In Saxon times, each class in the community was assigned a wergild and, in the event of murder or malicious injury, this was the amount of compensation payable by the malefactor or his family to the family of the injured or murdered person. A coerl's wergild was valued at 200*s* and that of a thane at 1,200*s*. The wergild for an unfree man (a serf) was paid to his master.
See also LAW *and* OATH HELPER

WESSEX The tribal kingdom of the West Saxons established in Hampshire in the early sixth century and gradually extended by conquest to include much of southern England (*see* KINGDOMS (ANCIENT)). Ultimately, under Alfred the Great and his successors, Wessex formed the nucleus of the Anglo-Saxon kingdom of England. The name was revived by the Dorset poet William Barnes (1801–86) and later in the Wessex novels of Thomas Hardy (1840–1928).

WESSEX CULTURE A flourishing early BRONZE AGE culture of Dorset and Wiltshire, characterized by numerous round barrows but few habitation sites. The area appears to have supported a substantial population engaged principally in agriculture, metallurgy and trade. Inhumation (and later cremation) was associated with grave goods, those of the richest burials being of such quality as to suggest a highly organized and hierarchical society, capable of undertaking the final remodelling of Stonehenge *c.* 1550 BC. The exotic style and execution of some grave goods also indicate a form of contact with contemporary European cultures. The comparatively abrupt demise of the Wessex Culture *c.* 1400 BC may indicate a decline in trade and deteriorating climatic conditions.

WETLANDS *see* RECLAMATION

WHEEL-HEAD CROSS A form of cross, with Celtic associations, in which the cross head is contained within, or overlays, a circle. This may have evolved from the practice of bracing the arms of a wooden cross or from the Mediterranean

Christian tradition of representing a cross within a circle. In ARMORY it is described as a *Celtic Cross*.
See also CHRISTIAN SYMBOLS *and* CROSSES

WHEELHOUSE (i) A farm building (*also* GIN-GANG, GIN-HOUSE, HORSE-GEAR, TRACK-SHED *and* WHEEL-RIG) *see* FARMSTEADS.
(ii) Scottish dwellings, dating from the third to the fifth centuries, often on or adjacent to the sites of BROCHS, which they appear to have superseded. Wheelhouses were circular stone-built dwellings with interior chambers partitioned by radiating masonry piers like the spokes of a wheel and with a hearth at the hub.

WHEEL WINDOW A circular window with a design of 'spokes' radiating from a central rim. This type of window is often confused with the ROSE WINDOW, which is also circular but contains a more complex design. Both are commonly found in medieval cathedrals, particularly in the end walls of nave and transepts.
See also GOTHIC ARCHITECTURE *and* WINDOWS

WHEELWRIGHT *see* WAGONS

WHIM *see* PORTLAND STONE

WHIPPING A punishment particularly imposed on women, who were either manacled to the parish whipping post or paraded through the streets and whipped at the tail of a cart. In 1740 London prostitutes were punished in this way.
See also PILLORY, PUNISHMENT *and* STOCKS

WHITE HORSES *see* HILL FIGURES

WICHERT *see* COB

WICK *and* **-WICK** A common place-name element from the Old English *wīc* (an early loan-word from the Latin *vicus*), meaning variously 'dwelling', 'farmstead', 'manor', 'hamlet' and 'quarter' (of a town). *Wīc* alone is found in Wick, Berkshire, and Wyke Regis, Dorset, both of which mean 'dairy farm'. As a first element it is often difficult to distinguish from other words (such as *wice*, meaning 'wych-elm') so that Wickham, Berkshire, means 'dwelling-place', while Wicklewood, Norfolk, means 'wych-elm wood'.
In the majority of cases, *wīc* is found combined with a descriptive first element to give, for example, Chiswick, Essex, 'a cheese farm', Shapwick, Dorset, 'a sheep farm' and Lenchwick, Worcestershire, an outlying hamlet of the village of Church Lench. Several *wīc* names are associated with manorial lords: Painswick, Gloucestershire, was the manor of Pain Fitzjohn (d.1137), and Wickwar, also Gloucestershire, was held by Roger le Warre in 1285. Many Wick and -wick names, derived from the Old Norse *vík*, meaning 'a bay', are to be found around the coasts of Scotland, though in England Scandinavian names such as Blowick ('dark bay') and Lowick 'leafy bay', both in Lancashire, are rare.

WICKET A small gate set into a fence or wall.

WIFE SELLING Until the end of the nineteenth century, there was a widespread belief that a wife was her husband's chattel and could therefore be sold. Newspaper reports tell of market-day auctions at which a wife was paraded with a halter, usually of plaited straw or ribbon, about her neck. The practice seems to have been of some antiquity, though references became more numerous with the increase in the circulation of newspapers in the nineteenth century. In 1782 a baptismal entry in the parish register of Purleigh in Essex refers to the mother as a bought wife. In the 1820s the French *Chargé d'Affaires* reported that the price for a wife in Smithfield market had recently doubled to 22*s*, while in Thomas Hardy's *The Mayor of Casterbridge*, Michael Henchard sold his wife for 5 guineas sometime towards the end of the same decade. Hardy obtained his information from the *Dorset County Chronicle*, from which he copied a number of instances in his notebook (*Commonplace Book 3*):

25 May 1826: *Sale of Wife*: Man at Brighton led a tidy-looking woman up to one of the stalls in the market, with a halter round her neck, and offered her for sale. . . . The woman has two children by her husband – one of whom he consents to keep, the other he throws

in as a makeweight to the bargain.

6 December 1827: *Selling Wife*: At Buckland nr. Frome, a labring [sic] man named Charles Pearce sold his wife to shoemaker Elton for £5 and delivered her in a halter in the public street. She seemed very willing. bells rang.

WILLOW Of the numerous varieties of willow growing in Britain, the most common are the native Crack Willow and White Willow. These common, or 'sally', willows were planted to conserve river banks and to provide materials for hurdles, poles, fences and fuel, 'provided it be sound and dry'. Most trees were pollarded (*see* POLLARD) to a height which prevented cattle eating the leaves.

Being tough, pliable and exceptionally light, willow is ideally suited to clubs, sticks and artificial limbs; and, being waterproof, to items such as the beating paddles used by washerwomen and slats for water-wheels. Cricket bats are made from a variety of the White Willow grown in Essex and neighbouring counties. Willow is also fairly heat-resistant, and kitchen bowls and utensils were often made of it, as were the brake blocks of carts. Pollard willows provided the wands for WATTLE AND DAUB building, 'kests' for bridge construction (cages containing solidified material for foundations), wattle fencing and a variety woven basket-work. Willow wands are pliable when moist, becoming harder and firmer but remaining resilient when dry.

Crack Willow is the tallest variety: it can grow to 27 metres (90 feet) and has a life span of about fifty years. The Goat Willow, which grows best on dryish soil, provided beautiful golden catkins which were scattered as 'palms' before the Corpus Christi processions. The osiers, or basketry willows, with their green or purple stems, are still grown in some areas, such as Sedgemoor in Somerset. Each summer the bunches of pliant young shoots, which rise from a pollarded willow stump to a height of *c*. 1.8 metres (6 feet), are harvested and either barked to give white willow or first boiled to dye them a bright buff colour. The Weeping Willow (which originated in China) was introduced at the beginning of the eighteenth century, seemingly at the same time as the first importation of 'Willow Pattern' china.

Willows are known by a variety of different names: osier, withy, palm, sallow and (in Scotland) saugh. Because willows often suffer from premature decay, a whipping with a willow rod was believed to stunt a child's growth and the willow of legend has a bitter taste because the Christchild is said to have been beaten with one.

WILLS *see* PROBATE

WINDBREAKS *see* SHELTER BELTS

WINDERS *see* STAIRCASES

WINDMILLS Early references to windmills are not always reliable, for many are contained in documents which were forged by medieval monastic houses in order to establish claims to ancient privileges which did not exist. The earliest authentic record is that of an 'adultarine' mill (one which operated unlawfully in direct competition to manorial mills) at Bury St Edmund's in 1191. It is likely that windmills were numerous by the end of the twelfth century and had been introduced from the continent of Europe by crusaders returning from the Holy Land. There are many (authentic) references to thirteenth-century mills in contemporary documents and several illustrations in manuscripts such as the *Windmill Psalter* of *c*. 1270.

The earliest windmills were primitive fixed structures which could only be operated when the wind was blowing from a particular quarter. These were followed by *post mills*, in which a weatherboarded body, on which the sails were carried, revolved on a strong central post so that it could be orientated to catch the wind. This was effected by means of a long tail pole and wheel which projected from the rear of the mill and was pushed into position by hand. This tail pole also increased the structure's equilibrium and sometimes carried a flight of steps by which the mill was entered. The central post was secured at the base by cross trees which were embedded within the raised mill-mound. Such

Ruined post-mill at Otwood, Surrey.

mounds may be mistaken for tumuli both in their configuration and their location, which was usually on an exposed or hilltop site. The machinery for driving the grinding stones was contained within the body of the mill and the trestles on which this was supported were later protected by the provision of a *roundhouse* which also provided storage space. The oldest surviving example of this type of mill is at Bourn in Cambridgeshire and dates from before 1636.

Towards the end of the medieval period, the roundhouse was often extended upwards to form a rigid structure on top of which a conical cap and sails revolved on a circular track. These *smock mills* were constructed of wood and were usually octagonal in plan, had battered (sloping) sides and were sometimes provided with a brick base, as at Cranbrook in Kent. They were particularly popular from the seventeenth century, as were *tower mills* which were constructed of brick or stone and were usually round in plan or occasionally octagonal. Like the smock mills they had revolving caps, though these were usually semi-spherical, and from 1745 fantails and gears were introduced into both types of mill so that the caps could be turned automatically and the sails directed into the wind.

There are three types of sail (*sweep*): *common sails*, the earliest type, consisted of sail-cloth stretched over a wooden framework; *spring sails*, which are series of movable shutters, pivoted at right angles to the length of the sweep, and connected by a rod to a spring which was adjusted by the miller so that the shutters opened automatically when the strength of the wind reached a pre-determined level; and *patent sails*, introduced from 1807, which also had movable shutters controlled by a system of weights and pulleys.

Regrettably, no medieval mills have survived, though there are many examples of the later types which may be seen both as ruins and as restorations. The oldest surviving tower mill is a decapitated fifteenth-century shell at Burton Dasset in Warwickshire and the oldest smock mill is the restored example at Lacey Green in Buckinghamshire, which dates from c. 1650.

Although steam-powered milling engines were introduced into several towns after 1784, many windmills were still operating commercially at the beginning of the twentieth century. But the widespread use on farms of portable milling engines, and the introduction in the 1870s of large-scale roller milling, hastened the windmill's decline, which was further exacerbated in 1916 by restrictions on the production of flour. About 350 mills were revived following the First World War but

these gradually ceased operations so that by 1953 there remained only twenty-one.

Wind power was used for purposes other than milling. In East Anglia, the Fens had been drained during the seventeenth century (*see* RECLAMATION) but environmental factors had been overlooked and *windpumps* (*marsh mills*) had to be introduced to lift water from one level to the next by means of 'scoop-wheels'. By the mid-eighteenth century, there were some 250 windpumps operating in the central Fens but these were replaced by steam-pumps from the 1820s. Several windmills have survived on the Norfolk Broads, where they were originally erected as windpumps, and at the Wicken Fen nature reserve in Cambridgeshire the only surviving windpump from the original Fen-land scheme has been re-erected and restored.
See also MILLS *and* WATER-MILLS

WINDOW GLASS *see* GLASS *and* STAINED GLASS

WINDOWS Saxon and early medieval windows were generally small and narrow. In part, this was for defensive reasons and because of the prohibitive cost of glazing (*see* GLASS), but of greater significance was the fact that contemporary builders, with a limited understanding of constructional techniques, were concerned that walls should not be weakened by large openings (*see* ARCH). Window openings were fitted with wooden shutters which could be barred at night, but although these helped to keep out the cold air in winter they also excluded the light so that semi-transparent materials, such as horn, were often used as cheap alternatives to glass. As the need for defence declined and building techniques improved so window openings became larger and wider.

The 'seemingly ethereal fragility' of late GOTHIC ARCHITECTURE was arrived at only after centuries of experimentation and innovation. The narrow-pointed *lancet windows* of the Early English period evolved through the mullioned and transomed lights of the Decorated and the ornate tracery of the Perpendicular (*see also* ROSE WINDOW *and* WHEEL WINDOW) to the broad, square-headed windows of the late fifteenth century.

The changing function of the medieval castle is also evident in rectangular mullioned windows inserted, somewhat incongruously at times, in the walls of solars and other domestic chambers. Domestic architecture of this late medieval period was characterized by elaborate bay and oriel windows. A *bay window* (or *compass window*) projects from a wall and rises from ground level through one or more stories, while an *oriel window* is of similar appearance but is cantilevered or supported on a corbel or bracket above ground level.

During the sixteenth century, windows continued to increased in size as a proportion of wall area. But large panes of glass were unable to withstand strong winds and windows were generally composed of small lozenge-shaped quarries (*leaded lights*), held together in a lattice-work of grooved lead bars (*canes*). Medieval windows were rarely intended to be opened and the canes of the leaded lights were secured by wire to iron bars (*saddle bars*) set within a stone or wood frame. Sometimes a hinged opening framework (*casement*) was provided within a window, and by the sixteenth century these had increased in size so that a large proportion of a window could be opened.

Seventeenth-century windows in the classical style (*see* CLASSICAL ARCHITECTURE) were square or round-headed and had rectangular panes secured within a framework of wooden bars (*glazing bars*) which replaced the medieval lead canes. Large circular or oval windows (*bull's eye windows*) are characteristic of churches of this period.

Curved *bow-fronted windows* became fashionable in terraces of the Regency period (*see* REGENCY ARCHITECTURE) and, in the eighteenth century, windows became taller, often extending the full height of a room. Semi-circular *Diocletian windows* were popular during the PALLADIAN period, as were *Venetian windows* (and doors) which were of tripartite design, with a central arched section between two lower flat-topped flanking lights.

By the end of the seventeenth century, *sash windows* had largely replaced casements. A sash window consists of two glazed frames running vertically in channels and counterbalanced by weights. When in 1597 Shakespeare wrote (in *Richard III*) 'Ere I let fall the windowes of mine eyes', he was referring to an early form of sash window which was held open not by counter-weights, but by stays. (Examples of these, dating from *c.* 1720, may still be seen in Wilkes Street, Spitalfields, in London.) The term itself (derived from the French *chassis*, meaning 'frame') was introduced into Britain from Holland and France in 1662, and the first recorded use of counter-weights appeared in the accounts of the Office of Works for 1669. 'Double sashes' (with both top and bottom sashes sliding) are recorded in Princess Mary's closet at St Jame's Palace, London, in 1672. A variation, the *Yorkshire sash*, in which the sashes slide horizontally without the use of weights, may be found throughout Britain, particularly on the rear elevations of houses. It is likely that window sashes were originally painted in

a stone colour but from the 1770s darker colours were preferred in imitation of the oak or mahogany sashes of the best quality houses.

As a general rule, earlier windows may be identified by thick glazing bars and substantial wooden-box framing. In London, eighteenth-century legislation required that sash frames should be concealed within the surrounding brickwork as a fire precaution. The practice became fashionable and, as a consequence, windows became larger and glazing bars thinner. As plate glass became more easily available, glazing bars were removed and single sheets of plate glass fitted within each sash. But the heavier glass, and the weakening of the structure by the removal of glazing bars, often resulted in sashes collapsing so that projecting 'horns' had to be added to the upper and lower edges of the sash to increase its structural strength. (Such horns on the windows of a pre-1840 house usually indicate that the original sashes have been replaced.)

The casement window was reintroduced in the early decades of the twentieth century, together with metal-framed windows. At first, these were of steel and, therefore, required painting, but from the 1930s they were available in aluminium.

Windows provide invaluable clues to the age of a house, though all too often the original windows have been replaced by ugly modern 'units' which are entirely unsympathetic to the architectural integrity of the building.

See also DORMER WINDOW *and* STAINED GLASS

WINDOW TAX Window Tax replaced HEARTH TAX in 1697 and was intended to defray the cost of 'making good the deficiency of the clipped money' by reminting the coin of the realm. The occupant (not the owner) of '. . . every dwelling house inhabited that now are or hereafter shall be erected within the kingdom of England, dominion of Wales and town of Berwick on Tweed (other than and except cottages)' was required to make an annual payment of 2*s*, with an additional payment of 8*s* for those who occupied dwellings with more than ten windows. In 1709 the rates were increased for larger houses though small dwellings, whose occupants did not pay poor or church rates, were exempt.

Unlike the hated Hearth Tax, assessments could be made without intruding on a household's privacy but the tax was nevertheless singularly unpopular and was described as a duty 'on fresh air, sunshine and health'. Householders would reduce their tax liabilities by blocking non-essential windows and as a result the yield gradually fell so that in 1747 new legislation was enacted and more detailed scales introduced. The flat rate of 2*s* was retained and those who occupied houses with between ten and fourteen windows were charged 6*d* per window, those with between fifteen and nineteen windows paid 9*d* per window and those with more than twenty windows paid 1*s* per window. As a consequence, the tax yield increased but so did the practice of blocking windows and during the 1750s and 1760s the rates were again increased, only to be doubled by Pitt in 1784.

From 1825, those with less than eight windows were exempt and the tax was abolished in 1851 to be replaced by an 'inhabited house duty'. The few Window Tax returns which have survived are usually kept in county record offices. Lists of names, addresses and taxes paid are to be found in the records of the Exchequer at the Public Record Office.

See also GLASS *and* TAXATION

WINDPUMPS *see* WINDMILLS

WINTERBORNE A common river name derived from the Old English *winterburna*, meaning 'intermittent stream', specifically one which is dry except in winter or during periods of unusually heavy rainfall. Several Dorset and Wiltshire villages are named after their winterbornes: Winterborne Kingston, for example, which was held by the king in 1086, and Winterborne Monkton, which once belonged to the abbey of Vaast in Arras. In parts of Yorkshire and Humberside, winterbornes are known colloquially as 'gipseys' and in Kent they are 'nailbournes', a corruption of 'eylebourns' from the Old English *ǣwell*, meaning 'spring'.

WIPPET STICK *see* SLATES

WITAN *see* MOOT

WITCHCRAFT The majority of witch-trials arose as the result of injury for which there was no apparent explanation other than the occult activities of someone who had acquired a sinister reputation or whose behaviour or appearance was in some way unusual. Indeed, the word 'sinister' (from the Latin *sinister*, meaning 'left') came to be applied to those who were left-handed or in some other way 'marked-out' and therefore invited suspicion.

During the Middle Ages, both the Church and intellectual opinion defined a witch as a heretic who obtained his or (more usually) her powers through a pact with the Devil. It was the act itself which attracted judicial punishment and in the majority of cases, when the deed or intent was not serious, the punishment was light: confinement in the STOCKS or PILLORY or a public penance in the parish church. But charges of political intrigue, Lollardy, heresy and treason were common in the fourteenth and fifteenth centuries and, in many cases, witchcraft and necromancy were added for good measure, often securing a conviction where the prosecution of other charges had failed.

A papal bull of 1484 resulted in fierce persecution which lasted for nearly one and a half centuries, the Old Testament denunciation 'Thou shalt not suffer a witch to live' (Exodus Ch. 22, v. 18) providing sufficient justification for more than 500 hangings. The Church's preoccupation with devil-worship reflected an intellectual conflict between late medieval concepts of heresy and popular superstition, and there can be little doubt that the situation was exacerbated by social pressures which encouraged allegations of witchcraft at a time when, in Protestant countries, the Church's traditional remedies (such as holy water) were no longer available.

It was during the reign of Henry VIII that witchcraft became a crime (defined as a compact with the devil to commit an evil act), and although the statute was repealed in 1547 (under Edward VI) a further act of 1563 made it a felony to invoke an evil spirit for any purpose, good or bad. In 1604 James I, who wrote a book on demonology, confirmed the availability of the death penalty in such cases and widened the scope of the law to include association with an evil spirit, regardless of intent. The Devil's Mark (often a wart) was looked for as confirmation of guilt and in Scotland the use of torture often produced bizarre confessions and a multiplicity of victims.

In 1645–6 a failed lawyer, Matthew Hopkins, became active as a professional witch-finder in the south-eastern counties of England, causing hysteria of epidemic proportions and using trial by ordeal (*see* LAW) to support otherwise unsustainable village prejudices and superstitions.

Witchcraft was gradually rejected by informed opinion during the late seventeenth century, though in rural areas it survived into the nineteenth century and beyond. The last witch was executed at Exeter in 1682 but the penalty was not abolished until the Witchcraft Act was repealed in 1951!

See also CONJUROR

WODEHOUSE (*also* **WODEWOSE**) A wild man of the woods, covered in green hair except where the flesh is visible in the face, elbows, knees, hands and feet. Several wodehouses are armed with clubs, as in the fifteenth-century effigy of Sir Robert

A wodehouse or wild man at the feet of the fifteenth-century effigy of Sir Robert Whittingham at Aldbury, Hertfordshire.

Whittingham at Aldbury, Hertfordshire. They are found in STAINED GLASS and carved in the capitals of pillars and on FONTS and MISERICORDS. Although apparently derived from a combination of silvan demon and Greek satyr, wodehouses symbolize strength and wholesomeness.

WODEN *see* GRIM

WODEWOSE *see* WODEHOUSE

WOLD *and* **WEALD** From the Old English *wald*, meaning 'woodland', the term is most often associated with windswept upland landscapes such as the Yorkshire Wolds and the COTSWOLDS of Gloucestershire, where 'At Stow-on-the-Wold the wind blows cold . . .'. Originally, the name described high forest land but following clearances it came to mean 'open upland country'. The Anglian form was also *wald*, but the Saxon-Kentish form was *weald*, hence the Weald of Kent, Surrey and Sussex, and of the lost *Andredes Weald* of Pevensey.

WOLVES Records suggest that wolves were extinct in Wales by 1000, in southern England by 1400 and in northern England by 1500. In the Highlands of Scotland, the last recorded sighting was in 1743, and in Ireland in 1786. But the Old English *wulf* is commemorated in place-names such as Wolford in Warwickshire and Woolmer Forest in Hampshire, and in the Romanesque carving found in many early churches such as Kilpeck and Castle Frome, Herefordshire.

WOODBANKS Medieval woodland was usually protected at its boundaries by substantial woodbanks which were intended both to prevent browsing animals from entering from surrounding fields and as a means of delineating the wood. A woodbank consisted of a massive earthen rampart with an outward-facing ditch. Some had double embankments and there is evidence to suggest that many carried a palisade or hedge or were faced with stone. There can be little doubt that the repair and maintenance of woodbanks was a considerable undertaking, one which reflected the commercial value of medieval woodland. Within the wood itself smaller woodbanks defined the various coppices which were cleared by rotation (*see* COPPICE). Many surviving woods are still contained within their ancient woodbanks, though the ramparts will almost certainly have been eroded and the ditches filled with accumulated debris so that they no longer perform any apparent function. Woodbanks may be confused with park pales (*see* DEER PARKS) or with the remnants of former hedgerows which have been taken into a more recent wood. But park pales enclosed very much larger areas of deer park while hedgebanks tend to be steeper and less massive than woodbanks and may still carry trees which have grown out of a former hedge.
See also POLLARD

'WOODLAND' COUNTRYSIDE *see* COUNTRYSIDE

WOODLAND Nearly 50 per cent of Britain's ancient woodland was lost in just four decades between 1947 and 1987. In the lowlands, ancient woods which once provided for the needs of entire communities have been cleared to create immense featureless prairies, and, encouraged by Common Market subsidies and tax incentives, many landowners continue to replace deciduous woodland with plantations of quick-growing, alien conifers as a means of obtaining more rapid returns on investment.

Except as cover for game, woodland is no longer profitable and yet for thousands of years managed woodland was an essential and profitable element of rural life. It invariably occupied land which was unsuitable for cultivation, and therefore complemented other areas of an estate. Unlike coniferous plantations, woodland is essentially self-perpetuating and, although STANDARDS were usually replaced with saplings after felling, the principle of natural regeneration formed the basis of effective woodland management. The underwood was a considerable resource which, when exploited to the full, could yield a higher income than adjacent ploughland or pasture (*see* COPPICE *and* POLLARD). Customary rights ensured that woodland also made provision for the day-to-day needs of communities (*see* COMMONS) and provided employment in the harvesting and manufacture of woodland products and in subsidiary crafts (*see* CHARCOAL).

It is unlikely that ancient woodlands were actually planted and most have occupied their existing boundaries since the early Middle Ages. From the Neolithic period, and through the Bronze and Iron Ages, extensive areas of wildwood were cleared for cultivation so that by the Roman occupation the landscape was probably even less wooded than it is today. In the centuries following the withdrawal of Rome, the so-called Dark Ages, much of the landscape reverted to natural woodland and heath, vast areas of which were later adopted as hunting FORESTS by the Norman and Angevin kings and their magnates. During the medieval period, the forest boundaries were gradually pushed back by assarting (*see* ASSART), and by the creation of WOOD PASTURE, and areas of woodland were enclosed by WOODBANKS and managed for the benefit of manorial lords and their tenants who enjoyed commoners' rights. From the Tudor period, substantial areas of ancient woodland were enclosed in DEER PARKS and incorporated into parkland, particularly during the seventeenth and eighteenth centuries, often re-colonizing cultivated land.

The invasion and decline of species, both through natural causes (such as climatic changes and the spread of disease) and as a result of man's intervention, is evident in most woods: the sycamore, for example, which was introduced in the sixteenth century, has subsequently flourished in many old woods, while the once prolific elm is rarely seen since the spread of Dutch elm disease in the 1970s. *See also* entries on specific trees

WOOD PASTURE As the name suggests, this was a form of land use which required a delicate balance to be maintained between grazing livestock and managed woodland, usually through pollarding (*see* POLLARD) and protected areas of coppice (*see* COPPICE). Although widespread during the Saxon and Norman periods (when it was described as *silua pastilis* in Domesday Book), there appears to have been a gradual reduction in the extent of wood pasture during the Middle Ages and following ENCLOSURE little remains today. Normally, the woodland belonged to the manorial lord, while grazing and other rights were exercised by the commoners (*see* COMMONS).

WOOL In the fourteenth century, Edward III commanded that in council his Chancellor should sit on a woolsack as a symbol of the pre-eminence of the wool trade. For more than four centuries, the manufacture and export of wool cloths dominated British commerce. The great medieval monastic houses (notably the CISTERCIANS) were 'built on wool', having acquired (usually through endowment) vast tracts of dry infertile land which although unsuitable for arable farming could be managed efficiently as sheep runs. Technically, the monasteries produced wool for their own needs but as these were minimal there was a massive surplus which was sold in Europe, together with the produce of manorial estates. But such a trade was wasteful of resources, and successive medieval governments imposed strict controls on the export of wool through TAXATION and the *Staple* system, while encouraging the production of wool cloth by introducing advantageous trading tariffs for English merchants and the immigration to England of expert weavers from Flanders.

In the Middle Ages, most wool, especially the finest coming from the Cotswolds, passed through London to Calais. This monopoly facilitated the collection of duties and enabled governments to regulate the flow of bullion. Indeed, under the Yorkist kings the Staple effectively became a department of state responsible for the maintenance of Calais. Each craftsman worked at home owning both equipment and materials. The weaver wove yarn bought from the spinner and sold cloth to the fuller who, having cleaned and thickened the cloth, sold it on to the merchant tailors. This independence was tempered by compulsory craft guilds which, in theory, controlled wages and working methods, and regulated prices and standards but in practice were often restrictive to enterprise and innovation. As a consequence, by the Tudor period entrepreneurs (*clothiers*) were producing wool cloth outside the incorporated towns. They purchased wool directly from the sheep farmers and sub-contracted the various processes (spinning, weaving, fulling, dyeing and finishing) to outworkers, many of whom were entirely dependent on a constant supply of work and were therefore vulnerable to exploitation. John Aubrey, a Wiltshire landowner, described the clothiers as 'keeping their spinners but just alive'.

Like the capitalists of the Industrial Revolution, Tudor and Stuart clothiers were socially ambitious. They married their children into the aristocracy, acquired coats of arms and built impressive houses for themselves, creating perhaps the most charming of all English settlements, the 'clothiers' towns', such as Painswick in the Gloucestershire Cotswolds. With the demise of the medieval guilds, many clothiers accepted with alacrity the rôle of their predecessors, endowing numerous churches, almshouses and schools as memorials to their prosperity and benevolence. In Yorkshire, however, the term 'clothier' had a very different meaning. These clothiers and their families produced unfinished 'white' cloth on lonely moorland farms and sold it on at market to merchants who had it dyed and finished. They did not enjoy the prosperity of the southern clothiers but from their labours grew the great Yorkshire woollen industry of the nineteenth century.

The process of converting the wool from a fleece into broadcloth (woven on a broad loom) varied little during these centuries. The sheered fleece was by custom handed over to women workers for rolling before being graded and packed into the woolsacks, which were of a statutory size. Each woolsack was suspended from a beam in the wool-barn so that it hung down to floor level and the two wool-packers stood inside it, skilfully 'footing' the fleeces into the corners and treading down the layers. When the last fleece was in place the packers stepped out backwards along the top, sewing up the sack as they did so. The woolsack was then lowered, eight 'holds' tied at the corners and the sacks in a consignment stamped with a distinctive mark (*see* MERCHANTS' MARKS). The wool was transported by wagons, covered as protection against the damp but ventilated so that the wool would not overheat. Woolsacks were sold by weight, not by the number of fleeces they contained, and were measured in *cloves* (3 kg/7 lb), *todds* (12.5 kg/28 lb) *weys* (82.5 kg/182 lb) and *packs* (109 kg/240 lb).

Once the fleece was 'broken', the product was called 'wool'. The raw wool was first sorted, according to length and quality, and washed. Sulphur bleaching (*stoving*) or blue-dying (using the leaves of the woad plant) was often carried out at this stage. After drying, the wool was oiled with Seville or Gallipoli oil or sometimes with butter or goose grease. Next the fibre was loosened (*carded*) or combed, and hand-spun by women outworkers until sufficient skeins of yarn had been reeled and sized to sell to a weaver as warp, which was threaded into the loom, or as abb (weft), which was wound onto quills which fitted inside the loom shuttles. After scouring, usually in stale urine to remove oil and size, the woven cloth was soaped, carefully folded and cleaned or 'fulled' under water, either by treading or beating under the wooden drop-hammers of fulling mills (*see* WATER-MILLS) and using a type of clay called *fuller's earth* as a mordant. The lengths of wet cloth, which would have shrunk from 49 to 36.6 metres (54 to 40 yards), were then brushed (*roughed*) to raise the nap, often with dried teasel-heads (*Dipsacus*) set into a handle, and taken to a 'tenting field' and stretched across a fence-like framework of upright poles to dry, the selvedges secured by 'tenter-hooks'.

Whites and 'medleys' were usually dyed in the wool (i.e. before weaving) and, until the sixteenth century, a large amount of undyed cloth was exported after fulling. But most cloth was dyed 'in the piece' and many areas acquired reputations for particular types or colours of cloth: Lincoln Green, for example, and Stroudwater Red, which was dyed exclusively for the scarlet uniforms of the British Army. The tenting fields of Stroud in Gloucestershire are commemorated in the red *billets* of the town's coat of arms, while a teasel in the arms of Frome in Somerset recalls its former wool trade.

WORKHOUSES Between 1723 and 1776, nearly 2,000 workhouses were built in England. These were provided by parishes and were financed out of the poor rates (*see* POOR LAW). By 1840, some 13.7 million of the 16 million inhabitants of England and Wales lived in areas where the reformed Poor Law was in force and where groups of parishes had been formed into unions to provide workhouses for the destitute.

Although the 1834 Poor Law Amendment Act had administrative and financial merits, it was in practice a singularly harsh piece of legislation. That 'fundamental document of Victorianism' was designed to remove from circulation those who were unable or unwilling to support themselves by refusing them outdoor relief and admitting them to the workhouse. This in turn was intended to reduce the supply of cheap labour, which had hitherto been subsidized by the rates, and to stimulate a rise in wages thereby encouraging the able-bodied to seek work.

For such a strategy to be effective it was necessary to ensure that life in the workhouse should be sufficiently unpleasant to deter the average labourer. It was not the intention of the legislation that the 'impotent and helpless poor' should be punished but in practice this is precisely what happened. Although outdoor relief remained the principal method of dealing with distress, the spectre of the workhouse inspired a pervasive dread of infirmity and destitution and many endured desperate cold and hunger before applying to a relieving officer for admission.

In the workhouse, husbands and wives were rigorously separated from each other and from their children and communication was forbidden. Even at meals, which generally consisted of gruel or broth, dry bread or potatoes, silence was maintained. Relatives could only be received by special permission and in the presence of the master or matron. Honest paupers and pregnant women shared the freezing, bare wards with consumptives, imbeciles and syphilitics: no distinction was made except by sex and age, only the youngest children being permitted to remain with their mothers. The male inmates were provided with occupations such as oakum-picking, stone-breaking and bone-grinding, and discipline was enforced by solitary confinement, penitential dress and a reduced diet. Although elementary education was available to the children, many of the 'teachers' were recruited from the paupers themselves and were often ineffectual and even brutal. The paupers were not prisoners: providing they gave notice of their intention to leave the workhouse they were free to do so. But once they had passed through its doors they could not remain in the neighbourhood without any visible means of support. To do so would invite arrest and imprisonment for vagrancy.

The worst workhouses were often those which had been established before 1834 and over which the Commissioners had exercised only minimal control.

Particularly bad conditions occasionally attracted publicity. At the Stockport Union near Manchester a man of seventy-two, who was suffering from a bad knee, refused to break stones and was ordered by a magistrate to spend fourteen days on the treadmill of Strangeways Prison. At Deptford in London a child of four was forced to spend three nights sleeping on the coffins in the workhouse mortuary. At St Asaph's workhouse in Clwyd a boy was flogged so severely that he died, and at Andover in Gloucestershire paupers fought over morsels of meat which still clung to the 'green' (still putrefying) bones they had been given to grind.

By far the worst case was that of the notorious Infant Pauper Asylum at Tooting in London. This housed some 1,400 children of between two and fifteen years of age and was the responsibility of a master called Drouet, who made substantial profits by exploiting his captive supply of cheap labour and maintained discipline through a regime of fear and brutality. Dormitories were infested and over-crowded, meagre meals were eaten while standing

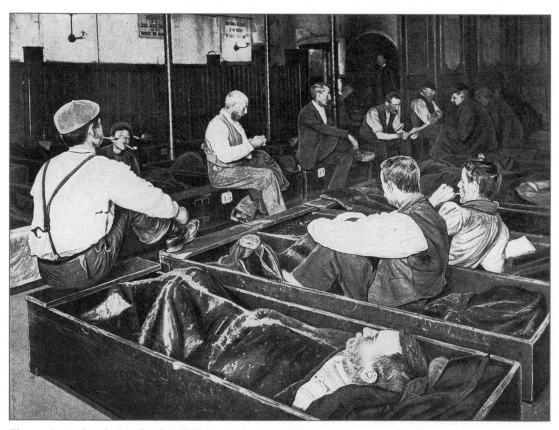

The men's ward at the Medland Hall Union in the early 1900s.

and there was insufficient drinking water so that those inmates who controlled the supply extorted tolls from the others. Complaints to visiting guardians were punished with thrashings, and visits by pauper parents were severely restricted. On one occasion in 1849 a mother was not informed of her child's death until several days after the funeral. Most significant was the attitude of the authorities. Official visitors, who at first expressed their outrage, subsequently 'reported most favourably' on conditions at the asylum. Perhaps Drouet was persuaded to share his profits?

One objective of the revised Poor Law was to facilitate the free movement of labour and consequently workhouses were required to accommodate 'casuals on the tramp' for one night in separate, secure premises where they could be kept firmly under control. These 'casuals' were often robust and disorderly characters who sometimes travelled in gangs and must have made life very difficult for the average rural or small-town workhouse master. In practice, there was often neither proper accommodation nor the means of maintaining discipline and in the 1850s most Poor Law boards deliberately ignored their obligation to admit 'casuals', a policy which was tacitly endorsed by the central authority. Each board was acutely aware of the need to avoid acquiring a reputation for laxity which would inevitably attract 'casuals' and other itinerants, including 'mouchers', a special breed of tramp which lived by scrounging, pilfering and assiduously avoiding the attentions of the constables. Parochial officers were past-masters in the art of obstruction and procrastination and it was only as a last resort that a genuinely destitute 'incomer' from another parish would be offered casual relief.

In 1913 workhouses became Poor Law Institutions and these were eventually superseded by the health and unemployment reforms which had been introduced in 1908–11, notably the National Insurance Act of 1911. Many surviving workhouse buildings have been adapted as hospitals and (the ultimate irony) as geriatric wards. Most are located on the outskirts of towns and are usually of an austere classical design with walled courtyards and radiating or extending wings.

The earliest workhouse records are contained in vestry minutes, while those of the post-1834 period will be found in the archives of the Guardians of the Poor which are usually held by county record offices. *See also* POOR HOUSES *and* SOCIAL WELFARE

WORT An Old English word meaning 'useful' and applied to plants which have culinary, medicinal and other beneficial properties, *woundwort* and *St John's wort*, for example.

-WORTH A very common place-name element derived from the Old English *worþ*, *worþig* and *worþign*, all originally meaning 'enclosure' but developing to imply an 'enclosure surrounding a homestead' and thence the 'homestead' itself. Turnworth, Dorset, is an early example, meaning 'enclosure of thorn bushes' (*þyrne* and *worþ*), whereas Bobbingworth, Essex, was the 'homestead of *Bubba's* people'. Variations include -worthy (*worþig*) as in Hamworthy, Dorset, and -wardine (*worþign*), which is commonly found in the southern Marches as in Bredwardine, Herefordshire, a 'hillside enclosure' (*brerd* meaning 'bank').

WRACK ROADS *see* SEAWEED LANES

WREATH *see* CREST

WRING HOUSE A room or shed containing a cider-press.

WYVERN *see* BEASTS (HERALDIC)

YALE *see* BEASTS (HERALDIC)

YARDLAND *see* OPEN FIELDS

YAT *see* GATE

YELMS *see* THATCHING

YEOMAN In thirteenth-century England, French and Latin terms (which had hitherto defined social class) were replaced by English ones, and those which had been founded on tenure and legal status were gradually superseded by terms indicating general social standing or economic function. Some terms were hardly affected by these changes: 'knight', for example, was used more often than the French *chevalier* or the Latin *miles*, but its meaning remained unchanged. Others, such as 'churl' (the

Old English *ceorl*) and 'villein', disappeared altogether or retained only a literary usage.

New terms were of diverse origin: some originated in the feudal household, 'esquire', for example, which in the fourteenth century came to denote the social rank immediately below that of knight (*see* ESQUIRE). This comparatively select number of esquires was but the senior stratum of a substantial group of free landowners (*valetti*) who, with the knights, represented their counties in Parliament during the first half of the fourteenth century. Those *valetti* below the rank of esquire were, in the late fourteenth century, described as 'franklins', men of substance and of gentle birth, many of whom no doubt aspired to armigerous status (*see* FRANKLIN). But by the early fifteenth century, the term 'franklin' had been superseded by two others: 'gentleman', which was applied to men of breeding who were not armigerous, and 'yeoman'.

By the mid-fifteenth century, therefore, local society comprised (in descending order) knights, esquires, gentlemen, yeomen and husbandmen, though franklins still made an occasional appearance. Of these, only knights and esquires possessed armigerous qualifications and, in common usage, several of the other terms were evidently interchangeable, despite the *Statute of Additions* of 1413 which required that plaintiffs in personal actions should describe precisely the status of their opponents. Fifteenth-century sumptuary legislation similarly propounded a strict hierarchy (*see* SUMPTUARY LAWS), and in 1445 it was determined that knights of the shire attending Parliament could include 'notable squires' and 'gentlemen of birth' but not those 'of the degree of Yeoman and bynethe'.

In the context of local society, a yeoman was therefore a freeholder below the status of gentleman but above that of most other copyhold tenants and was eligible to serve on juries and to vote in county elections. However, the term *valetti* was also used in official documents to describe those officers in royal and magnatial households who, although of lower status than knights, were often drawn from gentle families. In the early fourteenth century, the *valetti* included esquires, but as the esquires acquired their own distinctive armigerous status, so the term *valetti* came to be translated into English as 'yeomen'. Geoffrey Chaucer (1342–1400) was a yeoman (*valet*) of the king's chamber in 1367 before becoming an esquire. The Yeomen of the Guard, the sovereign's personal bodyguard, was formed by Henry VII in 1485 from his 'private guard of faithful fellowes'.

YEW TREES Yews are renowned both for their longevity and their mystical power. The oldest wooden weapons yet discovered are made of yew and it cannot be by chance that one of the letters of the runic alphabet is also the Old English name for the yew (*see* RUNES).

Evergreen, hard-timbered and poisonous, yews prefer well-drained limestone soils and were once much more widespread than they are now. Relics of ancient yew woods may often be identified in place-names such as Uley, Gloucestershire, Ewhurst, Surrey and Iwerne Minster, Dorset. Such woods must have been singularly eerie places: even today the mist-shrouded 'primeval yews and oaks of The Chase' (Hardy) endow a landscape such as that of Cranborne Chase on the Dorset–Wiltshire border with a character strongly evocative of the distant past.

See also CHURCHYARDS, where the yew is discussed at greater length.

YNYS In the Welsh, an island or water meadow, as in Ynys Enlli (Bardsey Island, Gwynedd), 'the isle of the race'. In Scotland, the same word is found as *inch* or *innis*; in Ireland *inch*, *innis* or *ennis*, and in Cornwall, *innis*. Ince, Cheshire, which forms an island on the low-lying southern bank of the River Mersey, is also derived from *ynys*.

See also -EY *and* HOLME

YSTRAD In the Welsh, 'a vale', as in Yystrad-fflur, Ceredigion, a Cistercian monastery known in English as Strata Florida or 'the Vale of Flowers'. In Scotland, the same word is found as the Gaelic *strath*.

APPENDIX I

ADDRESSES

The addresses of local history societies may be obtained from record offices which are listed under counties

Advisory Council on Public Records, *see* Public Record Office (PRO)
Air Historical Branch, Ministry of Defence, Lacon House, Theobalds Road, London WD6 1EJ www.raf.mod.uk/history
Ancient Monuments Society, St Ann's Vestry Hall, 2 Church Entry, London EC4V 5HB
    www.ancientmonumentssociety.org.uk
Anglesey County Record Office, Shire Hall, Glanhwfa Road, Llangefni LL77 7TW www.ynysmon.gov.uk
Angus Archives, Montrose Library, 214 High Street, Montrose, Angus DD10 8HE www.angus.gov.uk
Antiquarian Booksellers Association, 31 Great Ormond Street, London WC1
Antiquarian Horological Society, New House, High Street, Ticehurst, Wadhurst, East Sussex TN5 7AL
Architectural Association, 34–6 Bedford Square, London WC1B 3ES www.arch-assoc.org.uk
Architecture Heritage Fund, Clareville House, 26–7 Oxendon Street, London SW1Y 4EL www.heritage.co.uk
Argyll and Bute Council Archives, Lockgilphead, Argyll PA31 8RT www.argyll-bute.gov.uk
Arms and Armour Society, 30 Alderney Street, London SW1 www.armourer.co.uk/arms.htm
Army Records Centre, Bourne Avenue, Hayes, Middlesex UB3 1RF
Ashmolean Museum, Beaumont Street, Oxford OX1 2PH www.ashmol.ox.ac.uk
Association for Heritage Interpretation (AHI), The Administrator, AHI, Cruachan, Tayinloan, Tarbert PA29 6XF
    www.heritageinterpretation.org.uk/index.htm
Association for Industrial Archaeology, The Wharfage, Ironbridge, Telford, Shropshire TF8 7AW www.industrial-
    archaeology.org.uk
Association for the Protection of Rural Scotland, Gladstone's Land (3rd Floor), 483 Lawnmarket, Edinburgh EH1 2NT
    www.aprs.org.uk
Association of Church Recorders, *see* National Association of Decorative and Fine Art Societies
Association of Family History Societies of Wales, Hafod el Wy, 32 Ystad Llewelyn, Denbigh LL16 3NR
    www.rootsweb.com/~wlsafhs
Ayrshire Archives, County Buildings, Wellington Square, Ayr KA7 1DR

Baptist Historical Society, 4 Southampton Row, London WC1 www.baptisthistory.org.uk
Baptist Missionary Society, PO Box 49, 129 Broadway, Didcot, Oxon OX11 8XA www.bms.org.uk
Baptist Union Library, *see* Baptist Historical Society
Bath and North East Somerset Record Office, Guildhall, Bath BA1 5AW www.bathnes.gov.uk
Bedfordshire and Luton Archives and Record Service, Record Office, County Hall, Bedford MK42 9AP
    www.bedfordshire.gov.uk
Belfast Central Library, Royal Avenue, Belfast BT1 1EA www.belb.org.uk
Berkshire Record Office, Shire Hall, Shinfield Park, Reading RG2 9XD
Birmingham and Midland Institute, 9 Margaret Street, Birmingham B3 3BS
Birmingham City Archives, Central Library, Chamberlain Square, Birmingham B3 3HQ
Bodleian Library, Oxford OX1 3BG www.bodley.ox.ac.uk
Bookplate Society, 20a Delorme Street, London W6 8DT
Borthwick Institute of Historical Research, St Anthony's Hall, Peasholme Green, York YO1 7PW www.york.ac.uk/inst/bihr

Brewery History Society, 10 Ringstead Court, Sutton, Surrey www.breworld.com/organisations/bhs.html

Bristol Record Office, 'B' Bond Warehouse, Smeaton Road, Bristol BS1 6XN www.bristol-city.gov.uk

British Academy, 20–1 Cornwall Terrace, London NW1 4QP www.britac.ac.uk

British Agricultural History Society, Rural History Centre, Whiteknights, University of Reading, Berkshire RG6 2AG www.bahs.org.uk

British Archaeological Association, 1 Priory Gardens, Bedford Park, London W4 1TT www.britarch.ac.uk/baa

British Archaeological Library:

    Drawings Collection, 21 Portman Square, London W1H 9HF

    Manuscripts and Archives Collection, 66 Portland Square, London W1N 4AD

British Archaeological Trust, 304 Eddison House, Grove End Road, London NW8

British Architectural Library, 66 Portland Place, London W1B 1AD www.riba-library.com

British Association for Local History, 25 Lower Street, Harnham, Salisbury, Wiltshire SP2 8EY www.balh.co.uk

British Association of Paper Historians, c/o Engineering Department, The Science Museum, London SW7 2DD

British Coal Archives, 200 Lichfield Lane, Mansfield, Nottinghamshire NG18 4RG

British Institute of Professional Photography, Fox Talbot House, Amwell End, Ware, Hertfordshire SG12 9HN www.bipp.com

British Library, 96 Euston Road, London NW1 2DB www.bl.uk

British Library Newspaper Library, Colindale Avenue, London NW9 5HE www.bl.uk/collections/newspaper

British Museum, Great Russell Street, London WC1B 3DG www.thebritishmuseum.ac.uk

British Records Association, London Metropolitan Archives, 40 Northampton Road, London EC1R 0HB

British Record Society Ltd, College of Arms, Queen Victoria Street, London EC4V 4BT

British Telecom Archives, 268–70 High Holborn, London WC1V 7EE www.bt.com/archives

British Telecom Museum, Baynard House, 135 Queen Victoria Street, London EC4 4AT

British Trust for Conservation Volunteers, 36 St Mary's Street, Wallingford, Oxford OX10 0EU www.btcv.org

Buckinghamshire Record Office, County Hall, Walton Street, Aylesbury HP20 1UA www.buckss.gov.uk

Burke's Peerage, Eden Street, Kingston-upon-Thames, Surrey www.burkes-peerage.com

Business Archives Council, The Clove Building, 4 Maguire Street, Butler's Wharf, London SE1 2NQ

Byways and Bridleways Trust, The Granary, Charlcutt, Calne, Wiltshire SN11 9HL

CADW, Cathays Park, Cardiff CF10 3NQ www.cadw.wales.gov.uk

Cambrian Archaeological Association, Halfway House, Pont y Pandy, Bangor, Gwynedd LL57 3DG

Cambridgeshire County Record Office, Shire Hall, Castle Hill, Cambridge CB3 0AP www.camcnty.gov.uk

Campaign for the Protection of Rural Wales, Ty Gwyn, 31 High Street, Welshpool, Powys SY21 7YD www.cprw.org

Canterbury Cathedral Archives, The Precincts, Canterbury CT1 2EH www.canterbury-cathedral.org

Carmarthenshire Record Office, County Hall, Carmarthen SA31 1JP www.carmarthenshire.gov.uk

Cathedrals Fabric Commission for England, Church House, Great Smith Street, London SW1P 3NZ

Catholic Archives Society, Innyngs House, Hatfield Park, Hatfield, Hertfordshire AL9 5PI.

Catholic Archives, Scotland, Columbia House, 16 Drummond Place, Edinburgh EH3 6PL

Catholic Record Society, 12 Melbourne Place, Wolsingham, Co. Durham DL13 3EH www.catholic-history.org.uk/crs

Central Council of Church Bell Ringers, 50 Cramhurst Lane, Witley, Godalming, Surrey GU8 5QZ www.cccbr.org.uk

Central Register of Air Photographs, Welsh Office, Crown Offices, Cathays Park, Cardiff CF1 3NQ

Centre for Kentish Studies, County Hall, Maidstone, Kent ME14 1XQ www.kent.gov.uk/e&l/artslib/archives/archcks.html

Centre for Scottish Studies, University of Aberdeen, Taylor Building, King's College, Old Aberdeen, AB9 2UB www.abdn.ac.uk/celtic

Centre for South-Western Historical Studies, c/o Devon and Exeter Institution, 7 The Close, Exeter EX1 1EZ www.ex.ac.uk/~RBurt/swhs/

Ceredigion Archives, Swyddfa'r Sir, Marine Terrace, Aberystwyth SY23 2DE www.llgc.org.uk/cac/cac0009.htm

Chapels Society, c/o Council for British Archaeology (Northern Office), The King's Manor, York YO1 2EP www.britarch.ac.uk/chapelsoc/

Charity Commission for England and Wales, St Albans House, 57–60 Haymarket, London SW1V 4QX www.charity-commission.gov.uk

Chartered Insurance Institute (Museum of), 20 Aldermanbury, London EC2V 7HY www.cii.co.uk

Cheshire Record Office, Duke Street, Chester CH1 1RL www.cheshire.gov.uk/recoff/home.htm

Chetham's Library, Long Millgate, Manchester M3 1SB www.chethams.org.uk

Chief Herald of Ireland's Office (Genealogical Office), The Castle, 2 Kildare Street, Dublin 2

Church Monuments Society, c/o Society of Antiquaries, Burlington House, Piccadilly, London W1J 0BE

Church of England Record Centre, 15 Galleywall Road, South Bermondsey, London SE16 3PB

Church of Jesus Christ of Latter-day Saints (Branch Library), Hyde Park Chapel, 64 Exhibition Road, London SW7 2PA

City of Westminster Archives Centre, 10 St Anne's Street, London SW1P 2DE www.westminster.gov.uk/el/libarch/archives

Civic Trust, 17 Carlton House Terrace, London SW1Y 5AS www.civictrust.org.uk

Close Society, c/o The Map Library, British Library (see above) www.charlesclosesociety.org.uk

College of Arms, Queen Victoria Street, London EC4V 4BT www.college-of-arms.gov.uk

Common Ground, 45 Shelton Street, London WC2H 9HJ www.commonground.org.uk

Commons, Open Spaces and Footpaths Preservation Society, see Open Spaces Society

Congregational Church of England and Wales, Memorial Hall, Farringdon Road, London EC1 www.congregational.org.uk

Connexional Archivist, Methodist Church, Central Buildings, Oldham Street, Manchester

Cornwall Record Office, County Hall, Truro TR1 3AY www.cornwall.gov.uk/council-services/ab-de10/cro09.htm

Corporation of London, Records Office, Guildhall, London EC2P 2EJ www.corpoflondon.gov.uk/archives/clro/

Costume and Fashion Research Centre, Bath Museums Service, 4 The Circus, Bath, Somerset BA1 2EW
www.museumofcostume.co.uk

Costume Society, St Paul's House, Warwick Lane, London EC49 4BN www.costumesociety.org.uk

Council for British Archaeology, Bowes Morrell House, 111 Walmgate, York YO1 9WA www.britarch.ac.uk

Council for the Care of Churches, Fielden House, 13 Little College Street, London SW1P 3SH

Council for the Protection of Rural England, Warwick house, 25 Buckingham Palace Road, London SW1W 0PP
www.cpre.org.uk

Country Houses Association, Suite 10, Aynhoe Park, Banbury, Oxon OX17 3BQ

Countryside Agency, John Dower House, Crescent Place, Cheltenham, Gloucestershire, GL50 3RA
www.countryside.gov.uk

Cromwell Association, c/o Cromwell Museum www.cromwell.argonet.co.uk

Cromwell Museum, Grammar School Walk, Huntingdon, Cambridge PE29 3LF edweb.camcnty.gov.uk/cromwell

Cumbria Record Office, The Castle, Carlisle CA3 8UR www.cumbria.gov.uk/archives/carec.asp

Debrett's Peerage, King's Court, 2–16 Goodge Street, London SW1P 1FF www.debretts.co.uk

Denbighshire Record Office, 46 Clwyd Street, Ruthin LL15 1HP www.llgc.org.uk/cac/cac0011.htm

Department of the Environment, Transport and the Regions, Eland House, Bressenden Place, London SW1E 5DU
www.detr.gov.uk

Derbyshire Record Office, New Street (correspondence to County Offices), Matlock DE4 3AG
www.derbyshire.gov.uk/azserv/libh010.htm

Devon Record Office, Castle Street, Exeter EX4 3PU www.devon.gov.uk/dro/homepage.html

Dorset Record Office, Bridport Road, Dorchester DT1 1RP www.dorset-cc.gov.uk

Dr Williams' Library, 14 Gordon Square, London WC1H 0AG

Drinking Fountain Association, 105 Wansunt Road, Bexley

Dry Stone Walling Association of Great Britain, PO Box 8615, Sutton Coldfield, West Midlands B75 7HQ
www.dswa.org.uk

Duchy of Cornwall, 10 Buckingham Gate, London SW1E 6LA www.princeofwales.gov.uk/about/duchy/

Duchy of Lancaster, Lancaster Place, Strand, London WC2E 7ED

Duke of Norfolk's Library and Archives, Arundel Castle, Arundel, West Sussex BN18 9AB

Dumfries and Galloway Archives, 33 Burns Street, Dumfries DG1 2PS
www.dumgal.gov.uk/services/depts/comres/library/archives.htm

Durham County Record Office, County Hall, Durham DH1 5UL
www.durham.gov.uk/durhamcc/usp.nsf/web/pages/durham+record+office+homepage

Early English Text Society, Lady Margaret Hall, Oxford OX2 6QA

East Kent Archives Centre, Enterprise Zone, Honeywood Road, Whitfield, Dover CT16 3EH www.kfhs-
deal/freeuk.com/EKArchives/EKAC.htm

East Riding of Yorkshire, Archive Office, County Hall, Beverley HU17 9BA

East Sussex, see Sussex

East Sussex Record Office, The Maltings, Castle Precinct, Lewes BN7 1YT www.eastsussex.gov.uk/archives/main.htm

Ecclesiastical History Society, Department of History, University of Glasgow, Glasgow G12 8QQ

Ecclesiological Society, 3 Sycamore Close, Court Road, London SE9 4RD www.ecclsoc.org

Economic History Society, Dept of Economic and Social History, London School of Economics, Houghton Street, Aldwych, London WC2 7AY www.ehs.org.uk

Edinburgh City Archives, City Chambers, High Street, Edinburgh EH1 1YJ www.edinburgh.gov.uk

English Folk Dance and Song Society, Cecil Sharp House, 2 Regents Park Road, London NW1 7AY www.efdss.org

English Heritage, Fortress House, 25 Saville Row, London W1S 2ET www.english-heritage.org.uk

English Place-name Society, University of Nottingham, Nottingham NG7 2RD
www.nottingham.ac.uk/english/research/EPNS

English Place-name Survey, Grey College, Durham DH1 3LG

English Surnames Series, Centre for English Local History, Marc Fitch House, 5 Salisbury Road, Leicester LE1 7QR
www.le.ac.uk/elh/names.html

Ephemera Society, 8 Galveston Road, Putney, London SE9 4RD www.ephemera-society.org.uk

Essex Record Office, County Hall, Chelmsford CM1 1LX www.essexcc.gov.uk/heritage/ero

Family Record Centre, 1 Myddleton Street, London EC1R 1UW www.familyrecords.gov.uk

Federation for Ulster Local Studies, 18 May Street, Belfast BT1 4NL http://dnausers.d-n-a.net/UlsterHistory/federation.htm

Federation of Family History Societies, The Benson Room, Birmingham and Midland Institute, Margaret Street, Birmingham B3 3BS www.ffhs.org.uk

Flintshire Record Office, The Old Rectory, Haywarden CH5 3NR www.flintshire.gov.uk/lib6.html

Folklore Society, c/o The Warburg Institute, Woburn Square, London WC1H 0AB www.folklore-society.com

Folly Fellowship, 7 St Catherine's Way, Fareham, Hants PO16 8R2 www.heritage.co.uk/follies

Franciscan Archives (English Province), 58 St Anthony's Road, London E7

Friends of Friendless Churches, St Ann's Vestry Hall, 2 Church Entry, London EC4V 5HB, *see*
www.ancientmonumentssociety.org.uk

Furniture History Society, 1 Mercedes Cottages, St John's Road, Hayward Heath, West Sussex RH16 4EH
www.iserv.net~plucas/fhsoc.htm

Garden History Society, 70 Cowcross Street, London EC1M 6EJ www.gardenhistorysociety.org/index.shtml

General Register Office for England and Wales, Smedley Hydro, Trafalgar Road, Southport PR8 2HH
www.statistics.gov.uk/nsbase/registration/general_register.asp

General Register Office for Northern Ireland, Oxford House, 49–55 Chichester Street, Belfast BT1 4HL
www.nisra.gov.uk/gro

General Register Office for Scotland www.gro-scotland.gov.uk:
For family history research: New Register House, 3 West Register Street, Edinburgh EH1 3YT
For census, population, vital statistics data: Ladywell house, Ladywell Road, Edinburgh, EH12 7TF

Georgian Group, 6 Fitzroy Square, London W1P 6DX www.heritage.co.uk/georgian

Glamorgan Record Office, The Glamorgan Building, King Edward VII Avenue, Cathays Park, Cardiff CF1 3NE (*see also* West Glamorgan) www.llgc.org.uk/cac/cac0026.htm

Gloucestershire Record Office, Clarence Row, Alvin Street, Gloucester GL1 3DW www.gloscc.gov.uk

Greater Manchester County Record Office, 56 Marshall Street, New Cross, Manchester M4 5FU www.gmcro.u-net.com

Guernsey: Island Archive Service, 29 Victoria Street, St Peter Port GY1 1HU http://user.itl.net/~glen/archgsy.html

Guild of One-name Studies, 14 Charterhouse Buildings, Goswell Road, London EC1M 7BA www.one-name.org

Guildhall Library, Aldermanbury, London EC2P 2EJ

Gwent Record Office, County Hall, Cwmbran NP44 2XH www.llgc.org.uk/cac/cac0004.htm

Gwynedd:
Caernarfon Area Record Office (correspondence to County Offices, Shirehall Street, Caernarfon LL55 1SH)
www.llgc.org.uk/cac/cac0053.htm
Merioneth Archives, Cae Penarlâg, Dolgellau LL40 2YB www.llgc.org.uk/cac/cac0030.htm

Hampshire Record Office, Sussex Street, Winchester SO23 8TH www.hants.gov.uk/record-office/index.html

Harleian Society, c/o College of Arms, Queen Victoria Street, London EC4V 4BT

Her Majesty's Customs and Excise (Library), King's Beam House, Mark Lane, London EC3R 7HE www.hmce.gov.uk

Her Majesty's Stationery Office (HMSO) *see* Stationery Office www.hmso.gov.uk

Heraldry Society of Ireland, Castle Matrix, Rathkeale, Co Limerick
Heraldry Society of Scotland, 25 Craigentinny Cresc., Edinburgh EH7 6QA www.heraldry-scotland.co.uk
Heraldry Society, PO Box 32, Maidenhead, Berkshire SL6 3FD
Hereford Record Office, The Old Barracks, Harold Street HR1 2QX
    www.herefordshire.gov.uk/records_office/pol_records_intro.htm
Hertfordshire Archives and Local Studies, County Hall, Pegs Lane, Hertford SG13 8EJ www.hertsdirect.org/hcc/CI
Highland Council Archive, Inverness Library, Farraline Park, Inverness IV1 1NH
    www.highland.gov.uk/cl/publicservices/archivedetails/highlandarchive.htm
Historic Buildings and Monuments Commission for England, *see* English Heritage
Historic Buildings Council for Scotland, *see* Historic Scotland
Historic Buildings Council for Wales, *see* CADW
Historic Churches Preservation Trust, Fulham Palace, London SW6 6EA www.cofe.anglican.org/about/hcpt.html
Historic Houses Association, 2 Chester Street, London SW1X 7BB www.hha.org.uk
Historic Royal Palaces, Hampton Court Palace, East Molesey, Surrey KT8 9AU www.hrp.org.uk
Historic Scotland, Longmore House, Salisbury Place, Edinburgh EH9 1SH www.historic-scotland.gov.uk
Historic Telephone Directory Library, 7th Floor, 211 Old Street, London EC1
Historical Association of Ireland, Department of History, University College, Belfield, Dublin 4
Historical Association, 59a Kennington Park Road, London SE11 4JH
Historical Metallurgy Society, 22 Easterfield Drive, Southgate, Swansea SA3 2DB www.hist-met.org
History of Education Society, University of London, Institute of Education, 20 Bedford Way, London WC1H 0AL
House of Lords Record Office (The Parliamentary Archives), Westminster SW1A 0PW www.parliament.the-stationery-
    office.co.uk/pa/paarchiv.htm
Huguenot Society and Library, University College, Gower Street, London WC1E 6BT

Imperial War Museum, Lambeth Road, London SE1 6HZ www.iwm.org.uk
Independent Methodist Churches Historical Society, Providence Independent Methodist Church, Albert Road, Colne, Lancashire
India Office at the British Library, 96 Euston Road, London NW1 2DB www.bl.uk/collections/oriental
Industrial Society, Customer Centre, Quadrant Court, 49 Calthorpe Road, Edgbaston, Birmingham B15 1TH
    www.indsoc.co.uk
Institute of Agricultural History, The Rural History Centre, University of Reading, PO Box 229, Whiteknights, Reading
    RG6 6AG www.ruralhistory.org
Institute of Archaeology (Conservation of Historic Buildings), University College of London, 31–4 Gordon Square,
    London WC1H 0PY www.ucl.ac.uk/archaeology
Institute of Dialect and English Folk Life Studies, School of English, University of Leeds
Institute of Field Archaeologists, University of Reading, 2 Earley Gate, PO Box 239, Reading RG6 6AU
    www.archaeologists.net
Institute of Heraldic and Genealogical Studies, 79–82 Northgate, Canterbury, Kent CT1 1BA www.ihgs.ac.uk
Institute of Historical Research, University of London, Senate House, London WC1E 7HU www.ihrinfo.ac.uk
Institute of Irish Studies, Queen's University of Belfast, 8 Fitzwilliam Street, Belfast BT9 6AW www.qub.ac.uk/iis
Irish Architectural Archive, 73 Merrion Square, Dublin 2 www.archeire.com/iaa
Irish Genealogical Association, 164 Kingsway, Dunmurry, Belfast BT17 9AD
Irish Genealogical Research Society, The Irish Club, 82 Eaton Square, London SW1W 9AJ
Irish Manuscripts Commission, 73 Merrion Square, Dublin 2 www.irmss.ie
Ironbridge Gorge Museum, The Wharfage, Ironbridge, Telford, Shropshire, TF8 7AW www.ironbridge.org.uk
Isle of Man Manx National Heritage Library, Manx Museum and National Trust, Douglas IM1 3LY www.gov.im/mnh
Isle of Man Public Record Office, Unit 3, Spring Valley Industrial Estate, Braddan, Douglas IM2 2QR
    www.gov.im/deptindex
Isle of Wight County Record Office, 26 Hillside, Newport PO30 2EB www.dina.clara.net/iowfhs/recoffic.htm

Jersey Archives Service, The Weighbridge, St Helier JE2 3NF
Jewish Historical Society of England, 33 Seymour Place, London W1H 5AP www.users.dircon.co.uk/~jhse
Jewish Museum www.jewmusm.ort.org:
    Raymond Burton House, 129–31 Albert Street, Camden, London, NW1 7NB
    The Sternberg Centre, 80 East End Road, London, N3 2SY

John Rylands Library, 150 Deansgate, Manchester M3 3EH http://rylibweb.man.ac.uk

Kelly's Directories Ltd, Dorset House, Stamford Street, London SE1

Lambeth Palace Library, London SE1 7JU www.lambethpalacelibrary.org
Lanarkshire (North) Archives, 10 Kelvin Road, Lenziemill, Cumbernauld G67 2BA
Lancashire Record Office, Bow Lane, Preston PR1 8ND www.lancashire.gov.uk/education/lifelong/ro/index.htm
Landmark Trust, Shottesbrooke, Maidenhead, Berkshire SL6 3SW www.landmarktrust.co.uk
Landscape Institute, 6–8 Bernard Mews, London SW11 1QU www.l-i.org.uk
Leicestershire Record Office, Long Street, Wigston Magna, Leicester LE18 2AH www.leics.gov.uk/museums/records/htm
Library Association, 7 Ridgmount Street, London WC1E 7AE www.la-hq.org.uk
Lincolnshire Archives, St Rumbold Street, Lincoln LN2 5AB www.lincolnshire.gov.uk/archives
List and Index Society, Public Record Office, Ruskin Avenue, Kew, Surrey TW9 4DU
Liverpool Record Office and Local History Service, Central Library, William Brown Street, Liverpool L3 8EW
    www.liverpool.gov.uk/htm/services/6leidir/lib/lib3.htm
Local Historian, The (magazine), c/o British Association for Local History (*see above*)
Local History Magazine, The Local History Press Ltd, 3 Devonshire Promenade, Lenton, Nottingham NG7 2DS
    www.local-history.co.uk
Local Population Studies Centre, 17 Rosebery Square, Rosebery Avenue, London EC1
Local Population Studies Society, Department of Anthropology, University of Durham, 43 Old Elvet, Durham
London Library, 14 St James's Square, London SW1Y 4LG webpac.londonlibrary.co.uk
London Metropolitan Archives Centre, 40 Northampton Road, London EC1R 0HB
    www.steeljam.dircon.co.uk/gnloclma.htm
Lord Chamberlain's Office, St James's Palace, London SW1A 1BG
Lord Lyon King of Arms and the Court of Lord Lyon, HM New Register House, Edinburgh EH1 3YT

Manchester Local Studies Unit, Archives, Central Library, St Peter's Square, Manchester M2 5PD
    www.manchester.gov.uk/libraries/arls/index.htm
Manorial Society, 104 Kennington Road, London SE11 6RE www.msgb.co.uk
Medieval Settlement Research Group, The Secretary, Heritage and Environment Section, Environmental Services Group,
    Bedfordshire County Council, County Hall, Cauldwell Street, Bedford MK42 9AP www.britarch.ac.uk/msrg
Merseyside Record Office, 4th Floor, Cunard Building, Liverpool L3 1EG
Methodist Archives and Research Centre, John Ryland's Library, University of Manchester, Deansgate, Manchester M3 3EH
    http://rylibweb.man.ac.uk/data1/dg/text/method.html
Midlothian Local Studies Centre, 2 Clerk Street, Loan Head, Midlothian EH20 9DR
    www.earl.org.uk/partners/midlothian/local.html
Military Historical Society, National Army Museum, Royal Hospital Road, Chelsea, London SW3 4HT
Mocatta Library (Jewish), *see* Jewish Historical Society
Modern Records Centre, University Library, University of Warwick, Coventry, West Midlands CV4 7AL
    www.warwick.ac.uk/services/library/mrc
Monumental Brass Society, Lowe Hill House, Stratford St Mary, Suffolk CO7 6JX
    http://home.clara.net/williamlack/mbs/page.htm
Museum of London (and Library), 150 London Wall, London EC2Y 5HN www.museum-london.org.uk
Museum of Welsh Life, St Fagan's, Cardiff CF5 6XB www.nmgw.ac.uk/mwl/index.en.shtml
Museums Association, 42 Clerkenwell Close, London EC1R 0PA www.museumsassociation.org

National Archives of Ireland, Bishop Street, Dublin 8 www.nationalarchives.ie
National Archives of Scotland, Historical Search Room, HM General Register House, 2 Princes Street, Edinburgh EH1
    3YY www.nas.gov.uk
National Army Museum, Department of Archives, Royal Hospital Road, Chelsea, London SW3 4HT www.national-army-
    museum.ac.uk
National Association of Almshouses, Billingbear Lodge, Carter's Hill, Wokingham, Berkshire RG40 5RU
    www.almshouses.org
National Association of Decorative and Fine Arts Societies (NADFAS), 8 Guilford Street, London WC1N 1DT

National Association of Mining History Organizations, c/o Peak District Mining Museum, The Pavilion, Matlock, Derbyshire DE4 3NR www.ap.pwp.blueyonder.co.uk/namho.htm

National Horse Brass Society, Orchard End, Farm Road, Sutton, Surrey

National Inventory of War Memorials, *see* Imperial War Museum

National Library of Ireland, Kildare Street, Dublin 2 www.nli.ie

National Library of Scotland, Department of Manuscripts, George IV Bridge, Edinburgh EH1 1EW www.nls.ac.uk/collections/manuscripts/index.html

National Library of Wales, Department of Manuscripts and Records, Aberystwyth SY23 3BU www.llgc.org.uk

National Map Centre, 22–4 Caxton Road, London SW1H 0QH www.mapstore.co.uk

National Maritime Museum, Romney Road, Greenwich, London SE10 9NF www.nmm.ac.uk

National Monuments Record Centre, Great Western Village, Kemble Drive, Swindon SN2 2GZ www.english-heritage.org.uk/knowledge/nmr/index.asp

National Monuments Record, (London search-room), 55 Blandford Street, London W1H 7HN, *see above*

National Museum of Labour History, 103 Princess Street, Manchester M1 6DD www.nmlhweb.org

National Postal Museum, *see* Postal Heritage Services

National Railway Museum Library, Leeman Road, York YO26 4XJ www.nrm.org.uk

National Register of Archives, Quality Court, Chancery Lane, London WC2A 1HP www.hmc.gov.uk/nra/nra2.htm

National Society of Master Thatchers, 20 The Laurels, Tetsworth, Thame, Oxon OX9 7BH http://nsmt.hypermart.net

National Sound Archive at the Recorded Sound Information Service, The British Library National Sound Archive, 96 Euston Road, London NW1 2DB, *see* collections at www.bl.uk

National Statistics Office, Government Buildings, Cardiff Road, Newport NP10 8XG www.statistics.gov.uk

National Trust for Scotland, 28 Charlotte Square, Edinburgh EH2 4ET www.nts.org.uk

National Trust, 36 Queen Anne's Gate, London SW1H 9AS www.nationaltrust.org.uk

National Waterways Museum, Llanthony Warehouse, Gloucester Docks, Gloucester GL1 2EH www.nwm.org.uk

Navy Records Society, King's College, The Strand, London WC2R 2LS

News Library and Cuttings Research Department, 292 Vauxhall Bridge Road, London SW1V 1AE www.pa.press.net/news/news-library.html

Norfolk Record Office, Gildengate House, Anglia Square, Upper Green Lane, Norwich NR3 1AX www.norfolk.gov.uk/council/departments/nro/nroindex.htm

North Yorkshire County Record Office, postal correspondence to County Hall, Northallerton DL7 8AF www.northyorks.gov.uk/education/archives.shtm

Northamptonshire Record Office, Wootton Hall Park, Northampton NN4 8BQ www.nro.northamptonshire.gov.uk

Northumberland Record Office, Melton Park, North Gosforth, Newcastle upon Tyne NE3 5OX; go to 'Service Finder' and 'Archives' at www.northumberland.gov.uk

Nottinghamshire Archives, County House, Castle Meadow Road, Nottingham NG2 1AG www.nottscc.gov.uk/libraries/Archives

Open Spaces Society, 25a Bell Street, Henley-on-Thames, Oxon RG9 2BA www.oss.org.uk

Open University History Society, 7 Cliffe House Avenue, Garforth, Leeds LS25 2BW

Oral History Society, Department of Sociology, Essex University, Colchester CO4 3SQ www.oralhistory.org.uk

Order of St John, Library and Museum, St John's Gate, St John's Lane, Clerkenwell, London EC1M 4DA

Orders and Medals Research Society, 123 Turnpike Link, Croydon CR0 5NU www.omrs.org.uk

Ordnance Survey, Romsey Road, Maybush, Southampton SO16 4GU www.ordsvy.gov.uk

Orkney Archives, Orkney Library, Laing Street, Kirkwall KW15 1NW

Oxfordshire Record Office, St Luke's Church, Temple Road, Cowley, Oxford OX4 2EX archives@oxfordshire.gov.uk

Pembrokeshire Record Office, The Castle, Haverfordwest SA61 2EF www.llgc.org.uk/cac/cac0002.htm

Phillimore & Co. Ltd, (local history publications) Shopwyke Manor Barn, Chichester, West Sussex PO20 6BG www.phillimore.co.uk

Pipe Roll Society, c/o Public Record Office (*see below*)

Police History Society, c/o Norfolk Constabulary, Martineall Lane, Norwich, Norfolk www.policemanslot.com/p18.html

Poseidon Fountain Restoration Society, 11 Lonsdale Road, Gloucester GL2 0TA witley@nifty.demon.co.uk

Postal Heritage Services, Freeling House, Phoenix Place, London WC1X 0DL

Postal History Society, *see* Postal Heritage Services

Powys County Archives Office, County Hall, Llandrindon Wells, Powys LD1 5LG http://archives.powys.gov.uk

Prehistoric Society, Museum Bookshop, 36 Great Russell Street, London WC1B 3PP www.britarch.ac.uk/prehist

Presbyterian Historical Society of Ireland, Church House, Fisherwick Place, Belfast BT1 6DW

Press Association, *see* News Library and Cuttings Research Department

Principal Probate Registry, Duncombe Place, York YO1 2EA

Principal Probate Registry, First Avenue House, 42–9 High Holborn, London WC1V 6NP

Printing Historical Society, St Bride Printing Library, St Bride Institute, Bride Lane, Fleet Street, London EC4Y 8EE
www.rdg.ac.uk/~ltssmimm

Private Libraries Association, Ravelston, South View Road, Pinner, Middlesex HA5 3YD www.the-old-school.demon.co.uk/pla.htm

Public Record Office (Northern Ireland), 66 Balmoral Avenue, Belfast BT9 6NY http://proni.nics.gov.uk

Public Record Office (PRO), Ruskin Avenue, Kew, Richmond, Surrey TW9 4DU www.pro.gov.uk

Railway and Canal Historical Society, 3 West Court, West Street, Oxford OX1 3QP www.bodley.ac.uk/external/rchs

Record offices, *see* individual counties

Richard III Society, 4 Oakley Street, Chelsea, London SW3 5NN www.richardiii.net

Roman Military Research Society, Midfield Court, Thorplands, Northampton www.romanarmy.net

Royal Agricultural Society of England, National Agricultural Centre, Stoneleigh Park, nr Coventry, Warwickshire CV8 2LZ www.rase.org.uk

Royal Air Force Museum (Research and Information Services), Grahame Park Way, Hendon, London NW9 5LL
www.rafmuseum.org.uk

Royal Archaeological Institute, c/o Burlington House, Piccadilly, London W1J 0BE www.britarch.ac.uk/rai/home1.html

Royal Archives, Saxon Tower, Windsor Castle, Windsor, Berkshire SL4 1NJ

Royal Commission on Historical Manuscripts, Quality House, Quality Court, Chancery Lane, London WC2A 1HP
www.hmc.gov.uk/main.htm

Royal Commission on Historical Monuments (England), *see* English Heritage

Royal Commission on the Ancient and Historical Monuments of Scotland, John Sinclair House, 16 Bernard Terrace, Edinburgh EH8 9NX www.rcahms.gov.uk

Royal Commission on the Ancient and Historical Monuments of Wales, Plas Crug, Aberystwyth SY23 1NJ www.rcahmw.org.uk

Royal Historical Society, University College London, Gower Street, London WC1E 6BT

Royal Institute of British Architects, 66 Portland Place, London W1B 1AD www.architecture.com

Royal Museum of Scotland, Chamber's Street, Edinburgh EH1 1JF www.nms.ac.uk

Royal Photographic Society, The Octagon, Milsom Street, Bath BA1 1DN www.rps.org

Royal Society of Antiquaries of Ireland, 63 Merrion Square, Dublin 2

Royal Statistical Society, 12 Errol Street, London EC1Y 8LX www.rss.org.uk

Rural History Centre, University of Reading, Whiteknights, PO Box 229, Reading RG6 6AG
www.museums.reading.ac.uk/merl

School of Oriental and African Studies, Thorhaugh Street, Russell Square, London WC1H 0XG helpdesk@soas.ac.uk

Science Museum, Exhibition Road, London SW7 2DD www.sciencemuseum.org.uk

Scots Ancestral Research Society, 29b Albany Street, Edinburgh EH1 3QN

Scottish Borders Archive and Local History Centre, Library Headquarters, St Mary's Mill, Selkirk TD7 5EW
www.scotborders.gov.uk/libraries/hist/history.htm

Scottish Church History Society, 39 Southside Road, Inverness IV2 4XA

Scottish Genealogical Society, 15 Victoria Terrace, Edinburgh EH1 2JL www.sol.co.uk/s/scotgensoc

Scottish History Society, 17 Buccleuch Place, University of Edinburgh EH8 9LN www.eusa.ed.ac.uk/societies/scothist/

Scottish Library Association (SLA) (Local Studies Information Database), Motherwell Business Centre, Coursington Road, Motherwell ML1 1PW www.slainte.org.uk/SLA/slashome.htm

Scottish Local History Forum, c/o Royal Museum of Scotland, Chamber's Street, Edinburgh EH1 1JF www.drymen-history.org.uk/forum.html

Scottish Record Office and National Register of Archives, HM General Register House, Edinburgh EH1 3YY
www.oz.net/~markhow/scotsros.htm

Scottish Record Society, Department of Scottish History, University of Glasgow, Glasgow G12 8QQ

Scottish Records Association, Glasgow City Archives, Mitchell Library, 201 North Street, Glasgow G3 7DN

Shropshire Records and Research Centre, Castle Gates, Shrewsbury SY1 2AQ www.shropshire-cc.gov.uk/research.nsf

Society for Army Historical Research, National Army Museum, Royal Hospital Road, London SW3 4HT

Society for Church Archaeology, Bowes Morrell House, 111 Walmgate, York YO1 2UA

Society for Clay Pipe Research, 13 Sommerville Road, Bishopston, Bristol BS7 9AD

Society for Medieval Archaeology, Institute of Archaeology, University College London, 31–4 Gordon Square, London WC1H 0PY www.medarchsoc.uklinux.net

Society for Post-Medieval Archaeology, 267 Kells Lane, Low Fell, Gateshead NE9 5HU www.britarch.ac.uk/spma

Society for the Interpretation of Britain's Heritage (SIBH), *see* Association for Heritage Interpretation (AHI)

Society for the Promotion of Roman Studies, Senate House, Malet Street, London WC1E 7HU www.sas.ac.uk/icls/Roman

Society for the Protection of Ancient Buildings, 37 Spital Square, London E1 6DY www.spab.org.uk

Society for the Study of Labour History, general correspondence to Ken Lunn, School of Social and Historical Studies, University of Portsmouth, Portsmouth PO1 3AS facstaff.uww.edu/sslh/home.html

Society of Antiquaries of London, Burlington House, Piccadilly, London W1J 0BE www.sal.org.uk

Society of Antiquaries of Scotland, Royal Museum of Scotland, Chamber's Street, Edinburgh EH1 1JF

Society of Architectural Historians, Honorary Secretary, 6 Fitzroy Square, London W1T 5DX. It may be more useful to contact the website at www.sahgb.org.uk

Society of Archivists, 40 Northampton Road, London EC1R 0HB www.archives.org.uk

Society of Friends Library, Friends House, Euston Road, London NW1 2BJ www.quaker.org.uk/library

Society of Genealogists, 14 Charterhouse Buildings, London EC1M 7BA www.sog.org.uk

Society of Glass Technology, Don Valley House, Savile Street East, Sheffield S4 7UQ www.sgt.org.uk

Society of Jesus Record Office, 114 Mount Street, London WC2Y 6AH

Soil Survey and Land Research Centre, Cranfield Institute of Technology, Silsoe, Bedfordshire MK45 4DT www.cranfield.ac.uk/sslrc

Somerset Archive and Record Office, Obridge Road, Taunton TA2 7PU www.somerset.gov.uk/archives/mainpage.htm

Staffordshire Record Office, County Buildings, Eastgate Street, Stafford ST16 2LZ www.staffordshire.gov.uk/archives

Standing Council of the Baronetage, 3 Eastcroft Road, West Ewell, Epsom, Surrey KT19 9TX

State Paper Office, Dublin Castle, Dublin 2 homepage.tinet.ie/~seanjmurphy/nai/spo.htm; *see also* 'Archives moved from Dublin Castle' at www.nationalarchives.ie/readers.html

Stationery Office Ltd, Customer Services Department, St Crispin's, Duke Street, Norwich NR3 1GN www.hmso.gov.uk

Stirling County Archives, Unit 6, Burghmuir Industrial Estate, Stirling FK7 7PY

Stone Federation, 82 New Cavendish Street, London W1M 8AD www.stone-federationgb.org.uk

Suffolk Record Office: www.suffolk.gov.uk/libraries-and-heritage

    Central Library, Clapham Road South, Lowestoft NR32 1DR

    Gatacre Road, Ipswich IP1 2LQ

    77 Raingate Street, Bury St Edmunds IP33 2AR

Sundial Society, 4 New Wokingham Road, Crowthorne, Berkshire RG45 7NR www.sundialsoc.org.uk

Surrey History Centre, 130 Goldsworth Road, Woking GU21 1ND www.surreycc.gov.uk/centre.html

Teesside Archives, Exchange House, 6 Marton Road, Middlesbrough TS1 1DB; go to 'The Council', then 'Libraries and Archives' at www.middlesbrough.gov.uk

Theatre Museum, 1e Tavistock Street, London WC2E 7PA www.theatremuseum.org

Thirties Society, 18 Comeragh Road, London W14

Tramway Museum Society, National Tramway Museum, Crich, Matlock, Derbyshire DE4 5DP www.tramway.co.uk

Transport Trust, Marylebone Station Offices, London NW1

Tyne and Wear Archives Service, Blandford House, Blandford Square, Newcastle upon Tyne NE1 6DD www.thenortheast.com/archives

Ulster Museum, Botanic Gardens, Belfast BT9 5AB www.ulstermuseum.org.uk

Unitarian Historical Society (UHS), c/o Revd Ann Peart, 34 Old Broadway, Withington, Manchester M20 3DF www.hibbert.org.uk/heritage/UHS.html

United Reformed Church History Society, The Administrator, Westminster College, Madingley Road, Cambridge CB3 0AA

Vernacular Architecture Group, 'Ashley', Willows Green, Chelmsford, Essex CM3 1QD www.worthingtonm.freeserve.co.uk/vag

Victoria and Albert Museum, Cromwell Road, South Kensington, London SW7 2RL www.vam.ac.uk

Victorian Society. The most useful address is the website at www.victorian-society.org.uk

Viking Society for Northern Research, Department of Scandinavian Studies, University College London, Gower Street, London WC1E 6BT www.nottingham.ac.uk/~aezjj/homepage.html

Village Lock-up Association, 7 Inch's Yard, Market Street, Newbury, Berkshire RG14 5DP

Wallpaper History Society, c/o Victoria & Albert Museum, South Kensington, London SW7 2RL

Warwickshire County Record Office, Priory Park, Cape Road, Warwick CV34 4JS www.warwickshire.gov.uk/general/rcindex.htm

Welsh Historic Monuments Office, *see* CADW

Wesley Historical Society, 34 Spiceland Road, Northfield, Birmingham B31 1NJ

West Glamorgan Archive Service, County Hall, Oystermouth Road, Swansea SA1 3SN swansea.gov.uk/archives

West Lothian Council Archives, 7 Rutherford Square, Brucefield, Livingston, West Lothian EH54 9BU www.wlonline.org/main/frames~1~34~274.htm

West Sussex, *see* Sussex

West Sussex Record Office, correspondence to County Hall, West Street, Chichester PO19 1RN www.westsussex.gov.uk/RO/home.htm

West Yorkshire Archive Service, Wakefield Headquarters, Registry of Deeds, Newstead Road, Wakefield, WF1 2DE www.archives.wyjs.org.uk

William Adam Trust, 179 Canongate, Edinburgh EH8 8BN

William Morris Society, Kelmscott House, 26 Upper Mall, London W6 9TA www.morrissociety.org

Wiltshire and Swindon Record Office, County Hall, Trowbridge BA14 8JG; go to 'Records and Archives' at www.wiltshire.gov.uk/heritage

Woodland Trust, Autumn Park, Dysart Road, Grantham, Lincolnshire NG31 6LL www.woodland-trust.org.uk

Worcestershire Record Office, Headquarters Branch, County Hall, Spetchley Road, Worcester WR5 2NP www.worcestershire.gov.uk/records

Workers' Educational Association, Temple House, 17 Victoria Park Square, London E2 9PB www.wea.org.uk

York City Archives Department, Art Gallery Building, Exhibition Square, York YO1 7EW www.york.gov.uk/learning/libraries/archives/index.html

York Minster Archives, Minster Library, Dean's Park, York YO1 7JQ www.york.ac.uk/services/library/guides/minster.htm

APPENDIX II

BIBLIOGRAPHY

Adams, C.V. *Re-thinking English Local History* (Leicester University Press, 1987)

Alcock, N.W. *Old Title Deeds: A Guide for Local and Family Historians* (Phillimore, 1995)

Archer, L. *Architecture in Britain and Ireland 600–1500* (The Harvill Press, 1999)

Aston, M. *Interpreting the Landscape* (Batsford, 1985)

Battey, J.H. *Church and Parish* (Batsford, 1987)

Beresford, M. *History on the Ground*, revised edn (Sutton Publishing, 1998)

——. *The Lost Villages of England*, revised edn (Sutton Publishing, 1998)

Black, J. *Historical Atlas of Britain: The End of the Middle Ages to the Georgian Era* (Sutton Publishing, 2000)

Brown, A. *Fieldwork for Archaeologists and Local Historians* (Batsford, 1987)

Campbell-Kease, J. *A Companion to Local History Research* (A & C Black, 1989)

Clark, A.J. *Seeing Beneath the Soil* (Batsford, 1990)

Collis, J. *Digging Up The Past* (Sutton Publishing, 2001)

Colwell, S. *Family Roots: Discovering the Past in the Public Record Office* (Weidenfeld & Nicolson, 1991)

Cokayne, G.E. *The Complete Peerage*, 6 vols (Sutton Publishing, 2000)

Currie, C.R.J., and Lewis, C.P. (eds). *English County Histories: a Guide* (Sutton Publishing, 1994)

Danbury, E. *Palaeography for Historians* (Phillimore, 1998)

Dunning, R. *Local History for Beginners* (Phillimore, 1980)

Dymond, D. *Writing Local History* (Phillimore, 1996)

——. *Researching and Writing History: A Practical Guide* (Phillimore, 1999)

Edwards, P. *Farming: Sources for Local Historians* (Batsford, 1991)

Ekwall, E. *The Concise Oxford Dictionary of Place-names* (Clarendon, 1990)

Emmison, F.G. *Introduction to Archives* (Phillimore, 1977)

English Place-Name Society, series of county volumes: *for* address *see* APPENDIX I

Friar, S. *Heraldry for the Local Historian and Genealogist* (Sutton Publishing, 1992)

——. *A Companion to the English Parish Church* (Sutton Publishing, 1996)

Gardiner, J., and Wendborn, N. (eds). *The History Today Companion to British History* (Collins & Brown, 1995)

Gelling, M. *Signposts to the Past: Place Names and the History of England* (Phillimore, 2000)

Hey, D. *The Oxford Companion to Local and Family History* (OUP, 1996)

Higgs, E. *Making Sense of the Census: the Manuscript Returns for England and Wales 1801–1901* (HMSO, 1989)

Hindle, P. *Maps for Historians* (Phillimore, 1998)

Hollowell, S. *Enclosure Records for Historians* (Phillimore, 2000)

Hoskins, W.G. *Local History in England* (Longman, 1984)

——. *The Making of the English Landscape*, revised C. Taylor (Hodder and Stoughton, 1989)

——. *Fieldwork in Local History*, 2nd edn (Faber and Faber, 1982)

Humphery-Smith, C. *The Phillimore Atlas and Register of Parish Registers* (Phillimore, 1995)

Iredale, D. *Enjoying Archives*, 2nd edn (Phillimore, 1985)

Iredale, D., and Barrett, J. *Discovering Local History* (Shire Publications, 1999)

Kain, R., and Prince, H. *Tithe Surveys for Historians* (Phillimore, 2000)

Kitching, C. *Archives: The Very Essence of our Heritage* (Phillimore, 1996)

Lewis, C. *Particular Places: An Introduction to English Local History* (British Library, 1989)

Marcombe, D. *Sounding Boards: Oral Testimony and the Local Historian* (University of Nottingham, 1996)

Moody, D. *Scottish Local History* (Batsford, 1986)

Morton, A., and Donaldson, G. *British National Archives and the Local Historian* (Historical Association, 1980)

Muir, R. *Reading the Landscape* (Michael Joseph, 1981)

Munby, L. *Dates and Time: A Handbook* (Phillimore, 1997)

Murphy, M. *Newspapers and Local History* (Phillimore, 1991)

Newman, R. with Cranstone, D., and Howard-Davis, C. *The Historical Archaeology of Britain, c. 1540–1900* (Sutton Publishing, 2001)

Norrington, V. *Recording the Present* (Phillimore, 1988)

Oliver, R. *Ordnance Survey Maps: a Concise Guide for Historians* (Close Society, 1993)

Pevsner, N., and Newman, J. *The Buildings of England* series of county volumes (Penguin)

Platt, C. *The Architecture of Medieval Britain* (Yale University Press, 1990)

Porter, S.C. *Exploring Urban History* (Batsford, 1990)

Rackham, O. *The History of the Countryside* (Dent, 1986)

Richardson, J. *The Local Historian's Encyclopedia*, 2nd revised and enlarged edn (Historical Publications, 1993)

Richardson, R.C. *The Changing Face of English Local History* (Ashgate Publishing, 2000)

Riden, P. *Local History: A Handbook for Beginners* (Batsford, 1983)

——. *Record Sources for English Local History* (Batsford, 1987)

Riley, D.N. *Aerial Archaeology in Britain*, 2nd edn (Shire Publications, 1996)

Rodell, W. *Church Archaeology*, revised (Batsford, 1989)

Rogers, C.D., and Smith, J.H. *Local Family History in England* (Manchester University Press, 1991)

Stephens, W.B. *Sources for English Local History* (Phillimore, 1994)

Stuart, D. *Manorial Records* (Phillimore, 1992)

——. *Latin for Local and Family Historians* (Phillimore, 1995)

Tarver, A. *Church Court Records* (Phillimore, 1994)

Tate, W. *The Parish Chest* (Phillimore, 1983)

Taylor, C. *Fields in the English Landscape*, 2nd edn (Sutton Publishing, 2000)

Tiller, K. *English Local History: An Introduction* (Sutton Publishing, 1992, rep. 2001)

Trice Martin, C. *The Record Interpreter* (Phillimore, 1994)

Wagner, Sir A. *English Genealogy* (Phillimore, 1983)

West, J. *Village Records* (Phillimore, 1997)

Williams, M. *Researching Local History: the Human Journey* (Longman, 1996)

Willis, A., and Proudfoot, K. *Genealogy for Beginners* (Phillimore, 1997)

Winterbotham, D., and Crosby, A. *The Local Studies Library* (Phillimore, 1999)

INDEX OF PLACE-NAMES

Page numbers in *italics* indicate illustrations; those in **bold** refer to colour plates.

INDEX

INDEX